Second Edition

The Great Republic

A History of the American People

Bernard Bailyn

HARVARD UNIVERSITY

David Brion Davis

YALE UNIVERSITY

David Herbert Donald

HARVARD UNIVERSITY

John L. Thomas

BROWN UNIVERSITY

Robert H. Wiebe

NORTHWESTERN UNIVERSITY

Gordon S. Wood

BROWN UNIVERSITY

D. C. HEATH AND COMPANY

Lexington, Massachusetts   Toronto

The
Great Republic

Second Edition

A History of the American People

Cover Illustration: "New York Ballance Drydock," 1877 by Jurgan Frederick Huge. (Collection of Mr. and Mrs. Jacob M. Kaplan. Photograph by Geoffrey Clements courtesy of Whitney Museum, New York)

Acquisitions Editor: Ann H. Knight

Developmental Editor: Louise M. Sullivan

Production Editor: Louise M. Sullivan

Photo Researcher: Sharon L. Donahue

Designer: Esther Agonis

Cover Designer: Herb Rogalski

Cartographer: Norman C. Adams

Published simultaneously in Canada.

Printed in the United States of America.

International Standard Book Number: 0-669-02753-7

Library of Congress Catalog Card Number: 80-81431

Publisher's Foreword

Seldom has an introductory textbook inspired such keen interest and enthusiasm as *The Great Republic.* Certainly the reception of the first edition has made it clear that a great many historians share the authors' belief that a basic American history text should not be merely a narration of unrelated facts. It must attempt to explain and synthesize the whole complex history of our country.

Our goal in revising the book was clear: to maintain the book's quality, its fresh scholarship and bold interpretations, and at the same time make the book more accessible to today's undergraduates.

Our general approach to the Second Edition has been to reduce the number of pages; to put more material into concrete terms; to order the arguments, when possible, in a chronological fashion; to expand coverage of the important events of American history; and to add many more in-text subheadings to help students identify and organize what they read. In addition, the text is now organized so that Volume I of the paperback edition ends with a chapter on Reconstruction, and Volume II begins with the same chapter.

We hope you will agree that the new *Great Republic* is not only a rich and authoritative account of American history but also an extremely effective teaching tool.

Acknowledgments

We are gratified, as are the authors of *The Great Republic,* that so many historians offered their reactions, responded to questionnaires, and took time to discuss the book with our representatives and editors on campus and at professional meetings.

We especially wish to thank those who are listed below for their sensitive and informed comments and suggestions during the preparation of the Second Edition of *The Great Republic:* Thomas G. Alexander, Brigham Young University; Richard Amundson, Columbus College; Michael C. Batinski, Southern Illinois University at Carbondale; Nancy Bowen, Del Mar College; Richard J. Hopkins, The Ohio State University; Richard L. Hume, Washington State University; David Nasaw, The College of Staten Island of The City University of New York; John K. Nelson, The University of North Carolina at Chapel Hill; Mark A. Stoler, The University of Vermont; Sue Taishoff, University of South Florida; James C. Turner, University of Massachusetts, Boston; and Ken L. Weatherbie, Del Mar College.

Introduction

This book is a history of the American people, from the earliest settlements in the New World to the present. We call our book "The Great Republic," adopting a phrase Winston Churchill used to describe the United States. No one can doubt the greatness of the American republic if it is measured in terms of the size of our national domain, the vastness of our economic productivity, or the stability of our government and basic institutions. Whether that greatness has been equaled in the realm of culture, in the uses of power, or in the distribution of social justice is more debatable; on these matters readers will make up their own minds. Our task has been to present the story of America as we understand it—a story of great achievement, of enormous material success, and of soaring idealism, but a story too of conflict, of tumultuous factionalism, of injustice, rootlessness, and grinding disorder.

Each of the six sections of the book contains its own thematic emphasis, set out in separate introductions. But there are two general themes that unify the book as a whole. The first theme is the development and constant testing of free political institutions in America. To understand the United States today, one must analyze the conditions of life in the colonial period that made popular self-government at first possible, then likely, in the end necessary. One must then see how the American Revolution expressed the longings of provincial Britons for a total reform of political culture and projected this idealism onto a nation of continental scale. One must discover how democratic institutions and practices expanded during the nineteenth century and received their crucial testing in the American Civil War. One must understand how urbanization and industrialization produced radical changes in American political life by the beginning of the twentieth century. And one must ask how free, democratic institutions have sustained themselves through recent decades of depression, international crises, and world wars, and what the legacy of this long, complex development has been to the present technological world. Only through understanding the origins and growth of popular self-government, from eighteenth-century republicanism to modern mass democracy, can sense be made of the history of the American people.

A second theme, which has persisted from the very earliest days, is the tension between divisive ambitions on the one hand and the good of the community at large on the other. From the beginning the New World provided a feast for individual aspirations. Its vast resources, open for exploitation by the talented, the shrewd, the enterprising, and the energetic, stimulated powerful ambitions that were often insensitive to the human costs of success and that helped produce a society constantly in danger of fragmentation. The huge geographical extent of the country nourished divisive interests of all kinds, and the admixture of peoples from every quarter of the world led to ethnic and cultural pluralism, at times so strong as to threaten the disintegration of the social fabric. At the same time, however, there have been, from the founding of the colonies to the present, forces that worked for social stability and agreement, and an ideology, bred in Judaeo-Christian and Enlightenment idealism, that generated concern for justice and civility, and respect for the dignity of man.

The Founding Fathers correctly recognized that the constant struggle between special interests and the general welfare posed a severe threat to the continuance of a self-governing democratic nation. They knew there would be no automatic harmonizing of regional, economic, and social ambitions, no easy reconciliation of competing needs and desires; they worried that minorities might become subject to the tyranny of majorities, and that the weak might be crushed by the strong. At the same time they feared a centralized government powerful enough to impose order on these conflicting and exploitative interests and to protect the weak against the forces of organized power. They hoped that public institutions sensitive to popular pressures would successfully reconcile these conflicts and somehow create a stable, nationwide agreement out of a tumult of clashing ambitions. And they hoped that reasonable people would find their own highest interest in the preservation of the rule of law.

Though the Founding Fathers did not wholly resolve this tension between the interest of the society as a whole and the special interests of its most ambitious and most powerful parts, the system they devised provided mechanisms for the mediation of the struggles and for the protection of human values. Often the balance has been precarious between the general welfare and the welfare of regions, states, and economic and social groups; between the power of majorities and the welfare of minorities. From time to time the balance has tipped, first in the one direction, then in the other, but only once, in the horrendous catastrophe of the Civil War, has it ever been completely upset. The nation's commitment both to social stability and to the rights of individuals remains intact—still effective after generations of complex adjustment.

The tracing of these two themes—the development of free political institutions in America and the struggle to protect the individual and the general welfare against powerful majorities and special interests—links together the six sections and gives an overarching unity to the book. The sections are further unified by the authors' shared view of the nature of history. We all believe that history is not simply the accumulation of information about the past. It is a mode of understanding. The historian is obliged not merely to describe what happened but to explain it, to make clear why things developed as they did. We share, too, an aversion to any deterministic interpretation of history. At certain junctures economic and demographic forces are dominant, but they are themselves shaped by cultural forces. Great political events are at times triggered by economic drives, but at other times they are responses to beliefs and to aspirations that are not a direct reflection of economic needs. Political decisions alter economic life, social organization, and even the way people think—yet economic, social, and intellectual forces change politics too.

History, we believe, falls into no predetermined pattern. The course of American history was not predestined; the nation did not have to develop as it did. Why it did, and hence what accounts for the condition of our national life now, must be explained historically, stage by stage. We have sought to provide that explanation in the pages that follow, as part of the narrative of American history. The book is therefore self-contained, in that it supplies the basic factual information and essential narrative that readers will need, and it presents that information within a framework of analysis and explanation.

We hope that *The Great Republic* will help readers understand why and how America developed as it did, and where, as a result of this historic evolution, we have arrived after more than three centuries of growth and two centuries of nationhood.

B.B.　　　J.L.T.
D.B.D.　　R.H.W.
D.H.D.　　G.S.W.

Contents

PART ONE
Shaping the Republic, to 1760

Bernard Bailyn

Introduction 2

CHAPTER 1
The Background of English Colonization 5

Points of Contrast: Spain in America 5
England's Overseas Expansion 16
Personnel and the Role of the State 22
Financial Limitations and the "Starving Times" 23
Chronology 26
Suggested Readings 27

CHAPTER 2
Transplantation 29

Virginia: Squalor, Struggle, and a New Way of
 Life 31
The Pilgrims' "Sweet Communion" 38
The Puritans: Power in the Service of God 42
A Catholic Refuge on the Chesapeake 48
The Failure of the Dutch 51
Royal Rewards: Carolina and the Jerseys 55

Pennsylvania: A Godly Experiment and a Worldly
 Success 61
Chronology 64
Suggested Readings 64

CHAPTER 3
Europe in the Wilderness: American Society in the Seventeenth Century 67

Population Growth and Structure 68
Economic Instability 70
Social Instability 76
Religion 82
Suggested Readings 91

CHAPTER 4
Elements of Change, 1660–1720 93

Empire 93
Anglo-American Aristocracy 100
Rebellion: The Measure of Social Strain 109
Provincial Culture 113
Chronology 119
Suggested Readings 120

CHAPTER 5
American Society in the Eighteenth Century 122

The New Population: Sources and Impact 122
A Maturing Economy and a Society in Flux 128
Religion: The Sources of American
 Denominationalism 135
The Origins of American Politics 141
Suggested Readings 147

CHAPTER 6

The Enlightenment's New World   150

"Rule Britannia"   150
The Alienation of the State   157
The American   161
Chronology   168
Suggested Readings   168

Color Essay: Embellishing the Wilderness
    Between 140 and 141

PART TWO

Framing the Republic, 1760–1820

Gordon S. Wood

Introduction   172

CHAPTER 7

Sources of the Revolution   174

The Changing Empire   174
The Reorganization of the Empire   185
American Resistance   188
The Popularization of Politics   198
Chronology   200
Suggested Readings   201

CHAPTER 8

The Revolution: Ideology and War   203

An Asylum for Liberty   203
The Imperial Debate   206
The War for Independence   209
Republicanism   221
Chronology   224
Suggested Readings   224

CHAPTER 9

The States and the Confederation   226

State Constitution-Making   226
The Articles of Confederation   228
Republican Society   232
The Betterment of Humanity   239
Democratic Despotism   243
Suggested Readings   246

CHAPTER 10

The Federalist Age   248

The Critical Period   248
The Federal Constitution   253
The Hamiltonian Program   258
The Republican Opposition   264
Chronology   272
Suggested Readings   272

CHAPTER 11

The Revolution Recovered   275

The Revolution of 1800   275
An Empire of Liberty   282
The Origins of Judicial Review   288
Republican Religion   291
Republican Diplomacy   295
The War of 1812   299
Chronology   303
Suggested Readings   304

Color Essay: The Rising Glory of America
    Between 268 and 269

PART THREE

Expanding the Republic, 1820–1860

David Brion Davis

Introduction   308

CHAPTER 12

Population: Expansion and Exploitation   311

Population Growth, Immigration, and
  Urbanization   312
Farmers and the Land   315
Indians   322
The Slave's World   327
Population Distribution and Opportunity   332
Suggested Readings   337

CHAPTER 13

Politics: Cohesion and Division   339

"A Fire Bell in the Night": The Missouri
  Compromise   341
The End of Republican Unity   344
Jackson's Rise to Power   346
The Threat of National Division: Tariffs,
  Nullification, and the Gag Rule   349
The Bank War, the Panic of 1837, and Political
  Realignments   352

Whigs and the Two-Party System   356
Chronology   361
Suggested Readings   362

CHAPTER 14

Attempts to Shape the American Character   364

"We Must Educate or Perish"   364
The Evangelical Age   369
The Cult of Self-Improvement   376
The Tensions of Democratic Art   379
Suggested Readings   382

CHAPTER 15

Dissent, Protest, and Reform   385

The Mormons as a Test Case   386
The Benevolent Empire   391
Radical Abolitionism   397
Feminism, Perfectionism, and Political
  Consolidation   402
Suggested Readings   408

CHAPTER 16

Expansion and New Boundaries   410

Industrialization and Economic Growth   410
The South as a "Slave Society"   415
Foreign Dangers, American Expansion, and the
  Monroe Doctrine   417
The Mexican War and Manifest Destiny   428
Chronology   435
Suggested Readings   435

CHAPTER 17

Compromise and Conflict   438

Free Soil and the Challenge of California   439
The Crisis of 1850   442
The Know-Nothing Upsurge and Collapse of the
  Whigs   445

The Confrontation Over Kansas   447
Dred Scott and the Lincoln-Douglas Debates   451
The Ultimate Failure of Compromise   456
Chronology   461
Suggested Readings   461

Color Essay: The Perils of Civilization
  Between 396 and 397

PART FOUR

Uniting the Republic, *1860–1877*

David Herbert Donald

Introduction   466

CHAPTER 18

Stalemate, *1861–1862*   468

The Rival Governments   468
Winning the Border States   471
Raising the Armies   476
Financing the War   480
Wartime Diplomacy   482
Battles and Leaders   486
Chronology   491
Suggested Readings   491

CHAPTER 19

Experimentation, *1862–1865*   493

Evolution of a Command System   493
The Naval War   497
The Wartime Economy   500
Inflation and Its Consequences   501
Conscription and Conflict   504
Steps Toward Emancipation   506
Europe and the War   510
Wartime Politics in the Confederacy   511
Wartime Politics in the North   512
Northern Victory   516
Chronology   522
Suggested Readings   522

CHAPTER 20

Reconstruction, *1865–1877*   524

Paths Not Taken   525
Constitutionalism as a Limit to Change   528
Laissez-Faire as a Limit to Change   532
Political Parties as a Limit to Change   536
Racism as a Limit to Change   544
The Restoration of "Home Rule"   550
Chronology   555
Suggested Readings   555

CHAPTER 21

National Problems, *1865–1877*   557

American Diplomacy   558
Indian Wars   561
Toward a National Economy   565
Politics in the Gilded Age   571
Tariff and Currency Controversies   574
Discontent Among Farmers and Laborers   577
Chronology   584
Suggested Readings   584

Color Essay: From Eden to Babylon
  Between 556 and 557

PART FIVE

Nationalizing the Republic, 1877–1920

John L. Thomas

Introduction 588

CHAPTER 22

Stabilizing the American Economy 590

The Foundations of the American Industrial
  Revolution 591
Business Fills a Vacuum 597
The Counterrevolution Fails 601
The Farmers' Fight Against Disorder 605
Workers and the Challenge of Organization 611
The Fruits of the Industrial Revolution 615
Chronology 616
Suggested Readings 617

CHAPTER 23

The Politics of Reform 619

The Politics of Equilibrium 621
The Lost Decade 626
Conditions Without Precedent—The Populist
  Revolt 632
The Great Reversal: The Election of 1896 636
Chronology 643
Suggested Readings 643

CHAPTER 24

The Progressive Impulse 645

Cities in Revolt—The Rise of Urban
  Progressivism 646
The Man with the Muckrake 655
Progressivism Invades the States 656
Theodore Roosevelt: The Progressive
  as Hero 661
"Wise Radicalism and Wise Conservatism"—
  The Square Deal 664
The Limits of Neofederalism 668
Chronology 670
Suggested Readings 670

CHAPTER 25

Progressives and the Challenge of Pluralism 673

Changing the Progressive Guard 674
Americans—New and Old 681
The Rise of Social Feminism 688
Paradise Lost: Socialism in America 695
The New Freedom 697
Chronology 700
Suggested Readings 701

CHAPTER 26

The Path to Power: American Foreign Policy, 1890–1917 703

The Origins of American Expansionism 704
President McKinley's "Wonderful Experience" 707
Open and Closed Doors: Progressive Foreign
  Policy Under Roosevelt and Taft 714
"The Organized Force of Mankind"—Wilsonian
  Diplomacy and World War 721
Chronology 727
Suggested Readings 728

CHAPTER 27

Progressivism and the Great War   *730*

Slaughter on the Western Front   *730*
War and the Health of the State   *733*
The Little Rebellion: Progressivism and the
    Challenge of Culture   *741*
Artists and Scientists: Critics of
    Progressivism   *746*
The Ordeal of Woodrow Wilson   *748*
Chronology   755
Suggested Readings   755

Color Essay: Art as Urban Experience
    Between 716 and 717

PART SIX

Modernizing the Republic, *1920 to the Present*

Robert H. Wiebe

Introduction   760

CHAPTER 28

The Emergence of the Modern State   *763*

Vicious Years, 1920–1924   *763*
The Modern Political Economy, 1920–1929   *767*
Divided Politics in the New Era, 1924–1929   *772*

A New International Order, 1920–1929   *776*
Depression, 1929–1932   *779*
Chronology   783
Suggested Readings   784

CHAPTER 29

The Modern State in Crisis   *786*

The New Deal Arrives, 1933–1934   *786*
The New Deal at the Crossroads, 1935–1936   *794*
The New Deal Loses Its Way, 1937–1939   *798*
International Disintegration, 1931–1939   *802*
World War, 1939–1941   *807*
Chronology   812
Suggested Readings   812

CHAPTER 30

A Global Setting for the Modern State   *815*

The Second World War, 1941–1945   *815*
Postwar International Planning for Peace, 1945   *825*
The Cold War, 1945–1950   *827*
Containment, 1950–1953   *833*
From Wartime Prosperity to Peacetime
    Management, 1941–1945   *837*
Local Politics Comes to Washington,
    1941–1954   *846*
Chronology   853
Suggested Readings   854

CHAPTER 31

Modern Culture   *857*

Modern Values   *858*
Modern Families and Careers   *860*
Response of the Traditionalists   *863*
Dangers to the Individual   *866*
Answers for the Individual   *871*
Suggested Readings   878

CHAPTER 32

The Consequences of Modernization   880

Unity and Progress   880
World Order   884
Presidential Leadership   889
The Crisis in National-Local Relations   893
The Decline of Containment   899
The Lament of the Individual   903
Counterattack   907
Chronology   910
Suggested Readings   910

CHAPTER 33

An Elusive Stability   913

A National-Local Balance   913
A Flexible Diplomacy   917
The New Diplomacy   920

A Stumbling Economy   922
A Cloudy Horizon   924
Chronology   931
Suggested Readings   931

Color Essay: Varieties of Reality
    Between 876 and 877

APPENDIX   i

Map of the United States of America   *ii–iii*
Declaration of Independence   *v*
Articles of Confederation and Perpetual Union   *vii*
Constitution of the United States of America   *xii*
Presidential Elections   *xxiii*
Presidents and Vice-Presidents   *xxvii*
Growth of U.S. Population and Area   *xxviii*

INDEX   *xxix*

Maps and Charts

Spanish Conquests in America   6

Spanish and Portuguese Empires in the New World   10

Spain's Imperial Government in the New World, 1550   11

Raleigh's Virginia, 1584–1590   21

The Arc of Empire in the 17th Century: Ireland and America   24

The Indian Paths of Pennsylvania   31

Jamestown, 1607–1612   32

Northern British Settlements, 1700   47

Southern British Settlements, 1700   56

English Origins of New England Settlers, 1620–1650   90

Hudson River Estates in Colonial New York   103

The French Wars, 1680–1713   105

German Settlements in 18th-Century America   125

Mount Vernon Plantation   130

18th-Century Atlantic Trade Routes   133

The French and Indian War, 1755–1760   153

North America in 1763   175

Frontier Expansion, 1760s   177

Concentration of Population in the Colonies, 1760   178

Trade between Britain and the Colonies, 1763–1776   192

Northern Campaigns, 1775–1776   212

Northern Campaigns, 1777   216

Yorktown and the Southern Campaigns, 1778–1781   219

State Claims to Western Lands and Cessions   231

Northwest Ordinance of 1785, Land Survey   233

The Treaty of Greenville, 1795   264

Density of Population, 1810   283

The United States, 1803–1807   285

American Foreign Trade, 1790–1812   297

The War of 1812—Major Campaigns   299

Population, 1820   312

Population, 1860   313

The United States, 1820–1860   315

Main Roads, Canals, River and Lake Transportation, 1840s   319

Indian Removal to Western Territories, 1820–1840   326

The Two-Party System   340

The Missouri Compromise, 1820–1821   343

The Election of 1828   347

The Election of 1840   360

The Mormon Trail   389

Principal Railroads, 1860   414

Geographical Distribution of Slaves in 1820   419

Geographical Distribution of Slaves in 1860   419

Continental Expansion, 1819–1848   421

Wagon Trails Westward, 1840   427

The Election of 1844   428

Major Campaigns of the Mexican War   432

The Compromise of 1850   444

The Kansas-Nebraska Act, 1854   449

The Election of 1860   459

Secession   474

Operations in the East, July 1861–November 1862   487

Operations in the West, February–April 1862   488

The Confederate Offensive in the West, August–October 1862   490

Operations in the East, December 1862–July 1863   495

Operations in the West, 1863, The Vicksburg Campaign   496

Operations in the East, May 1864–April 1865   517

Sherman's March to the Sea   518

Reconstruction   541

Black Population, 1880   546

Hayes-Tilden Disputed Election of 1876   551

Westward Expansion and Indian Wars
  1864–1876 *564*
Principal Railroads, 1890 *593*
The U.S. Economy, 1873–1900 *598*
Passing of the Frontier, 1870–1890 *606*
The Election of 1880 *622*
The Election of 1884 *622*
The Election of 1896 *642*
The Election of 1912 *679*
Old and New Immigration, 1871–1920 *681*
The Lower East Side *684*
Woman Suffrage Before the 19th Amendment *694*
The Spanish War in the Philippines, 1898 *714*
The Spanish War in the Caribbean, 1898 *714*
The United States in the Pacific *715*
The United States in the Caribbean *717*

Major U.S. Operations on the Western Front,
  1918 *732*
The Election of 1928 *775*
Index of Common Stock Prices, 1924–1932 *779*
The Election of 1932 *787*
Tennessee Valley Authority (TVA) *793*
World War II, Europe and North Africa *820*
World War II in the Pacific *821*
The Shifting Front in Korea *834*
Recovery of the National Economy *840*
The Election of 1948 *842*
Black Population, 1920–1930 *848*
The Election of 1960 *891*
Vietnam and Southeast Asia *901*
The Election of 1968 *916*

PART ONE

Bernard Bailyn

Shaping the Republic

to 1760

The American Republic was created only in a legal sense in 1776. In a deeper and more general sense it was the product of a century and a half of development that preceded the establishment of American independence. The ultimate origins of this "Great Republic," as Winston Churchill called the American nation, lie far back in time—in desperate gambles of hard-pressed sixteenth- and seventeenth-century merchants involved in overseas trade; in the visions of Elizabethan dreamers who conceived of a western passage to the vast wealth of the Far East; in the courage and single-mindedness of religious refugees determined to carve a new life for themselves in the wilderness rather than compromise their beliefs; in the lifelong labors of a quarter of a million Africans transported in bondage to the New World; and in the everyday struggles of five generations of transplanted Europeans and their descendants, farmers and tradesmen for the most part, who sensed, however vaguely, that theirs was a new world, more generous to human aspirations, freer, more supportive of human dignity, and richer—for those whose risks succeeded—than any land known before.

These multitudes in colonial North America did not seek to transform the world. Though adventurous, more often than not they were conservative by instinct or became conservative as they sought to establish familiar forms of life in an unfamiliar environment. But traditions could not be maintained in wilderness communities whose basic conditions were so different from those elsewhere, and a new pattern of life slowly evolved in the course of five generations. Gradually, without theory, as matters of fact and not of design, the character of community life as it had once been known—its demographic foundations, economic processes, social organizations, religion, and politics—all of this was transformed.

Yet not by desire or will—not in an effort to attain an ideal or realize a theory. Change, in the years before the Revolution, was suspect by some, resisted in part, and confined in its effects as the colonists sought to emulate the pattern of more traditional, cosmopolitan societies. Their own provincial world was seen not as a model but as a regression to a more primitive mode of life. Behavior had changed—had had to change—with the circumstances of everyday life, but habits of mind and the sense of the rightness of things lagged behind. Many felt that the changes that had taken place in the years before the Revolution were *away from,* not *toward,* something; that they represented deviance; that they lacked, in a word, legitimacy.

For most Americans this divergence between ideals, habits of mind, and belief on the one hand, and experience and patterns of behavior on the other, was ended at the Revolution. An upheaval that destroyed the traditional sources of public authority called forth the full range of advanced and enlightened

Overleaf: "A South Prospect of Ye Flourishing City of New York," 1717. Engraving by John Harris after William Burgis. *(New York Public Library)*

ideas. Long-settled attitudes were jolted and loosened. Suddenly it was seen that the slow erosion in patterns of social life that had taken place in the colonial period had been good and proper. In the context of Revolutionary beliefs, these changes were conceived of as steps in the direction of a new ideal—the ideal of a simpler, less encumbered existence, in which the individual would count for more and the state less; in which the weight of burdensome social institutions would be permanently lifted; in which the blight of privilege and of the misuse of power would forever be destroyed; in which corruption would be exposed before it could sap the nation's strength; and in which, as a result of all of this, the ordinary person's desire for personal fulfillment could at long last be satisfied.

Such at least were the ideals of the Revolution, formulated by a generation of brilliant political thinkers convinced that it was their great historic role to set the world on a new course. And in the context of these ideals—which, however modified, are still the highest aspirations of the American people—the changes of the colonial years took on a new meaning. The settlement of the colonies and their subsequent development, John Adams wrote, could now be seen as "the opening of a grand scene and design in providence for the illumination of the ignorant and the emancipation of the slavish part of mankind all over the earth." The glass was half-full, not half-empty; and to complete the work of fate and nature, further thought must be taken and changes accelerated rather than restrained.

Social change and social conflict took place during the Revolutionary years, but the beliefs and aspirations of the founders of the American nation, unlike those of the leaders of the French and Russian revolutions, did not require the destruction and remaking of society. The Revolution did not create new social and political forces; it released forces and intensified changes that had been developing from the day the first settlers set foot on Jamestown. Modern America—a massively developed, affluent, and tumultuous technological society of over 200 million people—is worlds away from the tiny farming hamlets and obscure port towns of the seventeenth century, huddled on the coastal fringe of an almost undeveloped continent. Yet there is a clear line of continuity in American history that links those quite primitive settlements to the sophisticated, dynamic world power of the late twentieth century. For modern America is not simply the product of modern forces—industrialism, political democracy, universal education, a consumer culture. It is the product too of the idealism of the eighteenth-century Enlightenment, reinforced and intensified by the openness and affluence of American life.

It is this powerful strain of idealism flowing from the very different world of the eighteenth century into all the complexities of modern America that is the most distinctive feature of the American Republic as it enters its third century of existence. How that ineradicable strain first entered American life, how it was nourished in the soil of a strangely altered society that grew from confused seventeenth-century origins, and how the characteristic American mixture of idealism and materialism was first compounded, reaching so soon, in the subtle figure of Benjamin Franklin, an apparently absolute and perfect form —how all this took place is the central theme of the colonial period of American history.

Far from being a quaint prologue to the main story, therefore, the history of the settlement and early development of American society is a critically important phase of our history. Without an understanding of the pre-Revolutionary era none of the rest of our history can be properly understood.

The Background of English Colonization

The United States evolved from the British settlements on the mainland of North America, first permanently established in 1607. But a century earlier a more powerful European power, Spain, had founded an empire in the Western Hemisphere that was in a high state of development when the British first entered the colonial world. The growth of the Spanish empire in the Western Hemisphere and of Spanish-American society forms a remarkable, and revealing, contrast to the evolution of the British empire and of Anglo-American society. In some ways, to be sure, Anglo-American society in British North America and Indo-Hispanic society in Central America and South America are so different as to be incomparable. But there is one area at least in which extremely illuminating contrasts may be drawn: the realm of government and politics.

By the early eighteenth century, politics in British North America was distinctive in its free competition and in the institutional and cultural conditions that made such open competition possible. Nothing quite like these unconfined, brawling struggles—faction against faction, groups against the state—existed in any other colonial region of the world. There was certainly nothing like this in Spanish America; yet at one stage, strangely enough, it seems that there might have been. It is worth attempting, therefore, at the very outset to explore the underlying reasons for the absence of a free competitive political system in Spanish America at the height of the colonial period, and in doing so to isolate by contrast forces and circumstances that would later shape the dynamic political society of British America as it existed on the eve of the Revolution.

Points of Contrast: Spain in America

There are important contrasts between Spanish and British America at every stage of development. The very origins of settlement were different. Whereas it took England half a century after its first contact with the Western Hemisphere to establish even a temporary colony there, Spain proceeded swiftly after

Spanish Conquests in America

MAJOR EXPLORATIONS

———————	Columbus 1492-1493
– – – – –	" 1493-1494
·········	" 1498-1500
–·–·–·–	" 1502-1503
··········	Balboa, 1513
–·–·–·–	De León, 1513
┼┼┼┼┼	Cortés, 1519
··········	De Soto, 1539-1542
– – – –	Cabeza de Vaca, 1528-1536
———————	Coronado, 1542
– – – –	Pizarro, 1524-1535
═══════	Valdivia, 1541

Columbus's world-transforming discovery of 1492 to exploit the territories it claimed. Led by the courageous, greedy, and often brutal *conquistadores*—adventurers for whom there are no equivalents in British experience—Spain's exploration of the Western Hemisphere, its conquest of the native peoples, and its establishment of a new civilization swept forward in three main waves.

The Spanish Conquests. Columbus himself explored much of the Caribbean on his four voyages (1492–1504), and within a generation of his death in 1506 Spanish adventurers seized possession of most of the coastal lands of Central America and South America. The conquest of the Caribbean basin climaxed in 1513 with Balboa's penetration of the Isthmus of Panama and his discovery of the Pacific, and

BATTLE FOR THE INCAN CITY OF CUZCO
An imaginative depiction by Flemish engraver Theodore
De Bry (1528–98). Never having seen either America or
an Indian, De Bry portrayed the natives as ancient
Greeks, innocent but savage, and dwelt almost sadisti-
cally on cannibalism and the brutalities of the conquest.
Cuzco appears as a Spanish-American walled city. *(Rare
Book Division, The New York Public Library)*

with Ponce de León's discovery of the Florida mainland.

The second principal wave of Spanish expansion
in America was stimulated by rumors of vast treasures
hidden in a highly civilized state deep in the interior,
and led to the conquest, in one of the most dramatic
and bloody adventures ever recorded, of the Aztec
empire of Montezuma in Mexico (1519–21) by the resourceful, ruthless, and incredibly energetic Hernando
Cortés. There are no heroes in this tale of slaughter
and conquest; there are only, on the one side, passionately determined adventurers, half-mad with greed,
who overcame fearful adversity to plunder and ultimately to destroy an ancient civilization, and on the
other side, equally courageous and brutal but bewildered and unsophisticated natives. Cortés's conquest
of the Mexican world was extended to the north by
others: by Cabeza de Vaca circling the northern periphery of the Gulf of Mexico and ultimately reaching
the Gulf of California (1528–36); by Coronado, seeking
El Dorado—the mythical city of gold and jewels—in
the mud villages of Arizona, New Mexico, Colorado,
Oklahoma, and Kansas; and by Hernando de Soto,
cutting through northern Florida and the later southeastern states to discover the Mississippi (1539–41).
While these conquerors were exploring and sub-
duing what would become the northern borderlands
of Spain's empire, other followers of Cortés swept
through Central America and established Spanish rule
in Honduras and Guatemala.

The third great thrust of Spanish conquest was
led by an illiterate adventurer, Francisco Pizarro, who
propelled a series of expeditions from Panama through
the jungles of Ecuador and northern Peru into the
heartland of the elaborate Incan empire, then weakened by civil war. By a ruse he managed to capture
the Incan emperor, whom he murdered after extracting
a ransom of over twenty tons of pure gold and silver,
and he destroyed much of the Indian army and nobility.
He then proceeded to strip city after city of their
treasures, to embroil both natives and conquerors in
devastating warfare, and to establish in 1535 the new
central city of Lima.

From the plundered Incan lands further expeditions were launched, first into Ecuador, then into
Chile and northern Argentina (1535–37), and finally
into Bolivia (1539). The full subjugation of Chile was
a vast epic in itself, the work of yet another almost
unbelievably determined and ruthless *conquistador*,
Pedro de Valdivia. His small troop of Spanish adventurers and Indian followers survived desert journeys,

near starvation, and attacks by natives to found Santiago, Concepción, and Valdivia before succumbing to native rebellion in 1553.

Radiating out from these three main lines of conquest (first, the subjugation of the Caribbean islands and coastal areas; then the reduction of Mexico and the exploration of southern North America; and finally the invasion of Peru, Chile, and northern Argentina), Spain's empire in America expanded in all directions. By 1607, when England established at Jamestown its first permanent settlement in America, Spain's American dominion extended nearly eight thousand miles, from southern California to the Strait of Magellan. Spain then possessed the largest empire the Western world had seen since the fall of Rome. Its only competitor in the Western Hemisphere had been Portugal, which had controlled the coastal areas of Brazil, until the union of the Spanish and Portuguese thrones (1580–1640) gave Spain legal jurisdiction even there. Spain's fabulous western empire was the result of sheer lust for adventure, greed, and a passion to convert the heathen people to Christianity; it was also the result of remarkable administrative skill.

The Spanish Empire. Despite the vast distances involved and all the technical impediments to the coherent management of so vast a territory, Spain's American empire was well organized. The structure of government that had evolved during the sixteenth century was elaborate, ingeniously contrived, and, except for periods when royal authority collapsed in Spain itself, successful. And it was utterly different from the imperial system that Britain would devise a century later. It was most elaborately *bureaucratic.* Full-time salaried officials enforced detailed decrees and and laws governing the behavior of rulers and ruled— regulations that reached down into the daily life of

THE WORLD THE SPANIARDS FOUND
The Aztec priest's skull mask was meant to be worn with an elaborate feather headdress and rich robes. It must have had a terrifying effect on worshipers. The gold Mixtec chest plate represented the god of death. Opposite, Macchu Pichu, Peru, last refuge of the Incan emperors in their flight from the Spaniards. *(Opposite, Braniff International Photograph; below left, National Museum of Anthropology, Mexico City; right, Copyright The British Museum)*

the meanest peasants in the most remote corners of the empire, half a world away from the central administrative agencies in Spain. And the system was *patriarchal.* That is, it was hierarchical in structure, all authority ultimately centering in the patriarchal figure of the monarch of Castile, whose rule in his kingdom of America was conceived of as personal, an extension of his dynastic and domestic authority.

This projection of monarchical power into overseas territory by means of a complex bureaucracy had been initiated almost immediately upon the report of Columbus's discovery—a response that contrasts sharply with that of the British government a century later. By 1503, the first of the major imperial institutions, the *Casa de Contratación* (board of trade),

had been created. The *Casa*—in Seville—licensed all equipment and operations engaged in trade with America, enforced the commercial laws and regulations, collected customs duties and colonial crown revenues, and kept the commercial accounts for the entire empire. By virtue of its power over colonial commerce and the flow of treasure that poured into Spain from America, the *Casa* became in effect a major branch of the royal exchequer. From this original agency, Spain's imperial government, flung over half the globe yet bound by hundreds of rules and regulations enforced by an army of officials, developed within a single generation.

Yet in all of this the *Casa* was subordinate to the chief regulating agency in Spain, the Council of the Indies (created in 1524), which held the decisive control, in the king's name, of both the legislative and the executive governance of the colonies, and which constituted a branch of the royal court. All colonial laws and decrees, civil and religious, were issued by the Council; and the officials, clerical and secular, who enforced the regulations were appointed by the Council. It exercised a special responsibility for the spiritual and physical welfare of the Indians; it served as a court of last resort for the entire judiciary system of the colonies; it censored all publications in America; and it audited the accounts of the colonial treasurers.

The government agencies and officials in America were in one way or another subordinates of this supreme royal council. The chief governmental unit in America was the viceroyalty, of which two were created in the sixteenth century: New Spain (1535), which included all Spanish territory north of the Isthmus of Panama; and Peru (1542), covering all to the south except the coast of Venezuela. These massive jurisdictions were ruled by viceroys endowed with large and somewhat ambiguous portions of royal power and established in seats of glittering splendor.

The next level was that of the *audiencias,* of which there were seven by 1550; five more were added by 1661. Originally they were royal courts with direct access to the Council of the Indies and subject to its veto only; but the *audiencias* soon acquired administrative and political authority also, and they shared,

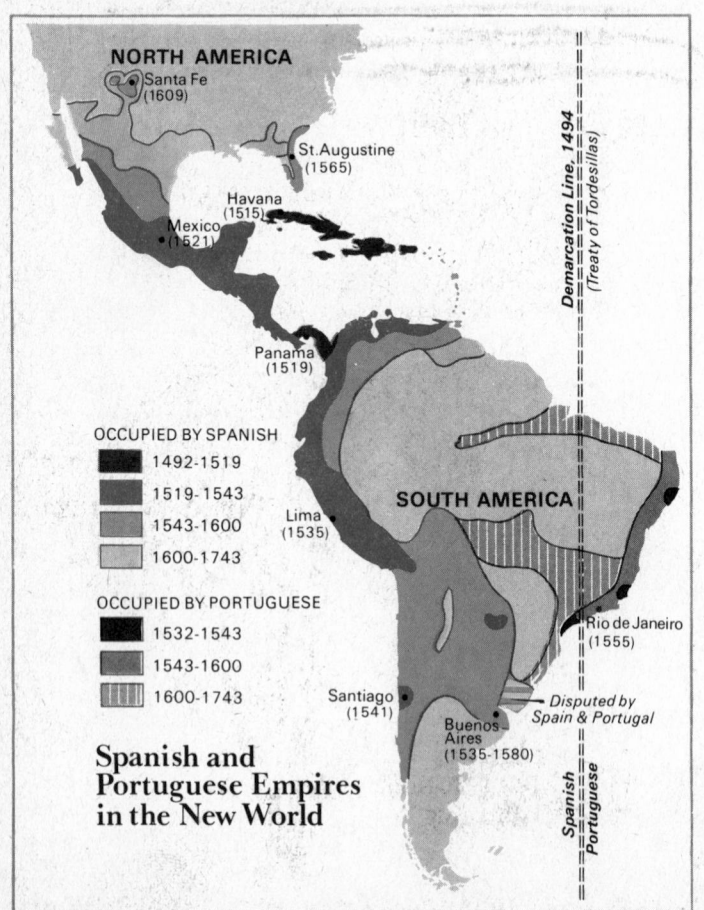

NORTH AMERICA
Santa Fe (1609)
St. Augustine (1565)
Havana (1515)
Mexico (1521)
Panama (1519)

Demarcation Line, 1494 (Treaty of Tordesillas)

OCCUPIED BY SPANISH
1492-1519
1519-1543
1543-1600
1600-1743

OCCUPIED BY PORTUGUESE
1532-1543
1543-1600
1600-1743

Lima (1535)

SOUTH AMERICA

Rio de Janeiro (1555)

Santiago (1541)
Buenos Aires (1535-1580)

Disputed by Spain & Portugal

Spanish
Portuguese

Spanish and Portuguese Empires in the New World

or contested, those powers with the viceroys. More clearly subordinate to the viceroyalties were lesser jurisdictions—*presidencias* and captaincies general—that were deliberately created as administrative subdivisions of the larger territorial governments.

These were the main jurisdictions. Below them lay a range of inferior units, whose chief officers were usually appointed by the viceroys or *audiencias*, with the approval of the Council of the Indies, and only occasionally by the crown itself. And below them, the lowest unit of civil government was the municipal corporation, or *cabildo*. Finally, in various lateral connections with the whole of this imperial hierarchy were various investigating and superintending officials appointed in Spain to strengthen the crown's authority throughout its American territories.

This elaborate structure of royal government was neither altogether rational in its construction, nor altogether efficient in its operation, nor altogether comprehensive in its reach. There were gaps and clumsy overlaps in authority. Subordinate jurisdictions, especially in the remote territories, found many ways of ignoring the superior authorities; and corruption was widespread, at least at the lower ranges of the hierarchy. Yet despite these weaknesses, the Spanish empire functioned for over three hundred years as a reasonably coherent state system, however inefficient its workings might appear to a modern analyst. And it was a system that was largely unchallenged. Of course there was resistance to this or that unpopular regulation and to the rule of any number of obnoxious officers sent out from Spain. But there was no openly organized political opposition to the state, only the passive refusal to comply with unacceptable or unenforceable crown orders, a pattern of action that was familiarly described by the formula, "I obey but I do not execute." Nor was there a body of ideas that would justify sustained opposition to the crown, nor political leaders experienced in challenging the authority of the state and motivated to do so. When in the end, more than three hundred years after its founding, Spain's empire in America succumbed to corruption, misgovernment, and rising democratic aspirations, there was no corps of native politicians capable of managing free governments and of creating responsible and stable self-government. And the doctrines that shaped the Latin American independence movement of the early nineteenth century were largely alien ideas that expressed only clumsily the particular needs of the Spanish-American people.

Contrast to the British Empire. In all of this, the contrast with British America could hardly be sharper or more significant. There was never an effective structure of imperial government in the Anglo-American empire. The authority of the British crown and of Parliament was scattered through half a dozen uncoordinated agencies of government, and it was never anything but superficial. It seldom penetrated much

Spain's Imperial Government in the New World, 1550

SEVILLE, FIRST CAPITAL OF THE SPANISH AMERICAN EMPIRE, BY ALONZO SANCHEZ COELLO
Linked by short river routes and canals to the Atlantic, Seville prospered enormously in
the sixteenth century. All shipping to and from America had to pass through the city. Its
Consulado, a gild of merchant houses, enjoyed a monopoly of Spanish trade with the New
World. In addition, the city was the seat of the *Casa de Contratación*. *(Museo de América,
Madrid; Mas/Art Reference Bureau)*

beyond the docks or the customs houses, and its control of the American political system was weak. Yet, paradoxically, there was organized resistance to this weak and scattered authority from the start. By the middle of the eighteenth century, resistance had grown into a sophisticated process of competitive politics and had bred politicians long experienced in local self-government. The transition to independence and to responsible self-government in British America was consequently smooth, and, once the War of Independence was concluded, entirely bloodless.

This stark contrast between the Spanish-American and the British-American patterns becomes even more vivid, and paradoxical, if one considers the fact that in the early years of the Spanish-American empire there had existed institutions that could have developed into bases for just the kind of competitive politics that developed in North America. But these institutions, instead of maturing into centers of open competition with the state, withered and disappeared. At the start, for example, the most powerful figures in Latin America were the *adelantados*, feudal lords granted extraordinary powers by the crown to subjugate the American frontiers—executive and judicial powers that were understood from the beginning to be essentially competitive with those of the crown. Yet few of the *adelantados* managed to transmit their authority to a second generation. Similarly, the *encomiendas*, which in the sixteenth century constituted another potential threat to the overall authority of the state, were eliminated as bases of political competition. Transferred as an institution from Spain to America in 1502, the *encomienda* was a grant of the labor of a specific number of native Indians—in effect a gift of slaves or serfs—and the land they occupied. The crown had intended to protect the natives by charging the grantees with responsibility for the Indians' spiritual and physical well-being, but the *encomiendas* quickly became the instrument of the most vicious oppression. The crown, determined to eliminate the institution, gradually succeeded in reducing the powers of the four thousand or so *encomenderos,* draining away their incomes and eliminating the heritability of the original grants. By the early eighteenth century the *encomienda* was no longer a political danger to the crown. In similar ways the threat of other, lesser competing political authorities—provincial assemblies and municipal corporations—was eliminated or reduced.

Why had all of these semi-independent agencies and institutions weakened or been absorbed into the state apparatus? Why had organized competitive politics died almost at birth in Spanish America while in British America it grew so quickly and so strongly? There is no simple explanation for this, but there were certain circumstances in Spanish America that form at least part of an explanation, and these circumstances contrast sharply with the conditions that shaped the development of the British American communities.

From the very start the crown—Ferdinand and Isabella in the first instance—actively and directly asserted its authority. Even before Columbus's discovery had been made, the monarchy had asserted its rule over lands conquered in its name, and not merely as commercial regulation but as territorial government in depth. The Spanish monarchs declared the whole of America to be a separate kingdom of the crown of Castile, its native peoples direct subjects of the crown, and its governmental jurisdictions subordinate agencies of the crown. This declaration was supported by the highest moral agency of the Western world, the papacy. Various papal bulls and encyclicals assigned the responsibility for the welfare of the natives, which meant primarily the task of converting them to Christianity, to the Castilian monarch. From that central Christian responsibility, jurists and theologians developed a massive body of legal, political, and theological commentary that strongly reinforced and justified the claims of the Spanish monarch to personal rule in America. And there were no competing intellectual

centers from which contrary ideas could develop. The Catholic church, conservative in doctrine and royalist in politics, dominated the intellectual life of Latin America. Far from Spanish America proving to be a legitimate refuge for religious dissenters, as British America would become, it developed into a more tightly controlled bastion of Catholic orthodoxy than Spain itself. Dissenters and heretics of all kinds were barred by law from emigrating to America.

Yet declarations and political theory do not in themselves create political realities. There was something in the situation in Spanish America that guaranteed a welcome for the crown's supremacy and that helped stifle competitive institutions at their birth. If one turns from institutions to population characteristics and asks what groups had the capacity to maintain an active opposition to the crown and would have had an interest in organizing such opposition, the situation becomes clearer.

The Spanish-American Population. There were four principal social categories in the Spanish-American population, of which the most numerous by far was that of the native Indians. The Aztecs, the Incas, and the other native Americans whom the Spanish encountered were advanced people in certain ways; but to Europeans of the time they were primitive, particularly in technology and weaponry, and they were helpless before the onslaught of the Spanish conquerers. People in good social discipline, numerous, and stable in location, the native Americans quickly became a mass laboring population, and they were incapable of organizing their own political institutions to speak against the state.

At the other extreme from the native Indians were the major imperial officeholders—the viceroys, *audiencia* judges, high church officials, and governors—who might most readily have created areas of independent authority. But the crown's policies in recruiting and controlling these officers prevented them from moving in that direction. The great majority of the high officers of church and state who served in Spanish America in the three hundred years of the colonial period were Peninsular Spaniards—that is, men born in the Iberian Peninsula, unaffiliated with American interests, and committed to returning to Spain after

TWO VIEWS OF THE FABULOUS SILVER MINE AT POTOSÍ
The external view appears in an atlas by Hermann
Moll, c. 1709–1720. The interior view (opposite) is an
imaginative depiction by De Bry which captures something of the degradation suffered by the Indian miners.
Thousands of these forced laborers perished in that
"mouth of hell" 16,000 feet above sea level. The wealth
produced at Potosí for over two centuries after the
mine's discovery in 1545 was stupendous, but the cost
in human suffering by whole populations of helpless
natives, slaving underground by dim candlelight for
days on end, was immeasurably greater. The city of
Potosí itself (in modern Bolivia) had a population of
120,000 by 1572 but remained a tumultuous mining
camp throughout the colonial period, swarming with
gamblers, prostitutes, and adventurers of all kinds.
(Above, Harvard College Library; opposite, Rare Book Division,
New York Public Library)

completing their tour of duty abroad. Further, controls were devised to limit any possible independence
these officials might have developed. Their tenure in
office was strictly limited; they were circulated within
the imperial system to prevent their acquiring too
strong an identification with any particular locality;
they were dependent on the crown treasury for their
salaries; and they were subjected to rigorous scru-
tinies of their conduct of office.

A third group was that of the Creoles, the American-born leaders of Spanish descent. Under favorable
conditions they might well have provided the initiative and organization for a vigorous political life,
for as opposed to the Indians they were politically
sophisticated, and as opposed to most high church
and state officers they were Americans, with American interests. And indeed, there were conflicts
between Creoles and Spanish officials, particularly
over officeholding and the enforcement of trade regulations. Further, late in the colonial period the sale
of public offices by the bankrupt Spanish state gave

descent, which distinguished them racially from the mass of the population. As a consequence, despite their local interests, they continued to identify themselves with Spain, which was the source of their status, wealth, and power.

Finally, there were two other groups in the Spanish-American population: the blacks, who were imported as slaves and who never acquired an active political role; and, politically more important, the large segment of the population that was racially mixed. By the 1570s the racially mixed elements constituted appoximately 2.5 percent of the entire populace. By the end of the colonial period that figure had risen to over 30 percent (another striking contrast to British America, where the racially mixed population was numerically insignificant). There was a great variety of racial combinations, but the most important element by far was the *mestizos*, those of mixed European and Indian ancestry. Yet, though numerous, the *mestizos* in general were felt to be socially inferior to the dominant Spanish elements and constituted a lower middle class of small farmers and shopkeepers. In a society where status, wealth, and power were controlled by those of pure Spanish heritage, *mestizos* avoided asserting their identities through politics and tended to escape by fitting themselves as inconspicuously as possible into the situation as it existed. It would take a profound cultural change to release their suppressed aspirations and free them to assume effective political roles. When that took place, and only then, the colonial era of Spanish-American history was over.

These population characteristics, utterly different from the characteristics of the British-American world, go far toward explaining the failure of a free competitive political system to develop in colonial Spanish America despite the availability of institutions that originally could have supported such politics. The small elite of high state officials was bound to Spain in every way. The Creoles were a small self-conscious ruling class whose well-being, in the great sea of native Indians, blacks, and racially mixed, depended on a continuing identification with the sources of authority in Europe. Only the racially mixed were disposed to move toward political autonomy, but

Creoles increasing access to public authority. But in general the Creoles' small numbers and their social situation shaped a dependent political role. Of the total population of more than 9 million in Spanish America in the 1570s, only 118,000 or 1.25 percent were Creoles. In the entire first century of Spain's colonial period, approximately 240,000 Spaniards emigrated to America. The contrast with British America is startling. In the equivalent period (to 1700), approximately 400,000 emigrants had left the British Isles for America alone, a yearly average two-thirds greater than that of the Spanish. The occupational character of the Creole population followed directly from their numbers. A thin overlay on a very large population of natives, these Americans of European descent never constituted the mass base of the social structure. They filled the upper strata of the American communities; they were landowners, clerics, army officers, and merchants. Their identity as a ruling class, and consequently their well-being, derived not from their American birth but from their European through most of three centuries they lacked the self-esteem, the numbers, and the experience to devise effective political weapons against the overwhelming Spanish establishment.

England's Overseas Expansion

England's entry into the Western Hemisphere was the very opposite of Spain's. Where Spain had been swift, England was slow; where Spain had been deliberate and decisive, England was muddled in purpose. For Spain, America almost immediately yielded immense wealth; for England, it created, at the start at least, more losses than profits. At no point were the differences more extreme and more consequential than at the very beginning of exploration and settlement.

PORTUGUESE CARRACKS OF THE EARLY SIXTEENTH CENTURY, PAINTING ATTRIBUTED TO CORNELIS ANTHONISZOON
These massive, high-built, unwieldy vessels designed for maximum freight capacity played a vital role in transoceanic shipping of the sixteenth century. The largest, over 1,800 tons, could carry 700 passengers and a cargo of 900 tons. *(National Maritime Museum, Greenwich)*

For no less than fifty years, while Spain was conquering and exploiting vast areas of Central America and South America, England did nothing to develop its claim to North America. That claim had been established in 1497-98 when John Cabot, commissioned by Henry VII, had discovered and begun the exploration of Newfoundland, Labrador, and Nova Scotia. His son Sebastian had continued the exploration into the Hudson Bay region of Canada in 1508-09, but throughout the reign of Henry VIII (1509-47) neither the crown nor private enterprise showed any interest in developing these distant territories. The only English contact with America that remained through these years was the work of fishermen from the west country of England—Cornwall, Devonshire, Dorsetshire—who, together with fishermen from France, Spain, and Portugal, had begun to exploit the wealth of the Grand Banks off Newfoundland and the coastal waters around the mouth of the St. Lawrence River. They became familiar with the southern Canadian and northern New England coasts and built crude shacks for their immediate convenience during the fishing seasons, but they made no attempt to establish permanent settlements or otherwise assert England's claim to the land.

Then suddenly, in the early 1550s, the situation was transformed, and in this sudden reversal are to be found the beginnings of British colonization. This development was complex, and it is as important to understand what did not happen as it is to know what did happen. For there was no sudden eruption of interest in overseas settlement as such, and there was no sudden determination on the part of England to assert its claim to America. Instead there were two basic shifts in orientation, both of which would eventually involve colonization but neither of which was originally directed to that goal. The first shift was in England's economy, the second in its international relations.

Economic and Diplomatic Changes. England's prosperity in the first half of the sixteenth century had been based on the growing European demand for its raw wool and woolen cloth, marketed largely in Antwerp, in what is now Belgium. Through the reign of Henry VIII more and more capital and labor had become involved in this dominant commercial enterprise, more and more arable land had been turned to pasturing sheep, and England's financial stability had become increasingly dependent on Antwerp. Then in the late 1540s this elaborate commercial structure began to weaken. By 1550 the Antwerp market was saturated, and in 1551 it collapsed. Cloth exports fell off 35 percent within a year, and the financial world was thrown into turmoil. The merchants were forced to reconsider the whole of their activities. New markets would have to be found, new routes of trade devised, and capital risked in ways that a previous generation wold have thought wildly speculative.

Changes in England's international position helped channel these suddenly mobilized energies. Antagonism with France had dominated England's policies through the reign of Henry VIII, and in this rivalry Spain had been England's natural ally. As a result England had been willing to respect Spain's claim to the whole of the Western Hemisphere, which had been set out in papal bulls in 1493 and in the Spanish-Portuguese Treaty of Tordesillas (1494), assuring Spain of its title to all of the Western Hemisphere 370 leagues west of the Cape Verde Islands. England had found it diplomatically useful to support this claim, at least tacitly, and the support was confirmed by the marriage of England's Queen Mary (1553–58) to Philip II of Spain.

But the accession of Queen Elizabeth in 1558 began a reversal in international relations as England's Protestantism began to dominate its foreign policy. By the 1560s it was clear that Spain threatened England's independence as a Protestant nation and that England's long-range interests in Europe lay in the support of the rebellious Protestants in France and of the Protestant Netherlands struggling to free themselves from Spanish rule. From an ally of Spain, England had become an enemy, and while England felt too weak until the 1580s to engage in open warfare with the great imperial power, the country had every reason to want to harass and plunder Spanish territories in any way possible.

Thus, impelled by a sudden economic need to break out of the safe, conservative commerce of earlier years, and no longer hesitant to attack Spain's

ELIZABETH I BY M. GHEERAERTS THE YOUNGER
As shrewd in politics as she was cautious in finance, Elizabeth sponsored England's overseas adventures by subtle means until she was ready to challenge Spain directly in 1585. *(National Portrait Gallery, London)*

overseas territories, England entered a new phase in its history—but not by plunging directly and immediately into colonization. Its response to the economic and diplomatic shifts took several forms, and only eventually, and almost incidentally, did it involve overseas settlement. In response to the new economic pressures foreign merchants were expelled from the realm, and English merchants were favored in the conduct of trade. Land that had been converted to sheep grazing was forced back into tillage; textile production was limited; and entry into trade by newcomers was restrained. Above all, the commercial community poured capital into a search for new kinds of overseas commerce and for new, distant markets independent of European middlemen. In 1555 enterprising merchants formed the Guinea Company for trade to Africa and the Muscovy Company for trade with Russia. In 1579 the Eastland Company organized English trade to the Baltic. In 1581 the Levant Company was created to control England's commerce with the Middle East. Finally, a series of contacts with India and Southeast Asia led to the creation of the East India Company in 1600.

These were legitimate and official enterprises. During the same years, risk capital, some of it drawn secretly from royal sources, went into semipiratical raids on Spanish commerce and Spanish shipping. These enterprises began in 1562 when John Hawkins of Plymouth broke into the Spanish trade monopoly of the West Indies and the South American mainland with the first of a series of illegal but highly lucrative peddling voyages, the third of which, in 1567, led to open conflict with the Spanish. Francis Drake took up the challenge at that point and began what proved to be twenty years of wildly adventurous raids on Spanish colonial properties, the culmination of which was his famous circumnavigation of the globe in 1577–80, a joint-stock enterprise which yielded, among other results, 4,600 percent profit to the shareholders.

By then English interest in the Western Hemisphere was rising—not primarily as a location for English colonies but as a route to Asian markets. The Cabots' explorations were recalled, and new information, commercial and geographical, flowed in to help justify the enthusiasm of a group of adventurers from the west of England. This group, led by Sir Humphrey Gilbert, determined to find a northwestern passage through the Western Hemisphere into the Far East. In 1565 the Privy Council heard a formal debate on possible new routes. The Muscovy merchants, naturally enough, urged endorsement of efforts to find an *eastern* passage, north of Siberia, and to exploit the Baltic hinterland. The westcountry gentry, long familiar with the North American coastal waters, urged

ESKIMO MAN, WOMAN, AND CHILD, BROUGHT BACK TO ENGLAND BY FROBISHER IN 1577

John White (see p. 20) accompanied Frobisher on his second voyage (1577) to Frobisher Bay, an inlet on the coast of Baffin Island, northeast of Hudson Bay, and probably sketched these three captured Eskimos on shipboard. The woman, whose child peeks out from within her hood, is tattooed in blue around the eyes. The Eskimos were sensations in Bristol, where they demonstrated the use of their kayak, but they died within a month of their arrival. Frobisher was convinced that the bay he found was the northwest passage leading to China and that ore picked up at the mouth of the bay contained gold. But his efforts to establish a mining settlement along the bay failed miserably even before it became clear that the ore contained no gold. *(Reproduced by courtesy of Trustees of the British Museum)* expeditions to the *west,* through the north of what is now Canada. Gilbert and the westerners were defeated in that debate, but with their support, in 1576–78, an enterprising mariner, Martin Frobisher, led three expeditions to the region northeast of Hudson Bay. He and his London backers, led by a merchant, Michael Lok, organized the short-lived Company of Cathay in response to the reports of gold—which later proved to be false—that were carried back. There were continuous frustrations for all of these western initiatives, but the search for the northwest passage went on, yielding in the end, after vain and desperate efforts to get through the ice and snow of the Canadian wilderness, a reasonably clear picture of that region of the globe.

First Attempts at Colonization. Gradually, within all of these overseas enterprises, the idea of colonization slowly developed. In his appearance before the Privy Council in 1565 Gilbert had suggested the value of colonies as way stations along the proposed routes to the Far East, and in 1578 he sought and received a crown charter for establishing a colony in America.

Gilbert's attempt in 1578 to establish a colony in New England or Nova Scotia—the first English effort to colonize in the Western Hemisphere—failed almost before it began. His small exploratory fleet was scattered by storms and diverted by the lure of privateering. Yet in the process of launching this first colonizing expedition, Gilbert acquired valuable experience in attempting to finance such ventures. He also engaged the enthusiasm of his gifted half-brother, Sir Walter Raleigh, in such ventures as these and drew into this realm of enterprise the two Richard Hakluyts, experts on overseas geography, who became important propagandists of colonization. The younger Hakluyt's *Discourse of Western Planting* (1584) shows the mingling of motives that existed in this advanced circle of enthusiasts. It was England's duty, Hakluyt argued, to Christianize the American pagans, especially since an American colony would provide a base for attacks on Spanish lands and Spanish treasure ships. More important would be the long-term economic gains from American colonies; they could supply England with exotic goods otherwise bought from Spain and create new markets for English consumer goods while at the

SIR WALTER RALEIGH AND HIS SON, 1602
Raleigh was an accomplished poet, soldier, courtier, and politician, and like many intellectuals of his time he was fascinated by geographical exploration and by the possibilities of overseas settlements—in Ireland as well as in America. He helped draw into the leadership of exploration and colonization the interrelated landed gentry of England's west country. The failure of his Roanoke settlement showed the impossibility of financing settlements in America by individual or family efforts. *(National Portrait Gallery, London)*

same time drawing off England's unemployed workers and turning their labor to advantage. New routes to Asia, new weapons against Spain, a new source of exotic supplies, and a new market for English goods as well as a new use for England's "surplus" population—all this would justify England's support for colonization.

Raleigh's and Hakluyt's ideas were not widely shared, and they did not become state policy. In 1584, after Gilbert had died on a voyage from Newfoundland, Queen Elizabeth transferred his patent to Raleigh, but she kept her government from directly supporting his plans for colonization. She made a minor contribution to financing a new expedition that he planned and gave his enterprise her personal blessing, but otherwise her government did nothing to help launch or sustain the famous "lost colony" that Raleigh established in America in 1585. This one English American settlement of the sixteenth century was thus of necessity almost entirely the *private* undertaking of a group of merchants and gentlemen from the west of England.

The history of this first English colony in the Western Hemisphere is quickly told. In three successive years separate groups of settlers were landed on Roanoke Island, a heavily wooded spot off the coast of North Carolina. The first group, 108 men, arrived there in 1585. They quickly fell out with the natives, ran through their food supplies as they explored the North Carolina coastal waters, and returned to England hurriedly the next year with Francis Drake when he unexpectedly appeared on his way home from a successful raid on the West Indies. Later that year—1586 —the second group, 18 men, was left behind by a party sent out to relieve the original group, but this forlorn and helpless crew was soon slaughtered by the Indians. The island was therefore deserted when, the next summer, 1587, the third and main contingent, consisting of 117 men, women, and children, arrived under Governor John White. What happened to this largest and best-equipped group of Raleigh's settlers has never been discovered. White was obliged to return quickly to England to speed on more supplies, but the threat of open war with Spain and the attractions of privateering kept relief vessels from reaching the colony. It was only in 1590 that White finally managed to return, to find the settlers gone. Apparently they had moved off to Croatoan Island, to the south in the outer banks of Pamlico Sound, and White could not follow them there. Their disappearance marks the end of Raleigh's efforts at colonization.

A fumbling, failing, almost pathetic affair, all of this, next to the bold and hugely successful first thrusts of the Spanish in America. Yet Raleigh's Roanoke venture is as revealing of the basic conditions that would later, in the seventeenth century, shape the successful English settlements as it is of the limitations that defeated colonization in the reign of Elizabeth.

INDIAN VILLAGE OF SECOTON AND A CHIEF'S WIFE AND DAUGHTER
These watercolors are from a portifolio of accurate and superbly colored scenes of Indian life and the natural environment made by John White on his voyages to Raleigh's "Virginia" in 1585 and 1587. Note the three plantings of corn, and the child's doll in English dress. *(Reproduced by Courtesy of the Trustees of The British Museum)*

Bay of
Chesepians

(Hampton
Roads)

(Cape Henry)

(Dismal

Swamp)

ATLANTIC

OCEAN

Chawan R.

Moratuc R. (Roanoke R.)

Trinitie Harbro
Inlet, 1585

(Kitty Hawk)

(Albemarle Sound) Occam

English Settlement
Roanoke I.

Inlets in 1585

(Cape Kanrick)
(Wimble Shoals)

Hatarask I.

Paquippe
Mattamuskeet
L.

Neus R.

Cipo (Pamlico R.)

M E N T S O
(Pamlico Sound)

Cape Hatteras
(Diamond
Shoals)

Croatoan I.

Approx. Shoreline,
1590

Inlet in 1585
(Okracoke Inlet)

Wococon Inlet
in 1585

Neus R.

Raleigh's Virginia, 1584-1590

♙ Indian Settlements

(Cape Henry) Modern Names in Parentheses

Outer Shorelines Approximate as in Raleigh's Time

0   10   20   30

Miles

Cape Feare
(Cape Lookout)

Lookout
Shoals

Modern Cape Fear is
50 Miles to the Southwest

Personnel and the Role of the State

Several things of permanent importance had become clear during these earliest and least successful years of English colonization in America. In England, there was a leadership group available for colonization quite different from the Spanish *conquistadores,* "drunk with a heroic and brutal dream," as a Spanish poet later described them. Where the Spanish conquerors were the sons of impoverished farmers and townsmen, many of them illiterate, the leaders of English overseas enterprise—Gilbert, Raleigh, Grenville, Hawkins, Drake—were the well-educated younger sons of the westcountry gentry, bred in secure landed establishments, familiar with the sea from childhood, barred by the laws favoring eldest sons from inheriting family properties, and eager somehow to reestablish themselves on the land in the same genteel condition they had known before.

Second, it was clear that there was in England a mass of laborers available for emigration to overseas colonies. London was swollen with unemployed workers (its population rose from 60,000 in 1500 to 200,000 in 1600). The countryside was swarming with migrant farmhands called by contemporaries "sturdy beggars"; and in the centers of the wool industry—the west country and East Anglia (Essex, Suffolk, and Norfolk)—underemployment was already generating the discontent that would express itself forcefully in the religious protest of Puritanism. Elizabethans spoke of the "multitude of increase in our people." Responsible officials were convinced that England was overpopulated and its well-being threatened by an idle labor force that consumed more than it contributed to the general fund of wealth: "Our land hath not milk sufficient in the breast thereof to nourish all those children which it hath brought forth." For many, the most attractive remedy was colonization and emigration. But though the population of England and Wales rose from just over 3 million in 1550 to just over 4 million in 1600 to 5.2 million in 1695, and in the next twenty-five years increased by another 800,000, there was, in fact, no absolute "surplus" of people, as seventeenth-century English analysts came to realize. The sense of overpopulation was created by the widespread displacement of a mass population and an exceptionally high

THE CHEAPSIDE-CORNHILL DISTRICT OF LONDON, 1658

From this swarming urban concentration came hundreds of emigrants, joining a multitude of others from the countryside to settle England's first colonies in America. *(From William Faithorne and Richard Newcourt's* Exact Delineation of the Cities of London and Westminster . . .*)*

degree of geographical mobility that resulted from rapid economic growth, from inflation, and from the commercialization of agriculture. But however they were perceived, these developments—which made available for recruitment a mass of ordinary farm and town workers—would prove to be crucial to the early peopling of British North America.

Third, it became evident that there was capital available in sizable amounts for investment in overseas ventures, as well as entrepreneurial interest in mobilizing that capital and directing it to profitable uses in colonization. The costs of financing the Roanoke voyages and the first efforts at colonization had been borne almost entirely by the westcountry gentry, but their resources were clearly inadequate to support further, larger-scale efforts. In 1589 Raleigh transferred control of the Virginia enterprise to a London business syndicate headed by Sir Thomas Smith, one of the most powerful merchants of the age. The capital available to these merchants was far greater than that of the westcountry gentry, and it would be these men of business who would launch the first new wave of colonization in the early seventeenth century.

It had become clear, too, that when efforts at colonization would be resumed (as plans and probes in the later years of Elizabeth's reign indicated they would be), the role of the crown would continue to be minimal. The crown would legalize exploration and settlement, and it would exert some supervision of the plans that were made, but it would initiate nothing and organize nothing, nor would it sustain or reinforce any enterprise that was undertaken. More important, the English crown had no desire to extend its direct rule over distant territories conquered or settled by Englishmen. Some form of government would be provided, but it would not be crown government in depth. The burden of governing colonies, like the burden of financing them, would be borne not by the crown but by the enterpreneurs of settlement or by the settlers themselves. Colonial government, at the start at least, would therefore of necessity be self-government of some sort, and the imperial organization as it evolved would be a superstructure, an overlay imposed on semi-independent units of local government.

JAMES I, PORTRAIT ATTRIBUTED TO JAN DE CRITZ, C. 1620
(National Maritime Museum, Greenwich)

Financial Limitations and the "Starving Times"

Peace with Spain in 1604 released the powerful expansionist impulses that had been building up in England for half a century. The resulting lunge into overseas enterprise in the reigns of James I (1603–25) and his son Charles I (1625–49) was spectacular. The famous settlements at Jamestown, at Plymouth, and around the Massachusetts Bay were only fragments of a great mosaic of efforts that reached into many parts of the globe, that involved hundreds of thousands of Englishmen of all descriptions, and that cost millions of pounds sterling. In this great expansion,

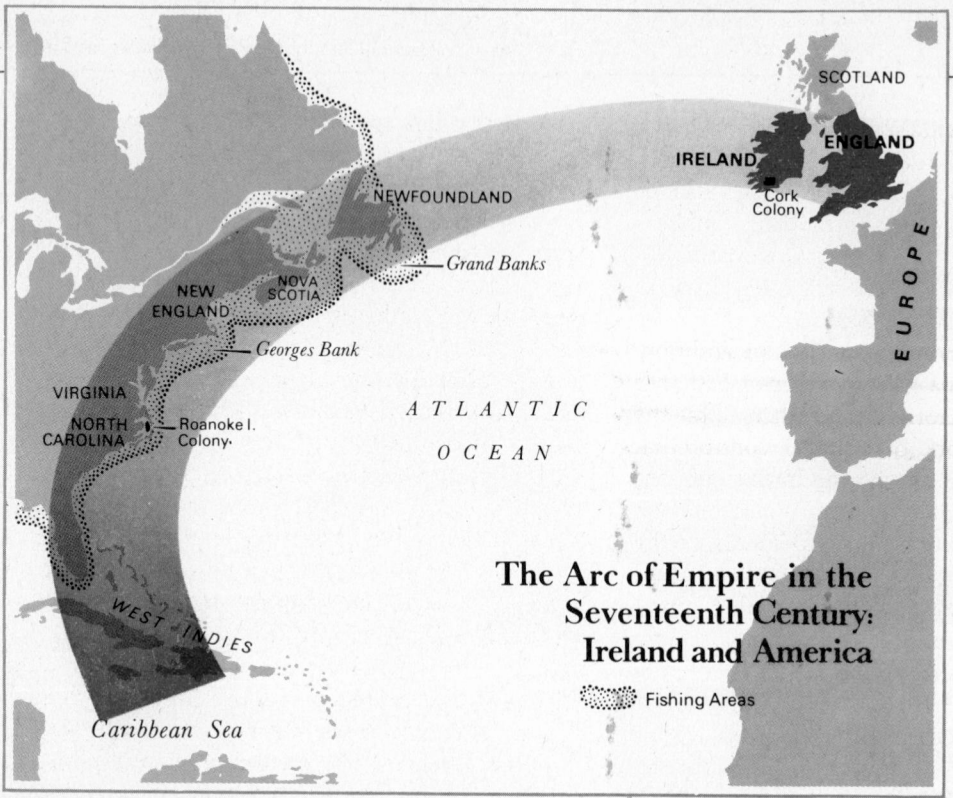

The Arc of Empire in the Seventeenth Century: Ireland and America

Fishing Areas

the chief center of colonization was not North America but Ireland, which had been the scene of England's first extensive and sustained efforts at overseas colonization. Henry VIII's failure to bind the Irish chiefs to him by feudal ties and gradually to infuse elements of English law and religion into his rebellious population had led, in 1566, to military conquest by the English. British communities were then transplanted to enclaves in southern Ireland which formed a "pale of settlement" against what were seen as utterly savage and ungovernable natives.

By 1604 Ireland and America were seen as equivalent centers of overseas expansion and they were linked geographically in Englishmen's minds. As they looked out at the world beyond England they saw a single arc of overseas territories suitable for colonization sweeping north and west from Britain, enclosing Ireland, Newfoundland, and the mainland coast of North America south to the Caribbean. It was therefore natural that nearby Ireland, which was described in a travel book of 1617 as "this famous island in the Virginia sea," would be the first and primary object of colonization in the explosion of

enterprise of the early seventeenth century. When in 1607 two of the most powerful Irish earls, resisting the authority of the English crown, fled from the British Isles, their vast properties, ultimately six of the nine counties of the northern province of Ulster, were confiscated. This immense territory was largely cleared of its native population and offered for sale to prospective "planters." London's city government and the largest gild corporations took up large grants. After the Irish rebellion of 1641 (which many linked to the Indian rebellion of 1622 in Virginia), 7 million more acres were cleared of their native inhabitants. Thousands of the native Irish were subjected to severe punishment for their involvement—proven or suspected—in the rebellion, and most of the Irish were driven beyond the English pale. Into these Irish plantations, in the same years that the North American settlements were being established, came a steady stream of English and Scottish emigrants. By 1642 an estimated 120,000 English and Scottish men, women, and children had settled in Ireland, a migration six times greater than the famous "Great Migration" that settled New England in the same period. Yet the Ulster plantation was only one, if the most extensive, of the colonization efforts of the time. Besides Ireland, and besides Virginia and Massachusetts, English settlements were established in Bermuda, in the Caribbean (Providence Island, Barbados, Saint Christopher, Nevis, Montserrat, Antigua), in Newfoundland, in Canada, in Nova Scotia, and on the mainland coast of South America. In addition, fragile contacts with India were developed first into flourishing trading "factories" and then into the beginning of the network of political control that would eventually cover much of the Indian subcontinent.

In this global context the first settlements on the mainland of North America were relatively small undertakings, and their early histories become understandable only in terms of the pattern of the greater whole. For while these American communities would ultimately acquire a unique historical importance, originally they shared characteristics common to the rest of these earliest seventeenth-century enterprises. And of these common characteristics none was more important than the way in which they were financed.

The Financing of the Colonies. Whatever their founders' ultimate dreams may have been, these earliest English colonies—whether in Newfoundland or Barbados, Ulster, Plymouth, or Virginia—were of necessity financed at the start by profit-seeking joint-stock companies. Eleven commercial companies bore the main financial burden of the settlements launched before 1640. They raised their capital (an estimated £13 million) by selling stock to a remarkably broad range of the English population. Thousands invested—landowners as well as merchants, people of ordinary means as well as those of wealth. And the management of the funds generated by these investments was, for the most part, in the hands of businessmen who worked not only within the usual constraints of business operations but also under two very special pressures; and these pressures explain much of the hardship and tragedy of life in the earliest American settlements.

First, the joint stocks—the initial capital funds —of these ventures were not expected to endure. Shareholders did not expect to leave their funds in

these companies and draw a steady income in dividends from them, but rather to benefit from the quick liquidation of the entire enterprise at the end of a single voyage or a set number of years, at which time the original capital plus whatever profits had accumulated would be distributed. Whether there would be any further investments beyond this initial one would depend on the business prospect when this complete division of the company's assets was made. The settlers, many of whom were in effect employees of these companies for a stated term of years, were consequently placed under great pressure to produce an immediate profit for the company. If they failed to ship back tangible proof of the financial value of the settlement, they would be cut off to fend for themselves as best they could. As a consequence, instead of searching carefully into the strange American environment, they spent time scrabbling for evidence of gold in every shallow stream, searching for routes to the Pacific Ocean around the bend of every broad river, and plunging almost suicidally into the backcountry to verify garbled Indian rumors of great cities or of vast sources of furs or precious metals.

The pressure on the settlers was further intensified by the technical fact that the legal liability of stockholders in these early joint-stock companies was unlimited. The backers of the settlements were personally liable, without limit, for any debts the settlement companies might incur, and they were therefore extremely sensitive to the possibility of failure. They had no choice but to abandon doubtful enterprises as quickly as possible.

The "Starving Times." The result was desperation and starvation, at times complete chaos, in these first colonies, and bankruptcy in the companies that first colonized mainland North America. For there were only three possible sources of quick profits: surface resources of great value in proportion to weight and bulk that might simply be lifted into boats and sent back to the investors; a docile native population that might be organized quickly into labor gangs to dig out less accessible resources; and the discovery of new routes to rich, exotic markets. None of these possibilities proved realistic on the coasts of North America, and as a consequence in the early years the life-sustaining supplies, after the first shipments, were withheld from the settlements, and one after another the companies failed. Sheer accident provided most of the profits that actually accrued at the start. In Bermuda, for example, ambergris, a secretion of whales used in making perfume and medicine, was found in large quantities; a shipment worth £10,000 saved the Bermuda Company, which later profited steadily from tobacco production. Similarly, the Providence Island Company had the good fortune to capture a Spanish treasure ship worth £50,000.

Such lucky accidents were rare, however. Almost every one of the companies that financed settlements in British North America failed, sooner or later, and as they did so the original investors sought desperately to find secondary sources of profit. Some of the stockholders, seeking to recover their losses, funded "magazines"—stores of goods to be sold at high prices to the desperate settlers. Some set up separately financed enterprises: glass and silk were favored in Virginia. Others attempted to develop "private plantations," that is, personal estates and jurisdictions in the new land given to them in place of the missing profits. The Virginia Company alone created fifty of these private domains. But few of these secondary enterprises succeeded. Perhaps the most successful subordinate joint stock created within the Virginia Company was the fund established to send over a hundred "maids" to Jamestown "to be made wives of." The investors in this venture realized 47 percent profit on their shares when they sold the women's work contracts to the colonists.

As the financial prospects dimmed, the investors withdrew altogether from the ventures. Often the colonists, cut off by their backers, found the transition to self-sustained community life desperately difficult. Even in the best of circumstances the first inhabitants of Jamestown or Bermuda or Plymouth would have had a shock in adjusting to the wilderness environment. Forced to search for sources of immediate profit while neglecting some of the most elemental provisions for survival, many found the struggle unendurable, and succumbed—to despair, to the ravages of disease, and to the harassment of hostile natives.

The narratives of the first settlements make painful reading. There was heroism, but there was murderous selfishness as well; there was industry, but also laziness and at times suicidal inertia. Death and misery were everywhere. It is perhaps not surprising that the best organized and most successful of the earliest communities were those dominated by passionate religious convictions. For only the transcendent goals, the fierce determination, and the inner certainty of the Pilgrim and Puritan leaders could withstand the disintegrating effects of the "starving times."

CHRONOLOGY

1492-1504	Columbus's four voyages to New World.
1494	Treaty of Tordesillas divides non-Christian world between Spain and Portugal.
1497-98	John Cabot explores Newfoundland, Labrador, and Nova Scotia, and establishes English claim to North America.
1503	Spain establishes board of trade, *Casa de Contratación.*
1508-9	Sebastian Cabot explores Hudson Bay region.
1509-47	Reign of Henry VIII.
1513	Balboa discovers Pacific Ocean after crossing Isthmus of Panama.
1513	Ponce de León discovers mainland of Florida.
1519-21	Cortés conquers Mexico.
1523	Verrazano explores coast of North America, establishing French claim.
1523-30	Spaniards conquer Honduras and Guatemala.
1524	Spain creates Council of the Indies.
1528-36	Cabeza de Vaca explores northern periphery of Gulf of Mexico, west to Gulf of California.
1532-35	Pizarro conquers Peru.

1534	Cartier's explorations establish French claim to St. Lawrence basin.	**1566**	England begins conquest of Ireland.
1535	Viceroyalty of New Spain created.	**1574**	Gilbert leads expedition to Hudson Bay.
1535-39	Initial Spanish conquest of Ecuador, Chile, northern Argentina, and Bolivia.	**1577-80**	Drake circumnavigates globe.
1539-41	De Soto explores southeastern United States and discovers the Mississippi.	**1578**	Gilbert fails to establish colony in North America.
1540-42	Coronado seeks legendary cities of wealth in North American Southwest.	**1584**	Richard Hakluyt (the younger) publishes *A Discourse on Western Planting.*
1540-53	Valdivia extends Spanish conquest of Chile.	**1585-87**	Raleigh fails to establish Roanoke Colony.
1542	Viceroyalty of Peru established.	**1585-98**	England colonizes Ireland.
1551	Antwerp market for English woolen goods fails.	**1603-25**	Reign of James I.
1553-58	Queen Mary reigns in England.	**1603-35**	In eleven voyages, Samuel de Champlain establishes French colonies in Canada.
1558-1603	Elizabeth's reign in England.	**1606**	Virginia Company chartered, includes two subcompanies.
1562-67	Hawkins trades and plunders in Spanish America.	**1607**	English colony established at Jamestown.

SUGGESTED READINGS

The discovery and conquest of Central and South America by Spain had been the subject of some of the greatest narrative histories written in the nineteenth century, notably William H. Prescott's *History of the Conquest of Mexico* (1843) and his *Conquest of Peru* (1847). This tradition of sweeping, dramatic narratives continues in our own time in the writings of Samuel E. Morison, particularly in his biography of Columbus, *Admiral of the Ocean Sea* (2 vol. and 1 vol. eds., 1942, condensed as *Christopher Columbus, Mariner,* 1956), and his *The European Discovery of America: The Southern Voyages, AD 1492-1616* (1974), a volume crowded with maps and photographs that was written after the author retraced the routes of the Spanish discoverers by ship and plane. John H. Parry has sketched the general development of European expansion, geographical discovery, and initial overseas settlements in two very readable books, *Europe and a Wider World, 1415-1715* (1949) and *The Age of Reconnaissance* (1963). And David B. Quinn has written a masterful summary of the first efforts of the Spanish, English and French to explore and settle North America in his *North America from Earliest Discovery to First Settlements* (1977).

There are several good introductory histories of Spanish America in the colonial period: Charles Gipson, *Spain in America* (1966); Hubert Herring, *A History of Latin America from the Beginnings to the Present* (3d ed., 1968), Parts I, II; Bailey W. Diffie, *Latin American Civilization: The Colonial Period* (1945); John H. Parry, *The Spanish Seaborne Empire* (1966); and Salvador de Madariaga, *Rise of the Spanish American Empire* (1947). An equivalent history of the Portuguese-American empire is C. R. Boxer, *The Portuguese Seaborne Empire, 1415-1825* (1969); on the French empire in America, see George M. Wrong, *The Rise and Fall of New France* (2 vols., 1928) and William J. Eccles, *Canada under Louis XIV* (1964) and *Canadian Frontier, 1534-1760* (1969). The best general account of the administrative and constitutional history of Spanish America is Clarence H. Haring, *The Spanish Empire in America* (1947). See also John L. Phelan, "Authority and Flexibility in the Spanish Imperial Bureaucracy," *Administrative Science Quarterly,* 5 (1960-61), 47-65; and for a theoretical analysis of the same subject in sociological terms, see Margali Sarfatti, *Spanish Bureaucratic-Patrimonialism in America* (1966). The underlying ideas of empire are described in John H. Parry, *The Spanish Theory of Empire in the Sixteenth Century* (1940).

On economic history, there are two classic works: Clarence H. Haring, *Trade and Navigation between Spain and the Indies . . .* (1918) and Earl J. Hamilton, *American Treasure and the Price Revolution in Spain, 1501–1650* (1934). In addition, see Peter J. Bakewell, *Silver Mining and Society in Colonial Mexico . . .* (1971); Woodrow W. Borah, *New Spain's Century of Depression (Ibero-Americana, 35, 1951);* and relevant chapters in John Lynch, *Spain under the Hapsburgs* (2 vols., 1964–69).

There are several studies that concentrate on the particular topics emphasized in this chapter. On race relations and population characteristics: essays by Magnus Mörner, Woodrow Borah, and Peter Boyd-Bowman, in Fredi Chiapelli, ed., *First Images of America* (1976), Vol II; Charles Gipson, *The Aztecs under Spanish Rule* (1964); John H. Rowe, "The Incas under Spanish Colonial Institutions," *Hispanic American Historical Review,* 37 (1957), 156–91; Lesley B. Simpson, *The Encomienda in New Spain* (1929); C. E. Marshall; "The Birth of the Mestizo in New Spain," *Hispanic American Historical Review,* 19 (1939), 161–84; James Lockart, *Spanish Peru, 1532–1560, A Colonial Society* (1968) and his *Men of Cajamarca* (1972); Charles Gipson, "The Transformation of the Indian Community in New Spain, 1500–1800," *Journal of World History,* 2 (1955), 581–607; Lyle N. McAlister, "Social Structure and Social Change in New Spain," *Hispanic American Historical Review,* 43 (1963), 349–70; Lewis Hanke, *The Spanish Struggle for Justice in the Conquest of America* (1949); and Silvio Zavala, *New Viewpoints on the Spanish Colonialization of America* (1943). Nathan Wachtel, *The Vision of the Vanquished* (1977) is an attempt to portray the trauma of the Spanish conquest from the Indians' point of view. On the dominance of Peninsular Spaniards in high office and the slow rise of Creoles through purchase of public office, see M. H. Burkholder and D. S. Chandler, *From Impotence to Authority* (1977) and J. H. Parry, *The Sale of Public Office . . .* (1953). For an extended comparison of the Spanish American and the British North American colonial empires, see James Lang, *Conquest and Commerce: Spain and England in the Americas* (1975). The Brazilian comparison is also relevant, in Richard R. Beeman, "Labor Forces and Race Relations: A Comparative View of the Colonization of Brazil and Virginia," *Political Science Quarterly,* 86 (1971), 609–36. Comparisons of slavery in North and South America have been worked out in books by Frank Tannenbaum *(Slave and Citizen),* Carl N. Degler *(Neither Black nor White),* Herbert S. Klein *(Slavery in the Americas),* and most comprehensively by David B. Davis *(The Problem of Slavery in Western Culture).*

The essential writings on England's involvement in geographical discovery and overseas settlement in the sixteenth century are by David B. Quinn. His *Roanoke Voyages, 1584–1590* (2 vols., 1955) contains every document related to that enterprise, a subject he has summarized in an excellent brief account, *Raleigh and the British Empire* (London, 1947). In addition, Quinn has edited the documents of the colonizing efforts of Sir Humphrey Gilbert (2 vols., 1940), written a biography of Gilbert, edited Hakluyt's writings, and discovered the Pilgrims' original plans to settle on the islands in the gulf of the St. Lawrence. Most aspects of his writing are brought together in a volume of his essays, *England and the Discovery of America, 1481–1620* (1974) and summarized in his *North America,* cited above. Samuel E. Morison's *The European Discovery of America: The Northern Voyages, A.D. 500–1600* (1971), covers in the same vivid fashion as *The Southern Voyages* the Cabots' voyages and all of the Elizabethan explorations, and it contains in addition an excellent account of the Roanoke expeditions. A more traditional summary is John B. Brebner, *The Explorers of North America, 1492–1806* (1933). G. R. Elton, *England under the Tudors* (1955), chap. xii is a very brief but useful summary of Elizabethan exploration and expansionism; chap. ix contains a good sketch of the economic background. A. L. Rowse's *The Expansion of Elizabethan England* (1955) and his *Elizabethans and America* (1959) are good reading.

The important role of Ireland in the origins of Elizabethan colonization and the connections between Irish and American settlement are best described in David B. Quinn, *The Elizabethans and the Irish* (1966). Quinn has analyzed the development of English ideas of colonization in the Irish context, particularly the concept of "plantation," in "Sir Thomas Smith (1513–1577) and the Beginnings of English Colonial Theory," *Proceedings of the American Philosophical Society,* 89, no.4 (Dec., 1945), 543–60, and in "Ireland and Sixteenth Century European Expansion," T. D. Williams, ed., *Historical Studies: I . . .* (1958). See also James Muldoon, "The Indian as Irishman," *Essex Institute Historical Collections,* 111 (1975), 267–289; and Nicholas P. Canny, "The Ideology of English Colonization: from Ireland to America," *William and Mary Quarterly,* 3d ser.,* 30 (1973), 575–98.

The masterwork on the financial history of sixteenth- and seventeenth-century English exploration and colonization is W. R. Scott, *The Constitution and Finance of English, Scottish and Irish Joint Stock Companies to 1720* (3 vols., 1912). Theodore K. Rabb, *Enterprise and Empire . . . 1575–1630* (1967), demonstrates statistically the broad social basis of investment in colonization. For the financial background of England's parallel colonization of Ireland in the seventeenth century, see Karl S. Bottigheimer, *English Money and Irish Land* (1971).

*This journal will be referred to hereafter as *Wm. and Mary Q.*

In 1600 the eastern coastal region of mainland North America, some 362,000 square miles from Maine to Georgia and west to the Appalachian Mountains, was largely uncultivated, much of it covered by forests, but it was by no means an unbroken wilderness. A native Indian population grouped in well-organized tribes and sharing approximately the same culture lived fairly sedentary lives, many in semipermanent villages of up to one thousand persons. Concentrated in the fertile coastal plain and the broad river valleys, they communicated readily along an intricate network of riverways and forest trails. They subsisted on a generally nutritious diet of fish and farm crops, principally maize, as well as on game and wild foods, and they rarely suffered famines.

But the Indians' hold upon the land was light. Large areas of the Atlantic woodland region were completely uninhabited (the New England coastal population was decimated by smallpox just before the first English settlers arrived). The average population density for the entire region east of the Appalachians in the early days of European settlement has been estimated by anthropologists at thirty-four persons per hundred square miles. In the most populous region, New England and coastal New York, with an estimated population of 72,000 in 1610, the average density was between four and five persons per square mile; in coastal Virginia the density was roughly two persons per square mile. Nowhere was more than one percent of all the land available for cultivation actually being farmed, and nowhere was possession of land conceived of in European terms. The Indians did not view land as parcels of property owned by individuals, but rather as a common resource that was inherited from ancestors, held in trust by tribal chiefs for future generations, and used by everyone for their daily needs. Nor was warfare thought of in European terms. Deadly personal and intertribal struggles were common, and the treatment of enemies was brutal; but the Indians did not undertake war to annihilate their enemies, to create utter devastation, or to engage in wholesale massacre. Finally, only in one area of the entire Atlantic coastal region were the native inhabitants organized into a political structure effective beyond the tribal level. And even in that one famous

Transplantation

and militarily important organization, the Iroquois Confederacy, control over the separate tribes was never secure.

By 1700 this vast coastal region had been transformed, and the foundations of British North American civilization established. The Indians had been eliminated from the seaboard lands—annihilated by the invading peoples in savage local wars and driven back beyond the western fringes of European settlement. The area now contained a quarter of a million transplanted Europeans and their children and grandchildren attempting to re-create the familiar pattern of European life in this undeveloped land. Recruited principally from two of the most dynamic and economically sophisticated nations of Europe, England and the Netherlands, they lived in communities that were parts of a commercial network spread across the entire Atlantic basin and that involved, directly or indirectly, all the nations of western Europe. Within this transplanted population, there were, mainly in Virginia and Maryland, over twenty thousand Africans bound in lifelong, heridtary, and debased servitude.

This transplanted population was organized into eleven provinces loosely controlled by an English government that was only beginning to understand the full importance of the colonial world it had acquired. A small proportion of the settlers, perhaps 8 percent, lived in the five main port towns (Boston, Newport, New York, Philadelphia, and Charleston) through which flowed most of the commerce and communications that linked this world to Europe. The rest lived in village communities numbering a few hundred souls, or on isolated family farms or "plan-

tations" modeled on European agricultural establishments but different from them in fundamental ways.

These tens of thousands of transplanted Europeans and Africans had arrived in no concentrated stream, under no centralized direction, and in no limited span of years. They had arrived, and in 1700 were continuing to arrive, irregularly, in various circumstances, their migration and settlement organized individually or by a variety of private organizations. The history of their migration and resettlement in America forms not one narrative but many. Yet these stories of colonization, for all their variety, follow a common pattern. They begin with high hopes and great plans—often utopian plans—designed by sponsoring individuals and groups whose imaginations

AN INDIAN SORCERER, 1585

Of this drawing by John White (see p. 20), Thomas Hariot, one of the Roanoke settlers of 1585, wrote: "They have sorcerers or jugglers who use strange gestures and whose enchantments often go against the laws of nature. For they are very familiar with devils, from whom they obtain knowledge about their enemies' movements." *(Reproduced by Courtesy of the Trustees of the British Museum)*

The map at far right is a composite reconstruction of all the trails known to have been used by the natives. It appears in Paul A. W. Wallace, *Indian Paths of Pennsylvania* (1965), which contains detailed descriptions of every path on the map.

were fired by the possibilities of starting the world anew, of creating new communities, and, usually, of profiting immensely by doing so. But contact with reality in an undeveloped land brought frustration, the failure of original high hopes, and disillusion. Thereafter, however, there was a creative adaptation by those who survived. This was the persistent pattern of English colonization in the seventeenth century: soaring expectations, disappointment, frustration, disaster or near disaster, and then a slow adjustment to the realities of life on the wilderness edge of the North American continent. Gradually, from this process, there emerged new forms of society made more complex by their superficial similarities to the familiar patterns of European life.

Virginia: Squalor, Struggle, and a New Way of Life

The settlement of Virginia is a classic case of high hopes shattered and a new world rescued from the ruins. It began in 1606 when the English crown chartered two Virginia Companies, one for Plymouth and one for London, incorporating the interests of the two main groups that had already been involved in western exploration and in the planning of American settlements: the gentry and merchants of the west country, and the London merchants to whom Raleigh had transferred his rights. The two groups were given separate though overlapping portions of the North American coast for settlement and instructed to ap-

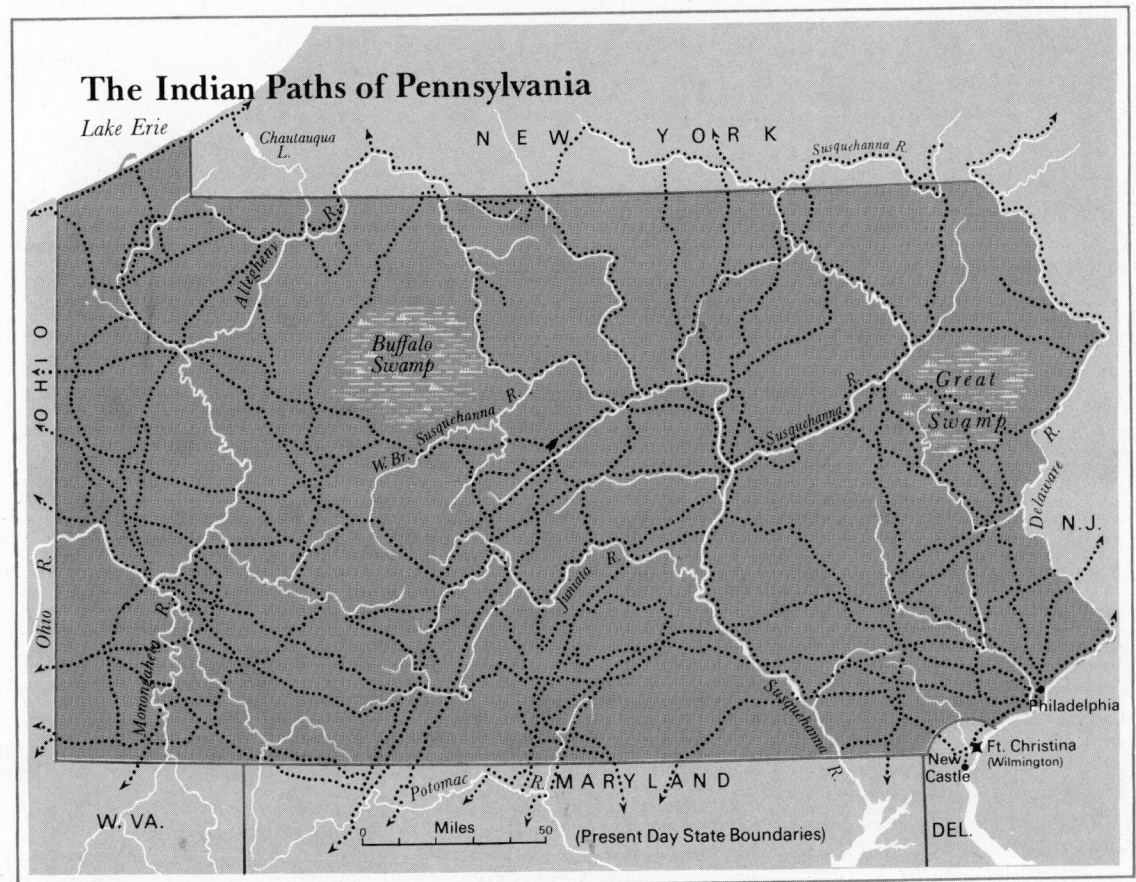

The Indian Paths of Pennsylvania

Jamestown, 1607-1612

point their own resident governments. In 1607 the Plymouth group, assigned the northern area between the Potomac River and the site of the present Bangor, Maine, attempted a settlement near the mouth of the Kennebec River (Sagadahoc, they called it), but everything went wrong. No sign of quick profits appeared, disease and Indian attacks decimated the small company huddled in the tiny fort, and within a year the effort was permanently abandoned.

Jamestown.   The London group, assigned the southern sector, was more ambitious and better financed. Its leaders, under Sir Thomas Smith, England's most powerful merchant, were extraordinarily energetic. In December 1606 they sent out three ships, the *Susan Constant*, the *Godspeed*, and the *Discovery*—tiny vessels scarcely able to hold the 144 people they carried, let alone survive a midwinter crossing of the Atlantic. It was April 1607 before they reached the Chesapeake,

and in May, on a low-lying island thirty miles upstream on the James River and close to the river bank, the 104 survivors of the voyage disembarked. On this spot, so permeated with stagnant water that no home site could be placed farther than 800 feet from malarial swamps, but safe from attack and believed to be close to passages through the continent to the Pacific, the Virginia Company of London established the first permanent British settlement in North America.

The colony survived, but only barely. During the eighteen years of the Virginia Company's existence (1606–24) Jamestown, the main settlement, was a disaster not only for those who lived there but for everyone in any way connected with it. Death was everywhere in the colony. Four out of five of the "planters" of the company years were victims of disease or of Indian attacks. That the company survived at all beyond its first two years was the result of the persistence of its leaders in pursuing delusive dreams of profits and of the financial support they were able to mobilize. Seldom has good money been thrown so extravagantly after bad; seldom have hard-headed businessmen been so mistaken in their expectations of success.

It quickly became clear that in Virginia there was neither easily extractable mineral wealth nor a discoverable passage through the continent, nor a useful native labor force. Hope came to rest on a new idea; that if the colony could be well populated and securely financed, it might produce more ordinary goods—grapes, sugar, tobacco, cotton, dye woods—which could be sold with substantial if not sensational profits in England. Once such a reliable foundation had been laid, the search for more dramatic and lucrative possibilities could then be resumed.

It was to establish the colony on this permanent basis that in 1609 the company in London obtained a revised charter and launched a new effort that gave the moribund colony hope for the future. Without the renewed effort of 1609, Jamestown would have followed Roanoke into oblivion—which it almost did in any case.

By the terms of the new charter, the company, hitherto financed by the contributions only of its incorporators and their personal acquaintances, was recast as a seven-year public joint-stock company. In February 1609 its books were opened for public subscriptions, and an elaborate publicity campaign was launched to stimulate the sale of these shares, especially in the form of pledges of personal service in the colony by prospective settlers. Such "adventurers of person" were given one or more shares of stock depending on their "quality" or special skills, each such share to be worth at least a hundred acres of land when in 1616 the company's total assets would be divided among the stockholders. At the same time, the stockholders were given more authority, and a new form of government was devised for the colony.

Under the first charter the resident government of the colony had consisted of an appointed council that elected its own president. The result had been wrangling among the leaders until Captain John Smith, a shrewd, hard-bitten, and commanding war veteran, seized power. It had been Smith—a romantic but intelligent adventurer—who by forceful leadership had kept the forlorn band from starving to death. He had managed too, by a combination of cleverness and brutality, to keep the neighboring Indian tribes cordial or at least intimidated, and he had made important explorations of the Chesapeake region and surveyed its economic possibilities. The lesson of his leadership was not forgotten. Under the new regulations of 1609 all authority in the colony was to be exercised by an appointed governor who was to be advised, not controlled, by a council and whose authority was to be limited only by the "liberties, franchises, and immunities" due all Englishmen and by the instructions that would be issued to him by the company.

The publicity campaign of 1609 was sensational. Colonization was preached from the pulpits of London, and the price of the company's stock rose on the merchant exchanges. Support of the Virginia Company became, for the moment, a national cause. As a result, in June 1609 the company was able to send out to Virginia a fleet carrying 500 men and 100 women with large quantities of equipment and supplies. But the whole expedition seemed doomed. The vessel that carried among its passengers the newly appointed officers of the colony was blown off course and ended as a wreckage in Bermuda—an episode that is echoed in Shakespeare's *The Tempest*. The 400 leaderless settlers who arrived in Jamestown were exhausted by the long voyage and debilitated by the putrid shipboard food. Disease was already spreading among them when they landed. Too weak at first to work, then deeply discouraged by the sordid prospects before them, shaken out of their normal social discipline and confused by the disordered life around them, they fell into fierce factional struggles, lethargy, and despair, and they failed to plant the crops they would need for the coming year. In the midst of a rich land they starved and, unable to withstand disease, died in droves, miserably. When the fearful winter of 1609–10 was over only some 60 of the settlers were still alive. In May the leaders finally arrived from Bermuda and found a scene of utter desolation. Jamestown's palisades were in ruins, the houses burnt for firewood, the last scraps of food—including cattle and domestic animals—consumed; and people spoke secretly of cannibalism.

THE INCONVENIENCIES

THAT HAVE HAPPENED TO SOME PERSONS WHICH HAVE TRANSPORTED THEMSELVES

from *England* to *Virginia*, vvithout provisions necessary to sustaine themselues, hath greatly hindred the Progresse of that noble Plantation: For preuention of the like disorders heereafter, that no man suffer, either through ignorance or misinformation; it is thought requisite to publish this short declaration: wherein is contained a particular of such necessaries, as either priuate families or single persons shall haue cause to furnish themselues with, for their better support at their first Landing in Virginia; whereby also greater numbers may receiue in part, directions how to prouide themselues.

Apparrell.	li.	s.	d.
One Monmouth Cap	00	01	10
Three falling bands	—	01	03
Three shirts	—	07	06
One waste-coate	—	02	02
One suite of Canuase	—	07	06
One suite of Frize	—	10	00
One suite of Cloth	—	15	00
Three paire of Irish stockins	—	04	—
Foure paire of shooes	—	08	08
One paire of garters	00	10	—
One doozen of points	—	00	03
One paire of Canuase sheets	—	08	00
Seuen ells of Canuase, to make a bed and boulster, to be filled in *Virginia* 8.s.	}		
One Rug for a bed 8. s. which with the bed seruing for two men, halfe is	} 08	00	
Fiue ells coorse Canuase, to make a bed at Sea for two men, to be filled with straw, iiij. s.	}		
One coorse Rug at Sea for two men, will cost vj. s. is for one	}	05	00
	04	00	00

Apparrell for one man, and so after the rate for more.

Tooles.	li.	s.	d.
Fiue broad howes at 2.s. a piece	—	10	—
Fiue narrow howes at 16.d. a piece	—	06	08
Two broad Axes at 3.s. 8.d. a piece	—	07	04
Fiue felling Axes at 18.d. a piece	—	07	06
Two steele hand sawes at 16.d. a piece	—	02	08
Two two-hand sawes at 5. s. a piece	—	10	—
One whip-saw, set and filed with box, file, and wrest	—	10	—
Two hammers 12.d. a piece	—	02	00
Three shouels 18.d. a piece	—	04	06
Two spades at 18.d. a piece	—	03	—
Two augers 6.d. a piece	—	01	00
Sixe chissels 6.d. a piece	—	03	00
Two percers stocked 4.d. a piece	—	00	08
Three gimlets 2.d. a piece	—	00	06
Two hatchets 21.d. a piece	—	03	06
Two froues to cleaue pale 18.d.	—	03	00
Two hand-bills 20. a piece	—	03	04
One grindlestone 4. s.	—	04	00
Nailes of all sorts to the value of	02	00	—
Two Pickaxes	—	03	—
	06	02	08

For a family of 6. persons and so after the rate for more.

VIRGINIA COMPANY BROADSIDE, 1622
This detailed list of items which emigrants should take to Virginia was published by the company in 1622 in response to an appeal by John Smith that they send only "well provided" workmen in the future. The list, which with the cost of transportation added up to a cost of £20, is said to be "the usual proportion that the Virginia Company does bestow upon their tenants which they sent." The headright system of land grants is explained at the bottom of the sheet. (*Rare Book Division, The New York Public Library*)

The ravaged settlement, still lacking the supplies that had been paid for by the subscription of 1609, seemed hopeless. On June 7, 1610, it was abandoned. The settlers sailed down the James in four small vessels en route to Newfoundland and home.

The Settlement Restored. The colony was saved by a coincidence, which contemporaries attributed to the providence of God. For by chance the departing settlers were met near the mouth of the James by a longboat from a fleet just arrived that carried 300 men and the new governor, Lord De la Warr. The despairing and fearful settlers were ordered back, and De la Warr began the slow process of restoring discipline and confidence, creating a sound agriculture, and establishing profitable relations with the Indians. At home the company, with somewhat despairing vigor, continued its fund-raising and sent further reinforcements of over 600 men with hundreds of domestic animals and shiploads of equipment. Emphasis was thrown now exclusively on the development of Virginia's agricultural, industrial, and commercial possibilities. A satellite settlement was founded at Henrico on the upper James (the site of Richmond), and two others were located at the mouth of the James. Social discipline was imposed harshly by a new code of laws published in 1612 as *Lawes Divine, Morall, and Martiall,* which organized the community into a quasi-military corps committed to compulsory service on common projects and subject to severe penalties for failure to work or to share military obligations.

Thus reinforced and thus disciplined, the colony slowly and painfully became marginally self-sustaining. Humble products—furs, timbers, sassafras, some experimentally produced iron, and beginning in 1614 small quantities of tobacco—began to fill the holds of the returning vessels. But these cargoes, though encouraging, were not profitable enough to stimulate sizable new investments in a company whose expenses were escalating dangerously with the succession of lifesaving supply ships. More funds would have to be raised. Subscribers were dunned for further contributions, unredeemed pledges were pursued in the courts, a public lottery was authorized and launched, more pamphlets were written on Virginia's glowing promise, and once again sermons were preached on the moral obligation to support this *Nova Britannia.* But even all this could not generate the necessary support. To popularize the organization further and to broaden its base, the company obtained a third charter (1612) that again increased the voice of the ordinary shareholders in the company's management. Still, the company's finances remained weak, so weak that in 1616, when the seven-year terminus of the 1609 joint stock was reached, the company was too poor to provide the surveys necessary to make the promised distribution of one hundred acres per share. By then the colony's population, despite all the recent reinforcements, was a mere 350.

One last, great effort had to be made if the company was to be saved and any profit at all realized from the tens of thousands of pounds that had been invested. In 1618 a new group of leaders headed by Sir Edwin Sandys took over control of the company from Smith and initiated the final phase of its history.

The company under Sandys's influence drew up a uniform and generous policy of land inducements for the "ancient planters" and for prospective investors and settlers. The "headright" system was devised whereby anyone who transported a settler to Virginia, including himself, would receive the right to locate, survey, and patent fifty acres of land. More important to the immediate fortunes of the company, shareholders were allowed to pool their landholdings into jointly owned tracts within the Virginia patent, and these, together with certain other large personal estates, were granted minor governmental powers.

The creation of these "private plantations," or "hundreds"—seventy of them were authorized by 1663—began the uncontrolled expansion of settled territory. The lower James valley became dotted with self-contained subcolonies. At the same time, the rigid military discipline of the *Lawes* of 1612 was

MARTIN'S HUNDRED, ONE OF THE "PARTICULAR PLANTATIONS" ALONG THE JAMES RIVER

A modern artist's sketch, based on archaeological excavations. Founded in 1619 by a company of London investors, the plantation of 21,500 acres was located 10 miles east of Jamestown and originally housed over 200 settlers. By 1622 it was reduced by famine and disease to 20 inhabitants and then almost completely destroyed in the Indian massacre. Depicted here: in the foreground, the company's compound, consisting of a longhouse on the right joined to a stable and a storehouse; in the background, the fort to which the settlers fled when attacked. The excavations have unearthed grisly remains of the massacre, including a corpse whose skull had been broken in by a blow with a cleaver or tomahawk and then smashed to pieces by further blows when the body had fallen to the ground. *(By Richard Schlecht. © National Geographic Society)*

A Declaration for the certaine time of dravving the great standing Lottery.

(Copyright Society of Antiquaries of London)

withdrawn in favor of a more normal system of civil courts bound by rules of common law, and a representative assembly—the first in American history—was provided for. At its first meeting in 1619 the assembly, consisting of the governor and his council sitting together with representatives of each of four projected "boroughs" and of the private jurisdictions, made clear that it would not only express popular grievances, as Parliament had done time out of mind, but also protect Englishmen's fundamental rights as they were known "at home."

In addition to all of this, the company launched a new economic program. Some 4,500 additional settlers were sent out to Virginia and through them an intense effort was undertaken to establish staple crops and products. Expert craftsmen began the manufacture of pitch, tar, ships, and other timber products, as well as iron, salt, and glass; and experiments were made with growing tropical and semi-tropical crops and with producing a salable wine and marketable silk.

It was all a colossal gamble by the energetic entrepreneurs who had taken over the company—and it was hopeless. Simply launching these enterprises drained all of the company's cash, most of it produced by the lottery, which became such a public nuisance that Parliament stopped it in 1621. Only a miraculous parlaying of small successes into basic security could rescue the company; and with no margin for error, a single disaster would mean the end.

Collapse and Legacy of the Virginia Company. In March 1622 the final disaster struck. The Indians, deprived of their lands, terrorized and brutalized in a hundred ways and fearful of the sudden growth of the English population, fell on the whole string of defenseless farms along the river and killed at least 347 of the inhabitants. Not only was the colony devastated physically, it was utterly demoralized. The settlers, fearful that the slaughter would be renewed and thirsting for vengeance, abandoned their fields at the start of the planting season and took up arms. The result was both a bloody reprisal and a crop failure in the fall that created a near famine. Hundreds who had escaped butchery by the Indians' arrows, knives, and clubs died of sickness in the winter. Two years later, in 1624, when the company's charter was finally annulled and the settlement became a dependency of the crown, there remained alive but 1,275 of the more than 8,500 souls who had ventured to settle in Virginia. In terms of its original purpose, the company was a complete failure.

Yet in a larger sense the Virginia Company had been successful. It had opened the North American mainland to British settlement; it had peopled a small portion of it—though at a fearful cost in wasted lives, both English and Indian. It had experimented with the economic possibilities of the Chesapeake region; and it had left behind a heritage of the rule of law, within the pale, and of the practice, however rudimentary, of colonial self-government. Above all, the company had set the pattern for Virginia's future development.

The general assembly, originally created by the company to rally support among the settlers, continued to exist when Virgina became a royal colony. Governor, council and representatives of the "burghs" (hence "burgesses") met together as a single group until, in the 1660s, the burgesses' interests became distinct enough from those of the council to justify their meeting as a separate body. This central government, plus county courts which were created in 1643, was the basic public authority that developed in this frontier community—a community whose everyday life was an unregulated response to the raw Chesapeake environment. By 1642, when Sir William Berkeley first arrived as governor—a position he would occupy for most of the next thirty-four years—the essential character of life in the first permanent British colony in America was clear.

This was no life of genteel ease on gracious "plantations," and there were no "cavalier" aristocrats. True, in the first years, when the settlement of Virginia was a sensational event promising all sorts of exotic rewards, the leadership of the colony had included intellectuals and sons of the nobility and of prominent churchmen and politicians. But by 1624 this early leadership had disappeared—casualties of the environment, victims of the Indians, disease, and discouragement. The new leaders established themselves by their sheer capacity to survive on rough, half-cleared tobacco farms and to produce material gains from the raw wilderness. Former servants, yeoman farmers, and adventurers of little social status or wealth, they lacked the attributes of social authority, but by brute labor and shrewd

manipulation they managed to prosper.

The leaders of Virginia in the generation after the company was dissolved were tough, unsentimental, quick-tempered, crudely ambitious men concerned with profits wrung from the soil and increased landholding, not the grace of life. They roared curses, drank exuberantly, and gambled extravagantly, sometimes betting their servants when other commodities were lacking. They asserted their interests fiercely. They wanted an aggressive expansion of settlement and trading enterprise and unrestricted access to land no matter what objections there might be from the Indians, and they sought from such governmental agencies as existed the legal endorsement of their hard-won acquisitions. They claimed large acreage; but it was cleared land that counted, and of that there was precious little for anyone. Because labor was in critically short supply, every effort was made to entice over from England workers whose labor could be counted on for periods specified in indentures (bonds of servitude). But though an average of 1,500 indentured servants arrived in the Chesapeake annually through most of the seventeenth century their terms of bonded service were short (normally four years) and most of them were quickly added to the general population of free tobacco farmers seeking to expand production and competing for hired labor.

Black "slave" labor (the meaning of the term was at first ambiguous) was known in Virginia as early as 1619. But black slaves were more expensive, in the short run at least, than white servants, and their absolute foreignness—in appearance, behavior, language, and skills—offended the English, who were indiscriminately suspicious of foreigners. A black labor force came into being only gradually. In 1640, only 150 blacks were reported in Virginia (not all of them slaves); in 1650, 300; in 1680, 3000; and in 1704, when the white population may have reached 75,600, there were roughly 10,000 blacks. And as the number of black laborers rose and as their importance to the developing economy became clear, a new status of bondage, "chattel slavery," took shape, something unknown hitherto in English law. As servitude for whites became progressively more limited in duration and less rigorous in demands, the laws began to specify that blacks would serve for life; that their offspring would automatically become the property of their masters; that conversion to Christianity would not lead to freedom; that nothing but discretion could limit the severity of penalties imposed upon them; that racially mixed marriages were forbidden; and finally that a "slave" was no longer, as heretofore, simply a servant of lowest condition but something absolutely different in the eyes of the law, a form of property to be bought and sold, a status applicable only and necessarily to blacks and to their descendants to the ultimate degree.

Such were the main provisions of the "slave codes" so devastating in their consequences for the whole of American history. The codes originated in the latter half of the seventeenth century in response to an acute need for labor, an elemental fear of foreignness, and an insensitivity to cruelty remarkable even for that callous age. But however peculiar the conditions that gave rise to these codes, once devised they became a fundamental part of the legal fabric of community life, and they intensified and perpetuated the racial fears and hostilities that had helped shape them. By 1700 it was becoming clear, to some at least, that chattel slavery, rising like some terrible germ-laden cloud, was poisoning the very soil and roots of human relations.

The Pilgrims' "Sweet Communion"

It is difficult, perhaps impossible, for twentieth-century Americans fully to recapture the state of mind of those who led the settlement of New England. The Puritans and Pilgrims are too easily caricatured: the former as God-intoxicated demons of self-righteousness or as intellectual gymnasts cogitating day and night on exquisite subtleties of theology; the Pilgrims as altogether simple Christians spotless in their uncompromising Biblicism. But as with most caricatures there is truth behind the obvious distortions. Both groups were products of the attempted reformation of the Elizabethan Church of England and of the desire for a more direct experience of God

than the church allowed. But otherwise they were very different. Their aims, their styles, their accomplishments were different, and their contributions to American life lie in altogether different spheres.

The Pilgrims were one of a series of radical "separatist" groups that first appeared in England in the 1570s. Loyal to the English state, they were determined to break altogether with the too ritualistic, too highly institutionalized, still too Catholic, Church of England. They formed their own pure and primitive churches—mere cells, conventicles, stripped bare of all ritual, unaffiliated with each other except for shared aspirations, and composed exclusively of true believers gathered voluntarily into covenanted brotherhoods. Defiant of persecution and without hope of forcing their views upon the world at large, yet never questioning the authority of the civil state, these fugitive groups of religious radicals were naturally drawn to the physical margins of the English world, where in isolation they might find peace to worship as they chose and yet still enjoy the protection of the English state.

The Separatists. One such conventicle of pious, humble, and stubborn believers, gathered in the village of Scrooby in Nottinghamshire, became famous as the Pilgrim Fathers. They had no desire to settle in America. To escape the corrupting English world, they fled first to Amsterdam, then to Leyden. But there was no escape, even in that tolerant Dutch university town. Their children, not steeled as they themselves had been in the fires of persecution, were attracted by the town's temptations, and would be lost to the true faith, the Pilgrims feared, if nothing were done. They would have to move again, to a less comfortable, more remote site, better suited to the establishment of a pure church of Christ. They considered various alternatives—elsewhere in the Netherlands, on the north coast of South America, on the islands in the gulf of the St. Lawrence River, which they had already investigated. Finally they settled on Virginia, with whose managers they had several contacts and which was then offering to groups such as theirs the semiautonomy of private plantations. By 1619 they had obtained approval from the Vir-

LEYDEN, IN THE NETHERLANDS, TO WHICH THE PILGRIMS FLED IN 1609

"A fair and beautiful city," Bradford wrote, where the Pilgrims "grew in knowledge and other gifts and graces of the spirit of God" but where their children were "drawn away by evil examples into extravagant and dangerous courses ... so that they saw their posterity would be in danger to degenerate and be corrupted." *(Rare Book Division, The New York Public Library)*

ginia Company to settle within its jurisdiction, a promise from the crown not to molest them in America, and financial help from an English investment group headed by one Thomas Weston. After many hesitations the Separatists willing to go to America sold their property to purchase shares in the joint undertaking with Weston, each planter's labor being reckoned as a single share of stock.

In July 1620, 35 of the 238 members of the Leyden congregation took leave of their brethren in a scene so poignant, so prayerful and tearful, that even casual Dutch onlookers wept. They sailed to Southampton on their own small vessel, the *Speedwell*, to join an English contingent of Separatists and the 180-ton *Mayflower*, which had been rented for them by the merchants. After two false starts that led them to abandon the unseaworthy *Speedwell* and that discouraged many from completing the voyage, the remaining Pilgrims and the laborers hired by the merchants crowded into the *Mayflower*, packed high with furniture, equipment, food, and animals, and on September 16 they set sail for Virginia.

There were 101 passengers in all, perhaps 87 of them Separatists or members of Separatist families. Outwardly they fared well on the overcrowded vessel: only one passenger died on the voyage, and two children were born on board. But the voyage lasted over nine weeks, and by the time Cape Cod was sighted (November 9) and they debarked at Provincetown at the tip of the cape (November 11), the entire party, crew and passengers, was ridden with disease, primarily scurvy, and so weakened by malnutrition that they were incapable of withstanding attacks of ordinary illnesses in the months that followed. The weather during this first winter in Plymouth, 1620–21, was quite mild for New England, but it proved to be one of the worst "starving times" recorded anywhere in British America. When spring at last arrived, half of those who had crossed on the *Mayflower* were dead.

They had settled, of course, in New England, though they carried with them a title to land in Virginia. But when they finally landed at Provincetown and "fell upon their knees and blessed the God of Heaven who had brought them over the vast and furious ocean and delivered them from all the perils and miseries thereof," they were determined to voyage no more and to ignore the legal problems that might arise. An exploring party found Plymouth Harbor on December 11, and there on a slope rising westward from the shore, probably the site of an abandoned Indian cornfield, they built the simple village of their desires.

Plymouth Plantation. Plymouth's history up to 1691, when it was absorbed into the more powerful Massachusetts Bay Colony, is a tale of modest triumphs—and a tale too of the defeat of human aspirations by the ravages of time, growth, and decay. All of it—the trials, the triumphs, and defeats—is recorded in Governor William Bradford's magnificent history, *Of Plymouth Plantation,* which he began in 1630 with a review of the earlier years and continued as a documentary journal and commentary covering the next sixteen years. It is one of the most moving and eloquent documents in the entire literature of American history. Its vivid Elizabethan imagery and its biblical cadences blend perfectly to express Bradford's hopes and struggles and finally his sense of tragedy and defeat.

Of the blessings he recorded, one was always paramount. At long last the Pilgrims were free, Bradford wrote, "to see, and with much comfort to enjoy, the blessed fruits of their sweet communion." The church was theirs, unfettered, unintimidated, and responsive to their ultimate desires. But there were troubles from the start. The first and most pressing was financial. For several years they failed as businessmen, and the merchants at home, bickering among themselves and fearful of mounting costs if they continued to resupply the settlers, sold out or simply abandoned their investments. By 1626 the company was bankrupt, but the Pilgrims, more honest than shrewd, continued to honor their original obligations. They struggled for years to squeeze enough profit from fur trading, fishing, and the sale of lumber, Indian corn, and wampum to pay off the original debts. By the time they succeeded, in 1648, many of the founders were dead.

More threatening than debts were the scattering

THE PLYMOUTH PLANTATION
Leyden Street, Plymouth, as it appears in the modern restoration. "The houses," a visitor wrote in 1628, "are constructed of clapboards, with gardens also enclosed behind and at the sides with clapboards, so that the houses and courtyards are arranged in very good order." *(Plimoth Plantation)*

of settlement and the dissipation of purpose which grew with the passage of years. A series of vessels had followed the *Mayflower* to Plymouth, and the population had risen steadily. By 1657, the year of Bradford's death, there were over 1,360 inhabitants. Plymouth no longer a single covenanted community but a colony of eleven towns that could not be enclosed within a single purpose, infused with a single spirit. Even if the gentle leaders had sought to impose discipline and control, they would have lacked the legal means to do so. Their original patent from the Virginia Company was worthless in New England, and a patent they received in 1621 from the Council for New England (which had taken over the legal rights of the old Virginia Company of Plymouth) was simply a vague land grant and an equally vague license to establish a local government. The government evolved slowly and uncertainly and was never sanctioned by charter or the approval of the crown.

The starting point was the Mayflower Compact, a document devised to control the restless noncommunicants while the Pilgrims were still at sea. It was simply an agreement—signed, on November 21, 1620, by 41 Pilgrims, hired laborers, and sailors—to obey whatever laws and officers the community would create. The signing of the Mayflower Compact in the cabin of the rocking vessel was a dramatic event. But the document was no constitution. The unsanctioned government that developed in Plymouth was primitive in organization. The freemen simply came together annually to choose a governor (Bradford was elected thirty times) and a group of assistants to support him; otherwise these electors met only on extraordinary occasions when called together by the governor.

So feeble was the colony's political structure, so weak the second and third generations' loyalty to Plymouth, that when the whole region was included within the boundaries of Massachusetts in the Bay Colony's second charter of 1691, the Pilgrims' colony slipped without a ripple into the larger jurisdiction. By then the erosion in the original purposes and piety was such that those who had inherited the leadership from Bradford could only rejoice that the government would at least continue to be in the hands of saints,

EDWARD WINSLOW, 1651
Winslow, the only Pilgrim of whom a portrait is known, was one of the better educated and more worldly wise of the group. His career illustrates the cosmopolitanism of the first generation of settlers in British America (see p. 113). His long years of service as Plymouth's chief business agent, Indian negotiator, and propagandist brought him often to England where in 1654 Cromwell engaged him on a diplomatic mission and then appointed him to head the expedition that seized Jamaica from the Spanish. Governor of Plymouth for three years, governor's assistant for over 20 years, he was largely responsible for setting up Plymouth's successful Indian trade and for exploring the adjacent territories. *(Courtesy, Plimoth Plantation)*

even if they were not saints of the Separatists' own persuasion.

But the essential destruction of the founders' utopia had taken place years before. Bradford's "sweet communion" in its fullest form had rested on deeply shared aspirations and on isolation from the corruptions of the changing world. When town begat town and the churches multiplied, and when the ordinary world was created within Plymouth itself by strangers and by children who failed to recapture their parents' piety, the Pilgrims' hopes were shattered.

Lacking all instinct for power, rejecting the world rather than seeking to reform it, and tolerant of the errors of others in their humble pursuit of personal piety, the Pilgrims were incapable of perpetuating the community they built, and their impact on American life was confined to the realm of ideals. For always, in the years that have followed the founding of their fragile utopia in Plymouth, the example of their selfless pursuit of an unattainable ideal and their rejection of the satisfactions of wealth, power, comfort, and self-glory in favor of deeper, spiritual rewards have been part of America's collective memory and part of its essential culture. But this model of life, though emulated in various ways at every stage of American history, has never been dominant. Far more vital in American culture has been the very different legacy of the Puritans.

The Puritans: Power in the Service of God

The Puritans shared with the Pilgrims a desire for a direct experience of religion free from the encumbrances of an elaborate church. They shared also certain theological views as well as a stubborn moral dignity.* But the Puritans, in America as in England, were proud and driving, and as demanding of themselves as they were of the world about them. They sought power—not for its own sake, to be sure, but for Christian purposes; and they sought it relentlessly, intolerantly, and successfully.

The decisions that led to this formative development in American history were made in stages within a hectic three-year period. In 1628 a group of around ninety active nonconformists, deeply troubled by the repressive tendencies of both church and state in England and well aware of the value of overseas settlements as refuges for people of their persuasion, came

*On Puritanism as a religious movement, see Chapter 3, pages 87–91.

together as the New England Company to obtain a land patent enclosing most of the present-day Massachusetts and New Hampshire. They sent out an advance party to rebuild a settlement on Cape Ann, north of Boston, that had recently been abandoned by a Puritan fishing company, but their anxieties continued to mount. Increasingly concerned about the future of nonconformity, they sought and obtained in 1629 a crown charter that created the Massachusetts Bay Company. This elaborate document, empowering them not only to trade and settle within the boundaries of their earlier land patent but "to govern and rule all His Majesty's subjects that reside within the limits of our plantation," was a legal bulwark behind which a powerful social movement could organize and develop.

The new corporation's efficiency was quickly demonstrated. Within weeks of its creation it sent off five vessels bearing more than two hundred settlers to join the earlier group then living in thatched cottages on the shores of Cape Ann. But far greater enterprises were stirring beneath the surface of the Massachusetts Bay Company. In the spring and summer of 1629 political and ecclesiastical conditions in England continued to worsen for critics of the Church of England, and in addition the Puritans learned of the defeat of Protestantism throughout Europe in the international war then raging. Moreover, the king dissolved Parliament, and with it went the hope of political remedies. On top of all of this, an economic depression created great distress in just the districts most prone to religious dissent.

The Great Migration. It was in this atmosphere of social, political, and economic panic in the spring and summer of 1629 that men of experience, ability, and established position turned their thoughts not merely to creating a refuge for people of their persuasion but to their own personal escape from England to some world apart, some fresh, uncorrupted realm. Within six months of the creation of the Massachusetts Bay Company a coalition of merchants, landed gentlemen, lawyers, and minor officials alienated from their own society, turned to the new Massachusetts Bay corporation and found in it a means of escape and of serving their own, and Puritanism's, higher purpose.

Only some of this gathering group of substantial Englishmen had been directly involved in the company before. Chief among the newcomers was John Winthrop, an intensely pious, well-connected forty-one-year-old Puritan landowner and attorney recently dismissed from his government position. Faced suddenly with unemployment and with the prospect of continuing harassment, and convinced that England was being overwhelmed by corruption, he came to see a providential significance in the work of the Massachusetts Bay Company. He was no mild and passive Pilgrim. Winthrop and the other leaders of the Massachusetts Bay Company were men of affairs, self-confident, energetic, and used to exercising authority. But their love of action in the ordinary world was disciplined by an equally powerful religious commitment. They loved the everyday world, but they loved it, as they liked to say, "with weaned affection." *In* the world but not *of* the world, they sought not to abandon the Church of England but to seize it, purge it of its corruptions, and reconstruct it in the image of a pure and unadorned Christianity, if not in England then in New England. And far from withdrawing from society, they sought to seize that too and transform it—to create, by persuasion if possible, by force if force were necessary and available to them, a society likely to gain God's approval. They were separatists only with respect to the English state, and this they made clear in the conclusion they reached at a momentous meeting in Cambridge late in August of 1629.

The twelve leaders who assembled secretly in Cambridge pledged themselves "ready in our persons" to join the migration to New England, taking with them their families and whatever provisions they could gather, and "to inhabit and continue in New England" —*provided* that the company officially transfer itself, its charter and government, to the colony. Three days later the corporation concurred, in effect voting itself out of business as a commercial organization and transforming itself into a rudimentary civil government. In October Winthrop was elected governor, and five months later, in March 1630, the great Puritan migration began. Before the year was out a fleet of seventeen ships had borne well over 1,000 settlers to Massachusetts. In all, during the years of the Puritan exodus, 1630–43, some two hundred

GOVERNOR JOHN WINTHROP
The leader of Puritan New England in its heroic age, a devout, able, and strong-willed leader, Winthrop directed his energies and talents to creating a pure version of the Church of England and a society directed to God's will. The set jaw, full but tightly drawn lips, and raised brows suggest intense self-discipline and resolution. (*American Antiquarian Society*)

vessels transported over 20,000 Englishmen to the Bay Colony.

No one community could contain them all. The original settlement, Salem on Cape Ann, became a staging area for groups moving south along the coast. First Charlestown, then Boston became the central settlement. From Boston groups moved on quickly to settle a ring of satellite towns immediately around the bay. Subsequently others founded a secondary ring of communities—Haverhill, Concord, Sudbury—some twenty or thirty miles inland. Finally, beginning in 1636, the migrating subgroups of the Puritan exodus broke contact altogether with the central settlement in Boston by establishing an independent cluster of towns—Hartford, Wethersfield, Windsor—on the Connecticut River over one hundred miles from Boston

Bay. By banding together politically, these towns became the colony of Connecticut, which formed its own government in 1639 and was chartered by the crown in 1662.

Church and Community. The dispersal of the Puritans into towns all over New England was remarkable for its speed; it was remarkable even more for the degree to which it carried forward the purposes of the Puritans. The dispersal of the colonists was no random scattering of people but a well-organized multiplication of church societies that became political bodies and land corporations as soon as they were founded. Groups that wished to establish towns sought the approval of the colony's legislature, the General Court. When the court's franchise was granted, it carried with it not only the legal right to create a limited governmental jurisdiction—a town—and to send representatives to the General Court; it also carried authority over a large parcel of land—a township—to be divided among the original heads of households in proportion to wealth or status. These town founders consequently not only owned their own individual shares of land but also, collectively, controlled the undistributed land as well. The same men, since they were the founding members of their covenanted church, controlled too the vital area of religion, and they constituted also the initial voting membership of the town's political meeting that regulated the mundane affairs of village life. Since all of these powers fell to the founders and not automatically to others who later joined the villages, these town fathers and their direct heirs controlled full participation in all the main spheres of life.

Their control was not resented, in the early years at least. Later there would be opposition and factionalism as newcomers found their way into these small farming villages and as the Puritans' fierce passion to reform the world faded into mere repressive austerity. But while the fires of the original faith still burned brightly and Puritanism was still a way of embracing the world, not of rejecting it, these oligarchic yet democratic villages remained cohesive bodies, closely bound into the larger Bible commonwealth.

The unity of the Massachusetts colony as a whole is remarkable when one considers the rapid and wide dispersal of the settlers. It reflects not only a widespread commitment to a particular way of life and to certain beliefs but also the founders' gift for self-government and their refusal to tolerate dissent.

The Massachusetts charter, being the articles of incorporation of a commercial organization, contained, of course, no provision for an independent civil government. It did, however, create the equivalent of a self-governing corporate borough, and the government that developed in Massachusetts emerged along the lines of that model. In John Winthrop the company, now the colony, had a duly elected governor; in the seven or eight available members of the company's board of directors there was a rudimentary council of magistrates, or governor's assistants; and in the adult male heads of households there were the "freemen," or voters, necessary to complete the membership of the transformed General Court. Soon the perpetuation of this government was provided for and basic rules laid down. In 1632 the freemen were given the power to choose not only the assistants but the governor and deputy governor as well. In 1634 it was agreed that taxes could be levied on the towns only by vote of the entire General Court and that in the future the entire body of freemen need not assembly in person for General Court meetings but could select representatives instead. These representatives, two or three from each town, were empowered to make laws, grant land, levy taxes, and transact whatever other business might come before the General Court.

Thus a civil government evolved from the organization of a commercial corporation. It was quickly completed. Since the representatives, or deputies, as they were commonly called, met together with the assistants or magistrates, they could conclude no business without the magistrates' agreement and hence had no distinct voice of their own and no impulse to develop their own rules and procedures. In 1644 this problem was overcome. In a sensational court case that pitted popular emotions against strict legality, the views of the more numerous representatives were vetoed by the minority votes of the mag-

THE OATH OF A FREE-MAN

I A.B. being by Gods Providence an Inhabitant and FREEMAN within the Iurisdiction of this Common wealth; doe freely acknowledge myselfe to be subject to the Government thereof.

AND therefore doe here sweare by the Great and Dreadful NAME of the Everliving GOD, that I will be true and faithfull to the same, and will accordingly yield affiftance & fupport thereunto with my perfon and eftate as in equity I am bound; and will alfo truly endeavour to maintaine& preferve all the liberties & priviledges thereof, fubmitting myfelfe to the wholefome Lawes & Orders made and eftablifhed by the fame. *** AND further that I will not Plot or practife any evill againft it, or confent to any that fhall fo doe: but will timely difcover and reveal the fame to lawfull authority now here eftablifhed, for the fpeedy preventing thereof.

MOREOVER I doe folemnly bind myfelfe in the fight of GOD, that when I fhall be called to give my voyce touching any fuch matter of this State in which FREEMEN are to deale *** I will give my vote and fuffrage as I fhall judge in mine own confcience may beft conduce and tend to the publicke weale of the body without refpect of perfon or favour of any man.

So help me GOD in the LORD IESVS CHRIST.

Printed at Cambridge in New England: by Order of the Generall Courte: Moneth the Firft - 1639

(American Antiquarian Society)

istrates. In the furor that resulted the two groups drew apart, permanently as it proved, into two separate houses, each capable of expressing itself independently of the other, though the agreement of both was still needed for legislative enactments. The lower house thereupon organized itself separately, electing a Speaker and working out parliamentary rules, a committee system, and other procedures modeled on those of the English House of Commons.

During the same years a court system was devised, largely copied from the local court system of England, and a code of laws agreed on. *The Lawes and Libertyes* of 1647 expressed not only the English common law in terms appropriate for life in the wilderness but also the Puritans' devotion to precepts of the Bible.

Puritan Control and Dissent. For despite all the involvements in such secular pursuits as clearing the wilderness and organizing towns, courts, and a general government, and despite the swift development of coastal and transatlantic commerce that also took place in these years, Massachusetts remained a Bible commonwealth. The legal device that secured the Puritan domination was not the clergy's control of government, for the clergy did not hold public office, but the restriction of the colony's electorate to the members of the church, a step that was taken in 1631. As a result of this measure, no matter how the population within the towns might change, or how the sources of immigration might shift, or how the people at large might drift away from the church, the central government of the colony would continue to represent primarily those loyal to the original Puritan purposes.

This arrangement was not challenged, for it expressed a broad consensus in the founding generation. The opposition to the Puritan establishment that did arise in these early years challenged not the basic religious character of the Puritan colony but specific points of doctrine; it flowed not from a deficiency of religious commitment but from an excess. Such opponents of the Puritan regime as Anne Hutchinson and Roger Williams were even more fanatical in their pursuit of religious truth, more relentless in their theology, more single-minded in their beliefs than the Puritan leaders themselves. In one way or another they went to extremes on issues the leaders felt obliged to keep in delicate balance.

Anne Hutchinson—passionate and inflexible in her convictions, brilliant in argument—was convinced that "justification," that is, the infusion of divine grace, the mysterious transfiguration by which sinful man becomes elect of God, was all that essentially mattered; "sanctification," that is, moral conduct, Christian behavior, piety, even prayer, was for her the mere husk of religion. And so, rejecting "works," rejecting in the end all ordinary worldly discipline and responsibility, and standing only for the ravishment of the soul by God, she gathered around her a band of followers, a church within a church, and thereby challenged the Puritan establishment to de-

RICHARD MATHER
Founder of a virtual dynasty of New England preachers and intellectuals, Mather is shown here in a woodcut by John Foster (c. 1670), which is probably the first print made in British America. Mather preached an austere Calvinism in Massachusetts for 34 years. (*American Antiquarian Society.*) In the background, notes taken on sermons heard in Boston by a spiritually tormented merchant, Robert Keayne. Convicted of overcharging and hence of greed and unchristian behavior, Keayne fell into an agony of protest and self-recrimination, which he expressed in an extraordinary fifty-thousand-word will. (*Massachusetts Historical Society*)

stroy her or destroy itself by tolerating her. But she could not be disposed of easily. In 1637 when the General Court tried her, it brought in a battery of ministers to assist in the prosecution, but in the dramatic trial that resulted, Anne Hutchinson held them off with astonishing skill, defending herself learnedly and wittily. But at last, in exhaustion and perhaps also in exaltation, she blurted out defiantly that her knowledge of God was "an immediate revelation," free of all institutions, independent of all earthly authority. This was the ultimate heresy, condemned as "antinomianism," an arrogance of such cosmic dimensions that the court could safely and in good conscience banish her from the colony and silence her followers thereafter.

Roger Williams was more learned than Anne Hutchinson and more respectable, but he was at least as "divinely mad" as she and as passionate in his beliefs. He could never accommodate himself to the halfway reforms of the nonseparating Puritan churches and to the colony's peculiar constitutional foundation. Not only did he denounce the validity of the colony's charter, but from his Salem pulpit he challenged the mingling of church and state that was the essence of the Bible commonwealth. Civil officers, he insisted, should have power only over the civil affairs of men, over their outward state and behavior, not over matters of conscience and religion. While it would only be in later years in England and in banishment in Rhode Island that Roger Williams would develop the doctrine of religious toleration for which he would become famous, he was clearly heading in that direction, and the mere approach to such a position was intolerable to the rulers of the colony. Beyond all of that, he condemned the colony's churches for their refusal to break altogether with the polluted Church of England. Church *reform* was not enough he insisted; purification was not enough. *Perfection* was the goal—a church of absolute purity, more "primitive" even than the church of the Separatists in Plymouth. Such a church was not to be had in Massachusetts. The colony's leaders regretfully—for Williams was a fine intellect and even to the Puritans a true Christian in his way—attempted to correct this wayward saint, then banished him too from the colony.

Later there would be other deviants from the Puritan way, other challengers, who were either silenced or ejected from the colony. Some of these dissidents moved south to Narragansett Bay where Roger Williams, certain followers of Anne Hutchinson, a few Quakers, and others unacceptable to Massachusetts were attempting to form communities in which they would be completely free to pursue their own special version of truth. But the scattered Narragansett villages were torn by discord; they splintered and regrouped repeatedly, until finally by the late 1640s four or five fairly stable communities emerged. Although the prosperous merchants who founded and dominated the island town of Newport were the most worldly of the Rhode Islanders, it was Roger Williams, the founder of Providence at the head of the bay, who recognized that only confederation of the towns and legal authorization from England would preserve the freedom of these

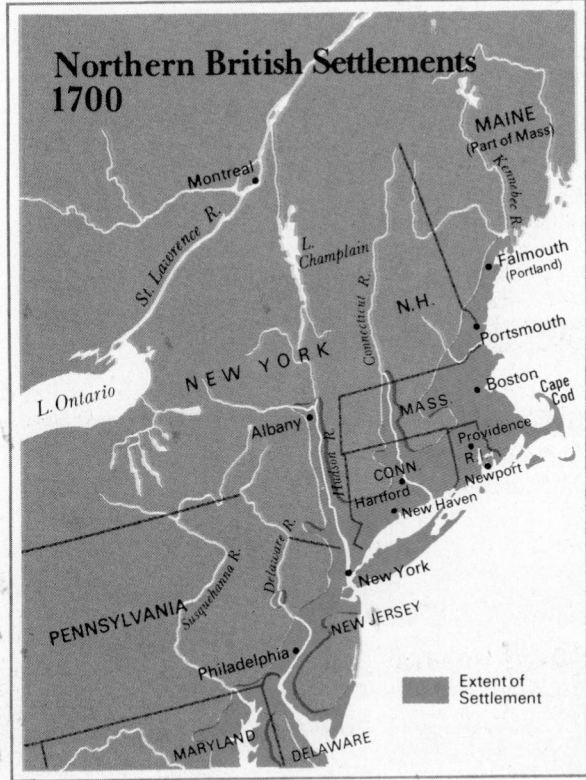

Northern British Settlements 1700

Extent of Settlement

tiny refugee settlements. And it was he who secured the refugee towns' independence by extracting from the English government first, in 1644, a patent creating "The Incorporation of Providence Plantations," and then, in 1663, a crown charter that legalized the permanent existence of the colony of Rhode Island.

Connecticut and Rhode Island were both products of the Massachusetts Bay Colony—the one a reproduction of the Puritans' culture, the other a rejection of it. Together, the central Puritan colony and its satellites to the west, south, and in scatterings north, formed the most vigorous transplanation of English life anywhere in the Western Hemisphere. At the heart of Puritan New England lay the determination to wipe out the corruptions of an old and oppressive world and create a new Jerusalem, in which power would not be rejected or despised but mobilized, and devoted to the service of the Lord.

A Catholic Refuge on the Chesapeake

How pervasive religion was in the establishment of British overseas settlements and how greatly America profited by England's willingness to allow its empire to develop as a refuge for religious minorities can be seen with special clarity in the founding of Maryland.

The refugee community in this case was not radical Protestant but Roman Catholic, more obnoxious to the Church of England than Protestant extremists. The dynamic force was a single family, the Calverts, ennobled in 1625 as the Lords Baltimore. This family, well connected with the rulers of England and only recently converted to Catholicism, had long been involved in overseas enterprises. In 1628–29 the first Lord Baltimore had traveled to the Chesapeake to investigate a possible asylum for refugee Catholics. Upon his return to England he had set in motion the elaborate process of obtaining a separate royal charter for a colony that would be safe for his co-religionists, and although he died just as the charter was being approved, his project was

carried through, and his ambitions fulfilled, by his twenty-six-year-old son, Cecilius Calvert, the second Lord Baltimore.

The key to much of what happened subsequently lies in the terms of the remarkable charter that was issued to the young Lord Baltimore in 1632 and in the use that the Calvert family made of the powers it bestowed. The charter granted Lord Baltimore the entire territory from the Potomac River north to the latitude of Philadelphia and west hundreds of miles to the Appalachian sources of the Potomac. The charter also gave Baltimore extensive governmental powers: the government was his to shape as he chose, and he was empowered to create a system of feudal relationships through land grants if that archaic practice appealed to him.

Significantly, it did. For in this case as in so many others the barrenness of America, its openness, challenged men's imagination and led them to project their desires and their fantasies in plans for new communities.

Toleration and Proprietary Plans. Success came quickly at first. The young Lord Baltimore, who was the proprietor of Maryland until his death in 1675, sent his brother Leonard to the colony as governor with detailed instructions on the management of the colony. Maryland, the proprietor made clear, was to be a Catholic refuge, but Catholics, Baltimore knew, could survive in the English world only as a tolerated minority, and they were therefore in no position to impose their will on others. Furthermore, he knew that the success of the colony would depend on the flow of immigrants into the area, and most of these prospective settlers would necessarily be Protestants. At the very start, therefore, Baltimore prohibited discrimination of any sort against Protestants. He also forbade Catholics from engaging in public controversies on religion, and ordered them to make every effort to live at peace not only with the colony's neighbors in Virginia but with the Puritans and Dutch to the north.

This much was necessary and realistic. Fantasy entered Lord Baltimore's thinking only as he contemplated his personal proprietorship of the land

and his extensive powers of government. How was one to use this princely domain and these extensive powers? What model could there be for such a vast personal estate and such extraordinary private authority? Feudalism, and its economic foundations in manorialism, provided a model of sorts for the Calverts to follow. Their provisions for land distribution, courts, and governance were the result of an effort to create some rough semblance of a feudal-manorial system. They designed proprietary manors of 6,000 acres complete with private courts, which were reserved to the blood relations of the Lord Proprietor, and ordinary manors limited to 3,000 acres. It was expected that all of these manors would be populated by tenants, whose labor would produce the rents and dues necessary to support the lords. The rest of the population would be landowning farmers and their dependents in various statuses, all appropriately submissive to the domination of the provincial nobility. It was a rational but hopelessly unrealistic design. Yet though the reality proved to be quite different from the blueprint, these original plans helped shape the community that in fact developed in Maryland.

In 1632 the Calverts set up a recruiting office for settlers on the outskirts of London, advertised their colony (though not their religion) widely, and were able to induce over two hundred settlers to join the first expedition. The prospective settlers arrived in the Chesapeake in March 1634, in good time for the year's planting and well equipped to survive the inevitable rigors of the first winter in a new colony. The Calverts located their main settlement, which they called St. Mary's, on a creek just north of the Potomac River. There they constructed a palisaded fort similar to that of early Jamestown. After the first winter in the fort, when it became clear that the colony would have supplies sufficient for its survival and that the neighboring Indians were friendly, the distribution of land began and the inevitable dispersal of population got under way.

Distribution of Land. As planned, the proprietor's relatives were given title to 6,000-acre tracts, and lesser manors were distributed to others, together with rights to private courts and other quasi-feudal

CECILIUS CALVERT, 2D LORD BALTIMORE (1605–1675)
Baltimore, who devoted his life to developing the colony that his father had planned, was never able to visit Maryland himself, governing instead through deputies. He is pictured here with his grandson, who had been born in Maryland and died at the age of 14, holding a "new map of Maryland" (*"Nova Terrae-Mariae Tabula"*) dated 1635 and attended by a handsomely dressed black servant. The boy's father, Charles, governor since 1661, succeeded as proprietor and 3rd Lord Baltimore upon Cecilius' death in 1675. *(Enoch Pratt Free Library. Photograph from the Maryland Historical Society)*

privileges. The manorial lords, in turn, as well as the proprietor himself, began selling parcels of land to those who could afford to pay for them and renting property to others. They reserved farms for their own use—"demesne" farms— and all the undivided property. But none of the manorial arrangements survived. The settlement of the countryside was in fact shaped by forces that were almost indistinguishable from those that had determined the development of Virginia.

As in Virginia, the primary cash crop in Maryland was tobacco, and the central difficulty in expanding production was similarly the shortage of labor. Every effort was made to stimulate the importation of laborers for the farms that spread out from several centers on the mainland and on the eastern shore of Chesapeake Bay. A series of laws required prospective manor lords to import at first five workers, then ten, then twenty. Virginia's headright system was introduced in Maryland in 1640, and independent householders who settled in the colony were given special land grants for themselves and the members of their families. The population rose rapidly, partly because migration continued and partly because the availability of fresh tidewater land attracted farmers from Virginia and other neighboring areas. By 1660 the population had probably reached 8,000 and was beginning to grow by natural increase. By 1670 it had grown to over 13,000, and a contemporary map identified 823 cultivated farms in the colony, scattered through a strip of settled territory along the lower shores of Cheaspeake Bay and the banks of the major rivers.

By then, forty years after the initial settlement, it was clear that the Calverts had created something quite different from a feudal–manorial regime. Maryland was dominated by a landholding oligarchy with an almost monopolistic control of public offices, set off from the bulk of the population by religion as well as by wealth and power.

In the earliest years the grants of large estates had meant little since the labor shortage allowed only small segments of these properties to be cultivated. As a result the terms of servitude were generous and freed servants acquired land and estab-

lished themselves as independent farmers with ease. But property values rose as the more fertile and accessible land came under cultivation and as a growing population competed more intensely for the best of the undistributed land. Freed servants found it more difficult to establish themselves in independent households and tended increasingly to serve, for a time at least, as tenants, their labor further increasing the value of the land they worked, to the ultimate advantage of the landlords. In this situation the original "manorial" grants became increasingly valuable simply as land, quite aside from the legal privileges that were supposed to accompany them. The original grantees and their heirs—especially those closely related to the Calverts—found themselves not manorial lords but well-to-do landowners in a world of tobacco farms, with control over properties valuable both for the rents they could produce and for the sale price they could ultimately command in a rising market.

The same men controlled the central offices in the government of the colony, which except for the years 1655–58 remained in the power of the proprietor, Lord Baltimore. He filled them with members of his family and their close associates, most of whom were Catholic. As in Virginia, the governor's council quickly became the central governing body. But in Maryland membership on the council was less the result of achieved prominence than of personal appointment by the lord proprietor. As a result the earliest political struggles in Maryland were not, as in Virginia, between the governor and the councillors but between the governor and the council on the one hand and the local representatives on the other. Fiercely competitive politics was part of the life of Maryland almost from the first years of settlement.

Leonard Calvert's instructions obliged him to call an assembly of freemen and to submit all laws to that body for approval. But he retained the right to summon, adjourn, and dismiss the assembly, and the exclusive right too of initiating all legislation, while the proprietor in England retained the power to veto any actions taken by the assembly. The first full meeting of the assembly (1638) was, like the first assemblies of Massachusetts and Virginia, a confused affair. Any freemen who chose to appear were seated. To free themselves from the dictatorial influence of the proprietary group, the representatives insisted that the assembly arrange itself like the House of Commons, take the power of convening and adjourning into its own hands, and adopt parliamentary rules. Gradually they won these demands, though the proprietor never relinquished the theoretical rights granted him in the charter. When the Long Parliament in England and the Civil War (1640–49) threw all Anglo-American relations into confusion, the assembly seized the power of initiating legislation, and the representatives forced the proprietor to allow them to meet independently of the council. Thereafter the representatives formed a separate lower house of the assembly.

By 1650 the structure of forces that would persist in seventeenth-century Maryland was fully evolved. The colony was governed by an absentee proprietor, his resident governor, and his appointed council, almost all of whom were Catholic. Together they monopolized the important public offices and the profits of office, and they were at the same time the major landlords. But the majority of the population, largely Protestant, had a legitimate voice in government through the lower house. They maintained a continuing battle, in the assembly and out, to force the proprietor and his followers to relinquish their special privileges. In no other colony, by the middle of the seventeenth century, was politics so sophisticated and so bitter as it was in the colony that had first been conceived as an oasis of manorial harmony.

The Failure of the Dutch

The founding of what would become New York differed radically from the pattern of the other British colonies. It was the Dutch, not the English, who founded this colony, which was not originally conceived of as a community at all. Its population from the start was culturally diverse. No legal system was effectively established and no government evolved comparable to the assemblies of Virginia and Maryland and to the General Court of Massachusetts Bay.

New Netherland, as the colony was called until its conquest by England in 1664, was an almost accidental creation of the Dutch West India Company, a trading organization centered in Amsterdam, that was founded in 1621. The colony was never the chief concern of this complex commercial company whose enterprises included trading forts on the Amazon River and establishments in West Africa and Brazil as well as in North America. The company set out, not to create a colony at all, but simply to exploit the fine fur supply and other resources of the middle Atlantic region that had been revealed by the explorations of Henry Hudson in 1609 and thereafter by voyages of a short-lived Dutch fur-trading company.

New Amsterdam. In 1624 the Dutch West India Company sent over thirty Dutch and Walloon (French-speaking Belgian) families to open settlements at Fort Orange and Esopus on the upper Hudson and at several points on the Delaware. Supplies, equipment, and a total of perhaps two hundred people followed in 1625. In that year too a blockhouse was built at the tip of Manhattan Island, which lies at the mouth of the Hudson River, to protect Dutch shipping and to serve as a convenient transfer point for shipments to and from the Hudson and Delaware river posts. The next year, 1626, the beginning of a regular village was constructed around the blockhouse on Manhattan Island—windmills for sawing wood and grinding corn and some thirty log houses spaced along the west side of the island. At the same time an energetic company officer, Peter Minuit, purchased the whole of the island from the native Manhates Indians and began to consolidate in this central village, called Fort Amsterdam or New Amsterdam, the main force of the scattered Dutch settlers. He withdrew some of the settlers from the distant and exposed posts on the upper Hudson and the Delaware, leaving only skeleton forces there to channel furs to New Amsterdam and to defend the Dutch claims. The population in New Amsterdam grew slowly, reaching only 450 in 1646 and perhaps 1,500 in 1664.

By midcentury the village of New Amsterdam consisted of the original blockhouse and windmills and a number of houses, all enclosed within a palisade, or wall (which became Wall Street), the whole compound surrounded by a canal. Scattered in the open area beyond the wall and canal were about fifty small farms (bouweries). In 1650 the village of New Amsterdam was a frontier community in which people of all sorts mingled, traded, and brawled. Men and women from half-a-dozen nations—Dutch, Walloons, French, English, Portuguese, Swedes, Finns, and Brazilian blacks—speaking, it was reported, eighteen different languages and professing every religious persuasion from Catholicism to Anabaptism, flocked to the settlement seeking to turn a profit on exchanges of furs, goods, produce, and land. It was as quarrelsome and disorderly a village as could be found in North America, torn by hostilities and constant disruption, constrained by no common purpose, disrespectful of the regulations that the company's loutish, blustering agents attempted to enforce, and above all neglected by the company that had sponsored the settlement and that remained legally responsible for its welfare.

For the company never doubted that whatever profits it was likely to make in North America would result from the fur cargoes that came in from the posts on the Hudson, Delaware, and Connecticut rivers, and from nothing else. The directors had no intention of throwing good money after bad, as the Virginia Company had done, in the vain hope of establishing a populous and prosperous agricultural and industrial community. They made no serious efforts to populate the colony, nor did they have available for that purpose as mobile a population as the English colonizers had had. To the company's directors, settlers meant private competition for their corporate control of the fur trade. They made every effort to monopolize that commerce, to impose heavy import and export duties on the colonists, and to lay taxes and fees in an effort to squeeze a profit from the settlements. Yet the profits that were made from the Dutch colony were made not by the company, which never recovered its initial investment, and not by the ordinary settlers, who lived little above the subsistence level in these early years, but by a few

NEW AMSTERDAM, ABOUT THE YEAR 1640
This view appeared as a miniature inset in a large map of New Netherland issued by Nicholas Visscher. *Legend: A:* Fort; *B:* Church of St. Nicholas; *C:* Jail; *D:* Governor's House; *E:* Gallows; *G:* West India Company's Stores; *H:* Tavern.

Dutch middlemen in New Amsterdam. These enterprising merchants and artisans fell in with the resident company officials to manipulate for their own benefit the monopolized sale of goods and supplies and the prices offered for furs and surplus farm products.

Contention and Indian Wars. At least one of the company's directors in the Netherlands, however, had a broader vision of the colony's future, and his strenuous efforts made a difference. Kiliaen Van Rensselaer, a wealthy Amsterdam jeweler, argued for the creation of large-scale private agricultural estates, like the proprietary manors in Maryland. These farming establishments, he claimed, would not only help stabilize the colony but would provide provisions, cattle, and other necessary supplies for the Dutch ships heading for the West Indies and elsewhere in the Western Hemisphere. His efforts resulted in the Charter of Freedoms and Exemptions issued by the company and confirmed by the Dutch government in 1629. The charter authorized the creation of "pa-

troonships," large estates that would be financed by groups of investors who would share in the profits but not in the management of these plantations, which would be controlled by the "patroons" alone.

Ten such investment groups were created, but only one patroonship, Rensselaerswyck, on both sides of the Hudson surrounding Fort Orange, developed in the form provided for in the charter and survived through the seventeenth century. To this huge estate Van Rensselaer, the patroon, sent a flow of goods, cattle, and equipment of all sorts, and he dispatched also at his own expense farmers and miscellaneous workers to populate the grant. By 1655 he had leased sixteen farms on the estate and had developed his personal manor efficiently despite all the confusions and difficulties of managing such property through deputies. And although it is doubtful that in the end Van Rensselaer recovered his heavy investment in the estate, he did establish on the upper Hudson a prosperous agricultural community.

The province of New Netherland as a whole, however, remained, as a contemporary wrote, "a wild country"—ill-organized, ill-managed, and contentious. The continuing disorder was partly the result of the uncontrolled multiplication of thinly populated villages, poorly organized and incapable of defending themselves. They appeared on all sides: on upper Manhattan (New Haarlem); in Westchester, across the Harlem River; on Staten Island; in New Jersey (Bergen); and especially on Long Island, where five Dutch towns appeared by the 1640s. The confusion in these border towns was compounded by the agitations of the neighboring English who moved in to New Netherland from the surrounding colonies. Attracted by the company's offer of freedom of worship, local self-government, and free land that would remain tax exempt for ten years, these migrants, while they helped populate the company's lands,

PETER STUYVESANT, c. 1660
Director-general of New Amsterdam for 17 years, this storming, peg-legged war veteran swore he would die before surrendering New Amsterdam to the English, but in fact he gave up the fort quietly in 1664 and retired peacefully to his farm in New York City. It had become his home, and there he died in 1672. *(Courtesy of The New-York Historical Society, New York City)*

created difficult administrative problems for the Dutch officials. In addition, these alien and discontented groups began agitating against the Dutch rule, advocating English conquest of the border areas if not of the whole colony. So acute were these border conflicts with the English that a formal treaty was drawn up between New Netherland and the confederation of New England colonies that had been created in 1643. The Treaty of Hartford (1650) set the Dutch-Connecticut boundary ten miles east of the Hudson River and eliminated Dutch claims beyond that line. But the New Englanders on Long Island continued to resist the Dutch authorities, and in the

South, on the Delaware River, Maryland challenged the Dutch openly. In the years preceding the English conquest of New Netherland the English settlers in the border areas had moved to open revolt.

None of these difficulties were eased by skillful management on the part of the Dutch officials or by the effectiveness of the colony's political institutions. Of the directors-general (governors) sent over by the company, only Peter Minuit (1626–31) was reasonably efficient and judicious. His two immediate successors were hopelessly inefficient, made more enemies than friends in the colony, and were finally removed from office in response to repeated charges that they were ruining the colony by their arrogance, corruption, indolence, and constant drunkenness. The second of them, Willem Kiefft (1638–47), personally set on foot a savage war against the neighboring Indians.

It began in 1642, after a number of Indian raids on outlying farms, with the slaughter of 110 unsuspecting and peaceful Indians encamped near New Amsterdam. This butchery was carried out with a barbarism that appalled even contemporary observers ("some came running to us from the country having their hands cut off; some lost both arms and legs; some were supporting their entrails with their hands, while others were mangled in other horrid ways, too horrid to be conceived"). All of this set the terms of a conflict that devastated New Netherland until, after three years, the Dutch hired the veteran English Indian fighter Captain John Underhill, who led 150 men in a midnight raid on an Indian village. Some 500 Indians were shot or burned alive in the conflagration that completed Underhill's victory. The peace that was concluded in 1646 was a peace not of reconciliation but of mutual exhaustion and fear of annihilation. When in 1647 the next, and last, director-general, Peter Stuyvesant, arrived, the colony was badly reduced in size, hard pressed by its competitive neighbors, and virtually abandoned by the failing company.

Stuyvesant, an autocratic ex-governor of the Dutch island of Curaçao, commissioned to oversee all Dutch interests in the Caribbean as well as to rule New Netherland, plunged into a hopeless tangle of contention. Given to fits of rage, savage in his efforts to wipe out all dissent from the colony's official Reformed Calvinism, and endowed with almost dictatorial executive powers, he made little headway in solving the colony's multiplying problems. By 1654 when the Dutch West India Company finally went bankrupt, all that remained to bear witness to the company's original hopes were a few wharves and bridges, a neglected fort, and a nondescript town hall and market area. In 1655 the Indians, in delayed vengeance, launched a new reign of terror on the faltering and battered settlements, and the colony's feeble resources were still further drained in the effort to survive. At the same time, the English in Connecticut laid plans to seize the colony and began more resolute encroachments on Dutch-claimed territory. By 1664, when an English fleet captured New Amsterdam, the colony as a whole was helpless, and in its desolation could only look to the new English authorities with hopes that had never been stirred by the Dutch West India Company or by such storming, hard-drinking martinets as William Kiefft and Peter Stuyvesant.

Royal Rewards: Carolina and the Jerseys

Thus by the 1640s—within a single generation of the chartering of the Virginia Company—large-scale, permanent colonies with a total population of over fifty thousand had been established along the Chesapeake Bay and the rivers of northern Virginia, at the mouth and along the banks of the Hudson River, and in central and southern New England. But no claim had yet been made to two great territories that adjoined these earliest European settlements: the mid-Atlantic region, between New Netherland and Maryland, and the land south of Virginia to the Spanish settlement at Saint Augustine, Florida. The settlement of these two major coastal regions—from one of which would be carved the Jerseys and Pennsylvania, and from the other the Carolinas and Georgia—took place in very different circumstances from those of the earlier settlements. Yet the earlier pattern of high hopes and imaginative designs followed by failure, disillusion,

CHARLES II
His return from exile and restoration to the throne (1660) marked a new phase in England's overseas expansion. He chartered the Carolinas, the Jerseys, and Pennsylvania, and his government enacted legislation that turned a collection of scattered settlements into a mercantile empire (Chapter 4). *(National Portrait Gallery, London)*

and then a slow emergence of communities in unexpected forms emerged in these later colonies as well.

Before these territories were settled, however, the greater world had been transformed. In the two decades after 1640 England was convulsed by civil war, by the execution of Charles I and the exile of Charles II, and by the creation of Oliver Cromwell's republican regime, which in the end became an autocratic "protectorate." In the midst of these domestic convulsions England engaged in two international wars: one with the Dutch, largely fought at sea (1652–54), and the other with Spain (1656–59), mainly in the Caribbean. By 1658, when Cromwell died, to be succeeded briefly as lord protector by his son, England was exhausted by the turmoil and eager for stability and reconciliation. When Charles II, now supported by disillusioned defectors from the conflict-torn Commonwealth, declared amnesty for all, liberty of conscience, and an endorsement of existing land titles, he was welcomed by a special parliamentary convention. He returned to England and to a restored monarchy in May 1660.

The Carolina Charter.   The main flow of colonization had been interrupted during these two tumultuous decades, but it was quickly resumed in the enterprising reign of Charles II (1660–85). While still in exile in France he and his followers, deprived of all

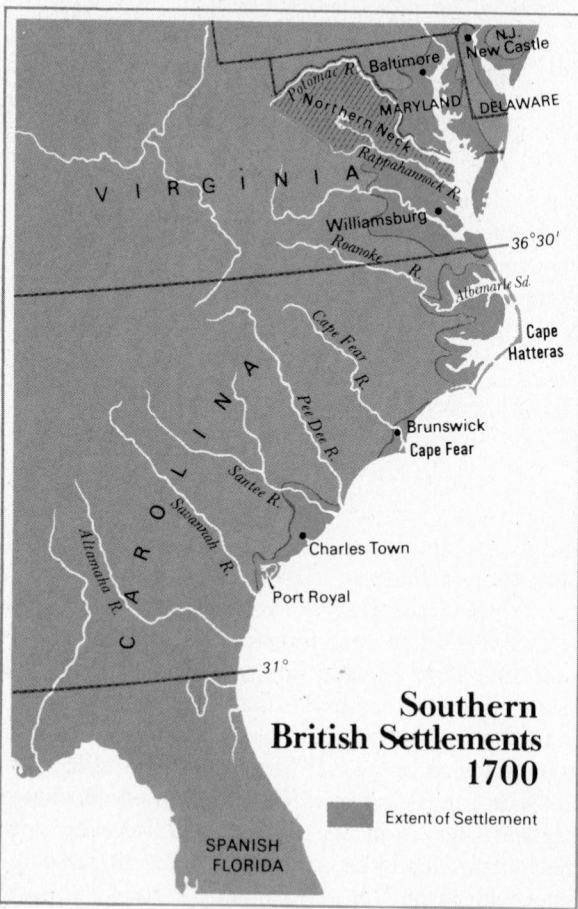

Southern British Settlements 1700

Extent of Settlement

other properties and prospects, had eyed the colonies as a rich field for exploitation. In 1649 the king had rewarded the loyalty of seven of his close followers with the proprietorship of the Northern Neck of Virginia, a domain of 5 million acres between the Potomac and the Rappahannock rivers. Once the court was reestablished in England, it turned its attention more fully to the colonies. In the competitive, exuberant atmosphere of Charles II's court, a syndicate of the most powerful courtiers was formed to promote the colonizing designs of an exceptionally enterprising plantation owner of the island of Barbados, Sir John Colleton.

Colleton, a well-connected royalist recently returned to London, knew that Barbados, the most profitable of England's West Indian islands, was producing a surplus population of land-hungry farmers displaced by the growth of slave plantations, and he knew too that Virginians and a few New Englanders were already attempting small experimental settlements in the lands just south of Virginia. He proposed to facilitate the settlement of this region, and quickly drew into his enterprise some of the most powerful figures of the realm. Among them were his kinsman the Duke of Albemarle, who had managed Charles' return to the throne; the Earl of Clarendon, Charles II's chief minister; Lord Berkeley, brother of the governor of Virginia, Sir William Berkeley; and above all, Sir Anthony Ashley Cooper, who as the Earl of Shaftsbury would become an important political power. For these imaginative and enterprising men Colleton's proposal was irresistible. No funds, time, or effort seemed to be required of them. Since settlement was already proceeding by spillovers from the older colonies, the proprietors had merely to design a system of government and land distribution, open a land office, appoint officials, and collect the rents.

The charter of Carolina that was issued to the eight partners in 1663 (extended in 1665) granted them title to all of the land lying between Virginia and Northern Florida and across the continent from sea to sea, and it gave them full rights of governance over this vast domain. The direct management of this immense territory did not interest them; they were not territorial imperialists. They had their eyes on the commercial possibilities of three tiny spots on the coastal fringe: first, a northern settlement safe behind the long spits of land that formed Albemarle Sound; second, a middle settlement at the mouth of the Cape Fear River where a cluster of New Englanders had already gathered; and third, a community at Port Royal, in the deeper south, close to what would later become the colony of Georgia. From these bustling nuclei would proliferate—the proprietors hoped—three well-populated, land-buying, rent-paying communities. They therefore divided the grant into three huge counties centered on these projected settlements. Then in "A Declaration and Proposals to All That Will Plant in Carolina" they designed governments patterned after the older British colonies, with veto powers retained by the proprietors. Freedom of religion was assured, as was a system of land distribution based on headrights of various dimensions, and large proprietary estates were reserved in every settlement.

It was a typical projection of enthusiastic colonial entrepreneurs, and it was typically unrealistic. The few Virginians in Albemarle were happy enough to organize an assembly to protest the terms of land allotment, but their settlement, from which would eventually develop the colony of North Carolina, was isolated from transoceanic commerce by coastal sand dunes and yielded not a penny of profit. And nothing, it seemed, could induce settlers in any numbers to remain on the swampy, sandy coastal land of Cape Fear, the proposed middle settlement, which was surrounded by hostile Indians. By 1669 the entire enterprise of Carolina was on the point of extinction, when it was suddenly taken over by Ashley, who rescued it from failure—though not in the way he planned.

With the assistance of the philosopher John Locke, who was his secretary, physician, and general counsel, Ashley reorganized the undertaking. He decided that funds would have to be raised from the sponsors themselves; that settlers would be sent out directly from England; and that the target would be the third, most southerly location, Port Royal, the site most favored by the Barbadians. With new capital raised from

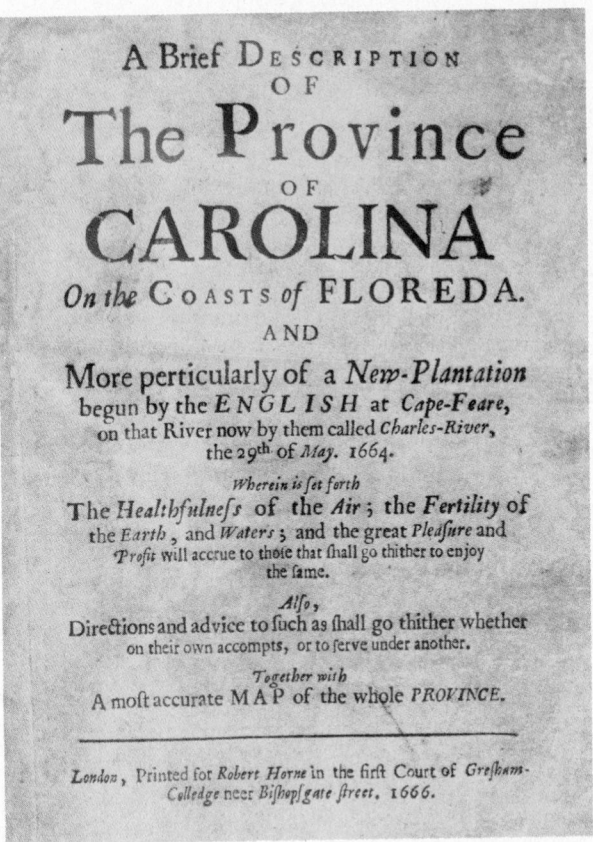

the original proprietors, Ashley was able to send out from England three vessels with about a hundred colonists and a large supply of equipment. The fleet was instructed to refit in Barbados and to recruit more settlers there, but misfortunes of every kind befell the expedition. Only a handful of settlers survived to establish a settlement, which they located not where one had been planned but much farther inland, out of reach of the Spanish. In 1670 that community, isolated from principal transportation routes, was still only a palisaded garrison surrounded by a few small subsistence farms. More vessels followed, however, especially from Barbados, and the leaders undertook a search for town sites suitable for the grand design of land distribution that had been set out by the proprietors. One of the promising sites they discovered, never contemplated by the proprietors, was Oyster Point, where the Ashley and Cooper rivers flow together, some sixty miles north of the original Port Royal. Gradually the superior attractions of this location, safe from coastal raids yet open to ocean commerce and at the hub of a network of river routes into the interior, overcame the proprietors' original plans for concentrated settlements. Family groups and individual farmers from the older mainland settlements and from Barbados began to move to this unplanned center of the colony and to establish claims to what quickly became valuable land along the banks of the rivers. By 1683 Oyster Point had been renamed Charles Town (a century later it would be called Charleston), and with a population of a thousand had become the center of a quickly growing colony. It was altogether different from the community at Albemarle, three hundred miles to the north, and altogether different too from anything that had been contemplated by the Carolina proprietors.

"Fundamental Constitutions." Of Ashley's and Locke's hopes and plans for Carolina after the reorganization of 1669 there is an extremely detailed picture in one of the most remarkable documents of the age, "The Fundamental Constitutions of Carolina," which they wrote in collaboration. It presented an elaborate blueprint for a hierarchical manorial world dominated by three orders of nobility—proprietors, "landgraves," and "caciques"—in which the association of landed property and public roles was designed to create stability. Utopian, intricately contrived, a mixture of nostalgic romanticism and hardheaded realism, the system that was detailed in the "Fundamental Constitutions," involving a legislative Council of Nobles and a system of manorial courts, was a dream that could never be put into effect. The government that in fact emerged in the first decades soon came to resemble that of the other proprietary colonies. In the eighteenth century, when the original Carolina charter was annulled, the colony's public institutions easily fell into the standard pattern of royal governments. Yet though the romantic notions that Ashley and Locke wrote into

their "Constitutions" died stillborn, a number of the document's provisions, which conformed to patterns of life that were otherwise developing in America, did become effective and did help shape the emerging community.

Religious toleration, provided for in the original Carolina charter, was reinforced and elaborated in the Ashley-Locke "Constitutions," and it contributed significantly to the development of the Carolinas. In addition, full naturalization of aliens was made extremely simple. Further, the "Constitutions" required that two-fifths of all the land of each county be granted in large estates to the nobility, and the way was thereby paved not so much for the creation of a landed nobility as for land speculation on a grand scale. Finally, the "Constitutions" established the rule of English law and outlined a structure of local administration similar to that of England—provisions that would remain fundamental to the exotic variant of British society that was developing at the end of the century in the southern part of the Carolina grant.

Carolina: Society and Economy. For what would become South Carolina *was* exotic, even in relation to the unusual communities that were elsewhere developing in mainland British America. Its quickly growing population, still a mere five to seven thousand by the end of the century, was peculiarly complex. It included not only New Yorkers, Puritan New Englanders, and Virginians, but also over five hundred English Presbyterians and Baptists and also a group of Presbyterian Scots. Recruitment of French Huguenots from their refuge in the Netherlands began in the earliest years and increased greatly after 1685 when these Protestant refugees lost all hope of returning to France; by 1700 at least five hundred Frenchmen were settled in the colony. But the dominant element from the start was the West Indians: several thousand tough, experienced frontier farmers displaced by the growth of the plantation economy in the sugar-producing islands and determined to establish themselves and prosper in this hot, fertile, unexplored land.

Experienced in the production of semitropical crops, experimental in their approach to agriculture, and familiar with slavery as a labor system, the West Indians, through the typical "starving times" of the early years, led the colony in the search for a staple crop. The first marketable products were familiarly British and held no great promise: timber, cattle, and foodstuffs, all of which had to be exchanged for sugar in the West Indies and in that form redeemed in the British markets. But gradually more exotic and more lucrative possibilities became clear. The first was the trade in furs, which remained a crucial element in the economic and social life of South Carolina for half a century. As early as the 1680s pack horses could be seen hauling into Charles Town and the other coastal villages animal skins bought through a series of exchanges from Indian hunters ranging deep in the wilderness south and west of the Savannah and Altamaha rivers. The Carolina fur traders, the least squeamish of men, working at the remote fringes of Western civilization, did not limit themselves to tracking down animals; they brought back humans as well. They led into Charles Town and the other villages troops of Indians captured from hostile tribes, and sold them into slavery at home and abroad.

Slavery—African, West Indian, American Indian—was a basic fact of life from the earliest days of South Carolina. There is evidence that in the early years of hardship, when survival was at stake, whites and blacks, freemen and slaves, worked together—"slaved" together—in conditions of relative equality. But that did not last. By the 1690s when the first successful experiments were made in the production of rice—the crop that, with indigo and the fur trade, would ultimately secure the colony's economy and require an ever-increasing work force of slaves—the condition of the blacks was reduced to absolute degradation. As early as 1708 blacks outnumbered whites in South Carolina, and by then the colony's black code, based on the savage slave laws of Barbados, was fully elaborated and rigorously enforced.

Such were the results of the enterprise of the Restoration courtiers who had been granted the great gift of Carolina in 1663. By the turn of the century South Carolina's survival was assured. The colony would prosper and grow—not as the utopia of balanced social orders that Locke and Ashley had dreamed of, but as a competitive world of rice plantations, savage race relations, land speculation, and commerce. Its most prominent families, as their fortunes rose, were increasingly eager for gentility, leisure, and the grace of life; but even more than the leaders of other colonies they were directly exposed to the wildness of the frontier and the barbarism of chattel slavery.

Settlement of the Jerseys. Of the Jerseys, founded at the same time as the Carolinas and under similar circumstances, less need be said. For there the proprietors' powers and claims almost immediately dissolved into an unchartable maze of divisions and subdivisions that left the territory open to largely unregulated settlement. There were, of course, high hopes at the start on the part of the two proprietors who in 1664 were granted the tract of approximately 5 million acres between the Delaware and Hudson rivers by the Duke of York, overlord of the territory conquered from the Dutch. But though these first proprietors of New Jersey, Lord John Berkeley and Sir George Carteret, both of whom were already proprietors of the Carolinas, issued grandiose plans modeled on the first Carolina designs, they had even less interest in managing this province than they had in governing the Carolinas.

In 1674 Berkeley sold his rights to a group of Quakers, setting in motion a bewildering exchange of shares, in the course of which, in 1676, the province was formally divided into two provinces, East Jersey and West Jersey. In the eastern sector heirs of Carteret attempted vainly to organize a coherent government out of the scattered settlements that had been founded by squatters. The new Quaker proprietors of the western portion attempted, amid paralyzing legal complications, to establish a refuge for their persecuted community. Harassed alike by the duke's governor in New York and the government at home, the Quaker leaders, among them William Penn, issued in 1677 an extraordinarily liberal and humane document "The Concessions and Agreements of the Proprietors, Freeholders and Inhabitants of ... West New Jersey in America," which guaranteed a democratically elected popular assembly, individual rights including absolute freedom of conscience, and adult male participation in local and provincial government. The first West Jersey assemblies of the early 1680s attempted, with uneven success, to enact all of this into law. But though groups of settlers appeared and began the cultivation of West Jersey, the Quakers' interests in colonization soon shifted to Pennsylvania, and West Jersey followed East Jersey into the hands of land speculators interested principally in the financial value of the proprietary claims. Scottish entrepreneurs led a Scots Presbyterian migration into East Jersey where they further compounded the mixture of peoples. Gradually, as farms and towns were built in both districts, a familiarly English pattern of local government emerged, in relation to which the proprietors were quite marginal. Yet title to the undistributed land remained in the proprietors' hands, even when the crown took temporary control of the two governments (1688–92) and after the two colonies were finally and permanently rejoined into the single crown colony of New Jersey (1702).

By then the territory that the Duke of York had so casually bestowed on his two followers contained a population of approximatley fourteen thousand, almost all of whom lived on one-family farms of from 50 to 150 acres. The ethnic and religious diversity was extraordinary, even for a British North American colony. Only New York was demographically more complex, but there a single group, the Dutch, predominated. In New Jersey no one group predominated. There were Africans, West Indians, Dutch, Germans, Huguenots, English, Scots, and Irish, worshiping as Congregationalists, Baptists, Quakers, Anglicans, Presbyterians, and Dutch and German Reformed. The colony had no particular

(Rare Book Division, The New York Public Library, Astor, Lenox and Tilden Foundations)

ADVERTISEMENT,

To all Tradeſ-men, Husbandmen, Servants and others who are willing to Tranſport themſelves unto the Province of New-Eaſt-Jerſy in America, a great part of which belongs to Scots-men, Proprietors thereof.

Whereas ſeveral Noblemen, Gentlemen, and others, who (by undoubted Rights derived from His Majeſty, and His Royal Highneſs) are Intereſted and concerned in the Province of *New-Eaſt-Jerſie*, lying in the midſt of the *Engliſh* Plantations in *America*, do intend (God-willing) to ſend ſeveral Ships thither, in *May, June,* and *July* enſuing, 1684. from *Leith, Montroſs, Aberdeen* and *Glaſgow.* Theſe are to give notice to all Tradeſ-men, Husband-men and others, who are willing and deſirous to go there, and are able to Tranſport themſelves and Families thither , upon their own Coſt and Charges, to a pleaſant and profitable Countrey, where they may live in great Plenty and Pleaſure, upon far leſs Stock, and with much leſs labour and trouble then in *Scotland*, that as ſoon as they arrive there, they ſhall have conſiderable quantities of Land, ſet out Heretably to themſelves and their Heirs for ever, for which they ſhall pay nothing for the firſt four or five years, and afterwards pay only a ſmall Rent yearly to the Owners and Proprietors thereof, according as they can agree. And all Tradeſ-men, Servants, and others, ſuch as, Wrights, Coupers, Smiths, Maſons, Millers, Shoe-makers, &c. who are willing to go there, and are not able to Tranſport themſelves, that they ſhall be carried over free, and well maintained in Meat and Clothes the firſt four years, only for their Service, and thereafter they ſhall have conſiderable quantities of Land, ſet out to themſelves and their Heirs for ever , upon which they may live at the rate of Gentlemen all their lives, and their Children after them: Their ordinary Service will be cutting down of Wood with Axes, and other eaſie Husband-Work, there being plenty of Oxen and Horſes for Plowing and Harrowing, &c. Let therefore all Tradeſ-men, Husband-men, Servants, and others who incline to go thither, and deſire further Information herein, repair themſelves to any of the Perſons underwritten, who will fully inform them anent the Countrey , and every other thing neceſſary, and will anſwer and ſatisfie their Scruples and Objections, and give them all other Incouragements according to their ſeveral abilities and capacities; viz.

At *Edinburgh* let them apply themſelves to the Lord Theſaurer-Deput, the Lord Regiſter, Sir *John Gordon*, Mr. *Patrick Lyon*, Mr. *George Alexander*, Advocates, *George Drummond* of *Blair, John Swintoun, John Drummond, Thomas Gordon, David Falconer, Andrew Hamilton*, Merchants; at *Braint-Iſland* to *William Robiſon* Doctor of Medecine; at *Montroſs*, to *John Gordon* Doctor of Medecine, *John Fullerton* of *Kinaber*, and *Robert* and *Thomas Fullertons* his Brothers; in the Shire of the *Mearns*, to *Robert Barclay* of *Urie*, and *John Barclay* his Brother ; at *Aberdeen*, to *Gilbert Moleſon, Andrew Galloway*, John and *Robert Sandilands, William Gerard* Merchants ; in the Shire of *Aberdeen*, to *Robert Gordon* of *Clunie*, and *Robert Burnet* of *Lethanty*; in the Shire of *Peirth* to *David Tiſbach* of *Monyvard* and Captain *Patrick Macgreiger*; In *Merſs* Shire, to *James Johnſton* of *Spoteſwood*; At *Keiſo*, to *Charles Ormiſton* Merchant ; In the *Lowes*, to *Kenith Mackenzie* younger of *Kildin*: And if any Gentleman or others be deſireous to buy or purchaſe any ſmall ſhares or portions of Land in the ſaid Province, they may repair to any of the foreſaid Perſons, who will direct them how they ſhall be ſerved, providing they do it timouſly, becauſe many more Perſons are dayly offering to buy, then can be cultural character or social organization, and its mixed farming economy was in no way distinctive in the agricultural world of the northern colonies.

Pennsylvania: A Godly Experiment and a Worldly Success

Of all the colonies, it is perhaps Pennsylvania that shows most vividly the contrast between soaring aspirations and mundane accomplishments. In part the vividness of the contrast was a consequence of the speed with which everything happened in Pennsylvania; in part too it was a reflection of the fame of the original plans and the force of the original hopes; and in part also it reflected the incongruous mixture of elements in William Penn's personality.

Quaker Immigrants. The founding of Pennsylvania was the accomplishment of one of the most radical religious sects of the seventeenth century. The Quakers, as religious extremists, had suffered severe persecution during their thirty years of existence as a group before the founding of Pennsylvania. Devoting themselves to finding the divine "inner light" within each soul, they practiced a religion free of all the encumbrances of church, clergy, and ritual. They were proud, courageous, and defiant of secular authority to the point of refusing to take ordinary oaths of loyalty. They advocated absolute freedom of conscience, were pacifists and political reformers.

By 1680 there were some fifty thousand members of this famous radical sect in Britain, largely among the poorest people, and there were smaller numbers scattered through continental Europe and North America. After the hysteria of the Popish Plot (1678), when it was alleged that England was being taken over by a French Catholic conspiracy led by the royal family, and after the Exclusion Crisis (1679–81), in which efforts were made to exclude the Catholic Duke of York from the succession to the throne, the English government launched savage attacks on all dissidents, especially such extremists as the Quakers. Some 1400 of these gentle but radical nonconformists were thrown in jail, and they were fined heavily both

for attending Quaker meetings and for failing to attend services of the Church of England. In default of payment (and most Quakers could not pay the fines) their goods—including their means of livelihood—were seized and destroyed or carted away. Victims of such persecution were crippled not only economically but spiritually as well, for Quakers regarded work as a divine calling, and the incapacity to pursue their vocations was a further inhibition of their religious life.

William Penn, though a well-educated son of one of England's most influential naval officers and a familiar and respected figure at the court of Charles II, shared in these disabilities as he did in all the fortunes of the Quakers whom he had joined as a young man. But his outlook was curiously complex. Convinced of the truth of the Quakers' tenets, he brought to the movement great energy, high-level contacts, a lawyer's shrewdness in polemics and court proceedings, and a businesslike approach to the endless controversies in which the group was embroiled. He was a radical—certainly in religion but also in politics—in that he sought every means of protecting the individual from the arbitrary power of the state and believed that government existed to improve the welfare of the masses. But he remained an aristocrat all his life. A political reformer and extremist in religion, he was nevertheless a monarchist. He continued to believe that the well educated and highly placed should have the decisive voices in public affairs, and though he suffered for his Quaker views, he managed to keep contact with the sources of his patronage at the court of Charles II.

Why Charles II granted this outspoken dissident a princely domain as a personal gift has never been fully explained. No doubt a long-standing crown debt to Penn's father was a factor, and the king may have thought he could get rid of the Quakers in this convenient way. But Penn's personal relations with the royal family were probably decisive, and of that very little is known. In any case, Charles II bestowed on Penn personally in 1681 the last unassigned portion of the North American coast. The grant encompassed the entire area between New York and Maryland, stretching west almost 300 miles from the New

Jersey border at the Delaware River—a total of 29 million acres, almost the size of England.

Penn was the outright owner of this territory, and he received also the authority to form a government, make most appointments to public office, and promulgate laws subject only to the approval of an assembly of freemen and the crown's right of veto. The charter established the supremacy of England's commercial regulations, but otherwise Penn was free to govern as he wished. He immediately set forth a Frame of Government—the first of a series, as it turned out. It is a strange document: in part a code of moral principles, including absolute freedom of worship and conscience; in part an intricate formulation of traditional arrangements for civil administration, reformed to satisfy Quaker ideals; and in part a blueprint for a remarkably *un*democratic government. A governor and a large council were to initiate and execute all laws, which the assembly, elected only by property owners, might accept or reject but not amend. Thus, amid striking statements of private and public morality and appeals to humanity and decency, Penn gave power not to the people at large but to their "natural" governors, though unlike the Calverts in Maryland he never thought of himself as a feudal overlord. From this fusing of benevolence and paternalism Penn expected a community of brotherly love to emerge, tolerant, free, secure, and above all peaceful. With those hopes in mind he turned with passion and skill to making his dreams come true.

In the end he was deeply disillusioned. Simply maintaining the legal title to his colony was an endless struggle, and his relations with the settlers were profoundly embittering. His colonizing efforts, however, were extraordinarily successful, especially at the start.

Growth of the Colony. Circulation of recruitment pamphlets through Britain and in translation in western Europe made Pennsylvania the best advertised

WILLIAM PENN'S MAP OF PHILADELPHIA, c. 1681
(Courtesy, Library Company of Philadelphia)

THE CITY OF PHILADELPHIA.

of all American colonies. A central "city of brotherly love," Philadelphia, was founded at an excellent site one hundred miles up the Delaware River where it meets the Schuylkill, and a well-designed street plan was laid out. A generous system of land distribution was set up. Land along the Delaware south of Philadelphia (the "lower counties") was added to Pennsylvania by the Duke of York to assure the colony's access to the sea. Quaker merchants invested heavily in the colony's expenses, and an assembly met within a year and composed a "Great Law" to serve as a temporary code of legislative and administrative principles and procedures. Above all, settlers arrived in large numbers.

By 1682, when Penn visited the province, the population was already 4,000—a remarkable swarming of people within a few months. There were Dutch, Swedes, and Finns from earlier settlements on the Delaware; West New Jerseyites; a large and influential influx of Welsh Quakers; Germans from the Rhineland who settled Germantown near Philadelphia; and above all English Quakers who flocked to the refuge Penn had provided for them. Fifty vessels brought 3,000 more settlers in 1683. By 1700 the colony's population was a remarkable 21,000. But by then Penn knew all the difficulties that his proprietorship entailed.

He was thoroughly embroiled with Lord Baltimore over the southern boundary of the province (a dispute that would be finally settled only with the drawing of the Mason-Dixon line on the eve of the Revolution). He was faced with stiff resistance to his authority by the settlers in the newly acquired "lower counties," a district that would ultimately form the state of Delaware; he was forced to allow them their own assembly in 1701. He was unfortunate in his choice of deputy governors and suffered from their clumsiness. Above all, he was faced with fierce opposition to his concept of government, an opposition that was led by some of the most deeply committed Quakers among the settlers.

From the beginning the colonial leaders insisted that the representative assembly, and not Penn or his deputy governors, have the determining voice in government. The house seized the power of initiating

legislation, and in 1696 forced Penn to concede that right. It insisted, against Penn's will, on amending bills presented to it by him, and it challenged his title to the undivided land. Pressure was maintained year after year in the 1690s until finally, after bitter disputes, and several revisions of the original Frame of Government, Penn agreed to an altogether new Frame. Written in 1701 by a joint committee of the council and the house, this charter of liberties, which would serve as the constitution of Pennsylvania until the Revolution, marked the final defeat of Penn's political ideals. It eliminated the council altogether from the legislative process, thus constituting the only unicameral government in British America. The king's veto of laws was retained but not Penn's, and the inhabitants were explicitly freed from any special allegiance to Penn or his descendants. What remained beyond dispute to the founder and his heirs was title to the undistributed land and the authority to appoint the resident governors. All the other chartered powers were either eliminated or challenged, and not by a democratic, populist majority of the population but by an oligarchy of Quaker politicians and representatives elected on a limited franchise, a quarrelsome, opinionated, ambitious clique that would dominate the colony's politics for the next half-century.

Penn had lost control of the province. But though Pennsylvania had failed to develop into the utopia of its founder's dreams, it was a fabulous worldly success. Contentious in politics but populous and prosperous from the start, open and attractive equally to penniless refugees and ambitious merchants, perfectly located and peopled for maximum economic growth, the distribution center for a mass population of laborers and yet a center too of provincial high culture, Pennsylvania became within a single generation the dynamic heart of the British North American world. It was with a sure instinct in 1723 that the ambitious seventeen-year-old Benjamin Franklin left Boston to seek his fortune in Philadelphia. William Penn was only five years dead, but his City of Brotherly Love had become a vigorous, prosperous community of ten thousand souls, a vital part of a colonial world that was evolving in unexpected ways.

CHRONOLOGY

1607 Virginia Company of London establishes settlement at Jamestown.

1609 Pilgrims flee to Holland to avoid religious persecution.

1609 Second charter of Virginia Company.

1612 Third charter of Virginia Company.

1619 First Africans arrive in Virginia. First North American representative assembly meets in Virginia.

1620 Mayflower Compact signed; Pilgrims establish Plymouth Colony.

1621 Dutch West India Company chartered.

1622 Indian rebellion in Virginia.

1624 Virginia Company charter annulled; English crown takes control of Virginia. First settlements in New Netherlands.

1625–49 Reign of Charles I.

1626 Dutch settle Manhattan.

1629 Massachusetts Bay Company chartered.

1630 Puritan emigration from England begins; continues until 1643.

1632 Cecilius Calvert, Lord Baltimore, receives charter for Maryland colony.

1634 First settlements in Maryland.

1635 Roger Williams banished from Bay Colony.

1636 Harvard College founded. First permanent English settlements in Connecticut and Rhode Island.

1638 Anne Hutchinson convicted of heresy in Massachusetts; flees to Rhode Island.

1639 Fundamental Orders adopted in Connecticut.

1642 Basic literacy law passed in Massachusetts Bay.

1642–48 Civil war in England.

1643 Confederation of New England colonies.

1644 Rhode Island receives patent.

1647 Law requiring towns to maintain schools passed in Massachusetts Bay Colony.

1649 Northern neck of Virginia granted to courtiers in exile.

1663 Carolina charter granted to eight proprietors; Rhode Island granted charter.

1664 English conquest of New Netherland; grant of New Jersey to two proprietors.

1681 Charles II issues Pennsylvania charter to William Penn.

SUGGESTED READINGS

There have been two recent efforts to summarize the English background of seventeenth-century colonization: Wallace Notestein, *The English People on the Eve of Colonization, 1603–1630* (1954) and Carl Bridenbaugh, *Vexed and Troubled Englishmen, 1590–1642* (1968). But more revealing than either of these general descriptions, which are based largely on literary sources, are studies that have nothing to do with colonization directly but make clear the disarray, mobility, and vitality of English society which underlay the extraordinary exodus of English men and women overseas: Peter Laslett, *The World We Have Lost* (1965); Peter Clark and Paul Slack, eds., *Crisis and Order in English Towns 1500–1700* (1972); John Patten, *English Towns, 1500–1700* (1978); Peter Spufford, "Population Mobility in Pre-Industrial England" (three essays in *Genealogists Magazine,* 1973–74); and the writings of W.G. Hoskins on English local history, most of which are listed in his *Local History in England* (1959). The best introduction to the economic history of pre-industrial England is Charles Wilson, *England's Apprenticeship, 1603–1763* (1965), two-thirds of which is on the seventeenth century; chaps. i–iii are particularly relevant.

The most comprehensive survey of the native North American population is the massive volume 15 (1978) of the Smithsonian Institution's new series, *Handbook of North American Indians.* This volume, subtitled *The Northeast,* summarizes all the available information—historical, an-thropological, and archaeological—concerning all the native tribes from Maine to North Carolina and west to the Great Lakes. T. J. Brasser's chapter on early Indian-European contacts, Christian Feest's on the Chesapeake and North Carolina tribes, and Elizabeth Tooker's on the League of the Iroquois are particularly valuable. Writings on the extremely difficult subject of the size, distribution, and structure of the Indian population are listed in H. F. Dobyns, *Native American Historical Demography* (1976) to which should be added S. F. Cook, *The Indian Population of New England in the Seventeenth Century* (1976) and several of the contributions to the *Handbook*, cited above. For a useful sketch of the seaboard Indians on the eve of European colonization see T. J. Brasser, "The Coastal Algonkians: People of the First Frontiers," in Eleanor B. Leacock and Nancy O. Lurie, eds., *North American Indians in Historical Perspective*, 1971. There are detailed accounts of the conflicts of races for only a few of the seventeenth-century colonies: Allen W. Trelease, *Indian Affairs in Colonial New York: The Seventeenth Century* (1960); Alden W. Vaughan, *New England Frontier: Puritans and Indians, 1620–1675* (1975); Douglas E. Leach, *Flintlock and Tomahawk: New England in King Philip's War* (1958); Nancy O. Lurie, "Indian Cultural Adjustment to European Civilization," in James M. Smith, ed., *Seventeenth-Century America* (1959); and Francis Jennings, *The Invasion of America* (1975). Jennings' book is a bitter outcry against the wrongs done the North American Indians by the Puritans (and in this, a criticism of Vaughan's more even-handed treatment) and a boiling polemic against historians' characterization of the Indians as sparse in numbers, hostile to Europeans, savage, heathen, and unsophisticated in agriculture, trade, and politics. What the Indians were, aside from the victims of Puritans and mythologizing historians, does not emerge. Jennings' bibliography is excellent. For a survey of the wars between the European settlers and the Indians in the seventeenth century, see Wilcomb Washburn's chapter in the *Handbook*.

The most detailed and comprehensive single narrative of the English settlements in the seventeenth century is Charles M. Andrews, *The Colonial Period of American History* (vols. I–III, 1934–37), which concentrates on constitutional history and the development of public institutions. A more up-to-date and broad-ranging account of the planting and early growth of the southern colonies is Wesley F. Craven, *The Southern Colonies in the Seventeenth Century, 1607–1689* (1949). The settlement stories are retold in briefer scope in John E. Pomfret, *Founding the American Colonies, 1583–1660*

(1970) and Wesley F. Craven, *The Colonies in Transition, 1660–1713* (1968), both of which contain extensive bibliographies. There are excellent essays on local government in the colonies in Bruce C. Daniels, ed., *Town and County* (1978).

On the founding of Virginia, there are, besides the relevant chapters of Andrews *Colonial Period*, vol. I, and Craven's *Southern Colonies*, a detailed narrative of public events in Richard L. Morton, *Colonial Virginia* (2 vols., 1960); an excellent short summary in Alden T. Vaughan, *American Genesis* (1975); a revealing account of the high culture of the initiators of settlement, in Richard B. Davis, *George Sandys* (1955); biographies of Pocahontas and John Smith by Philip L. Barbour; and two excellent collections of documents: L. G. Tyler, ed., *Narratives of Early Virginia, 1606–1625* (1907) and Warren M. Billings, ed., *The Old Dominion in the Seventeenth Century . . .* (1975). Sigmund Diamond's provocative essay, "From Organization to Society: Virginia in the Seventeenth Century," *American Journal of Sociology*, 63 (1958), 457–75,[1] interprets the founding as the transformation of a quasi-military organization into a fully formed society of multiple relationships. Bernard Bailyn, "Politics and Social Structure in Virginia," in Smith, ed., *Seventeenth-Century America*, pp. 90–115,* considers the development of politics in its relation to the evolving social structure. Edmund Morgan considers the human cost of the colony's success in terms of the exploitation of labor in "The First American Boom: Virginia 1618–1630," *Wm. and Mary Q.*, 18 (1971), 169–98,* a topic discussed in a broader context in his *American Slavery, American Freedom* (1975).

The labor problem in Virginia involves the difficult question of the origins of chattel slavery. The modern debate on that question was initiated and framed by a brilliant article by Oscar and Mary F. Handlin, "Origins of the Southern Labor System," *Wm. and Mary Q.*, 7 (1950), 199–222,* reprinted as chap. i of Handlin's *Race and Nationality in American Life* (1957). Handlin's view is that chattel slavery in British America was a unique institution, different from slavery in any other form or place; that the concept of "slavery" in its American meaning was created in the seventeenth-century Chesapeake; and that it arose as a legal condition, in response not so much to race prejudice

---

[1] This essay and several mentioned in the references that follow have been reprinted in an excellent collection, *Colonial America: Essays in Politics and Social Development* (Stanley N. Katz, ed., 2d ed., Boston, 1976). Essays and selections from books that appear in this volume are indicated by an asterisk(*).

as to an effort to attract voluntary white labor by debasing the condition of involuntary black labor. For differing views, emphasizing race prejudice, the fear of foreignness, and religious differences, see Winthrop Jordan, *White over Black* (1968), Part I*, and Carl N. Degler, "Slavery and the Genesis of American Race Prejudice," *Comparative Studies in History and Society,* 2 (1959), 49–66. For a listing of recent writings on the subject, see Vaughan, *American Genesis*, p. 198.

On the Pilgrims and Plymouth, see George D. Langdon, Jr.'s general account, *Pilgrim Colony* (1966) and John Demos's social analysis, *A Little Commonwealth* (1970). George F. Willison's *Saints and Strangers* (1945) is a breezy, amusing interpretation. Bradford's great history, *Of Plymouth Plantation*, is available in a modern edition prepared by Samuel E. Morison (1952).

On the founding and early development of the Puritan colonies in New England, see, besides Andrews' chapters in *The Colonial Period*, Edmund S. Morgan's short biography of John Winthrop, *Puritan Dilemma* (1958); Darrett Rutman's *Winthrop's Boston* (1965); Samuel E. Morison's *Builders of the Bay Colony* (1930); Raymond P. Stearns, *The Strenuous Puritan: Hugh Peter* (1954); and above all, Winthrop's own *Journal . . . 1630–1649* (J. K. Hosmer, ed., 2 vols., 1908). For a theatrical and psychological account of Anne Hutchinson's career, see Emery Battis, *Saints and Sectaries* (1962), and on Roger Williams there are books by S. H. Brockunier, Perry Miller, and Edmund S. Morgan. On seventeenth-century Connect-icut, besides Andrews, see Isabel M. Calder, *The New Haven Colony* (1934) and Mary J. A. Jones, *Congregational Commonwealth* (1968). On Rhode Island, see Sydney V. James, *Colonial Rhode Island* (1975), and on Maine and New Hampshire, Charles E. Clark, *The Eastern Frontier* (1970), Part I.

Maryland is well covered in Andrews' and Craven's general books, but in the case of New York the general accounts should be supplemented by Thomas J. Condon, *New York Beginnings* (1968); Van Cleaf Bachman, *Peltries or Plantations* (1969); and the early chapters of Michael Kammen, *Colonial New York* (1975). M. Eugene Sirmans, *Colonial South Carolina* (1966) and Peter H. Wood, *Black Majority* (1974) are essential on South Carolina. Hugh T. Lefler and Albert R. Newsome, *North Carolina* (1954) is a good summary of that colony's early history. Wesley F. Craven, *New Jersey and the English Colonization of North America* (1964) is the best short book on that colony, though there are a number of more detailed studies by John E. Pomfret. The most recent history of the founding of Pennsylvania is Edwin B. Bronner's *William Penn's "Holy Experiment"* (1962); on the colony's early political history, see Gary B. Nash, *Quakers and Politics . . . 1681–1726* (1968). Catherine O. Peare, *William Penn* (1957) narrates the essential facts of the founder's life in a somewhat exclamatory fashion; Mary M. Dunn, *William Penn, Politics and Conscience* (1967) is an excellent study of Penn's ideas and religious beliefs.

Thus, through these many agencies—commercial companies, religious organizations, individual entrepreneurs, syndicates of courtiers—communities of Europeans were established on mainland North America. By 1700 these colonies formed an almost continuous line of seaboard settlements from New Hampshire to South Carolina and westward irregularly a hundred miles or so to the first falls of the coastal rivers. The total population of some 250,000 Europeans and Africans and their descendants, most of them English-speaking, were by no means spread evenly through this broad area. They clustered along river valleys to take advantage of the fertile soil and easy lines of communication, and they left behind large pockets of unsettled land. Even in the oldest communities of Massachusetts and Virginia this was still a frontier world, fundamentally shaped by its continuing encounter with the wilderness. Yet there were areas populated by native-born children of native-born parents—a third generation in America. For them, home was the colony, however much they might acknowledge a greater "home" abroad. Though they did not think of themselves as peculiarly "American," they lived settled lives in communities familiar to them from birth, and these were communities whose distinctive characteristics were becoming clear.

Newcomers to the colonies in 1700 (and immigration continued in all areas, though least in New England) were no longer faced with the bewildering disarray that earlier settlers had known. But neither did they find themselves in communities quite like any seen before. By 1700 the British colonies had acquired distinctive characteristics. There were great variations region by region and settlement by settlement, but despite the differences, common elements of a re-ordering of European life could be found in these communities.

This re-ordering of social life was not the result of design, or planning, or intent. Planning, as we have seen—elaborate designs and soaring dreams—there had been in abundance. But none of these original plans had been fulfilled; all had been quickly destroyed or slowly dissolved upon contact with the harsh reality. The deviations from European life

Europe in the Wilderness
American Society in the Seventeenth Century

that had developed by 1700 were products of the impact of circumstance upon the culture of essentially conservative immigrants, most of whom sought personal satisfactions, personal freedoms, and security within familiar patterns of life. For many, the changes that took place were felt to be regressions rather than advances. Change was more often resisted than pursued. Only later would the alterations in community life be seen as advances toward an ideal—the ideal, expressed in the Enlightenment goals of the Revolution, of a freer, more fulfilling way of life.

Population Growth and Structure

American society in the seventeenth century was shaped in large part by demographic characteristics. Because the first American population was an immigrant population and because life in the colonies was harsh and was known to be harsh, the society that resulted was no evenly balanced re-creation of the social structure of Europe. The upper strata of traditional society were absent from the start. Of Europe's ruling nobility, there were no representatives at all. There were few even of what might loosely be called the aristocracy or of the upper gentry, few even of professional upper middle class, if one may use these modern terms. For then, as now, society's leaders and those who were well established did not easily tear up their roots, migrate, and struggle to secure themselves in an undeveloped land.

The Free Population. Most of the free population in mainland North America was recruited from the lower working population of England and the Netherlands—not for the most part the lowest, not destitute vagrants and outcasts, but farm workers, industrial workmen, tradesmen, and artisans. In the immigrant lists of the time, the two occupations most commonly entered were "yeoman," or "husbandman" (a farm worker, usually with some degree of independence) and artisan, or tradesman. Outside of New England, between one-half and two-thirds of all white immigrants were indentured servants. They were bound, for four years or more, to serve some master faithfully in exchange for their transatlantic passage, care and protection, and "freedom dues," which often included a small parcel of land. Averaging approximately 1,500 arrivals a year between 1630 and 1700, these immigrants to the Chesapeake, originally bound in various conditions of servitude, totaled more than 100,000 by 1700.

Further, the free population as it emerged from the seventeenth century was peculiarly mobile. The population was originally recruited, and continued to be recruited, from groups already dislodged from secure roots. Often for these people resettlement in America was not a unique transplantation but a second or third uprooting. And outside of New England, institutional or legal restraints on mobility, so vital a part of life in traditional European societies, scarcely existed at all. People were free to move where they would. The large majority of the indentured servants in the Chesapeake region survived servitude to enter the community free of involvement, commitment, or obligation, free to follow the attractions of security, profit, or congeniality wherever they might be found.

More important still, the free population of the northern colonies in the seventeenth century, and of the southern colonies too by the early eighteenth century, was unusual in the speed of its growth. The information that historians have recently gathered on the demographic characteristics of early New England reveals a society that was remarkably fertile. In an era in which most of European society was scarcely reproducing itself, the most prolific of the settled communities in America may have reached the extraordinary growth rate of 5 to 6 percent a year. Until the 1650s, it is true, Virginia and Maryland seem to have remained a death trap of disease. A random list of ninety-nine adult deponents before one Virginia county court shows an average age at death of only 48 in the years between 1637 and 1664. These were mostly men; the life expectancy of women aged 20 in the same region was only 40. In Maryland the population began to reproduce itself only in the 1680s; before then only the constant flow of immigrants, highly vulnerable to the diseases common to the Chesapeake region, accounted for population growth. But the death rate in the Chesapeake colonies fell rapidly in the later seventeenth century as the proportion of native-born in the population, who developed immunities to the prevalent diseases early in life, increased. The population of Virginia, supplemented by constant immigration, rose rapidly: it stood at 8,000 in 1644, quadrupled to 32,000 in the next thirty years, and then more than doubled once again in the next thirty years, reaching an estimated 75,600 in 1704.

In New England, once the initial immigration was completed, the population grew during the seventeenth century at an average rate of 2.6 or 2.7 percent a year, which meant that the settled population, quite aside from further immigration, was doubling approximately every twenty-seven years. And whatever else may be said about such a phenomenon as this, it meant that all other social changes were intensified by sheer demographic pressure.

How can this extraordinary growth rate be explained? Not, apparently, by an unusual birthrate. The birthrates available for selected American communities are similar to birthrates in French and English villages of this period. The root of the difference apparently lies in the lower death rate in the American colonies, once the original "starving times" were over and once the deadly "seasoning" times in the southern colonies came to an end. In Plymouth, Massachusetts, the life expectancy of men who survived to the age of 21 was 69.2 years, and in Andover, Massachusetts, the average age at death of the first settlers was 71.8 years; for their sons the average was 65.2. In that same village community, life expectancy at birth for males in the seventeenth century was longer by 12.6 years than it would be for men in England two hundred years later.

This rapidly growing population was unusual too in its age structure, which is associated with population growth. The American population was youthful. Most of the tens of thousands of indentured servants were between 18 and 24 years of age when they arrived. In Bristol, Rhode Island, 54 percent of the population were children; in seventeenth-century England the equivalent figure is 42.6 percent.

ALICE MASON, 1670

This forthright, unpretentious portrait by an unknown artist illustrates not only the appearance of children in the seventeenth century but attitudes toward children and childhood. This is not a child but a miniature adult, an individual who happens to be short and deficient in certain important ways, especially in the capacity to enjoy full religious experience, but for the most part fully endowed and responsible for her actions. The modern concept of childhood was a later development. *(U.S. Department of the Interior, National Park Service. Adams National Historic Site, Quincy, Massachusetts)*

The American population, being youthful, was less vulnerable to the ravages of disease than a more evenly age-distributed population would have been. The survival rate reflects too a higher proportion of women who were in the years of fertility, 15–45, and in addition a younger average age at marriage, at least in the northern colonies, especially for women.

In England, where 15 percent of the population were servants constrained from marrying young and where socioeconomic circumstances made establishing new households difficult for those without inheritances, it appears that the average age at first marriage was 28 for men and 24 for women. For one Massachusetts community that has been closely studied (Dedham), the equivalent figures are 25.5 and 22.5. In Plymouth the average age at first marriage for women at the end of the seventeenth century was 22.3; in Bristol, R.I., before 1750, the average age for women's first marriages was 20.5. As a result of these younger marriages women commonly bore children from their very early twenties until they were in their mid-forties. Younger marriages also assured a higher survival rate of children since the offspring of such marriages in preindustrial societies seem to have been more resistant to disease.

Finally, of the population characteristics that distinguish the emerging American communities from the parent communities abroad, there was an altered sex ratio. In England through these years, as in most settled societies, there were more women than men. The figures for England in the period 1574–1821 are 91.3 men to every 100 women. In the early years of settlement in America the figures are wildly inverted. In Virginia in 1625, over 75 percent of the settlers were men, and by midcentury the proportion was still approximately 6 to 1. Even in New England, where immigration by family was more common, there were 3 men for every 2 women in the middle of the century (a ratio reached in Virginia only in 1700), and while the proportion tended to level out as the century progressed, the traditional preponderance of women was by no means reached by 1700.

The Black Population. All of this pertains to the free white population. No such precise figures can be given for the growing black population. We know only that of the 250,000 inhabitants of British North America in 1700, perhaps 10 percent were blacks, almost all of them slaves. Most had arrived from Barbados or elsewhere in the West Indies. It was only in 1674 that the Royal African Company brought the first shipment direct from Africa. Thereafter, as the flow of white indentured servants from Britain slackened due to changes in the English labor market and to the growing attractions of the nonplantation colonies, shipments of slaves from Africa increased steadily. The decisive turning point—a landmark in American history—was the mid-1680s when black slaves for the first time outnumbered white servants in the southern labor force. When in 1698 the Royal African Company lost its monopoly, a flock of small operators entered the grim but profitable trade in human lives, and the floodgates were open: 10,000 slaves arrived in the Chesapeake colonies in the years 1698–1709.

In the seventeenth century, however, the number of blacks was still small, and partly because of that they lived lives of extreme degradation on the southern plantations. Family life—any kind of dignified existence—was impossible in a population of slaves, predominantly male, torn from their homes and brutalized in an utterly alien world where disease devastated infants and childbearing women, and where plantations were so small, isolated, and primitive that there were no tasks except the most degrading kinds of field labor. Often slaves lived not even in small huts or sheds in which a semblance of family life or familiar culture might be constructed, but in laborers' barracks. A measure of relief would come only a generation later, when an American-born black population was settled long enough to develop a more balanced sex ratio; when plantation life had evolved to the point where the need for artisanship and household help would allow escape for some of the slaves from the worst kind of field drudgery; and when stable communities of blacks were large enough to nourish a distinctive subculture, mingling African and American traditions—a subculture that would persist and flourish and in the end help shape the national culture of the American people.

Economic Instability

As American society emerged in the early eighteenth century, economic life, social organization, and the practice of religion varied greatly from region to region and from colony to colony. But running through all these major areas of life was a common characteristic, namely, the glaring difference between the colonists' assumptions, ideals, and expectations on the one hand, and on the other hand the actualities of life as it was experienced in America. In considering each of these three areas, one may most profitably start by isolating the colonists' assumptions and expectations, the ideal by which the reality would instinctively be measured. Against this background the departures of American life stand out most clearly, and their impact on the inner experiences of settlers seeking to re-create a familiar and controllable world may most clearly be assessed.

Assumptions and Expectations. The dominant view of the economy that the colonists brought with them was that of a stable system through which a more or less constant supply of goods and services flowed for the benefit of a population of relatively unchanging needs and desires. The object of individual effort in such a system was to secure oneself within it and to help preserve its organization. Difficulties, when they arose, were assumed to be disturbances in the established relations among the producing, distributing, and consuming elements, and remedies were sought that would bring the elements back into their established and proper proportions. The object of primary concern was the consumer not the producer, and a consumer of fixed, not growing, wants. Controls were assumed to be necessary to keep the economy in proper working order, especially to prevent greed or accidents from disturbing the system. And controls were not assumed to be solely those of the state. Lesser bodies, such as gilds and municipal governments, which stood between the individual and the state, were assumed to be proper agencies of economic regulation.

Such were the ordinary assumptions and the ideal expectations of colonists still close to late medieval culture, still far from the modern world of dynamic economic systems in which an ever-rising production and the manipulation of consumption are essential keys to success. How well did the developing colonial economies conform to these tradi-

tional assumptions? The economies that developed north and south violated these expectations on every point, and in doing so created a sense of jarring disarray until, ultimately, the American economic system became established and familiar, and Americans learned to accommodate themselves to the high instability that lay at the heart of this new system.

New England's Economy. In New England there had originally been little desire to create a commercial system that would link the Bay Colony's small port towns to an intricate network of Atlantic commerce and involve the Puritans in the greater world they had left behind. The original goal was economic self-sufficiency, the condition most likely to preserve the Bible commonwealth free of corruption and contamination. But by the late 1650s circumstances had led the Puritans to create the peculiarly complex economic system, closely involved with Atlantic commerce, that would continue basically unchanged until the Revolution.

The failing effort to perpetuate the Bay Colony's economic independence, once the capital of the original settlers had been exhausted, took two main forms. First, Puritan entrepreneurs, with the active support of the colony's government, sought to produce locally the supplies needed by the settlers, which meant establishing manufactures of iron goods and cloth. An elaborate scheme set on foot by John Winthrop, Jr., the governor's son, resulted in the establishment in Saugus, Massachusetts, of a complete ironworks. It was the product of prodigious efforts by a few devoted entrepreneurs, of the investment of over £12,000 by English businessmen, and of gifts from the General Court of land, tax exemption, and a monopoly of the local markets. But the Saugus Works flourished only briefly and then collapsed into bankruptcy, the victim of a destructive squeeze between inescapably high costs and low profits.

Similarly ineffective was the colony's effort to establish a local cloth industry. A Massachusetts law of 1656 hopefully but quite unrealistically ordered all idle hands in the Bay Colony to busy themselves with spinning and weaving and assessed every family an amount of cloth proportionate to the number of avail-

SAUGUS IRONWORKS
In this restoration of the works as they existed in 1650, the forge is at the left, the rolling and slitting mill at the right. *(Richard Merrill, photographer)*

able "spinners" in the household. But there were no "idle hands" in this labor-short society. Every available "hand" could find more than enough employment in the fields of the newly opened towns. There was no effective response to the government's demands and exhortations.

But if neither of the two basic manufactures—iron goods and cloth—could be locally produced, self-sufficiency of a sort might yet be created by discovering a small, lightweight, and highly valuable commodity which might be exchanged directly in England for the needed goods. For a few years in the early economic history of New England it seemed as though this would be the ultimate solution. The settlers found a rich supply of fur-bearing animals in the coastal region and just beyond, and they began

a quick exploitation of this highly profitable resource. The easily available beavers, otters, and raccoons were taken by the hundreds and their pelts shipped home in direct exchange for manufactures. But furs proved to be a limited resource. The animals reproduced themselves far more slowly than they were killed, and by the 1650s the supply in the immediate coastal region was exhausted. The New Englanders then pressed west against the Dutch on the Hudson who blocked them from contact with the sources of furs in northern New York and the Great Lakes region. Some furs continued to flow into Boston from trading posts on the Maine coast and the upper Connecticut River, but furs as a basis for the economy, after a decade of wonderful promise, faded from the economy of New England.

Failing to create economic independence or a direct exchange with England, a generation of small merchants in the Bay Colony worked out a system of exchanges throughout the Atlantic world that would produce the needed imports of finished goods. Increasingly, as the population grew, foodstuffs, fish, and timber products became available and the commercial possibilities they created became clear. These products could be sold not in England, which also produced them, but in Catholic Europe (France, Spain, and the Wine Islands of Madeira, the Azores, and the Canaries). These markets could use all the fish that could be sent, and the West Indies could absorb not only fish and other food supplies needed to feed the labor force but also timber for buildings and horses to help work the sugar mills. From the West Indies in turn sugar products could be obtained for sale elsewhere in America and in the English markets; and from Madeira, the Azores, and the Canary Islands wine could be procured for sale in the Atlantic ports. And other contacts could be made. Tobacco could be picked up in the Chesapeake, fish in Newfoundland, and various agricultural products in New York and later in Pennsylvania. An intricate circuit of exhanges could be created—horses and fish for sugar, sugar for bills of exchange, wine, tobacco or locally produced goods.

The purpose of these series of exchanges, which might go on for months or even years before being concluded, was the eventual establishment of credits in the ledgers of some merchant in London or Bristol. The credits would finance the purchase of manufactures to be imported to the colony for profitable sale. These profits would in turn make possible bigger shipments in the next cycle and perhaps investment in shipbuilding as well.

So the commercial system evolved in New England, to be re-created with variations in all the northern colonies. Each colony's system was distinctive, but all were interlocked and had common characteristics. These were no stable, easily controllable commercial flows. They were highly unstable, driven by uncertainty and inescapable risks. Everything conspired to make this commercial world dynamic and erratic.

COD FISHING ON THE GRAND BANKS AND THE NORTH AMERICAN SHORE
This French print of 1705 shows all stages of the fishing industry, from catching the fish (*C*) to gutting and scaling (*F,G*) and drying and packing (*V,Q*). Fish at the upper left are being carted away for salting, and the press at lower left (*R*) is extracting oil from the cod livers, the waste draining into the tub (*S*), the oil into the barrel (*T*). *(Library of Congress)*

For, to begin with, the local production of salable commodities was unreliable and irregular. Not only were there ordinary crop failures but the hinterland farmlands were still being opened and their location and volume of production were still experimental. Even less reliable were the West Indian and Atlantic island markets, which might easily be glutted by a few shipments and from whom it was impossible to obtain reliable market information before cargoes were sent. Further, this commerce was managed not by a few big

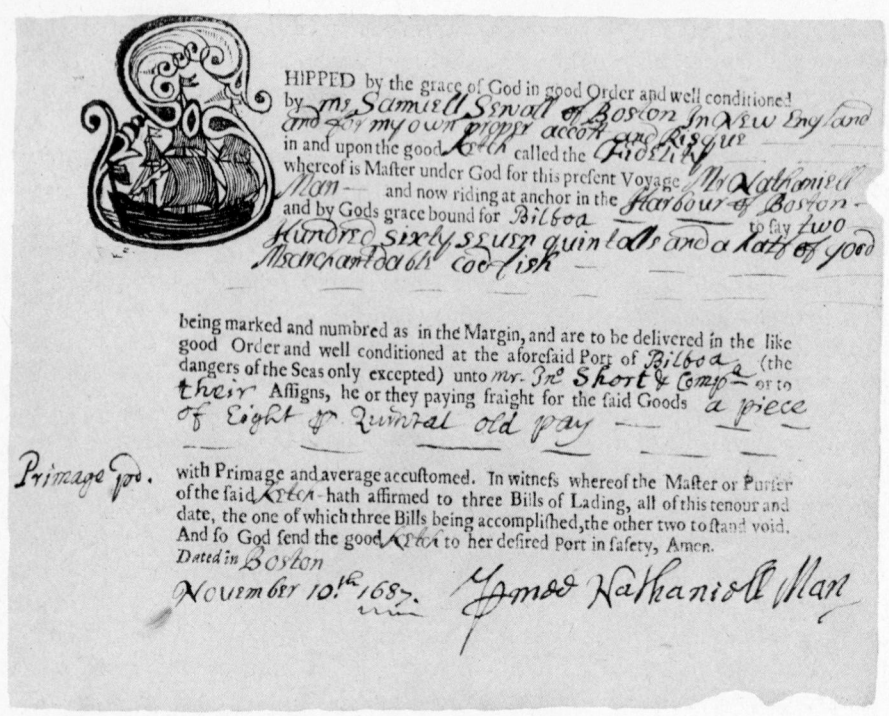

SHIPPING MANIFEST, 1687
(*Massachusetts Historical Society*)

firms whose decisions and agreements might stabilize the system, but by many small and highly competitive merchants. Finally, specialization for any of these small merchant entrepreneurs was virtually impossible if only because a chronic money shortage led to the necessity for payment in goods, with the result that every merchant had to be prepared to sell—or barter—almost any commodity at any time in any market he could find.

As a result of all these conditions, it was nearly impossible to match available goods to available markets. Between the initial shipment of goods and their arrival at an ultimate destination, the entire commercial picture could change. The merchants ventured largely into the dark and were victims of sudden gluts and unpredictable famines and of vicious price fluctuations. There was no fixed geometry of trade. There was no rigid "triangular" trade, in the seventeenth century or after. There were only constantly shifting polygons, forming and reforming as merchants undertook what were in effect peddling voyages up and down the North

American coast and in the Caribbean and Atlantic commercial lanes.

Overseas trade proved to be a highly competitive, risky business, in which success was the result of speculative venturing, intelligent risk-taking, and driving entrepreneurship. The principle of success was not the completion of safe, carefully planned exchanges but the almost limitless accumulation of exchanges of all sorts of commodities in a great variety of markets. It was a dynamic system, impelled by powerfully expansive forces.

For over a century this commercial system provided the northern colonies with the goods they needed and helped produce the material basis for a flourishing provincial culture. And from this system important social consequences flowed. In such a commercial world there could be no hard and clear definition of a merchant "class." The situation encouraged the participation of newcomers, starting with very little, who would have been rejected as interlopers in English commercial towns. There were no effective institutional boundaries that might confine the group. Neither gilds nor municipal corporations developed to limit the merchant community or to regulate its activities. Anyone's contribution to the struggling commercial economy was valuable, and the purpose of government intervention could only be to stimulate innovation, not limit it. A dynamic, unstable, unpredictable yet successful commercial system had produced a fluid merchant group, constantly recruiting newcomers from among successful tradesmen and farmers and seeking security and wealth in a system whose essence was risk.

The Southern Economy. No less risky, competitive, and unstable was the economic system that developed in the Chesapeake region around the production and marketing of the staple crop of tobacco. The details are of course altogether different from those of the northern commercial system, but here too success would come not from sharing in regular production and a stable process of distribution but from involvement in runaway cycles of production and a lurching, unpredictable distribution system. And in the South as in the North, a dynamic economy produced uncontrollable social consequences.

Originally there had been little enthusiasm for producing tobacco, which was considered harmful to health and was associated with general immorality. In the reign of James I (who himself wrote *A Counterblaste to Tobacco* in 1604), tobacco pipes were used as doorsigns of brothels. But then as now, however harmful it was to health, tobacco sold, and it sold extremely well in England, originally as an expensive luxury item imported from Spain. Once Americans began to sell tobacco in England they worked diligently to exploit the market, and quickly flooded it. By the late 1630s the price of tobacco in England had dropped precipitously, to a point less than the cost of production. There was a mild recovery of prices in the early 1640s and then further collapses in the 1660s as production rose still further in the Chesapeake colonies. By the end of the century, prices were still low, and a pattern of recoveries and collapses had emerged that would persist throughout the colonial period.

The low prices and the uncontrollable cycles were symptoms of profound problems in the tobacco economy. The primary problem was overproduction. By the end of the 1630s, little more than a decade after the first marketable crop had reached England, the Chesapeake colonies were producing 1.5 million pounds of tobacco a year. By 1700 the figure had risen to about 38 million pounds annually. In addition, the Chesapeake industry suffered from serious competition. Spain continued to send the best-quality crop, which commanded the highest prices, and sizable shipments also arrived from the Caribbean Islands. England too was a competitor, since tobacco was a well-established crop in Gloucestershire. To compound the troubles further, as production rose, American tobacco deteriorated in quality, and the middlemen assumed that it would fetch the lowest prices. Perhaps even more important were the technical difficulties of marketing this product of the scattered Chesapeake farms.

The tobacco specialists who appeared quickly within the London merchant community worked out a marketing procedure that survived for a century. In this "consignment" system the English merchants were primarily selling agents. The planters sent their crops to these merchants, usually on the merchants' vessels, for sale through them in the English and European markets. The English merchants advanced funds for all the necessary charges—freight, fees, taxes, storage, and so on—and repaid themselves, with profit, when the crop was eventually sold. In addition, they advanced goods to the planters charged against the eventual tobacco sales, and so they became the planters' bankers and creditors as well as merchandisers. There was a rough efficiency in this system, but it victimized the planters by involving them in endless debt cycles. Any given crop was in effect mortgaged long before it was sold. Further, the planters had no control whatever over the sale of their crops; they had no choice but to rely entirely on the merchants' goodwill. Finally, it was impossible, by this system, ever to adjust production to demand. Often two years would go by between shipment and and news of eventual sale, by which time several new crops would have been produced and disposed of. The net result of this system was constant debts and an unmanageable rigidity in the economic process that governed the planters' lives.

As if overproduction, keen competition, deteriorating quality, and a rigid marketing system were not burdens enough, there was the decisive problem of breaking into the markets of continental Europe. England could absorb relatively little of the enormous Chesapeake production. Of the approximately 38 million pounds of tobacco exported to England in 1700, 25 million pounds were reexported to the continent. Thus these ultimate markets were crucial to the prosperity of the American tobacco farmers.

At first the continental countries banned American tobacco altogether; then they imposed high duties; and finally they established "farms," that is, state-controlled or state-owned and state-operated monopolies of imports, which determined how much tobacco would be imported, what grades would be allowed in, and what prices would be charged. And as this mechanism matured and the political complexities of tobacco marketing in Europe multiplied, Dutch middlemen became increasingly important in transmitting the commodity to the ultimate markets. And so still another burden was added to the already heavily encumbered trade.

Such was the array of problems that developed in the seventeenth century as the southern economy took shape. Throughout the century strenuous efforts were made to overcome these problems, with only partial success. The English government taxed Spanish tobacco out of the English markets and rooted out tobacco planting in Gloucestershire; at the same time, the West Indian producers withdrew from this increasingly competitive industry. But Dutch shippers were shrewd competitors, and until the force of the Navigation Acts was felt toward the end of the century, they remained effective participants in the shipping trade. And neither the English nor the colonial governments could force the individual American tobacco growers to limit their production. Quite the contrary. Most planters were ever more convinced that the more they produced the greater would be their income; and as a consequence the system was propelled forward as if by a powerful internal accelerator. Production continued to expand, and so too did the area of land under cultivation.

The social consequences of this risky and unstable economy were profound. The constant expansion of the area of settlement went forward without regard for the Indians, who were driven back behind ever-expanding frontiers. As the planters pressed deeper into the interior in search of fresh lands, they forced even the friendly Indians into hostility. There were frontier skirmishes long before the full-scale race war broke out that touched off Bacon's Rebellion (1676).*

Further, the tobacco economy generated a desperate need for a large labor force. Hired or indentured servants were never available in sufficient numbers, and as a result the tobacco farms remained relatively small (an average of 250 acres). Slavery was an obvious solution to the labor problem even if its capital costs were greater than those of a free labor system. By the end of the century it was clear that the demands of the tobacco economy were inexorably enlarging the slave labor force and thereby compounding one of the greatest evils of American life.

The peculiar economy of tobacco, finally, eliminated the possibility that an urban society would develop to the south of Pennsylvania. The organization of the tobacco trade prevented local merchants from developing into independent entrepreneurs since the commercial processes were provided for in England. As a consequence the secondary activities that ordinarily develop around "entrepreneurial headquarters" (shipbuilding, service trades, brokerage, and shopkeeping) were frustrated from the start. On the eve of the Revolution, Williamsburg had a total population of but two thousand, and even that small population was largely the result of the government's residence in the town. Baltimore and Norfolk, with populations of six thousand each, developed not in the heart of the tobacco country but at the borders of more diversified economies.

Social Instability

No aspect of community life came under more intense pressure than social organization. The genera-

---

*On Bacon's Rebellion, see pp. 109–10.

tion that settled in America in the years before 1660 was still close to the Elizabethans, who in a period of rapid social change had spelled out clearly the traditional assumptions of an ideal community structure. The Elizabethans, and their colonizing descendants, assumed that society was not a miscellaneous collection of people pursuing their separate goals and relating to each other haphazardly. For them, society was a disciplined organism, a fabric closely "knit together," as they liked to say, whose overall character was more meaningful than any of the separate parts that composed it. Specifically, they assumed that society would display at least three essential characteristics.

They expected, first, that the parts of a community would complement each other and fit together harmoniously to compose the commonwealth as a whole. They expected, too, that the structure of society would be essentially hierarchical, organized into distinct levels of inferiority and superiority, levels not of "class" but of status and dignity, characteristics related to occupation and wealth but not defined by them. And they assumed, third, that the hierarchy of society was a unitary structure in which people of superior status in one aspect of life would be superior in all others. Thus the rich would be politically powerful, educated, and dignified; leadership in public and private affairs would fall to the highborn, the firstborn, the natural leaders, equipped to rule by all the attributes of social superiority.

These were characteristics of all coherent societies, the Elizabethans believed, and those among them who voyaged to America had no intention of recasting or rejecting such fundamental notions. But in fact the world that emerged in mainland North America did not conform to these ideals. To be sure, there was no total breakdown, once the horrors of the "starving times" were overcome; there was no instant transformation into a different mode of life. But from the first years of settlement there were acute stresses and strains that made social life in the colonies tense, strange, and difficult.

The sources of some of these problems were obvious. The colonists were well aware that the political and economic leadership of the communities was being assumed by people who, though capable of dealing with the raw environment, lacked the traditional social attributes of command—a sense of natural superiority, habitual dignity, personal authority. The respect due to the leading figures was not, as a result, automatically forthcoming. Political and economic leaders were vulnerable to criticism and challenged in ways their social superiors would not have been.

Puritanism and Social Order. In New England this general problem was peculiarly compounded. Within the Puritans' distinctive status system purity of religion, piety, and rectitude were decisive in establishing distinction. At the same time, every effort was made to perpetuate a traditional social structure. Allotments of land in the newly opened townships, for example, were by common agreement made larger for persons of wealth, position, and professional training. Even so vague a distinction as "ability" was materially rewarded. But the conflict with religious values could not be avoided.

The problem was at least clearly understood. One of the Puritans' most influential English leaders, Lord Say and Sele, considered joining the Great Migration in 1636, but then paused. Was it not true, he wrote the Reverend John Cotton in Boston, that men could attain the franchise in Massachusetts simply by being accepted into the church, no matter what their social condition might be? If so, what certainty was there that people like himself would be able to play their proper roles? Cotton tried to reassure him. Everyone knew that "monarchy and aristocracy are both of them clearly approved and directed in scripture" and that God never ordained democracy to be "a fit government either for church or commonwealth." So His Lordship need have no fear of finding in New England a world turned upside down. Still, Cotton had to admit, the Puritans *were* committed to the service of the Lord; religious considerations in the end would prevail and *should* prevail. For is it not better, he asked, "that the commonwealth be fashioned to the setting forth of God's house, which is his church, than to accommodate the church frame to the civil state?" The noble lord read the message correctly and stayed home. The Bay Colony's tumults in the founding years continued to reflect the

NEW ENGLAND HOUSES OF THE SEVENTEENTH CENTURY

Below, the Ironmaster's House, Saugus, built in the 1630s and enlarged 20 years later, is an exceptionally imposing residence for the period. The ordinary workers at Saugus lived in thatch-roofed cottages even simpler than the houses in Plymouth (p. 40). *Left*, the Paul Revere house in Boston, 1680. The overhanging second story and heavily leaded casement windows are typical of the substantial artisans' houses of the time. *(Below, Mark Flannery, photographer)*

strange confusion and intermixture of religious and social distinctions.

Social Structure and Family Life. Everywhere in the colonies there were difficulties and confusions in maintaining a traditional social order in the raw wilderness world. On the farms, whether in New England, New York, the Chesapeake colonies, or Carolina, it was physically impossible to maintain the expected differences in styles of life—differences not merely between masters and servants who labored side by side, but between field workers on the one hand and preachers, teachers, and doctors on the other. Laboring side by side day after day, masters and servants found their life-styles approaching each other until the differences rested only on a legal statement, a scrap of paper establishing the servants' dependency, a formality whose force, deprived of material sanction, grew weaker with time. There were few luxuries anywhere, and nowhere was there the material basis for leisure. The few people of professional training lived far more primitive lives than their education and occupational roles would traditionally have assured them.

In the towns the problems of maintaining traditional status differentiation were especially dramatic. The standard refrain through the century was that the free workers—the handicraftsmen, shipwrights, carpenters, shoemakers, tailors—had lost all respect for traditional roles and social distinctions. The wages they claimed were astronomical, it was commonly said; their social pretensions insufferable. They flaunted their prosperity outrageously, and aped their superiors in ways that offended all sense of decency and social order. Every effort was made to contain the social disorder that they created by eliminating the causes of this alleged misbehavior or by limiting its effects. Occasionally when the problem became acute, the assemblies sought to limit wages in order to restrict the workers' ambitions and protect the public against their apparent greed. But such laws could not be enforced. The workers' services were indispensable; people would pay almost anything they demanded. And the workers' arguments were convincing too: prices, they said, were rising;

they had expenses to meet. Let prices be fixed if wages were. But price fixing was as futile as wage fixing, and what a later generation would call "escalator clauses" were tried with only temporary effect on the demands and behavior of the free, self-employed workers.

By 1660 the effort to eliminate the source of the workers' extravagance had clearly failed, and it was left for the assemblies to try to discipline behavior itself, to try to confine dress and social intercourse to appropriate forms of decency. Sumptuary legislation restricted the wearing of finery, limited display, and lectured an apparently disordered population on the confusion of the times. The Massachusetts Bay Colony's sumptuary law of 1651 is perhaps the most eloquent testimony of the age to the founders' pervasive sense of disarray. The General Court declared its

utter detestation and dislike, that men or women of mean condition should take upon them the garb of gentlemen, by wearing gold or silver lace, or buttons, or points at their knees, or to walk in great boots, or women of the same rank to wear silk or tiffany hoods or scarves which, though allowable to persons of greater estates or more liberal education, yet we cannot but judge it intolerable in persons of such like condition.

The times were deeply disordered, the court said, and it therefore ordered

that no person within this jurisdiction, . . . whose visible estates shall not exceed the true and indifferent value of £200 shall wear any gold or silver lace, or gold and silver buttons, or any bone lace above 2 shillings per yard, or silk hoods or scarves, upon the penalty of 10 shillings for every such offense.

And then, in a devilishly clever provision, the court decreed that if the town selectmen found anyone they judged "to exceed their ranks and abilities in the costliness or fashion of their apparel," they were to increase the offender's tax rate to the level of wealth he or she pretended to—all of this *provided*, the General Court added in an afterthought that illuminates the unstable social landscape like a flare, that the law *not* apply to any of the colony's magistrates or their families, to any regular military officers or soldiers

JOHN FREAKE AND HIS WIFE ELIZABETH AND CHILD, 1674
Freake was one of the successful merchants who arrived in Boston well after the original Puritan migration and brought with him a "corrupting" luxuriance of style. His buttons are silver, his collar fine lace, his sleeves puffed muslin, and his gold brooch studded with precious stones. His wife's embroidered petticoat is carefully revealed. *(Worcester Art Museum)*

on active duty, or to anyone else *"whose education and employment have been above the ordinary degree, or whose estates have been considerable, though now decayed."*

"*Though now decayed*"—the phrase echoes a profound sense of disordered change, of a decline of standards. And in no aspect of life was this sense more acute than in the realm of the family. Here, it was felt, the erosion went deepest, the disorder was most manifest. The Puritan magistrates repeatedly denounced the loosening of family ties and the defiance of authority in this most intimate and fundamental of all social units. Repeatedly they commanded parents to do their duty to their children and to themselves, and ordered children to respect and obey their parents and to fulfill their family obligations. The laws grew more stringent as the years passed. In New Hampshire, Massachusetts, and Connecticut, in conformity with the biblical injunction, death was de-

creed for children who struck or cursed their parents (the law was invoked at least once, though never enforced). In Massachusetts, tithingmen were made responsible for the good order of groups of ten families, and the church synod of 1679, blaming the evils of the time on "defects of family government," commanded the tithingmen to redouble their efforts to reinforce the failing discipline of weak-willed parents.

In fact, of course, the family was not being destroyed. On the surface, at least, the institution was little weaker at the end of the century than it had been at the start. But something *had* happened. There *were* problems, and those problems, if properly understood, help explain the outcries, the sense of disarray, and the efforts to remedy what was felt by many to be a disastrous decline in the traditional good order of family life.

To understand these problems, it is necessary to

note that families in the seventeenth century were considered the archetype of all social order. In this micro-community, it was believed, all order began, all patterns of inferiority and superiority took shape. The political commonwealth was but an enlargement of the family. Rulers were conceived of as patriarchs whose dominance as heads of commonwealths was justified by God the father of all. All of this was a cliché of the age, but a cliché that, like most common-places that pass unchallenged, was essentially real-istic. For most Englishmen experienced a larger, more highly structured, more complex, and more disci-plined family unit than now exists in the Western world, but not because the nuclear family (parents and children) was significantly larger than it is now. Most completed families in seventeenth-century England contained only two or three children, though many more were born and died young. The sense of complexity, structure, and discipline grew from the fact that family meant or implied the household—all those who lived together under one roof—and almost all Englishmen at some time in their lives had expe-rienced the household-family as a complex and dis-ciplined institution. For servants were traditionally part of this artificially extended family, and servitude was remarkably widespread. Something like a third of all English families had servants; at any one time, between 10 and 15 percent of the entire English pop-ulation was serving in another's household—and serv-ing not merely as day workers exchanging limited services for wages but as family members committed to total employment in exchange for maintenance, protection, and to some extent education. In addition, free children of other families circulated as guests, often for long periods, in more affluent households or even in households of equivalent social position. As a result, at least 45 percent of all English people lived in households of six or more members. Consequently most people, at least in their youth, experienced families as complex, to some extent even partriarchal, units.

In traditional settings, material circumstances reinforced and helped perpetuate these household-families. Young people found it difficult to break away and establish new independent households. For eco-nomic independence was largely made possible in this predominantly agricultural world by the pur-chase, or the long-term lease, of plots of arable land, and it was extremely difficult to make such transac-tions in the absence of available public land. As a result, many servants found themselves obliged to remain dependent beyond the time of their contrac-tual obligations; marriages were delayed, since mar-ried couples were expected to live in their own establishments and not within other households; and family discipline developed naturally and remained a familiar, accepted fact of life.

In the colonies of seventeenth-century America these material reinforcements of traditional family life were either greatly weakened or eliminated. Where land was far more freely available than in England, the establishment of independent households, though difficult physically, became a relatively easy matter economically. What is remarkable in these circum-stances is not that the average age at first marriage fell, but that it did not fall even further and faster than it did, and that there was not more pressure against tra-ditional family organization than there was.

But the availability of land was only one of the alterations in reinforcement of traditional family life in the colonies. The acute and continuing labor short-age, which shifted the dependency relations within the family and household, meant that parents and mas-ters depended on their children and servants as never before. They needed them, sometimes desperately, to provide critically necessary labor. In this sense, the parents became dependents—but not only in this sense. The young learned to cope with the environment more rapidly than their seniors; they adapted to change more easily; and in the end they inevitably became lifelines to the world for their elders. They became, in effect, their parents' teachers, despite the unquestioned and continuing assumption of parental superiority.

In the Chesapeake region through most of the seventeenth century the common disorder of family life was greatly increased by the fearful death rate. Where only half the people born would live to age 20, and where two out of every three marriages were broken by the death of one of the partners (more often the husband), family and household life was chaotic.

Widows, left with several children in a rough frontier society where there were many more men than women, remarried quickly, if only for survival. Often their husbands brought children from earlier marriages, and the households, in which wives acquired greater importance and authority than was normal for the age, were crowded with half-siblings and stepchildren. And there were orphan children everywhere.

The consequences of the tensions and widespread disarray ran deep. Gradually the law responded to these altered circumstances. Primogeniture—the legal requirement that real property descend only to the eldest son so that the family estate would remain intact—was commonly ignored where land was plentiful. The common practice was to divide property among the members of a family, perhaps with double portions for the wife and eldest son. Orphan courts appeared in the South to protect the interests of children otherwise uncared for. And the law became more responsive to the interests of women. In Massachusetts laws were passed that prohibited husbands from striking their wives—"unless it be in his own defense." Women, north and south, acquired new rights to own, administer, and legally protect property; to conduct business; and to represent themselves in court. And they were treated more equitably by the courts in divorce proceedings. In general, women enjoyed a higher social status in seventeenth-century America than they did in England, where the traditionally severe subordination of females, inherited from the medieval past, continued largely unchanged.

The legal position of bonded servants also improved. In some places the severity of punishment was limited by law; in others, working conditions were improved; and in all the colonies every effort was made to use the law to keep servants at work despite the liberating forces that surrounded them. A case is recorded in which a servant ran away after being punished for attempting to rape his master's ten-year-old daughter—the suit being filed not to punish the culprit but to get him back and to force him to complete his term of service! Everywhere the conditions of contractual obligations grew lighter as the ease of transition to personal independence was recognized.

Social order was not destroyed in the seventeenth-century colonies, nor was the world transformed. But on this western frontier of European civilization, society had acquired new instabilities, along with new freedoms for traditionally subordinated elements in the nonslave population. In calmer years and in more settled circumstances, some of these changes would recede into more traditional forms, but most would become part of a permanently altered way of life.

Religion

Religion was inevitably involved in the larger social changes, for the colonists' culture was still profoundly Christian and churches were still the preeminent cultural institutions as well as vital social agencies. The seventeenth century was an age of intense religious controversy; men and nations struggled savagely over differences in religious opinion. Yet a few nearly universal presumptions were shared by almost all religious groups—presumptions that illuminate the history of religion in early America particularly well.

Christians, save for the most extreme radicals, generally assumed that there was a universally true religion and that a plurality of beliefs should not be encouraged. However much most seventeenth-century Christians differed on what doctrines were orthodox, they assumed that *some* doctrines were absolutely right and others wrong and that the effort to eradicate, or at least to heavily constrain, heresy and to extend orthodoxy was altogether legitimate. Equally axiomatic was the belief that religion was not simply a spiritual matter nor of concern only to the church. The agencies of the state were understood to have a major responsibility to supervise religion and to enforce orthodoxy. Finally, as overseas emigration became a prominent part of the life of western Europe, it was assumed that church institutions established in the colonies would follow familiar organizational patterns and fit somehow into some larger pattern of religious institutions. No one expected that churches established in the frontier borderlands would become institutions with special characteristics.

The history of religion in the first two or three generations can be seen as the story of the violation of these presumptions and the struggle to retain them in the face of adversity. Christianity in more or less familiar outward form of course survived, but it survived with significant alterations that were forced into being, not by will or doctrine, but by intractable circumstances. Not for another century would these changes be fully accepted and incorporated into the deliberate design of religious organization and practice. But the seeds of what would later evolve into America's distinctive denominational organization of religion were planted and nourished in the complex social history of the seventeenth century.

The Anglican Church in Virginia. The most revealing example of the way in which environment shaped the development of Christianity in America lies in the history of the Church of England in Virginia. Here the sense of orthodoxy was strong and free from pressures of reform and from doctrinal conflicts; here the fullest re-creation of traditional forms was attempted; and here the failure of expectation was particularly severe.

The Virginia Company and the government that followed it assumed that the Church of England in its established form would simply be reproduced in the settlements along the James River, and that these local branches of the church would be easily incorporated into the national church. But there were severe problems from the start, most of which flowed from the difficulty of devising a workable economic basis for the newly founded church institutions. In England churches were usually supported by land endowments, gifts of income-producing property donated by patrons. In Virginia the company, and subsequently the crown, took over the role of patron to the newly founded parishes. In 1618 the company set aside as church land 100 acres (later increased by the crown to 200 acres) in each of the still vague "boroughs." The income from this land, to be produced by the labor of tenants, was to support a minister and the upkeep of the church. But tenants were not easily obtainable in Virginia, and the land was worthless until some kind of labor could be provided. This left two alternatives for the support of the church. First, the clergy could become almost full-time farmworkers and produce

ST. LUKE'S CHURCH, ISLE OF WIGHT COUNTY, VIRGINIA (LATE SEVENTEENTH CENTURY)
A typical Anglican parish church, with its bell tower, arched windows, and buttresses. *(Courtesy, Virginia State Travel Service)*

the expected income, a prospect that in itself discouraged the recruitment of well-trained clergymen. Alternatively, a new kind of support would have to be forthcoming. This new form—taxation—was anticipated by the company when it ordered parishioners to supplement the income of the church land until its yield equaled £200 a year. Such supplements quickly became common, then universal. It soon became standard practice for the parishioners' governing body, the vestry, to vote funds for the church as an annual tax rate.

Once taxation became the financial basis of the church, the size of the parish became a critical problem. If the parish were to be defined by the number of people, with the standard set by the population of the usual English parish, the resulting territory would spread so widely along the colony's creeks and rivers that proper ministrations would be impossible. On the other hand, if the geographical size of the parish were kept small so that the parishioners could gather easily

COLLEGE OF WILLIAM AND MARY, PICTURED IN THE 1730s

Founded in large part to educate Virginians for the Anglican ministry, it was built to the plans of Christopher Wren. The central building was erected by the end of the century but had to be rebuilt after a fire of 1705. *(Library of Congress)*

and ministers could be in constant communication with flocks, the per capita cost of support would be extremely high. The inevitable result, in the under-developed and struggling economy, was a pattern of unworkably large parishes and, because of variations in population density and wealth, great variations in the support of the clergy.

By the end of the first generation, the dilemma facing the church was officially recognized. In 1662 the assembly tried to make all church salaries uniform at £80 a year. But this figure had to be translated into set amounts of tobacco, which was the medium of exchange, and when the real value of tobacco fell, so too did the real worth of the ministers' salaries. In any case, being paid in tobacco, the clergy were at the mercy of local variations in quality and were dependent too on the goodwill of their parishioners for the selection of tobacco that was made.

From this simple and fundamental economic problem flowed profoundly important consequences in the lives of the clergy and in the life of religion in general. By English standards the ministers were almost everywhere grossly underpaid, and they were faced with next-to-impossible conditions of work. Further, they were stripped of economic independence because of their reliance on annual gifts of the parish. Nor did they acquire security of tenure. In England the patrons (or their heirs) who endowed the churches nominated ministers for lifetime appointment as rectors, and the bishops confirmed them in office. In Virginia, the patrons, given the tax base of the ministers' salaries,

proved to be the vestries, the self-perpetuating bodies of lay leaders of the church in each parish. The vestries were instructed by the church officers in England to present their nominees to the governors for formal induction into office. But in most cases they refused (only 10 percent of the Virginia clergy in the seventeenth century were ever formally inducted into their offices), claiming that the available candidates were so inferior in quality that they did not deserve permanency of tenure.

It was a self-intensifying problem. The vestries refused to present candidates for formal induction to permanent tenure because the quality of the clergy was too low to justify such confidence and respect; but their refusal was an important reason why well-qualified candidates refused to settle in Virginia. The declining spiral fell lower and lower. Many well-qualified and able young clergymen were present in Virginia in the early years, but by the end of the century their numbers had declined to insignificance. Recruitment seemed to come from the dregs of the ecclesiastical barrel. Efforts of church missionaries and later of the Church's Society for the Propagation of the Gospel in Foreign Parts (founded in 1701) led to a series of proposals to remedy the situation. One of the early proposals resulted in the chartering of the College of William and Mary in 1693 to provide a means of educating Virginians locally for the ministry. But it was extremely difficult to improve the situation. By 1724 the reputation of the clergy in Virginia had become so scandalous that the following almost farcical proposals were included in a comprehensive plan of reform submitted to the Bishop of London, whose jurisdiction included the American colonies.

And to prevent the scandals of bad life in the clergy, let it be enacted that whatsoever minister shall be found guilty of fornication, adultery, blasphemy, ridiculing of the Holy Scriptures, or maintaining . . . any doctrine contrary to the 39 Articles shall . . . lose his living [income] and be suspended from all exercise of the ministerial function for three years. . . . And because drunkenness is one of the most common crimes and yet hardest to be proved . . . let it be enacted that the following proof shall be taken for a sufficient proof of drunkenness, viz., first, let the signs of drunkenness be proved such as sitting an hour or longer in the company where they were a drinking strong drink and in the meantime drinking of healths or otherwise taking his cups as they came around like the rest of the company; striking, challenging, threatening to fight, or laying aside any of his garments for that purpose; staggering, reeling, vomiting, incoherent, impertinent, obscene, or rude talking. Let the proof of these signs proceed so far till the judges conclude that the minister's behavior at such a time was scandalous, indecent, and unbecoming the gravity of a minister.

The debasement of the clergy was one aspect of the general transformation of the Church of England in Virginia. Another development, in the long run equally important, was the destruction of the hierarchical structure of the church. This came about as a result of the distance from higher controls in England and by the local vestries' assumption of absolute power in church affairs. Control fell to the parish level, and the result was in effect a congregational institution, despite the official affiliation with the Church of England, which was governed by bishops and archbishops. Further, the practice of religion was simplified, even secularized to some extent. Since most ministers could not reach all areas of their parishes, lay readers were appointed to fulfill certain ministerial functions. The general simplicity of life and the lack of funds for embellishments meant that the sacraments were administered without the proper vestments or ornaments of church ritual. The dead were buried in private cemeteries more often than in parish burial grounds; the holy days were neglected; and marriage was performed in private residences under lay auspices. Further, the church as a judicial body declined into insignif-

icance, for the members of the vestries and of the local civil courts were often the same people. It was more reasonable, in view of the weakness of the church, for cases of moral offenses to be brought before the civil courts than before the church courts. And it was the civil courts rather than the weak parish institutions that became the repositories for vital statistics.

No one, of course, doubted that the Church of England had been established in Virginia, but it was a strange establishment indeed. Conditions had led the church as an institution toward what might be called nonseparating Congregationalism—institutionally the position adopted in New England—not as a matter of doctrine but as a matter of social and institutional fact.

Toleration in Catholic Maryland. Maryland shared the same environmental conditions, and its religious institutions would have conformed to the same pattern except for two basic facts: first, the government of the colony was in the hands of a Catholic proprietor who conceived of the colony as a Catholic refuge; and second, the great majority of those available for settlement in the colony were Protestants, and the success of the colony depended on the success of recruitment. The proprietor's Catholic interests would have to be handled with the greatest care.

At the start, the Calverts issued to their governors instructions they thought would satisfy the conflicting demands. They ordered the Maryland officials to give no offense to Protestants because of their religion; to see to it that Catholicism was practiced as privately as possible; and to leave those who professed Christianity in any form free to worship as they chose. It was a vague, pragmatically liberal position, and it was promptly attacked both by the Jesuits who had accompanied the settlers, demanding that Catholicism be established far more substantially than this, and by the Protestants in the colony, whose opposition to Catholic rule erupted into open rebellion in the early years of the English Civil War. It was to stabilize the situation in the face of these cross pressures and to protect Maryland's charter that the Calverts issued in 1649 their famous Act Concerning Religion.

This document, though remarkable for its era, is not an act for full freedom of religion. It begins, in fact, by ordering the death penalty for any non-trinitarian Christians who insisted on professing their religion in Maryland. But it goes on to say that, in order to assure public tranquility—and for that reason alone—all trinitarian Christians were guaranteed the right to profess and practice their religion. Nothing in this document, which remained in effect through the century, challenged the prevailing idea of orthodoxy. It contained no hint of the principles of the separation of church and state, or of freedom of conscience and worship as good in themselves—no hint of any of the soaring ideals of liberty of thought and conscience that would later find expression in Jefferson's great Statute of Religious Freedom. The Calverts' act specified toleration on the narrowest possible ground—for just those groups whom it was expedient to tolerate: Catholics, Anglicans, and moderate Protestant dissenters. Yet it was a significant departure, if limited and pragmatic, and it fitted perfectly the decentralization of religion that was otherwise developing in the colony. For in Maryland as in Virginia the necessary tax base of church support meant full control by local authorities, in most places by the vestries. This, together with the official toleration of most differing groups, meant the emergence in this colony of a multi-denominational Christianity whose institutional form was essentially congregational.

The Dutch Church in New York. The same result in even more extreme form emerged in New York. The Dutch, like the English, assumed at the start that their national church, Dutch Reformed Calvinist, would be re-created in America, and that it would be controlled by that church's ruling body, the Classis of Amsterdam. But from the earliest years, New Netherland was complex in its religious character, and there were no effective controls from the home country. Besides Dutch Calvinists, Jews, and a broad range of sectarian radicals that included Anabaptists and Quakers, there were Lutherans, whose insistence on the right to public worship led to their suppression and persecution by Stuyvesant. The Dutch West India Company's policy was to permit *private* worship of any kind, so long as the Dutch church was officially recognized and supported by universal taxation. The Lutherans, however, insisted on the right to public worship. The question remained unsettled, the source of fierce animosities, until after the English conquest. Then, in 1665, the freeholders of each community in New York were ordered to vote for some one Protestant church, which would then be locally established. Once chosen, the denomination would be supported by general taxation, though private worship was allowed to continue.

The Dutch church remained dominant, of course, since most of the colonists were Dutch, and in this situation of local option it sought to perpetuate its heritage and mode of worship. But here as in the Chesapeake colonies settlements were scattered, the recruitment of properly qualified ministers was extremely difficult, and proper ministrations proved impossible to perform. Here too lay readers presided when ordained ministers were unobtainable, and there was a radical decline in the outward quality of religious life. Worse still, after the English conquest the Dutch church became a branch of an alien national church. How could this American branch relate to the home body? If the Dutch settlers in New York acknowledged the supremacy of the Dutch church fully, they would in effect be challenging the supremacy of the English crown; if they did not make that challenge, implicitly at least they would not be faithful to their own religious profession. It was

SYMBOLISM ON PURITAN GRAVESTONES
Folk art (see color section) was never absent from the colonies. In Puritan New England it took particularly imaginative form in the portrayal of death, sin, and salvation in gravestone carvings. *Far right,* the John Foster stone, Dorchester, Massachusetts, 1681, depicts Time holding back the hand of Death from extinguishing the flame of life atop the globe. The allegory was copied from an illustration in *Hieroglyphiques of the Life of Man* (1638) by Francis Quarles, a popular English poet. *Right,* panel of a stone of 1692 in which a naked imp of the underworld carries both Time's hour glass and Death's dart. *(Both photographs, Allan Ludwig)*

a dilemma that could not be resolved but might be endured if the issue was never pressed.

New England Puritanism. In the context of these unexpected developments elsewhere in the colonies, the outward form of religion that became established in New England is perhaps not so unique. Everywhere the hierarchy of church organization had failed to develop, ritual had become simplified, sacramental functions of the church were reduced, and laymen shared pulpits with ordained ministers. None of this, however, had been the consequence of doctrine or belief or intent. All of it had developed in response to the circumstances of life in the new American colonies. In New England the same developments were small parts of a general plan of religious reform that was pursued almost fanatically and fortified by a theological position whose refinement was the work of men of subtle mind and great intellectual energy. But Puritanism was not only an intellectual system and it did not satisfy only the needs of theologians. It was a social movement as well as an intellectual movement, and it performed, in New England

as in Old England, a notable social function.

The central character of New England Puritanism emerges most clearly if one defines it precisely; and its social role becomes apparent if one concentrates on the question of why its force continued once the original settlements were stabilized.

New England Puritanism was one specific expression within a broad protest movement against the religious conservatism of the Church of England as it existed under Elizabeth. Those who would later be known as Puritans felt that England's break with the Roman Catholic Church under Henry VIII had not gone far enough. The differences between the Puritan reformers and the conservative churchmen did not lie in central theological points. Both groups were predestinarian: both believed that human salvation was ultimately determined by decisions of a mysterious God. The differences lay in two questions concerning the nature and function of the church as an institution.

The first was the question of how effective the church could be in assisting people in their search for salvation. The Anglican churchmen, like Catholics, believed that the church could be instrumental in bridging the world of ordinary, physical humanity and that of men in a state of God's grace. The difference between physical existence and true sanctity was not, the church insisted, total and absolute, bridgeable only by God's gift of spiritual rebirth; qualified priests and the procedures and rituals of the church could assist in the great search for salvation. With this, the Puritans disagreed. The gap between nature and grace was for them absolute and total, and could be mediated only by God in direct contact with an open and willing soul and by the Bible, which contained God's recorded words. The church's institutions and its ritual—all such outward "works"—merely interfered with the essential experience of religion, which for the Puritans was the experience of man struggling to make contact with an inscrutable God.

The second question that came to define Puritanism concerned the visibility of God's church. Orthodox Anglicans felt that it was impossible ever truly to tell who had achieved a state of grace and who had not. This was the ultimate mystery, and therefore the church existed for everyone, in the hope that its good offices would help some to achieve a better life and would be a natural home for those who were already members of God's elect. For Anglicans the membership of the "visible" church (that is, the worldly institution of the church) should include the whole of society; people should be born into the church as a fact of their mortal existence. The Puritans disagreed vehemently with this position. They felt that it was possible though difficult to distinguish the elect from ordinary mortals. Tests could be devised and signs detected that would dis-

FIRST PARISH MEETING HOUSE, HINGHAM, MASS. 1681
This famous building, whose exterior is largely the work of the eighteenth century, retains much of the original seventeenth-century interior. Lacking models for the spacious but austere building they had in mind and spurning all architectural embellishments, the ship carpenters hired for the occasion simply built a ship's keel in reverse to form the interior roof. *(Photos by Arthur B. Mazmanian from his* The Structure of Praise © The Beacon Press)

tinguish these "saints" from unredeemed humanity and make it possible to confine full church membership to those visibly sanctified people. Church membership should not include everyone in society, the Puritans felt; it should be a gathering of saints. The visible church, they said, and God's church of the elect should, as far as possible, be one.

These two key issues defined the protest movement of the late sixteenth century which in the broadest sense was Puritanism. But Puritanism in this broadest sense includes a wide range of positions on the question of the church's relation to society, only one of which was established in the Bay Colony. The Massachusetts Puritans believed that church membership should be limited to the elect of God, but they also continued to believe that the church, even so reduced, should control society as a whole and be responsible for creating conditions favorable to the search for salvation. For them there could be no denial of responsibility for the everyday world as it existed. The condition of all people was the responsibility of the saints, and the church, though only of the saints, must somehow be active in the affairs of the unredeemed.

How such a program could be effected was a matter of endless discussion and writing both in England and in America. But in England the Congregational Puritans' energies had been absorbed in the struggle for survival against an authoritarian church determined to eliminate active dissent. In Massachusetts and Connecticut, however, the Puritans, protected from interference by the charters, could work out fully the implications of their "nonseparating," Congregationalist position.

Because profoundly committed Puritans were in full charge of the community in Massachusetts and Connecticut, and because their beliefs hinged on the identification of the visible and invisible churches, the passage into full church membership took on a significance it had nowhere else. For in England, where the Congregationalist Puritans were a persecuted minority, there was no scramble on the part of ordinarily religious but unsanctified people to gain membership in these congregations. Only the fully committed and utterly sincere would have wished to join a group so embattled politically and

so demanding in its practices. In New England the situation was altogether different. Here the Congregational Church leaders held all the powers; they *were* the government, and the resources and power available in the community were at their disposal. Where the Congregational Church was fully established and where social rewards were attached to membership in the church, the passage into full church affiliation became a critical issue for the society as a whole. Quickly, therefore, procedures were devised that opened access to the population at large but allowed in only those who objectively demonstrated superiority in spiritual gifts.

Candidates were obliged to make a public "profession"—to give an open account of the act of saving grace that had brought them to the condition of redemption that justified membership in the church. This was followed by a public interrogation by church officials and experienced laymen, an inquisition, often exceedingly subtle in its demands, in which these public professions could be challenged for their authenticity and defenses made to these challenges. Finally, if this exhibit and defense had been successful, a formal ritual of acceptance was devised by which membership was officially conferred.

This was no casual procedure. Gaining entrance to the church was the central event in religious life of the Puritan communities. The subsequent history of the church in New England would be shaped by the fate of these procedures.*

Defining the process of entering into the church was one side of the central problem of the Bible commonwealth. The other side was how to justify the rule of the saints to those who were not church members, those excluded from the social rewards the church could bestow. The *intellectual* justification of the rule of the elect was never in doubt. A central idea of the Puritans was the doctrine of the covenant, which asserted the obligation of the saved to do whatever mortals could do to pave the way for the unregenerate to attain salvation. According to the covenant, the elect were obliged to expose ordinary men to truth, to remove impediments to their redemption, and to urge them to seek an ultimate salvation.

*See Chapter 5, pp. 135–36.

But theories do not answer people's urges and longings, their fears and aspirations. A mass population will not accept an elite rule obnoxious to them merely because a theory urges them to. No one can be argued into a willing subservience. There is every reason to believe that the mass of the settlers accepted, indeed welcomed, the rule of the saints. We do not know exactly how many New Englanders in the first two generations reached full membership in the church. One informed estimate is 47 percent, though that is probably too high. We do know that of the twenty thousand or so immigrants of the Great Migration, few returned to England, and there were no rebellions against the religious zeal of the Puritan leaders. Such protests as there were mainly took the form of differing opinions on specific points of doctrine, and most often were led by individuals—Roger Williams, Anne Hutchinson—even more zeal-

English Origins of New England Settlers, 1620-1650
(Based on a sample of 2,646 emigrants)

ous in religion than the Winthrops.

The explanation for the Puritans' success, in psychological and sociological terms, is related to the sources of the Great Migration. The mass of the settlers were husbandmen and artisans drawn primarily from East Anglia and the west country of England, which were not merely the chief centers of Puritanism but the centers too of economic distress in the 1620s and 30s. Crop failures and an extended depression in the cloth industry, whose two main centers were in these regions, created a mass of discontent and severe social dislocation. Puritanism fed on these disturbed conditions. Its teachings offered an explanation in moral terms of what was happening in the lives of this apprehensive and unrooted population. For the Puritans' social views were medieval rather than modern. They were suspicious of the life of trade, feared the effects of greed on the flow of necessary goods, and urged the necessity of subordinating the individual to the welfare of the community. Though the personality traits that Puritanism fostered—diligence, accountability, self-denial, and the scrupulous use of every God-given moment of time—would later serve to stimulate the development of an unqualified capitalism, its social doctrines confined these characteristics to goals set by the good of the whole. Puritanism stimulated acquisitiveness but at the same time preached the control of greed and self-satisfaction, and it sought to create a society in which social controls in behalf of the community good would predominate.

The thousands of unregenerate found in Puritanism not tyranny but a source of security for which they longed. Uprooted and buffeted by economic upheaval and social dislocation, they found in New England a society that officially restrained economic appetites and translated the incomprehensible workings of the marketplace into familiar moral language. More than that, they found in close-knit village communities a system of group controls that would effectively eliminate the threat of arbitrary economic fluctuations and create the security that was one of the main goals of their existences.

By the end of the century this vital function of Puritanism was losing its power as the third generation, born secure, lost contact with the original aims of the Great Migration. But for a moment in history—two lifetimes, more or less—Puritanism had been a comfort and not an affliction, a source of security otherwise unattainable by ordinary victims of social change.

No more in religion than in social organization or economic life was this a world transformed. But everywhere, in these small and obscure but swiftly growing communities, there were instabilities, uncertainties, and changes that had not yet settled into permanent new forms.

SUGGESTED READINGS

There is no single comprehensive and detailed history of American society in the seventeenth century. The subject has only recently been conceived of in the terms discussed in this chapter, and the student must draw for details on a scattering of publications. This is especially true of the first topic discussed in this chapter: population. There has recently been an extraordinary burst of interest in the field of historical demography, especially for the seventeenth century, in large part stimulated by innovating studies of the French and English populations of the same period. Their influence on early American history is summarized in Philip J. Greven, Jr., "Historical Demography and Colonial America," *Wm. and Mary Q.*, 24 (1967), 438–54. Of the older publications, two are still useful: the compilation of contemporary population estimates in Evarts B. Greene and Virginia D. Harrington, *American Population before the Federal Census of 1790* (1932) and Abbot E. Smith, *Colonists in Bondage* (1947), a study of immigrant convicts and indentured servants. The new writings, based on statistical analysis of small communities, originally concentrated on New England; the most recent and most elaborate of these studies relate to the Chesapeake region. A summary of New England's extraordinary growth rate appears in Daniel S. Smith, "The Demographic History of Colonial New England," *Journal of Ecomonic History*, 32 (1972), 165–83. Other important writings on population growth are Philip J. Greven, Jr., *Four Generations . . . Andover, Massachusetts* (1970); John Demos, "Notes on Life in Plymouth Colony," *Wm. and Mary Q.*, 22 (1965), 264–86;* and the same author's *A Little Commonwealth* (1970). The contrasting high death rate in the earliest years in Virginia and the eventual recovery and rapid growth of population there too are discussed in Edmund S. Morgan, *American Slavery, American Freedom* (1975). Most of these studies reveal the distorted age structure and sex ratio in the settlement years, but there is important additional information on both in John Demos, "Families in Colonial Bristol,

R.I. . . . ," *Wm. and Mary Q.*, 25 (1968), 40–57; in Irene W. D. Hecht, "The Virginia Muster of 1624/5," *ibid.*, 30 (1973), 65–92; and in Herbert Moller's occasionally fanciful "Sex Composition and Correlated Culture Patterns of Colonial America," *ibid.*, 2 (1945), 113–53. On migration to early New England, see T. H. Breen and Stephen Foster, "Moving to the New World . . . ," *ibid.*, 36 (1973), 189–223, and Charles Banks, *Planters of the Commonwealth* (1930); on the spread of population, see Lois K. Mathews, *The Expansion of New England* (1909), chaps. ii–iii. On the peopling of the Chesapeake area, the most notable writings are found in two collections of essays: A. C. Land, L. G. Carr, and E. C. Papenfuse, eds., *Law, Society, and Politics in Early Maryland* (1977); and T. W. Tate and D. L. Ammerman, eds., *The Chesapeake in the Seventeenth Century* (1979). Essays in J. M. Smith, ed., *Seventeenth-Century America* (1959) and Wesley F. Craven, *White, Red, and Black* (1971) are also useful.

There are two valuable sketches of the overall development of the early American economy: Stuart Bruchey, *Roots of American Economic Growth, 1607–1861* (1965) and George R. Taylor, "American Economic Growth before 1840," *Journal of Economic History*, 24 (1964), 427–44. The world context of American commercial development is well presented in Ralph Davis, *Rise of the Atlantic Economies* (1973).

The growth of the commercial economy in early New England is traced in Bernard Bailyn, *The New England Merchants in the Seventeenth Century* (1955) and in Bernard and Lotte Bailyn, *Massachusetts Shipping, 1697–1714* (1959). The psychological turmoils of a Puritan merchant, caught between entrepreneurial and pietistic impulses, emerge in Bailyn, ed., *The Apologia of Robert Keayne* (1965). Curtis P. Nettels, *The Money Supply of the American Colonies before 1720* (1934) covers various aspects of American and Atlantic commerce as well as monetary history. For a social description of the emerging port towns, see Carl Bridenbaugh, *Cities in the Wilderness* (1938).

Many aspects of the southern economy are described in Lewis C. Gray, *History of Agriculture in the Southern United States to 1860* (2 vols., 1933), and there is still value in Philip A. Bruce's *Economic History of Virginia in the Seventeenth Century* (2 vols., 1896). The master historian of the tobacco economy, however, is Jacob M. Price; it is from his writing particularly that one learns of the worldwide commercial network that shaped the lives of the Chesapeake farmers. In his *The Tobacco Adventure to Russia . . . 1676–1722* (*Transactions of the American Philosphical Society,* 1961), Price traces the failure of the London tobacco merchants to market Chesapeake tobacco in Russia, an effort which, if it had succeeded, would have transformed the economy and society of the American South. Price also discusses the French-American tobacco trade in *France and the Chesapeake* (2 vols., 1973).

Traditional ideals of social organization are depicted in E. M. W. Tillyard, *Elizabethan World Picture* (1943) and in Gordon J. Schochet, *Patriarchalism in Political Thought* (1975); the latter has an excellent chapter on the ideals and actuality of the family in seventeenth-century England, a subject discussed at length by Peter Laslett in *The World We Have Lost* (1965) and in his introduction to *Household and Family in Past Time* (1972). Many of the new community-demographic studies cited above, particularly those of Greven and Demos, make clear the difficulty of maintaining traditional forms in the wilderness setting. See also Sumner C. Powell, *Puritan Village* (1963) and Edmund S. Morgan, *Puritan Family* (1944). Kenneth A. Lockridge, *New England Town: Dedham . . .* (1970) locates the disarray only at the end of the seventeenth century. On social mobility there are several important writings: William A. Reavis, "The Maryland Gentry and Social Mobility, 1637–1676," *Wm. and Mary Q.,* 14 (1957), 418–28; Russell R. Menard, "From Servant to Freeholder," *ibid.,* 30 (1973), 37–64; Linda A. Bissell, "From One Generation to Another," *ibid.,* 31 (1974), 79–110; and Menard *et al.,* "Opportunity and Inequality," *Maryland Historical Magazine,* 69 (1974), 169–84. The political consequences of social mobility and conflict are depicted in Bernard Bailyn, "Politics and Social Structure in Virginia,"* James M. Smith, ed., *Seventeenth-Century America* (1959). On the altered role of women in seventeenth-century America, see Roger Thompson, *Women in Stuart England and America* (1974); on children and childhood, see R. W. Beales, Jr., "In Search of the Historical Child," *American Quarterly,* 27 (1975), 379–98. Philip Greven has sketched the history of child-rearing in early America in terms of shifting patterns of family life, religious experience, and self-identity in *The Protes-*

tant Temperament (1977).

On religion, Sydney E. Ahlstrom, *Religious History of the American People* (1972), surveys generally the European background as well as the transplantation of European institutions, ideas, and beliefs to the North American continent. For a particularly thoughtful overall interpretation, stressing the colonial period, see Sidney E. Mead, *The Lively Experiment* (1963). For the seventeenth century, the subject has been dominated by the prolific scholarship on Puritanism. The master scholar in that subject has been Perry Miller. His two-volume *New England Mind* (*The Seventeenth Century,* 1939; *From Colony to Province,* 1953); his many essays, collected in *Errand into the Wilderness* (1956) and *Nature's Nation* (1967); and his and Thomas H. Johnson's anthology of sources, *The Puritans* (1938) have made New England Puritanism one of the most absorbing subjects of modern historiography. Miller's books set in motion a flood of writing on Puritanism, which is surveyed in Michael McGiffert, "American Puritan Studies in the 1960's," *Wm. and Mary Q.,* 27 (1970), 36–67. The closest approach to a new general interpretation of Puritan thought since Miller's *New England Mind* is David D. Hall, *The Faithful Shepherd: A History of the New England Ministry in the Seventeenth Century* (1972). Among the many other important writings on Puritanism are Alan Simpson, *Puritanism in Old and New England* (1955); Edmund S. Morgan, *Visible Saints* (1963); James F. MacLear, "The Heart of New England Rent," *Mississippi Valley Historical Review,* 42 (1956), 621–52; Emil Oberholzer, Jr., *Delinquent Saints* (1955); and Timothy H. Breen, *The Character of the Good Ruler* (1970). Darrett B. Rutman, *American Puritanism* (1970) is an interesting essay of interpretation. Most recently Sacvan Bercovitch, *The Puritan Origins of the American Self* (1975) has shown the enduring impact of Puritan ideals on American self-imagery and culture.

No other religious community of the seventeenth century has received even remotely comparable study. On Anglicanism, in general, see George M. Brydon, *Virginia's Mother Church* (1947) and Elizabeth H. Davidson, *Establishment of the English Church in the Continental American Colonies* (1936); on the efforts to reform the Anglican Church in the late seventeenth and early eighteenth centuries, see Parke Rouse, Jr., *James Blair of Virginia* (1971). On the Catholics, see John T. Ellis, *Catholics in Colonial America* (1965); on the Dutch Reformed, Frederick J. Zwierlein, *Religion in New Netherland* (1910); and on the Baptists, William G. McLoughlin, *New England Dissent, 1630–1833* (2 vols., 1971).

*See footnote on page 65.

Thus, the founding of British America is the story of the efforts of private groups and individuals to profit in some way from the exploitation of the North American continent. The leading organizers had various motives. For some, the predominant goals were economic, for others, religious. For most, however, there was a mingling of religious, economic, and patriotic interests stimulated by discontent at home, lure of adventure, and the hope that in an open land, free of inherited encumbrances, their fortunes would improve. This scattering of private enterprises, some of them protected in their independence by crown charters, had developed without overall plan or general organization. By 1660 there was little sense on either side of the Atlantic that these settlements together formed an effective empire.

In the two generations that followed the restoration of the Stuarts to the throne of England (1660), efforts were made to draw these unrelated settlements into an overall governmental organization, to impose regulation and control of some sort over this miscellaneous collection of towns, villages, and farms. The way this was done, and the way in which these efforts at regulation interacted with the natural growth and maturing of the American communities, had a permanent effect on the character of American life.

Empire

Three interest groups, dominant at the Restoration court of Charles II (1660–85), account for the extension of the authority of the British government to America. The first were courtiers, the most active of them the Carolina proprietors, who had assisted in restoring Charles II to the throne and had remained his key advisers. Their stake in America deepened as the possibilities of extracting profit from the settlements became more realistic. And to advance their interests in the colonies most of these courtiers were willing to share in the work of devising appropriate administrative machinery and to serve as members of the agencies that were created.

A second and ultimately more influential group was composed of the merchants and their allies in government who marketed American products and sold

Elements of Change
1660–1720

JAMES II AT THE TIME OF HIS ACCESSION
James's stubborn insistence on imposing a Catholic
regime on a Protestant nation and his autocratic disre-
gard of political realities led to his downfall in the
Glorious Revolution (1688) and to a great advance in
British liberalism. *(National Portrait Gallery, London)*

royal family itself, particularly those of the king's
brother, James, Duke of York, and his private entourage. As proprietor of New York, an expert on naval
affairs, and an unusually energetic administrator,
James made clear soon after the Restoration that he
would be a leading figure in designing an empire
from among the scattered American settlements.

It was the combination of these three groups—
courtiers, merchants, and the royal family, particularly
James—all with stakes in the colonies, that accounts
for the organization of the British empire at the end of
the seventeenth century. Their goals were not identical, and there was no coordinated planning, but their
interests converged in efforts at three levels.

Administration. Together they created, first, through
a fumbling, pragmatic process of evolution, a network
of administrative controls. Immediately after the Restoration, the king's Privy Council began appointing
committees of its own members, occasionally supplemented by others, to deal with colonial problems as
they arose. The volume and importance of the business that came before these committees soon justified
the appointment of a standing committee, called the
Lords of Trade (1675), composed only of members of
the Privy Council. This committee, irregular in its
efforts and lacking reliable staff, was a bridge to the
permanent supervisory body, the Board of Trade and
Plantations, which was created in 1696.

As an independent agency the Board of Trade,
consisting of eight high state officials and eight paid
members, remained the central pivot of the British imperial administration throughout the eighteenth century. But as a "Council of the Indies," it had notable
weaknesses. First, the range of its duties was unrealistically broad. It was expected effectively to supervise
all the trade of Britain, its fisheries, and the care of the
poor throughout Britain, as well as all colonial matters.
In dealing with the colonies it was expected to have a
special responsibility for reviewing all crown appointments in America and all the legislation that emerged
from the colonies. Yet despite these responsibilities,
the board's actual power proved to be severely limited.
Other, better-established branches of government
took over some measure of the control of colonial af-

manufactured goods to the colonists. These merchants
were aware that a significant part of the English economy would become involved in the colonies, and they
became leaders in the growing movement to assert
British control over the American settlements—not
for the sake of power, glory, and "empire" in some
abstract sense, but for the sake of trade and England's
economic growth.

Finally, there were the personal interests of the

fairs, and the board's power failed to mature.

The essential conflict lay between the board and the secretary of state for the Southern Department, in whose geographical jurisdiction the Western Hemisphere fell. This secretary of state was one of the chief executive officers of the government, with particular responsibility for international relations. The center of his concerns was not the struggling settlements on the coast of North America but the glittering court of Louis XIV in Paris. Nevertheless, by 1704 the secretary of state for the Southern Department successfully challenged the Board of Trade for executive authority over the colonies, and the result was a fundamental weakness at the heart of the British overseas administration. The Board of Trade remained an information-gathering body, in effect the colonial office of that era, in charge of a substantial flow of information to and from the colonies; but it lacked the power to enforce regulations, make appointments, or otherwise direct the course of events. It could advise, counsel, admonish; but orders came from the secretary of state's office which might or might not have available to it the board's voluminous files and which tended to view colonial affairs in the context of western European diplomacy.

That significant division of authority was not the only source of administrative confusion as the empire took shape. Almost every major branch of the central government discovered some interest in the colonies and managed to secure some corner of control. The Treasury took responsibility for the colonial customs administration. The Admiralty successfully claimed jurisdiction over naval stores and other colonial products vital to the British navy, and took responsibility for patrolling the coastal waters to enforce the growing body of commercial regulations. Further, the War Office took charge of army operations on the North American mainland during the many years when European international conflicts involved overseas territories. The army's contracting, like that of the navy, had a powerful influence on the economic development of the colonies, and its strategic planning involved American manpower as well. Weaving through all of these ill-assorted jurisdictions was the authority legitimately exercised by England's attorney general, solic-

itor general, and several auditors and collectors of the king's revenues.

By the early eighteenth century an imperial administration had taken shape in the British world. But it was a very different structure from the Spanish American empire. There was no central authority equivalent to the Spanish Council of the Indies, which had at its disposal both information and executive authority and drew together all the other agencies of government that had a finger in colonial matters. The various British agencies conflicted with each other. There were overlaps in jurisdiction, and also significant gaps in authority. As a result, there was a minimum of effective central control.

Yet for Britain this administrative inefficiency was not acutely distressing. For the guiding principles behind the organization of the British empire did not require tight administrative efficiency in the years before 1760, and it did not require territorial government in depth. The colonies could largely be left alone so long as certain minimal expectations were met, and these expectations centered almost entirely on the regulation of commerce.

Mercantilism and Commercial Regulation. Britain's was a mercantilist empire. It came together as an extension of England's commercial growth. Its guiding principles were derived from mercantilism, the ancient doctrine that the state must intervene to regulate economic activity for the public welfare. In the heated commercial rivalries of the seventeenth century, mercantilists made two assumptions that framed the regulations of Britain's American empire: first, that the economic universe was composed of competing national states; and second, that there was a fixed amount of wealth ultimately available. According to mercantilist theory, the purpose of commercial regulation for each nation-state was to secure economic self-sufficiency and, by maintaining a favorable balance of trade, to avoid falling into dependence on rival states. In this competition among nations, the colonies were fundamentally important. If they did not provide Britain with needed colonial products, these commodities would have to be purchased from other nations and hence wealth would be drained by the rival states. It followed that every effort would have to be made to direct the flow of valuable colonial products to Britain alone. Further, the colonies, as markets for the sale of manufactured goods, were to be monopolized by Britain, for every purchase of goods from a rival state meant some small drainage in the national treasure.

It was to put these ideas into effect that the famous navigation acts were passed by Parliament in three main groups beginning soon after the Restoration. The first of these enactments (1660) restricted the shipping and marketing of all colonial goods to British subjects. England alone, it was decreed, would enjoy the profits of shipping and reexporting colonial goods. Further, a special list was prepared of "enumerated" commodities that could be shipped only to England or other British ports. The basic list included all the goods that England would otherwise have had to buy from other imperial powers: sugar, tobacco, cotton, indigo, ginger, certain dyes, and special wood products. Later other commodities were added to the original list: rice and molasses in 1704; naval stores in 1705 and 1729; copper and furs in 1721.

The act of 1660 was the basic law governing colonial trade. Two others completed the pattern of mercantilist regulation. The so-called Staple Act of 1663 gave England a monopoly of the sale of European manufactures to the American colonies. European goods, the law stated, could not be shipped directly to America from Europe, even if the ships that carried them were British. These goods would have to be sent first to England, unloaded there, and reshipped to the colonies. Thus valuable customs duties would be produced for the English Treasury and at the same time foreign merchants would be put at a disadvantage. Certain exceptions were made, either because, like salt, they were necessary for American industry, or because like servants, horses, and provisions from Scotland and Ireland, or wines from Madeira or the Azores, they involved no competition with English production. A supplementary law, that of 1673, quite technical and the source of endless confusion, sought to plug gaps created by the wording of the earlier legislation.

Thus, out of the convergent interests of courtiers, merchants, and the royal family had come the beginning of an imperial system operating at three levels: as an administrative unit; as a doctrine (mercantilism);

and as a set of commercial regulations. It was, by 1700, an empire of world importance; but its government was decidedly limited in effectiveness. It was limited administratively because of the ill-coordinated jumble of agencies that governed it. It was limited in theory by the mercantilist doctrines that prevailed—doctrines that demanded not territorial governance in depth but only regulation of external commerce. And it was limited also by the intricacy of the governing legislation and the great difficulty of enforcing these laws three thousand miles from home. By the early eighteenth century no one could doubt that the American colonies were part of an empire; but neither could anyone conceive of the ill-managed, superficial administration as a centralized dominion. The passion for territorial rule was not there, nor the drive of dynastic ambition.

James II and the Dominion of New England.   The limits of the British imperial system become particularly clear when one considers the efforts that were made later in the seventeenth century to turn the empire into something more powerful than this—something more effective than it ever in fact became. For there was one person at the center of the English government who did have ambitions akin to those of continental monarchs, and who also had the instincts of an efficient administrator and a personal entourage capable of managing an efficient system.

The instincts that led the Duke of York, subsequently James II (1685–88) to seek to expand and deepen the controls of empire can be traced back to his childhood training as a military leader in the autocratic court of France; to his desire, as a royal refugee, to exercise the power that had been denied him; and to the fortunate position he found himself in when his brother, Charles II, returned to the throne. As Lord High Admiral with a loyal following of war-seasoned officers, James took command of garrisons all over England and appointed as governors those hungry veterans who had merged their fortunes with his. For him the colonial world was but an extension of the realm. Soon his captains turned up as governors and other high officers in the Caribbean and North American governments. His base on the mainland was New York, which he ruled as proprietor from the time it was captured from the Dutch. Slowly he expanded this center into a larger imperial dominion, his efforts coinciding with the more general efforts the English government was then making to restrict the private jurisdictions that had been created in the early years of colonization.

For in the later seventeenth century and continuing into the early years of the eighteenth century, the British government, as part of its elaboration of empire, undertook to cut back the chartered powers of the private jurisdictions in America. Progress was slow, erratic, and in the end incomplete. Virginia, when the company failed in 1624, and New York, when James II acceded to the throne in 1685, both automatically became crown colonies. Also, it was not difficult to separate New Hampshire from Massachusetts (1680) and assign it a royal governor. But for the rest, the charters created serious problems, and they had to be attacked directly. Between 1684 and 1691 the charters of Massachusetts, Connecticut, Rhode Island, New Jersey, Pennsylvania, Maryland, and Carolina were confiscated.

It was in the early years of this campaign against these partly independent jurisdictions that James's grand and ill-fated design unfolded. As king, his ultimate ambition, it seems, was to create two centralized viceroyalties in America which would be ruled by crown-appointed governors and councils. The Delaware River at 40 degrees latitude (the division between the two original Virginia companies) was apparently seen as the boundary between the two great domains. During his short and tumultuous reign James focused his attention on the northern section, which became known as the Dominion of New England.

In a legal sense, the Dominion came together easily after 1685. To the core colony of New York were added New Hamphire, Massachusetts, Connecticut, Rhode Island, and New Jersey as each of their charters was annulled or suspended. To rule the Dominion, in place of the existing officials, James sent over one of his closest allies and former comrades in arms, Edmund Andros, who had served him well in several other positions, particularly as governor of New York (1674–81). To assist Andros at his headquarters in Boston, James appointed a royal council which included a majority of recently arrived merchants who had struggled against the Puritan establishment, hitherto with little effect. Together, royal governor and royal council moved to work out the implications of direct and full territorial government similar to that of the Spanish crown in the Southern Hemisphere.

To the horror of the Puritans throughout New England, Andros declared toleration for all groups, and confiscated Boston's Old South Church for the use of Church of England services. Equally offensive was his disregard of the ancient principles of English self-government. He continued by mere executive declaration taxes that had originally been levied in Massachusetts by the representative General Court. Worse still was Andros's land policy. He commanded that all town lands be regranted in the name of the king and be subject to the payment of annual quitrents to the crown, and that the towns' undistributed common lands be placed at the council's disposal. Finally, to complete the destruction of the local jurisdictions, he limited the activities of the town meetings to electing officials who would help collect taxes.

Andros's efforts never reached beyond Massachusetts, indeed scarcely beyond Boston and the coastal towns. But their implications were widely known and they stimulated ferocious opposition. His tax policy provoked an open rebellion in the town of Ipswich, led by the Reverend John Wise, and to the imprisonment of that outspoken preacher and four of his followers. Resistance grew among the Puritan leaders and the landholders throughout New England. By the time Andros's royal master was deposed in the Glorious Revolution in England, the royalist regime in Boston was so universally hated and so isolated that the rebellion that rose against it and that imprisoned the governor and his closest allies took place, in April 1689, almost without a struggle.

All of James's colonial plans disappeared with his fall from power. When this high tide of imperial ambition fell back, the more permanent forms of Anglo-American relations emerged as the charters were restored, though with qualifications, and the slow, partial elimination of private jurisdictions continued. The two Jerseys were reunited into a single royal colony in 1702. In the Carolinas a popular rebellion against the proprietors (1719) and constant pressure against them in England led in 1729 to the formal separation of the two districts into two royal colonies. The one residue of the Carolinas' proprietary origins was the retention of one of the eight original shares by the diplomat and politican the Earl Granville, heir of Sir George Carteret. When consolidated in 1745, his inheritance, the so-called Granville District, constituted title to the undistributed land of fully half of North Carolina on which lived perhaps two-thirds of the colony's population. The charters of Pennsylvania and Maryland were restored to the Penn and Calvert families; but in both cases the selection of the governor had thereafter to be approved by the crown, and all legislation was subject to review by the crown's legal officers.

The British American Empire. The results of these developments after the collapse of James's Dominion was a return to the limited and superficial empire that had existed long before 1685, modified by the reduction of chartered privileges in several colonies. In its decentralization and ineffiency, Britain's empire was far different from Spain's, but it was still a visible, extensive empire. Its visibility, by the early eighteenth century, appeared most dramatically to most Americans not so much in law enforcement or in recast institutions as in the increasing number of officials sent to America to manage the new system. In most port towns there were customs collectors appointed by the Treasury who brought with them small teams of assistants. There were auditors and surveyors of the king's revenues. And there were officers of the vice admiralty courts created by the law of 1696—subordinate arms of the admiralty court system that held jurisdiction over maritime law in Britain. The judges and clerks of these "prerogative" courts (operating without juries and by rules different from those of the common law courts) were part of the imperial presence, as were, indirectly and for the limited purpose of enforcing the navigation laws, the governors and lieutenant governors of all of the royal colonies.

The importance of these officials, most of whom were newcomers to America at the end of the century, cannot be exaggerated. They represented—indeed embodied—the empire. The way they approached their work, the attitudes they brought to Anglo-American relations, and the ways in which they related to the local communities became matters of importance in the life of the American people. They affected not only the actuality of government but the image of government and of political authority more generally.

These officials were not efficient imperial bureaucrats, and they were seldom committed to promoting the strength of the empire. Their offices were minor parts of the patronage system of the English government, and hence were seen as a kind of private property parceled out by political leaders to their deserving followers. Appointees were expected to profit by their positions through fees, gifts, and perquisites, as well as through salaries. Appointments were made almost randomly with respect to administrative ability or interest in public affairs. What counted were connections and the applicant's capacity to force his patron to reward loyalty and previous service.

At times the appointments were bizarre, even those at the highest level. The governor of New York from 1701 to 1708 was a rapacious transvestite, Lord Cornbury, a member of the Clarendon family, who traipsed around the colony in women's clothes and squeezed profit from anything he could lay his hands on. The governor of Virginia from 1705 to 1737 was the Earl of Orkney, who never had the slightest intention of setting foot in America, and never did. He had been a war companion of William III and was the Duke of Marlborough's leading infantry commander. His appointment was a reward too, however, for somewhat less heroic service. He had made what may have been a supreme sacrifice by marrying William III's mistress, Elizabeth Villiers.

Orkney's career as absentee governor of Virginia is revealing in many ways. The stated salary of the position was £2,000 a year. Orkney in effect sold the office for £1,200 to a series of lieutenant governors who served in his place, with the understanding that they were entitled to make as much out of the job as they could. He selected, as it happens, some able men: Robert Hunter, 1706 (who, because of accidents at sea and his wife's connections, ended up governor not of Virginia but of New York, a post he filled with distinction); Alexander Spotswood, in 1709; and William Gooch, in 1727. These three had only one thing in common: they had all fought as officers under Orkney and Marlborough. No less than nine veterans of the battle of Blenheim received colonial governorships for their service.

Under these conditions, what is surprising is not that colonial offices were occasionally filled by avaricious deviants like Cornbury or by psychological cripples like Sir Danvers Osborn, who hanged himself in a fit of melancholy a week after his arrival as New York's governor, nor that lesser posts were frequently held by altogether unqualified hacks. What is remarkable is that some appointees were in fact conscientious and honest, and sought dutifully to serve the imperial interest as well as the local population.

Still, it is the randomness of these appointments, the disregard of the incumbents' ability and experience, and hence in the end the arbitrariness of the system, that had the deepest effect on American life. The consequences were profound.

First, these appointments to offices in the colonies served to increase the existing superficiality of the British imperial system. Officeholders, always insecure in tenure, knew that the same arbitrary movement of the patronage system that put them in office could easily eject them. Sooner or later, they knew, quite without regard to the quality of their work, they would be replaced by someone closer to the levers of power. Consequently they were highly susceptible to compromises and vulnerable to local pressures. If the situation required speed in making a profit from office, they would be quick about it, at the expense, if need be, of the strict execution of their duties.

Further, British officialdom, as it emerged from these formative years, inculcated in Americans a sense that government, far from being a seamless web uniting high and low through a series of responsible links, was essentially a structure composed of two distinct and antagonistic levels, a level of local,

LORD CORNBURY, GOVERNOR OF NEW YORK, IN FEMALE DRESS Of Lord Cornbury, a cousin of Queen Anne, an eighteenth-century historian wrote that he used "to dress himself in a woman's habit and then to patrol the fort in which he resided. Such freaks of low humor exposed him to the universal contempt of the people." His avarice led the Assembly to assert its control over tax revenues, and his zealous Anglicanism resulted in broader religious toleration. *(New-York Historical Society, New York City)*

internal government that expressed the dominant interests of the local community, and a superior, external authority which was in its nature hostile to local interests. Often the external power became identified with executive authority and the local and benevolent authority with legislative power. Such a sharp distinction between these functions of government was extraordinary for the time and was destined to have a continuing importance in American history.

Even more general still, among the consequences of British officialdom, was the growth on the part of politically active Americans of a kind of cynicism to all government, an attitude of anti-authoritarianism stimulated by the character and behavior of these officials. These officeholders represented a nation that was revered by most of the colonists; but in themselves these officers were often incompetent, poor, and supercilious, a bad enough combination made worse by their easy corruptibility. Americans could only wonder whether the power such people represented deserved automatic compliance.

Beyond all of this lay the sense, as the imperial officialdom developed, that the social and political worlds were far from unified, that social and political leadership at the highest level was dissociated. The native social leaders of the colonies did not represent the state. In fact, when local leaders competed with strangers for high office in their own colony, they did so often on unequal terms, and their failures were embittering. Thus William Byrd II, a second-generation American who spent fifteen years being educated and making contacts in England before taking over the family property in Virginia, failed in his bid to buy the lieutenant governorship of his native colony from Orkney and spent years struggling with his successful rival, Spotswood, who had no original stake in the colony and no knowledge of it when he arrived on the scene. Byrd finally acquired a seat on the colony's council, but only after ten years of diligent effort.

What made all of these consequences of the growth of officialdom especially important was the fact that they coincided with the natural emergence of local elites in the mainland colonies. The dominance of these local leaders within the maturing communities could not be doubted, and their demands for recognition—in politics as in other spheres of life— could not easily be ignored.

Anglo-American Aristocracy

The rise of a provincial aristocracy toward the end of the seventeenth century and in the early eighteenth century was the result of the exploitation, by skillful, energetic, and ambitious men, of opportunities that suddenly became available. These opportunities were created by basic developments in social and economic life.

Land as the Basis of Aristocracy.   The material basis for most social distinctions in the colonies, as in England, was the ownership or control of land. The thirty years that bridged the turn of the century, 1690–1720, saw a significant shift in this basic relationship. Between these two dates the land area under active cultivation remained approximately the same, because of Indian wars and the difficulty of overcoming natural barriers in the way of westward expansion. But during these same years the population more than doubled: it rose from approximately 210,000 to 460,000. Land was still far easier to acquire in the colonies than it was in England, but the increasing population pressure created significant changes in social relations, and in itself accounts for the emergence of new social elites.

In New England the emergence of a landowning aristocracy in the long-settled towns was marked by dramatic conflicts almost everywhere. In its original form the New England town had been a kind of democracy of male heads of households, all of whom were full church members, freemen in the town meeting, and landowners with shares in the undivided common land. As time passed and migration among towns grew while immigration into the colonies continued, questions arose about how newcomers would share in these original privileges. Certain answers came quickly. Access to membership in the church was controlled by a procedure calculated to make the entry of newcomers possible but still highly selective. Access to participation in the town meeting was less easily determined but in the end was opened to all respectable male inhabitants. But there was no easy resolution of the question of control of the undivided land. The heirs of the original grantees had no desire to share their inheritances with newcomers, and they closed ranks against the claimants.

Without originally intending to do so, these second- and third-generation colonists began to form exclusive companies of landholders. Challenged in the town meeting by those excluded from sharing in the common property, they drew apart and met separately, only to have their rights to the undivided land challenged at law. In certain towns they sought compromises by allocating plots—often dismissed as bribes—to conspicuous opponents or to those with special claims. Most often, however, confrontation could not be evaded. The challenges went up to the General Court, whose decisions, after a period of uncertainty, favored the heirs of the original grantees.

As a result, not only did the fortunate heirs continue to enjoy the increasingly valuable property, but they shared control of the still undivided common land. With this inherited capital, they were in the best possible position to build fortunes out of real estate. Those shrewd or enterprising enough to take full advantage of the opportunities that lay at hand broadened out their operations from small local transactions to large-scale land speculation. Some moved into trade through successes in commercial farming; the most enterprising did both. In Connecticut the most successful became known as River Gods because of their valuable properties along the colony's main waterway. Everywhere in New England land claims proved a rich ore available for refinement into gold, prestige, and power.

The same was true in the South; but there, as tobacco cultivation spread westward, profits from the land were intimately tied up with the problem of labor, and that increasingly meant slavery. It was in the later seventeenth century that the critical importance of slavery first emerged in southern society. A great revolution in social relations as well as in the economy was created by the spread of slavery and the growth of the black population. Slavery accounted not only for the introduction of a major component of the American population but also for a basic source of social stratification within the white population. The logic of this development quickly became clear.

With profits from tobacco production small and at times nonexistent, the *extensiveness* of planting seemed increasingly important. Land was available for expansion, but labor was not. The immigration of white indentured servants from England declined sharply after 1660 because of a slackening in England's population growth and an improved English labor market, especially in the London area. Slaves alone, it seemed, provided an answer to the labor problem, and they were increasingly available as the British slave trade entered a period of expansion and

increasing efficiency. Slaves *in the long run* were cheap. Their upkeep, averaged over a lifetime of labor, was perhaps £1 per year, as opposed to a servant's annual maintenance cost of £2–£4. But if slaves were cheaper than servants in the long run, they were more costly in the short run because they required a higher initial investment. And cost were rising constantly. Average slave prices doubled between 1660 and 1750, and by the Revolution they had tripled. In 1700 a newly imported "prime field hand" cost £20 in Virginia; in 1750, £30. Nevertheless their numbers continued to rise as their importance in the spreading tobacco culture became clearly understood. An estimated 20,000 slaves were brought to British North America in the two decades after 1700; 50,000 arrived in the subsequent two decades. In 1715 blacks formed a quarter of Virginia's total population, by the '30s 40 percent. In South Carolina blacks outnumbered whites by 1708; by 1720 the ratio was almost 2 to 1, and the black population was growing at a faster rate than the white.

The growth of the slave labor force, which made possible a significant increase in tobacco cultivation and eventually in rice and indigo production, created a deepening social distinction within the white population. Capital was the critical determinant. Since profits depended on the extent of cultivation and since that in turn depended on slave labor which required high capital outlays, the line between those who had capital available and those who did not, or between those who could acquire it and those who could not, became crucial. Those with greater assets formed a new class of "great planters" in a society that as late as 1700 consisted almost entirely of farm operations of small and medium size. In Lancaster County in northern Virginia in 1716, a majority of taxpayers owned slaves, but few had more than 2 or 3; only four owned over 20; one, however—Robert Carter—had 126. At his death in 1732 Robert "King" Carter—planter and above all land agent and speculator, son of a settler of 1649 who had brought capital with him and had accumulated the land claims of no less than five wives—was said to possess 300,000 acres and £10,000 in cash. Capital and inherited land claims, in a world of steeply rising land values, deter-

INDIGO CULTURE IN SOUTH CAROLINA
The plants of the blue dyestuff are being carried to fermenting vats, and the resulting liquid flows down the sluice at left into containers. *(Charleston Library Society)*

mined who would succeed and who would not, who would control the land and who would not, and who would live like princes on the land—bourgeois, enterprising princes, to be sure, desperately concerned with markets, prices, and the humblest details of farming—but princes nevertheless.

Trade as the Basis of Aristocracy. In the main commercial centers the merchant community as a whole remained open, free of the formal limitations of gilds and other artificial barriers to entrance. But toward the end of the seventeenth century, and increasingly in the early eighteenth century, significant differences within the merchant group appeared nevertheless, and a mercantile aristocracy of sorts began to make its appearance.

As the commercial system settled into its com-

plex pattern of oceanic routes covering the North Atlantic basin, certain portions of the network proved crucial and dominated the others. Entrance into this primary route became more and more difficult to achieve, and the colonial merchants who controlled it became dominant figures. For as the magnitude of imports from England increased and as the marshaling of colonial products in ever larger quantities made greater and greater demands on colonial entrepreneurs, the English specialists in North American trade began to concentrate their shipments to a few ports and to a relatively few merchants. They sought commercial correspondents who could be relied on to send payments quickly in good bills of exchange or salable commodities. Once involved in these primary circuits of trade, through which flowed the all-important "dry goods" (iron products and textiles, primarily) a merchant had a cumulative advantage over others. The main profits of the commercial system tended to center in these major importers, while the smaller merchants, confined to local routes, fell more and more clearly into subordinate roles.

In the large port towns the dominant entrepreneurs who were in direct contact with the English merchants and in control of the critical goods formed an aristocracy of sorts. It was an aristocracy that was still limited in affluence, fluid in membership, and insecure, but it was a visible elite nevertheless, and its fortunes rested on the primary flows of commerce.

Political Influence as the Basis of Aristocracy. Thus economic developments—in the ownership of land in New England, in the expansion of the tobacco economy in the Chesapeake, and in the maturing of commerce in the main centers in the North—underlay the development of native elites. But the forces behind this development were not only economic. They were political as well. As the colonial governments took firm shape in the middle and later years of the century, the value of political patronage and the yields of the public office became unmistakably clear. The possibilities were seen first in Virginia, where what might be called the first "court house gang" took form during the long governorship of Sir William Berkeley (1641–52, 1659–77).

The appointments that Berkeley could make gave him power over many aspects of the colony's life. In addition to appointing justices of the peace, sheriffs, and tax collectors, he could nominate members of the council, who not only enjoyed considerable prestige but benefited materially from the privileges available to them. Over the twenty-nine years of his administration Berkeley, through his appointments, formed a clique of officials loyal to himself to whom he channeled these benefits. A similar little oligarchy developed simultaneously around the proprietary interest in Maryland.

It was not in Virginia or in Maryland, however, but in New York that these possibilities were most dramatically revealed. There in the 1690s a new land-owning elite was created almost overnight, largely by a single governor attempting to make his own fortune and the fortunes of his followers as quickly as possible. In New York's tumultuous and competitive politics at the end of the century, the ruthless partisanship of Governor Benjamin Fletcher (1692–97) was extraordinarily effective. Personally rapacious, surrounded by a mercenary gang of petty plunderers whom he had brought with him, Fletcher—and Cornbury after him—proceeded to buy the loyalty of the dominant group of local powers by bestowing on them enormous grants of land and confirming others previously made.

He did not invent the procedure. One patroonship had survived in flourishing shape from the Dutch period—Rensselaerswyck, a manor of close to a million acres on both sides of the Hudson—and several other great estates had been granted subsequently. Of these, the most important was Livingston Manor, a grant of 160,000 acres that had been extracted from the Dominion government by a particularly supple Scottish-Anglo-Dutch politician, Robert Livingston—a man Fletcher said, who began as "a little bookkeeper" but who "screwed himself into one of the most considerable estates in the province, . . . never disbursing sixpence but with the expectation of twelve." It was just such sharp-eyed opportunists and hustling politicians, scrambling in the bonanza land grab of late seventeenth-century New York, whose appetites Fletcher fed. The estates he parceled out in Dutchess and Westchester counties varied in size and in legal and political privileges, but almost all exceeded 100,000 acres. Some grants were literally open-ended: sixteen miles, commonly, along a river bank running back indefinitely into the unsurveyed countryside.

Profits from the French and Indian Wars. The results of political influence were not limited to landholding. Politics also affected the development of trade and the establishment of the merchant leadership, for at the end of the century government contracting, political in its essence, became a prime source of economic advancement, especially during war years. The colonies became involved in both of the international wars in which England fought during these years: the inconclusive War of the League of Augsburg (1689–97), in which England led a coali-

tion against France's effort to dominate central Europe, and the more consequential War of the Spanish Succession (1702–13) in which England and Holland joined to block Louis XIV's claim to the crown of Spain. Both of these wars, whose main operations spread over large areas of Europe, led to hostilities between the English colonies and the French in southern Canada. The slow-growing colony of New France had been settled at the same time as the English colonies; but, limited in its development by religious restrictions on immigration, rigid systems of land distribution and of social relations, and a tightly controlled colonial bureaucracy, it had achieved a population of only 6,000 by 1660 and perhaps 15,000 by 1700. Nevertheless, the French had been aggressive fur traders, trappers, and fishermen from the beginning, and for years there had been minor clashes between them and the English settlers, especially in Nova Scotia. Those clashes escalated into savage border warfare and extended struggles for inland territories during the two international wars that spanned the years 1689–1713. Both of these wars involved the English colonists as much economically as militarily.

In the first, known as King William's War in the colonies, the French, with Indian support, fought the English for control of Hudson Bay, and in 1690 fell on the exposed northern borders of English settlement with devastating raids on an arc of towns from Portland, Maine, to Schenectady, New York. The Anglo-American efforts concentrated on capturing Port Royal in Nova Scotia, which was taken but then lost by Massachusetts troops in 1690–91, and on an elaborate attack on the center of French Canada, which failed miserably.

The same pattern was repeated in the second of these wars, known in the colonies as Queen Anne's War. Once again the Maine settlements were raided; and Deerfield, Massachusetts, was destroyed. In retaliation the colonists razed Nova Scotian villages and attacked Port Royal twice before finally taking that fortress. And far to the south during the same war, a force of Carolinians and Indians burned St. Augustine and destroyed the string of Spanish missions that linked the Spanish coastal settlements to French Louisiana. By the Treaty of Utrecht (1713),

James Bay

HUDSON'S BAY COMPANY

In Dispute Between French & British Trade Competition

NEWFOUNDLAND

St. John's

1711

CAPE BRETON

Louisbourg

1690

Quebec

1711

Port Royal

NOVA SCOTIA

1711

Montreal

1710

Falmouth

1690

L. Frontenac

1690

Schenectady

Albany

Deerfield

Boston

Hartford

Newport

Ft. Detroit

New York

Ft. St. Louis

Philadelphia

Williamsburg

Edenton

New Bern

English, French, Spanish Traders in Competition

Charles Town

1702

FLORIDA

St. Augustine

GULF OF MEXICO

NEW FRANCE

LOUISIANA

Mississippi R.

Wabash R.

Ohio R.

St. Lawrence R.

→ English Advance
← French Advance
⇐ Indian Advance
←--- Spanish Advance
• Settlements
✕ Forts or Trading Posts
✕ Indian Wars

EUROPEAN POSSESSIONS AFTER TREATY OF UTRECHT, 1713

- English
- French
- Spanish
- Claimed by England and France
- Claimed by England and Spain

The French Wars, 1680–1713

whose main provisions marked a significant British victory in Europe, Britain secured permanent title to Newfoundland, Acadia (Nova Scotia), and Hudson Bay, though not all the boundaries were clear, and won a thirty-year contract to supply Spanish America with 4,800 slaves and a cargo of goods annually.

All of the American efforts in these wars of the European powers made great demands on the fragile colonial economies and accounted for significant inflows of funds. Troops had to be mobilized, housed, transported, and fed; ships had to be built, equipped, and manned; and native sources of naval supplies had to be exploited. The management of these efforts during these two decades of war fell into the eager hands of a few colonial merchants. Some were experienced. Andrew Belcher, once a Cambridge innkeeper, had made his first successes in trade as

PETER FANEUIL (1700—43)
Nephew and heir of the Huguenot refugee Andrew Faneuil, who made a fortune in trade in Boston in the early 18th century, Peter devoted himself to commerce and public affairs. In 1740 he gave the city its famous Faneuil Hall, which became a cockpit of Revolutionary activity. *(Massachusetts Historical Society)*

a supplier to the Massachusetts government during its brief and bloody war against the local Indians, King Philip's War (1675–76). In the international conflicts that followed, Belcher became the colony's principal contractor. By his profits he established a family that would rise to the governorship and to other important offices and would enjoy grand tours of Europe and the acquaintance of monarchs. The Faneuil family, Huguenot refugees from France, also established itself partly through wartime contracting. In New York another Huguenot, Stephanus De-Lancey, and the Schuyler brothers in Albany, all active in many enterprises, used government con-

tracting as a major source of profits. Through that business, political in its origins, these contractors established families as important in New York as the Belchers and Faneuils were in Massachusetts.

The Limits of Social Distinction. So in these many ways the situation made possible, toward the end of the century, the growth of local elites. Enterprising merchants like Belcher and Faneuil, landowning squires like the Connecticut River Gods, planters like the Fitzhughs, the Carters, and the Byrds, and manorial "lords" like the Livingstons of New York formed an aristocracy of sorts, a leadership group distinguished by wealth or substantial claims to wealth, political influence, and a superior style of life. But if this was an aristocracy, it was a limited aristocracy indeed. The limitations of their distinctions, the essential weakness of their positions, and the instability of the membership of these groups were as important as the eminence that they had achieved.

They formed, to begin with, no "class"—that is, no body of corporate interests, known and acknowledged, that dominated individual or family interests. The concerns of these striving merchants, hustling land speculators, and hard-pressed planters were personal, local, and immediate. They identified their interests not with the stable concerns of a particular stratum of society that had existed before them and would persist after them and that defined each member's particular welfare. Their interests were their own, only occasionally and erratically merging with the concerns of others in similar situations to form common commitments and a common program of public action.

Further, these emerging elites were distinguished from most of their contemporaries by wealth alone, and wealth of a particularly fragile kind. In education, in race, in ancestry, in cultural disposition, in speech and personal style, they were largely indistinguishable from hundreds of others who competed with them openly. They had achieved, simply, a degree of wealth, and wealth, in the colonial situation, was remarkably insecure. There was almost no way to invest a fortune securely. "Urban" properties provided perhaps the steadiest yields but were limited in scale and availability. Most capital was tied up in daily trading or planting operations or in land bought on speculation, and momentary upsets could prove to be disasters. Bankruptcies were common occurrences. Repeatedly names rose from obscurity only to disappear back into the population at large.

Even when wealth was maintained, however, it could provide no institutional protection for distinctions once they were achieved. There were no legal barriers or institutional forms that could protect these fragile aristocracies—no system equivalent to ennoblement, no institution like a House of Lords, no estate of nobles, no organization of any kind, secured in law, by which membership once created could be fixed and transmitted across the generations. The colonial councils were political bodies, and while membership in them expressed an enviable status, seats were not legally heritable and membership remained open not merely to local competition by every striving merchant, planter, and

landowner, but to officials sent from abroad.

Of all the limitations in the distinctions of new elites, however, the most striking was the lack of visible distance between them and the bulk of the population from which they had emerged. They had not traveled very far; in so short a time they had not been able to create a world set far apart. They built manor houses, town houses, and plantation "seats" that had some style, and they shared in other efforts to establish the outward forms of a superior way of life. But the scale, the magnitudes, of all their efforts was yet modest—lavish, perhaps, by the standards of frontier tobacco farmers and petty shopkeeper-merchants, but incomparable to the establishments of aristocracies abroad. The Van Cortlandt's manor house on their estate on the Hudson was a modest one-and-one-half story wooden building—a pleasant summer house, a farmhouse more or less, improved for middle-class comfort but hardly suitable for an affluent country gentleman in England. "Westover," the Byrds' estate in Virginia, was more elegant and

VAN CORTLANDT MANOR HOUSE, CROTON-ON-HUDSON, NEW YORK
The manor, granted to Stephanus Van Cortlandt in 1697, originally included 86,123 acres. The restored manor house, shown here, was built around an even simpler structure by Stephanus's grandson, Pierre, over a period of years beginning in 1749. (Courtesy, Sleepy Hollow Restorations, Tarrytown, New York)

WILLIAM BYRD II, HIS WIFE MARIA, AND HIS ESTATE, WESTOVER

Son of a successful Virginia trader and planter, Byrd spent about 20 years in England before settling down to his inheritance. The present house was the third erected on that site, and became one of the showpieces of colonial Virginia. *(Top, The Library of Congress; left, The Virginia Historical Society; right, The Metropolitan Museum of Art, Fletcher Fund, 1925)* more substantial, with pretentions to a higher, more sophisticated style in its carved interior woodwork and up-to-date exterior brick façades. But much of its ultimate beauty was acquired gradually, in successive additions and refinements. In its original form it was a square abode of eight main rooms and like so many of the other proud houses of the time it was solidly middle class. So too the most elegant and famous house in Boston in this period, built by the merchant John Foster between 1689 and 1692 and destined to descend in the Hutchinson family, seemed an immense achievement by the standard of the place and time, but it would have been indistinguishable from the ordinary town houses of prosperous tradesmen in any of the major cities of Europe. There was nothing anywhere in America to compare with the great urban residences and palatial country houses of the truly rich, or even the middling rich, of Europe—nothing to compare with the more modest "seats" of the lesser aristocracy which were then being built with fine taste in England.

The heights achieved by the Van Cortlandts, the Hutchinsons, the Belchers, and the Byrds were within the reach of many and never free from competition. Conversely, the surrounding ordinary world enjoyed a remarkably high level of general well-being. There was, to be sure, poverty in early eighteenth-century America. There was indigence and misery as there has been in every society that has ever existed; but among the ordinary free population there was a degree of affluence that was unique for the time. Land remained available, even if it was increasingly difficult for freed servants to rise to full independence and public influence; and entrance to wholesale trade, though narrower than before, remained open to competition. If there were a few great landlords, there were a great many independent farmers. If there were a few suddenly rich merchant "princes," there was a large number of others who had some share in the profits of trade. In the years of Queen Anne's War, one-third of the entire adult male population of Boston (544 individuals) were part owners of some seagoing vessel. And no fewer than 207 of these investors—12 percent of the adult male population of the town—called themselves "merchants."

Rebellion: The Measure of Social Strain

It was the sudden emergence of these new elites—proud but still striving and well within the range of rivals close behind—that explains the intensity of the rash of rebellions that occurred in the American colonies in the later 1600s. These are very small events in the scale of Western history, but seen within the context of the rapid maturing of Anglo-American society, they are extremely revealing. They show the inner seams, the strains and tensions, of communities whose social structure was still forming and in which no group's dominance and no individual's eminence were safe from effective competition.

There were five outbreaks, and their dates are significant:

Virginia	Bacon's Rebellion	
Carolina	Culpeper's Rebellion	1677
Massachusetts	Rebellion against Andros and the Dominion of New England	1689
New York	Leisler's Rebellion	1689
Maryland	The Protestant Association	

The origins of three of these rebellions—those in Massachusetts, New York, and Maryland—coincided with the arrival of news of the Glorious Revolution in England. In all three cases the insurgents explicitly associated themselves with that rebellion in England, which forced James II into exile and destroyed the threat of his autocratic rule. But the parallels, while not altogether fanciful, are superficial. None of the basic accomplishments of the Glorious Revolution were duplicated in the colonies. In England a king was deposed and sovereignty was shown to lie not in anointed monarchs and not in popular mobs, but in Parliament and the consensus of political and social leaders. Further, in England the supremacy of law—statute law and common law—had been established above any action of executive and crown, and judges had been made independent of "the pleasure of the prince." The legislature, finally, had declared the independence of its existence; its elections and its convenings were fixed in regular schedules and altogether disengaged from dictates of the crown. The American rebellions duplicated none of this. Sovereignty was in no way an issue in these provincial upheavals; the American executives retained the arbitrary powers that were eliminated in England; judges remained subordinate to "the pleasure of the prince"; and the existence and convening of the representative assemblies remained subject to executive decree.

The colonial insurrections were events of a different order. They differed greatly in their immediate causes. But whatever the original incitements may have been, once in process they expressed the social strains of communities in which social controls and political dominance were subjects of controversy, objects of challenge and continuous struggle.

Bacon's Rebellion. Thus Bacon's Rebellion began, in a period of economic distress, as an unauthorized war against the Indians on Virginia's northwestern frontier. Governor Berkeley's policy had been to stabilize the boundaries between Indians and whites and to protect the natives from land-hungry settlers. Although it was a sincere attempt to deal with a difficult problem, it was also a conservative policy, favoring the well-established planters and especially Berkeley's supporters and beneficiaries. As such, it was offensive to newcomers like Nathaniel Bacon, who had quarreled with the governor and had been denied the monopoly of the Indian trade he sought, and to Bacon's chief ally, Giles Bland, who had arrived in the colony in 1671 as customs collector but had been fined by the governor for "barbarous and insolent behaviors," then arrested, and finally dismissed from his post.

Around Bacon and Bland an opposition group formed. Victims of Berkeley's new establishment and increasingly resentful of the benefits that clique had acquired, they demanded land, without regard to the rights or needs of the border Indians squeezed between the double pressure of rival tribes behind them and white settlers before them. A violent conflict between Indians and the settlers in the border area that Bacon sought to control provided an excuse to launch a full-scale war, which became a civil war in 1676

when Berkeley repudiated Bacon and his allies and sought to bring them to justice. The rebels, having suppressed the border Indians in bloody battles, turned back upon the colony, seized the government, defeated and scattered Berkeley's forces, and burned Jamestown to the ground. But they could not sustain the insurrection. Bacon died of exposure and exhaustion in the midst of a confused military campaign. Deprived of his leadership, the rebellion faded out, and Bacon's chief allies were soon hanged for treason.

In all this turmoil the Baconites' voice rose loud and clear. Who are these men "in authority and favor," they demanded to know in their "Manifesto," to whose hands the dispensation of the country's wealth has been committed? Note, they cried, "the sudden rise of their estates compared with the mean quality in which they had first entered the country,"

. . . and let us see whether their extractions and education have not been vile, and by what pretense of learning and virtue they could [enter] so soon into employments of so great trust and consequence; let us . . . see what sponges have sucked up the public treasure and whether it hath not been privately contrived away by unworthy favorites and juggling parasites whose tottering fortunes have been repaired and supported at the public charge.

But these challengers were themselves challenged. For another element in the upheaval, expressed in the laws of "Bacon's Assembly" of 1676, was the discontent among the ordinary settlers at the *local* privileges of some of the same newly risen county magnates—the Baconites—who assailed the privileges of Governor Berkeley's inner clique. At both levels, local and central, the rebellion challenged the stability of newly secured authority.

The wave of rebellion in Virginia, which broke suddenly and spread quickly, soon subsided. By the end of the century the most difficult period of adjustment had passed and the colonists generally accepted the fact that certain families were indeed distinguished from others in riches, in dignity, and in access to political authority, and were likely to remain so. There had never been a challenge to British supremacy or to the idea that some people would inevitably be "high and eminent in power and dignity; others mean and in subjection." Protests and upheaval had resulted from the discomforts of discovering who was, in fact, which, and what the particular consequences of "power and dignity" were.

Culpeper's Rebellion. More confused than Bacon's Rebellion was the almost comic-opera insurrection that took place in 1677 in Albemarle, the northern sector of Carolina. There some three thousand farmers struggled to survive in the swampy, sandy coastal lands and to profit from smuggling tobacco with the help of a few enterprising New England merchants. When the proprietor's group, no less hard-drinking, ill-tempered, and profiteering than their opponents, attempted to collect customs, they were set upon by a gang of rivals led by a belligerent malcontent named John Culpeper who accused them of malfeasance and treason, jailed them, seized the government, and sent charges against them to England. After endless confusion and an almost farcical series of attacks and counterattacks between the two groups, the Carolina proprietors finally managed to restore order. But the rebellion died slowly, partly because the legal proceedings in England were protracted but in greater part because of the continuing uncertainty of legitimate leadership in the rough, tumultuous backwoods community.

Leisler's Rebellion. In New York the struggle between an emerging establishment and a resentful opposition was clearer than it was in the South, but also more bitter and more permanently consequential in politics.

When word of the Glorious Revolution arrived in New York, the lieutenant governor, Francis Nicholson, decided to strengthen Manhattan's garrison with militia troops. One of the captains of the militia was a well-to-do, cantankerous merchant, Jacob Leisler. Relations between the militia and Nicholson's regular troops grew difficult, then explosive, especially since Nicholson's legal status was unclear once James II had been deposed. In June 1689 the militia, led by Leisler, seized the fort in the name of the new English monarchs, William and Mary, and Nicholson sailed for England. In December William III's message to the chief officer of government arrived, instructing him to retain his post, and Leisler interpreted this directive as addressed officially to himself as the colony's acting governor. He drew around him what was at first a large group of supporters, who proceeded to parcel out the colony's offices and run the government, including its feeble war effort. In 1691 when the next royal governor, the well-named Henry Sloughter, arrived and demanded that Leisler surrender the city and the government, Leisler, whose support had steadily eroded in two years of erratic rule and who by then scarcely controlled any of the colony outside the city walls, refused. Sloughter's superior power prevailed, Leisler and his followers surrendered, and after a quick and legally dubious trial he and his chief assistant, his son-in-law Jacob Milbourne, were hanged for treason and their property confiscated.

But these savage sentences, which Parliament legally annulled in 1695, hardly ended the struggle. By the time Leisler's regime had ended, the political leadership of the colony was broken into two violently antagonistic parties, the Leislerians and the anti-Leislerians, who thereafter alternated in power with successive governors, each party attempting literally to annihilate the other when the opportunity arose, or failing that to crush them politically so that they would never regain power. Again, the social background is crucial. Behind this see-sawing political conflict lay a latent struggle that had been in progress since the English conquest. During those years an Anglo-Dutch leadership group had taken form under governors sent out by the Duke of York. The colony's official patronage had come to center on this small group of families, whose ultimate rewards would come in the land grants of Benjamin Fletcher. Gradually this Anglo-Dutch cabal—the Bayards, Van Cortlandts, Philipses, Livingstons, and Schuylers—had made arrangements that satisfied their interests: a flour milling and exporting monopoly for New York City, which in effect gave them control of that vital industry; a New York City monopoly for shipping on the Hudson; and an Albany monopoly of the colony's Indian trade.

The offices had been theirs, and so too was the colony's economy, to the increasing resentment of those excluded. Gradually a combination of alienated factions had taken shape. Led by the merchants, especially those of Dutch origins, who were denied access to these privileges, it had included the city artisans, who were indirect victims of the junto's monopolies, and the Long Island townsmen, most of whom had migrated from Connecticut. Increasingly, the focus of this rising discontent had centered on Leisler, who had fought the Anglo-Dutch leaders on several issues, had been jailed in a religious controversy in Albany, had thereafter refused to pay customs, and had defied all efforts to bring him into court. His associates had had similar careers.

It had been this group of alienated, resentful, and enterprising outsiders, many of whom, under the Dutch, had been in positions of authority, who had sparked the opposition to Nicholson and turned it into a rebellion against the new Anglo-Dutch establishment. In principle, Leisler and his followers were no more "democrats" than were the Baconites in Virginia, but they found in the language of the Glorious Revolution a "Protestant" program—against monopolies, against autocracy, in favor of open access and a broad sharing of benefits—that served their interests well.

The Protestant Association. In Maryland, resentment, long-smoldering against the Calverts' Catholic ascendency, had erupted as early as 1676 in an obscure rebellion in Calvert County. When news of the Glorious Revolution arrived, the same small group of insurgents, further antagonized by a particularly obnoxious proprietary governor, led two hundred and fifty of the settlers to seize the colony's government. Calling themselves the Protestant Association, they issued a declaration condemning the proprietary party for excessive fee-taking, for resisting royal authority, and for arbitrary taxation; they identified telltale signs of an incipient papal plot; and they petitioned the crown to take over the government from the Calverts, which was promptly done.

It was only in 1715 that the Calverts' control of Maryland was returned to them, but by then the family had turned Protestant and the government had been drawn into the general pattern of colonial governance which required crown approval of executive appointments and of the colony's legislation. The rebellion

PETER SCHUYLER, MAYOR OF ALBANY, 1686–94 BY NEHEMIAH PARTRIDGE
Also for many years chief English negotiator with the Indians, Schuyler is pictured here in 1718, eight years after he took four Iroquois chiefs to London where they were received with honor by Queen Anne. *(Collection City of Albany, New York)*

had sprung out of the jostling instability of late seventeenth-century animosities, and while the proprietary group thereafter still dominated the executive government, it could no longer block the advance of the planter aristocracy or ignore a legislative body whose influence was built into the structure of government.

The Downfall of Andros. Though in Massachusetts there were special, local peculiarities in the rebellion that took place, there was also a similar underlying conflict. The continuing dominance of the Puritan regime, protected by the original charter, delayed the characteristic struggle of social groups. But after the confiscation of the charter in 1684 and the establishment of the Dominion, the pattern seen elsewhere quickly developed. Almost immediately, the favors of patronage and power began to flow to a small group of speculators and merchant insiders, some of them in Andros's entourage, some of them adventurous natives who gravitated to the new establishment. For four years this newly dominant group enjoyed a feast of privilege and in the process generated resentments among others that found expression in an uprising made especially bitter by the Puritan animosities that fueled it.

These rebellions are obscure events, and they are confused events, especially the last three in which the rebels claimed association with the successful revolutionaries in England. Everywhere the insurgents sought to identify themselves with the struggle for English liberty and against various forms of tyranny. None, however, questioned the basis of public authority; all submitted to legitimate crown power when it appeared; none fought for the full range of liberties that would be set out in the English Bill of Rights (1689) and the Act of Settlement (1701), which concluded the revolution in England. They did not question the nature of government but its control; not its structure and essential character, but its personnel; not what and how, but who. Enclosed in their provincial world, they sought, above all, equity in the actions of government that properly reflected the balance of society as it had emerged through a period of rapid growth and change.

Provincial Culture

These insurrections of the late seventeenth century were not only obscure events in the scale of Western history; they were also—significantly—provincial events. And as such they were characteristic of Anglo-American culture generally as it emerged in the early 1700s. For that culture had greatly changed in its relations to the parent culture from which it had developed. In the early years the settlements, however small, distant, and isolated, had been part of a vital movement in the forefront of western European life. The key figures were products of the European world. They were isolated physically in America but not psychologically or intellectually or spiritually. They never lost the sense that they were engaged in a momentous enterprise, something that mattered in an important way to the world they had left behind. They felt they could easily return, and when they did, they found themselves enhanced, not diminished, by their sojourn in the exotic frontier west. Thus the poet, traveler, and scholar George Sandys, son of the Archbishop of York, slipped back easily into Lord Falkland's literary circle after his stay in Virginia, having made good progress on his translation of Ovid's *Metamorphoses*. So Roger Williams returned to Cromwell's council of state, and Winthrop's nephew George Downing, sent off to Harvard College to improve his morals and manners, became Cromwell's chief intelligence officer, was knighted, and ended as England's ambassador to Holland. The settlements had been relevant and vital to the most forward-looking minds of the time.

By 1700 none of this was true. As the colonies grew, they grew apart, into a separate world of their own—connected with the greater world beyond, but still fundamentally removed. The success or failure of the colonists' daily affairs no longer mattered as they once had. The settlers no longer made news; they listened for it, intently, from abroad, and imitated what they could of styles of thought, of ways of living and patterns of behavior. They knew themselves to be provincials in the sense that their culture was not self-contained; its sources and superior expressions were to be found elsewhere than in their

JOHN WINTHROP, JR., BY AN UNKNOWN 17TH CENTURY PAINTER

Sophisticated, learned, and enterprising, the younger Winthrop was more versatile and more genial than his austere father and less passionately committed to the Puritans' spiritual quest. The features of the two Winthrops' faces are strikingly similar (see p. 43), but their expressions are entirely different, reflecting quite different life experiences and outlooks. *(Courtesy, Harvard University Portrait Collection)*

own land. They must seek it from afar; it must be acquired, and once acquired, be maintained according to standards externally imposed, in the creation of which they had not shared. The most cultivated of the colonists read much, purposefully, determined to retain contact with the greater world at home. The diary of William Byrd II with its record of daily stints of study is a stolid testimonial to the virtues of regularity and effort in maintaining standards of civilization set abroad.

This basic transformation can be seen particularly well in the later career of the gifted and learned son of the patriarch John Winthrop. John, Jr., was educated at Trinity College, Dublin, and in London at the lawyers' Inner Temple. As a young man he had helped manage an English overseas military expedition, and had traveled in the Mediterranean and the Middle East. A physician, amateur scientist, and imaginative entrepreneur who served as governor of Connecticut for eighteen years, he struggled to maintain contact with the Royal Society in London of which he was the first American member. There was "a current of loneliness, almost pathos," the younger Winthrop's latest biographer writes, "in his anxiety to stay in touch." He wrote letter after letter to the society's secretary; he sent over scientific specimens—rattlesnake skins, birds' nests, plants, crabs, strange pigs; he studied the society's *Transactions* so as not to fall too far behind; and to those concerned with the propagation of the gospel he dispatched John Eliot's Algonquian translation of the Bible and two essays written in Latin by Indian students at Harvard. But these were failing efforts. In the end loneliness and isolation overcame him. He died in 1676, venerated in the villages along the Connecticut River—themselves changing like autumn leaves from vital, experimental religious communities to sere, old-fashioned backwoods towns—but forgotten in the greater world at home. His sons, however, provincial land speculators and petty politicians, had no such memories as their father had had, and no such aspirations; they suffered therefore, no such disappointments. They were native to the land, and their cultural horizons had narrowed to its practical demands.

This was a silent drama—of a high culture, temporarily transferred, becoming permanently provincial; and it was a drama played out most vividly in the field of education. For education, in its broadest sense, serves more than any other social process to liberate people from local, parochial environments and bring them into contact with larger worlds and broader horizons. Education is perhaps the most sensitive index to the changing character of American life as it developed in these transition years. It is also one of the most difficult subjects to interpret. For there were great accomplishments, but there were also great defeats; soaring ambitions, but serious neglect.

Education. Certain things, however, are clear. In New England the founding generation made a remarkable effort not only to perpetuate education as it was then known but to improve it—to spread it more widely and more effectively through the entire population than it was even in England, where formal education was extraordinarily widespread for the time. The Puritans' efforts in education stemmed primarily from their religious convictions, specifically their insistence that every person, saint or sinner, have personal access to the Holy Scriptures, which meant the capacity to read. That was a mere beginning, however, for to the Puritans the truly religious person was a student not only of the Bible but also of commentaries on the Bible, including those intricate oral commentaries preached at prodigious length from every pulpit in the land. To perpetuate this biblical culture in the population at large would require schooling that went beyond the normal Elizabethan assumption that the goal of formal education was training in vocational roles. For the Puritans, there was only one essential vocation, and that was spiritual. Though true salvation was in the end a God-given grace, the preparation for grace—the opening of the mind and soul to such a possibility—was a matter of education, knowledge, and will.

It was not this central religious commitment alone, however, that led the Puritans to their remarkable efforts in education. Partly too they were driven by a sense that in their wilderness condition the family, which traditionally had borne so much of the burden of transmitting the elements of culture across the generations, had weakened and was failing in its duty and capacity. This fear bore heavily on the minds of the founding elders.* They looked ahead to the future and noted that if extraordinary precautions were not made in time they would leave behind not a Bible commonwealth but a tribe of rustic barbarians. If family discipline were loose, if parents were slack

*For pressures on family life in the seventeenth century, see pp. 79–82.

in their responsibilities, the public—the government, the magistrates—would have to provide for the future.

Ambitious, therefore, not merely to perpetuate education but to extend it, the Puritans turned instinctively to the willingness of people voluntarily to establish and support formal institutions of education. For they knew that the recent wave of educational foundations in England had been accomplished by private philanthropy; by gifts from institutions (gilds, universities) and even more from individual donors, usually in the form of land endowments. And in the first fifteen years, the records of six towns show that a number of relatively rich inhabitants *did* attempt to establish schools with the traditional endowment base. But the land was wild, tenants were scarce, and endowments were worth nothing if they produced no rents. Other forms of financing would have to be found. In place of pleas to the rich, there must be commands. The towns ordered the wealthy to volunteer, then took to group action, assigning some of the towns' common land to schools. But the hoped-for income failed for lack of reliable tenants. In the end, there was only one resource: taxation. It began as a supplement to private gifts and ended as almost the sole and universal basis of elementary education.

So for a decade and more the Puritans struggled with the problem of education, experimented, and came to fear that their whole endeavor would fail unless some uniform provisions were made, some universal standards set, and facilities provided that would guarantee the survival of their hopes into the future. In the 1640s they made their great departure in two famous laws. By a law of 1642, the Massachusetts General Court charged all parents and ministers with the responsibility for the "calling and employment of their children, especially of their ability to read and understand the principles of religion and the capital laws of this country." Five years later, in 1647, the legislative provisions were completed: the General Court ruled that all towns of 50 families must provide for the maintenance of elementary schools, and all towns of 100 families must support Latin grammar schools. These laws became models for the rest of Puritan New England. Connecticut followed with similar provisions in 1650, and Plymouth in two stages, 1658 and 1677. Wherever these enactments remained on the books they were innovative and creative. But they are easily misunderstood.

For these laws do *not* provide for public education as it has been known since the nineteenth century. The concept of a strict distinction between "private" and "public" did not exist in the seventeenth century. Neither of these laws of the 1640s specified "public" moneys as the financial basis of the community's schools; neither made formal schooling obligatory at any level. What they *did* do was, first, to establish a minimum level of educational accomplishment (not schooling) by specifying masters' and parents' obligations and reinforcing these obligations with sanctions of fines and the threat of removing children to other households. Second, the laws required that schooling, at both elementary and secondary (Latin grammar) levels, be made universally *available* for those who wished to take advantage of it. Third, these laws established a community-wide obligation to support formal institutions of education without reference to the benefits any individual or family derived from these schools. Finally, the laws made clear that the government's role in the whole area of education would not be merely supplementary or supportive or supervisory, but positive and compelling.

All of this, written into these innovating American laws on education, was highly creative. But these famous laws are the beginning, not the end, of the historical development. The question is not merely what was hoped for and what was provided for, but what happened to these hopes and these provisions in later years. What effect did these remarkable provisions have on the lives of the people?

By the end of the seventeenth century it was clear that the hopes of the Puritans were not being evenly and satisfactorily fulfilled. Fines against delinquent towns were common. Subsequent revisions and codifications of the laws cite continuing neglect on the part of masters, parents, and towns. The old fears not only continued but seemed to grow more intense. In Massachusetts in 1671 the fines on towns that neglected to maintain grammar instruction were

doubled. In 1689 Cotton Mather, third generation scion of a great clerical dynasty and self-appointed guardian of the ancestral hopes, bemoaned his people's fate. He doubted, he declared in a sermon of that year, if New England suffered "under an iller symptom than the too general want of education in the rising generation." If not overcome, this neglect, he said, would "gradually and speedily dispose us to that sort of Creolean degeneracy observed to deprave the children of the most noble and worthy Europeans when transplanted into America."

But even Mather's magisterial voice could not halt the movement of change. In 1718 the General Court, again increasing the delinquency fines, condemned the "many towns that not only are obliged by law but are very able to support a grammar school, yet choose rather to incur and pay the fine and penalty than maintain a grammar school." As settlements spread throughout the countryside, as contact with the centers of high culture grew thin, and as the original fires of Puritanism cooled, the instinct somehow to modify the law or adjust it to the realities of everyday life grew bolder, stronger, and more effective, though the laws remained on the books and magistrates sought to enforce them. Sometimes there was outright evasion. A town would obey by hiring a teacher who knew no Latin to teach that subject "as far as he was able." More commonly, a new institution was used, the "moving school," which satisfied the law by providing for a schoolmaster and his equipment but distributed his services on a circuit that moved through the town's lands in proportion to the spread of population. Thus Gloucester, Massachusetts, had a Latin grammar school, but the teacher and his books moved about in a cycle of three years, settling in seven places in the following monthly proportions: 9, 7, 5½, 5½, 4½, 3, 1½. Thus even the most remote corner of the township had contact with the "moving school," but it was available for children in that most isolated area only one and a half months every three years.

Finally, by the mid-eighteenth century the towns found a permanent solution: the district school. The towns were now formally divided into school districts, each district drawing its proportionate share of the available funds and using it as its own local school committee decided. Schools thus existed in almost every town; but the variations were great. For the management of the schools was now entirely in the hands of the localities, some of them limited, isolated localities, incapable of and uninterested in transcending their narrow environments. Some schools were excellent, some poor, some dismal. Often the Latin grammar school proved to be a common school in which children of all ages were taught at their own levels. Uniformity was lost, but the "Creolean degeneracy" that Mather had feared had failed to take hold. New England emerged in the eighteenth century still a literate culture, still open to a high level of cultural attainment.

All of this was a flame, sparked by the original creators of the Bible commonwealth, that burned fitfully at times but never failed. How remarkable an accomplishment it was may be seen by the contrast with the slow and irregular development of education elsewhere in the colonies, where the churches and a few generous individuals sought to provide for schooling. In 1671 Governor Berkeley of Virginia wrote about his colony, "I thank God there are no free schools nor printing," these being sources, he declared, of "disobedience and heresy and sects." By 1689 there were still only six schools of various kinds in Virginia. In the same year Maryland had one school. New York, mainly through the efforts of the Dutch church, may have had eleven.

The Colleges. That education at the elementary and secondary levels developed as it did in New England was in part the result of the reinforcement it received from higher education, established in the same years, which too became closely bound to the immediate needs of these provincial communities.

There can be little doubt about the Puritans' primary reason for founding in 1636 the institution that became Harvard College. They dreaded, they said, "to leave an illiterate ministry to the churches when our present ministers shall lie in the dust." There were other motives too, especially the hopes

LT. GOV. WILLIAM STOUGHTON OF MASSACHUSETTS
In the background is the building that this dour, wealthy, old-fashioned Puritan gave to his alma mater, Harvard, in 1699. It was the first American college building donated by an alumnus. *(Courtesy of the Harvard University Portrait Collection, Gift–John Cooper, 1810)*

of those who sought an instrument for propagating the gospel to the native Indians through preachers trained at the college who would go out to deliver the word. But though the gospel mission failed miserably amid the general failure of civilized relations between Indians and whites, the effort to maintain a college primarily for training preachers and secondarily for educating gentlemen in the liberal arts

COLONIAL COLLEGES

College	Colony	Founded
Harvard College	Massachusetts	1636
College of William and Mary	Virginia	1693
Yale College	Connecticut	1701
College of New Jersey (Princeton University)	New Jersey	1746
College of Philadelphia (University of Pennsylvania)	Pennsylvania	1754
King's College (Columbia University)	New York	1754
College of Rhode Island (Brown University)	Rhode Island	1764
Queen's College (Rutgers University)	New Jersey	1766
Dartmouth College	New Hampshire	1769

took root and flourished. By the time the College of William and Mary, the second English colonial college, was chartered in 1693 as part of the effort to improve the condition of the Anglican clergy in Virginia, Harvard College, named after its first private benefactor, John Harvard, was a stable institution. Its influence, through its graduates, was great and its continued existence, written into the terms of the colony's second charter of 1691, was firmly guaranteed.

Yet like so much else in American life, this college, and those that would follow it, grew apart from the models on which they were based and became something different. The Puritan founders intended to create a familiar university-college, a residential institution whose ownership and direction would lie in the hands of the teachers—the resident tutors and professors. But the colonial colleges did not develop in that way. Instead, by an intricate process of evolution, ownership of the property and the ultimate government of the colleges came to rest not in the teachers but in boards of trustees external to the educational process, who hired the teachers and supervised the work of the colleges on behalf of the founding community. For the central impulse in creating these colleges was the community's desire to perpetuate a learned clergy and to advance learning in the wilderness setting. Later in American history the nature of the founding community

would shift—to denominations serving their particular concerns and to states reconizing the need for experts in technical fields and seeking to provide for the public's general education. But from the establishment of the first college in 1636 onward, the initiating impulse and the resources have come from groups outside the profession of teaching and learning, and the governance of higher education has reflected the groups' insistence on seeing that the institutions fulfill these community mandates. In this sense all the American colleges and universities have been community schools—products not so much of the world of education and learning as of desires and decisions of the community at large. Control has therefore rested with the founding communities, and as, in the colonial period, the horizons of the communities narrowed, the mandates of the colleges narrowed too. A learned clergy was indeed perpetuated, and higher education made generally available, not only in Massachusetts, Virginia, and Connecticut, but in New Jersey, Pennsylvania, New York, Rhode Island, and New Hampshire. Through these institutions the pursuit of learning and the cultivation of the arts were advanced and transmitted across the generations. But at the root of their foundations lay not so much a love of learning for its own sake as the parochial concerns of communities of limited horizons, determined to sustain their founders' commitments to serving local, provincial needs.

CHRONOLOGY

1660   Restoration of Stuart monarchy (Charles II, 1660–85).
Basic navigation law, monopolizing colonial trade and shipping for Britain, passed by Parliament; includes "enumeration" clause.

1662   Massachusetts Bay ministers sanction halfway convenant.
Colony of Connecticut chartered by crown.

1663   New royal charter issued to Rhode Island.
New navigation act (Staple Act) passed, channeling colonies' importation of European goods through England.
Charter of Carolina given to eight courtiers.

1664   England conquers New Netherland, which becomes proprietary colony of Duke of York.
New Jersey charter issued to two courtiers.

1665   Duke's Laws for New York promulgated.

1669   Fundamental Constitutions of Carolina issued.

1673   New navigation act imposes "plantation duties."

1675   Lords of Trade appointed as committee of Privy Council.

1675–76   King Philip's War in New England.

1676   Bacon's Rebellion in Virginia.
New Jersey divided into East and West Jersey.

1677   West New Jersey's Concessions and Agreements issued.
Culpeper's Rebellion in Carolina.

1680   New Hampshire given royal charter.

1681   Pennsylvania charter granted to William Penn; first settlements in 1682.

1684   Massachusetts Bay charter annulled by crown (charters of Connecticut, Rhode Island, New Jersey, Pennsylvania, Maryland, and Carolina abrogated in following years, to 1691).

1685–88   Duke of York becomes James II; his accession royalizes New York.

1686   Dominion of New England established.

1688   Glorious Revolution in England drives out James II in favor of William and Mary.

1689   Successful rebellion in Boston against Dominion of New England.
The Protestant Association in Maryland rebels.

1689–91   Leisler's Rebellion in New York.

1689–97   King William's War (colonial phase of Europe's War of the League of Augsburg).

1691   Massachusetts Bay Colony gets new charter.

1692   Witchcraft hysteria in Salem, Massachusetts; twenty "witches" executed.

1693   College of William and Mary founded.

1696   English government establishes Board of Trade and Plantations.
Passage of comprehensive navigation act, extending admiralty court system to America.

1699   Woolen Act passed by Parliament.

1701   Yale College founded.
New and permanent Frame of Government adopted in Pennsylvania.

1702–13   Queen Anne's War (colonial phase of Europe's War of the Spanish Succession), concluded in Treaty of Utrecht.

1702   West and East New Jersey formed into single royal colony.

1702–14   Reign of Queen Anne.

1708   Saybrook Platform adopted in Connecticut.

1714–27   Reign of George I, beginning Hanoverian dynasty.

1719   Rebellion against proprietors in Carolina.

SUGGESTED READINGS

The fullest account of the origins of the British imperial system, in both theory and institutions, is Charles M. Andrews, *The Colonial Period of American History,* IV (1938). On the theory of empire, see in addition Richard Koebner, *Empire* (1961) chap. iii; on the all-important customs administration in the colonies, Thomas C. Barrow, *Trade & Empire* (1967); and on the difficulty in the late seventeenth century of imposing regulations on the scattered settlements, see Michael G. Hall, *Edward Randolph and the American Colonies* (1969). On the influence of the Duke of York (James II) and his entourage on the evolution of empire and the importance of his and his lieutenants' military background, see Stephen S. Webb, ". . . The Household of James Stuart in the Evolution of English Imperialism," *Perspectives in American History,* 8 (1974), 55–80. On the patronage sources of colonial appointments and other aspects of the politics of the early empire, see Webb's "Strange Career of Francis Nicholson" and "William Blathwayt, Imperial Fixer," *Wm. and Mary Q.,* 23 (1966), 513–48; 26 (1969), 373–415—a subject presented in full in Webb's *The Governors-General* (1979). On James II's ill-fated effort to organize a territorial government, see Viola F. Barnes, *The Dominion of New England* (1923).

The emergence of a native Anglo-American aristocracy is traced generally, in the case of Virginia, in Bernard Bailyn, "Politics and Social Structure in Virginia,"* James M. Smith, ed., *Seventeenth-Century America* (1959) and Louis B. Wright, *First Gentlemen of Virginia* (1940); in the case of commercial New England, in Bernard Bailyn, *New England Merchants in the Seventeenth Century* (1955); in the case of New York, in Thomas Archdeacon, *New York City, 1664–1710* (1976); and in the five main port towns, in Carl Bridenbaugh, *Cities in the Wilderness* (1938). The origins of rural aristocracies in New England, rooted in the shifting relations between population and land, are described in Roy H. Akagi, *The Town Proprietors of the New England Colonies* (1924) and probed analytically in Richard L. Bushman's thoughtful *From Puritan to Yankee* (1967) and in the individual community studies listed in the references to chapter III. For the reflection of this development in government, see Kenneth A. Lockridge and Alan Kreider, "Evolution of Massachusetts Town Government, 1640–1740," *Wm. and Mary Q.,* 23 (1966), 549–74. For case studies of the emergence of the southern aristocracy, see the essays on social mobility in the Chesapeake area cited for the previous chapter; Louis B. Wright's edition of Byrd's diaries and literary writings; and Richard B. Davis, ed.,

William Fitzhugh and His Chesapeake World, 1676–1701 (1963). The political aspects of a rising aristocracy are analyzed in the case of New York in Patricia U. Bonomi, *A Factious People* (1971), chaps. ii, iii; in Archdeacon's *New York City;* and in Lawrence H. Leder, *Robert Livingston* (1961).

The late seventeenth-century wars (the subject of Francis Parkman's dramatic classics, *Count Frontenac and New France under Louis XIV,* 1877; and *A Half-Century of Conflict,* 1892) are sketched briefly in Howard H. Peckham, *The Colonial Wars, 1689–1762* (1964), but their deeper significance for the development of Anglo-American politics, trade, and society is suggested in G. M. Waller, *Samuel Vetch, Colonial Enterpriser* (1960).

The colonial rebellions of the late seventeenth century are described, insofar as they relate to the English rebellion against James II, in David S. Lovejoy, *The Glorious Revolution in America* (1972); there is a documentary collection related to these events in a book of the same title edited by Michael G. Hall, Lawrence H. Leder, and Michael G. Kammen. But as social events these uprisings are to be associated with Bacon's Rebellion, which is described generally in Wilcomb E. Washburn, *The Governor and the Rebel* (1957) and analyzed in social terms in Bailyn, "Politics and Social Structure"*; in Wesley F. Craven, *Southern Colonies in the Seventeenth Century* (1949); and in Edmund Morgan, *American Slavery, American Freedom* (1975). For the social background of Leisler's Rebellion, see Archdeacon's book cited above (excerpted into essay form as ". . . The Age of Leisler in New York City,"*) and Jerome R. Reich, *Leisler's Rebellion* (1953), which exaggerates the "democratic" impulses of the rebels. On Boston's rebellion, see Barnes, *Dominion of New England.* The most exhaustive study of the social background of any of these rebellions, however, is Lois G. Carr and David W. Jordan, *Maryland's Revolution of Government 1689–1692* (1974).

The deepening provincialism of American culture in the late seventeenth century emerges in the colonists' writings, analyzed with subtlety in the opening chapter of Kenneth S. Lynn, *Mark Twain and Southwestern Humor* (1959); in the careers of third-generation Anglo-Americans such as the Winthrops (Richard S. Dunn, *Puritans and Yankees: The Winthrop Dynasty of New England, 1630–1717,* 1962, Bk. III) and the Mathers (Robert Middlekauff, *The Mathers: Three Generations of Puritan Intellectuals, 1596–1728,* 1971, Bk. III); in the missionary efforts of the Anglicans (Parke Rouse, Jr., *James Blair of Virginia,* 1971; Leonard W. Cowie, *Henry Newman: An American in London, 1708-43,* 1956); in travelers' accounts (Jasper Danckaerts [1679-80], pub. 1867; the Frenchman Durand [1687], pub. 1923; Sarah Knight [1704], latest pub. 1972); and above all in education.

For a comprehensive, detailed, and broadly conceived account of early American education, see Lawrence A. Cremin, *American Education: The Colonial Experience, 1607-1783* (1970), Parts I-III; for a general interpretation of the social role of colonial education, see Bernard Bailyn, *Education in the Forming of American Society* (1960); and for the deepening localization of standards, described in the text, Harlan Updegraff, *Origin of the Moving School in Massachusetts* (1907). Robert Middlekauff has traced the persistence of the classical tradition in the face of provincial difficulties in *Ancients and Axioms* (1963). James Axtell, *The School upon a Hill* (1974) shows through education in the broadest sense, how New England's culture was transmitted across the generations.

On the origins of higher education, see Samuel E. Morison's magisterial works, *The Founding of Harvard College* (1935) and *Harvard College in the Seventeeth Century* (2 vols., 1936), both summarized in his *Three Centuries of Harvard: 1636-1936* (1936). Though these learned and highly readable books remain fundamental, Morison's general interpretation has been challenged: by Winthrop S. Hudson, "The Morison Myth Concerning the Founding of Harvard College," *Church History,* 8 (1939), 148-59; and by Jurgen Herbst, "The First Three American Colleges: Schools of the Reformation," *Perspectives in American History,* 8 (1974), 7-52, in which parallels are drawn between Harvard, Yale, and William and Mary on the one hand and the "*gymnasia illustria,* academies, or *Gelehrtenschulen* on the Continent" on the other. Yale's origins have recently been detailed with great care by Richard Warch in *School of the Prophets: Yale College, 1701-1740* (1973) and William and Mary's in Rouse, *Blair*. All aspects of education and artistic expression are discussed in Richard B. Davis, *Intellectual Life in the Colonial South, 1585-1763* (3 vols., 1978).

*See footnote on page 65.

CHAPTER 5

American Society in the Eighteenth Century

The end of the War of the Spanish Succession in 1713 and the creation of a stable political regime in England under Sir Robert Walpole, prime minister from 1721 to 1742, introduced a period of great expansion in all spheres of Anglo-American life. In the two generations that followed the war, despite minor involvements in other international conflicts and repeated cycles of commercial recession, the American colonies grew so rapidly and matured so fully that they came to constitute an important element not only in British life but in the life of the Atlantic world generally. Developing on scattered seventeenth-century foundations, becoming more and more distinctive though outwardly seeking to conform to the normal patterns of European life, and drawn more and more elaborately into the ill-organized structure of empire, the colonies acquired characteristics that would remain permanent in American life.

The New Population: Sources and Impact

Fundamental to all aspects of eighteenth-century American history was the phenomenal growth of the population. In 1700 the population was approximately 250,000; by 1775 it had grown tenfold, to 2.5 million, which was fully a third of the size of the population of England and Wales (6.7 million). A fifth of the American people were black, almost all of them slaves, nine-tenths of whom lived south of Pennsylvania. They constituted two-fifths of the population of Virginia and almost two-thirds of the population of South Carolina.

Bu the 1760s the settlements formed an almost unbroken line along the seaboard, from Maine to Florida, and they reached deep into the interior. In New England, groups moving up the Connecticut River and the coastal streams penetrated into New Hampshire and Vermont. In New York, settlements spread through the rich Hudson, Mohawk, and Schoharie valleys, and in Pennsylvania and the Carolinas extended back to the Appalachians. In a few places, especially southwestern Pennsylvania, the Appala-

chian mountain barrier had been breached by frontiersmen who were actively opening fresh lands to
cultivation in Indian territories.

The population was almost entirely rural. Of the
towns, the most populous was Philadelphia, with approximately 35,000 inhabitants. The five largest communities (Philadelphia, New York, Boston, Charleston, and Newport, Rhode Island) had a combined
population of 90,000, or 3.6 percent of the total. Fifteen smaller towns, ranging from New Haven, Connecticut, with 8,000 to Savannah, Georgia, with 3,200,
account for another 77,500; but very few of the total
town population of approximately 167,500 lived in
circumstances that can be called "urban" in a modern
sense.

The rapid increase in the size of the population
—it almost doubled every twenty-five years—was in
large part the result of natural growth. But it was
the result too of new flows of immigration. While the
basic recruitment from England continued, though
at a reduced rate, and while between 250,000 and
300,000 Africans were imported directly or indirectly from their homelands, new groups began to
make important contributions. Religious persecution in France led to the immigration of several thousand Huguenots (French Protestants, forced to flee
after 1685 when the tolerant Edict of Nantes was
revoked); and from Scotland came groups of Jacobites
(those faithful to the exiled James II and his son)
after their military defeat by the English in 1715. But
the main new flows came from two quite different
sources, which together supplied approximately 20
percent of the total American population when the
first national census was taken in 1790.

The Irish. The first new source was Ireland—not
Catholic Ireland but Protestant northern Ireland,
which had been the first overseas colony of the English people. The efforts of the English in the early
seventeenth century to colonize a great "plantation"
in Ulster, the six northern counties of Ireland, had
attracted to that region a large migration from Scotland, where social and religious conditions throughout the seventeenth century were unsettled. By 1715
perhaps 150,000 Scots had crossed the Irish Sea to

settle on Irish estates where rents were originally
low. From this heartland of "Scotch-Irish" Presbyterianism a large migration to America took place
in the eighteenth century. How many were involved
we do not know exactly, but the best estimate is a
yearly average of 4,000 through most of the century,
totaling nearly a quarter of a million. It was said by
W. E. H. Lecky, Ireland's greatest historian, that the
loss of so great a number of Irish Protestants to America in the eighteenth century ended forever the hope
of balancing the religious communities in that tormented island.

The Germans. The other new source of the American population was the upper Rhine valley, in southwestern Germany. This area, especially the district
west of the Rhine, which formed the Rhenish Palatinate, had been badly ravaged in the religious wars
of the seventeenth century and then, in 1688–89,
devastated by French armies. In addition, Catholic
princes, particularly the Palatinate's ruling Elector,
had begun to persecute the increasingly numerous
Protestant sects. When, further, crop disasters in
1708 and 1709 reduced much of the same population
to beggary and a new English naturalization law
made British territory an attractive refuge, a movement of peoples began that ended in furnishing a
major component of the American population. William Penn had begun recruiting settlers in the Rhineland as early as the 1680s, and it was to his colony
eventually that the greatest number of German-
speaking people came. These "Pennsylvania Dutch"
(from *Deutsch:* that is, Germans, not Hollanders) comprised one-third of that colony's population by 1775.
The census of 1790 showed almost as many German-
born or German-descended Americans (9 percent of
the population) as there were Scotch-Irish, and their
influence was at least as important in the development of American society.

For in the end it is not only the numbers involved that account for the importance of migrations
like these. More important are the attitudes, apti-
tudes, and ambitions of the immigrants and their
influence on the development of the community's
life. In the case of these two groups, the impact was

GERMAN PIETIST EMIGRANTS

The man carries in one hand the orthodox Lutheran "Augsburg Confession" and in the other Johann Arndt's classic of pietistic devotion, *Vom Wahren Christentum* (1605; republished in Philadelphia in 1751). His pack bears the motto, "God is with us in need," hers, "God has done great things for us"; and between the two in the original print was the caption "Nothing but the gospel drives us into exile. Though we leave the fatherland, we remain in God's hand." In the background is a German servant's indenture dated 1736, a year in which a large number of Salzburg emigrants, such as the two depicted here, were fleeing religious persecution. *(Foreground: Library of Congress. Background: Photo by Pennsylvania Historical and Museum Commission, Harrisburg, Pa.)*

profound. Both were alienated groups—alienated from authority both civil and ecclesiastical. Both groups were hostile to all establishments, stubborn in defense of their rights, and ambitious for economic security. Both contributed powerfully to the shaping of American social and political life.

Attitudes of the New Immigrants. For the Scotch-Irish, resentment if not hatred of the English establishment had long been a way of life. Britain had excluded Irish products from sale elsewhere in British territory and thereby blighted Ireland's economic growth. Further, the Anglo-Irish landlords, mainly absentees, had increased rents whenever leases fell due, and in addition the Scotch-Irish, being Presbyterian nonconformists, were victimized by the Anglican religious establishment, which they were obliged to support by special taxes. In 1704 a sacramental test excluded Presbyterians from all public offices, and marriages solemnized in their churches were declared invalid. As a result of all of this, the first wave of Scotch-Irish immigrants, arriving in Boston and the Delaware ports between 1717 and 1720, carried with it a burning resentment of the English establishment in all its forms. Those who followed, attracted by enthusiastic letters promising "liberty and ease as the reward of ... honest industry," freedom from escalating rents, and access to public office, shared these attitudes in varying degrees and carried these resentments through the length and breadth of the colonies.

The Germans, legally aliens, had no natural affinity with the British establishment and no political contacts to help protect them in this exploitative world. Further, their legal position was weak. Before 1740, they could become British subjects only by specific deeds of "denization" or by naturalization granted by the colonial governments. Both were generous in the rights they bestowed, but both were revocable; neither bound the *British* government (hence locally naturalized Germans could not qualify as "British" subjects under the Navigation Acts); and neither was automatically accepted in any colony but the original. Many of these problems were eliminated by Parliament's general Naturalization Law of 1740, which permitted aliens who had resided continuously for seven years in any of the British colonies to become naturalized subjects of all colonies. But naturalization by this process was time consuming; excluded Catholics; involved an oath offensive to Jews, Quakers, and certain other Protestants; and did not carry over fully to England itself, where naturalized colonists were not automatically entitled to own land or hold crown office.

Alienated from, if not actively hostile to, the British government, these Scotch-Irish and German

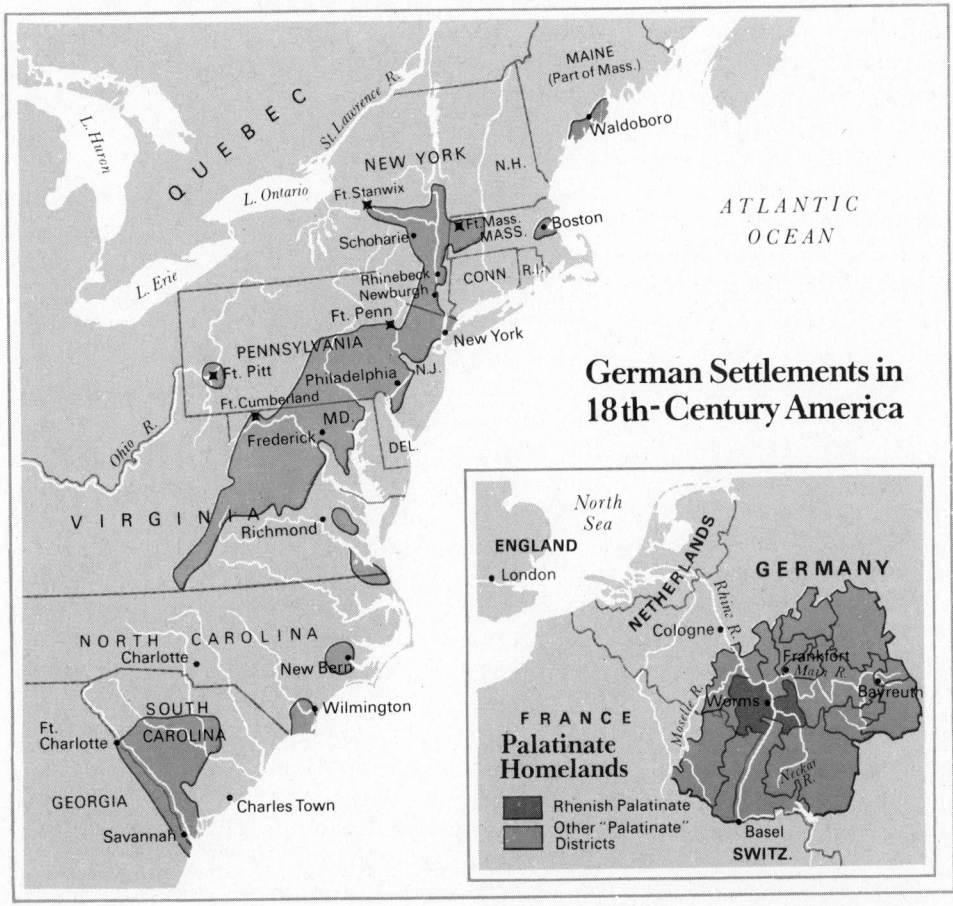

German Settlements in 18th-Century America

Palatinate Homelands

Rhenish Palatinate
Other "Palatinate" Districts

newcomers had little reason to feel close to the colonial governments either, or to the groups that dominated these governments. As settlers they were often physically remote from the capitals, taking up land in backcountry areas far distant from the seats of power. At times they did not even know which governmental jurisdiction they belonged to as they moved through the backcountry. Often their arrival preceded that of the local government, whose agents therefore appeared as exploiters. And in addition, the immigrants were often deliberately exploited, not merely by land speculators and managers of the infamous trade in German "redemptioners" (those who had to sell their labor for a term of years in order to cover the costs of transportation) but almost officially by the colonial governments.

The Blacks and Slavery. If these two major new elements in the American population, the Scotch-Irish and the Germans, were in various ways alienated from the Anglo-American establishment, they at least had access to the processes of law and ultimately of politics by which to express their grievances. But for the black population there were no such possibilities of relief and assimilation. Their separateness was rigidly fixed by the alienation of race and by the debasement of slavery.

How this large population of black people accommodated themselves to North American life, the fearful human cost of that accommodation, and the character of their resistance to the brutal system that dominated their lives we do not fully know, and probably never will know. There are no documents that record directly the blacks' feelings and the intimate details of their personal lives. But from the indirect evidence that has been assembled, one catches glimpses not only of degradation but of bewildering ambiguities and paralyzing tensions in human relations, as well as heroic efforts to maintain some measure of human dignity.

Slavery as it developed in the eighteenth century had many shadings, many variations. Only 10 percent of the slave population lived north of Maryland, constituting 4 to 5 percent of the population of that region. Spread thinly through the northern colonies, their highest concentration was in New York City, where they may have formed as much as 17 percent of the population. Working side by side with white field servants in the countryside and as laborers in the towns, they mingled with the poorest elements among the whites, formed stable families, and even managed to accumulate small sums on the side when they were "hired out" by their masters to work for others. These northern blacks—field hands, town laborers, and factory workers—were native-born Americans for the most part, and they formed part, though a severely deprived part, of the general Anglo-American world.

The opposite was true of the tens of thousands of transplanted Africans (a third of all the North American blacks) who lived in the Carolinas and Georgia. The worst conditions were those on the fearful rice and indigo plantations of South Carolina. There, in tropical heat, laboring half the year knee-deep in the muck of the rice fields, the slaves lived unspeakably wretched lives, utterly isolated from the dominant society and alienated from the roots of their own culture. In the face of the appalling mortality in the disease-ridden environment, they grew in numbers only by the continuous addition of new importations—thousands upon thousands of newly enslaved Africans who had survived the 20 percent death rate on the transatlantic voyage and had been sold like animals in the great Charleston slave market. On these isolated plantations in the Deep South, the blacks' culture remained closer to that of West Africa than it did anywhere else in British North America.

The Chesapeake tobacco plantations, on which over half the black population lived, were quite different. By the 1760s some of the plantations had become large enough to support slave quarters that constituted well organized communities. Family life was relatively stable, and the population grew by natural increase. Further, the need for house servants and artisans of all kinds relieved a sizable percentage of the black population from the worst kind of field work. Here, in this long-established tobacco world, where black kinship groups of second- and third-generation American natives spread across

CHARLESTOWN, *April* 27, 1769.

TO BE SOLD,

On WEDNESDAY the *Tenth Day of* MAY *next*,

A CHOICE CARGO OF

Two Hundred & Fifty

NEGROES:

ARRIVED in the Ship COUNTESS of SUSSEX, THOMAS DAVIES, Mafter, directly from GAMBIA, by

JOHN CHAPMAN, & Co.

** THIS is the *Veffel* that had the *Small-Pox* on Board at the *Time* of her *Arrival* the 31ft of *March* laft : Every neceffary *Precaution* hath fince been taken to cleanfe both *Ship* and *Cargo* thoroughly, fo that thofe who may be inclined to purchafe need not be under the leaft *Apprehenfion* of Danger from *Infection*.

The *NEGROES* are allowed to be the likelieft *Parcel* that have been imported this *Seafon*.

1769

(American Antiquarian Society)

groups of plantations, a stable Afro-American culture, distinctive in religion, folk art, and social patterns, developed most fully. But the civility of the slaves' lives, where it existed at all, was extremely superficial. However assimilated they may have been in the North, and however involved they may have been in kinship networks in Virginia and Maryland, slaves everywhere were debased by the bondage that confined them. Humane masters might create plantations akin to biblical patriarchies, and wise masters might discover the economic value of allowing blacks to enjoy a modicum of leisure, a degree of independent activity, and the dignity of family

life; but everywhere brutality was never far below the surface. And everywhere there was resistance of some sort.

On the plantations in the South, untrained slaves fresh from Africa were most often sent off to outlying plots of land where they lived out their lives in unending field work. Still bearing, often, the ritual face scars of their earlier tribal life, where they had learned companionship and cooperation and where they had thought of time not in terms of hourly routines but of seasonal cycles, they found it extremely difficult, at times impossible, to adjust to the grueling labor. Some ran off, seeking to return to Africa or to set up villages to re-create the life they had known. A few, in the early years, found refuge in "maroon" (fugitive) encampments in the Carolina swamps and deep in frontier forests, but most of the fugitives were returned exhausted, half-starved, and in rags after long exposure in the woods and swamps, to continue their inescapable "seasoning." In time, however, these field hands found effective means of resistance, not in hopeless efforts to escape but in malingering, wasting equipment, damaging crops, and silently disobeying. Their rebelliousness, directed at the plantation and only occasionally at their overseers or masters, could have no long-term results, but at least it gave immediate relief to their feelings.

More complex and more self-damaging was the resistance of the American-born slaves employed as personal servants in and around the planters' houses. Enclosed within households of patriarchal discipline, they were forced into continuous close contact with masters who were made tense and insecure by the blacks' constant presence and whose domestic lives were poisoned by the helpless availability of slaves of both sexes. Commonly the slaves perfected techniques of petty harassment that increased their masters' insecurity. Convenient personality disguises (the seemingly obedient "Sambo") minimized the likelihood of clashes with masters whose tensions could be released in sadistic rages.

The most openly rebellious of the eighteenth-century slaves were the most thoroughly assimilated, the highly skilled artisans, whose talents gave them a measure of independence and who could deal with the environment as effectively as the whites. They were the most likely to survive as fugitives, and the most capable of easing their everyday burdens by shrewd manipulation. Closest to the white-man's world, these skilled workmen understood the full meaning of their bondage, and while they lived somewhat more comfortably, they may have even suffered more. Everywhere slavery meant profound degradation and constant fear—for the whites as well as for the blacks.

A Maturing Economy and a Society in Flux

The single most distinctive fact of the American economy as a whole in the eighteenth century was the broad spread of freehold tenure—the outright ownership of land—throughout the free population. In contrast, all of the land of England in the mid-eighteenth century was owned only by one-tenth of all heads of households; 400 great landlords, representing a mere 3/100 of 1 percent of all families, held between 20 percent and 25 percent of all the land of the realm. Over 80 percent of the land was worked by tenants, whose rent constituted the income upon which the owners of the land lived. The social experience of the great majority of the English people was based on tenancy; it shaped the structure of English society and the organization of politics, for both rested on the existence of a leisured aristocracy supported by the income that others produced from the land. And the unspoken assumption that the more land one owned the greater one's income would be—an assumption based on the scarcity of arable land relative to the available labor—was the force behind all agrarian enterprise.

The situation in the American colonies was entirely different. From the beginning the great attraction had been the availability of free land, and that attraction had not proved false. Though there were important regional variations, the large majority of nonslave farmworkers owned the land they worked, even if only at the end of their working lives and

even if not in the form and quantities they desired. This dominant fact of eighteenth-century American life created conditions altogether different from those that existed elsewhere. How unusual the resulting situation was may perhaps best be seen by examining the apparent *exceptions*—situations, that is, where a re-creation of the traditional life of landlords would appear to have taken place.

The Great Landowners. Thus the population growth and the resulting increase in land values led those who had proprietary claims to large tracts of land derived from the seventeenth-century charters to cash in on them if at all possible. Four such claims were particularly imposing: those of the Penn family to the undistributed land of Pennsylvania; those of the Calvert family to Maryland's residual land; those of Earl Granville, the heir of Sir George Carteret, to one share of the original Carolina grant, a claim that was calculated to cover most of the northern half of the present state of North Carolina; and those of Lord Fairfax, as the heir to the Northern Neck of Virginia, the 5 million acres between the Potomac and the Rappahanock rivers that had originally been granted by Charles II in 1649. By the mid-eighteenth century these colossal properties were no longer wild land but territories being opened to cultivation, and they were suddenly becoming valuable to their owners. But with the exception of Fairfax, who lived in Virginia after 1753, none of these great landowners were resident landlords and none were personally engaged in managing and developing landed estates worked by permanent tenants in the familiar European pattern. Their greatest profits came less from steady rents than from sales in rising land markets.

The operations of these great proprietary landowners were not essentially different from those of lesser land speculators throughout the colonies. Since the land was originally wild, the owner had the choice either of making a high capital investment to clear the land, improve it, and otherwise make it rentable at a profit, or of letting it out at low or no rent, and benefiting from the increase in value created by the labor of the tenants as they cleared and worked the land. The former was clearly uneconomic. Investments in many other forms of enterprise were more profitable than preparing wild land for lucrative rentals. The best strategy was to rent the land at low fees to tenants who would break it open to cultivation and who looked forward themselves to becoming the ultimate purchasers. Profits from such land sales, based on the initial labor of tenants, could be huge, and also continuous, since the purchasers often bought the farms on loans from the original landowners secured by mortgages on the land itself.

In a few places in the colonies, however, there were landowners, who *did* seek to establish themselves as landlords in a traditional sense, and they encountered sharp and at times even violent opposition. On a few estates along the Hudson, and in New Jersey to a lesser extent, many of the traditional forms of landlordism were re-created: high perpetual rents, incidental taxes and fees, and insecurity of tenure. These burdens could be enforced because of the landlords' political influence; because of a recording system that carefully protected their land claims; and because of the landlords' control of the courts through which the tenants would normally have sought relief. But the result was not in the end the re-creation of a traditional landlord system. It was trouble—more trouble than could be easily handled. Many of the tenants simply refused to accept the burdens. They protested continually, and resorted to all sorts of devices to destroy the landlords' control. They commonly acquired dubious titles to the land they worked from Indians or from New England land speculators and sought to validate these claims legally.

By the 1750s the situation on the tenanted estates in eastern New York and in New Jersey was explosive. The tenants refused to pay rents and duties, and when the courts tried to extract the payments due, the tenants formed an armed insurrection. The climax came in 1766 in a wave of rioting. Tenants simply renounced their leases and refused to get off the land when ordered to do so. In Westchester County in New York, rebellious farmers, declared to be "levellers" by the landlords, formed mobs, opened the jails, and stormed the landlords' houses. It took a regiment of regular troops with militia auxiliaries to put down the insurrection. Yet even then

tenancy could not be uniformly enforced. Many of the farmers simply moved off to the nearest vacant land, particularly in Vermont, which as a result of this exodus from the Hudson River estates and of a parallel migration of discontented New Englanders was opened to settlement for the first time.

Plantations in the South. To the extent, then, that landlordism on the Hudson River estates was an exception to the general American pattern, it was one that could be sustained only with great difficulty. A more glaring exception to the rule of freehold tenure was in the South, where plantations worked by slave labor would seem, in some measure at least, to have created the economic basis of a landed aristocracy. But the southern aristocracy of the eighteenth century lived in a completely different world from that of the English gentry and aristocracy whom they sought to emulate. There were large estates in the South (though not a great many: in Maryland only 3.6 percent of all estates were worth over £1,000), and they did support an aristocracy of sorts. But the plantation estates in the South were far different from the tenanted estates of the English aristocracy, quite aside from the obvious fact that the labor force was composed of slaves rather than of legally free tenants.

An English estate was not a single unit of production: it was a combination of many separate producing farms managed by individual tenants. A plantation in the eighteenth-century American South, on the other hand, was a single unit of production—a unified agricultural organization of considerable size under a single management. The whole enterprise was operated as a unit in managing labor and in planning production. From these basic conditions flowed the central characteristics of the life of the southern gentry.

No more in the eighteenth century than in the seventeenth were the southern planters leisured landowners living comfortably on profits produced by others. They were actively drawn into the process of crop management, land use, and labor direction, and they thus became active producers of their own income. Even if overseers were the immediate super-

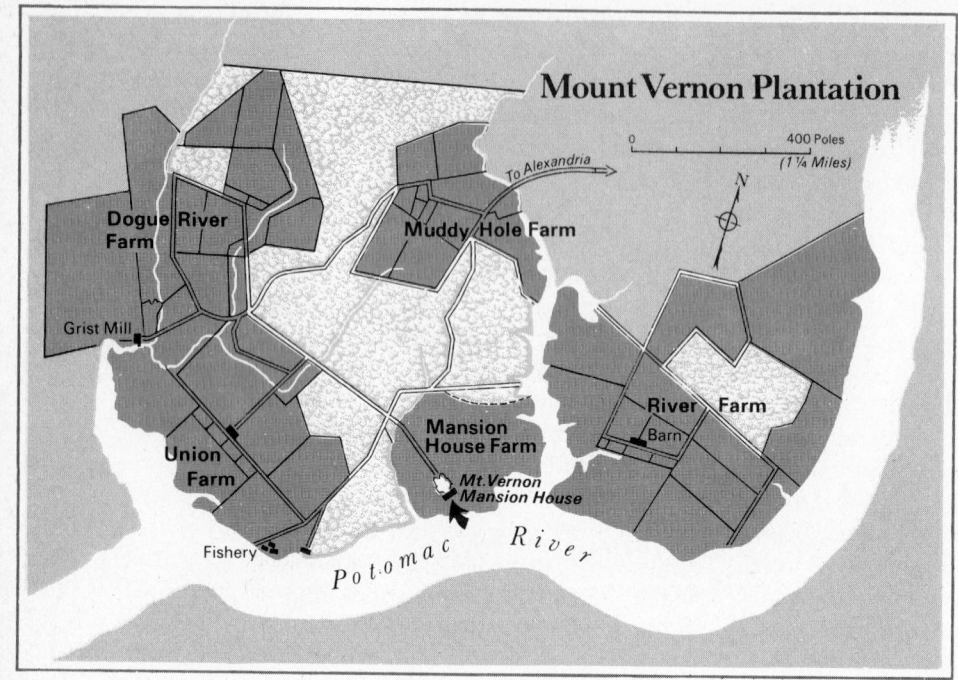

Mount Vernon Plantation

Dogue River Farm

Grist Mill

Muddy Hole Farm

To Alexandria

River Farm

Barn

Mansion House Farm

Union Farm

Mt. Vernon Mansion House

Fishery

Potomac River

0   400 Poles
           (1¼ Miles)

N

MOUNT VERNON PLANTATION, ABOUT 1787
The plantation, which occupied about 10,000 acres, consisted of four working farms and the mansion house property. It was a largely self-sufficient community, containing, besides the slave quarters and agricultural buildings on the farms, a coach house and stables, a smoke house, a spinning house, a spring house, a wash house, carpenter's, tailor's, shoemaker's, and blacksmith's shops, and vegetable gardens.

visors of work on the plantations, the planters discovered at their cost that the managerial responsibility was theirs. A glance at such vivid documents as Landon Carter's diaries shows, not what Edmund Burke correctly called the prime requisite of a true aristocracy, "uncontending ease, the unbought grace of life," but the worried concerns of hard-pressed agrarian businessmen, absorbed in ledgers, profit margins, and the endless difficulties of farm production and labor management. Though the plantation owners attained a certain graciousness in style of living, that elegance was a light veneer over a rough-grained life of land dealing, ministering to the physical needs and managing the disciplinary problems of a partially dehumanized and latently rebellious slave labor force, and attempting to steer a profitable course through a commercial world that was largely insensitive to the pressures the planters might bring to bear.

Plantations in the South differed from European estates in that the increase in the size of the unit of ownership did not increase the income available to the owner. The larger the plantation, the more ex-

posed the owner was to economic dangers and the more precarious the profits he might secure. For the larger the estate, the larger the fixed charges of maintaining slaves and equipment. These expenses remained constant or grew in size no matter what the marketing situation might be, and in bad years debts could rise drastically. Indeed, once started, a marketing depression tended to deepen rapidly and uncontrollably as unsold goods carried over from one season to the next, enlarging the glut to catastrophic size.

In such periods of reversal, planters, far from enjoying the "unbought grace of life," struggled desperately to cut overhead costs or otherwise compensate for the marketing losses. Some concentrated on attaining self-sufficiency in the production of food and clothing so that indebtedness would not mean actual penury. Others turned to crop diversification. Starting on the eastern shore of the Chesapeake in the 1720s and continuing west rapidly, planters began converting to the production of grains and livestock, though the preponderance of tobacco production was never eliminated. And still others took what benefit they could from a new form of marketing introduced by Scottish entrepreneurs, whose investments in the southern American economy in the eighteenth century were a significant new development.

The Scottish merchants and bankers, principally in Glasgow, concentrated on developing the interior of the Chesapeake region. In the backcountry the units of tobacco production tended to be smaller than they were in the East, there was very little capital to start with, and there was no direct contact with ocean shipping. The old consignment system of marketing tobacco was therefore inappropriate for the development of this region. In an effort to reduce freight charges and to increase efficiency, the Scottish firms established stores in the backcountry that were managed by "factors." These agents bought tobacco crops outright, stored them, and in the end shipped them to central distribution points where vessels sent from Scotland could take up cargoes as fast as they could load.

From the merchants' point of view, this system had the advantage of eliminating the waiting time that vessels otherwise would have in collecting a cargo, and hence meant a material reduction in shipping costs. For the planters, it offered somewhat greater control, since they were in a position to oversee the actual sale of their crops without having to account for the complexities of the European tobacco markets. Like the tidewater planters, these inland tobacco growers also accumulated debts to the merchants, but their debts were less for consumption than for production: they took the form of loans for the purchase of slaves, equipment, and the other costs of initiating production. In organizing this trade and in making these investments the Scots became the financiers of the development of the western tobacco lands. It was estimated that in 1765 Glasgow firms had £500,000 of credits outstanding in the Chesapeake. And by then their "factors" had become prominent figures—usually unpopular figures—in the region's society.

In none of this was there a reproduction of the economic basis of a traditional landlord class. In all areas and in every subcategory of the agricultural economy, something new had evolved, and what appeared to be traditional was not. The few princely properties of the heirs of the original proprietary families were not so much tenanted estates as the capital of personal land companies whose greatest profits came from the sale of the land. The southern planters did not form a leisured aristocracy but were active, hard-pressed farm and labor managers whose profits were as likely to be threatened as to be enhanced by an increase in their holdings. In this world of widespread freehold tenure, attempted recreations of traditional landlord systems led not to reliable incomes and a life of agrarian gentility but

ISAAC ROYALL, JR., AND HIS FAMILY, BY ROBERT FEKE (1741) This painting, one of the earliest by the self-taught American painter Feke and one of the earliest group portraits painted in America, shows (right to left) Royall, his wife and child, his sister-in-law, and his sister. Royall, then 22 years old, had inherited a fortune from his father, an Antiguan sugar planter who moved to Massachusetts in 1732 and settled his family on a handsome estate in Medford. The younger Royall, who served on the Massachusetts Council for over 20 years, was a loyalist during the Revolution; his estate was confiscated, and he died in England in 1781. *(Harvard University Law School Collection)*

to controversy, even violent conflict. There were peaceable tenants, it is true, in many areas; but tenancy, far from being the normal pattern of life for those who worked the land, was an exceptional and often transitory condition and its economic function was ordinarily different from what it traditionally had been. Above all, land speculation—the use of land as a salable commodity rather than as an income-bearing property—was an almost universal occupation.

The World of Commerce. The commercial sector of the economy was equally distinctive. Its focus lay in the larger port towns, comparable in size to the second and third rank English provincial cities. All of them but Boston (whose population was stable at around 16,000) continued to grow quickly. Though visitors often noted their outward resemblance to such cities as Edinburgh and Bristol, they noted too some of the differences, which resulted from the fact that they were products of a frontier economy. There was of course, in all of these towns, a laboring population, but most of the urban workers were self-employed artisans or workmen in small-scale, often family-sized, businesses. There was a small though growing number of casual laborers—dock hands, laborers in shipbuilding enterprises, and others—who picked up what employment they could in menial tasks around the towns. They formed a volatile element in these communities, and they suffered in times of depression. But there is no evidence of mass destitution. The number of those who received charity, while it increased, never approached the figures of the dependent poor in Europe. In England at times one-third of the population was impoverished, and in the cities, where beggars crowded the cellars and attics, massed in back alleys, and overwhelmed the charitable institutions, another third was poor enough to be rendered destitute by the repeated economic crises. But Philadelphia did not even build an almshouse until 1732; New York built one only in 1736. Rarely before 1760 were more than one hundred people supported by poor relief in Philadelphia. At no time during those years did as much as 1 percent of the population of New York and Philadelphia receive charity in any form.

A series of close statistical studies of the British mainland North American colonies in the 1700s re-

SEA CAPTAINS CAROUSING IN SURINAM, BY JOHN GREENWOOD (1758) Surinam (Dutch Guiana) on the northern coast of South America was a favorite port of call for American merchants who exchanged horses and tobacco there for sugar products. Greenwood, a Bostonian who lived in Surinam, painted in the faces of several well-known Rhode Island merchants. *(The St. Louis Art Museum)*

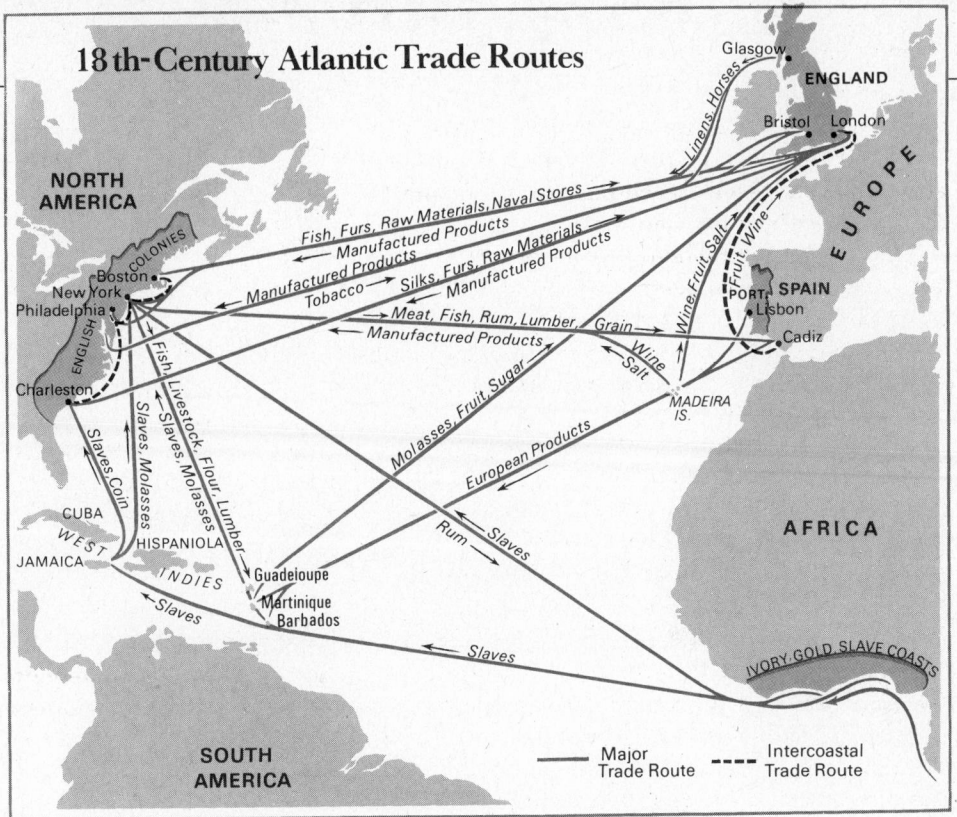

18th-Century Atlantic Trade Routes

NORTH AMERICA

Glasgow
ENGLAND
Bristol • London •

EUROPE

Fish, Furs, Raw Materials, Naval Stores
Manufactured Products
Manufactured Products
Tobacco
Silks, Furs, Raw Materials
Manufactured Products

COLONIES
Boston •
New York •
Philadelphia •

Linens, Horses

Fruit, Wine
Wine, Fruit, Salt

PORT. SPAIN
Lisbon •
Cadiz •

Meat, Fish, Rum, Lumber
Manufactured Products
Grain
Wine
Salt

ENGLISH

Charleston •

Fish, Livestock, Flour, Lumber
Slaves, Molasses
Slaves, Molasses
Slaves, Coin

Molasses, Fruit, Sugar

MADEIRA IS.

European Products

AFRICA

CUBA
JAMAICA
WEST INDIES
HISPANIOLA
Guadeloupe
Martinique
Barbados

Rum
Slaves

Slaves

IVORY, GOLD, SLAVE COASTS

SOUTH AMERICA

Slaves

Slaves

——— Major Trade Route
- - - - Intercoastal Trade Route

veals a level of living that "was probably the highest achieved for the great bulk of the population in any country up to that time," and that was as true in the towns as in the countryside. Though a relatively small part of the urban population controlled an increasing proportion of the total wealth, and though the gulf between rich and poor deepened, "the fact remains that not only were the rich getting richer but the poor were too, albeit at a slower rate." There was poverty in the pre-Revolutionary towns, but no mass starvation; there were riots, but no "bread riots"; and the "mobs" that became highly visible were not spearheads of a desperate proletariat inflamed by utopian aspirations and seeking to transform the structure of society. They were crowds of young apprentices, dock workers, and seamen temporarily idle between voyages, usually led by lesser merchants or independent craftsmen.

It would have been surprising had it not been so, for the society of the commercial towns retained the characteristics of a pioneer world. Labor remained relatively scarce, which meant that wages remained high enough to make small savings possible. Day laborers in Boston were paid twice as much as their equivalents in London. Furthermore, in the typical small-scale enterprise the distance between employer and employee remained narrow, both objectively (in terms of life-style and function) and subjectively (in terms of feelings of superiority or alienation). The typical artisan worked closely with his employer, and their activities were not unbridgeably different. Labor troubles took a quite different form from those in modern society. Strikes were protests not by urban workers against conditions or wages but by master workers, employers, and independent artisans against price levels set by the community for the sale of their products, or efforts to stop widespread infiltration by outsiders into licensed trades. Town workers were periodically distressed by the movements of the economy, which lurched through repeated phases of bust and boom, but there was no permanently alienated "proletariat."

The urban communities were dominated by the merchants, who in this period became figures of importance throughout the Atlantic world. The merchant

BALTIMORE IN 1752

Aquatint by William Strickland, done in 1817 after a sketch made by John Mole, Esq., in 1752. *(I. N. Phelps Stokes Collection, The New York Public Library)*

group as a whole developed between two quite opposite sets of pressures, two conflicting tendencies. During the early and middle years of the eighteenth century there were forces that tended to limit and stabilize the mercantile leadership—to make of these leading figures an elite merchant aristocracy. But at the same time there were other forces tending to upset the dominance of all would-be merchant elites, and these forces were related to the deepest elements of the developing economy.

A significant degree of stability was created in the merchant group of the early eighteenth century in part by political stability in England. The secure arrangement of politics, patronage, and influence devised by the prime minister Robert Walpole in the 1720s helped stabilize the organization of Atlantic commerce, involved as it was with politics and government contracting. At the same time, specialization within the English mercantile establishment increased through the period, and the specialist wholesalers who controlled shipments to the colonies restricted their trade to selected American correspondents. And there were technical improvements in trade and finance, particularly the development of marine insurance, that helped make possible growing concen-

tration of commercial capital and entrepreneurial control.

All of these developments, plus the general fact that large operators could effect economies of scale, meant that the commercial community was acquiring elitist characteristics. Yet despite this emergence of dominant groups, the merchant community as a whole, and commerce as a whole, remained highly competitive and fluid in membership. For, first, as raw frontier areas matured into settled agricultural producing regions, successful farmers branched out into marketing, became inland traders, and ultimately merchants. Prosperous market farmers, particularly those located at transfer points on the rivers or inland trade routes, parlayed their advantages in goods and location into trading operations and drifted into commercial pursuits, combined often with land speculation.

But it was not only a matter of old settled areas producing surpluses from which market farmers could build careers in commerce. Wholly new hinterlands developed almost overnight, and from them emerged new men who proved effective competitors indeed.

In 1720 the chief agricultural producing areas were located northeast of the Hudson and in the Chesapeake region. Thereafter the preponderance shifted to the middle colonies, the area between the Hudson and Chesapeake Bay. Surplus goods, chiefly grain, flowed to the swiftly growing port of Philadelphia from the Pennsylvania backcountry, from New Jersey, and from parts of Maryland; and this flow enriched a new mercantile aristocracy, particularly of Quakers, in Philadelphia. By the 1760s the value of their trade with England exceeded that of all of New England. Similar developments took place in other regions. Within a space of only ten years in the 1740s and 1750s Baltimore rose from a wilderness village to a thriving urban center serving the marketing needs of a new hinterland area, and within a single generation Baltimore's merchants became important figures in the commercial world.

The result of all these movements in agriculture and trade was a highly dynamic mercantile world. Although conditions made possible the stabilization of a merchant leadership group, the rapid development of the economy in long-settled areas and the constant opening of new areas of agricultural production created a continuous recruitment of new merchants and a continuous tension of competition between established figures and newcomers. There was a widespread sense that certain merchant families, established by the 1760s for two, three, or even four generations, were forming into an oligarchy; but at the same time there were always new faces, new families, capable of taking the same successful risks that had once served to establish the older families.

Religion: The Sources of American Denominationalism

The tensions within the commercial world were moderate next to those that developed in religion. Since American culture in the mid-eighteenth century was still largely religious in its orientation, these tensions lay at the heart of the social world everywhere in the colonies, north and south, seaboard and inland.

The central event in the history of religion in America in the eighteenth century was the Great Awakening, the revivalist eruptions of the late 1730s and the 1740s, which roared through the colonies like a sheet of flame and left behind a world transformed. In part this wave of passionate evangelicalism was a typical expression of a general movement that swept through much of the Western world. The Great Awakening coincided with an outpouring of Anglican evangelicalism—which would become Methodism—in England and Wales and with a wave of Pietism in the German-speaking world. There were direct connections between the American revivalists and their European counterparts, but there was something unique too in the American evangelical movement, and it produced quite distinctive results.

Religion and Society in New England.   In New England the background and sources of the Awakening came closest to the European pattern of such evangelical waves. By the early eighteenth century the Congregational churches had experienced the draining away of inner fervor and of emotional commitment that is typical of all long-established churches and that characteristically gives rise to evangelical searchings and outbursts. It is paradoxical that this should have been so since Puritan Congregationalism had itself originally been a protest against a formal church establishment, the Church of England, and it had contained two essential characteristics that had distinguished it from any established church. First, membership in the Congregational churches had not been an automatic consequence of physical birth but had resulted from individual acts of deliberate association based on an inner experience; and second, church institutions had been decentralized into Congregational units.

These original characteristics of New England Puritanism did not survive unchanged into the eighteenth century. By the mid-seventeenth century the New England churches had faced a crisis that arose from the failure of the second and third generations to duplicate the spiritual experiences of the founders and to come forward into membership through an act of saving grace. The founders' children had been baptized in the church on the basis of their parents' profession and the likelihood of their own ultimate conversion; but full membership awaited the childrens' own personal "calling." In fact, many were never converted. Should, then, the children of these baptized but unconverted members of the church also be baptized?

This was the agonizing problem that had faced the Puritans in the mid-seventeenth century. If the answer had been Yes, then the church as a body of converted Christians would have been destroyed. But if the answer had been No, then, as conversions became fewer and fewer, the church would have grown apart from the society as a whole; it would have become a mere sect, without the basis for social control that was so fundamental a part of Puritan life. The solution came in a convention of ministers that met in 1657 whose decision was confirmed by a synod of 1662. By the arrangement devised then, which became known as the "halfway covenant," unregenerate members *could* transmit membership in the church automatically to their children, but only a *halfway* membership: such children would be baptized, but they would not be offered the sacrament of communion, nor would they be entitled to vote as members of the church. As halfway members, they would be required to make a public pledge to obey the rulings of the church and to bring up their children as proper Christians. Still, they were members, if only partial, and the distinction between them and the full members who sat with them in church week after week was thin, and grew thinner and more technical as the years passed.

The "halfway covenant" was an unstable compromise that deeply eroded the Puritans' original concept of the church as a body of proven saints. Conservatives and liberals alike found the halfway distinction illogical and unmanageable, turned to baptizing all, and sought to bring everyone to communion who was willing to accept it.

It was partly in an effort to control such permissive innovations that the more orthodox Puritan churches moved toward institutional centralization and away from congregational autonomy. In Massachusetts regional ministerial associations were formed which sought to impose certification and disciplinary powers over the clergy and over the general management of church affairs. Though in 1705 the effort to create such an organization in civil law was defeated, informal communication among the churches was

strengthened. In Connecticut a parallel effort succeeded completely. There, the so-called Saybrook Platform of 1708 became a public law, creating county "consociations" of the Congregational churches with disciplinary powers, regional associations of ministers, and a colony-wide general association of delegates of the ministers.

By all of these developments—a slackening in religious fervor, a growing identity of church and society, and the spread of general controls over originally independent congregational bodies—the Puritan churches increasingly approached the condition of a formalized establishment. The process had obvious limits. In the eyes of British law, Congregational churches were nonconformist and therefore their advantages as an established group in British territory could never have the full sanction of law behind them. The Church of England, paradoxically a dissenting body in New England, led all opposition groups in claiming the privileges accorded nonconformists in England. And in this they were successful. In the 1720s Anglicans, Quakers, and Baptists gained full rights of worship in Congregational New England and of using their church taxes for their own support. They were free, too, to hold office and to attend all institutions of learning. But they still remained *tolerated* groups, obliged to register with the authorities. No one was free of the obligation to support religion, and no group but these three was allowed the privileges of dissent.

New England Congregationalism was thus a loose establishment, but it was an establishment nevertheless, and one in which religion as an inner experience had tended to fade and in which formal observance and institutional ritual had grown increasingly important. Less and less did the churches satisfy people's inner yearnings; more and more were these churches vulnerable to the charge of excessive formalism and of a deadening complacency.

Religion and Society South of New England. Even less were the churches in the other colonies capable of satisfying the deeper needs of a still generally religious society. In Virginia the long-standing inability of the Church of England to serve the needs of the com-

Prospect of the City of New-York

1 Fort George	6 The Prison.	11 Old Dutch Church	16 Quaker's Meeting
2 Trinity Church	7 New Brick Meeting	12 Jew's Synagogue	17 Calvinist Church
3 Presbyter. Meeting	8 King's College	13 Lutherian Church	18 Anabaptist Meeting
4 North D. Church	9 St. Paul's Church	14 The French Church	19 Moravian Meeting
5 St. George's Chapel	10 N.Dutch Cal.Church	15 New Scot's Meeting	20 N. Lutheran Church

(Department of Rare Books and Special Collections, Princeton University Library)

munity was now compounded by its ambiguous relationship to the new settlers, almost all non-Anglicans, who moved into the backcountry in the 1720s and 1730s. Maryland too, after 1702, had an established Anglican church, but the Anglican community in that colony was numerically small, and its hold on the population at large was even looser than that of the Church of England in Virginia.

Elsewhere the institutional character of religious life was so chaotic and so volatile that it eludes clear description. In the Carolinas and Georgia (the latter settled in 1732 by Anglican philanthropists as a refuge for England's paupers and as a buffer against Spanish Florida), there were Anglican establishments of sorts. Nonconformists were welcomed, however, and little effort was made to regulate religious life as a whole, which in many areas was overwhelmingly non-Anglican. Pennsylvania, Rhode Island, and New Jersey had no established churches at all. In Pennsylvania and Rhode Island the very idea ran against the principles of the influential Quakers, and in New Jersey the religious diversity was so extreme and the Anglican community so small that no agreement on a privileged religion could be reached. And in New York, where dissenters outnumbered Anglicans by at least 15 to 1, the only flourishing Anglican institution was New York City's Trinity Church, which Governor Fletcher had endowed with an independent source of income.

The overwhelming fact, amid the institutional confusion of religion in eighteenth-century America, was that the dominant churches, no matter what their definition, were failing to minister effectively to the needs of a people for whom religion continued to be a primary emotional and cultural experience. It is significant that the most vigorous branch of the Church of England in eighteenth-century America was its missionary arm, the Society for the Propagation of the Gospel in Foreign Parts. Originally formed to bring the Christian gospel to the Indians, it had instead devoted itself to guaranteeing the survival of the Anglican Church in America and strengthening it in every possible way. Under its first leader, the Reverend Thomas Bray (1656–1730), the SPG, as it was called, launched missionary expeditions to likely points throughout the colonies, helped maintain existing parishes and organize new ones in the great desert of American nonconformity, and in its activities created the church's only effective organization above the parish level.

The Great Awakening. *revival* It was into this ill-served, parched, and questing religious world that the evangelicalism of the Great Awakening fell like a blazing torch. The revival did not begin all at once. There were early stirrings in the Connecticut River valley, touched off by the remarkable young minister of Northampton, Massachusetts, Jonathan Edwards.

He was heir to a famous ecclesiastical tradition.

JONATHAN EDWARDS, BY JOSEPH BADGER
Painted a few years before Edwards was expelled from
his Northampton pulpit for insisting on conversion as a
basis for church membership and for attempting to
discipline children of leading families. After seven years
as a missionary to the Indians, Edwards was chosen
president of the College of New Jersey (Princeton) but
died after a few months in office, at the age of 55. *(Yale
University Art Gallery. Bequest of Eugene Phelps Edwards)*

Grandson of the powerful "Pope" Solomon Stoddard of Northampton, whom he eventually succeeded,
Edwards, from the time of his graduation from Yale
at the age of seventeen, devoted himself to the central philosophical and theological problems of the
age. While preaching and fulfilling his other pastoral duties, he worked out a body of thought so
subtle and so original that it has established him
as one of the powerful thinkers of the eighteenth
century. His chief professional task, however, was
more ordinary: it was to bring sinful men to a knowledge of God and to the experience of spiritual rebirth. Stoddard had stirred local revivals in the 1720s;

and in 1734 and 1735 Edwards, to his own great surprise and gratification, suddenly found his own people responding overwhelmingly to his closely reasoned sermons on justification by faith. Northampton
was overcome with religious enthusiasm. Dozens
of once complacent parishioners went through tumultuous passions of regeneration.

Word of a providential revival spread swiftly
through the farming hamlets of the Connecticut
River valley and then eastward along Long Island
Sound, touching off similar outbreaks as it went.
By the time Edwards published an account of his
local revival, his *Faithful Narrative of the Surprising Work
of God* (1737), the wave had passed, but it had become famous throughout the colonies and in Great
Britain as well. It had stirred ministers everywhere to
new exertions in bringing sinful people to an experience of God's grace, and it had created a brimming
expectancy that some vast outpouring of religious
zeal, if not the actual establishment of God's kingdom on earth, was about to take place. By 1740, when
George Whitefield, the brilliant English preacher
who had already stirred successful revivals on two
tours through the middle and southern colonies, appeared in New England, anticipation was spilling
over into fulfillment. It was Whitefield, following
in the wake of Edwards's revival, who finally threw
open the floodgates and let loose an outpouring of
soul-shaking evangelicalism that flooded New England for four tumultuous years.

Whitefield's tour of New England was spectacular. In Boston, preaching first to hundreds who
jammed the churches until they could hold no more,
then to thousands in open-air meetings, the young
impassioned orator transfixed listeners used to hearing scholarly sermons read to them from carefully
prepared texts. He was equally successful in a series
of meetings in northern New England, and then in
the West. In Northampton his preaching was so affecting that Jonathan Edwards, Whitefield reported,
"wept during the whole time of exercise." After stops
south along the valley towns that had already experienced the revival, Whitefield ended his tour in
New York.

His preaching, he correctly reported, had made
a great difference in the North. So too did that of the

second great leader of the Awakening, Gilbert Tennent. This second-generation Scotch-Irish minister for a decade had led the "New Light" (evangelical) party within the growing Presbyterian communities of New Jersey and New York. He had been educated in his father's "Log College" in Neshaminy, Pennsylvania, devoted to propagating the principles of

GEORGE WHITEFIELD PREACHING, BY JOHN WOLLASTON. (1741, WHEN WHITEFIELD WAS 27)

He appeared, a Connecticut farmer recalled, "almost angelical; a young, slim, slender youth before thousands of people with a bold, undaunted countenance, . . . he looked as if he was clothed with authority from the Great God, . . . and my hearing him preach gave me a heart wound." "What a spell he casts over an audience," Jonathan Edwards' wife wrote, "by proclaiming the simplest truths of the Bible. I have seen upwards of a thousand people hang on his words with breathless silence, broken only by an occasional half-suppressed sob." *(National Portrait Gallery, London)*

"experimental" religion—that is, deeply experienced rather than intellectual and doctrine-bound religion. Tennent's tour through southern New England lasted three months in the fall and winter of 1740–41. They were tumultuous months of mass excitement, profound emotional upheaval, and inner transformation.

Elsewhere too the revival continued its blazing progress. It tore through the Presbyterian and Dutch Reformed communities of the middle colonies, splitting them into conservative and evangelical wings. The "New Side" evangelical Presbyterians of Pennsylvania and New Jersey formed their own synod in 1741 and sent out their own itinerant preachers to invade districts dominated by the "Old Side." It was these revivalist Presbyterians moving southward from Pennsylvania who had the greatest impact in Virginia. Their most effective preacher, Samuel Davies, sustained in Hanover County the most important of the southern revivals, and in the process spurred the Anglican authorities to take repressive measures against nonconformity by fining unlicensed preachers. Even more influential in the southern colonies were the evangelical Baptists. They reached out more effectively than any other church or sect to the unchurched common people of the backcountry, and most successfully proselyted among the new settlers on the southern frontier. And at the end of the colonial period, evanglicals of the Church of England led by the Reverend Devereux Jarratt, who would soon organize as the Methodist Church, also began to share in the work of extending the Awakening to the settlers on the expanding frontier.

Effects of the Great Awakening. Such was the greatest event in the history of religion in eighteenth-century America. Its effects were more revolutionary by far than those of the parallel movements in Europe—Pietism in Germany and Methodism in England and Wales. The differences are revealing. The revivals in America were not, as elsewhere, distinctively lower class affairs that gave new voice to the aspirations of the socially deprived. Nor were they limited to any particular geographical group: they were as successful in the large towns as in the countryside. Their impact could not be confined. At least four areas of American social life were irreversibly affected by the great revivalist wave.

First, the authority and status of the clergy were permanently weakened. The revivalists cared little for offices, formal status, education, learning, or even, within reasonable limits, outward behavior. For them, qualification for religious leadership was gained only by force of inner experience and by the ability to unlock parishioners' spiritual aspirations. It followed naturally that they would challenge the authority of established educational institutions like Yale and Harvard whose training for the ministry seemed to them to be intellectual and formalistic. When Connecticut barred from the ministry anyone not trained at Yale, Harvard, or a foreign Protestant university, the Presbyterian New Lights not only formed a new synod devoted to evangelical preaching but in 1746 created a new college, the College of New Jersey (later Princeton) which would emphasize religion of the emotions, of the spirit, as well as of the mind. Rutgers, Brown, and Dartmouth also were founded in response to the revival movement, for the Awakening, which challenged all preachers to justify their authority by their own spiritual gifts and by their power to reach into other souls, could not tolerate merely formal qualifications of any kind.

Second, the Awakening tended to destroy the identification of churches with specific territorial boundaries. The revivalists believed their call extended not to the few people who happened to have employed them as preachers but to anyone anywhere who would heed their word, and especially to all those whose ministers were unconverted. They therefore naturally became "itinerants," invading established parishes. If welcomed, they preached officially as visiting ministers: if not, they set up in barns or open fields and preached to anyone who came. The establishment vehemently objected to such invasions, and "itineracy" became one of the central controversies of the revival. But it could not be stopped, and where it occurred it tended to free the churches from specific territorial foundations, released them into a universe of competing groups.

Related to this was a third effect of the Awakening, nothing less than the near destruction of institutional religion as the organizing framework of small-group society. For in all the new settlements, and continuously on the disorganized frontiers, the church had provided a vital center for society itself. When the Awakening hit the more vulnerable communities, a series of splits most often occurred. A split-off of a New Light faction from a stubborn Old Light majority could severely rupture a community; and even if the splinter group eventually returned, it did so more or less free of general control. Often there was no point at which the disintegration could be stopped. Whole units simply disappeared in the course of successive splinterings, ending in a mere cluster of family-sized factions, free of all constraints of church organization.

Finally, the Awakening put unsupportable pressures on what remained of church-state relations, not in doctrine but in practice. The revivalists did not believe themselves to be unorthodox. Quite the contrary. They claimed that they alone represented the true orthodoxy in Protestant Christianity and denounced the establishments for their deviations. In so doing they created new grounds for challenging the practical right of any church to claim a privileged place in the eyes of the law. They thereby moved closer to the conclusion that the very notion of an establishment of religion was false and that the only safe and correct course was to deny any and all privileges of the state to any religious group.

Denominationalism. From all of the developments in religion that had been in motion from the time of the first English settlements in North America—developments now greatly intensified and compounded by the Great Awakening—religion in America acquired a new character. It became essentially voluntaristic—an activity one was free to join or not to join—even for the high church groups whose official doctrines assumed an inescapable identification of church and society enforced by the state. Organized religion had also developed an emphasis on persuasion as its essential activity. The churches, lacking the sanction of the state to guarantee membership, lacking, too, secure institutional structures and effective group discipline, swung their efforts toward

View of Savannah, 1734. *The I. N. Phelps Stokes Collection, The New York Public Library*

Embellishing the Wilderness

The European settlement of North America was an intrusion into the wilderness, a struggle to impose the familiar forms of an advanced civilization into an environment that was almost totally unredeemed from its natural, uncultivated state. The awareness of this struggle was as vivid to those who settled the last British colony, Georgia, and who pictured Savannah in 1734 as a tiny clearing at the edge of a vast forest as it had been to the settlers of Virginia a century and a quarter earlier. The struggle took its toll. Not only were there significant modifications in the conduct of everyday life —regressions and simplifications, it seemed—but at the margins there were complete surrenders to the wilderness. There were always frontiersmen who spent months drifting from one isolated primitive encampment to another, and emerging from time to time to buy with animal skins what they needed for survival and to tell remarkable tales of worlds beyond the mountains and the swamps. But these wandering semi-primitives were rare in British America—much rarer than they were in French Canada, where half-savage trappers and woodsmen (the famous *coureurs de bois* who roamed the wilderness for years at a time) formed a significant part of the population.

British America from the beginning was a bourgeois society. The wilderness exerted no fatal seduction; it proved to be a challenge to the arts of cultivation, to the nesting instinct, to the impulse to domesticate and to embellish. Beauty, in European terms, was sought from the start, transferred at first from "home" and then imitated, however crudely, by local craftsmen. The artifacts of daily living had to be made from materials that lay at hand, by men whose task it was to provide the necessities of life, not the refinements. But though the products were often rough, they were rarely primitive. Occasionally, even in the earliest years, some striking embellishment, some special grace of line, balance, or proportion, some flash of vivid and

(*Above*) Massachusetts press cupboard, late seventeenth century. *Courtesy, Museum of Fine Arts, Boston. Gift of Mr. and Mrs. William R. Robinson*

(*Left*) Spindled chair, 1640–1660. *Courtesy, Museum of Fine Arts, Boston. Photo by Richard Cheek*

(*Opposite*) Queen Anne chair from Philadelphia.

harmonious color, emerged to mark the point at which craft turned to art.

So furniture was crafted in the seventeeth century from local woods, its bare, hard surfaces as uncomfortable as they were serviceable and durable; but sometimes even in the earliest years the furniture was embellished too, with a conscious style, decorated and beautified. Spindled oak pieces like the Ipswich, Massachusetts, press cupboard were stained with vegetable dyes to give them tone, and their ornaments painted black to simulate ebony; the result was a complex, dappled black-brown surface. Later such embellishments grew more sophisticated as the Queen Anne chair reveals; and by the early 1700s japanned highboys

(Above) Crewel petticoat border, mid-eighteenth century. *Courtesy, Museum of Fine Arts, Boston. Gift of Mrs. J. R. Churchill*

(Right) Japanned chest, early eighteenth century. *Courtesy, Metropolitan Museum of Art, Purchase 1940, Joseph Pulitzer Bequest*

were being produced with structural designs in classical modes and oriental scenes in brilliant color. Quite independently the Dutch in New York and the Germans in Pennsylvania developed from their own folk traditions a distinctive pattern of decoration. And everywhere craftsmen learned to produce not only beautifully designed wooden furniture in contemporary styles but upholstered pieces that were colorful as well as solid and comfortable.

Textile embellishments took many forms, from embroidered chair seats and petticoat borders to crewel bed hangings and draperies. And the skill of the silversmiths developed quickly too. By the end of the seventeenth century intricately designed and handsomely worked silver bowls, tankards, coffee pots, and sugar boxes were seen on tables in the South as in the North. Craftsmen like John Coney were creating objects in silver that would delight their users and viewers for generations to come.

(Left) Silver tankard, late seventeenth century. *Courtesy, Museum of Fine Arts, Boston. Gift of Mr. and Mrs. Dudley Pickman*

(Below) Sugar box, by John Coney, 1680–1690. *Courtesy, Museum of Fine Arts, Boston, Elliot Fund*

THE SWAINS SHALL WONDER WHEN THEY READ
THO MONG ON ALL THE GROUE
THAT HEAUEN ITSELE CAME DOWN AND BLED
TO WIN A MORTALE LOUE

Everyday life was visibly enhanced—not transformed into a wonder world of aristocratic ostentation but simply embellished, decorated, elevated above mere practicality. Clock faces and inlaid rifle stocks became minor works of art, the clock cases and gun grips beautifully worked wood. Door frames were improved by conscious imitation of metropolitan models. Glassware evolved in unexpected forms, and metal workers produced weathervanes that had the animated beauty of modern mobiles.

(Opposite) Bed hangings, c. 1745. *Old Goal Museum, York, Maine*

(Above) Glass sugar bowl, late eighteenth century. *Courtesy, The Henry Francis du Pont Winterthur Museum*

(Right) Doorway of Fowler Tavern, mid-eighteenth century, Westfield, Massachusetts. *Courtesy of the Metropolitan Museum of Art, Rogers Fund, 1916*

Raleigh Tavern, Williamsburg, Virginia. *Colonial Williamsburg Foundation*

The wilderness remained—a threat to European civilization and a constructive challenge to creativity in a people conscious both of the simplicity of their lives and of the richness of their cultural heritage. Young men like Jefferson grew up in a borderland world, looking out from Queen Anne rooms of spare elegance onto a wild, uncultivated land.

promotion and outward activity and away from the purification of doctrine and the maintenance of internal order. Finally, the role of individual decision shifted. Where in traditional situations involvement with a dominant religion was automatic, the momentous decision was to break with the association into which one was born. As a consequence, religious indifference could go hand in hand with extensive church membership. In the colonies the opposite was true: to do nothing was likely to mean to have no affiliation at all, and the momentous decision involved joining, not severing, a religious association. As a result, broad waves of religious enthusiasm could go hand in hand with low church membership.

By the end of the colonial period these characteristics were taking on a patterned and stable form, which would later be called Denominationalism. Products of the intractable realities of the colonial situation, these characteristics would find expression in theory, law, and formal doctrine during the Revolution and in the years that followed.

The Origins of American Politics

The key to much in pre-Revolutionary America was the gap that developed between expectation and reality. This discordant pattern was more extreme and more consequential in politics and government than in any other area of life. For not only did the discrepancy between theory and expectation on the one hand and actuality on the other shape the character of American public life, but it laid the basis for the transformation of the relations between Britain and the colonies.

The Structure of British Politics.   All formal notions of public life in the British world rested on the belief that the British political system of the mid-eighteenth century was the freest and best that existed, and that the colonial governments and political systems were more or less imperfect replicas of that world-famous model. In theory, balance was the key to the British constitution. From classical antiquity had come the notion, reaffirmed in the Renaissance

and in seventeenth-century England, that there were three pure forms of government. Any one of these if properly maintained could serve the people properly but all tended to degenerate into evil forms that created oppression. Monarchy, the rule by one, degenerated into tyranny; aristocracy, the rule of a few, became oligarchy; and democracy, the rule of the whole political population, declined into the rule of the mob. The challenge to political thinkers had long been the problem of devising a balance among these forms that would stabilize government and bring the degenerative processes to a halt. The British constitution, it was generally agreed, had achieved precisely such a stable balance of pure forms, its balance embodied in the competition among the crown, representing monarchy; the House of Lords, representing the nobility or aristocracy; and the House of Commons, representing the democracy.

Such was the theoretical explanation of the working of the British constitution in the mid-eighteenth century, a theory that was almost universally believed to explain the stability and freedom that had been achieved in Britain. Yet, as a description of the actual working of the British government, it was misleading. The balance of these elements was more apparent than real. The supposed preserves of the elements of the constitution were thoroughly infiltrated by the others, and their functioning was different from the idealized description. In fact the source of the political stability of mid-eighteenth century Britain lay not in the supposed balance of these socioconstitutional orders, which Americans sought to emulate, but in two sets of special conditions, both highly relevant to an understanding of the peculiar form of politics that developed in eighteenth-century America.

The main underlying condition that made Britain's stability possible was the fact that the great constitutional issues of the seventeenth century had been settled in the Glorious Revolution of 1688: the problem of the extent of crown authority and the problem of the relation of church and state. As to the first, the terms of settlement of the Glorious Revolution stipulated that the monarch would not create courts without statute or dismiss judges without formal impeachment; would not impose taxes without grant of Parliament; and would not maintain a standing army in peacetime or engage in wars for foreign territory without Parliament's consent. The crown had been forced to agree further not to limit unduly or extend the existence of a Parliament or interfere with its regular meetings—elections and convenings being placed on a regular calendar schedule. In addition, it was understood, at least after 1707, that the king would not veto acts of Parliament.

As to the religious settlement after the Glorious Revolution, the established Church of England continued to enjoy the privileges and benefits of the state, and all who did not explicitly reject it were considered to be members of its community. But the desire for an enforced uniformity was abandoned. Dissent was tolerated, though penalized. The great majority of nonconformists were permitted to worship as they pleased; they enjoyed almost full civil rights, and in the course of the century attained most political rights as well.

These underlying conditions made stability possible. That stability was actually achieved was the result of the informal accommodation that was worked out between the crown and the House of Commons. A working relationship between the two was achieved by a set of operating conventions so fundamental as to comprise in effect a private, informal constitution. The ministry, acting for the crown, disciplined and manipulated the House, in part by managing elections into the House through its control or outright ownership of "rotten boroughs" or other easily dominated constituencies, and in part by distributing crown patronage to Members so as to assure safe majorities on controversial issues. In the mid-eighteenth century about 200 of the 558 Members of the House of Commons held crown appointments or gifts of one sort or another, and another 30 or 40 were more loosely tied to government by awards of profitable contracts. A fluctuating num-

THE HOUSE OF COMMONS IN THE MID-EIGHTEENTH CENTURY

The facing benches, separated only by the speaker's table and the few feet of open floor space, encouraged direct debate. Like so much of British political life, this seating arrangement was widely imitated in the colonies (see p. 145).

ber of other Members was bound to the administration less directly, particularly by the gift or promise of one or more of the 8,000 excise offices available.

It was this use of "influence" in managing elections and in controlling votes in the two Houses that, together with the settlement of the main policy questions, explains the stability of English political life in the mid-eighteenth century. There were certain technical requirements for such stabilizing control: an abundance of patronage available for disposal by the ministry; a small electorate, for the larger the voting population the greater the difficulty of control; and a system of representation that was not related to the shift and growth of the population or closely bound to the wishes of a broad electorate.

Differences in the Colonies. All of these conditions existed in eighteenth-century Britain, but none of them existed in anything like the same measure in the mainland colonies of British North America. Yet the similarity between the British government and the separate colonial governments was an axiom of political thought in eighteenth-century America. As bicameral legislatures developed in the colonies during the seventeenth century, with the lower houses more and more clearly standing for local, popular interests and the Councils appearing to approximate the classical houses of the aristocracy, the assumption grew that the colonial governments were miniatures of the British government. Dr. William Douglass of Boston explained in his *Summary, Historical and Political . . . of the British Settlements in North America* (1749–51) that, by the governor,

representing the King, the colonies are monarchical; by the Council, they are aristocratical; by a House of Representatives or delegates from the people, they are democratical: these three are distinct and independent of one another . . . the several negatives being checks upon one another. The concurrence of these three forms of government seem to be the highest perfection that human civil government can attain to in times of peace.

Such irregularities and exceptions as there were in the American replicas, Douglass said, "doubtless in time will be rectified."

But while in England the mixed and balanced constitution produced a high degree of political harmony, similar institutions in the colonies produced the opposite. Conflict, so intense at times that it could lead to a total paralysis of government, was common in American politics. There was conflict, first, between the branches of government—between the executive on the one hand and the legislatures on the other. But it was not only a matter of conflict between branches of government. There was, besides this, factionalism that transcended institutional boundaries and at times reduced the politics of certain colonies to an almost unchartable chaos of competing groups. Some were personal groups, small clusters of relatives and friends that rose suddenly at particular junctures and faded quickly, merging into other equally unstable configurations. Others were economic, regional, and more generally social interest groups, some quickly rising and quickly falling, some durable, persisting through a generation or more, though never highly organized and only intermittently active, and continually shifting in personnel. Still others (though these were fewer) were groups formed to defend and advance programs that transcended immediate personal and group interests. Most were vocal and difficult to control; and while in certain colonies at certain times political life attained the hoped-for balance and tranquility, most governors in the eighteenth century at one time or another echoed the weary question and the anguished plea of William Penn to the political leaders of the City of Brotherly Love soon after it was founded: "Cannot more friendly and private courses be taken to set matters right in an infant province? . . . For the love of God, me, and the poor country, be not so *governmentish!*"

But Pennsylvania remained, in Penn's words, "noisy and open in [its] dissatisfactions," and so did most of the other colonies during the three generations that preceded the Revolution. For beneath the apparent similarities in the formal constitutions of government in England and America, there were basic differences in the informal structure of politics. The similarities in government were superficial, the differences in politics so profound as to seem almost an inversion of the universally admired British model.

WEATHERVANE, BY SHEM DROWNE
(MID-EIGHTEENTH CENTURY)
Swivelling atop the cupola of the Massachusetts Province
House with its glass eyes flashing in the sun, this 4½-
foot gilded weathervane was the work of an untutored
craftsman. The visual and symbolic effect of the almost
life-sized American archer swinging vigilantly year after
year over the residence of the royal governors, always
aiming an arrow to fly with the wind, was striking. It
"bedazzled the eyes of those who looked upward,"
Nathaniel Hawthorne wrote in a story inspired by
Drowne, "like an angel of the sun." (*Massachusetts
Historical Society*)

The settlement of the Glorious Revolution had
not extended to the colonies. The governors in all
but the chartered colonies of Rhode Island and Connecticut had the executive authority to veto legislation, which could also be disallowed by the Privy
Council or the proprietors in England. The royal

governors, in addition, had the authority to delay
sittings of the lower houses of the assemblies or dissolve them at will, and they quickly became accustomed to using those powers. As a result, the lower
houses were as dependent on executive will for their
existences as the House of Commons had been under
the Tudor and Stuart monarchs. Nor was the judiciary
in the colonies protected as it was in England. Judges
at all levels, from justices of the peace to the chief
justices of the supreme courts, were appointed on
nomination of the governors and dismissible by the
executives' will. Similarly, the governors in all but
the three charter governments could create courts
without note of the legislature, and did so repeatedly,
especially chancery courts, which sat without juries
and were concerned with such unpopular matters as
collecting arrears of quitrents. Associated with these
"prerogative courts" in the colonists' minds were the
vice admiralty courts, which operated over maritime
matters, also without juries, with a jurisdiction
broader than that exercised by equivalent courts in
England.

Lesser powers that had been eliminated in England were also accorded the executive in America:
power over the election of the Speakers of the House;
power over church appointments; power over fees.
But it was in the more consequential areas primarily—
the vetoing of colonial legislation, dismissing and
dissolving legislative bodies, and firing judges and
creating courts—that the legal power of the executive
was felt to be the most threatening and a source of
danger to liberty and to the free constitution.

But what distinguished the American colonial
governments from the British even more than the
exaggeration of executive authority was an array of
other circumstances that radically reduced, sometimes eliminated, the force of that "influence" by
which the executive in England disciplined dissent
and conflict in the political community and maintained its supremacy in government.

To begin with, the colonial executives lacked the
flexibility they needed for successful engagement in
politics. The royal governors arrived in the colonies
not merely with commissions that outlined their
duties, but with instructions that filled in the details

so minutely and with such finality that in some of the most controversial and sensitive public issues the executive was politically immobilized. Further, the armory of political weapons so essential to the successful operation of the government of Walpole was reduced in the colonies to a mere quiverful of frail and flawed arrows. Very little political patronage—gifts of public office, contracts, honors, or other benefits of government—was available to the colonial governors by which to buy off opposition and maintain their dominance over the legislatures. Further, the highly irregular, inequitable, and hence easily manipulated electoral system was absent in America.

There were no rotten boroughs in the colonies. No assembly seats were owned outright by the government, and there were no defunct constituencies easily manipulated by the administration, for there had been no gradual accumulation of "liberties" bestowed in ancient times in recognition of once active but long since extinct political forces. While in England the House of Commons was frozen in composition throughout the eighteenth century, most of the colonial assemblies had been created at a stroke on general principles—so many delegates per unit of local government—and were continually expanding. So normal had the expectation of expansion become by midcentury that when governors, fearing the total eclipse of their influence in the legislatures because of the increasing numbers of representatives, tried to stop the multiplication of constituencies and seats they found themselves involved in serious political struggles. What is important is not that by enlightened twentieth-century standards apportionment was here and there inequitable in the colonial legislatures, but that by normal eighteenth-century standards it was so well-adjusted to the growth and spread of population and so insensitive, as a consequence, to pressure from embattled executives.

Other practices created additional problems for the governors. From the earliest years it had been common in Massachusetts for towns to instruct their representatives on how to vote in the General Court in regard to controversial issues, and this practice continued irregularly into the eighteenth century, used when the localities were committed to particular

views they wished to have represented no matter what influence was brought to bear against them. Elsewhere, too, representatives were instructed on delicate issues, and often when delegates were not instructed they themselves postponed acting until—as in New York in 1734—"they had taken the sentiments of their constituents." Further, delegates were often required to be residents of the communities they represented at the time of their incumbency. The result, the eighteenth-century historian William Smith wrote, was that the assemblies seemed to be composed "of plain, illiterate husbandmen, whose views seldom extended farther than to the regulation

THE VIRGINIA HOUSE OF BURGESSES
As in the British House of Commons (p. 142), the speaker's chair (rear, under the center window) and table separate the facing benches. The room is small, and the arrangements encouraged intimate discussion. *(The Colonial Williamsburg Foundation)*

of highways, the destruction of wolves, wildcats, and foxes, and the advancement of the other little interests of the particular counties which they were chosen to represent." Residential requirements were not universal in the eighteenth-century colonies, but they were common enough to contribute measurably to the enfeeblement of "influence."

But of all the underlying characteristics that distinguished politics in America from the English model, the sheer number of those who could vote was perhaps the most dramatic. A broad franchise had not originally been planned or desired. Most colonies sought to do no more than re-create, or adapt with minor variations, the forty-shilling freehold qualification (the ownership that is, of real estate worth 40s. a year in rents), which had prevailed in the county constituencies of England for three hundred years. But if ownership of land worth 40s. a year was a restrictive qualification in England, it was permissive in the colonies where freehold tenure was widespread among the white population. So ineffective was this traditional franchise definition that most colonies went on to specify the restriction more elaborately. But everywhere the effect was to broaden the franchise, rather than to restrict it. Some colonies defined the requirements for voting in terms of acreage: in Virginia 100 acres unsettled, or 25 acres settled; in North Carolina and Georgia, 50 acres whether settled or unsettled. In other colonies permanent or even lifetime leases were declared to be as valid for the franchise as freehold property, and in some, personal property of any description was allowed to serve as qualification. Inflation of local currency values further eased the restrictions of franchise qualification. In Rhode Island a £400 property "restriction," measured in local paper money, opened the franchise to 75 percent of the colony's adult males. To the disgusted Governor Thomas Hutchinson in Massachusetts, it seemed that "anything with the appearance of a man" was allowed to vote.

Generalizing across the variety of statutory provisions and practices of the various colonies, one can safely say that 50 to 75 percent of the adult male white population was entitled to vote—far more than could do so in Britain, and far more too, it appears, than wished to do so in the colonies themselves.

Apathy in elections was common. Yet however neglected, the broad franchise was potentially a powerful weapon, certain to work against the ability of the executives to control elections and voting in the assemblies for the interest of the state.

The Pattern of Colonial Politics. The overall configuration of early American politics was a patchwork of contradictions. There was a firmly rooted belief that the colonial constitutions corresponded in their essentials to the English model of mixed government. That assumption was violated, however, first, by what were believed to be excessive powers in the hands of the executive, and second, by the absence in the colonies of the devices by which in Britain the executive maintained discipline, control, and stability in politics. Swollen claims and shrunken powers, especially when they occur together, are always sources of trouble, and the political trouble that resulted from this combination can be traced through the history of eighteenth-century politics.

But the structure of American politics in the eighteenth century is not wholly revealed in this. The nature of leadership too was a source of controversy. Americans, like all Britons—indeed, like all Europeans of the eighteenth century—assumed that political leadership was only one of a number of expressions of leadership within society, and that in the nature of things those who enjoyed superiority in one sphere would enjoy and exercise it in another. In a society of stratified "dignities" (if not classes), political leadership was expected to rest with the natural social leaders of the community, whose identity, it was assumed, would be steadily and incontestably visible. And so indeed it was in America—in *some* of the colonies, in *certain* respects, at *certain* times.

In Virginia in the three generations that followed Bacon's Rebellion, a hierarchy of the plantation gentry emerged in stable form, dominated by social and economic leaders whose roots could be traced back to the 1650s and whose dominance in politics was largely uncontested. So too in Connecticut, a landed gentry of "ancient" families consolidated its control in the early eighteenth century and came to dominate the political life of the colony. But even in these extreme examples there were premonitions of disturbances to come—in Virginia, in the expansion of settlement in the west and the establishment there of new figures of potential power and of distinctive religious interests; in Connecticut, in the growth of religious radicalism, especially in the eastern counties, which were already disturbed as a result of the leanness of the agricultural economy and of the frustrated desire for geographical expansion.

Yet Virginia and Connecticut were colonies of the greatest stability. In most of the colonies the identity of the natural political leaders remained as it had been in the late seventeenth century, a matter of controversy, at times the source of political struggles. New figures appeared overnight everywhere in the colonies, and always there were alien elements introduced into the top of the political hierarchy in the form of officials sent from England in positions of high authority.

These were the shaping elements of those "noisy dissatisfactions" that so plagued the tranquility of governors in eighteenth-century America. The political system was contentious—a factional system in which the will and dignity of the ill-organized imperial state were openly attacked by opposition groups. It was a free competitive politics that was the very opposite of the immobile, bureaucratized state system that prevailed in the colonies of Spain's American empire.

Such was American society in the eighteenth century, a strange society caught between traditional institutions and ways of thinking and unexpected circumstances. A polyglot population drawn from many sources in Europe, Africa, and the West Indies lived in communities that did not recognize cultural pluralism or conceive of ways by which an alien race could coexist with the dominant British except in constant conflict or absolute subjection. While one-fifth of the population was held in chattel slavery and enjoyed no more of the world's goods than well-cared-for animals, the rest enjoyed a level of affluence unknown to any other large population in the Western world. Social institutions that presumed a stable and well-ordered population were subjected to extreme pressures of population growth and mobility. Land was widely distributed in freehold tenure, though efforts were repeatedly made to re-create a traditional landlord class, and tenancy was just as likely to foster land speculation as to provide income for a leisured landed gentry. Transoceanic commerce was increasingly dominated by a merchant class tied securely to a traditional commercial oligarchy in Britain, but the established merchants were beset on all sides by irrepressible competition generated by the swift, uneven growth of an uncontrolled economy. Religious organization, still traditional in concept and doctrine, was so deeply eroded by altered circumstance that it seemed transformed even before the Great Awakening reduced what remained of familiar forms to an almost unrecognizable disorder. And politics was an open competition for place, profit, and power fought out within a culture that condemned factionalism as seditious and that assumed that the state was in some sense sanctified and above mere factional contention.

It was a strange world, full of incongruities, but it was moving toward a resolution of its most glaring inconsistencies.

SUGGESTED READINGS

There are several useful general surveys of eighteenth-century American society. The most valuable introduction, combining narrative and analysis, remains James T. Adams, *Provincial Society, 1690–1763* (1927); though out of date on certain matters, it touches on all major topics, includes a great deal of basic information, and conceives of society in structural and organizational terms. Lawrence H. Gipson's *British Empire before the American Revolution,* vols. II and III (1939) provides a comprehensive description from literary sources of the colonies in the years 1748–1754 and includes a full bibliography in the annotation. Volumes IV and V (1939–1942) survey the frontier areas in dispute with Spain and France and also the Caribbean colonies. An effort, the first of its kind, to bring together into a general picture the recent findings on social organization and economic development is James A. Henretta, *The Evolution of American Society, 1700–1815* (1973), chaps. i–iv. Daniel J. Boorstin's *The Americans: the Colonial Experience* (1958) is a highly personal analysis of eighteenth-century American culture, styles of life, learning, and artistic expression. Boorstin's analysis of the professions in colonial America is particularly valuable. Max Savelle, *Seeds of Liberty* (1948) is a survey of intellectual history and the fine arts.

On the eighteenth-century population, see Robert V. Wells, *The Population of the British Colonies in America before 1776* (1975), which analyzes the surviving censuses. Information in Greene and Harrington, *American Population* (referred to for chap. 3) and in Stella H. Sutherland, *Population Distribution in Colonial America* (1936) remains useful. Of the new immigrations, the Irish are described in R. J. Dickson, *Ulster Immigration to Colonial America* (1966) and Wayland F. Dunaway, *The Scotch-Irish of Colonial Pennsylvania* (1944); the Germans in Albert B. Faust, *The German Element in the United States* (2 vols., 1909), F. R. Diffenderfer, *The German Immigration . . .* (1900), and Gillian L. Gollin, *Moravians in Two Worlds* (1967); and the Scottish in Ian C. C. Graham, *Colonists from Scotland* (1956). On the legal incorporation of foreign peoples into British America, see James H. Kettner, *The Development of American Citzenship, 1608-1870* (1978).

A reliable and detailed picture of the life of the black population and of slavery in the eighteenth century has only recently begun to appear and is still very incomplete. An attempt to summarize all the recent writing is Ira Berlin, "Time, Space, and the Evolution of Afro-American Society on British Mainland America,"*American Historical Review,* 85, no. 1 (February 1980), 44-78. There are useful articles devoted entirely to colonial slavery in special issues of two journals: *Wm. and Mary Q.,* 35 (1978), no. 2; and *Southern Studies,* 16 (1977), no. 4. Peter Wood, *Black Majority* (1974) is an excellent account of slavery in South Carolina to 1739; Gerald W. Mullin, *Flight and Rebellion* (1972) traces slave resistance in Virginia. Two articles by Allan Kulikoff on slavery in the Chesapeake region are also useful: *Journal of Southern History,* 45 (1979), 513-40; and in A. C. Land *et al.,* eds., *Law, Society, and Politics in Early Maryland* (1977). Winthrop D. Jordan, *White over Black* (1968), Parts I, II, scrutinizes white attitudes toward blacks.

On landowning and agriculture, see Lewis C. Gray, *History of Agriculture in the Southern United States to 1860* (2 vols., 1933) and Percy W. Bidwell and John I. Falconer's parallel book on the North. A broad survey of the opening of new frontier lands in the tradition of Frederick Jackson Turner is Ray A. Billington, *Westward Expansion* (1949), chaps. v-viii, which contains an exhaustive bibliography of writings on the westward movement. A case study of the opening of new townships in New England, contradicting the Turner view on many points, is Charles S. Grant, *Democracy in the Connecticut Frontier Town of Kent* (1961). On the opening of the land in Pennsylvania, see James T. Lemon, *The Best Poor Man's Country* (1972); on land utilization in North Carolina, Harry R. Merrens, *Colonial North Carolina* (1964); on land and population in Virginia, Carville V. Earle, *The Evolution of a Tidewater Settlement System* (1975).

Of the exceptions to freehold tenure discussed in this chapter, there is an excellent essay on the old proprietary estates: Rowland Berthoff and John M. Murrin, "Feudalism, Communalism, and the Yeoman Freeholder . . . ," Stephen G. Kurtz and James H. Hutson, eds., *Essays on the American Revolution* (1973). On tenancy, see Willard F. Bliss, "Rise of Tenancy in Virginia," *Virginia Magazine of History and Biography,* 58 (1950), 427-41; Clarence P. Gould, *Land System in Maryland, 1720-1765* (1913); Gregory A. Stiverson, *Poverty in a Land of Plenty* (1977); Sung Bok Kim, *Landlord and Tenant in Colonial New York* (1978); and Patricia U. Bonomi, *A Factious People* (1971), chap. vi. Plantation life and the harassed role of the large planters are vividly portrayed in Jack P. Greene, ed., *Diary of Colonel Landon Carter* (2 vols., 1965). The condition of ordinary planters is described in Aubrey C. Land, "Economic Behavior in a Planting Society . . . ," *Journal of Social History,* 33 (1967), 469-85 and "Economic Base and Social Structure . . . ," *Journal of Economic History,* 25 (1965), 639-54.* On the role of the Scottish merchants in transforming the marketing of tobacco, see Jacob M. Price, "The Rise of Glasgow in the Chesapeake Tobacco Trade," *Wm. and Mary Q.,* 11 (1954), 179-99, and on marketing in general, "Economic Growth of the Chesapeake and the European Markets, 1697-1775," *Journal of Economic History,* 24 (1964), 496-511, as well as Price's *France and the Chesapeake* (2 vols., 1973).

On commerce generally, besides Emory R. Johnson *et al., History of Domestic and Foreign Commerce* (1915), see James F. Shepherd and Gary M. Walton, *Shipping, Maritime Trade, and the Economic Development of Colonial North America* (1972), a technical study with elaborate statistics on 1768-72. Arthur L. Jensen, *Maritime Commerce of Colonial Philadelphia* (1963) is an excellent account. Richard Pares, *Yankees and Creoles* (1956) and Richard B. Sheridan, *Sugar and Slavery . . . the British West Indies, 1623-1775* (1974) cover the Caribbean trade; on the timber trade and fisheries, see Joseph J. Malone, *Pine Trees and Politics* (1964) and Harold A. Innis, *The Cod Fisheries* (1940). Perhaps the best insight into the working of commerce is provided by studies of individual merchants. There are accounts of the Hancocks of Boston by W. T. Baxter, of the Beekmans of New York

*See footnote on page 65.

by Philip L. White, of the Pepperrells of Maine and New Hampshire by Byron Fairchild, and of the Browns of Rhode Island (a particularly vivid example of social and occupational mobility) by James B. Hedges. Life in the port towns is described in Carl Bridenbaugh, *Cities in the Wilderness* (1938), *Cities in Revolt* (1955), and *Rebels and Gentlemen: Philadelphia . . .* (1942); in Richard B. Morris, *Government and Labor in Early America* (1946); and in Gary B. Nash, "Urban Wealth and Poverty in Pre-Revolutionary America," *Journal of Interdisciplinary History,* 6 (1976), 545–84. Alice H. Jones has published the wealth estimates referred to in the text, in *Economic Development and Cultural Change,* 18, no. 4, Part II (1970) and *Journal of Economic History, 32* (1972), 98–127.

Eighteenth-century religion is summarized in Sydney E. Ahlstrom, *Religious History of the American People* (1972), Part III. Sidney E. Mead, *The Lively Experiment* (1963), traces the development of American denominationalism. Major religious currents in New England are described in Perry Miller, *New England Mind: From Colony to Province* (1953); Robert G. Pope, *The Half-Way Covenant* (1969); Robert Middlekauff, *The Mathers* (1971); Ola Winslow, *Meeting-house Hill* (1952), and James W. Jones, *The Shattered Synthesis* (1973). There is a large literature on the Great Awakening, much of it brought together into a single brief book, J. M. Bumsted and John E. Van de Wetering, *What Must I Do to Be Saved?* (1976), which contains a good bibliography. The major works are: Edwin S. Gaustad, *Great Awakening in New England* (1957); Wesley M. Gewehr, *Great Awakening in Virginia* (1930); Charles H. Maxson, *Great Awakening in the Middle Colonies* (1920); Richard L. Bushman, *From Puritan to Yankee* (1967); C. C. Goen, *Revivalism and Separatism* (1962); and William G. McLoughlin, *New England Dissent* (2 vols., 1971). Excellent also on the complicated awakenings in the middle colonies are Leonard J. Trinterud, *Forming an American Tradition . . . Presbyterianism* (1949) and Martin E. Lodge, "The Crisis of the Churches in the Middle Colonies, 1720–

1750," *Pennsylvania Magazine of History and Biography,* 95 (1971), 195–220. There are documentary collections on the awakenings by Richard L. Bushman and by Alan Heimert and Perry Miller; biographies of Jonathan Edwards by Miller (1949), Ola E. Winslow (1940), and Edward H. Davidson (1968); of Whitefield, by Stuart C. Henry (1957); and of the importance Baptist leader Isaac Backus, by William G. McLoughlin (1967). Evarts B. Greene, *Religion and the State* (1941) and William G. McLoughlin, "Isaac Backus and the Separation of Church and State," *American Historical Review,* 72 (1968), 1392–1413 show the colonial origins of American church-state relations.

The operation of the imperial government is described fully in Leonard W. Labaree, *Royal Government in America* (1930) and Jack P. Greene, *The Quest for Power* (1963); but politics, though intimately related to government, is a different matter. Bernard Bailyn, *Origins of American Politics* (1968) is an effort at a general interpretation, stressing the relations between formal and informal organizations and between political activities and political beliefs. The role of colonial offices in the British patronage system is explained from the British point of view in James A. Henretta, "*Salutary Neglect*" (1972) and in Alison G. Olson and Richard M. Brown, eds., *Anglo-American Political Relations, 1675–1775* (1970) and from the American point of view in Stanley N. Katz, *Newcastle's New York* (1968). Michael Kammen, *Empire and Interest* (1970) is an exceptionally imaginative effort to show the changing ways in which the British political system accommodated the interests of economic and political groups in Britain and America.

Of the many thorough studies of the politics of individual colonies, several are outstanding: Bonomi, *A Factious People;* Robert Zemsky, *Merchants, Farmers, and River Gods* (1971); Charles Barker, *Background of the Revolution in Maryland* (1940); and M. Eugene Sirmans, *Colonial South Carolina* (1966). J. R. Pole, *Political Representation* (1966) covers both England and America throughout the eighteenth century.

CHAPTER 6

The Enlightenment's New World

In 1760, when the young George III ascended the throne of Great Britain, Americans like Britons everywhere joined in the celebrations enthusiastically. Not only had the nonslave population of the colonies enjoyed with Britain the freest political conditions of the Western world, and not only had the colonists shared, though erratically, in Britain's rising prosperity, but they had participated too in Britain's recent military victories over the perennial enemy, France. Now, released from the immediate pressure of frontier wars and aware as never before of the richness of the land that lay to the west, they glimpsed a future that could be prosperous and free beyond all earlier expectations. One could reasonably conceive, the Boston preacher Jonathan Mayhew wrote in 1759, of "a mighty empire" in British America "(I do not mean an independent one) in numbers little inferior perhaps to the greatest in Europe, and in felicity to none." One could picture, he wrote, cities "rising on every hill ... happy fields and villages ... [and] religion professed and practiced throughout this spacious kingdom in far greater purity and perfection than since the times of the apostles."

Mayhew's buoyant sense of America's prospects as part of the British world was shared in varying degrees by many others. But beneath the glowing surface there were dark undertones in Anglo-American relations that had been developing through all the years of mutual growth and pragmatic accommodation. These countercurrents had no predictable or inevitable outcome. They could as reasonably have grown into a pattern of stable and peaceable relations as become sources of serious disruption. The future would depend on the ability of men in power to understand and manage the complex problems that faced them. In retrospect, however, one thing is clear. These antagonisms, rooted at three levels in the subsoil of Anglo-American life, were like buried traps: to ignore them was to risk disaster.

"Rule Britannia"

At the most obvious level were the antagonisms generated by the war efforts of the mid-eighteenth century.

War of Jenkins' Ear. During the years after 1713, Britain engaged in three wars with European powers, and the colonies were involved in varying degrees in all of them. The first, the so-called War of Jenkins' Ear (1739–42) was fought with Spain over trading rights in the Caribbean and Central America. In the peace treaty of 1713 that ended the War of the Spanish Succession Britain had been granted the privilege of selling a limited number of slaves and a specified quantity of goods in the Spanish West Indies. The legitimate presence of British trading vessels in these otherwise closed markets had encouraged smuggling, which was countered by mutual rights of search. Spain's brutal handling of these shipboard searches had been no more improper or illegal than the British smuggling, but it had outraged British public opinion. When a certain Captain Robert Jenkins presented to a parliamentary committee one of his ears, which he said had been cut off by the Spanish seven years earlier as a punishment for smuggling, Parliament demanded a war of revenge for such atrocities, which the head of the government, Robert Walpole, who wished to avoid war, could not refuse.

The war, which ranged widely, was fought at first in the Western Hemisphere. A makeshift army of South Carolina and Georgia troops invaded Florida but failed to capture St. Augustine or to relieve the pressure on the southern frontier, and the action turned to the Caribbean. There the main effort was an assault on the Spanish town of Cartagena, on the Colombian coast, for which an American regiment of 3,500 men was recruited, to serve under British commanders. That campaign, in 1740, was a ghastly failure. A hopelessly slow and ill-mounted attack on the fort led to the butchery of the American troops, which was succeeded by an epidemic of yellow fever and a loss of supplies. After further failures in Cuba, the remains of the expedition, which had been largely financed as well as manned by the colonies, staggered home. The losses were shocking. Only 600 Americans survived, and they brought back with them a bitter resentment of the callousness, incompetence, and superciliousness of the British military commanders. Years later Americans still recalled the agonies their countrymen had endured on this senseless campaign and the appalling waste of lives and goods.

King George's War. In 1740 the Spanish war had broadened into a general European conflict when Prussia seized the Austrian province of Silesia. Britain went to Austria's aid, and France joined Spain. Thereupon Britain, ever fearful of a single continental power controlling Europe, concluded peace with Spain (1742), and in 1744 declared war on France. This complicated series of struggles, which had begun with the Prussian invasion of Silesia, was known in Europe as the War of the Austrian Succession (1740–48) and in America as King George's War (1744–48). While its conclusion in the Treaty of Aix-la-Chapelle was no more than a truce to allow for recuperation, that arrangement left yet another source of resentment between Britain and the colonies in Britain's abandonment of an important American victory.

The focus of conflict in the Western Hemisphere during King George's War was the French naval station at Louisbourg, a massive fortification on Cape Breton Island just north of Nova Scotia, which guarded the entrance to the St. Lawrence River, sheltered French privateers, and controlled the rich fishing waters between mainland North America and Newfoundland. When Governor William Shirley of Massachusetts heard that its garrison was undermanned and dispirited and its fortifications in disrepair, he rallied support from the Massachusetts merchant community and persuaded the General Court to finance an expedition to capture the citadel. Equipment and troops were gathered from all over New England and from colonies as far south as Pennsylvania, arrangements were made for British naval support under a New Yorker, Commodore Peter Warren, and the troop command was given to a popular Maine merchant and militia colonel, William Pepperrell.

As the transports, warships, supplies, and men gathered in Boston, the campaign, in the aftermath of the Great Awakening, took on the air of a festive crusade. The clergy preached fire and destruction to the French "papists" and their pagan Indian allies. In April 1745 four thousand New England troops

SIR WILLIAM PEPPERRELL, 1747, BY JOHN SMIBERT
Pepperrell is posed on a hill overlooking Louisbourg, to
which he points and into which two cannon balls are
gracefully falling. An engraving of this painting of the
popular hero was promptly made for wide distribution.
(Courtesy, Essex Institute, Salem, Mass.)

amphibious force to take the partly demolished fortress, the French, hopelessly outnumbered and lacking food supplies and naval support, surrendered. On June 17 the "Gibraltar of the New World" was handed over to Pepperrell.

For New England, indeed for all of America, it was a glorious victory. Warren, who made a fortune from his capture of French merchant ships, was promoted to admiral; Pepperrell was knighted. But the war was far from over. Disease decimated the troops occupying Louisbourg, and the frontiers from Maine to New York were set aflame in savage raids. Border garrisons in Vermont, western Massachusetts, and New York were attacked, captured, retaken, and attacked again. Massachusetts, promised repayment by Parliament for its expenses in capturing Louisbourg, planned a massive assault on Quebec but then abandoned it when news arrived of a large French expedition moving to recover Louisbourg. And though that French fleet, scattered by storms and swept by disease, never made contact with the fortress, and though another French fleet on the same mission was captured by Warren, the border raids continued and spilled over into Nova Scotia. The war disintegrated into miscellaneous violence. Isolated towns and farmhouses were burned and their inhabitants slaughtered, though the butchery could make no possible difference to the outcome. Prisoners were taken, then exchanged. Grand campaigns were hatched with Indian allies then dissolved before any action could be taken and for reasons that could not be clearly explained. Spain's raids on several forts along the southern British coast were equally inconclusive and equally ill-designed to affect the outcome of the war.

Nothing substantial had been accomplished when in December 1748 news arrived that peace had been concluded in Europe. It brought relief from bloodshed, but in exchange for the return of Madras in India, which France had taken, England returned Louisbourg, the symbol of American military pride, to the French. Five hundred Americans had died in action to accomplish nothing, and twice that many had been killed by disease, exposure, and accidents. The return of Louisbourg would be recalled along

landed safely near the fortress of Louisbourg, turned the cannons of a captured defense battery against the central fortification, and attacked, not by sea, as the French had expected, but by weakly defended land approaches. The French held off the attackers through all of April and May while the New Englanders—who were not soldiers but undisciplined farmers, fisherman, and town workers—bumbled and stumbled their way to control of the harbor islands. Just as Warren was preparing to land an untrained with bitter memories of the Cartagena expedition—and with the memories of another famous episode of King George's War.

In 1747 Commodore Knowles's naval press gangs had attempted, in the fashion of the time, to shanghai likely recruits for the royal navy on the streets of Boston. But Boston, he discovered, was not London. To his amazement, his men were fought off by an incensed mob in one of the most violent town riots of the pre-Revolutionary years. The townsmen's rampage against this flagrant though traditional invasion of civilian rights lasted for four days, and it remained a living memory for a generation to come.

The French and Indian War. The third and last of these pre-Revolutionary wars followed in part the pattern of the others. This time, however, America was the central theater of war, not a marginal one; and this time the outcome was conclusive, and the resentment generated between Britain and the colonies was of a different order of magnitude.

The immediate cause of the Seven Years' War (1756–63), known in the colonies as the French and Indian War, was a series of clashes between French army units on the one hand and Virginians on the other. The French units were trying to secure the Ohio River valley for France by establishing a string of forts there. The Virginians had claims to this territory that went back to the original charter, and these were now being advanced by a powerful group of land speculators. The French repulsed the Virginians' efforts to found a British fort at the strategic junction of the Ohio, Allegheny, and Monongahela rivers and early in 1754 established their own Fort Duquesne there instead. A small force under the twenty-two-year-old Major George Washington failed to dislodge them and was itself then defeated at a stockaded encampment called Fort Necessity.

FRANKLIN'S SNAKE DEVICE, 1754
This famous emblem, first published by Franklin just before the meeting of the Albany Congress, was reprinted with variations throughout the colonies and became a symbol of resistance to Britain in the years preceding the Revolution. (*Historical Society of Pennsylvania*)

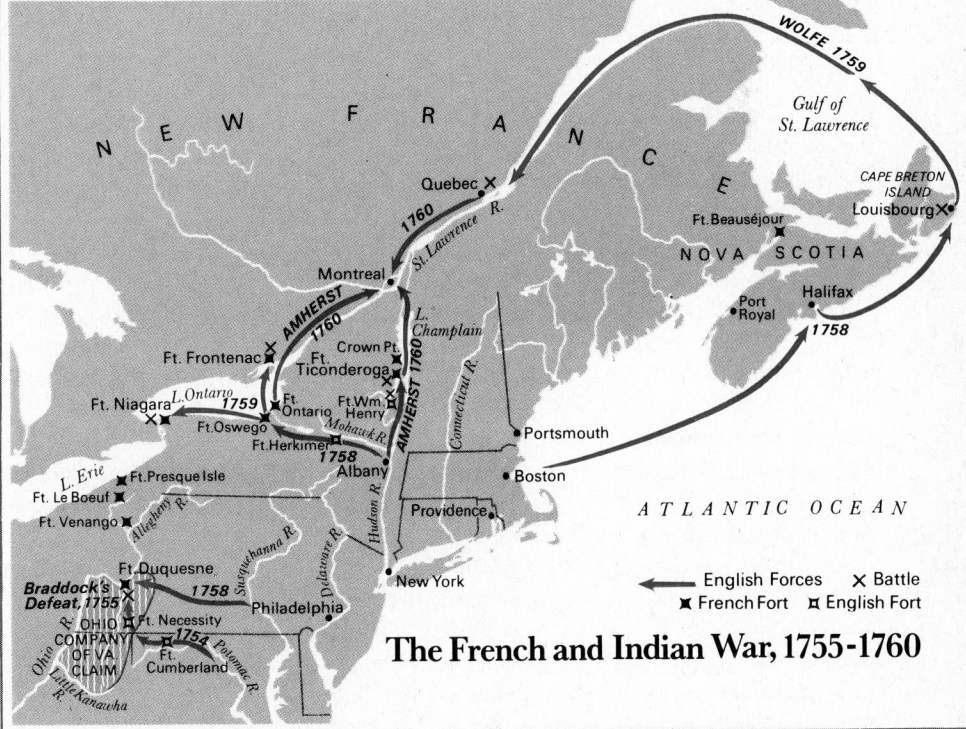

The French and Indian War, 1755-1760

Shortly after this engagement, representatives of seven colonies, anticipating a larger conflict than any of the previous wars, met at Albany in a fruitless effort to coordinate defense plans among themselves and with their Indian allies. Though they adopted in principle Benjamin Franklin's proposal for a political and military union of the colonies, they could not convince a single colonial assembly to ratify the plan for a general government that was drawn up. Meanwhile the British government moved ahead with a design for a large-scale war that involved dispatching a sizable army to America, enlisting colonial troops, and collecting in America quantities of provisions and equipment. Early in 1755, Major General Edward Braddock, an arrogant disciplinarian with little sympathy for difficult colonials and no sense of how to handle them, arrived with the advance regiments. He undertook, in the wilderness of western Pennsylvania, the first engagement in a war that was not formally declared until May 1756 but that, once declared, spread quickly to all points of contact among the major European powers—not only in Europe, America, and the Caribbean but in Africa, India, and the Philippines as well.

For two years the British suffered defeat after defeat. Braddock's army, moving west to eliminate Fort Duquesne, fell into confusion at the first, accidental contact with the enemy and was almost annihilated by a small French and Indian force hidden along the sides of the road. There were 1,000 casualties in an army of 1,400; only 23 of 86 officers survived. Washington, who helped lead the pell-mell retreat, buried Braddock in the road to keep his grave from being discovered. To the north, Nova Scotia, whose boundaries were disputed and whose native Acadians were either pro-French or unreliably neutral, had to be retaken by the British; 6,000 of the Acadians were rounded up and deported south to the thirteen colonies. But though this action isolated Cape Breton and its fortress of Louisbourg, the effort by the new commander in chief, Lord Loudoun, to capture that citadel in 1757 failed. So too did Governor Shirley's ambitious effort to force the French from the arc of forts that formed the northwest boundaries of the British colonies. Instead of the British taking the two French forts—Frontenac and Niagara—on Lake Ontario, the

French under the adroit commander Montcalm took the British fort, Oswego, on the eastern side of that lake. Then, secure in Crown Point on Lake Champlain, the French moved deeper into New York by establishing Fort Ticonderoga ten miles to the south on Champlain. Finally, in August 1757 they seized Fort William Henry even farther to the south, on Lake George, and captured with it 2,000 British troops. But even this was not the end of the disasters. While in Europe, where Austria and Prussia had reversed sides, French and Austrian armies overran Britain's client state Hannover and threatened Prussia, the French on the western American frontier penetrated to Fort Herkimer on the Mohawk River, murdering noncombatant German farmers along the way. The whole of central New York and western New England was exposed; Albany seemed doomed.

It was at this absolute low point in British fortunes that the planning of that strange, brilliant, imaginative, and neurotic war minister, William Pitt, began to have its effect. Appointed secretary of state in 1757 and possessing a vision of imperial greatness that was unique for the time, Pitt conceived of something akin to a total war. He demanded huge government expenditures, heavy subsidies for the European allies to neutralize the continental zone, and large commitments by the colonies, to be financed by Parliament. He conceived of an American army of 24,000 British regulars and 25,000 colonial troops—a very large force for the time.

Passing over established but ineffective generals in favor of younger and more energetic commanders, he launched a series of efforts to break the French arc of forts north and west of the mainland colonies. The first of his plans—an attack on Ticonderoga in July 1758—failed miserably. But that was his only failure. Later the same month, a force of 9,000 regular army troops and 500 colonials under the young General Jeffrey Amherst and the thin, sickly, but tigerish Brigadier James Wolfe, only thirty-one years old, took Louisbourg. A month later, in a swift raid, the British swept over the critical supply depot of Fort Frontenac, the link between the St. Lawrence River and the French posts to the farther west and south, and with it seized control of Lake Ontario. In November a mixed force led by three excellent commanders including

Colonel Washington finally redeemed Braddock's defeat by forcing the French from Fort Duquesne, thereby seizing for Britain the entire upper Ohio Valley.

By early 1759, the year of Britain's greatest victories, the iron ring around the northern British colonies had been broken at three critical points: on the east (Louisbourg and Nova Scotia), the west (Frontenac and Lake Ontario), and the south (Duquesne). And there were successes not only in America but in India and Africa and at sea. Then Pitt, riding the crest of great popularity at home, planned the kill. Canada was to be sealed off in the far west by the capture of Fort Niagara; General Amherst was to invade Canada by way of Lake Champlain and the St. Lawrence Valley; and Wolfe was to take Quebec in an amphibious expedition moving west up the St. Lawrence River. For all of this, a fortune in supplies, transports, and firearms, in addition to three large armies with substantial naval support, was required.

Somehow, these great demands were met. In July 1759 Fort Niagara, which linked New France to the far west, was captured. At the same time, the French withdrew from Ticonderoga and Crown Point, leaving them to Amherst. By the time his troops had rebuilt these forts it was too late for him to proceed with the planned thrust into Canada from the south. But Wolfe, in one of the best-organized, most daring, and luckiest exploits in British military history, succeeded in his assigned task in Pitt's strategy.

Moving almost 10,000 men in over 200 warships and transports through the St. Lawrence to Quebec without serious loss, Wolfe fumbled for over seven weeks seeking a way to penetrate the heavily fortified city built atop the 150-foot cliffs that form the north shore of the St. Lawrence at that point. Finally, on the night of September 12, 1759, he led 4,500 men up the cliff along a diagonal roadway he discovered and into battle formation on the Plains of Abraham, just west of the city. When the French, without waiting for reinforcements, charged the carefully disposed British army rather wildly, they were met with a dis-

A VIEW OF THE TAKING OF QUEBEC, SEPTEMBER 13, 1759
This detail of a print of 1760 telescopes the debarking of the troops, their dislodging of the French defenders of the cliffside trail, and the final battle on the Plains of Abraham. *(Royal Ontario Museum, Toronto)*

ciplined and efficient barrage that broke their ranks, and they were driven from the field defeated. Among the relatively few British casualties (60 dead, 600 wounded) was Wolfe; among the French, Montcalm. On September 17, Quebec surrendered.

A year later Amherst's army, moving north and east from the lakes, converged on Montreal and with contingents from Quebec forced the French governor to surrender the whole of New France. In the final peace treaty of 1763, Britain gained undisputed possession of all of North America east of the Mississippi save for New Orleans, including all of Nova Scotia and all of Canada. Furthermore, Spain, which had entered the war only in 1762, was forced to concede Florida to Britain in exchange for the return of Cuba, which a British expedition had captured in 1762. Spain's compensations were New Orleans and the land west of the Mississippi, which France had rashly pledged to Spain as a reward for its entry into the war.

It was a great triumph of British arms, and it was matched by other British successes all over the world. But there were serious hidden costs. The most obvious was the huge debt that England acquired in prosecuting the war, which set in motion a reaction against grand and costly overseas adventures and would lead the government of George III to consider new forms of taxation. Less obvious was the immediate effect of the war on Anglo-American relations. While Americans rejoiced in the victory and for the first time in their history were relieved of the threat of French and Spanish stimulation of Indian attacks on the frontiers, they learned to fear the presence of large professional armies and to insist that militias alone were forces compatible with liberty. They learned, too, to an extent they had not before, that, though they were British, they were somehow a separate people, yet not an inferior people as the army commanders under whom they fought so often seemed to assume. For through all these wars—from the catastrophe before Cartagena to the triumph on the Plains of Abraham—they experienced the arrogance, indifference, and often the stupidity of an officer class that was a traditional part of European life but was alien, abrasive, and in the end intolerable in America.

Beyond all of that there were resentments at the imperial regulations—some of them newly devised, some newly enforced during the French and Indian War. As part of his program for a total national effort, Pitt sought to eliminate all violations of the navigation acts, all smuggling, indeed all commercial contact with the enemy that might bolster his economy or help supply his troops. It was not an altogether new effort. As early as 1756, the Privy Council had ordered the colonial governors to enforce the strict letter of the law and to eliminate the trade with the enemy that was well known to be taking place in neutral ports. In pursuit of these goals and in support of the efforts of the customs officials, the highest colonial courts had issued writs of assistance to customs officials. These general warrants, authorizing customs officers to command the assistance of court officials in searching for smuggled goods, were granted by the high court of Massachusetts in 1755, 1758, 1759, and 1760, and were valid throughout the lifetime of the reigning sovereign. They served their purpose well, but they were deeply resented by the merchant community, which was determined to seek relief when the opportunity arose.

Pitt's insistence on enforcing the letter of the law elevated all of these efforts to a new level. In the course of his brief but powerful ministry (he was forced to resign in 1761), he issued stringent orders that closed loopholes in the regulations, brought the complex rules together into an integrated whole, and fixed responsibility for negligence. Governors were drawn directly into the business of imperial law enforcement, and the navy became a more effective police arm than it had been before. Conflict was implicit in all of this. Well before 1763 certain colonial merchants and politicians who were antagonistic to the imperial establishment were beginning to question the value of a connection of which they suddenly seemed to be victims.

Yet all of this was but the tip of an iceberg. Attempts to enforce the mercantilist system during the last colonial war brought to the surface of public controversy other conflicts in imperial relations that had hitherto been submerged.

The Alienation of the State

Long before Pitt became involved in public affairs, three problems had arisen in Anglo-American relations that had not been solved but merely put off, patched up with makeshift solutions, and then ignored. They could be ignored because they had developed largely as a consequence of the mercantilist system, and as long as that system was not rigidly enforced the pressure of these problems was slight. The problems remained, nevertheless, and there was a price to be paid for evasion and neglect. Even in their moderated form they created a distance, an alienation, between Britain and America, and that alienation was as much a part of the Anglo-American world in 1760 as the universal welcome accorded the young monarch, George III.

Smuggling and the Balance of Payment. The first of these problems arose from the fact that the rapidly increasing American population created a growing market for British goods which was not matched by an equivalent growth of a market within Britain itself for the products that the colonies could sell. By the 1730s American consumption of British goods rose well beyond the colonists capacity to pay for them through direct exchanges with Britain. By the late 1760s the colonists were running a trade deficit with Britain of £1,800,000 a year, over 90 percent of it incurred by the northern and middle colonies.

The deficit had been largely made up by invisible earnings such as shipping services and by the profits of trade with southern Europe and the West Indies. The West Indies trade was particularly important in maintaining the colonies' solvency, and exchanges with the *foreign* West Indies—especially with the French sugar islands of Guadeloupe, Martinique, and Santo Domingo—had become a vital part of that trade. Dealings with the French islands, where the American merchants could buy cheaply and sell at unusually high rates, were particularly important in making up the deficits in payments to Britain and thus in keeping the commercial colonies solvent. But that trade was increasingly resented by the British West Indian

SUGAR CANE AND THE ART OF MAKING SUGAR, FROM A PRINT OF 1749
(Library of Congress)

planters and their merchant associates in England. They recognized that the more successful this foreign trade was, the higher the cost of provisions would be on their own plantations and the lower the price they could obtain for their own products.

The issue became embattled as early as 1730. The British planters and merchants moved to protect themselves against French competition by seeking to establish high duties on foreign sugar products imported into the mainland colonies. The American merchants and the colonial agents in London rose in opposition, claiming that such duties were more than the trade could bear and that they would wreck the Anglo-American commercial system and bankrupt the northern colonies. A fierce debate raged in the newspapers and pamphlets and in the House of Commons, but the result, given the power of the West Indian lobby in London, was foreordained. In 1733 Parliament passed the so-called Molasses Act, which imposed prohibitive import duties on foreign sugar products.

This established the terms of the problem as it existed in 1760. For the Molasses Act set in motion the development of a network of illegal importations. Customs officers in the North American ports were systematically bribed, and became accustomed to ignoring the strict letter of the law and settling for a certain percentage of the legal duties. Techniques for smuggling were perfected, and gradually a large part of the northern commercial economy developed a stake in the systematic corruption of the law—law that seemed arbitrary, the product of a distant, alien, and hostile government.

Conflict Over Manufactures. Something of the same sense developed from a second problem in Anglo-American economic relations that arose during the same years. The mercantile system was based on the assumption that colonial areas were producers of exotic goods and raw materials and that they were consumers, not producers, of finished goods. Large-scale manufacturing, it was assumed, was an activity reserved to the home country, and the law reflected that assumption by prohibiting the manufacture of certain basic goods in the colonies. English statutes

from the end of the seventeenth century forbade the export from England of machines or tools used in the clothing industry. The Woolen Act (1699) prohibited the export of American wool or woolen products from any one colony to another. A law of 1718 forbade the free emigration of skilled artisans from Britain, and the Hat Act (1732) barred the exportation of American-made hats from the colony where they were manufactured.

Yet increasingly, as the American economy developed, investments in manufactures seemed attractive and proved to be lucrative as small accumulations of capital appeared in various areas. The sums were not large by English standards, but what surplus capital was available in the colonies was peculiarly disposed to such investments. For other outlets were limited. Some profits could be plowed back into expansion of commercial enterprise. Surpluses could be invested too in urban properties, in financing land speculation, in English government bonds, in personal loans or in equipment for business. But most such investments were limited to face-to-face transactions; there were no investment institutions that could broaden the range and magnitude of the money market. In a society not prone to extravagant consumption, those who controlled the slowly growing surplus turned more and more to manufactures. There were adverse conditions that restricted what could be done: a continuing labor shortage, a poor overland transportation system, and limited markets. But wherever these disabilities were to some degree overcome, the results were impressive.

In shipbuilding the problems of both transportation and markets were eliminated, since England's need for merchant vessels was continuous and heavy. By the late colonial period almost 40 percent of all British-owned merchant vessels were built in the thirteen colonies. About 100 vessels were sold to Britain annually, worth at least £140,000. Iron production presented greater difficulties which were only partly overcome by dispersal into small producing units and the use of slave labor. Nevertheless iron production too rose remarkably, not only in the large Principio works in Maryland and the Hasenclever plants in New Jersey but in dozens of smaller establishments scattered through the colonies. At the end of the colonial period there were 82 blast furnaces and 175 forges in the colonies (more than existed in England and Wales), and they produced 30,000 tons of crude iron a year. This product was less than half of Britain's, but it was an imposing achievement nevertheless.

Of the products manufactured in the colonies, only ships and rum were produced in such quantities that the colonists' needs were filled. But the manufacture of other goods was increasing steadily, and British authorities recognized the danger this posed to the principles of mercantilism. Britain's restrictive legislation grew more elaborate. The manufacture or export from the colonies of specific textiles was outlawed in 1750. And in that year too the most famous restrictive enactment, the Iron Act, was passed. Though it removed duties on the importation of pig and bar iron into Britain, this act prohibited the erection of finishing plants for iron goods in all the colonies.

The effect of these laws in economic terms is difficult to gauge. Surplus wealth available for investment in manufactures was never large, and there were other factors, quite aside from restrictive legislation, that tended to impede industrial growth. But in the less measurable area of attitudes to the authority responsible for such legislation, the impact of restrictive legislation was significant. It further heightened the colonists' awareness of hostile interests in the government "at home" and deepened their feelings of hostility and alienation.

Currency and Banking. The same effect resulted from the handling of the money problem, which remained an acute issue through most of the mid-eighteenth century. The problem was created by the virtual absence of specie, or coin, as a medium of exchange. The coinage of money, being a sovereign prerogative, was prohibited in the colonies after the confiscation of the charter of Massachusetts, under whose jurisdiction the "pine tree shilling" had been minted in the seventeenth century. The colonists made every effort thereafter to attract Spanish coin to the British colonies, but the negative balance of trade made their efforts unsuccessful. The solution

was paper money—unusual in the eighteenth-century —which entered into the economy in two forms.

The first form was bills of credit that were issued by the colonial governments to repay debts the governments owed to merchant contractors. Massachusetts began this practice in 1690, and in the years that followed before 1760 almost every other colony did the same. These bills, which were in effect IOUs to be redeemed eventually by the governments, were declared legally valid as payment for taxes. As a consequence, they entered into general circulation, their value maintained by the expectation of eventual redemption. But these bills were not generally made full legal tender (that is, valid for payment of all debts, public and private), and they continued to be thought of as wartime expedients. The quantity available depended less on the needs of the economy than on the occasional demands for public expenditure.

The second form of paper money was that issued by land banks, which were in effect public loan agencies. They were created to issue money to individuals at 5 percent interest, repayable gradually and secured against default by mortgages on land or other real property. The success of these banks, which by 1750 were in existence in every colony but Virginia, was striking. They injected a badly needed flow of currency; they reduced taxation (through the income produced from the interest on the loans); they created a source of low-interest credit needed for agricultural development; and they built up purchasing power that may have helped soften the effects of depressions. Further, as opposed to bills of credit, the land banks put funds at low interest directly into the hands of the farmers; bills of credit went first to the merchants, who translated them into credit for the farmers on less generous terms. Both, however, provided a needed medium of exchange and, despite their experimental character, were on the whole successful. Bills of credit were especially sound in the middle colonies where both merchants and officials backed the issues and limited them carefully.

In parts of New England and the South, however, there was overissuance and serious depreciation. In these areas creditors feared they would be repaid in paper money that had lost value since the debts had been incurred. Even more apprehensive were the English merchants, who feared severe losses if their credit were in any way affected by the cheapening of currency. Together, creditors in the colonies and in England pressured the British government to send strict orders to the colonial governors not to allow bills to be issued as full legal tender and to insist that the currency laws state the times of redemption clearly, and that these specifications be honored to the letter.

But such strict controls were difficult to enforce, and a crisis arose in New England in the 1730s. Rhode Island's bills flooded the region (that colony issued £100,000 worth of paper bills in 1733 alone), and the Boston merchants refused to honor them. The pressure for more issues continued, however, and in 1739 a group of Massachusetts merchants formed a *private* land bank, which was authorized by the

General Court to issue £150,000 worth of bills at 3 percent interest. Many members of the business community were greatly alarmed at this, especially since repayment was allowed in commodities of uncertain value, and they formed in opposition to the land bank what was called a silver bank, which would issue notes redeemable in silver, not commodities. The two groups fought bitterly, and in the end the governor and council declared the land bank's bills invalid, although £50,000 had already been placed in circulation. The leading land bankers organized public protests, which became riotous. There were arrests and jailings, and in the end the British government adopted repressive measures. In 1741 the so-called Bubble Act was extended to the colonies, which outlawed all joint-stock companies not authorized by Parliament (in effect outlawing all private banks). Years of litigation followed in Massachusetts as creditors who had already accepted payment in the

COLONIAL PAPER MONEY
The Massachusetts paper penny bears the signature of Thomas Hutchinson, the future loyalist governor, then a member of a committee in charge of issuing bills of credit. The issue of 1750 was a victory for Hutchinson's hard money policy. Based on £180,000 of silver that Parliament sent in repayment of wartime expenses, it replaced all of the colony's inflated currency in circulation. (*American Antiquarian Society*)

bank's bills demanded repayment in valid money. It was the worst upheaval in the Bay Colony between the establishment of the Dominion of New England in the 1680s and the early years of the Revolution. Samuel Adams's father was one of the local officials removed from office for continuing to support the land bank.

But the more traditional *public* land banks continued to exist, and the value of their issues continued to fluctuate. In Massachusetts, paper was discounted from par at a ratio of 9 to 1. In Rhode Island, nine issues of paper were in circulation in 1750, representing a par value of £465,000, and in addition there was £60,000 worth of bills of credit legally available. But by then more comprehensive legislation was being drafted. In 1751 Parliament passed the Currency Act, directed to the New England colonies alone. By its terms, no new land banks could be created in New England; no paper money could

thereafter be made full legal tender; all bills were to be retired on the strict schedule of the original legislation; and bills could be issued to pay for government expenses only if provision were made for their redemption by taxes within two years.

Though the Currency Act applied only to New England, it constituted a warning and threat to all the colonial governments against allowing any looseness in the management of paper money. Orders went out from London severely restricting the use of this currency in all the colonies, though it had become an essential part of the American economy and though those responsible for the paper issues were by no means wildcat inflationists. Every knowledgeable merchant knew the value of sound paper money, and many, like Franklin, correctly saw that its controlled expansion could be a stimulus to the entire economy. In this case also, as in the prohibitive taxation of the trade with the foreign West Indies and in the restriction of American manufactures, the action of the British government was seen to be not merely unfairly competitive but hostile. The action seemed arbitrary and unreasonable—an imposition that called into question the grounds of loyalty. To obey such laws as these was a form of humiliation exacted by a government that seemed distant, alienated from the people it governed and unresponsive to their needs.

The American

The antagonisms between Britain and the colonies that resulted from their uneasy collaboration in wartime and the resentments created by Britain's seemingly arbitrary and hostile legislation were problems largely of policy and management. Potentially, at least, they were within the realm of political control. A deeper and less manageable source of distance and alienation between Britain and America lay in the area of cultural perceptions—the sense Americans had of who they were in relation to the other peoples of the world, of what their life was like, and who, in contrast, the British were within the same set of considerations. These attitudes and perceptions are facts which in the end are as important as battles and laws and political campaigns, although they are more difficult to establish, to measure, and to describe.

Through the two generations of growth and expansion that preceded the accession of George III, Americans had gradually acquired a sense of themselves as a separate people—separate not in law or politics or constitution, but in character and culture. It was a complex image, composed of many strands, and it could be seen as positive or negative depending on the context or point of view. It was an image of a simple, rustic, innocent, uncorrupted, and unsophisticated people, an appropriate self-image for a colonial people, perhaps, but no simple reflection of reality. For it was, first, a compound of several intellectual traditions and influences; it was, in addition, a reflection of the ideas and attitudes of Europe's enlightened thinkers; and it was, finally, a product of certain specific political ideas of great potential power.

In its origins this image can be traced back to the ambiguous picture that Europeans formed of the American Indians soon after their first contact with the Western Hemisphere, a picture compounding simplicity and savagery, vigor and barbarism, innocence and paganism. By the eighteenth century this mingled image in the case of British North America came to be applied as much to the Creoles—that is, natives of European descent—as to the Indians, whom the English had long since come to think of as unredeemably savage, if not satanic. This transfer of traits from the natives to the European colonists was facilitated by the common belief that the colonists had deliberately copied certain practices and skills from the Indians and as a result had acquired from them certain peculiar characteristics. Infants strapped to boards, for example, were thought to develop like Indians whatever their race or culture; American women, like Indians, were believed to be taller than European women and to suffer fewer miscarriages. This notion was reinforced by the "scientific" arguments of the environmentalists, an influential group of continental European thinkers who believed that life in all its forms was determined by the material conditions in which it was lived. It seemed reasonable to believe, from this point of view, that what

had long been true of the Indians in the great American laboratory of nature would eventually, if it did not already, apply to the colonists too.

But more practical and immediate influences were also at work detailing the Americans' simplicity, innocence, and rusticity. The image of the American colonists—their own view of themselves as well as the view that others had of them—was shaped too by the recruiting propaganda that had circulated throughout Europe and America for over a century. All of these publications, from the advertisements of the Virginia Company to the publications of the German "newlanders" operating along the Rhine and the pamphlets distributed in Ireland by American land speculators, stressed the idyllic wonders of a simple, loosely institutionalized, benign society where land was free, where government scarcely existed, and where religion was practiced in absolutely uncontested freedom.

Perhaps the greatest influence of all in propagating the image of British America as a land of simple, innocent, independent, and virtuous folk was the widespread knowledge of the kinds of people who had in fact gone there—self-respecting servants, ambitious artisans, sturdy yeoman, Puritans—and above all, and most sensationally, Quakers. The symbolic importance of the Quakers to the world at large was overwhelming. In the seventeenth century they had been thought of principally as exotic radicals. They were famous throughout Britain and France for their fanatical independence of mind and their absolute refusal to respect mere earthly authorities (hence their practice of addressing people of all ranks with the familiar "thee" and "thou"). In the more tolerant atmosphere of the early eighteenth century their reputation had shifted from that of defiant and fanatical seekers of religious freedom to that of genial advocates of pacifism, toleration, simplicity in religion, and ordinary human rights in the face of aristocratic and authoritarian power. It was this cluster of traits that attracted Voltaire to them during his stay in England (1726–29) and that led him to praise them extravagantly again and again. For this powerful figure of the European Enlightenment, the Quakers as a group were the embodiments of civic virtue; and the essence of their virtues, he believed,

THE EUROPEAN IMAGE OF AMERICA: VOLTAIRE ON PENNSYLVANIA AND THE QUAKERS.
Voltaire's account of Anglo-American life, which first appeared in English translation in 1733, was published in France in 1734 as *Lettres Philosophiques* and promptly condemned to be burnt by the hangman as "likely to inspire a license of thought most dangerous to religion and civil order." The book nevertheless circulated widely. This passage on Penn as a great lawgiver, on Pennsylvania as a utopia, and on the Quakers as humble people of civic virtue and peace was taken over almost verbatim into the great French *Encyclopédie* (1751–1780), the massive summary of European liberal thought, and hence entered the mainstream of the Enlightenment. *(Reproduced by permission of Houghton Library, Harvard University)*

could be seen in Pennsylvania, where all their dreams and the dreams of all mankind, he thought, had reached fulfillment. Here, Voltaire wrote, an enlightened republican lawgiver had created a human paradise. Philadelphia, he wrote in one of his *Philosphical Letters* (1734), was so prosperous that people flocked to it from all over the continent; Penn's laws were so wise that no one of them had ever been changed; the Indians had been won over to friendship; there was equality and religious freedom without priests; and there was peace everywhere. "William Penn might glory," he wrote, "in having brought down upon the earth the so much boasted golden age, which in all probability never existed but in Pennsylvania."

The world, it seemed, agreed. Montesquieu, perhaps the most widely respected and influential political analyst of the age, called Penn the greatest lawgiver since classical antiquity. The monumental French *Encyclopédie* of enlightened ideas included Penn among the cultural heroes of Europe. And in addition to all of this, every informed person in the Western world knew something about Pennsylvania, and about America in general, through the extraordinary figure of Benjamin Franklin.

BENJAMIN FRANKLIN, BY ROBERT FEKE, AND "POOR RICHARD'S ALMANAC"

The portrait was painted about the time of Franklin's retirement from business. Thirty years later Franklin's image was completely transformed (see p. 166). *(Left, Fogg Art Museum, Harvard University; below, The Historical Society of Pennsylvania)*

Poor Richard, 1733.

AN

Almanack

For the Year of Chrift

1733,

eing the Firft after LEAP YEAR:

And makes fince the Creation	Years
By the Account of the Eaftern *Greeks*	7241
By the Latin Church, when ☉ ent. ♈	6932
By the Computation of *W. W.*	5742
By the *Roman* Chronology	5682
By the *Jewifh* Rabbies	5494

Wherein is contained

he Lunations, Eclipfes, Judgment of the Weather, Spring Tides, Planets Motions & mutual Afpects, Sun and Moon's Rifing and Setting, Length of Days, Time of High Water, Fairs, Courts, and obfervable Days.

itted to the Latitude of Forty Degrees, and a Meridian of Five Hours Weft from *London,* but may without fenfible Error, ferve all the adjacent Places, even from *Newfoundland* to *South-Carolina.*

y RICHARD SAUNDERS, Philom.

PHILADELPHIA:

inted and fold by *B. FRANKLIN,* at the New Printing Office near the Market.

The Third Impreffion.

Franklin and the Image of America. Franklin, the most famous American of the eighteenth century and one of the most famous and influential Americans who has ever lived, was born in Boston in 1706, the son of a candle and soap maker. At the age of seventeen he ran away to Philadelphia, where he eventually prospered as a printer and an organizer of printing establishments in several colonies. At the age of forty-two he retired from business to devote himself to public causes, to writing, and to scientific experimentation. He corresponded with English scientists and intellectuals, particularly Peter Collinson, a Quaker merchant and a member of the Royal Society, on the problems of electricity, and it was in the form of letters to Collinson that he published the results of his studies, *Experiments and Observations on Electricity* (1751). This book was one of the great sensations of the eighteenth century. It went through five editions in English, three in French, one in Italian, and one in German before 1800, and it elevated Franklin to the highest ranks of Western thinkers. Buffon, the greatest French naturalist of the age, himself arranged for the French edition; the encyclopedist Diderot declared Franklin to be the very model of the modern experimental scientist.

And who was Franklin? A simple, unsophisticated product of the primitive society of British North America—yet he had outdone the most sophisticated intellectuals of Europe in their own field of endeavor. The implications were sensational. In the context of the great wave of reform thinking that is called the Enlightenment, Franklin's mere existence as a successful intellectual conveyed a powerful message. It reinforced the arguments of reformers everywhere and demonstrated conclusively the validity of their challenge to the establishment.

Though Enlightenment thought was complicated in its details, in its essence it was clear and simple. At its heart lay discontent with the condition of life as it was known and a general approach to improvement. All enlightened thinkers in one way or another pictured human nature as good, or if not good, then at least capable of great improvement and of far greater happiness than was commonly experienced.

The evils of the world that reduced people to misery were seen mainly as artifacts—constructions of men and women themselves. To Voltaire, the chief evils were the great public institutions, especially the church and a corrupt and dogmatic priesthood. To the physiocrats, the French economic reformers who believed that agriculture alone produced wealth, the great evil was the irrational constraints on agricultural production and marketing; to Locke, it was the arbitrary, authoritarian state; to Rousseau, it was civilization itself. For all, the cruelties and miseries of life were products of constructions that people themselves had made, and the solution was the reform of these structures so that human nature would be released to attain the happiness of which it was capable.

But there were powerful counter-arguments. These great imposing institutions—the state, the church, the regulated economy, and the social structures that gave power to a hereditary aristocracy—were, after all, the guardians of social order and stability; they were also the carriers of high culture and the sponsors of the finest human achievements. To eliminate them or change them radically might create not freedom but anarchy, not a higher civilization but barbarism. What was needed by all the enlightened thinkers was an example, not of thuggish primitivism but of civilized simplicity—a Christian society free from the encumbrances of rigid and powerful institutions, a society in which reason had been used in fashioning public institutions and in which, despite the simplicity of life, high culture was maintained and advanced. In British North America generally, in Pennsylvania more specifically, and above all in the figure of Franklin—apparently an untutored genius, a simple and unaffected but accomplished virtuoso of science, letters, and statecraft—they had the example they wanted. If Franklin had never existed it would have been necessary for the philosophers of the Enlightenment to invent him—a fact which Franklin understood perfectly, which he shrewdly played upon, and which he expressed most clearly in the *Autobiography* that he wrote in the later years of his life.

FRANKLIN, THE ENLIGHTENMENT'S PHILOSOPHER

Top, a painting by John Trumbull. It expresses perfectly the image Franklin had projected to the enlightened world ever since the publication of his experiments. *Bottom,* the popularization of Franklin's image. A box cover, probably of the 19th century, showing the great triumvirate of the Enlightenment—"The Light of the Universe" —Voltaire, Rousseau, and Franklin. *(Top, Yale University Art Gallery; bottom, The Metropolitan Museum of Art, Gift of William H. Huntington, 1883)*

To much of the Western world, Franklin *was* America; he was the American incarnate. Caught up in the imagery of simplicity and natural gifts demanded by Enlightenment aspirations, he demonstrated the meaning of the New World to the Old, and thereby helped shape Americans' self-awareness as well as Europe's perception of the provincial society beyond the sea.

America and the Grounds of Political Freedom.   Inevitably Franklin played on the theme of the social and moral grounds of political freedom, for it was in this area that American self-imagery came into its sharpest focus and acquired its greatest relevance for the affairs of the everyday world. It was universally believed that in the end the success of Britain's celebrated constitution, or of any constitution that protected the people's liberties, depended on the virtue of the political population. To maintain the balance of forces in government that prevented the misuse of power required eternal vigilance. Freedom from oppression rested on the ability of the people to resist the encroachments of a priviliged and arrogant aristocracy and on the capacity of the aristocracy to resist the corruptions of profit and power and to continue to use its privileges for the good of the whole. If the people's will to protect their own liberties weakened, or if Britain's aristocracy succumbed to sloth and self-indulgence as had the aristocracies of continental Europe, freedom would be destroyed by the predictable encroachments of arbitrary power.

The signs, for Americans of the late provincial period, were worrisome. Repeatedly they found reason to question the moral qualities of English society, to doubt the independence of "the democracy" in Britain and the impartiality and responsibility of the British aristocracy. American visitors to England sent back disturbing reports. John Dickinson of Pennsylvania, in England in the election year 1754, wrote home that he was "filled with awe and reverence" by his contact with scenes of ancient greatness and by the sophistication and variety of life in London. But he was shocked too by the corruption of English politics. Over £1 million, he reported to his father, was spent in efforts to manipulate the election.

WATCH PAPERS ENGRAVED BY NATHANIEL HURD, 1762
These circular portraits were designed to fit inside the cover of a pocket watch. *(American Antiquarian Society)*

If a man cannot be brought to vote as he is desired, he is made dead drunk and kept in that state, never heard of by his family or friends till all is over and he can do no harm. The oath of their not being bribed is as strict and solemn as language can form it, but is so little regarded that few people can refrain from laughing while they take it. . . . Bribery is so common that it is thought there is not a borough in England where it is not practiced. . . . We hear every day in Westminster Hall leave moved to file information for bribery, but it is ridiculous and absurd to pretend to curb the effects of luxury and corruption in one instance or in one spot without a general reformation of manners, which everyone sees is absolutely necessary for the welfare of the kingdom. Yet Heaven knows how it can be effected. It is grown a vice here to be virtuous.

This was not simply provincial prudery. English writers too decried the loss of virtue, warning of its implications for politics, and their voices were clearly heard in America. James Burgh's *Britain's Remembrancer* (1746) denounced "our degenerate times and corrupt nation"; the British people, he said, were wallowing in "luxury and irreligion . . . venality, perjury, faction, opposition to legal authority, idleness, gluttony, drunkenness, lewdness, excessive gaming, robberies . . . a legion of furies sufficient to rend any state or empire . . . to pieces." Burgh's pamphlet was reprinted first by Franklin in 1747, then by another Philadelphia printer in 1748, and again in Boston in 1759. So too Dr. John Brown's blistering attack on English corruption, *An Estimate of the Manners and Principles of the Times* (1757), found an eager audience in America—an audience convinced of the superiority and virtue of its own uncorrupted manners and of its own moral capacity to satisfy the demands of freedom if freedom were ever challenged.

So the American people entered the age of George III. Their prospects were excellent despite the troubles that lay beneath the surface of Anglo-American life and the doubts they had of the moral quality of the British people and the responsibility of the British leaders. Conscious of their characteristics as a colonial people—provincial but vigorous, unsophisticated but uncorrupted, contentious but free, undeveloped in all the main institutions of society but more prosperous than any large population in the Western world—they saw themselves growing powerful and mature as part of an enriching imperial connection.

CHRONOLOGY

1727–60 Reign of George II.

1729 Separate royal colonies, North and South Carolina, created.

1732 Georgia established to furnish buffer against Spanish and as philanthropic effort to relocate England's paupers.

1733 Molasses Act restricts colonial importation of sugar goods from French West Indies.

1734–35 Jonathan Edwards touches off evangelical revival in Northampton, Massachusetts, and throughout Connecticut River valley.

1735 New York jury acquits John Peter Zenger of charge of seditious libel on ground that printing truth can be no libel.

1739–40 George Whitefield tours America and ignites major phase of Great Awakening.

1739–42 War of Jenkins' Ear, fought with Spain principally in Caribbean and Central America.

1740–41 Private land bank created in Massachusetts; outlawed by Parliament.

1744–48 King George's War (colonial phase of Europe's War of the Austrian Succession, 1740–48); concluded in Treaty of Aix-la-Chapelle.

1745 New England troops take fortress of Louisbourg on Cape Breton Island (returned to France at end of war).

1750 Iron Act, limiting production of finished iron goods in colonies, passed by Parliament.

1751 Currency Act, restricting issuance and currency of paper money in New England colonies, passed by Parliament.
Publication of Franklin's *Experiments and Observations on Electricity*.

1754 Albany Congress and Plan of Union.

1754–63 French and Indian War (colonial phase of Europe's Seven Years' War, 1756–63.)

1759 Quebec falls to British army.

1760 George III accedes to throne.

SUGGESTED READINGS

The eighteenth-century colonial wars were the subject of Francis Parkman's most dramatic narratives—still immensely readable—in his nine-volume series, *France and England in North America*. His *Half-Century of Conflict* (2 vols., 1892) covers King George's War, and his *Montcalm and Wolfe* (2 vols., 1884) the French and Indian War. A modern, technical, scholarly work covering the same ground in greater detail but lacking Parkman's narrative style is Lawrence H. Gipson's *British Empire before the American Revolution*, vols. VI–VIII (1946–53). Excellent also among the general works on the pre-Revolutionary military events are Stanley Pargellis, *Lord Loudoun in North*

America (1933) and John Shy, *Toward Lexington* (1965), chaps. i–iii. Howard H. Peckham, *The Colonial Wars, 1689–1762* (1964) provides a brief introduction to the whole subject.

On the three problems of Anglo-American relations discussed in the second section of the chapter, the balance of payments and commerce with the West Indies are discussed in James F. Shepherd and Gary M. Walton, *Shipping, Maritime Trade, and the Economic Development of Colonial North America* (1972), esp. App. IV; Richard B. Sheridan, "The Molasses Act and the Market Strategy of the British Sugar Planters," *Journal of Economic History*, 17 (1957), 62–83 and *Sugar and Slavery* (1974); Richard Pares, *Yankees and Creoles* (1956) and *War and Trade in the West Indies, 1739–1763* (1936); and Thomas C. Barrow, *Trade and Empire* (1967). On manufactures: Victor S. Clark, *History of Manufactures in the United States* (3 vols., 1929); Eleanor L. Lord, *Industrial Experiments in the British Colonies . . .* (1898); Curtis P. Nettels, "The Menace of Colonial Manufacturing, 1690–1720," *New England Quarterly*, 4 (1931), 230–69; Arthur C. Bining, *British Regulation of the Colonial Iron Industry* (1933); Shepherd and Walton, *Shipping* (cited above), esp. App. VI. And on the money supply and banks, see E. James Ferguson, "Currency Finance . . .," *Wm. and Mary Q.*, 10 (1953), 153–80; Theodore G. Thayer, "The Land Bank System in the American Colonies," *Journal of Economic History*, 13 (1953), 145–59; Andrew M. Davis, *Currency and Banking in . . . Massachusetts Bay* (2 vols., 1901); Richard

A. Lester, *Monetary Experiments . . .* (1939); and George A. Billias, *Massachusetts Land Bankers of 1740* (1959). For a general assessment of the importance of the colonies' trade and manufactures to Britain's economy, see Jacob M. Price, "Colonial Trade and British Economic Development, 1660–1775," *Lex et Scientia*, 14 (1978), 106–26.

On cultural relations between the colonies and Europe, see, besides the Boorstin and Savelle books cited for chapter 5, Michael Kraus, *The Atlantic Civilization: Eighteenth-Century Origins* (1949); Sacvan Berkovitch, *The Puritan Origins of the American Self* (1975); Durand Echeverria, *Mirage in the West . . . the French Image of American Society to 1815* (1957); Gilbert Chinard, "Eighteenth Century Themes on America as a Human Habitat," *Proceedings of the American Philosophical Society*, 91 (1947), 25–57; Howard M. Jones, *O Strange New World* (1964); and Bernard Bailyn, *Ideological Origins of the American Revolution* (1967), chaps. ii–iii. On Franklin's extraordinary role in cultural relations between Europe and America, see Alfred O. Aldridge, *Franklin and His French Contemporaries* (1957); Antonio Pace, *Franklin and Italy* (1958); I. Bernard Cohen's edition, *Benjamin Franklin's Experiments* (1941) and his *Franklin and Newton* (1956); and Charles C. Sellers, *Benjamin Franklin in Portraiture* (1962). The full standard biography is Carl Van Doren, *Benjamin Franklin* (1938); a shorter but well-rounded account is Verner W. Crane, *Benjamin Franklin and a Rising People* (1954).

PART TWO

Gordon S. Wood

Framing the Republic

1760–1820

*T*he American Revolution is the single most important event in American history. Not only did it create the United States, but it defined most of the persistent values and aspirations of the American people. The noblest ideals of Americans—the commitments to freedom, equality, constitutionalism, and the well-being of ordinary people—were first defined in the Revolutionary era. The Revolution gave Americans the belief that they were a people with a special destiny to lead the world toward liberty. The Revolution, in short, gave birth to whatever ideology Americans have had. The United States was the first nation in the modern world to make political and social principles the foundation of its existence. A society composed of so many different races and peoples from so many different places could not be a nation in any traditional sense of the term. It was the Revolutionary experience and the ideals and beliefs flowing from it that have held Americans together and made them think of themselves as a single people.

The origins of such a momentous event necessarily lay deep in America's past. A century and a half of dynamic developments in the British continental colonies of the New World had fundamentally transformed inherited European institutions and customary patterns of life and had created the basis for a new society. Suddenly in the 1760s Great Britain thrust its imperial power into this changing world with a thoroughness that had not been felt in a century, and precipitated a crisis within the loosely organized empire. American resistance turned into rebellion; but as the colonists groped to make sense of the peculiarities of their society this rebellion became a justification and idealization of American life as it had gradually and unintentionally developed over the previous century and a half. In this sense, as John Adams later said, "The Revolution was effected before the war commenced." It was a change "in the minds and hearts of the people."

But this change was not the whole American Revolution. The Revolution was also part of the great transforming process that carried America into modernity. Despite the corrosive and disruptive effects of the wilderness that by 1760 had fundamentally altered the institutions and lives of the American colonists, mid-eighteenth-century society still retained, along with powdered

Overleaf: "Globe Village" by Francis Alexander c. 1882. (Courtesy of the Jacob Edwards Library, Southbridge, Massachusetts)

wigs and knee breeches, many traditional habits of behavior and social relationships that separated it from the more fluid, bustling, individualistic world of the early nineteenth century. Although by 1760 much had changed, more remained to be changed.

The Revolution released and intensified forces that, by the early years of the nineteenth century, helped create in America a society unlike any that had existed before, a society almost as different from America in 1760 as colonial America had been from eighteenth-century England. This complicated Revolution developed through several phases. Although its origins went back to the seventeenth-century settlements and its consequences are with Americans still, the Revolution can be essentially encompassed between 1760 and 1820. Some Americans thought the Revolution was over in 1776 with the Declaration of Independence and the creation of new state governments. Others, however, believed the Revolution ended only with the reconstruction of the national government in 1787; and still others thought it was not finished until the new central government was infused with strength and energy in the 1790s. Yet many other Americans saw these later centralizing developments as a repudiation of the original Revolution and thus sought to recover the spirit of 1776. For them the election of Thomas Jefferson as president of the United States in 1800 was the real fulfillment of the Revolution, a fulfillment that required ratification by another war against Great Britain in 1812.

By the end of that second war against Britain, the central impulses of the Revolution had run their course. At last the future and stability of the Republic seemed secure. Democracy and equality were no longer issues to be debated; they had become articles of faith to be fulfilled. The ideological antagonisms that the Revolution had aroused had finally petered out. In place of a collection of little more than 2 million monarchial subjects huddled along the Atlantic coast, America by 1820 had become a huge, expansive nation of nearly 10 million republican citizens, active, energetic, and filled with the sense of great possibilities that lay before them.

CHAPTER 7

Sources of the Revolution

In 1763 Great Britain straddled the world with the greatest and the richest empire since the fall of Rome. From India to the Mississippi its arms had been victorious. The Peace of Paris that concluded the Seven Years' War gave Britain unrivaled dominance over the northern and eastern half of North America. From the defeated powers, France and Spain, Britain acquired huge chunks of territory in the New World—all of Canada, East and West Florida, and millions of fertile acres between the Appalachians and the Mississippi. Since Spain received the territory of Louisiana from France in compensation for losing the Floridas, France, Britain's most fearsome enemy, was removed altogether from the North American continent.

Yet at the moment of Britain's ascendancy there were powerful forces at work that would soon, almost overnight, change everything. In the aftermath of the Seven Years' War British officials found themselves having to make long-postponed decisions concerning the colonies that set in motion a train of events that ultimately shattered the empire.

The Changing Empire

Since the formation of the empire in the late seventeenth century, there always had been some royal officials and bureaucrats interested in reforming the awkwardly imposed imperial structure and in expanding royal authority over the colonists. But most of their schemes had been thwarted by English ministries more concerned with the patronage of English politics than with colonial reform. These ministers were anxious to keep disruptive colonial issues out of Parliament, where they might be readily exploited by opposition politicians. Under such circumstances, the empire had been allowed to grow haphazardly without much control from London. People from all countries had been encouraged to settle in the colonies, and land had been freely dispensed.

Although few imperial officials had ever doubted that the empire was supposed to be a hierarchical structure and that the colonies were inferior to and dependent upon the mother country, in fact it had

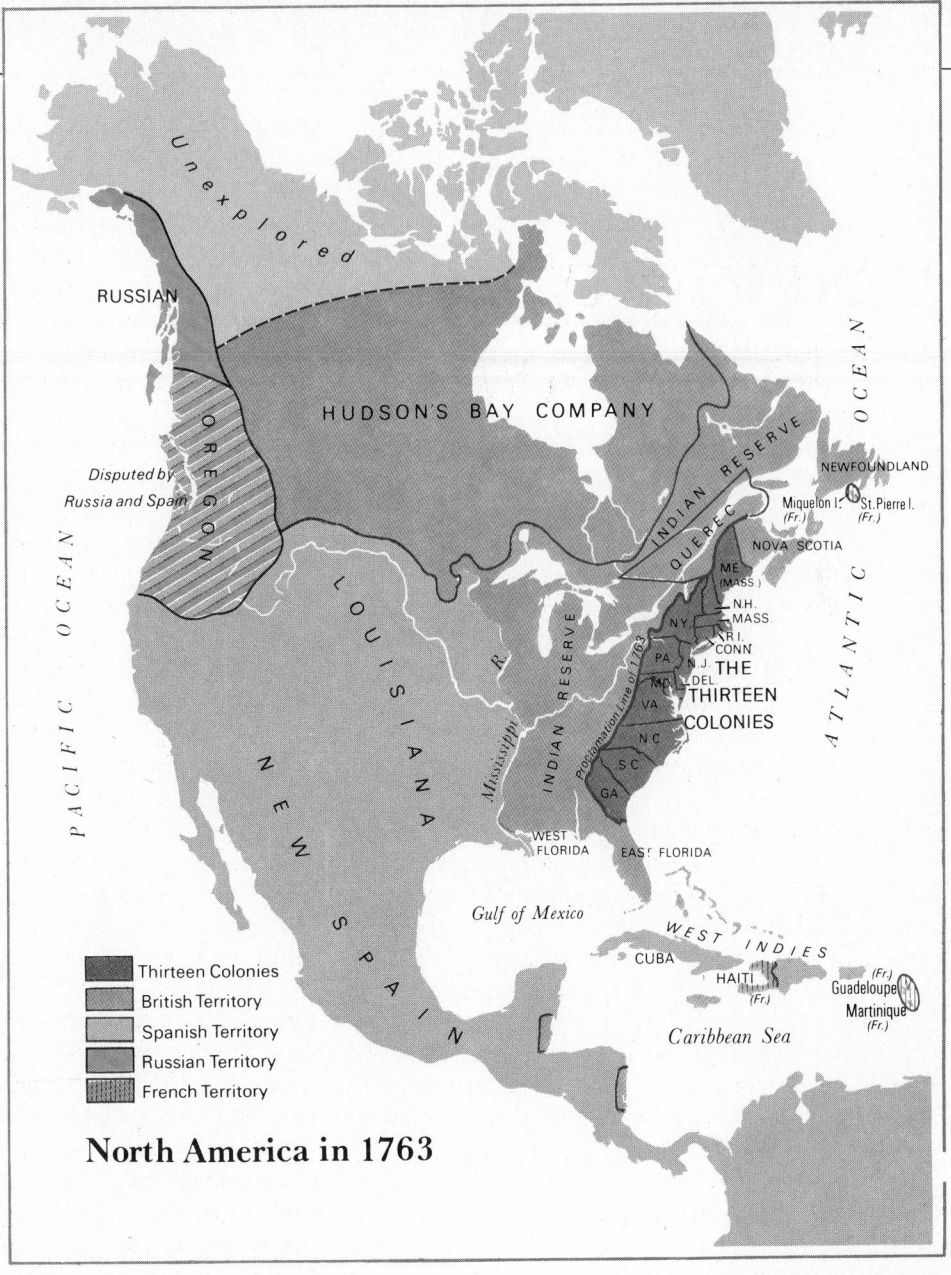

North America in 1763

Legend:
- Thirteen Colonies
- British Territory
- Spanish Territory
- Russian Territory
- French Territory

not worked that way. The relationship that had developed was based on the irrationalities and inefficiencies of the imperial system—on the variety of offices, the diffusion of power, and the laxity of organization. Even in the regulation of trade, which was the empire's main business, the inefficiency, the loopholes, and the numerous opportunities for corruption prevented the imperial authority that did exist from interfering substantially with the colonists' pursuit of their own economic and social interests.

By the middle of the century, however, new circumstances began compelling changes in this irrational but working relationship. The British colonies —there were twenty-two of them in the Western Hemisphere in 1760—were becoming too important to be treated as casually as the mother country had treated them in the first half of the century. Dynamic developments throughout the greater British world demanded that the mother country pay more attention to her North American colonies.

Population Growth and Movement. The most basic of these developments was the growth and movement of people. Throughout the whole English-speaking world—in the home islands and colonies alike—the population in the middle decades of the eighteenth century was increasing at unprecedented rates and redistributing itself in massive movements of people. From virtual stagnation during the first half of the eighteenth century, England's population in the 1740s suddenly began to increase. The populations of Ireland and Scotland had been moving steadily upward since the beginning of the century. That of the North American colonies was growing even faster—virtually exploding—and had been doing so since the beginning of the settlements. Indeed, the colonists continued to multiply more rapidly than any people in the Western world. Between 1750 and 1770 they doubled in numbers, from a million to over 2 million, and thereby became an even more important part of the British world. In 1700 the American population had been only one-twentieth of the British and Irish combined; by 1770 it was nearly one-fifth, and such far-sighted colonists as Benjamin Franklin were predicting that sooner or later the center of the British empire would shift to America.

Everywhere the burgeoning British population was in motion, moving from village to village and from continent to continent. In Britain in a matter of decades, growing numbers of migrants created the new industrial cities of Birmingham, Manchester, and Leeds, and made London the largest urban center in the Western world. Many continued to move from the British Isles across the Atlantic to the New World. The migration of Protestant Irish and Scots that had begun early in the century increased after the French and Indian War. Between 1764 and 1776, 125,000 people left the home islands for the American colonies. From the colonial port towns, particularly Philadelphia, these British migrants together with Germans from the Rhine Valley joined with increasing numbers of uprooted colonists to move through a variety of routes over half a continent.

For nearly a century and a half the colonists had been confined to a several-hundred-mile-wide strip along the Atlantic coast. Now in the middle decades of the eighteenth century they began to feel the pressures from the increasing density of population. Over-cultivated soil in the East was becoming depleted. The number of tenants, particularly in the Chesapeake areas, was visibly growing. Older towns, especially in New England, now seemed crowded, and young men coming of age could no longer count on obtaining parcels of land as their fathers had done. Throughout the colonies more and more people were on the move, many drifting into the small colonial cities that were ill-equipped to handle them. By 1772 in Philadelphia the percentage of poor was eight times greater than it had been twenty years earlier, and almshouses were being constructed and filled as never before. Most of these transient poor, however, saw cities like Philadelphia only as way stations in their endless search for land on which they might re-create the stability they had been forced to abandon.

Now that the French had been conquered, people eager to take advantage of the newly acquired land in the interior set out in all directions. In 1759 speculators and settlers moved into the area around Lake Champlain and westward along the Mohawk into central New York. Between 1749 and 1771 New York's population grew from 73,348 to 168,007. Tens of thousands of colonists and new immigrants pushed into western Pennsylvania and south into the Carolinas along routes on each side of Virginia's Blue Ridge. Along these roads strings of towns—from York, Pennsylvania, to Camden, South Carolina—quickly developed to service the travelers and to distribute produce to distant markets. The growth of settlement was phenomenal. In Pennsylvania twenty-nine new localities were created between 1756 and 1765—more in these few years than in the entire previous history of the colony. North Carolina increased its population sixfold between 1750 and 1775 to become the fourth largest colony.

New frontiers appeared everywhere simultaneously throughout British North America. By the early 1760s hunters and explorers like Daniel Boone began

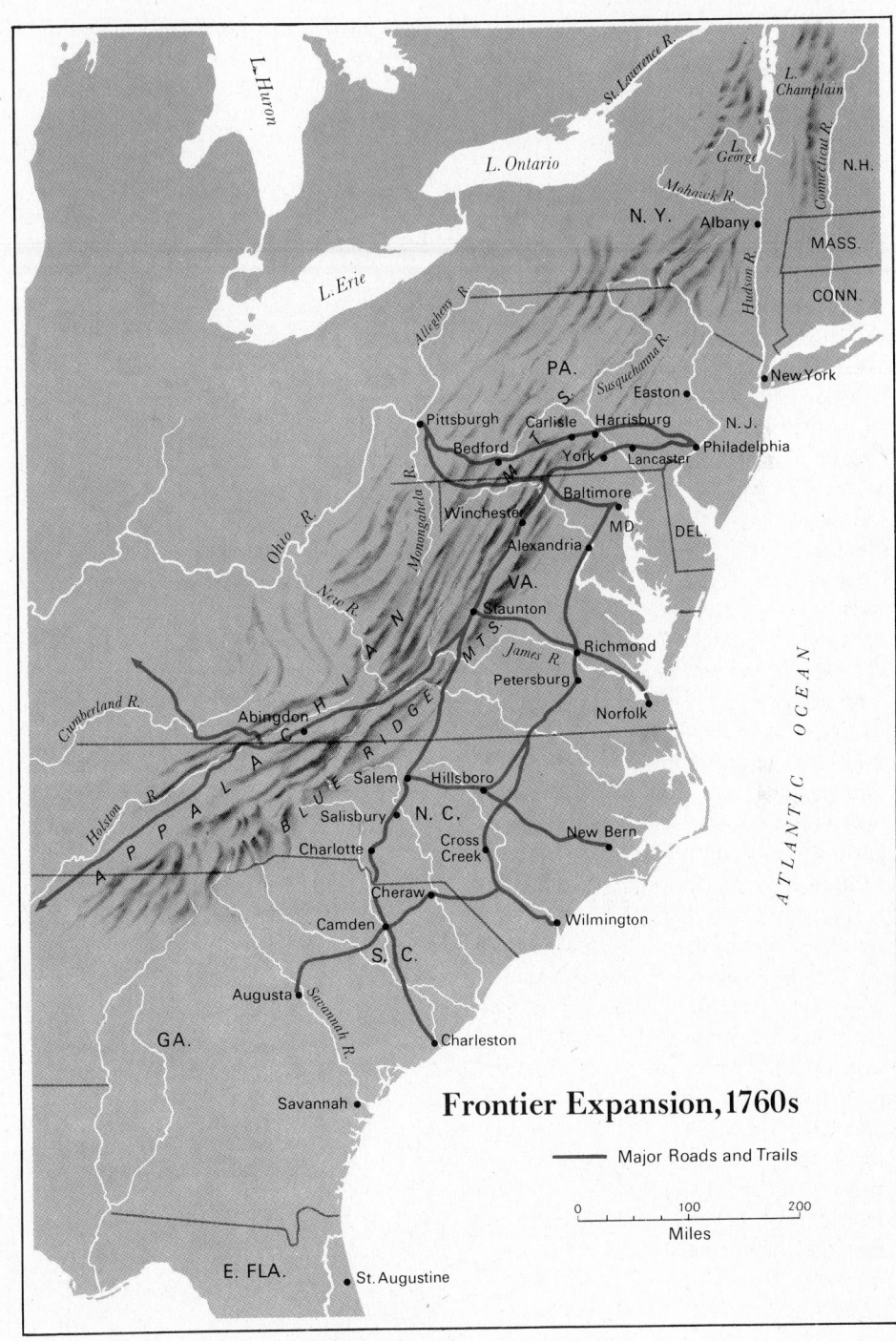

Frontier Expansion, 1760s

—— Major Roads and Trails

0   100   200
Miles

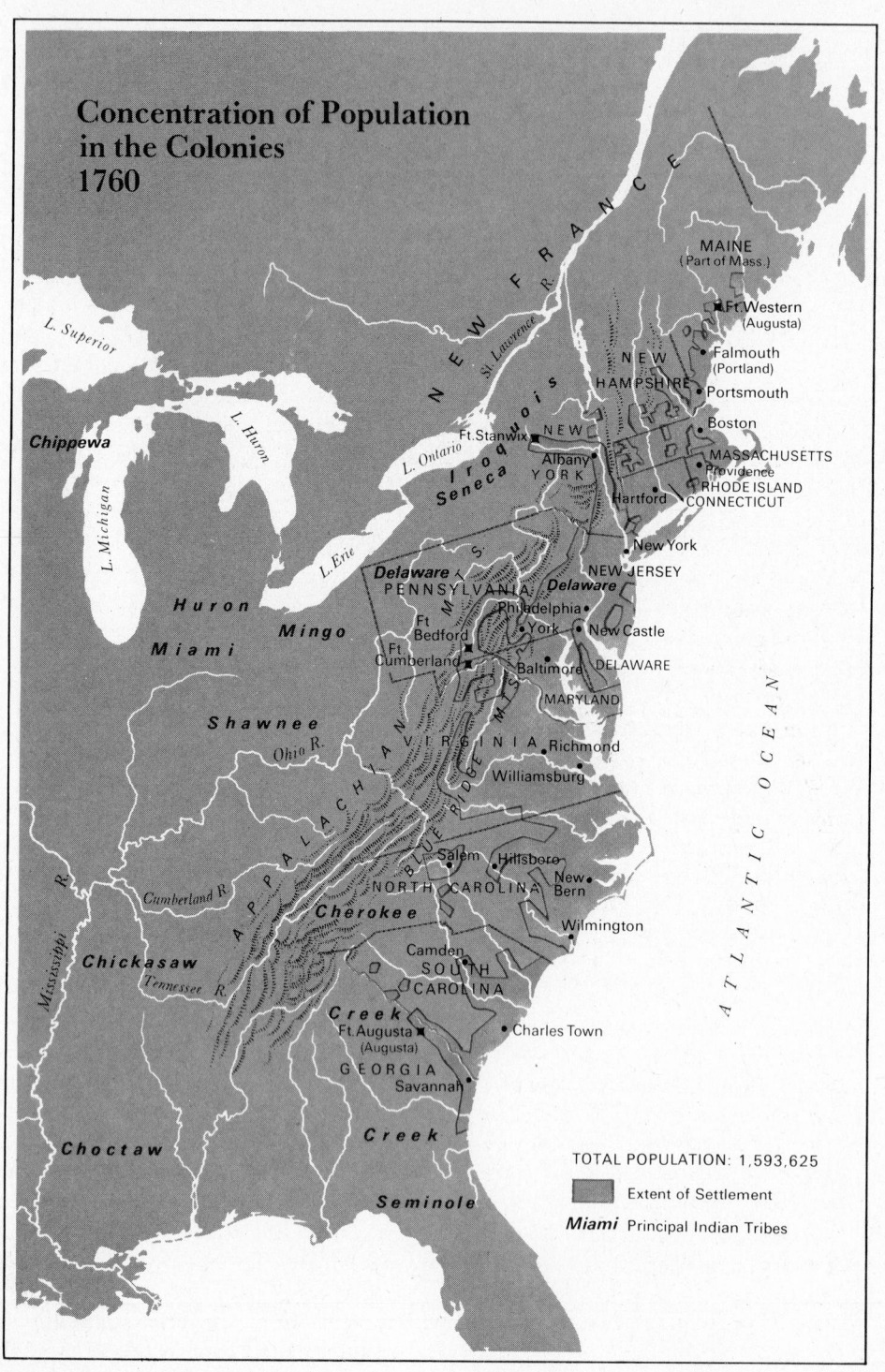

Concentration of Population in the Colonies 1760

L. Superior

L. Huron

L. Michigan

L. Erie

L. Ontario

Chippewa

NEW FRANCE

St. Lawrence R.

MAINE
(Part of Mass.)

Ft. Western
(Augusta)

Falmouth
(Portland)

Portsmouth

NEW HAMPSHIRE

Ft. Stanwix

Iroquois

Seneca

NEW YORK

Albany

Boston

MASSACHUSETTS

Providence

RHODE ISLAND

Hartford

CONNECTICUT

New York

Huron

Mingo

Miami

Delaware

PENNSYLVANIA

NEW JERSEY

Delaware

Philadelphia

New Castle

Ft. Bedford

York

Ft. Cumberland

Baltimore

DELAWARE

MARYLAND

Shawnee

Ohio R.

VIRGINIA

Richmond

Williamsburg

Cumberland R.

APPALACHIAN

BLUE RIDGE

Salem

Hillsboro

New Bern

NORTH CAROLINA

Cherokee

Wilmington

Chickasaw

Tennessee R.

Mississippi R.

Camden

SOUTH CAROLINA

Creek

Ft. Augusta
(Augusta)

Charles Town

GEORGIA

Savannah

Choctaw

Creek

Seminole

ATLANTIC OCEAN

TOTAL POPULATION: 1,593,625

Extent of Settlement

Miami Principal Indian Tribes

opening up paths westward through the Appalachians. Settlers, mostly small farmers, soon followed. Some moved southward to the valley of the Holston and the headwaters of the Cumberland and Tennessee rivers, and others spread northwest into the Ohio Valley and Kentucky basin. Some drifted down the Ohio and Mississippi rivers to join overland migrants from the southern colonies in the new province of West Florida, and thus completed a huge encirclement of the new western territory.

During the decade and a half before Independence, New England throbbed with movement. New towns were created by the founding of new settlements and the division of existing ones. By the early 1760s the number of transients drifting from town to town throughout the region multiplied dramatically, in some counties doubling and more than tripling the numbers of the previous decade. Many farmers gave up searching for opportunities within established communities and set out for distant places on the very edges of the expanded empire. Massachusetts and Connecticut colonists not only trekked to northern New England and Nova Scotia but traveled to areas as far away as the Susquehanna in Pennsylvania and the lower Mississippi. Indeed, the largest single addition to the population of West Florida came from the settlement of four hundred families from Connecticut in 1773–74. In the late 1760s the migration to the Wyoming Valley in Pennsylvania of people from Connecticut was so massive that in 1774 Connecticut annexed these Pennsylvania settlements and made them part of one of its counties. Between 1760 and 1776 some twenty thousand people from southern New England moved up the Connecticut River into New Hampshire and what would later become Vermont. In that same period migrants from Massachusetts streamed into Maine and founded 94 towns. In all, during the years between 1760 and 1776, 264 new towns were established in northern New England.

So momentous was this explosion of peoples in search of land that British and colonial authorities could scarcely comprehend what was happening. The colonists, one astonished official observed, were moving "as their avidity and restlessness incite them. They acquire no attachment to place: but wandering about seems engrafted in their nature; and it is a weakness incident to it that they should forever imagine the lands further off are still better than those upon which they are already settled." Land fever infected all levels of the society. While someone like Ezra Stiles, minister at Newport, Rhode Island, and later president of Yale, bought and sold small shares in places all over New England and in Pennsylvania and New York, more influential figures like Benjamin Franklin were concocting gargantuan speculative schemes in the vast unsettled terrain of the West.

All of this movement had far-reaching effects on American society and its place in the British empire. The fragmentation of households, churches, and communities increased, and the colonial governments lost control of mushrooming new settlements. In the backcountry, lawlessness and vagrancy became more common, and disputes over land claims and colonial boundaries increased sharply. But the most immediate effect of this rapid spread of people, and the most obvious to imperial officials in the 1760s, was the pressure the migrations placed on the Indians.

Indians. At the beginning of the Seven Years' War the problems of the Indians in the West compelled the British crown for the first time to assume direct control of Indian affairs from the colonies. Two British Indian superintendents, one each for the northern and southern regions, now had the task of pacifying tribes of Indians who were, as one superintendent said, "the most formidable of any uncivilized body of people in the world." New England had few Indians left, but New York had 2,000 warriors, mostly fierce Senecas, remaining from the once powerful Six Nations of the Iroquois. In the Susquehanna and Ohio valleys were a variety of tribes, mostly Delawares, Shawnees, Mingos, and Hurons, who claimed about 12,000 fighting men. On the southern frontiers the Indian presence was even more forbidding. From the Carolinas to the Yazoo River were some 14,000 warriors, mainly Cherokees, Creeks, Choctaws, and Chickasaws. Altogether this native population formed an imposing barrier to British western expansion.

After French authority had been eliminated from

INDIANS

The story of Indian-white relations in North America is a tragic one. Already by the middle of the eighteenth century many of the Indian tribes had become dependent on the white man's goods, including tools, weapons, and liquor. Thus not only were the Indians losing their lands to the whites but they were inadvertently collaborating in the corruption and destruction of their culture. *Top*: "Cherokee Indians brought to London, 1730" by Alexander Cuming; *center*, Choctaw burials, (*both, Smithsonian Institution, National Anthropological Archives*); *right*, "Outewas Indian, 1759," by George Townshend (*National Portrait Gallery, London*)

Canada and Spanish authority from Florida, the Indians were no longer able to play one European power off against the other. Britain now had sole responsibility for regulating the lucrative fur trade and for maintaining peace between whites and Indians. The problems were awesome: not only were many whites prepared to use brandy and rum to achieve their aims, but they had conflicting interests. Traders competed among themselves: some favored regulation of the fur trade; most did not. But all traders wanted Indian reservations established in the West which settlers could not invade, and they drew upon the support of humanitarian groups concerned with the fate of the Indians. Land speculators, however, wanted to push back the Indians and open the West to settlement. Confused, lied to, and cheated of their land and their furs by greedy white traders and land-hungry migrants, the Indians retaliated with atrocities and raids. Some tribes attempted to form coalitions and wage full-scale war.

Thus the end of the Seven Years' War did not end violence on the frontier. From the devastating Cherokee War in 1759–61 in South Carolina to the assault on the Shawnees in 1774 by Lord Dunmore, the royal governor of Virginia, British officials repeatedly had to resort to troops to put down the Indians' resentment at white encroachments on their lands and the deceitful practices of the traders. The biggest Indian uprising of the period occurred in 1763 following the British takeover of the former French forts in the West. In just a few weeks Indians from several tribes under the leadership of an Ottawa chief named Pontiac surprised and destroyed all but three of the British posts west of the Appalachians. Before they were defeated by British troops, the angry warriors had penetrated eastward into the backcountry of Pennsylvania, Maryland, and Virginia and had killed more than two thousand colonists. No wonder then that many royal authorities in the 1760s concluded that only the presence of regular troops of the British army could maintain peace in the American borderlands of the empire.

Backcountry Disorder. The rapid growth and spread of peoples in the mid-eighteenth century affected more than white-Indian relations on the frontier.

Thousands of migrants flowed into the backcountry beyond the reach of the colonial governments. So removed from authority were the settlers that sometimes only vigilante groups were able to impose order. In South Carolina in the 1760s, backcountry people organized vigilante "Regulators" to put down roving gangs of thieves, but these illegal posses often turned raiders themselves. By the early 1770s the Green Mountain Boys of Vermont under the leadership of Ethan Allen and his brother were terrorizing all who submitted to New York's jurisdiction, and Connecticut Yankees were fighting Pennsylvanians for control of the settlements along the Susquehanna River. Sometimes out of necessity frontiersmen in these trans-Appalachian areas joined to form compacts of government for their raw societies, which often consisted of little more than "stations" or primitive palisaded forts surrounded by huts.

Everywhere in the backcountries the rapid influx of people weakened the legitimacy of existing authority. In the rapidly growing interiors of both Pennsylvania and North Carolina, settlers in the 1760s rose in arms against what they believed was exploitation by remote eastern governments. In western Pennsylvania, Scotch-Irish settlers led by the Paxton Boys rebelled against their underrepresentation in the pacifist, Quaker-dominated legislature. In 1763–64, they killed Indians who were under the government's protection, and then marched on Philadelphia. Only the diplomacy of Benjamin Franklin and the promise of a greater voice in the colonial assembly turned the rebels back. In North Carolina not only was the backcountry underrepresented in the provincial legislature but its local government was under the corrupt management of carpetbagging officials and lawyers from the east. In 1767 a group of western vigilantes, assuming the familiar title of "Regulators," erupted in violence, took over the county courts, and petitioned the North Carolina government for more equitable representation, lower taxes, and local control of their affairs. Although at the so-called battle of the Alamance in 1771 two thousand of these "Regulators" were dispersed by the North Carolina governor and his force of eastern militia, the deeply rooted fears among many Americans of the dangers of inequitable representation and remotely wielded political power

ACONOSTOTA (CUNNE SHOTE) (?–1785)
Cherokee Indian chief who repaid white treachery in South Carolina with his own. In 1760 he led Cherokee warriors against Carolina frontier settlements and massacred the defenders of Fort Loudoun. During the Revolution he fought for the British.   (*The Thomas Gilcrease Institute of American History & Art, Tulsa, Oklahoma*)

JOSEPH BRANT (1742–1807)
This chief of the Mohawks was educated by English Indian Superintendent Sir William Johnson, sent to London, and presented to the Court. He fought effectively on the British side during the Revolution. As an Anglican convert he translated the New Testament and the Prayer Book into his native tongue.

could not be so easily dispelled by royal officials. Indeed, these Westerners were only voicing toward their own colonial governments the same attitudes Americans in general had about British power.

Economic Expansion.   All of these consequences flowing from the increased numbers and movement of people in North America were bound to heighten Britain's interest in its colonies. But not merely demographic forces were at work reshaping British attitudes toward the colonies and transforming American society. Equally important was the related expansion of the Anglo-American economy that took place in the middle decades of the eighteenth century.

By 1750 the immediate origins of what would soon become the Industrial Revolution were already visible in Britain. British imports, exports, and industrial production of various sorts—all the major indicators of economic growth—were rapidly rising. Americans were deeply involved in this sudden economic expansion of the mother country, and by the 1760s were feeling its reverberating effects everywhere.

In the years after 1745 colonial trade with Great Britain grew dramatically and became an increasingly important segment of the English and Scottish economies. Nearly half of all English shipping was engaged in American commerce. The North American mainland alone was absorbing 25 percent of England's exports, and Scottish commercial involvement with the colonies was growing even faster. From 1747 to 1765 the value of colonial exports to Britain doubled, from about £700,000 to £1,500,000, while the value of colonial imports from Britain rose even faster, from about £900,000 to over £2 million. For the first time in the eighteenth century Britain's own production of foodstuffs could not meet the needs of its suddenly rising population; by 1760 Britain was importing more grain than it exported.

This increasing demand for foodstuffs—not only in Great Britain but in southern Europe and the West Indies as well—meant soaring prices for American exports. Between the 1740s and the 1760s the price of American wheat sent to the Caribbean increased nearly 60 percent, flour 54 percent, pork 48 percent. Even tobacco prices went up 34 percent in the same period. This heightened demand and rising prices for American exports enticed more and more ordinary farmers into producing for distant markets. By the 1760s remote trading centers in the hinterland such as Staunton, Virginia, and Salisbury, North Carolina, were shipping large quantities of tobacco and grain eastward along networks of roads and towns to the sea. Port cities like Baltimore, Norfolk, and Alexandria grew up almost overnight to handle this swelling traffic.

These soaring prices for agricultural exports meant rising standards of living for more and more Americans. It was not just the great planters of the South and the big merchants of the cities who were getting richer, but ordinary Americans too were now buying luxury items—what were increasingly called "conveniences" that had traditionally been purchased only by the gentry—from Irish linen and lace to matched sets of Wedgwood dishes.

Although nineteen out of twenty Americans were still engaged in agriculture, the rising levels of taste and consumption drew more colonists into manufacturing, at first mostly crude textiles and shoes. Transportation and communications rapidly improved as roads were built and regular schedules were established for stage coaches and packet boats. In the 1750s the post office under the leadership of Benjamin Franklin, the British deputy postmaster general, cre-

ated weekly mails between Philadelphia and Boston and cut the delivery time in half, from six to three weeks. The growing population, better roads, more reliable information about markets, and the greater variety of towns, all encouraged domestic manufacturing for regional and intercolonial markets. By 1768 colonial manufacturers were supplying Pennsylvania with eight thousand pairs of shoes a year. Areas of eastern Massachusetts were becoming more involved in manufacturing: in 1767 the town of Haverhill, with fewer than three hundred residents, had forty-four workshops and nineteen mills. By this date many colonial artisans and would-be manufacturers were more than eager to support associations to boycott English imports.

But most colonists still preferred British goods. Since by the mid-1760s Americans were importing from Britain about £500,000 worth of goods more than they were exporting to the mother country, the trade deficit with Britain that had existed earlier in the century continued to vex the colonists. Part of this deficit in the colonists' balance of payments with Britain was made up by the profits of shipping, by British wartime expenditures, and by increased sales to Europe and the West Indies. But a large part was also made up by liberal extensions to the colonists of English and Scottish credit. By 1760 colonial debts to Britain amounted to £2 million; by 1772 they had jumped to over £4 million. After 1750 a growing proportion of this debt was owed by colonists who earlier had been excluded from direct dealings with British merchants. Small tobacco farmers in the Chesapeake gained immediate access to British credit and markets through the spread of Scottish factors or stores in the hinterlands of Virginia and Maryland. By 1760 it was not unusual for as many as 150 petty traders in a single port to be doing business with a London merchant house.

These demographic and economic forces had a corrosive effect on the traditional structure of colonial society. The ties of kinship and patronage that held people together, never strong in America to begin with, were now further weakened. Even in Virginia, one of the most stable of the colonies, the leading gentry planters found their authority challenged by

"ATTEMPT TO LAND A BISHOP IN AMERICA"

By 1768 proposals for establishing an Anglican bishop in America had become identified with British efforts to deprive the colonists of their liberties.

small farmers cut loose from older dependent economic relationships. During the middle decades of the eighteenth century, ordinary people of Virginia left the established Church of England in growing numbers and formed new evangelical religious communities that rejected the high style and luxury of the dominant Anglican gentry. Within a few years,

succeeding waves of enthusiastic New Light Presbyterians, Separate Baptists, and finally Methodists swept up new converts from among the common farmers of the Chesapeake. Between 1769 and 1774 the number of Baptist churches in Virginia increased from seven to fifty-four.

The Virginia gentry blamed this growth of religious dissent on the long-existing laxity of the Anglican clergy, who in turn accused the lay vestries of Anglican planters of not supporting them. Amid these mutual recriminations, the Virginia House of Burgesses passed acts in 1755 and 1758 that fixed the standard of value of tobacco used to meet debts and public obligations at two pence a pound. Since tobacco prices were rising rapidly, this legislation, known as the "Two Penny Acts," penalized creditors and those public officials like the clergy who were used to being paid in tobacco. British merchants and the Virginia clerical establishment protested and were able to get the king's Privy Council to invalidate the act of 1758 passed by the House of Burgesses. In 1763 in one of the Virginia clergy's legal suits for recovery of wages lost by the Two Penny Act, known as the Parsons' Cause, a rising young lawyer, Patrick Henry, first made his reputation. Henry argued that, because he had disallowed the act, the king "from being the father of his people [has] degenerated into a Tyrant, and forfeits all rights to his subjects' obedience." In similar ways in all the colonies authority, both local and imperial, was being placed under increased pressure.

It is doubtful whether anyone anywhere in the mid-eighteenth century knew how to control these powerful social and economic forces at work in the Anglo-American world. Certainly the flimsy administrative arrangement that governed the British empire was unable to manage this dynamic world. By mid-century many British officials realized that some sort of overhaul of this increasingly important empire was needed. But few understood the explosive energy and the sensitive nature of the people they were tampering with. The empire, Benjamin Franklin warned, was like a fragile Chinese vase that required delicate handling indeed.

The Reorganization of the Empire

After 1748 imperial reforms of one sort or another were in the air. The eye-opening experience of fighting the Seven Years' War amid colonial evasion and corruption of the navigation laws had provoked Pitt and other royal officials into strenuous but piecemeal reforms of the imperial system. But these beginnings might have been stifled, as others had been, if it had not been for the enormous problems created by the Peace of Paris in 1763.

The most immediate of these problems was the disposition of the new territory acquired from France and Spain. New governments had to be organized; the Indian trade had to be regulated; land claims had to be sorted out; and something had to be done to keep the conflicts between land-hungry white settlers and the restless Indians from exploding into open warfare.

Even more unsettling was the huge expense confronting the British government. By 1763 the war debt totaled £137 million; its annual interest alone was £5 million, a huge figure when compared with an ordinary yearly British peacetime budget of only £8 million. There was, moreover, little prospect of military costs declining. Since the new acquisitions were virtually uninhabited by Englishmen, the government could not rely on its traditional system of local defense and police. Lord Jeffrey Amherst, commander in chief in North America, estimated that he would need ten thousand troops to maintain order among the French and Indians and to deal with squatters, smugglers, and bandits. Thus at the outset of the 1760s the British government made a crucial decision—a decision that no subsequent administration ever abandoned—to maintain a standing army in America. This peacetime army was more than double the size of the army that had existed in the colonies before the Seven Years' War, and the costs of maintaining it quickly climbed to well over £400,000 a year.

Where was the money to come from? The landed gentry in England felt pressed to the wall by taxes; a new English cider tax of 1763 actually required troops to enforce it. Under the circumstances—with the tales of American prosperity brought back by returning British troops, with the benefits of the new land and the peace apparently accruing to the colonists—it seemed reasonable to the British government to seek new sources of revenue in the colonies and to make the navigation system more efficient in ways that royal officials had long advocated. A half century of "salutary neglect" had to come to an end.

George III and British Politics. Disruptions within the delicate balance of the empire were therefore inevitable. But the accession in 1760 of a new monarch, the young and impetuous George III, aggravated the changing Anglo-American relations. George III was only twenty-two, shy and inexperienced in politics, but he was stubbornly determined to rule personally in a manner distinctly different from that of the earlier Hanoverian monarchs. Influenced by his inept Scottish tutor and "dearest friend," Lord Bute, George aimed to purify English public life of its corruptions and factionalism and to substitute duty to crown and country for party intrigue. The results of George's good intentions were the greatest and most bewildering fluctuations suffered by English politics in a half-century—all at the very moment the long-postponed reforms of the empire were to take place.

Historians no longer depict George III as a "tyrant" seeking to undermine the English constitution by choosing his own ministers against the wishes of Parliament. But there can be little doubt that men of the time felt that George III, whether he intended to or not, was violating the political conventions of the day. When he chose Lord Bute, his Scottish favorite who had little political strength in Parliament, to head his government and excluded such Whig ministers as William Pitt and the Duke of Newcastle, who did command political support in Parliament, the new king may not have been acting unconstitutionally, but he certainly was acting against customary political realities. Bute's retirement in 1763 did little to ease the opposition's apprehensions that the king was seeking the advice of Tory favorites "behind

GEORGE III (1783–1820)
George III had one of the longest reigns in English history. He was sincere but slow-witted, and suffered from a hereditary disease that eventually caused him spells of madness. The artist, Benjamin West, was an American who became in 1772 historical painter to the king and later president of the Royal Academy. (*The Cleveland Museum of Art, Gift of Mr. and Mrs. Lawrence S. Robbins.*)

NORTH (1732–1792)
North was the first political leader George III found who could organize a stable government. He had the political skills to manage the House of Commons but he had no knowledge of waging war. Despite his repeated talk of resigning, he lasted as prime minister from 1770 to 1782. (*Library of Congress.*)

the curtain" and attempting to impose decisions upon the leading political groups in Parliament rather than governing through them. By diligently attempting to shoulder his constitutional responsibility for governing in his own stubborn, peculiar way, George III helped to increase the political confusion of the 1760s.

A decade of short-lived ministries in the 1760s contrasted sharply with the stable and long-lasting Whig governments of the previous generation. It almost seemed as if the headstrong king trusted no one who had the support of Parliament. After Pitt and Newcastle had been dismissed, and Bute had failed, the king in 1763 turned to George Grenville, Bute's protégé, because he could find no one else acceptable to him to be his chief minister. Although Grenville was responsible for the first wave of colonial reforms, his resignation in 1765 resulted from a

personal quarrel with the king and had nothing to do with colonial policy. Next, the Whigs connected with the Marquess of Rockingham, for whom Edmund Burke was spokesman, formed a government; but this Whig coalition never had the confidence of the king, and lasted scarcely a year. In 1766 George at last called upon the aging Pitt, now Lord Chatham, to head the government, but Chatham's illness (gout in the head, critics said) and the bewildering parliamentary factionalism of the late 1760s turned the ministry into a hodgepodge, which Chatham scarcely ruled at all.

By 1767 no one seemed to be in charge. Ministers shuffled in and out of offices, exchanging positions and following their own inclinations even against the wishes of their colleagues. Amid this confusion only Charles Townsend as chancellor of the exchequer gave any direction to colonial policy, and he died in 1767. Not until the appointment of Lord North as prime minister in 1770 did George find a politician whom he trusted and who also had the support of Parliament.

Thus in 1763 the British government was faced with the need to overhaul its empire and gain revenue from its colonies at the very time when the English political situation was more chaotic and confused than it had been since the early decades of the eighteenth century. No wonder it took only a bit more than a decade for the whole shaky imperial structure to come crashing down.

The Proclamation of 1763 and the West. The government began its reform of the newly enlarged empire by issuing the Proclamation of 1763. This crown Proclamation created three new royal governments— East and West Florida and Quebec—and enlarged the province of Nova Scotia. It turned the vast trans-Appalachian area into an Indian reservation, and prohibited all private individuals from purchasing Indian lands. The aim was to maintain peace in the West and to channel the migration of peoples northward and southward into the new colonies. There, it was felt, the settlers would be in closer touch with both the mother country and the mercantile system and more useful as buffers against the Spanish and the remaining French.

But circumstances undid these royal blueprints. Not only were there bewildering shifts of the ministers in charge of the new policy, but news of Pontiac's Indian rebellion in the Ohio Valley in 1763 forced the government to rush its program into effect. The demarcation line along the Appalachians that closed the West to white settlers was hastily and crudely drawn, and some colonists suddenly found themselves living in the Indian reservation. The new trading regulations and sites were widely ignored and created more chaos in the Indian trade than had existed earlier. So confusing was the situation in the West that the British government could never convince the various contending interests that the Proclamation was anything more than, in George Washington's words, "a temporary expedient to quiet the

minds of the Indians." The unsteady British governments, beset by hosts of speculators and lobbyists, were compelled to negotiate a series of Indian treaties shifting the line of settlement westward. But each modification only whetted the appetites of the land speculators and led to some of the most grandiose land schemes in modern history. The climax of this speculative frenzy was reached in 1769 when a huge conglomerate, the Grand Ohio Company, whose membership involved prominent figures on both sides of the Atlantic, petitioned the crown for the rights to millions of acres in the Ohio Valley.

The British government finally tried to steady its dizzy western policy with parliamentary help in the Quebec Act of 1774. This act transferred the land and the control of the Indian trade in the huge area between the Ohio and Mississippi rivers to the province of Quebec and allowed its French inhabitants French law and Roman Catholicism. As enlightened as this act was toward the French Canadians, it managed to anger all American interests—speculators, settlers, and traders alike. This arbitrary alteration of provincial boundaries threatened the security of all colonial boundaries and frightened American Protestants into believing that the British government was trying to erect a hostile popish province in the North and West.

The Sugar and Stamp Acts. The new colonial trade policies were more coherent than Britain's western policy, but no less provocative. The Plantation Act, or Sugar Act, of 1764 was clearly a major successor to the great navigation acts of the late seventeenth century. It prescribed a series of regulations designed to tighten the navigation system and in particular to curb the colonists' smuggling and corruption. Absentee customs officials were ordered to their posts and given greater authority and protection. The jurisdiction of the vice-admiralty courts in customs cases was broadened. The navy was granted greater power in inspecting American ships. The use of writs of assistance (or search warrants) was enlarged. To the earlier list of enumerated colonial products like tobacco and sugar that had to be exported directly to Britain were added skins, iron, timber, and others.

A TEST IMPRESSION OF ONE OF THE STAMPS THE BRITISH
GOVERNMENT PLANNED TO USE IN THE COLONIES IN 1765.

These British reforms, which threatened to upset the delicately poised patterns of trade built up in the previous generations, could be regarded as part of Britain's traditional authority over colonial commerce. But the next step in Britain's new imperial program could not. Grenville's ministry, convinced that the customs reforms could not bring in the needed revenue, was determined to try a decidedly different method of getting at American wealth. In March 1765 Parliament by an overwhelming majority passed the Stamp Act, which levied a tax (to be paid, like all duties, in British sterling, not in colonial paper money) on legal documents, almanacs, newspapers, and nearly every form of paper used in the colonies. Although stamp duties had been used in England since 1694 and by several colonies in the 1750s, such a parliamentary tax, directly touching the everyday affairs of Americans, exposed the nature of political authority within the empire in a way no other issue in the eighteenth century ever had.

American Resistance

The atmosphere in the colonies could not have been less receptive to these initial efforts by the British government to reorganize the empire. In the early 1760s, with the curtailing of wartime spending, the commercial boom collapsed. Between 1760 and 1764 American markets were glutted with unsold goods at the same time that bumper tobacco crops (the result, in part, of new independent producers) drove tobacco prices down by 75 percent. Such developments threatened the entire credit structure, from London and Scottish merchant houses to small farmers and shopkeepers in the colonies. As a result, business failures and bankruptcies proliferated. By the middle 1760s the colonial market economy was in confusion, beset by an adverse balance of trade, severe restrictions on credit, low prices, and a shortage of currency. Aggravating the collapse was the large number of small merchants who had been enticed into participating in the market during the previous decade or so.

And finally the requirements of American shippers for posting bonds and obtaining certificates of clearance were so greatly increased that nearly all colonial merchants, even those involved only in the coastwise trade, found themselves enmeshed in a bureaucratic web of bonds, certificates, and regulations.

To these frustrating rigidities now built into the navigation system were added new customs duties, which raised the expenses of American importers in order to increase British revenue. The Sugar Act imposed duties on foreign cloth, sugar, indigo, coffee, and wine imported into the colonies and eliminated the refunds of duties hitherto made in England on foreign goods reexported to America. Most important, the Sugar Act reduced the supposedly prohibitory duty of sixpence a gallon on foreign molasses, set by the Molasses Act of 1733, to threepence a gallon; in 1766 the duty was further reduced to one penny a gallon on all molasses. The government assumed that with the smaller duty it would be cheaper for American merchants to import molasses legally than to resort to smuggling and bribery. The lower duty would therefore earn money for the crown.

It is not surprising that the victims of the collapse sought to blame their shifting fortunes on the distant government in England. In fact the British government's response to the financial crisis could not have been more clumsy and provocative. In 1764 Parliament passed a new Currency Act, which extended to all the colonies the 1751 prohibition against New England's issuing of paper money as legal tender. This sweeping and simple-minded resolution of a complicated problem was only one of the many ways in which British power in these years brought to the surface the latent antagonisms between the colonies and the mother country.

The Sugar Act, coinciding with this postwar depression, created particularly severe problems for all those who depended on trade with the French and Spanish West Indies. Paying the duty on foreign molasses, the colonists feared, would make it too expensive to import. Yet without foreign sugar products the northern rum industry would be ruined, the export trade in fish and foodstuffs to the Caribbean would be curtailed, and America's ability to pay indirectly for English imports would be endangered. These fears, together with hostility to all the new trade regulations accompanying the Sugar Act, stirred up opposition and boycotts by merchants in the northern ports and provoked the first deliberately organized intercolonial protest. The assemblies of eight colonies drew up and endorsed formal petitions pleading economic injury from the Sugar Act and sent them to royal authorities in England.

Britain's next step, however, Grenville's stamp tax of 1765, excited not a protest, but a firestorm that swept through the colonies with a force that amazed everyone. This parliamentary tax, however fiscally justifiable it may have been, posed such a distinct threat to the jurisdictions of the colonial legislatures and the liberties of the colonists that Americans could no longer contain their opposition within the traditional channels of remonstrance and lobbying.

When word reached America that Parliament had passed the Stamp Act without even considering any colonial petitions against it, the colonists reacted angrily. Merchants in the principal ports formed protest associations and pledged to stop importing British goods in order to bring economic pressure on the British government. Newspapers and pamphlets, the number and like of which had never appeared in America before, carried articles that seethed with resentment against what one New Yorker called "these designing parricides" who had "invited despotism to cross the ocean, and fix her abode in this once happy land." At hastily convened meetings of towns, counties, and legislative assemblies, the colonists' anger boiled over in fiery declarations.

This torrent of angry words could not help but bring the constitutional relationship between Britain and her colonies into question.* In the spring of 1765 the Virginia House of Burgesses adopted a series of resolves denouncing parliamentary taxation and asserting the colonists' right to be taxed only by their elected representatives. These resolves were introduced by Patrick Henry, who at age twenty-nine had just been elected to the legislature. Henry had already made a name for himself in a county court house two years earlier during the Parsons' Cause. Now in the more august setting of the House of Burgesses Henry dared to repeat his earlier challenge to crown authority by declaring that, as Caesar had his Brutus, and Charles I his Cromwell, so some American would undoubtedly stand up for his country. He was stopped by the Speaker for suggesting treason, and some of his resolves, including one proclaiming the right of Virginians to disobey any law not enacted by the Virginia assembly, were too inflammatory to be accepted by the legislature. Nevertheless, colonial newspapers printed them all as though they had been endorsed by the Virginia assembly and convinced many that Virginians had virtually asserted their legislative independence from Great Britain.

Such boldness was contagious. The Rhode Island assembly declared the Stamp Act "unconstitutional" and authorized the colony's officials to ignore it. In

*For a full discussion of the constitutional issues, see Chapter 8, pp. 203–11.

PATRICK HENRY (1736–1799)
Unlike most of the other Revolutionary leaders, Henry left almost no writings. What he did leave were vivid memories of his impassioned oratory. He introduced to the political world of the Virginia gentry the fervor and style of an evangelical preacher. (*Library of Congress*)

October 1765 thirty-seven delegates from nine colonies met in New York in the Stamp Act Congress and drew up a set of formal declarations and petitions denying Parliament's right to tax them. But remarkable as this display of colonial unity was, the Stamp Act Congress, with its opening acknowledgment of "all due Subordination to that August Body the Parliament of Great Britain," could not fully express American hostility.

Ultimately it was the eruption of violence designed to prevent the stamps from being distributed that nullified the Stamp Act in America. On August 14, 1765, a crowd destroyed the office and attacked the home of Andrew Oliver, the stamp distributor for Massachusetts. The next day Oliver promised not to enforce the Stamp Act. Twelve days later a mob gutted the home of the person who seemed to be responsible for defending the Stamp Act in Massachusetts, Oliver's brother-in-law, Lieutenant Gover-

nor Thomas Hutchinson. As news of the rioting spread to other colonies, similar violence and threats of violence spread with it. From Newport, Rhode Island, to Charleston, South Carolina, local groups organized for resistance. In many places fire and artillery companies, artisan associations, and other fraternal bodies formed the basis for these emerging local organizations, which commonly called themselves "Sons of Liberty." Led mostly by members of the middling ranks—shopkeepers, printers, master mechanics, small merchants—these Sons of Liberty burned effigies of royal officials, forced stamp agents to resign, compelled businessmen and judges to carry on without stamps, developed an intercolonial network of correspondence, and generally enforced nonimportation and managed antistamp activities throughout the colonies.

British Reactions.   In England, with the Rockingham Whigs now in charge of the ministry, the British government was prepared to retreat. Not only were the Whigs eager to disavow Grenville's policies, but they had close connections with British merchants hurt by American economic boycotts. In February 1766 Parliament repealed the Stamp Act. Yet British anger over the rioting in America and the constitutional issue raised by colonial protests forced the Rockingham Whigs to couple the repeal with a Declaratory Act stating that Parliament had the right to legislate for the colonies "in all cases whatsoever."

Despite the British government's attempt to offset its repeal of the Stamp Act by this declaration of parliamentary supremacy, after 1765 the imperial relationship and American respect for British authority—indeed, for all authority—would never again be the same. The crisis over the Stamp Act aroused and unified Americans as no previous political event ever had. It stimulated bold political and constitutional writings throughout the colonies, deepened political consciousness and participation, and produced new forms of organized popular resistance. By compelling the resignation of stamp agents and obedience to popular measures, the people, through "their riotous meetings," as Governor Horatio Sharpe of Maryland observed in 1765, "begin to think they

Thursday, *October* 31, 1765.

THE

PENNSYLVANIA JOURNAL;

AND

WEEKLY ADVERTISER.

NUMB. 1195.

EXPIRING: In Hopes of a Refurrection to LIFE again.

OPPOSITION TO THE STAMP ACT

In Philadelphia, newspaper publisher William Bradford announced the suspension of publication of his *Pennsylvania Journal,* while in Massachusetts a local stamp agent was hung in effigy to protest the new tax. (*Historical Society of Pennsylvania; The Metropolitan Museum of Art, Bequest of Charles Allen Munn, 1924*)

can by the same way of proceeding accomplish anything their leaders may tell them they ought to do."

The British government could not satisfy with mere declarations its continuing need for more revenue. Since the colonists evidently would not stomach "direct" and "internal" taxes like the stamp tax, British officials concluded that the government would have to gather revenue through the more traditional "indirect" and "external" customs duties. After all, the colonists as a result of the Sugar Act were already paying duties on molasses, wine, and several other inported products. Consequently, in 1767 Parliament led by Chancellor of the Exchequer Charles Townshend imposed new levies on glass, paint, paper, and tea imported into the colonies. Although all the new customs duties, particularly the lowered molasses

duty of 1766, began bringing in an average yearly revenue of £45,000—in contrast to only £2,000 a year collected before 1764—the yearly sums raised were scarcely a tenth of the annual cost of maintaining the army in America.

Convinced that something more drastic had to be done, the British government reorganized the executive authority of the empire. In 1767–68 the government created an American Board of Customs, located in Boston and reporting directly to the Treasury, and erected three new superior vice-admiralty courts at Boston, Philadelphia, and Charleston, besides the one already at Halifax. To cap the entire structure, in belated recognition of the importance of the colonies, it established a new secretaryship of state exclusively responsible for American affairs. At the same time, for the sake of economy, the government decided to pull back much of the army from its costly deployment in the West and to close many of the remote posts. The army was now to be stationed in the coastal cities, where, according to the new parliamentary Quartering Act of 1765, the colonists would be responsible for its housing and supply. Not only did this withdrawal of the troops eastward away from the French and Indians contribute to the chaos in the western territory, but concentrating a standing army in peacetime amid a civilian population blurred the original mission of the army in America and heightened the colonists' fears of British intentions.

By 1768 there was a new determination among royal officials to put down the unruly forces that seemed to be loose. Amid the ministerial squabbling of the late 1760s some officials were suggesting that British troops be used against American rioters. Revenue from the Townshend duties was earmarked for the salaries of royal officials in the colonies so that they would be independent of the colonial legislatures. The colonial governors were instructed to maintain tighter control of the assemblies and not to agree to acts that increased popular representation in the assemblies or the length of time the legislatures sat. Some royal officials toyed with more elaborate plans for remodeling the colonial governments, proposing that the Massachusetts charter be revoked and that the royal councils be strengthened. Some even suggested introducing a titled nobility into America to sit in the colonial upper houses.

The Townshend Crisis in America.   In the atmosphere of the late 1760s, these measures and proposals were not simply provocative; they were explosive. After the Stamp Act crisis, American sensitivities to all forms of English taxation were thoroughly aroused. With the passage of the Townshend duties, the earlier pattern of resistance reappeared and expanded. Pam-

TRADE BETWEEN THE COLONIES AND BRITAIN, 1763–1776

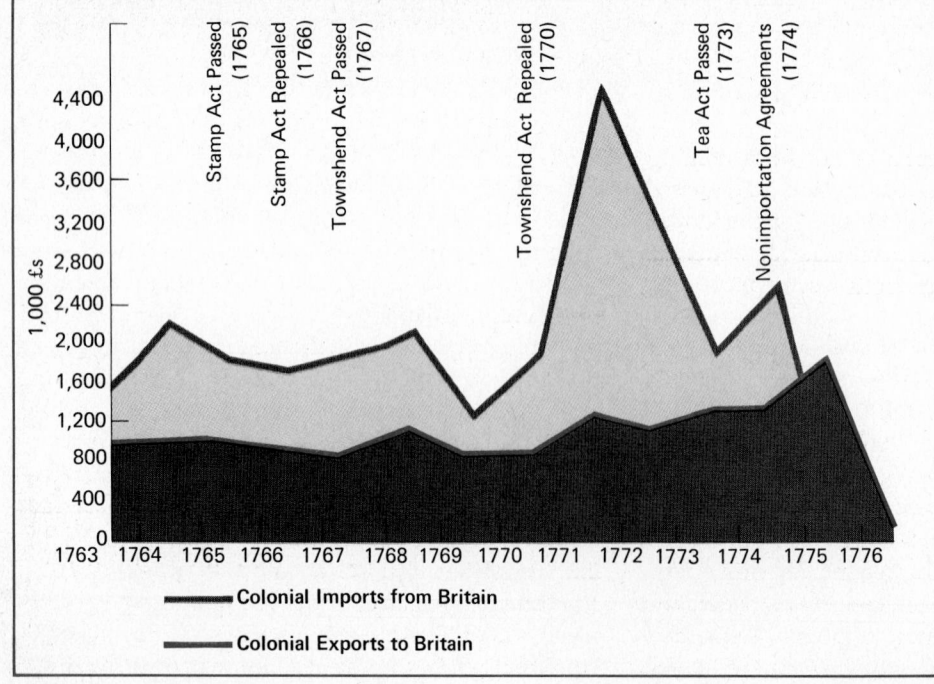

phleteers and newspaper writers again leapt to the defense of American liberties. The cultivated Philadelphia lawyer John Dickinson, in his *Letters from a Farmer in Pennsylvania*, the most popular pamphlet of the 1760s, disavowed all parliamentary taxation, whether "internal" or "external," and called for reviving the nonimportation agreements that had been so effective in the resistance to the Stamp Act. Following Boston's lead in March 1768, merchants in the colonial ports again formed associations to boycott British goods. Despite much jostling among different groups of merchants and jealousy between the ports, by 1769–70 these nonimportation agreements had cut British sales to the northern colonies by nearly two-thirds. The wearing of homespun cloth was encouraged, and in New England villages "Daughters of Liberty" held spinning bees. By now more Americans than ever were involved in the resistance movement. Extralegal groups and committees, usually but not always restrained by popular leaders, emerged to inspect tobacco in Maryland, punish importers in Philadelphia, mob a publisher in Boston, or harass customs officials in New York.

Nowhere were events more spectacular than in Massachusetts. There the situation was so inflammatory that every move triggered a string of explosions that widened the gap between the colonists and royal authority. Forty-six-year-old Samuel Adams, with his puritanical zeal, organizational skill, and abiding hatred of crown authority, soon became a dominant political figure. It was later said that 1768 was the year Adams decided on independence for America. Given the events in Massachusetts during that year, it is easy to see why.

In February 1768 the Massachusetts House of Representatives issued a "Circular Letter" to the other colonial legislatures denouncing the Townshend duties as unconstitutional violations of the principle of no taxation without representation. Lord Hillsborough, the secretary of state of the newly created American Department and a hardliner on controlling the colonies, ordered the Massachusetts House to rescind its Circular Letter. When the House defied this order by a majority of 92 to 17 (thereby enshrining the number "92" in patriot rituals), Gov-

SAMUEL ADAMS, BY JOHN SINGLETON COPLEY
Of all the American leaders, Sam Adams came closest to being a professional revolutionary, selflessly devoted to the cause. As "one of Plutarch's men," Adams took seriously the spartan severity of classical republicanism. (*Courtesy, Museum of Fine Arts, Boston*)

ernor Francis Bernard dissolved the Massachusetts assembly. With this legal means for redressing grievances silenced, mobs and other unauthorized groups in the colony erupted. Boston, which was rapidly becoming a symbol of colonial resistance, ordered its inhabitants to arm and called for an extralegal convention of town delegates. Beset by mobs, customs officials in Boston found it impossible to enforce the navigation regulations, and they pleaded for military help. When a British warship arrived at Boston in June 1768, customs officials promptly seized John Hancock's ship *Liberty* for violating the trade

"THE BOSTON MASSACRE" ENGRAVED BY PAUL REVERE

This print was scarcely an accurate depiction of the "Massacre." It aimed for rhetorical and emotional effect and became perhaps the most famous piece of antimilitary propaganda in American history. *(Library of Congress)*

acts. Since Hancock and his great wealth were prominently associated with the resistance movement, the seizure was intended to be an object lesson in royal authority. Its effect, however, was to set off one of the fiercest riots in Boston's history.

Hillsborough, believing virtual anarchy existed in Massachusetts, dispatched two regiments of troops from Ireland. They began arriving in Boston on October 1, 1768, and their appearance marked a crucial turning point in the escalating controversy: for the first time the British government had sent a substantial number of soldiers to enforce British authority in the colonies. By 1769 there were nearly four thousand armed redcoats in the crowded seaport of fifteen thousand inhabitants. Since the colonists shared traditional English fears of standing armies, relations between townspeople and soldiers deteriorated. On March 5, 1770, British troops fired upon a threatening crowd and killed five civilians. The "Boston Massacre," especially as it was depicted in Paul Revere's engraving, aroused American passions and inspired some of the most sensational rhetoric heard in the Revolutionary era.

This resort to troops to quell disorder was the ultimate symptom of the ineffectiveness of the British government's authority, and many Britishers knew it. Such coercion, it was argued in Parliament and in the administration itself, only destroyed the goodwill on which the colonists' relation to the mother country must ultimately rest. Indeed, throughout the escalation of events in the 1760s many of the ministers remained confused and uncertain. "There is the most urgent reason to do what is right, and immediately," wrote Lord Barrington, secretary at war, to Governor Bernard in 1767, "but what is that right and who is to do it?" English officials advanced and retreated, cajoled and threatened in ever-more desperate efforts to enforce British authority without aggravating the colonists' hostility. In the winter of 1767–68 the British responded to the disorder in Massachusetts with a series of parliamentary resolutions and addresses to the king, condemning Massachusetts' denial of parliamentary supremacy and threatening to bring the colonial offenders to England for trial. Yet strong minority opposition in the House of Commons and the ministry's unwillingness to precipitate further crises made these resolutions empty gestures. The government was content now to wage only what one Englishman called "a paper war with the colonies."

By the end of the 1760s British plans for reorganizing the empire were in shambles. Colonial legislatures and royal governors were at loggerheads; Britain's authority was denounced daily in print; and mobs were becoming increasingly common in the countryside as well as in city streets. Customs officials under continuous intimidation quarreled with merchants, naval officers, and royal governors.

The customs officials' entanglement in local politics made efficient or even-handed enforcement of the trade acts impossible. What enforcement there was thus appeared arbitrary and discriminatory, and drove many merchants, like the wealthy South Carolinian Henry Laurens, who had earlier been contemptuous of the Sons of Liberty, into bitter opposition.

The financial returns to the British government from the customs reforms seemed in no way commensurate with the costs. By 1770 less than £21,000 had been collected from the Townshend duties, while the loss to British business from American nonimportation movements during the previous year was put at £700,000. It was therefore not surprising that the British government now abandoned the hope of securing revenue from the duties and labeled the Townshend program, in Lord Hillsborough's words, "contrary to the true principles of commerce." In 1770, after years of ministerial chaos, reorganization of the king's government under Lord North prepared the way for repeal of the Townshend duties. Only the duty on tea was retained, in Lord North's words, "as a mark of the supremacy of Parliament, and an efficient declaration of their right to govern the colonies."

Yet the stabilization of English politics with the formation of North's ministry and the repeal of the Townshend duties could scarcely undo what had already been done. Whatever ties of affection had earlier existed between the colonists and Great Britain were fast being destroyed by irritation and suspicion. Many Americans were coming to believe that their interests and their hopes, their rights and their liberties, were threatened by British power. Although politicians on both sides of the Atlantic were by the early 1770s calling for a return to the situation before 1763, going back was clearly no longer possible.

For two years there was a superficial tranquility. Then the struggle began again. In 1772 Rhode Islanders, angry at the imperious enforcement of the navigation acts, boarded the British naval schooner *Gaspée*, sank it in Narragansett Bay, and wounded its captain. A royal commission, empowered to send all suspects to England for trial, was dispatched from England to inquire into the sinking. This authority seemed to fulfill earlier British threats to bypass regular judicial procedures, and it provoked Virginia into calling for the creation of legislative committees of correspondence, to which five assemblies responded.

Massachusetts towns, under Boston's and particularly Samuel Adams's leadership, had already begun organizing committees of correspondence. In the fall of 1772 the town of Boston published an inflammatory document, *The Votes and Proceedings* of its town meeting, which listed all the British violations of American rights. These included taxing and legislating for the colonists without their consent; introducing standing armies in peacetime; extending the powers of vice-admiralty courts, which used no jury trials; restricting colonial manufacturing; and threatening to create an Anglican episcopate in America. The publication was sent to the 260 towns of Massachusetts, and more than half responded positively in the greatest outpouring of common local opinion the resistance movement had yet seen. By the end of 1773 independence was being discussed freely in colonial newspapers. Since the North government was determined to uphold the sovereignty of Parliament, an eventual confrontation seemed unavoidable.

The Climax: The Tea Act and Coercive Acts. Parliament provided the occasion in 1773 by granting the East India Company the exclusive privilege of selling tea in America. Although the North government intended this Tea Act only to be a means of saving the East India Company from bankruptcy, it set off the final series of explosions. Not only did the act allow colonial radicals to draw attention once again to the unconstitutionality of the existing tax on tea, but it also permitted the company to grant monopolies of selling tea to particular merchants in the colonies, thus angering those traders who were excluded. An alarm was spread throughout the colonies. In several ports ships were prevented from landing the company's tea. In Boston, when that

happened, Governor Thomas Hutchinson, whose mercantile family was one of those consigned a right to sell tea, refused to allow the ships carrying tea to leave without unloading their cargo. In response, on December 16, 1773, a group of patriots disguised as Indians dumped about £10,000 worth of tea into Boston harbor. "This is the most magnificent movement of all," exulted John Adams, an aspiring young lawyer from Braintree, Massachusetts. "This destruction of the tea is so bold, so daring, so firm, intrepid and inflexible, and it must have so important consequences, and so lasting, that I can't but consider it an epocha in history."

Adams was right. To the British the Boston Tea Party was the ultimate outrage. Angry officials and much of the political nation of Great Britain clamored for a retribution that would squarely confront America with the issue of Parliament's right to legislate for the colonies. "We are now to establish our authority," Lord North told the House of Commons, "or give it up entirely." In 1774 Parliament passed a succession of laws that came to be known as the Coercive Acts. The first closed the port of Boston until the destroyed tea was paid for. The second altered the Massachusetts charter and reorganized the government: the Council was made appointive, town meetings were restricted, and the governor's power of appointing judges and sheriffs was strengthened. The third allowed royal officials charged with capital offenses in the colonies to be tried in England or another colony to avoid a hostile jury. The fourth gave the governor power to requisition private buildings instead of using barracks for the quartering of troops. At the same time, Thomas Gage, commander in chief of the British army in America, was made governor of the colony of Massachusetts.

The First Continental Congress. The Coercive Acts provoked open rebellion in America. Whatever royal authority was left in the colonies dissolved. In many areas local communities, with a freedom they had not had since the seventeenth century, attempted to put together new popular governments from the bottom up. Mass meetings that sometimes attracted thousands of aroused colonists endorsed resolutions and called for new political organizations. Committees of different names and sizes—committees of safety, of inspection, of merchants, of mechanics, of Fifty-One, of Nineteen, of Forty-Three —vied with each other for political control. In the various colonies royal government was displaced in different ways, depending on how extensive and personal previous royal authority had been. In Massachusetts, where royal authority had reached into the villages and towns through appointments of justices of the peace, the displacement was greater than in Virginia, where royal influence had scarcely touched the planters' oligarchic control of the counties. But everywhere there was a fundamental transfer of authority that opened new opportunities for new men to assert themselves.

By the end of 1774 in many of the colonies local associations were controlling and regulating various aspects of American life. Committees overawed voters, directed appointments, organized the militia, managed trade, intervened between creditors and debtors, levied taxes, issued licenses, and supervised the courts or closed them. Royal governors stood by in helpless amazement as new informal governments gradually grew up around them. These new governments ranged from town and county committees and newly created provincial congresses (which often duplicated but sometimes greatly enlarged the former assemblies) to a general congress of the colonies —the First Continental Congress—which convened in Philadelphia in September 1774.

In all, fifty-five delegates from twelve colonies (all except Georgia) participated in the First Continental Congress. Some colonists, and even some royal officials, hoped that this Congress might work to reestablish imperial authority. Those who were eager to break the bond with Great Britain, however, won the first round. Led by the cousins Samuel and John Adams from Massachusetts, and by Patrick Henry and Richard Henry Lee from Virginia, the Congress endorsed the inflammatory Resolves of Suffolk County, Massachusetts, which recommended outright resistance to the Coercive Acts. But Congress was not yet ready for independence. It came very close—failing by the vote of a single colony—to considering further and perhaps adopting a plan of union between Britain and the colonies proposed by Joseph Galloway, leader of the Pennsylvania assembly and spokesman for the conservative congressional delegates from the middle colonies. Galloway's plan was radical enough as it was; it envisioned a grand colonial council along the lines earlier proposed by the Albany Congress of 1754. Enactments by either the American grand council or the British Parliament were to be subject to mutual review and approval.

By 1774, however, too many colonists had determined that Parliament had no more right to make laws for them than it did to tax them. The Congress in its Declaration and Resolves of October 14, 1774, said as much, conceding that the colonists were willing to abide by parliamentary regulation of their external trade, but only "from the necessity of the case." By this date it was unlikely, even if the Congress had adopted Galloway's plan, that it could have reversed the transfer of authority that was taking place in the colonies. In the end, the Continental Congress simply recognized the new local authorities in American politics and gave them its blessing by adopting the Continental Association. This continentwide organization put into effect the nonimportation, nonconsumption, and nonexportation of British goods that the Congress had agreed on. Committees in all the counties, cities, and towns were now ordered by the Congress "attentively to observe the conduct of all persons," to condemn publicly all violators as "enemies of American liberty," and to "break off all dealings" with them.

With the new sanction of the Congress expressed in this Association, the local committees, speaking in the name of "the body of the people," proceeded with the political transformation taking place. Groups of men, from a few dozen to several thousand, marched through villages and city streets searching out enemies of the people. Such suspected enemies were often forced to recant unfriendly words or designs against the public, to sign confessions of guilt and penitence, and to swear new oaths of friendship to the people. In all the colonies there were signs of an emerging new political order.

WOODEN FIGURE OF "VIRTUE"
CARVED BY SIMEON SKILLIN (C. 1790)

With the creation of the United States, republican Americans replaced the image of the Indian maiden with a classical goddess, often depicted bearing a liberty cap, which since antiquity had been a symbol of men newly freed from slavery. (*Yale University Art Gallery. The Mabel Brady Garvan Collection*)

The Popularization of Politics

These remarkable political changes were not simply the product of the colonists' resistance to British imperial reform. Britain's attempts to reorganize its empire took place not in a vacuum but in complicated, highly charged situations existing in each colony. In some cases these local political conditions had as much to do with the escalation of the controversy between the colonies and the mother country as did the steps taken by the British government three thousand miles away. Everywhere in the 1760s there were colonial gentry eager to exploit popular resentment against the British reforms for local political advantage with little or no appreciation of the ultimate consequence of their actions.

Thus in New York, for example, political factions led by the well-to-do families of Livingstons and DeLanceys vied with each other in whipping up opposition to the imperial legislation, in seeking the support of extralegal popular groups like the Sons of Liberty, and in generally expanding the rights and the participation of the people in politics. They did this not with the aim of furthering electoral democracy but only for the tactical purpose of gaining control of the elective assemblies. While this sort of unplanned popularization of politics had gone on in the past, particularly in urban areas, the inflamed atmosphere that the imperial crisis generated gave it a new cutting edge with new and unpredictable implications.

In colony after colony local quarrels, often of long standing, became so entangled with imperial antagonisms that they reinforced one another in a spiraling momentum that brought into question all governmental authority. Even those authorities not directly exercised by Great Britain, such as the proprietary governments of Pennsylvania and Maryland, were victimized by the imperial crisis. Thus in Maryland in 1770, a proclamation by the proprietary governor setting the fees paid to government officials seemed to violate the principle of no taxation without representation made so vivid by the imperial debate. This executive proclamation provoked a bitter local struggle that forced Daniel Dulany, wealthy councillor and former opponent of the Stamp Act, into defending the governor. In the end the controversy destroyed the governor's capacity to rule and made Dulany a loyalist to the British cause.

By the 1770s, all these developments, without anyone's clearly intending it, were revealing a new kind of politics in America. The rhetoric of liberty now quickened long-existing popular political tendencies. Various craftsmen and religious minorities were no longer willing to have wealthy gentlemen speak for them and were demanding explicit representation of their members in political organizations. Politicians in some colonies called for a widened suffrage, the use of the ballot, legislatures opened to the public, printed legislative minutes, and recorded legislative divisions—all in an effort to enlarge the political arena and limit the power of those who clung to the traditional ways of private arrangements and personal influence. Everywhere in the colonies "incendiaries," as royal officials called them, were taking advantage of the people's resentments against the British regulations to compete for political leadership. More and more "new men" were using electioneering to short-circuit the narrow and controlled channels of politics.

Changes in Public Rhetoric. As more Americans became literate, political consciousness broadened and deepened. This development could be seen and heard in the public rhetoric. Throughout the eighteenth century and at the outset of the imperial controversy, most newspaper essays and pamphlets were written by gentlemen, and most speeches in legislative and other public bodies were spoken by gentlemen for restricted audiences of educated men like themselves. Their speeches and writings were often stylized by rhetorical rules and were usually embellished with Latin quotations and references to the literature of Western culture. The gentry's speeches and writings did not have to influence directly and simultaneously all the people but only the leaders, who in turn would bring the rest of the people with

them. By the time of the Revolution, however, this world was beginning to change.

The astonishing popularity of Patrick Henry's oratory and Thomas Paine's writing epitomized this change. Both these Revolutionary agitators emerged from obscurity in these years. Henry, although the son of a locally important planter of Hanover County, Virginia, was a failure as a planter and storekeeper. At age twenty-three he taught himself law and in the 1760s became the gentleman-spokesman for poor and middling farmers and religious dissenters of southwestern Virginia. Paine, a onetime English corsetmaker and schoolmaster and a twice-dismissed excise officer, only arrived in the colonies at the end of 1774, thirty-seven years old and filled with rage at the establishment that had pressed him down. Within little more than a year he had written *Common Sense,* the most incendiary and popular pamphlet of the entire Revolutionary era; it went through twenty-five editions in 1776 alone.

As agitators, both Henry and Paine sought to reach out to wider audiences. Like the evangelical preachers he listened to as a youth, Henry was a master of the oral culture in which most ordinary people still exclusively lived. Paine, for his part, looked for readers everywhere, but especially in the artisan- and tavern-centered worlds of the cities. Believing that existing conventions of speech and writing would not allow them to express to ordinary people new feelings of revulsion and aspiration, both men deliberately rejected the traditional methods of persuasion and thus aroused the awe and consternation of the gentlemanly elite. Both lacked formal schooling, both were accused of using ungrammatical language and coarse imagery, and both relied on their audiences knowing only one literary source, the Bible. Both Henry and Paine aimed to break through the usual niceties and forms of rhetoric; and in their public expression, they meant to declare—in the words of one contemporary, speaking of Henry—that "it was enough to feel." Fancy words, Latin quotations, and learned citations no longer mattered as much as honesty and sincerity and the natural revelation of feelings. With this change in values, new sorts of men who held at once deep animosities and high hopes for bettering the world released their passions and enthusiasms into public life.

Men who, like Thomas Hutchinson, had been reared in the old ways and benefited from them stood bewildered and helpless in the face of these popularizing developments. They possessed neither the psychological capacity nor the political sensitivity to understand, let alone to deal with, this kind of popular politics and the moral outrage and fiery zeal that lay behind it. They intrigued and schemed, and tried to manipulate those whom they thought were the important people in the opposition (in 1768, for example, offering John Adams the office of advocate-general in the Massachusetts admiralty court). And they accused those individuals of demagoguery or ridiculed them as upstarts. Frightened by the increased violence, they struck out furiously at the kinds of popular politics they believed were eroding authority and causing the violence. Such traditional and prudent men could not accept a new and different world, and after the Declaration of Independence they either fell silent or became "loyalists," determined to remain faithful to the king and support the society that had bred them.

CHRONOLOGY

1760   George III accedes to throne.

1763   Treaty of Paris ends Seven Years' War between Great Britain, and France and Spain.
Pontiac's rebellion, uprising of Indians in Ohio Valley.
Proclamation line drawn along Appalachians by British forbids settlement in West by whites.
Parsons' Cause, resulting from efforts by Anglican clergy in Virginia to recover salaries lost from Two Penny Acts.
Paxton uprising by Scotch-Irish settlers in western Pennsylvania.

1764   Sugar Act passed by Parliament, reducing duty on foreign molasses.
Currency Act prohibits issues of legal-tender currency in the colonies.
Brown University founded.

1765   Stamp Act passed.
Stamp Act Congress meets in New York.

1766   Stamp Act repealed by Parliament, which adopts Declaratory Act asserting its authority to bind the colonies "in all cases whatsoever."
Antirent riots by tenant-farmers in New York.

1767   Townshend duties passed.
American Board of Customs established.
John Dickinson's *Letters from a Farmer in Pennsylvania*.
Organization of the Regulators in backcountry of South Carolina.

1768   Secretary of State for the Colonies established in England—first executive department with exclusively colonial concerns.
Circular Letter of Massachusetts House of Representatives.
John Hancock's ship *Liberty* seized.
British troops sent to Boston.

1769   American Philosophical Society reorganized, with Benjamin Franklin as president.

1770   Lord North's ministry formed.
Townshend duties repealed, except for duty on tea.
Boston Massacre.

1771   Benjamin Franklin begins his *Autobiography*.
Battle of Alamance, North Carolina, between western Regulators and eastern militia led by the governor.

1772   British schooner *Gaspée* burned in Rhode Island.
Boston Committee of Correspondence formed.

1773   Tea Act imposed.
Boston Tea Party.

1774   Coercive Acts.
Continental Congress meets in Philadelphia.
Galloway's Plan of Union.
Continental Association.

SUGGESTED READINGS

A convenient guide to the historical literature on the American Revolution can be found in Jack P. Greene, ed., *The Reinterpretation of the American Revolution, 1763–1789* (1968). Although there are many short accounts of the Revolution, the student ought to begin with R. R. Palmer's monumental *The Age of the Democratic Revolution: A Political History of Europe and America, 1760–1800* (2 vols; 1959, 1964), which places the American Revolution in a Western perspective. Stephen G. Kurtz and James H. Hutson, eds., *Essays on the American Revolution* (1973); Alfred F. Young, ed., *The American Revolution* (1976); and the five volumes from the Library of Congress, *Symposia on the American Revolution* (1972–76) are collections of original essays on various aspects of the Revolution.

Among the early attempts to treat the coming of the Revolution from an imperial viewpoint, George Louis Beer, *British Colonial Policy, 1754–1765* (1907), is still informative. Charles M. Andrews summarized his ideas on the causes of the Revolution in *The Colonial Background of the American Revolution* (1931). The most detailed narrative of the political events leading up to the Revolution, written from an imperial perspective, is Lawrence H. Gipson, *The British Empire before the American Revolution* (15 vols., 1936–70). Gipson has summarized his point of view in *The Coming of the Revolution, 1763–1775* (1954). Merrill Jensen, *The Founding of a Nation* (1968), is the fullest single volume of the pre-Revolutionary years written from an American perspective; it is especially rich in its description of the factional struggles within the separate colonies. An ingenious but sound study that combines the views of a British and an American historian on the causes of the Revolution is Ian R. Christie and Benjamin W. Labaree, *Empire or Independence, 1760–1776* (1976).

The appropriate chapters of James A. Henretta, *The Evolution of American Society, 1700–1815* (1973), discuss American society on the eve of the Revolution. Jackson T. Main, in *The Social Structure of Revolutionary America* (1965), has attempted to describe the distribution of wealth and the nature of "classes" in American society. Carl Bridenbaugh, *Cities in Revolt* (1955), attributes the Revolutionary impulse to the cities. Gary B. Nash, *The Urban Crucible: Social Change, Political Consciousness, and the Origins of the American Revolution* (1979), stresses urban class conflict in bringing on the Revolution. The extent of westward migration is ably recounted in Jack M. Sosin, *Revolutionary Frontier, 1763–1783* (1967). Carl Bridenbaugh, *Mitre and*

Sceptre (1962), describes the growth of Anglicanism and the effort to establish an American episcopacy in the decades leading up to the Revolution. For the American reaction to these efforts, see Charles W. Akers, *Called unto Liberty: A Life of Jonathan Mayhew, 1720–1766* (1964).

The opening years of the reign of George III have been the subject of some of the most exciting historical scholarship in the twentieth century—largely the work of Sir Lewis Namier and his students. Namier and his followers have exhaustively demonstrated that George III was not seeking to destroy the British constitution, as nineteenth-century historians had argued, and that in 1760 party government with ministerial responsibility to Parliament lay very much in the future. Namier's chief works include *The Structure of Politics at the Accession of George III* (2d ed., 1957), and *England in the Age of the American Revolution* (2d ed., 1961). For detailed studies of British politics in the Revolutionary era, see P. D. G. Thomas, *British Politics and the Stamp Act Crisis* (1975); Paul Langford, *The First Rockingham Administration: 1765–1766* (1973); John Brooke, *The Chatham Administration, 1766–1768* (1956); Bernard Donoughue, *British Politics and the American Revolution: The Path to War, 1773–1775* (1964). The best biography of George III is John Brooke, *King George III* (1972). An excellent summary of British politics is George H. Guttridge, *English Whiggism and the American Revolution* (2d ed., 1963); but for a more recent study that reconciles the Whig and Namierite interpretations, see John Brewer, *Party Ideology and Popular Politics at the Accession of George III* (1976).

Other important studies of British imperial policy in the period 1760–1775 include Jack M. Sosin, *Whitehall and the Wilderness . . . 1763–1775* (1961); Michael Kammen, *A Rope of Sand: The Colonial Agents, British Politics, and the American Revolution* (1968); and Franklin B. Wickwire, *British Subministers and Colonial America, 1763–1783* (1966). On the military in America, see John Shy, *Toward Lexington: The Role of the British Army in the Coming of the American Revolution* (1965); and Neil R. Stout, *The Royal Navy in America, 1760–1775* (1973).

On American resistance, see especially Edmund S. Morgan and Helen M. Morgan, *The Stamp Act Crisis* (1953), which emphasizes the colonists' appeal to constitutional principles. Pauline Maier, *From Resistance to Revolution* (1972), stresses the limited and controlled character of American opposition. But see Dirk Hoerder, *Crowd Action* in *Revolutionary Massachusetts, 1765–1780* (1977). Oliver M. Dickerson, *The Navigation Acts and the American Revolution* (1951), argues that Americans accepted the navigation system until "customs racketeering" was introduced in the late 1760s. For a more balanced view of the navigation system, see Thomas C. Barrow, *Trade and Empire: The British Customs Service in Colonial America, 1660–1775* (1967).

On other irritants and incidents in the imperial relation, see Joseph A. Ernst, *Money and Politics in America, 1755–1775* (1973); Carl Ubbelohde, *The Vice-Admiralty Courts and the American Revolution* (1960); M. H. Smith, *The Writs of Assistance Case* (1978); Hiller Zobel, *The Boston Massacre* (1970); Benjamin W. Labaree, *The Boston Tea Party* (1964); and David Ammerman, *In the Common Cause: American Response to the Coercive Acts of 1774* (1974). Arthur M. Schlesinger, *The Colonial Merchants and the American Revolution, 1763–1776* (1918), schematically traces the responses of an important social group.

The loyalist reaction is analyzed in William H. Nelson, *The American Tory* (1961); Robert M. Calhoon, *The Loyalists in Revolutionary America: 1760–1781* (1973); and Bernard Bailyn, *The Ordeal of Thomas Hutchinson* (1974). A vitriolic account by a loyalist of the causes of the Revolution is Peter Oliver, *Origin and Progress of the American Rebellion*, ed. Douglass Adair and John A. Schutz (1961).

Among the many local studies of American resistance are Carl Becker, *The History of Political Parties in the Province of New York, 1760–1776* (1909); David S. Lovejoy, *Rhode Island Politics and the American Revolution, 1760–1776* (1958); Theodore Thayer, *Pennsylvania Politics and the Growth of Democracy, 1740–1776* (1954); Richard Ryerson, *The Revolution Is Now Begun: The Radical Committees of Philadelphia, 1765–1776* (1978); Patricia Bonomi, *A Factious People: . . . New York* (1971); Jere R. Daniel, *Experiment in Republicanism: New Hampshire Politics and the American Revolution, 1741–1794* (1970); Richard H. Brown, *Revolutionary Politics in Massachusetts* (1970); Stephen E. Patterson, *Political Parties in Revolutionary Massachusetts* (1973); and Ronald Hoffman, *A Spirit of Dissension: Economics, Politics, and the Revolution in Maryland* (1973). For biographical analyses of some of the leading Revolutionaries, see John C. Miller, *Sam Adams* (1936); Richard R. Beeman, *Patrick Henry* (1974); Merrill Peterson, *Thomas Jefferson and the New Nation* (1970); Eric Foner, *Tom Paine and Revolutionary America* (1976); Peter Shaw, *The Character of John Adams* (1976); and John R. Howe, Jr., *The Changing Political Thought of John Adams* (1966).

The Revolution: Ideology and War

Within the short span of a dozen years or so following the introduction of the imperial reforms, Americans who had celebrated the accession of George III were in open rebellion against Great Britain. The speed with which Americans moved into rebellion astonished their contemporaries, and it has astonished historians ever since. A series of trade acts and tax levies, however far-reaching in their implications, do not seem to justify revolution. Yet many Americans by 1776 agreed with John Adams that the colonists were "in the very midst of a revolution, the most complete, unexpected, and remarkable, of any in the history of nations." What accounts for this revolution? How was it justified?

It was not the particular acts of the British government in themselves but the meaning the colonists gave to those acts that explains the Revolution. From the outset of the controversy, Americans sought to understand the intentions of the British government and to determine their rights and liberties. The result was an outpouring of political writings and an interest in political ideas unequaled in the nation's history. The colonists' extraordinary efforts to discover the meaning of what was happening made the Revolution an unusually intellectual affair and ultimately gave it worldwide importance.

An Asylum for Liberty

Throughout their writings, American patriot leaders insisted they were rebelling, not against the principles of the English constitution, but on behalf of them. They invoked historic English party designations and called themselves "Whigs," and branded the supporters of the crown "Tories" in order to express their continuity with the great struggles for political liberty in seventeenth-century England. By emphasizing that it was the letter and spirit of the British constitution that justified their resistance, Americans could easily believe they were simply preserving what Englishmen had valued from time immemorial; they thereby gave a conservative coloring to their Revolution.

Yet the colonists were mistaken in believing that they were struggling only to return to the essentials

AN ENGLISH RADICAL

John Wilkes was the most popular hero of the age in the Anglo-American world. Although a gentleman himself, he came to symbolize for middling and lowly sorts of people all their pent-up hostilities toward established authority. Note the references in the engraving to the seventeenth-century libertarian philosophers, John Locke and Algernon Sidney. Silver bowl by Paul Revere (1735–1818), Boston, 1768. Note No. 45, Wilkes and Liberty engraving. (*Print: American Antiquarian Society; Bowl: Courtesy, Museum of Fine Arts, Boston*)

of the English constitution. The historical traditions of the English constitution they invoked were not the principles held by English officials in the mid-eighteenth century, but were in fact, as the Tories and royal officials tried to indicate, "revolution principles" outside the mainstream of English thought. Since the colonists seemed to be reading the same literature as other Englishmen, they were hardly aware that they were seeing the English heritage differently. Amid their breadth of reading and references, however, was a concentration on a strain of thought that ultimately implicated them in a peculiar conception of English life and in an extraordinary radical perspective on the English constitution they were so fervently defending.

The Country-Whig Tradition of Opposition. The heritage of liberal thought the colonists drew upon was composed not simply of the political treatises of notable philosophers like John Locke but also of the writings of such influential coffee-house pamphleteers as John Trenchard and Thomas Gordon. Many

of these pamphleteers were on the extreme edges of the political spectrum and wrote out of a deep and bitter hostility to the great political, social, and economic changes taking place in England during the first half of the eighteenth century. These critics thought that the general commercialization of English life, seen in the rise of the Bank of England, powerful trading companies, stock markets, and the huge public debt, was corrupting traditional values and threatening England with ruin. Believing that the crown was ultimately responsible for these changes, such writers promoted a so-called "country" opposition to the deceit and luxury of the "court" party associated with the crown. They were obsessively fearful of the capacity of executive or state power—particularly as it had operated under the ministries of Sir Robert Walpole—to corrupt Parliament and English society. Throughout the first half of the eighteenth century these defenders of political liberties made ringing proposals to reduce and control what seemed to be the enormously inflated powers of the crown in order to recover the rights of the people and the original principles of the English constitution.

Many of the reforms they proposed were ahead of their time for England—reforms that advocated the right to vote for all adult males and not just well-to-do property-holders, more liberty for the press, and greater freedom of religion. Other suggested reforms aimed at prohibiting salaried government puppets ("placemen") from sitting in the House of Commons, at reducing the public debt, and at obtaining such popular rights as equal representation for more people, the power to instruct members of Parliament, and shorter Parliaments. All of these reform proposals combined into a widely shared conception about how English life should ideally be organized. In this ideal nation, the parts of the constitution would be independent of one another, and members of Parliament would be independent of any connection or party. In other words, there would exist a political world in which no one would be controlled by anyone else.

The colonists had long felt the relevance of these "country" ideas more keenly than the English themselves. These ideas had made good sense of both the simple character of American life in contrast with a sophisticated England and of the colonists' antagonism to royal power; and during the conflicts between their assemblies and governors during the first half of the eighteenth century Americans had invoked these ideas off and on. Now, however, in the years after 1763 the need to explain the growing controversy with Britain gave this country-opposition ideology a new and comprehensive importance. It not only prepared the colonists intellectually for resistance but offered them a powerful justification of their many differences from a decayed and corrupted mother country.

A Conspiracy Against Liberty. These inherited ideas contained an elaborate set of rules for political action by the people. How were the people to identify a tyrant? How long should the people put up with abuses? How much force should be used? The answers to these questions came logically as events unfolded and led the colonists almost irresistibly from

resistance to rebellion. Step by step the colonists became convinced that the obnoxious efforts of crown officials to reform the empire were not simply the result of insensitivity to peculiar American conditions or mistakes of well-meant policy but were rather the intended consequences of grand tyrannical design. In Thomas Jefferson's words, the British reforms by 1774 were nothing less than "a deliberate systematical plan of reducing us to slavery."

America, the colonists believed, was the primary object of this tyrannical conspiracy, but the goals of this conspiracy ranged far beyond the colonies. Americans were involved not simply in a defense of their own rights but in a worldwide struggle for the salvation of liberty itself. The crucial turning point came in the late 1760s. Americans had earlier read of the prosecution of the English radical John Wilkes for criticizing His Majesty's government in his *North Briton* No. 45 and had made Wilkes and the number "45" part of their political symbolism. Then in 1768 Wilkes's four successive expulsions from the House of Commons, despite his repeated reelections by the voters of Middlesex outside London, seemed to many Americans to mark the twilight of representative government in Great Britain. Everywhere liberty seemed to be in retreat before the forces of tyranny. As Americans learned of the desperate struggles of the Sons of Liberty in Ireland and the failure of the freedom fighter Pascal Paoli to establish the independence of Corsica, they became convinced that America was the only place where a free popular press still existed, the only place where the people could still elect representatives who spoke for them and them only.

By 1776 their picture of the immensity of the struggle they were involved in was complete. And they could respond enthusiastically, as lovers of mankind and haters of tyranny, to the passionate appeal of Thomas Paine's *Common Sense* to stand forth for liberty:

Every spot of the old world is overrun with oppression. Freedom hath been hunted round the globe. Asia and Africa have long expelled her. Europe regards her like a stranger, and England hath given her warning to depart. O! receive the fugitive, and prepare in time an asylum for mankind.

THOMAS PAINE, BY JOHN WESLEY JARVIS
Paine was probably the first detached "intellectual" in
American history. He belonged to no country, lived
by his pen, and saw his role as the stimulator of revolutions. (*The National Gallery of Art, Washington, D.C.*)

The Imperial Debate

The belief that America was destined to redeem and
make free not just its own people but the entire world
helped to create a distinctive identity that is still an
important part of American awareness. Indeed, much
of what Americans believe about themselves, their
governments, and their rights and liberties derives
from the Revolutionary experience. The Revolutionary era was the most creative period in the history
of American political thought. During three decades
of intense controversy, intricate argument, and political experimentation, Americans made lasting contributions to constitutional thought everywhere. The
immediate origins of this rich intellectual achievement lay in the debate that accompanied the colonists'
rising resistance to British authority. This debate
compelled the colonists to put into words for the

first time their own peculiar political experience and
to lay the intellectual foundations for their subsequent constitution-making.

Virtual vs. Actual Representation. With the Stamp
Act, the first unmistakable tax levy by Parliament,
American intellectual resistance was immediately
elevated to the highest plane of principle. "It is insep-
arably essential to the freedom of a people, and the
undoubted rights of Englishmen," the Stamp Act
Congress declared in 1765, "that no taxes should be
imposed on them, but with their own consent, given
personally, or by their representatives." And since
"the people of these colonies are not, and from their
local circumstances, cannot be represented in the
House of Commons in Great Britain," the colonists
could only be represented and taxed by persons,
known and chosen by themselves, in their respective
legislatures. This statement defined the American
position at the outset of the controversy, and despite
subsequent confusion and stumbling this essential
point was never shaken.

Once the British ministry sensed a stirring of
colonial opposition to the Stamp Act, a group of English government pamphleteers set out to explain and
justify parliamentary taxation of the colonies. Although the arguments of these writers differed, they
all eventually agreed that the Americans, like all
Englishmen everywhere, were embraced by acts of
Parliament through a system of "virtual" representation. It was this concept of virtual representation, as
distinct from actual representation, these writers argued, that gave Parliament its supreme authority or
sovereignty. Even though the colonists, like "nine-
tenths of the people of Britain," did not in fact choose
any representative to the House of Commons, one
government pamphleteer wrote, they were undoubtedly "a part, and an important part of the Commons
of Great Britain: they are represented in Parliament
in the same manner as those inhabitants of Britain
are who have not voices in elections." During the
eighteenth century, England's electorate comprised
only a tiny proportion of its population. Since English
electoral districts were a hodgepodge left over from
centuries of history, ancient "rotten boroughs," completely depopulated by the eighteenth century, con-

tinued to send members to Parliament while newer large cities like Manchester and Birmingham sent none. What made such peculiarities intelligible to Englishmen was the assumption, classically voiced by Edmund Burke in 1774, that each member of Parliament represented the whole community, not just a particular locality. Hence representation in England was proper and effective not because of the process of election, but rather because of the mutual interests presumably shared by members of Parliament and the Englishmen for whom they spoke, including those, like the colonists, who did not actually vote for them.

The Americans immediately and emphatically rejected these British claims that they were "virtually" represented in the House of Commons in the same way that the nonvoters of cities like Manchester and Birmingham were. In the most notable colonial pamphlet written in opposition to the Stamp Act, *Considerations on the Propriety of Imposing Taxes* (1765), Daniel Dulany of Maryland conceded the relevance in England of virtual representation, but denied its applicability to America. For America, he wrote, was a distinct community from England and thus could hardly be represented by Members of Parliament with whom it had no common interests. Others pushed beyond Dulany's argument, however, and challenged the very idea of virtual representation. If the people were to be properly represented in a legislature, many colonists said, they not only had to vote directly for the members of the legislature but had to be represented by members whose numbers were proportionate to the size of the population they spoke for. What purpose is served, asked James Otis of Massachusetts in 1765, by the continual attempts of Englishmen to justify the lack of American representation in Parliament by citing the examples of Manchester and Birmingham who returned no members to the House of Commons? "If those now so considerable places are not represented, they ought to be."

In the New World, electoral districts were not the products of history going back to time immemorial but recent and regular creations related to changes in population and the formation of new towns and counties. As a consequence, many Americans had come to believe in a very different kind of representation from that of the English. Their belief in "actual" representation made election not incidental but central to representation; it stressed the closest possible connection between the local electors and the elected agent. For them it was only proper that representatives be residents of the localities they spoke for and that people of the locality have the right to instruct their representatives; and it was only fair that localities be represented in proportion to their population. In short, the American belief in actual representation pointed toward the fullest and most equal participation of the people in the process of government that the modern world had ever seen.

"THE BRUTAL TREATMENT OF JOHN MALCOMB. . . ."
This print from a London paper shows John Malcomb, commissioner of customs at Boston, being tarred and feathered in 1774 for trying to collect customs duties. Note the number "45" on the patriot's hat, a symbol of liberty since John Wilke's imprisonment for printing the *North Briton* No. 45. (*The John Carter Brown Library, Brown University*)

THE PATRIOTIC AMERICAN FARMER.

J—N D·K·NS—N, Esq; BARRISTER at LAW.

Who with Attic Eloquence, and Roman Spirit, hath af-
ferted the Liberties of the BRITISH Colonies in America.

'Tis nobly done to Stem Taxations Rage,
And raife the Thoughts of a degenerate Age,
For Happinefs and Joy, from Freedom fpring;
But Life in Bondage is a worthlefs Thing.

**JOHN DICKINSON'S
"THE PATRIOTIC AMERICAN FARMER"**

In the 1760s Dickinson was the most famous patriot-
writer in all America. But by 1776 his unwillingness
to endorse American independence diminished his reputation, which posterity has not yet restored.
(*American Antiquarian Society*)

The Problem of Sovereignty. Yet while Americans
were denying Parliament's right to tax them because
they were not represented in the House of Commons,
they knew that Parliament had exercised some authority over their affairs during the previous century,
and they groped to explain what that authority should
be. What was the "due subordination" that the Stamp
Act Congress admitted Americans owed Parliament?

Could the colonists accept parliamentary legislation
but not taxation—"external" customs duties but not
"internal" stamp taxes? In his famous *Letters from a
Pennsylvania Farmer* (1767–68), John Dickinson repudiated the idea that Parliament could rightly impose
"external" or "internal" taxes, and made clear once
and for all that the colonists opposed *all* forms of
parliamentary taxation. Dickinson recognized nevertheless that the empire required some sort of central
regulatory authority, particularly for commerce, and
conceded Parliament's superintending legislative
power so far as it preserved "the connection between
the several parts of the British empire." The empire,
it seemed to many colonists, was a unitary body for
some affairs but not for others.

To all of these halting and fumbling efforts to
divide parliamentary authority, the British offered a
simple, formidable argument. Since they could not
conceive of the empire as anything but a single,
homogeneous community, they found absurd and
meaningless all these American distinctions between
trade regulation and taxation, between "external" and
"internal" taxes, or between separate spheres of authority. If Parliament even "in one instance" was as
supreme over the colonists as over the people of England, then, wrote William Knox in a crucial ministerial pamphlet of 1769, the Americans were members
"of the same community with the people of England."
On the other hand, if Parliament's authority over the
colonists were denied "in any particular," then it
must be denied in "all instances" and the union between Great Britain and the colonies dissolved. "There
is no alternative," Knox concluded; "either the colonies are part of the community of Great Britain or
they are in a state of nature with respect to her, and
in no case can be subject to the jurisdiction of that
legislative power which represents her community,
which is the British Parliament."

What made this British argument so powerful
was its basis in the widely accepted doctrine of sovereignty—the belief that in every state there could be
only one final, indivisible, and uncontestable supreme
authority. This was the most important concept of
English political theory in the eighteenth century;
and it became the issue over which the empire was
finally broken.

This idea that every state had to have in the end one single supreme undivided authority somewhere had been the basis of the British position from the beginning. The concept of sovereignty was best expressed in the Declaratory Act of 1766, which, following the repeal of the Stamp Act, affirmed Parliament's authority to make laws binding the colonists "in all cases whatsoever." But now in the early 1770s its implications were drawn out fully. In 1773 Massachusetts Governor Thomas Hutchinson was provoked into directly challenging the radical movement and its belief in the *limited* nature of Parliament's power. In a dramatic and well-publicized speech to the Massachusetts legislature, Hutchinson attempted to clarify the central constitutional issue between America and Great Britain once and for all and to show the colonists how unreasonable their views were. "I know of no line," he declared, "that can be drawn between the supreme authority of Parliament and the total independence of the colonies, as it is impossible there should be two independent legislatures in one and the same state."

By then many Americans despaired of trying to divide what royal officials told them could not be divided. The Massachusetts House of Representatives had a simple answer to Hutchinson's position. If there were no middle ground between the supreme authority of Parliament and the total independence of the colonies from Parliament, as Governor Hutchinson said, then, the House declared, there could be no doubt that "we were thus independent." The logic of sovereignty therefore forced a fundamental shift in the American position. By 1774 the leading colonists, including Thomas Jefferson and John Adams, were arguing that sovereignty resided only in the separate American legislatures. Thus Parliament had no final authority over America, and the colonies were connected to the empire solely through the king. The most the colonists would concede was that Parliament had the right to regulate their external commerce, as the Declaration and Resolves of the First Continental Congress put it, "from the necessity of the case, and a regard to the mutual interest of both countries." But the British government remained committed to the principle of the Declaratory Act, which no leader of the Revolution could any longer take seriously.

The War for Independence

However necessary ideas were in making events meaningful and in mobilizing people into resistance and rebellion, they could not by themselves achieve independence. Once Britain determined to enforce its authority with troops, Americans had to take up arms to support their beliefs.

By the beginning of 1775, the English government was already preparing for military action. In February Lord North got Parliament to pass what he regarded as a conciliatory measure. He proposed that any colony contributing its proportionate share to the common defense would not be subject to parliamentary taxation. But since the British government did nothing to resolve the issues raised by the Coercive Acts and the declarations of the Continental Congress, the colonists regarded North's efforts at reconciliation as an insidious attempt to divide them. By this date North's supporters and the king himself saw no alternative to force in bringing the colonists back into line. George III had told North as early as November 1774, "Blows must decide whether they are to be subject to the Country or Independent." The British government thus increased the army and navy and began restraining the commerce first of New England and then of the other colonies.

In May 1775 delegates from the colonies met in Philadelphia for the Second Continental Congress to take up where the First Congress left off. Outwardly the Congress continued the policy of resolves and reconciliation. In July, at the urging of John Dickinson, Congress in an Olive Branch Petition professed loyalty to the king and humbly asked him to disavow his "artful and cruel" ministers who were blamed for the oppressive measures. At the same time, the Congress issued a "Declaration of the Causes and Necessities of Taking Up Arms" (largely the work of Dickinson and Thomas Jefferson), in which the colonies denied they had any "ambitious design of separating from Great Britain, and establishing independent states." As this superb summary of the American case against Britain demonstrated, the time for paper solutions had passed. Fighting had broken out at Lexington and Concord, Massachusetts, in April 1775, and the Second Congress now had to assume some

THE BATTLE OF CONCORD, MASSACHUSETTS

In their march to and from Concord on April 19, 1775 73 British soldiers were killed and 200 wounded out of a total force of 1800. Of the nearly 4000 colonial militia who fought sometime during the day, 49 were killed and 46 were wounded. *(State Street Trust Company)*

of the responsibilities of a central government for the colonies. It created a continental army, appointed George Washington of Virginia as commander, issued paper money for the support of the troops, and formed a committee to negotiate with foreign countries.

By the summer of 1775 the escalation of actions and reactions was out of control. On August 23, George III, ignoring the colonists' Olive Branch Petition, proclaimed the colonies in open rebellion. In October he publicly accused them of aiming at independence. By December the British government declared all American shipping liable to seizure by British warships. As early as May 1775, American forces had captured Fort Ticonderoga at the head of Lake Champlain. Out of a desire to bring the Canadians into the struggle against Britain, the Congress ordered makeshift forces under Richard Montgomery and Benedict Arnold to invade Canada. Although by the beginning of 1776 no official American body had as yet formally endorsed independence, the idea was obviously in the air. It was left to Thomas Paine to express in January 1776 in his *Common Sense* the accumulated American rage against George III, whom Paine now called the "Royal Brute." In the early spring of 1776, the Congress threw open America's ports to the world and prepared for the Declaration of Independence, which it formally approved on July 4, 1776. In this famous thirteen-hundred word document, largely written by the graceful hand of Jefferson, the king, as the only remaining link between the colonists and Great Britain, was now held accountable for every grievance suffered by Americans since 1763. The reign of George III, Americans declared "to a candid world," was "a history of repeated injuries and usurpations, all having in direct object the establishment of an absolute Tyranny over these States."*

The Declaration of Independence was not an American call to arms but a consequence of arms already taken up. For over a year, beginning with the hostilities in Massachusetts in the spring of 1775 and including the ill-fated American attack on Quebec in the winter of 1775–76, the American and British forces had been at war. It was a war that would eventually go on for nearly eight years—the longest war in American history, until that of Vietnam two centuries later.

*For the Declaration of Independence, see Appendix.

The War in the North, 1775–1776. This war for independence passed through a series of distinct phases, growing and widening until what had begun in British eyes as a breakdown in governmental authority in a section of their empire became in time a world struggle. Great Britain found itself for the first time in the eighteenth century diplomatically isolated and at one point, in 1779, even threatened with French invasion. The war for American independence thus eventually became an important episode in Britain's long struggle with France for global supremacy, a struggle that went back a century and would continue for another generation into the nineteenth century.

The British military actions of 1775 grew logically out of the coercive policies of 1774, for both rested on the assumption by the British government that Boston was the center of the disruption and needed to be isolated and punished. The British thought at first that they were dealing with mobs led by a few seditious instigators who had to be arrested and tried and

"THE DECLARATION OF INDEPENDENCE," BY JOHN TRUMBULL

The committee that drafted the Declaration of Independence included from left to right; John Adams, Roger Sherman, Robert R. Livingston, Thomas Jefferson, and Benjamin Franklin. (*Copyright Yale University Art Gallery*)

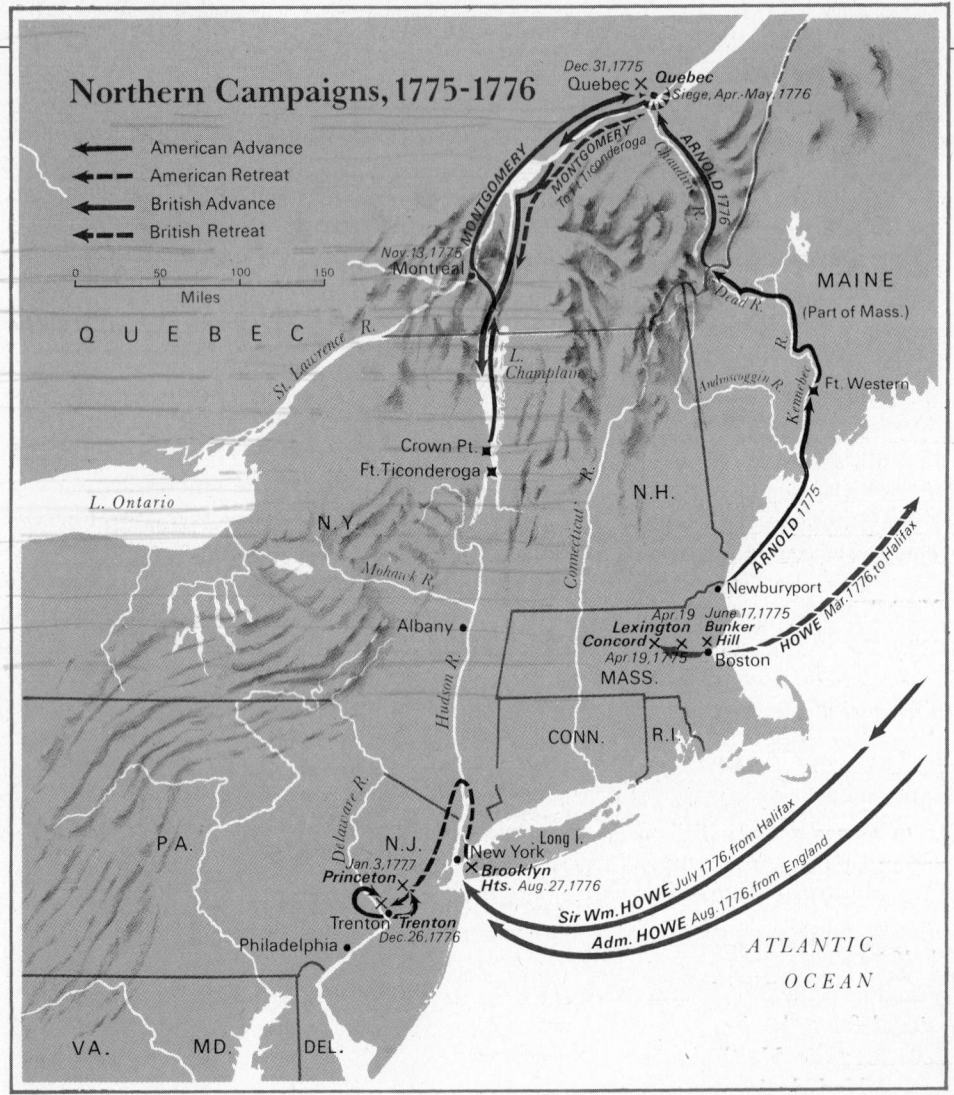

Northern Campaigns, 1775-1776

→ American Advance
⟵⟵⟵ American Retreat
→ British Advance
⟵⟵⟵ British Retreat

0   50   100   150
Miles

Dec. 31, 1775
Quebec ✕ Quebec
  ● Siege, Apr.-May, 1776

MONTGOMERY

MONTGOMERY
Tent.Ticonderoga

ARNOLD 1776

Chaudière R.

Nov. 13, 1775
Montreal ●

MAINE
(Part of Mass.)

Dead R.

St. Lawrence R.

L. Champlain

Kennebec R.

Androscoggin R.

Ft. Western

L. Ontario

Crown Pt. ■
Ft.Ticonderoga ■

N.H.

ARNOLD 1775

Connecticut R.

HOWE Mar.1776,to Halifax

N.Y.

Mohawk R.

● Newburyport

Apr. 19   June 17, 1775
Lexington   Bunker
Concord ✕ ✕ ✕ Hill
Apr.19,1775
           Boston ●

Albany ●

Hudson R.

MASS.

CONN.   R.I.

Long I.

P.A.

Delaware R.

N.J.   New York ●
Jan. 3,1777   ✕ Brooklyn
Princeton ✕   Hts. Aug.27,1776

Trenton Trenton
         Dec. 26,1776

Philadelphia ●

Sir Wm. HOWE July 1776, from Halifax
Adm. HOWE Aug.1776, from England

ATLANTIC
OCEAN

VA.   MD.   DEL.

whose bases of insurgency had to be broken up. This view of the situation led General Gage on April 19, 1775, to attempt to seize rebel munitions stored at Concord, Massachusetts. As a result the colonial militia was called out. It stopped the British at Lexington and harassed them on their march back to the besieged town of Boston. By surrounding Boston from positions in Charlestown and Dorchester Heights, the colonists raised doubts that all that was required to quell the struggle was police action.

Two months later in June 1775, British soldiers attempted to dislodge American fortifications on a spur of Bunker Hill in Charlestown overlooking Boston. Assuming, in General John Burgoyne's words, that no numbers of "untrained rabble" could ever stand up against "trained troops," the British under General William Howe attempted a series of frontal assaults on the American position that were eventually successful but only at a terrible cost of one thousand British casualties, over 40 percent of Howe's troops. In this battle at Bunker Hill—the first formal engagement of the Revolution—the British suffered their heaviest losses of the entire war. This experience convinced the British government that it was not simply a New England mob they were up against, and it swept away almost every objection among the ministers to a conquest of the colonies.

The appointment of generals by the Continental Congress, the organization of a Continental field army under George Washington in the summer of 1775, and the American expedition to Canada were evidence to the British that they were involved in a military rather than a police action, which in turn dictated a conventional eighteenth-century policy of maneuver and battle. This change of strategy required that the British evacuate Boston in favor of New York, with its presumably more sympathetic population, its superior port, and its central position. Accordingly, in the summer of 1776 Howe, who replaced Gage as commander in chief of the British army in North America, sailed into New York harbor with a force of over 30,000 men. Howe aimed to cut New England off from the other rebels and to defeat Washington's army in a decisive battle. It was a plan that Howe was to spend the next two frustrating years trying to realize.

On the face of it, a military struggle seemed to promise all the advantage to Great Britain. Britain was the most powerful nation in the world with a population of about 11 million, compared with only 2.5 million colonists. The British navy was the largest in the world, with nearly half its ships initially committed to the American struggle. The British army was a well-trained professional force, having at one point in 1778 nearly 50,000 troops in North America alone; to this force were added during the war over 30,000 hired German mercenaries. To confront this military might the Americans had to start from scratch, creating eventually a small continental army numbering at times less than 5,000 troops, supplemented by state militia units of varying sizes. The whole motley collection was led mostly by inexperienced, amateur officers. The commander in chief, Washington, for example, had been only a regimental colonel on the Virginia frontier, and had little first-hand knowledge of combat. Not surprisingly, then, most British officers thought that the Americans would be no match for His Majesty's troops. A veteran of many North American campaigns told the

GEORGE WASHINGTON, BY CHARLES WILSON PEALE

Washington's genuis lay not in his military expertise in the field but in his coolness and determination and in his extraordinary political skills. Although he lost most of his battles, he never lost the support of his officers or the Congress. (*The Brooklyn Museum, Dick S. Ramsay Fund*)

House of Commons in 1774 that with 5,000 regulars he could easily march from one end of the country to the other.

Yet such a contrast of numbers was deceptive, for the British disadvantages were immense and perhaps overwhelming, even at the beginning when their opportunities to put down the rebellion were greatest. Great Britain not only had to carry on the war three thousand miles across the Atlantic with consequent problems of communications and logistics, but also had to wage a different kind of war from any other the country had fought in the eighteenth century. A well-trained army might have been able to conquer the American forces, but, as one French officer observed at the end, America itself was unconquerable. The great breadth of territory and the wild nature of the terrain made conventional maneuverings and operations difficult and cumbersome. The fragmented and local character of authority in America inhibited decisive action by the British; there was no nerve center anywhere whose capture would destroy the rebellion. In such circumstances the prevalence of amateur militia and the weakness of America's organized army made the Americans more dangerous than if they had a trained professional army. The British never clearly understood what they were up against—a revolutionary struggle involving widespread support in the population. Hence they continually underestimated the staying power of the rebels and overestimated the strength of the loyalists. And in the end, independence came to mean more to the Americans than reconquest did to the English.

From the outset, the English objective could never be as simple and clear-cut as the Americans' desire for independence. Conquest by itself could not restore political relations and imperial harmony. Many people in England were reluctant to engage in a civil war, and several officers actually refused out of conscience to serve in America. Although the bulk of the Parliament and the English ministry were intent on subjugating America by force, the British commanders appointed in 1775, Sir William Howe and his brother Admiral Richard, Lord Howe, in charge of the navy, never shared this overriding urge for outright coercion. The brothers, particularly Lord Howe, saw themselves not simply as conquerors but also as conciliators. They interrupted their military operations with peace feelers to Washington and the Continental Congress, and they tried to avoid plundering and ravaging the American countryside and ports out of fear of destroying all hope for reconciliation. Such "a sentimental manner of waging war," as Lord George Germain, head of the American Department, called it, weakened the morale of British officers and troops and left the loyalists confused and disillusioned.

The Howes' policy was not as ineffectual initially as it later appeared. After defeating Washington at Brooklyn Heights on Long Island in August 1776 and driving him in the fall of 1776 from New York City, General Howe drove Washington into pell-mell retreat southward. Instead of pursuing Washington across the Delaware River, Howe resorted to a piecemeal occupation of New Jersey, extending his lines and deploying brigade garrisons at a half-dozen towns around the area with the aim of gradually convincing the rebels of British invincibility. Loyalist militiamen emerged from hiding and through a series of ferocious local struggles with patriot groups began to assume control of northern New Jersey. Nearly 5,000 Americans came forward to accept Howe's

RECRUITING FOR THE AMERICAN CAUSE

Privateers were privately-owned armed vessels sailing under license (letters of marque) issued by a state or by the Continental Congress. There were more than 2,000 of them during the Revolution. Enemy vessels captured by privateers became the captors' "prizes." (*American Antiquarian Society*)

The YANKEY's return from CAMP.

FATHER and I went down to camp,
    Along with Captain Gooding,
There we fee the men and boys,
    As thick as hafty pudding.
        Yankey doodle keep it up,
Chorus.   Yankey doodle, dandy,
        Mind the mufic and the ftep,
        And with the girls be handy.
And there we fee a thoufand men,
    As rich as 'Squire David ;
And what they wafted every day,
    I wifh it could be faved.
        Yankey dooole, &c.
The 'laffes they eat every day,
    Would keep a houfe a winter :
They have as much that I'll be bound
    They eat it when they're a mind to.
        Yankey doodle, &c.
And there we fee a fwamping gun,
    Large as a log of maple,
Upon a ducid little cart,
    A load for father's cattle.
        Yankey doodle, &c.
And every time they fhoot it off,
    It takes a horn of powder—
It makes a noife like father's gun,
    Only a nation louder.
        Yankey doodle, &c.
I went as nigh to one myfelf,
    As 'Siah's underpining ;
And father went as nigh again,
    I tho't the deuce was in him.
        Yankey doodle, &c.
Coufin Simon grew fo bold,
    I tho't he would have cock'd it :
It fcar'd me fo, I fhrink'd it off,
    And hung by father's pocket.
        Yankey doodle, &c.
And captain Davis had a gun,
    He kind of clapt his hand on't,

and ftuck a crooked ftabbing iron
    Upon the little end ou't.
        Yankey doodle, &c.
And there I fee a pumpkin fhell
    as big as mother's bafon,
And ev'ry time they touch'd it off,
    They fcamper'd like the nation.
        Yankey doodle, &c.
I fee a little barrel too,
    The heads were made of leather,
They knock'd upon't with little clubs,
    And call'd the folks together.
        Yankey doodle, &c.
And there was captain Wafhington,
    and gentlefolks about him,
They fay he's grown fo tarnal proud,
    He will not ride without 'em.
        Yankey doodle, &c.
He got him on his meeting clothes,
    Upon a flapping ftallion,
He fet the world along in rows,
    In hundreds and in millions.
        Yankey doodle, &c.
The flaming ribbons in their hats,
    They look'd fo taring fine, ah,
wanted pockily to get,
    To give to my Jeminah.
        Yankey doodle, &c.
I fee another fnarl of men
    a digging graves, they told me,
So tarnal long, fo tarnal deep,
    They 'tended they fhould hold me.
        Yankey doodle, &c.
It fcar'd me fo, I hook'd it off,
    Nor ftop'd, as I remember,
Nor turn'd about 'till I got home,
    Lock'd up in mother's chamber.
        Yankey doodle, &c.

(*American Antiquarian Society*)

offer of pardon and to swear loyalty to the crown. American prospects at the end of 1776 were as low as they ever would be during the war. These were, as Thomas Paine wrote, "times that try men's souls."

The Howes' policy of leniency and pacification, however, was marred by plundering by British troops and by loyalist recriminations against the rebels. But even more important in undermining the British successes of 1776 were Washington's brilliant strokes in picking off two of General Howe's extended outposts, at Trenton on December 26, 1776, and at Princeton on January 3, 1777. With these victories Washington forced the British to withdraw from the banks of the

Delaware and to leave the newly formed bands of loyalists to fend for themselves. Patriot morale soared, oaths of loyalty to the king declined, and patriot militia moved back into control of local areas vacated by the withdrawing British troops. The British again had to reconsider their plans.

Burgoyne and Saratoga, 1777.   The British strategy for 1777 involved sending an army of 8,000 under General John Burgoyne southward from Canada through Lake Champlain to recapture Fort Ticonderoga. Near Albany, Burgoyne was to join a secondary force under Lieutenant Colonel Barry St. Leger

Quebec

Ottawa R.

Q U E B E C

St. Lawrence R.

Montreal

× Ft. St. John

MAINE
(Part of Mass.)

ST. LEGER

BURGOYNE

L. Champlain

L. Ontario

NEW YORK

Ft. Ticonderoga

L. George

ST. CLAIR

N.H.

Ft. Oswego

Aug. 23
Ft. Stanwix

Saratoga
Burgoyne surrenders
Oct. 17, 1777

Manchester

STARK
Aug. 16

Newburyport

Oriskany ×
Aug. 6, 1777

Ft. Herkimer

ARNOLD

GATES

× Bennington

Albany

Connecticut R.

MASS.

Boston

Oct. 15, 1777
Kingston

Hudson R.

CONN.

R.I.

Ft. Montgomery
Oct. 6

CLINTON

PENNSYLVANIA

Susquehanna R.

Delaware R.

WASHINGTON

Jan. 3 1777
Princeton ×
Princeton

Long I.

New York

Oct. 4 1777
Germantown
Valley Forge ● ×

Trenton

N.J.

Brandywine ×
Sept. 11

Philadelphia

ATLANTIC

OCEAN

Wilmington

MARYLAND

HOWE

DEL.

HOWE *Aug. 1777*

American Advance
American Retreat
British Advance

Chesapeake
Bay

0   50   100   150
Miles

VIRGINIA

Northern Campaigns, 1777

moving eastward through the Mohawk Valley, and General Howe, advancing northward from New York City through the Hudson Valley. The ultimate aim of the campaign was to isolate New England and break the back of the rebellion. It was assumed in England that General Howe would join with Burgoyne. But Howe continued to believe that there was widespread loyalist support in the middle states and decided to

capture Philadelphia, the seat of the Continental government. He moved on Philadelphia by sea, landing after much delay at the head of Chesapeake Bay at the end of August 1777. Washington, believing he should not give up the Continental capital without a struggle, confronted Howe at Brandywine and later at Germantown and was defeated in both battles. But his defeats were not disastrous; they proved that the

American army was capable of organized combat, and they prevented Howe from moving north to help Burgoyne. Howe's capture of Philadelphia demonstrated that loyalist sentiment reached only as far as British arms, and it scarcely justified what happened to Burgoyne's army in the North.

After St. Leger's force was turned back at Oriskany, New York, in the summer of 1777, Burgoyne and his huge slow-moving entourage from Canada increasingly found their supply lines stretched thin and their flanks harassed by patriot militia from New England. While Burgoyne's slow advance gave the American forces in the Hudson Valley needed time to collect themselves, the British army was diminishing. When 900 of Burgoyne's men attempted to seize provisions from a patriot arsenal in Bennington, Vermont, they were overcome and destroyed by 2,000 New England militia under John Stark. Another 900 British redcoats were detached to garrison Ticonderoga. Burgoyne determined to press on. On September 13–14 he crossed to the west side of the Hudson, cutting off communications with his rear. When he reached Saratoga, he confronted a growing American force of over 10,000 men under General Horatio Gates. Two bloody battles convinced Burgoyne of the hopelessness of his situation, and in October 1777 he surrendered his entire army to the Americans.

Saratoga was the turning point. It suggested that reconquest of America might be beyond British strength. It brought France openly into the struggle. And it led to changes in the British command and a fundamental alteration in strategy.

From the beginning of the rebellion France had been secretly supplying money and arms to the Americans in the hope of revenging its defeat by Britain in the Seven Years' War. By 1777 French ports had been opened to American privateers, and French officers were joining Washington's army. It seemed only a matter of time before France recognized the new republic. The British ministry realized at once the significance of Burgoyne's surrender, and by appointing the Carlisle Commission early in 1778 made new efforts to negotiate a settlement. The British government now offered the rebels a return to the imperial status before 1763, indeed everything the Americans had originally wanted. These British over-

HORATIO GATES (1728–1806)
This low-born former officer in the British army was appointed Washington's adjutant-general in 1775. After his victory at Saratoga, some members of Congress and several officers, including General Thomas Conway, thought about replacing Washington with Gates. These suggestions, which became known as the "Conway Cabal," were stifled by Washington's political shrewdness. (*Library of Congress*)

tures, which Franklin skillfully used in Paris to play on French fears of an Anglo-American reconciliation, led Louis XVI's government in February 1778 to sign two treaties with the United States: one a commercial arrangement, the other a military alliance pledged to American independence. In 1779 Spain, in hopes of recovering its earlier losses from England, especially Gibraltar, became allied with France. And in 1780 Russia formed a League of Armed Neutrality to which nearly all of the maritime states of Europe eventually acceded—leaving England diplomatically isolated for the first time in the eighteenth century.

The War in the South, 1778–1781.   After 1778, putting down the rebellion became secondary to Britain's global struggle with France and Spain. The center of the war effort in America shifted seaward and southward as Britain sought to protect its stake in the West Indies. General Howe was replaced by Sir Henry Clinton, and a more ruthless policy was adopted, including the bombardment of American ports and marauding expeditions in the countryside. Philadelphia was abandoned, and the British assumed a defensive position from their northern bases in New York and Rhode Island. From its concentration in the West Indies, the British force now aimed to secure military control of ports in the American South, restore civil royal government with loyalist support, and then methodically move the army northward as a screen behind which the gradual pacification of rebel territory by local loyalists would proceed. This strategy was based on an assumption that the South, with its scattered, presumably more loyalist population living in fear of Indian raids and slave uprisings, was especially vulnerable to the reassertion of British authority.

At the end of 1778, the British captured Savannah, and on May 12, 1780, with the surrender of General Benjamin Lincoln and an American army of 5,500 men, the British took Charleston. It was the greatest American loss of soldiers in the entire war. A new, hastily assembled American southern army under General Gates—the victor of Saratoga—rashly moved into South Carolina to stop the British advance. On August 16, 1780, at Camden, South Carolina, Gates suffered a devastating defeat, which destroyed not only his new American army but his military reputation as well. But the British were not able to consolidate their gains and give the loyalists the military protection they needed to pacify the countryside. Loyalist retaliations against Whigs for past harsh treatment and British depredations, particularly those by Colonel Banastre Tarleton, drove countless Georgians and Carolinians into support of the Revolution. Irregular bands of patriots, sometimes organized under colorful leaders like Francis Marion, "the Swamp Fox," harassed the loyalists and the British army, and turned the war in the Lower South into a series of guerrilla skirmishes.

Lord Cornwallis, now in command of the British forces in the South, was impatient with the gradual policy of pacification and was eager to demonstrate British strength to the undecided by dramatically carrying the war into North Carolina. With his army constantly bedeviled by patriot guerrillas, he had just begun moving north when word of the destruction of his left flank at King's Mountain on October 7, 1780, forced him to return to South Carolina. In the meantime, the Americans had begun organizing a third southern army under the command of a thirty-eight-year-old ex-Quaker from Rhode Island, Nathanael Greene, recently quartermaster general of the Continental army. Shrewdly avoiding a direct confrontation with Cornwallis, Greene compelled the British to divide their forces. On January 17, 1781, at Cowpens in western South Carolina a detached corps of Greene's army under Daniel Morgan defeated "Bloody" Tarleton's Tory Legion and changed the course of British strategy in the South. Cornwallis cut his ties with his base in Charleston and set out after the elusive American army. After an indecisive battle with Greene at Guilford Courthouse on March 15, 1781, Cornwallis's tired and battered soldiers withdrew to Wilmington on the coast of North Carolina with the intention of moving the seat of war northward into Virginia. Thus ended the British experiment with a thorough program of pacification. During the spring and summer of 1781, patriot forces regained control of the entire Lower South except for a narrow strip between Charleston and Savannah.

Although marauding by British forces in the summer of 1781 frightened Virginians and humiliated Governor Thomas Jefferson, Cornwallis could not convince his commander in chief, Clinton, in New York to make Virginia the center of British military

Yorktown and the Southern Campaigns 1778-1781

N.Y.
CONN.
New York
PA.
N.J.
York
Philadelphia
MD.
Aug.-Sept., 1781
DEL.
Mt. Vernon
GRAVES & HOOD
BARRAS *From Newport*
HOOD
WAYNE
LAFAYETTE
WASHINGTON & ROCHAMBEAU
VA.
Charlottesville
Chesapeake Bay
James R.
Richmond
Yorktown
Yorktown *Oct.19, 1781*
Sept. 5, 1781
Ohio R.
Kanawha R.
PROCLAMATION LINE OF 1763
Potomac R.
Susquehanna R.
Delaware R.
DE GRASSE *From the West Indies*
GREENE
Guilford C.H.
Guilford Court House Mar.15, 1781
CORNWALLIS
MORGAN
Oct.7,1780
Kings Mt.
Charlotte
N.C.
Roanoke R.
CORNWALLIS *April, 1781*
GATES *1780*
Cape Fear R.
Cowpens Jan.17,1781
MORGAN
TARLETON
Winnsboro
S.C.
Aug.16,1780
Camden
Camden
Pee Dee R.
Santee R.
Wilmington
ATLANTIC OCEAN
Savannah R.
Charleston *May 12,1780*
CLINTON & CORNWALLIS *From New York*
LINCOLN
GA.
CAMPBELL *From New York*
Savannah *Dec.29, 1778*

FRANCO-AMERICAN FORCES
Advance
BRITISH FORCES
Advance
Retreat

0   50   100   150
Miles

JOHN TRUMBULL'S "SURRENDER OF LORD CORNWALLIS"
General Benjamin Lincoln of Massachusetts leads the surrendered British troops between the French and American forces. Rochambeau and Washington, the two allied commanders in chief, are on horseback to the rear. Lafayette is the second figure from Washington's left. To Lafayette's immediate left is Baron von Steuben, the Prussian army captain who in 1778 was made a major-general in the Continental Army. (*Courtesy of Yale University Art Gallery*)

operations. The haggling between the two generals enabled the Americans to bolster their Virginian troops under the command of the dashing French nobleman, the Marquis de Lafayette, who had been in the struggle since 1777. Cornwallis's withdrawal to the Virginia coast and his eventual isolation at Yorktown gave the combined American and French army of nearly 17,000 men under Washington and the Comte de Rochambeau the opportunity it was looking for. The French fleet under Admiral de Grasse moved into Chesapeake Bay and blocked Cornwallis's plans to escape by sea. Thus surrounded and bombarded in Yorktown, Cornwallis was forced to surrender his army of 8,000 troops to Washington in October 1781. The British policy since 1778 of spreading their control along the entire Atlantic seaboard depended on maintaining naval superiority; and when this superiority was temporarily lost in

1781, the entire plan collapsed. Although the war dragged on for several months, everyone knew that Yorktown meant American independence.

The Peace Treaty. The peace, nevertheless, still had to be won. The main objective of the new nation —independence from Great Britain—was clear and straightforward. But this objective and others concerning America's territorial boundaries and its rights to the Newfoundland fisheries had to be reconciled with the aims of America's ally, France, and with the aims of France's ally, Spain, which had been at war with Great Britain since 1779. The United States and France had pledged in 1778 not to make a separate peace with Britain. But since France was bound to Spain against Britain until Gibraltar was recovered, there was great danger of American interests' getting lost in the machinations of the European powers.

Despite the desire of France and Spain to humiliate Britain, neither monarchy really wanted a strong and independent American republic. Spain in particular feared the spread of republicanism among its South American colonies and sought to protect its interests in the Mississippi Valley.

Although Franklin, John Adams, and John Jay, the American negotiators in Europe, were only "militia diplomats," in Adams's words, they wound their way through the intricate problems of international politics with professional diplomatic skill. Despite instructions from the Congress to do nothing without consulting the French, the American diplomats decided to negotiate with Britain alone. By hinting at the possibility of weakening the Franco-American alliance, they induced Great Britain to recognize the independence of the United States and to agree to generous boundaries for the new country: on the west, the Mississippi River; on the south, the thirty-first parallel; and on the north, roughly the present boundary with Canada. The American negotiators then presented this preliminary Anglo-American treaty to France as an accomplished fact and persuaded the French to accept it by suggesting that allies must conceal their differences from their enemies. The prospect of American peace with Britain now compelled Spain to abandon its demands for Gibraltar and to settle for Minorca and East and West Florida. In the final treaty signed on September 3, 1783, the United States, by shrewdly playing off the mutual fears of the European powers, gained independence and concessions that stunned the French and indeed all of Europe.

Republicanism

From 1775, when independence and hence the formation of new governments became imminent, and continuing throughout the war, nearly every piece of writing about the future of the new states was filled with extraordinarily idealistic hopes for the

PRELIMINARY PEACE NEGOTIATIONS WITH GREAT BRITAIN, BY BENJAMIN WEST

Although history painter to George III, the American-born Benjamin West actually toyed with the idea of painting the great events of the American Revolution. But this unfinished picture of the peace negotiators was the only one he attempted. The picture includes John Jay, John Adams, Benjamin Franklin, Temple Franklin (Franklin's grandson and secretary to the delegation), and Henry Laurens, who did not sign the final treaty. (*Courtesy, The Henry Francis du Pont Winterthur Museum*) transformation of America. Americans had come to believe that the Revolution meant nothing less than the reordering of eighteenth-century politics and society—a reordering summed up in the conception of republicanism.

This republicanism was in every way a radical ideology, comparable in the eighteenth century to Marxism in the nineteenth. It meant more than simply eliminating a king and instituting an elective system of government. It added a moral and indeed utopian dimension to the political separation from England—a dimension that promised a fundamental shift in values and a change in the very character of American society.

Republicanism intensified the radicalism of the "country" ideology Americans had borrowed from opposition groups in English society and linked it with older and deeper European currents of thought. This republican tradition reached back through the brief commonwealth period in seventeenth-century England and the writings of James Harrington, John Milton, and Algernon Sidney to its classical beginnings in antiquity. By the eighteenth century this republican tradition had become a kind of counter-culture for many dissatisfied Europeans. In countless writings and translations, eighteenth-century European and English intellectuals evoked the image of an earlier Roman republican world of simple yeomen-citizens enjoying liberty and pastoral virtue. They viewed this idealized ancient world as an alternative to the sprawling monarchies, with their hierarchies, pervasive luxury, and corruption, that they had come to despise in their own time.

In the excitement of the Revolutionary movement, these classical republican values merged with the long-existing image of Americans as a simple, egalitarian, liberty-loving people to form one of the most coherent and powerful ideologies the Western world had yet seen. Many of the ambiguities Americans had felt about the rustic provincial character of their society were now clarified. What some people had seen as the crudities and deficiencies of American life could now be viewed as advantages for republican government. Independent American farmers who owned their own land were now regarded not as primitive folk living on the edges of European society and in the backwaters of history, but as citizens naturally equipped to realize the republican values intellectuals had espoused for centuries.

Independent Citizens. Inevitably then the new American states in 1776 became republics. Everyone knew that these new republics with their elective systems had not only political but moral and social significance. Republicanism struck directly at the traditional society in which heredity, patronage, and dependency were essential. Believing that the social evils of the Old World—encrusted privilege, inflated aristocracy, and pervasive poverty—all flowed from the abuses of government, republican liberals aimed to reduce if not destroy government's overarching power. They were determined that government no longer be able to squeeze money from the people, create titles of distinction, grant monopolies, shore up religious establishments, dispense offices, and do all those other things that ate away at the moral vitality of the people. In place of strong government, republicanism promised a society in which relations would be based on natural merit and the equality of independent citizens linked to one another in harmony. Although republicanism was based on individual property-holding, it repudiated a narrow, selfish individualism and stressed a morality of social cohesion and devotion to the common welfare. Several of the states, Massachusetts, Pennsylvania, and Virginia, in 1776 even adopted the designation "commonwealth" to express better this new dedication to the public good.

Such republican communities of independent citizens presented an inspiring ideal. But history had shown republics to be the most unstable kind of state, highly susceptible to faction and internal disorder. Theorists thus concluded that republics had to be small in territory and homogeneous in character. The only existing European republican models —the Netherlands, and the Italian and Swiss city-states—were small and compact. When a large country attempted to establish a republic, as England had tried to do in the seventeenth century, the experiment was sure to end in some sort of dictatorship, like that of Oliver Cromwell. Unlike monarchies, whose executive power and numerous dependent ranks maintained public order even over a large and diverse population, republics had to be held together from below, by the people themselves.

The Need for Virtue. Republicanism was radical precisely because it demanded an extraordinary degree of moral virtue in the people. If only the society could be organized so as to allow the moral strength of people to express itself, then there would be little need for excessive monarchlike government. But if the society developed in such a manner as to lessen the people's virtue, if the people became selfish and luxury-loving as the ancient Romans had, then the society's ability to sustain a republic would be lost and the transformation of the republican state into a monarchy or dictatorship would inevitably follow.

Americans, however, seemed naturally virtuous and thus ideally suited for republican government. Did they not possess the same hardy egalitarian character that the ancient republican citizens had had? Were not the remarkable displays of popular order in the face of disintegrating royal governments in 1774–75 evidence of the willingness of the American people to obey their governments without coercion? The Revolutionary leaders exhorted the American people to act patriotically, telling them, as Samuel Adams did, that "a Citizen owes everything to the Commonwealth." The citizen was in fact, as the Philadelphia physician Benjamin Rush said, "public property. His time and talents—his youth—his manhood—his old age—nay more, life, all belong to his country."

Republican citizens, in short, had to be patriots, and patriots were not simply those who loved their country but those who were free from the control of others. As Jefferson wrote in his *Notes on Virginia,* "Dependence begets subservience and venality, suffocates the germ of virtue, and prepares fit tools for the designs of ambition." Hence the sturdy independent yeomen, Jefferson's "chosen people of God," were regarded as the most incorruptible and the best citizens for a republic.

The individual ownership of property, especially land, was essential for a republic, both as a source of independence and as evidence of a permanent attachment to the community. Those who were propertyless and dependent, like women and servants, could thus be justifiably denied the vote because they could have no wills of their own. In Europe, corruption and dependency were common because only a few people possessed property. But, as one Carolinian wrote in 1777, "The people of America are a people of property; almost every man is a freeholder." Jefferson was so keen on this point that he proposed in 1776 that the new commonwealth of Virginia grant fifty acres of land to every citizen who did not have that many.

Equality. At the heart of this republican emphasis on virtue and independence lay equality, the most powerful and influential concept in American history. Equality was the necessary basis for the anticipated harmony and public virtue of the New World. The incessant squabbling over position and rank and the bitter contentions of factional politics in the colonies had been due, it was said, to the artificial inequality of colonial society, created and nourished largely through the influence and patronage of the British crown. In a republic individuals were no longer doomed to be what their fathers had been. It was ability not birth that mattered. But republican equality did not mean the elimination of distinctions. Republics would still have an aristocracy, said Jefferson, but it would be a natural not an artificial one. A republican elite would resemble not the luxury-loving, money-mongering lackeys of the British court but the stoical and disinterested heroes of antiquity—men like George Washington, who seemed to Americans to embody perfectly the classical ideal of a republican leader.

Obviously these ideals of Revolutionary republicanism could not be wholly realized. Much of its communitarian emphasis flew in the face of the surging individualism of American life. Yet whatever the practical results, republicanism as it was idealized by Jefferson's generation colored the entire Revolutionary movement. Eventually it would come to shape much of what Americans believe and value.

CHRONOLOGY

1775 Battle of Lexington and Concord.
Fort Ticonderoga taken by American forces.
Second Continental Congress meets in
Philadelphia.
George Washington appointed commander in
chief of Continental army.
Battle of Bunker Hill.
Congress adopts its "Declaration of the Causes
and Necessities of Taking Up Arms."
George III proclaims colonists in open
rebellion.
American forces fail to take Quebec; General
Montgomery killed.
Pennsylvania Quakers form first antislavery
society in world.

1776 Thomas Paine's *Common Sense.*
British troops evacuate Boston.
Congress calls on colonies to suppress all
crown authority and establish governments
under authority of the people.
Declaration of Independence.
Battle of Long Island, New York; Americans
defeated by General Howe.
British take New York City.
Battle of Trenton.
New Hampshire, New Jersey, Pennsylvania,
Delaware, Maryland, Virginia, North Carolina,
and South Carolina write state constitutions.
Rhode Island and Connecticut change their
colonial charters.

1777 Battle of Princeton.
Battle of Monmouth, New Jersey. Although
outcome indecisive, Washington's troops stand
up to British regulars.
Battle of Brandywine, Pennsylvania;
Washington defeated.

British occupy Philadelphia.
Battle of Germantown, Pennsylvania; Howe
repulses Washington's attack.
Burgoyne surrenders at Saratoga.
Articles of Confederation adopted by
Continental Congress, but not ratified by all
states until 1781.
Washington retires to Valley Forge for winter.
New York and Georgia write state constitutions.

1778 United States concludes military alliance and
commercial treaty with France. First and only
military alliance by United States until North
Atlantic Treaty Organization, 1949.
British evacuate Philadelphia.
British seize Savannah, Georgia.

1779 Spain enters the war against Britain.
George Rogers Clark captures Vincennes and
ends British rule in Northwest.

1780 Americans surrender 5,500 men and the city
of Charleston, South Carolina.
Battle of Camden, South Carolina; Gates
defeated by Cornwallis.
Battle of King's Mountain, South Carolina;
British and Tories defeated.
Creation of Massachusetts constitution.

1781 Battle of Cowpens, South Carolina; British
under Tarleton defeated by Morgan.
Battle of Guilford Courthouse, North Carolina;
outcome indecisive, but Cornwallis withdraws
to coast.
Cornwallis surrenders to Washington at
Yorktown, Virginia.

SUGGESTED READINGS

Modern interest in the ideas of the Revolution dates back to the 1920s and 1930s with the studies of constitutional law and natural rights philosophy by Carl Becker, *The Declaration of Independence* (1922); Charles H. McIlwain, *The American Revolution: A Constitutional Interpretation* (1923); Randolph G. Adams, *Political Ideas of the American Revolution* (1922); William S. Carpenter, *The Development of Amer-*ican Political Thought* (1930); and Benjamin F. Wright, Jr., *American Interpretations of Natural Law* (1931). While these books emphasized formal political theory, others explicitly treated the ideas as propaganda. See Philip Davidson, *Propaganda and the American Revolution, 1763–1783* (1941); and Arthur M. Schlesinger, *Prelude to Independence: The Newspaper War on Britain, 1764–1776* (1958).

In the 1950s serious attention was paid to the determinative influence of ideas in Clinton Rossiter, *Seedtime of the Republic* (1953); and especially in Edmund S. Morgan and Helen M. Morgan, *The Stamp Act Crisis* (1953). The Morgan book focuses on parliamentary sovereignty.

Only in the 1960s, however, did historians comprehend the Revolutionary ideas as ideology and begin to recover the distinctiveness of the late eighteenth-century world. The starting point now for analyzing the ideology of the Revolution—as a configuration of ideas giving meaning and force to events—is Bernard Bailyn, *The Ideological Origins of the American Revolution* (1967). Bailyn's book, which appeared initially as the introduction to the first of a four-volume edition of *Pamphlets of the American Revolution, 1750–1776* (1965–   ), was partly based on the rediscovery of the radical Whig tradition by Caroline Robbins, *The Eighteenth-Century Commonwealthmen* (1959). J. G. A. Pocock, *The Machiavellian Moment* (1975); J. R. Pole, *Political Representation in England and the Origins of the American Republic* (1966); Trevor H. Colbourn, *The Lamp of Experience: Whig History and the Beginnings of the American Revolution* (1965); and Isaac F. Kramnick, *Bolingbroke and His Circle* (1968), have further contributed to an understanding of the sources of the Revolutionary tradition. Pauline Maier, *From Resistance to Revolution* (1972), details the escalation of American fears of British policy between 1765 and 1776.

On the military actions of the Revolutionary War, the best brief account is Willard M. Wallace, *Appeal to Arms* (1951). Don Higginbotham, *The War of American Independence* (1971), and John Shy, *A People Numerous and Armed: Reflections on the Military Struggle for American Independence* (1976), best appreciate the unconventional and guerrilla character of the war. Two books edited by George A. Billias, *George Washington's Generals* (1964) and *George Washington's Opponents* (1969), contain excellent essays written by various historians on the military leaders of both sides. Eric Robeson, *The American Revolution in Its Political and Military Aspects, 1763–1783* (1955), has some

penetrating chapters on the conduct of the war. For naval operations, see Gardner W. Allen, *A Naval History of the American Revolution* (2 vols., 1913). The fullest account of British strategy is Piers Mackesy, *The War for America, 1775–1783* (1964). On the British commanders in chief, see Ira Gruber, *The Howe Brothers and the American Revolution* (1972); and William Willcox, *Portrait of a General: Sir Henry Clinton in the War of Independence* (1964). Paul H. Smith, *Loyalists and Redcoats* (1964), describes British attempts to mobilize the loyalists.

On diplomacy the standard account is Samuel Flagg Bemis, *The Diplomacy of the American Revolution* (1935). See also William C. Stinchcombe, *The American Revolution and the French Alliance* (1969). Richard B. Morris, *The Peacemakers* (1965), is a full study of the peace negotiations.

For a summary of the history writing covering the eighteenth-century tradition of republicanism, see Robert E. Shalhope, "Toward a Republican Synthesis: The Emergence of an Understanding of Republicanism in American Historiography," *Wm. and Mary Q.*, 3d. ser., 29 (1975). Studies emphasizing the peculiar character of this tradition include Bernard Bailyn, *The Ideological Origins of the American Revolution* (1967); J. G. A. Pocock, *The Machiavellian Moment* (1975); Franco Venturi, *Utopia and Reform in the Enlightenment* (1971); Gerald Stourzh, *Alexander Hamilton and the Idea of Republican Government* (1970); and Gordon S. Wood, *The Creation of the American Republic, 1776–1787* (1969). Garry Wills, *Inventing America: Jefferson's Declaration of Independence* (1978), stresses the importance of Scottish moral sense philosophy and the natural sociableness of people in Jefferson's thought. On the origins of the Americans' conception of the individual's relationship to the state, see James H. Kettner, *The Development of American Citizenship, 1608–1870* (1978). For the influence of antiquity, see Richard Gummere, *The American Colonial Mind and the Classical Tradition* (1963); and Meyer Reinhold, ed., *The Classick Pages* (1975). For the way in which many Europeans viewed the New World in the eighteenth century, see Durand Echeverria, *Mirage in the West* (1957).

CHAPTER 9

The States and the Confederation

"How few of the human race have ever enjoyed an opportunity of making an election of government," rejoiced John Adams, like many others in 1776. Indeed, it was in the spirit of being able to control their own destiny that the Revolutionaries approached the immense task ahead of them. They had an acute sense that the entire world was watching to see how they would put their ideals into practice when they established governments for the new country. Their investigations into the abuses of power and the protection of liberty that had begun during the imperial debate now shaped the new governments they formed, in what proved to be the most creative period of constitutionalism in American history.

State Constitution-Making

From the time royal authority disintegrated, Americans began thinking about creating new governments. During the summer of 1775 Samuel Adams and John Adams of Massachusetts, together with the Virginia delegation to the Continental Congress led by Richard Henry Lee, worked out a program for independence. They made plans to establish foreign alliances, to create a confederation, and most important, to frame new state governments. The climax of their efforts came with the congressional resolutions of May 1776, advising the colonies to adopt new governments "under the authority of people," and declaring "that the exercise of every kind of authority under the . . . Crown should be totally suppressed." Even before the Declaration of Independence, the Congress had created a committee to form a confederation, and some of the states—New Hampshire, South Carolina and Virginia—had begun working on new constitutions. With the May resolves and the Declaration of Independence, the other states followed successively; by the end of 1776 New Jersey, Delaware, Pennsylvania, Maryland, and North Carolina had formed new constitutions. Because the corporate colonies, Rhode Island and Connecticut, were already republics in fact, they simply confined themselves to the elimination of all mention of royal authority in their existing charters. Because of war conditions Georgia and New York delayed their constitution-making until 1777. Massachusetts had recovered its old charter that the British had abrogated, and was busy preparing to write a more permanent constitution.

In 1776–77, most of the Americans' attention and much of their energies were concentrated on establishing these new state constitutions. The states, not the central government or Congress, were to test the Revolutionary hopes. In fact, forming new state governments, as Jefferson said in the spring of 1776, was "the whole object of the present controversy." For the aim of the Revolution had become not simply independence from British tyranny, but the prevention of future tyrannies.

Constitutions as Written Documents.   It was inevitable that Americans would embody their constitutions in written documents. By the word "constitution," most eighteenth-century Englishmen meant not a written document but the existing arrangements of government, that is, laws, customs, and institutions, together with the principles they embodied. Americans, however, had come to view a constitution in a different way. From the seventeenth century, they had repeatedly used their colonial charters as defensive barriers against royal authority; and during the debate with Britain, they had been compelled to recognize that laws made by Parliament were not necessarily constitutional, or in accord with fundamental principles of rightness and justice. If the constitutional principles were to be asserted against a too powerful government, then somehow they had to be lifted out of the machinery of government and set above it. The Americans' new state constitutions would therefore have to be fixed plans—written documents as the British constitution never had been—presciding the powers of government and specifying the rights of citizens.

Fear of Executive Power.   As they wrote these new state constitutions, the Americans set about to institutionalize all that they had learned from their colonial experience and from the recent struggle with England.

Although they knew they would establish republics, they did not know precisely what forms the new governments should take. Their central aim was to prevent power, which they identified with the rulers or governors, from encroaching upon liberty, which they identified with the people or their representatives in the legislatures. Only the Americans' deep fear of executive power can explain the radical changes they made in the authority of their now elected governors.

In their desire to root out tyranny once and for all, the members of the state congresses who drafted the new constitutions reduced the governors' powers to a pale reflection of those that had been exercised by the royal governors. No longer would governors have the authority to create electoral districts, control the meeting of the assemblies, veto legislation, grant lands, erect courts, issue charters of incorporation, or in some states pardon crimes. All the new state governors were surrounded by controlling councils elected by the assemblies. These governors were to be elected annually, generally by the assemblies, limited in the number of times they could be reelected, and subject to impeachment.

However radical these changes in executive authority may have been, many Americans believed that they did not get to the heart of the matter. They did not destroy the most insidious and dangerous source of despotism—the executive's power of appointment to office. Since in a traditional, monarchical society the disposal of offices, honors, and favors affected the social order, American republicans were determined that their governors would never again have the capacity to dominate public life. Exclusive control over appointments to executive and judicial offices was now wrested from the traditional hands of the governors and shared with the legislatures. This change was justified by the familiar principle of "separation of powers." This emphasis in the new state constitutions on keeping the executive, legislative, and judicial parts of the government separate and distinct was invoked in 1776, not to protect each power from the others, but to keep the judiciary and especially the legislature free from executive manipulation, the very kind of manipulation that had corrupted the English Parliament. Hence the new constitutions categorically barred all executive office-holders and those receiving salaries from the government from sitting in the legislatures. As a consequence, parliamentary cabinet government such as existed in England was forever prohibited in America, and constitutional development moved off in a direction independent of the former mother country.

Strengthening of the Legislatures.   The powers and prerogatives taken from the governors in the new state constitutions of 1776 were granted to the legislatures. This marked a radical shift in the responsibility of government. Traditionally in English history the "government" had mainly been identified with the executive; representative bodies had generally been confined to voting taxes and passing corrective and exceptional legislation. But the new American state legislatures, in particular the lower houses of the assemblies, were no longer to be merely adjuncts of governmental power or checks on it. They were now given powers formerly reserved to magistrates, including the making of alliances and the granting of pardons.

To ensure that the state legislatures fully embodied the will of the people, the ideas and experiences behind the Americans' view of representation were now drawn out and implemented. The Revolutionary state constitutions put a new emphasis on actual representation and explicit consent: on equal electoral districts, on annual elections, on a broadened suffrage, on residential requirements for both electors and elected, and on the right of constituents to instruct their representatives. The royal authority's prohibition against extending representation to newly settled areas was now dramatically reversed. Towns and counties, particularly in the backcountry, were granted either new or additional representation in the state legislatures, in a belated recognition of the legitimacy of the western uprisings of the 1760s. Some of the new constitutions even explicitly recognized the principle that population was the basis of representation. Five states wrote into fundamental law specific plans for periodic adjustments of their representation, so that, as the New York constitution of 1777 stated, it "shall for ever remain proportionate and adequate."

In light of what would happen in the coming dec-ade, the confidence of the Revolutionaries in 1776 in their representative legislatures was remarkable. Except for some disgruntled Tories, few people expected these state legislatures to become tyrannical; for in the Whig theory of politics it did not seem possible for the people to tyrannize over themselves. Of course the people were apt to be licentious or headstrong; hence the republics needed not only governors but upper houses in the legislatures to counterbalance the popular lower houses of representatives. All the states, except Pennsylvania, Georgia, and the new state of Vermont, therefore provided for upper houses or senates, the designation taken from Roman history. The senators in these bicameral state legislatures were not to be a legally defined nobility but the wisest and best members of the society, who would revise and correct the well-intentioned but often careless measures of the people represented in the lower houses.

This Revolutionary state constitution-making was an extraordinary achievement. Nothing quite like it had occurred before in modern history. Foreign intellectuals thought that the new American state constitutions were concrete realizations of Enlightenment ideas. In the decade following Independence the state constitutions were translated, published, and republished in France and other European countries, and their features were avidly examined and debated. More than anything else in 1776 these new written state constitutions gave people everywhere a sense that a new era in history was beginning.

The Articles of Confederation

At the same time that the Revolutionaries were creating their state constitutions, they were drafting a central government. Yet in marked contrast to the rich and exciting public explorations of political theory accompanying the formation of the state constitutions, there was little discussion of the plans for a central government. In 1776 the loyalties of most people were still concentrated on their particular provinces. The Declaration of Independence, drawn up by the Continental Congress, was actually a declaration by "thirteen united States of America" proclaiming that as "Free and Independent States, they have full Power to levy War, conclude Peace, contract Alliances, establish Commerce, and to do all other Acts and Things which independent States may of right do." Despite all the talk of union, few Americans in 1776 could conceive of creating a single full-fledged Continental republic.

Still, the Congress needed some legal basis for its authority. Like the various provincial conventions, it had been created in 1774 simply out of necessity, and was exercising an extraordinary degree of political, military, and economic power over Americans. It had adopted commercial codes, established and maintained an army, issued a Continental currency, erected a military code of law, defined crimes against the union, and negotiated abroad. With the approach of Independence it was obvious to many leaders that a more permanent and legitimate union of the states was necessary. Although a draft of a confederation was ready for consideration by the Congress as early as mid-July 1776, not until November 1777, after heated controversy, did Congress present a document of union to the states for their separate approval or rejection. It took nearly four years, until March 1781, for all the states to accept this document and thereby legally establish the Articles of Confederation.

The Nature of the Union. The Articles created a confederacy, called "The United States of America," that was essentially a continuation of the Second Continental Congress. Delegates from each state were to be sent annually to the Congress, and each state delegation was to have only a single vote. In Article 9 Congress was granted the authority to determine diplomatic relations, requistion the states for men and money, coin and borrow money, regulate Indian affairs, and settle disputes between the states. While a simple majority of seven states was needed for minor matters, a larger majority, nine states, was required for important matters, including engaging in

PAPER CURRENCY ISSUED BY THE CONTINENTAL CONGRESS
(American Antiquarian Society)

war, making treaties, and coining and borrowing money. There was no real executive but only congressional committees with fluctuating memberships.

This union was stronger than many people expected. The states were specifically forbidden to conduct foreign affairs, make treaties, or declare war. The citizens of each state were entitled to the privileges and immunities of the citizens of all states. All travel and discriminatory trade restrictions between the states were eliminated. Judicial proceedings of each state were honored by all states. These stipulations, together with the substantial grant of powers to the Congress, made the United States of America as strong as any similar republican confederation in history. The Articles marked a big step toward a genuine national government.

Nevertheless, the Americans' fear of distant central authority, intensified by a century of experience in the British empire, left no doubt that this Confederation would remain something less than a full national government. Under the Articles, the crucial powers of commercial regulation and taxation, indeed all final lawmaking authority, remained with the states. Congressional resolutions continued to be, as they had been under the Continental Congress, recommendations which, it was assumed, the states would enforce. And should there be any doubts of the decentralized nature of the Confederation, Article 2 stated bluntly that "each State retains its sovereignty, freedom and independence, and every power, jurisdiction, and right, which is not by this confederation expressly delegated to the United States, in Congress assembled."

The "United States of America" thus possessed a literal meaning that is hard to appreciate today. The Confederation, based on equal representation of each state, necessarily resembled more a treaty among closely cooperating sovereign states than a single government. It was intended to be and remained, as Article 3 declared, "a firm league of friendship" among states jealous of their individuality. Not only ratification of the Articles of Confederation but any subsequent changes in it required consent of all states.*

*For the Articles of Confederation, see Appendix.

State Rivalries and the Disposition of the Western Lands. The local self-interests of the states prolonged the congressional debates over the adoption of the Articles and delayed its unanimous ratification until 1781. The major disputes—over representation, the apportionment of the states' contribution to the union, and the disposition of the western lands—involved concrete state interests. Large populous states like Virginia argued for proportional representation in the Congress, but had to give way to the small states' determination to maintain equal representation. The original draft of the Articles provided that each state's financial contribution to the general treasury be based on its population, including slaves. Strenuous opposition from the southern states, however, forced the Congress to shift the basis for a state's financial contribution to the value of its land. This was done against the wishes of the New England states where land values were high.

The states' rivalries were most evident in the long controversy over the disposition of the western lands between the Appalachians and the Mississippi. The Articles sent to the states in 1778 for ratification gave Congress no authority over the unsettled lands of the interior, and this delayed its approval. While states like Virginia and Massachusetts with charter claims to this western territory wanted to maintain control over the disposal of their land, states like Maryland and Rhode Island without such claims wanted the western land pooled in a common national domain under the authority of Congress. By March 1779, however, all the states had ratified the Articles except Maryland, which, under the influence of land speculators, refused to join the union until all the states had ceded their western lands to the central government. When Virginia, the state with charter rights to the largest amount of western territory, finally agreed on January 2, 1781, to surrender its claims to the United States, the way was prepared for other land cessions and for ratification of the Articles of Confederation by all the states. But the Confederation had to promise, in return for the cession of claims by Virginia and the other states, that this huge national domain in the West would "be settled and formed into distinct republican states."

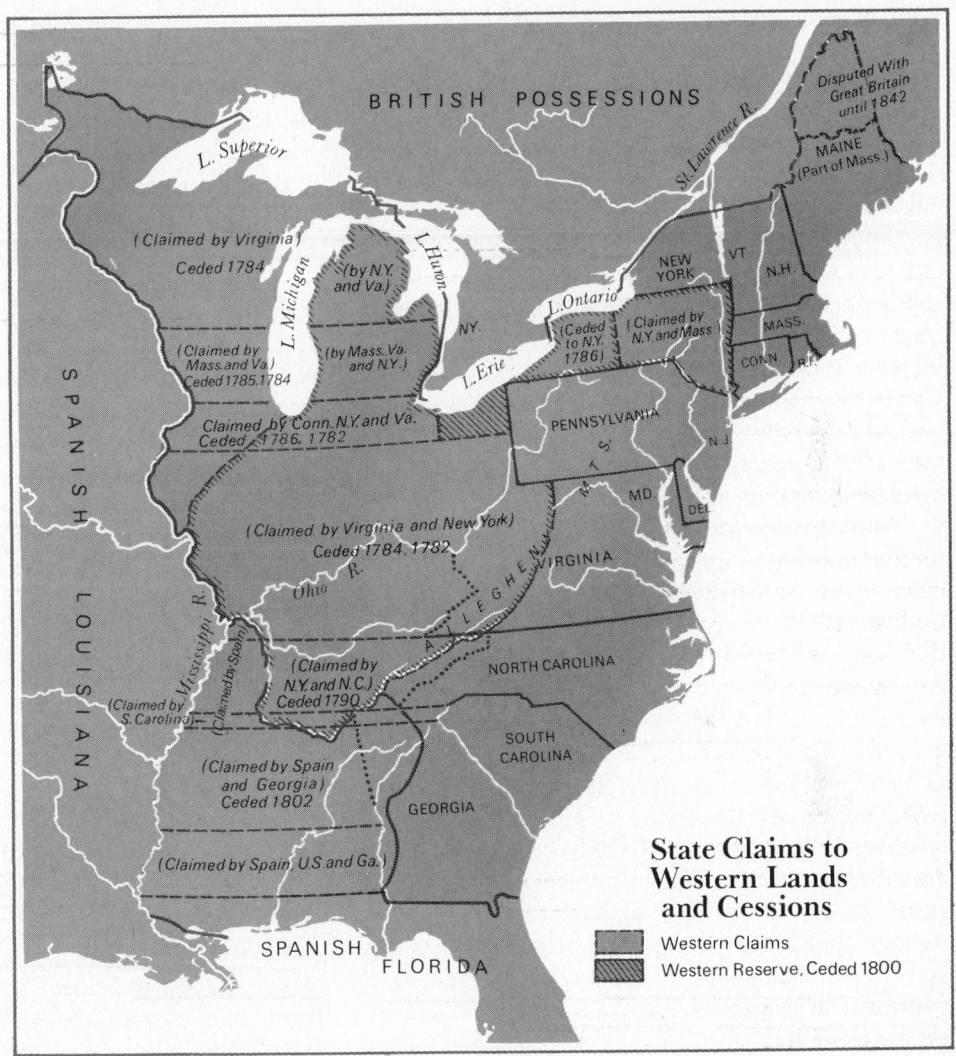

State Claims to
Western Lands
and Cessions

Western Claims
Western Reserve, Ceded 1800

Ordinances for the West.

The Congress drew up land ordinances in 1784 and 1785, and in 1787 it adopted the famous Northwest Ordinance which acknowledged, as the British in the 1760s had not, the settlers' destiny in the West. The land ordinances of 1784 and 1785 provided for the land north of the Ohio River and west of the Appalachians to be surveyed and formed into townships of six miles square along lines running east–west and north–south. Each township was divided into thirty-six numbered lots, or sections of 640 acres. The Confederation favored speculators and large groups by providing for the sale of the land by auction and by stipulating that a section was to be the smallest unit purchased, at a price of no less than a dollar an acre. In each township Congress retained four sections for future sale and set aside one other for the support of public education. The Ordinance of 1787 dealt with the political organization of the Northwest. It guaranteed to the settlers basic political and legal rights and arranged for the area to be divided into not less than three nor more than five territories. When each territory reached a population of 60,000 it was to be admitted to the Union on equal terms with the existing states.

These remarkable ordinances were the greatest achievement of the Confederation outside of winning the war. They solved at a stroke the problem, which Britain had been unable to solve, of relating "colonies" or dependencies to the central government. In the succeeding decades the Land Ordinance of 1785 and the Ordinance of 1787 remained the bases for the surveying, sale, and the political evolution of America's western territories. Settlers could leave the older states assured that they were not abandoning their political liberties and know that they would be allowed eventually to form new republics as sovereign and independent as the other states in the Union. Thus even the organization of this great national landed resource by the Congress was immediately devoted to the dispersion of central authority by the anticipated creation of more states, the only political units most Americans seemed to value.

Republican Society

At the same time that efforts to establish governments and constitutions were being made, unsettling changes in American society were taking place. To be sure, there was no immediate collapse of the social order and no abrupt and wholesale destruction of familiar social institutions. But everywhere there were alterations in the way people related to government, to the economy, and to each other. Many of these changes were the results of deeply rooted forces long in motion, some since the beginning of the colonial period. But others were the sudden effects of the Revolution itself.

The Departure of the Loyalists. One such sudden effect was the departure of tens of thousands of loyalists. The loyalists may have numbered close to half a million, or 20 percent of white Americans. Nearly twenty thousand of them fought for the crown in regiments of His Majesty's army, and thousands of others served in local loyalist militia bodies. As many as sixty to eighty thousand loyalists, it is estimated, left America during the Revolution for Canada and

Great Britain, although many of these returned after the war and were reintegrated into American society. Although the loyalists came from all ranks and occupations of the society, a disproportionate number of them belonged to the upper political and social levels. Many had been officeholders and overseas merchants involved with government contracting; in the North, most were Anglicans. Their regional distribution was likewise uneven. In New England and Virginia they were a tiny minority. But in western frontier areas, where hostility to eastern encroachment went back to the pre-Revolutionary times, and in the regions of New York, New Jersey, and Pennsylvania, and the Deep South where the British army offered protection, loyalists made up a considerable part of the population. Their flight, displacement, and retirements created a vacuum at the top that was rapidly filled by patriots. The effects were widespread. Crown and Tory property and lands valued at millions of pounds were confiscated by the Revolutionary governments and almost immediately thrown onto the market. The resulting speculation accentuated the sudden rise and fall of fortunes during the Revolutionary years.

Economic Effects of the Revolution. Economic disruptions created the most social disorder. Suddenly Americans found themselves outside the protective walls of the British mercantile empire which had nurtured their commercial life for over a century. Exports dropped drastically. Traditional markets in Britain, and especially in the British West Indies, were closed. Bounties paid on particular colonial products were now gone. Colonial ships could no longer be sold to Britain and prewar sources of credit were upset. Such changes were devastating to particular groups and individuals, but overall the results of the break from Britain were beneficial and stimulating. Simply by destroying old encrusted habits and relationships the Revolution released new energies.

The South suffered the greatest dislocations from the war. Not only did it lose established markets for its tobacco and other staples, but tens of thousands of its slaves were freed by the British and taken out of the country. Indeed, the British army was perhaps the greatest single instrument of emancipation in

The land to the north of the Ohio River was to be surveyed and marked off in a rectangular pattern before any of it was sold. Congress's land ordinance provided for east-west base lines, north-south "ranges," and townships with sides paralleling the ranges and base lines.

Although Indian resistance and meager land sales limited the number of ranges actually surveyed under the Land Ordinance of 1785 to seven in southeastern Ohio, the policy of surveying in rectangular units remained the basis of the United States' land system. The Ordinance of 1785 and the Land Act of 1796 provided for settlers' purchasing a definite, previously surveyed tract—section 35 in township 2, for example—and thus ended the confusion that had resulted from vague colonial land boundaries and from the southern warrant system in which settlers gained title to plots they had laid out themselves.

"THE TONTINE COFFEE HOUSE," BY GUY FRANCIS, 1797

During the Revolution fire had ravaged much of the commercial section of New York. In the following years New York's merchants enlarged the harbor facilities and rebuilt the business district, including this busy corner of Wall and Water streets. By 1797 New York had surpassed rival Philadelphia in both imports and exports. (*Courtesy of The New-York Historical Society, New York City*)

America until the Civil War. But these dislocations only accelerated an agricultural diversification that had begun before the Revolution. The Upper South in particular recovered rapidly. Tobacco production in the 1780s equaled prewar levels, and involved many new participants and new marketing arrangements.

In the North divisions within the merchant communities that had been apparent before the Revolution now widened, and merchants who had previously been on the periphery of economic activity were granted new opportunities at the center of things. In Massachusetts, for example, provincial families like the Higginsons, Cabots, and Lowells quickly moved into Boston and formed the basis of a new Massachusetts elite. The same process was duplicated

less notably but no less importantly elsewhere. New merchants pushed out in all directions in search of new markets, not only into the restricted colonial areas of the West Indies and South America, but throughout Europe and even as far away as China.

After the war trade with Great Britain quickly reached its earlier levels; by the 1780s aggregate figures show an amazing recovery of commerce. Yet such gross statistics do not do justice to the extent of change involved; for in all the states there were new sources of supply, new commercial configurations, and new and increased numbers of participants in the market. Although exports soon surpassed their prewar levels, they now represented a smaller part of America's total economic activity. The wartime collapse of British imports had encouraged domestic manufacturing, and though purchasing of British goods resumed with the return of peace, societies were now formed to promote American manufacturing and to secure protective legislation. Already the economy was beginning to turn inward with a remarkable spread of interstate and interregional trade that would soon generate demands for new roads and canals. In these changing circumstances, towns without hinterlands to exploit began a relative decline. Newport, Rhode Island, for example, had been a flourishing colonial port but, without an inland area for supply and marketing, it rapidly slipped into insignificance.

The Revolutionary War itself was at once a disrupting and a creative force. Like all wars, it destroyed familiar channels of trade and produced new sources of wealth. Almost overnight the machinery of governmental finance was overhauled. During the war the Congress and the states became gigantic borrowers and buyers and dominated economic life in ways that were unfamiliar to eighteenth-century Americans. Since there were no mechanisms for assessing and taxing wealth, and since Congress did not even have the legal authority to tax, American governments had to rely largely on borrowing to pay for the war. But government borrowing could scarcely raise the sums needed. Both the Congress and the state governments therefore resorted to the extensive printing of noninterest-bearing paper currency, which took on the character of forced loans. These bills of credit, which the governments promised to redeem by taxes at some future time, were given to citizens in return for supplies and services.

This currency issued by the congressional and state governments eventually totaled nearly $400 million in paper value and led to a socially disintegrating inflation. By 1781, $167 of congressional paper money was worth only $1 in specie, and the depreciation of the states' bills was nearly as bad. While creditors, wage earners, and those on relatively fixed incomes were hurt by this inflation, many of those who were most active in the economy, buying and selling goods rapidly, were able to profit. These circulating government bills enabled countless commodity farmers and traders to break out of a barter economy and to specialize and participate more independently in the market. Throughout the war, government buying was generally a commercial stimulant; army purchasing agencies became new centers of economic activity and breeding grounds for both petty entrepreneurs and powerful postwar capitalists.

(American Antiquarian Society)

Long-Range Social Change. These were the immediate social and economic effects of the war. But there were other, deeper, and more long-lasting conditions that were greatly affected by the Revolution and by republicanism. Despite a slackening of immigration and the loss of tens of thousands of loyalist emigrés, the population continued to grow. The 1780s saw the fastest rate of demographic growth of any decade in American history. This swelling population, after being delayed for several years in the late 70s by intermittent warfare against the British and Indians, resumed its movement westward. By the early 1780s there were over twenty thousand inhabitants in the Kentucky territory; within a decade it had become more populous than most of the colonies had been at the time of the Revolution.

This spectacular growth and movement of people further weakened the traditional forms of social organization. Such a mobile population, one Kentuckian told James Madison in 1792, "must make a very different mass from one which is composed of men born and raised on the same spot. . . . They see none about them to whom or to whose families they have been accustomed to think themselves inferior." And the ideology of republicanism intensified these tendencies. In a republic, declared a writer in 1787 in the *American Museum* (the most important of several new American magazines founded in the postwar years), "the idea of equality breathes through the whole and every individual feels ambitious to be in a situation not inferior to his neighbour."

This republican equality became a rallying cry

FRONTIER FARM IN 1793

Even at the end of the eighteenth century, many American farmers continued to grow their crops Indian style, girdling and burning trees, planting between tree stumps, and allowing the fields to revert to forest when their fertility gave out. Such wasteful and shifting methods of agriculture shocked foreign observers but made sense where land was so abundant. (*Harvard College Library*)

NICHOLAS BOYLSTON, BY JOHN
SINGLETON COPLEY, 1760

Boylston represented those wealthy and fashionable
circles surrounding royal authority that ambitious men
like John Adams simultaneously admired and resented.
"Dined at Mr. Nick Boylstones . . . ," Adams in 1766
confided to his diary with wide-eyed excitement. "An
elegant dinner indeed! Went over the house to view
the furniture, which alone cost a thousand pounds sterling. A seat it is for a noble man, a prince, the turkey
carpets, the painted hangings, the marble tables, the
rich beds with crimson damask curtains and counter-
panes, the beautiful chimney clock, the spacious garden,
are the most magnificent of any thing I have ever seen."
(*Fogg Art Museum, Harvard University*)

for people in the aspiring middle ranks who were
now more openly resentful than ever before of those
who presumed to be their social superiors. The formation in 1783 of the hereditary Order of the Cincinnati by Revolutionary army officers aroused partic-

ularly bitter hostility. Some fervent citizens attacked
distinctions of all kinds, including membership in
private social clubs and the wearing of imported
finery. Gentlemen in some areas of the North found
that the traditional attributes of social authority—
breeding, education, gentility—were becoming liabilities for political leadership. In this new republican
society no one would admit being dependent on anyone else. Every citizen now claimed for himself or herself the titles that had once belonged only to the gentry—"Mr." and "Mrs." Foreign visitors were stunned
by the unwillingness of American servants to address
their masters and mistresses as superiors and by the
servants' refusal to admit they were anything but
"help." For many Americans, never having to doff
one's cap to anyone was what living in a free country
meant.

This growing egalitarianism did not mean that in
post-Revolutionary America wealth was distributed
more equitably. On the contrary: the inequality of
wealth was greater after the Revolution than before.
What it did mean was that the way people related to
one another was being transformed. Relationships
came to be based on money rather than on social
position. Towns, for example, stopped assigning seats
in their churches by age and status and began auc-
tioning the pews to the highest bidders. Self-earned
wealth gave men the independence that republicanism
celebrated and seemed a more appropriate source of
achievement than patronage or influence. For many
Americans wealth soon became the sole and, in the
new republican society, the proper means of distinguishing one person from another.

By the end of the eighteenth century the character
of all sorts of former paternalistic dependencies was
changing. Many apprentices no longer became "children" in the master's family but were trainees in a
business, now often conducted outside the household. Paternalism in labor relations was now replaced
by impersonal cash payments, and journeymen moved
more frequently from one master to another. Both
masters and journeymen in many of the crafts were
beginning to perceive their interests as more distinct
and conflicting than they had before; and as employers and employees they were forming new class-con-
scious organizations to protect these interests. Be-

tween 1786 and 1816 at least twelve strikes by various craftsmen occurred (the first major strikes by employees against employers in American history), and masters were now resorting more and more to the courts to enforce what had once been seen largely as a mutual and personal relationship.

The Destruction of Corporate Privilege.   Many of the individual and face-to-face relationships of the older society gradually gave way to larger and more impersonal business associations. While only a half-dozen business charters had been granted in the entire colonial period, in the years after the Revolution corporate grants rapidly multiplied. The republican states created private banks, insurance companies, and manufactures, and licensed entrepreneurs to operate bridges, roads, and canals.

Eleven charters of incorporation were issued by the states between 1781 and 1785, 22 between 1786 and 1790, and 114 between 1791 and 1795. Between

PLEDGE OF SOLIDARITY

This pledge of solidarity between worker and employer in 1795 represented the tradition of the past when journeymen and masters of a particular craft worked together in the same shop. Already, the interests of artisan employers and employees were becoming separate and distinct.   (*Library of Congress*)

PAUL REVERE, BY JOHN SINGLETON COPLEY

Urban artisans and craftsmen like the silversmith Paul Revere were the most important social group in the cities that emerged into political consciousness during the Revolutionary era. (*Courtesy, Museum of Fine Arts, Boston. Gift of Joseph W., William B., and Edward H. R. Revere*)

1800 and 1817 the states granted nearly 1,800 corporate charters; the single state of Massachusetts had more corporations than existed in all of Europe. If one town had an incorporated bank, it seemed that every town wanted one, and the annually elected popular legislatures of the states, beset by hosts of new interests, were readily pressured into granting them.

This rapid creation of corporations typified the increasingly fragmented nature of the public interest under popularly elected governments. As far back as the Virginia Company, at the time of the original settlements, governmentally chartered corporations had been instruments by which the state harnessed private enterprise to carry out such desirable public goals as founding a colony, maintaining a college, or building a bridge. In the new republican society, however, not only had such forms of legal privilege become suspect, but it had become no longer clear to whom the state ought to grant its legal authority. So mistrusted was legal privilege in the egalitarian atmosphere of the early republic that such corporate monopolies could only be justified by making them available to practically everybody. This practice, of course, destroyed their exclusiveness. If nearly everyone had access to these corporate powers granted by the state, then what had once been a privilege now became a right. And as rights, these corporate charters, even though issued by state legislatures, were immune from future legislative tampering—a view eventually endorsed by the Supreme Court in the *Dartmouth College* case of 1819.

In this famous case the Court decided that the charter of Dartmouth College, although it was originally granted by the New Hampshire legislature and had a public purpose, was a private contract that could not be violated by the legislature. The states in the post-Revolutionary years therefore not only parceled out their legal authority to individuals and groups in the society but at the same time lost control of what they dispersed. Unexpected and disturbing as these disintegrating developments were to devout republicans like Jefferson, they were only the logical consequence of the Revolution's promise to break up politically supported privilege in order to allow the free expression of individual talent and energy.

The Betterment of Humanity

The republicanism of the Revolutionary era was not just exhilarating; it was contagious as well. Its optimistic liberalism, its promise of beginning everything anew, could not be confined to governmental reform or to the invigoration of manufacturing and commerce; inevitably it spilled out into all areas of American life.

In the years following the Revolution there was a suddenly aroused enthusiasm for putting the humanitarian hopes of the Enlightenment into practice. Drawing upon the thoughts of the great seventeenth-century English philosopher John Locke, eighteenth-century liberals stressed the capacity of human nature to be shaped by experience and external circumstances. People were not born to be corrupt. Placed in a proper republican environment, people could develop in healthy ways that the encrusted society of the Old World had not permitted. From these enlightened assumptions flowed the reforming liberalism that would affect the Revolutionary era and all subsequent American history as well.

Educational and Social Reform. Since republicanism depended upon a knowledgeable citizenry, the Revolution immediately inspired educational efforts of every conceivable sort. American leaders formed scores of scientific organizations and medical societies, and produced many scholarly magazines. Gentlemen-scientists and amateur philosophers gave lectures and wrote essays on everything from raising Merino sheep to expelling noxious vapors from wells. They compiled geographical and historical studies of the states. And they concocted elaborate plans for educational structures ranging from elementary schools to a national university.

Although by 1776 there were only nine colleges in America, by 1800 sixteen more had been founded; and by the early nineteenth century colleges—mostly religiously inspired and short-lived—were being created by the dozens. Yet in the decades immediately following the Revolution most of the high hopes of the Revolutionary leaders for the establishment of publicly supported educational systems were not fulfilled, largely because of penny-pinching legislatures and religious jealousies. Even in New England, which had a long tradition of public education, privately endowed academies sprang up in the post-Revolutionary years to replace the older town supported grammar schools. Nevertheless, the republican ideal that the state had a fundamental responsibility to educate all its citizens remained alive to be eventually realized by the Common School movement during the second quarter of the nineteenth century.

Not only education but all social institutions were affected by this Revolutionary idealism. Americans grasped at the possibility that they might change their environment, even their natural environment, and thus their character. When the fast-growing

BENJAMIN RUSH, 1745-1813

One of the most versatile figures of the American Enlightenment, Rush was a physician, scientist, and humanitarian reformer of unbounded optimism. By the early nineteenth-century however, his earlier confidence in liberal rationalism was gone. The country's reliance on liberty "has already disappointed the expectations of its most sanguine and ardent friends." "Nothing but the gospel of Jesus Christ" could save republicanism. (Courtesy, Pennsylvania Hospital)

cities were afflicted by epidemics of yellow fever, Americans cleaned the streets and built public water works for sanitation. If the heat and cold of America's climate were too excessive, they cleared forests and drained marshes, and congratulated themselves on having moderated the weather. They now regarded virtually every sort of social victim as salvageable. Societies for assisting widows, immigrants, debtors, and other distressed groups were formed in the cities. More such philanthropic organizations were established in the decade and a half following Independence than in the entire colonial period. Revolutionary leaders like Jefferson drew up plans for liberalizing the harsh penal codes inherited from the colonial period. Pennsylvania led the way in the 1790s in abolishing the death penalty for all crimes other than murder, and began the experiment of confining criminals in specially designed penitentiaries instead of, as in the past, publicly punishing their bodies by whipping, mutilation, and execution.

The Family and Women. Republicanism even affected the transformation of the family that was taking place in many parts of the Western world at the end of the eighteenth century. In a republican society children could no longer be regarded simply as a means of making money for and bringing honor to the family; everyone in the family had to be treated individually and equally. Thus the new Revolutionary state governments struck out against aristocratic colonial laws that had confined the inheritance of property to the eldest sons (primogeniture) and to special lines of heirs (entail). Family-arranged marriages increasingly gave way to ties based on romantic love, and writings and novels in the post-Revolutionary years stressed the importance of raising children to become rational and independent citizens.

Republicanism also enhanced the status of women. It was now said that women as wives and mothers had a special role in cultivating in their husbands and children the moral feelings—virtue and social affection—necessary to hold a sprawling and competitive republican society together. Although some American leaders like the physician and humanitarian Benjamin Rush concluded that republi-

ABIGAIL ADAMS, BY MATHER BROWN
Though unschooled, the wife of John Adams was a
confident, intelligent and widely-read woman. Occasionally she expressed her resentment at the circumscribed role allowed to women in the eighteenth century, playfully urging John in 1776 to "remember the
ladies" in his plans for enhancing liberty. But generally she was very willing to sacrifice herself for her
husband and to accept her femininity "as a punishment
for the transgression of Eve." *(New York State His-*
torical Association, Cooperstown, New York)

MERCY OTIS WARREN (1728–1814), BY JOHN SINGLETON COPLEY
Warren, a sister of James Otis and the wife of the
Massachusetts patriot James Warren, was an important
intellectual figure in her own right. She wrote a number of satiric plays and a three-volume devoutly republican history of the Revolution. *(Courtesy, Museum of*
Fine Arts, Boston)

canism required women to be educated along with
men, others feared that female education would lead
only to vanity and a false ornamental gentility. Besides, asked Timothy Dwight, president of Yale, if
women were educated, "Who will make our pud-
dings?"

At the same time that a distinct sphere of domestic usefulness was being urged on women, they were
becoming more economically important and independent. Economic developments made it possible for
women to earn their own incomes by working in
handicrafts at home, hence enabling them to purchase
more and more "conveniences." Once they had become more independent by earning money at home,
women found it easier to work outside the household,
in factories and later as teachers. Although the development of a new sphere of domestic usefulness for
women may seem regressive by modern standards,

it was at the time liberating, and it intensified the advance begun in the colonial period over the dependent, inferior position traditionally held by women.

Antislavery. Perhaps the institution most directly and substantially affected by the liberalizing spirit of republicanism was chattel slavery. To be sure, the enslavement of nearly a half a million blacks was not eradicated at the Revolution, and in modern eyes this failure, amid all the high-blown talk of liberty and equality, becomes the one glaring and hypocritical inconsistency of the Revolutionary era. Nevertheless, the Revolution did suddenly and effectively end the social and intellectual climate that had allowed black slavery to exist in the colonies for over a century without substantial questioning. The colonists had generally taken slavery for granted as part of the natural order of society and as one aspect of the general brutality and cheapness of life in those premodern and prehumanitarian times. Bondage and servitude in many forms had continued to exist in pre-Revolutionary America, and the colonists had felt little need to question or defend slavery any more than other forms of debasement. Now, however, republican citizenship suddenly brought into question all kinds of personal dependency. For the first time

THE OLD PLANTATION, c. 1774–1794

"On Sundays," wrote a British visitor to the Chesapeake in 1774, "the slaves generally meet together and amuse themselves with Dancing to the Banjo. This musical instrument . . . is made of a Gourd something in imitation of a guitar, with only four strings. . . . Their Dancing is most violent exercise, but so irregular and grotesque. I am not able to describe it." (*Abby Aldrich Rockefeller Folk Art Center, Williamsburg*)

Americans were compelled to confront the slavery in their midst, to recognize that it was an aberration, a "peculiar institution," and, if they were to retain it, to explain and justify it.

Even before the Declaration of Independence, the colonists' struggle against political "slavery" had exposed the contradiction of tolerating chattel slavery. The initial efforts to end the contradiction were directed at the slave trade. In 1774 the Continental Congress urged abolishing the slave trade, and a half-dozen states quickly followed this advice. In 1775 the Quakers of Philadelphia formed the first antislavery society in the world, and soon similar societies were organized elsewhere, even in the South. During the war Congress and the northern states together with Maryland gave freedom to black slaves who enlisted in their armies. In various ways the Revolution worked to weaken the institution.

In the North, where slavery of a less harsh sort than existed in the South had been widespread but not deeply rooted in the society or economy, the institution was susceptible to political pressure, and it slowly began to recede. In the decades following the Revolution, most of the northern states moved to destroy slavery. By 1830 there were less than 3,000 slaves out of a northern black population of over 125,000. The Revolutionary vision of a society of independent freeholders led Congress in the 1780s to forbid slavery in the newly organized Northwest Territory between the Appalachians and the Mississippi. The new federal Constitution of 1787 promised an end to the slave trade after twenty years (1808), which many hoped would cripple the institution.

In the South, however, despite initial criticism by Jefferson and Madison and other enlightened social thinkers, slavery was too entrenched to be legislatively or judicially abolished. Southern whites who had been in the vanguard of the Revolutionary movement and among the most fervent spokesmen for its liberalism now began to develop a self-conscious sense of difference from the rest of America that they had never had before. By the 1790s the South was living with a growing realization, fed by the black insurrections in Santo Domingo, that the American presumption that people everywhere had a right to seek their freedom meant all people, white or black.

Democratic Despotism

Post-Revolutionary America was not all exhilaration and optimism however. Despite the victory over Great Britain and the achievement of independence, many of the Revolutionary leaders soon became disillusioned in the 1780s with the way the Revolution was developing. The very success of the Revolution in opening up opportunities for economic prosperity to new elements of the population made the 1780s a critical period for some members of the Revolutionary elite. Some even thought the entire experiment in republicanism was in danger. Too many ordinary people, some felt, were perverting republican equality, defying legitimate authority, and confounding those natural distinctions that all gentlemen, even republican gentlemen, thought essential for social order. Everywhere, even among the sturdy independent yeomen farmers—Jefferson's "chosen people of God"—private interests, selfishness, and money-making seemed to be eclipsing social affection and public spirit and indicating that Americans lacked the qualities required of republicans. If this were true, America, some feared, was doomed to share the fate that had befallen the ancient republics, Britain, and other corrupt nations. Americans, William Livingston, governor of New Jersey concluded in 1787, "do not exhibit the virtue that is necessary to support a republican government." This unrepublican character of the people seemed most clearly revealed in the behavior of the greatly strengthened state legislatures.

Democratization of the State Legislatures. The radical changes in representation that accompanied the Revolution had democratized the state assemblies by increasing the number of members and by altering their social character. Men of more humble, more rural origins, and less educated than those who sat in the colonial legislatures, now became representatives. In New Hamshire, for example, in 1765 the colonial house of representatives had contained only thirty-four members, almost all well-to-do gentry from the coastal region around Portsmouth. By 1786 the state's house of representatives had increased to eighty-eight members. Most of these men were ordinary farmers or men of moderate wealth, and many were from the western areas of the state. In other states, the change was much less dramatic but no less important. It was reflected in the shifts, or in the attempted shifts, of many of the state capitals from their former colonial locations on the eastern seaboard to new sites in the interior—from Portsmouth to Concord, from New York to Albany, from Williamsburg to Richmond, from New Bern to Raleigh, from Charleston to Columbia, from Savannah to Augusta.

Everywhere electioneering and the open competition for office increased, along with demands for greater popular access to governmental activities. Assembly proceedings were opened to the public, and a growing number of newspapers, which now included dailies, began to report legislative debates. Self-appointed leaders, speaking for newly aroused groups and localities, took advantage of the enlarged suffrage and the annual elections of the legislatures (a radical innovation in most states) to seek membership in the assemblies. New petty entrepreneurs like Abraham Yates, a part-time lawyer and cobbler of Albany, and William Findley, a Scotch-Irish ex-weaver of western Pennsylvania, bypassed the traditional social hierarchy and vaulted into political leadership in the states. The number of contested elections and the turnover of legislative seats multiplied.

Local Factionalism. Under these circumstances many of the state legislatures could scarcely fulfill what many Revolutionaries in 1776 had assumed was their republican responsibility to promote the general good. In every state decisions had to be made about what to do with the loyalists and their confiscated property, about the distribution of taxes among the citizens, and about the economy. Yet with the general political instability, the common welfare in the various states was increasingly difficult to define. By the 1780s James Madison concluded that "a spirit of *locality*" in the state legislatures was destroying "the aggregate interests of the community,"

and that this localist spirit was "inseparable" from elections by small districts and towns. Each representative, said Ezra Stiles, president of Yale College, was concerned only with the special interests of his electors. Whenever a bill was read in the legislature, "every one instantly thinks how it will affect his constituents."

Such narrow-interest politics was not new to America. But the multiplication of economic and social interests in the post-Revolutionary years and the heightened sensitivity of the enlarged popular assemblies to the conflicting demands of these interests now dramatically increased its intensity and importance. Debtor farmers urged low taxes, the staying of court actions to recover debts, and the printing of paper money. Merchants and creditors called for high taxes on land, the protection of private contracts, and the encouragement of foreign trade. Artisans pleaded for price regulation of agricultural products, the abolition of mercantile monopolies, and tariff protection against imported manufactures. And entrepreneurs everywhere petitioned for legal privileges and corporate grants.

All this political scrambling among contending interests made lawmaking in the states seem chaotic. Laws, as the Vermont Council of Censors said in 1786 in a common complaint, were "altered—realtered—made better—made worse; and kept in such a fluctuating position, that persons in civil commission scarce know what is law." As James Madison pointed out, more laws were enacted by the states in the decade following Independence than in the entire colonial period. Many of them were simply private acts for individuals or resolves that redressed minor grievances. Every effort of the legislatures to respond to the excited pleas and pressures of all the various groups alienated as many as it satisfied and brought lawmaking itself into contempt.

By the mid-1780s many American leaders had come to believe that the state legislatures, not the governors, were the political authority to be most feared. Not only were some of the legislators violating the individual rights of property through their excessive printing of paper money and their various acts on behalf of debtors, but in all the states the assemblies pushed beyond the generous grants of legisla-

MASSACHUSETTS STATE HOUSE AND MEMORIAL COLUMN, 1795-1798
Charles Bulfinch (1763-1844) was one of the first Americans to move from being a leisured gentleman with an amateur interest in building to becoming a professional architect. Everything about his State House, one of many public buildings he designed, celebrates the new classical grandeur of republican America. (*The Bostonian Society*)

tive authority of the 1776 Revolutionary constitutions and were absorbing numerous executive and judicial duties. It began to seem that the legislative power of the people was no more trustworthy than the detested royal power had been. Legislators were supposedly the representatives of the people who annually elected them; but "173 despots would surely be as oppressive as one," wrote Jefferson in 1785 in his *Notes on Virginia.* "An *elective despotism* was not the government we fought for."

Revision of the State Constitutions. Such growing fears of tyrannical legislatures forced many leaders to have second thoughts about their popularly elected assemblies. Indeed, the ink was scarcely dry on the Revolutionary state constitutions before some were suggesting that they needed to be revised. Beginning with the New York constitution in 1777 and proceeding through the constitutions of Massachusetts in

1780 and New Hampshire in 1784, constitution-makers now sought a very different distribution of powers of government from that made in 1776.

Instead of placing all power in the legislatures, particularly in the lower houses, and draining all power from the governors as the early state constitutions had done, these later constitutions strengthened the executives, senates, and judiciaries. The Massachusetts constitution of 1780 especially seemed to many to have recaptured some of the best characteristics of the English constitutional balance, which had been forgotten during the popular enthusiasm of 1776. The new Massachusetts governor, with a fixed salary and elected directly by the people, now assumed more of the independence and some of the powers of the old royal governors, including those of appointing to offices and vetoing legislation.

With the Massachusetts constitution as a model, other constitutional reformers worked to revise their own state constitutions. The popular legislatures were reduced in size and their authority curbed. Senates or upper houses were instituted where they did not exist, as in Pennsylvania, Georgia, and Vermont; and where they did exist, they were made more stable by lengthening their terms and by requiring higher property qualifications for their members. The governors were freed of their dependence on the legislatures, and given a clearer responsibility for government. And judges became independent guardians of the constitutions. By 1790 Pennsylvania, South Carolina, and Georgia had reformed their constitutions along these more conservative lines; New Hampshire, Delaware, and Vermont soon followed in the early 1790s.

At the same time that political leaders were trying to restrengthen the authority of governors, senators, and judges that had been diluted in the state constitutions created in 1776, they also were trying to limit the powers of the legislatures by appealing to the fundamental law that was presumably embodied in these written documents. Since many of the constitutions had been created by simple legislative act, the distinction between fundamental and ordinary law was not easily sustained. At first several of the states had grappled with various devices to ensure the fundamentality of their constitutions. Some simply declared their constitutions to be fundamental; others required a special majority or successive acts of the legislature for amending the constitution. But none of these measures proved effective against recurrent legislative encroachments.

Out of these kinds of pressures, both logical and political, Americans gradually moved toward institutionalizing the belief that if the constitution was to be truly immune from legislative tampering, it would have to be created, as Jefferson said in 1783, "by a power superior to that of the ordinary legislature."

For a solution, Americans fell back on the institution of the convention. In 1775–76, the convention had been merely a legally deficient legislature made necessary by the crown's refusal to call together the regular representatives of the people. Now, however, the convention became a special alternative representation of the people with the exclusive authority to frame or amend a constitution. When Massachusetts and New Hampshire came to write new constitutions in the late 1770s and early 1780s the proper pattern of constitution-making and constitution-altering had become clear. Constitutions were formed by specially elected conventions and then placed before the people for ratification.

With this idea of a constitution as fundamental law immune from legislative encroachment firmly in hand, some state judges during the 1780s began cautiously moving in isolated cases to impose restraints on what the assemblies were enacting as law. In effect they said to the legislatures, as George Wythe, judge of the Virginia supreme court, did in 1782, "Here is the limit of your authority; and hither shall you go, but no further." These were the hesitant beginnings of what would come to be called "judicial review." But as yet many leaders were unwilling to allow appointed judges to set aside laws made by the people represented in democratically elected legislatures. It appeared obviously unrepublican.

As vigorously as all these state reforms were tried in the 1780s, however, to many they did not seem sufficient. By the mid-eighties some reformers were thinking of shifting the arena of constitutional change from the state to the nation and were considering some sort of modification of the structure of the central government as the best and perhaps only answer to America's political and social problems.

SUGGESTED READINGS

The fullest account of state constitution-making and politics is Allan Nevins, *The American States during and after the Revolution, 1775–1789* (1924). Elisha P. Douglass, *Rebels and Democrats* (1955), is important in emphasizing the radical and populist impulses in the states. Among the

most significant of the state studies are Philip A. Crowl, *Maryland during and after the Revolution* (1943); Richard P. McCormick, *Experiment in Independence: New Jersey in the Critical Period, 1781–1789* (1950); Irwin H. Polishook, *Rhode Island and the Union, 1774–1795* (1969); Robert J. Taylor,

Western Massachusetts in the Revolution (1954); and Alfred F. Young, *The Democratic Republicans of New York: The Origins, 1763–1797* (1967). Jackson T. Main, *The Sovereign States, 1775–1783* (1973), describes state affairs during the war. J. R. Pole, *Political Representation in England and the Origins of the American Republic* (1966), has some excellent chapters on state politics during the Revolutionary and immediate post-Revolutionary years. Merrill Jensen, in *The Articles of Confederation . . . 1774–1781* (1940), and *The New Nation . . . 1781–1789* (1950), describes the political and social conflicts within the Confederation government and stresses the achievements of the Articles. H. James Henderson, *Party Politics in the Continental Congress* (1974), emphasizes a sectional rather than a social division among the delegates to the national government. The best history of the congress is Jack N. Rakove, *The Beginnings of National Politics* (1979).

The starting point for appreciating the social changes of the Revolution is the short essay by J. Franklin Jameson, *The American Revolution Considered as a Social Movement* (1926). The last two chapters of James A. Henretta, *The Evolution of American Society, 1700–1815* (1973), summarize the social effects of the war and the Revolution. J. Kirby Martin, *Men in Rebellion: Higher Government Leaders and the Coming of the American Revolution* (1973); Jackson T. Main, *The Upper House in Revolutionary America, 1763–1788* (1967); and Main, "Government by the People: The American Revolution and the Democratization of the Legislatures," *Wm. and Mary Q.*, 3d ser., 28 (1966), document the displacement of elites in politics during the Revolution. Chilton Williamson, *American Suffrage from Property to Democracy, 1760–1860* (1960), describes the expansion of voting rights. A neat account of Concord, Massachusetts in the Revolution is Robert A. Gross, *The Minutemen and Their World* (1976).

A helpful survey of American social history is Rowland Berthoff, *An Unsettled People* (1971). But it has not replaced the encyclopedic History of American Life Series edited by Arthur M. Schlesinger and Dixon Ryan Fox. The two volumes covering the Revolutionary era are Evarts B. Greene, *The Revolutionary Generation, 1763–1790* (1943); and John Allen Krout and Dixon Ryan Fox, *The Completion of Independence, 1790–1830* (1944). Population developments are summarized by J. Potter, "The Growth of Population in America, 1700–1860," in David Glass and D. E. Eversley, eds., *Population in History* (1965). An important social history that goes well beyond its title is David J. Rothman, *The Discovery of the Asylum: Social Order and Disorder in the New Republic* (1971).

Two surveys of economic life are useful: Stuart Bruchey, *The Roots of American Economic Growth, 1607–1861* (1965); and Douglass C. North, *The Economic Growth of the United States, 1790–1860* (1961). To understand the interrelated nature of the social, economic, and political processes in this period, the student can find no better work than Oscar Handlin and Mary Handlin, *Commonwealth: A Study of the Role of Government in the American Economy: Massachusetts, 1774–1861* (rev. ed., 1969). It is especially important for its analysis of the changing nature of the corporation.

On the commercial effects of the Revolution, see Curtis P. Nettles, *The Emergence of a National Economy, 1775–1815* (1962); and Robert A. East, *Business Enterprise in the American Revolutionary Era* (1938). On the plight of the loyalists, see Wallace Brown, *The Good Americans* (1969), and Mary Beth Norton, *The British-Americans: The Loyalist Exiles in England, 1774–1789* (1972).

On the Enlightenment, see Henry May, *The Enlightenment in America* (1976) and Henry S. Commager, *Empire of Reason* (1977). The standard survey is Russel B. Nye, *The Cultural Life of the New Nation, 1776–1830* (1960). See also Joseph J. Ellis, *After the Revolution: Profiles of Early American Culture* (1979). A particularly important study of education is Carl F. Kaestle, *The Evolution of an Urban School System* (1973). See also Rush Welter, *Popular Education and Democratic Thought in America* (1962), and Douglas Sloan, *The Scottish Enlightenment and the American College Ideal* (1971). On women, see Mary Beth Norton, *Liberty's Daughters: The Revolutionary Experience of American Women, 1750–1800* (1980); and Nancy Cott, *The Bonds of Womanhood* (1977). Benjamin Quarles, *The Negro in the American Revolution* (1961), is the best study of the contribution of blacks to the Revolution. On slavery and opposition to it, see Winthrop Jordan, *White over Black: American Attitudes toward the Negro, 1550–1812* (1968); and David Brion Davis, *The Problem of Slavery in the Age of Revolution, 1770–1823* (1975). On the abolition of slavery in the North, see Arthur Zilversmit, *The First Emancipation* (1967).

CHAPTER 10

The Federalist Age

*T*he American Revolution, like all revolutions, could not fulfill all the highest hopes of its leaders. Within a decade after the Declaration of Independence was signed many of the Revolutionary leaders had come to doubt the direction America was taking. Not only were they anxious to lessen the power of the state legislatures, but at the same time they were becoming increasingly aware that the Confederation Congress was too weak to accomplish its tasks both at home and abroad. In the mid-1780s frustration with piecemeal changes in the Articles of Confederation came together with mounting concern over the political and social conditions in the states to produce a powerful momentum for drastic constitutional change. The federal Constitution of 1787 was the result.

This new national Constitution, which supplanted the Articles of Confederation, both limited the authority of the states and created an unprecedented concentration of power. Many Americans could only conclude that this new Constitution represented as radical a change as the Revolution itself. At last, in the eyes of some, the inauguration of a new federal government promised the harmony and stability that would allow America to become a great and glorious nation.

The Critical Period

Even before the Articles of Confederation were ratified in 1781, the experiences of the war had exposed the weakness of the Congress and encouraged some Americans to think about making changes in the central government. By 1780 the war was dragging on longer than anyone had expected, and the skyrocketing inflation of the paper money used to finance it was unsettling commerce and business. Congressional delegates were barred from serving more than three years in six, and leadership in the Confederation was fluctuating and confused. The states were ignoring congressional resolutions and were refusing to supply their allotted financial requisitions to the federal government. The Congress stopped paying interest on the public debt. The Continental army was smoldering with resentment at the lack of pay and was falling apart through desertions and even outbreaks of mutiny. All these circumstances were forcing mercantile and creditor interests, especially those centered in the mid-Atlantic states, to seek to add to the powers of the Congress—by broad interpretation of the Articles; by direct amendment, which required the consent of all states; and even by the threat of military force.

Domestic Weakness of the Confederation. A shift in congressional leadership in the early 1780s expressed the increasing influence of these concerned groups. Older popular radicals such as Richard Henry Lee and Arthur Lee of Virginia and Samuel Adams of Massachusetts were replaced by younger men such as James Madison of Virginia and Alexander Hamilton of New York, who were more interested in authority and stability than popular liberty. Disillusioned by the ineffectiveness of the Confederation, these nationalists in the Congress set about reversing the localist and power-weakening thrust of the Revolution. They strengthened the regular army at the expense of the militia and promised pensions to the Continental army officers. They reorganized the departments of war, foreign affairs, and finance in the Congress and appointed individuals in place of committees to run them.

The key individual in the nationalists' program was Robert Morris, a wealthy Philadelphia merchant who was made superintendent of finance and virtual head of the confederacy in 1781. Morris undertook to stabilize the economy and to involve financial and commercial groups with the central government. He induced Congress to recommend to the states that paper money laws be repealed and to require that the states' contributions to the general expenses be paid in specie. And he sought to establish a bank and to make federal bonds more secure for investors.

This nationalist program depended upon amending the Articles so that the Confederation would have the power to levy a five percent duty on imports. Once Congress had adequate revenues independent of the states, the Confederation could pay its debts and would become more attractive to prospective

ROBERT MORRIS
Morris, a wealthy Philadelphia merchant, has been called "the financier of the Revolution." Land speculation in the 1790s ruined him, and he ended his career in debtors prison. (*National Portrait Gallery, Smithsonian Institution, Washington, D.C.*)

buyers of its bonds. Although Morris was able to induce Congress to charter the Bank of North America, the rest of the nationalists' economic proposals narrowly failed. Not only did the states refuse to grant the unanimous consent required for the tax amendment, but many were delinquent in supplying requisitioned funds to Congress. Nor was Congress able to get even a restricted authority to regulate commerce.

After the victory at Yorktown in October 1781 and the opening of peace negotiations with Great Britain, interest in the Congress declined and some individuals became desperate. The prospect of Congress's demobilizing the army without fulfilling its promises of back pay and pensions created a crisis that brought the United States as close to a military coup d'état as it has ever been. In March 1783 the officers of Washington's army encamped at Newburgh on the Hudson issued an address to the Congress concerning their pay, and actually considered some sort of military action against the Confederation. Only when Washington personally intervened and refused to support a movement designed, as he said, "to open the floodgates of civil discord, and deluge our rising empire in blood" was the crisis averted.

News of the peace in 1783 shattered much of the unionist sentiment that had existed during the war. By December 1783 the Congress, in Jefferson's opinion, had lost much of its usefulness. "The constant session of Congress," he said, "can not be necessary in time of peace." After clearing up the most urgent business, the delegates should "separate and return to our respective states, leaving only a Committee of the states," and thus "destroy the strange idea of their being a permanent body, which has unaccountably taken possession of the heads of their constituents."

Congressional power, which had been substantial during the war years, now began to disintegrate, and delegates increasingly complained how difficult it was even to gather a quorum. Congress could not even agree on a permanent home for itself, but wandered from Philadelphia to Princeton, to Annapolis, to Trenton, and finally to New York. The states reasserted their authority and began taking over the payment of the federal debt that many had earlier hoped to make the cement of union. By 1786 nearly one-third of the federal securities had been converted into state bonds, thus creating a vested interest among

public creditors in the sovereignty of the individual states. Under these circumstances the influence of those, in Hamilton's term, "who think continentally" rapidly declined, and the chances of amending the Confederation piecemeal declined with them. The only hope of reform now seemed to lie in some sort of convention of all the states.

International Weakness of the Confederation.　In Europe the reputation of the United States dwindled as rapidly as did its credit. Loans from the Dutch and French were extracted only at extraordinary rates of interest. Since American ships now lacked the protection of the British flag, they were seized by the Barbary states in the Mediterranean and their crews sold as slaves. Congress had no money to pay the

THE OLD STATE HOUSE OF PENNSYLVANIA (UNTIL 1799) LATER CALLED INDEPENDENCE HALL.

Both the Second Continental Congress and the federal Convention of 1787 met here. The tower was added in the middle of the eighteenth century to house the Liberty Bell. (*By permission of the Houghton Library, Harvard University*)

necessary tribute and ransoms to these North African pirates.

Amid a world of hostile empires it was even difficult for the new republican confederacy to maintain its territorial integrity. Britain refused to send a minister to the United States and ignored its treaty obligations to evacuate its military posts in the Northwest, claiming that the United States had not honored its commitments. The treaty of peace had stipulated that the Confederation would recommend to the states that loyalist property confiscated during the Revolution be restored and that neither side would make laws that obstructed the recovery of prewar debts. When the states flouted these treaty obligations, the impotent Confederation could do nothing.

Britain was known to be intriguing with the Indians and encouraging separatist movements in the Northwest and in the Vermont borderlands, and Spain was doing the same in the Southwest. Spain in fact refused to recognize American claims in the territory between the Ohio River and Florida. In 1784, in an effort to influence the American settlers moving into Kentucky and Tennessee, Spain closed the Mississippi to American trade. Ready to deal with any government that could ensure access to the sea for their agricultural produce, many of the westerners were, as Washington noted in 1784, "on a pivot. The touch of a feather would turn them any way."

In 1785–86 John Jay, a New York aristocrat and the secretary of foreign affairs, negotiated a treaty with the Spanish minister to the United States, Diego de Gardoqui. By the terms of this agreement Spain was opened to American trade in return for America's renunciation of its right to navigate the Mississippi for several decades. Out of fear of being denied an outlet to the sea in the West, the southern states prevented the necessary nine-state majority in the Congress from agreeing to the treaty. But the willingness of a majority of seven states to sacrifice western interests for the sake of northern merchants brought long-existing sectional jealousies into play and threatened to shatter the Union.

Toward the Philadelphia Convention. The inability of the Confederation to regulate commerce finally precipitated reform of the Articles. Jefferson, Madison, and other agrarian-minded leaders feared that if American farmers were prohibited from selling their surplus crops freely in Europe not only would the industrious character of the farmers be undermined, but the United States would be unable to pay for manufactured goods imported from Europe and would therefore be compelled to enter into large-scale manufacturing for itself. This in turn would eventually destroy the yeoman-citizenry on which republicanism was based and create in America the same kind of corrupt, stratified, and dependent society that existed in Europe.

Yet, in the 1780s, despite strenuous diplomatic efforts like those of John Adams in Britain and Jefferson in France to develop new international commercial relationships involving the free exchange of goods, the mercantilist empires of the major European nations remained generally closed to the new republic. The French were unwilling to take as much American produce as expected, and Britain effectively closed its markets to competitive American goods while recapturing American consumer markets for its own goods. The Confederation lacked any authority to retaliate with trade regulations, and several attempts to grant Congress a restricted power over commerce were lost amid state and sectional jealousies. The Confederation Congress watched helplessly as the separate states attempted to pass conflicting navigation acts of their own; by the mid-eighties Connecticut was laying heavier duties on goods from Massachusetts than on those from Great Britain.

By 1786 these accumulated pressures made some sort of revision of the Articles inevitable. Virginia's desire for trade regulation led to a convention of several states at Annapolis in September 1786. Those who attended this meeting quickly realized that commerce could not be considered apart from other problems and called for a larger convention in Philadelphia the following year. After several states agreed to send delegates to Philadelphia, the Confederation Congress belatedly recognized the approaching convention and in February 1787 authorized it to revise and amend the Articles of Confederation.

DANIEL SHAYS AND JACOBB SHATTUCKS
Shays and Shattucks, former militia officers, were leaders of the uprising of aggrieved western Massachusetts farmers in 1786. The farmers, calling themselves "Regulators," protested the shortage of money and the foreclosures of mortgages and imprisonments for debt. Shays's Rebellion had a powerful effect on conservative leaders and helped compel reform of the national government. (*National Portrait Gallery, Smithsonian Institution, Washington, D.C.*)

Although by 1787 nearly all of America's political leaders agreed that some reform of the Articles was necessary, few expected what the Philadelphia Convention eventually created—a new Constitution that utterly transformed the structure of the central government and promised a radical weakening of the power of the states. The extraordinarily powerful national government that emerged from Philadelphia went well beyond what was demanded in additional congressional powers by the difficulties of credit and commerce and the humiliations in foreign affairs. Given the Revolutionaries' loyalty to their states and their deep-rooted fears of centralized governmental authority, the formation of the new Constitution was a truly remarkable achievement that cannot be explained simply by the obvious weaknesses of the Articles of Confederation.

In the end it was the problems within the separate states during the 1780s that made constitutional reform of the central government possible. The confusing and unjust laws coming out of the state governments, Madison informed Jefferson in 1787, had become "so frequent and so flagrant as to alarm the most stedfast friends of Republicanism." It was these state vices, said Madison, that "contributed more to that uneasiness which produced the Convention, and prepared the public mind for a general reform, than

those which accrued to our national character and interest from the inadequacy of the Confederation to its immediate objects."

In 1786 a rebellion of nearly two thousand debtor farmers threatened with foreclosure of their property broke out in western Massachusetts. This rebellion, led by a former militia captain, Daniel Shays, confirmed many of these anxieties about state politics. For the insurrection, which temporarily closed the courts and threatened a federal arsenal, occurred in the state considered to have the best balanced constitution. Although Shays's insurgents were defeated by militia troops, his sympathizers were victorious at the polls early in 1787, and they enacted debtor relief legislation that added to the growing fears of legislative tyranny.

Thus by 1786–87 the reconstruction of the central government was being sought as a means of correcting not only the weaknesses of the Articles but the internal political vices of the states. A new central government, some believed, could save both Congress from the states and the states from themselves. And new groups joined those already working to invigorate the national government. Urban artisans hoped a stronger national government would prevent competition from British imports. Southerners, particularly in Virginia, wanted to gain representation

in the national government proportional to their growing population. And most important, gentry up and down the continent momentarily submerged their sectional and economic differences in the face of what seemed a threat to individual liberty from the tyranny of legislative majorities within the states. Creating a new central government was no longer simply a matter of cementing the Union, or of standing up strong in foreign affairs, or of satisfying the demands of particular creditor, mercantile, and army interests. It was now a matter, as Madison declared, that would "decide forever the fate of republican government."

The Federal Constitution

The convocation of the Philadelphia Convention that drafted the federal Constitution in the summer of 1787 was very much a revolutionary movement. Yet such were the circumstances and climate of the post-Revolutionary years in America that the sudden calling of a constitutional convention and the creation of an entirely new and different sort of federal republican government in 1787 seemed remarkably natural and legitimate.

Fifty-five delegates representing twelve states attended the Philadelphia Convention in the summer of 1787. (Rhode Island refused to have anything to do with efforts to revise the Articles.) Although many of the delegates were young men—their average age was forty-two—most were well educated and experienced members of America's political elite. Thirty-nine had served in Congress at one time or another, eight had worked in the state constitutional conventions, seven had been state governors, and thirty-four were lawyers. One-third were veterans of the Continental army, that "great dissolvent of state loyalties," as Washington once called it. Nearly all were gentlemen, "natural aristocrats," who took their political superiority for granted as an inevitable consequence of their social and economic position. Washington was made president of the Convention. Some of the outstanding figures of the Revolution were not present: Samuel Adams was ill; Jefferson and John Adams

were serving as ministers abroad; and Richard Henry Lee and Patrick Henry, although selected by the Virginia legislature, refused to attend the Convention, Henry saying, "I smelt a rat." The most influential delegations were those of Pennsylvania and Virginia, which included Gouverneur Morris and James Wilson of Pennsylvania and Edmund Randolph, George Mason, and James Madison of Virginia.

The Virginia Plan. The Virginia delegation took the lead, presenting the Convention with its first working proposal. This, the Virginia Plan, was largely the effort of the thirty-six-year-old Madison, who

JAMES MADISON, 1751–1836

Madison was the greatest political thinker of the Revolutionary era and perhaps of all American history. His was the most critical and undogmatic mind of the Revolutionary leaders. More than anyone else he formulated the theory that underlaid the new expanded republic of 1787. (*The Thomas Gilcrease Institute of American History and Art, Tulsa, Oklahoma*)

more than any other person deserves the title "father of the Constitution." Short, shy, and soft-spoken, habitually dressed in black, trained to no profession but widely read and possessing an acute and questioning mind, Madison devoted his life to public service. He understood clearly the historical significance of the meeting of the Convention, and it is because he decided to make a detailed private record of the Convention debates that so much is known of what was said that summer in Philadelphia.

Madison's initial proposals for reform were truly radical. They were not, as he pointed out, mere expedients or simple revisions of the Articles; they promised "systematic change" of government. What Madison had in mind was to create a general government that would not be a confederation of independent republics but a national republic in its own right. It would operate directly on individuals and be organized as the state governments had been organized, with a single executive, a bicameral legislature, and a separate judiciary.

This national republic would be superimposed on the states, which would now stand to the central government, in John Jay's words, "in the same light in which counties stand to the state of which they are parts, viz., merely as districts to facilitate the purposes of domestic order of good government." Thus the radical Virginia Plan provided for a two-house national legislature with the authority to legislate "in all cases to which the states are incompetent" and "to negative all laws passed by the several states, contravening in the opinion of the national legislature, the articles of union." If the national government had the power to veto all state laws, Madison believed, it could then play the same role the English crown had been supposed to play in the empire—that of a "disinterested umpire" over clashing interests.

The New Jersey Plan.   For many in the Philadelphia Convention, however, this Virginia Plan was much too extreme. Most delegates were prepared to grant substantial power to the federal government, including the right to tax, regulate commerce, and execute federal laws; but many did not want to allow such a weakening of state authority as the Virginia Plan proposed. Opponents of the nationalists, led by dele-

gates from New Jersey, Connecticut, New York, and Delaware, countered with their own proposal, the New Jersey Plan (so-called because William Paterson of New Jersey introduced it). This plan essentially amended the Articles of Confederation by increasing the powers of Congress but at the same time maintained the basic sovereignty of the states. With two such opposite proposals before it, the Convention, in the middle of June 1787, approached a crisis.

Provisions of the Constitution.   During the debate that followed, the nationalists, led by Madison and Wilson, were able to retain the basic features of the Virginia Plan. Although the Convention refused to grant the national legislature a blanket authority "to legislate in all cases to which the separate States are incompetent," it granted the Congress (in Article I, Section 8, of the Constitution) a list of enumerated powers, including the powers to tax, to borrow and coin money, and to regulate commerce. Instead of giving the national legislature the right to veto harmful state laws, as Madison wanted, the Convention forbade the states to exercise particular sovereign powers whose abuse lay behind the crisis of the 1780s. In Article I, Section 10, of the final Constitution the states were barred from carrying on foreign relations, levying tariffs, coining money, issuing bills of credit, passing *ex post facto* laws (which punished actions that were not illegal when they were committed), or doing anything to relieve debtors of the obligations of their contracts.*

In contrast to the extensive fiscal powers given to the Congress, the state governments were rendered nearly economically impotent. Not only did the new federal Constitution prohibit the states from imposing customs duties—the eighteenth century's most common and efficient form of taxation—but it denied the states the authority to issue paper money and succeeded in doing what the British government's several currency acts had earlier tried to do.

The Convention decided on a strong and single executive. The president stood alone, unencumbered by an executive council except of his own choosing.

*For the Constitution, see Appendix.

With command over the armed forces, with the authority to direct diplomatic relations, with power over appointments to the executive and judicial branches, and with a four-year term of office and perpetual eligibility for reelection, the president was a magistrate who, as Patrick Henry later charged, could "easily become king."

To ensure the president's independence, he was not to be elected by the legislature, as the Virginia Plan had proposed. Since the framers of the Constitution believed that only a few presidential candidates in the future would be known to the people throughout the country, they provided for local elections of "electors" equal in number to the representatives and senators from each state. These electors would cast ballots for the president, but if any candidate failed to get a majority—which in the absence of political parties and organized electioneering was normally expected—the final selection from the five candidates with the most votes would be made by the House of Representatives, with each state delegation having one vote.

The Virginia Plan's suggestion of a separate national judiciary to hold office "during good behavior" was accepted without dispute; the structure of the national judiciary was left to the Congress to devise. The right of this judiciary, however, to nullify acts of the Congress or of the state legislatures was as yet by no means clear.

The nationalists in the Convention reluctantly gave way on several crucial issues, particularly on the national legislature's authority to veto state legislation. But they fought longest and hardest to hold on to the principle of proportional representation in both houses of the legislature, and almost stalemated the Convention. It was decided that both taxation and representation, at least in the House of Representatives, would be based not on states as such or on landed wealth, but on population, with the slaves each counting as three-fifths of a person. The nationalists like Madison and Wilson, however, wanted representation in the Senate also to rest on population. Any semblance of representing the separate sovereignty of the states smacked too much of the Articles of Confederation. Hence they came to regard the eventual "Connecticut Compromise" by which

ROGER SHERMAN, BY RALPH EARL

Roger Sherman (1721–1793) began as a cobbler, but well before the Revolution he had become a lawyer, merchant, and substantial Connecticut official. He is best known for his introduction in the Philadelphia Convention of the "compromise" granting each state two senators. (*Yale University Art Gallery, Gift of Roger Sherman White*)

each state secured two senators in the upper house of the legislature as a defeat.

Although Madison and Wilson lost the battles over the congressional veto of state laws and proportional representation in both houses, the Federalists (as those who supported the Constitution came to call themselves) had won the war even before the Convention adjourned. Once the New Jersey Plan, which embodied the essentials of the Articles of Confederation, was rejected in favor of the Virginia Plan, the opponents, or Antifederalists, found themselves forced, as Richard Henry Lee complained, to accept "this or nothing."

Although the Articles of Confederation stipulated that amendments be made by the unanimous consent of the state legislatures, the delegates to the Philadelphia Convention decided to bypass the state legislatures and submit the Constitution to specially elected state conventions for ratification. Approval of only nine of the thirteen states was necessary for the new government to take effect. This transgression of earlier political principles was only one of many to which the Antifederalists objected.

The Federalist-Antifederalist Debate. The federal government established by the Philadelphia Convention seemed severely to violate the maxims of 1776 that had guided the Revolutionary constitution-makers. Not only did the new Constitution provide for a strong government with an extraordinary amount of power given to the president and the Senate, but it created a single republican state that would span the continent and encompass all the diverse and scattered interests of the whole of American society—an impossibility for a republic, according to the best political science of the day.

During the debates over ratification in the fall and winter of 1787-88, the Antifederalists seized on these Federalist violations of the earlier Revolutionary assumptions. They charged that the new federal government with its concentration of power at the expense of liberty resembled a monarchy, and that because of the extensive and heterogeneous nature of the society it was to govern, it would have to act tyrannically. Inevitably America would become a single consolidated state, with the individuality of the separate states sacrificed to a powerful government. And this would happen, the Antifederalists argued, because of the logic of sovereignty—that powerful principle of eighteenth-century political science, earlier maintained by the English in the imperial debate, that said that no society could long possess two legislatures but must inevitably have one final, indivisible, lawmaking authority. The Antifederalists argued that if the new national government was to be more powerful than the state governments, and the Constitution was to be the "Supreme Law of the Land," then, according to the doctrine of sovereignty, the legislative authority of the separate states would eventually be annihilated.

Despite these formidable Antifederalist arguments, the Federalists did not believe that the Constitution repudiated the Revolution and the prin-ciples of 1776. During the decade since Independence the political world had been transformed. Americans, it now appeared clear, had effectively transferred the location of this final lawmaking authority called sovereignty from the institutions of government to the people at large.

In the years since the Revolution many Americans had continued to act outside of all official institutions of government. During the 1780s they had organized various committees, conventions, and other extralegal bodies of the people as they had during the Revolution, to voice grievances and to seek political goals. Vigilante actions of various kinds had done quickly and efficiently what the new state governments often were unable to do, whether it was controlling prices, preventing profiteering, or punishing Tories. Everywhere people had drawn out the logic of "actual" representation and had sought to instruct and control the institutions of government. By 1787-88 all of this activity of the people at large tended to give reality to the idea that sovereignty in America resided in the people, and not in any institution of government. Only by believing that sovereignty was held by the people outside of government could Americans make theoretical sense of their recent remarkable political inventions—their conception of a written constitution immune from legislative tampering, their special constitution-making conventions, and their unusual ideas of "actual" representation.

The Federalists were now determined to use this new understanding of the ultimate power of the people to meet all the Antifederalist arguments against the Constitution. True, they said, the Philadelphia Convention had gone beyond its instructions to amend the Articles of Confederation; it had drawn up an entirely new government, and had provided for its ratification by special state conventions. But had not Americans learned during the previous decade that legislatures were not competent to create or change a constitution? If the Constitution were to be truly a fundamental law, then, Federalists like Madison argued, it had to be ratified "by the supreme authority of the people themselves." Hence it was "We the people of the United States," and not the

The Federal Plan Most Solid & Secure
Americans Their Freedom Will Ensure
All Arts Shall Flourish in Columbias Land
And All Her Sons Join as One Social Band

SOCIETY of PEWTERERS

SOLID AND PURE

SILK BANNER OF
SOCIETY OF PEWTERERS
The pewterers, like other artisans, favored the new Constitution and in several cities
in July 1788 joined in huge
parades celebrating the birth
of the new federal government. Such craftsmen were
worried about imported foreign manufactures and thought
the new national government
could better levy tariffs than
the separate states. Their support of the Constitution was
important for ratification in
several northern states. (*Courtesy of The New York Historical
Society, New York City*)

states, that ordained and established the Constitution.

By locating sovereignty in the people rather than in any particular institution, the Federalists could now conceive of what had hitherto been a contradiction in politics—two legislatures operating simultaneously over the same community—and could thus answer the principal objection to the Constitution. Only by making the people themselves the final law-making authority could the Federalists explain this emerging conception of federalism, or that peculiar division of legislative responsibilities between the national and state governments that still amazes the world.

This new understanding of the relation of the society to government now enabled the Federalists to explain the expansion of a single republican state over a large continent of diverse groups and interests. Seizing on the English philosopher David Hume's radical suggestion that a republican government might operate better in a large territory than in a small one, the Federalists, and in particular James Madison, ingeniously turned upside down the older assumptions about the appropriate size of a republic.

Experience in America after 1776 had demonstrated that no republic could be made small enough to avoid the clashing of rival parties and interests (tiny Rhode Island was the most faction-ridden of all). The extended territory of the new national republic, Madison wrote in a series of publications, especially in his most famous piece, *The Federalist* No. 10, was actually its greatest source of strength.* In a large society, Madison concluded, there were so many interests and parties that no one faction could triumph and the threat of majoritarian tyranny would be eliminated. Furthermore, election by the people

The Federalist was a series of eighty-five essays published in New York in the winter of 1787–88 in defense of the Constitution. They were written under the pseudonym "Publius" largely by Madison and Alexander Hamilton, with five essays contributed by John Jay. The essays were quickly published as a book and became the most famous work of political philosophy in American history, labeled by Jefferson in 1788 as "the best commentary on the principles of government, which ever was written."

in the large districts of the national government would inhibit demagoguery and crass electioneering. If the people of a state—New York, for example—had to select only ten men to the federal Congress in contrast to the sixty-six they elected to their state assembly, they were more likely to ignore ordinary men and elect those who were experienced, well educated, and well known. In this way the new federal government would avoid the problems the states had suffered from in the 1780s.

In the ratifying conventions held in the states throughout the fall, winter, and spring of 1787–88, the Antifederalists were little match for the arguments and the array of talents that the Federalists gathered in support of the Constitution. Many of the Antifederalists were state-centered men with local interests and loyalties, politicians without the influence and education of the Federalists, and often without social and intellectual confidence. They had difficulty making themselves heard because they had very few influential leaders and because much of the press was closed to them: out of a hundred or more newspapers printed in the late 1780s only a dozen supported the Antifederalists.

Many of the small states—Delaware, New Jersey, Connecticut, and Georgia—which were commercially dependent on their neighbors or militarily exposed, ratified immediately. The critical struggles took place in the large states of Massachusetts, Virginia, and New York, and acceptance of the Constitution in these states was achieved only by narrow margins and by the promise of future amendments. North Carolina and Rhode Island rejected the Constitution, but after New York's ratification in July 1788 the country was ready to go ahead and organize the new government without them.

Despite the difficulties and the close votes in some states, the country's eventual acceptance of the Constitution was nearly preordained, for the alternative was governmental chaos. Yet in the face of the preponderance of wealth and respectability in support of the Constitution, what in the end remains extraordinary is not the political weakness and disunity of Antifederalism but its strength. That

large numbers of Americans could actually reject a plan of government created by the leaders of the nation and backed by George Washington and nearly the whole of the "natural aristocracy" of the country said more about the changing character of American politics and society than did the Constitution's acceptance. It was indeed a portent of what was to come.

The Hamiltonian Program

The Constitution created only the outline of the new government; it remained for Americans to fill in the details of the government and make something of it. During the succeeding decade the government leaders, that is, the Federalists—who clung to the name used by the supporters of the Constitution—sought to build a consolidated empire that few Americans in 1776 had ever envisioned. The consequence of their efforts was to make the 1790s the most awkward decade in American history, bearing little relation to what went on immediately before or after.

Because the Federalists stood in the way of democracy as it was emerging in the United States, everything seemed to turn against them. They despised political parties, yet parties nonetheless emerged, shattering the remarkable harmony of 1790 and producing one of the most divisive and passionate eras in American history. They sought desperately to avoid conflict with England to the point where they appeared to be compromising the independence of the new nation. In the end the war with Great Britain that they sought to avoid had to be fought anyway in 1812. By the early nineteenth century Alexander Hamilton, the brilliant leader of the Federalists, who more than anyone else pursued the heroic dreams of the age, was not alone in his despairing conclusion "that this American world was not made for me."

Organizing the Government.   There was more consensus when the new government was inaugurated in 1789–90 than at any time since the Declaration of Independence. Regional differences were temporarily obscured by a common enthusiasm for the new Constitution. And the unanimous election of Washington as the first president gave the new government an immediate respectability. Washington, with his tall, imposing figure and his Roman nose and stern, thin-lipped face, was already at age fifty-eight an internationally famous classical hero. Like Cincinnatus the Roman conqueror, he had returned to his farm at the moment of military victory. He was understandably reluctant to take up one more burden for his country and thus risk shattering the reputation he had so painstakingly earned as commander in chief; yet his severe sense of duty made refusal of the presidency impossible. He possessed the dignity, patience, and restraint that the untried but potentially powerful office needed at the outset. Despite the strong-minded, talented people around him, particularly Hamilton as secretary of the treasury and Jefferson as secretary of state, Washington was very much the leader of his administration.

Immediately Madison, as the government's leader in the House of Representatives, sought to fulfill earlier promises to the Antifederalists and quiet their fears by proposing amendments to the Constitution. He beat back Antifederalist efforts to change fundamentally the character of the Constitution and extracted from the variety of suggested amendments those least likely to sap the energy of the new government. To the chagrin of some former Antifederalists, the ten amendments that were ratified in 1791 —the Bill of Rights—were mostly concerned with protecting from the federal government the rights of *individuals* rather than the rights of the *states*. They included the guarantees of freedom of speech, press, religion, petition, and assembly and a number of protections for accused persons. Only the Tenth Amendment, reserving to the states or the people powers not delegated to the United States, was a concession to the main Antifederalist fear.*

With the inauguration of Washington and the establishment of the new government, many Americans began to feel a sense of beginning anew, of

*For the fist ten amendments, see Appendix.

EDWARD SAVAGE'S "LIBERTY"

This 1796 engraving combines the two most important symbols of the early Republic, the goddess "Liberty" giving support to the eagle, representing power and unity. The print was very popular and for years appeared in a wide variety of adaptations, including embroidery. Note the liberty cap on the flag staff in the background. (*Library of Congress*) putting the republican experiment on a new and stronger foundation. They talked of benevolence, glory, and heroism, and foresaw the inevitable westward movement of the arts and sciences across the Atlantic to the New World. The outlook was cosmopolitan, liberal, and humanitarian; America was entering a new age.

Yet despite all this optimism the Americans of the 1790s never lost their Revolutionary sense of the novel and fragile nature of their boldly extended republican government. Except in the epic poems of a few excited patriots such as Joel Barlow and Timothy Dwight, America in the 1790s was far from being a consolidated nation in any modern sense. Already separatist movements in the West threatened to break up the new country. Some Westerners even considered an allegiance to Spain in return for access to the Gulf of Mexico. The entire Mississippi River basin was susceptible to exploitation by ambitious adventurers willing to sell their services to European nations, including William Blount, senator from Tennessee and George Rogers Clark, frontier hero during the Revolution. Fear of this kind of intrigue and influence led to the hasty admission into the Union during the 1790s of Vermont, Kentucky, and Tennessee. But the danger of splintering remained.

Only in this context of uncertainty and awesome responsibility for the future of republican government can the Federalist aims and the conflicting passions they aroused be properly appreciated. The very character of America's emerging republican state was at issue in the 1790s. The Federalist leaders sought to maintain the momentum that had begun in the late 1780s when the Constitution was formed. In place of the impotent confederation of chaotic states, they envisioned a strong, consolidated, commercial empire led by an energetic government composed of the best men in the society.

In order to bolster the dignity of the new republic with some of the ceremony and majesty of monarchy, some Federalists in the Senate, led by Vice-President John Adams, tried to make "His Highness" the proper title for addressing the president. Because the future of the new republic was so unformed and problematical, such an issue seemed loaded with significance and occupied the Congress in a month of debate. Although the Federalists lost this monarchical title to the republican simplicity of "Mr. President," they drew up elaborate rules concerning government receptions and the proper behavior at what soon came to be called the "republican court" located in New York and, after 1790, in Philadelphia. At the same time, plans were begun for erecting a monumental "federal city" as the permanent capital. Always acutely sensitive to the precedents being established, the Federalists also worked out the relations between the president and the Congress. Before the end of the first session of the Congress in 1789, the sparse frame of government provided by the Constitution had been filled in. Congress created the executive departments of state, war, and treasury, and a federal judiciary consisting of the Supreme Court and a hierarchy of inferior courts.

Hamilton's Financial Program. Alexander Hamilton, then thirty-five years old, was the moving force in the new government. As a military aide to Washington during the Revolutionary War, he had earned the president's admiration. In fact, despite his short stature, Hamilton impressed everyone who met him. Unlike Washington, he was quick-witted, excitable, and knowledgeable about public finance. Born in the West Indies an illegitimate son of a Scottish merchant, Hamilton was anxious to enter and enjoy the polite world of the rich and wellborn. But despite his concern for the commercial prosperity of the United States he cannot be regarded simply as a capitalist promoter of America's later business culture. He was willing to allow ordinary men their profits and property, but it was fame and honor he wanted for himself and for his country. As the secretary of the treasury he was now in a crucial position to put his ideas into effect.

Since British "country-opposition" groups had traditionally considered the treasury as the source of political corruption, the new secretary of the treasury was regarded by the first Congress with some suspicion, and with good reason. The treasury was by far the largest department, with dozens of officers and well over two thousand customs officials, revenue agents, and postmasters; and although Congress limited the capacity of these officials to engage in business or trade or to buy public lands or government securities, they were an important source of patronage and influence. Hamilton, in fact, saw his role in eighteenth-century English terms—as a kind of prime minister to President Washington. Hamilton felt justified in meddling in the affairs of the other departments and of the Congress and in taking the lead in organizing and administering the government. While denying that he was creating a "court" party, he set out to duplicate the great financial achievements of the early eighteenth-century English governments that had laid the basis for England's stability and commercial supremacy.

Hamilton worked out his program in a series of four reports to the Congress in 1790–91, on credit, on duties and taxes, on a national bank, and on manufactures. Nearly everyone admitted that the new government needed to put its finances in order and to settle the Revolutionary War debts of the United States. Hamilton was determined to establish the credit of the United States, but he was not at all interested in paying off what the American governments, state and national, owed their citizens and others in the world. Instead of extinguishing these public debts, which in 1790 totaled $42 million for the federal government and $21 million for the several state governments, Hamilton proposed that the United States government "fund" them, that is, collect all the government bonds and loan certificates, both federal and state, into a single package and issue new federal securities in their place.

In this way the central government would create a consolidated and permanent national debt that would strengthen America in the same way that the English national debt had strengthened England. Regular interest payments on the refunded debt were to be backed by the new government's revenues from customs duties and excise taxes; indeed, over 40 percent of these revenues in the 1790s went to pay interest on the debt. These interest payments not only would make the United States the best credit risk in the world, but would create a system of investment

ALEXANDER HAMILTON (1757–1804)
Hamilton is the most controversial of the Founding Fathers. Certainly he was the least taken with radical Whig ideology and the most adventurous and heroic. As Gouverneur Morris said, "he was more covetous of glory than of wealth or power." His talents, his energy, and his clear sense of direction awed his contemporaries, friends and enemies alike. (*Library of Congress*)

for American moneyed groups who lacked the stable alternatives for speculation that Europeans had.

Besides giving investors a secure stake in the new national government, these new bonds would become the basis of the nation's money supply. Not only would the securities themselves be negotiable instruments in business transactions, but Hamilton's program provided for their forming two-thirds of the capital of a new national bank patterned on the Bank of England. This Bank of the United States and its branches (to be established in select cities) would serve as the government's depository and fiscal agent and act as a central control on the operation of the state banks, which numbered thirty-two by 1801. But most important, it would create paper money.

The Bank would issue its notes as loans to private

FIRST BANK OF THE UNITED STATES, PHILADELPHIA

Designed by an unsuccessful businessman from New Hampshire, Samuel Blodget, this building was essentially a three-story New England brick house with a classical portico, decorated, the *Gazette of the United States* reported excitedly, in the style of "Palmyra and Rome when architecture was at its zenith in the Augustan age." (*Library of Congress*)

citizens, and these notes along with those of the state-chartered banks would become the principal circulating medium for a society that lacked an adequate supply of specie, that is, gold and silver coin. Above all, Hamilton wanted a paper money that would hold its value in relation to specie. By guaranteeing that the federal government would receive the Bank's notes at face value for all taxes, holders of the notes would be less likely to redeem them in coin. The notes would pass from hand to hand without depreciating, even though only a fraction of their value was available in specie at any one time. Although many American leaders continued to believe, as John Adams did, that "every dollar of a bank bill that is issued beyond the quantity of gold and silver in the vaults, represents nothing, and is therefore a cheat upon

somebody," these multiplying bank notes quickly broadened the foundation of the nation's economy.

In his final report, that on manufactures, Hamilton laid out plans for eventually industrializing the United States. He and some other Federalists hoped to transform America from an agricultural nation into precisely the complicated and stratified country that agrarians such as Jefferson and Madison feared. He proposed incentives and bounties for the development of large-scale manufacturing that would be very different from the small household industry most Americans were used to. Yet because the Federalist government needed the revenue from customs duties on imported manufactures, and because most businessmen's energies were still absorbed in overseas shipping and land speculation, these proposals for stimulating manufacturing went unfulfilled. The rest of Hamilton's extraordinary financial program, however, was adopted by Congress early in the 1790s.

Hamilton's Political Program. As much as Hamilton and other Federalist leaders planned for and celebrated the commercial prosperity of the United States, their ultimate goals were more political than economic. Like many other Federalists, Hamilton had no faith in the idealistic hopes of the Revolutionaries that American society could be held together solely by "virtue," by the people's willingness to sacrifice their private interests for the sake of the public good. Instead of virtue and the natural sociability of men, Hamilton saw only the ordinary individual's selfish pursuit of his own private happiness. Social stability therefore required the harnessing of this self-interest. The Federalists thus tried to use the new economic and fiscal measures to re-create in America traditional kinds of eighteenth-century connections to knit the sprawling society together.

In effect, Hamilton sought to reverse the egalitarian thrust of the Revolutionary movement. He and other Federalists believed that the national government could influence and manipulate the economic and social leaders of the country, and these leaders in turn would use economic interest to bring along the groups and individuals dependent upon them in support of the new central government. Not only did the Federalists expect the new national financial program to draw people's affections away from the now economically weakened state governments, but they deliberately set out to "corrupt" the society (in the language of eighteenth-century opposition thinking) into paying allegiance to the central government. In local areas they exploited previous military camaraderie and the Society of the Cincinnati, the organization of Revolutionary War officers; they appointed important and respectable individuals to the federal judiciary and other federal offices; they carefully managed the Bank of the United States and other parts of the national economic program; and they had President Washington in 1791 make a regal tour of the country.

By 1793, through the shrewd use of these kinds of influence or "corruption" on key individuals, the Federalists had formed groups of "friends of government" in most of the states. The lines of connection of these centers of economic and political patronage ran from the various localities through the Congress to the federal executive, and created a vested interest in what opponents called "a court faction"—the very thing that Madison in *The Federalist* No. 10 had deemed unlikely in an expanded republic.

Ultimately Hamilton believed, as he declared in 1794, that "government can never [be] said to be established until some signal display has manifested its power of military coercion." From the beginning many Federalists, such as Secretary of War Henry Knox, regarded a cohesive militia and a regular army as "a strong corrective arm" necessary for the federal government to meet all crises "whether arising from internal or external causes." In 1791 the Federalists imposed a federal excise tax on whiskey—a profitable and transportable product for many inland grain farmers—to ensure that all citizens, however far-removed from the seaports, felt the weight of the new national government. When in 1794 some western Pennsylvania farmers rebelled against this hated internal tax, they seemed to fall into the government's plans, as Madison charged, to "establish the principle that a standing army was necessary for enforcing the laws." The national government raised nearly fifteen thousand militia troops to meet this Whiskey Rebellion. Such an excessive show of force was essential, President Washington declared, because "we had given no testimony to the world of being able or willing to support our government and laws."

Dealing with external problems was not as easy as putting down internal rebellions. Both Great Britain and Spain maintained positions on the borderlands of the United States and traded and plotted with the Indians, who still occupied huge areas of the trans-Appalachian West. From its base in Canada, Britain encouraged the Indians to join forces and resist American encroachments. In the South, Spain held the Floridas, New Orleans, and the Louisiana territory, refused to recognize American boundaries,

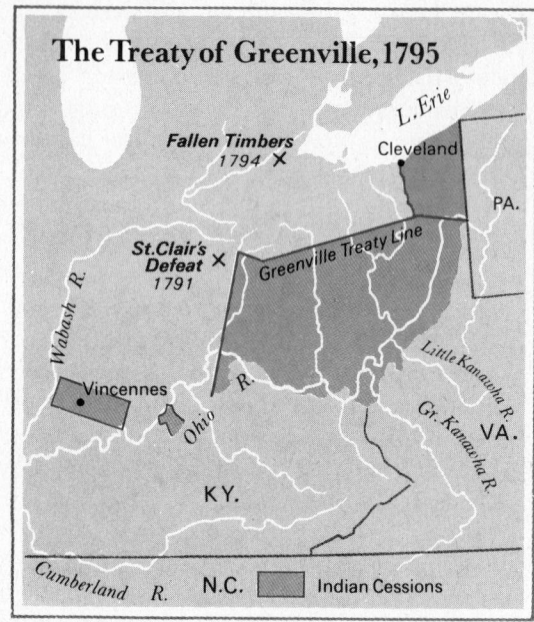

The Treaty of Greenville, 1795

Fallen Timbers 1794 ✕

Cleveland

L. Erie

PA.

St. Clair's Defeat ✕ 1791

Greenville Treaty Line

Wabash R.

Vincennes

Ohio R.

Little Kanawha R.

Gr. Kanawha R.

VA.

KY.

Cumberland R.   N.C.   Indian Cessions

controlled navigation down the Mississippi, and offered protection to the Creeks and Cherokees of the Southwest. Much of the diplomacy of the early Republic was devoted to the removal of these barriers to western expansion.

Major breakthroughs came in 1795. In 1790–91 the Indians of the Northwest inflicted several defeats on American soldiers, mostly militia, in the area along the present boundary between Ohio and Indiana, climaxing in November 1791 with the annihilation of a motley collection of troops under the command of Arthur St. Clair, the territorial governor of the Northwest. These devastating defeats gave the Federalists the opportunity to overhaul the War Department and to create the regular standing army that many of them wanted.

With a reorganized professional army, General Anthony Wayne in 1794 smashed the Indians at Fallen Timbers, near present-day Toledo, Ohio, and temporarily broke Indian resistance and British influence in the Old Northwest. In the Treaty of Greenville in 1795 the Indians ceded much of the Ohio territory to the United States and made inevitable

the British evacuation of the Northwest posts that was promised in a treaty negotiated by John Jay and ratified in 1795.

In another treaty that Thomas Pinckney negotiated in the same year, Spain finally recognized American claims to the Florida boundary and to navigation of the Mississippi. Both Jay's and Pinckney's treaties thus secured the territorial integrity of the United States in a way the diplomacy of the Confederation had been unable to do.

But the United States was still far from being a world power. Measuring American strength by European standards, the Federalists were acutely conscious of the country's weakness in the world, and this consciousness largely determined their foreign policy. Unlike England and France, the United States as yet lacked the essential elements of state power and greatness—commercial strength and military might. Since to build the United States into a strong and prosperous nation rivaling the powers of Europe might take fifty years or more, the new nation had to buy time by maintaining harmonious relations with Great Britain.

Britain was the only power that could seriously hinder American development; duties on British imports supplied the national revenue on which Hamilton's entire financial program depended. Until the United States could stand up to Great Britain, the Federalists believed that the country ought to concentrate on acquiring or controlling the New World possessions of a decrepit Spain and on dominating the Western Hemisphere. The Federalists' policy of reconciliation with Britain thus became another means toward the ultimate fulfillment of their grandiose dreams of American glory.

The Republican Opposition

Opposition to the Federalist program was slow in developing. Since the only alternative to the new national government was the prospect of disunity and anarchy, Alexander Hamilton and the Federalists were in a position to build up their system without great difficulty. During the first year of the new government (1789–90), James Madison acted as congressional leader of those anxious to counteract Antifederalist sentiment and eager to build a strong and independent executive. Not only did Madison write President Washington's first inaugural address, but he argued for the president's exclusive power to remove executive officials and worked hard to create a Treasury Department with a single head. Indeed, Hamilton, thinking of the collaborative atmosphere of 1787–88 in which he and Madison had written *The Federalist* papers, was so confident of Madison's nationalism and that of the southern representatives in the Congress that he felt betrayed when they did not unquestionably support his program.

On the refunding of the debt and on the national assumption of the states' debts Madison broke with the administration. On the refunding issue he urged some sort of discrimination between the original purchasers of the federal bonds and their present, often northern, speculative holders who had bought them cheaply. Madison was also convinced that national assumption of the outstanding state debts would penalize those states, particularly Virginia, that had already liquidated a large portion of their debts. Yet in 1790 congressmen who were opposed to these measures were still capable of compromising for the sake of federal union. Jefferson, Madison, and other southern representatives were even willing to support national assumption of state debts in return for locating the new federal city on the Potomac on the border between Virginia and Maryland.

With the government's effort to charter the Bank of the United States in December 1790, the opposition began to assume a more strident and ideological character. Madison in the House of Representatives and Jefferson in the cabinet as secretary of state both urged a strict construction of the Constitution as a defense against what seemed to have become the dangerous consolidating implications of Hamilton's program. They argued that the Constitution had not expressly granted the federal government the authority to charter a bank. Washington, after asking the opinions of his cabinet members on the constitution-

ality of the Bank, rejected Jefferson's view in favor of Hamilton's broad construction of the Constitution. Hamilton argued that Congress's authority to charter a bank was implied by the clause in the Constitution that gave Congress the right to make all laws "necessary and proper" to carry out its delegated powers. But this presidential decision in favor of the Bank did not quiet the opposition.

By 1791 a "republican interest" was emerging in the Congress and in the country, with Madison and Jefferson as its spokesmen. By 1792 this "interest" had begun to form into a Republican "party." This Republican party now saw itself representing the "country opposition" of the people against the corrupt influence of the Federalist "court." It was the 1760s and 1770s all over again.

The Republican Party. The Republican party was composed of and supported by a variety of social elements. Foremost were southern planters who were becoming increasingly conscious of the distinctiveness of their section of the country and more and more estranged from the business world Hamilton's system seemed to be generating. Unlike Federalist gentlemen in the North these southern gentry retained the earlier Whig confidence in what Jefferson called the "honest heart" of the common man. Part of this faith in democracy shared by Jefferson and his southern colleagues came from their relative insulation from it. With the increasing questioning of black slavery in the North and throughout the world, small white farmers in the South found a common identity with large planters. Most of the leading planters therefore did not feel threatened by the democratic electoral politics that was eating away popular deference to "the better sort" in the North.

In the North, especially in the rapidly growing middle states, ambitious individuals and new groups without political connections were finding that the Republican party was a means by which they could challenge entrenched leaders. Therefore, while the Republican opposition to the Federalist program in the South was largely the response of rural gentry committed to a nostalgic image of independent free-

He in a trice struck Lyon thrice
Upon his head, enrag'd, sir.

Who seiz'd the tongs to ease his wrongs,
And Grifwold thus engag'd, sir.

Congress Hall.
in Philadᵃ Feb. 15, 179?
S. E. Cor. 6ᵗʰ & Chestnut

CARTOON LAMPOONING THE LYON-GRISWOLD TANGLE IN CONGRESS IN 1797

With the wrestling on the floor of the House of Representatives in 1797 between Republican Matthew Lyon of Vermont and Federalist Roger Griswold of Connecticut, followed by Lyon's "outrageous" and "indecent" defense (he was reported in the *Annals* of Congress to have said, "I did not come here to have my —— kicked by everybody"), some members concluded that Congress had become no better than a "tavern," filled with "*beasts,* and not gentlemen," and contemptible in the eyes of all "polite or genteel" societies. (*New York Public Library*)

holders, the Republican party in the North was the political expression of new egalitarian social forces released and intensified by the Revolution. Such rising entrepreneurs were in fact the principal contributors to the very kind of world the southern Republicans were coming to fear.

These diverse and ultimately incompatible sectional and social elements were brought together in a national Republican party by a comprehensive and common ideology. This Republican ideology, involving a deep hatred of bloated state power and of the political and financial mechanisms that created such power, had been inherited from the English "country-opposition" tradition, sharpened and Americanized during the Revolutionary years. Now, during the 1790s, it was given a new and heightened relevance by the policies of the federal administration.

To those steeped in country-Whig ideology, Hamilton's system threatened to re-create the kind of government and society Americans had presumably eradicated in 1776—a society of patronage connections and artificial privilege sustained by executive powers that would in time destroy the independence of the republican citizenry. Hamilton appeared to be another Walpole, using the new economic program to corrupt the Congress and the country and create a swelling phalanx of "stock-jobbers and king-jobbers" (in Jefferson's words) in order to build up executive power at the expense of the people.

Once the Republicans grasped this ideological pattern, all the Federalist measures fell into place. The high-toned pageantry of the "court," the aristocratic talk of titles, the defense of corporate monopolies, the enlargement of the military forces, the growth of taxes, the reliance on the monarchical president and the aristocratic Senate, all pointed toward a systematic plan, as Caroline County of Virginia declared in 1793, of "assimilating the American government to the form and spirit of the British monarchy." Most basic and insidious of all was the Federalist creation of a huge perpetual federal debt, which, as George Clinton, the Republican governor of New York, explained, not only would poison the morals of the people through speculation, but would "add an artificial support to the administration, and by a species of bribery enlist the monied men of the community on the side of the measures of government. . . . Look to Great Britain."

The French Revolution. The eruption of the French Revolution in 1789 and its subsequent expansion in 1792 into a European war pitting monarchical Britain and republican France against one another added to the quarrel Americans were having among themselves over the direction of their society and government. The meaning of the American Revolution and the capacity of the United States to sustain its grand republican experiment now seemed tied to the fate of Britain and France.

President Washington proclaimed America's neutrality in the spring of 1793. The United States quickly tried to take advantage of its position and to gain recognition of its neutral rights by the belligerents. Unable to control the seas, France threw open its empire in the West Indies to American commerce, and American merchants soon developed a profitable shipping trade between the French and Spanish West Indies and Europe. Britain retaliated by invoking what was called the Rule of 1756. This rule, first set forth during the Seven Years' War, enabled British prize courts (that is, courts that judged the legitimacy of the seizure of enemy ships or goods) to deny the right of neutral nations in time of war to trade with belligerent ports that had been closed to them in time of peace. During 1793 and 1794 Britain seized over three hundred American merchant ships.

Although Washington had proclaimed the United

States' neutrality, the Federalists and their Republican opponents both sought to favor whichever power—Britain or France—they thought would better promote American interests. The Federalists attempted strenuously to overcome the natural sympathy most Americans had for France, their former Revolutionary ally and new sister republic. Citizen Genêt, the new French minister to the United States, in 1793 began arming privateers in the United States for use against the British and seemed to be appealing over the head of the government to the American people for support. These clumsy actions helped the Federalists win over many Americans otherwise sympathetic to the French Revolution. Aided by the increasing fears of antireligious sentiments and of social upheaval, both associated with the French Revolution, the Federalists recruited growing numbers of Protestant clergy and conservative groups to their cause. While the Republicans were calling for stiff commercial retaliation against Britain for its seizing of American ships and sailors and for its continued occupation of posts in the Northwest, the Federalists hoped to head off war with Britain by negotiation. In the spring of 1794 Washington appointed John Jay, chief justice of the Supreme Court, to be a special minister to Great Britain.

Jay's Treaty. The treaty negotiated by Jay with Britain diplomatically expressed both the Federalist fears of France and the Federalist reliance on the British connection. In the treaty Britain finally agreed to evacuate the Northwest posts, to open parts of her empire to American commerce, and to set up joint arbitration commissions to settle the outstanding issues of prewar debts, boundaries, and compensation for illegal seizures. The United States was compelled to abandon principles concerning freedom of the seas and broad neutral rights that it had promoted since 1776. The treaty in effect recognized the British Rule of 1756. Moreover, by granting Britain more favorable trade conditions than it gave to any other nation, the United States ceded the power to make any future commercial discrimination against Britain, the one great weapon the Republicans counted on to weaken the former mother country's hold on American commerce.

The Republicans were aghast at the treaty. Jay was burned in effigy, and Republicans in the House of Representatives tried to prevent implementation of the treaty, which the Senate reluctantly ratified in 1795 after a bitter struggle. Although the Republicans thought that Britain had conceded to America little more than peace, for most Federalists this was enough. War with Britain would end the imports of English goods and the customs revenues on which Hamilton's financial program depended and would only increase the influence of what Federalist Senator George Cabot of Massachusetts called "French principles [that] would destroy us as a society."

The Quasi-War with France. Washington's decision to retire from the presidency at the end of his second term created an important precedent for the future. The New Englander and vice-president John Adams was widely regarded as Washington's natural successor, but he was elected in 1796 by only a narrow margin of electoral votes, seventy-one to sixty-eight, over the Republican leader, Thomas Jefferson, who became vice-president. Before Washington left office, he with the aid of Hamilton prepared a Farewell Address that became an important political testament of American history, laying the basis for later American "isolationism." In the address, Washington urged Americans "to steer clear of permanent alliances" with any foreign power. Republicans rightly thought that Washington was rejecting the idea that the United States and France were naturally linked in the common cause of bringing revolutionary republicanism to the world.

The Federalist government's pro-British policies expressed in Jay's treaty now drove the embattled French into a series of attacks on American shipping and a refusal to deal with the United States until the new American connection with Britain was broken. President Adams dealt with the crisis in 1797 by sending a special mission to France. The French government, using agents designated as X, Y, and Z,

JOHN ADAMS (1735-1826)
Adams is perhaps the most neglected of the Founding Fathers; he certainly felt himself to be. He seemed to court unpopularity with his displays of jealously, vanity, and pomposity. Yet as his diaries reveal, he was at heart a vulnerable, amiable, and very likeable person. (*The Metropolitan Museum of Art. Gift of William H. Huntington, 1883*)

tried to extort a payment from the American diplomats as a precondition for negotiations. This humiliating "XYZ Affair" further aroused American antagonism to France and led to the repudiation of the Franco-American treaties of 1778, the outbreak in 1798 of an undeclared "quasi-war" on the seas with France, and the opportunity for some extreme Federalists led by Hamilton to strengthen the central government once and for all.

Jefferson, as the leader of the Republican party, saw the world differently. Whether in or out of office, he never let the growing anti-French atmosphere weaken his faith in the cause of the French revolu-

"The Gore Children" c. 1753 by John Singleton Copley. Courtesy, The H. F. du Pont Winterthur Museum

The Rising Glory of America

Late eighteenth century American gentry were confident that the United States would eventually exceed Europe in artistic grandeur and taste. Yet the fine arts had so long been associated with European court life and social decadence that many Americans thought them incompatible with republican simplicity and virtue. Hence any art that Americans developed would have to be a peculiarly republican one.

Americans found the sources for such a republican art in a revolutionary artistic movement that swept through Europe in the latter half of the eighteenth century. This movement, later called neoclassicism, sought to emulate the severe and rational standards of classical antiquity and to infuse art with new moral seriousness and idealistic virtue. Drawing its subjects from history, art would become an instrument for public reform and refinement. Artists would no longer be craftsmen amus-

ing a few rich aristocratic patrons; they would become philosophers instructing a whole society eager to uplift its taste and cultivate its manners.

John Singleton Copley (1738–1815) of Boston had longed to express these new ideas in his art, but the provinciality of colonial society had compelled him to devote his immense talent to painting portraits of the colonial gentry. In 1774, in frustration, he sailed for England. He left a moment too soon, for the Revolution changed everything.

"The Battle of Bunker's Hill" by John Trumbull. Copyright Yale University Art Gallery

John Trumbull (1756–1843), member of a distinguished Connecticut family, quickly grasped that the Revolution was as much a cultural as a political event. He knew only too well that being an artist, "as it is generally practiced, is frivolous, little useful to society, and unworthy of a man who has talents for more serious pursuits. But, to preserve and diffuse the memory of the noblest series of actions which have ever presented themselves in the history of man"—that was a task that "gave dignity to the profession" and justified any gentleman's devotion.

Trumbull's use of the grand style and his attempt at an ennobling effect from history painting can be seen vividly in his *The Battle of Bunker's Hill* (1786). Trumbull thought he would make a

fortune from the sale of engravings of his paintings of the Revolution, but after an initial encouraging reception, subscriptions soon ceased. Early nineteenth-century Americans were not much interested in history paintings, and Trumbull even had trouble getting Congress to pay for the huge commemorative scenes of the Revolution he painted in the rotunda of the Capitol.

No one responded to neoclassical ideas about art with more enthusiasm than did Thomas Jefferson. Since architecture to Jefferson was "an art which shows so much," it was particularly important for the new republican nation that appropriate inspirational forms be used. He cursed the Georgian buildings of colonial Virginia as barbaric, and aimed, through a new symbolic architecture, "to improve the taste of my countrymen, to increase their reputation, to reconcile to them the respect of the world and procure them its praise." He wanted Americans to emulate a classical art that "has pleased universally for nearly 2000 years," even at the expense of functional requirements. From France in the 1780s Jefferson badgered his Virginia colleagues into erecting as the new state capitol a magnificent copy of the Maison Carrée, a Roman temple at Nîmes from the first century A.D., and thus almost singlehandedly introduced the classical style to American public buildings. In fact there was nothing like this use of a Roman temple anywhere in the world. No matter that Richmond was still a backwoods town with mud-lined streets. No matter that a model of a Roman temple was hard to heat and acoustically impossible. For Americans other considerations counted more. By 1820 Roman and Greek revival architecture had become the official style of public buildings in the new nation.

Detail of Virginia State Capitol. *Library of Congress*

View of Richmond from Bushrod Washington's Island in the James River *by Benjamin Henry Latrobe. The Papers of Benjamin Henry Latrobe, Maryland Historical Society*

Excited by the new ideas about art, the Revolutionaries created a sudden outpouring of iconographic works. Statues and monuments were planned; plays, prints, and pageants were employed in support of the Revolution and the new republic. The Revolutionaries continually interrupted their constitution-making and military campaigning to design all sorts of emblems and commemorative medals and to sit for long hours having their portraits painted for history's sake.

When compared to the later extravagant French Revolutionary achievement, under the direction of Jacques Louis David, of putting the arts into the service of republicanism, the American artistic efforts seem pale and feeble. But given America's provincialism and its lack of artists and artistic experience, the Revolutionaries' aims and accomplishments are astonishing. That a monumental city like Washington, D.C., with its sweeping scale, its huge boulevards, and its magnificent parks, could have been conceived and begun in the midst of a swampy wilderness is an extraordinary tribute to the neoclassical aspirations of the Revolutionary leaders.

Yet the classical spirit that inspired Washington, D.C., the ancient place names, the Roman and Greek buildings, and the many emblems and devices was being lost even as these things were being created. Soon few Americans would know the meaning behind the Latin mottoes and the Masonic pyramid and eye appearing on the Great Seal. Indeed, many of the cultural artifacts that Americans inherited from the Revolutionary and early republican eras remain only as awkward reminders of the brevity of America's classical age.

Plan of Washington, D.C., 1791, by Pierre Charles L'Enfant (Library of Congress); Great Seal of the United States of America, front and back; House of Representatives colonnade and design for female figure for the Capitol, drawn by Benjamin Latrobe, 1815 (Library of Congress); Capitol building, east and west wings, drawn by W. Thornton, 1794 (Library of Congress).

SACRED

to the Memory of

WASHINGTON

Ob. 14 Dec. 1799

Æt. 68

The symbol-making of American neo-classical art reached its height with the various depictions of Washington, who came to represent all the great republican virtues Americans ought to value. This oil painting on glass shows the great hero, no longer a man but a symbol, being borne to heaven in a dramatic apotheosis. Such pictures were supposed to fill viewers with awe and inspiration and make them conscious of their national identity.

The concept of art as high-minded moral instruction lingered into the new democratic age of the 1820s. Like earlier American artists, Samuel F. B. Morse (1791–1872) sought to escape from the vulgarity of painting portraits. Instead he wanted to "elevate and refine public feelings by turning the thoughts of his countrymen from sensuality and luxury to intellectual pleasures" by painting great historical subjects, like his *The Old House of Representatives* (1821). The canvas measured nearly seven feet by twelve feet and cost Morse a year of labor. Although the painting was photographic in its meticulous detail, in its emphasis on classical sobriety, dignity, and decorum, it hopelessly idealized the brawling and rowdy House of Representatives that had emerged by the 1820s. Morse put the painting on tour, but the public would not pay to see its elected officials, and Congress would not buy it. In disillusionment Morse eventually turned to photography and the invention of the telegraph and the code which bears his name.

(Opposite) Oil painting on glass, made in China. *Courtesy, The Henry Francis du Pont Winterthur Museum*

(Below) "The Old House of Representatives" by Samuel F. B. Morse. *In the collection of the Corcoran Gallery of Art*

"Pat Lyon at the Forge"
by John Neagle. Courtesy
of Museum of Fine Arts,
Boston

This new kind of republican portrait reveals just how far behind early nineteenth-century America had left its patrician colonial hierarchy. Although Lyon by 1826 was a rich and prominent businessman, he wanted his portrait, as he said, to depict his humble origins as a blacksmith in Philadelphia, "at work at my anvil, with my sleeves rolled up and a leather apron on." The artist, John Neagle (1796–1865), was himself something of a self-made man. His father came from County Cork and his mother was a New Jersey yeoman's daughter. He managed, however, to marry the stepdaughter of the well-known and successful portrait painter, Thomas Sully (1783–1872).

As different as the new bourgeois leaders of the early republic were from the eighteenth-century gentry, in wanting from art mainly pictures of themselves they were much the same. By the 1820s many American intellectuals were still anxiously awaiting the long-predicted westward transit of the arts across the Atlantic.

T H E

COLUMBIAN MAGAZINE,

For A P R I L, 1789.

Embellished with two COPPER-PLATES, representing,

I. Six Specimens of FOSSILS found in the United States.
II. A Prospect of the PAYSAIC FALLS, in New-Jersey.

CONTENTS.

History of the American war, [continued] 209
Answers to queries on the present state of husbandry and agriculture in the Delaware state, [concluded] 217
Remarks on a passage in Brydone's Travels, 220
Life of William Penn, founder of Pennsylvania 223
Description of certain American fossils 228
Address of John Doe, ib.
Description of the Dismal Swamp in Virginia; with proposals for, and observations on the advantages of draining it; by the hon. William Byrd, 232
Account of a free setlement of Negroes at Sierra Leona; in a letter from Granville Sharpe, esq; to doctor Lettsom, 234
Directions for expelling noxious vapours from wells, 240

Dissertation on the influence of the mother on the fœtus, 241
Improvement in the culture of hemp, and fitting it for use: by John Read, esq; of Massach setts, 246
Essay on genius, [continued] 249
The Retailer, No. IX. 252
An original anecdote, 255
Literary intelligence, an account of new medical books, ib.
Recipe, 256

THE COLUMBIAN PARNASSIAD.
Sonnet on a wall-flower, 257
The happy pair, ib.
Cantata for St. Andrew's day, 259
Ossian's address to the sun, 261

THE CHRONICLE,
Containing foreign and domestic intelligence, 262
Marriages, 268
Deaths, ib.

TO WHICH ARE PREFIXED,

Tables of METEOROLOGICAL OBSERVATIONS, viz. two for the months of FEBRUARY and MARCH, made in Charleston, South-Carolina; and one for the month of FEBRUARY, made at Spring-Mill, Pennsylvania: ——also,

The PRICES CURRANT of MERCHANDIZE and PUBLIC SECURITIES, and the COURSE of EXCHANGE.

PHILADELPHIA:

PRINTED FOR JAMES TRENCHARD.

America! with Peace and Freedom blest,
Pant for true Fame, and scorn inglorious rest:
Science invites; urgil by the Voice divine,
Exert thy self, till every Art be thine.

PAGES FROM "COLUMBIAN MAGAZINE"

Between 1775 and 1795 twenty-seven learned and gentlemanly magazines like this one were begun, six more than in the entire colonial period. The creation of these new journals was a remarkable testimony to the cultural promise of the Revolution. (*American Antiquarian Society*)

of what they called the "petty electioneering arts" of the Republican opposition, they were not comfortable with the new democratic politics. They saw themselves in traditional eighteenth-century terms as gentleman leaders to whom ordinary people, if they were only left alone, would naturally defer. The Federalists attributed the difficulties and disorder of the 1790s to the influence of newspapers, demagogues, and extralegal political associations. Republican upstarts and factions, they believed, were stirring up the people against their natural rulers. They spread radical French principles, interfered with the

electoral process, and herded the people, including recent immigrants, into political activity. New kinds of writers and publishers, like the former indentured servant and now congressman and editor Matthew Lyon of Vermont, were reaching out to influence an audience as obscure and ordinary as themselves. Through the coarse language and slander of their publications they were destroying the governing gentry's personal reputation for character on which popular respect for the entire political order was presumably based.

By the late 1790s, amid an economic depression

and the "quasi-war" with France, all these Federalists' fears climaxed in their desperate repressive measures of 1798—measures which more than anything else have tarnished the historical reputation of the Federalists. In control of both the executive and the Congress, the Federalists contemplated various plans for strengthening the Continental union. They sought to broaden the power of the federal judiciary, to increase the transportation network throughout the country, and to enlarge the army and navy. Above all, the Federalists aimed to end the Republicans' political exploitation of new immigrants and to stop the flow of Republican literature that was poisoning the relations between rulers and ruled.

In 1798 the Federalist-dominated Congress enacted Alien and Sedition Acts, which lengthened the naturalization process for foreigners, gave the president extraordinary powers to deal with aliens, and provided the central government with the authority to punish as crimes seditious libels against federal officials. At the same time, the Congress ordered the immediate enlistment of a new regular army of twelve thousand and laid plans for provisional armies numbering in the tens of thousands. Washington was to be called out of retirement as commander in chief of the new army, but Hamilton was to be actually in command. Presumably all this was done to meet the threat of a French invasion, but some people believed that it was to deal with the domestic disorder of the United States. When the United States army quickly suppressed an armed rebellion of several northeastern Pennsylvania counties led by John Fries in protest against the new federal tax on houses, land, and slaves, the advantages of federal strength were confirmed in some Federalist eyes.

For their part, the Republicans in 1798–99 thought the very success of the American Revolution was at stake. In response to the Federalist repression, particularly the Alien and Sedition Acts, the Virginia and Kentucky legislatures issued resolutions, drawn up by Madison and Jefferson respectively. These resolutions proclaimed the right of the states to judge the constitutionality of federal acts and to interpose themselves between the citizenry and the unconstitutional actions of the central government. Although the other states declined to support Virginia and Kentucky, the stand taken by the two states opened a question about the nature of the union that would trouble the country for many years to come.

By the end of the decade several developments brought a measure of reconciliation. Both Madison and Jefferson were unwilling to resort to force to support their resolutions. British Admiral Horatio Nelson's naval victory over the French at the Battle of the Nile in October 1798 lessened the threat of a French invasion of either England or America. But most important in calming the crisis was the action of President John Adams.

Adams's presidency had been contentious, and he was never in command of his own cabinet, let alone the government. This short, puffy, and sensitive man, who wore his heart on his sleeve, was much too honest, impulsive, and independent-minded to handle the growing division among the Federalists over the military buildup; but he had an abiding fear of standing armies and a stubborn courage. In 1799 against the wishes of his advisers he decided to send another peace message to France despite the humiliating failure of his earlier effort in the XYZ Affair. France, now under Napoleon as first consul, agreed to make terms, and in 1800 signed an agreement with the United States that brought the quasi-war to a close.

Adams's independent action irreparably split the Federalist leadership between the moderates who supported the president and the High Federalists who supported Hamilton, and thus crippled Adams's chances of winning the presidential election of 1800. Adams, always ready to bemoan his country's neglect of his achievements, considered his decision to negotiate with France "the most disinterested, most determined and most successful of my whole life." His controversial decision ended the war crisis and undermined the attempts of the extremist Federalists to strengthen the central government and the military forces of the United States. Although the worst was over, that was not yet clear to everyone at the time. In 1800 the British ambassador still thought the "whole system of American Government" was "tottering to its foundations."

CHRONOLOGY

1781 Articles of Confederation ratified.
Congress establishes Bank of North America.

1782 Fall of Lord North's ministry.

1783 Newburgh conspiracy of American army
officers.
Society of Cincinnati founded.
Pennsylvania Evening Post, first daily newspaper
in United States, begins publication.
Treaty of Peace with Britain signed.

1785 Land Ordinance for Northwest Territory
adopted by Congress.

1786 Jay-Gardoqui Treaty; rejected by Congress.
Virginia Statute for Religious Freedom.
Shays's Rebellion in western Massachusetts.
Annapolis Convention; adopts plan to meet in
Philadelphia to revise Articles of Confederation.

1787 Federal Constitutional Convention meets in
Philadelphia and drafts Constitution.
Northwest Ordinance enacted by Congress.
The Federalist papers begun by Madison,
Hamilton, and Jay.

1788 Ratification of United States Constitution by
all the states except Rhode Island and
North Carolina.

1789 First session of Congress meets.
Washington inaugurated as first president.
Capitol at Richmond, Virginia, built from
model of Maison Carrée supplied by Jefferson.
Outbreak of French Revolution.

1790 Hamilton's Report on Public Credit; Funding
Bill; Assumption Bill.
Father John Carroll made first Roman Catholic
bishop of United States with See in Baltimore.

1791 Bank of the United States established.

First ten amendments to Constitution
(Bill of Rights) adopted.
Defeat of General Arthur St. Clair by
Ohio Indians.

1793 Execution of Louis XVI and outbreak of
European war.
Washington inaugurated for second term.
Proclamation of Neutrality by Washington.
Citizen Genêt Affair.
Samuel Slater erects first cotton mill at
Pawtucket, Rhode Island.
Eli Whitney applies for patent on cotton gin.
Yellow fever epidemic in Philadelphia.

1794 Whiskey Rebellion in western Pennsylvania.
Battle of Fallen Timbers, Ohio; General
Anthony Wayne defeats Indians.
Philadelphia-Lancaster turnpike completed.

1795 Jay's Treaty with Britain.
Treaty of Greenville, between United States
and Indians of Northwest.
Pinckney's Treaty with Spain.

1796 Washington's Farewell Address, warning
against foreign entanglements and domestic
factionalism.
John Adams elected president.

1798 XYZ Affair reported by Adams to Congress.
Quasi-war with France on high seas.
Alien and Sedition Acts enacted by Federalists
in Congress.
Virginia and Kentucky resolutions.
Eleventh Amendment to Constitution ratified.

1799 *American Review and Literary Journal*, first
quarterly literary review in America, established
by the novelist Charles Brockden Brown.
Fries uprising in Pennsylvania.

SUGGESTED READINGS

John Fiske, *The Critical Period of American History* (1888), popularized the Federalist view of the Confederation for the nineteenth century. Merrill Jensen, *The New Nation* (1950), minimizes the crisis of the 1780s, and explains the movement for the Constitution as the work of a small but dynamic minority. E. James Ferguson, *The Power of the Purse . . . ,1776—1790* (1961), also stresses the nationalists' efforts to strengthen the Confederation. Clarence L. Ver Steeg, *Robert Morris, Revolutionary Financier* (1954), is the major study of that important figure. Forrest McDonald, *E Pluribus Unum: The Formation of the American Republic, 1776-1790* (1965), describes the commercial scrambling by Americans in the 1780s. The best account of the army and the Newburgh Conspiracy is Richard H. Kohn, *Eagle and Sword: The Federalists and the Creation of the Military Establishment in America, 1783–1802* (1975). Frederick W. Marks III, *Independence on Trial* (1973), analyzes the foreign problems contributing to the Constitution. The best short survey of the Confederation period is still Andrew C. McLaughlin, *The Confederation and the Constitution, 1783–1789* (1905).

Charles Beard's *An Economic Interpretation of the Constitution* (1913) sought to explain the Constitution as something other than the consequence of high-minded idealism. It became the most influential history book ever written in America. Beard saw the struggle over the Constitution as "a deep-seated conflict between a popular party based on paper money and agrarian interests and a conservative party centered in the towns and resting on financial, mercantile, and personal property interests generally." While Beard's particular proof for his thesis—that the Founders held federal securities that they expected would appreciate in value under a new national government—has been demolished, especially by Forrest McDonald, *We the People* (1958), his general interpretation of the origins of the Constitution still casts a long shadow. Jackson T. Main, *Political Parities before the Constitution* (1974), finds a "cosmopolitan"-"localist" split within the states over the Constitution. Gordon S. Wood, *The Creation of the American Republic, 1776–1787* (1969), working through the ideas, discovers a similar social, but not strictly speaking a "class," division over the Constitution.

For a different emphasis on the origins of the Constitution, see Robert E. Brown, *Reinterpretation of the Formation of the American Constitution* (1963); and Benjamin F. Wright, Jr., *Consensus and Continuity, 1776–1787* (1958). The best history of the Convention is still Max Farrand, *The Framing of the Constitution of the United States* (1913), which sees the Constitution as "a bundle of compromises" designed to meet specific defects of the Articles. Irving Brant's third volume of his biography of *James Madison* (6 vols., 1941–61) has a sure-footed description of the Convention.

Max Farrand, ed., *The Records of the Federal Convention of 1787* (4 vols.; 1911, 1937); and Jonathan Elliot, ed., *The Debates in the Several State Conventions on the Adoption of the Federal Constitution* (5 vols., 1876), are collections of the important documents. Jacob Cooke, ed., *The Federalist* (1961), is the best edition of these papers. Two sympathetic studies of the Antifederalists are Jackson T. Main, *The Antifederalists . . . , 1781–1788* (1961); and Robert A. Rut-

land, *The Ordeal of the Constitution* (1966). See also Robert A. Rutland, *The Birth of the Bill of Rights, 1776–1791* (1955). The papers of the Founders—Jefferson, Franklin, Hamilton, John Adams, Madison, and others—are currently being published in mammoth scholarly editions.

Politics in the 1790s is ably summarized in John C. Miller, *The Federalist Era, 1789–1801* (1960). Richard Buel, Jr., *Securing the Revolution: Ideology in American Politics, 1789–1815* (1972), however, better recaptures the distinctiveness of the age and the problematical character of the new national government. John C. Miller, *Alexander Hamilton, Portrait in Paradox* (1959), is the fullest biography; but Gerald Stourzh, *Alexander Hamilton and the Idea of Republican Government* (1970), better places this leading Federalist in an eighteenth-century context. In this respect, see also the collected essays of Douglass Adair, *Fame and the Founding Fathers* (1974). A concise study is Forrest McDonald, *The Presidency of George Washington* (1974). For single-volume biographies of Washington, see Marcus Cunliffe, *George Washington: Man and Monument* (1958); and James Thomas Flexner, *Washington: The Indispensable Man* (1974).

Leonard D. White, *The Federalists: A Study in Administrative History* (1948), is the standard account of the creation of the governmental bureaucracy. See also Carl Prince, *The Federalists and the Origins of the U.S. Civil Service* (1978). Lisle A. Rose, *Prologue to Democracy* (1968), describes the formation of Federalist influence in the South during the 1790s. Richard H. Kohn, *Eagle and Sword: The Federalists and the Creation of the Military Establishment in America, 1783–1802* (1975), is important for understanding the Federalist goals. On foreign policy, see Samuel Flagg Bemis, *Jay's Treaty* (1923), and *Pinckney's Treaty* (1926). Jerald A. Combs, *The Jay Treaty* (1970), is broader than its title would suggest. A good survey is Lawrence S. Kaplan, *Colonies into Nation: American Diplomacy, 1763–1801* (1972).

Much of the literature on the history of the 1790s treats the opposition of the Republicans as ordinary party activity. See William N. Chambers, *Political Parties in a New Nation . . . , 1776–1809* (1963); and Noble E. Cunningham, Jr., *The Jeffersonian Republicans: The Formation of Party Organization, 1789–1801* (1957). Notable exceptions are Richard Buel, Jr., *Securing the Revolution* (1972), and Lance Banning, *The Jeffersonian Persuasion* (1978). See also John Zvesper, *Political Philosophy and Rhetoric: A Study of the Origins of American Party Politics* (1977). On the formation of extralegal organizations, all we have is Eugene P. Link, *Democratic Republican Societies, 1790–1800* (1942). There are a number of studies of the growth of the Republican party in the separate states. See especially Paul Goodman, *The*

Democratic Republicans of Massachusetts (1964); Alfred F. Young, *The Democratic Republicans of New York* (1967); Sanford W. Higgenbotham, *The Keystone in the Democratic Arch: Pennsylvania Politics 1800–1816* (1952); Carl E. Prince, *New Jersey's Jeffersonian Republicans* (1967); and Norman K. Risjord, *Chesapeake Politics, 1781–1800* (1978). On the Whiskey Rebellion, see·Leland D. Baldwin, *Whiskey Rebels* (1939).

On the foreign crisis of the late 1790s, see Alexander De Conde, *The Quasi-War: Politics and Diplomacy of the Undeclared War with France, 1797–1801* (1966). Manning J. Dauer, *The Adams Federalists* (1953), captures some of the desperation of the Federalists in 1798. The fullest study of the Alien and Sedition Acts is James Morton Smith, *Freedom's Fetters* (1956); but for a proper appreciation of the special eighteenth-century context in which freedom of speech and of the press has to be viewed, see Leonard W. Levy, *Legacy of Suppression* (1960). Stephen G. Kurtz is solid on *The Presidency of John Adams . . . , 1795–1800* (1957).

The Revolution Recovered

The Federalist world, born in the reaction to the excesses of Revolutionary populism, could not endure. It ran too much against the grain of fast-moving social developments. The Federalists of the 1790s refused to recognize that the people's position in American politics was no longer a debatable issue. Convinced that people feared disunion so much that almost any sort of strong national government within a republican framework would be acceptable, the Federalists tried to revive some of the energy and authority of executive government that had been lost in the turbulence of the Revolution. America was increasingly more prosperous, and the Federalists counted on this to justify both their program and their reliance on rule by a traditional gentlemanly elite. But so out of touch were they with the rapid developments of American life, so counter to the impulse of the Revolutionary ideology was their program, that they provoked a second revolutionary movement that threatened to tear the Republic apart.

Only the electoral victory of the Republicans in 1800 ended this threat and brought, in the eyes of many Americans, the entire Revolutionary venture of two and a half decades to successful completion. Indeed, "the Revolution of 1800," as the Republican leader and third president of the United States, Thomas Jefferson, described it, "was as real a revolution in the principles of our government as that of 1776 was in its form."

The Revolution of 1800

Thomas Jefferson was an unlikely popular radical. He was a well-connected and highly cultivated southern planter who never had to scramble for his position in Virginia. The wealth and leisure that made possible his great contributions to liberty were supported by the labor of a hundred or more slaves. He was tall, gangling, red-haired, and unlike his fellow Revolutionary John Adams, whom he fought and befriended for fifty years, he was reserved, self-possessed, and incurably optimistic. He disliked personal controversy and was always charming in face-to-face relations with both friends and enemies. But at a distance

THOMAS JEFFERSON, ARCHITECT; MONTICELLO; AND SKETCH OF THE ROTUNDA OF THE UNIVERSITY OF VIRGINIA

"Architecture," Thomas Jefferson once said, "is my delight, and putting up and pulling down one of my favorite amusements." Even as a young man, Jefferson was absorbed in designing and building his home at Monticello. He went at architecture with a mathematical precision; no detail of building—from the chemistry of mortar to the proper technique of laying bricks—was too insignificant for his attention. *(Portrait by R. Peale. Courtesy, The New-York Historical Society, New York City; Monticello, Massachusetts Historical Society)* he could hate, and thus many of his opponents concluded that he was two-faced. He was undeniably complicated. He mingled the most lofty visions with astute backroom politicking. He was a sophisticated man-of-the-world, who loved no place better than his native Virginia. This complex slaveholding aristocrat became the most important apostle for democratic idealism in American history.

Thomas Jefferson's narrow victory in the presidential election of 1800 confirmed the changing course of national developments. Jefferson received seventy-three electoral votes, to the sixty-four of the Federalist candidate, John Adams, who was opposed by the Hamiltonians within his own party. For a moment even that close victory was in doubt. Because the Constitution did not provide that the electors distinguish between their votes for president and vice-president, both Jefferson and the Republican vice-presidential candidate Aaron Burr had received the same number of electoral votes, thus throwing the election into the House of Representatives. After thirty-five deadlocked ballots, Hamilton and other Federalist leaders, preferring Jefferson to Burr and thinking they had assurances from Jefferson to continue Federalist policies, allowed the acknowledged Republican leader to become president. To avoid a repetition of this electoral impasse, the country adopted the Twelfth Amendment to the Constitution, which allowed the electors to designate the president and vice-president separately in their ballots.*

In these confused electoral circumstances it is difficult to see the bold and revolutionary character of Jefferson's election. It was one of the first popular elections in modern history that resulted in the peaceful transfer of governmental power from one "party" to another. At the outset Jefferson himself struck a note of conciliation: "We are all republicans—we are all federalists," he said in his inaugural address. Many Federalists were soon absorbed into the Republican cause. And the Republican administration did subsequently deviate from strict Republican principles. Thus the continuities are impressive, and the Jeffersonian "Revolution of 1800" has blended nearly im-

*For the Twelfth Amendment, see Appendix.

THOMAS JEFFERSON'S VICTORY BANNER, 1800
(Ralph E. Becker Collection, Smithsonian Institution, Division of Political History)

perceptibly into the main democratic currents of American history. However, when compared with the consolidated state the Federalists tried to build in the 1790s, what the Republicans did after 1800 proved that a real revolution—as Jefferson said it was—took place.

Government Without Power. Believing that most of the evils afflicting mankind in the past had flowed from the abuses of political establishments, the Republicans in 1800 set about deliberately to carry out what they rightly believed was the original aim of the Revolution—to reduce the overawing and dangerous power of government. They wanted to form a national republic based on the country-Whig opposition ideology and formed in the image of the Revolutionary state governments of 1776. They envisioned a central state whose authority would resemble that of the old Articles of Confederation more than that of the

European type of state the Federalists had thought essential. They wanted in fact to create a general government that would rule without the traditional attributes of power.

From the outset Jefferson was determined that the new government would lack even the usual rituals of power. At the very beginning he purposefully set a new tone of republican simplicity in contrast to the stiff formality and regal ceremony with which the Federalists, in imitation of European court life, had surrounded the presidency. Since the Federalist presidents, like the English monarchs, had personally delivered their addresses to the legislature "from the throne," Jefferson chose to submit his in writing. Unlike Washington and Adams, he made himself easily accessible to visitors, all of whom, no matter how distinguished, he received, as the British chargé reported, "with a most perfect disregard to ceremony both in his dress and manner." Much to the shock of foreign dignitaries, at American state occasions he replaced the protocol and distinctions of European court life with the egalitarian rules of what he called "pell-mell."

While Jefferson's dignity and gentlemanly tastes scarcely allowed any actual leveling in social gatherings, his transformation of manners at the capital harmonized with changes in society. For the Republican revolution soon brought to the national government men who, unlike Jefferson, were without the attributes of gentlemen, who did not know one another, and who were decidedly not at home in polite society. During the following years of the early nineteenth century, life in the national capital became steadily vulgarized by the growing presence in drawing rooms of muddy boots, unkempt hair, and the constant chawing and spitting of tobacco.

Even the removal of the national capital in 1800 from Philadelphia, the bustling intellectual and commercial center of the country, to the rural wilderness of the "federal city" on the Potomac accentuated the transformation of power that was taking place. It dramatized the Republicans' attempt to separate the national government from intimate involvement in the society and their aim to erect the very kind of general government Hamilton, in *The Federalist* No.

27, had warned against, "a government at a distance and out of sight" that could "hardly be expected to interest the sensations of the people." The new and remote capital, Washington, D.C., utterly failed to attract the population, the commerce, and the social and cultural life needed to make it what its original planners had boldly expected, the Rome of the New World. By 1820 Washington was an out-of-the-way village of less than ten thousand inhabitants whose principal business was keeping boardinghouses. Situated in a marsh, the federal city fully deserved the gibes of the visiting Irish poet, Thomas Moore:

> This embryo capital
> where Fancy sees
> Squares in Morasses,
> obelisks in trees.

Political Reform The Republicans in fact meant to have an insignificant national government. The federal government, Jefferson declared in his first message to Congress in 1801, was "charged with the external and mutual relations only of these states." All the rest—the "principal care of our persons, our property, and our reputation, constituting the great field of human concerns"—was to be left to the states. Such a limited national government required turning back a decade of Federalist policy. The Sedition Act of 1798 was allowed to lapse, a new liberal naturalization law was adopted, and rigorous economy was invoked to root out Federalist corruption.

The inherited Federalist governmental establishment was minuscule by modern standards and was small even by eighteenth-century European standards; in 1801 the headquarters of the War Department, for example, consisted of only the secretary, an accountant, fourteen clerks, and two messengers; and the attorney general did not have even a clerk. Nevertheless, in Jefferson's eyes, this tiny federal bureaucracy had become "too complicated, too expensive," and offices under the Federalists had "unnecessarily multiplied." Thus the roll of federal officials was severely cut back. All tax inspectors and collectors were eliminated. The diplomatic establishment was reduced to three missions—in Britain,

REPUBLICANS

Turn out, turn out and save your Country from ruin !

From an *Emperor*—from a *King*—from the iron grasp of a *British Tory Faction*—an unprincipled banditti of British speculators. The hireling tools and emissaries of his majesty king George the 3d have thronged our city and diffused the poison of principles among us.

DOWN WITH THE TORIES, DOWN WITH THE BRITISH FACTION,

Before they have it in their power to enslave you, and reduce your families to distress by heavy taxation. Republicans want no Tribute-liars—they want no ship Ocean-liars—they want no Rufus King's for Lords—they want no Varick to lord it over them—they want no Jones for senator, who fought with the British against the Americans in time of the war.—But they want in their places such men as

Jefferson & Clinton,

who fought their Country's Battles in the year '76

(Courtesy of the New-York Historical Society, New York City)

France, and Spain. The Federalist dream of creating a modern army and navy in emulation of Europe disappeared; the military budget was cut in half. The army, stationed only in the West, was left with 3,000 regulars and only 172 officers. The navy had but a half-dozen frigates, and by 1807 these were replaced with several hundred gunboats designed only to defend the coast or to deal with the Barbary pirates in the Mediterranean. The benefits of a standing military establishment, the Jeffersonians believed, were not worth the cost either in money or in the threat to liberty such an establishment posed.

Since Hamilton's financial program had formed the basis of the heightened political power of the federal government, it above all had to be dismantled. All the internal excise taxes the Federalists had designed to make the people feel the energy of the national government were eliminated. For many citizens the federal presence was now reduced to the delivery of the mails.

Although Jefferson's extremely able secretary of the treasury, Albert Gallatin, persuaded the reluctant president to keep the Bank of the United States, the government was under continual pressure to reduce the Bank's influence. The growing numbers of state banking interests were resentful of the privileged and restraining authority of the national Bank. By 1811 state bankers and southern planters, who hated all banks, eventually prevented a renewal of the Bank's charter. The federal government then distributed its patronage among twenty-one state banks and effectively diluted its authority to control by that means either the society or the economy. It was in fact the proliferation of these state-chartered banks and their issuing of notes that enabled the states to have paper money after all, in spite of the Constitution's prohibition against the states' issuing bills of credit.

Just as Hamilton had regarded the permanent federal debt as a principal source of support for the federal government, so the Republicans were determined to pay off the debt, and quickly. By 1810 the federal debt had been reduced to nearly half of the $80 million it had been when the Republicans took office. Jefferson's lifelong desire to reduce the government's debt was not simply a matter of prohibiting a present generation from burdening posterity, but a matter of destroying what he considered an insidious and dangerous instrument of political influence. His aim was to create a new kind of government, one without privilege or patronage.

Perhaps nothing illustrates Jefferson's radical conception of government better than his problems with patronage. Not all Republicans took his assault on patronage as seriously as he did, and many were often reluctant to join a government in which they would have no sources of influence. Time and again Jefferson found himself caught between his conscientious determination to avoid any semblance of Hamiltonian political patronage or "corruption" and the pressing demands of his fellow Republicans that he give them a share in the government and oust the enemy. Once the Federalists were replaced by Republicans, however, there was no need for compromise on this issue. Removals from office for political reasons came to an end. By the end of the administrations of Jefferson's Republican successors, James Madison (1809–17), James Monroe (1817–25), and John Quincy Adams (1825–29) the holders of government appointments had become a permanent officialdom of men grown old in their positions. Until the Jacksonian revolution of 1828 patronage as a means of influence in government virtually ceased.

Republican Politics.   Jefferson, through a combination of this initial patronage and some improvised forms of political influence (in particular his nightly legislative dinner parties and the use of confidential legislative agents), was able personally to direct the Congress and the Republican party to an extraordinary degree. Yet Jefferson's personal strength and his notable achievements as president cannot hide the remarkable transformation in the traditional meaning of government that the Republican revolution of 1800 created. During the opening three decades of the nineteenth century, particularly after Jefferson retired from the presidency, the United States government was weaker than at any other time in its national history.

The alignments of politics became increasingly confused. The Federalists in 1800–1801 surrendered the national ruling authority without a fight. Because the Federalist leaders considered themselves gentlemen for whom politics was not an exclusive concern, they were prepared to retire to their businesses and private lives and await what they assumed would soon be the people's desperate call for the return of the "wise and good" and the "natural rulers." But the popular reaction they expected to the Republican revolution never came. Some, like John Jay and John Adams, retired to their country estates. Others, like John Quincy Adams, the son of the former president, eventually joined the Republican movement. Others, like Robert Goodloe Harper of South Carolina, clung to their principles and their minority status in politics. And still others, like Timothy Pickering, secretary of state under Adams, dreamed of revenge and fomented separatist plots in New England. But as a national party Federalism slowly withered under the relentless democratization of American society.

Although the Federalists and Republicans continued to compete for election and worked successfully to increase voter participation, neither was a party in any modern sense; and it is probably anachronistic to call their electoral competition, as many historians have done, "the first party system." Though the Federalists continued to put up presidential candidates, their electoral strength was generally negligible and mostly confined to New England. In 1820 they were too weak even to nominate a candidate.

While the declining Federalist gentry regarded themselves less as a party than as dispossessed rulers, the Republicans saw themselves as leaders of a revolutionary movement eager to incorporate the bulk of the opposition into their fold. Only as long as the Federalists posed a threat to the principles of free government could the Republicans remain a unified party. Therefore as the possibility of a Federalist resurgence receded, the Republican party gradually fell apart. A variety of Republican factions and groups arose in the Congress and in the country organized around particular individuals (the "Burrites," the "Clintonians"), around states and sections (the "Pennsylvania Quids," the "Old Republicans" of Virginia), or around ideology ("the Principles of '98," the "Invisibles," the "War Hawks"). Individual politicians continued to pride themselves on their independence from influence of any sort, and "party" remained a disparaging term. In fact, until the Jacksonian era nothing approaching a stable party system developed in the Congress.

By the end of Jefferson's presidency in 1809 the balance of governmental power had slipped to the Congress, which was unequipped to exercise it. Because of the great increase in the size of Congress and its growing disintegration into diverse voting blocs, neither Madison nor Monroe was able to use any of the personal presidential charm and influence that Jefferson had used. By 1808 caucuses of Republicans within the Congress had taken over nomination of the party's candidates for the presidency, and Republican presidential aspirants soon became dependent on the legislature in the way governors in the Revolutionary state constitutions of 1776 had been.

While Secretary of State James Madison was able with Jefferson's private blessing to secure the Republican nomination in 1808 and again in 1812 against only some divided opposition, in 1816 Madison's secretary of state, James Monroe, had to contend strenuously with Secretary of War William H. Crawford of Georgia for the nomination. By the early 1820s Secretary of State John Quincy Adams, Secretary of

War John C. Calhoun, and Secretary of the Treasury Crawford were all feuding with one another and seeking support in the Congress for the presidential nomination. If such political realities did not dictate presidential subservience to the legislature, Republican ideology did. Except in foreign affairs, both Presidents Madison and Monroe, the second and third members of the "Virginia Dynasty," regarded Congress as the rightful determinant of the public will, free of executive influence.

As the Congress in Madison's and Monroe's administrations (1809–25) gathered up the power passing from the executive, it sought to organize itself into committees in order to initiate and supervise policy. But the rise of the committee system only further fragmented the government into contending interests. The executive authority itself broke apart into competing departments, each seeking its own support in the Congress and becoming a rival of the president. Congress now fought with the president for control of the cabinet and connived with executive department heads behind the president's back. At one point the Congress actually forced Madison to accept a secretary of state who was plotting against him, and its meddling drove Monroe into bitter hostility against his secretary of the treasury, with whom he stopped speaking. Until the congressional caucus system of presidential nomination collapsed in 1824 and a new kind of democratic presidency emerged in 1828 with the election of Andrew Jackson, the energy of the national executive remained weak.

But despite this concentration on strict republican principles there were by the second decade of the nineteenth century many Americans who sought to reclaim and reenact some of the abandoned Federalist measures. A new generation of politicians, less attached to the ideology and fears of the eighteenth century and with none of Hamilton's dream to create a consolidated European-like state, now began urging a new national bank, protective tariffs, and a federally sponsored program of internal improvements. By 1815 the nation had grown faster than anyone had expected, and new states, new interests, and new outlooks had to be taken into account. By then it was becoming clear that the future of the country lay in the West.

(Abby Aldrich Rockefeller Folk Art Center, Williamsburg, Virginia)

An Empire of Liberty

While Hamilton and the Federalists had looked eastward across the Atlantic to Europe for their image of the destiny of the United States, the Republicans from the beginning had had their eyes on the West. Only by moving westward, Jefferson thought, could Americans maintain their republican society of independent yeomen-farmers and avoid the miseries of the concentrated urban working classes of Europe. Jefferson was indeed the most expansionist-minded president in American history. He dreamed of Americans endowed with republican principles eventually swarming over the continent and creating an "empire of liberty." Yet even Jefferson did not anticipate how suddenly and chaotically Americans would scatter westward.

The population grew from almost 4 million in 1790 to over 7 million in 1810 and nearly 10 million by 1820, and much of it was moving west. By the 1790s the population in some of the tidewater counties of the Chesapeake already was declining. The advance over the Allegheny Plateau that had been a trickle before the Revolution and had swelled during the 1780s now became a flood. Within a single generation following the Revolution more territory was occupied than during the entire colonial period. By 1810 westward-moving Americans had created a great triangular wedge of settlement to the Mississippi. The northern side ran from New York along the Ohio River, the southern side from east Georgia through Tennessee, and the two lines met at the tip of the wedge at St. Louis. Within this huge triangle of settlement people were distributed haphazardly, and huge pockets remained virtually uninhabited.

National leaders had expected migration westward, but not the way it happened. The carefully drawn plans of the 1780s for the orderly surveying and settlement of the West were simply overwhelmed by the massive and chaotic movement of people. Many settlers ignored land ordinances and titles, squatted on the land, and claimed rights to it. For decades beginning in 1796 the federal government steadily lowered the price of land, reduced the size of purchasable tracts, and relaxed the terms of credit in ever-more desperate efforts to bring the public land laws into line with the speed with which they were being settled. There was more land than people could use, and still they kept moving; some moved three and four times in a lifetime. Speculators and land companies that had counted on land values rising through neat and orderly settlement, as in colonial days, were now wiped out. Many of the most prominent and wealthy Revolutionary leaders, including Robert Morris, financier during the Confederation, Henry Knox, Washington's secretary of war, and James Wilson, justice of the Supreme Court,

Density of Population, 1810

Salem
Boston
Newport
Providence
New York
Newark
Philadelphia
Baltimore
Washington
Charleston
Savannah
New Orleans

People per Square Mile
- Over 90
- 45 to 90
- 18 to 45
- 2 to 18
- Under 2
- • Major Cities

MERIWEATHER LEWIS (1774–1809)
President Jefferson in 1801 made this soldier and explorer his private secretary and thought so highly of his scientific as well as military qualifications that he appointed him the leader of the long-planned expedition to the Pacific. Together with his friend William Clark, Lewis led a party of fifty in a two-year exploration of western North America. It is one of the great heroic events of American history. *(National Portrait Gallery, Smithsonian Institution, Washington, D.C.)*

speculated heavily in land and ended their careers in bankruptcy. Even Washington died with his estate tied up in speculative land that no one would pay for.

The Louisiana Purchase. Nothing in Jefferson's administration contributed more to this astonishing expansion than his sudden acquisition in 1803 of the entire Louisiana territory, which, extending from the Mississippi to the Rockies, doubled the size of the United States. For decades Jefferson and other American leaders had foreseen that this young and thriving nation would expand naturally and "piece by piece" take over the feebly held Spanish possessions in North America. Some even thought that British-held Canada would eventually pass to the United States. When the Revolutionary War ended in 1783, Jefferson was already dreaming of explorations to the Pacific. And when he became president, well before he had any inkling that America would purchase the whole Louisiana territory, he laid plans for scientific—and also military and commercial—expeditions into the foreign-held trans-Mississippi West. The most famous of these expeditions was that of Lewis and Clark, eventually undertaken in 1803–06.

When in 1800, in the Treaty of San Ildefonso, a weak Spain ceded back to a powerful France the Louisiana territory, including New Orleans, it had formerly held west of the Mississippi these dreams of expansion were suddenly placed in doubt. The livelihood of the western farmers depended on the free navigation of the Mississippi, and Jefferson was determined to maintain it. He immediately began strengthening fortifications in the West and preparing for the worst. "The day that France takes possession of New Orleans," he informed his American minister to France, Robert Livingston, in April 1802, "we must marry ourselves to the British fleet and nation." This prospect of an American-British alliance threatened the French; Napoleon was already appraising the difficulties of reestablishing the French empire in the New World if war should break out again in Europe. As a result, in 1803 the French government decided to sell to the United States not just New Orleans, which Jefferson had sought to purchase, but all of Louisiana for $15 million.

The United States, 1803-1807

Lewis and Clark, 1804-1806
Pike, 1805-1806
Pike, 1806-1807
Freeman, 1805

Jefferson hesitated over what to do; he feared that the purchase of Louisiana by the federal government would exceed the limited powers granted to it by the Constitution. He considered amending the Constitution in order to acquire this new territory, but finally and regretfully, under intense pressure, he allowed his constitutional scruples to be passed over in silence. Despite its fulfillment of his grandest dreams for America, Jefferson's agonized decision did not suggest that he was conceding in any way to a broad Federalist interpretation of the Constitution. His hesitation only showed the extreme seriousness with which he took his strict construction of the Constitution.

The purchase of Louisiana was the most popular and momentous event of Jefferson's presidency. Not only did it end the long struggle for control of the Mississippi's outlet to the sea, but it also, as Jefferson exulted, freed America from Europe's colonial entanglements and prepared the way for the eventual dominance of the United States in the Western Hemisphere. Its most immediate consequence, however, was to raise fears once again of the country's splitting apart. The borders of the new territory were so vague, the Spanish hold on Mexico and the Floridas so weak, and the rough and unruly frontier inhab-

VIEW OF NEW ORLEANS, 1803

"There is on the globe one single spot, the possessor of which is our natural and habitual enemy," said President Jefferson in 1802. "It is New Orleans, through which the produce of three-eighths of our territory must pass to market." It was the American desire to control this port that led to the Louisiana Purchase. *(Chicago Historical Society)*

itants so captivated by the dreams of America's destined expansion that adventurers, filibustering expeditions, and rumors of plots and conspiracies flourished throughout the South and the West.

The Burr Conspiracy. The most grandiose of these schemes was that of 1806–7. It involved Aaron Burr, Jefferson's former vice-president, and (until he turned state's evidence) General James Wilkinson, commanding general of the United States Army secretly in the pay of the Spanish government and one of the most unscrupulous and skillful adventurers in American history. In the summer of 1806 Burr and sixty men in flatboats floated down the Ohio and Mississippi toward New Orleans to make contact with the Spanish. When Burr learned that Wilkinson had

denounced him, he fled toward Florida, probably on his way to Europe, but was captured and brought east to be tried for treason. Although Burr was acquitted because no overt act of treason could be constitutionally proved, he undoubtedly had had in mind some sort of conspiracy, involving a number of American military and civil officials, directed toward an attack on Mexico or a separation of the western areas of the United States. These kinds of activities and the danger of the country's splintering caused the Congress to incorporate into the Union as fast as possible the underdeveloped frontier territories of Ohio (1803), Louisiana (1810), Indiana (1816), Mississippi (1817), Illinois (1818), and Alabama (1819). These new western states were firmly Republican and created constitutions that were more democratic than those of the older eastern states. Most provided for weak executives, white adult male suffrage, annually elected legislatures, no property qualifications for officeholders, and popular election for a host of offices, including judges.

Indians. The Indians in these western territories were no match for the hordes of advancing settlers. By 1800 Ohio had 45,000 inhabitants; by 1810 it had over 230,000 and was already bursting its boundaries. Although the Greenville Treaty of 1795 had drawn a definite line between Indians and whites, most Americans, including President Jefferson, assumed that the vast Indian hunting grounds between Ohio and the Mississippi must sooner or later belong to the advancing Americans. Jefferson expected the Indians willingly to cede their lands to the United States and either become farmers and partake of the blessings of republican civilization or move west beyond the Mississippi.

American pressure on the Indians to surrender their lands was immense, and under Presidents Jefferson and Madison fifty-three treaties of land cession were made. Finally in 1805 the Shawnee Chief Tecumseh and his brother The Prophet attempted to halt this steady encroachment of whites by forming an Indian confederacy. This tribal effort at organized resistance was broken by the governor of the Indiana Territory, General William Henry Harrison, in a battle between 600 Indians and a mixed force of 1,000 American army troops and Kentucky frontiersmen at Tippecanoe in 1811. Sporadic Indian fighting and raiding in the Old Northwest continued, however, but it did not stop the waves of settlers. By 1815 the Indiana Territory had nearly 60,000 settlers.

In the southwestern territories the Indian presence was even more formidable. Still, by 1810, the Mississippi Territory (much of present-day Alabama and Mississippi) had over 40,000 people, including 17,000 slaves, mainly clustered along the Mississippi River counties south of Natchez, which was fast becoming a bustling trade center. In 1810 the Territory of Orleans (modern Louisiana) had over 76,000 inhabitants, more than half of whom were slaves. New Orleans with its mixture of Spanish, French, and

other nationalites in a population of over 10,000 was by far the largest and most flamboyant city of the Mississippi Valley and on its way to becoming one of the great ports of the country. By 1810 pioneers were rapidly pushing beyond the Mississippi River into what are now the states of Arkansas and Missouri, leaving behind huge pockets of Indians—Creeks in

TECUMSEH (c. 1768–1813)
Tecumseh, a Shawnee chief, was perhaps the most extraordinary Indian leader in American history. Together with his brother, the Prophet, he attempted in the early nineteenth century to organize a huge confederation of Indians in the Northwest. The Indians were to refuse to cede any more lands to the Americans and were to abandon the white man's ways and goods. But after the battle of Tippecanoe in 1811, organized Indian resistance gave way to sporadic warfare. Tecumseh was killed fighting for the British at the battle of the Thames (1813). *(Courtesy, Field Museum of Natural History, Chicago)*

Georgia, and Cherokees in Tennessee. By 1815 the Missouri Territory had over 20,000 people.

All the while eastern Federalists expressed alarm at this expanding "empire of liberty." With their vision of the United States as a homogeneous and integrated nation-state like those of Europe, the Federalists found it inconceivable that such a gigantic republic could long hold together. To the Republicans, however, who thought of the United States as a loosely bound confederation of states, the huge expanse of territory posed no problems. "Who can limit the extent to which the federative principle may operate effectively?" asked Jefferson in his second inaugural address. Jefferson's "empire of liberty" was always one of like principles, not of like boundaries; and he was at times remarkably indifferent to the possibility that a western confederacy might break away from the eastern United States. What did it matter? he asked in 1804. "Those of the western confederacy will be as much our children and descendants as those of the eastern."

The Federalists called it "a most visionary theory," and believed the consequence would eventually be anarchy. But in the Republican conception, Americans were creating new bonds of social cohesion, not the virtue of classical republicanism perhaps, but, as Jefferson said, "that progress of opinion which is tending to unite them in object and in will."

The Origins of Judical Review

At Jefferson's election in 1800 no institution of the national government was more detested by the Republicans than the judiciary. The appointed federal judges were less susceptible to popular rule than were other government officials, and during the 1790s the Federalists had consciously tried to strengthen the federal courts in order to extend the central government's presence among the people. Since there was not a single Republican judge in the entire national judiciary during the 1790s, Republican newspaper editors had often been brought before the federal courts on charges of sedition. Moreover, Federalist land speculators with interests that spanned

state lines had used the more sympathetic federal courts to resolve their conflicting claims, often to the anger of Republican-controlled state courts. Even after the Federalists had lost the election of 1800, the lame duck Congress dominated by Federalists had passed a new judiciary act creating a system of circuit courts and broadening the jurisdiction of the federal courts. And before surrendering the presidency to Jefferson, John Adams had hastily appointed a number of judges, including John Marshall as chief justice of the United States. This convinced Jefferson that "the remains of federalism" had "retired into the judiciary as a stronghold . . . , and from that battery all the works of republicanism are to be beaten down and erased."

To complete "the revolution," therefore, as a fellow Virginian told Jefferson, "the enemy" had to be routed from "that strong fortress." After a bitter debate in the Congress, the Republicans repealed the Federalist Judiciary Act of 1801. They thus destroyed the newly created circuit courts and for the first and only time in United States history revoked the tenure of federal judges as well. In order to bring the entire judicial establishment under greater congressional control, some Republicans proposed amending the Constitution. Others, however, fixed on impeachment for "high crimes and misdemeanors" as the best constitutional device available for removing obnoxious Federalist judges. The Republicans in the House of Representatives first impeached and the Senate then convicted John Pickering, an alcoholic and insane judge of the federal district court of New Hampshire, even though he had committed no crimes or misdemeanors.

With this broad construction of the criminal meaning of impeachment in hand, the most rabid Republicans under the leadership of John Randolph of Virginia, next attempted to bring down Supreme Court Justice Samuel Chase, the most overbearing Federalist on the Court. However, this perversion of the impeachment process into a mode of removal was too much for some Republicans. While a majority of the Senate in 1805 found Chase guilty, the Republicans could not muster the necessary two-thirds majority. Not only did Chase's acquittal hurt

JOHN MARSHALL, 1755–1835, BY CEPHAS THOMPSON
Marshall is the most famous Chief Justice of the Supreme Court in American history. During his long tenure on the Court from 1801 to his death, this Virginia Federalist participated in more than 1,000 decisions, writing over half himself. In effect Marshall created for America what came to be called constitutional law and transformed the meaning and role of the Supreme Court. (*The Bettmann Archive, Inc.*)

Randolph's reputation, driving him to the extremist edges of the Republican party, but it ended any further direct assault by the Republicans on the national judiciary.

Marbury v. Madison. In the meantime John Marshall from his position as chief justice of the Supreme Court managed to drain some of the bitterness from the controversy over the judiciary. Marshall was the most important chief justice in American history. During his long career (1801–35), which spanned the administrations of five presidents, he laid the foundations both for the Court's eventual independence and for the constitutional supremacy of the national government over the states.

In 1801, however, the Court was very weak. Although Marshall solidified the Court by making one justice's opinion, usually his own, stand for the decision of the whole Court, he had to move very cautiously. Instead of confronting the Republicans head-on by declaring the Congress's repeal of the Judiciary Act of 1801 unconstitutional, as many Federalists had urged, Marshall chose to act indirectly. In the case of *Marbury* v. *Madison* (1803), the Marshall Court decided that Marbury, one of the "midnight judges" President Adams had appointed, was entitled to his commission, which Secretary of State Madison had withheld. Yet if unenforced by the president, such a bold decision would obviously have discredited the Court. Marshall avoided a losing clash with the executive branch by going on to state that, although Marbury deserved his commission, the Court had no authority to order the president to grant it. The provision of the earlier Federalist-enacted Judiciary Act of 1789 that gave the Court such original authority, he said, was unconstitutional. Thus Marshall obliquely asserted the Court's role in overseeing the Constitution without the serious political repercussions involved in opposing the Republicans. Since the American people regarded their written Constitution as "the fundamental and paramount law of the nation," wrote Marshall for the Court, then it followed that "a law repugnant to the Constitution," such as part of the Judiciary Act of 1789, "is void; and that courts, as well as other departments, are bound by that instrument."

Although Marshall's decision in *Marbury* v. *Madison* has since taken on immense historical significance as the first judicial assertion by the Supreme Court of its right to declare acts of Congress unconstitutional, few in 1803 saw its momentous implications. Such a right was nowhere explicitly recognized in the Constitution, and it was by no means established in American thinking at the end of the eighteenth century. To be sure, some like Hamilton in *The Federalist* No. 78 tried to justify this ultimate judicial authority by invoking the supremacy of the Constitution created by the sovereignty of the people and protected by the courts.

By asserting in the *Marbury* decision that the

Court had a right and duty to declare what the fundamental law was, Marshall obviously drew upon this earlier thinking. But he did not say unequivocally that the Court was the only part of the national government with such a right and duty. Indeed, Marshall's assertion of judicial authority in the *Marbury* decision was limited and ambiguous and implied that the other departments in the government had an equal obligation with the courts to construe the law in accord with the Constitution. Jefferson certainly believed that the executive and the legislature had the same ultimate right as the judiciary to interpret the Constitution, and he always explicitly denied the "exclusive" authority of the judiciary to decide what laws were constitutional. Such a monopoly of interpretative power, he said in 1804, "would make the judiciary a despotic branch." *Marbury* v. *Madison* was in fact the only time in Marshall's long tenure in which the Supreme Court declared an act of Congress unconstitutional.

Constitutional Nationalism. What the Marshall Court did do in its long career was declare a large number of *state* judicial interpretations and *state* laws in violation of the federal Constitution. In a series of decisions beginning with the *United States* v. *Peters* (1809) and proceeding through *Martin* v. *Hunter's Lessee* (1816) and *Cohens* v. *Virginia* (1821), the Supreme Court established its right to review and reverse decisions of state courts involving interpretations of federal law and the federal Constitution. At the same time, following the first test in *Fletcher* v. *Peck* (1810), the Court overturned a series of state laws that interfered with private contracts and hence violated the Constitution.

Marshall, however, was not content merely with these negative restraints on state power; he sought positively to enhance the supremacy of the national government. In the greatest decision of his career, *McCulloch* v. *Maryland* (1819), Marshall upheld the right of Congress to charter a national bank even though that right was not expressly mentioned in the Constitution. The power to charter a bank, said Marshall, was implied by the "necessary and proper" authority the Constitution granted to Congress to carry its delegated powers into effect. Hence the

attempt by the Maryland legislature to destroy the Bank by taxation was unconstitutional. No decision of Marshall's was more important to the future of America and none asserted the supremacy of the Constitution more unequivocally. By 1820 the Court had already become—even for James Madison—something resembling that "disinterested umpire" he had wanted in 1787 the entire federal government to be.

The Manipulative Tradition of American Law. Yet as important as Marshall's decisions were in establishing that the Court had final authority over the states to interpret the Constitution, they do not by themselves explain the origins of the extraordinary authority wielded by all American judges. Nineteenth-century Americans inherited an unusual manipulative attitude toward law from the colonial period. Since the colonists had derived their law haphazardly both from their colonial legislatures and courts and from various English sources, they tended to equate law not with what English judges and legal authorities said it was, but with what made sense in America's local circumstances. Time and again eighteenth-century Americans had justified minor deviations and irregularities in their laws in the name of reason, justice, or utility. They thus developed a particularly pragmatic attitude toward law that became stronger in the decades that followed the Revolution.

In the emerging business society of early nineteenth-century America, the desired predictability of law came not from strict adherence to precedent but from rapid adaptability to changing commercial circumstances. To mold the law to fit the needs of America's expanding enterprise, judges increasingly abandoned the customs and technicalities of the inherited English common law and replaced them with useful and prudent regulations. By the second decade of the nineteenth century, American law was coming to be thought of as a man-made creative instrument of social policy. And judges under fast-moving economic pressures were becoming the chief agents of legal change. The judicial interpretative power inherent in the flexibility of American law from the beginning was now starkly revealed and liberally expanded.

Despite continued efforts in the early nineteenth

century to weaken this remarkable judicial authority, law in America maintained its pliable and instrumental quality. Although judges continued to deny that they made law in the way legislatures did, it was obvious that they did something more than simply discover it in the precedents and customs of the past. Law in America, rooted in the consent and sovereignty of the people, was designed to serve the needs of that people, and when it did not, it was the obligation of judges to construe it in such a way that it did. In fact, if neither legislatures nor judges could act fast enough to shape the law to changing circumstances, then some Americans thought that the people themselves, in extralegal groups and "mobs," had the right to take the law into their own hands and mold it as their situation demanded. The peculiarly American practices of judicial review and vigilantism were actually two sides of the same legal coin.

Republican Religion

Although politics and constitutionalism dominated the Revolutionary era, most ordinary Americans still conceived of the world in religious terms. Hence the Revolution and even republicanism had a religious dimension. Indeed, the Revolution marked an important point in the history of American religion. It endorsed the Enlightenment's faith in liberty of conscience, severed the already tenuous connection between church and state, and advanced America into a religious world of competing denominations that was unique to Christendom.

Religious Liberty in the Revolution.   From the outset of the Revolutionary controversy, Americans had argued that the dark forces of civic tyranny and religious tyranny were linked. All the new Revolutionary constitutions of 1776 in some way affirmed religious freedom. Yet the constitutional declarations "that all men have a natural and unalienable right to worship Almighty God according to the dictates of their own consciences" did not necessarily mean that the state would abandon its traditional role in religious matters. To be sure, the establishment of the Church of England that existed in several of the colo-

nies was immediately eliminated. But the Maryland, South Carolina, and Georgia Revolutionary constitutions authorized their state legislatures to create in place of the Anglican church a kind of multiple establishment using tax money to support "the Christian religion."

Virginians especially were divided over the meaning of their 1776 declaration of religious liberty. Liberals like Jefferson and Madison joined growing numbers of Presbyterian and Baptist dissenters to oppose the Anglican clergy and planters in a fierce but eventually successful struggle for the complete disestablishment of the Church of England. In 1786 this Virginia struggle was climaxed by the passage of Jefferson's memorable Act for Establishing Religious Freedom. Many of the states, however, retained some vague or general religious qualifications for public office, and both Connecticut and Massachusetts continued to maintain their modified Congregational establishments.

In short, unlike the church in Europe, the American churches, developing as they had in the colonial period, perceived no threat from revolution or republicanism. Except for the Anglican clergy, Protestant ministers were in the vanguard of the Revolutionary movement. In fact, it was the clergy who made the Revolution meaningful for most common people. For every gentleman who read a scholarly pamphlet and delved into Whig and ancient history for an explanation of events, there were dozens of ordinary people who read the Bible and looked to their ministers for an interpretation of what the Revolution meant. Evangelical Protestantism blended with republicanism in a common effort to rid America of sin and luxury and to build a new society of benevolence and virtue.

Despite these hopes, however, the immediate effect of the Revolution on church organization was devastating. The Revolution destroyed churches, scattered congregations, and led to a sharp decline in church membership. By the 1790s perhaps only one in twenty Americans was affiliated with a church. The earlier revivalistic enthusiasm receded under the pressure of a spreading religious rationalism, or deism, which sought to substitute reason for revelation and the science of Newton for the mysteries of

LEMUEL HAYNES, 1753–1833, FIRST BLACK MINISTER OF THE CONGREGATIONAL CHURCH IN AMERICA

Haynes fought in the Revolutionary War, and after he was ordained in 1785 he became minister of the west parish of Rutland, Vermont, where he remained for thirty years. *(Museum of Art, Rhode Island School of Design, Gift of Lucy T. Aldrich)*

traditional Christianity. In 1784 Ethan Allen published his deistic work *Reason the Only Oracle of Man*, which boldly attacked the Bible and the clergy and defended natural religion. With Thomas Paine's *Age of Reason* (1794), the Comte de Volney's *Ruins of Empire* (1791), and Elihu Palmer's attempts to organize deistic societies among urban workingmen in the 1790s, it seemed to many religious leaders that republicanism was breeding infidelity.

As long as the enlightened deism of Jefferson and the other Revolutionary leaders had been confined to the drawing rooms of the gentry and was not publicized, it had posed little threat to Protestant orthodoxy. But with the dissemination of rational and natural religion among ordinary people at the time of

the French Revolution, the clergy, especially the older Calvinistic clergy, became alarmed and began a countermovement on behalf of orthodox Christianity. So identified with the excesses of the French Revolution and hence the Republican party was this rational deism that even Hamilton toyed with the idea of enlisting Christianity on behalf of the beleaguered Federalists. In the end this countermovement by conservative Congregationalists and Presbyterians in the 1790s transcended its creators. It became an eastern version of the revivalism that had continued throughout the South and West during the Revolutionary era, and it eventually fused into the early nineteenth-century evangelical movement known as the Second Great Awakening.

The Second Great Awakening. The Second Great Awakening was a radical expansion and extension of the earlier eighteenth-century revivals. It did not simply intensify the religious feeling of existing church members; more important, it mobilized unprecedented numbers of hitherto unchurched people into religious communions. By popularizing religion as never before and by bringing Christianity into the remotest areas of America, this great revival marked the beginning of the republicanizing and nationalizing of American religion. Thousands upon thousands of ordinary people found in evangelical religion new sources of order and community.

In the decades following the Revolution the various Protestant churches reorganized themselves nationally and entered a period of denominational rivalry. With the decline in the number of college graduates among the gentry now willing to enter the ministry, the older Calvinist churches, Presbyterians and Congregationalists, were forced to form separate colleges and seminaries for the professional education of clergymen and to recruit increasing numbers of their ministers from lower social levels. The newer denominations, the Methodists and the Baptists, recruited their preachers even more informally. Rejecting as they did the idea of a settled and learned ministry, they were more capable than the older churches of speaking the language of the common people they sought to evangelize. By 1820 the Baptists and Methodists had become the largest denominations in America.

Although evangelism spread throughout America, it was most successful in the West, where the dynamic process of revivalism was better able to deal with a mobile population than were the traditional churchly institutions. In the first twelve years of the nineteenth century the Methodists in Tennessee, Kentucky, and Ohio grew from less than 3,000 to well over 30,000. In the short period between 1800 and 1802 the Baptists in Kentucky alone increased from 4,700 to 13,500. In these fast-growing new territories the need for some kind of community, however loose and voluntary, among isolated men and women was most intense; there the need for building barriers against barbarism and licentiousness was most keenly felt.

In the summer of 1801 at Cane Ridge, Kentucky, unbelievable numbers of these Westerners, together with dozens of clergymen of several denominations, came together in what some thought was the greatest outpouring of the Holy Spirit since the beginning of Christianity. Crowds estimated at 12–25,000 participated in a week of frenzied conversions. The heat, the noise, and the confusion were overwhelming: ministers shouted sermons from wagons and tree stumps; people fell to the ground moaning and wailing in remorse, and they sang, laughed, barked, rolled, and jerked in excitement. This gigantic camp meeting at Cane Ridge immediately became a symbol of the promises and the excesses of the new kind of evangelical Protestantism spreading throughout the South and West. Although the conservative Presbyterians and Congregationalists in the East did not hold camp meetings, they too were compelled to adopt some of the new revivalistic methods. By 1820 there were already clearly revealed a number of basic and interrelated characteristics of American religious life whose roots went back to the colonial period and which underlay the emerging Evangelical Age.

Evangelical Denominationalism. First, the number of religions multiplied, and whatever lingering sense of orthodoxy there was disintegrated; the legal residues of establishment in Connecticut (1818) and Massachusetts (1833) were eliminated. American religions became denominations and abandoned once and for all the traditional belief that any of them could be the true and exclusive church for the society. Each religious association, called or *denominated* by a particular name, now saw itself simply as one limited and imperfect representative of the larger Christian community; each denomination was equal to and in competition with the others. No other society in the world had ever conceived of religion in this way.

By abandoning all expectation of maintaining any special identity with the society, religion in America became an entirely personal and voluntary affair in which all individuals who wished to could bring about their own salvation. Even the Calvinists, who believed that God had already chosen those who were to be saved, nevertheless managed to stress the responsibility of each individual for his or her own conversion. Sin was no longer thought of as inherent in human beings but as a kind of failure of individual will. Thus each person was fully capable of eliminating sin through his or her individual exertion. With such an assumption the numbers who could be saved were no longer limited by God's election, and all the denominations began to sound remarkably like the new denomination, the Universalists, who democratically promised salvation for everyone.

Since religion was now clearly personal and voluntary, people were free to join and change religious associations whenever they wished. This meant that the churches were less capable than they had been in the eighteenth century of reflecting the variety of social ranks within their own community. Particular denominations became identified with particular social classes; for example, the Episcopalians (the former Anglicans) and the Unitarians (liberal Congregationalists) became largely the preserve of social elites. If the role of the denominations was to contend with one another for souls in the religious marketplace, then it was important that each denomination be as united, tightly organized, and homogeneous as possible. Dissenters and schismatics were thus allowed to go their separate ways without the struggles that had marked earlier American religious life. The consequence was a further splintering of religion and the proliferation of new, peculiar religious groups, like the Stonites and Campbellites, with no connection whatever to the Old World.

The divisive effects of this fragmentation were offset by a conscious blurring of theological distinctions among the competing denominations. Some extreme evangelicals urged the creation of a simple Christian religion based only on the gospel. They denounced in the name of the American Revolution all the paraphernalia of organized Christianity, including even the clergy, and claimed the right of every individual to be his own theologian. Within a few decades some of these fundamentalist Christians came together as the Disciples of Christ, which soon emerged as the third-largest Protestant religious group in nineteenth-century America.

Despite the competition among them, all the denominations identified themselves with the nation and worked to unify American culture under evangelical Protestantism. Clergymen were determined to prove that America's separation of church and state would not result in the infidelity and religious neglect that most Europeans expected. Evangelicals emphasized over and over that America, though without a state supported church, was nonetheless a nation of God. Throughout the early nineteenth century, religious groups resisted the secularizing effects of the Enlightenment and the First Amendment, and urged the Republic to recognize its basis in Christianity by instituting chaplains in Congress, proclaiming days of fasting and prayer, and ending mail delivery on the Sabbath. Clergymen, said Nathaniel William Taylor of Connecticut, the most important theologian of the Second Great Awakening, had no intention of creating a new governmental establishment or denying the rights of conscience. "We only ask for those provisions in law . . . in behalf of a common Christianity, which are its due as a nation's strength and a nation's glory."

By 1800 the fate of Christianity and the fate of the nation were tied together by a belief in millennialism. Many evangelical clergymen had come to believe that America was leading humanity into earth's final thousand years of glory and happiness before the Second Coming of Christ and the Day of Judgment predicted in the Bible. The apocalyptic hopes of these clergymen focused on contemporary historical events occurring in America as signs of the approaching age of perfection. The millennium thus became more than a vague promise of Christian theology; it was to be an actual phase in the history of the American republic. Every advance in America's worldly progress—even new inventions and canals—was interpreted in millennial terms. By giving the millennium such a concrete temporal and material character and by identifying the Kingdom of God with the prospects of the United States, the Protestant clergy contributed greatly to nineteenth-century Americans' growing sense of mission. By improving and prospering, the United States—it was thought—was destined to redeem the world.

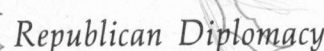

Republican Diplomacy

The dramatic culmination of the Republicans' revolution of 1800 came in the War of 1812. It was an unusual war, a war on which the entire experiment in free government seemed to rest. It was a war that few wanted but that many had made inevitable. It was a war that in the end solved nothing, but that was widely regarded as a glorious American victory.

The origins of the War of 1812 lay in the American principles of foreign relations first expressed at the time of the Revolution. The American Revolution had been centrally concerned with power, not only power within a state, but power among states in their international relations. Throughout the eighteenth century liberal intellectuals had looked forward to a rational world in which corrupt monarchical diplomacy and secret alliances, balances of power, and dynastic conflicts would be eliminated. In short, they had dreamed of nothing less than an end of war and a new era of peace based on natural commercial relations among nations. If the people of the various nations were left alone to exchange goods freely among themselves, it was believed, then international politics would become republicanized and pacified.

Suddenly in 1776, with the United States isolated outside the European mercantile empires, the Americans had an opportunity and a need to put these liberal ideas about the free exchange of goods into practice. Thus commercial interest and Revolutionary idealism blended to form the basis for American thinking about foreign affairs that lasted until well into the first half of the twentieth century. America first expressed these principles during discussions over the prospective treaty with France at the time of Independence. Many in the Congress in 1776 at-

BUILDING THE FRIGATE "PHILADELPHIA"

All seven of the frigates of the United States Navy that fought the War of 1812 were built in the 1790s, when war with France threatened. The Federalists also wanted to build some ships of the line, which had more decks and nearly twice as many guns as frigates. Although the Federalists acquired timber and six navy yards, the accession of the Republicans in 1801 ended their plans for enlarging the Navy. (*I. N. Phelps Stokes Collection, The New York Public Library*) tempted to work out a model treaty to be applied to France and eventually to other states that would avoid the traditional kinds of political and military commitments and focus instead on exclusively commercial connections. Although in the treaties of 1778 with France the United States was unable to implement its desired commercial plan, and in fact had to settle for a customary European kind of military alliance, many Americans never lost their enlightened hope that international politics might be made over by new liberal commercial relationships.

By the 1790s, however, the Federalists had rejected many of these enlightened dreams for international relations. Hamilton in particular denied the liberal assumptions that republics were naturally peaceful and that commerce was an adequate substitute for the power politics of traditional diplomacy. He put no stock in the idealistic Republican conviction that Britain's great power could be dealt with solely by a policy of commercial discrimination and economic coercion.

The Republicans therefore emerged as the preservers of the visionary principles of diplomacy they identified with the Revolution of 1776. In contrast to the Federalists, who thought the only way to prepare for war was to build up the government and armed forces in a European manner, the Republicans believed that the United States did not need, nor could safely afford, enlarged state power and a traditional army and navy; it did not even need an elaborate diplomatic establishment. While some Republicans in the 1790s urged eliminating all American diplomatic posts except those in London and Paris, others favored replacing the entire American representation abroad with consuls, who were all that were required to handle matters of international trade. At times Jefferson even talked wistfully of abandoning all international commerce so that the United States might "stand, with respect to Europe, precisely on the footing of China." More often, however, he and other Republicans saw American commerce not simply as something to be protected by national policy, as the Federalists did, but as a political weapon to be used as an alternative to war in the way the colonists had used nonimportation in the pre-Revolutionary crisis with Great Britain.

Republicans and the War in Europe.   When the conflict between Britain and France resumed in 1803, the Republicans, now in control of the national government, at last had an opportunity to put their policies to a test. Since Britain was unable to contest on land Napoleon's domination of the continent of Europe, it was determined to exploit its supremacy on the seas to blockade France into submission.

American commerce, once again caught between these two Goliaths, prospered magnificently. Ever since the outbreak of the European war in the early 1790s, American merchants had gained access to the European mercantile empires formerly barred to them and had made the United States the largest neutral carrier of goods in the world. Between 1793 and 1807 American ship tonnage tripled, and the value of American exports increased fivefold. Particularly profitable was the growth of America's wartime shipping between the Spanish and French possessions in the New World and Europe. The value of this trade increased from $300,000 in 1790 to nearly $60 million by 1807. This commerce, however, violated the British Rule of 1756, which prohibited neutrals in time of war to trade within a mercantile empire closed to them in time of peace. To protect this carrying trade, therefore, American merchants developed a legal fiction. By carrying belligerent goods from, say, the French West Indies to American ports, unloading and paying duties on them, then reloading and getting a rebate on the duties before taking them on to France, American traders broke their voyages and thus technically conformed to the British Rule of 1756. The British now resolved to put a stop to this reexport trade. The *Essex* decision of 1805, in which a British admiralty court held that belligerent goods reexported in this fictitious manner were liable to seizure, opened the way to increased British attacks on American shipping.

At the same time, Britain expanded its impressment, or the forcible removal, of seamen from American vessels on the grounds that they were British subjects. Many of these seamen were deserters from the British navy, and since Great Britain refused to recognize the right of expatriation, which was an essential right for a nation of immigrants, conflict over the nationality of American seamen was inevita-

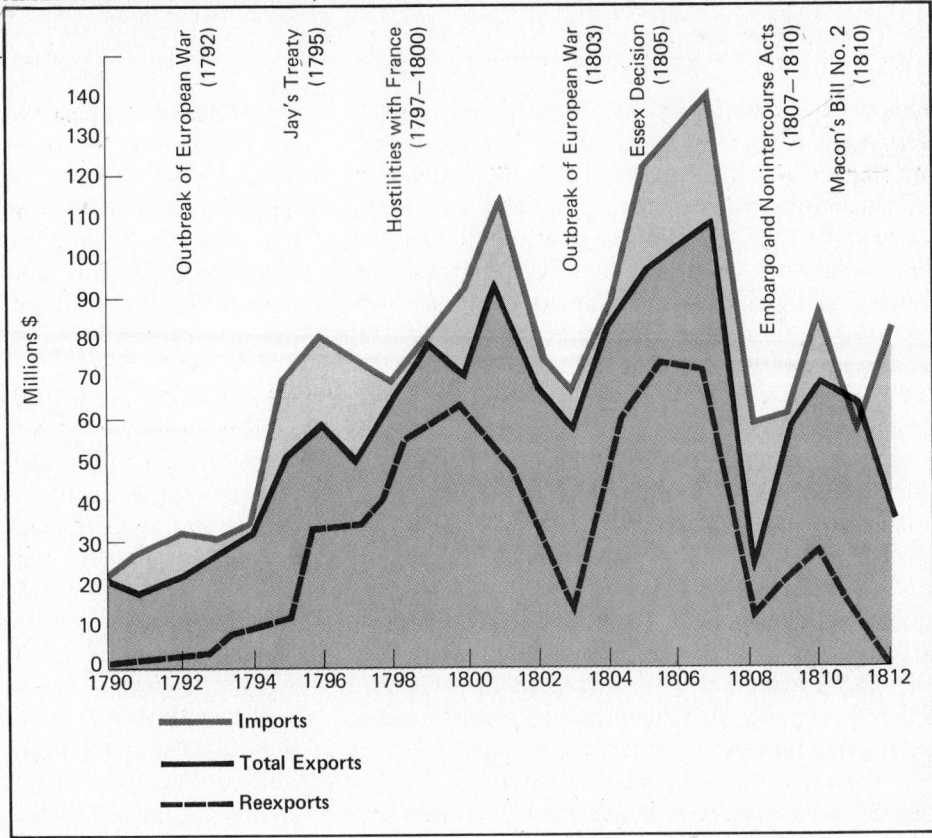

ble. "This authorized system of kidnapping upon the ocean," as John Quincy Adams called it, continued until it was ended by the general European peace of 1815 and resulted in an estimated ten thousand sailors being forcibly taken from American ships. Such provocative practices now dissolved the cordial relations between Britain and America that had begun with Jay's Treaty in 1795.

Napoleon responded to the British blockade with commercial restrictions of his own—a "continental system" designed essentially to deprive England of markets in Europe. In his Berlin Decree of 1806, he ruled that any neutral vessel stopping at an English port would be denied access to all European ports under French control. The British retaliated by requiring all neutral ships trading in the blockaded zones of Europe to stop at English ports to secure licenses. Napoleon then countered with his Milan Decree of 1807, which declared that all neutral ships submitting to British search or entering British ports

to secure licenses would be confiscated by the French. The net effect of these belligerent regulations was to render all neutral commerce illegal and liable to seizure by one power or the other. Although by 1807 the French were rigorously confiscating American ships in European ports, Britain's greater ability to capture American vessels (it was plundering about one of every eight American ships that put to sea) and its humiliating practice of impressment made Britain appear the greater culprit in American eyes. British regulations seemed to strike at the heart of American independence. "They assume the principle," said John Quincy Adams in 1808, "that we shall have no commerce in time of war, but with her dominion, and as tributaries to her."

The immediate response of the Jeffersonian administration to the British seizures was the Nonimportation Act of 1806, threatening a prohibition of certain British imports unless an Anglo-American agreement could be reached. Jefferson refused to send to the Senate for ratification a treaty with Britain that William Pinckney and James Monroe had negotiated in December 1806, not only because its commercial provisions scarcely went beyond Jay's Treaty in opening the British empire to American trade, but, more important, because it did not renounce the British practice of impressment.

Almost immediately thereafter, in June 1807, the British man-of-war *Leopard* fired upon the American warship *Chesapeake* as it sailed out of Norfolk, killing several seamen; the British then boarded the American ship and impressed four sailors, including three Americans alleged to be deserters from the British navy. Waves of patriotic indignation swept through the United States and brought Anglo-American relations to the breaking point. "Never since the battle of Lexington," said Jefferson, "have I seen the country in such a state of exasperation as at present." Although the United States was emotionally primed for war, the Republican leaders were reluctant as yet to abandon their idealistic principles of diplomacy.

The Embargo. All of the strains of idealism and utopianism present in American Revolutionary thinking were now brought to a head with the Republicans' resort to a general embargo. In 1807 Congress passed a sweeping prohibition of all American shipping with the outside world. Jefferson determined to see this "candid and liberal experiment" in "peaceful coercion" through to the end. From December 1807 to March 1809 in the face of mounting opposition, particularly from New England, Jefferson's government desperately stuck by—indeed, used ever-harsher measures to enforce—its embargo policy.

While Britain and France showed few ill effects from this self-imposed stoppage of American shipping, American commerce was thrown into disarray. The American export and reexport trade, which between 1805-7 had doubled to over $108 million in value, suddenly fell to $22 million during 1808; and American imports declined in value from $138 million to $56 million. Yet the economic effects were far from disastrous. Not only did numerous loopholes and violations—especially toward the end of 1808—mitigate the embargo's depressing effect on the economy, but America's growing reliance on its own do-

mestic manufacturers and its internal markets was strengthened by the cutbacks in international trade. Yet while many areas of the United States could fall back on their domestic overland and coastwide trade, the New England ports, such as Boston, Salem, and Providence, with their relatively meager hinterlands and their disproportionate investment in the overseas carrying and reexport trade, were badly hurt by the embargo.

In New England the embargo had the political effect of temporarily reviving Federalism. With hundreds of New England petitions flooding in on the government, with some New Englanders on the verge of rebellion, and with the Federalist governor of Connecticut claiming the right of the state to interpose its authority between the federal government and its citizens, some sort of retreat from the embargo became a matter of time. Hopeful of salvaging something from their policy of peaceful coercion, the Republicans on March 1, 1809, replaced the embargo with the Nonintercourse Act, which prohibited trade with just France and Britain and provided that if either belligerent canceled its blockade against American shipping, then nonintercourse would be maintained only against the other.

President Madison was just as determined as Jefferson had been to maintain this Republican experiment in commercial warfare, but difficulties in enforcing the Nonintercourse Act and growing governmental deficits from the loss of duties on trade forced the Madison administration to turn its commercial restrictions inside out. Macon's Bill No. 2, which passed Congress in May 1810, once again opened American shipping with both Britain and France, with the provision that if either belligerent revoked its restrictions on neutral commerce, nonintercourse would be restored against the other. Signs of a change in Napoleon's policy against American shipping and Madison's eagerness to prove the workability of the experiment in peaceful coercion led the Republican administration in March 1811 into a hasty invocation of nonintercourse against Great Britain.

If the United States had to go to war, the Republicans thought, then better to fight the country that had symbolized resistance to the experiment in popular self-government from the beginning. Despite some strong misgivings over Napoleon's dictatorship and some weak suggestions that America fight both belligerents simultaneously, it was virtually inconceivable that the Republicans would have gone to war against France. The threat of Federalist "monarchism" tied to Great Britain was still so real to Republicans that war with Britain became a necessary product of the Republican revolution of 1800 and thus of the original Revolution itself. "We are going to fight for the re-establishment of our national character," declared Andrew Jackson.

The War of 1812

War was declared in June 1812, and it was strictly a Republican party war. The congressional vote for war was solidly opposed by the Federalists and it temporarily unified the splintered Republican party. Many Republican congressmen newly elected in 1810, such as Henry Clay of Kentucky, Felix Grundy of Tennessee, and John C. Calhoun of South Carolina, were so eager to fight that they earned the label of "War Hawks." Although many of the Republican congress-

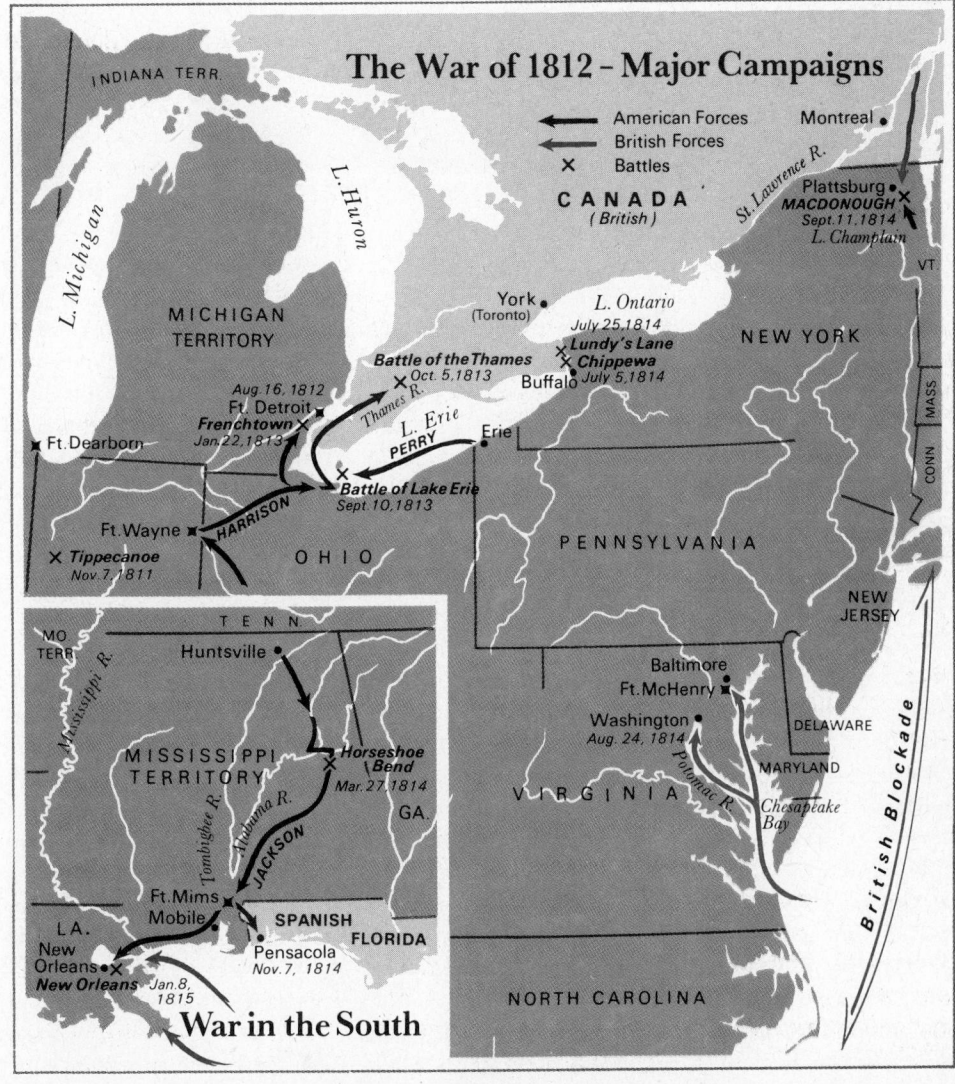

The War of 1812 – Major Campaigns

War in the South

PERRY'S VICTORY ON LAKE ERIE, BY AN UNKNOWN ARTIST
Oliver Hazard Perry (1785–1819) commanded a fleet of nine vessels built in Erie, Pa., to challenge British control of the Great Lakes in the War of 1812. During the battle on Sept. 10, 1813 Perry's flagship was disabled, and, as the painting depicts, he transferred to the *Niagara.* Then he sailed directly into the British line and destroyed the British ships, inspiring his famous dispatch: "We have met the enemy and they are ours." *(New York State Historical Association, Cooperstown, N.Y.)*

men came from areas far removed from the eastern trading ports, they represented farmers who were interested in commerce and in the marketing of their agricultural produce. Moreover, many backcountry Americans deeply resented British and Spanish intrigue among the Indians of the Northwest and Southwest and were convinced, especially by the recent battle with Tecumseh's Indians at Tippecanoe in November 1811, that the frontier would never be at peace until the British and Spanish bases in Canada and Florida were eliminated. War offered an opportunity to do just that.

Yet in the end the war came because the Republicans' foreign policy left no alternative. America had been engaged in a kind of war with the European belligerents since 1806. The actual fighting of 1812 was only the logical consequence of the failure of "peaceful coercion." Still, many Republicans hesitated to commit the United States to a traditional sort of military conflict. They realized, as Jefferson had warned in 1806, that "our constitution is a peace establishment—it is not calculated for war." War, they feared, would lead to a Hamiltonian enlargement of taxes, debt, military forces, and the executive branch; far from saving the Jeffersonian revolution of 1800, war might ultimately destroy republican principles. Therefore, even as the Republicans moved inevitably

toward war, many of them opposed all efforts to strengthen the government's capacity to wage it. While Nathaniel Macon of North Carolina, for example, reluctantly conceded the necessity of war, he like other Republicans urged reduction of the navy, indeed suggested abolition of the army, opposed raising taxes, and resisted all efforts to add two assistant secretaries to the War Department. Not only was the regular army cut back in favor of the militia, but the Bank of the United States, the government's chief financial agency, was allowed to expire in 1811 on the eve of hostilities. With such deliberate lack of preparation the war was bound to be very different from any known before.

The Invasions of Canada. Though woefully unprepared for war, many Americans in 1812 were confident of victory. Since two out of every three persons in Upper Canada (present-day Ontario) came from America, Canada seemed ripe for American "liberation." It would be, said Jefferson, "a mere matter of marching." But the American militia campaigns against Canada in 1812 were all dismal failures; General William Hull surrendered his entire army at Detroit without a fight. William Henry Harrison, the hero at Tippecanoe, was then appointed commander of the northwestern army; but before he could get very far, part of his army was wiped out at French-town near Detroit in January 1813.

In April 1813 invading Americans captured York (present-day Toronto), the capital of Upper Canada, and burned its public buildings; but within two months the American forces were in retreat once again. After Oliver Perry secured naval control of Lake Erie, Harrison finally defeated combined British and Indian forces on the Thames River north of the Lake in October 1813. Although this victory broke up the Indian confederacy, American leaders thought it was too far west to have any strategic significance and did not follow it up. During the summer of 1814 Americans tried to invade Canada again, but withdrew after several tough but indecisive battles in the Niagara region. After two years of repeated forays, the American position on the Canadian frontier remained what it had been at the beginning.

On the sea American frigates, including the U.S.S. *Constitution*, initially won some notable single-ship engagements, and American privateers, the navy's militia, captured more than thirteen hundred British merchant vessels. Eventually, however, Britain's great naval superiority made itself felt, and by 1813 most of the American warships were bottled up in their ports and American commerce was effectively blockaded. When Napoleon abdicated early in 1814, Britain was able to concentrate its military attention on America. It planned several major assaults, one designed to move down the Lake Champlain route that Burgoyne had followed in the Revolutionary War, and another aimed at New Orleans. During the summer of 1814 a British marauding force landed in the Chesapeake, entered Washington, and burned the Capitol and the White House. The government's credit collapsed and the nation's finances were thrown into chaos. Without a national bank the government was unable to transfer funds across the country or to pay its mounting bills.

The Treaty of Ghent. Despite these humiliating circumstances, however, the American peace commissioners sent to negotiate with the British in August 1814 in Ghent, Belgium, were unwilling to make any concessions. The British, learning that their invasion from Canada had turned back as a result of an American naval victory on Lake Champlain in September 1814 and increasingly anxious about the shifting situation in Europe, came to realize once again that a decentralized government and a spacious continent were not easily conquered. The peace signed on Christmas Eve, 1814, restored the status quo as it was before the war and said nothing about impressment and maritime rights. Andrew Jackson's smashing victory over the British invasion at New Orleans at the beginning of 1815 came after the treaty was signed and clinched it. Although the Americans had gained nothing tangible from the war, it was widely and rightly regarded as a great success for the Republican party and the nation.

URBAN SOCIETY
"Worldly folk" questioning chimney sweeps and their master before Christ Church, Philadelphia, by Pavel Petrovich Svinin. *(The Metropolitan Museum of Art, Rogers Fund, 1942)*

The Hartford Convention and the End of the Federalists.

The peace effectively destroyed Federalism as a national movement. The northeastern Federalists had repeatedly obstructed the war, refusing to comply with federal militia requisitions and discouraging loans to the United States government. Some New England extremists talked of separating from the Union. Other Federalists were convinced that the Republican failures in the war would justify their opposition and that a disillusioned people would catapult the Federalists back into national dominance.

Hence the Federalist convention that met in Hartford, Connecticut, at the end of 1814 disavowed secession and contented itself with proposing a series of amendments to the Constitution. These amendments were designed to curb the power of the South in the federal government by eliminating the three-fifths representation of slaves; to prevent the admission of new states, future embargoes, and declarations of war without a two-thirds majority of Congress; and to end Virginia's dominance of the executive by prohibiting the president from serving two terms and the same state from providing two presidents in succession. The national exuberance following the Treaty of Ghent and Jackson's victory discredited these Federalist hopes and led to the enthusiastic election in 1816 of still another Republican and Virginian president, James Monroe. Thus was vindicated the Republicans' remarkable experiment in governing a huge country and fighting a war without the traditional instruments of power.

Although the war seemed to settle nothing, actually it settled everything. "Notwithstanding a thousand faults and blunders," John Adams told Jefferson in 1817, Madison's administration had "acquired more glory, and established more Union than all his three predecessors, Washington, Adams, Jefferson, put together." The Revolution, which had begun nearly a half century earlier, at last seemed to be over and to have succeeded. The Federalist attempt to build a strong central government had been halted. The new national government the Republicans had created was unlike any the eighteenth century traditionally understood to be a government. Its capital was isolated from the main social and economic cen-

DETAIL OF "ELECTION DAY AT THE STATE HOUSE," PENCIL BY JOHN LEWIS KRIMMEL, 1813.
(*Historical Society of Pennsylvania*)

ters of the country; its influence was diffused throughout a rapidly expanding geographical sphere; and its effect on the daily lives of its citizens was negligible.

By 1817–18 Jefferson was exultant. "Our government," he wrote in those years to his old French ally, the Marquis de Lafayette, "is now so firmly put on its republican tack, that it will not be easily monarchised by forms." The War of 1812 and the disgrace of the Federalists, he said, had ended the need for his revolutionary party, and had in fact resulted in the "complete suppression of party." In the new "Era of Good Feelings" symbolized by Monroe's uncontested election to the presidency in 1820, the ideological passions and divisions aroused by the Revolution could at last subside. Americans could begin celebrating their own common national identity.

CHRONOLOGY

1800 Washington, D.C., becomes capital.
Library of Congress established.
Convention of 1800, supplanting treaties of 1778 with France.
Thomas Jefferson elected president.

1801 Plan of Union between Presbyterians and Congregationalists to bring religion to frontier.
War with Barbary states.
Cane Ridge, Kentucky, revival meeting.
John Marshall becomes chief justice.

1802 Republican Congress repeals Judiciary Act of 1801.

1803 *Marbury* v. *Madison*, Supreme Court upholds right of judicial review.
Louisiana Purchase.
War resumed in Europe.
Lewis and Clark expedition begun.

1804 Hamilton killed by Vice-President Aaron Burr in duel.
Impeachment of judges Pickering and Chase.
Twelfth Amendment to Constitution ratified.
Jefferson elected for second term.

1805 Pennsylvania Academy of Fine Arts formed.
Essex decision by British prize court increases British seizures of American neutral ships.

1806 Monroe-Pinckney treaty with Britain, which Jefferson refuses to send to Senate for ratification.
Burr conspiracy.

1807 *Chesapeake-Leopard* affair.
Embargo Act.
Robert Fulton's steamboat *Clermont* travels on Hudson River from Albany to New York in 30 hours.

1808 Congress prohibits Americans from participating in African slave trade.

1809 James Madison elected president.
Embargo repealed; Nonintercourse Act passed, prohibiting trade with Britain and France.

1810 Macon's Bill No. 2 passed, restoring trade with Britain and France, but providing for trade restrictions to be reimposed on one of the powers if other should abandon its seizure of American ships.
Connecticut Moral Society formed to combat infidelity and drinking.
West Florida annexed by Madison.
American Board of Commissioners for Foreign Missions formed.
In *Fletcher* v. *Peck*, Supreme Court invalidates state law re *Yazoo* land claims because of impairment of contracts.

1811 Madison, believing Napoleon has removed restrictions on American commerce, prohibits trade with Britain.
Battle of Tippecanoe, Indiana, in which William Henry Harrison defeats Tecumseh and prevents formation of Indian confederacy.
Charter of the Bank of the United States allowed to lapse by Congress.

1812 Congress declares war against Britain.
Americans surrender Detroit to British.
Madison elected for second term.

1813 Battle of Lake Erie, in which Captain Oliver Perry defeats British naval forces.
Battle of the Thames, in which General Harrison defeats British and their Indian allies.

1814 Battle of Horseshoe Bend, Alabama; General Andrew Jackson defeats Creek Indians fighting for British.
British burn Washington, D.C.
Commander Thomas Macdonough defeats British fleet on Lake Champlain; invading British turned back at Plattsburgh, New York.
Hartford Convention of Federalist delegates from New England states meets.
Treaty of Ghent signed between United States and Great Britain.

1815 Battle of New Orleans; Jackson defeats British.
North American Review founded in Boston; soon becomes leading literary review in America.

1816 Second Bank of the United States chartered by Congress.
American Bible Society founded.
Protective tariff passed.
James Monroe elected president.

1817 Bonus Bill establishing fund for building roads and canals vetoed by Madison.
American Tract Society formed to circulate religious literature in the West.
Seminole War on Georgia-Florida border.

1818 General Jackson invades Florida to end Seminole War.

Rush-Bagot convention between Britain and United States establishes American fishing rights and boundary between United States and Canada.

1819 Commercial panic with many bank failures.

Adams-Onis Treaty signed between United States and Spain; Spain cedes Florida to the United States and recognizes the western limits of the Louisiana Purchase.

Dartmouth College case.

McCulloch v. *Maryland*.

1820 Missouri Compromise.

James Monroe reelected president.

SUGGESTED READINGS

The classic account of the Republican administrations is Henry Adams, *History of the United States of America during the Administration of Thomas Jefferson [and] of James Madison* (9 vols., 1889–1891). It is artful, but its obsession with the ironic turn of Jeffersonian policies subtly distorts the period. Marshall Smelser, *The Democratic Republic, 1801–1815* (1968), is a one-volume survey. Daniel Sisson, *The American Revolution of 1800* (1974), tries to recapture the radical meaning of Jefferson's election; but it does not succeed as well as James S. Young, *The Washington Community, 1800–1828* (1966), which despite an unhistorical focus rightly stresses the Republicans' fear of power. On the Republican party, see Noble E. Cunningham, Jr., *The Jeffersonian Republicans in Power: Party Operations, 1801–1809* (1963). Richard Hofstadter, *The Idea of a Party System: The Rise of Legitimate Opposition in the United States, 1740–1840* (1969), is a lucid essay that tries but does not quite break from the party conception of the secondary sources on which it is based. David Hackett Fischer, *The Revolution of American Conservatism: The Federalist Party in the Era of Jeffersonian Democracy* (1965), is an important book that compels a new look at the Republicans as well as the Federalists. A tough-minded study is Forrest McDonald's *The Presidency of Thomas Jefferson* (1976). See also James H. Broussard, *The Southern Federalists, 1800–1816* (1979). On the Republicans' dismantling of the Federalist bureaucracy, see Leonard D. White, *The Jeffersonians: A Study in Administrative History, 1801–1829* (1951). See also Noble E. Cunningham, Jr., *The Process of Government under Jefferson* (1979), and Robert M. Johnstone, Jr., *Jefferson and the Presidency* (1979). On Jefferson and Madison, see the monumental multivolumed biographies by Dumas Malone and Irving Brant.

Daniel Boorstin, *The Lost World of Thomas Jefferson* (1948), describes the rigidities of intellectual life in Republican circles, while Linda K. Kerber analyzes the Federalists' cultural problems in *Federalists in Dissent* (1970).

On the development of the West, see Reginald Horsman, *The Frontier in the Formative Years, 1783–1815* (1970). On the new cities of the West, see Richard C. Wade, *The Urban Frontier* (1959). Beverley W. Bond, *The Civilization of the Old Northwest: A Study of Political, Social and Economic Development, 1788–1812* (1934) is a good compilation. Land policy and land laws are covered in Malcom J. Rohrbough, *The Land Office Business . . . 1789–1837* (1968).

On the Louisiana Purchase, see Alexander De Conde, *The Affair of Louisiana* (1976); and the appropriate chapters of George Dangerfield, *Chancellor Robert R. Livingston of New York, 1746–1803* (1960). On Indian affairs, see Reginald Horsman, *Expansion and American Indian Policy, 1783–1812* (1967). For the tragic irony in the story of American relations with the Indians, see Bernard W. Sheehan, *Seeds of Extinction: Jeffersonian Philanthropy and the American Indian* (1973). A good, short, though unsympathetic, account of the Burr conspiracy can be found in Thomas Abernathy, *The South in the New Nation, 1789–1819* (1961).

On the politics of the judiciary, see Richard E. Ellis, *The Jeffersonian Crisis* (1971). The best biography of Marshall is still Albert J. Beveridge, *The Life of John Marshall* (4 vols., 1919). The origins of judicial review are treated in Edward S. Corwin, *The "Higher Law" Background of American Constitutional Law* (1955); and Charles G. Haines, *The American Doctrine of Judicial Supremacy* (1932). But despite all that has been written, the sources of judicial review remain perplexing. Understanding the problem requires less work on the Supreme Court and more on colonial jurisprudence. For a significant study of changes in law during the Revolution, and after, see William E. Nelson, *Americanization of the Common Law: The Impact of Legal Change on Massachusetts Society, 1760–1830* (1975); and Morton J.

Horowitz, *The Transformation of American Law, 1780–1860* (1977).

On religion and the Revolution, see William W. Sweet, *Religion in the Development of American Culture, 1765–1840* (1952). On the varying definitions of the American Enlightenment and its relation to Protestantism, see the superb study by Henry F. May, *The Enlightenment in America* (1976). The opening chapters of Perry Miller, *The Life of the Mind in America* (1965), are very helpful for understanding the emergence of evangelicism. The essays collected in Elwyn A. Smith, ed., *The Religion of the Republic* (1971), are important in relating evangelical Protestantism and republicanism. Older studies that need updating are Catherine C. Cleveland, *The Great Revival in the West, 1797–1805* (1916); and Oliver W. Elsbree, *The Rise of the Missionary Spirit in America, 1790–1815* (1928). See also John Bole, *The Great Revival in the South, 1787–1805* (1972); Howard Miller, *The Revolutionary College: American Presbyterian Higher Education, 1707–1837* (1976); and especially Donald G. Mathews, *Religion in the Old South* (1977). For secular-minded approaches to evangelicism, see Charles I. Foster, *An Errand of Mercy: The Evangelical United Front, 1790–1837* (1960); and Clifford S. Griffin, *Their Brothers' Keepers: Moral Stewardship in the United States, 1800–1865* (1960). On the changing role of the ministry, see Donald M. Scott, *From Office to Profession: The New England Ministry, 1750–1850* (1978). On deism, see Gustav A. Koch, *Republican Religion* (1933); and Herbert M. Morais, *Deism in Eighteenth-Century America* (1934). On millennialism, see Ernest Lee Tuveson, *Redeemer Nation: The Idea of America's Millennial Role* (1968); James W. Davidson, *The Logic of Millennial Thought* (1977); and Nathan O. Hatch, *The Sacred Cause of Liberty* (1977).

The underlying eighteenth-century liberal assumptions about international politics are explored in Felix Gilbert, *To the Farewell Address: Ideas of Early American Foreign Policy* (1961). Lawrence S. Kaplan, *Jefferson and France: An Essay on Politics and Political Ideas* (1967), captures the idealism of Jefferson. The best discussion of the diplomatic steps into war is Bradford Perkins, *Prologue to War: England and the United States, 1805–1812* (1961). Burton Spivak, *Jefferson's English Crisis: Commerce, Embargo and the Republican Revolution* (1979), is the best study of the embargo. Julius W. Pratt, *Expansionists of 1812* (1925), stresses how the desire of Westerners and Southerners for land caused the war. However, A. L. Burt, *The United States, Great Britain and British North America* (1940), emphasizes the issues of impressment and neutral rights. Roger H. Brown, *The Republic in Peril: 1812* (1964), and Norman K. Risjord, *The Old Republicans* (1965), offer the best perspective on the logic of the Republicans' foreign policy that led to war.

Harry L. Coles, *The War of 1812* (1965), and Reginald Horsman, *The War of 1812* (1969), are good brief surveys. Irving Brant, *James Madison: The Commander in Chief, 1812–1836* (1961), defends Madison's wartime leadership, but Ralph Ketcham, *James Madison* (1971), is better in recovering the peculiar character of Madison's republican aims. On the Treaty of Ghent, see Bradford Perkins, *Castlereagh and Adams: England and the United States, 1812–1823* (1964). James M. Banner, *To the Hartford Convention: The Federalist and the Origins of Party Politics in Massachusetts, 1789–1815* (1970), superbly describes the Federalists' attitudes and stresses their conservative purposes in calling the Convention.

PART THREE

David Brion Davis

Expanding the Republic

1820–1860

The end of the American Enlightenment also marked the end of attempts to model American society on European blueprints. By the 1820s it was becoming clear that the American people would quickly overleap restraints and limits of every kind. Expansive, self-assertive, extravagantly optimistic, they believed they had a God-given right to pursue happiness. In a nation of supposedly infinite promise, there could be no permanent barriers to the people's aspirations for wealth and self-improvement.

This absence of barriers, of distinctions of rank, and of prescribed identities was what Alexis de Tocqueville meant by "the general equality of condition among the people." Nothing struck Tocqueville more forcibly when he visited the United States in 1831 than this leveling of ancient and inherited distinctions of rank. He took it to be "the fundamental fact" about American society from which all other facts seemed "to be derived." Tocqueville was aware of the economic and racial inequalities of American society. Indeed, he suggested that it was precisely the lack of traditional restraints, such as those associated with a landed aristocracy, that opened the way for racial oppression and for a new kind of aristocracy created by business and manufacturing.

All societies require a system of rules, restraints, and limits. In a traditional, premodern society, such as the feudal regime to which Tocqueville looked back with some nostalgia, there was a certain stability to the territorial boundaries of a kingdom, an estate, or a people. Similarly, few people questioned the customary rules that defined social rank, the rights and duties of lords and peasants, the inheritance of land, the limits of political power and economic enterprise, and the expectations appropriate for each individual. Men and women knew what they had been born to, what place they had been assigned by fate. A close relation prevailed between the narrow boundaries of the physical environment and the social boundaries that political, legal, and religious institutions imposed.

The United States, as Tocqueville repeatedly emphasized, had thus far managed to avoid anarchy while greatly expanding most people's possibilities of life. From the time of the first colonial settlements, Americans had evolved institutions that had ensured a degree of order and stability to social life, protecting the public good from the worst excesses of acquisitive self-interest. By the early nineteenth century, however, there was a growing faith that the public good would best be served by allowing maximum freedom to the individual pursuit of self-interest.

In the period 1820–60 this drive for individual self-betterment led to an unprecedented economic and territorial expansion, to the migration of millions

Overleaf: "View of Baltimore from Federal Hill, 1850" by Fitz Hugh Lane. (Courtesy, Shelburne Museum, Shelburne, Vermont)

of Europeans to America, and to the settlement of millions of Americans in the new states and territories of the West. Much of the nation's foreign policy was devoted to extending territorial boundaries and to preventing European attempts to impose future barriers to American influence and expansion in the Western Hemisphere. Federal land policy encouraged rapid settlement of the West. Both national and state governments committed a large share of public resources to the construction of roads, canals, and railroads that surmounted the barriers of mountains and increasing distance. Government at all levels actively sought to stimulate growth and economic opportunity. Much of the political ideology of the period was directed against forces and institutions, such as the Second Bank of the United States, which could be portrayed as restricting individual opportunity.

But for many thoughtful Americans, reformers as well as conservatives, there was a danger that these expansive energies would erode all respect for order, balance, and community purpose; that the competitive spirit would lead to an atomized society ruled by the principle, "Every man for himself and the devil take the hindmost"; that the American people would become enslaved to money, success, and material gratification; and that the centrifugal forces of expansion would cause the nation to fly apart.

Most of the proposed remedies centered on the critical need to shape and reform individual character. Instead of looking to political institutions and governmental programs, most Americans sought social change through the moral reformation of individuals. They believed that if self-interest could be enlightened by a sense of social responsibility, the nation could be saved from the dehumanizing effects of commercialism and competitive strife. This was the great goal of the public schools, the religious revivals, and most of the new reform movements. It was a mission that gave a new importance and an educational role to mothers and to the middle-class home. In one sense, these efforts at shaping character embodied a nostalgic desire to restore a lost sense of community and united purpose. But the crusades for moral improvement were also instruments of modernization that encouraged predictable and responsible behavior and that aimed at ennobling and legitimating a market-oriented society.

It was the issue of Negro slavery that finally dramatized the conflict between self-interest and the ideal of a righteous society—a society that could think of itself as "under God." And it was the westward expansion of Negro slavery that ultimately became the testing ground for defining and challenging limits—the territorial limits of slavery, the limits of federal power, and the limits of popular sovereignty and self-determination. For most of the period an ambiguity on all these matters allowed the North and South to expand together and to resolve periodic conflicts by compromise. By the 1850s, however, southern leaders insisted that the equal rights of slaveholders would be subverted unless the federal government guaranteed the protection of slave property in the common territories. Northern leaders, including eventually many moderates who had always favored compromise, drew a firm line against imposing slavery on a territory against the wishes of the majority of settlers. To paraphrase the poet Robert Frost, the territorial question came down to what Americans were willing to wall in or wall out. In one form or another, Americans had to face the question whether, in a free society, any limits could be imposed on the total dominion of one person over another.

Population: Expansion and Exploitation

To understand American experience during the four decades preceding the Civil War, one must grasp the dimensions of demographic and economic change. Other nations have undergone periods of rapid growth and industrialization, accompanied by painful cultural adjustment and social conflict. In general, however, this modernizing experience has occurred in long-settled communities with traditions, customs, and class interests that served at once as barriers to change and as stabilizers of society. What distinguished American history, in the period 1820–60, was that a modern market economy emerged in conjunction with the rapid settlement of virgin land and the unprecedented expansion of the western frontier.

There were few barriers to this double process, and the American people were determined to test, push back, and overcome what barriers there were. The American economy showed a remarkable freedom in the flow of goods, people, and capital in response to market forces. No laws restricted the influx of European and Asian laborers. The Constitution ruled out any taxes on American exports. Thanks largely to southern pressure, the federal government gradually lowered protective tariffs on imports. The federal government's sale and donation of immense tracts of public land were intended to encourage individual enterprise in a free and unregulated market. Political stability, even in the rapidly created new states, helped to guarantee the security of private property and the legal enforcement of contracts. The states themselves actively promoted economic growth, but no other society had imposed so few fiscal, political, religious, and social restraints on the marketplace. No other society had been so confident that market forces constituted the "invisible hand" of a higher, cosmic order. No other society had become so committed to the goals of maximizing individual profits by increasing productivity and lowering costs.

The result of this extraordinary freedom from limitations, along with the availability of land, labor, and capital, was extremely rapid economic growth. As perceived and experienced by living human beings, however, this growth was both liberating and extremely disruptive. It destroyed family self-sufficiency, pride in craftsmanship, and personal and family ties that unified residential communities with local economic markets. Though the growth of national markets broadened the range of individual choice for businessmen, there was little choice for the Indians, slaves, unskilled laborers, landless farmers, and domestic servants; in short, for all those who were excluded by force or circumstance from the benefits of the market. Despite a generally rising standard of living, Americans in the pre-Civil War decades witnessed growing economic inequalities. Moreover, the nation's triumphs in economic and territorial expansion depended on two forms of outright racial exploitation: the coercive removal of the Indian people from the rich land east of the Great Plains; and the forced labor of black slaves who produced invaluable exports, mainly cotton, that helped finance America's economic growth.

Population Growth, Immigration, and Urbanization

From 1820 to 1860 America's population maintained the extraordinary rate of growth that had characterized the colonial and early national periods. The average increase by decade amounted to nearly 35 percent; the total population continued to double every twenty-three years. The United States sustained this high rate of growth until the 1860s. During the nineteenth century no European nation achieved a growth rate one-half as high as America's for even two decades.

America's population growth cannot be attributed to any single, consistent cause. Before the mid-1840s most of the population growth resulted from the remarkable fertility of the American people, reinforced by a relatively low rate of infant mortality. Like many countries in modern Africa and South America, the United States literally swarmed with children. In 1830 nearly one-third of the total white population was under the age of ten. Yet in most parts of the country the birthrate had actually begun to decline before 1810 and continued to fall throughout the century. By the 1840s it was only the influx of European immigrants, who accounted for one-

quarter of the total population increase in that decade, that maintained the previous rate of national growth.

Imigration was partly the result of economic distress in Europe. Few Europeans would have left their homes if population growth had not pressed hard on available supplies of land, food, and jobs, and if they had not been displaced and defined as expendable by the forces of a market economy. The disastrous failure of Ireland's potato crop in 1845, followed by five years of famine, gave many Irish little choice but to emigrate or starve. And the British landlords who controlled Ireland helped to subsidize emigration in the hope of reducing taxes for the support of workhouses, which were spilling over with starving laborers evicted from the land. In parts of Germany and Scandinavia, governments encouraged emigration as a way of draining off unemployed farmers and artisans, who had been displaced by the modernization of agriculture and by competition from imported machine-made goods.

But the most important stimulus to immigration

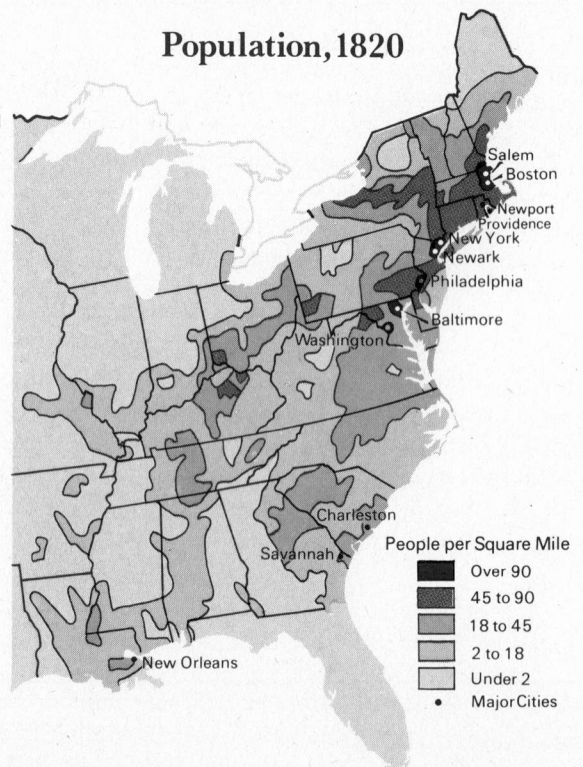

Population, 1820

People per Square Mile

- Over 90
- 45 to 90
- 18 to 45
- 2 to 18
- Under 2
- • Major Cities

was the promise of jobs in America. Immigration rose to high levels during America's years of greatest prosperity, and lagged during years of economic recession. Mass emigration from Europe was a direct response to the sudden demand in America for labor in construction and manufacturing, and to the supposedly limitless opportunity for land ownership in the West. American promoters, representing shipping firms, labor contractors, manufacturers, and even the governments of western states, enticed Europeans with glowing accounts of the United States. More persuasive were the reports of fellow villagers or family members who had already crossed the Atlantic and tested the terrain. In the 1830s when northwestern Europe became aware of America's economic boom, of the North's shortage of labor, and of the opening of vast tracts of farmland in the West, the number of immigrants rose to nearly 600,000, approximately a fourfold increase over the previous decade. In the 1840s the number soared to about 1.5 million, and in the 1850s to about 2.8 million.

The swelling stream, although it originated almost entirely from northwestern Europe, was anything but homogeneous. It included illiterate peasants from Germany and Ireland, highly skilled artisans from England, Germany, Belgium, and Switzerland, political refugees escaping the repression that followed the abortive European revolutions of 1830 and 1848, and Jews and other victims of religious discrimination. The Germans amounted to about 1.3 million immigrants, and many had sufficient funds to purchase farms in the West or at least to make their way to thriving German communities in Cincinnati, St. Louis, and Milwaukee. The Irish, numbering some 1.7 million, had few skills and often arrived penniless, traveling steerage in the holds of westbound ships that had carried American lumber, grain, cotton, and other bulk products to Europe. Cast off by Britain as an unwanted population, the Irish peasants were in effect dumped in the northeastern port cities or sometimes in Canada, from which they migrated southward. Gradually they found employment in heavy

Population, 1860

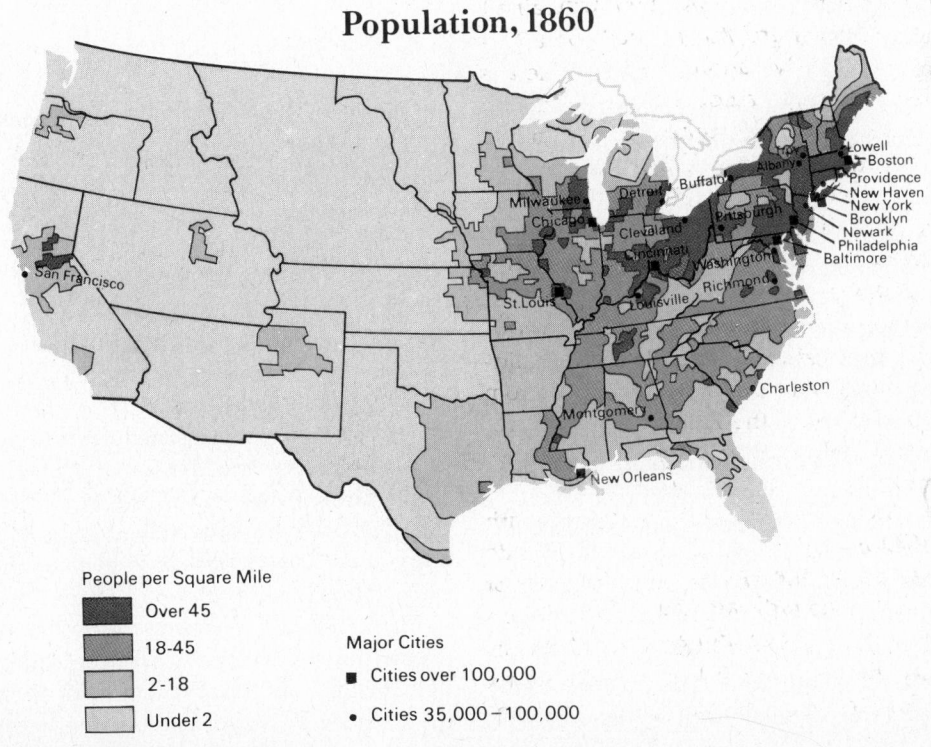

People per Square Mile

- Over 45
- 18-45
- 2-18
- Under 2

Major Cities

- ■ Cities over 100,000
- • Cities 35,000 – 100,000

EMIGRATION AGENT'S OFFICE

By the 1840s the expansion of transatlantic commerce had greatly reduced the westbound steerage fare from Europe to America. Nevertheless, many emigrants, such as the Irish portrayed here, had to depend on loans, charitable gifts, or funds sent from relatives in America. *(Library of Congress)*

construction work, in foundries and factories, and in domestic service, though for a time they enormously swelled the ranks of paupers and recipients of public and private welfare.

Before the Civil War the proportion of foreign-born in the population as a whole never rose above 15 percent, but in Boston and New York City by the 1850s the figure had climbed to over 50 percent. Over half the foreign-born lived in Ohio, Pennsylvania, and New York. This concentration of immigrants greatly accelerated the growth of cities in the Northeast and towns and villages along the Great Lakes and the Ohio and Mississippi rivers.

In 1860 four out of five Americans still lived in rural environments, that is, on farms or in settlements of less than 2,500. Nevertheless, by 1850 over half the populations of Massachusetts and Rhode Island lived in urban centers, a proportion the nation at large did not reach until the 1920s. By 1860 eight American cities, three of them west of the Appala-

chians, had more than 150,000 inhabitants, a population exceeded at that time by only seven cities in industrial England. Although America could boast of no metropolis equivalent to London, in 1860 the combined populations of Manhattan and Brooklyn exceeded 1 million. New York City, endowed with a superior harbor and with the Hudson River, which provided deep-water navigation into the interior, had won a further competitive advantage over other seaboard cities when in 1818 its merchants established the first regular, scheduled sailings to Europe. Seven years later the Erie Canal opened cheap access to the Great Lakes and to the markets of the West. Immigrants arrived and stayed in New York because it was America's great seaport and commercial center, a crucible of risk and opportunity.

Overall, the declining birthrate resulted in a slightly higher average age for the American population, but the influx of immigrants greatly enlarged the number of Northeasterners between the ages of twenty and thirty. In 1850 over 70 percent of the American people were still under thirty, a figure that takes on greater meaning when compared with the 63 percent for England and the 52 percent for France. Before the Civil War the Americans remained an extraordinarily youthful people, a circumstance that helps to account for their restlessness, their venturesomeness, and their impatience with boundaries of any kind.

Alexis de Tocqueville echoed the amazement of many Europeans at the "strange unrest" of a people who could be seen "continually to change their track for fear of missing the shortest cut to happiness":

In the United States a man builds a house in which to spend his old age, and he sells it before the roof is on . . . he brings a field into tillage and leaves other men to gather the crops; he embraces a profession and gives it up; he settles in a place, which he soon afterwards leaves to carry his changeable longings elsewhere . . . and if at the end of a year of unremitting labor he finds he has a few days' vacation, his eager curiosity whirls him over the vast extent of the United States, and he will travel fifteen hundred miles in a few days to shake off his happiness. Death at length overtakes him, but it is before he is weary of his bootless chase of that complete felicity which forever escapes him.

This sense of limitless possibility helps to explain the feverish westward rush of population. By 1860 the settled area of the United States was five times what it had been in 1790, and nearly half the people lived beyond the 1790 boundaries of settlement. As late as 1820 many Americans had thought it would take at least a century to settle the vast territory west of the Mississippi. In 1860 the United States had firmly established its present continental boundaries, except for Alaska. No other nation had populated so much new territory in so short a time or absorbed so many immigrants. No other had combined rapid urbanization with the dramatic expansion of an agricultural frontier.

Farmers and the Land

Before the Civil War the majority of American families made their livings by supplying the primary human needs for food and clothing. Agriculture dominated the economy and provided the commodities for most of the nation's domestic and foreign trade. Even in towns and cities families customarily kept a vegetable garden and perhaps a pig, a cow,

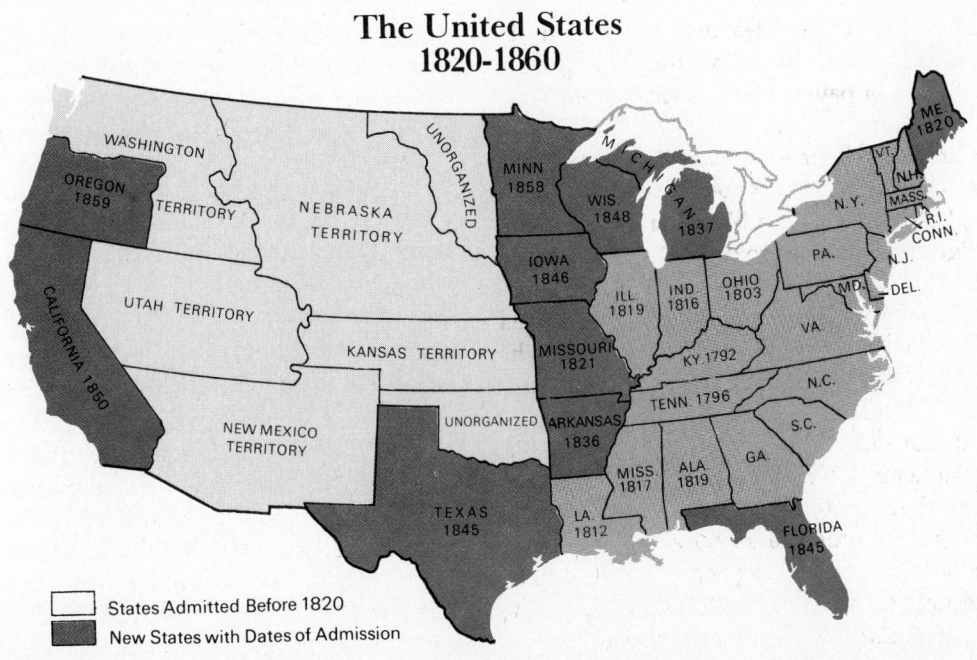

The United States 1820-1860

States Admitted Before 1820
New States with Dates of Admission

and chickens. Many of the most seasoned urbanites could at least remember the smell of a barnyard from their childhoods.

Agricultural Expansion. What distinguished the period 1820–60 were two trends that might seem at first to be contradictory. On the one hand, the quickening pace of urbanization and industrialization brought a decisive shift toward nonagricultural employment. This shift had actually begun in the late eighteenth century but had started to slow before 1820, when approximately 79 percent of the labor force was gainfully employed in agriculture. By 1850, however, the proportion had fallen to 55 percent. This was the most rapid structural change in the economy during the entire nineteenth century. On the other hand, the same period saw a phenomenal expansion of agriculture into the "virgin lands" of the West and Old Southwest, accompanied by revolutionary changes in transportation and marketing. The two trends were intimately related. The urban East provided the capital and markets that made the agricultural expansion possible. The food and fiber of the West and Old Southwest were indispensable for the industries and urban growth of the East. Western farming, fur trapping, mining, and lumbering were the spearheads of an expansive capitalist economy increasingly integrated with the great markets of the world.

A nation of farmers is almost by definition a nation at an early stage of economic development. Yet in nineteenth-century America, agriculture did not suggest a conservative way of life limited by the entrenched customs of a feudalistic past. Farming increasingly took on the characteristics of a speculative business. The very isolation of individual farms, posted like sentries along lonely country roads, indicated that Americans placed efficiency above community solidarity. The individual family, practically imprisoned near the fields it worked and usually owned, had proved to be the most effective unit of production.

Four central conditions shaped America's unprecedented expansion of cultivated land. First, public policy continued to favor rapid settlement of the im-mense public domain, amounting to a billion acres if one includes the territorial acquisitions of the 1840s. There was no countervailing interest in conserving resources and future revenue. Second, despite population growth, agricultural labor remained scarce and expensive, especially in frontier regions. Most farm owners had to rely on an occasional hired hand to supplement the labor of their own families or of tenant families. In the South the price of slaves continued to rise. Third, the dispersion of settlement made farmers heavily dependent, for many decades, on navigable rivers and waterways for transportation. Fourth, the real estate mentality of earlier periods burgeoned into a national mania as the westward movement and the mushrooming of towns brought spectacular rises in land values. Great land companies and private investors, representing eastern and European capital, purchased virtual empires of western land and then used every possible device to promote rapid settlement. Even the small farmers saw that it was more agreeable to make money by speculating in land than by removing stumps or plowing up the resistant bluestem grass of the prairies.

From one point of view the pioneering outlook was progressive. There can be no doubt that Americans who moved west were inventive, hardy, and willing to take risks. Often moving ahead of roads and organized government, the frontier farmers engaged in a struggle by trial and error to succeed in the face of unfamiliar climate, insects, soil conditions, and drainage. In time they experimented with different crops, livestock, and transportation routes, searching for the commodity and market that would bring a predictable cash return. Although the federal government supplied little direct information to farmers, it continued Jefferson's tradition of promoting land surveys and sending expeditions into land west of the Mississippi to collect information on flora and fauna, geology, watersheds, and Indians. This enterprising spirit, evident in both public and private endeavors, led to the discovery and exploitation of undreamed of resources, confirming Tocqueville's judgment that "Nature herself favors the cause of the people."

But the quest for immediate returns also led to a

ruthless stripping of natural resources. In the absence of national legislation and national power, the timber, grasses, and minerals of the public domain invited a headlong scramble by the pioneers to cut trees, graze their cattle, and dig for ore. The government actually bought gold and silver that miners took from public property. European visitors were astonished at the American conviction that forests were a hostile element to be destroyed without regard for need. Trees, like the buffalo and beaver of the West, seemed so plentiful that few Americans could foresee a time of diminishing supply.

The soil itself, the most valuable of all resources, fared no better. Americans generally lacked the incentives and patience to conserve the soil by using fertilizers and carefully rotating crops. They tended to look on land as a temporary and expendable resource that should be mined as rapidly as possible. This attitude, especially prevalent in the South and the West, reflected the common need to produce the most profitable single crop, whether wheat, corn, rice, tobacco, or cotton, in order to pay for land that they had purchased or settled on credit.

The entrepreneurial character of American agriculture owed much to the way new lands were originally settled. For Americans of the late twentieth century it is difficult to grasp the significance of the fact that the chief business of the federal government, before the Civil War, was the management and disposal of public land. The government, wanting revenue as well as rapid settlement, hastily surveyed tracts of western land, which were then sold to the highest bidder at public auction; the remainder was offered at the minimum price of $1.25 per acre. Since there was no limit to how many acres an individual or company might buy, investors eagerly bought blocks of thousands of acres. The great peaks of speculation coincided with the expansion of bank credit in the early 1830s and in the mid-1850s. The profitable resale of such land depended on promoting settlement.

Speculators and Squatters. Speculators had always helped to shape the character of American agriculture. The great theme of American settlement was the continuing contest of will between absentee owners and the squatters who first developed the land and who often had some partial claim of title. Although squatters often sold their own claims to succeeding waves of migrants, they tended to picture wealthier speculators as rapacious vampires. Yet the large speculators played a key role in financing the rapid settlement of the public lands. Pooling private capital, they loaned money to squatters, often at illegally high interest rates, to finance the purchase of tools, livestock, and supplies. They extended credit for buying farms. They pressured local and national governments to subsidize canals and railroads. Such speculation often involved considerable risk; the returns on investment depended on the speculators' ability to predict business conditions accurately and on how fast settlement took place.

Squatters for their part yearned for economic independence. They successfully agitated for state "occupancy laws" favoring the claims of actual settlers and guaranteeing them compensation, if evicted, for their cabins, fences, outbuildings, and other improvements. Squatters also pressed for a lowered minimum in the amount of public land that could be purchased, a restriction that had fallen by 1832 to 40 acres. Above all, squatters called on the federal government to sanction squatting, formally allowing settlers to clear and cultivate tracts of public land prior to purchase. This policy of preemption, developed in limited acts in the 1830s and finally established in a general law of 1841, gave squatters the chance to settle land and then purchase as much as 160 acres at the minimum price in advance of public auction.

In practice the federal land system was a compromise between the interests of farmers and those of speculators. Government measures did nothing to curb speculators, who were in fact favored by the requirement, beginning in 1820, of full cash payment for public land; by lavish donations of land to military veterans, railroads, and state governments; and by eventual pricing of land long unsold for as little as 12.5¢ an acre. Federal land policy allowed speculators to amass great private fortunes by acquiring valuable tracts of the public domain. Yet the wide dispersion of freehold farms gave some substance to the myth that any American could become an owner of property and an independent producer for the capitalist market.

Southern agriculture remained strikingly distinctive, though it was influenced by the same public land policies that applied to the rest of the country and the same democratic pressures for widespread property ownership in the form of family farms. As in the North, owners of family farms tried to combine relative self-sufficiency with a cash income from marketable staples. By 1820 the long depression in tobacco prices had induced many planters in the coastal area of Virginia and Maryland to shift to the cultivation of wheat and corn. Having suffered a relative decline in income during the decades following Independence, white Southerners had led the way in the rush for western land.

Demand for Better Transportation.   Access to growing markets was the overriding concern of the com-

mercial farmer. Unlike southern cotton, most of the North's commercial crops were perishable and had to be marketed fairly quickly. Yet the teams of horses that hauled wagons of freight over the nation's turnpikes averaged no better than two miles an hour. The craze during the early nineteenth century for building turnpikes, bridges, and plank roads failed to reduce significantly the cost of long-distance freight. It was not until canals began to link together other inland waterways that northern farmers could think of concentrating on the production of corn and wheat for distant markets.

The Erie Canal, completed in 1825, united Northeast and West by providing a continuous waterway from Lake Erie to the Atlantic. In 1817 it had cost 19.2¢ per mile to ship a ton of freight overland from Buffalo to New York. By the late 1850s the cost per mile, via the canal, had dropped to 0.81¢. New York State had directed and financed this prodigious undertaking, by far the longest canal in the world, and

THE JUNCTION OF THE ERIE AND NORTHERN CANALS, c. 1830–1832
Although canals greatly reduced the cost of overland freight, it was a slow and arduous task negotiating multiple locks and pulling barges by rope from the "tow path" alongside.   *(Courtesy of the New-York Historical Society, New York City)*

Main Roads, Canals, River and Lake Transportation, 1840s

— Roads === Canals ····· Navigable Rivers

soon reaped spectacular rewards. Foreign capital quickly flowed into the country to meet the demand of other state and municipal governments, setting off a canal-building mania that soon linked Pittsburgh with Philadelphia, and the Ohio River with the Great Lakes. The high cost of building this network of waterways, undertaken for the most part by the states themselves, severely strained the credit of Ohio, Pennsylvania, and Indiana. But by dramatically lowering the costs of transport, the most successful canals had an enormous effect on northern agriculture and industry.

By the mid-1830s the basic pattern of internal transportation began to shift away from the traditional routes that had led from the Ohio and upper Mississippi valleys to New Orleans and ocean shipment via the Gulf of Mexico. Ohio Valley farmers would continue to ship grain and pork down the Mississippi by flatboat. The richest markets, however, lay east of the Great Lakes, and for a time the richest commercial agriculture developed in regions accessible by canal to Lake Erie. By 1840 Rochester, New York, had become the leading flour-milling center of the country. The marketing of grain became more efficient as brokers and other middlemen began to arrange for storage, transport, sale, and credit. This transformation preceded the East–West railroad connections of the early 1850s.

Rise of the Cotton Kingdom.   From 1820 on, Southerners benefited from three advantages unavailable in the North. First, the climate and soil of large parts of the South were ideally suited to growing cotton, the indispensable raw material for the Industrial Revolution. The perfection of the cotton gin and screw press, devices for extracting cotton from the plant and compressing it into bales, provided Southerners with benefits of technological innovation that northern agriculture did not begin to approximate until the late 1850s. Second, the rapid improvement and wide use of steamboats opened the way to upriver navigation on the Mississippi and the rich networks of other southern waterways, thereby lowering transportation costs even more dramatically than the northern canals did. Third and most important, southern agriculture could exploit the labor of black slaves, whose numbers increased from 1.5 million in 1820 to nearly 4 million in 1860. A self-reproducing labor force had long distinguished the South from other slave societies in the New World, which remained dependent on the continuing importation of slaves from Africa. It was the unprecedented natural increase in the slave population that enabled white Southerners to clear and settle the vast Cotton Kingdom extending from Georgia to Louisiana, Arkansas, and eventually, eastern Texas.

While the economics of slavery is still subject to much dispute, one must begin by emphasizing the shortage of white labor as a crucial condition affecting both northern and southern agriculture. All American farmers wanted the independence and relative security of owning their own land. Since land was generally accessible, especially in the West, this meant that it was difficult to hire nonfamily labor in order to expand production and take advantage of a rising demand for cash crops, such as wheat, cotton, and corn.

In the North, this labor shortage led to improved transportation, labor-saving machinery, and promotional schemes to attract immigrants. But in the South, black slaves provided a highly mobile and elastic supply of labor. Large planters and speculators could quickly transport an army of involuntary workers to clear rich western land, or sell slaves to meet the labor demands of expanding areas. Even prospering family farmers could buy or rent a few slaves in order to increase their output of cotton or other cash crops. The flexibility of the system also enabled planters to allocate needed labor to raising livestock and growing foodstuffs for domestic consumption; and when market conditions improved, to increase the proportion of time devoted to cotton or other staples.

These various advantages also meant that slaves became the major form of southern wealth, and slaveholding the means to prosperity. Except for the bustling port of New Orleans, great urban centers failed to appear, and internal markets languished. European immigrants, having no wish to compete with slave labor, generally shunned the region. Investment flowed mainly into the purchase of slaves, whose soaring price reflected an apparently limitless demand.

There can be no doubt that investment in slaves brought a profitable return, or that the slave economy continued to expand throughout the pre-Civil War decades. Yet, essentially, the system depended on the world's demand for cotton as it entered the age of industrialization, led by the British textile industry. At times the South's production of cotton outran international demand; cotton prices fell sharply following the Panics of 1819 and 1837. But until the Civil War, the world market for cotton textiles grew

"GEESE IN FLIGHT"

This imaginative painting by Leila T. Bauman captures some of the mid-nineteenth-century excitement over movement and improved transport—the steam from the train and riverboat harmonizing with the movement of horses, geese, and wind. *(Courtesy, National Gallery of Art)*

at such a phenomenal rate that both southern planters and British manufacturers thought only of infinite expansion. By 1840 the South grew over 60 percent of the world's cotton; during the pre-Civil War boom, more than three-fourths of the South's cotton was exported. Much of it went to Britain, amounting to over 70 percent of that country's cotton imports. In addition, the South also shipped cotton to the rising industries of continental Europe, including Russia. Throughout the antebellum period cotton accounted

for well over half the value of all American exports, and thus paid for the major share of the nation's imports. A stimulant to northern industry, cotton also contributed to the growth of New York City as a distributing and exporting center that drew income from commissions, freight charges, interest, insurance, and other services connected with the marketing of America's number one commodity.

Neither American sellers nor British buyers felt comfortable over such a single source of prosperity.

British manufacturers searched unsuccessfully for alternative sources of high-grade cotton. Though the South continued to export large quantities of rice, tobacco, and other staples, southern commercial conventions unsuccessfully called for a more balanced economy. In Louisiana wealthy sugar planters expanded production by using new technology for the processing of cane. Planters effectively applied slave labor to cultivating hemp, corn, and grain; to mining and lumbering; to building canals and railroads; and even to manufacturing textiles, iron, and other industrial products. Yet the South's economic growth and prosperity depended ultimately on foreign markets.

Paradoxically, no other American region contained so many farmers who merely subsisted on their own produce; yet in no other region had agriculture become so speculative and commercial—for small cotton famers who could not afford slaves as well as for the planter elite. Like some of the later Third World regions where involuntary labor produced raw materials for industrial nations, the South was intimately connected with industrial capitalism and yet cut off from its liberalizing and diversifying influences.

Indians

This rapid expansion in agriculture, North and South, depended initially on the displacement of the native population. The white Americans, determined to go where they pleased and to seize any chance for quick profit, regarded the millions of acres of western land as a well-deserved inheritance that should be exploited as quickly as possible. But in 1820 the prairies and forests east of the Mississippi still contained approximately 125,000 Indians. Although millions of acres had been legally cleared of Indian occupancy rights, the physical presence of the Indians blocked the way to government sale of much public land that could lead to increased revenue, to profits from land speculation, and to the creation of private farms and plantations.

The Indians, hopelessly outnumbered by an invader with superior technology, had little room for maneuver. Though they had long sought trade and alliances with whites, Indians had learned that advancing white settlements undermined tribal culture and destroyed the fish and game on which their economy depended. If the Indians had little understanding of the whites' conceptions of private property and competitive individualism, the whites were just as blind to the diversity and complexity of Indian cultures, to the natives' traditions of mutual obligation and communal ownership of land, and to the peculiarly advanced position of Indian women. Iroquois women, for example, played a crucial role in political and economic decisions. Such cultural barriers made it easier for whites to think of Indians in terms of negative stereotypes—as deceitful and bloodthirsty savages or as a weak and "childlike" race doomed to extinction. In fact, the Indian responses to white encroachments were complex, ranging from skillful warfare and stubborn negotiation to resigned acquiescence in the face of treachery and superior force.

The Indians had proved to be the major losers in the War of 1812. This war, by ending the long conflict between Western settlers and European sovereigns, had removed the Indians' last hope of finding white allies who could slow the advance of white America. The decisive victories of William Henry Harrison over the Shawnees in the Old Northwest, and of Andrew Jackson over the Creeks in the Old Southwest, had also shattered the hope of a union between northern and southern Indian confederations. These triumphs opened the way for exploiting tribal divisions and for gradually abandoning what Jackson termed "the farce of treating with Indian tribes" as units. Jackson thought that all Indians should be required as individuals to submit to the laws of the states, like everyone else, or to migrate beyond the Mississippi, where they could progress toward civilization at their own pace.

Federal Indian Policy.　The land-hungry frontiersmen faced the constraints of a federal Indian policy that had evolved from imperial, colonial, and early national precedents. This makeshift policy rested on four premises that were becoming increasingly contradictory. First, in line with Old World legal concepts the federal government continued to acknowledge that Indian tribes, while lacking many of the attributes of sovereignty, were in some sense independent nations that had acquired rights of possession by prior occupancy of the land. The continuing efforts to negotiate treaties, to purchase land, and to mark off territorial boundaries demonstrated that legitimate settlement by whites required at least symbolic consent from Indians. The same Old World model allowed the United States to punish "aggressor" tribes by demanding the cession of land as a legal indemnity for the damages of war.

The second premise, a product of New World experience, was that Indian "occupancy" must inevitably give way to white settlement. White Americans, like the heirs of a dying relative, had an "expectancy"—to use Jefferson's phrase—in the property that Indians held. In theory this preemptive claim did not infringe on the existing property rights of Indians. It simply gave the American government an exclusive right to purchase Indian lands, thereby blocking any future imperial designs by European powers. In practice, however, the doctrine of preemption led to the third premise of supreme federal authority over Indian affairs. Knowing the dangers of alliances between hostile Indians and foreign nations, the federal government had from its beginning assumed powers that would have been unthinkable in any other domestic sphere. It subjected all trade with Indians to federal licensing and regulation. It invalidated any sale or transfer of Indian lands, even to a state, unless made in accordance with a federal treaty. It guaranteed that Indians would be protected from encroachments on unceded land. Unfortunately, no federal administration had the will or military power to protect Indian rights while supervising the equitable acquisition of land by whites. In a government increasingly attuned to the voice of the people, the Indians had no voice of their own.

The fourth premise, which Jefferson had articulated and which gained momentum after the War of 1812, was that Indian culture, or "savagery," and American civilization could not permanently coexist. President James Monroe expressed the common conviction in a letter of 1817 to Andrew Jackson: "The

hunter or savage state requires a greater extent of territory to sustain it, than is compatible with the progress and just claims of civilized life, and must yield to it." The government actively promoted schools, agriculture, and various "useful arts" among the Indians, hoping to convert nomadic hunters into settled farmers. This hope drew nourishment from the progress of the more populous southern tribes, particularly the Cherokees, whose achievements in agriculture, in developing a written alphabet, and in adopting white technology seemed to meet the American tests of capability. But the government also pressured the Cherokees into ceding tracts of valuable eastern land in exchange for lands west of the Mississippi. By 1824 it was becoming clear that the five southern confederations—Cherokees, Creeks, Choctaws, Chickasaws, and Seminoles—could not survive as even temporary enclaves without federal protection against white exploiters. The southern tribes occupied western Georgia and North Carolina, and major portions of Tennessee, Florida, Alabama, and Mississippi, including the heart of the future Cotton Kingdom. In 1825 President Monroe officially proposed that these and all other remaining tribes should be persuaded to move west of the Mississippi, a plan that Jefferson and others had long regarded as the only way of saving America's original inhabitants from ultimate extinction.

Conflict of Federal and State Laws. In Georgia, white speculators, squatters, and gold miners had no desire to see civilized Indians living on choice ancestral land. In 1828, when the Cherokees adopted a constitution and claimed sovereign jurisdiction over their own territory, the state declared them to be mere tenants on state land, subject to the state's laws and authority. In 1832, in the case of *Worcester* v. *Georgia*, Chief Justice John Marshall ruled against the state. Georgia, he said, had no right to extend state laws to the Cherokees or their territory. "The several Indian nations," he maintained, were "distinct political communities, having territorial boundaries, within which their authority is exclusive, and having a right to all lands within those boundaries, which is not only acknowledged, but guaranteed by the United

CATLIN'S AMERICAN INDIANS

Although Americans were continually reminded of the Indians' acts of cruelty, as in this scene of initiation rites in a Mandan tent, there was also a growing fascination with Indians as representatives of the exotic. Even by the early 1830s George Catlin had created a prototype for the commercial Wild West show. An accomplished painter of Plains tribesmen, Catlin also created the heroic image of Osceola, the Seminole chief who had been captured by American treachery and who posed for this portrait in prison, shortly before his death. For over two centuries Anglo-American settlers had magnified Indian violence in order to justify their own aggression against Indians. The Seminole War presented the opportunity for dramatizing the ultimate racial nightmare—the specter of supposedly docile blacks uniting with Indians to slaughter "defenseless" whites. Such images appealed to deep-seated racial fears and helped to justify the most extreme measures for removing "wild" Indians far beyond the geographic boundaries of a "civilized" slave society. *(Top left, courtesy of the American Museum of Natural History; top right, National Portrait Gallery, Smithsonian Institution; bottom, American Antiquarian Society; opposite page, Library of Congress)*

States." But President Jackson, who had already withdrawn the federal troops earlier sent to protect Cherokee lands from intrusion, had no intention of enforcing the Supreme Court's decision.

Jackson firmly believed that Indians should be subject to state law and to the forces of a free market economy. To deal with tribes as privileged corporate groups, he thought, was simply to reinforce the power of corrupt chiefs and cunning half-breeds, who prevented tribesmen from following their own best interest. Jackson had no doubt that the vast majority of Indians, when liberated from tribal tyranny, would willingly emigrate to the West. The civilized few would be free to cultivate modest tracts of land and become responsible citizens of state and nation.

Jackson's denial of federal protection provided the needed incentives for a supposedly voluntary migration. Following Georgia's lead, other southern states harassed Indians with laws that few tribesmen could comprehend. White traders and lawyers descended like locusts on Indian lands, destroying tribal unity and authority. In 1830 Congress supported Jackson's policy by appropriating funds that would enable the president to negotiate treaties for the removal of all Indian tribes then living east of the Mississippi. The government still considered it necessary to purchase title to Indian land and to grant allotments of land to individual tribal leaders who could prove a legitimate claim. Federal officials even sought to protect Indians by supervising private contracts for sale. The majority of Indians, however, had no concept of land as a measurable and salable commodity. A few of the more experienced Chickasaws and other tribesmen secured good prices for rich cotton land, but white speculators, who swiftly cornered between 80 and 90 percent of southern allotments, reaped windfall profits.

The government thus furthered its goal of removal by dispossessing the Indians of their land. Victims of wholesale fraud, chicanery, and intimidation, the great mass of southern Indians had no choice but to follow the "Trail of Tears" to the vacant territory of Oklahoma. Subjected to disease, starvation, and winter cold, thousands died along the way.

Massacre of the Whites by the Indians and Blacks in Florida.

The above is intended to represent the horrid Massacre of the Whites in Florida, in December 1835, and January, February, March and April 1836, when near Four Hundred (including women and children) fell victims to the barbarity of the Negroes and Indians.

Military force gave a cutting edge to removal deadlines; in 1838 federal troops herded fifteen thousand Cherokees into detention camps. Meanwhile, Indians north of the Ohio River had earlier been demoralized as whites had cut down the supply of game, negotiated treaties with the more acculturated factions of certain tribes, and ensnared primitive societies with unfamiliar mechanisms of debt and credit. In 1832 the government crushed the resistance of Sac and Fox Indians in Illinois and Wisconsin, and in 1835 launched a long and costly war against the Seminoles in Florida. By 1844, except for a few remaining pockets mainly in the backcountry of New York, Michigan, and Florida, the mission of removal had been accomplished.

In his Farewell Address of March 4, 1837, Jackson applauded Indian removal as a great humanitarian achievement that had also happily removed the main impediment to America's economic growth:

While the safety and comfort of our own citizens have been greatly promoted by their removal, the philanthropist will rejoice that the remnant of that ill-fated race has been at length placed beyond the reach of injury or oppression, and that paternal care of the General Government will hereafter watch over them and protect them.

The Beginning of Indian Reservations. Ten years later, however, the government had recognized the impossibility of a "permanent Indian barrier" west of the Mississippi. Having defeated all Indian attempts to build dikes against the tides of westward migration, the government now began moving toward

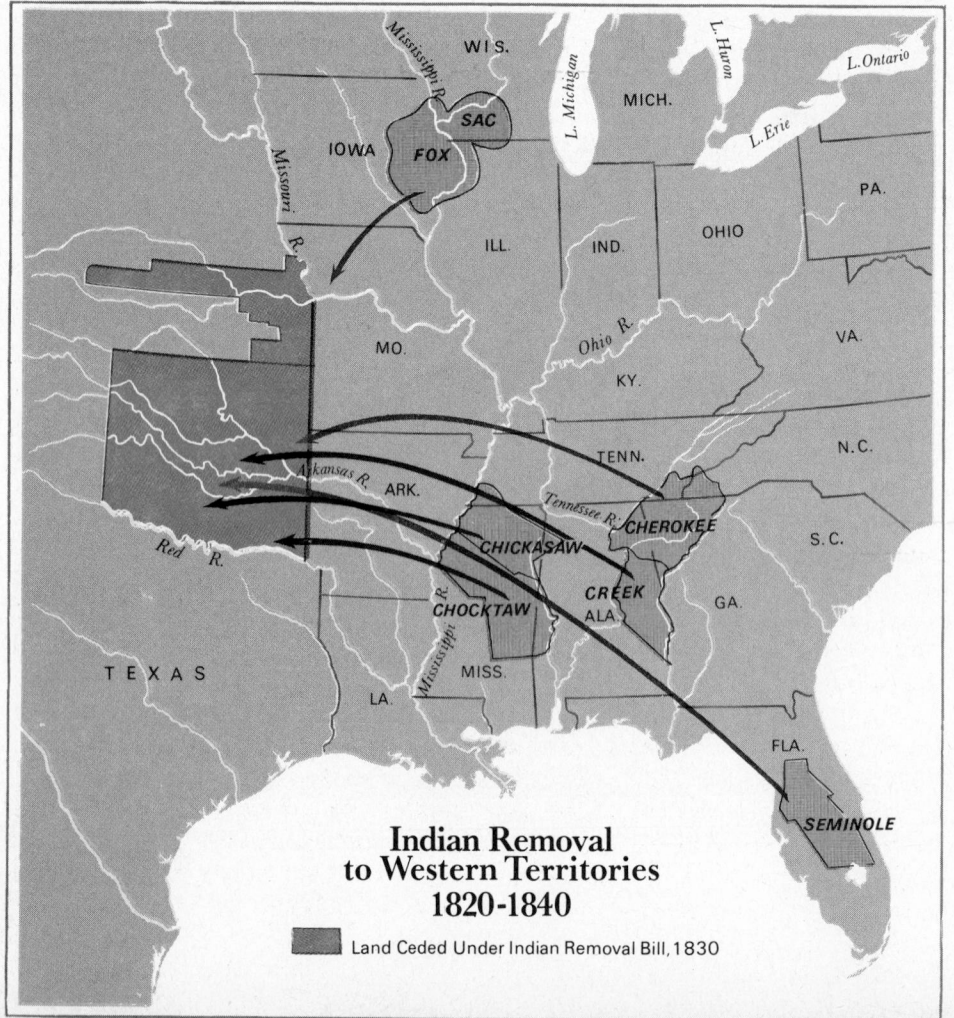

Indian Removal
to Western Territories
1820-1840

Land Ceded Under Indian Removal Bill, 1830

a policy of fencing Indians within specified "reservations" and opening the otherwise boundless territory of the great West to wagon trains, cavalry, miners, farmers, surveyors, and railroads. Even in the 1820s a few perceptive Indian chieftains had foreseen that western lands would be no more invulnerable than the lands in the East, a conclusion soon confirmed by the destruction of tribal game reserves and by the purchase of remaining Indian lands in Missouri and Iowa. The Anglo-Saxon settlers in Texas, who won independence from Mexico in 1836, asserted the unprecedented claim that Indians had no right whatever to possession of the land. Texas reaffirmed this doctrine after being annexed as a state in 1845, and even demanded that some twenty-five thousand Apaches and other tribesmen be removed or face extermination. Years of border warfare finally led in 1854 to the Texans' acceptance of Indian reservations under federal jurisdiction. But the federal government found that it could not protect Texas tribes from being slaughtered by marauding whites, and therefore authorized their removal to the territory north of the Red River.

Meanwhile, from 1846 to 1860 government policy began to settle the fate of the strong western tribes that had previously been free to roam prairies and mountain parks without concern for the conflicting claims of white nations. The American invasion and occupation of New Mexico, in the Mexican War, led to brutal punitive expeditions against the Navajo. In 1851 Congress passed the critically important Indian Appropriations Act, designed to consolidate western tribes on agricultural reservations, thereby lessening the danger to the tens of thousands of emigrants streaming toward California and Oregon and also to the proposed transcontinental railroad.

The degradation reached its climax in California, in the 1850s, where federal restraints on white aggression disappeared. Whites molested the Diggers and other primitive Indians, shooting the males for sport and enslaving the women and children. Farther east, the Apaches and powerful Plains tribes would continue to offer sporadic and sometimes spectacular resistance. The famed encounters between Indians and the United States Cavalry came after the Civil War. But even by 1860 the western tribes had been demoralized, their economy had been fatally weakened when buffalo and other game became depleted, and increasing numbers of Indians had been herded into compounds with boundaries that moved only inward.

The Slave's World

The native Americans were not the only or the most numerous racial victims of the nation's expansion in the pre-Civil War years. Millions of black laborers were even more systematically exploited in the expansion of southern agriculture.

The Slave Masters. In theory, the southern slaveholder possessed all the power of any owner of chattel property. This power was limited only by state laws, which were generally unenforceable, protecting slaves from murder and mutilation; setting minimal standards for food, clothing, and shelter; and prohibiting masters from teaching slaves to read or allowing them to carry firearms or roam about the countryside. These slave codes acknowledged that bondsmen were human beings who were capable of plotting, stealing, fleeing, or rebelling, and who were likely to be a less "troublesome property" if well cared for under a regimen of strict discipline. Yet the laws also insisted that the slave was a piece of property that could be sold, traded, rented, mortgaged, and inherited. They did not recognize the interests and institutions of the slave community, or the slave's right to marry, to hold property, or to testify in court.

In practice, it proved impossible to treat human beings as no more than possessions or as the mere instruments of an owner's will. Most masters were primarily motivated by the desire for profit. They wanted to maximize their slaves' productivity while protecting the value of their capital investment, a value that kept rising with the generally escalating trend in slave prices. Accordingly, it made sense to provide a material standard of living that would promote good health and a natural increase in the size of slave families, and thus increase capital gains. It also made sense to keep the morale of slaves as high as possible, and to encourage them to do willingly

COTTON PLANTATION, BY C. GIROUX
Although southern slaves cultivated sugar, rice, hemp, tobacco, and other crops, it was the cotton plantation that gave a distinctive stamp to nineteenth-century American slavery. *(Courtesy, Museum of Fine Arts, Boston)*

and even cheerfully the work they would be forced to do in the last resort. Convinced of the moral legitimacy of the system, most planters sincerely believed that their own best interests were identical with their slaves' best interests. They therefore sought to convince slaves of the essential justice of slavery, and expected gratitude for their acts of kindness, indulgence, and generosity, or even for their restraint in inflicting physical punishment.

But slaves were not passive, compliant puppets who could be manipulated at will. As human beings they had one overriding objective: self-preservation at a minimal cost of degradation and loss of self-respect. To avoid punishment and win rewards, they carried out with varying degrees of thoroughness their owners' demands. But black slaves became cunningly expert at testing their masters' will. They learned how

to mock while seeming to flatter; how to lighten unending work with moments of spontaneity, song, intimacy, and relaxation; how to exploit the whites' dependence on black field drivers and household servants; and how to play on the conflicts between their masters and white overseers. In short, they learned through constant experiment and struggle how to preserve a core of dignity and self-respect.

Although slavery "worked" as an economic system, its fundamental conflict of interests created a highly unstable and violent society. The great sugar planters in Louisiana and cotton planters in the delta country of Mississippi, often employing over one hundred slaves on a productive unit, tried to merge Christian paternalism with a kind of welfare capitalism. They provided professional medical care, offered monetary rewards for extra productivity, and granted a week or more of Christmas vacation. Yet these same plantations were essentially ruled by terror.

Even the most humane and kindly planters knew that only the threat of violence could force gangs of field hands to work from dawn to dusk "with the discipline," as one contemporary observer put it, "of a regular trained army." Frequent public floggings reminded every slave of the penalty for inefficient labor, insubordination, or disorderly conduct. Bennet H. Barrow, a particularly harsh Louisiana planter, maintained discipline by ordering occasional mass whippings of all his field hands, by chaining offenders or ducking them under water, and even by shooting a black who was about to run away. Barrow also distributed generous monetary bonuses to his slaves and bought them Christmas presents in New Orleans. The South could point to far gentler masters who seldom inflicted physical punishment. Slaves understood, however, that even the mildest of whites could become cruel despots when faced with the deception or ingratitude of people who, regardless of pretenses to the contrary, were kept down by force.

Masters also uneasily sensed that circumstances might transform a loyal and devoted slave into a vengeful enemy. It is true that white Southerners could congratulate themselves on the infrequency of serious insurrections, especially when the South was compared with Brazil and most of the Caribbean. Yet the French colony of St. Domingue had enjoyed an even more secure history than the American South until 1791, when the greatest of all slave revolts had led to the creation of the black republic of Haiti. Toussaint L'Ouverture, the brilliant Haitian military leader, was until the age of forty-five the trusted, docile, and privileged slave of an unusually kind and indulgent master. The record showed that the South had no magic immunity from slave revolts. In 1822 South Carolina hanged thirty-five blacks after uncovering Denmark Vesey's plot for a full-scale insurrection, a plot that involved some of Charleston's most trusted household servants. Nine years later Nat Turner led some seventy slaves on a bloody rampage through Southampton County, Virginia. To the outside world Southerners presented a brave façade of self-confidence, and individual planters reassured themselves that their own slaves were happy and loyal. But rumors of arson, poisoning, and suppressed revolts continued to flourish. Alarmists frequently warned that outside agitators were secretly sowing discontent among the slaves. This widespread fantasy at least hinted at the truth; slavery not only had little sanction in the outside world, but the institution ultimately depended on the sheer weight of superior force.

The difficulties in generalizing about the slave's world are compounded by the geographic, climatic, and cultural diversities of the "South"—a region in which mountain highlands, pine forests, and swampy lowlands are all frequently traversed within a few hundred miles.

Almost half of the southern slaveholders owned fewer than five slaves; 72 percent owned fewer than ten. The typical master could thus devote close personal attention to his human property. Many small farmers worked side by side with their slaves, an arrangement that might have been far more humiliating for the slaves than working in a field gang under black "drivers." From the slave's point of view, much depended on the character of an owner, on the norms of a given locality, on the accidents of sale, and on the relative difficulty of harvesting cotton, rice, tobacco, or sugar.

Slave experiences covered a wide range from remarkable physical comfort and lack of restraint to the most savage and unrelieved exploitation. But to dwell on contrasting examples of physical treatment is to risk losing sight of the central horror of human bondage. As the Quaker John Woolman pointed out in the eighteenth century, no human is saintly enough to be entrusted with total power over another. The slave was an inviting target for the hidden anger, passion, frustration, and revenge from which no human is exempt; a slave's work, leisure, movement, and daily fate depended on the will of another person.

Moreover, despite the numerical predominance of small slaveholders, most southern slaves were concentrated on large farms and plantations. Over half belonged to owners who held twenty or more slaves; one-quarter belonged to productive units of over fifty slaves. In the South, slave ownership was the primary route to wealth, and the most successful planters cornered an increasing share of the growing but limited human capital. Therefore, most slaves experienced fairly standardized patterns of plantation life.

Life on the Plantation. By sunrise black drivers had herded gangs of men and women into the fields. The older children served as water carriers or began to learn the lighter tasks of field work. Slaves too old for field work tended small children, along with the stables, gardens, and kitchens. This full employment of all available hands was one of the economies of the system that increased the total output from a planter's

SCULPTURED FIGURE
Excavated at the site of a plantation forge in Virginia, this iron figure is an excellent example of eighteenth-century Afro-American sculpture. *(Collection Adele Earnest)*

AFRO-CAROLINIAN FACE VESSEL
Recent research in art history has demonstrated a profound African influence on the folk sculpture of American slaves in such states as Georgia and South Carolina. This cultural continuity was always modified by the slaves' gift for improvisation and by their need to respond expressively to a new physical and social environment. *(Courtesy Augusta Richmond County Museum)*

capital investment. Nevertheless, slaves often succeeded in maintaining their own work rhythm and in helping to define the amount of labor a planter could reasonably expect. Bursts of intense effort required during cotton picking, corn shucking, or the eighteen-hour-a-day sugar harvest were followed by periods of festivity and relaxation. Even in relatively slack seasons, however, there were cattle to be tended, fences mended, forests cleared, and food crops planted.

Black slaves were saved from becoming mere robots in the field by the strength of their own community and evolving culture. There has long been controversy over the survival in North America of African cultural patterns. In contrast to Brazil, where continuing slave importations sustained a living bond with African cultures, the vast majority of southern blacks were removed by several generations from an African-born ancestor. Yet recent research has uncovered striking examples of African influence in the southern slaves' oral traditions, folklore, songs, dances, language, sculpture, religion, and kinship patterns. The question at issue is not the purity or even persistence of distinct African forms. In the New World all imported cultures have undergone blending, adaptation, and synthesis. The point is that slaves created their own Afro-American culture, which preserved the most crucial areas of life and thought from white domination. Within such a culture, sustained by strong community ties, slaves were able to maintain a sense of apartness, of pride, and of independent identity.

African kinship patterns seem to have been the main vehicle for cultural continuity. As in West Africa, children were frequently named for grandparents, who were revered even in memory. Kinship patterns survived even the breakup of families. Strangers often took on the functions and responsibilities of grandparents, uncles, and aunts. The fictional portrayals of Uncle Tom and Aunt Jemima were not figments of the imagination; many younger slaves were cared for and protected by "aunts" and "uncles" who were not blood kin. These older teachers and guardians passed on knowledge of a historical time, before the fateful crossing of the sea, when their ancestors had not been slaves. This historical awareness inspired hope in a future time of deliverance, a deliverance that slaves associated with the Jews' biblical flight from Egypt, with the sweet land of Canaan, and with the Day of Jubilee. In the words of one spiritual:

> Dear Lord, dear Lord, when slavery'll cease
> Then we poor souls will have our peace;—
> There's a better day a-coming,
> Will you go along with me?
> There's a better day a-coming,
> Go sound the jubilee!

Historians have recently recognized how important the slave family was as a refuge from the dehumanizing effects of being treated as chattel property. The strength of family bonds is suggested by

MOSS PICKERS, SAVANNAH, GEORGIA
This remarkable photograph of American-born slaves depicts generational continuity from childhood to old age and also suggests the kind of household utensils and living quarters that could be seen in antebellum Georgia. *(Courtesy, Lightfoot Collection)*

the thousands of slaves who ran away from their owners in search of family members separated by sale. The myth of weak family attachments is also countered by the swarms of freedmen who roamed the South at the end of the Civil War in search of their spouses, parents, or children, and by the eager desire of freedmen to legalize their marriages.

Nevertheless, the slave family was a highly vulnerable institution. Though many slaveholders had moral scruples against separating husbands from wives or small children from their mothers, even the strongest scruples frequently gave way to economic need. The forced sale of individual slaves in order to pay a deceased owner's debts further increased the chances of family breakups. In some parts of the South, it was common for a slave to be married to another slave on a neighboring or even distant plantation, an arrangement that left visitation at the discretion of the two owners.

In sexual relations there was a similar gap between moral scruples and actual practice. White planter society officially condemned miscegenation, and tended to blame lower-class whites for fathering mulatto children. Yet there is abundant evidence that many planters, sons of planters, and overseers took black mistresses or sexually exploited the wives and daughters of slave families. This abuse of power was not as universal as abolitionists claimed, but it was common enough to humiliate black women, to instill rage in black men, and to arouse shame and bitterness in white women. At best, slave marriage was a precarious bond, unprotected by law and vulnerable to the will of whites.

The larger slave community provided some stability and continuity for the thousands of blacks who were sold and shipped to new environments. On the larger plantations one could find conjurers whose magic powers were thought to ward off sickness, soften a master's heart, or hasten the success of a courtship. There were black preachers who mixed Christianity with elements of West African religion and folklore. In the slave quarters particular prestige was attached to those who excelled at the traditional memorizing of songs, riddles, folktales, superstitions, and herb cures—who were carriers, in short, of Afro-

American culture. These forms of oral communication allowed free play to the imagination, enabling slaves to comment on the pathos, humor, absurdity, sorrow, and warmth of the scenes they experienced. Together with the ceremonial rituals, especially at weddings and funerals, the oral traditions preserved a sanctuary of human dignity that enabled slaves to survive the humiliations, debasement, and self-contempt that were inseparable from human bondage.

Population Distribution and Opportunity

As we have seen, America's spectacular expansion in agriculture, which fueled other forms of economic growth, depended in large measure on the dispossession of Indians and on the exploitation of black slave labor. There can be no question that the nation's overall economic growth brought impressive gains in income and standard of living. By 1860, in per capita income, the United States was well ahead of western Europe; even the South was richer than most nations of Europe. But much is yet to be learned about the actual distribution of wealth in the pre–Civil War decades, to say nothing of the opportunity to acquire property or to move upward in status and occupation.

Discussions of America's economic opportunities generally omit three groups: the Indians; the black slaves; and the free blacks in both North and South whose small economic gains in various skilled trades and service industries were severely damaged by competition from white immigrants. Even excluding these oppressed minorities, one finds many indications that economic inequality increased substantially from 1820 to 1860.

The Rich Grow Richer, 1820–1860. According to the best recent estimates, by 1860 the upper 5 percent of families owned over half the nation's wealth. The disparity was far greater than this in parts of the South, where the wealth of the average slaveholder was growing far more rapidly than that of the average nonslaveholder. The average slaveholder was not only more than five times as wealthy as the average

FIVE POINTS, NEW YORK CITY, 1827

For many decades the region around "Five Points," the intersection of five streets in lower Manhatten, epitomized the worst of urban degradation: poverty, prostitution, crime, drunkenness, and mob violence. Fashionably dressed gentlemen and racially mixed crowds mingled with prostitutes and pigs. *(Brown Brothers)*

Northerner, but more than ten times as wealthy as the average nonslaveholding southern farmer. Even in the relatively egalitarian farming country of the eastern North Central states, the upper 10 percent of landholders owned nearly 40 percent of taxable wealth. The national centers of inequality, however, were the growing urban regions from Boston to New Orleans. Although much statistical research remains to be done, it is clear that between 1820 and 1860 the big cities led the nation toward the increasing dominance of the very rich. By 1860, according to one estimate, Philadelphia's richest 1 percent of population owned half the city's wealth; the lower 80 percent of the city's population had to be content with 3 percent of the wealth. According to a relatively modest estimate, the richest 5 percent of American families in 1860 received between 25 and 35 percent of the national income. While these figures indicate an inequality far greater than that estimated for modern America, they are roughly comparable to the inequalities in northern Europe in the late nineteenth century.

This conclusion would not be startling if America's pre–Civil War decades had not been claimed and almost universally accepted as "the age of the common man." American politicians and journalists eagerly expanded on the theme "equality of condition," supposedly confirmed by the observations of Alexis de Tocqueville and other European travelers. On closer inspection, however, Tocqueville and other travelers claimed only that American fortunes were "scanty" compared with fortunes in Europe; that in America "most of the rich men were formerly poor"; and that in America "any man's son may become the equal of any other man's son." In other words, American inequalities were thought to be temporary and to enhance the incentives of a race to success in which all were free to compete.

This belief in America's unique fluidity was especially reassuring by 1850, when European industrialism had produced undeniable evidence of misery, class conflict, and seething revolution. By that date American leaders could not hide their alarm over similar contrasts of wealth and squalor, particularly when the urban poor congregated in slums beyond the reach of traditional religious and social discipline. Yet affluent Americans persuaded themselves that the poor were free to climb the ladder of success, and that the wealthiest citizens were, in the words of Senator Henry Clay, "enterprising self-made men, who have whatever wealth they possess by patient and diligent labor."

In truth, however, the fortunes of John Jacob Astor and other leading American families compared favorably with the fortunes of the richest Europeans. Notwithstanding a few astonishing examples of rags-to-riches achievement, the great majority of America's rich and successful men had benefited from inherited wealth, an affluent childhood, or a prestigious family tradition. Between 1820 and 1860 there was a marked persistence of family wealth; in effect, the rich grew richer. In the cities, at least, they constituted an elite that became increasingly segregated by exclusive clubs, high social life, intermarriage, foreign travel, and business alliances.

At the other end of the spectrum was the mass of unskilled day laborers, who took what temporary jobs they could find and whose wages, even if regular, could not possibly support a family unless supplemented by the income of wives and children. No one knows the size of this unskilled, propertyless population, which drifted in and out of mill towns, flocked to the construction sites of canals and railroads, and gravitated to urban slums. In the 1840s and 1850s the largest cities attracted the chronic failures and castoffs who had no other place to turn. They jammed themselves into the attics and dank, windowless basements of Boston's Half Moon Place, where as many as one hundred people might share the same overflowing privy; or into New York's notorious Old Brewery, a noxious tenement that supposedly housed over a thousand beggars, pickpockets, whores, robbers, alcoholics, and starving children. In contrast to mid-nineteenth-century England, the relatively unstructured society of America provided very few public agencies that could enforce minimal standards of health, welfare, and safety.

Social Mobility.   The extremes of wealth and poverty tell little about the amount of upward movement from one class to another. Thus far, however, the available evidence indicates that the odds were heavily against an unskilled laborer's acquiring a higher occupational status. The overwhelming majority of unskilled workers remained unskilled workers. It is true that in the 1850s many of the sons of unskilled workers moved into semiskilled factory jobs. But this generational advance was almost always limited to the next rung on the ladder. It was extremely rare for the children of manual workers, even skilled manual workers, to rise to the levels of clerical, managerial, or professional employment.

Despite growing signs in the pre–Civil War decades of semipermanent boundaries between occupational groups, there were remarkably few expressions of class consciousness or class interest. Historians have sometimes been misled by the labor rhetoric of the Jacksonian period, a time when the rich felt it necessary to prove their humble origins and when everybody who could do so laid claim to the proud title of "workingman." The labor leaders of the era were typically artisan proprietors and small businessmen intent on fixing prices and reducing the hazards of interregional competition. This is not to deny the importance of immigrant British artisans who had been displaced by the British factory system, who reinforced the preindustrial craft traditions in the United States, and who were schooled in the techniques of secret organization and industrial warfare. Nor can one deny the courage of union organizers who faced conspiracy trials in the 1820s and 30s, who saw their gains wiped out by the depression of 1837–42, and who finally formed city federations of craft unions and national trades unions in the 1850s. Yet the great strikes for higher wages and for the ten-hour day were staged by skilled printers, typographers, hatters, tailors, and other artisans. Employers, who were mostly supported by the courts and who benefited from fresh supplies of cheap immigrant labor, had little difficulty in breaking strikes. Although the Massachusetts Supreme Court led the way, in *Commonwealth* v. *Hunt* (1842), in ruling that trade unions were not in themselves conspiracies in restraint of trade, in 1860 only 0.1 percent of the American labor force was organized.

Even by the 1840s America's relative freedom from class consciousness and class conflict evoked considerable comment. According to Karl Marx and other European observers, the explanation could be found in the fresh lands of the American frontier, which provided an outlet for surplus population. In America, George Henry Evans's National Reform Association referred to the West as a "safety valve" that could and should provide an escape for workers whose opportunities were limited in the East. Evans contended in the 1840s that the nation owned enough land in the West to guarantee every family a farm. In the 1850s Horace Greeley, editor of the enormously influential New York *Tribune*, popularized the Republican party's slogan, "Vote yourself a farm." More than a generation later, the historian Frederick Jackson Turner and his followers evolved a detailed historical theory that pictured the frontier as both a safety valve for the pressures of the industrializing East and a wellspring of rejuvenating opportunity.

The theory, in its simplest and crudest form, has been thoroughly demolished. The eastern laborer, earning a dollar a day or less, could not afford to travel to the frontier and borrow funds for a farm and tools, even if he possessed the skills for western farming. The evidence shows that western land sales lagged in hard times, when a safety valve would be most needed, and increased when prosperity drove up the prices of wheat and cotton. Except for a few cooperative settlement associations and a few hundred wage earners sent by antislavery groups to settle Kansas, there are no records to show that industrial workers were transformed into frontier farmers.

On the other hand, the westward surge of millions of Americans intensified and dramatized the central fact of American life: physical mobility. Wages in the Northeast might well have been lower if the farmers, shopkeepers, artisans, and small businessmen who did go West had stayed put. Some of these aspiring adventurers might have been forced to seek factory employment. Some might have become America's counterparts to Europe's labor organizers. Ironically, since young males predominated in the migration away from industrial New England, an increasing number of women had no prospect for marriage and thus became part of a permanent industrial labor force. These women found themselves living permanently on the low wages from jobs they had taken while awaiting marriage.

Intense geographic mobility reinforced the myth of America's boundlessness, of America's infinite promise. By 1850 one-quarter of the entire population born in New England had moved to other states. The South Atlantic states experienced a no less striking westward drain of whites and of black slaves. In each decade the northern cities, towns, and factories witnessed an extraordinary inflow and outflow of population. Although few of these mobile Americans had a chance to acquire farms, they moved because they had hope of finding it better someplace else. And the hope may have been more significant than the reality they found. For unskilled laborers the reality was often grim, but the factories and towns they left behind had no need to worry about their accumulating grievances. The more fortunate and competitive movers could not doubt that Illinois was preferable to Ohio, or that New York City offered

VICTUALLERS IN PHILADELPHIA

Victuallers were licensed suppliers of food, drink, and provisions. This parade of Philadelphia victuallers was typical of the ceremonial processions of various trades and crafts, proud of their ancient emblems and symbols of public service, but concerned, even by the 1820s, over economic changes which threatened their distinctive identity. *(Courtesy, The Historical Society of Pennsylvania)*

more opportunities than the rocky hillsides of Vermont.

It was obvious that the condition of most white Americans, except for the floating population of impoverished laborers, was improving. Even the lowliest Irish laborers in a factory town like Newburyport, Massachusetts, found that they could accumulate property if they stuck to their jobs for a decade or more. To maintain a savings account or eventually to buy a house required discipline, frugality, and multiple income from family members at the expense of education and leisure. The Irish put a greater premium on home ownership than on education or occupational achievement. The Jews, on the other hand, tended to make every sacrifice for their children's education. The gains, particularly for the families of manual workers, were extremely limited. But these gains engendered pride in achieving what others had not achieved, and were sufficient to prevent even a permanent working class from becoming a permanent and propertyless proletariat.

The incessant turnover of population, the lack of physical roots, also gave force to the ideology of an open and boundless society—an ideology repeatedly stressed by newspapers, sermons, and political speeches. Who could tell what had become of all one's former neighbors and fellow workers? No doubt some had hit it rich. The mystery of everyone's past made it believable that most men's positions had been won according to talent and performance—that in America, where the only limits were individual will and ability, most men got what they were worth. If in time a manual worker could finally boast of a savings account of $300, of owning the roof over his head, or of a son who had moved up to the next rung on the ladder, why should he doubt the common claim, "This is a country of self-made men," where most of the rich had once been poor?

SUGGESTED READINGS

For informative surveys and detailed bibliographies, see George Dangerfield, *The Awakening of American Nationalism, 1815–1828* (1965); Glyndon G. Van Deusen, *The Jacksonian Era* (1959); Edward Pessen, *Jacksonian America: Society, Personality, and Politics* (1969); and Russel B. Nye, *Society and Culture in America, 1830–1860* (1974). Louis Hartz, *The Liberal Tradition in America* (1955), presents a brilliant and provocative interpretation of America's divergence from Old World norms. Hartz, like most interpreters of the period, draws heavily on Alexis de Tocqueville's classic work, *Democracy in America,* of which there are many editions. Daniel J. Boorstin's *The Americans: The National Experience* (1965), also emphasizes America's uniqueness. The period is illuminated in different ways by Yehoshua Arieli, *Individualism and Nationalism in American Ideology* (1964); Rowland Berthoff, *An Unsettled People: Social Order and Disorder in American History* (1971); and Fred Somkin, *Unquiet Eagle: Memory and Desire in the Idea of American Freedom, 1815–1860* (1967). An anthology of primary source material, accompanied by extensive commentary, is David B. Davis, ed., *Antebellum American Culture: An Interpretive Anthology* (1979).

Population growth is analyzed by J. Potter, "The Growth of Population in America, 1700–1860," in *Population and History. . . ,* eds. D. V. Glass and D. E. C. Eversley (1965); and Richard A. Easterlin, *Population, Labor Force, and Long Swings in Economic Growth: The American Experience* (1968). Maldwyn A. Jones, *American Immigration* (1960), is a useful introduction to the subject; it should be supplemented by Marcus L. Hansen, *The Atlantic Migration, 1607–1860* (1940); Oscar Handlin, *Boston's Immigrants* (1959); Charlotte Erickson, *Invisible Immigrants;* Robert Ernst, *Immigrant Life in New York City, 1825–1863* (1949); Kathleen N. Conzen, *Immigrant Milwaukee, 1836–1860* (1977); and Carl Wittke, *The Irish in America* (1956). For urbanization, see Sam Bass Warner, Jr., *The Urban Wilderness* (1972); Richard C. Wade, *The Urban Frontier* (1964); and Paul Boyer, *Urban Masses and Moral Order in America, 1820–1920* (1978).

The best introduction to current views of economic growth can be found in W. Elliot Brownlee, *Dynamics of Ascent* (1974), and Stuart Bruchey, *Growth of the Modern American Economy* (1975). For a fascinating discussion of the economic thought of the pre–Civil War period, see Joseph Dorfman, *The Economic Mind in American Civilization.* Vol. 2 (3 vols., 1946–49).

The best introduction to Indian removal is Wilcomb E. Washburn, *The Indian in America* (1975). Francis P. Prucha, *American Indian Policy in the Formative Years* (1962), is sympathetic to government policy-makers. Ronald N. Satz, *American Indian Policy in the Jacksonian Era* (1975), provides an informative account of the subsequent period. The most recent and comprehensive study of the so-called civilized tribes is Charles Hudson, *The Southeastern Indians* (1976); for the Far West, see Sherburne F. Cook, *The Conflict between the California and White Civilization* (1976). An outstanding work which corrects the mythology regarding the relation between Indians and western pioneers is John Unruh, *The Plains Across: The Overland Emigrants and the Trans-Mississippi West* (1979). There are three valuable related works in intellectual history: Roy H. Pearce, *The Savages of America* (1965); Richard Slotkin, *Regeneration through Violence: The Mythology of the American Frontier, 1600–1860* (1973); and Roderick Nash, *Wilderness in the American Mind* (1967).

Ray A. Billington, *Westward Expansion* (1974), presents an excellent survey of western history as well as a comprehensive bibliography. The fullest histories of agriculture are Percy W. Bidwell and John I. Falconer, *History of Agriculture in the Northern United States, 1620–1860* (1925), and Lewis C. Gray, *History of Agriculture in the Southern United States to 1860* (2 vols., 1933). A briefer and outstanding survey is Paul W. Gates, *The Farmer's Age: Agriculture, 1815–1860* (1960), which can be supplemented by Clarence H. Danhof, *Change in Agriculture in the Northern United States, 1820–1870* (1969).

The classic study of transportation is George R. Taylor, *The Transportation Revolution, 1815–1860* (1951). A monumental work, confined to New England, is Edward Kirkland, *Men, Cities, and Transportation* (2 vols., 1948). For canals, see Harry N. Scheiber, *Ohio Canal Era* (1969), and R. E. Shaw, *Erie Water West* (1966).

Eugene D. Genovese, *Roll, Jordan, Roll* (1974), is a monumental study of Negro slavery in the South. Herbert G. Gutman, *The Black Family in Slavery and Freedom, 1750–1925* (1976), is no less impressive and innovative. For a briefer and illuminating discussion of the slaves' society, based mainly on slave narratives, see John W. Blassingame, *The Slave Community* (rev. ed., 1979). Two rich collections of source material are Willie Lee Rose, ed., *A Documentary History of Slavery in North America* (1976); and John W. Blassingame, ed., *Slave Testimony* (1977). As an overall survey of slavery as an institution Kenneth Stampp's *The Peculiar Institution* (1956) has not been superseded.

A highly controversial work on the economics of Negro slavery is Robert W. Fogel and Stanley L. Engerman, *Time on the Cross: The Economics of American Negro Slavery* (1974). For important criticisms of this work, as well as for new information, see Paul A. David *et al., Reckoning with Slavery* (1976), and Herbert G. Gutman, *Slavery and the Numbers Game* (1975). An excellent survey of the more traditional literature is Harold D. Woodman, ed., *Slavery and the Southern Economy* (1966). For the use of slaves in nonagricultural employment, see Robert S. Starobin, *Industrial Slavery in the Old South* (1970). The synthesis of African and Christian religious forms is carefully studied in Albert J. Raboteau, *Slave Religion: The "Invisible Institution" in the Antebellum South* (1978). A brilliant and comprehensive study of black folklore and culture is Lawrence W. Levine, *Black Culture and Black Consciousness: Afro-American Folk Thought from Slavery to Freedom* (1977).

A pioneering study of social and economic mobility is Stephan Thernstrom, *Poverty and Progress* (1964). For disparities in the distribution of wealth and income, see Edward Pessen, *Riches, Class, and Power before the Civil War* (1973), and Lee Soltow, "Economic Inequality in the United States in the Period from 1790 to 1860," *Journal of Economic History,* 31 (December 1971), 822–839. The discovery of poverty is analyzed in Robert H. Bremner, *From the Depths* (1956), and Raymond A. Mohl, *Poverty in New York, 1783–*

1825 (1971). On working-class culture, the best guides are Alan Dawley, *Class and Community: The Industrial Revolution in Lynn* (1977); James Henretta, "Families and Farms: Mentalité in Pre-Industrial America," *Wm. and Mary Q.,* 3d. ser., vol. 35 (1978); Bruce Laurie, *The Peoples of Philadelphia* (1973); Paul Faler, "Cultural Aspects of the Industrial Revolution: Lynn, Massachusetts, Shoemakers and Industrial Morality, 1826–1860," *Labor History,* 15 (Winter 1974); Herbert G. Gutman, *Work, Culture, and Society in Industrializing America* (1976); Howard M. Gitelman, *Workingmen of Waltham* (1974); Peter R. Knights, *The Plain People of Boston* (1971); and Norman Ware, *The Industrial Worker, 1840–1860* (1959). For labor movements and protests, see David Montgomery, "Workers' Control of Machine Production in the Nineteenth Century," *Labor History,* 17 (1976); David Montgomery, "The Shuttle and the Cross: Weavers and Artisans in the Kensington Riots of 1844," *Journal of Social History* (Summer 1972); Joseph Rayback, *A History of American Labor* (1966); Walter Hugins, *Jacksonian Democracy and the Working Class* (1960). Two good studies of the ideology of the self-made man, Irvin G. Wyllie, *The Self-Made Man in America* (1954), and John G. Cawelti, *Apostles of the Self-Made Man* (1965), should be supplemented by Daniel T. Rodgers, *The Work Ethic in Industrial America, 1850–1920* (1978). Though dealing with a later period, Richard Weiss, *The American Myth of Success* (1969), also sheds light on the earlier history of the subject.

The generation that came to maturity in the early nineteenth century carried a unique burden. As "children of the Founding Fathers," they could not achieve immortal fame by winning independence from British tyranny. Instead, their assigned mission was vigilant preservation—the preservation of what the famous lawyer Rufus Choate called the "beautiful house of our fathers" against divisive ambition, corruption, and arbitrary power.

For a time it seemed that Liberty and Union could be preserved by patriotic rhetoric honoring hallowed figures like Thomas Jefferson and John Adams (who both died on July 4, 1826, exactly fifty years after the adoption of the Declaration of Independence) and by electing "Virginia Dynasty" presidents. The last in that succession, James Monroe, still appeared in public dressed in his Revolutionary War uniform. The collapse of the Federalist party, after the War of 1812, fostered the illusion of an "Era of Good Feelings" in which a single national party would guarantee republican simplicity, order, and self-restraint. President Monroe, in his second inaugural address (1821), invoked the image of harmony. The American people, he affirmed, constituted "one great family with a common interest." Four years later President John Quincy Adams, also a Republican, voiced similar sentiments and happily observed that "the baneful weed of party strife" had been uprooted. Most Americans still associated political parties with the self-serving, aristocratic factions that had dominated British politics. In a republican nation, as in a republican family, no room could be allowed for selfish alliances representing separate interests.

This ideal of family unity was, however, far removed from social and economic realities. Between 1819 and 1821 Congress faced the most dangerous crisis it had yet experienced when northern and southern representatives deadlocked over the admission of Missouri as a new slave state. Simultaneously, the financial panic of 1819, followed by a severe depression, aroused widespread hostility toward banking corporations and other groups that had used political influence to gain economic privilege. Economic recovery and expansion only intensified demands for equality of opportunity, as various competing classes, localities, and social groups became

CHAPTER 13

Politics: Cohesion and Division

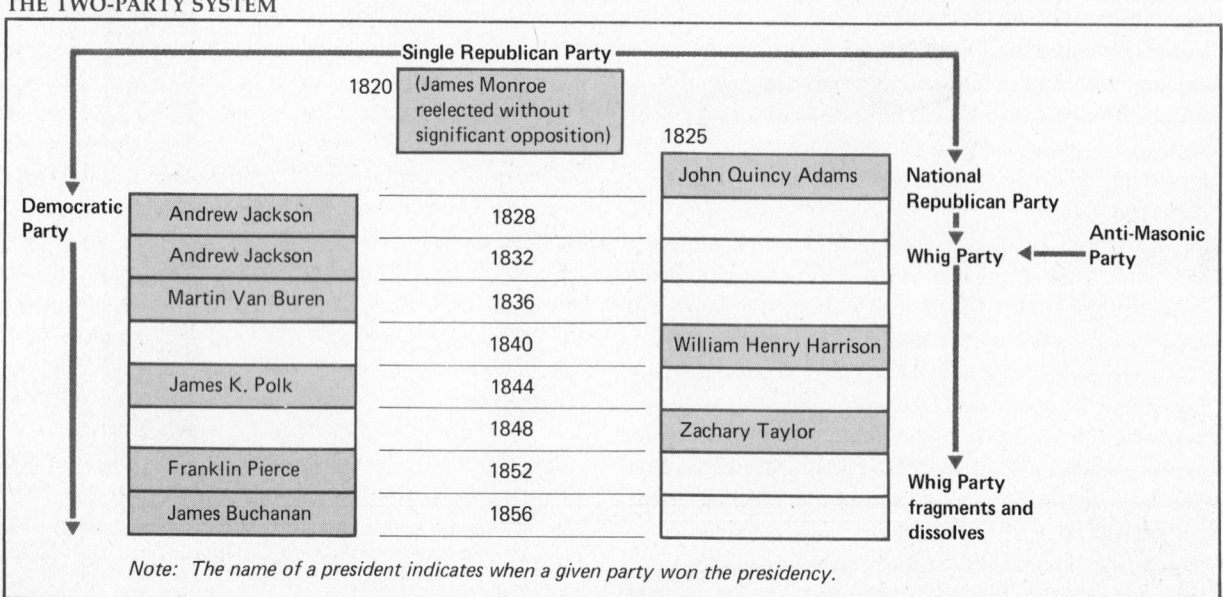

GEORGE CALEB BINGHAM'S "VERDICT OF THE PEOPLE"

Politics became the Americans' major public ritual. Like religious revivals, political events provided the occasion for sociability and for emotional expression. But politics also evoked the excitement that springs from looking upon or touching the levers of power. *(Courtesy, The Boatman's National Bank of St. Louis)*

THE TWO-PARTY SYSTEM

	Single Republican Party		
1820	(James Monroe reelected without significant opposition)	1825	
		John Quincy Adams	National Republican Party
Democratic Party	Andrew Jackson — 1828		Whig Party ← Anti-Masonic Party
	Andrew Jackson — 1832		
	Martin Van Buren — 1836		
	— 1840	William Henry Harrison	
	James K. Polk — 1844		
	— 1848	Zachary Taylor	
	Franklin Pierce — 1852		Whig Party fragments and dissolves
	James Buchanan — 1856		

Note: The name of a president indicates when a given party won the presidency.

increasingly aware of the unequal effects of government policies concerning tariffs, banking and currency, and public land sales. By the mid-1820s it was becoming painfully clear that widening opportunities for some Americans meant constricting opportunities for others. Paradoxically, the post-Revolutionary generation found a way of containing the many factions that had arisen by *institutionalizing* division in the form of political parties. From the early 1830s to the early 1850s, this two-party system helped preserve national cohesion. The Democrats and the National Republicans—succeeded later by the Whigs— were national coalitions of sectional, class, economic, ethnic, and religious interests, held together by compromise and cooperation. To maximize votes, politicians had to find ways of arousing the apathetic on more than immediate local issues. The basic political style that emerged in antebellum America, in the South and West as well as in the North, centered on the portrayal of some self-serving, privileged interest that had secretly consolidated power and had begun to shut off equal access to the rewards of national growth. In an era of relative security from foreign dangers, politicians continued to portray their opponents as heirs of the British and Tories who were seeking to undermine American liberties and betray the heritage of the Founding Fathers. The Democrats and Whigs survived as national coalitions as long as they drew significant support from both the slaveholding and nonslaveholding states. But when black slavery, the institution that most flagrantly subverted liberty and opportunity, was seriously questioned in a national forum, the unifying force of the parties was destroyed.

"A Fire Bell in the Night": The Missouri Compromise

From the time of the Continental Congress, American leaders had realized that a serious dispute over slavery could jeopardize their bold experiment in self-government. Beginning with the Constitutional Convention, the entire structure of national politics had been designed to prevent any faction from directly threatening southern slaveholders and thereby subverting common national interests. It is therefore not surprising that before 1819 slavery never became a central issue in national politics. But it was an issue that sat like an unactivated bomb in the minds of the foremost political leaders.

The agreement to keep the bomb unactivated rested on two unwritten understandings: the North would recognize the property rights of southern slaveholders and the South would recognize slavery as an evil that should be discouraged and eventually abolished whenever it became safe and practicable to do so. Changing circumstances, including the shifting balance of sectional power, forced repeated challenges to these understandings. The challenges took the form of clashes in Congress, during which representatives from the Lower South threatened to dissolve the Union and even hinted at the possibility of civil war. On each occasion the resulting compromise strongly favored the South. This political process demonstrated the Americans' remarkable ability to make pragmatic adjustments in the interest of national stability. Yet these successful compromises depended on the dangerous assumption that southern threats of disunion would always be met by northern concessions.

The militancy of the Lower South's congressional leaders rested on a realistic estimate of the future. For a time the North could afford to make concessions because slavery seemed to endanger no vital northern interests. But after 1815, humanitarian causes had increasing appeal in the North and more and more Northerners expressed moral and patriotic misgivings over the westward expansion of slavery. Sooner or later, as Southerners like John Randolph predicted, such northern antislavery sentiments would become strong enough to create new sectional parties. Even by 1820, as a result of rapid population growth in the North, the major slaveholding states held only 42 percent of the seats in the House of Representatives. Only the Senate could provide a firm bulwark against potential northern encroachments, and the key to the Senate was new slave states. In the Senate, following the admission of Mississippi and Alabama (1817, 1819), eleven slave states balanced eleven free states.

Sectional Conflict. The Missouri crisis erupted in February 1819, when the House was considering a bill that would enable the people of Missouri to draft a constitution and be admitted as a slave state. Slaves constituted nearly one-sixth of the territory's population. James Tallmadge, Jr., a New York Jeffersonian Republican, offered an amendment that prohibited the further introduction of slaves into Missouri and provided for the emancipation, at age twenty-five, of all children of slaves born after Missouri's admission as a state. After a prolonged and often violent debate, the House approved Tallmadge's amendment by an ominously sectional vote. The Senate, after equally violent debates, passed a Missouri statehood bill without any restrictions on slavery. The issue seemed hopelessly deadlocked.

Virginia now took the lead in militancy, trying to arouse a generally apathetic South to a common peril. "This momentous question," Jefferson announced from Monticello, where he had retired, "like a fire bell in the night, awakened and filled me with terror." Along with Madison and other Virginia statesmen, Jefferson was convinced that the attempt to exclude slavery from Missouri was part of a Federalist conspiracy to create a sectional party and destroy the Union.

The Missouri crisis was aggravated by a sense that understandings had been broken, veils torn off, and true and threatening motives exposed. The congressional debates rekindled the most divisive issues that had supposedly been settled in the Constitutional Convention, and thus raised the hypothetical question of disunion. This reenactment of 1787 was underscored by the prominence in the congressional debates of two of the Convention's surviving antagonists —Charles Pinckney of South Carolina, who now insisted that Congress had no power to exclude slavery from even the unsettled territories; and Rufus King of New York, the alleged leader of the Federalist conspiracy, who now announced that any laws upholding slavery were "absolutely void, because [they are] contrary to the law of nature, which is the law of God."

It was a new generation of Northerners, however, who had to reaffirm or reject the kinds of compromises over slavery that had created the original Union. Like the Founders, the northern majority in Congress could do nothing about slavery in the existing states. But there had been an understood national policy, they believed, enshrined in the Northwest Ordinance, committing the government to restrict slavery in every feasible way. This understanding had seemingly been confirmed by southern avowals that slavery was an evil bequeathed by the past. The North had accepted the original slave states' expectations that migrating slaveholders would not be barred from bringing their most valuable property into the territories south of the Ohio River and east of the Mississippi. But Missouri occupied the same latitudes as Illinois, Indiana, and Ohio (as well as Kentucky and Virginia). To allow slavery to become legally entrenched in Missouri might thus encourage its spread throughout the entire West, to the detriment of free labor and industry. Southerners had long argued, however illogically, that if slavery were diffused over a large geographical area, it would weaken as an institution and the likelihood of slave insurrections would diminish. In 1820 Daniel Raymond, a prominent political economist, gave the obvious reply: "Diffusion is about as effectual a remedy for slavery as it would be for the smallpox, or the plague."

Southerners were particularly alarmed by the argument of northern congressmen that the constitutional guarantee to every state of "a Republican Form of Government" meant that Missouri could not be admitted as a slave state. The argument implied that Virginia and other southern states fell short of "a Republican Form of Government" and would therefore not be admissible to a new Union. If this were true, the southern states would be reduced to a second-class status. If they accepted the northern definition of a republican form of government, they had no choice but to take steps toward abolishing slavery or to face, like colonies, the punitive measures of an imperial authority.

The Terms of Compromise. Henry Clay, the Speaker of the House of Representatives, by exerting all the powers of his office and of his magnetic personality, finally achieved a compromise. A small

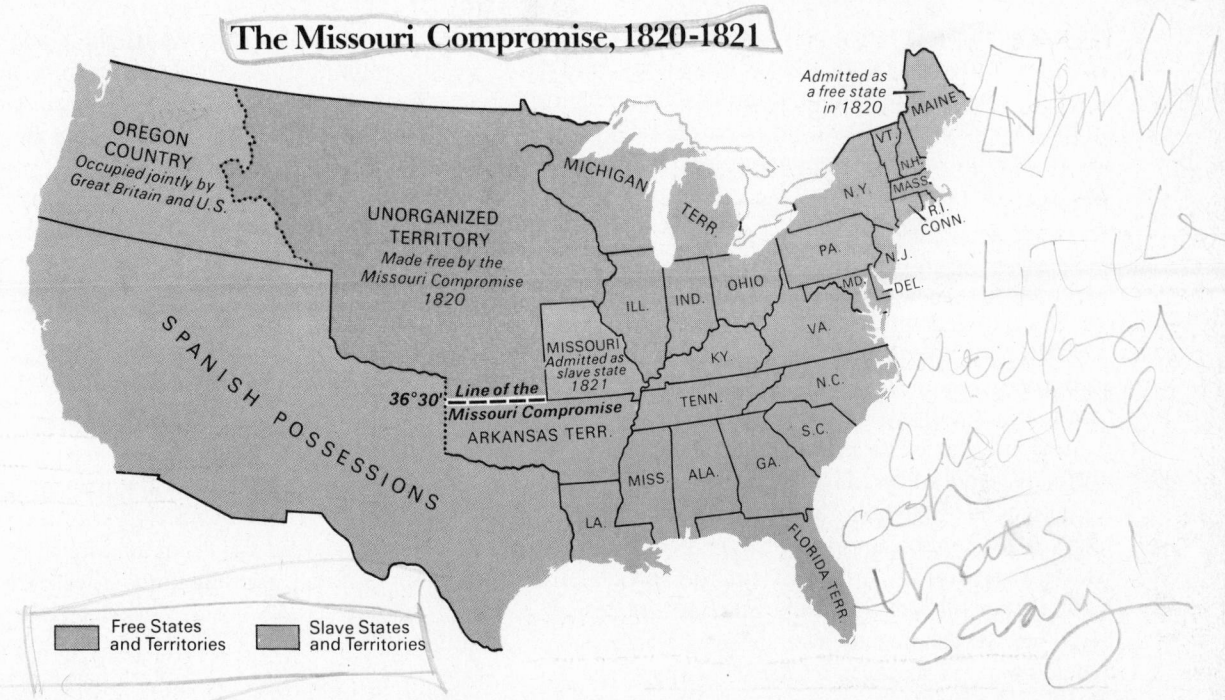

The Missouri Compromise, 1820-1821

OREGON COUNTRY
Occupied jointly by Great Britain and U.S.

UNORGANIZED TERRITORY
Made free by the Missouri Compromise 1820

SPANISH POSSESSIONS

Admitted as a free state in 1820 — MAINE

MICHIGAN TERR.

VT. N.H. MASS. R.I. CONN.

N.Y.

PA.

N.J.

MD. DEL.

ILL. IND. OHIO

VA.

MISSOURI
Admitted as slave state 1821

KY.

36°30' Line of the Missouri Compromise

ARKANSAS TERR.

TENN.

N.C.

S.C.

MISS. ALA. GA.

LA.

FLORIDA TERR.

■ Free States and Territories   ■ Slave States and Territories

minority of northern congressmen agreed to drop the antislavery provision for Missouri, while a small minority of Southerners agreed that slavery should be excluded from the remaining and unsettled portions of the Louisiana Purchase north of latitude 3°30', the same latitude as the southern border of Missouri. In effect, this measure limited to Arkansas and the future territory of Oklahoma any further expansion of slavery within the Louisiana Purchase. Given the sectional balance of power, the swing vote favoring these concessions was sufficient to carry the compromise. The way was now opened for admitting Maine as a free state, since the Senate had refused to accept Maine's statehood until the House had abandoned efforts to restrict slavery in Missouri.

The press and legislatures of the North generally interpreted the Missouri Compromise as a victory for the South. A new hope arose that public pressure could force Missouri to adopt a constitution providing for gradual emancipation. But the defiant Missourians drafted a constitution that prohibited the state legislature from emancipating slaves without the consent of their owners and that barred free blacks and mu-

lattoes from entering the state. Since free blacks had been recognized as citizens by some of the eastern states, this second provision violated the constitutional guarantee that "the Citizens of each State shall be entitled to all Privileges and Immunities of Citizens in the several States." Northern congressmen now stood firm in rejecting the Missouri constitution and in effect the entire compromise. Eventually, in 1821, Clay's skillful manipulation of committees produced a second compromise prohibiting Missouri from discriminating against citizens of other states—an abstract resolution that still left citizenship undefined. The country applauded Clay for saving the Union.

But the Union would never be the same. In southern eyes the uninhibited debates on slavery had opened a Pandora's box of dangers. The free blacks of Washington had packed the galleries of the House and had listened intently to antislavery speeches. In 1822, during the trial of the conspirators associated with Denmark Vesey, a Charleston slave testified that Vesey had shown him an antislavery speech delivered by Rufus King, "the black man's friend." The link between the Missouri debates and a sizable slave conspiracy stunned South Carolina, confirming its worst fears. The cumulative effect was twofold: to unite all whites in the suppression of dangerous discussion, and to strengthen the hand of states' rights extremists and of the defenders of slavery as a positive good.

The End of Republican Unity

The Missouri crisis alerted politicians to the perils of sectional division. The North's unexpected outrage over the admission of a new slave state convinced many Southerners that they needed to cultivate rising northern leaders like Martin Van Buren, whose faction of young "Bucktails" had captured control of the New York Republican party by 1820. Van Buren, whose shrewdness, ambition, and personal charm made up for his lack of family prestige and connections, viewed the clamor over slavery as evidence of a dangerous breakdown in party loyalty. New national organizations were needed that could prevent sectional conflict. Party distinctions, he said, were infinitely safer than geographic ones. If party distinctions were suppressed, "geographical differences founded on local instincts or what is worse, prejudices between free and slaveholding states" would inevitably take their place.

The Van Buren faction also stated a new conception of political parties as agencies of the people. When the Bucktails were attacked by their opponents as the "Albany Regency," a label suggesting the oppressive British regency of the Prince of Wales (1811–20), they replied with a strong defense of political parties, a defense that later Democrats and Whigs would echo. In America, they claimed, political parties drew their power from the people instead of from kings or aristocratic cliques; therefore, the American people could safely extend their loyalty to parties. American parties, far from being self-serving, required a selfless submission to the will of the organization. This respect for party discipline was later summed up by a prominent Whig who declared that he "would vote for a dog, if he was the candidate of my party." In theory, the excesses of one party would inevitably be exposed by the other party, and public opinion would decide between them. Responsiveness to the people would thus be ensured as each party strove to win the largest possible mandate from the people.

Van Buren's appeal for disciplined national parties came at an opportune time. As early as 1821 it was evident that the Virginia Dynasty of presidents would end in 1825 with Monroe's second term. The Republicans, no longer confronted by Federalist opponents, were splintering into personal and sectional factions. One group responded to the vibrant nationalism of Henry Clay's "American System"—a policy for economic expansion based on protective tariffs, a national bank, and federal aid for internal improvements. Other "Old Republicans," including Van Buren, viewed government intervention in the economy as a revival of the kinds of alliances between political power and special privilege that had corrupted Britain. By the early 1820s many Americans, especially in the South and West, had ample grounds for fearing that a northeastern elite would gain economic control of the nation's banks and system of credit.

Election of 1824.   Monroe's second administration was dominated by political maneuvering to determine who would be his successor. Three of the leading contenders—William H. Crawford, John Quincy Adams, and John C. Calhoun—were nationally distinguished members of Monroe's cabinet. Crawford, secretary of the treasury during several administrations, a Georgian born in Virginia, would be heavily favored in any congressional party caucus. He had won prestige as America's minister to France during the War of 1812 and as an advocate of state rights and limited federal power, he was supported by the aged Thomas Jefferson and other influential Virginians. Van Buren led the Crawford forces in Congress. But the skeleton congressional caucus that nominated Crawford carried little weight, and an incapacitating illness further diminished his chances.

The other leading candidates bypassed the established procedure of nomination by congressional party caucus and sought support from state legisla-

HENRY CLAY

Henry Clay's campaign posters stressed national economic growth and public welfare, goals to be directly fostered by protective tariffs and a national bank. *(Library of Congress)*

tures. Three of the remaining aspirants were closely associated with the economic nationalism that had alienated the Old Republicans. John Quincy Adams, the secretary of state and the nation's most experienced diplomat, could expect solid support from his native New England but would always be aloof from the rough-and-tumble electioneering of the South and West. John C. Calhoun, the secretary of war, had little support outside his native South Carolina. A graduate of Yale and a product of America's first small law school, in Connecticut, Calhoun was one of the few political leaders of his time who could be described as an "intellectual." Calhoun withdrew from the presidential race before the election, assuming that his almost certain choice as vice-president would help him win the highest office in 1828. Henry Clay, the popular "Harry of the West," had won national prestige as a parliamentarian and engineer of compromise in the House of Representatives. It was expected that if no candidate should win the electoral majority, the House would elect Clay president. But despite his appeal in Kentucky and other western states, Clay ran fourth in electoral votes and was therefore excluded by the Twelfth Amendment from further consideration.

The fifth candidate, Andrew Jackson, entered the contest unexpectedly and at a late stage. Unlike the other candidates, he had taken no clear stand on the controversial issues of the day, and his brief terms in the House and Senate had been undistinguished. Jackson's national fame arose from his victory over the British at the Battle of New Orleans in the War of 1812, and from his unswerving efforts to clear the West of Indians, thus promising limitless opportunity for white Americans. But "Old Hickory" was a good bit more than a military hero and an Indian fighter. Born on the Carolina frontier and orphaned at age fourteen, Jackson had studied law and had finally emigrated to Nashville, Tennessee, where he became attached by marriage and business connections to the local network of leading families. He prospered as an attorney, land speculator, and planter, and became the owner of over one hundred slaves. The Tennessee leaders who originally promoted Jackson for the presidency did not take his candidacy seriously, hoping only to use his popularity for their own local purposes. In 1823 Jackson's backers were astonished when the movement caught fire in Pennsylvania and other states. The Old Hero turned out to be an astute politician, who perfectly gauged the national temper and who, once launched on the road to the presidency, skillfully took charge of his own campaign.

In the election of 1824 Jackson won a plurality of both the popular and the electoral votes, and could therefore legitimately claim to be the choice of the people. But because no candidate had won an electoral majority, the responsibility of electing a president fell to the House of Representatives. There, Clay threw his decisive support behind Adams, who was elected president and who soon appointed Clay secretary of state. This so-called corrupt bargain deeply embittered Calhoun, who was already beginning to defect from his former colleagues' economic nationalism. It also infuriated Jackson, who almost immediately launched a campaign to unseat Adams in 1828.

John Quincy Adams as President.   This final collapse of Republican unity proved to be a disaster for Adams's presidency. Adams inaugurated his administration by proposing a sweeping program of federal support for internal improvements, science, education, and the arts. For example, he hoped that Congress would subsidize western explorations and an astronomical observatory. He soon discovered, however, that he lacked the mandate and the power for even the simple tasks of government. One of the most intelligent and farseeing presidents, Adams was also one of the least successful. Unfairly accused of being a monarchist with arrogant contempt for the people, he had the misfortune of inheriting the presidency when it had fallen into decay. His own experience with the realities of American political life helped to make him the unmourned victim, in 1828, of the first modern presidential contest.

Jackson's Rise to Power

Andrew Jackson, the leader of the rising Democratic coalition, precisely fitted the need for a popular national political leader. His stately bearing and natural dignity befitted one of "nature's noblemen," someone who had risen to greatness without benefit of family, formal education, or subservience to any faction. Jackson's promoters disseminated the roman-

J. Q. ADAMS, BY THOMAS GIMBREDE
John Quincy Adams personified the intellectual as statesman. A man of learning and of wide diplomatic experience, he was more at home in the courts and capitals of Europe than in the caucuses and public forums of American politics.   *(National Portrait Gallery, Smithsonian Institution, Washington, D.C.)*

tic mythology by every conceivable means: ballads, broadsides, barbecues, liberty pole-raisings, local committees, and militia companies. In contrast to the office-grubbing politicians and to the austere, highly cultivated John Quincy Adams, here was a frontiersman, a truly self-made man, a soldier of iron will who personified the will of the people, a man without artifice or pretension who moved decisively in the light of simple moral truths. The Jackson image, in short, was an image of reassuring stability in the face of bewildering social and economic change.

Jackson also fitted the need for a leader who

comprehended the new meaning of party politics. Against the Adams-Clay alliance he molded a coalition that included among other groups the followers of Calhoun (who became his running mate in 1828), Virginia's Old Republicans, influential Westerners who had become disillusioned with Clay, former Federalists who had lost office in New Jersey, and Van Buren's powerful Albany Regency. This new Democratic party appealed to many urban workers and immigrants, to frontier expansionists and Indian haters, to many southern planters, and to various northeastern editors, bankers, and manufacturers who built local Democratic machines as the means of gaining or preserving power.

The "Tariff of Abominations."   Jackson's state organizers, looking ahead to 1828, bypassed the local ruling gentry and concentrated for the first time on mobilizing the necessary popular vote to capture the full electoral vote of critical states. Because the new coalition contained Pennsylvanians who clamored for higher tariffs and South Carolinians who detested tariffs, keeping unity required delicate manipulation. In 1828 Jackson's leaders in Congress helped to pass the so-called Tariff of Abominations, an opportunistic bill which made arbitrary concessions to various groups demanding protection. They assumed that southern support for Jackson was secure, that the new duties on raw materials would win votes from northern and western protectionists, and that the most objectionable provisions could be blamed on the Adams administration. The subsequent outrage in the South suggested that Jackson as president could no longer get by with vague statements favoring a "judicious" tariff. Yet Southerners knew that a Jackson-Calhoun alliance was far more promising than the economic nationalism of Adams and Clay, who were now known as National Republicans.

The Election of 1828.   In a general sense, the election of 1828 affirmed the people's rejection of policies that seemed to encourage special privilege, except for the privilege of owning slaves and counting three-fifths of the slave population for purposes of representation. In the South, Jackson's 200,000 supporters,

accounting for 73 percent of that section's vote, gave him 105 electoral votes; in the North, where he won only slightly more than half the popular vote, his 400,000 supporters gave him only 73 electoral votes. The election also proved the effectiveness of campaign organization and of the promotional techniques that Jackson's managers, particularly Van Buren, had perfected.

Once in power, the Democrats soon adopted two instruments that solidified popular support for party rule. The first was a system of patronage, or "spoils," which continued practices begun during previous administrations and tried to give them legitimacy. Jackson ardently defended the theory that most public offices required no special abilities or experience, that they should frequently rotate among loyal deserving party workers, and that party rule should prevent the establishment of a permanent and parasitic class of civil servants. In fact, however, he actually removed no more than one-fifth of the surviving federal officeholders.

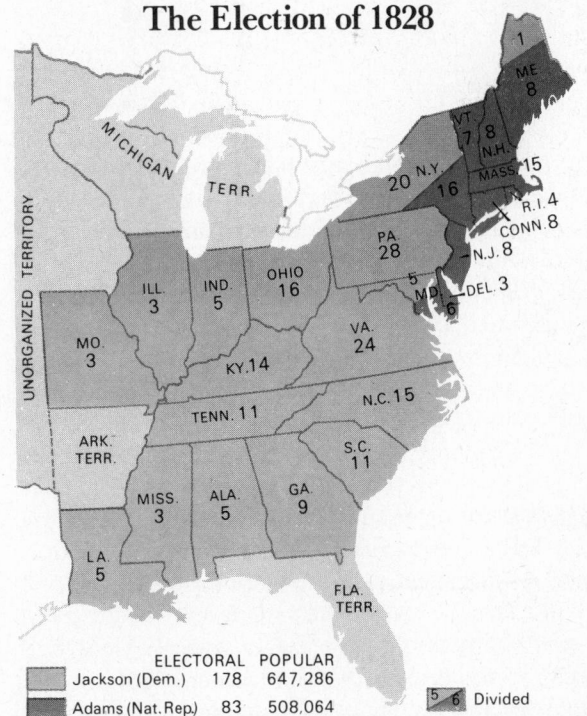

The Election of 1828

	ELECTORAL	POPULAR
Jackson (Dem.)	178	647,286
Adams (Nat. Rep.)	83	508,064

5 6 Divided

JACKSON TICKET

Honor and gratitude to the man who has filled the measure of his country's glory—Jefferson

FOR THE ASSEMBLY
GEORGE H. STEUART,
JOHN V. L. McMAHON.

JACKSON POSTER, 1828
In the presidential campaign of 1828, Andrew Jackson appeared as a symbol of patriotism, military honor, and faithful preservation of the ideals of the Founding Fathers. *(Library of Congress)*

The second mechanism was the national party convention, which, like various Jacksonian measures, had earlier been initiated by anti-Jacksonian forces. As an alternative to nomination by legislative caucus, the "convention," by its name, suggested a return to fundamental law, to the direct voice of the people assembled in a constitution-framing body. Although party conventions could do no more than frame partisan platforms and nominate partisan candidates, they pretended to represent the true interests of the people. In theory, since they drew representatives from a broad spectrum of society, they were more democratic than legislative caucuses. In practice, they were more subject to manipulation by political machines. But like the partisan spoils system, the party convention symbolized the central appeal of Jackson's party. It promised to break the congealing crust of privilege and eliminate all institutional barriers to individual opportunity. It also provided the assurance of solidarity with a party headed by a man of the people, a man who magnified the idealized self-image of millions of Americans.

Certain principles and aspirations distinguished the Jacksonian Democrats from their National Republican (later Whig) opponents. Jackson had long given voice to the West's demand for territorial expansion as a way to ensure economic opportunity. As the first Westerner elected to the presidency, he symbolized a geographical shift in political power. Of course, not all Westerners supported Jackson. Those who understood that western economic expansion depended on access to eastern markets and on investment capital from the East and Europe favored federal aid for internal improvements, a program that Henry Clay championed. But though Jackson vetoed the Maysville Road Bill, which authorized funds to build a road in Kentucky, suggesting that federal support for internal improvements was unconstitutional, he did not lose the majority of western voters. Many Westerners had come to view federally supported internal improvements as sources of waste and corruption. Others learned that despite Jackson's pronouncements federal support for roads and canals continued to pour in from a Congress less concerned with constitutional theory than with constituents' needs. On the whole, the West cheered for Jackson because it had come to see itself as the repository of values that Jackson fought for: an agrarian society of independent farmers, committed to individual enterprise and local self-determination.

To say Jacksonian Democrats were advocates of laissez-faire is accurate but insufficient. They knew that on the local and state levels, economic opportunity hinged on political power. And Jackson was the most forceful and aggressive president since Washington. During preceding administrations the chief executive's powers had been siphoned off by cabinet rivals and a jealous Congress. With the aid of party discipline, Jackson soon exerted his dominance over Congress by an unprecedented use of vetoes and pocket vetoes (the refusal to sign a bill during the last ten days of a congressional session). Except for Van Buren, whom he chose as secretary of state,

ANDREW JACKSON
In this homey carving President Jackson appears as a gaunt, stern, rough-hewn man of the people, a democratized Washington. *(Museum of the City of New York)*

Jackson treated his cabinet in the manner of the army's commander in chief. Unlike his predecessors, Jackson escaped the coercion of disloyal and powerful cabinet members by relying on a group of informal advisers, the so-called Kitchen Cabinet, who could be trusted or dismissed at will.

The Threat of National Division: Tariffs, Nullification, and the Gag Rule

Protective Tariffs. Tariffs and fiscal policy were obvious testing grounds for defining the role of the federal government in national economic life. Because the economy was still more regional than national and because the national government had so few functions, the critical issues of the era grew out of the commitment to protective tariffs and a national bank that had resulted from the War of 1812. The Middle Atlantic states, the most vulnerable to competition from European manufactured goods, had long been the political stronghold of protectionism. During the 1820s, as New England's economy became increasingly dependent on the production of wool and on textile manufacturing, Daniel Webster and other New England leaders abandoned their traditional defense of free trade and portrayed protective tariffs as the key to economic growth and individual opportunity. Simultaneously, the Lower South became increasingly hostile to tariffs that threatened to raise the price of manufactured goods and to curtail foreign markets for rice and cotton. For a time the Democrats successfully arranged compromises among the various interests and regions represented in the party. In 1832, however, Congress passed a tariff bill that was unresponsive to the demands of the Lower South. South Carolina thereupon defied federal authority and sought to arouse the rest of the slaveholding South to the dangers of being victimized economically by the federal government. South Carolinians believed that acceptance of such dependence would reduce the state to the status of a colony and deprive it of any effective protection against antislavery ideas.

South Carolina's sudden threat of disunion severely tested the American political system, and it involved issues that went far beyond the protective tariff. In no other state had a planter aristocracy succeeded so well in commanding the allegiance of small farmers, both slaveholding and nonslaveholding, and in preventing the development of an effective two-party system. Despite continuing conflicts between the coastal and upcountry regions, there were few checks on state-rights extremists who were able to exploit fears of slave insurrection and anger over persisting agricultural depression, high consumer prices, and sagging prices for rice and cotton in foreign markets.

Moreover, of all the southern states South Carolina had the closest historical, geographical, and cultural ties with the British West Indies. Like those British colonies, South Carolina had a dense concentration of slaves, and its merchants and planters had continued to import African slaves until 1808, when the slave trade was prohibited by federal law. South Carolinians were acutely aware that in Britain a seemingly innocuous movement to end the slave trade had been transformed, by 1823, into a crusade for slave emancipation. And they knew that the West Indians, though still a powerful faction in Parliament, had found no way of countering commercial policies that had hastened their economic decline. The lesson was clear. The West Indian colonies had once been far richer and more valued than Canada or New England; in 1832 they faced possible devastation—a massive slave revolt broke out in Jamaica after Christmas 1831—and certain economic ruin.

Theory of Nullification.

South Carolina could escape a similar fate, the state's leaders believed, only by reasserting state sovereignty and insisting on the strict limitation of national power. The tariff issue made an ideal testing ground for the defense of slavery without risking the explosive effects of debating the morality of slaveholding. Because the power to tax and regulate trade could also be used to undermine slavery, the two questions had been linked in the Constitutional Convention of 1787 and in the Missouri debates. Conversely, a state's power to nullify a tariff would be a guarantee not only against economic exploitation but also against direct or in-

JOHN C. CALHOUN, 1782–1850
(National Archives)

direct interference with slavery. Calhoun, in his anonymous *Exposition* (1828), refined the theoretical arguments that were being put forth by South Carolina's most militant leaders. According to Calhoun the ultimate appeal, in any dispute between federal and state interests, must be directed to a state convention, the same power that originally enabled the state to ratify the Constitution. Otherwise, a national majority, controlling the federal courts as well as Congress, would have unlimited power. The tyranny of the majority could be curbed only if each state retained the right to consent or to nullify, within its own jurisdiction, the national majority's decisions. Calhoun carefully distinguished nullification from secession. He looked for means by which states might exercise an authentic, though limited, sovereignty while remaining within the Union.

The nullification controversy was complicated by the shifting pressures of state, sectional, and national politics. Calhoun, the vice-president, hoped to succeed Jackson as president, and many South Carolinians still believed they could achieve their goals through the Democratic party. Calhoun did not divulge his authorship of the *Exposition* until 1831, when he had split with Jackson over various personal and political issues. When Jackson purged Calhoun's followers from his cabinet and administration, Van Buren became in effect the president's chosen successor. Nevertheless, Calhoun continued to aspire to the presidency. He believed nullification would be a means of satisfying South Carolina's "fire-eater" extremists and of establishing the Union on a more secure basis, while still preserving his own national following.

By 1832, however, South Carolina had become increasingly isolated from the rest of the South and had also failed to unite the West against an alleged northeastern conspiracy to discourage western settlement. Though many Southerners detested protective tariffs and maintained that states had a right to secede from the Union, southern legislatures turned a stony face to nullification. As a result, there was no regional convention of southern delegates that might have moderated South Carolina's suicidal course by reinforcing the hand of the South Carolina unionists who risked their lives and reputations in a violent and losing struggle with the extremists. In the fall of 1832 South Carolina held a state convention that directly challenged federal authority by making it unlawful after February 1, 1833, to collect tariff duties within the state.

South Carolina chose the wrong president to test. Andrew Jackson was a wealthy slaveholder but he was also a shrewd politician. Though his maturing views on tariffs and internal improvements were close to those of South Carolina's oligarchy, he had fought for the military supremacy of the United States, crushing British and Indian armies; had hanged English meddlers in Spanish Florida; and had ordered the execution of an unruly teenage soldier. He was probably the toughest of America's presidents. When South Carolina nullified the tariff of 1832, the old

general privately threatened to lead an invation of the state and to have Calhoun hanged. He sent reinforcements to the Federal forts in Charleston harbor, but publicly sought to avoid armed conflict by relying on civilian revenue agents to enforce the law and by warning that armed resistance would be punished as treason.

As in 1820, the crisis ended in a compromise which failed to resolve fundamental conflicts of interest and ideology. In an attempt to head off civil war, Henry Clay, assisted by Calhoun, secured the passing of a compromise bill that would gradually reduce tariff duties over a period of nine years. But this measure was accompanied by a "force bill," reaffirming the president's authority to use the army and navy when necessary, to enforce Federal laws. South Carolina's fire-eaters continued to call for armed resistance; the governor recruited a volunteer army. Early in 1833, however, the state convention repealed its earlier nullification of the tariff and, to save face, nullified the force bill. Jackson ignored this defiant gesture. He had already proscribed as unlawful and unconstitutional the claim that any state could annul the laws of the United States. In effect, he had told rebellious states that secession was their only escape, and that secession would be met with armed force.

"Gag Rules." The compromise did not allay South Carolina's suspicions and anxieties. The nullification controversy had failed to provide the assurance of constitutional safeguards against a hostile national majority. Southern extremists demanded ironclad guarantees that would permanently bar the abolitionists' "incendiary publications" from the mails and prevent Congress from receiving petitions calling for the abolition of slavery in the District of Columbia. In actuality, the Democratic party fulfilled these objectives in a less formal way. The Jackson and Van Buren administrations, dependent on the large Democratic vote in the South, encouraged federal postmasters to stop abolitionist literature at its point of origin. Despite continuing protest from northern Whigs, northern Democrats also provided southern congressmen of both parties with enough votes to maintain "gag rules" from 1836 to 1844, a procedure that automatically tabled abolitionist petitions in Congress and helped prevent explosive debates on the subject of slavery. Many Northerners were outraged by these infringements on civil and political liberties. But South Carolinians were also dissatisfied with pragmatic mechanisms for security that depended on the continuing support of the national Democratic party. Without further constitutional protections, they feared that a shift in northern opinion might induce Congress to withdraw all federal sanction and protection for slavery.

The Bank War, The Panic of 1837, and Political Realignments

The Bank War.   Meanwhile, President Jackson had enhanced his national popularity by declaring "war" on the Second Bank of the United States (BUS). Jackson had long harbored a mistrust of banks in general, especially of the BUS. Van Buren, Senator Thomas Hart Benton of Missouri, Amos Kendall of the Kitchen Cabinet, and other key presidential advisers shared these sentiments. To understand their "hard-money" position, it is important to remember that the national government issued no "paper money" like that in circulation today. Payment for goods and services might be in gold or silver coin (specie) or, more likely, in paper notes issued by private commercial banks. The value of such paper currency fluctuated greatly. The hard-money Democrats realized that large commercial transactions could not be carried on with specie. But they believed that the common people, including small businessmen as well as farmers and wage earners, should not be saddled with the risk of being cheated by a speculative currency. They also knew that a policy favoring the greater circulation of gold and silver coin, which seemed magically endowed with some fixed and "natural" value, would win votes for the party.

To a large degree, however, the reserves and transfers of specie were controlled by the BUS. The BUS performed many of the functions of a truly national bank. Its own notes could be exchanged for specie, and they were accepted by the government as legal payment for all debts to the United States. Because the BUS had large capital reserves and because it limited the issue of its own highly stable notes, it occupied a creditor position relative to the hundreds of state-chartered banks throughout the country. It served as a clearinghouse and regulatory agency for their money, refusing to accept notes that were not backed by sufficient reserves of specie. By promoting monetary stability, the BUS helped to improve the public reputation of banks in general and eased the difficulties of long-distance transfers of goods and credit. It also mobilized a national reserve of capital on which other banks could draw. Consequently most state banks favored congressional renewal of the BUS charter, which was scheduled to expire in 1836.

Opponents of the bank feared the concentration of so much economic power in a few hands and worried that the federal government had practically no control over the bank, although it provided one-fifth of the bank's capital. The bank's critics complained that, even under the expert presidency of Nicholas Biddle, this partly public institution was far more oriented to the interests of its private investors than to the interests of the general public. Senator Daniel Webster, the main lobbyist for rechartering the BUS, not only was the director of the Boston branch (the BUS headquarters was in Philadelphia), but relied heavily on Biddle for private loans and fees for legal and political services. In Jackson's eyes the BUS had become a "monster institution," unconstitutionally diverting public funds for private profit.

The celebrated "Bank War" erupted into open conflict in 1832, when Webster and Clay launched a legislative offensive, partly to prevent Jackson's reelection. Knowing that they could win support from many Democrats for the passage of a bill rechartering the BUS, they were confident that the president could not veto the measure without fatally damaging his chances for reelection in the fall. Jackson took up the challenge. In a masterful veto message he spelled out the principles that would be a touchstone for "Jacksonian democracy" and for populist politics in the decades to come. He denounced the BUS as a

"THE DOWNFALL OF MOTHER BANK"
In this popular cartoon Jackson's removal of federal deposits from the Bank of the United States carries overtones of Christ's chasing the money lenders from the ancient temple. Biddle, in the form of the devil, flees along with Webster, Clay, and the various minions of the Money Power. *(Library of Congress)*

priviliged monopoly, and vowed to take a stand "against all new grants of monopolies and exclusive privileges, against any prostitution of our Government to the advancement of the few at the expense of the many." Jackson in no way favored leveling wealth or other distinctions derived from "natural and just advantages." "Equality of talents, of education, or of wealth," he affirmed, "cannot be produced by human institutions." But government should provide "equal protection, and, as heaven does its rains, shower its favors alike on the high and the low, the rich and the poor." The BUS, he declared, represented a flagrant example of government subsidy to the privileged, of laws that made "the rich richer and the potent more powerful." Jackson also warned of the dangerous provisions that allowed foreigners to buy BUS stock and thus to acquire influence over American policy. In

defiance of the Supreme Court's decision in *McCulloch v. Maryland* (1819), he argued that the BUS was unconstitutional.

Although Webster and other conservative leaders immediately cried that the president was trying "to stir up the poor against the rich," the election of 1832 decisively vindicated Jackson's bold leadership and political shrewdness. Old Hickory would have won a sweeping victory even if the opposition votes had not been divided between Henry Clay, the National Republican candidate, and William Wirt, the reluctant leader of the Anti-Masons. Confident now that the supporters of the BUS could never override his veto, Jackson vowed to defang the "monster institution" by removing all of the deposits placed in the bank by the federal government.

This aggressive policy was opposed by many of

DANIEL WEBSTER, 1782–1852
(*Culver Pictures, Inc.*)

ever, without adding to popular hostility to the bank. In the winter of 1832–33 Biddle did retrench, but the constriction of credit was not serious enough to shake Jackson's resolution. The president also gained political leverage through his discriminating choice of pet banks. Many bankers who had earlier hoped to keep clear of the political struggle were eager for interest-free federal funds that would allow them to expand loans and other commercial operations. Jackson's victory was fairly complete by the spring of 1834.

Jackson's Hard-Money Policy. Like many triumphs, the destruction of the BUS enmeshed the victors in a web of problems. The Democrats claimed that by slaying the "monster," they had purged the nation of a moral evil. Yet the deposit of federal funds in pet banks encouraged the expansion of credit, and in the mid-1830s the nation reeled from the intoxication of a speculative boom. Some of the orthodox Jacksonian officials even bemoaned the growing federal surplus—an unimaginable phenomenon to later generations who have only known federal deficits and mounting public debts—because there seemed to be no place to put the funds that would not corrupt the Republic. Whatever the administration did invited trouble. On the one hand, if it distributed funds to the states, it fed the speculative boom by encouraging further construction of roads and canals and other kinds of "improvements." On the other hand, if it kept the funds in the pet banks, these banks clearly had to be regulated by the federal government, lest they too feed inflation by issuing vast quantities of paper money based on this reserve.

Slowly Jackson and his successor, Van Buren, who was elected in 1836, moved toward a policy of hard money. They tried to reduce or eliminate the circulation of small-denomination bank notes and to set a minimal requirement for the pet banks' specie reserves. In 1836 Jackson also issued an executive order, the so-called "specie circular," requiring payments in specie for purchase of public land. The specie circular represented a direct federal effort to curb speculation and thus to manage the fluctuations of the economy. This controversial measure signaled the

the president's advisers, since the BUS already appeared to be doomed. The removal policy also raised new problems. According to Jackson's plan, which his secretary of the treasury, Roger B. Taney, soon put into execution, federal funds would be dispersed among chosen state-chartered banks that were soon dubbed "pet" banks. For the policy to succeed, Jackson had to persuade the banking community that decentralization would not bring economic disaster. Nicholas Biddle, on the other hand, needed to produce a minor financial panic to underscore the powerful role of the BUS in maintaining financial stability. Biddle could not exert his full financial powers, how-

"THE TIMES"

This complex cartoon portrays the allegedly disastrous results of the Democratic rule: the government's hard money policy leads to a run on the bank, which has suspended specie payments; the custom house is deserted; debtors are herded into the sheriff's office; beggars and unemployed artisans crowd the streets; scenes of drunkenness are linked with the unruliness of immigrants and Locofoco radicals. *(Library of Congress)*

growing dominance of the antibank and hard-money factions in the Democratic party. The subsequent nomination and election of Van Buren strengthened the hand of those Democrats who found hostility to all banks politically effective.

The Panic of 1837. In 1837 a banking panic brought an abrupt end to the speculative boom, and by 1839 a severe depression had developed that persisted to the mid-1840s. This painful downturn in investment, prices, and employment was mainly the product of a business cycle still tied to agriculture (especially cotton), and related to English demand, English in-

vestment, and the international flow of silver. In many respects the American economy still resembled that of a colony or underdeveloped nation dependent on foreign investment and on raw material exports. Hence it was vulnerable to sudden contractions of British credit coupled with temporary drops in the British demand for cotton. As bankruptcies multiplied, the business community blamed the widespread suffering on Jacksonian fiscal policies which had first fueled reckless expansion by destroying the BUS and then had suddenly curtailed credit by requiring specie for the purchase of public land. But as bankers and businessmen deserted the Democratic party, the reigning hard-money, laissez-faire faction argued that the economic collapse proved the folly of government partnership with even pet banks.

After three years of bitter intraparty struggle, President Van Buren finally achieved a "divorce of bank and state" with the passage of the Independent Treasury Act (1840). By locking federal funds in "independent" subtreasuries of the United States government insulated from the banking community, this measure deprived the banking system of reserves that might have encouraged loans and aided economic recovery.

Laissez-faire Capitalism.   In summary, the Democrats' program can be illuminated by pointing to two inconsistencies. First, their economic policies did little to aid the groups of farmers and artisans the Democrats claimed to represent. If the political attacks on special privilege served to revitalize democratic ideology, the ultimate beneficiaries were the southern planters who were aided by Indian removal, lowered tariffs, and the suppression of antislavery literature and petitions. Moreover, the policy of economic laissez-faire seemed to offer the South assurance that the federal government would not interfere with the interstate movement of slave labor. By 1838 Calhoun and his followers, who had earlier seceded from the Democratic party, returned to the fold, and as it turned out, Calhoun's return paved the way for southern domination of the party in the two decades to come.

Second, the nation's banking continued to grow into an integrated system, and the nation's economy continued to grow with serene disregard for the fluctuations of politics. The attempts of Jackson and Van Buren to withdraw the government from what they saw as a corrupting economy had little effect on the general trends of economic development.

Whigs and the Two-Party System

For most of the thirty years following Jackson's 1828 victory the Democrats ruled the White House. Between 1828 and 1856 their presidential nominees defeated every opposition candidate except William Henry Harrison (1840) and Zachary Taylor (1848), both of whom died in office. John Tyler, the vice-president who succeeded Harrison only a month after the latter's inauguration, soon returned to his original Virginia Democratic loyalties and principles. Millard Fillmore, Zachary Taylor's successor, was a genial but colorless Whig party hack who began his political career as an Anti-Mason and ended it by running for president in 1856 on the nativist and anti-Catholic "Know-Nothing" or American party ticket.

But the Democrats' dominance of the presidency is deceptive. By the late 1830s Whigs could match Democratic strength in most parts of the country. Though the South has commonly been pictured as a preserve for state-rights Democrats, Whigs predominated as the South's representatives in three out of five Congresses elected between 1832 and 1842. Whig strength was particularly evident on local, county, and state levels. For the viability of the two-party system depended essentially on vigorous local conflict—on the ability of a second party to challenge incumbents by convincing voters that a genuine alternative was available. To maintain partisan loyalties, leaders tried to exploit or manufacture conflicts, to dramatize party differences, and to be responsive enough to public demands to convince voters that their grievances could be resolved through the ballot. Whigs, like the Democrats, claimed to represent the interests of the *excluded* people against a privileged and self-serving "power." Since no incumbent party could possibly avoid patronage, the game of two-party politics consisted of proving that incumbents were partial to their friends and thus insincere in professing to serve the common good. In effect, both parties were torn between a desire to battle for the special interests of their permanent constituency and a need to advocate bland, lofty goals that would attract the widest possible national following.

Webster, Clay, and Calhoun.   Like the Democratic party, the Whigs were a wholly new coalition. They were not, as the Democrats charged, simply Federalists in disguise—the Democrats themselves recruited an impressive number of ex-Federalist leaders. In

BORN TO COMMAND

OF VETO MEMORY

HAD I BEEN CONSULTED

KING ANDREW THE FIRST.

"KING ANDREW THE FIRST"
The Whig image of Jackson as an autocratic king, brandishing the veto and trampling the Constitution under foot. *(Library of Congress)*

Congress the Whigs first began to emerge in a legislative rebellion against Jackson's "Executive Usurpation." During the summer of 1832 Jackson's veto of the bill rechartering the BUS led to the temporary coalition of three of the most formidable senators in American history. All three longed for the presidency. By 1832 they had won fame as three mythical gods, deliverers of Olympian oratory that dazzled aspiring young men.

Daniel Webster struck the keynote when he attacked "King Andrew" as a reincarnation of the French monarch who had declared, "I am the State." A man of humble New Hampshire origins and aristocratic Boston tastes, Webster had risen in the legal

profession by emulating and paying deference to New England's commercial elite. He was a heavy drinker, given to extravagant living and continual debt. His sonorous voice and commanding physical presence could never quite convey the moral sincerity that most northeastern Whigs expected of their leaders. Yet Webster upheld their traditional mistrust of divisive parties and their traditional ideal of government by "disinterested gentlemen." He succeeded in blending this conservative tradition with a celebration of material and moral progess. As the agent of commercial and manufacturing interests in Massachusetts, he was flexible enough to shift his style of argument from the forums of the Supreme Court and the Senate to the stump of popular politics, always pleading for the natural harmony of interests that the Democratic party threatened to undermine.

Henry Clay considered himself a Jeffersonian Republican and the leader of the National Republicans, the label originally applied to Jackson's opponents. The author of the American System, designed to maximize federal support for industry, economic growth, and national self-sufficiency, Clay joined Webster's assaults on Jackson's alleged despotism. Clay was a Kentuckian of Virginia birth, and had also risen from humble origin. Like Webster, he was notorious for extravagant living, though Clay's self-indulgence took the typically southern forms of gambling, dueling, and horse-racing. A slave-owning planter and brilliant courtroom lawyer, Clay assumed two contradictory political roles. He competed with Jackson as a western man of the people, a coonskin man of nature. But Clay had also helped to negotiate the Treaty of Ghent ending the War of 1812; he had been Adams's secretary of state; and he represented the western business and commercial interests that demanded federal aid for internal improvements. One of the greatest political manipulators in nineteenth-century America, Clay had talents unequaled in caucuses, committee rooms, and all-night boardinghouse negotiations.

The most unpredictable member of the anti-Jackson triumvirate was John C. Calhoun, who had shifted in the 1820s from militant nationalism to a militant defense of slavery and state rights, and who had been Jackson's nominal ally until personal conflicts had provoked a fatal split. Despite Calhoun's dramatic turnabouts, contemporaries admired the clarity and logical force of his arguments and respected his earlier distinguished service as secretary of war. But Calhoun's role in the nullification controversy made him a dangerous ally in the developing Whig coalition. Most southern Whig leaders shared the economic and nationalistic views of their northern brethren; Calhoun did not.

Whig Philosophy.   The Whig outlook on the world was almost too diffuse to be termed an ideology. Like the Democrats, Whigs gloried in the dream of America's future as the greatest nation the world had ever seen, and they found confirmation for that dream in the measurable growth of population, wealth, and power. Far more than the Democrats, they associated the "spirit of improvement" with concrete technological and social inventions. They assumed that steam power, the telegraph, railroads, banks, corporations, prisons, factories, asylums, and public schools all contributed to an advancing civilization and to an increasing equality of opportunity. On both social and individual levels, they advocated saving from income, capital accumulation, budgetary planning, and fiscal responsibility. They opposed aggressive territorial expansion as a cure-all for economic problems. They insisted that America's expansion and power should be harnessed to social ends and stabilized by publicly acknowledged moral boundaries. Alarmed by the excesses of rampant individualism, they expressed continuing and sometimes hysterical concern over the loss of community—over the demagogues who won support by inciting the poor against the rich, children against parents, wives against husbands, and geographic section against geographic section.

Whigs thought of themselves as conservatives and often invoked European theories that stressed the organic unity of society and the necessity of balancing human rights with social duties. Yet the Whig ideal of government was essentially optimistic and progressive. In 1825, long before the Whig party began to coalesce, John Quincy Adams advanced the

central Whig proposition that the Constitution had given the central government both the duty and the necessary powers to promote "the progressive improvement of the condition of the governed."

On a popular level the Whig party began to appear by 1834 as a loose coalition of state and local groups opposed to Jacksonian Democrats. Reluctant to allow the Jacksonians a monopoly of the popular label "democrat," the anti-Jacksonians sometimes called themselves Democratic Whigs. The final acceptance of the term "Whig" was significant. Superficially the label suggested an identity with the British "country" party which had allegedly defended the British constitution against the despotism of the pro-Catholic Stuart kings and the later executive encroachments of George III. This imagery linked "King Andrew" with the various reactionary and demagogic monarchs of Europe. Such parallels may seem farfetched, but the very act of drawing parallels with Europe contained a deeper significance. Unlike the Democrats, the Whigs tended to deny the uniqueness of the American experience and to place less faith in political institutions than in economic and cultural progress. They also tended to look on Britain, despite its monarchic and aristocratic institutions, as a model of economic and cultural progress. For the most thoughtful Whig spokesmen, America was less a revolutionary departure from the rest of the world than a testing ground for progressive forces that were universal and depended essentially on moral character.

The Whig Constituency.   In all parts of the country Whigs attracted a broad cross section of the electorate, a cross section, however, often weighted in favor of the wealthy, the privileged, and the aspiring, but including—paradoxically—the victims of overt discrimination. In the North this constituency included most of the free blacks; British and German Protestant immigrants; manual laborers sympathetic with their employers' interests; business-oriented farmers; educators, reformers, and professional people; well-to-do merchants, bankers, and manufacturers; and active members of the Presbyterian, Unitarian, and Congregationalist churches. In the South the party had particular appeal to urban merchants, editors, bankers, and to those farmers and planters who associated progress with expanding commerce, capital accumulation, railroads, and economic partnership with the North.

During their initial stages of organization the Whigs faced three formidable problems. First, in the populous northern states like New York, Pennsylvania, and Massachusetts they had to find strategies for uniting the economic interests of the National Republicans with the moral and cultural aspirations of various groups alienated by the incumbent Democrats. Second, they had to get rid of the elitist stigma that had been fastened on John Quincy Adams and then on the defenders of the BUS, and somehow prove that they were better democrats than the Democrats. Finally, they had to find delicate maneuvers for bypassing senatorial prima donnas like Webster and Clay and selecting less controversial presidential candidates who could appeal to the nation without arousing dissension and jealousy among the various state party organizations.

The way these problems were met is well illustrated by the career of Thurlow Weed of New York, who became the prototype of the nineteenth-century political boss and manipulator. A self-made man, Weed first acquired a voice in New York politics as editor of the Rochester *Telegraph* and as a bitter foe of Van Buren's Albany Regency. In 1827 Weed and his young protégé William H. Seward took up the cause of Anti-Masonry as a means of embarrassing the ruling Van Buren machine. In western New York, Anti-Masonry had suddenly erupted as a kind of religious crusade after the abduction and probable murder of a former Freemason who was thought to have divulged the secrets of the fraternal society. The crusade expressed widespread popular resentment against an organization that knit many of the wealthier and more powerful urban leaders of the state into a secret brotherhood pledged to mutual aid and support. Weed and Seward succeeded in portraying the Van Buren regime as the agent of Freemasonry—a "monster institution"—intent on suppressing legal investigation and prosecution of the alleged murder, and on disguising statewide links between Masonic political influence and economic privilege. This antielitist rhetoric helped to counteract the Democrats' claims of being the true champions of the people against the unpopular Adams administration in Washington. By 1830 Anti-Masons captured approximately one-half the popular vote in New York State. When the movement showed increasing signs of strength in other northern states, Weed and other strategists worked to absorb the National Republicans into a new anti-Jackson coalition.

But though the Anti-Masons organized the first national political convention in American history, Weed began to sense that the movement could be no more than a springboard for a successful national party. Weed launched his powerful Albany *Evening Journal* as an Anti-Masonic organ, but he increasingly downplayed Masonry and combined blistering attacks on the Albany Regency with the advocacy of various social reforms. To his political cronies and businessmen backers Weed kept insisting that the Jacksonians could never be beaten so long as they continued to persuade the people that they represented "the principle of democracy ... the poor against the rich." By 1834 Weed had abandoned Anti-Masonry and had succeeded in organizing a New York Whig coalition.

In 1836, when the Whigs tried to broaden their appeal by nominating various regional candidates for president, including Daniel Webster of Massachusetts and Hugh White of Tennessee, it was Weed's candidate, William Henry Harrison of Ohio, who won the most electoral votes. "Old Tippecanoe," famous for his military defeat of the Shawnee Indians in 1811, appealed to many former Anti-Masons and won strong support in the South as well as in New York, Ohio, and Pennsylvania. After years of patient organizing, wire-pulling, and passing out cigars, Weed finally came into his own in 1838 when he succeeded in getting Seward elected governor of New York. As the master of patronage, the official state printer, and the "dictator" of the New York machine, Weed was now in a position to challenge his old archrival Van Buren, who claimed to be the president of the common people.

TIPPECANOE ROARER

By 1840 the Whigs could match the Democrats as a popular people's party with their own distinctive songs, clubs, and political symbols. *(Courtesy, The Cincinnati Historical Society)*

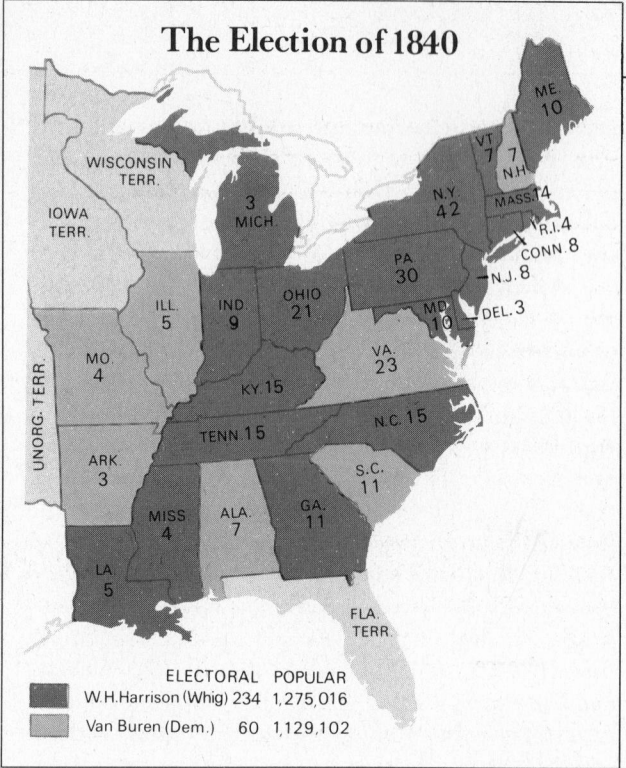

The Election of 1840

	ELECTORAL	POPULAR
W.H.Harrison (Whig)	234	1,275,016
Van Buren (Dem.)	60	1,129,102

The Election of 1840. In 1840 Weed played a key role in blocking the Whigs' nomination of Clay and in opening the way for Harrison. Weed's young protégé, Horace Greeley, edited the Whigs' most influential paper, *The Log Cabin,* which set the pace by attacking President Van Buren as an affected dandy who had transformed the White House into a palace of effeminate luxury. Greeley and others cast Harrison as a frontiersman of simple tastes; his symbols were a barrel of cider (whether hard or soft depended on the locality), and a log cabin with a welcoming

coonskin at the door. Harrison's victory seemed to show that strategists like Weed had overcome the Whigs' political liabilities. They could rival the Democrats in populistic appeals, in carnival-like hucksterism, and above all, in grass-roots organization.

Nevertheless, the Whigs never found a magnetic national leader who, like Jackson for the Democrats, could become a unifying symbol for their party. John Tyler, the vice-president who succeeded Harrison, soon betrayed the economic principles of the party. In 1844 Clay went down to defeat for a third time, after which the Whigs returned to the tested expedient of nominating apolitical military heroes, Zachary Taylor in 1848 and Winfield Scott in 1852.

The Whigs' difficulties went beyond the weakness of their presidential candidates. Despite their political pragmatism and impressive party discipline, the Whigs contained a militant, reform-minded element that resented the compromises necessary for a national party. Anti-Masonry had been one of the early expressions of such reformist and issue-oriented politics, and many of the Anti-Masons who joined the Whigs had never been comfortable with the opportunism of leaders like Thurlow Weed, who placed victory above principle. In addition to the Anti-Masons, the Whig party became the uneasy lodging place for people who wanted laws enforcing a stricter Sabbath, laws prohibiting the sale of alcohol, laws barring slavery in the territories and abolishing slavery in the District of Columbia, and laws prolonging the time before an immigrant could be naturalized or allowed to vote. These causes were nourished by the spread of Protestant religious revivals in the North. Among southern Whigs and hard-headed supporters of Clay's American System they had little appeal.

Limitations of the Two-Party System.   Nevertheless, while a national party's strength depended on a continuing sensitivity to the needs of its constituent groups, it also served as a disciplining and educational force, imposing definite limits to individual, local, and regional self-assertion. The political issues of the 1840s tended to reinforce such party loyalty.

The majority of state legislators adhered to a strict Whig or Democratic vote even when a different position might have harmonized more with local or personal interests. The appointment of loyal party men to positions in local land offices, post offices, and customhouses established Whig or Democratic nerve centers at the grass-roots level. Until the early 1850s, when voters became disillusioned with traditional alternatives and when the Whig party began to fall apart, the two-party system worked as a powerful cohesive force in American society. Unfortunately this political stability rested on the illusion of consistent and sharply defined differences between two parties which were intended to represent the interests of only white Americans. If the existence of national parties succeeded in moderating sectional conflict, it was at the cost of suppressing alternatives to the expansion of slavery and of stifling national debate over America's most dangerous conflict of interest.

CHRONOLOGY

1820   Missouri Compromise.
Maine admitted as 23rd state.
Reelection of James Monroe without opposition symbolizes "Era of Good Feelings."

1821   Henry Clay effects "Second Missouri Compromise."
Missouri admitted as 24th state.

1822   Denmark Vesey's conspiracy to lead massive slave uprising in South Carolina exposed.

1824   John Quincy Adams elected president by House of Representatives after failure of any candidate to win electoral majority.

1827   Thurlow Weed takes up cause of anti-Masonry

1828   John C. Calhoun's anonymous *South Carolina Exposition and Protest.*
Congress passes "Tariff of Abominations."
Election of Andrew Jackson as president brings triumphant victory to new Democratic party.

1830   Jackson vetoes Maysville Road Bill.
Anti-Masonic party holds first national party convention.

1832   Beginning of Jackson's "war" against Second Bank of the United States (BUS).
Special convention in South Carolina nullifies new protective tariff.
Jackson reelected president.

1833   Congress provides for a gradual lowering of tariffs, but passes Force Bill authorizing Jackson to enforce federal law in South Carolina.

1836   Jackson's "specie circular."
Martin Van Buren elected president.

1837   Financial panic brings many bank failures and suspension of specie payment.

1839   A major depression begins, leading to widespread bankruptcies and default of several states.

1840   Congress passes Van Buren's Independent Treasury Act.
William H. Harrison elected president; Whigs in power.

1841   John Tyler becomes president upon Harrison's death.

SUGGESTED READINGS

Arthur M. Schlesinger, Jr., *The Age of Jackson* (1945), should be used with caution, but is still an indispensable introduction to political democratization. Other studies that illuminate the same subject are Shaw Livermore, Jr., *The Twilight of Federalism* (1962); Chilton Williamson, *American Suffrage: From Property to Democracy* (1960); Henry Christman, *Tin Horns and Calico: A Decisive Episode in the Emergence of Democracy* (1945); David M. Ludlum, *Social Ferment in Vermont* (1939); and Marvin E. Gettleman, *The Dorr Rebellion* (1973).

Lee Benson, *The Concept of Jacksonian Democracy: New York as a Test Case* (1961), challenges the traditional historical categories of liberalism and conservatism. Richard P. McCormick, *The Second American Party System: Party Formation in the Jacksonian Era* (1966), also deemphasizes political issues and ideology. These pioneering works should be supplemented by Richard Hofstadter, *The Idea of a Party System* (1969); Ronald Formisano, *The Birth of Mass Political Parties: Michigan, 1827–1861* (1971); Joel Silbey, ed., *Transformation of American Politics, 1840–1860* (1967); Douglas T. Miller, *Jacksonian Aristocracy: Class and Democracy in New York, 1830–1860* (1967); and Michael F. Holt, "The Antimasonic and Know-Nothing Parties," and Holt, "The Democratic Party," in *History of U.S. Political Parties*, ed. Arthur M. Schlesinger, Jr., Vol. 1 (1789–1860: *From Factions to Parties*), (4 vols., 1973). Michael F. Holt, *The Political Crisis of the 1850s* (1978), while dealing mainly with a later period, points to connections between political ideology and the working of the party system.

For the election of 1828, see R. V. Remini, *The Election of Andrew Jackson* (1963). Two imaginative studies of Jacksonian ideology are Marvin Meyers, *The Jacksonian Persuasion* (1957); and John W. Ward, *Andrew Jackson: Symbol for an Age* (1955). For a comprehensive portrait of Jackson's early years, see R. V. Remini, *Andrew Jackson and the Course of American Empire* (1977); for his presidency, see Richard B. Latner, *The Presidency of Andrew Jackson: White House Politics* (1979). Informative essays on all of the presidential elections can be found in Arthur M. Schlesinger, Jr., ed., *History of American Presidential Elections, 1789–1968*. Vol. 1 (4 vols., 1971)

The standard work on the tariff issue is Frank W. Taussig, *The Tariff History of the United States* (1931). The best introduction to the banking controversy is R. V. Remini, *Andrew Jackson and the Bank War* (1967). The main authorities on the history of banking are Bray Hammond,

Banks and Politics in America from the Revolution to the Civil War (1957); J. Van Fenstermaker, *The Development of American Commercial Banking, 1782–1837* (1965); and Fritz Redlich, *The Molding of American Banking* (2 vols., 1947–51). Thomas P. Govan, *Nicholas Biddle* (1959), presents a strong defense of the president of the Bank of the United States. The wider political ramifications of the controversy are examined in William G. Shade, *Banks or No Banks: The Money Question in Western Politics* (1972), and John M. McFaul, *The Politics of Jacksonian Finance* (1972).

On the Missouri crisis of 1820, Glover Moore, *The Missouri Controversy* (1953), is still the most thorough and convincing account. William W. Freehling, *Prelude to Civil War* (1966), presents a masterful interpretation of South Carolina's growing militancy, and of the nullification and gag-rule controversies. For the general question of sectionalism, see William J. Cooper, *The South and the Politics of Slavery, 1828–1856* (1978).

There is still no adequate history of the Whig party and its antecedents, but Daniel W. Howe, *The Political Culture of the American Whigs* (1980), brilliantly illuminates the Whig ideology. See also Lynn L. Marshall, "The Strange Stillbirth of the Whig Party," *American Historical Review*, 62 (January 1967), 445–68; Charles G. Sellers, Jr., "Who Were the Southern Whigs?" *American Historical Review*, 59 (January 1954), 335–46; Glyndon G. Van Deusen, "Some Aspects of Whig Thought and Theory in the Jacksonian Period," *American Historical Review*, 63 (January 1958), 305–32; and Thomas H. O'Connor, *Lords of the Loom: The Cotton Whigs and the Coming of the Civil War* (1968).

Political history is always illuminated by the biographies of influential figures. Richard Hofstadter, *The American Political Tradition* (1948), provides brilliant sketches of a number of pre–Civil War leaders. Among the best biographies are Martin Duberman, *Charles Francis Adams, 1807–1886* (1961); Samuel F. Bemis, *John Quincy Adams and the Foundations of American Foreign Policy* (1949), and *John Quincy Adams and the Union* (1956); W. N. Chambers, *Old Bullion Benton: Senator from the New West* (1956); William E. Smith, *The Francis Preston Blair Family in Politics* (2 vols., 1933); Richard N. Current, *John C. Calhoun* (1966); C. M. Wiltse, *John C. Calhoun: Nationalist, 1782–1828* (1944); *Nullifier, 1829–1839* (1949); *Sectionalist, 1840–1850* (1951); Clement Eaton, *Henry Clay and the Art of American Politics* (1957); Marquis James, *Life of Andrew Jackson* (1938); Harry Ammon,

James Monroe: The Quest for National Identity (1971); Charles G. Sellers, Jr., *James K. Polk: Jacksonian, 1795–1843* (1957); *Continentalist, 1843–1846* (1966); Robert Dawidoff, *The Education of John Randolph* (1979); Glyndon G. Van Deusen, *William Henry Seward* (1967); David H. Donald, *Charles Sumner and the Coming of the Civil War* (1960); Carl B. Swisher, *Roger B. Taney* (1935); Holman Hamilton, *Zachary Taylor* (1951); William Y. Thompson, *Robert Toombs of Georgia* (1966); James P. Shenton, *Robert John Walker: A Politician from Jackson to Lincoln* (1961); Robert F. Dalzell, Jr., *Daniel Webster and the Trial of American Nationalism, 1843–1852* (1973); Sydney Nathans, *Daniel Webster and Jacksonian Democracy* (1973); Glyndon G. Van Deusen, *Thurlow Weed: Wizard of the Lobby* (1947); and John W. DuBose, *The Life and Times of William Lowndes Yancey* (2 vols., 1892).

Of the many editions of diaries and collected papers, the following deserve special notice: C. F. Adams, ed., *The Memoirs of John Quincy Adams* (12 vols., 1874–77); Thomas Hart Benton, *Thirty Years' View* (1857); Allan Nevins, ed., *The Diary of Philip Hone, 1828–1851* (2 vols., 1927); Allan Nevins and Milton H. Thomas, eds., *The Diary of George Templeton Strong* (4 vols., 1952); Horace Greeley, *Recollections of a Busy Life* (2 vols., 1868); Milo M. Quaife, ed., *The Diary of James K. Polk* (4 vols., 1910); and J. C. Fitzpatrick, ed., *The Autobiography of Martin Van Buren* (1920).

CHAPTER 14

Attempts to Shape the American Character

During the pre–Civil War decades political and religious leaders repeatedly warned that the fate of free institutions depended on the moral and intellectual character of the American people. Religious beliefs continued to differ about man's sinfulness or inherent capacity for love and social harmony. But Americans of various persuasions agreed that human nature was much like clay that can be molded to any shape before it hardens.

This conviction could be inspiring. In 1823, for example, Charles Jared Ingersoll, a Philadelphia lawyer and former congressman, delivered the influential *Discourse Concerning the Influence of America on the Mind.* Ingersoll was confident that the average American, as a result of the free and republican environment, stood far above the average European in both intelligence and virtue. He promised that American achievements in the arts and sciences would soon show the world the full potentialities of human nature when it was not hobbled by despotism and aristocratic privilege.

But a capacity for infinite improvement might also be a capacity for infinite corruption. Even the optimists tended to worry over the growing inadequacy of local religious and social institutions in the face of America's sensational expansion. The need to shape or change individual character gave a new social importance to educators, religious revivalists, popular essayists, phrenologists, and other promoters of self-improvement.

"We Must Educate or Perish"

Shaping character, whether by school, church, prison, or asylum, seemed to be the only means of ensuring moral stability in an expansive and increasingly individualistic society. Lyman Beecher, best-known today as the father of Harriet Beecher Stowe but in his own day the most prominent Protestant minister in the North, viewed the rapid settlement of the West with a mixture of exhilaration and alarm. By 1835 the states west of the Appalachians had grown so rapidly that he could predict a population of 100 million by 1900: "A day which some of our children may live to see." As a "young empire of mind, and power, and wealth, and free institutions," the West, Beecher believed, contained the potential for nothing less than "the emancipation of the world." Beecher had no doubts about the West's material progress. The danger was "that our intelligence and virtue will falter and fall back into a dark minded, vicious populace—a poor, uneducated reckless mass of infuriated animalism." Aroused particularly by the supposed threat of Catholic immigrants, whom he pictured as the agents of foreign despots intent on subverting republican institutions, Beecher urged an immediate crusade to evangelize and educate the West: "For population will not wait, and commerce will not cast anchor, and manufacturers will not shut off the steam nor shut down the gate, and agriculture, pushed by millions of freemen on their fertile soil, will not withhold her corrupting abundance. We must educate! We must educate! or we must perish by our own prosperity."

The State of Education. Educational reformers had some reason for alarm. Even Massachusetts, which in 1837 established the nation's first state board of education, suffered from dilapidated school buildings, untrained and incompetent teachers, and dependence on unequal and unpredictable local funding. The one-room country schoolhouse, often idealized in later years, was not only dirty, drafty, and overheated, but commonly packed with children of all ages, some old and rowdy enough to inflict beatings on male teachers and to prompt some women teachers to hide a pistol in a desk drawer. The soaring growth of eastern cities made middle-class citizens suddenly aware of begging street urchins, teenage prostitutes, gangs of juvenile delinquents, and vagrant children who, like Mark Twain's Huckleberry Finn, had little desire to be "civilized."

Until the second quarter of the nineteenth century, the education of Americans was informal, unsystematic, and dependent on parental initiative and ability to pay. Even so, compared with most Europeans, white American males had always enjoyed a high rate of literacy, especially in New England. During the 1790s a surprising number of artisans and skilled laborers had sent their children to the "common pay schools" in New York City, where children of rich and poor backgrounds mingled. By the early nineteenth century illiteracy was rapidly disappearing among white females. Boys and girls frequently attended the same schools, despite prejudices against sexual integration. Some "free" schools expected parents to pay a small fee, and most tax-supported schools were intended only for the children of paupers. Aside from school attendance, apprenticeship long served as a noteworthy educational institution, providing the vocational skills that could not be learned in any school. Not until the mid-nineteenth century—and in the South not until after the Civil War—did education become increasingly confined to specialized institutions segregated from the mainstreams of adult social life.

Working-Class Demands. Middle-class religious reformers were not the only ones to demand educational reform. In 1828 the organized mechanics and journeymen of Philadelphia, most of whom were skilled artisans and craftsmen who had served their apprenticeship, began to protest. As in other northeastern cities, these workers were angered by depressed wage levels, by the substitution of temporary child "apprentices" for skilled adult labor, and by the erosion of the traditional craft system that allowed apprentices and journeymen to rise within a given trade. The Philadelphia Working Men's party pressed for a broad range of economic and social reforms. "The original element of despotism," proclaimed a committee in 1829, "is a monopoly of talent, which consigns the multitude to comparative ignorance, and secures the balance of knowledge on the side of the rich and the rulers."

The demand for free tax-supported schools became a rallying cry for the workingmen's parties and associations that sprang up in New York, Boston, and dozens of small towns throughout the country. A group of New York workers expressed the typical rhetoric when they asked in 1830 "if many of the monopolists and aristocrats in our city would not consider it disgraceful to their noble children to have them placed in our public schools by the side of poor yet industrious mechanics?" Though many of the

"POPERY UNDERMINING FREE SCHOOLS"
A typical example of anti-Catholic iconography. While the American eagle hovers over the schoolhouse, this bulwark of democratic institutions is being literally undermined by sappers working under the directions of a priest, who in turn is executing the orders of the pope, pictured here as a foreign potentate. *(American Antiquarian Society)*

leaders of these groups were not manual laborers, the short-lived workingmen's movement reflected an authentic desire for equal educational opportunity on the part of skilled laborers whose economic and social condition had begun to deteriorate.

For most workingmen economic grievances soon took precedence over education. The economic growth of the pre–Civil War decades called for more and more unskilled laborers, but not for a significant increase in the number of skilled and nonmanual workers who might benefit materially from an education beyond the "Three Rs." In New York City, where the proportion of nonmanual and professional jobs changed very little from 1796 to 1855, many working-class parents questioned whether they should sacrifice family income in order to educate their children for jobs that did not exist.

As early as 1832 the New York Public School Society pointed out: "The labouring classes of society will, to a great extent, withhold their children from school, the moment they arrive at an age that renders their services in the least available in contributing to the support of the family." Later evidence indicated that children under fifteen earned as much as 20 percent of the income of working-class families in Newburyport, Massachusetts. For such families compulsory attendance laws often threatened an unbearable drop in already subsistence-level income. Not surprisingly, 40 percent of Newburyport's laborers admitted to the census takers of 1850 that their school-age children had not been enrolled in any school during the previous year. And many children who were enrolled could not attend regularly.

Moreover, by the 1840s the working class in the Northeast was becoming increasingly Roman Catholic. Though the public schools were theoretically secular—in New York and elsewhere denominational schools had been deprived of public funding—the values and teachings of the schools were unmistakably Protestant. Most Americans in the mid-nineteenth century still regarded Americanism as synonymous with Protestantism. Protestant clergymen played a critical role on school committees and in school reform. They saw nothing sectarian about public school teachers reading aloud from the King James Bible or teaching that the Protestant Reformation represented a liberation from Popish despotism. Bishop John Hughes and other Catholic leaders saw the matter differently. In 1840 New York Catholics launched a political offensive against the Protestant monopoly of public education. As a result of this conflict, the Catholic church decided to construct its own separate system of schools, a costly program that took many decades to complete.

For many immigrants, Catholics, and working-class parents the Protestant school reformers threatened to impose a uniform set of values on all segments of American society. Resistance also arose from local authorities who feared any centralizing interference from a state board of education. Many conservatives insisted that parents should pay for education, if they could afford it, just as they would for any other service or commodity. Others, brought up on the tradition of church schools, feared that the teaching of value-laden subjects would be catastrophic if guided only by a vaguely Protestant and nondenominational spirit.

Educational Reformers. These obstacles to the expansion of public education were finally overcome by reformers like Horace Mann, who as the chief officer of the Massachusetts Board of Education from 1837 to 1848 became the nation's leading champion of public schools. An ascetic, humorless puritan, Mann denounced intemperance, profanity, and ballet dancing along with ignorance, violence, and Negro slavery. Having personally struggled with the terrors of his New England Calvinist heritage, he had finally concluded that children were capable of infinite improvement and goodness. As a kind of secular minister, still intent on saving souls, he insisted that there must have been a time in the childhood of the worst criminal when, "ere he was irrecoverably lost, ere he plunged into the abyss of infamy and guilt, he might have been recalled." Mann offended the religiously orthodox by winning the fight in Massachusetts against specific religious instruction in the public schools. He outraged conservatives by asserting that private property is not an absolute right but rather

a trusteeship for society and future generations. Trained as a lawyer, he decided as a young man that "the next generation" should be his clients. In pleading the cause of generations to come, he held that school taxes were not a "confiscation" from the rich, but rather a collection of the debt the rich owed to society.

Reformers placed a stupendous moral burden on the public schools. Horace Mann proclaimed the common school to be "the greatest discovery ever made by man." "Other social organizations are curative and remedial," he said; "this is a preventive and antidote." This characteristic argument suggests that the schools were to be a bulwark against undesirable change, preserving the cherished values of a simpler, more homogeneous America. Educators spoke of the frenzied pace of American life, of the diminishing influence of church and home. They held that the school should thus serve as a substitute for both church and home, preventing American democracy from degenerating into what Mann called "the spectacle of gladiatorial contests." The school, representing the highest instincts of society, could alone be counted on for cultivating decency, cooperation, and a respect for others. Women, it was believed, were best suited as teachers because they exemplified the noncombative and noncompetitive instincts. Because they also could be employed for lower wages than men, women teachers soon predominated in New England's elementary schools.

The character traits most esteemed by educational reformers were precisely those alleged to bring material success in a competitive and market-oriented society: punctuality, cheerful obedience, honesty, responsibility, perseverance, and foresightedness. Public schools seemed to promise opportunity by providing the means of acquiring such traits. In the words of one school committee, the children "entered the race, aware that the prize was equally before all, and attainable only by personal exertion." The famed McGuffey's "Eclectic" series of readers, which after 1836 were used in countless schoolrooms and of which well over 100 million copies were eventually sold, taught young readers that no possession was more important for getting on in the world than reputation, or "a good name." On the other hand, the readers held out little hope of rags-to-riches success. When the good little poor boy sees other children "riding on pretty horses, or in coaches, or walking with ladies and gentlemen, and having on very fine clothes, he does not envy them, nor wish to be like them." For he has been taught "that it is God who makes some poor, and others rich; that the rich have many troubles which we know nothing of; and that the poor, if they are but good, may be very happy."

From a present-day viewpoint, the educational reformers were often insensitive to the needs of the non-Protestants, non-Christians, nonwhites, and women. Throughout the North, except in a few scattered communities, the public schools excluded black children. Many localities made no provision for blacks to be educated. Other towns and cities, including New York and Boston, distributed a small portion of public funds to segregated and highly inferior schools for blacks. By 1850 blacks constituted no more than 1.5 percent of Boston's population,

REGULATIONS

OF THE

FEMALE CLASSICAL SEMINARY, BROOKFIELD.

THE Principal expects of the young Ladies attending his Seminary,

1. That they will attend at the Academy, regularly and punctually, at the hours appointed by the Principal.

2.—That all noise and disorder in the house, before the Principal arrives, and after the exercises are closed, will be carefully avoided.

3.—That, during the hours of instruction, they will give constant and diligent attention to the exercises prescribed, avoiding every thing which would be an interruption to the teacher or pupils.

4.—That, during the recitations, all the members of a class will close their books, except the nature of the recitation requires their being open.

5.—That the young Ladies will constantly attend public worship on the Sabbath.

6.—That they will always board in those families, which have the approbation of the Principal.

7.—That they will not attend balls, assemblies, or other parties for the indulgence of frivolous mirth.

8.—That the social visits of the young Ladies, among the families of the village, will be arranged by the Principal, whenever invitations are extended.

9.—That they will avoid walking or riding, with persons of the other sex, at unseasonable hours.

10.—That they will not leave town, without permission from the Principal.

11.—That they will be subject in all respects to the superintendence and direction of the Principal, while belonging to his school.

TUITION, for each term. Arithmetic, Grammar, or Geography, $3,50.— Rhetoric, History, or Latin, $4,50.——Geometry, Natural Philosophy, Chemistry, Algebra, Euclid, Logic, Intellectual Philosophy, or Moral Philosophy, $5,00.——French, Music, and Painting will probably be taught the ensuing spring.
Sept. 1825.

E. AND G. MERRIAM, PRINTERS, BROOKFIELD.

EDUCATING WOMEN
The pre-Civil War decades opened unprecedented opportunities for middle-class girls to advance beyond an elementary level of education. The price of this opportunity, however, was a system of strict discipline and of constant supervision of manners and morals. *(Left, American Antiquarian Society; Right, The Metropolitan Museum of Art, Gift of I. N. Phelps Stokes, Edward S. Hawes, Alice Mary Hawes, and Marion Augusta Hawes, 1937)*

but it still required a prolonged struggle on the part of militant blacks and white abolitionists to achieve legal desegregation. In 1855 Massachusetts became the single state in which no applicant to a public school could be excluded on account of "race, color or religious opinions." In marked contrast to the public schools, Oberlin, Harvard, Bowdoin, Dartmouth and some other private colleges opened their doors to a few black students. In 1837 Oberlin also became America's first coeducational college. In general, however, American women had no opportunities for higher education except in female seminaries and, by the 1850s, in a few western state universities.

By the 1850s Massachusetts had acquired all the essentials of a modern educational system: special "normal schools" for training female teachers; the grading of pupils according to age and ability; standardized procedures for advancement from one grade to another; uniform textbooks; and a bureaucracy extending from the board of education to superintendents, principals, and teachers. Although Massachusetts led the nation, by the 1850s it was possible for a New York City male child to proceed from an "infant school" to a college degree without paying tuition. Educational reformers, many of them originally New Englanders, had helped to create state-supported and state-supervised school systems from Pennsylvania to the new states of the Upper Mississippi Valley. In the 1850s the same cause made some headway in the South, particularly in Virginia and North Carolina.

Whatever prejudices and blind spots the public school movement may have had, it aroused the enthusiasm of hundreds of idealistic men and women who devoted time and energy to the cause. Northern legislators committed an impressive proportion of public spending to the education of succeeding generations. The movement, particularly in the 1850s, trained a young generation of teacher-missionaries, who in time would descend on the devastated South, equipped with an ideology for "reconstruction." Above all, the movement reinforced the American faith that social problems could be solved by individual enterprise, a diffusion of knowledge, and a reconstruction of moral character.

The Evangelical Age

Americans continued to look on the church, no less than the public school, as a decisive instrument for shaping the national character. As in the early national period, religion appeared to thrive the more it achieved independence from the state.* Despite the officially secular stance of American governments, evangelical Protestantism became increasingly identified with patriotism, democracy, and America's mission in the world. Despite the continuing division and competition among religious denominations, Americans increasingly appealed to religion as the only adhesive force that could preserve a sense of community and united purpose.

Religious Revivals. Between 1820 and 1860 religious revivalism became a powerful organizing and nationalizing force, permeating all parts of American life, in the South as well as the North, in the cities as well as on the western frontier. Although church membership figures can be misleading, since many people who regularly attended church could not meet the religious or financial obligations required for formal membership, it has been stated that by 1835 as many as three out of four adult Americans maintained some nominal relationship to a church. Most foreign observers agreed with Tocqueville that by the 1830s there was no country in the world in which the Christian religion retained "a greater influence over the souls of men."

For the majority of adults evangelical Protestantism provided a common language and a common frame of reference. It explained not only the nature and destiny of man but the meaning of democracy and of American nationality. In the words of a non-church member, a young self-made man and future president of the United States, Andrew Johnson, "Man can become more and more endowed with divinity; and as he does he becomes more God-like in his character and capable of governing himself." Like millions of other Americans, Johnson believed

---

*In 1833 Massachusetts became the last state to give up an established church.

CAMP MEETING, ca. 1835
The religious camp meeting, originally associated with the boisterous and unruly West, became an established and well-organized institution throughout rural America. *(Courtesy of the New York Historical Society, New York City)*

that Christianity and political democracy were together elevating and purifying the people, working toward the day when it could be proclaimed: "The millennial morning has dawned and the time has come when the lion and the lamb shall lie down together, when . . . the glad tidings shall be proclaimed . . . of man's political and religious redemption, and there is 'on earth, peace, good will toward men.'"

In some ways this evangelical vision transcended boundaries of class and section. Although it is possible to think of America as undergoing a single Great Revival during the six decades preceding the Civil War, the revival's social significance differed according to time and place. Some socioeconomic groups were more susceptible to religious enthusiasm than others. Some personality types were likely to view revivalists as self-righteous zealots who threatened to remove all fun from life. Others were likely to

seize the chance to profess faith in Christ crucified, to announce repentance for their sins, to experience the liberation of rebirth, and as the popular hymn put it, to "stand up, stand up for Jesus!" For many Americans religion provided the key to social identity. It was not that people flocked to churches to meet the right kind of people, although some no doubt did. It was rather that the "right" kind of religion, as defined by employers, slaveholders, and other wielders of power, was often considered to bestow the "right" kind of character.

Religious revivalism depended on sensitivity to the community's norms and vital interests. In the South leaders of various denominations discovered that any open criticism of slavery could threaten the very survival of a church. The Baptist and Methodist churches thus gradually retreated from their cautious antislavery pronouncements of the late eighteenth century, which had supposedly bred discontent if not insurrection among Negro slaves. By the 1830s the most influential southern churches had begun to deny that there was any moral contradiction between slavery and Christianity. They also insisted that Christianity, rightly understood, posed no danger to "the peculiar institution."

As a result of the evangelical revivals, southern planters increasingly promoted the religious conversion of their slaves. Even by the first decades of the nineteenth century, a growing number of churchmen and planters had argued that religious instruction would make slaves more obedient, industrious, and faithful. The ideal Christian master would treat his slaves with charity and understanding. The ideal Christian slave would humbly accept his assigned position in this world, knowing that his patience and faithfulness would be rewarded in heaven. Servitude, in short, could be softened, humanized, and perfected

by Christianity. The reality of slavery fell far short of the ideal. Religion may have induced many masters to take a sincere interest in their slaves' welfare, but it could not eliminate the cruelty and injustice inherent in the system.

No white preachers could entirely purge Christianity of its subversive overtones, or prevent black preachers from converting it into a source of self-respect, dignity, and faith in eventual deliverance—the longed-for Day of Jubilee. In both North and South, free blacks responded to growing racial discrimination by forming their own "African" churches, usually Baptist or Methodist. And despite the efforts by whites to control every aspect of their slaves' religion, the slaves created their own folk religion and shaped it to their own needs and interests. As one ex-slave from Texas recalled, "The whites preached to the niggers and the niggers preached to theyselves."

MEETING IN THE AFRICAN CHURCH

Although most illustrators tended to caricature American blacks, this wood engraving conveys some of the fervor and emotional intensity of the black churches, the churches that did so much in preserving a sense of hope and communal identity.
(Library of Congress)

Civilizing the West. Revivalism also served as a socializing force in the nonslaveholding West, but the context and consequences were different. In the opinion of Easterners, the West was both lawless and sinful. From the lumber camps of Wisconsin to the mining camps of California, the image of Westerners was essentially the same: rough dirty men who swore, gambled, got drunk, frequented houses of prostitution, and relished savage eye-gouging, knife-slashing fights. Although the stereotypes were exaggerated, there was no doubt that frontier communities were a challenge to nineteenth-century notions of decency and civilization.

The challenge of the West could not be met simply by building churches where none had existed before. When Theron Baldwin, a member of a Yale missionary group, arrived in Illinois in 1830, he was horrified by the ignorance of the settlers. Even in Vandalia, the state's capital, Baldwin discovered that most of the pupils in his Sunday school class were illiterate. Nor could he find a literate adult in over half the families he visited in the region. Religion, Baldwin concluded, could make no headway without education and an institutional rebuilding of society. Appealing for funds from the East, he expressed the New England ideal: "We wish to see the school house and church go up side by side and the land filled with Christian teachers as well as preachers." He added, significantly, that young men could come there "and in a short time get enough by teaching to purchase a farm that would ever after fill their barns with plenty and their hands with good things." Baldwin himself worked to secure from the legislature a charter for the first three colleges in the state. As a result of the labors of Baldwin and other young missionaries, the Old Northwest became dotted with academies, seminaries, and small denominational colleges.

Easterners who still thought of churches as fixed institutions within an ordered society did not understand that religious revivals were an effective instrument for shaping and controlling character. The frank emotionalism and homespun informality of the western and southern revivals disguised the fact that even the camp meetings were soon stabilized by rules, regulations, and the most careful advance planning. And camp meetings were by no means the most important tool of the revivals. The power of the movement flowed from the dynamic balance between popular participation and the control of leaders. According to the evangelical message, every man and woman, no matter how humble or mired in sin, had the capacity to say "Yes!" to Christ's offer of salvation—to reject what was called "cannot-ism," and along with it an unsatisfying identity. Even for the poor and uneducated, consent opened the way for participation and decision-making.

Peter Cartwright, for example, grew up in one of the most violent and lawless regions of Kentucky; his brother was hanged for murder, and his sister was said to have "led a life of debauchery." At the age of sixteen Cartwright repented his sins at a Methodist camp meeting; at seventeen he became an exhorter; at eighteen a traveling preacher; at twenty-one a deacon; and at twenty-three a presiding elder of the church. Each upward step required a probationary period, followed by an examination of the candidate's conduct, ability, and purity of doctrine. The Methodists showed particular skill in devising a system that encouraged widespread participation and upward mobility under hierarchical authority. But all the evangelical churches displayed the great American gift for organization. Revivals, they believed, could not be had by waiting for God to stir human hearts. Revivals required planning, efficient techniques, and coordinated effort. The need was not for educated theologians but for professional promoters.

Christianity and the Social Order. While revivalism was an organizing and socializing movement, it was also by definition selective. The people most likely to be converted were those who had some Christian upbringing or those who were already disturbed by excessive drinking, gambling, fighting, disorder, and irresponsibility. Conversion itself reinforced crucial social distinctions. For one part of the community, religion became more than a matter of going to church on Sunday. The obligations of a new religious life required sobriety and responsibility from friends, family, employees, and business associates. The weekly "class meetings" and "love feasts" provided fellowship and helped to prevent backsliding. No doubt the solidarity of the converted brought order and discipline to the community at large. But if the evangelicals always insisted that every man and woman could say "Yes!", there were always those who said "No!" The congregations that loved to hear their preachers "pouring hot shot into Satan's ranks" knew that Satan's ranks were concentrated on the other side of the tracks.

Religious revivals could accentuate social distinctions by forging an alliance among the more ambitious, self-disciplined, and future-oriented members of a community. In the fall of 1830, for example, the leaders of Rochester, New York, invited Charles Grandison Finney to save that booming city from sin. By far the most commanding and influential evangelist of the pre–Civil War period, Finney was a tall, athletic spellbinder, a former lawyer who had undergone a dramatic religious conversion in 1823. Though lacking formal seminary training, Finney had been ordained as a Prebyterian minister and in 1825 had begun a series of highly unorthodox and spectacular revivals along the route of the newly constructed Erie Canal.

In 1831 Finney's triumphs in Rochester stunned Christian America; communities from Ohio to Boston appealed to him to save their collective souls. Finney's converts in Rochester were largely manufacturers, merchants, lawyers, shopkeepers, master artisans, and skilled journeymen. He appealed to people who had profited from the commercial revolution initiated by the building of the Erie Canal but who had become deeply disturbed by the immense influx of young transient laborers looking for work. Rochester's leaders had no control over the behavior of these youths. Significantly, during Rochester's revival years church membership declined among the hotel proprietors and tavern keepers who catered to the floating population of young males traveling the Erie Canal. Rochester's Protestant churches, interpreting the revival as a sweeping popular mandate, launched a crusade to purge the city of its dens of vice and unholy amusement. They also offered a "free church" —free of pew rents and other financial obligations—

to the workers on the canal. Increasingly Rochester became divided between a Christian minority dedicated to education and upward advancement and an essentially nonpolitical, free-floating majority of disoriented and unskilled young men.

Philadelphia differed from Rochester in important respects, but there, too, religious revivals eventually redefined the boundaries of respectable and "modern" behavior. Unlike Rochester, which grew by 512 percent in the 1820s, Philadelphia was not a new boom town. An old city by American standards, Philadelphia was relatively resistant to religious enthusiasm. Revivalism had little appeal to the wealthy Quakers and conservative Presbyterian clergy who dominated the city's religious life. Evangelical morality was even less appealing to Philadelphia's workingmen, who preserved and cherished a traditional artisan, preindustrial culture. Largely because of irregular and undeveloped transportation to interior markets, Philadelphia workers suffered periodic layoffs. This forced leisure allowed them to enjoy traveling circuses, cockfights, drinking and gambling at the local taverns, and above all, the boisterous comradeship of voluntary fire companies. Until 1837 neither the revival nor the closely related temperance movement made much headway among Philadelphia's manual workers. The people who reformed their drinking habits and who joined the reform-minded wing of the Presbyterian church were the professional and business groups who were ushering in the new industrial order. But in 1837 the financial panic and subsequent depression began to undermine the traditional habits and culture of the working class. Waves of religious revivalism, often Methodist in character, reached working-class neighborhoods. A new and more powerful temperance movement developed spontaneously from the ranks of master craftsmen, journeymen, shopkeepers, and the most ambitious unskilled laborers. In Philadelphia, as in Rochester, the decision to abstain from all alcohol was the key symbol of a new morality and of a commitment to self-improvement. By the 1840s the evangelical workingmen could contrast their own sobriety and self-discipline with the moral laxity of mounting numbers of Irish immigrants. Not surpris-

RIOT IN PHILADELPHIA

In 1844 anti-Catholic violence reached a climax in Philadelphia, where the Catholic bishop had persuaded school officials to allow the use of both the King James and Latin vulgate Bibles. After Protestant mobs had burned two Catholic churches, a full-scale riot required the intervention of state militia. *(The Library Company of Philadelphia)*

ingly, the revivalism that bolstered the self-respect of blue-collar native workers also contributed to virulent anti-Catholicism and to nativist prejudice against a population that seemed to threaten the newly won dignity of manual labor.

Revivalism and Economic Prosperity.   Revivals appeared to be the only hopeful counterforce against rampant individualism, self-serving politics, and corrupting luxury. As Finney put it, "the great political and other worldly excitements" of the time distracted attention from the interests of the soul. He held, accordingly, that these excitements could "only

be counteracted by *religious* excitements." Only revivals could prevent the United States from sliding into the decay and collapse of ancient Greece and Rome, and prepare the nation "to lead the way," in Lyman Beecher's phrase, "in the moral and political emancipation of the world."

Revivalism was fed by the moral doubts that inevitably accompanied rapid economic growth, the disruption of older modes of work and responsibility, the sudden accumulation of wealth, and the appearance of new class divisions. Revivalist preachers denounced atheism far less than "mammonism," the greedy pursuit of riches. They voiced repeated concern over the frantic pace of American life, the disintegration of family and community, and the worship of material success.

But revivalism seldom led to ascetic withdrawal or to spiritualistic contemplation. Evangelical religion was above all activist, pragmatic, and oriented toward measurable results. The fame of Finney and the other great exhorters depended on the body count, or soul count, of converts. Finney proclaimed: "The results justify my methods"—a motto that could as well have come from John D. Rockefeller or other entrepreneurs in more worldly spheres. Finney confidently predicted: "If the church will do her duty, the millennium may come in this country in three years." He knew, however, that a millennium would require no revivals, and that as a revivalist, though dedicated to virtue, he needed sin much as a soldier needs war.

There was a close relation between the revivals and America's expansive economy. The exuberant materialism of American life furnished revivalists with continuing targets for attack and with vivid symbols of communal strife and moral shortcoming. Without moral crises there would be no cause for national rededication, and calls for rededication have long been America's way of responding to social change. But on another level, the revivalists had merged their cause with America's secular destiny. They had repeatedly warned that without religion, American democracy would speedily dissolve into "a common field of unbridled appetite and lust." Yet instead of dissolving, the nation continued to prosper, expand, and reveal new marvels. Sometimes clergymen hailed the achievements as signs of national virtue and divine favor. More important, as a reflection of their increasing respect for efficient methods and material results, they applauded technological improvements as the instruments that God had provided for saving the world.

The telegraph, railroad, and steamship all quickened the way for spreading the gospel around the world, and could thus be interpreted as portents of the coming millennium. But America's technology and rapid westward expansion could be justified only if America took seriously the burdens of a missionary nation. Samuel Fisher, the president of Hamilton College, elaborated on the message in an address to the American Board of Commissioners for Foreign Missions:

Material activity, quickened and guided by moral principle, is absolutely essential to the development of a strong and manly character. . . . The product of this devotion to material interests is capital diffused through the masses; and capital is one of the means God uses to convert the world.

The diffusion of capital through the masses seemed to falter in 1857, when a financial crash brought a severe depression and unprecedented unemployment among factory workers. Economic insecurity formed the backdrop of what many took to be "the event of the century," the great urban revival of late 1857 and 1858. What distinguished the event from earlier religious revivals was the absence of revivalists. In Philadelphia and New York thousands of clerks and businessmen began to unite spontaneously for midday prayer. The New York *Herald* and the New York *Tribune* devoted special issues to the remarkable events—wealthy stockbrokers praying and singing next to messenger boys; revivals in the public high schools; joint services by Methodists, Episcopalians, Presbyterians, Baptists, and even the traditionally antirevivalist Unitarians. The spirit rapidly spread to manufacturing towns throughout the Northeast. Unscheduled and unconventional religious meetings sprang up in small towns and rural areas from Indiana to Quebec. "It would seem," wrote one enthusiast, "that the mighty crash was just what was wanted . . . to startle men from their golden dreams." Americans had become too overbearing, too self-confident, too complacent in their success. Yet if God had shown His displeasure, as countless interpreters maintained, He had also chosen means that underscored America's promise. He had punished Americans with economic loss, which even the hardest head among the business community could understand.

The great revival of 1858 gave a new sense of unity to Northerners who had become increasingly divided by class and religious conflict, to say nothing of the issue of slavery. It also signified the maturity of an urban, industrial Protestantism committed to material progress and self-improvement. For good or for ill, the revivals reinvigorated America's official ideal of *Novus Ordo Seclorum*—a phrase stamped on every dollar bill, conveying the message that a new social order is to exist, that Americans carry the high burden of helping to create a better world.

The Cult of Self-Improvement

What made public schools and religious revivals seem so indispensable by the 1830s was the relative absense of authoritative institutions that could define social roles, rules of conduct, and models of character. There was no standing army, for example, that could train a military class or enforce unpopular public policy. The disestablishment of the churches gave semiliterate evangelists the same official status as college-trained theologians. Some states guaranteed any citizen, regardless of training, the right to practice law in any court. Increasingly Americans showed little respect for any intellectual elite, religious or secular, or for any group of self-perpetuating masters who claimed to preserve and monopolize a body of knowledge that the public at large could not understand.

Not only had American law rejected Old World notions of privileged social orders, but as time went on courts swept away most of the legal barriers that had restrained individuals from entering into certain kinds of risky or inequitable agreements. In other words, the law assumed that all society was a market of competitive exchange in which each individual calculated the probable risks of a given choice of action. This burden of individual freedom and responsibility placed an enormous premium on acquiring effective skills and up-to-date knowledge. Continuous self-improvement became the great ideal of the age.

Lyceums and Learning.   To Americans of the late twentieth century there is nothing novel about fads, cults, and nostrums that promise the solution to life's problems. But in the 1830s and 1840s the cult of self-improvement was unprecedented in both the bold-

ness and variety of its appeals. Some conservatives expressed alarm over the credulity of public opinion, assuming that fads and quackery posed a threat to public order. But the pervasive desire of the people was not for restructuring society but for self-knowledge and self-advancement. Numerous respectable societies and institutes for adult education and "mutual improvement" began to spread in the 1820s from England to the United States. Tens of thousands of adults, first in New England and then in the Old Northwest, grew accustomed to attending lyceums—public lectures, concerts, and cultural events. Lyceum lectures covered a vast range of subjects, but tended during the early years of the movement to concentrate on "useful knowledge" associated with moral improvement and popular science.

Americans generally equated the advance of science with the advance of human liberty, a linkage that was part of the heritage of the European Enlightenment. They believed that everyone could benefit from the scientific method; the marvels and secrets of nature were open to all. But what most impressed and fascinated American audiences were lectures and books on the applications of science, demonstrating the ingenious ways that human beings could master nature. As early as 1829 Jacob Bigelow's *Elements of Technology* not only helped to popularize a

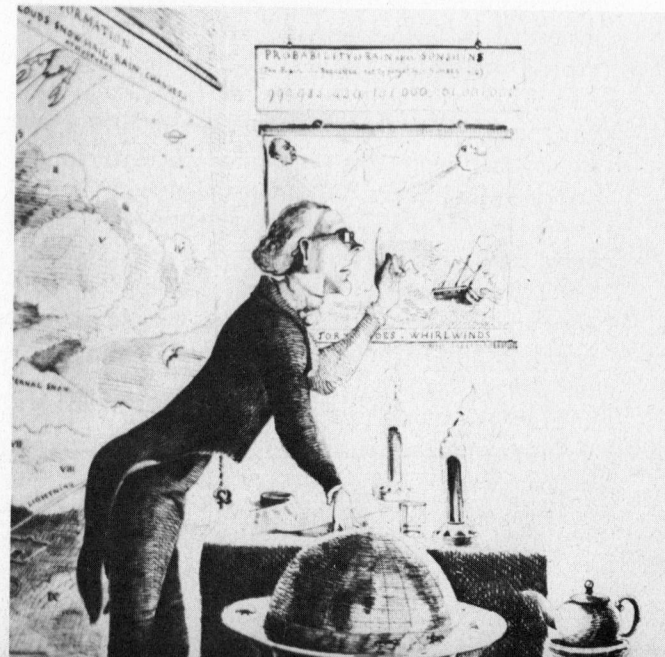

new word but gave impetus to the general public's growing inclination to see invention as the key to national progress. Excitement over the uses of technology and steam power was matched by a new curiosity about the human mind, which had shown that it could unlock nature's secrets.

Mind Control. The gap between public ignorance and the achievements of science could be bridged if someone invented the supreme technology, a technology for controlling the human mind. The quest for such power united many of the popular cults and fads. Mesmerists, for example, claimed to have discovered the laws of magnetic attraction and repulsion that governed relations between people. Spiritualists convinced hundreds of thousands that they had found techniques and apparatus for communicating with the dead and probing the laws of the occult. Even the manuals on self-improvement and character building, directed mainly at the young, presumed definitive knowledge of the mechanics of the brain. The Reverend John Todd's *Student's Manual* (1835), which sold by the hundreds of thousands, maintained that mental power depends on a strict conservation of bodily and especially sexual energies. Todd's thesis, repeated by countless physicians and other experts, was that masturbation or sexual excess of any kind posed the

gravest threats to sanity, social order, and individual achievement. Self-improvement required the rigorous avoidance of unwholesome thoughts and tempting situations.

Phrenology. Phrenology, however, was the most ambitious and institutionalized science of the mind. The invention of Franz Joseph Gall, a Viennese physician, phrenology identified the supposed physical location in the brain of a large assortment of human "faculties," such as firmness, benevolence, acquisitiveness, destructiveness, and platonic love. Phrenologists claimed that they could precisely measure character from the form and shape of a head. Americans first responded to phrenology as a promising medical breakthrough. Gall's leading disciple, Johann Gaspar Spurzheim, became the first missionary for the cause. On a visit to America in 1832, he was lionized by New England dignitaries, including Justice Joseph Story and the Yale chemist Benjamin Silliman. For a time the support of Horace Mann, the famous Unitarian preacher William Ellery Channing, and business leaders like Abbott Lawrence gave phrenology intellectual prestige. As usual, however, the American public displayed far more interest in practical application than in theory. Two skillful promoters, Orson and Lorenzo Fowler, helped to convert

LYCEUM LECTURE
A caricature of the early man-of-science, pontificating to an audience of attentive women and to a few apparently inattentive men. (*Museum of the City of New York*)

PHRENOLOGY CHART
This widely circulated bust of Dr. Johann Spurzheim illustrated the physical location of an amazing assortment of abilities, inclinations, and character traits. *(Library of Congress)*

phrenology into a major business enterprise. In the cities audiences of thousands paid fees for lengthy lecture series expounding the new science. Thousands more flocked to salons to have their characters analyzed. Itinerant lecturers and mail-order courses enlightened the countryside. By the mid-1850s the *American Phrenological Journal* had a circulation of over fifty thousand.

In many ways phrenology perfectly suited the needs of a people devoted to technique and uncertain of their own character. In an expansive and socially disruptive economy, it provided a new set of guidelines that reduced the fear of risk. Employers, for example, no longer able to rely on long-term apprenticeships, on personal knowledge of an employee's family, or even on a worker's reputation in the community, could request a phrenological examination. Young men who dreamed of many careers but who could decide on none welcomed a science that would measure their talents and capabilities. The great message of phrenology was individual adjustment. In a world of confusing and fluid expectations, it furnished boundaries and specific identities. It told the individual which traits to cultivate and which to restrain. For the faithful it also made life more predictable. Criminologists not only found a physical explanation for deviant behavior, but discovered a new hope for preventing crime by identifying potential criminals and by teaching convicts to control their overdeveloped antisocial faculties. Although Americans gradually came to realize that the results of phrenology could not substantiate its high promise, they had expressed an ardent desire, which would continue to our own time, for a popular science of human behavior.

Emerson. Like phrenology, the essays and lyceum lectures of Ralph Waldo Emerson, who came closer than anyone else to being America's official philosopher of the nineteenth century, offered something for everyone and thus nourished hope for reduced friction and for social harmony. While there is no way of knowing how much influence Emerson actually had on American thought and culture, he helped to stimulate the great literary renaissance of the 1850s. For decades to come his writing was a source of inspiration for reformers, businessmen, and countless ordinary folk. It can be argued that Emerson's worship of power and of self-improvement provided the spiritual backdrop for the entire progressive era of the early twentieth century.

Yet Emerson's thought eludes all attempts at classification or categorization. His words awakened reformers but he wrote the most penetrating critiques of reform of his generation. He was at once the most homespun, down-to-earth, and yet stratospheric of American thinkers. An ardent champion of cultural independence, he defined the mission of native artists and writers, yet exploited his knowledge of the newest currents of German and English thought. He was the leading figure in a group that domesticated German idealistic philosophy, usually referred to by Immanuel Kant's awkward term "Transcendentalism"; but he championed an extreme form of individualism and never felt comfortable as a member of any association. His pithy maxims on self-reliance were quoted by anarchists and yet were framed on the walls of the nation's business leaders.

Emerson's spongelike capacity to absorb ideas and the common attitudes of his time, and his empathy for all sides and commitment to none, had much in common with America's greatest weaknesses and strengths. To various audiences he proclaimed that "who so would be a man, must be a noncon-

RALPH WALDO EMERSON, 1803–1882
(Library of Congress)

formist." To the youth of America he delivered the reassuring thought: "We but half express ourselves, and are ashamed of the divine idea which each of us represents. . . . Trust thyself: every heart vibrates to that iron string." He upbraided Americans for their single-minded pursuit of wealth and fame, for their obsession with material things. But the point of this protest against materialism and conformity—which became clearer as both Emerson and his audiences grew older—was the need for a continuing reshaping and reinvigoration of the American character.

To Emerson the great peril that threatened the American people was not injustice but a fragmentation of soul: "The reason why the world lacks unity and lies broken and in heaps, is because man is disunited with himself." The essential problem, then, was one of reconstituting character, of recovering a sense of the whole. By self-reliance Emerson really meant a detachment from society in order to achieve the sense of wholeness that flowed from unity with God, or as Emerson put it, "the Oversoul." This notion that every "private man" possesses infinite and godlike capacities was an inspiring ideal, perfectly suited to the fantasies and aspirations of many Americans. At times, however, this doctrine meant that Emerson had no standard beyond power and success: "Power is, in nature, the essential measure of right."

The Tensions of Democratic Art

The continuing democratization of American culture produced a profound ambivalence about the artistic standards and precedents of European culture. On the one hand, American writers and artists felt the need to proclaim their independence from Europe and to create a genuinely native art, stripped of aristocratic associations. On the other hand, by the 1820s it was becoming clear that political independence did not guarantee cultural independence and that republican institutions would not automatically give birth to the Great American Masterwork. Improved transportation, coupled with a prolonged period of peace in Europe, made it easier for Americans to cross the Atlantic in search of inspiration and training.

"THE GREEK SLAVE" AT THE DUSSELDORF GALLERY
The traveling exhibition of Hiram Powers's "The Greek Slave" created the greatest artistic sensation of the pre-Civil War decades. The daring—and to some, immoral—display of female nudity was justified by the "ideality" of the form and by the assumption that the enslaved girl had been immodestly stripped by her brutal Turkish captors. *(The New York Public Library)*

LOOKING NORTH TO KINGSTON
An example of the Hudson River School of landscape painting in which human settlement and transport are blended into a dreamy, spiritualized Nature. *(Courtesy, Smith College Museum of Art)*

Even the more ardent cultural nationalists viewed Europe with awe and fascination. Often shocked by European contrasts between elegance and squalor, they were also dazzled by the great cathedrals, castles, spacious parks, monumental public buildings, museums, and villas. From Washington Irving's *Alhambra* (1832) to Nathaniel Hawthorne's *Marble Faun* (1860), American writers expressed their enchantment with castles and ruins, with places that had been steeped in centuries of history. Whatever its evils, Europe teemed with associations that fed the imagination. It was the continent of mystery, of beauty, of romance, and in short, of culture. For many American artists it was also at least a temporary refuge from the materialism, vulgarity, and hurried pace of life they found in the United States. It is significant that Washington Irving was living in England when he created the classic American tales "Rip Van Winkle" and "The Legend of Sleepy Hollow" (1819–20). James Fenimore Cooper was living in Paris when he wrote *The Prairie* (1827). Horatio Greenough, America's first professional sculptor and a champion of democratic artistic theory, completed his gigantic, half-draped statue of George Washington, a statue commissioned by the United States government, in his studio in Florence.

It would be a mistake, however, to think of American art of the period as slavishly imitative. Although Americans tended to express native subject matter in conventional artistic forms, they became increasingly skilled and sophisticated in their mastery of the forms. The choice of native material also affected the total character of a work. For example, space, nature, and the wilderness took on new qualities as Thomas Cole, Asher B. Durand, and other painters of the Hudson River school sought to idealize the American landscape. Cooper's five "Leatherstocking Tales," *The Pioneers* (1823), *The Last of the Mohicans* (1826), *The Prairie* (1827), *The Pathfinder* (1840), and *The Deerslayer* (1841), were far more than American versions of Sir Walter Scott's "Waverley novels." Like William Gilmore Simms's tales of the southern frontier and backcountry, they gave imaginative expression to a distinctively American experience with Indians, violence, the law, and the meaning of social bonds in a wilderness setting. The popular New England poets and men-of-letters chose homey, unpretentious sub-

jects that disguised both their literary skill and erudition. Thus Henry Wadsworth Longfellow, a translator of Dante and a master of meter, celebrated the village blacksmith. John Greenleaf Whittier sang of the barefoot boy. The highly cultivated James Russell Lowell delivered political satire in the homespun Yankee dialect of an imaginary Hosea Biglow.

Art as Product. By the 1820s it was becoming clear that art in America would have to be marketed like any other commodity, and that the ideal of the dabbling gentleman amateur would have to give way to the reality of the professional who wrote, carved, or painted for a living. Federal, state, and local governments did award a few commissions for patriotic and historical subjects, but political squabbles over art (including the seminudity of Greenough's Washington) dampened artists' desire for government patronage. The need to compete for middle-class customers and audiences helps to explain the dominant patriotic, didactic, and sentimental themes of popular American culture.

Art as Character Shaper. A self-consciously democratic art, as opposed to the remnants of folk art that it began to replace, had to justify itself by serving such essentially nonartistic needs as shaping of character. Before the Civil War, both literature and the so-called fine arts claimed to perform educational, quasi-religious functions. They provided models to imitate, they trained and refined the emotions and they taught that sin is always punished and virtue rewarded. Art promoted patriotism by glorifying the American Revolution and deifying George Washington. It defined idealized sex roles by identifying the American male as the man of action and conquerer of nature—hunter, trapper, scout, mountain man, sea-faring adventurer—and by associating the American female with refinement of emotions—physical frailty, periods of melancholy, and a sensitivity expressed by sudden blushing, paleness, tears, and fainting—and confinement in a home. Above all, art furnished models of speech, manners, courtship, friendship, and grief that helped to establish standards of middle-class respectability.

A few writers achieved the imaginative indepen-

THE TALCOTT FAMILY
This "primitive" watercolor of the Talcott family by Deborah Goldsmith captures the ideal of the home as a private refuge, surrounded by trees and green space. Note that the father and mother share the responsibilities of parenthood, and that the grandmother seems detached in space as well as by her old-fashioned dress. *(Courtesy, Abby Aldrich Rockefeller Folk Art Center, Williamsburg, Virginia)*

dence to interpret character and sensibility in new ways. Edgar Allan Poe, who strove for commercial success while remaining committed to the ideal of art as an autonomous craft, gave a dark transmutation to the stock themes of sentimental poetry and fiction. In a different way Nathaniel Hawthorne subtly transcended the conventions of sentimental moralism in *The Scarlet Letter* (1850), *The House of the Seven Gables* (1851), and *The Blithedale Romance* (1852). This period of creativity, later termed the American Renaissance, included Walt Whitman's *Leaves of Grass* (1855), which not only celebrated the boundless potentialities of American experience but took joy in defying the conventional limits of poetic language. Herman Melville's *Moby Dick* (1851), one of the world's great

novels, also fused native subject matter with new and distinctively American artistic forms. Henry David Thoreau's *Walden* (1854) stated a goal that could be applied to many of the best works of the period. Thoreau had nothing but contempt for the conventional efforts to shape character in the interest of social conformity. But Thoreau's decision to live by himself on Walden Pond was an experiment in self-improvement. The goal of his experiment, and of the art it produced, was to break free from the distractions and artificialities that disguised "the essential facts of life"—"to drive life into a corner, and reduce it to its lowest terms." "For most men, it appears to me," he said, "are in a strange uncertainty about it, whether it is of the devil or of God."

SUGGESTED READINGS

An excellent collection of source material on children can be found in the first volume of Robert H. Bremner, ed., *Children and Youth in America: A Documentary History* (1970–71). Two recent studies of the history of juvenile delinquency are Joseph M. Hawes, *Children in Urban Society* (1971), and Robert M. Mennel, *Thorns and Thistles* (1973).

Michael Katz, *The Irony of Early School Reform* (1968), sharply challenges the self-congratulatory tradition of educational history. Two important studies, also critical but more balanced, are: Carl F. Kaestle, *The Evolution of an Urban School System: New York City, 1750–1850* (1973), and Stanley K. Schultz, *The Culture Factory: Boston Public Schools, 1789–1860* (1973). Rush Welter, *Popular Education and Democratic Thought in America* (1962), presents a more traditional approach, and so does the excellent biography by Jonathan Messerli, *Horace Mann* (1972). Among the special studies of note are Bernard Wishy, *The Child and the Republic: The Dawn of Modern American Child Nurture* (1968); Marianna C. Brown, *The Sunday School Movement in America* (1961); Ruth Elson, *Guardians of Tradition: American Schoolbooks of the Nineteenth Century* (1964); Vincent P. Lannie, *Public Money and Parochial Education* (1968); and Merle Curti, *The Social Ideas of American Educators* (1935). The best introduction to higher education is Frederick Rudolph, *The American College and University* (1962), which can be supplemented by Theodore R. Crane, ed., *The Colleges and the Public, 1767–1862* (1963), and by Richard Hofstadter and Wilson Smith, *American Higher Education: A Documentary History* (2 vols., 1961).

The most imaginative treatment of revivalism is the first section of Perry Miller, *The Life of the Mind in America* (1965). William G. McLoughlin, Jr., *Modern Revivalism* (1959), gives a more detailed and systematic account of individual revivalists and more recently McLoughlin has written a stimulating interpretive essay, *Revivals, Awakenings, and Reform: An Essay on Religion and Social Change in America, 1607–1977* (1978). Charles A. Johnson, *The Frontier Camp Meeting* (1955), is the standard history of the subject. The wider social impact of revivalism in New York State is brilliantly traced in Whitney Cross, *The Burned-Over District* (1950), but this must now be supplemented by Paul E. Johnson's *A Shopkeeper's Millennium: Society and Revivals in Rochester, New York, 1815–1837* (1978).

The fullest general history of American religion is Sydney E. Ahlstrom, *A Religious History of the American People* (1972). A provocative study analyzing the cultural alliance between Protestant ministers and middle-class women is Ann Douglas, *The Feminization of American Culture* (1977). Among the special studies of unusual interest are Henri Desroche, *The American Shakers from Neo-Christianity to Pre-Socialism* (1971); Nathan Glazer, *American Judaism* (1957); Daniel W. Howe, *The Unitarian Conscience* (1970); Martin Marty, *The Infidel: Freethought in American Religion* (1961); William G. McLoughlin, Jr., *The Meaning of Henry Ward Beecher* (1970); Theodore Maynard, *The Story of American Catholicism* (1960); Ernest L. Tuveson, *Redeemer Nation:*

The Idea of America's Millennial Role (1968). D. H. Meyer, *The Instructed Conscience: The Shaping of the American National Ethic* (1972); T. D. Bozeman, *Protestants in an Age of Science: The Baconian Ideal and Antebellum American Religious Thought* (1977); and Winton U. Solberg, *Redeem the Time: The Puritan Sabbath in Early America* (1977).

Perry Miller, *Life of the Mind in America* (1965), contains a brilliant analysis of legal thought in America. A masterly interpretive work is James W. Hurst, *Law and Social Order in the United States* (1977), which should be contrasted with the challenging and highly innovative work by Morton J. Horwitz, *The Transformation of American Law, 1780–1860* (1977). An important aspect of constitutional development is traced in Bernard Schwartz, *From Confederation to Nation: The American Constitution, 1835–1877* (1973). Leonard W. Levy, *The Law of the Commonwealth and Chief Justice Shaw* (1957), is an outstanding study of a leading jurist. The standard biographies of Marshall and Taney are Albert J. Beveridge, *The Life of John Marshall* (4 vols., 1916–19), and Carl B. Swisher, *Roger B. Taney* (1936).

On science, the last section of Perry Miller's *Life of the Mind* contains important insights. The best general work is George Daniels, *American Science in the Age of Jackson* (1968). For medicine, see Richard H. Shryock, *Medicine and Society in America* (1960); and Martin Kaufman, *Homeopathy in America: The Rise and Fall of a Medical Heresy* (1971). Among the best biographies of individual scientists are Edward Lurie, *Agassiz: A Life of Science in America* (1960), and Frances Williams, *Matthew Fontaine Maury* (1963).

John D. Davies, *Phrenology: Fad and Science* (1955), is highly informative. Carl Bode treats the popularization of knowledge in *The American Lyceum* (1956), and reveals popular taste and culture in *The Anatomy of American Popular Culture* (1959).

The most illuminating studies of Emerson's thought are Joel Porte, *Representative Man: Ralph Waldo Emerson in His Time* (1979), and Stephen Whicher, *Freedom and Fate: An Inner Life of Ralph Waldo Emerson* (1953). O. B. Frothingham, *Transcendentalism in New England* (1876), conveys a young participant's memories of the liberating excitement of the Transcendentalist movement. Perry Miller, ed., *The Transcendentalists* (1950), is a difficult but magnificent anthology. Walter Harding's *Thoreau: Man of Concord* (1960), and Joseph W. Krutch, *Henry David Thoreau* (1948), can be supplemented with profit by Richard Lebeaux, *Young Man Thoreau* (1977). For individual Transcendentalists, see Charles Crowe, *George Ripley* (1967); Odell Shepard, *Pilgrim's Progress: The Life of Bronson Alcott* (1937); and Arthur M. Schlesinger, Jr., *Orestes A. Brownson* (1939). F. O. Matthiessen, *American Renaissance* (1941), is a brilliant and unsurpassed study of Emerson, Thoreau, Hawthorne, Melville, and Whitman.

Of the numerous studies of important literary figures, the following have special value for the historian: Richard Chase, *The American Novel and Its Tradition* (1957); Joel Porte, *The Romance in America: Studies in Cooper, Poe, Hawthorne, Melville, and James* (1969); Charles Feidelson, Jr., *Symbolism and American Literature* (1953); A. N. Kaul, *The American Vision: Actual and Ideal Society in Nineteenth-Century Fiction* (1963); R. W. B. Lewis, *The American Adam: Innocence, Tragedy, and Tradition in the Nineteenth Century* (1955); and David Levin, *History as Romantic Art* (1959). For Whitman, see Gay Allen, *The Solitary Singer* (1967). The best introduction to Poe is Edward Wagenknecht, *Edgar Allan Poe: The Man Behind the Legend* (1963). Newton Arvin has written two fine literary biographies: *Herman Melville* (1950); and *Longfellow: His Life and Work* (1963). For Hawthorne, see Edward Wagenknecht, *Nathaniel Hawthorne: Man and Writer* (1961).

Van Wyck Brooks, *The Flowering of New England, 1815–1865* (1936), is still highly readable and informative. On the South, the best guide is Jay B. Hubbell, *The South in American Literature, 1607–1900* (1954). Henry Nash Smith, *Virgin Land: The American West as Symbol and Myth* (1950), is a brilliant study of the imaginative portrayal of the West. The early publishing industry is analyzed in William Charvat, *Literary Publishing in America, 1790–1850* (1959). For popular literature, see James Hart, *The Popular Book in America* (1950); Herbert R. Brown, *The Sentimental Novel in America, 1798–1860* (1940); and Frank L. Mott, *Golden Multitudes: The Story of Best Sellers in the United States* (1947). Mott, *American Journalism* (1962), is the standard source on newspapers. The first volume of Mott's monumental *A History of American Magazines* (5 vols., 1957), is a mine of information. For folk songs, see Alan Lomax, *The Folk Song in North America* (1969).

Oliver W. Larkin, *Art and Life in America* (1949), is the fullest study of the early history of art and architecture. On painting it should be supplemented by Barbara Novak's superb study, *Nature and Culture: American Landscape and Painting, 1825–1875* (1980), as well as David C. Huntington, *Art and the Excited Spirit: America in the Romantic Period* (1972); and James T. Flexner, *That Wilder Image: The Painting of America's Native School from Thomas Cole to Winslow Homer* (1962). Neil Harris, *The Artist in American Society: The Formative Years, 1790–1860* (1966), is a sensitive study of art as a profession. Arthur H. Quinn, *American Drama* (2 vols., 1955), is a comprehensive introduction to the theater. A more imaginative work is David Grimstead, *Melodrama Unveiled* (1968). On architecture, see Talbot F. Hamlin, *Greek Revival Architecture in America* (1944); and Wayne Andrews, *Architecture in America* (1960). The best guides to early American music are Gilbert Chase, *America's Music* (1955); H. Wiley Hitchcock, *Music in the United States* (1969); and Dena J. Epstein, *Sinful Tunes and Spirituals: Black Folk Music through the Civil War* (1977).

Dissent, Protest, and Reform

*T*he desire to transform character lay at the heart of American reform. Like other Americans, reformers rejoiced in the nation's freedom from kings and nobles, from aristocratic institutions, and from status and roles defined at birth. They were cheered by the absence or removal of traditional barriers to human progress. But in pursuing the good life that had supposedly been made accessible by the sacrifices of the Founders, Americans had somehow created a society of astounding moral and physical contrasts—a society of luxury and of squalor, of spiritual uplift and of degradation, of freedom and of bondage. In the eyes of dissenters and reformers, it often seemed that America was ruled only by the principles of ruthless self-interest and power.

The spirit of dissent and reform centered in the Northeast and particularly in New England. During the years before the Civil War, this region spawned numerous crusades to regenerate the social order—to substitute love, harmony, and cooperation for what William Ellery Channing termed the "jarring interests and passions, invasions of rights, resistance of authority, violence, force" that were deforming the entire society. Whether these movements were religious or secular, most of them sought to orient American culture to a "higher law," "the moral government of God," as a means of preventing anarchy. Though reformers differed in their specific objectives, they shared a common desire to channel spiritual aspirations into the secular world of power.

Their procedures—the character of the reform movement of the pre–Civil War period—were unique. Throughout the ages religious reformers had sent out missionaries to convert the heathen, and had sought to provide the world with models of ascetic life, dietary discipline, and selfless commitment. But they had never created the kind of highly professional reform organizations that began to spring up in Britain and America in the early nineteenth century. These organizations were devoted to various goals—to abolishing slavery, to building model penitentiaries, to persuading people to abstain from alcoholic drinks. The objectives were uncompromising, and the systematic techniques for mobilizing public opinion and exerting pressure on public officials were altogether novel.

Nevertheless, these reform movements usually embodied a nostalgia for a supposedly simpler and more harmonious past. Members of the movements believed that the evils they combated had multiplied because of an alarming disintegration of family authority and community cohesiveness and of traditional morality. The various programs, therefore, had a dual objective for change and improvement. On the one hand, they attacked institutions, lifestyles, and traditional social roles that seemed to limit individual opportunity and to block the path of progress. On the other hand, they attempted to restore and revitalize a sense of purity, simplicity, and wholeness which had been lost in the headlong pursuit of modernity and material improvement.

The Mormons as a Test Case

The history of the Mormons is seldom included in discussions of American dissent and reform. Yet, not only was Mormonism America's first truly indigenous religion, it began as a radical expression of dissent—so radical that Mormons found that they could survive only by building their own asylum in the remote deserts of the Far West. Because the early history of Mormonism exemplifies so many of the aspirations and difficulties of other dissenters—who wished to live in their own ways in accordance with a higher moral law, free from the religious and political contaminations of their time—the Mormon experience can serve as an introduction or "test case." What the Mormons tested, essentially, were the outermost limits of permissible dissent, and the ability of any group or subculture to withstand the pressures of American secular society.

Joseph Smith, Founder.   In 1830 Joseph Smith, Jr., published The Book of Mormon in Palmyra, New York. He said the work was a translation of mysterious golden plates containing the history of an ancient Christian civilization in the New World. It also portrayed the American Indians as the degenerate but salvageable descendants of an ancient Hebrew tribe, and foresaw a new American prophet who would

discover the lost history and reestablish Christ's pure and undefiled kingdom in the New World. In 1830 Smith was an athletic, gregarious, cheerful, intensely imaginative man of twenty-four, who was subject to visions and claimed revelations. He was the son of one of America's many families of drifters, debtors, and habitual losers, whose poverty worsened as they drew closer to belts of commercial prosperity. Smith had been born in the hills of Vermont, and his parents had migrated to that caldron of progress and poverty, of religious revivalism and new social movements, in upstate New York that was soon to be known as the "Burned-Over District." Shortly after the publication of The Book of Mormon, Smith organized the Church of Christ, which in 1834 would be renamed the Church of Jesus Christ of Latter-Day Saints.

Faced from the outset with religious persecution, Smith knew that the saints must ultimately move westward and build their city of Zion at some divinely appointed spot near the Indian tribes they were commissioned to convert. As he was told to do in his revelations, he dispatched missionaries to scout out the Missouri frontier. In 1831 a few Mormons established an outpost near Independence, Missouri, which Smith designated as the site of the New Jerusalem, and which was then the eastern entry to the Santa Fe Trail. During the same year Smith and his New York followers migrated to Kirtland, Ohio, near Cleveland, where Mormon missionaries had converted an entire community.

Persecution of Mormons.   By 1839 the Mormons had met defeat in both Ohio and Missouri and were fleeing to a refuge of swampy Illinois farmland that Smith had bought along the eastern shore of the Mississippi. In Ohio the Mormons had experimented with communal ownership of property and with an illegal, wildcat banking venture that had brought disaster during the Panic of 1837. In Missouri prosouthern mobs, hostile to any group of nonslaveholding Yankees, and infuriated by reports that Mormons intended to bring free blacks into the state, had destroyed the settlements around Independence. A series of armed encounters, beginning with an attempt to bar Mormons from voting, led to outright warfare and to Governor L. W. Boggs's proclamation that the Mormons had to be treated as enemies, and "had to be exterminated, or driven from the state." At Haun's Mill a band of Missourians massacred nineteen Mormon men and boys. Smith himself was convicted of treason and sentenced to be shot. But he managed to escape, and in Illinois the Mormons finally built their model city of Nauvoo, which the legislature incorporated in 1840 as a virtually independent city-state. The Mormon's political power derived from the decisive weight they could throw in state elections that were fairly evenly balanced between Whigs and Democrats. Beginning in 1840 their numbers grew not only as the result of missionary work in the East, but as the result of the immigra-

tion of thousands who had been converted to Mormonism in the manufacturing districts of England. The English converts' route to the American Zion was eased by the church's highly efficient planning authority that took care of the details of travel.

By the early 1840s visitors to Nauvoo marveled at the city's broad streets, carefully laid out in neat squares; at the steam sawmills and flour mill, the factories, hotel, and schools. Though the Nauvoo temple, supported by thirty gigantic pillars and walls of hewn stone, was not yet complete, it promised to be, in the words of the poet John Greenleaf Whittier, "the most splendid and imposing architectural monument in the new world." Dressed in the uniform of a lieutenant general, Smith presided over a Nauvoo legion of 2,000 troops. In 1843 he dictated the official

JOSEPH SMITH, REVIEWING TROOPS
While this painting exaggerates the machine-like discipline of the Nauvoo legion, it suggests why many non-Mormons could feel concern over Joseph Smith's private army. *(Church Archives, The Church of Jesus Christ of Latter-Day Saints)*

revelation, which he never made public, justifying the practice of plural marriage or polygamy. In 1844 he established the secret Council of Fifty, a secular authority independent of the church, and gave it the mission of building a world government that would prepare the way for Christ's kingdom.

But Smith felt the American world closing in on him and his fellow Mormons. Sensing that the surrounding society would not long tolerate Mormon power, he unsuccessfully tried to persuade the new Republic of Texas to sponsor an independent Mormon colony along the contested border with Mexico. While also sending secret diplomatic missions to Russia and France, he tried to influence the established order through normal political channels. But neither the federal government nor the 1844 presidential candidates would defend the Mormons' claims against Missouri outlaws who had seized thousands of Mormon farms and buildings. As a gesture of protest, Smith finally announced his own candidacy for the highest office in the land. But long before the election, Smith ordered the destruction of a printing press set up by Mormon dissidents who had declared: "We will not acknowledge any man as king or lawgiver to the church." Illinois then charged Smith with treason and locked him and his brother in the Carthage jail. On June 27, 1844, a "mob" that included many prominent non-Mormon citizens stormed the jail and killed them both.

To the Mormons the Prophet's martyrdom brought shock, division, and a struggle for power. It also temporarily appeased the aggression of anti-Mormons and gave Smith's followers time to plan an exodus. Brigham Young, like Smith a man of humble Vermont origin, soon emerged as the leader of the church and as one of the nineteenth century's greatest organizers. Aided by the elite Quorum of the Twelve Apostles and the Council of Fifty, he preserved order and morale while considering and rejecting possible refuges in British and Mexican territory. Before the end of 1845, the Mormon leadership had decided to send an advance company of 1,500 men to the valley of the Great Salt Lake, then still part of Mexico. As a result of mounting persecution and harassment, the Mormons soon concentrated

their energies on evacuating Nauvoo, on selling property at tremendous sacrifice, and on setting up refugee camps from eastern Iowa to Winter Quarters, a temporary destination in eastern Nebraska. The last refugees crossed the Mississippi at gunpoint, leaving Nauvoo a ghost town. During the summer of 1846 some 12,000 Mormons were on the road; 3,700 wagon teams stretched out across the prairies of Iowa.

In the summer of 1847 Brigham Young led a vanguard of picked men across the barren wastes of Nebraska and Wyoming to the Great Salt Lake Valley of Utah. In September a second party of 2,000 weary Mormons found home in the new Zion. During the same year the American defeat of Mexico brought Utah within the dominion of the United States. The Mormons had contributed a battalion of 500 men who had marched with the American army across New Mexico to southern California, and whose pay had helped to finance the migration to Utah. Yet by 1848 the Mormons occupied an inland mountain fortress, a thousand miles beyond the Kansas frontier, and seemed at last to be the masters of their own destiny. When federal judges and other officials arrived in the territory, they found that the Mormons had held a census, adopted a constitution, elected Young governor, and established a "State of Deseret," complete with its own currency and army. The theocratic government was responsible for the remarkably rapid and orderly settlement of the valley, for the collective labor and central economic planning that brought irrigation to the dry but fertile land, and for the coordinated expansion that planted ninety-six colonies in ten years, extending in a corridor from Salt Lake City to San Diego.

Ten years before the time when South Carolina defied federal authority by firing on Fort Sumter and thus precipitating the Civil War, federal officials fled from Utah, denouncing Young's government as a theocracy fundamentally disloyal to the United States. Although the Mormons professed loyalty to the Constitution and acknowledged their territorial status, they intended to pay little attention to authorities sent from Washington. When Young publicly proclaimed the sacred doctrine of polygamy, which Mormon leaders had privately practiced for over a

MORMONS EXPELLED FROM NAUVOO

Despite its inaccuracies, this romanticized view of the Mormons being expelled from Nauvoo conveys the reality of white American families being driven out of the city they built. The building on the horizon is the famous Nauvoo temple. *(Church Archives, The Church of Jesus Christ of Latter-Day Saints)*

BRITISH POSSESSIONS

OREGON TERRITORY

MINNESOTA TERRITORY

WISCONSIN

NEW YORK
Palmyra
1830

INDIAN

Missouri R.

IOWA
Winter 1846-48
Quarters

Kirtland 1831-37
PENNSYLVANIA

Great Salt L.   Ogden
Virginia City
Salt Lake City
1847
Carson City
UTAH TERRITORY

ILLINOIS
Nauvoo
1840-45
Carthage

INDIANA   OHIO

COUNTRY

Platte R.

(Omaha)

CORRIDOR
Cedar City

Ohio R.

Colorado R.

Las Vegas

Independence
1831-39   MISSOURI

Los Angeles

MIGRATION
San Bernardino
1851

San Diego

NEW MEXICO TERRITORY

Phoenix

Gila R.

Colorado R.

ARKANSAS

Mississippi R.

Red R.

CALIFORNIA

TEXAS

Rio Grande

MEXICO

The Mormon Trail

⬅ Mormon Migrations 1830-1851

⊙ Mormon Settlements

▢ Projected State of Deseret

0   Miles   400

decade, he presented a ready-made issue to outraged reformers, clergymen, and politicians. President Buchanan felt the need of appeasing this popular clamor and of forcibly establishing federal authority in Utah. In 1857 he dispatched a regular army force of 2,500 men to impose federal law on the Mormons; they were led, in an irony of history, by Albert Sidney Johnston, who would soon be a Confederate general resisting an invasion by the United States.

Fortunately for the Mormons, winter snows trapped the expedition in the Rocky Mountains, allowing time for behind-the-scenes negotiations. Governor Young proclaimed martial law and threatened to burn Salt Lake City to the ground and "to utterly lay waste" the land if Utah were invaded. State-rights Democrats had little enthusiasm for setting precedents that might be turned against southern slavery, and though Buchanan had sworn that he would "put down the Mormon rebellion," he decided early in 1858 to proclaim a "pardon" to the inhabitants of Utah if they would obey United States laws and cooperate with federal officials. To prove their strength, however, the Mormons evacuated Salt Lake City. Johnston's army entered a deserted city, greeted only by squads of tough police, "glowering from beneath their hat-brims, with clubs in their hands, and pistols ready slung at their belts." The later withdrawal of federal troops concluded the so-called Mormon War, which brought no change in the actual government of Utah. When Buchanan's successor, Abraham Lincoln, was asked what he proposed to do about the Mormons, he answered, "I propose to let them alone." Lincoln, of course, had other problems on his hands.

No story in American history is more incredible. From the outset, Mormonism embodied the longings and aspirations of people who had not shared in the growing prosperity and social modernization of the early nineteenth century. The poet Whittier observed, after listening to a Mormon service in Massachusetts: "They speak a language of hope and promise to weak, weary hearts, tossed and troubled, who have wandered from sect to sect, seeking in vain for the primal manifestation of the divine power." The new church recruited most of its members from the more remote

BRIGHAM YOUNG, 1801–1877
(Library of Congress)

and isolated parts of New England; from the sparsely populated southern districts of New York and adjacent parts of Pennsylvania; from the rural backcountry of the Upper South and frontier Midwest; and eventually from both rural and manufacturing districts of Wales, Lancashire, and Scandinavia. Few of these converts were well-to-do, well educated, or well established in settled communities. They were mainly small farmers who had been displaced by commercial agriculture, and footloose tradesmen and mechanics who had been bypassed by expanding markets, a people already uprooted and highly mobile, long engaged in a search for communal and religious security.

The Meaning of Mormon Dissent. Because the Mormon search for authority took religious form, it is easy to miss its radical challenge to American secular values and institutions. Against a pluralistic permissive, and individualistic society, the Mormons pitted a higher authority that rested on a rock of unswerving certainty and conviction. Their institutions, based on divine authority, cast doubt on the legitimacy of popular sovereignty, secular law, and established government. The claim that divine revelation sanctioned such a practice as polygamy challenged the basic premises of secular law and morality. And according to their enemies, the Mormons' communal economy subverted private property, encouraged wholesale theft, and excluded non-Mormon enterprise from Utah. Far worse, the Mormons had shown little Christian forbearance in response to persecution. If like the earliest Christians they had looked for strength from the blood of their martyrs, they had also promised retaliation, or "blood atonement," to their enemies.

But the Mormons were not revolutionaries. Despite many points of dissent, Mormonism had much in common with the developing culture of pre–Civil War America. No other American denomination so fully incorporated the "Protestant ethic" of work, or the rule of abstaining from tobacco and all alcoholic drinks as a symbol of their own self-discipline and modernized values. In many respects, the Mormons' theocratic ideal was an extreme version of the ideal of Lyman Beecher, the New England revivalist reformer, and of countless other evangelists who insisted that rampant democracy must be guided by a higher moral force.

In sum, Mormonism was both a radical protest against the values of an individualistic, competitive, uprooting, and disinheriting world, and a vehicle of solidarity and authority that enabled its members to adjust to that world. During the pre–Civil War decades no other movement, with the exception of the southern crusade to vindicate black slavery, posed so serious a challenge to the ideology of the industrializing, urbanizing, and modernizing North. The Mormons probed the outermost limits of tolerance, the violent limits where dissent verged on treason, and finally established their own fragile asylum beyond— but soon within—America's geographical frontiers. Unlike the South, they escaped the major confronta-

tion of civil war. But their unique success required a prolonged accommodation and ultimate capitulation to the civilization against which the South finally waged civil war.

The Benevolent Empire

Like the founders of Mormonism, the reformers of the early nineteenth century were responding to the breakdown of social rules and moral authority associated with a traditional society. To restore "the moral government of God" was the supreme goal of the so-called Benevolent Empire—an informal coalition of home and foreign missionary societies, the American Tract Society, the American Sunday School Union, the American Society for the Promotion of Temperance, the American Colonization Society, the Prison Discipline Society, and the General Union for Promoting the Observance of the Christian Sabbath. Even William Lloyd Garrison, who later came to symbolize radical abolitionism and a defiance of both church and state, began his career in the 1820s as a lowly but ardent champion of these seemingly conservative reform organizations. Like many clergymen and wealthy philanthropists, young Garrison deplored the rising "mobocracy," the "lawless multitude" who enjoyed liquor, violence, profanity, sexual vice, and vulgar entertainment. American social reform originated in the crusade to purify public morals and to find new means, such as the asylum and penitentiary, for instilling habits of regularity, sobriety, obedience, and responsibility.

The Reform of Society. Ideals of purification and the exclusion of undesirables dominated the activities of the Benevolent Empire. Having already provided for the abolition of slavery in the northern states, many antislavery reformers wanted to send the free blacks back to Africa, an idea that had gained increasing support during the early nineteenth century, especially among missionary groups who assumed that American blacks would help to Christianize the land of their ancestors. Drunkards were to be banished from the sight of respectable society.

STATE PENITENTIARY,
PENNSYLVANIA
The early nineteenth century
witnessed the creation of asylums—totally planned and
manipulated environments—
which were intended to cure
the insane, reform criminals,
and liberate the handicapped
from the effects of deafness
and blindness. Whether liberating or repressive, these institutions exemplified the prevailing faith in the malleability
of human nature. *(Courtesy,
The Pennsylvania Prison Society)*

Criminals and deviants of various kinds were to be
walled off in prisons and asylums, where in the words
of some New York reformers of 1822, "their stubborn
spirits are subdued, and their depraved hearts softened, by mental suffering." When deviants were institutionalized, they could neither disturb nor con-
taminate a society that needed to concentrate on
business and moral virtue. Some enthusiastic prison
reformers even argued that society itself should be
modeled on "the regularity, and temperance, and
sobriety of a good prison."

Unlike the Mormons, these reformers aspired to
be leaders and transformers of the dominant secular
society. Although they sought to gather together like-
minded promoters of virtue, they originally gave no
thought to withdrawing from a sinful society in order
to practice virtue. Most of the leaders of the Benevolent Empire were men of economic and educational
attainment. They could think of themselves, under
"normal" circumstances, as the natural leaders of
their communities. They tended to idealize the New
England heritage of ordered and homogeneous communities governed by educated clergy and magistrates. Above all, they looked increasingly to Britain

for models of "practical Christianity" and organized
reform.

Organized philanthropy had a long history in
Britain, but during the Napoleonic wars (1798–1815)
it grew dramatically. A vast campaign was set afoot
in Britain to reform public morals, to Christianize
the world, and to unite rich and poor by an affec-
tionate bond of philanthropy that would replace the
traditional deference to the upper classes that even
in England had begun to decay. The British and Foreign Bible Society, founded in 1804, became the
model for nonsectarian organizations committed to
the ideal of "Christian unity." The Bible Society also
became a pioneer in highly specialized organization
as it acquired women's auxiliaries, skilled professional agents, and teams of "visitors" assigned to
specific towns, districts, and streets to collect funds,
interview poor families, and distribute Bibles. This
kind of systematic division of labor, later to form the
core of Mormon community organization in Utah,
was soon adopted by hundreds of British societies.

There were societies to promote Christianity
among the Jews, observance of the Christian Sabbath, universal peace, and the abolition of slavery;

societies to suppress immorality, infidel publications, juvenile delinquency, and cruelty to animals; societies to aid the indigent blind, the industrious poor, orphans of soldiers and sailors, and "Poor, Infirm, Aged Widows, and Single Women, of Good Character, Who Have Seen Better Days." The English, who seem to have outdone the Americans as a nation of joiners, even launched the Society for Returning Young Women to Their Friends in the Country.

By the 1820s Britain appeared suddenly to have moved into the vanguard of humanitarianism. The evangelical reformers won particular prestige from the leadership they took in the successful campaign to abolish the African slave trade. Most Americans, however, remembering the British invasions of the United States during the War of 1812, continued to think of England as a nation of tyranny and political corruption, and remained suspicious of any alleged humanitarian change of heart. But the New England clergy welcomed any news of England's moral transformation. Confronted by the collapse of Federalist political power, by the growing political force of public opinion, and by irresistible demands for the separation of church and state, many New England clergymen seized on the organizational apparatus of British benevolence as a means for securing control of American culture. With the aid of allies from other parts of the Northeast, these New England ministers and reformers succeeded in capturing and Americanizing the British evangelical spirit and in institutionalizing it in New York City, Philadelphia, and regions stretching west to Illinois.

From about 1810 to 1830 the Benevolent Empire developed gradually as local societies for the reformation of morals enlarged their objectives through various interstate and interlocking personal networks. A remarkable number of the original promoters of benevolent societies were students or recent graduates of Andover Theological Seminary in Massachusetts, founded by Congregationalists in 1809 in opposition to Harvard's drift toward liberal, rationalistic religion (Unitarianism). Andover was a seedbed for missionary work in Asia, Africa, and the American West. Many of the seminary's alumni took up such secular causes as black colonization, prison reform, and the suppression of intemperance. Louis Dwight, for example, who traveled the country as an agent for the American Bible Society, was so shocked by the squalor and disorder of jails that he became a leading crusader for the penitentiary system of total silence, close surveillance, and solitary confinement at night used in the Auburn, New York, prison. This Auburn system, Dwight maintained, "would greatly promote order, seriousness, and purity in large families, male and female boarding schools, and colleges."

These Andover reformers worked closely with serious-minded young ministers and laymen who had attended Yale or Princeton, as well as with rich and pious businessmen like Edward C. Delavan, Gerrit Smith, and the Tappan brothers. Delavan, a former wine merchant and Albany real estate magnate, contributed a fortune to the temperance cause. Gerrit Smith, a land baron in upstate New York, promoted innumerable reforms ranging from Sunday schools, penitentiaries, and temperance to radical abolitionism, women's rights, and world peace. Arthur and Lewis Tappan, who were wealthy importers and retail merchants in New York City, contributed money and leadership to a whole galaxy of local and national reform societies.

The Sabbatarian Movement. The movement to enforce the Christian Sabbath reveals some of the basic concerns of the Benevolent Empire as well as the obstacles that prevented the emergence of a much hoped-for "Christian party in politics." In 1810 Congress had passed a law requiring the mail to flow seven days a week, in order to meet the critical business demands for faster communication. Sunday mail service immediately drew fire from Lyman Beecher and other New Englanders, and subsequently provoked national debate. For devout Christians the Sabbath evoked memories of a less hurried, agrarian past. This was true even for some harried merchants who were uneasy over their own success and total immersion in worldly pursuits; the silent Sabbath became a reassuring symbol of spiritual goals which justified the previous six days of worldly cares and ambition.

It is significant that Sabbatarian reform orig-

"GO YE INTO ALL THE WORLD"
A certificate given to contributors to the Presbyterian Board of Foreign Missions. At the left are pictured a New England church and factories; at the right, scenes from Burma, the site of the most publicized early American mission. *(American Antiquarian Society)*

inated in the boom town of Rochester, not in the long-settled urban areas of the seaboard. Rochester's established clergy had come from New England and New Jersey, where a quiet Sabbath had been enforced by custom and law. But the Erie Canal passed directly under the windows of Rochester's First Presbyterian Church, and the rowdy boatmen made no effort to lower their voices during the hours of Sunday prayer. In 1828 the town's leading ministers, real estate magnates, and entrepreneurs enlisted Lyman Beecher and Lewis Tappan in a national crusade to persuade

Congress to enforce the laws of God. Although unsuccessful, the movement was historically important because it polarized "serious Christians" against the multitude; because it prepared the way for collaboration between wealthy New York philanthropists and social activists inspired by the revivals of Charles Grandison Finney; and because it marked the transition between distributing Bibles and resorting to direct political and economic action. It should also be emphasized that Rochester lay at the heart of the Burned-Over District and that the Sabbatarian movement coincided with the anti-Masonic crusade, Finney's revivals, the perfection and extension of the Auburn penitentiary system, and the birth of Mormonism.

Although the various causes taken up by the Benevolent Empire appear conservative when compared with later abolitionism, feminism, and perfectionism, they challenged vested interests and provoked immediate and furious resistance. The Sabbatarian movement, for example, threatened loss to owners of boat lines, ferries, taverns, theaters, and stores, much as the temperance movement threatened not only brewers, distillers, and distributors but also thousands of grocers and storekeepers whose customers expected a free pick-me-up as a sign of hospitality. Like the more militant temperance reformers, the Sabbatarians urged true Christians to boycott offending proprietors. Between Buffalo and Albany they also established their own six-days-a-week Pioneer Stage Line, a counterpart of the special temperance hotels and of the abolitionist shops that sold only produce made by free labor. These "anti"-institutions, which were almost uniformly unsuccessful, were intended to be sanctuaries—virtuous, disciplined environments set off from a chaotic and corrupting society—and models for the world to imitate. But like other reformers, the Sabbatarians were also committed to an imperial mission. Setting a precedent for later abolitionists, they organized a great petition campaign to persuade Congress to stop the Sunday mails. Like the abolitionists, they warned that unless Congress acknowledged a "higher law," the nation had little chance for survival:

If this nation fails in her vast experiment, the world's last hope expires; and without the moral energies of the Sabbath it will fail. You might as well put out the sun, and think to enlighten the world with tapers . . . as to extinguish the moral illumination of the Sabbath, and break this glorious mainspring of the moral government of God.

As the Mormons later discovered, many Americans were suspicious of people who laid claim to the moral government of God. By 1831 the Benevolent Empire had failed in its most daring and secular missionary efforts to regenerate society. Lyman Beecher

had early defined the supreme goal of the missionary and benevolent societies: to produce "a sameness of views, and feelings, interests, which would lay the foundation of our empire upon a rock." But this purpose smashed against the rocklike resistance of people who refused to be homogenized, especially under Yankee direction. In response to the Sabbatarians' petitions, Congress agreed with a Kentucky senator who drafted a report stating that the national legislature was not "a proper tribunal to determine the laws of God." The colonization movement—the movement to send free blacks to Africa—did much to unite northern urban blacks, who angrily affirmed that they would not accept a foreign asylum as a substitute for justice: "We will never separate ourselves voluntarily from the slave population of this country." "Let not a purpose be assisted which will stay the cause of the entire abolition of slavery." Resistance to the Benevolent Empire also appeared in the South and Southwest, paradoxically, where an antimission movement appealed to "Hard-Shell" Baptists and rural Methodists. These groups found no biblical sanction for benevolent societies and bitterly resented any attempts to bring religious instruction to the blacks. Further, as one Baptist declared, "our backwoods folks" simply could not understand the pretentious talk of the "young men come from the eastern schools."

The Benevolent Empire solved no social problems. It received no credit for legislative triumphs of the magnitude of Britain's abolition of the slave trade (1807) and gradual emancipation of West Indian slaves (1833). By 1837, moreover, internal conflicts had shattered all hope of a united front among evangelical reformers. Growing divisions over slavery simply intensified suspicions and grievances that had long been festering on every level. Sectarian rivalry weakened the supposedly nondenominational societies that northern Presbyterians and Congregationalists had always controlled. In 1837, when the Presbyterian church separated into conservative Old School and liberal New School camps, the economic depression also sharply reduced philanthropic gifts and thus further weakened the various organizations of the Benevolent Empire. The major Protestant churches, however, continued much of the work under denominational auspices.

Waging the War.   It can be argued that the true revolution in American reform began in the 1820s with the militancy, the dedication, the towering expectations, and the phenomenal organization of the nonsectarian, evangelical societies. It began, that is, when an agent of the Sunday School Union, addressing the well-to-do members of the Bible Society, repeated a British motto: "Not by exactions from the opulent but by the contributions from all"; when the organizers of foreign missions called for a "vast body like a host prepared for war"; and when the benevolent societies developed the techniques of modern fund-raising campaigns. The real revolution began with the mass production of literally millions of moralistic tracts, priced cheaply enough to undersell all commercial publications and marketed by discounts and other techniques that were far ahead of commercial practice. By 1830, in short, the evangelicals had devised all the apparatus needed for a massive conquest of American culture.

Although the conquest had ethnic, class, and geographical boundaries, few invading armies or political revolutions have had such a far-reaching effect on an entire society as the Benevolent Empire did. In 1834 the Temperance Society estimated that they had over 1.25 million members; in 1836 the American Tract Society alone sold over 3 million publications. In 1843, in response to the depression that had filled New York City's streets with thousands of beggars and vagrants, the New York Association for Improving the Condition of the Poor imitated the earlier models and sent teams of agents to gather information district by district and to distribute food, fuel, and clothing. The needy recipients could not help but be influenced, one way or another, by the association's links with the temperance movement, its conviction that poverty was a problem of individual morality, and its commitment to make the poor "respectable." If the reformers harbored little sympathy for sinners who refused to be saved, their ideology rested on a belief in human perfectibility, strongly laced with hopes for an American millennium.

The reformers' confidence in human perfectibil-

ity inspired a multitude of efforts, especially in the 1840s, to liberate individuals from all coercive forces and institutions. Perfectionism—the belief that people are capable of unlimited moral improvement—took both religious and secular forms. Suddenly new things seemed possible, new ways of thinking and acting seemed worth trying. The nation had never before witnessed such frothy experimentation, such gusty defiance of traditional wisdom, or such faith in spontaneous love and harmony. Some reformers won fame for their success in emancipating individual victims of deafness, blindness, and insanity. Samuel Gridley Howe, best known for his pioneering work with the blind and deaf-blind, expressed the growing view that even criminals were "thrown upon society as a sacred charge." "Society," Howe said, "is false to its trust, if it neglects any means of reformation." Prison reformers tried, with little success, to transform penitentiaries into communities of rehabilitation and to persuade society of the need for parole, indeterminate sentences, and sympathetic care for discharged convicts. Nativists, who were alarmed by the increasing number of Catholic immigrants, publicized cases of Catholic women who had escaped from supposedly tyrannical and immoral nunneries, and demanded laws that would liberate Catholic laymen from the control of their priests.

Temperance.   The temperance movement, a direct outgrowth of the Benevolent Empire, illustrates this mixture of humanitarianism, intolerance, progressivism, and self-righteousness. Though sometimes portrayed as religious cranks and killjoys, the temperance reformers were responding to a genuine social problem. During the early nineteenth century, per capita consumption of hard liquor far exceeded even the highest twentieth-century levels; alcohol abuse undoubtedly contributed to family discord and child abuse, to public disorder, and to lowered productivity and rising social costs of all kinds. By the mid-1830s various groups of urban artisans and northern free blacks endorsed temperance as a prerequisite for self-improvement. At the same time, middle-class champions of total abstinence became embroiled in bitter disputes over biblical sanctions for drinking wine.

"Fur Traders Descending the Missouri" *by John Caleb Bingham. The Metropolitan Museum of Art, Morris K. Jesup Fund, 1933*

By the second quarter of the nineteenth century a growing number of artists were giving imaginative expression to the changing American experience. Some of these artists drew on the rich resources of primitive painting and popular folklore; an increasing number had received formal training in Europe and in the new artistic academies of the East. Apart from training and talent, American artists were becoming more sensitive to the opportunities and coercions of a market economy in which art competed with other luxuries. They were becoming more responsive to the exotic and romantic fashions of the time, largely derived from Europe and, above all, to America's dramatic expansion, which seemed at once exhilarating and dangerous. For the central legacy of Old World culture, running like a blinking danger light from the ancient Greeks to Shakespeare and Milton, was the message that destruction inevitably follows excessive human pride, arrogance, or a defiance of

The Perils of Civilization

the boundaries that God and nature had imposed on humankind.

Nature became the central theme of American art in the pre–Civil War era. It was still a nature that stood above and apart from humankind—a source of inspiration, a force to be conquered, but not a *resource* to be preserved in parks or commemorated in museums. George Caleb Bingham, who grew up on the frontier, could portray the penetration and exploitation of nature as an idyllic moment of harmony. He depicts fur traders descending the great Missouri River (not fishermen or hunters in a protected game preserve). The boat

"Death Struggle" by Charles Deas. Shelburne Museum, Inc., Shelburne, Vt.

is laden with pelts and a live fox is chained to the bow. The young trapper lounges over his gun and a dead waterfowl. The colorful detail and sharp, angular lines of the men and boat stand out against the feathery trees in the background. Yet Bingham has skillfully blended the human forms with the watery reflections and mist of the wild landscape. His trappers are less intruders upon nature than converts to its serenity.

Even when conflict became explicit, nature re-

tained a sense of transcendence or "otherness." Civilization had not yet won supremacy. In Charles Deas's melodramatic painting, *Death Struggle*, a white trapper, still clutching a mink he has caught in a trap, is locked in combat with an Indian. In contrast to Bingham's peaceful mist and mirror-like river, nature now assumes the beautiful awe and terror that romantics termed the "sublime"—a boiling conflict between light and darkness that recalls nineteenth-century illustrations of Dante's

Divine Comedy and Milton's *Paradise Lost*. Deas's painting also echoes the themes of the contemporary *Leather-Stocking Tales* of James Fenimore Cooper. Deas's trapper, like Cooper's heroes, is in dire peril, but the white audience can confidently assume that his Indian foe will plunge into the dark abyss below.

Yet there was open space in the West that remained unconquered. The first pictorial images of conquest focused on trading posts that enclosed small fortified spaces in the midst of boundless plains and barren mountains. Alfred Jacob Miller's views of Fort Laramie represented a compromise between the harmonious blending of Bingham and the stark combat of Deas. Miller, enlisted in 1837 as the official artist for an expedition led by a British explorer and army officer, made the first on-the-spot paintings of the Rocky Mountains fur-

trapping region. Fort Laramie had been built on the North Platte River (northeast of the later town of Laramie, Wyoming), at the crossroads of Indian trading routes and in the direct path of the future Oregon Trail. Miller depicted it as an outpost of white civilization, a protected space filled with rectangular lines and jutting towers reminiscent of medieval European castles. A secure oasis for tens of thousands of future overland emigrants, it was also surrounded by the tepees of nomadic Oglala Sioux. As portrayed here in *The Interior of Fort Laramie* by Miller, the fort stakes off a physical space for controlled intercourse between whites and Indians—the Indians who were sometimes allowed to enter the gate, trade, stare at the cannon, and be exploited, sexually and otherwise, by a superior power.

"The Interior of Fort Laramie" *by Alfred Jacob Miller. Walters Art Gallery, Baltimore*

For pre–Civil War Americans, the Far West represented only one aspect of nature, a raw nature that sometimes seemed to threaten the moral and psychological foundations of civilization. East of the Mississippi, where civilization faced no more than a mopping-up operation, the victors could afford a certain nostalgia for the wilderness landscape that was being transformed and enclosed. Most of the East was still woodland, swamp, and pasture, but "nature," in the sense of an environment that affects man more than it is affected by man, seemed increasingly vulnerable. It could therefore be enshrined and for a time preserved in its precarious autonomy by landscape painting, a form of art that enjoyed increasing popularity. The reverent imagery of the so-called Hudson River School suggested a divine spirit within hills, brooks, forests, rocks, clouds, and illuminated skies. Building on this tradition, Martin Heade evolved an eerie realism that captured fleeting moments of changing light and atmosphere, often set off by wide horizons where civilized land gives way to a wild and ominous sea. In his *The Coming Storm*, the luminous sailboat and human figures seem almost frozen in place, yet threatened by the distant flash of lightning and heavy rain clouds. In the works of Heade and other landscape painters, nature could startle viewers, bringing a delight of recognition as well as a moment of humility. As the symbol of something beyond human reach, nature could thus serve as an aesthetic counterweight to civilization's demands for predictability, mastery, and control.

"The Coming Storm" by Martin J. Heade. The Metropolitan Museum of Art, Gift of Irving Wolf Foundation

"The Láckawanna Valley" by George Innes. The National Gallery of Art, Washington, D.C., Gift of Mrs. Huttleston Rogers

In a way, however, American culture demanded that nature somehow assimilate and give legitimacy to the machine. This demand was most imaginatively met by George Innes, who in 1854 accepted a commission from the Lackawanna Railroad Company to paint such unorthodox subjects as a railroad roundhouse and steam locomotive. In Innes's *The Lackawanna Valley,* a pastoral landscape seems to embrace and merge with civilization's smoke and iron. A lone spectator, similar to the contemplative figure in Heade's *The Coming Storm,* looks out upon a peaceful valley. The train's plume of smoke is echoed by a distant wisp beyond the church steeple. The curving track links the background hills with the tall tree in the foreground. Despite the stumps, despite the signs of encroaching industry, the human intrusion on nature appears to be in harmony with nature's rhythms.

But antebellum artists evolved no similar formula for romanticizing the city, a subject they generally shunned. A few anonymous painters did succeed in documenting the squalor, moral degradation, and jostling confusion of New York's growing slums. It was Thomas Cole, however, the original leader of the Hudson River School and the painter who did the most to popularize the American landscape, who expressed the era's most striking vision of the consequences of "overcivilization."

Cole painted his five canvases on *The Course of Empire* after returning from a residence in Europe, where he had contemplated the ruins of antiquity. His choice of classical imagery had special meaning for a modern republic that had taken so many of its moral and aesthetic models from classical Rome. Cole's first two canvases show the evolution from primitive origins of a pastoral, creative, classical society. In *The Consummation of Empire*, however, chasteness and innocence have given way to luxurious decadence. The scene represents a total subjugation and defiance of nature. Except for a jutting cliff in the background, the landscape has become wholly encrusted with marble temples and monuments. An imperial procession on the bridge suggests the arrogance of unlimited power. The sinuous fountain and voluptuous setting at the lower right suggest moral decay.

"The Consummation of Empire" by Thomas Cole. Courtesy of the New York Historical Society, New York City

"The Destruction of Empire" by Thomas Cole. Courtesy of the New York Historical Society, New York City

In *The Destruction of Empire* the viewer's perspective has shifted to the right and rear. The jutting cliff is still visible in the distance, and is the only landmark certain to survive the catastrophic destruction. Civilization is engulfed in a storm of flame and swirling smoke. People spill like ants from the bridge, while in the foreground the statue of a gigantic headless warrior holds his helpless shield above the scene of pillage and rape. On the base of the statue Cole inscribed the large numbers "1836," which was not only the date of the painting but a year when financial panic caused many Americans to ponder the future course of their own empire.

Cole's final canvas presents lifeless ruins and rubble covered by creeping vegetation—a view of nature unperturbed by the extinction of civilization. A similar theme of catastrophism, qualifying the exuberant optimism of antebellum society, was not uncommon in American literature and art. It drew on traditions of religious millennarianism as well as on the fear that any republic, no matter how virtuous its origins, might share the fate of Rome. Both models suggested the spasmodic anxieties of a people who continued to defy the limits and boundaries of their Old World heritage.

In 1840 the movement took a new direction when groups of reformed alcoholics began organizing "Washingtonian Societies" that appealed to working-class people and to members of subcultures that had not been reached by the traditional and elitist temperance organizations. At Society meetings former drunkards told rapt audiences what hell was really like, sometimes reenacting the agonies of delirium tremens. Old guard temperance leaders tried to use and patronize the Washingtonians, much as some white abolitionists tried to use and patronize fugitive slaves. But the middle-class societies never felt comfortable with the former victims of intemperance, or with the boisterous showmanship that induced thousands of disreputable-looking people to pledge themselves, at least temporarily, to total abstinence.

Faith in "moral suasion," or individual conversion to abstinence, disintegrated in the face of hundreds of thousands of German and Irish immigrants who had little taste for Yankee moralism. The celebrated "Maine law" of 1851, which outlawed the manufacture and sale of alcoholic beverages, marked the maturing of a new campaign for legal coercion in the form of statewide prohibition. On both local and state levels, bitter political conflicts erupted over the passage, repeal, and enforcement of prohibition laws. For temperance reformers of the 1850s, it was no longer safe to rely on the individual's mastery of temptation. The crucial act of will was now to be made by the state, which would attempt to remove the temptation. In less than thirty years one of the crucial goals of the Benevolent Empire had been consigned to the realm of political power; faith in moral influence and liberation had yielded to what the *American Temperance Magazine* hailed as the only force that drunkards could comprehend—"the instrumentality of the law."

Radical Abolitionism

Black slavery was the first issue to expose the limitations of the Benevolent Empire. Even by 1830 there was a striking discrepancy between the public optimism of the evangelical philanthropists and their whispered despair concerning black slavery. Harsh facts made the discrepancy increasingly noticeable. Despite the legal prohibition in 1808 of slave imports from Africa, the natural increase of the American slave population exceeded all earlier expectations. The number of slaves in the United States increased from approximately 1.5 million in 1820 to over 2 million in 1830. This figure represented almost one-sixth of the total United States population and more than twice the number of slaves in the British and French West Indies. The number of free blacks grew during the 1820s from about 234,000 to 320,000.

Failure of Black Colonization. In 1830 the American Colonization Society transported a total of only 259 free blacks to Liberia, the West African colony that the society had established as a refuge for American blacks. Yet most reformers still regarded colonization as the only solution: "We must save the Negro," as one missionary put it, "or the Negro will ruin us." Racial prejudice permeated the Benevolent Empire, and was by no means foreign to later radical abolitionists. But the new and significant fact was the rising tide of virulent racism among the working classes of the North. Prejudiced as they may have been, many leaders of the colonization movement were sincere opponents of slavery who abhorred the growing racism of the northern masses and who saw deportation as the only realistic means for preventing racial war in the North and for inducing southern planters to free their slaves.

A series of events reinforced the realization that white America could not solve its racial problem by shipping a few hundred free blacks each year to Liberia. In 1829 David Walker, a Boston black who belonged to the Massachusetts General Colored Association, published his revolutionary *Appeal to the Colored Citizens of the World*, which justified slave rebellion and warned white Americans that if justice were delayed blacks would win their liberty "by the crushing arm of power." The pamphlet created a furor and copies soon appeared among blacks in the Deep South. Then in 1831 Nat Turner, a trusted Virginia slave, led the bloodiest slave revolt the South had yet experienced. At the end of the same year a far larger insurrection rocked the British colony of Jamaica. In Britain, mass demonstrations continued to demand the immediate and unconditional emancipation of West Indian slaves. When Parliament responded in 1833 with monetary compensation to slaveowners to cover part of the financial loss of emancipation, and with an apprenticeship plan to prepare slaves for freedom, a few Americans concluded that effective political action of any kind required a mammoth mobilization of public opinion.

The Ethical Basis of Abolitionism. To the young abolitionists who began to appear in the early 1830s, black slavery was the great national sin. Theodore Dwight Weld, the son of a Connecticut minister and a convert and close associate of Charles Grandison Finney in upstate New York, personally symbolized the fusion of American revivalism with British anti-slavery influence. His most intimate friend and religious model was Charles Stuart, a visiting British reformer who worked with Finney's disciples in the Burned-Over District and then in 1829 returned to England to throw himself into the battle for slave emancipation. After being urged by Stuart to take up the cause in America, Weld shifted from temperance and educational reforms to abolitionism, becoming one of the most fearless and powerful lecturers in the area from Ohio to Vermont. Early in 1833 he wrote a letter to William Lloyd Garrison, whom he knew only by reputation, illuminating the meaning of slavery as sin:

That no condition of birth, no shade of color, no mere misfortune of circumstances, can annul the birth-right charter, which God has bequeathed to every being upon whom he has stamped his own image, by making him a *free moral agent,* and that he who robs his fellow man of this tramples upon right, subverts justice, outrages humanity, unsettles the foundations of human safety, and sacrilegiously assumes the prerogative of God; and further, tho' he who retains by force, and refuses to surrender that which was originally obtained by violence or fraud, is joint partner in the original sin, becomes its apologist and makes it the business of every moment to perpetuate it afresh, however he may lull his conscience by the vain plea of expediency or necessity.

Weld's statement sums up an ethical imperative that sprang from three fundamental convictions: that

all men and women have the ability to do what is right, and are therefore morally accountable for their actions; that the intolerable social evils are those that degrade the image of God in man, stunting or corrupting the individual's capacities for self-control and self-respect; and that the goal of all reform is to free individuals from being manipulated like physical objects. As one Garrisonian put it, the goal of abolitionism was *"the redemption of man from the dominion of man."*

That abolitionists like Weld were almost wholly concerned with ideals was at once their greatest strength and greatest weakness. America was supposedly a nation of doers, of practical builders, framers, drafters, organizers, and technicians. The overriding question, in abolitionist eyes, was whether the nation would continue to accommodate itself to a social system based on sheer violence. To propose rational plans or to get embroiled in debates over the precise means and timing of emancipation would only play into the hands of slavery's apologists. What the times required, therefore, was "an original motive power" that would shock and awaken public opinion, create a new moral perspective, and require legislators to work out the details, however imperfectly, of practical emancipation. In 1831 William Lloyd Garrison admitted: "Urge immediate abolition as earnestly as we may, it will alas! be gradual abolition in the end. We have never said that slavery would be overthrown by a single blow; that it ought to be we shall always contend."

The Abolitionists. On one level, the abolitionists realistically saw that the nation had reached a dead end on slavery. Instead of gradually withering away, as earlier optimists had hoped, the evil had grown and had won increasing acquiescence from the nation's political leaders and most powerful institutions. Therefore, the abolitionists took on the unpopular role of agitators, of courageous critics who stood outside the popular refuges of delusion, hypocrisy, and rationalization. In 1830 Garrison went to jail for writing libelous attacks against a New England merchant who was shipping slaves from Baltimore to New Orleans. After Arthur Tappan had paid his fine and

THE LIBERATOR

OUR COUNTRY IS THE WORLD---OUR COUNTRYMEN ARE ALL MANKIND.

WILLIAM LLOYD GARRISON, 1805–1879
(Harvard College Library)

secured his release, Garrison in 1831 founded the newspaper *The Liberator* in Boston, hurling out the famous pledge: *"I will be* as harsh as truth, and as uncompromising as justice. . . . I am in earnest—I will not equivocate—I will not excuse—I will not retreat a single inch—AND I WILL BE HEARD."

Although *The Liberator* had an extremely small circulation and derived most of its support from black subscribers in the Northeast, Garrison succeeded in being heard. In the South especially, newspaper editors seized the chance to reprint specimens of New England's radicalism, accompanied by their own furious rebuttals. Even before the end of 1831, the Georgia legislature proposed a reward of $5,000 for anyone who would kidnap Garrison and bring him south for trial. Garrison also championed the free blacks' grievances against the Colonization Society, which he had once supported, and mounted a blistering attack against the whole conception of colonization. He pointed out that the hope for colonization confirmed and reinforced white racial prejudice and that it was racial prejudice that was the main barrier the abolitionists faced in the North. Largely as a result of Garrison's early and independent leadership, the American Anti-Slavery Society, founded in 1833, committed itself to at least a vague legal equality of whites and blacks and to a total repudiation of colonization.

Even though they had practically declared war

against the values, institutions, and power structure of Jacksonian America, the abolitionists continued to think of their reform societies as simple extensions of the Benevolent Empire. They assumed that they could quickly win support from churches and ministers; that they could persuade the pious, influential, and respectable community leaders that racial prejudice was as harmful as intemperance. Then, after mobilizing righteous opinion in the North, they could shame the South into repentance. Abolitionists did not think of themselves as provokers of violence and disunion. Rather, it was slavery that had brought increasing violence and threats of disunion. A national commitment to emancipation, they believed, would ensure harmony and national union.

Like the wealthy British philanthropists, Arthur and Lewis Tappan moved from various benevolent causes to the cause of immediate emancipation. By 1833 philanthropists in Great Britain had won the support of the established order as well as of middle-class public opinion. But in America, precisely because the Tappans had wealth and prestige, they were viciously attacked for encouraging radicals like Garrison and for betraying the common interests that had allowed leaders in different sections to do business with one another. Mass rallies in the South pledged as much as $50,000 for the delivery of Arthur Tappan's body, dead or alive. In New York City, business leaders vainly pleaded with the two brothers, whose lives were being repeatedly threatened by 1834, to give up their radical activities. In that year, prominent New Yorkers cheered on a mob of butcherboys and day laborers who smashed up Lewis Tappan's house and burned the furnishings. Only the unexpected arrival of troops prevented an armed assault on the Tappans' store.

Antiabolitionists played on popular suspicions of England, charging that men like George Thompson, an English friend of Garrison's, had been sent "to foment discord among our people, array brother against brother . . . to excite treasonable opposition to our government . . . to excite our slave population to rise and butcher their masters; to render the South a desert, and the country at large the scene of fraternal war." Abolitionists continually invoked the ideals of

JACK, A SLAVE DRIVER
This remarkable photograph portrays "Jack," an African-born driver on B. F. Taylor's South Carolina plantation. It was recently discovered, along with other daguerreotypes of African-born slaves, at Harvard's Peabody Museum of Archaeology and Ethnology. The pictures were originally commissioned in 1850 by Louis Agassiz, a celebrated Swiss-born scientist eager to prove that God had created Africans as a distinct and separate species. It is ironic that Agassiz, who wanted to give scientific support to the enemies of abolitionism, could gather documents that were far more eloquent indictments of slavery than any of the literary evidence available to abolitionists. *(Peabody Museum, Harvard University)*

the Declaration of Independence and portrayed themselves as fulfilling the Revolution's promise. But their enemies styled themselves as Minute Men defending American liberties. The mob riots of the Revolutionary periods appeared to sanction the antiabolitionist riots that spread across the North in the 1830s. For the most part this mob violence was carefully planned, organized, and directed toward specific goals, such as the destruction of printing presses and the intimidation of free blacks. The leaders were "gentlemen of property and standing"—prominent lawyers, bankers, merchants, doctors, and local political leaders of both parties. In most towns and cities the white abolitionists and free blacks had little protection from the forces of law and order. The colonizationists, already weakened by financial difficulties and internal division, took the lead in accusing the abolitionists of being "amalgamationists" who would not stop short of encouraging black men to woo the daughters of white America.

Abolitionism and Freedom of Speech. It was this bugaboo that brought the northern crowds into the streets and that also lay behind the abolitionists' most dramatic break with the Benevolent Empire. Lane Theological Seminary, in Cincinnati, was meant to be one of the Empire's crowning achievements, a beachhead of benevolence on the Ohio River, a staging ground for the missionary conquest of the West. Arthur Tappan paid Lyman Beecher's salary as president of the seminary. He also paid the way for Theodore Weld, then thirty-one, to attend the school as a student. Early in 1834 Weld conducted at Lane an eighteen-day soul-searching revival on the question of slavery. After converting many students and nonstudents to the doctrine of immediate emancipation, Weld led his band into the slums where the black residents of Cincinnati lived. There they set up libraries, conducted evening classes, and fraternized with the city's "untouchable" caste. In Weld's view, educational institutions had a duty to train minds for the new "era of disposable power and practical accomplishment."

To the Tappans' dismay, Lane's board of trustees voted to get rid of Weld and the other antislavery leaders, and Lyman Beecher, who was still a supporter of colonization, acquiesced in the decision. Various leaders of American higher education agreed that antislavery agitation endangered the fundamental purposes of American colleges. In response, almost all the Lane students walked out of the seminary with

Weld. Some ended up in Arthur Tappan's newly financed college, Oberlin. But many joined Weld as traveling agents for the American Anti-Slavery Society, of which Arthur Tappan was president, braving showers of rotten eggs and stones in order to address the American people.

As a product of the Benevolent Empire, abolitionism drew on and perfected techniques of mass communication that gave the nation its first taste of modern "public relations." By 1835 the new steam printing press and other technological improvements had reduced the cost and increased the volume of mass publication. In 1834 the Anti-Slavery Society distributed 122,000 pieces of literature; in 1835 the figure rose to 1.1 million. President Jackson and various national and local authorities expressed alarm over this attempt to apply the methods of the Bible and tract societies to a revolutionary purpose—a purpose that threatened one of the nation's chief capital investments as well as a national system for racial control. But though the government encouraged the destruction of abolitionist mail, it could do nothing about the itinerant abolitionist lecturers in the North, the "antislavery bazaars" held to raise funds and distribute literature, the auxiliary societies for ladies and children, or the flood of propaganda in the form of medals, emblems, broadsides, bandannas, chocolate wrappers, songs, and children's readers.

The rapid growth of abolitionist societies, coupled with violent efforts to suppress them, led to sharp divisions of opinion over abolitionist principles and tactics. One turning point was the celebrated martyrdom in 1837 of Elijah P. Lovejoy, a New England abolitionist who, like the Mormons, had been driven out of Missouri and had established a refuge in Illinois. While trying to defend a new printing press from an antiabolitionist mob, Lovejoy was shot and killed. His violent death dramatized the issue of civil liberties and won new support for the abolitionists; it also forced abolitionists to debate the proper response to violence, since Lovejoy and his men had used arms in self-defense.

Nonresistance. Garrison, who had nearly been lynched in 1835 by a Boston mob, had become convinced that violence was a disease infecting the entire body of American society. Whenever the nation faced any issue of fundamental morality, such as the treatment of Indians, blacks, or dissenters, it resorted to the principle that might makes right. The only Christain response, Garrison maintained, was to renounce all coercion and adhere to the perfectionist ideal of absolute nonresistance. If abolitionists tried to oppose power with power, as Lovejoy had done, they were certain to be crushed. They would also dilute their moral argument, since the essence of slavery was the forcible dominion of man over man. In 1838 Garrison and his followers formed the New England Non-Resistance Society, a group which condemned every kind of coercion including not only defensive war and capital punishment, but lawsuits, prisons, and insane asylums, unless designed solely for "cure and restoration."

What began to emerge in New England abolitionism, then, was a radical repudiation of all limits imposed on the individual by the threat of force. Negro slavery and racial oppression were merely extreme manifestations of an evil embodied in the patriarchal family, the criminal law, and the police power of the state. By 1843 Garrison concluded that the majority rule was simply the rule of superior power, with no protection for human rights, that the Union had always been a compact for the preservation of slavery, and that the Constitution was therefore "a covenant with death, and an agreement with Hell." The Garrisonians demanded withdrawal from corrupt churches and from all complicity with the corrupt government. Calling for disunion with the South, they also crossed the threshold of symbolic treason and declared themselves enemies of the Republic.

In interesting ways the Garrisonians' rhetoric paralleled the rhetoric of the Mormons. "The governments of the world," Garrison announced in 1837, "are all anti-Christ." Yet by 1845 he also cast off the Old Testament, arguing that God could never have sanctioned slavery and violence. Instead of moving beyond the geographic frontiers, as the Mormons had done, to establish the kingdom of God, Garrison defended his own fortress of moral independence within a hostile society.

Feminism, Perfectionism, and Political Consolidation

Radical abolitionism was part of a much broader protest against forms of oppression and inequality that had long been accepted as inevitable. In the 1830s abolitionism became intertwined with attacks against the traditional subordination of women. The founders of the feminist movement, like the male abolitionists, had mostly served apprenticeships in the moral reform and temperance societies of the Benevolent Empire.

Women were not only deprived of higher education, barred from the professions, and denied the right to vote; most women upon marriage also surrendered any legal right to their own earnings and property. Harriet Robinson, who began working in a Massachusetts textile mill at age eleven and who participated in 1836 in one of the first women's strikes against wage-cutting, recalled that many workers were "fugitives" from oppressive husbands and had thus assumed false names in order to prevent their husbands from legally seizing their wages. Such conditions evoked mounting protest from writers like Catharine Beecher, a daughter of Lyman Beecher and sister of Harriet Beecher Stowe. While conceding that women should not infringe upon the "male sphere" of business and politics, Catharine Beecher exposed the oppression of mill girls, fought for improved female education, and attempted to enlist thousands of American women as teachers in a vast crusade "to secure a proper education to the vast multitude of neglected American children all over our land." Such agitation focused attention on women's collective interests, problems, and responsibilities, and thus contributed to a new feminist consciousness.

Female Abolitionists. Abolitionism provided female reformers with an egalitarian ethic and with a public forum for attacking entrenched injustice. From the outset, the Garrisonian movement attracted a group of exceptionally talented writers and lecturers such as Maria Weston Chapman, Lydia Maria Child, Abby Kelly, and Lucretia Mott. Among Garrison's most important converts were Sarah and An-

HARRIET BEECHER STOWE, 1811–1896
The daughter of Lyman Beecher, Harriet Beecher Stowe, *above,* suddenly became not only the most famous member of an illustrious family but also the world's most admired and hated woman. Bitterly attacked in the South, she was lionized in England and soon became an international literary celebrity. *(The Metropolitan Museum of Art. Gift of I. N. Phelps Stokes, Edward S. Hawes, Alice Mary Hawes, and Marion Augusta Hawes, 1937)*

ELIZABETH CADY STANTON
In 1840 she traveled to London with her husband, abolitionist Henry Brewster Stanton, to the first World's Antislavery Convention where the issue of women's participation sharply divided the convention. Subsequently, she and Lucretia Mott led the first women's rights convention in the United States held at Seneca Falls, New York, in July, 1848. *(American Antiquarian Society)*

gelina Grimké, two articulate sisters who had abandoned their father's South Carolina plantation and had then been converted to Quakerism and abolitionism in Philadelphia. Because they could speak of southern slavery from personal experience, the Grimkés had a striking effect on New England audiences. In 1837 they boldly lectured to mixed audiences of men and women, an offense that outraged clergymen and conservative reformers who believed that women should move within a precisely limited "sphere." The Grimkés attacked the hypocrisy of conservative abolitionists who scoffed at biblical justifications for slavery but who invoked the Bible when defending female subservience. The Garrisonians convinced the Grimkés that the Christian "principles of peace" were at the root of all reform; the Grimkés helped to convince the Garrisonians that the same principles applied to the "domestic slavery" of women to men.

In 1840 the issue of women's participation in abolitionist conventions brought an irreparable split in the American Anti-Slavery Society, which the more conservative Tappan faction abandoned to the Garrisonian radicals. Female abolitionists increasingly stressed the parallels between their own powerlessness and the legal status of slaves. In 1848 Elizabeth Cady Stanton and Lucretia Mott finally organized at

Seneca Falls, New York, the first convention in history devoted to women's rights. The convention's Declaration of Sentiments, modeled on the Declaration of Independence, proclaimed that "the history of mankind is a history of repeated injuries and usurpations on the part of man toward woman, having in direct object the establishment of an absolute tyranny over her." Among the list of specific grievances, Stanton insisted on including the exclusion of woman from "her inalienable right to the elective franchise."

Despite this demand for political rights, the National Women's Rights conventions of the 1850s devoted more attention to legal and economic disabilities, and to challenging the clergy's insistence that the Bible defined a subordinate "sphere" for the "weaker sex." "Leave woman," Lucy Stone, a radical feminist leader, demanded, "to find her own sphere."

Although abolitionism provided the feminists with a sympathetic audience and with ready-made channels of communication, the relationship was also limiting in the sense that women's rights were always subordinate to the seemingly more urgent cause of slave emancipation. This dependence is evident even in the rhetoric of radical feminists who compared the prevailing system of marriage to a private plantation in which every woman was a slave breeder and a slave in the eyes of her husband.

Communitarianism. The quest for social equality led some reformers, including radical abolitionists, to join experimental communities where they could escape from the coercions and frustrations of competitive labor and of the private, isolated family. Some of these communities were inspired by secular social theories. In the 1820s, for example, the socialist experiment at New Harmony, Indiana, was based on the doctrines of Robert Owen, a wealthy Scottish philanthropist. In the 1840s a wide scattering of projects drew on the theories of Charles Fourier, a French social philosopher. The most successful communities, however, were those of religious sects like the Rappites and Shakers, or those disciplined by the authority of extraordinary leaders such as John Humphrey Noyes.

THE FUGITIVE SLAVE'S SONG, 1845
Frederick Douglass's escape from slavery was celebrated in a popular song. The illustration, however lacking in skill, is notable because it broke away from the standard racist caricature of blacks. *(American Antiquarian Society)*

Noyes, who had studied theology at Andover and Yale, was a perfectionist who believed that the millennium had already begun and that the time had arrived for "renouncing all allegiance to the government of the United States, and asserting the title of committees could help a small number of fugitives find their way to Canada and relative security—and blacks were the main conductors on the so-called Underground Railroad—but except in Massachusetts, black abolitionists had little leverage for loosening the rocklike edifice of discriminatory law. Instead, white abolitionists kept pressuring blacks to keep a low profile, to act the part assigned them by white directors, who presumably knew the tastes of an all-white audience, and to do nothing that might spoil the show.

In the 1840s black leaders gradually cast off the yoke that had bound them to a white man's cause and tried to assert their own leadership. In 1843, at the Convention of the Free People of Color held at Buffalo, Garnet openly called for a slave rebellion, arguing that it was a sin to submit voluntarily to human bondage. Douglass adhered to his own version of nonresistance until 1847, when he broke with Garrison over the propriety of founding a black abolitionist newspaper, the *North Star.* In the same year Garrison sadly reported that Remond had proclaimed that "the slaves were bound, by their love of justice, to RISE AT ONCE, en masse, and THROW OFF THEIR FETTERS." *oooh—kinky!!*

But speeches were one thing, action another. Black abolitionists had always looked to voting, a right few blacks possessed, as the most promising route to power. For the most part, therefore, they supported the Liberty party in 1840 and 1844, and the Free Soil party in 1848. The drift of antislavery politics, however, was away from black civil rights in the North and emancipation in the southern states and toward a walling off of the western territories—a walling off, in all probability, of free blacks as well as slaves. It is not surprising that by 1854 a few black leaders like Martin Delaney were talking of a separate black nation, or that blacks who had proudly defended their American heritage and right to American citizenship were beginning to reconsider voluntary colonization.

But by 1854 many northern whites had also con-cluded that the Slave Power had seized control of America's manifest destiny, thereby appropriating and nullifying the entire evangelical and millennial mission.* Moreover, the Fugitive Slave Law of 1850, requiring federal agents to recover fugitive slaves from their sanctuaries in the North, directly challenged the North's integrity and its new self-image as an asylum of liberty. The arrival of federal "kidnappers" and the spectacle of blacks being seized in the streets invited demonstrations of defiance and civil disobedience. Increasing numbers of former moderates echoed Garrison's rhetoric of disunion, and an increasing number of former nonresistants called for a slave insurrection or predicted that the streets of Boston might "yet run with blood." Wendell Phillips, a Boston aristocrat and the most powerful of all abolitionist orators, rejoiced in the knowledge "that every five minutes gave birth to a black baby," for in its infant wail he recognized the voice that should "yet shout the war cry of insurrection; its baby hand would one day hold the dagger which should reach the master's heart."

In the 1850s northern abolitionists finally concluded that if the Slave Power were not crushed by insurrection or expelled from the Union, it would surmount every legal and constitutional barrier and destroy the physical ability of Northerners to act in accordance with the moral ability that had been the main legacy of revivals. The western territories were thus the critical testing ground that would determine whether America would stand for something more than selfish interest, exploitation, and rule by brutal power. All of the aspirations of the Benevolent Empire, of evangelical reformers, and of perfectionists of every kind could be channeled in a single and vast crusade to keep the territories free, to confine and seal in the Slave Power, and thus to open the way for an expansion of righteous liberty and opportunity that would transcend all worldly limits.

*For this critical contest over admitting Kansas as a slave state, see Chapter 17, pp. 447–51.

SUGGESTED READINGS

David B. Davis, ed., *Ante-Bellum Reform* (1967), presents differing interpretations of reform and also an annotated bibliography. Though out of date, Alice F. Tyler, *Freedom's Ferment* (1944), is the only comprehensive survey. Whitney R. Cross, *The Burned-Over District* (1950), analyzes the origins of secular reform as well as of Mormonism and other religious movements.

Thomas F. O'Dea, *The Mormons* (1957), is the best introduction to Mormonism. Fawn M. Brodie, *No Man Knows My History: The Life of Joseph Smith* (1945), is also indispensable. Klaus J. Hansen, *Quest for Empire* (1967), is a brilliant account of the Mormons' efforts to prepare for a worldly Kingdom of God. Robert B. Flanders, *Nauvoo: Kingdom on the Mississippi* (1965), is a fascinating study of the Mormons' city-state in Illinois. A dramatic and authoritative narrative of the westward migration is Wallace Stegner, *The Gathering of Zion: The Story of the Mormon Trail* (1964). Leonard J. Arrington's two works, *Great Basin Kingdom* (1958) and *Building the City of God: Community and Cooperation among the Mormons* (1976), are masterly accounts of the Mormon settlement of Utah. On polygamy, see Kimball Young, *Isn't One Wife Enough?* (1954). Norman F. Furniss, *The Mormon Conflict, 1850–1859* (1960), covers the so-called Mormon War.

There are no satisfactory general works on the relation between religion and secular reform. Important aspects of the subject are examined in Carroll Smith-Rosenberg, *Religion and the Rise of the American City: The New York Mission Movement* (1971); Paul E. Johnson, *A Shopkeeper's Millennium: Society and Revivals in Rochester, New York, 1815–1837* (1978); Charles I. Foster, *An Errand of Mercy: The Evangelical United Front* (1960); Clifford S. Griffin, *Their Brothers' Keepers: Moral Stewardship in the United States* (1960); Timothy L. Smith, *Revivalism and Social Reform* (1957); and Bertram Wyatt-Brown, "Prelude to Abolitionism: Sabbatarian Politics and the Rise of the Second Party System," *Journal of American History*, 58 (1971), 316–41. The temperance movement, a critical link between evangelical religion and secular reform, is well described in John A. Krout, *The Origins of Prohibition* (1925). For American drinking habits, see W. J. Rorabaugh, *The Alcoholic Republic: An American Tradition* (1979).

The literature on abolitionism is voluminous. The historical precedents and background are covered in David B. Davis, *The Problem of Slavery in Western Culture* (1966); and *The Problem of Slavery in the Age of Revolution,* *1770–1823* (1975). The best brief account of later abolitionism is James B. Stewart, *Holy Warriors: The Abolitionists and American Slavery* (1976). Gilbert H. Barnes, *The Anti-Slavery Impulse* (1933), is a dramatic and readable study, emphasizing the role of Theodore Weld and the Lane Seminary rebels. For an opposing and brilliantly argued view, see Aileen S. Kraditor, *Means and Ends in American Abolitionism: Garrison and His Critics on Strategy and Tactics* (1967). A similarly powerful and creative work is Lewis Perry, *Radical Abolitionism: Anarchy and the Government of God in Antislavery Thought* (1973). Provacative new approaches can be found in Lewis Perry and Michael Fellman, eds., *Antislavery Reconsidered: New Perspectives on the Abolitionists* (1979). Leonard L. Richards, *"Gentlemen of Property and Standing": Anti-Abolition Mobs in Jacksonian America* (1970), keenly analyzes antiabolition violence. Concerning civil liberties, see Russel B. Nye, *Fettered Freedom: Civil Liberties and the Slavery Controversy* (1963); and Thomas O. Morris, *Free Men All: The Personal Liberty Laws of the North, 1780–1861* (1974).

For the politics of antislavery, see Richard H. Sewell, *Ballots for Freedom* (1976), as well as the following biographical studies: Bertram Wyatt-Brown, *Lewis Tappan and the Evangelical War against Slavery* (1969); Betty Fladeland, *James Gillespie Birney: Slaveholder to Abolitionist* (1955); James B. Stewart, *Joshua R. Giddings and the Tactics of Radical Politics* (1970); Richard H. Sewell, *John P. Hale and the Politics of Abolition* (1965); Frank O. Gatell, *John Gorham Palfrey and the New England Conscience* (1963); Ralph V. Harlow, *Gerrit Smith* (1939); Edward Magdol, *Owen Lovejoy, Abolitionist in Congress* (1967); and David Donald, *Charles Sumner and the Coming of the Civil War* (1960). William Lloyd Garrison, who tried to abstain from political involvement, is the subject of two fine biographies: John L. Thomas, *The Liberator: William Lloyd Garrison* (1963); and Walter M. Merrill, *Against Wind and Tide: A Biography of William Lloyd Garrison* (1963).

Benjamin Quarles, *Black Abolitionists* (1969), is a pioneering study of a subject long neglected by historians. An important recent work is Jane H. Pease and William H. Pease, *They Who Would Be Free: Blacks' Search for Freedom, 1830–1861* (1974). For Frederick Douglass, see Arna Bontemps, *Free at Last: The Life of Frederick Douglass* (1971), and Douglass, *Life and Times of Frederick Douglass, Written by Himself* (1881).

An original work that is indispensable for understanding the changing status of women and the origins of feminism is Nancy F. Cott, *The Bonds of Womanhood: "Woman's Sphere" in New England, 1780–1835* (1977), which should be supplemented by Barbara J. Berg, *The Remembered Gate: Origins of American Feminism—The Woman and the City, 1800–1860* (1977) and Keith M. Melder, *Beginnings of Sisterhood: The American Woman's Rights Movement, 1800–1850* (1977). Aileen S. Kraditor, ed., *Up from the Pedestal: Selected Writings in the History of American Feminism* (1968), is an excellent anthology. The best overall survey is Carl N. Degler, *At Odds: Women and the Family in America from the Revolution to the Present* (1980). Other useful works are Ellen C. DuBois, *Feminism and Suffrage: The Emergence of an Independent Women's Movement in America, 1848–1869* (1978); W. L. O'Neill, *Everyone Was Brave: The Rise and Fall of Feminism in America* (1970); Andrew Sinclair, *The Better Half: The Emancipation of the American Woman* (1965); and Page Smith, *Daughters of the Promised Land* (1970). For individual biographies, see Alma Lutz, *Created Equal: A Biography of Elizabeth Cady Stanton* (1973); Otelia Cromwell, *Lucretia Mott* (1971); Katharine Du Pre Lumpkin, *The Emancipation of Angelina Grimké* (1974); and Gerda Lerner, *The Grimké Sisters from South Carolina: Rebels against Slavery* (1967).

David S. Rothman, *The Discovery of the Asylum* (1971), is a brilliant interpretation of reformatory institutions. The most imaginative study of early prisons is W. David Lewis, *From Newgate to Dannemora: The Rise of the Penitentiary in New York* (1965). Black McKelvey, *American Prisons* (1936), is a more comprehensive reference. On the insane, the best guides are Helen E. Marshall, *Dorothea Dix: Forgotten Samaritan* (1937); and Gerald N. Grob, *Mental Institutions in America: Social Policy to 1875* (1973). For the reformer who did most for the deaf and blind, see Harold Schwartz, *Samuel Gridley Howe* (1956).

The classic work on the peace movement is Merle Curti, *The American Peace Crusade, 1815–1860* (1929), which should be supplemented by Peter Brock, *Pacifism in the United States: From the Colonial Era to the First World War* (1968).

On communitarian settlements, the best general works are Mark Holloway, *Heavens on Earth* (1951), and the relevant chapters in Donald D. Egbert and Stow Persons, *Socialism and American Life* (2 vols., 1952). The communitarian phase inspired by Robert Owen is masterfully covered by J. F. C. Harrison, *Quest for the New Moral World: Robert Owen and the Owenites in Britain and America* (1969). For the New Harmony experiment, see also William Wilson, *The Angel and the Serpent* (1964); and Arthur Bestor, *Backwoods Utopias* (1950). The best introduction to the Oneida community is Maren L. Carden, *Oneida: Utopian Community to Modern Corporation* (1969); Robert D. Thomas, *The Man Who Would Be Perfect: John Humphrey Noyes and the Utopian Impulse* (1977). Three other studies of unusual importance are Lawrence Veysey, ed., *The Perfectionists: Radical Social Thought in the North, 1815–1860* (1973); Michael Fellman, *The Unbounded Frame: Freedom and Community in Nineteenth-Century Utopianism* (1973); and William H. Pease, *Black Utopia: Negro Communal Experiment in America* (1963).

Expansion and New Boundaries

The 1840s marked the beginning of a new era. In the North, recovery from a long depression was accompanied by rapid urban growth, the extension of machine production and of the factory system, the influx of hundreds of thousands of immigrants, and the construction of vast railway networks linking western farms with eastern markets. In the South, the remarkable profitability of cotton and sugar plantations confirmed a whole region's unapologetic commitment to slave labor. The moral discomforts that had troubled Jefferson's generation of Southerners had finally given way to a proud and self-conscious identity as a "progressive slave society." This sectional confidence was bolstered not only by the world's demand for cotton but by the annexation of Texas. The resulting Mexican War, which extended America's boundaries to the Pacific, led some southern leaders to dream of a vast tropical empire based on the slave labor of an "inferior race." These spectacular fulfillments of trends and aspirations that had been developing since the War of 1812 posed grave challenges to governmental policy and to the nation's sense of its own character.

Industrialization and Economic Growth

There is still much controversy over the stages of America's economic growth. Some economists have advanced the theory of a dramatic "takeoff" starting in the 1840s, in which the growth of the nation's productivity shot dramatically ahead of the growth of population. The best recent evidence suggests that a pattern of long-term accelerated growth preceded significant industrialization and probably originated in the 1820s from the interaction between urbanization and western agriculture. In those years manufacturing still mostly conformed to the literal meaning of the word—goods that were made by hand in households and in small shops or mills. Blacksmiths, coopers, cobblers, curriers, hatters, tailors, weavers—these and other artisans and apprentices worked in central shops, mills, and stores, or moved as itinerants through the more sparsely settled countryside. Yet the 1820s marked the beginning of rapid urbanization, a decisive shift toward nonagricultural employment, and perhaps the fastest economic growth of the pre–Civil War era.

Manufacturing. As had happened in England, cotton textiles became the leading industrial innovation. Aided somewhat by protective tariffs, a group of wealthy Boston merchants pooled their capital and in the 1820s extended the Waltham system of large-scale factory production to new manufacturing centers like Lowell and Chicopee, in Massachusetts. The Waltham system, which had been created by New England merchants when the War of 1812 had curtailed international trade, exploited the latest English technology, such as the power loom, and continued to draw on the expertise of immigrant English artisans.

If their products were to compete successfully with imported English textiles, New England manufacturers had to lower the cost and increase the efficiency of labor. Traditionally, American manufacturers had cut costs by employing children or families including children who increased the labor force without increasing wages. It soon became apparent, however, that children could not handle the frequent breakdowns of the new machinery or conform to the regimen necessary for increased labor productivity.

By the late 1840s immigrants had begun to ease the general shortage of factory labor. But for a few decades the Boston merchants relied on the unique expedient of employing adult young women who were attracted to the factories by chaperoned dormitories and various cultural amenities. The merchant-manufacturers desired, no doubt sincerely, to avoid the moral degradation that had stigmatized the English factory system. As economy-minded entrepreneurs, they also hoped to exert influence over their employees' leisure time, preventing the binges and self-proclaimed holidays that had always led to irregular work habits and absenteeism among the preindustrial folk. New England farm girls could also be hired for less than half the wages of male factory hands, since they were secondary earners for their families and since the factory was virtually the only possible liberation from the farm.

From 1815 to 1833 the cotton textile industry increased average annual output at the phenomenal rate of 16 percent. Although slackening demand soon reduced the annual rate of growth to about 5 percent, textile producers, including wool and carpet manufacturers, continued to be pioneers in mechanization, in efficiency, and in the use of steam power.

New England also gave birth to the so-called "American system of manufacturing." This innovation consisted of imaginatively applying and reaping the benefits from a machine-tool technology that had first been developed in England. Unlike the English, American manufacturers could not draw on a plentiful supply of highly skilled craftsmen with many years of training in an established craft tradition. They therefore encouraged the perfection of light machine tools that not only eliminated many hand operations but also allowed ordinary mechanics to measure within one-thousandth of an inch and to mill or cut metal with great precision. At the English Crystal Palace exhibition of 1851, American machinery astonished European experts. In 1854 one of the English commissions sent to study American achievements exclaimed over "the extraordinary ingenuity displayed in many of their labour-saving machines, where automatic action so completely supplies the place of the more abundant hand labour of older manufacturing countries."

The English investigators understood the significance for the future of such seemingly prosaic devices as a machine that produced 180 ladies' hairpins every minute. As early as 1853 an exuberant writer for the *United States Review* could predict that within a half-century machines would liberate Americans from the restraints of work: "Machinery will perform all work —automata will direct them. The only tasks of the human race will be to make love, study and be happy."

In 1860 American industry was still at an early stage of transition, showing sharp contrasts according to product and level of regional development. The American iron industry, despite an impressive expansion in output, was not, for example, nearly as successful as the cotton textile industry in adopting and improving the latest English technology. The continued use of small blast furnaces that used charcoal to produce malleable iron has been explained by the cheapness and availability of wood for charcoal; by the absence of bituminous coal east of the

Engraved for the "Pennsylvania" Magazine.
By Christopher Tully, who first Made and Introduced this
Machine into this Country

Newly invented Machine, for Spinning of Wool or Cotton.

INDUSTRY IN NEW ENGLAND

Americans expressed an absorbing interest in diagrams of new machines, such as Christopher Tully's eighteenth-century spinning machine for wool; even young boys became expert in grasping the principles by which gears transmitted power to moving rollers and other parts. The woman tending a machine in the illustration at right is weaving cloth on a power loom. The lithograph of the Pontoosuc Woolen Mills in Pittsfield, Massachusetts, dramatizes the rural setting of early American industry. *(Top left, American Antiquarian Society; others, Merrimack Valley Textile Museum)*

Alleghenies; by the belated discovery and use of anthracite; and by the particular needs of local blacksmiths. Whatever the reasons, American industry in the 1850s heavily depended on imported English wrought iron and railroad rails, and lagged far behind England in exploiting coal, iron, and steam.

In the West, manufacturing often reverted to preindustrial methods that had almost disappeared in the East. But even in the Northeast many goods were produced not in factories but by merchants who still relied on the "putting-out" system, distributing raw materials to laborers who often owned their own tools and worked at home. Other merchant capitalists hired laborers essentially as instruments of production—they had no share in the ownership of tools and machines, in managerial decisions, in the risks of marketing, or in the industrial product.

In 1860 American manufacturing still depended largely on water power, not steam. The typical firm employed a handful of workers, was unincorporated, and engaged in the small-scale processing of raw materials. Few industries processed the products of other industries. The nation's largest industries included some that were thoroughly mechanized, such as the production of cotton goods, flour, and meal; some that were partly mechanized, such as the manufacture of boots and shoes; and some that were characterized by premodern technology and low labor productivity, such as lumbering and the making of men's clothing.

Agriculture. The expansion and commercialization of agriculture, in both North and South, provided the impetus for the economy's accelerated growth and modernization.* During the 1840s the United States began to export an increasing proportion of its agricultural output, partly in response to poor harvests in Europe and to England's repeal of the protective "Corn Laws" that had excluded American and other

*See Chapter 12, pp. 315–22.

foreign grain. This outflow helped to pay for America's imports of manufactured products and the immense interest charges on foreign investment in American land, cotton, and railroads. Much of America's economic expansion depended on the ability to attract such investment from Europe. By preventing glutted domestic markets, agricultural exports also helped to raise the price of domestic farm products, thereby encouraging the further expansion of cash crops.

Continuing improvements in transportation enabled agricultural regions to specialize in the search for competitive advantages in response to the pressures of an increasingly national market. In the states of the Old Northwest, north of the Ohio River, farmers began to buy trademarked tools and machines from authorized distributors. Steel plows, invented in the 1830s but widely accepted only in the 1850s, made it possible to break the tough sod and cultivate the rich but sticky soil of the prairies. Mechanical reapers had also been invented in the 1830s, but only in the 1850s did Cyrus McCormick's Chicago factory begin large-scale production and employ modern techniques of advertising and promotion. As the Old Northwest proved its superiority in producing wheat and other grains, along with wool, corn, pork, and beef, farmers in the East, no longer able to compete with their western counterparts, had to be content to produce hay for horses and perishable foodstuffs for urban markets.

Railroad Building. The great railroad boom of the late 1840s and 1850s dramatized the growing links between agriculture and industry. Although the nation's railroads equaled the canals in mileage as early as 1840, canal barges and river steamboats continued to carry a significant proportion of freight throughout the antebellum period. By providing speedy access to isolated farms and distant markets, railroads opened new horizons and extended the risks and promises of a commercial society.

The development of railway networks was long delayed by primitive technology, a high incidence of breakdowns and accidents, and construction costs that required unprecedented amounts of capital investment. As early as 1828, Baltimore promoters began building the first trans-Appalachian railroad to compete with New York's Erie Canal, which threatened to channel much of the western trade toward New York City. But it was not until 1853 that this Baltimore and Ohio road reached the Ohio River. As late as 1860 there were still hundreds of small, independent lines with different widths of track. Nevertheless, by the early 1850s construction engineers were improving rails, roadbeds, bridges, and locomotives. Railroad corporations had amassed immense

reserves of capital, and their managers were learning how to administer complex bureaucracies that employed thousands of workers and required instant interstate communication by means of the recently perfected electric telegraph. By 1854 tracks extended from New York City to the Mississippi, and, by 1860, to the Missouri at St. Joseph. This burst of western railroad construction led to the beginning of consolidation into trunk lines that further cemented economic ties between the West and the Northeast. By 1860 railroads had become the nation's

**Principal
Railroads
1860**

first billion-dollar industry, spawning the first giant corporations, linking cash-crop farming with the production of iron, coal, lumber, and machine tools.

Panic of 1857.   There were dark shadows, however, in this overall picture of growth and economic integration. The mid-1850s brought a slowing down of investment and of industrial production, culminating in the financial panic of 1857. For the first time the business cycle seemed to be primarily geared to the fluctuations of nonagricultural forces, such as speculative investment in railroads, in the domestic economy. Significantly the South suffered little from the essentially industrial depression of the late 1850s. Southern leaders could not refrain from gloating over the economic vulnerability of northern industry and the insecurities of "wage slavery." Northern leaders angrily accused the South of contributing to the depression by defeating northern moves for protective tariffs and free homesteads. Slave-grown cotton remained an important contributor to the North's industrial growth. But many Northerners perceived the South as a vestige of colonial dependency—a dependency on English markets that blocked the way to national self-sufficiency.

The South as a "Slave Society"

By the 1830s the institution of black slavery had come to dominate all aspects of southern society. Apologies for slavery as an unfortunate though necessary evil were beginning to give way to aggressive self-justification. Paradoxically, as the South became increasingly isolated from the free-labor ideology of the Western world, the expansion of cotton cultivation helped to assure southern leaders that slavery was indispensable to northern and British industry. Accordingly, slaveholders regarded their critics as ungrateful hypocrites who would bite the hand that fed them.

The meaning of the term "slave society" is best illustrated by the West Indian colonies of the eigh-

teenth and early nineteenth centuries. There Negro slaves typically made up 90 percent or more of an island's population; political and social life was wholly dominated by large planters, their managers and agents, and the merchants who lived off the system. On the question of black slavery there was almost no dissent.

Parts of the South almost approximated this model: the swampy lowcountry of South Carolina and the Sea Islands; the fertile Black Belt, extending from Georgia to Mississippi; the delta counties of Mississippi and the sugar parishes of Louisiana. But unlike the small and isolated West Indian islands, the sprawling South was anything but a uniform and monolithic society. In 1860 roughly 10,000 families belonged to the planter aristocracy, out of a white population of some 8 million. Fewer than 3,000 families owned over one hundred slaves. Barely one out of four white Southerners owned a slave or belonged to a family that did. There were extensive regions of eastern Tennessee and western Virginia where blacks, slave or free, were a rarity. Slavery had declined sharply in most of the Upper South (by 1860 fewer than 2,000 slaves remained in Delaware). Nor could most of the nonslaveholding majority be classed as hillbillies and poor whites. In addition to artisans, factory workers, and professionals, there were millions of small farmers in the South who worked their own land or who grazed herds of cattle, pigs, and horses in the forests and open range of the public domain.

Nevertheless, except for a few isolated pockets, the South did become a slave society dominated politically and ideologically by a planter oligarchy. Throughout the period, slaveholding remained the most widespread and obvious route to wealth and status. By 1860 millions of nonslaveholders believed that any serious threat to slavery was sufficient justification for southern independence; many of them, especially in the Southwest, had reasonable hopes of acquiring land and becoming planters. And small farmers often depended on a neighboring planter's cotton gin or political patronage; they knew that in turn he depended for security on their services as armed patrols that searched the countryside for any unauthorized movement of blacks.

Dominance of the Planter Class.   The planter class could also draw on a rich tradition of political leadership. In the South—but not in the North—the eighteenth-century connection between wealth and personal political power endured. Political leadership sprang directly from the ownership of slaves, which was supposed to provide leisure, a concern for public order, and a certain paternalistic self-assurance in exercising authority. The planter elite demonstrated skill in commanding the loyalty of nonslaveholding whites and also in disciplining dissent within the white population. By the 1830s numerous southern abolitionists and Southerners with simply a strong distaste for slavery had emigrated to the North or West after abandoning hope of challenging the dogma that Negro slavery was a necessary evil that should be discussed as little as possible. They left behind them a planter elite solidified in its defense of slavery and militantly intolerant of dissent.

The key to southern white unity was race. The South was an amorphous society dedicated to the ideal of equality of opportunity as long as the ideal applied only to whites. It was also a region that depended economically on a system of labor exploitation that was difficult to square with republican and libertarian principles. Racial doctrine, the supposed innate inferiority of blacks, became the primary instrument for justifying the persistence of slavery, for rallying the support of nonslaveholding whites, and for defining the limits of dissent.

Southern Free Blacks.   The key to racial policy was the status of free blacks. Before the nineteenth century this status had been ambiguous, and the number of free blacks was insignificant. By 1810, however, as a result of the emancipations that had accompanied and followed the Revolution, there were 100,000 free blacks and mulattoes in the southern states. This group, the fastest growing element in the southern population, was beginning to acquire property, to found "African" churches and schools, and to assert its independence, especially in the Upper South. In

response, white legislators tightened restrictions on private acts of freeing slaves in an effort to curb the growth of an unwanted population. A rash of new laws, similar to the later black codes of Reconstruction, reduced free Negroes almost to the status of slaves without masters. The new laws regulated their freedom of movement; prohibited their fraternization with slaves; subjected them to surveillance and discipline by whites; denied them the legal right to testify against whites; required them to work at approved employments; and threatened them with penal labor if not actual reenslavement. Paradoxically, in the Deep South free blacks continued to benefit from a more flexible status because they were fewer than elsewhere in the South and, as in the West Indies, could serve as valued intermediaries between a white minority and a slave majority. Racial discrimination was most flagrant in the Upper South, precisely because slavery was economically less secure in that region.

Decline of Antislavery in the South.   From the time of the Revolution a cautious, genteel distaste for slavery had been fashionable among the planters of the Upper South. This Jeffersonian tradition persisted even after the more militant abolitionists had been driven from the region and after Methodist and Baptist leaders had backtracked on various resolutions encouraging gradual emancipation. The desire to find some way of ridding the South of its "burden" or "curse," as the Jeffersonian reformers called it, was perpetuated by some of the sons of affluent planters who went to the North or to Europe to study.

The hope of removing the South's burden also won assent from a few cosmopolitan planters, mostly Whigs, who were troubled by the soil depletion and economic decline of eastern Virginia and Maryland, and by the continuing loss of population to the Southwest. In 1832 the belief that slavery was "ruinous to the whites" received unexpected support in the Virginia legislature from nonslaveholders who lived west of the Blue Ridge and who had various motives for challenging the political control of tidewater planters. But in the end, their arguments, in a notable legislative debate of 1832 which arose in response to Nat

Turner's insurrection, demonstrated the power of racism. Even the nonslaveholding rebels acknowledged that bondage had benefits for blacks, and that its detrimental effects on white society could be ended only by gradually freeing and deporting the entire black population. The antislavery delegates failed even to carry a resolution that would have stigmatized slavery as an evil to be dealt with at some future time.

The Proslavery Argument.   By the 1840s—less than a decade later—such a public debate would have been inconceivable in any southern state. By then regional loyalty, intensified by sectional conflict, required that Southerners believe slavery to be a "positive good." The proslavery argument ranged from appeals to ancient Greek and Roman precedents to elaborate biblical interpretations designed to prove that slavery had never been contrary to the laws of God. Drawing on the romantic and chivalric literary fashions of the time, southern writers represented the plantation as a feudal manor blessed with human warmth, reciprocal duties, knightly virtues, and a loyalty to blood and soil.

The most striking part of the proslavery ideology was its indictment of liberalism and capitalism, its well-documented charge that the prevailing rule in so-called free societies, as George Fitzhugh put it, was "every man for himself, and the devil take the hindmost." In his *Sociology for the South* (1854) and *Cannibals All!* (1857), Fitzhugh incisively criticized the philosophic premises of an individualistic, egalitarian society. He also examined the destructive historical consequences of dissolving the social and psychological networks that had once given humanity a sense of place and purpose. Fitzhugh, the most rigorous and consistent proslavery theorist, presented the master-slave relation as the only alternative to a world in which rampant self-interest had subjected propertyless workers to the impersonal exploitation of "wage-slavery." He was consistent enough to renounce *racial* justifications for actual slavery and to propose that the benefits of the institution he boasted of be extended to white workers. But these arguments, however interesting theoretically, only showed

how far Fitzhugh had moved from social reality. Racism lay at the heart of the South's unity; the enslavement of whites was unthinkable, and in the 1850s the South even rejected extremist proposals for expelling or reenslaving a quarter-million free blacks. Fitzhugh's theories did more to expose the moral dilemmas of free society than to illuminate the actual complexities and contradictions of the South.

It is true that moral doubts persisted, especially in the Upper South. But after the 1830s such doubts were more than counterbalanced by the conviction that emancipation in any form would be a disaster, for blacks as well as whites. Southerners channeled their moral concern into dedicated efforts to reform, improve, and defend the peculiar institution. To own slaves, according to the reigning dogma, meant to have a sense of duty and a burden—a duty and a burden that defined the moral superiority of the South; a duty and a burden nonslaveholders in the South respected and were prepared to defend with their lives. That, perhaps, was the ultimate meaning of a "slave society."

Foreign Dangers, American Expansion, and the Monroe Doctrine

America's foreign policy had always presupposed a commitment by the national government to protect and support the South's peculiar institution. It is true, however, that American foreign policy reflected many other interests and motives, and that until 1844 protecting slavery was not explicitly acknowledged as a vital objective. The overriding objective in the early nineteenth century, as in the post-Revolutionary period, was to prevent England or France from acquiring a foothold in the increasingly vulnerable Spanish territories of North America. But those territories, including Cuba, East and West Florida, and Texas, were a threat mainly to the slaveholding South. The War of 1812 made clear that possession of the Floridas was essential for the security of the entire Lower South. From bases in supposedly neutral Spanish Florida, the British had incited Indian raids, had encouraged slave desertions, and had originally planned to launch an invasion inland to cut off New Orleans from the rest of the United States. The Haitian revolution of 1791–1804 had also shown that war could ignite a massive slave insurrection and totally destroy a slaveholding society.

Decline of New World Slavery.   One of the consequences of the Napoleonic wars was the fatal weakening of slaveholding regimes in most parts of the New World. Not only did France lose Haiti, the richest sugar colony in the world, but Napoleon's seizure of Spain opened the way for independence movements in the immense Spanish territories from Mexico to Chile. The prolonged wars of liberation undermined the institution of slavery and committed the future Spanish American republics to programs of gradual emancipation. After the British abolished the slave trade to their own colonies, they embarked on a long-term policy of suppressing the slave trade of other nations. By 1823, when little remained of the former Spanish, Portuguese, and French New World empires, slavery was a declining institution except in Brazil, Cuba (still a Spanish colony), and the United States.

This wider context dramatizes a momentous paradox of American foreign policy from the time of Jefferson's presidency to the Civil War. The extension of what Jefferson termed an "empire for liberty" was also the extension of an empire for slavery and thus a counterweight to the forces that threatened to erode slavery throughout the hemisphere. Jefferson himself initiated the policy of trying to quarantine Haiti, economically and diplomatically, to end the contagion of black revolution. In 1820, in the midst of the Missouri crisis and in response to Spain's delay in ratifying the Transcontinental Treaty of 1819 ceding East Florida, Jefferson privately assured President Monroe that the United States could soon acquire not only East Florida but Cuba—then on the road to becoming the world's greatest producer of slave-grown sugar—and Texas. Texas, he confidently predicted, would be the richest state of the Union, partly because it would produce more sugar than the country could consume.

There is no reason to think that American statesmen consciously plotted to create a vast empire for slavery—at least until the 1840s. From the annexation of Florida (1821) to the annexation of Texas (1845), the United States acquired no new territory that could upset the balance between free states and slave states achieved by the Missouri Compromise. The Old Southwest contained immense tracts of uncleared and uncultivated land, and many Southerners feared that reckless expansion would lead to excessive production that would lower the price of cotton and other staples.

Slavery and Territorial Expansion.   The connections between slavery and national expansion were more indirect. They involved two basic and continuing premises that governed foreign policy. The first premise was that territorial expansion was the only means of protecting and extending the principles of the American Revolution in a generally hostile world. "The larger our association," Jefferson had predicted, "the less will it be shaken by local passions." According to this nationalist view, Americans could deal with domestic imperfections once the nation had achieved sufficient power to be secure. Thus for ardent nationalists like John Quincy Adams any personal misgivings over slavery had to give way to the need for a united front against the monarchic despots of Europe. During the Missouri crisis the antislavery forces could never overcome the unfair charge that they were serving Britain's interests by fomenting sectional discord and blocking the westward expansion of the United States.

The second premise, held with passionate conviction by every president from Jefferson to Polk, was that England was America's "natural enemy," a kingdom ruled by selfish interest, filled with a deep-rooted hatred for everything America represented, and committed to the humiliation and subjugation of her former colonies. Anglophobia had much to do with the swift demise of the Federalist party. It was nourished by contemptuous anti-American essays in British periodicals and by unflattering descriptions by English travelers which were widely reprinted in the United States. Many Americans blamed England for the eco-

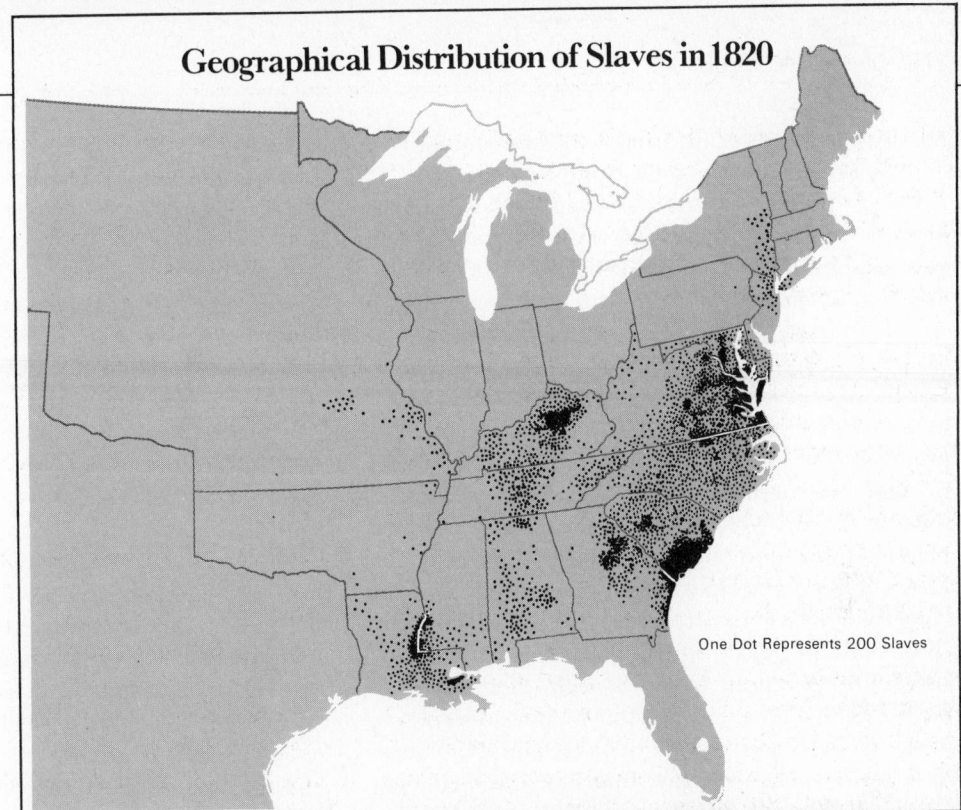

Geographical Distribution of Slaves in 1820

One Dot Represents 200 Slaves

Geographical Distribution of Slaves in 1860

One Dot Represents 200 Slaves

nomic depressions of 1819 and 1837. Irish immigrants regarded the English as their hereditary enemies. No American politician could risk even the suspicion of being an unintentional agent of British interests. It was thus an unhappy coincidence that British interests veered increasingly toward antislavery which American leaders interpreted, not without some reason, as a cloak for new forms of economic and ideological imperialism.

It was the takeover of Florida that established the precedents for the future and that also coincided with the dramatic southwestward expansion of cotton and slavery. As early as 1786 Jefferson had warned against pressing "too soon on the Spaniards." He held that East and West Florida could not be in better hands. He feared, however, that the Spanish were, as he said, "too feeble to hold them till our population can be sufficiently advanced to gain it from them piece by piece." By 1810 there were enough American settlers in the Baton Rouge district of West Florida to stage an armed rebellion against Spanish rule. President Madison, affirming that West Florida was part of the Louisiana Purchase, promptly annexed the section of the Gulf coast extending eastward to the Perdido River. To prevent any possible transfer of West Florida to England, Congress sanctioned Madison's annexation but balked at plans to seize East Florida during the War of 1812.

The Transcontinental Treaty of 1819.

The postwar negotiations with Spain involved not only Florida but the entire western boundary of the United States. Spain had never recognized the validity of Napoleon's sale of Louisiana, a sale prohibited by the treaty transferring the territory from Spain to France. Luis de Onís, the Spanish minister, tried to limit American claims to the narrowest strip possible west of the Mississippi. But as the negotiations dragged on, the South American wars of independence increasingly undermined Spain's position. Secretary of State John Quincy Adams proved to be a tough and skillful bargainer, and in 1818 Andrew Jackson, then the American military commander in the South, immensely strengthened Adams's hand. Without official authorization, Jackson invaded East Florida, captured

the main Spanish forts, deposed the governor, and hanged two English troublemakers. The excuse was that Florida had become a refuge for fugitive slaves and a base for Seminole Indian raids on American settlements.

Faced with the temporary seizure of his main bargaining card and fearful that the United States would begin aiding the rebellious Spanish colonies, Onís, agreed in the Transcontinental Treaty of 1819 to cede the Floridas to the United States in return for America's relinquishing the questionable claim that Texas was part of the Louisiana Purchase. In actuality, Onís had been desperate enough to give up most of Texas. But as President Monroe assured General Jackson, "We ought to be content with Florida, for the present, and until the public opinion . . . [in the Northeast] shall be reconciled to any further change."

For Adams the Transcontinental Treaty (or Adams-Onís Treaty, ratified in 1821) was "a great epoch in our history." Not only did it transfer the Floridas to the United States, but it extended American territorial claims to the Pacific Ocean. Spain ceded to the United States her rather weak claims to the Pacific Northwest, and agreed to an international boundary that extended from the Sabine River, dividing Texas from Louisiana, westward along the Red and Arkansas rivers to the Rocky Mountains, and then along the forty-second parallel to the Pacific. Spain had hardly ratified this momentous treaty before the burden of defending its boundaries fell upon an independent, weak, and war-torn Mexico.

Events Leading to Monroe Doctrine.

The collapse of the Spanish empire led directly to the Monroe Doctrine. By 1823 it was clear that Spain could never reduce her rebellious colonies to their former status, and Britain and America shared a common interest in preventing Europe's Holy Alliance of autocratic nations from intervening in Spain's behalf. Under pressure from the Russian czar, France was about to invade Spain, where a revolution had established a constitutional monarchy, in order to restore the absolutist regime of Ferdinand VII. The French foreign minister was known to have grandiose schemes for extending to the New World the Holy Alliance's

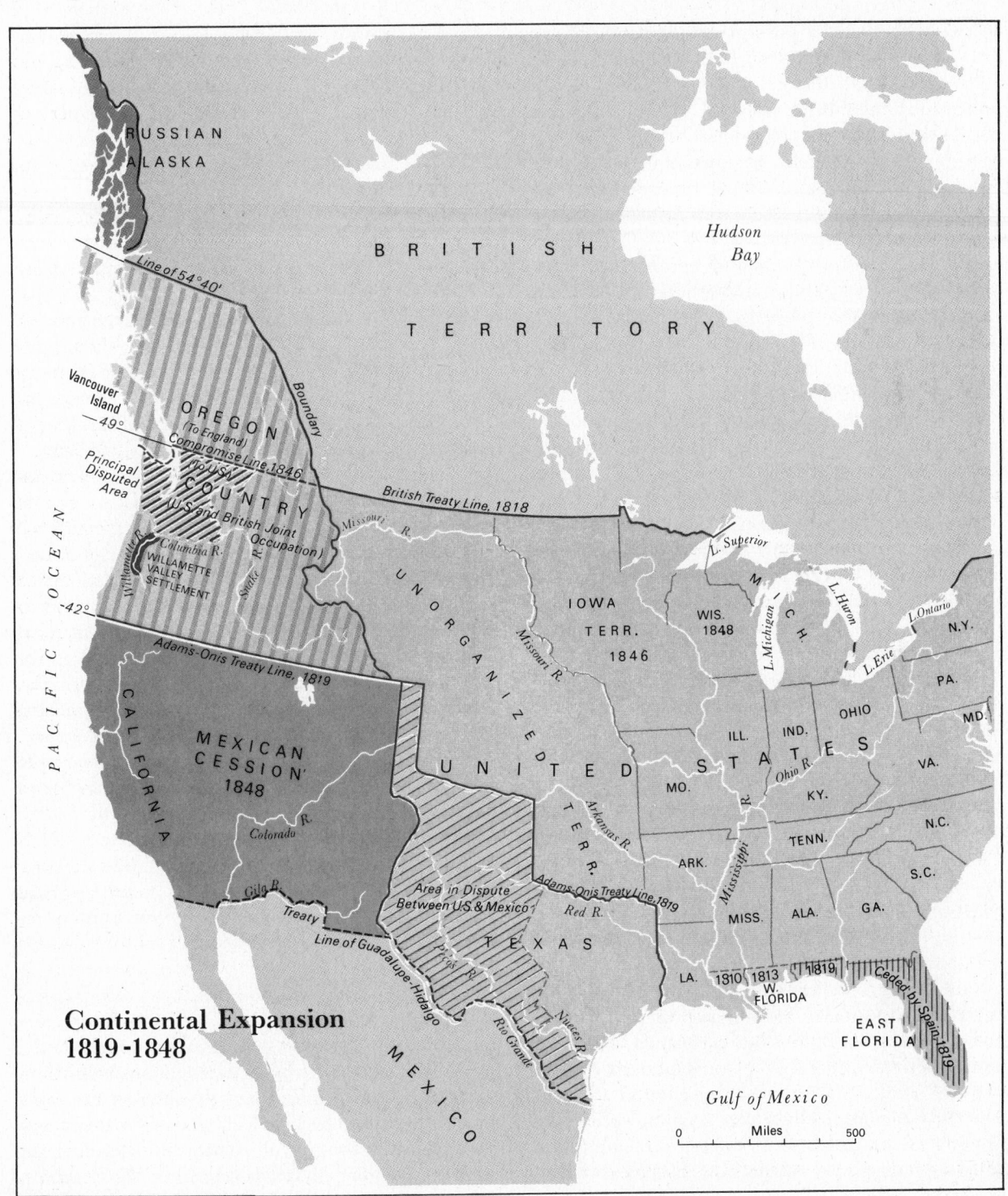

RUSSIAN ALASKA

B R I T I S H

T E R R I T O R Y

Hudson Bay

Line of 54°40'

Vancouver Island

49°

OREGON
(To England)
Compromise Line 1846
(To U.S.)

C O U N T R Y
(U.S. and British Joint Occupation)

Boundary

British Treaty Line, 1818

Principal Disputed Area

42°

Columbia R.
WILLAMETTE VALLEY SETTLEMENT

Snake R.

Willamette R.

Missouri R.

Adams-Onis Treaty Line, 1819

P A C I F I C   O C E A N

CALIFORNIA

MEXICAN CESSION 1848

Colorado R.

Gila R.

Treaty

Line of Guadalupe-Hidalgo

U N O R G A N I Z E D

T E R R.

U N I T E D

Missouri R.

Arkansas R.

Adams-Onis Treaty Line 1819

Red R.

Area in Dispute Between U.S. & Mexico

Pecos R.

T E X A S

Rio Grande

Nueces R.

M E X I C O

IOWA TERR. 1846

WIS. 1848

L. Superior

M I C H.

L.Michigan

L.Huron

L. Erie

L.Ontario

N.Y.

PA.

MD.

ILL.

IND.

OHIO

Ohio R.

VA.

MO.

KY.

S T A T E S

Mississippi R.

TENN.

N.C.

ARK.

S.C.

MISS.

ALA.

GA.

LA.

1810   1813   1819
W. FLORIDA

EAST FLORIDA

Ceded by Spain 1819

Gulf of Mexico

Continental Expansion 1819-1848

0   Miles   500

crusade for monarchic government. England, though not willing to risk war, strongly opposed this French intervention in Spain. And while not a promoter of independent republics, England also had no intention of allowing antirevolutionary zeal to interfere with her growing commercial dominance in the former Spanish empire. George Canning, the English foreign minister, therefore proposed a joint British-American declaration that would disavow any British or American designs on former Spanish territory and that would warn other nations against intervention.

The British offer presented the Monroe administration with a serious dilemma. The United States was the only nation that had begun to recognize the independent republics of Spanish America, but only Britain could deter a Franco-Spanish expeditionary force from trying to subdue them. Moreover, in 1821 Russia, which was leading the crusade to reestablish monarchic rule and which had earlier expanded from Siberia into Alaska, had issued a decree claiming a monopoly over the North Pacific. Russian traders were becoming more active in the Oregon country, a region that England and the United States had agreed to occupy jointly at least until 1828. Although accepting Canning's offer to issue a joint declaration would have the drawback of temporarily preventing America's annexation of Cuba, the idea appealed to the elder statesmen, Jefferson and Madison, as well as to Monroe and most of his cabinet.

The question was complicated further by the forthcoming presidential election of 1824. The nationalist, anti-English vote was much on the minds of the leading candidates. John Quincy Adams, the secretary of state, was already being portrayed by his rivals as a former Federalist and secret Anglophile. Despite his proved nationalism and loyal service to Republican administrations, Adams was vulnerable to such charges because of his New England and Federalist background. He was also the only candidate who was not a slaveholding planter. He knew that as secretary of state he would bear the largest share of political liability resulting from any Anglo-American alliance. He had long gone out of his way to publicize his resistance to English pressure for an antislave trade treaty. Adams now insisted on a uni-

lateral declaration against European intervention in the New World, much as he insisted on a unilateral policy against the slave trade. It would be more candid and dignified, Adams pointed out, to declare United States principles directly to Russia and France than "to come in as a cock-boat in the wake of the British man-of-war."

Adams's arguments prevailed, and the famous Monroe Doctrine reaffirmed America's diplomatic independence from Europe. By disavowing any American interference in the "internal concerns" of European states, Monroe in effect repudiated the popular clamor for aiding various revolutionary struggles against despotism, including the Greek war for independence from Turkey. But America's warning to Europe against future colonization in the New World extended to Britain as well as to Russia and France. And the Monroe Doctrine in no way precluded America's own expansion in the New World.

For some time the Monroe Doctrine had little practical consequence, except perhaps in vindicating Adams's reputation as a nationalist and thus in helping him win the presidency. Regardless of American pronouncements, it was British naval power that ensured the independence of Spanish America. Yet the Monroe administration, by spurning an Anglo-American alliance, also set a precedent for opposing any foreign attempts to limit the expansion of slavery. No doubt Monroe was thinking only of monarchic institutions when he warned that the United States would consider any European attempt to extend "their system" to any portions of the Western Hemisphere dangerous to America's peace and safety. By the 1830s, however, antislavery was an integral part of the British "system," and many Southerners regarded the expansion of slavery as vital to America's "peace and safety."

Annexation of Texas.   The Texas issue eventually tested this point and led to a proslavery reformulation of the Monroe Doctrine. For abolitionists in both Britain and the United States it was not inevitable that Texas should become a slave state. In 1829 Mexico abolished slavery in all provinces (including California), providing loopholes only for the stubborn

SAM HOUSTON, 1793–1863
Leader of the badly outnumbered Texans whose spectacular victory at San Jacinto in 1836 secured Texas's independence from Mexico, Houston went on to become president of the new republic, then senator from the new state. In 1861 as governor, Houston's stand against Texas's secession from the Union forced him out of office. *(Library of Congress)*

Anglo-American settlers in Texas. By 1830 the Mexican government had become alarmed by the growing autonomy of the Anglo-American settlements, by the intrigue accompanying the American government's secret efforts to purchase Texas, and by the agitation for annexation in the Jacksonian press. Consequently in 1830 the Mexican government tried to prohibit the further immigration of Anglo-Americans as well as the further importation of slaves, and sought to promote the colonization of Europeans as a buffer against encroachments from the United States. Since Negro slavery had only begun to take root in Texas, English reformers were beginning to look on the province as a promising site for cultivating cotton with free labor. Benjamin Lundy, an American Quaker abolitionist, even tried in the early 1830s to establish an asylum in Texas for free blacks from the United States.

But during his travels in Texas Lundy found evidence of growing proslavery sentiment and of various plots to throw off Mexican rule and annex Texas to the United States. The Mexican government was in fact incapable of either governing or satisfying the needs of the Anglo-Texans. In 1836, after President Antonio López de Santa Anna had succeeded in abolishing Mexico's federal constitution and in asserting centralized rule, the Texans proclaimed their independence. Their new constitution, modeled on the United States Constitution, specifically legalized Negro slavery. Meanwhile, Santa Anna's army had wiped out a small band of Texas rebels at San Antonio's Alamo Mission, thereby provoking cries for revenge in the American press. Aided by a great influx of volunteers from the officially neutral United States, the Texans, led by General Sam Houston, crushed the Mexican army at San Jacinto, captured Santa Anna, and soon voted overwhelmingly to join the United States.

As late as 1835 President Jackson had tried to buy not only Texas but all the Mexican territory stretching northwestward to the Pacific; his main object was to secure "within our limits the whole bay of St. Francisco." By then Americans had long been engaged in trade along the Santa Fe Trail and settlers were beginning to arrive by sea in sparsely populated California. After the Texan Revolution, however, Jackson knew that a premature attempt at annexation would in all likelihood bring on a war with Mexico, which refused to acknowledge Texan independence. It would also arouse the fury of the Northeast and lead to a sectional division within the Democratic party in the election year of 1836. But Jackson knew that California was important to the whaling and

McKAY'S SHIPYARD

Donald McKay's shipyard in East Boston, established in 1845, constructed some of the fastest, most graceful, and most beautiful sailing ships ever made. McKay's clipper, the *Flying Cloud*, made San Francisco in less than 90 days from New York. The *James Baines* set a world record of 12 days 6 hours from Boston to Liverpool. McKay's best clippers could average more than 400 nautical miles in a day.   *(Courtesy, Richard Parker Collection. Photograph from George Eastman House)*

"THE SPLENDID, A1 CLIPPER SHIP"

An advertisement for the highly competitive clipper ship travel to San Francisco.   *(Museum of the City of New York.)*

Merchants' Express Line of Clipper Ships for San Franc

THE SPLENDID A 1 CLIPPER SHIP

W. B. DINSMOR

FOSTER Commander,

IS LOADING AT PIER 13 EAST RIVE

D. S. STETSON & CO.,

Agents in San Francisco.
Messrs. De Witt, Kittle & Co.

maritime interests of the Northeast. New England whalers and cargo ships had begun to make portions of the Pacific an American preserve. Jackson therefore secretly advised Texans to bide their time and to establish a claim to California, "to paralyze the opposition of the North and East to Annexation." He assumed that such opposition would wane as soon as Northerners concluded that annexing Texas would lead to the acquisition of California.

The passage of time, however, encouraged the hopes of American and British opponents of slavery. Jackson's Democratic successor, Martin Van Buren, was too dependent on northeastern support to risk agitating the public with the question of annexation. John Quincy Adams's eloquent speeches in the House of Representatives, in which he served for seventeen years after he retired as president, popularized the view that the southern Slave Power had engineered the Texas Revolution and the drive for annexation. In 1838 Adams carried on a three-week filibuster, presented hundreds of antislavery petitions, and finally defeated a move to annex Texas by joint resolution. The rebuffed Texan leaders withdrew their formal proposal for annexation and began to think seriously of building an independent empire. As time went on, they looked to Britain and France for financial support and for diplomatic aid in ending the perilous state of war with Mexico.

The spring and summer of 1843 marked a decisive turn of events. John Tyler, who had been elected as Harrison's vice-president in 1840 and had then become president after Harrison's death, had been disowned by the Whig party. He was therefore courting southern Democrats and searching for an issue that would win him reelection. Daniel Webster, the last of the Whig cabinet members, finally resigned as secretary of state after negotiating with Britain the Webster-Ashburton Treaty; this treaty settled disputed borders with Canada, provided for cooperative measures in suppressing the Atlantic slave trade, and was immediately attacked by Democrats for betraying America's interests. Through Calhoun's influence, Webster was replaced by Abel P. Upshur, a Virginian who had defended slavery as a "positive good." For the first time, an entire administration was in the hands of ardent proslavery Southerners who saw territorial expansion as the key to southern security.

Britain and Texas. Although British leaders did not want to antagonize the South, on which England depended for cotton, they were sensitive to one abolitionist argument. An independent Texas might begin importing slaves from Africa, thereby adding to Britain's difficulties in suppressing the Atlantic slave trade. The British had evidence that American officials in Cuba were conniving with slave smugglers and that American ships predominated in the illegal trade to Cuba. Texas might open another rich market for the same interests. Therefore, when Britain offered Texas a treaty of recognition and trade, it included a secret agreement to outlaw the slave trade. Otherwise, under close questioning from a delegation of abolitionists, Lord Aberdeen, the foreign secretary, conceded only two points: that in serving as mediator between Texas and Mexico, Britain hoped that any peace agreement would include a commitment to slave emancipation; and that as everyone knew, the British public and government hoped for the abolition of slavery throughout the world.

In Washington these words brought anger and alarm. The Tyler administration was convinced that West Indian emancipation had proved to be an economic and social disaster. The British, according to the prevailing southern theory, were now determined to undermine slavery in other nations to improve the competitive advantage of their own colonies, including India. But Southerners never comprehended the depth of antislavery sentiment among the British middle class. Having subsidized West Indian emancipation by paying £20 million in compensation to planters, British taxpayers wanted assurance that Britain's short-term sacrifices would not lead to the expansion of plantation slavery in neighboring regions of the Caribbean and Gulf of Mexico.

Regardless of the truth, however, Southerners had long been predisposed to believe that British antislavery was part of a long-term diplomatic plot to seal off and contain the United States within a crescent of British influence extending from Cuba and Texas to California, Oregon, and Canada. In 1843 this conviction was seemingly confirmed by the exaggerated reports of Duff Green, an intimate of Calhoun's and President Tyler's secret agent in England and France. According to Green, the British government was about to guarantee interest on a loan to Texas on the condition that Texas abolish slavery. The plan would make Texas a British satellite and an asylum, like Canada, for fugitive slaves from the United States. The British, by erecting a barrier of freedom across the southwestern flank of the slaveholding states, could effectively join northern abolitionists in destroying both slavery and the federal Union.

Like many myths, this elaborate fantasy rested on a thin foundation of truth. It interpreted every event as part of a master plan, and justified national desires that were otherwise difficult to justify. It furnished the pretext for the grand strategy that would govern American expansionist policy for the next five years. In response to an appeal for advice from Secretary of State Upshur, Calhoun in 1843 secretly spelled out the steps for implementing this policy. He called for private assurances to Texas that as soon as a propaganda campaign had been launched to soften northern opposition, the administration would secure annexation. In order to win support from the land-hungry farmers of the Old Northwest, Calhoun also suggested linking Texas annexation with the assertion of American claims to Oregon. As a preliminary step toward this plan, he wanted to demand a formal explanation from Britain for policies that threatened "the safety of the Union and the very existence of the South."

Calhoun himself soon had the power to begin implementing this grand design. Early in 1844 Upshur was killed in an accident, and Calhoun succeeded him as secretary of state. Soon afterwards a Whig newspaper revealed that the administration had been engaged for months in secret negotiations with Texas and that Tyler was about to sign an annexation treaty. In response to growing northern furor, Calhoun seized on and made public the British government's private avowal that Britain "desires, and is constantly exerting herself to procure, the general abolition of slavery throughout the world."

By skillfully distorting and publicizing the British diplomatic notes, Calhoun tried to identify the anti-annexation cause with a British plot to destroy the Union. He lectured the British on the blessings of Negro slavery, employing faulty statistics from the census of 1840 to argue that emancipation in the North had produced Negro insanity, crime, suicide, and degeneracy. He also informed Mexico that because of the British conspiracy to subvert southern slavery, the United States was forced to annex Texas in self-defense.

The Expansionist Issue and Election of 1844. This open defense of slavery by an American secretary of state marked the beginning of a sectional conflict over slavery and expansionism that severely tested the party system. President Tyler's defection from the Whigs, in addition to Calhoun's presidential ambitions and independence from party discipline, complicated the political maneuvering that set the stage for the 1844 campaign. With an eye to northern votes, both Henry Clay and Van Buren, the leading Whig and Democratic contenders, felt compelled by April 1844 to express their opposition to the immediate annexation of Texas.

In the Senate the Missouri Democrat Thomas Hart Benton led the onslaught against the duplicity of Tyler and Calhoun. Seven other Democratic senators, all Northerners, joined the Whigs in decisively rejecting the annexation treaty. Yet the Whig opposition to expansion encouraged the Democratic party to close ranks and rally behind patriotic demands for the "reannexation of Texas" (which assumed that Texas had been part of the Louisiana Purchase), and the "reoccupation of Oregon" (which assumed that Britain had never had legitimate claims to the region south of 54°40', the border of Russian Alaska). The issue of expansion diverted attention from the Democrats' internal disputes over banking and fiscal policy, and also enabled a southern-dominated coalition to defeat Van Buren and nominate James K. Polk, a Jacksonian expansionist from Tennessee, as the Democratic candidate.

As Calhoun had predicted, the Oregon question became an ideal means for exploiting national Anglophobia and winning northern support for national expansion. For decades the British Hudson's Bay Company had ruled the region north of the Columbia River, although the United States had strong claims to the Columbia itself and to the territory extending southward to latitude 42°. New England ships had long frequented the entire Pacific Northwest in search of sea otter furs for the China trade, and since the 1820s American trappers had developed a thriving trade in beaver and other furs within the region west of the Rockies. As American traders challenged the political and judicial authority of the powerful Hudson's Bay Company, it became more difficult to resolve conflicting Anglo-American claims. Moreover, in 1827, when the two nations had renewed a "joint occupation" agreement that simply deferred any settlement of national boundaries, no one could fore-

see the future appeal of the fertile Willamette Valley to farmers in the Old Northwest. Glowing reports from American missionaries to the Indians of the rich farmland there helped to spread the "Oregon fever" of the 1840s, inducing thousands of families to risk the perils and hardships of overland travel to the Pacific. In 1843 the first of the great overland wagon migrations along the Oregon Trail took place, and the resulting claims to "All Oregon" acted as a political balance wheel for the annexation of Texas.

In 1844, as in other elections of the time, voter preference depended less on issues than on ethnic, religious, and party loyalty. And so, concerned about the crucial swing vote, Clay, the Whig candidate, retreated from his earlier stand against Texas annexation. His last-minute gestures for southern support persuaded thousands of northern Whigs to vote for

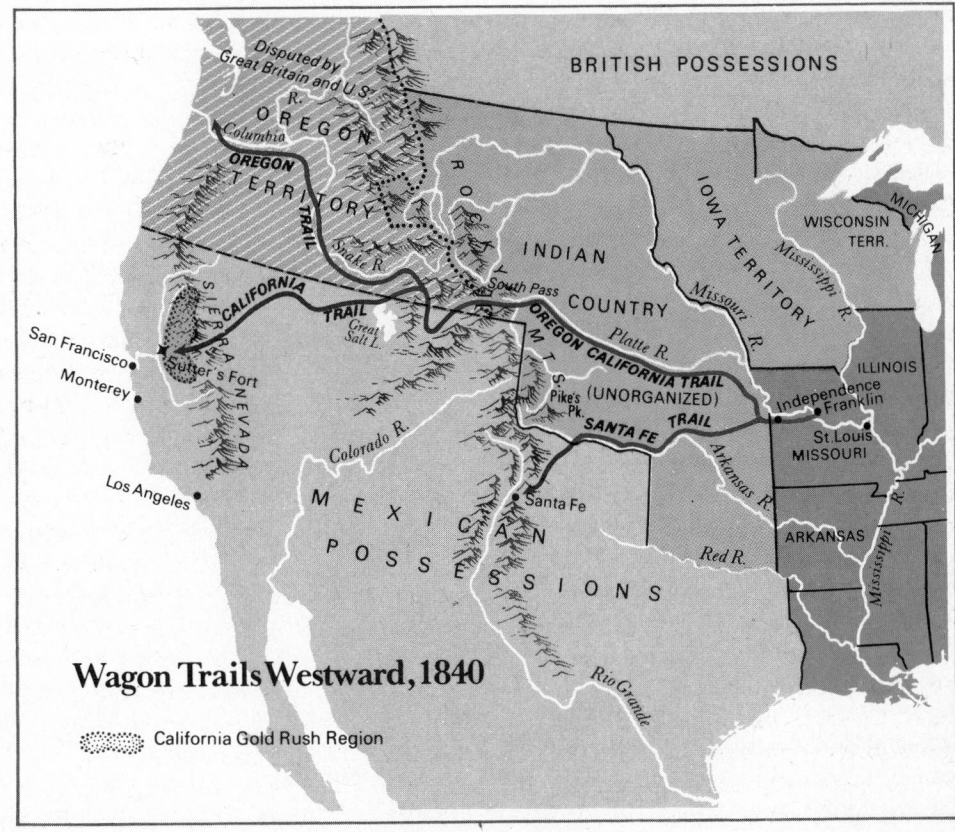

Wagon Trails Westward, 1840

:::::::: California Gold Rush Region

James G. Birney, the Liberty party candidate, who stood firm against annexation. More popular votes were actually cast against Polk than for him, and although he won the election, he would certainly have lost it if Birney's votes in New York and Michigan had gone to Clay.

Nevertheless, the incumbent President Tyler and the triumphant Democrats interpreted the election as a mandate for immediate annexation. The Democrats in Congress united in championing the new expansionism, allowing the retiring Tyler administration to secure annexation by joint resolution of both houses of Congress. After a tense period of international intrigue, the Republic of Texas rejected offers of peace from Mexico and mediation from Britain. In December 1845, having bypassed territorial status, Texas entered the Union as a new slave state.

The Mexican War and Manifest Destiny

The admission of Texas coincided with President Polk's aggressive reformulation of the Monroe Doctrine. In his annual message of December 2, 1845, Polk warned that henceforth the United States would not tolerate any kind of European interferences designed to limit the spread of the American form of government or the right of any of the peoples of North America "to decide their own destiny," by which Polk meant the right to be annexed to the United States. In the case of Texas, whose boundaries were still extremely controversial, such annexation meant a federal commitment to support the restoration of slavery in a region in which it had earlier been outlawed by Mexico. Only the future could determine the fate of Cuba, California, and Oregon—provinces that Polk had very much in mind. And the future too would determine precisely how the people would "decide their own destiny," an ideal soon to be known as "popular sovereignty."

Oregon and California. President Polk's warnings about European interference were directed mainly at Britain. He emphasized that the danger of British

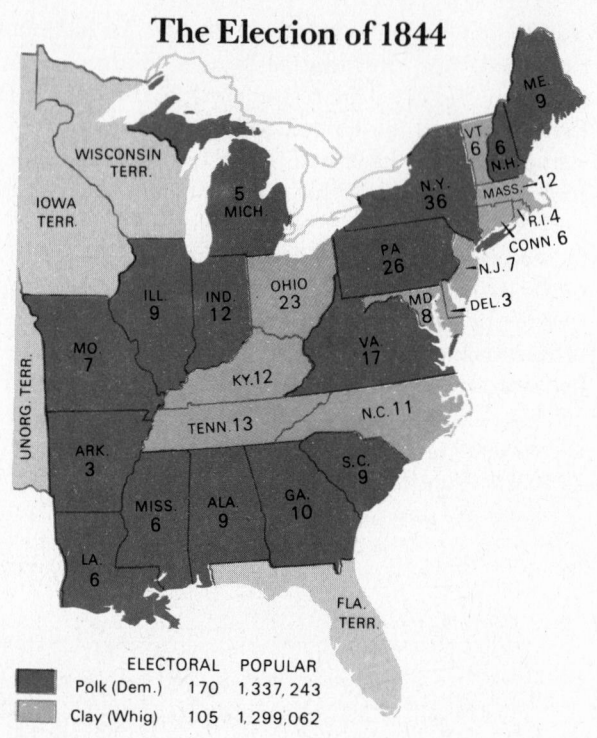

The Election of 1844

	ELECTORAL	POPULAR
Polk (Dem.)	170	1,337,243
Clay (Whig)	105	1,299,062

economic or political interference, even apart from physical colonization, justified an indefinite expansion of America's boundaries. He also spurned further negotiation with Britain over the Oregon question and asked Congress to give notice of the termination of the 1827 joint occupation agreement. The dismayed British government ignored the belligerent rhetoric but commissioned new steam warships and ordered a naval force to the northeast Pacific.

While Polk hoped to force concessions from Britain on Oregon, his primary objective was California. In 1845 a British consul correctly observed that California, which contained no more than ten thousand white inhabitants, was at the mercy of whoever might choose to take possession of it. Polk feared that the British might appropriate the province as compensation for Mexican debts. Months before his December message, orders had been sent to the commodore of the American Pacific Squadron, instructing him to seize San Francisco and other ports if he could "ascertain with certainty" that Mexico had declared war against the United States.

Polk's secretary of state, James Buchanan, also sent secret instructions to Thomas Larkin, the American consul at Monterey, telling him to foil British plots and to foment, as cautiously as possible, a spirit of rebellion among the Spanish Californians. Finally, only days after Polk's belligerent message, America's dashing "Pathfinder," Captain John C. Frémont, arrived in California at the head of a "scientific expedition" of heavily armed engineers. Frémont had been exploring the Mexican West without permission from Mexico, and would soon defy the Mexican authorities in California and encourage the Anglo-American settlers in an uprising, supposedly in their own self-defense.

Slidell's Mission. December 1845 also marked the arrival in Mexico City of Polk's secret minister, John Slidell, who had orders to win Mexican acceptance of the Rio Grande River as the new border with the United States, and to purchase as much of New Mexico and California as possible. The instructions emphasized the determination of the United States to

A DRUGSTORE, A BOOKSTORE, AND AN "INTELIGENCE" OFFICE: SONORA, CALIFORNIA
In such outposts as Sonora, California, the general store was a gathering place for people of all classes and occupations. *(Wells Fargo Bank History Room, San Francisco)*

prevent California from becoming a British or French colony, and authorized Slidell to offer Mexico as much as $25 million for the territories desired, with the additional proviso that the United States would assume the debts owed by Mexico to American citizens.

The Mexican government had earlier shown a willingness to settle the Texas dispute, but by December, when one of Mexico's numerous revolutions was about to erupt, the unstable government could not dare recognize an American envoy who made such sweeping demands, demands that had already been leaked to the American press. Mexican nationalists considered Texas a "stolen province," and especially resented the wholly unfounded claim that Texas extended to the Rio Grande. In 1816 Spain had designated the Nueces River, 130 miles north and east of the Rio Grande, as the boundary between Tamaulipas and the province of Texas; this was the boundary that appeared on American and European maps. In 1836, however, when the Texans had captured the Mexican president, Santa Anna, he had been forced to agree to the Rio Grande boundary as a condition for his release. The Mexican government had promptly repudiated this extortionary agreement. By the end of 1845, Mexican nationalists, hoping for European support, were eager for a war of revenge against American imperialists.

War with Mexico.   On learning of Slidell's failure, the Polk administration was also eager for war but wanted a pretext that would justify seizing California. In January 1846 the president ordered General Zachary Taylor, who had been poised for the move, to march to the Rio Grande. Without opposition, American ships blockaded the river and Taylor took up a position across from the Mexican town of Matamoros, toward which he aimed his cannons. By early May, however, Washington had heard no news of hostilities and the impatient president and cabinet decided that Mexico's unpaid debts and the rebuff to Slidell were sufficient grounds for war. Then just as Polk had drafted a war message to Congress, news arrived that a minor skirmish had occurred between Mexican and American patrols. Polk could now indignantly

inform Congress that war already existed. He said, "Notwithstanding all our efforts to avoid it [war] exists by the act of Mexico herself. [Mexico] has passed the boundary of the United States, has invaded our territory and shed American blood upon the American soil."

By any objective interpretation, Americans had crossed the Mexican boundary and had shed Mexican blood on Mexican soil. For American expansionists, however, the protests from Europe simply substantiated the fact that the growth of the United States was a blow to political and religious tyranny. It was America's mission to liberate the peoples of California, Mexico, Cuba, Central America, and even Canada, allowing them to share in the blessings of republican government, religious freedom, and modern technology. In 1845 an influential Democratic editor had coined the electric phrase "manifest destiny," while denouncing the policy of other nations of

hampering our power, limiting our greatness and checking the fulfillment of our manifest destiny to overspread the continent allotted by Providence for the free development of our yearly multiplying millions.

But the crusade to prevent Europe from imposing a "balance of power" in North America strained the fragile balance on which the Union had always depended, the balance of power between North and South. In the Northeast and particularly in New England the Mexican War provoked thunderous outrage. It was denounced from press and pulpit as a war of brutal aggression, plotted by the Slave Power to extend slavery and secure permanent control over the free states. The Massachusetts legislature went so far as to proclaim the war unconstitutional.

The war remained unpopular with the great majority of Whig leaders, even in the South, who objected to Polk's devious tactics and to the way in which Congress had been stampeded into a declaration of war in order to rescue Zachary Taylor's army, which was erroneously said to be endangered.

Settlement of Oregon Controversy.   By June 1846, a month after the war began, even the prowar western Democrats were angered when Polk allowed the

AMERICAN SOLDIERS HEADING SOUTH
General Thomas John Wood, a member of Zachary Taylor's staff, leads American troops through the streets of Saltillo, the capital of Coahuila province in northern Mexico. *(Yale University Library)*

Senate to assume full responsibility for approving a treaty that gave Britain Vancouver Island and all of the Oregon country north of the forty-ninth parallel. As the western expansionists rightly suspected, Southerners had never been enthusiastic about adding probable free states in the Pacific Northwest, and Polk had no wish to risk war with England when he was intent on dismembering Mexico.

Yet the nation as a whole supported the war. Mindful that opposition to the War of 1812 had split and destroyed the Federalist party, Whigs in Con- gress dutifully voted for military appropriations and congratulated themselves on the fact that the army's two leading generals, Zachary Taylor and Winfield Scott, were also Whigs. Taylor was the first to win glory. Within a few months, and with incredibly few American casualties, he defeated Mexican armies much larger than his own, crossed the Rio Grande, and captured the strategic town of Monterrey, thereby commanding northeastern Mexico. According to Democratic critics, he then settled down to prepare for the presidential campaign of 1848, which he won. In

February 1847, however, in the battle of Buena Vista, Taylor crushed another Mexican army over three times the size of his own. It was led by Santa Anna, who had earlier been exiled from Mexico. Polk had allowed Santa Anna to enter Mexico from Cuba because he believed that this self-styled Napoleon of the West would persuade Mexico to sue for peace.

Meanwhile, by early 1847 Polk's professed objectives had been achieved. Mexico's defense of California collapsed so rapidly that the only serious conflicts stemmed from the rival and uncoordinated American onslaughts: Consul Larkin's efforts to mobilize the restive Spanish Californians; Frémont's leadership of the Anglo-American settlers; the American navy's capture of the port towns; and the arrival of an overland force, led by Stephen W. Kearny, which conquered New Mexico on the way to San Diego.

But the war was far from over. What the Mexicans lacked in leadership and modern armament, they made up for in national pride and determination. The United States could hardly claim an efficient military machine, but the army sparkled with talent. The roster of young officers read like a gallery of later Union and Confederate heroes: Lee, Grant, Sherman, Meade, McClellan, Beauregard, Stonewall Jackson, and even Jefferson Davis. For Europeans, whose memories of Napoleonic battles had receded into more than thirty years of romantic haze, the American triumphs were stupendous—without parallel, according to the Manchester *Guardian,* "except in that of Alexander the Great through Persia, Hannibal from Spain

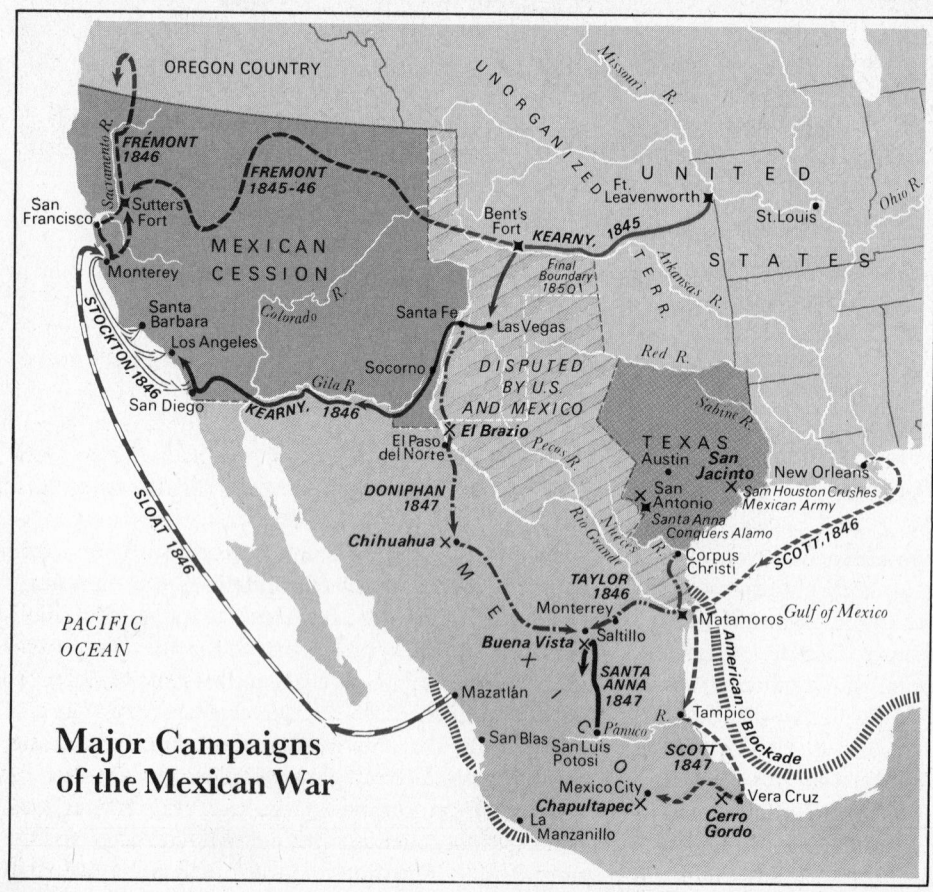

Major Campaigns of the Mexican War

"THE OCCUPATION OF THE CAPITAL OF MEXICO BY THE AMERICAN ARMY" BY P.S. DAVAL
Americans enter the historic square, or Zocalo, of Mexico City, March 1847. *(American Antiquarian Society)*

to the gates of Rome, or Napoleon over the Alps into Italy." Instead of one Napoleon, America had them "by the dozen."

Treaty of Guadalupe Hidalgo. The events that astonished even hostile Europeans began with General Scott's invasion of central Mexico in March 1847. By September, after winning a series of hotly contested battles, American troops had captured Mexico City and were relaxing in the halls of the Montezumas. Still, the Mexicans refused to surrender. In the United States Americans were becoming increasingly divided over the meaning of Manifest Destiny. As the American army pushed upward to the Mexican plateau, in the caustic words of James Russell Lowell, "our Destiny higher an' higher kep' mountin'." Some Southerners believed that slavery could be extended at least into the northern states of Mexico; some antislavery Northerners believed that Mexico would be

a force for freedom, and therefore favored annexing the whole country. In general, however, the Democratic leaders—Polk, Buchanan, Lewis Cass, Stephen Douglas, Sam Houston, Jefferson Davis—demanded and expected to get no less than a third of the country south and west of the Rio Grande. They were therefore outraged when Nicholas Trist, whom Polk had angrily recalled as America's negotiator, proceeded to conclude the unauthorized Treaty of Guadalupe Hidalgo. Instead of capitalizing on America's conquests, Trist settled for the same terms that Slidell had been prepared to offer before the war: the United States was to pay Mexico $15 million and assume up to $3.25 million in Mexican debts to American citizens in return for California, New Mexico, and the Rio Grande boundary. Polk would have liked to repudiate the treaty, but feared that further war and prolonged negotiations would split the Democratic party in an election year. Alarmed by the growing antiwar and Free Soil movement among northern Democrats, he reluctantly submitted the treaty to the Senate, which approved it in March 1848.

Attempts to Acquire Cuba.   But Polk had other cards up his sleeve. In 1848 the Democratic expansionists launched an intense propaganda campaign to annex the Yucatán Peninsula, a rebellious province that had seceded from Mexico and that contained white inhabitants in danger of being exterminated by hostile Indians. Polk, fearing British intervention and mindful of the virtually unemployed American army in Mexico, invited Congress to act. But enthusiasm waned when news arrived that the Yucatán racial crisis had subsided.

Polk was actually far more interested in acquiring Cuba. Like the Yucatán Peninsula, Cuba guarded access to the Gulf of Mexico; its traditional strategic importance would be increased by any future canal, about which there was already much discussion, connecting the Gulf of Mexico with the Pacific. In 1848 England was on the verge of war with Spain, and might at any time gain control of Cuba. Many of Cuba's sugar planters, resenting England's growing interference with their labor system and fearing the continuing spread of emancipation in the West Indies, believed that annexation to the United States was their only guarantee of remaining a prosperous slave society.

The Polk administration knew, however, that the North would not approve the use of military force to acquire over one-third of a million additional Negro slaves. Polk's only alternative was to try, with the utmost caution and secrecy, to persuade Spain that $100 million was a good price for a colony that was about to rebel or be lost to England. But Spain greatly prized the only rich remnant of her once great empire, and contemptuously rejected the bungled overtures of Polk's minister. The prospects for annexing Cuba were further dashed when, in the fall of 1848 Lewis Cass, the Democratic candidate who favored the purchase of Cuba and the annexation of Yucatán, was defeated for the presidency by the nonexpansionist Zachary Taylor.

Southern hopes for acquiring Cuba now turned to encouraging a Cuban revolution against Spain. Groups of Cuban emigrés, aided by American expansionists, led a series of "filibustering" invasions to liberate the Cuban people. By 1850, however, the anxieties of Cuban planters had subsided and their desire to be taken over by the United States had waned. In 1851, in an episode that strangely anticipated the Bay of Pigs disaster in 1961, Cubans captured the entire expedition of Narciso Lopez, a southern hero, and executed him and fifty of his American followers.

Serious efforts to acquire Cuba revived under the Democratic administration of Franklin Pierce (1853–57), which contained many of Polk's more ardent expansionists. In 1854 the diplomatic intrigues culminated in the secret meetings of America's ministers to Spain, France, and England, who drafted a long memorandum to the State Department justifying the forcible seizure of Cuba if the island could not be purchased from Spain. Labeled the Ostend Manifesto, the secret memorandum was leaked to the American public at a moment of explosive sectional conflict, confirming the conviction of many Northerners that the Slave Power would continue to expand unless checked by political might. One of the authors of the Manifesto, the minister to Britain, was James Buchanan. His platform, as the Democratic presidential candidate in 1856, openly called for annexing Cuba. By this time, however, the heated controversy over legalizing slavery in Kansas had diverted attention from further national expansion.

CHRONOLOGY

1819 Transcontinental (Adams-Onís) Treaty. Spain renounces claims to the Floridas and Pacific Northwest; United States renounces claims to Texas.

1823 President issues Monroe Doctrine.

1829 Mexico abolishes slavery.

1831 Nat Turner's slave insurrection in Virginia.

1832 Virginia legislative debates whether to allow a committee to report on future abolition of slavery.

1836 Texas proclaims its independence from Mexico. Martin Van Buren elected president.

1838 John Quincy Adams's filibuster defeats move to annex Texas.

1841 John Tyler becomes president on death of Harrison.

1842 Webster-Ashburton Treaty settles disputed U.S.-Canada boundary; provides for extradition of fugitives.

1843 "Oregon Fever"; first overland caravans to Oregon.
Duff Green, Calhoun, and others begin planning imperial expansion to thwart British plots to undermine American slavery.

1844 Senate rejects Calhoun's Texas annexation treaty. James K. Polk elected president.

1845 Texas enters Union as slave state.
Polk gives aggressive reformulation to Monroe Doctrine.
John Slidell's unsuccessful mission to Mexico to negotiate purchase of New Mexico and California.

1846 Beginning of Mexican War. General Zachary Taylor invades Mexico from the north.
Treaty with Britain divides Oregon Territory along 49th parallel.

1847 General Winfield Scott captures Vera Cruz and Mexico City.

1848 Treaty of Guadalupe Hidalgo ends Mexican War, establishes Rio Grande as border.
Secret attempts to purchase Cuba from Spain.
Zachary Taylor elected president.

1854 Ostend Manifesto favors U.S. purchase or annexation of Cuba.
Railroads link New York City with the Mississippi River.
George Fitzhugh's *Sociology for the South.*

1857 Financial panic and depression.

SUGGESTED READINGS

For overviews of antebellum economic growth, see W. Elliot Brownlee, *Dynamics of Ascent* (1974), and Stuart Bruchey, *Growth of the Modern American Economy* (1975). A more technical but useful summary of the new economic history is Lance E. Davis *et al.*, *American Economic Growth: An Economist's History of the United States* (1972). Douglass C. North, *The Economic Growth of the United States, 1790–1860* (1961), stresses the importance of international trade. Peter Temin, *The Jacksonian Economy* (1969), challenges many of the traditional beliefs of historians.

For the general subject of transportation, see George R. Taylor, *The Transportation Revolution, 1815–1860* (1951). For railroads, see Albert Fishlow, *American Railroads and the Transformation of the Ante-Bellum Economy* (1965); Alfred D. Chandler, Jr., ed., *The Railroads: The Nation's First Big Business* (1965); and Thomas C. Cochran, *Railroad Leaders, 1845–1890* (1953). The organization and management of railroad corporations is masterfully analyzed in Alfred D. Chandler, Jr., *The Visible Hand: The Managerial Revolution in American Business* (1977). The role of government is treated in Carter Goodrich, *Government Promotion of American Canals and Railroads, 1800–1890* (1960); Louis Hartz, *Economic Policy and Democratic Thought* (1954); and Oscar Handlin and Mary F. Handlin, *Commonwealth: A Study of the Role of Government in the American Economy* (1969).

The best works on maritime trade are Robert G. Albion, *The Rise of New York Port* (1939), and Samuel E. Morison, *Maritime History of Massachusetts, 1789–1860* (1921). For the clipper ships, see C. C. Cutler, *Greyhounds of the Sea* (1930), and A. H. Clark, *The Clipper Ship Era* (1910). L. H.

Battistini, *The Rise of American Influence in Asia and the Pacific* (1960), treats an important aspect of America's commercial expansion.

On manufacturing, Victor S. Clark, *History of Manufactures in the United States, 1607–1860* (3 vols., 1929), remains indispensable. The best specialized studies are Peter Temin, *Iron and Steel in Nineteenth-Century America* (1964); Caroline F. Ware, *The Early New England Cotton Manufacture* (1931); Arthur H. Cole, *The American Wool Manufacture* (2 vols., 1926); and Nathan Rosenberg, ed., *The American System of Manufactures* (1969). Siegfried Giedion, *Mechanization Takes Command* (1948), contains a fascinating account of American technological innovation. A brilliant study of the significance of the new technology is Merritt R. Smith, *Harpers Ferry Armory and the New Technology: The Challenge of Change* (1977). H. J. Habakkuk, *American and British Technology in the Nineteenth Century* (1962), places American invention in a larger context, as does Carroll W. Pursell, Jr., *Early Stationary Steam Engines in America: A Study in the Migration of Technology* (1969). For a comprehensive reference work, see Melvin Kranzberg and Carroll W. Pursell, Jr., eds., *Technology in Western Civilization* (2 vols., 1967). The ideological impact of technology is imaginatively treated in John F. Kasson, *Civilizing the Machine: Technology and Republican Values in America, 1776–1900* (1976). The social implications of industrialization are admirably traced in Alan Dawley, *Class and Community: The Industrial Revolution in Lynn* (1977).

The best general guide to sectional conflict and the coming of the Civil War is David M. Potter, *The Impending Crisis, 1848–1861* (completed and edited by Don E. Fehrenbacher, 1976). Allan Nevins, *Ordeal of the Union* (2 vols., 1947), is a highly readable and informative survey of the same subject.

A comprehensive picture of the South as a slave society can be found in Clement Eaton, *A History of the Old South: The Emergence of a Reluctant Nation* (1975); and Eaton, *Freedom of Thought in the Old South* (1940). The growth of sectional feeling is outlined in more detail in Charles S. Sydnor, *The Development of Southern Sectionalism, 1819–1848* (1948); and Avery O. Craven, *The Growth of Southern Nationalism, 1848–1861* (1953). Carl N. Degler, *The Other South: Southern Dissenters in the Nineteenth Century* (1974), traces the decline of antislavery protest. H. Shelton Smith, *In His Image, But . . .* (1972), is a fine study of the growing racism in the southern churches. Frank Owsley, *Plain Folk of the Old South* (1949), contains valuable information on the nonslaveholding whites. A penetrating study of the mythology of the Old South, often northern in origin, is

William R. Taylor, *Cavalier and Yankee* (1961). C. Vann Woodward's essays in *The Burden of Southern History* (1960) and *American Counterpoint* (1971) are indispensable for understanding the South. The mind of the planter class is brilliantly illuminated by two accounts contemporary with the period: Mary B. Chestnut, *A Diary from Dixie* (1949); and Robert M. Myers, ed., *The Children of Pride: A True Story of Georgia and the Civil War* (1972).

The standard work on proslavery thought is William S. Jenkins, *Pro-Slavery Thought in the Old South* (1935), which can be supplemented by Harvey Wish, *George Fitzhugh* (1943), and Drew Gilpin Faust, *A Sacred Circle: The Dilemma of the Intellectual in the Old South, 1840–1860* (1977). Ira Berlin, *Slaves without Masters* (1975), is a superb analysis of free blacks in the South. John H. Franklin, *From Slavery to Freedom* (1974), is the best introduction to the history of the blacks. George M. Fredrickson, *The Black Image in the White Mind: The Debate on Afro-American Character and Destiny, 1817–1914* (1971), is a brilliant study of racism in America. More specialized works of importance are Eugene H. Berwanger, *The Frontier against Slavery: Western Anti-Negro Prejudice and the Slavery Extension Controversy* (1967); and William Stanton, *The Leopard's Spots: Scientific Attitudes toward Race in America, 1815–1859* (1960).

The fullest history of the origins of the Monroe Doctrine is Dexter Perkins, *The Monroe Doctrine, 1823–1826* (1927). Ernest R. May, *The Making of the Monroe Doctrine* (1975), stresses the importance of domestic politics preceding the presidential election of 1824. For the European background, see E. H. Tatum, Jr., *The United States and Europe, 1815–1823* (1936); and C. C. Griffin, *The United States and the Disruption of the Spanish Empire* (1937). For a general introduction to American foreign policy, see Lloyd C. Gardner et al., *Creation of the American Empire* (1973); and for a more traditional view, Samuel F. Bemis, *A Diplomatic History of the United States* (1965). The standard work on Asia is A. Whitney Griswold, *The Far Eastern Policy of the United States* (1938).

Ray A. Billington, *Westward Expansion* (1974), covers every aspect of America's westward expansion and contains an encyclopedic, relatively up-to-date bibliography. Albert K. Weinberg, *Manifest Destiny* (1935), is a fascinating study in intellectual history, but it should be supplemented by Edward M. Burns, *The American Idea of Mission: Concepts of National Purpose and Destiny* (1957). In three outstanding, revisionist studies, Frederick W. Merk reemphasizes the importance of slavery and the fear of British encroachments on the West: *Manifest Destiny and Mission in American History: A Reinterpretation* (1963); *The Monroe Doctrine and*

American Expansionism, 1843–1849 (1966); and *Slavery and the Annexation of Texas* (1972). For a detailed treatment of the diplomatic history, see D. M. Pletcher, *The Diplomacy of Annexation: Texas, Oregon and the Mexican War* (1973).

On Texas two of the standard works are by William C. Binkley: *The Texas Revolution* (1952); and *The Expansionist Movement in Texas, 1836–1850* (1925). Much can still be learned from the older, nationalistic studies: J. H. Smith, *The Annexation of Texas* (1911); and E. C. Barker, *Mexico and Texas, 1821–1835* (1928). For a meticulous portrayal of the Mexican point of view, see Gene M. Brack, *Mexico Views Manifest Destiny, 1821–1846* (1976).

Frederick W. Merk has written several superb essays on the Anglo-American diplomacy regarding Oregon: *Albert Gallatin and the Oregon Problem* (1950); and *The Oregon Question: Essays in Anglo-American Diplomacy and Politics* (1967). For general histories of the Northwest, see Norman A. Graebner, *Empire on the Pacific* (1955); Oscar O. Winther, *The Great Northwest* (1947); and Earl Pomeroy, *The Pacific Slope: A History* (1965).

Ray A. Billington, *The Far Western Frontier, 1830–1860* (1956), is a lively and scholarly survey of the exploration and settlement of the Great West. By far the best account of the overland emigration to the Far West is John D. Unruh, Jr., *The Overland Emigrants and the Trans-Mississippi West, 1840–1860* (1979). The fascinating story of govern-ment exploration is described with admirable care in William H. Goetzmann, *Army Exploration in the American West, 1803–1863* (1959). Gloria G. Cline, *Exploring the Great Basin* (1963), is an invaluable study. H. M. Chittenden, *The American Fur Trade of the Far West* (3 vols., 1935), is still the most comprehensive story of the fur trade, although important new work has long been in progress. Though sometimes scorned by professional historians, Bernard DeVoto's *Across the Wide Missouri* (1947), which deals with the Mountain Men and fur trade, and DeVoto's *The Year of Decision, 1846* (1943), which deals with the political, social, and cultural events surrounding America's war with Mexico, are exciting, readable, and basically accurate accounts of the early West.

J. H. Smith, *The War with Mexico* (2 vols., 1919), remains the fullest account of the Mexican War. Of the studies listed at the end of the previous chapter, Gene M. Brack, *Mexico Views Manifest Destiny* (1976), deserves special mention for its insight into the Mexican motives for war. The best recent account of the military campaigns is K. Jack Bauer, *The Mexican War, 1846–1848* (1974). For Mexican-American relations, see G. L. Rives, *The United States and Mexico: 1821–1848* (2 vols., 1913). John H. Schroeder, *Mr. Polk's War: American Opposition and Dissent, 1846–1848* (1973), is an excellent study of antiwar sentiment.

CHAPTER 17

Compromise and Conflict

On the surface the two-party system resolved the dangerous sectional conflicts unleashed by the annexation of Texas, the Mexican War, and the acquisition of a new continental empire. By the early 1850s cohesion and compromise seemed to have triumphed over division. Americans, more prosperous than they had ever been before, were able for the most part to ignore or rationalize evidence of continuing injustice and exploitation. Public interest in further empire building waned, despite attempts by Democratic leaders to revive the people's enthusiasm. There was sufficient challenge, it seemed, in building railroads, settling a continent, and extending American commerce. In 1854, for example, Commodore Matthew C. Perry, through diplomatic tact and a display of naval power, persuaded the rulers of Japan to open that country to trade and Western influence. In the opinion of political realists, the North had neither the will nor the desire to interfere with slavery in the South; nor was there any reason for the North to fear that slavery would expand beyond its "natural limits" in Missouri, Arkansas, and Texas.

There were hazards, however, in this very triumph of moderation. The stormy passions that culminated in the Compromise of 1850 gave way to political apathy and disenchantment. Voters complained that Whigs and Democrats were indistinguishable in their self-serving lust for office, in their mouthing of stale rhetoric on stale issues, and in their unresponsiveness to public needs and fears. For reasons that varied in each state and locality, significant numbers of voters abandoned their former party allegiance. One consequence of this realignment was the rapid disintegration of the Whigs, especially in the South. By 1855 the anti-Catholic Know-Nothing party had replaced the Whigs as the dominant anti-Democratic alternative in the Northeast. In all sections the weakening of balanced national parties opened the way for new and more extreme appeals to resist the encroachments of some supposedly antirepublican "power."

The American fear of unchecked power was deeply rooted in the colonial and Revolutionary past. The fear acquired new dimensions, however, as the restraints of local customs, traditions, and privileges gave way to individual enterprise and the dominance of market forces. For a time the party system succeeded in channeling and moderating public alarm over the rise of various "powers," such as Freemasons, the "Monster Bank," the "Money Power," Jackson's "monarchic" presidency, and the alleged British conspiracy to block American expansion. By the mid-1850s, however, the controversy over slavery in the territories began to distract attention from anti-Catholic nativism, and the Americans' diffuse fears of unchecked power became grounded in the concrete conflict of interests between free and slave societies.

Like a magnetic field, Negro slavery polarized opposing clusters of values, interests, and aspirations. Southerners believed that any withdrawal of federal sanction and protection for slavery would expose private property to the tyranny of a national majority, undermine the equal sovereignty of states, and lead America in the direction of European "wage-slavery" and class warfare, to say nothing of black insurrection and racial amalgamation.

By the mid-1850s a growing number of Northerners had become convinced that black slavery, by supporting "idle planters" and by associating work with servility, undermined the dignity of labor. As an alternative to the whips and chains of the South, the North offered an idealized vision of prosperity and progress without exploitation—a vision of industrious farmers and proud artisans, of schoolhouses, churches, town meetings, and self-made men. The vast territories of the West, unfenced and jointly owned by the American people, would thus become the critical testing ground for two competing versions of the American dream.

Free Soil and the Challenge of California

Once the vast Mexican territories were acquired, national decisions had to be made. These decisions reactivated all the constitutional issues as well as the political and moral arguments of the Missouri crisis of 1819–21. Would the South be able to maintain its balance of power in the Senate? What was the precise nature of congressional power over territories and the creation of new states? Would the government impose limits on the further expansion of slavery? Or would it adopt a policy of noninterference? Or would it, perhaps, openly sanction slavery by guaranteeing all free Americans equal protection if they took into the common territories property, such as slaves, protected by the laws of their former states?

The Wilmot Proviso. It was predictable that a move would be made in Congress to prohibit slavery in any of the territories acquired by the Mexican War; similar moves had been made since 1784 concerning the trans-Appalachian West, Mississippi, Louisiana, Arkansas, and Missouri. In 1846 the motion came from David Wilmot, a Pennsylvania Democrat, in the form of a proposed amendment to an appropriation bill. The Wilmot Proviso was extraordinarily significant because it was used to challenge "Mr. Polk's War" and all that it signified. The legislatures of fourteen free states eventually endorsed the Proviso's principle; and while many northern senators ignored the instructions of their states, the House of Representatives several times approved the measure, which antislavery members continued to offer.

From 1847 to 1850 this sectional insistence that the territories ceded by Mexico remain "free soil" raised a challenge to Whig and Democratic party unity. Many southern Whigs denounced any proposal for excluding slavery from the territories as a direct violation of southern rights and of state equality. The more extreme Calhounites tried to erode national party loyalty by uniting all Southerners in defense of sectional rights and in opposition to any candidate who failed to repudiate the Wilmot Proviso. In the North in the election of 1848 both Whigs and Democrats suffered losses to the new Free Soil party, which nominated Martin Van Buren for president. "Conscience Whigs," centered in Massachusetts, refused to vote for Zachary Taylor, the former general and Louisiana slaveholder nominated by the Whigs. They claimed that moral protest against the further expansion of slavery should take precedence over the material and political advantages of a united Whig party.

POSTER FOR FREE SOIL RALLY
(American Antiquarian Society)

Free Soil Democrats were led by New York "Barnburners," politicians who had been angered when the Democrats rejected Van Buren in 1844 and had then been further alienated when Polk's administration had favored rival Democratic factions in distributing patronage.

But this upsurge of sectional politics proved to be singularly unsuccessful in undermining the two-party system. Both the Whig and the Democratic parties evaded official commitment on the territorial issue and unashamedly made contradictory appeals to northern and southern voters. In the election of 1848 Van Buren received only 14 percent of the popular vote in the North and won no electoral votes for his Free Soil party. Taylor carried even Massachusetts, where the Whig defections seemed most threatening; Whigs actually gained strength in the South. As a result of this defeat, Van Buren and most of his Democratic followers returned to the national party which now shared common interests in opposing a new Whig administration. The Conscience Whigs, for their part, mostly returned to their uneasy alliance with the "Cotton Whigs," led by such powerful New England textile manufacturers as Abbott Lawrence and Nathan Appleton, who looked to a continuation of their profitable trade relations with the cotton-producing South. Early in 1849 it became clear that the Calhounites had little hope of winning support for a new southern rights coalition.

The survival of national parties did nothing, however, to resolve the territorial issue or to break the congressional deadlock over the Wilmot Proviso. Northern Democrats had favored either extending the Missouri Compromise line of 36°30′ to the Pacific, or leaving the question of slavery to territorial legislatures (popular sovereignty) without congressional interference. President Taylor, on the other hand, tried to prevent further sectional confrontations by urging California and New Mexico to draft constitutions and apply for immediate statehood. This strategy would have avoided congressional action either sanctioning or banning slavery. Both Taylor and his southern opponents recognized that the inhabitants of the Far West, if allowed to organize state governments, would almost certainly vote to exclude Negro slavery. These settlers, most of whom had lived in the intensely racist states of the Old Northwest, cared little about the fate of the slaves in the South, but feared the competition of slave labor in a "land of promise" supposedly reserved for aspiring whites.

Suddenly antiblack feeling became acute in California. The great gold rush of 1849 brought tens of thousands of settlers who resented the prolongation of ineffective military government and who clamored for instant statehood. It also brought a small number of southern masters and slaves and of free black prospectors who, according to hostile whites, were "proverbially lucky." White miners considered it unfair to compete with slave labor, and also considered it degrading "to swing a pick side by side with the Negro," whether free or slave. Fear and hatred of blacks, particularly in the mining regions, led the California constitutional convention of 1849 to copy the sections of the newly written Iowa constitution that prohibited slavery.

In Oregon, which was organized as a separate territory south of the Columbia River, the fusion of

SLUICI
Gold
"long
Aubu
(Court
Library

racism ... more clear-cut. Thoug ... e region by 1844, the pr ... d the models of the Ol ... removal of both slaves ... succeeded in delaying ... orial status until 1848, a ... a concerted drive to lega ... Territory. After heated ... m decisively rejected s ... more decisively the cons ... black settlers—a measure ... rt of the state's constitut

By 1849, ... tended to construe even such dubious forms of antislavery as abolitionism in disguise. Most southern leaders, whether Whig or Democrat, had moved from a defensive policy of censorship and gag rules to an aggressive hostility toward any barrier, however theoretical, to the expansion of slavery. They feared that enactment of the Proviso would swing the full weight of the federal government against an institution it had always protected. By 1849 Free Soil and antislavery congressmen had already linked the Proviso with demands for abolishing slavery in the District of Columbia, which, like the territories, was subject to federal legislation. The new personal liberty laws of the northern states raised the prospect that the North would become as secure a refuge for runaway slaves as British Canada, to which a small number of blacks had successfully escaped.

Indeed, for a growing number of southern diehards, the Northeast of the late 1840s was becoming a perfect replica of the British enemy that had first exploited her own slave colonies, and then ruined them under the influence of misguided philanthropy, finally using antislavery as a mask of righteousness in assuming commercial and ideological domination of the globe. The Northeast, like England, was attracting millions of immigrant wage earners, was developing vast urban centers, and was gaining mastery over the mysterious sources of credit and investment capital. Unless Dixie made her stand, she would therefore share the fate of the exploited, debt-ridden, and ravaged West Indies. If the South were deprived of land and labor for expansion, its boundaries pushed back from the west and the Gulf of Mexico as well as from the north, it would then be subjected by a tyrannical government to slave emancipation and racial amalgamation.

The Crisis of 1850

The Taylor administration faced a succession of problems that exposed irreconcilable divisions within the Whig party. Zachary Taylor was a recent convert to Whiggery (previously, he had never even voted) who had run for president as a military hero and as a man "above party." As president he aggravated the mistrust of Old Whigs when, seeking to broaden the administration's constituency, he bypassed party stalwarts in distributing patronage. Taylor also seemed to betray traditional Whig principles when he tried to build a broad coalition that could compete with the Democrats, who were gaining enormous strength from the votes of recent immigrants.

The preceding Polk administration had reestablished the Independent Treasury, reaffirming the Democrats' opposition to any alliance between government and banks. It had also enacted the Walker Tariff that drastically reduced the duties Whigs had established in 1842. To the dismay of Old Whigs, Taylor balked at proposals to repeal the treasury and tariff acts and advocated compromises that would avoid unnecessary conflict. Simultaneously southern Whigs who had thought they could trust a Louisiana planter were shocked to discover that the president had no objections to admitting California as a free state. In fact, Taylor even dumbfounded his powerful Georgia backer, Robert Toombs, by saying that if Congress saw fit to pass the Wilmot Proviso, "I will not veto it."

When the Thirty-First Congress convened in December 1849, there was a prolonged and ominous conflict over electing the Speaker of the House. It soon became clear that Taylor's program for admitting California and New Mexico as states would receive no support from southern Whigs or even from such party chieftains as Clay, Webster, and Seward. Tensions were heightened by the knowledge that all northern legislatures, with one exception, had instructed their senators to insist on the Wilmot Proviso in any agreement respecting the territories. Also, a growing number of southern legislatures were ap-

pointing delegates to a convention at Nashville in June 1850 to consider potentially revolutionary measures for the defense of southern rights.

Clay's Resolutions.   In January 1850 the aging Henry Clay temporarily recovered leadership of the Whig Party by offering a series of compromise resolutions to the Senate. As an alternative to the Wilmot Proviso and to the popular southern plan which would extend the Missouri Compromise line to the Pacific, Clay favored admitting California as a free state. He also proposed that no restrictions on slavery be imposed in the rest of the territory acquired from Mexico. Clay also attempted to resolve the critical Texas issue. Texas claimed a western boundary that included more than half of the present state of New Mexico. As a result there was an imminent danger of border conflict between the armed forces of Texas and the United States, a conflict that could easily escalate into civil war. Further, when Texas became an American state it had lost its former customs revenue, which was a matter of considerable concern to the influential holders of Texas bonds. To resolve these problems, Clay proposed that the government assume the Texas debt—which promised windfall profits to Texas bondholders—as compensation for Texas's acceptance of New Mexico's territorial claims.

In a gesture to northern sensibilities, Clay recommended that Congress prohibit professional slave trading in the District of Columbia, and thereby rid the national capital of the moral eyesore of slave pens and public auctions. But he also urged that Congress should allay southern fears of an abolitionist "entering wedge" by formally denying that it had authority to interfere with the interstate slave trade and by promising that slavery would never be abolished in the District of Columbia without the consent of its citizens as well as the consent of neighboring Maryland. Finally, Clay proposed that Congress adopt a fugitive slave law that provided severe punishment for anyone who obstructed the efforts of slave owners to recover runaway slaves in any part of the United States.

Such was Clay's contribution to the Compromise

of 1850. The ensuing congressional struggle took place on two distinct levels. On the loftiest level, the Senate became a public forum for some of the most famous and eloquent speeches in American history, speeches that clarified conflicting principles, conflicting political philosophies, and conflicting visions of America's heritage, mission, and destiny. Calhoun, so ill and so near death that he could not personally deliver his farewell address to the nation, argued that a tyrannical northern majority had gradually excluded Southerners from 1.25 million square miles of territory. No further compromises could save the South from a continuing loss of power or prevent the day when a hostile and increasingly centralized government would execute the demands of the abolitionists. The Union might be preserved if the North agreed to open all the territories to slaveholders and to restore, by constitutional amendment, an equal and permanent balance of sectional power. Otherwise, self-preservation would require the South to separate, and to fight if the North refused to accept secession in peace.

Daniel Webster, in his famous reply on March 7, insisted: "There can be no such thing as a peaceable secession." Recoiling in horror from the prospects of disunion and fratricidal war, he pleaded for compromise and for a charitable spirit toward the South. He concurred with southern complaints against the abolitionists, and supported Clay's demand for an effective fugitive slave law. The territorial issue, he claimed, should be no cause for further discord. Convinced that slave labor could never be profitable in the western territories, Webster saw no need for a further legal exclusion that could only antagonize the South.

On March 11 the growing antislavery audience in the Senate found a spokesman in William H. Seward, the New York Whig leader who had helped engineer Taylor's candidacy but who now failed to support the president's plan. Seward, whom Webster described as "subtle and unscrupulous" and bent "to the one idea of making himself president," gave political force to the traditional abolitionist doctrine concerning the territories: "There is a higher law than the Constitution, which regulates our authority over the domain . . . the common heritage of mankind."

The Compromise of 1850. These and other great speeches raised momentous issues; but it is likely that they changed few votes. The second level of struggle involved political infighting that ranged from bribes and lobbying by speculators in Texas bonds to patient and tireless work by committees of experts committed to American political procedures and to the technicalities of constitutional law. Apart from the moderating influence of powerful banking and business interests, which stood to gain by national unity, four circumstances contributed to the final congressional approval of the compromise of 1850.

First, despite signs of an ominous sectional division of parties, Stephen Douglas rallied a core of Democrats, particularly from the Old Northwest and border states, who could counteract the combined pressures of southern and northern extremists. Second, Douglas's drive to win southern support for a railroad connecting Chicago with the Gulf of Mexico (the Illinois Central) demonstrated the rewards that could be gained through sectional cooperation. Third, under Douglas's leadership the Senate wisely abandoned an "Omnibus Bill" that combined most of the compromise in one package. This move allowed both houses of Congress to form sectional alliances that were just barely strong enough to carry each measure —the North overcoming southern resistance to the admission of California and the abolition of the slave trade in the District of Columbia; the South, thanks to many northern abstentions, having its way in enacting the new Fugitive Slave Law. Finally, President Taylor, who had shown no sympathy for the compromise, suddenly died in July. Millard Fillmore, his successor, was close to Webster and Clay and threw the full weight of his administration behind the compromise. Fillmore also skillfully defused the explosive crisis over the Texas–New Mexico boundary. In September much of the nation sank back in relief, assuming that the adoption of Clay's and Douglas's proposals marked the end of serious sectional conflict.

Thus the Compromise of 1850 was made up of the following points: (1) the admission of California as a free state; (2) the organization of the rest of the Mexican cession into two territories, New Mexico and Utah, without federal restriction on slavery; (3) adjustment of the Texas–New Mexico boundary; (4) the award of $10 million to Texas as compensation for the land yielded to New Mexico; (5) prohibition of the slave trade but not of slavery itself in the District of Columbia; and (6) a stringent fugitive slave law. This complex congressional agreement created the illusion of peace; but there was no real consensus on any of the critical issues. In the District of Columbia, trading and selling of slaves continued, though not as openly as before. Blacks, and particularly Indians, continued to be held as slaves on the supposedly free soil of California. The Fugitive Slave Law, which deprived accused blacks of a jury trial and of the right to testify in their own defense, dramatized the agonizing consequences of enforcing a national compromise for which the North had little taste.*

*For the northern reaction to the Fugitive Slave Law, see Chapter 15, page 407.

One of the northern responses to this law was the serial publication in 1851 of Harriet Beecher Stowe's *Uncle Tom's Cabin,* a novel that soon reached millions in book form and in stage presentations. Mrs. Stowe's popular classic, today often underrated as a work of literary persuasion, interpreted the moral and psychological evils of slavery in terms perfectly attuned to the culture of northern evangelical Protestantism. It encouraged every reader who sympathized with the fictional fugitives, in their harrowing ordeal of escape, to share the guilt of a compromise that gave national sanction to slave catchers.

Popular Sovereignty. It was on the territorial issue that the Compromise of 1850 seeded the worst storm clouds of the future. The compromise was deliberately ambiguous concerning the territories. Congress appeared to reaffirm its authority to prohibit slavery in the territories, for it delegated this authority to the legislatures of Utah and New Mexico, subject to the possible veto by a federally appointed governor or by Congress itself. To appease the South, however, Congress publicly registered doubts about the constitutionality of this authority, which could be determined

The Compromise of 1850

Free State or Territory
Slave State or Territory
Territory Open to Slavery

only by the Supreme Court. In effect, Congress invited slaveholders to challenge the constitutionality of any restrictions territorial governments might make on their property rights before the state governments had been established. Most Southerners reluctantly accepted "popular sovereignty" because it at least left the doors open to slavery. Northern moderates—"doughfaces" to their antislavery enemies— were convinced that popular sovereignty would ultimately guarantee free states while avoiding a congressional showdown that would lead to the South's secession.

To pragmatists like Daniel Webster and Stephen Douglas it seemed inconceivable that national policy of any kind could reverse the dominant western pattern of free-labor settlement. Cultivating cotton was too profitable and the value of slaves too great to encourage risky experiments in the semiarid West. It is true that in 1852 Utah legally recognized slavery and that in 1857 New Mexico adopted a slave code. Yet neither territory acquired more than a handful of Negro slaves. Southerners, long accustomed to the security of slave patrols and local law-enforcement agencies, were fearful of taking valuable human property into a region where courts might invoke the old Mexican law prohibiting slavery and where legislatures might at any time be swayed by the convictions of a free soil and anti-Negro majority. Moderates like Douglas advertised the Compromise of 1850 as a "final settlement," but in fact it narrowed the area of further acceptable compromise. The belief grew in the South that disunion would be the inevitable, and the only honorable, response to any further northern threats.

The Know-Nothing Upsurge and Collapse of the Whigs

Between 1853 and 1856 the two-party system rapidly disintegrated as the Whigs literally disappeared and as the Democrats suffered disastrous losses in the North while acquiring unassailable dominance in the South. The reasons for this dramatic political transformation are still a matter of controversy. Even in 1852 the Whigs were seriously divided as a result of the Compromise of 1850. In deference to southern demands, the party's platform of 1852 endorsed this essentially Democratic "final settlement" of the slavery issue. Southern Whigs, however, were infuriated by the party's refusal to renominate Fillmore, who was viewed by many Northerners as a puppet of the Slave Power. Winfield Scott, the military hero who was finally nominated, showed signs of becoming a Seward protégé like Zachary Taylor.

The Election of 1852. Because Southerners no longer trusted northern Whigs as reliable allies in the defense of slavery, the party suffered a devastating defection of southern voters in the election of 1852. In the North, simultaneously, a distinctive Whig identity was blurred. The Whig platform was very similar to the Democratic platform, and Whigs made clumsy and unsuccessful attempts to compete with the Democrats for the votes of immigrant Catholics. This strategy alienated the growing number of Whig nativists—as well as many native-born Democrats of Protestant background—who believed that the professional politicians' hunger for votes had betrayed America's heritage of republicanism, Protestantism, and independence from foreign influence, including that of the Catholic pope.

The remarkable upsurge of political nativism, expressed in 1854 by the Know-Nothing party, was symptomatic of a widespread popular hostility toward the traditional parties. On the one hand, the decisive victory in 1852 of Franklin Pierce, a bland northern Democrat from New Hampshire, could be interpreted as confirmation of a national desire for compromise and mediocrity. On the other hand, the results of state and local elections showed that voters felt that the existing parties were unresponsive to the people's needs. Anti-Catholic nativism suddenly became the vehicle for asserting previously vague grievances.

Know-Nothing Victories. Though anti-Catholicism had been deeply embedded in the American colonial experience, until 1854 this prejudice had lacked national political focus. The Order of the Star-Spangled Banner, the nucleus of the Know-Nothing party, remained an obscure secret society until the local spring elections of 1854 when entire tickets of secret Know-Nothing candidates were swept into office by write-in votes. Local dignitaries of the traditional parties, often confident that they were uncontested, found themselves thrown out of office by men they had never heard of. In Massachusetts the Know-Nothings won 63 percent of the popular vote. By 1855 the Know-Nothings, officially called the American party, had captured control of most of New England. They had become the dominant party opposing the Democrats in New York, Pennsylvania, California, and the border states. They had made striking inroads in Virginia, North Carolina, Georgia, and other southern states, and for a time held the balance of power in Congress. In much of the Northeast the Know-Nothings had defeated or prevented the spread of the new Republican party, which had been founded in 1854 to prevent the extension of slavery into the western territories. In effect, in two years the Know-Nothings had replaced the Whigs as a national political force.

The causes of this revolutionary realignment are difficult to assess. The religious revivals of the 1820s and 1830s had cultivated the belief that the survival of republican government depended on the liberating and unifying force of Protestantism. Protestant revivalists had repeatedly attacked any cohesive corporate group, such as the Freemasonic order or the Mormon or Catholic churches, which supposedly put institutional loyalty above individual moral choice. Prominent northern clergymen, mostly Whigs, had saturated the country with lurid and often hysterical anti-Catholic propaganda. This had contributed to mob violence and church burning, which culminated in a bloody Philadelphia riot in 1844.

Between 1845 and 1854 this traditional prejudice was greatly intensified by the arrival of nearly 3 million immigrants, the majority of whom were Catholics. These newcomers, with their divergent values and life-styles, threatened the Whig dream of an ordered, morally progressive, and homogeneous society—or what one Know-Nothing congressman referred to as a "unity of character and custom." For their part, such Catholic leaders as Archbishop John Hughes of New York made no apologies for their own mobilization of political power or for their own vision of a Catholic America. As Hughes launched a counteroffensive against Protestant indoctrination in the public schools, nativists warned that immigrant voters slavishly obeyed the orders of their priests who, as the agents of European despotism, sought to undermine America's republican institutions. The fact that the Catholic church had opposed the European revolutionary movements of 1848 reinforced many people's fear of antirepublican subversion.

Disintegration of National Party System. The Know-Nothing movement also reflected more immediate ethnic and economic conflicts, especially as native-born workers began blaming immigrants for low wages and unemployment. Though there was little foundation for this belief, nativism had special appeal for artisans and manual workers who associated immigrants with a new and threatening America —an America of increasing urban poverty, of factories and railroads, of rising prices and abruptly changing markets. In the South and in the border states, people also hoped that the Know-Nothing movement would finally end the "needless" sectional disputes over slavery.

In 1856 Millard Fillmore ran as the candidate of the combined American and Whig parties and received nearly 44 percent of the popular vote in the slaveholding states. Nativism was weaker in the Old Northwest, where there was a greater tolerance for immigrants. Yet there the Republicans capitalized on a similar disenchantment with the old parties, often at the expense of the Democrats. In 1854 the Democrats suffered irretrievable losses throughout the North—their representatives in Congress fell from ninety-one to twenty-five. These sudden defections to the Know-Nothing and Republican parties meant that, henceforth, northern Democrats would have little leverage within the restructured national party.

The Know-Nothing movement is significant because it helped to destroy the existing party system. Once in power, the Know-Nothings failed to restrict immigration or to lengthen the traditional five years' residence required for naturalized citizenship. Like other parties, the short-lived American party proved

BROADSIDE FOR A KNOW-NOTHING LECTURE
(American Antiquarian Society)

to be vulnerable to political ambition and compromise. But before being absorbed by the Republicans, the Know-Nothings brought about a massive shift in voter alignments, undermined national party discipline, and hastened the total disappearance of the Whigs. The importance of this ominous development cannot be exaggerated. When the discipline of the party system was swept away, sectional conflict could no longer be suppressed or safely contained.

The Confrontation over Kansas

Stephen Douglas had long been interested in the organization and settlement of the Nebraska Territory—the vaguely defined region west and northwest of Missouri and Iowa, an immense portion of the Louisiana Purchase that had been reserved for Indians and was legally exempt from white settlement. As a senator from Illinois, Douglas had a frank interest in transcontinental railway routes, which, he expected, would make Chicago the hub of mid-America. He was also an ardent patriot and expansionist, convinced that America had been commissioned to free the world from despotism. He thought that the only serious obstacle to this mission was England, which had instigated the subversive activities of American abolitionists, who in turn had provoked the militancy of southern extremists. These Southerners had then blocked the organization of territories north of the Missouri Compromise line of 36°30'.

By 1854, when Douglas was chairman of the Senate Committee on Territories, he had concluded that the Missouri Compromise must be modified to overcome southern fears if the Nebraska country was to be opened to settlement, if the nation was to be bound together by transcontinental railroads and telegraph, if Americans were to fulfill their mission of driving Great Britain from the continent, and if Douglas himself was to reunite and lead the fractured Democratic party. He therefore drafted a bill that applied to Nebraska the popular sovereignty provision that Congress had already applied to Utah and New Mexico under the terms of the Compromise of 1850. This unexpected move destroyed nearly four years of relative sectional peace.

The Kansas-Nebraska Act. Douglas tried at first to play down the contradiction between popular sovereignty and the slavery prohibition of 1820, which applied to all the Louisiana Purchase territory north of the present state of Oklahoma. In 1850 Congress had left it to the courts to resolve any conflicts between popular sovereignty and the unrepealed Mexican law prohibiting slavery in Utah and New Mexico, and Douglas hoped to bypass the Missouri Compromise in the same way. But William Seward and other antislavery Whigs plotted to make the Nebraska bill as objectionable as possible. At the same time, a powerful group of southern senators, the disciples of Calhoun, conspired to make repeal of the Missouri Compromise a test of Democratic party loyalty.

After a series of caucuses Douglas recognized that the Nebraska bill could not pass unless Southerners were assured that all territories would be legally open to slaveholders. Aided by his southern allies, he helped to persuade President Pierce to throw administration support behind a new proposal that would declare the Missouri Compromise "inoperative and void" because it was "inconsistent with the principles of nonintervention by Congress with slavery in the States and Territories, as recognized by the legislation of 1850." This new bill would also provide for the organization of two separate territories, Kansas and Nebraska. By simply affirming that the rights of territorial governments were "subject only to the Constitution of the United States," Douglas's new bill evaded the critical question whether popular sovereignty included the right to exclude slavery. In this form the Kansas-Nebraska bill of 1854 won almost unanimous support from southern Whigs and Democrats and from enough northern Democrats to pass both houses of Congress.

Southern leaders, no less than Stephen Douglas, were astonished by the outrage that exploded across the North. Opponents interpreted the bill as the violation of a "sacred compact," the Missouri Compromise, and as a shameless capitulation to the Slave Power. The legislatures of five northern states passed resolutions condemning the Kansas-Nebraska Act. When Douglas was traveling by rail, he saw so many figures of himself hanging from trees and burned in effigy that he joked, "I could travel from Boston to Chicago by the light of my own effigy." According to the law's defenders, the cries of betrayal were sheer hypocrisy, for antislavery Northerners themselves had repudiated the principle of the Missouri Compromise by refusing to extend the compromise line to the Pacific coast. Yet the breach of faith, however interpreted, led to a rapid dissolution of other shared understandings and political restraints. For the first time, antislavery and proslavery moderates began to perceive each other as more dangerous than the extremists.

Rise of the Republican Party.   What most alarmed proslavery moderates was the sudden appearance of a new and wholly sectional party, scornfully termed the "Black Republicans." This party, in the eyes of its enemies, professed moderation but tried to use the goal of excluding slavery from the territories as a means of capturing control of the federal government. Instead of being satisfied that California was free and that the number of free states was certain to increase, the self-styled Republicans (who had resurrected Jefferson's party label) seemed even to moderate Southerners to be intent on humiliating the South and on reducing the slave-holding states to the status of a colony.

By the mid-1850s Southerners were keenly aware of the growing discrepancy in wealth between their own rural economy and the economy of the urbanizing North. The great cotton boom of the 1850s had proved that even unparalleled southern prosperity could not narrow the gap. Picturing themselves as the nation's true producers of wealth, slaveholders blamed northern middlemen, epitomized by Wall Street bankers and merchants, for siphoning off their just rewards. The new Republican party represented the final and fatal spearhead of the conspiracy as it allied Free-Soilers, antislavery Democrats, and remnants of powerful Whig combines such as the Seward and Weed machine of New York. Whereas the earlier Liberty and Free Soil parties had never had a chance of success, the Republicans in 1856, hardly two years after their appearance, carried eleven of the sixteen free states. General John C. Frémont, the Republican presidential candidate, amassed an astonishing popular vote and would have won over Buchanan, the Democrats' candidate, if he had carried Pennsylvania and Illinois.

The Crisis over Kansas.   Even for antislavery moderates, however, the events in Kansas following passage of the Kansas-Nebraska Act showed that compromise had only encouraged proslavery conspirators to begin to take over the western territories. The Republicans believed that unless drastic countermeasures were taken, America's free white workers would be deprived of the land and opportunity that was their birthright. Congress, by failing to provide definite legal measures for excluding slavery from the territories, had guaranteed that the issue would be decided by numerical and physical force.

The crisis over Kansas was actually the result of complex rivalries and aspirations. The government opened the territory to settlement before Indian treaties had been ratified and before Indian tribes, many of them recently removed to Kansas from the East, had been dispossessed and pushed onto reservations. In 1854 thousands of white settlers began the scramble for Kansas land, searching for the best town sites and the likely railroad routes of the future. Kansas, even without the slavery issue, would have been the scene of a speculative mania and a shameless defrauding of the Indians.

But the passions generated by slavery swept aside the last fragile restraints, such as the frontier's customary rules against "jumping," or disregarding,

prior land claims. According to Missouri's fiery Senator David R. Atchison, a free Kansas would inevitably lead to the demise of slavery in Missouri: "We are playing for a mighty stake, if we win we carry slavery to the Pacific Ocean; if we fail we lose Missouri, Arkansas, and Texas and all the territories; the game must be played boldly." Atchison thus helped to organize bands of "Border Ruffians" to harass settlers from the free states. On the opposite side, New Englanders organized an emigrant aid crusade with the purpose of colonizing Kansas with free-state settlers. Although Stephen Douglas referred to the Emigrant Aid Society as "that vast moneyed corporation," the movement was in fact poorly financed, and it succeeded in transporting barely one thousand settlers to Kansas. But the movement's sensational promotion fed the fantasies of Missourians and Southerners that eastern capitalists were recruiting armies of abolitionists and equipping them with Sharps rifles.

The Kansas-Nebraska Act, 1854

The acts of terrorism reached a climax in 1856 and became, in effect, a civil war. Antislavery newspapers declared that war had actually begun when a large proslavery force, supposedly acting under the authority of law enforcement officials, sacked the free-state town of Lawrence. The revenge for such proslavery outrages was even more savage. Even fervid southern alarmists had not imagined anything as brutal as John Brown's retaliatory massacre at Pottawatomie Creek. Brown, a wild and messianic ne'er-do-well with an abolitionist background and abolitionist connections, who thought of himself as an agent of God's vengeance, led four of his sons and two followers in a night attack on an unprotected settlement. They brutally executed five men and boys who were vaguely associated with the proslavery party.

In Congress all pretense of civility collapsed. In 1856 speakers became inflamed, personal, malicious. Senator Charles Sumner of Massachusetts, after denouncing "the crime against Kansas" and "the rape of a virgin territory, compelling it to the hateful embrace of slavery," delivered studied insults to the elderly Andrew Butler, a senator from South Carolina. On the Senate floor Butler's cousin, Preston Brooks, later savagely attacked the seated Sumner with a cane, leaving him unconscious and seriously injured. This triumph of "Bully" Brooks, a congressman from South Carolina, won applause from much of the South. For many Northerners, Sumner's Senate seat, which remained empty for over three years during his prolonged recovery, was a silent warning that Southerners could not be trusted to respect any codes, agreements, or sets of rules.

The same warning on a larger scale seemed to come out of the chaos of Kansas politics. By 1857 there could be no doubt that the overwhelming majority of Kansas settlers opposed admitting the territory as a slave state. Like the white settlers in California and Oregon, they also wanted to exclude free blacks along with slaves. For most Kansans these were in themselves minor issues compared to the disposal of Indian lands, squatter rights, rival railroad routes, and the desirability of free homesteads. What made slavery an explosive question in Kansas, and what made Kansas a detonating fuse for the na-

tion, was the federal government's effort to bypass the people's will.

The Pierce and Buchanan administrations made a series of miscalculations. In the first tumultuous stage of settlement, the Pierce administration had legally recognized a proslavery territorial legislature established by wholesale fraud; some seventeen hundred Missourians had crossed the border to cast illegal votes. Many moderates hoped that the flagrant acts of this provisional legislature—such as making it a felony to question the right to hold slaves in Kansas—would soon be repealed by a more representative body. But the free-state settlers chose to boycott the elections that the "legal" proslavery government authorized and to establish their own extralegal government and constitution.

The Lecompton Constitution.   In 1857 the Buchanan administration was thus committed to support the outcome of an official election of delegates to a constitutional convention, in Lecompton, Kansas, in preparation for statehood, even though only one in twelve eligible voters went to the polls. By then, the South had become convinced that the security of the slave system hinged on making Kansas a slave state. Buchanan had become equally convinced that the survival of the Democratic party hinged on appeasing the South (in 1856, 119 of his 174 electoral votes had come from slave states). In Kansas, there were no moderating pressures on the proslavery convention that drafted the convention's "Lecompton constitution." In Washington, the declining power of the northern Democrats gave a similarly unrestrained hand to the southern Democrats who dominated Buchanan's administration.

For Stephen Douglas the vote in Kansas on the proslavery Lecompton constitution was a total subversion of popular sovereignty. The voters, instead of being allowed to accept or reject the constitution as a whole, were asked only to approve the article guaranteeing for the future the right of property in slaves. If the article were rejected, the Constitution would still protect the legal status of slaves already in the territory. Although the free-state majority again registered their protest by abstaining from this vote, Buchanan exerted the powers of his office to pressure

Congress into admitting Kansas as a slave state. This policy brought a bitter break with Douglas, who denounced Buchanan's attempt to "force this constitution down the throats of the people of Kansas, in opposition to their wishes." In 1858, as in 1854, Congress became the scene of a violent sectional struggle. But this time Douglas led the antiadministration forces. Buchanan stood firm, sacrificing much of his remaining Democratic support in the North. In the end, in 1858, the Buchanan administration suffered a crushing defeat when the free state party forced a popular vote in Kansas on the whole of the Lecompton constitution. The territory's electorate rejected the constitution by a vote of nearly 10 to 1, though at the cost of indefinitely postponing statehood. (As it turned out, Kansas became a free state in 1861.)

Dred Scott and the Lincoln-Douglas Debates

The Lecompton struggle contributed to a fatal split in the Democratic party. The Democratic party had survived a stormy period which had led to the sectional division of the largest Protestant churches and benevolent societies, to say nothing of the collapse of the Whigs. The party had given the South a disproportionate access to national power, but an access dependent on winning the support of northern allies. As the number of such allies began to dwindle, they were partly replaced by southern Whigs. Thus as the Democratic party became more southern in character, there were fewer restraints on attempts to test the party loyalty of northern Democrats and to adopt an avowedly proslavery program. The Lecompton constitution was actually the second critical test imposed on northern Democrats. The first test was the *Dred Scott* decision.

The Dred Scott Decision. The Southerners who dominated the Supreme Court decided to use the *Dred Scott* case as a way to resolve critical issues that Congress had long evaded. From the time that the Court received the case, late in 1854, to its long-delayed decision in 1857, the paramount issue was whether Congress had the constitutional right to prohibit slavery in any territory or to delegate such a right to territorial governments, as implied by Stephen Douglas's formula of "popular sovereignty." In the recently disputed territories of New Mexico, Utah, and Kansas, no judicial cases involving the exclusion of slavery had yet arisen.

There had been many previous suits for freedom by slaves who had lived with their masters as temporary residents of free states. Even southern courts had sometimes granted freedom to such slaves, but the decisions had depended on complex technical issues that mostly involved state law. What distinguished Dred Scott, a Missouri slave who sued the state for his freedom, was that he and his master, an army surgeon, had lived together for several years not only in the free state of Illinois but in a part of Wisconsin Territory where slavery had been *federally* prohibited by the Missouri Compromise. Despite this clear violation of federal law, Scott's initial trials in Missouri courts were confined to narrower issues.

In 1854 technical complications allowed Scott's lawyers to transfer his suit for freedom to the United States Circuit Court for the District of Missouri. This first federal trial raised a preliminary question that courts had never resolved and that affected the enforcement of the Fugitive Slave Law of 1850. Were any blacks citizens to the extent of being qualified by the Constitution to bring suit in a federal court? After years of debate and postponement in the United States Supreme Court, this jurisdictional question enabled Chief Justice Roger Taney to link Scott's individual claim with momentous constitutional issues. For if blacks were not citizens entitled to constitutional rights and privileges, Dred Scott would be subject only to the laws of Missouri, and blacks seized under the provisions of the Fugitive Slave Law of 1850 would have no recourse to federal courts. The *Dred Scott* case also involved a second question of enormous significance. The court also had to decide if Congress had exceeded its powers in 1820 when it had outlawed slavery in the Louisiana Purchase north of 36'30°. If so, Dred Scott was still a slave and therefore could not bring suit in federal court.

By the end of 1856 the *Dred Scott* case had received widespread national publicity, with newspapers summarizing the opposing arguments delivered before the Court. Although informed observers anxiously awaited a verdict that might have explosive political consequences, they generally expected the Court to deny its jurisdiction on narrow technical grounds, thus confirming the judgment of lower courts that Scott was still a slave. When the decision was finally announced, in 1857, seven of the justices rejected Scott's claim to freedom but all nine wrote separate opinions. There is still controversy over what parts of the "Opinion of the Court," written by Chief Justice Taney, represented the opinion of a majority of the justices.

Taney's opinion arrived at three sweeping conclusions: first, Taney held that at the time the Constitution of the United States had been adopted, blacks had "for more than a century been regarded as beings of an inferior order . . . so far inferior that they had no rights which the white man was bound to respect; and that the negro might justly and lawfully be reduced to slavery for his benefit." Taney further contended that neither the Declaration of Independence nor the privileges and immunities of the Constitution had been intended to apply to blacks, whether slave or free. Even if later free blacks in certain states had been granted citizenship, Taney said, they were not citizens "within the meaning of the Constitution of the United States." They were not entitled to the rights and privileges of a citizen in any other state, nor could they sue in a federal court.

Second, after denying the Court's jurisdiction over Dred Scott, Taney reinforced his argument by moving on to the substantive issues. As for Scott's residence in Illinois, the Court had already recognized the principle that the status of a slave taken to a free state should be determined by the laws of the slave state to which he had returned. On Scott's residence in the federal territory north of 36°30', Taney ruled that the Missouri Compromise had been unconstitutional, since Congress had no more power in a federal territory than in a state to deprive a citizen of his property. Finally, having argued that slaves could not be differentiated from other forms of property

protected by the Fifth Amendment, Taney concluded that Congress could not give a territorial government powers that exceeded those of the federal government: "It could confer no power on any local Government, established by its authority, to violate the provisions of the Constitution." This judgment struck directly at Douglas's interpretation of popular sovereignty, and affirmed the extreme southern view that the people of a territory could not legally discriminate against slave property until they acquired the sovereignty of statehood.

Reaction to the Decision.   Both the South and President Buchanan were jubilant. Despite vigorous dissenting opinions from Justices John McLean and Benjamin R. Curtis, the highest court in the land had ruled that excluding slavery from the territories, the goal that had brought the Republican party into existence, was unconstitutional. Republican newspapers like the New York *Tribune* scornfully replied that the decision was "entitled to just as much moral weight as would be the judgment of a majority of those congregated in any Washington bar-room." Stephen Douglas, the leading contender for the Democratic presidential nomination in 1860, remained silent for many weeks. He wholly agreed with the denial of black citizenship and took credit for the congressional repeal of the Missouri Compromise. Yet his relations with Buchanan and the South were already strained, and he knew that his future career hinged on finding a way to reconcile the southern version of limited popular sovereignty, embodied in the *Dred Scott* decision, with his own constituents' demand for genuine self-determination.

In an important speech at the Illinois statehouse, in May 1857, Douglas presented his response to the *Dred Scott* decision. He argued that the constitutional right to take slaves into a territory was a worthless right unless sustained, protected, and enforced by "police regulations and local legislation." By contrasting an empty legal right with the necessary public support to enforce such a right, Douglas denied any meaningful contradiction between the *Dred Scott* decision and his own principle of popular sovereignty. Two weeks later Abraham Lincoln gave his reply to

Douglas before the same forum. Terming the *Dred Scott* decision erroneous, Lincoln reminded his audience that the Supreme Court had frequently overruled its own decisions, and promised: "We shall do what we can to have it to over-rule this."

Since 1854, when he had attacked the Kansas-Nebraska Act, Lincoln had begun making a new career by pursuing Stephen Douglas. Elected to Congress as a Whig in 1846, he had suffered politically from his opposition to the Mexican War. Lincoln was a self-educated Kentuckian, shaped by the Indiana and Illinois frontier. In moral and cultural outlook, however, he was not far from the stereotyped New Englander. He abstained from alcohol, revered the idea of self-improvement, dreamed of America's technological and moral progress, and condemned slavery as a moral and political evil. "I have always hated slavery," he told a Chicago audience in 1858, "I think as much as any Abolitionist. . . . I have always hated it, but I have always been quiet about it until this new era of the introduction of the Nebraska Bill began. I always believed that everybody was against it, and that it was in course of ultimate extinction."

The Kansas-Nebraska Act taught Lincoln that men like Douglas did not care whether slavery was "voted *down* or voted *up*." It also allowed him to exercise his magnificent talents as a debator and stumpspeaker, talents which had already distinguished him as a frontier lawyer, a state legislator, and an attorney and lobbyist for such corporations as the Illinois Central Railroad. Lincoln's humor, his homespun epigrams, his unaffected self-assurance, all diverted attention from his extraordinary ability to grasp the central point of a controversy and to compress an argument into its most lucid and striking form. In 1856, after a period of watchful waiting, Lincoln played an important part in the belated organization of the Illinois Republican party. Two years later the Republican state convention unanimously nominated him to succeed Douglas as United States senator.

The Lincoln-Douglas contest was unprecedented both in form and in substance. At this time senators were still elected by state legislatures, and no party convention had ever nominated a candidate. In an acceptance speech on June 16, 1858, Lincoln concisely and eloquently stated the arguments he would present directly to the people, appealing for a Republican legislature that would then be committed to elect him to the Senate. Since Douglas had unexpectedly repudiated the Lecompton constitution and had joined the Republicans in fighting it, Lincoln needed to persuade the electorate that Douglas's own crusade for popular sovereignty had rekindled the slavery agitation and had led directly to the *Dred Scott* decision and the Lecompton constitution. According to Lincoln, Douglas's moral indifference to slavery disqualified him as a leader who could stand firm against the future aggressions of the Slave Power. For Lincoln was wholly convinced that the conflict over slavery would continue until a crisis had been reached and passed. As he said in his famous "House Divided" speech:

"A house divided against itself cannot stand.
I believe this government cannot endure, permanently half *slave* and half *free*.
I do not expect the Union to be *dissolved*—I do not expect the house to *fall*—but I *do* expect it will cease to be divided.
It will become *all* one thing, or *all* the other.
Either the *opponents* of slavery, will arrest the further spread of it, and place it where the public mind shall rest in the belief that it is in course of ultimate extinction; or its *advocates* will push it forward, till it shall become alike lawful in *all* the States, *old* as well *as new*—North as well as *South*.
Have we no *tendency* to the latter condition?"

The "House Divided" speech signified a turning point in American political history. Lincoln stated that expediency and a moral neutrality toward slavery had undermined the Founders' expectation that slavery was "in the course of ultimate extinction." If the North continued to make compromises and failed to defend a boundary of clear principle, the South was certain to dictate "a second Dred Scott decision," depriving every state of the power to discriminate against slave property. In Lincoln's view, Douglas's Kansas-Nebraska Act had been part of a master plan or conspiracy, which Lincoln compared to "a piece of *machinery*" that had been designed to legalize slavery, step by step, throughout the United States. In asserting that "the people were to be left 'perfectly free' 'subject only to the Constitution,'" Douglas had provided "an exactly fitted *niche,* for the Dred Scott decision to afterwards come in, and declare the perfect freedom of the people, to be just no freedom at all."

Lincoln was not an abolitionist. He was convinced that prohibiting the further spread of slavery would be sufficient to condemn it to "ultimate extinction," a belief shared by many southern leaders. Yet he insisted on a public policy aimed at that goal—a public policy similar to that of England in the 1820s or, in Lincoln's eyes, to that of the Founders. For Lincoln, repudiating popular sovereignty was the same as repudiating the moral indifference exemplified by Douglas; and this was the first step toward national redemption.

The Lincoln-Douglas Debates. Because Douglas seemed to be the nation's most likely choice for president in 1860, his struggle with Lincoln for reelection to the Senate commanded national attention. Making full use of newly constructed railroads, the two candidates traveled nearly ten thousand miles in four months. They crisscrossed Illinois, their tireless voices intermingling with the sound of bands, parades, fireworks, cannon, and cheering crowds. Each community tried to outdo its rivals in pageantry and in winning the greatest turnout from the countryside. Lincoln and Douglas agreed to participate in seven face-to-face debates, which are rightly regarded as classics in the history of campaign oratory. Douglas tried to make the most of his experience as a seasoned national leader (at forty-five he was four years younger than Lincoln), and to portray his opponent as a dangerous radical. According to Douglas, Lincoln's "House Divided" speech showed a determination to impose the moral judgments of one section on the other. Lincoln's doctrines threatened to destroy the Union and to extinguish the world's last hope for freedom. Douglas also exploited the racial prejudice of his listeners, drawing laughter from his sarcastic refusal to question "Mr. Lincoln's conscientious belief that the negro was made his equal, and hence his brother."

Lincoln searched for ways to counteract the image of a revolutionary. Always insisting on the moral and political wrong of slavery, he repeatedly acknowledged that the federal government could not interfere with slavery in the existing states. He opposed repeal of the Fugitive Slave Law. He wholly rejected the idea of "perfect social and political equality with the negro." He did maintain, however, that blacks were as much entitled as whites to "all the natural rights enumerated in the Declaration of Independence, the right to life, liberty and the pursuit of happiness." If the black was "perhaps" not equal in moral or intellectual endowment, "in the right to eat the bread, without leave of anybody else, which his own hand earns, *he is my equal and the equal of judge Douglas, and the equal of every living man.* [Great applause.]"

The election in Illinois was extremely close. The Republicans did not win enough seats in the legislature to send Lincoln to the Senate, but the campaign immediately elevated him to national prominence. Lincoln had succeeded in articulating and defending a Republican antislavery ideology that combined a fixity of purpose with a respect for constitutional restraints. Lincoln had also magnified the gap that separated the Republicans from Douglas and other anti-Lecompton Democrats. He had further isolated Douglas from proslavery Democrats in the South who were already embittered by Douglas's "treachery" with regard to the Lecompton constitution. They were then outraged by Douglas's response to Lincoln in the debate at Freeport, Illinois, where he had maintained that regardless of what the Supreme Court might decide about the constitutionality of slavery in a territory, the people had the "lawful means to introduce it or exclude it" as they pleased. Repeating his familiar point that slavery could not exist "a day or an hour anywhere" unless it was supported by local police regulations, Douglas emphasized that the "unfriendly legislation" of a territorial government could effectually prevent slavery from being introduced. As Lincoln quipped, this was to say, "A thing may be lawfully driven from a place where it has a lawful right to stay."

In 1859 the breach between Douglas and the South could no longer be contained. The people of

STEPHEN A. DOUGLAS, 1813–1861
Wooden folk sculpture of Stephen Douglas, who opposed Abraham Lincoln in the epic senatorial election of 1858 as well as in the presidential election of 1860. At left, the "Little Giant" in his prime. *(Below: Courtesy, National Portrait Gallery, Smithsonian Institution, Washington, D.C.; left: Brady Collection, National Archives)*

Kansas ratified a new constitution prohibiting slavery, thereby giving bite to Douglas's "Freeport Doctrine." In the Senate, where Douglas had been ousted from his chairmanship of the Committee on Territories, he led the fight against the demand for a federal slave code protecting slave property in all the territories. During a tour of the South, Douglas became alarmed by the growing movement, led by young proslavery "fire-eaters," to revive and legalize the African slave trade. Looking ahead to the Democratic convention of 1860, Douglas issued what amounted to an ultimatum about the party platform. Northern Democrats, he insisted, would not allow the party to be used as a vehicle for reviving the African slave trade, securing a federal slave code, or pursuing any of the other new objectives of southern extremists. Douglas warned that Northerners would not retreat from defending genuine popular sovereignty, even though popular sovereignty was clearly running against the interests of the South.

The Ultimate Failure of Compromise

By 1860 a multitude of hitherto separate fears, aspirations, and factional interests had become polarized into opposing visions of America's heritage and destiny. Traditional systems of trust and reciprocity had collapsed.

John Brown's Raid. John Brown, who had warred against slavery in Kansas, was a key symbol of this polarization. Since 1857 Brown had been lionized by the most eminent New England reformers and literary figures. Backed financially by a secret group of abolitionists, Brown also cultivated intimate ties with free black communities in the North. On the night of October 16, 1859, he and some twenty heavily armed white and black followers seized part of the federal arsenal at Harpers Ferry, Virginia. Brown hoped to begin the destruction of slavery by igniting a slave insurrection and creating in the South a free-soil asylum for fugitives. After resisting federal troops for two days, Brown surrendered; he was tried for conspiracy, treason, and murder, and was hanged.

During his trial Brown claimed to have acted under the "higher law" of the New Testament, and insisted, "If I had done what I have for the white men, or the rich, no man would have blamed me." For Brown the higher law was not a philosophical abstraction but a moral command to shed blood and die in the cause of freedom. In the eyes of sedentary reformers and intellectuals, Brown's courage to act on his principles made him not only a revered martyr but a symbol of all that America lacked. Democratic editors and politicians, however, saw Brown's criminal violence as the direct result of the irresponsible preaching of William H. Seward and other "Black Republicans." The New York *Herald* reprinted Seward's speech on the "irrepressible conflict" alongside news accounts from Harpers Ferry. Many Southerners came to the stunned realization that Brown's raid could not be dismissed as the folly of a madman, since it had revealed the secret will of much of the North. A Virginia senator concluded that Brown's "invasion" had been condemned in the North "only

because it failed." In the words of Jefferson Davis, a Mississippi senator who had been Pierce's secretary of war, the Republican party had been "organized on the basis of making war" against the South.

Paradoxically both the Republicans and southern extremists agreed that slavery must expand under national sanction if it were to survive. They also agreed that if the *Dred Scott* decision was valid, the government had an obligation to protect slave property in all the territories. This denial of any middle ground made it logical for southern fire-eaters to argue that a revived African slave trade would allow more whites to own slaves and would thus help to "democratize" the institution. Above all, both the Republicans and southern extremists rejected popular sovereignty as Douglas had defined it. For Southerners, the Constitution prohibited either Congress or a territorial legislature from depriving a settler of his slave property. For Republicans, the Constitution gave Congress both the duty and power to prevent the spread of an institution that deprived human beings of their inalienable right to freedom.

Because these positions were irreconcilable, the northern Democrats held the only keys to possible compromise in the presidential election of 1860. But like the Republicans, the Douglas Democrats had drawn their own firm limits against further concessions to southern extremists. Early in 1860 Jefferson Davis challenged those limits by persuading the Senate Democratic caucus to adopt a set of resolutions committing the federal government to protect slavery in the territories. For Davis and other southern leaders, a federal slave code was the logical extension of the *Dred Scott* decision, and the principle of federal protection of slave property an essential plank in the forthcoming Democratic platform. The Douglas Democrats knew that such a principle of guaranteed protection would completely undercut their reliance on legislation "unfriendly" to slavery in a territory, and that such a plank would guarantee their defeat in the North.

Division of Democratic Party. In April 1860 the fateful Democratic national convention met at

It cant stop me for I built it

How can I get over this Rail Fence.

You find me in dis yer Fence, Massa Duglis.

THE ELECTION OF 1860
A cartoonist's view of the presidential race between Lincoln, the tall railsplitter, and Douglas, who is carrying a jug of liquor and whose record on slavery in the territories constitutes an insuperable obstacle (black man waiting in fence to stop Douglas). *(Library of Congress)*

Charleston. When a majority of the convention refused to adopt a platform similar in principle to Davis's Senate resolutions, the delegates from eight southern states withdrew, many of them assuming that this disunionist gesture would force the Douglas faction to compromise. Douglas held firm to his principle of popular sovereignty and as a result could not muster the two-thirds majority required for nomination. In a surprise move the northern Democrats then agreed to adjourn the convention and to reconvene six weeks later in Baltimore.

There the Democratic party finally destroyed itself as a national force. Delegates from the Lower South again seceded, and this time adopted an extreme proslavery platform and nominated John C. Breckinridge of Kentucky for president. The northern remnants of the party remained loyal to popular sovereignty, however it might be modified in practice

by the *Dred Scott* decision, and nominated Douglas.

Meanwhile, the division of the Democrats at Charleston had given the Republicans greater flexibility in nominating a candidate. In 1858 Douglas had portrayed Lincoln as a flaming abolitionist, and the South had accepted the image. To the North, however, Lincoln appeared more moderate and less controversial than the better-known Senator Seward of New York. Unlike Seward, Lincoln was not popularly associated with the higher-law doctrines that had led to Harpers Ferry. Although Lincoln disapproved of Know-Nothing nativism, he was more discreet than Seward and thus stood less chance of losing the nativist vote in critical states like Pennsylvania. If some Northerners regarded him as a crude buffoon from the prairies, he appealed to many Northerners as the tall rail-splitter of humble origins, a man of the people, an egalitarian. Except for his general endorsement

THE UNION MUST AND SHALL BE PRESERVED

FREE SPEECH.
FREE HOMES,
FREE TERRITORY.

PROTECTION TO AMERICAN INDUSTRY

FOR PRESIDENT
ABRAHAM LINCOLN
OF ILLINOIS

FOR VICE PRESIDENT
HANNIBAL HAMLIN
OF MAINE

LITH.BY W.H.REASE   COR.4TH & CHESTNUT STS.PHILADA.

CAMPAIGN POSTER
The Republican candidates for president and vice president in 1860. *(Library of Congress)*

of the Homestead Act, protective tariffs, and a transcontinental railroad—all programs that were popular in the North and West and that had been blocked in Congress by the South—Lincoln was associated with few issues and had made few enemies. In May, at the Republicans' boisterous convention in Chicago, Lincoln finally overcame Seward's early lead and received the nomination.

The presidential campaign of 1860 was filled with the noisy hucksterism and carnival atmosphere that had been standard since 1840. The Republicans tended to discount the warnings of serious crisis, and contemptuously dismissed southern threats of secession as empty bluff. The Breckinridge Democrats tried to play down such threats and to profess their loyalty to the Constitution and Union. Yet various groups of moderates realized that both the Constitution and Union were in jeopardy. This was the message of the new Constitutional Union party, which was led largely by former Whigs and which won many supporters in the Upper South. And this was the message that Stephen Douglas repeated bravely and incessantly—in the South as well as in the North—in the first nationwide speaking campaign by a presidential candidate.

The Election of 1860. In November the national popular vote was divided among four candidates, and Lincoln received only 40 percent of the national total. Yet he received 180 electoral votes, 57 more than the combined total of his three opponents. He carried every free state except for New Jersey, and won 4 of New Jersey's 7 electoral votes. In ten of the slave states, however, he failed to register a single popular vote. Breckinridge, the southern Democrat, captured all the states of the Lower South as well as Delaware, Maryland, Arkansas, and North Carolina. John Bell, the leader of the once powerful Whig party in Tennessee and the candidate of the Constitutional Union party, carried Tennessee, Kentucky, and Virginia. Though Douglas received approximately 525,000 more popular votes than Breckinridge, and trailed Lincoln by only 491,000, he won 12 electoral votes (9 from Missouri and 3 from New Jersey). In many respects it was not really a national election. In the North it was essentially a contest between Lincoln and Douglas; in the South between Breckinridge and Bell.

For the South the worst fears and predictions of forty years had come true. The United States had never had an administration avowedly hostile to black slavery. Lincoln's reassurances regarding the constitutional protection of slavery in the existing states could not mitigate the crucial facts. The election had proved that the North was populous enough to bestow national power on a minority party that had no support in the South. The Republican party was committed to free-labor ideology and to the proposition that slavery was a moral wrong. Slaveholders would have to take Lincoln's professions of restraint on good faith. If he or his successors should become more militant, they could not be checked by a balance of political power. A dominant sectional party would control federal patronage, the postal service and mili-

The Election of 1860

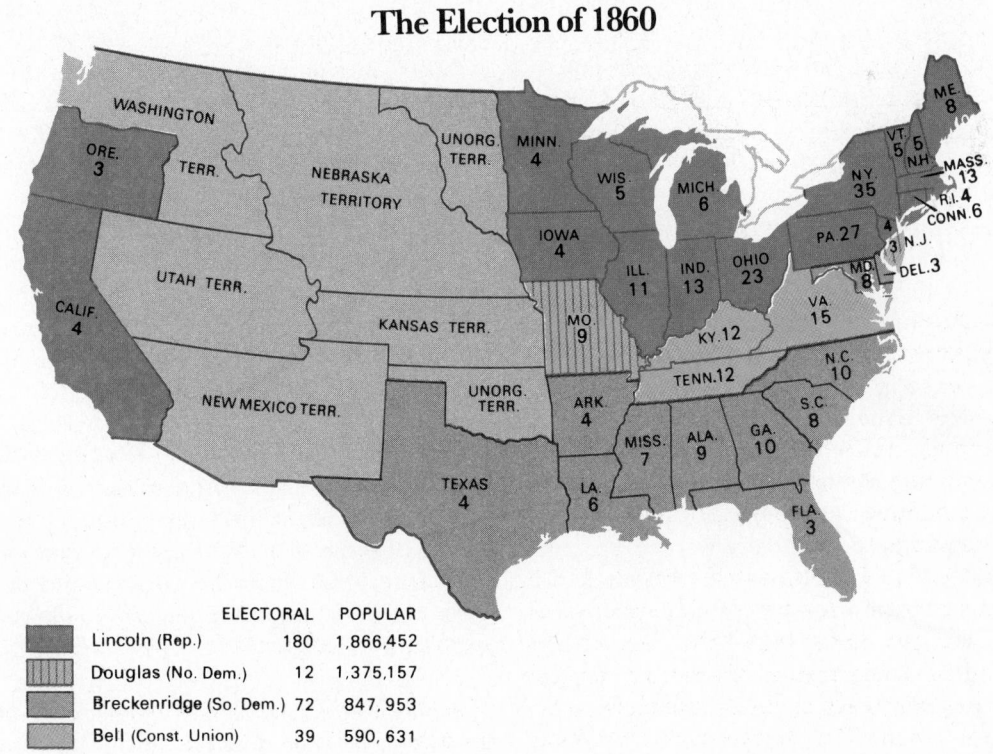

	ELECTORAL	POPULAR
Lincoln (Rep.)	180	1,866,452
Douglas (No. Dem.)	12	1,375,157
Breckenridge (So. Dem.)	72	847,953
Bell (Const. Union)	39	590,631

tary posts, the appointment of federal judges and other officeholders. Such considerations strengthened the hand of secessionists. On December 20, 1860, South Carolina crossed the threshold that had been so closely approached during the nullification crisis. A special convention repealed the state's ratification of the Constitution and withdrew South Carolina from the Union. Unlike Jackson when faced with similar defiance, President Buchanan maintained that the federal government could do nothing to prevent the move.

Unionists mounted stiffer resistance to secession in the other states of the Lower South. The chief controversies, however, involved timing—whether to follow the stampede of the fire-eating militants or to wait until Lincoln had shown his true colors. By February 1, 1861, the militants had triumphed in Mississippi, Florida, Alabama, Georgia, Louisiana, and Texas. Inevitably the shock produced reflex actions toward the traditional saving compromise. Senator John Crittenden of Kentucky initiated the first of such moves two days before South Carolina officially seceded. Though Crittenden's proposed amendments to the Constitution were defined as moderate, they matched the most extravagant southern demands of a few years before. Even so, the leaders of the Lower South knew that no "compromise" would be secure unless the Republican party miraculously repudiated its antislavery principles. Most Republicans could not publicly approve Crittenden's "unamendable" amendment guaranteeing the permanent security of slavery. Nor could they return to the old Democratic proposal for extending the Missouri Compromise line to the Pacific. The 1850s had shown that federal commitment to establishing and protecting slavery south of that line would only encourage southern ambitions in the Caribbean and Latin America. As Lincoln confidentially warned William Kellogg, his mouthpiece in Congress: "Entertain no proposition for a compromise in regard to the *extension* of slavery. The instant you do, they have us under again; all our labor is lost, and sooner or later must be done over. . . . The tug has to come and better now than later."

By 1860 the North and South had moved beyond the reach of compromise. The United States had originally emerged from an act of secession, from a final rejection of compromise with England. Even after independence had been won, Americans continued to perceive Britain as a conspiratorial power threatening to hold back the nation's expansive energies. But despite this threat, America continued to prosper and expand. The period from 1820 to 1860 witnessed a progressive extension of limits, an overleaping of boundaries of every kind. History seemed to confirm the people's wish for total self-determination. The American people, like the American individual, seemed to be free from the burdens of the past and free to shape their own character. The one problem their ingenuity could not resolve was Negro slavery, which the Founding Fathers had seen as an unwanted legacy of British greed. Paradoxically the South increasingly came to regard Negro slavery as the necessary base on which freedom must rest. For the North a commitment to slavery's ultimate extinction was the test of freedom. Each section detected a fatal change in the other, a betrayal of the principles and mission of the Founding Fathers. Each section feared that the other had become transformed into a despotic and conspiratorial power very similar to the original British enemy. And both sections shared a heritage of standing firm against despotism.

It was not accidental that the greatest novel of the period, Herman Melville's *Moby Dick* (1851), tells of the destruction that inevitably flows from denying all limits, rules, and boundaries. The novel concerns Captain Ahab's relentless and stubborn pursuit of a great white whale, a "nameless, inscrutable, unearthly thing" that becomes a symbol for all the opposing, unknown forces of life. Ahab, who commands a crew containing most of the races and types of mankind, thinks that he can become the master of his own fate. Ignoring a series of warnings and portents, he is incapable of admitting that he might be wrong or that there might be forces beyond his control.

Melville's novel is full of rich and universal meaning concerning the heroic yet impossible quest to know the unknowable. Since Americans of the

1850s believed that men were born free and that God would ensure the triumph of democracy in the world, they could not accept Melville's brooding skepticism. Nevertheless, there was a lesson for pre–Civil War America in this tale of a highly rational but half-crazed captain—a captain who becomes so obsessed with his mission that he finally throws his navigation instruments overboard, so that he can steer only toward the visible spout of the whale. Captain Ahab seeks liberation in an unswerving pursuit and conquest of limits. In the end he dooms himself and his ship to destruction.

CHRONOLOGY

1846 Wilmot Proviso fuses question of slavery's expansion with consequences of Mexican War.
Walker tariff, adopted for revenue only, eliminates principle of protection.

1848 Gold discovered on American River in California.
Van Buren, running for president on Free-Soil ticket, receives 10 percent of popular vote.
Zachary Taylor elected president.

1850 In Congress, violent sectional debate culminates in Compromise of 1850.
Fugitive Slave Law requires federal agents to recover escaped slaves from sanctuaries in the North.
Taylor's death makes Millard Fillmore president.

1851 Herman Melville's *Moby Dick.*

1852 Franklin Pierce elected president.
Harriet Beecher Stowe's *Uncle Tom's Cabin.*

1853 Upsurge of political nativism, the Know-Nothings.

1854 Spectacular Know-Nothing election victories.
Collapse of Whigs.

1854 New Republican party emerges.
Commodore Perry opens Japan to American trade.
Kansas-Nebraska Act rekindles sectional controversy over slavery.

1856 John Brown's murderous raid at Pottawatomie Creek.
James Buchanan elected president.

1857 Dred Scott decision.
In Kansas, proslavery Lecompton constitution ratified as free-state men refuse to vote.

1858 Lincoln-Douglas debates.

1859 John Brown's raid on Harpers Ferry.

1860 Democratic party deadlocked at Charleston convention finally divides along sectional lines at Baltimore.
Abraham Lincoln elected president.
South Carolina secedes from the Union.

1861 Mississippi, Florida, Alabama, Georgia, Louisiana, and Texas secede.

SUGGESTED READINGS

David M. Potter, *The Impending Crisis, 1848–1861* (1976), continues to be the best guide to the topics discussed in the present chapter. See also William J. Cooper, *The South and the Politics of Slavery 1828–1865* (1978). The titles on the causes of the Civil War, listed at the end of Chapter 18 in Part Four are also highly relevant.

On California, the best general guide is Andrew F.

Rolle, *California: A History* (1969). For the California gold rush and western mining in general, see Rodman W. Paul, *California Gold: The Beginning of Mining in the Far West* (1947); and Paul, *Mining Frontiers of the Far West, 1848–1880* (1963). Kevin Starr, *Americans and the California Dream, 1850–1915* (1973), presents brilliant vignettes of early California history. For the experiences of blacks in California, see Rudolph M. Lapp, *Blacks in Gold Rush California* (1977). Chinese immigration and anti-Chinese sentiment is admirably treated in Alexander Saxton, *The Indispensable Enemy: Labor and the Anti-Chinese Movement in California* (1975).

Holman Hamilton, *Prologue to Conflict* (1964), is the most detailed and accurate account of the Compromise of 1850. For the preceding presidential election, see Joseph G. Rayback, *Free Soil: The Election of 1848* (1970). Stanley W. Campbell, *The Slave Catchers: Enforcement of the Fugitive Slave Law, 1840–1860* (1968), traces the consequences of the most unpopular provision of the Compromise of 1850. Stephen Douglas's motives for introducing the Kansas-Nebraska Act are judiciously weighed in Robert W. Johannsen, *Stephen A. Douglas* (1973). This definitive biography is also an excellent source on the later Kansas controversy and the Lincoln-Douglas debates. Roy F. Nichols, "The Kansas-Nebraska Act: A Century of Historiography," *Mississippi Valley Historical Review,* 43 (September 1956), 187–212, is an invaluable guide to the controversial issues. The tangled local conflicts over land and railroad sites are illuminated in Paul W. Gates, *Fifty Million Acres: Conflicts over Kansas Land Policy, 1854–1890* (1954); and James C. Malin, *The Nebraska Question, 1852–1854* (1953). For Harriet Beecher Stowe's world-famous response to the Kansas controversy, see Philip van Doren Stern, *Uncle Tom's Cabin, an Annotated Edition* (1964); and Charles H. Foster, *The Rungless Ladder: Harriet Beecher Stowe and New England Puritanism* (1956).

The political realignment of the 1850s has been reinterpreted in Michael F. Holt, *The Political Crisis of the 1850s* (1978). Ray Billington, *The Protestant Crusade, 1800–1860* (1938), provides an outstanding overview of anti-Catholic nativism. For the intellectual ties between nativism and other movements, see David B. Davis, "Some Themes of Counter-Subversion," *Mississippi Valley Historical Review,* 47 (September 1960), 205–24. The best studies of political nativism are Michael F. Holt, "The Politics of Impatience: The Origins of Know-Nothingism," *Journal of American History,* 60 (September 1973), and Holt, *Forging a Majority: The Formation of the Republican Party in Pittsburgh* (1969).

The best brief account of the origins and early history of the Republican party is Hans L. Trefousse, "The Republican Party, 1854–1864," in *History of U.S. Political Parties,* ed. Arthur M. Schlesinger, Jr., Vol. 2, 1141–72 (4 vols., 1973). See also Trefousse, *The Radical Republicans* (1969). Eric Foner, *Free Soil, Free Labor, Free Men: The Ideology of the Republican Party before the Civil War* (1970), is a penetrating

study of the Republicans' thought and values. The definitive study of the *Dred Scott* decision is Don E. Fehrenbacher, *The Dred Scott Case: Its Significance in American Law and Politics* (1978).

John Brown, a man of violence, has been the subject of violently conflicting interpretations. For traditional and hostile views, see James C. Malin, *John Brown and the Legend of Fifty-Six* (1942); and the brilliant essay by C. Vann Woodward in *The Burden of Southern History* (1960). More sympathetic evaluations can be found in Stephen B. Oates, *To Purge the Land with Blood: A Biography of John Brown* (1970); Benjamin Quarles, *Allies for Freedom: Blacks and John Brown* (1974); and Louis Ruchames, ed., *John Brown: The Making of a Revolutionary* (1969).

Johannsen's biography of Douglas, listed above, treats the Lincoln-Douglas debates and a penetrating analysis can be found in Don E. Fehrenbacher, *Prelude to Greatness: Lincoln in the 1850s* (1962). The debates themselves are presented in an authoritative edition by Paul M. Angle, ed., *Created Equal? The Complete Lincoln-Douglas Debates of 1858* (1958). Harry V. Jaffa, *Crisis of the House Divided: An Interpretation of the Issues in the Lincoln-Douglas Debates* (1959), gives the brilliant, far-reaching, and somewhat eccentric interpretation of a conservative political philosopher.

Most of the biographical studies of Lincoln listed in Part Four, at the end of Chapter 18, are relevant to this chapter. Fehrenbacher's *Prelude to Greatness* is an important source, and mention should be made of James G. Randall, *Lincoln, the Liberal Statesman* (1947); Benjamin Quarles, *Lincoln and the Negro* (1962); and above all, Allan Nevins, *The Emergence of Lincoln* (2 vols., 1950).

The climactic impasse between North and South is imaginatively presented in two major studies: Roy F. Nichols, *The Disruption of American Democracy* (1948); and David M. Potter, *Lincoln and His Party in the Secession Crisis* (1942). Avery O. Craven, *The Coming of the Civil War* (1942), stresses the importance of propaganda and irrationality. For the hopes and fears of contemporaries, see J. Jeffrey Auer, ed., *Antislavery and Disunion, 1858–1861: Studies in the Rhetoric of Compromise and Conflict* (1963). No one has yet written a wholly satisfactory account of the secessionist movements in the South. For conflicting interpretations, see William L. Barney, *The Secessionist Impulse: Alabama and Mississippi* (1974); Steven A. Channing, *Crisis in Fear: Secession in South Carolina* (1970); Charles B. Dew, "Who Won the Secession Election in Louisiana?" *Journal of Southern History,* 36 (February 1970), 18–32; Dwight L. Dumond, *The Secession Movement, 1860–1861* (1931); William J. Evitts,

A Matter of Allegiances: Maryland from 1850 to 1861 (1974); and R. A. Wooster, *The Secession Conventions of the South* (1962).

Two works that give a fascinating picture of the northern response to secession are Kenneth M. Stampp, *And the War Came: The North and the Secession Crisis, 1860–61* (1950); and Howard C. Perkins, ed., *Northern Editorials on Secession* (2 vols., 1942). For the election of 1860, see Elting Morison, "Election of 1860," in *History of American Presidential Elections, 1789–1968,* ed. Arthur M. Schlesinger, Jr., Vol. 2, 1097–1122 (4 vols., 1971). On the futile gestures for compromise, see Albert J. Kirwan, *John J. Crittenden: The Struggle for the Union* (1962); and Robert G. Gunderson, *Old Gentlemen's Convention: The Washington Peach Conference of 1861* (1961).

PART FOUR

David Herbert Donald Uniting
the Republic
1860–1877

*T*hese [Northern] people hate us, annoy us, and would have us assassinated by our slaves if they dared," a Southern leader wrote when he learned that a "Black Republican," Abraham Lincoln, would certainly be elected president in 1860. "They are a *different* people from us, whether better or worse and *there is no love* between us. Why then continue together?" The sectional contests of the previous decades suggested that Americans had become members of two distinct, and conflicting, nationalities. By 1860, Northerners and Southerners appeared not to speak the same language, to share the same moral code, or to obey the same law. Compromise could no longer patch together a union between two such fundamentally different peoples. "I do not see how a barbarous and a civilized community can constitute one state," Ralph Waldo Emerson gravely concluded for many Northerners. "The North and the South are heterogeneous and are better apart," agreed the New Orleans *Bee*. "We [Southerners] are doomed if we proclaim not our political independence."

On first thought, the four-year civil war that broke out in 1861 seems powerfully to confirm this idea that the Union and the Confederacy were two distinct nations. Yet the conduct of the war suggested that Northerners and Southerners were not so different as their political and intellectual leaders had maintained. At the beginning of the conflict both governments tried in much the same ways to mobilize for battle their invertebrate, unorganized societies. As the war progressed, both Union and Confederacy adopted much the same diplomatic, military, and economic policies. By the end of the war both governments were committed to abolishing slavery, the one institution that had most clearly divided the sections in 1860.

Overleaf: Mathew Brady's photograph of the ruins of Richmond, Virginia, April, 1865. *(Library of Congress)*

The events of the postwar period gave further evidence that the inhabitants of the North and South were—what they had always been—part of the same nationality. Though some Republicans wanted a radical revolution in the social and economic system of the conquered Confederacy, there were relatively few, and only limited, social experiments or political innovations during Reconstruction. In both the North and the South, shared beliefs in limited government, in economic laissez-faire, and in the superiority of the white race blocked drastic change, while shared economic interests and national political parties pulled the sections back into a common pattern of cooperation.

During the decade after the Civil War other tensions in American society, largely ignored during the long period of sectional controversy, began to be evident. Anti-expansionists clashed with expansionists. Native Americans tried to defend their tribal lands from white encroachments. Small businesses fought to keep from being swallowed up by monopolies. Farmers struggled to break the power of the railroads and the grain elevators that controlled their access to markets. Seeking fairer wages, hours, and conditions of work, labor came into conflict with capital.

These issues not merely diverted attention from the old controversies between North and South, between white and black; they helped place those controversies in perspective. They made it evident that the Civil War had been not so much a contest between two separate nations as one of a series of continuing struggles within the American nation to define a boundary between the centralizing, nationalizing tendencies in American life and the opposing tendencies toward localism, parochialism, and fragmentation.

CHAPTER 18

Stalemate

1861–1862

During the first two years of the Civil War, as the Union and the Confederacy grappled with each other inconclusively, it seemed that two distinct and incompatible nations had emerged from the American soil. Certainly the aims announced by their leaders were totally inconsistent. President Abraham Lincoln announced that the United States would "constitutionally defend, and maintain itself"; the territorial integrity of the nation must remain inviolate. For the Confederate States, President Jefferson Davis proclaimed that his country's "career of independence" must be "inflexibly pursued." As the rival governments raised and equipped armies, attempted to finance a huge war, and sought diplomatic recognition and economic assistance abroad, the people of the two nations increasingly thought of each other as enemies: "Yankees" and "Rebels." It is easy to understand why Lord John Russell, the British foreign minister, concluded: "I do not see how the United States can be cobbled together again by any compromise. . . . I suppose the break-up of the Union is now inevitable."

A shrewder observer might have reached the opposite conclusion. Perhaps the most striking thing about the war in America was the fact that both sides carried it on through virtually identical methods. The Union and the Confederate governments faced the same wartime problems and arrived at the same wartime solutions. Northerners and Southerners on the battlefields found each other not two alien peoples but mirror images. That identity made the conflict truly a brother's war.

The Rival Governments

The government of the Confederate States was in most respects a duplicate of that of the United States, from which the Southern states had just withdrawn. Framed by delegates from six states of the Lower South (delegates from Texas, which seceded on February 1, 1861, arrived late), the Constitution largely followed the wording of the one drawn up in Philadelphia in 1787. To be sure, the new charter recognized the "sovereign and independent character" of that document, it used no euphemism about persons "held to Service or Labour" but recognized explicitly "the right of property in negro slaves." Otherwise, the two documents were substantially and intentionally identical. As secessionist Benjamin H. Hill of Georgia explained, "We hugged that [United States] Constitution to our bosom and carried it with us."

Inaugurating the Presidents. For president of the new republic, the Montgomery convention chose Jefferson Davis, of Mississippi, who had ardently defended Southern rights in the United States Senate but who had only reluctantly come to advocate secession.* If the crowds that thronged the streets of Montgomery on February 18, 1861, hoped to hear a stirring inaugural from the new Southern head of state, they were disappointed. Stepping forward on the portico of the Alabama statehouse, Davis gave a long, legalistic review of the acts of Northern aggression that had led to the formation of the new state. While Davis pledged he would, if necessary, "maintain, by the final arbitrament of the sword, the position which we have assumed among the nations of the earth," he spoke in a tone more melancholy than martial. He saw himself as the leader of a conservative movement. "We have labored to preserve the Government of our fathers in its spirit," he insisted.

Just two weeks later, from the portico of the yet unfinished Capitol in Washington, another conservative took his inaugural oath. The capital was thronged, as Nathaniel Hawthorne wrote, with "office-seekers, wire-pullers, inventors, artists, poets, prosers (including editors, army correspondents, attachés of foreign journals, and long-winded talkers), clerks, diplomatists, mail contractors, [and] railway directors." On public buildings along the route of the

INAUGURATION OF JEFFERSON DAVIS
On February 18, 1861, Jefferson Davis, standing in front of the state capitol at Montgomery, Alabama, took the oath of office as the first—and, as it proved, only—President of the Confederate States of America. Davis is the thin, tall figure behind the lectern. To his right is William L. Yancey, a leading secessionist; to his right, Howell Cobb, president of the Confederate Senate, who administered the oath. *(Library of Congress)*

the constituent states, but it also announced that they were forming "a permanent federal government," and it listed most of the same restrictions on state action included in the United States Constitution. Unlike

*The Montgomery convention drew up a provisional constitution of the Confederacy, constituted itself the provisional legislature of the new republic, and named Jefferson Davis the provisional president. It also drew up a permanent constitution, which was submitted to the states for ratification. After that, regular elections were held in the fall of 1861 both for members of the Confederate Congress and for president. Reelected without opposition, Davis was formally inaugurated as the first and only regular president of the Confederate States on February 22, 1862.

inaugural procession, sharpshooters were strategically placed, to prevent any pro-Southern interruption of the proceedings. Abraham Lincoln's inaugural address was similar in tone to Davis's. Vowing that the Union would be preserved, Lincoln gave a low-keyed version of the previous sectional quarrels, explained his personal views on slavery, and pledged that he contemplated "no invasion—no using of force" against the seceded states. In a warning softened by sadness, he reminded his listeners of the oath he had just taken to preserve, protect, and defend the government of the United States and entreated his Southern fellow citizens to pause before they assailed it. "In *your* hands, my dissatisfied fellow-countrymen," he concluded, "and not in *mine,* is the momentous issue of civil war."

Organizing the Two Administrations. In the weeks immediately following the two inaugurations, the central problem confronting both Davis and Lincoln was not so much whether either should start a civil war but whether they could form viable governments. In Davis's Confederacy, everything had to be started afresh. Even the most routine legal and governmental matters could not be taken for granted. For instance, it was not certain, until the Confederate Congress passed an act, whether the laws of the United States passed before 1861 and the decisions of the United States courts were binding in the seceded states. The new nation had to choose a flag—over the opposition of some purists who claimed that the Confederacy, representing the true American spirit, ought to retain the Stars and Stripes and let the Union look for a new banner.

In selecting his cabinet advisers, President Davis theoretically had a free hand, but in fact his range of choice was severely limited. No man of doubtful loyalty to the new government could be permitted a place in his cabinet; no Southern Unionist in the tradition of Henry Clay, John J. Crittenden, and John Bell was invited. On the other hand, because Davis wanted the world to see that the Confederacy was governed by sober, responsible men, he excluded from his council all the most conspicuous Southern fire-eaters. Then, too, he had to achieve some balance

between former Whigs and former Democrats, and he felt obliged to secure a wide geographical spread by appointing one member of his original cabinet from each of the seven Confederate states, except Mississippi, which he himself represented. As a result of these elaborate calculations, Davis's cabinet consisted neither of his personal friends nor of the outstanding political leaders of the South, except for Secretary of State Robert Toombs, of Georgia, who served only briefly.

Such a cabinet might have sufficed in a country where administrative procedures and routines were firmly rooted. Instead in the Confederacy there was everywhere a lack of preparation, a lack of resources for running a government. Typical was the Confederate Treasury Department, which initially consisted of one unswept room in a Montgomery bank, "without furniture of any kind; empty . . . of desks, tables, chairs or other appliances for the conduct of business." The secretary of the treasury had to pay for the first rickety furniture out of his own pocket.

Disorganization and improvisation also characterized Lincoln's government in Washington. The Union had the advantage of owning the Capitol, the White House, and the permanent records of the United States government, and it had a recognized flag and a postal system. But in other respects it was thoroughly demoralized. Lincoln's government had no clear mandate from the people, for the president had received less than 40 percent of the popular vote in the 1860 election. It had an army of only 14,657 men, and every day army and navy officers announced that they were defecting to the South. Its treasury was empty. Some of the most experienced clerks in the Washington offices were leaving to join the Confederacy, and others who remained were of suspect loyalty. Adding to the confusion was the fact that Lincoln's was the first Republican administration and under the prevailing spoils system, party workers who had helped elect the Republican candidate now flocked to Washington, expecting to oust Democratic officeholders. Accompanied by their representatives or senators and bearing huge rolls of recommending letters, the office seekers besieged Lincoln in the White House. Wryly the president compared himself to an innkeeper whose clients demanded that he rent rooms in one wing of his hotel while he was trying to put out a fire in the other.

To add to the confusion, not one member of the Lincoln administration had previously held a responsible position in the executive branch of the national government, and many, including the president himself, had no administrative experience of any sort. Like Davis, Lincoln made no attempt to form a coalition government; for his cabinet he did not choose leaders of the Douglas Democracy or the Constitutional Union party. Nor after a few unsuccessful efforts did he name Unionists from the South. Instead, all members of his cabinet were Republicans. That fact, however, scarcely gave his government unity, for several of Lincoln's cabinet appointees had themselves been candidates for the Republican nomination in 1860 and hence were rivals of Lincoln and of each other. The most conspicuous member was Secretary of State William H. Seward, wily and devious, extravagant in utterance but cautious in action, who felt that he had a duty to save the country through compromise and conciliation despite its bumbling, inexperienced president. Seward's principal rival in the cabinet was Secretary of the Treasury Salmon P. Chase, pompous and self-righteous, who had an equally condescending view of Lincoln's talents and who lusted to become the next president of the United States. The other members, with whom Lincoln had had only the slightest personal acquaintance, were appointed because they were supposed to have political influence or to represent key states.

Winning the Border States

Desperately needing time to get organized, these two shaky rival administrations immediately confronted a problem and a crisis, which were intimately interrelated. The problem concerned the future of the eight remaining slave states, which had not yet seceded. Though tied to the Deep South by blood and sentiment and fearful of abolitionist attacks upon their "peculiar institution" of slavery, these states had refused to rush out of the Union. In January 1861,

ABRAHAM LINCOLN
"Probably," wrote Walt Whitman, "the reader has seen physiognomies ... that, behind their homeliness or even ugliness, held superior points so subtle, yet so palpable, making the real life of their faces almost as impossible to depict as a wild perfume or fruit taste ... such was Lincoln's face—the peculiar color, the lines of it, the eyes, mouth, expression. Of technical beauty it had nothing—but to the eye of a great artist it furnished a rare study, a feast, and fascination." *(Library of Congress)*

Virginia had elected a convention to consider secession, but it dillydallied and did nothing. In February, North Carolinians and Tennesseans voted against holding secession conventions. When the Arkansas and Missouri conventions did meet in March, they voted not to secede. Up to April 1861, Kentucky, Maryland, and Delaware held no elections or conventions. But the loyalty of all these states to the Union was clearly conditional upon the policy Lincoln's government adopted toward the Confederacy.

Crisis Over Fort Sumter.   The crisis was the first test of that policy. It concerned the fate of the United States installations in the seceded states that still remained under Federal control. At Fort Pickens in Pensacola Bay, an uneasy truce held between the Union troops in the garrison and the Confederate force on the mainland. The real trouble spot was Fort Sumter, in the harbor of Charleston, South Carolina. Its garrison, which consisted of about seventy Union soldiers and nine officers under the command of Major Robert Anderson, was no serious military threat to the Confederacy, but its presence at Charleston, the very center of secession, was an intolerable affront to Southern pride. Confederates insisted that President Davis demonstrate his devotion to the Southern cause by forcing Anderson and his men out immediately. Many Northerners, who had despairingly watched during the final months of the Buchanan administration as fort after fort was turned over to the Confederates, also saw Sumter as a test of the strength and will of the Lincoln administration.

Despite these pressures, there were in both governments powerful voices that urged compromise or at least delay. All but two members of Lincoln's cabinet initially thought that Sumter should be evacuated. Davis's secretary of state was equally adverse to hasty action. When the Confederate cabinet discussed attacking Fort Sumter, Toombs solemnly warned: "The firing upon that fort will inaugurate a civil war greater than any the world has yet seen."

But Anderson's situation made some action necessary. After Charleston authorities prohibited further sale of food to the troops in the fort, his men faced starvation. The day after Lincoln was inaugurated he learned that the garrison, unless supplied, could hold out no longer than April 15. Since Lincoln had just pledged that he would "hold, occupy, and possess" all places and property belonging to the government, he promptly directed his secretary of the navy to begin outfitting an expedition to provision Fort Sumter. At the same time, recognizing how dangerously explosive the Charleston situation was, he explored alternatives. One possibility was to reinforce Fort Pickens, in the relatively calm area of Florida; that would allow Lincoln to demonstrate his firmness of purpose, even if he was obliged to withdraw Anderson from the Charleston harbor. But the naval expedition sent to Florida miscarried, the Union commander at Pickens misunderstood his orders, and the planned reinforcement could not be completed in time for Washington to know about it before Anderson's deadline for surrender. Another possibility was to consent to a peaceable withdrawal from Fort Sumter in return for assurances that the still vacillating border states would remain in the Union. "If you will guarantee to me the State of Virginia, I shall remove the troops," Lincoln confidentially promised a prominent Virginia Unionist. "A State for a fort is no bad business." But the Virginians delayed, a rainstorm kept a delegation of Unionists from reaching Washington, and they could give no firm promises. Seeing no other possible course, Lincoln let the expedition bearing food and supplies sail for Sumter.

President Davis understood that in merely supplying Fort Sumter Lincoln was not committing an act of aggression. Indeed, he predicted that for political reasons the United States government would avoid making an attack so long as the hope of retaining the border states remained. But the Confederate president's hand was forced too. Hot-headed Governor Francis Pickens and other South Carolina extremists, impatient with Davis's caution, prepared to attack the fort. Rather than let Confederate policy be set by a state governor, Davis ordered General P. G. T. Beauregard, in command of the Confederate forces at Charleston, to demand the surrender of Fort Sumter. Anderson responded that he would soon be starved out, but he failed to promise to withdraw by a definite date. Beauregard's officers felt they had no alternative but to reduce the fort. At 4:30 A.M. on April 12 firing began. Outside the harbor the relief expedition Lincoln had sent watched impotently while Confederates bombarded the fort. After thirty-four hours, with ammunition nearly exhausted, Anderson was obliged to surrender.

Promptly Lincoln called for 75,000 volunteer soldiers to put down the "insurrection" in the South. On

May 6 the Confederate Congress countered by formally declaring that a state of war existed. The American Civil War had begun.

Both at that time and later there was controversy about the responsibility for precipitating the conflict. Critics claimed that Lincoln by sending the expedition to provision Fort Sumter deliberately tricked the Confederates into firing the first shot. Indeed, some months after the event Lincoln himself told a friend that his plan for sending supplies to Major Anderson had "succeeded." "They attacked Sumter," he explained; "it fell, and thus, did more service than it otherwise could." That statement clearly reveals Lincoln's wish that if hostilities began, the Confederacy should bear the blame for initiating them, but it does little to prove that Lincoln wanted war. It is well to remember that throughout the agonizing crisis the Confederates took the initiative at Sumter. It was Charleston authorities who cut off Anderson's food supply; it was Confederate authorities who decided that, though the fort offered no military threat, Anderson must surrender; and it was the Southerners who fired the first shot. Writing privately to the Confederate commander at Fort Pickens, President Davis acknowledged that there would be a psychological advantage if the Southerners waited for the Federal government to make the initial attack; but, he added, "When we are ready to relieve our territory and jurisdiction of the presence of a foreign garrison that advantage is overbalanced by other considerations." These other considerations impelled Davis to demand the surrender of Fort Sumter.

Decisions in the Border States. If intent can be tested by consequences, it is evident that, initially at least, it was the Confederacy, not the Union, that benefited from the attack upon Fort Sumter. The slave states still in the Union had now to make a choice of allegiances, and for a time it seemed that all would join the Confederacy. Virginia Governor John Letcher spurned Lincoln's call for troops as a bid "to inaugurate civil war," and on April 17 the state convention hastily passed a secession ordinance. Technically it was subject to popular ratification, but in actuality it immediately linked to the Confederacy the most populous and influential state of the Upper South, with its long tradition of leadership, its vast natural resources, and its large Tredegar Iron Works.

Other border slave states acted only a little less precipitously. On May 6 the Arkansas convention voted, with only five dissenters, to withdraw from the Union. When Lincoln's call for troops reached Governor Isham Harris of Tennessee, he replied haughtily: "In such an unholy crusade no gallant son of Tennessee will ever draw his sword," and began private negotiations with Confederate officials. On May 7 the Tennessee state legislature ratified the arrangements Harris had already made and voted to secede. On May 20 the North Carolina convention, under pressure from pro-Confederate newspapers to withdraw forever from the "vile, rotten, infidelic, puritanic, negro-worshipping, negro-stealing, negro-equality . . . Yankee-Union," unanimously adopted a secession ordinance.

Far to the west, the Confederacy scored another victory in the Indian Territory (later to become the state of Oklahoma). Confederate Commissioner Albert Pike had little success with the Plains Indians there, but he won over most of the so-called civilized tribes, many of whom were slaveholders. The Confederacy agreed to pay all annuities that the United States government had previously provided, and it allowed the Choctaws, Chickasaws, Creeks, Seminoles, and Cherokees to send delegates to the Confederate Congress. In return these tribes promised to supply troops for the Confederate army. Most of them loyally supported the Southern effort throughout the war, and the Cherokee chief, Brigadier General Stand Watie, did not formally surrender until a month after the war was over. A rival faction among the Cherokees, headed by Chief John Ross, and most of the Plains Indians favored the Union cause.

Elsewhere along the border, the Confederacy fared less well. Though it was a slave state with sentimental ties to the South, Delaware never really contemplated secession. Much more painful was the decision of Maryland, a state bitterly divided. On April 19 a pro-Confederate mob in Baltimore fired upon a Massachusetts regiment en route to Washington, and communications were then cut between

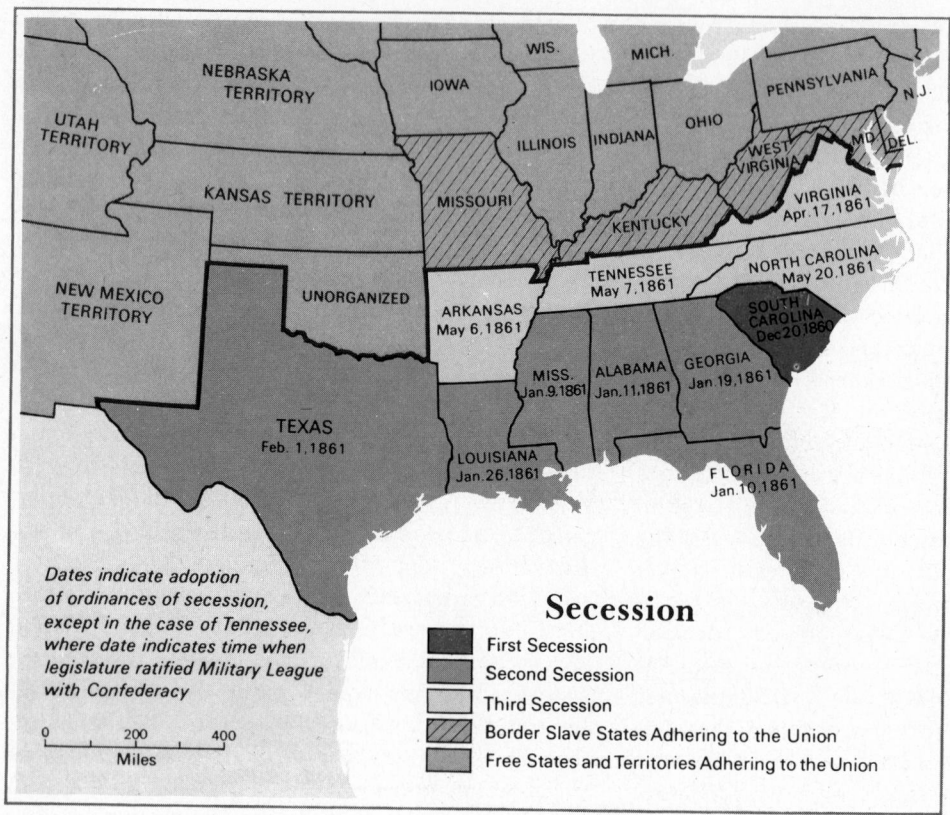

NEBRASKA TERRITORY
UTAH TERRITORY
WIS.
MICH.
IOWA
PENNSYLVANIA
N.J.
ILLINOIS
INDIANA
OHIO
WEST VIRGINIA
MD.
DEL.
KANSAS TERRITORY
MISSOURI
VIRGINIA Apr.17,1861
NEW MEXICO TERRITORY
UNORGANIZED
KENTUCKY
TENNESSEE May 7,1861
NORTH CAROLINA May 20,1861
ARKANSAS May 6,1861
SOUTH CAROLINA Dec.20,1860
MISS. Jan.9,1861
ALABAMA Jan.11,1861
GEORGIA Jan.19,1861
TEXAS Feb. 1,1861
LOUISIANA Jan.26,1861
FLORIDA Jan.10,1861

Dates indicate adoption of ordinances of secession, except in the case of Tennessee, where date indicates time when legislature ratified Military League with Confederacy

0   200   400
Miles

Secession

- First Secession
- Second Secession
- Third Secession
- Border Slave States Adhering to the Union
- Free States and Territories Adhering to the Union

the Union capital and the rest of the country. For a time it seemed highly probable that Maryland would secede. But Lincoln arranged for further shipments of Union troops to bypass Baltimore until passions could cool. By May, Baltimore was back under Federal control, and the mayor, along with nineteen members of the state legislature, was unceremoniously arrested and jailed without trial. In the 1861 fall elections, Maryland chose an uncompromising Unionist as governor, and thereafter there was no further question of secession.

In Missouri the Union cause was managed with less skill. Though the pro-Southern governor denounced Lincoln's call for troops as "illegal, unconstitutional, revolutionary, inhuman, [and] diabolical," public opinion was so evenly divided that no steps toward secession probably would have occurred had not Union Commander Nathaniel Lyon precipitated

hostilities by overrunning an encampment of pro-secessionist militia near St. Louis. Confederate sympathizers rallied to protect them, and for two days there was bloody street fighting in the city. Open warfare followed. Union forces controlled the area around St. Louis; secessionists commanded by Sterling Price, most of the rest of the state. After General John C. Frémont became commander of the department of the West, with his headquarters in St. Louis, the territory under Union control was gradually extended. During the next three years, guerrilla warfare devastated the Missouri countryside, as neighbor fought neighbor. The bitterness was further aggravated when free-soil men from Kansas, remembering how Missouri "border ruffians" had once tried to extend slavery into their state, crossed the border to take revenge upon secessionist sympathizers. In turn, Confederate gangs, the most notorious led by the horse thief and murderer William C. Quantrill, preyed upon Missouri Unionists.

Far more skillful was Lincoln's handling of Kentucky, which was his native state as well as that of Jefferson Davis. As in Missouri, the governor was an outright secessionist, but strong Unionist sentiment prevented the calling of a state convention. Out of this statemate rose the anomalous situation of Kentucky declaring itself neutral in any conflict between the United States and the Confederacy. Between May and September of 1861 both the Lincoln and the Davis governments ostensibly acquiesced in this policy of neutrality; at the same time, each tried quietly to strengthen the hands of its partisans in Kentucky. Finally, suspecting that Federal forces were about to seize a position in Kentucky, the Confederates moved first and took Columbus. Union troops then entered Paducah, and neutrality was dead. These months of indeterminate status gave Kentucky Unionists a chance to plan and organize, so that the state did not, like Tennessee, join the Confederacy nor, like Missouri, become a fierce battleground. In bringing about this outcome, Lincoln himself played a large role, for he gave Kentucky affairs close attention and took pains to assure prominent Kentuckians in private interviews that he "intended to make no attack, direct or indirect, upon the institution or property [meaning slavery] of any State."

Although most Virginians favored the Confederacy, the Union had loyal supporters in the western counties of that state, long disaffected from the planter oligarchy of the tidewater region and little interested in slavery. When the Virginia convention voted for secession, a sizable minority of the delegates, mostly from these western counties, were opposed, and they went home vowing to keep their state in the Union. A series of exceedingly complex maneuvers followed, including the summoning of several more or less extralegal conventions and the creating of a new government for what was termed "reorganized" Virginia, rivaling that at Richmond. This "reorganized" government then gave permission—as required by the United States Constitution—for the counties west of the mountains to form a new and overwhelmingly Unionist state of West Virginia. Not until 1863, when all these steps were completed, was the new state admitted to the Union. Thus by that date there were no fewer than three state governments on Virginia soil: the pro-Confederate government at Richmond; the "reorganized" pro-Union government, which had only a small constituency and huddled under the protection of Federal guns at Alexandria; and the new Union government of West Virginia.

In summary then, after the firing of Fort Sumter, the border slave states divided. Virginia, Arkansas, Tennessee, and North Carolina went with the Confederacy; Delaware, Maryland, Missouri, and Kentucky remained in the Union, where they were presently joined by West Virginia.

Importance of the Border States.   It is impossible to exaggerate the importance that these decisions, made early in the conflict, had upon the conduct of the Civil War. For the Confederacy, the accession of states from the Upper South was essential. For all the brave talk at Montgomery, the Confederacy was not a viable nation so long as it consisted only of the seven states of the Deep South. So limited, its population was only one-sixth of that of the remaining states of the Union. In all the Gulf states in 1861 there was not a foundry to roll heavy iron plate or to cast cannon, nor a large powder works, nor indeed a single factory of importance. But when Virginia, North Carolina, Arkansas, and Tennessee joined the Confederacy, they almost doubled its population. What is more, they brought to the new nation the natural resources, the foundries and factories, and the skilled artisans that made it possible to rival the Union. To recognize the economic and psychological strength added by these states of the Upper South—and also to escape the sweltering summer heats of Montgomery—the Confederacy in May 1861 removed its capital from Montgomery to Richmond.

If the states of the Upper South brought the Confederacy strength they also limited its freedom of action. So important were Richmond and Virginia that defending this area became the passion of the Confederate government, so absorbing that it neglected the vital western theaters of military operations.

For Lincoln's government, too, the border states were vital. If Maryland had seceded, the capital at Washington would have been surrounded by enemy territory, cut off from the Union states of the North and the West. Confederate control of Kentucky would have imperiled river transportation along the Ohio, and the secession of Missouri would have endangered Mississippi river traffic and cut off communication with Kansas and the Pacific coast. While Lincoln grieved over the secession of the states that joined the Confederacy, he could take comfort in the fact that by keeping four slave states in the Union he was preventing the Southern armies from recruiting from a population that was three-fifths as large as that of the original Confederacy.

So important were the border states for the Union government that special pains had to be taken not to disturb their loyalty. In particular, Lincoln saw that there must be no premature action against slavery. European nations might fail to understand the nature of the American Civil War and Northern abolitionists might denounce their president as "the slave-hound from Illinois," but Lincoln knew that to tamper with slavery would result in the loss of the border states, particularly Kentucky. "I think to lose Kentucky is nearly the same as to lose the whole game," he wrote to a friend. "Kentucky gone, we cannot hold Missouri, nor, as I think, Maryland. These all against us, and the job on our hands is too large for us. We would as well consent to separation at once, including the surrender of this capitol."

Raising the Armies

While Lincoln and Davis were moving in parallel fashion to win the support of the border states, ordinary folk, North and South, were rallying around their flags. On both sides the firing on Fort Sumter triggered a rush to enlist. "War! and volunteers are the only topics of conversation or thought," an Oberlin College student reported when the news reached Ohio. "The lessons today have been a mere form. I cannot study. I cannot sleep, I cannot work, and I don't know as I can write." An Arkansas youth recorded identical emotions: "So impatient did I become

for starting that I felt like a thousand pins were pricking me in every part of the body and [I] started off a week in advance of my brothers."

The Rush to Volunteer.   Ordinarily a volunteer offered to enlist in one of the regiments that was being raised in his community. Wealthy citizens and prominent politicians usually took the lead in recruiting

UNITED STATES VOLUNTEERS
In both the Union and the Confederacy the first step in raising a regiment was often the publication of a broadside like this one *(shown right)* calling for volunteers. *(Library of Congress)*

PRIVATE JOHN WERTH, RICHMOND HOWITZER BATTALION, C.S.A. *(below)* AND AN ILLINOIS VOLUNTEER OF 1861 *(lower right)*
As soon as volunteers were sworn in and received their uniforms and equipment, most rushed to photographers' studios to have pictures made for their loved ones. *(Below, The Museum of the Confederacy, Richmond; right, Library of Congress)*

these companies. Inevitably these regiments displayed a wide variety of arms, ranging from rusty flintlocks to the latest sharpshooting rifles. Often their uniforms bore distinctive insignia; for instance, a Louisiana battalion recruited from the daredevil New Orleans roustabouts called themselves the Tigers, and their scarlet skullcaps bore mottoes like "Tiger on the Leap" and "Tiger in Search of a Black Republican." Perhaps the most colorful, and impractical, uniforms were those of the Northern Zouave regiments, dressed in imitation of the French troops in North Africa. These soldiers, wearing their red fezzes, scarlet baggy trousers, and blue sashes, were magnificent in a military review, but when they had to wade across a stream, their baggy garments ballooned around them and they floated down the current like so many exotic waterlilies. When a regiment's ranks were filled, there was invariably a farewell ceremony, featuring hortatory addresses, lengthy prayers, and the presentation of the regimental flag, often hand-sewn by patriotic wives and sweethearts of the enlisted men. Then, loaded with hams, cakes, and sweetmeats provided by fond mothers and wives, the men went off to war.

Wartime Maladministration. Neither Union nor Confederate War Departments knew what to do with this flood of volunteers. Leroy P. Walker, the first Confederate secretary of war, had had no military training and no administrative experience. An amiable Southern gentleman, fond of prolonged conversation with visitors, of writing discursive three-page business letters, and of filing his correspondence by piling it in a chair after he had read it, Walker was wholly unable to cope with the situation. Complaining that he lacked equipment and arms, he refused the services of regiment after regiment. Perhaps 200,000 Confederate volunteers were thus rejected during the first year of the war.

The Northern war office was equally chaotic. Simon Cameron, the secretary of war, had been forced upon Lincoln as part of a political bargain. Cameron's main objective was to become the undisputed boss of Pennsylvania politics. There is no evidence that he used his cabinet position to line his own pockets, but he did employ his huge patronage to strengthen his faction of Pennsylvania Republicans. Lacking administrative talents, Cameron like Walker, simply could not deal with the flood of volunteers, nor could he supervise the hundreds of contracts his office had to make for arms, ammunition, uniforms, horses, and dozens of other articles for the army. Inevitably there was haste, inefficiency, and corruption. For instance, in October 1861, General Frémont, desperately needing mounts for his cavalry in Missouri, contracted to purchase 411 horses. Subsequent investigation proved that 350 of the beasts supplied him were undersized, under or overaged, ringboned, blind, spavined, and incurably unfit for service; 5 were dead. Unable to equip the Union volunteers as they rushed to defend the flag, Cameron thought it was his principal duty "to avoid receiving troops faster than the government can provide for them."

As the war wore on, the initial enthusiasm for volunteering abated, and many of the men rejected by Walker and Cameron in the early months of the conflict were never available again. Soon even those whose services had been accepted began to exhibit less enthusiasm for the war. Most had expected the army to be like the peacetime militia, to which all able-bodied white men belonged; the monthly militia rallies had been the occasion for fun and frolic, punctuated by a little, uneven military drill, a considerable amount of political oratory, and a great deal of drinking. Now they discovered that war was not a lark. Belonging to the army meant discipline, spit-and-polish cleaning of equipment, and hours of close-order drill. A soldier's life was one of endless monotony, punctuated occasionally by danger from enemy bullets and more frequently by disease resulting from inadequate food and clothing, lack of vaccination, filthy drinking water, and open latrines. By the end of 1861, many Union volunteers were beginning to count the weeks until the end of their three-year term of enlistment. Confederate regiments, which had been enrolled for twelve months, were about ready to disband in the spring of 1862.

Reorganization and Conscription. Of necessity, then, Lincoln and Davis moved, almost simultaneously, to strengthen their War Departments in order to give more central direction to their armies. In January 1862, having persuaded Cameron to become American minister to Russia, Lincoln named a former Democrat, Edwin M. Stanton, to the War Department. Brusque and imperious, Stanton quickly reorganized the War Department, regularized procedures for letting war contracts, and investigated frauds. Standing behind an old-fashioned writing desk, looking like an irritable schoolmaster before a willful class, Stanton heard all War Department business in public. Patronage seekers, even when accompanied by congressmen, he brusquely dismissed; contractors had to state their prices in clear, loud voices; and even a petitioner bearing a letter of introduction from the president might be abruptly shown the door. Working incessantly, Stanton saw to it that the Union army became the best supplied military force the world had ever seen.

It took a bit longer for Davis to find a war secretary to his liking. When Walker, to everyone's relief, resigned in September 1861, Davis replaced him briefly with Judah P. Benjamin, who subsequently became Confederate secretary of state, and then with George Wythe Randolph, who did much to see that Robert E. Lee and Thomas J. ("Stonewall") Jackson had the necessary arms and supplies for their 1862 campaigns. But when Randolph and Davis disagreed over strategy, the secretary had to go, and in November 1862 James A. Seddon succeeded Randolph. Sallow and cadaverous, looking, as one of his clerks remarked, like "an exhumed corpse after a month's interment," Seddon was nevertheless diligent and efficient. Moreover, he had the good sense to give solid support to subordinates of great ability. Perhaps the most competent of these was General Josiah Gorgas, head of the Confederate ordnance bureau. Thanks to Gorgas's exertions, the Confederacy, which in May 1861 had only about 20 cartridges for each musket or rifle, by 1862 built powder plants capable of producing 20 million cartridges—enough to supply an army of 400,000 men for twelve months.

While both presidents were strengthening their War Departments, they also moved, in 1862, to take a more active role in recruiting troops. Because the twelve-month period of enlistment of Confederate troops expired in the spring, Davis warned that the Southern army would be decimated just as Federal forces were approaching Richmond. Uncomfortably ignoring the principle of state sovereignty proclaimed in the Confederate Constitution, the Southern Congress on April 16, 1862, passed a national conscription act, which made every able-bodied white male between the ages of eighteen and thirty-five subject to military service. This first conscription law in American history, however, allowed for numerous exemptions, ranging from druggists to Confederate government officials; and a subsequent law excused from military service planters or overseers supervising twenty or more slaves. The purpose of the Con-

federate conscription act was less to raise new troops than to encourage veterans to reenlist. If the men stayed in the army, the law provided, they could remain in their present regiments and elect new officers; if they left, it threatened, they could be drafted and assigned to any unit that needed them.

Lincoln's government moved toward conscription a little more slowly. After the bloody campaigns in the summer of 1862, volunteering all but stopped, and the army needed 300,000 new men. Union governors suggested to the president that a draft would stimulate volunteering, and on July 17 the Federal Congress passed a loosely worded measure authorizing the president to set quotas of troops to be raised

PRESENTATION OF COLORS, 1ST MICHIGAN INFANTRY, MAY, 1861

Regiments were raised under state, not national, auspices. Before a regiment left home to join the Union or Confederate army, there was usually a formal ceremony, where the governor or some other high-ranking state official made a patriotic speech and presented the fighting men with their regimental flag. *(Courtesy of the Burton Historical Collection of the Detroit Public Library)* by each state and empowering him to use Federal force to draft them if state officials failed to meet their quotas. Intentionally a bogeyman, which the governors used to encourage enlistments, this first Union conscription law brought in only a handful of men.

Financing the War

If it became hard for both the Union and the Confederate governments to raise troops, it was even harder to supply and pay them. Though the United States in 1860 was potentially one of the great industrial nations of the world, it was still primarily an agricultural country, with five out of six of its inhabitants living on farms. The factories that would be called upon to supply vast armies were mostly small in scale. Some 239 companies manufactured firearms in 1860; their average invested capital was less than $11,000. Textile mills, especially for the manufacture of woolens, were larger, but ready-made clothing was still sewn in small shops. The country produced an abundance of foodstuffs, but there was no effective wholesale marketing system for meat and grain. Maps showed that by 1860 the country was crisscrossed by 30,000 miles of railroads, but most of these were in fact short spans, each under its own corporate management, often not connected to other lines at common terminals and even having different rail gauges. The sending of a boxcar from, say, Baltimore to St. Louis was an undertaking that required diplomacy, improvisation, frequent transshipment, long delays, and a great deal of luck. Commercial transactions were impeded by the fact that the United States in 1860 had no national bank; indeed, it did not even have a national currency, for the bills issued by the numerous state banks, depreciating at various rates, formed the principal circulating medium.

Problems of the Treasury Departments. Yet Union and Confederate leaders had somehow to mobilize this invertebrate economy so that it could support an enormous war effort. Both governments relied primarily upon privately owned factories to supply their armies, rather than upon government-operated ones. Necessity more than a theoretical preference

for free enterprise lay behind this choice. If individual businessmen and corporations had little experience in the large-scale production of goods, the civil servants at Washington and Richmond had even less. Where it seemed useful, both governments supplemented the output of private undustry with production from government-owned plants. While the Lincoln administration was purchasing firearms from Colt, Remington, and dozens of other manufacturers, it continued to rely upon its own armories, especially the one at Springfield, Massachusetts, for some of its best weapons. Because the South was even more largely rural and agricultural than the North, it had to be more active in establishing government-owned plants, the most successful of which was the huge powder factory at Augusta, Georgia. But both governments contracted with private individuals and corporations for most of the arms, clothing, and other equipment needed for the armies.

It was easier to contract for supplies than it was to pay for them. Both Union and Confederacy began the war with empty treasuries. When Secretary of the Treasury Chase took up his duties in Washington, he was horrified to discover that between April and June 1861 the expenses of the Union government would exceed its income by $17 million. Inexperienced in financial matters, Chase, whose reputation had been built on his work as an antislavery lawyer and politician, desperately cast about for solutions.

Chase's difficulties were nothing compared to those of his Confederate counterpart, Christopher G. Memminger, who had to make bricks without clay as well as without straw. Like Chase, Memminger had no extensive experience in financial matters, and his neat, systematic mind was troubled by the free and easy ways of government finance during wartime. He did what he could to bring about order—by requiring Confederate Treasury employees to keep regular 9–to–5 hours, by outlawing drinking on the job and by insisting that his visitors curb their customary garrulity and state their business. Such measures, however, did little to solve Confederate financial difficulties.

Sources of Revenue. Neither secretary seriously thought of financing the war through levying taxes.

26TH NEW YORK INFANTRY AT FORT LYON, VIRGINIA
Once accepted into the Union or Confederate army, volunteers found they had a great deal still to learn before they were soldiers. These New York volunteers, manning the fortifications surrounding Washington, were receiving lessons in close-order drill. *(Library of Congress)*

For either the Union or the Confederacy to impose heavy taxation in 1861 might well have killed the citizens' ardor for war. Americans simply were not used to paying taxes to their national government; there had been no federal excise duties during the thirty-five years before the war. In 1860 the United States Treasury had no internal revenue division, no assessors, no inspectors, and no agents. Since tariffs were a more familiar method of raising revenues, both secretaries hoped for large customs receipts. But when Republicans in the Union Congress passed the highly protective Morrill Tariff in 1861 and raised rates even higher in 1862, they effectively killed that source of revenue. Similarly, the Union blockade of the South reduced the amount and value of goods brought into Confederate ports and cut the Southern income from tariffs. In desperation the Union government resorted to a direct tax (levied upon each state in proportion to population) of $20 million in August 1861; much of it was never collected. The same month the Confederates imposed a "war tax" of 0.5 percent on taxable wealth. Davis's government, like Lincoln's, had to rely upon the states to collect this tax, and most of them preferred issuing bonds or notes rather than levying duties upon their people.

In neither country was borrowing a realistic possibility for financing the war. Products of the Jacksonian era with its suspicion of paper certificates of indebtedness, Americans of the 1860s were a people who preferred to hoard rather than invest their surplus funds. The rival Union and Confederate governments themselves shared this same suspicion of paper and this trust in specie. In the North, Secretary Chase insisted that the banks of New York, Philadelphia, and Boston subscribe to a $150 million federal bond issue, but he was unwilling to take anything but gold or silver in payment. The drain on the banks' reserves, coupled with uncertainty over the course of the war, forced Northern banks to suspend specie payment for their notes in December 1861. Nor was Chase more successful in his early attempts to sell Union bonds directly to small investors. The Confederacy followed much the same course in its borrowing. An initial loan of $15 million was quickly subscribed to, with the result that Southern banks, including the strong institutions of New Orleans, were obliged to give up virtually all their specie to the new government; consequently they could no longer redeem their notes in gold or silver. Memminger's attempt to sell subsequent Confederate bonds directly to the Southern people ran into the difficulty that nobody had any specie. Urged by Vice-President Alexander H. Stephens and other Confederate orators, planters in the fall of 1861 subscribed tobacco, rice, cotton, and other commodities to purchase bonds. Since the Union blockade cut off the market for these products, the Confederate government realized little from the loan.

CONFEDERATE PAPER MONEY

Both the Confederacy and the Union were obliged to resort to paper money in order to finance the war. In the South engravers were few and incompetent. As a result the likenesses they produced of President Davis and other Confederate officials were so unprepossessing as to raise doubts about the artists' loyalty to the Southern cause.

Recourse to Paper Money.   In consequence, by early 1862 both governments moved to the issue of paper money, backed only by the promise that it would some day be redeemed in specie. Both Treasury secretaries came reluctantly to this policy. Memminger, a prominent hard-money advocate before the war, was obliged to resort to the printing presses in 1861. The Confederacy issued $100 million in paper money in August 1861, and the next year it printed millions of dollars more. Having denounced "an irredeemable paper currency, than which no more certainly fatal expedient for impoverishing the masses and discrediting the government of any country, can well be devised," Chase found it even more embarrassing than Memminger to resort to treasury notes. But by January 1862 he had no alternative. Declaring that an issue of paper money was now "indispensably necessary," he persuaded Congress to authorize the printing of $150 million in non-interest–bearing United States treasury notes (which were promptly dubbed "greenbacks," because of their color). Rarely does history provide such a tidy illustration of how huge impersonal forces overrule the preference and will of individual statesmen.

Wartime Diplomacy

In diplomacy as in economic policy the Union and the Confederacy moved along parallel paths during the first two years of the war. Neither Lincoln nor Davis had much knowledge of diplomacy or took an active role in the conduct of foreign policy. Both, however, had difficulties with their secretaries of state. Seward, Lincoln's principal adviser, would ultimately rank as one of the greatest secretaries of state, but in the early stages of the Civil War he gave evidence of wild eccentricity, coupled with personal ambition. At the height of the Sumter crisis, he submitted to Lincoln a private memorandum complaining that the government as yet had no policy for dealing with secession, announcing his readiness to take over the president's function and shape a suitable policy, and suggesting that the proper course for the administration was to "change the question before the public from one upon slavery . . . for a question upon union or disunion" by precipitating a confrontation with foreign powers. If allowed, Seward would "seek explanations from Great Britain and Russia"— for what offenses he did not specify; he "would demand explanations from Spain and France, categorically, at once," presumably over their threatened intervention in the affairs of Santo Domingo and Mexico; and if Spain and France did not respond forthwith, he would urge a declaration of war against these powers. Lincoln, to his enduring credit, quietly filed away this memorandum, refrained from dismissing a secretary who planned to bring on a world war, and allowed Seward time to return to his senses.

Despite Lincoln's reticence, word of Seward's bellicosity leaked out in conversation at Washington dinner tables, and diplomats at the capital soon had a pretty good idea of what was in the secretary's mind. From the diplomatic dispatches, European governments during the first two years of the war learned to view all Seward's policies with skepticism, even after the secretary had returned to sobriety and moderation. Perhaps, however, the awareness of Seward's hair-trigger temper did something to make those governments more cautious in their relations with the United States and less willing to recognize the Confederacy.

Davis, too, had trouble with his state department. Robert Toombs, the first Confederate secretary of state, was as ambitious and overbearing as he was able. It was a relief when he decided that the path to glory lay on the battlefield rather than in the cabinet and resigned to take a commission in the Southern army. His successor, R. M. T. Hunter, was equally ambitious, and—perhaps with an eye on the 1868 Confederate presidential election—he too promptly resigned, to become senator from Virginia. In March 1862, Davis finally found his man in Judah P. Benjamin, who had already been Confederate attorney general and secretary of war. Serving until the end of the war, Benjamin cleverly reflected the changing moods of his chief, but he was not an innovator in foreign policy. In the words of a critical Northerner who visited Richmond during the war, Benjamin had a "keen, shrewd, ready intellect, but not the stamina to originate, or even to execute, any great good, or great wickedness."

Union and Confederate diplomatic appointments abroad were rather a mixed lot. If Lincoln lacked tact in appointing Carl Schurz, considered a "red republican" for his participation in the German revolution of 1848, as minister to conservative, monarchical Spain, Davis showed a total failure to understand British antislavery sentiment by sending William L. Yancey, the most notorious Southern fire-eater, as first Confederate commissioner to London. On the positive side, the Union minister to Great Britain, Charles Francis Adams, exhibited the patience and restraint required in his difficult assignment; and the pride, the chilly demeanor, and the punctiliousness of this son and grandson of American presidents made him a match even for the aristocratic British foreign minister, Lord John Russell. Of the Confederate emissaries abroad, probably John Slidell of Louisiana proved ablest; wily, adroit, and unscrupulous, he was perfectly at home in the court of Napoleon III.

European Neutrality. Much to the disappointment of Americans on both sides, the attitudes of European powers toward the Civil War were not primarily shaped by the actions of American ministers, secretaries of state, or even presidents. Nor, during 1861 and 1862, were they shaped by appeals to economic self-interest. Southerners, firmly believing that cotton was king, expected that pressure from British and French textile manufacturers would compel their governments to recognize the Confederacy and to break the blockade. But as it happened, European manufacturers had an ample stockpile of cotton, purchased before the outbreak of hostilities, and were therefore not much affected when Southern cotton was cut off in 1861. By 1862 cotton mills in both Britain and France were suffering, but Union and Confederate orders for arms, ammunition, and other equipment counterbalanced these losses. There was great hardship among the workers in the cotton mills, especially in the Lancashire district of England, where unemployment was high, but their complaints were relatively ineffectual since Britain still did not allow these men to vote.

Northerners were equally disappointed by the attitude of European governments. Knowing the strength of the antislavery movement abroad, particularly in Great Britain and France, they expected the European powers to condemn the slaveholding Con-

COTTON IN THE STOCKS.

M. Mercier :—"HOW MUCH LONGER IS THIS TO LAST? OR ARE YOU WAITING UNTIL WE INTERFERE?"

"COTTON IN THE STOCKS"

The Union blockade sealed off Southern exports of cotton and helped produce severe hardships in the textile-producing regions of Great Britain and France. This 1862 cartoon shows the French minister to Washington, Henri Mercier, threatening Uncle Sam with European intervention if the blockade is not lifted. *(Library of Congress)*

federacy. Their hope was unrealistic because, during the early years of the war, the Union government took no decisive steps toward emancipation. Indeed, Lincoln pledged that he would not interfere with slavery where it existed, Seward branded the abolitionists and "the most extreme advocates of African slavery" as equally dangerous to the Union, and Union generals helped Southern masters reclaim their runaway slaves. It was scarcely surprising that European opponents of slavery were confused and could do little to influence the attitudes of their governments toward the war in America.

What Northerners and Confederates alike failed to understand was that the policy of European states toward the Civil War would be determined largely by considerations of national self-interest. Since the Crimean War, an uneasy balance of power had prevailed in Europe, and no nation was eager to upset it by unilateral intervention in the American conflict. But concerted action by the European powers was always difficult because of mutual suspicion, and in the 1860s it was virtually impossible because of the nature of the British government. The British prime minister, Lord Palmerston, who was nearly eighty years old, headed a shaky coalition government, which was certain to fall if it undertook any decisive action. With the British government immobilized, the Russians favorable to the Union cause, and the Prussians and the Austrians mostly indifferent to the conflict, the inclination of the ambitious Napoleon III to meddle in favor of the Confederacy was effectively curbed.

As a result, European nations announced their neutrality early in the war. Queen Victoria's proclamation of May 13, 1861, was typical in recognizing that a state of war existed between the United States and "the states styling themselves the Confederate States of America" and in declaring British neutrality in that war. None of these proclamations recognized the Confederacy as a nation—that is, no one declared that it was a legitimate, independent power, entitled to send ambassadors and ministers abroad and to receive those from other nations, to enter into treaties with other powers, or, in general, to be treated just like any other sovereign state. But the proclamations did recognize the Confederates as belligerents. That meant that the Southerners were not to be considered simply as a group of riotous or insurrectionary individuals but as participants in a systematic, organized effort to set up their own independent government. Recognition as a belligerent, under international law, entitled the Confederacy to send out privateers without their being considered pirate ships. Recognition that a state of war existed in America also meant that the Union government could not simply declare Southern ports closed to foreign ships; to exclude foreign shipping it would have to maintain an effective blockade of the Confederacy. Initially these proc-lamations seemed a great Confederate sucess. In fact, however, they were both necessary and warranted by international law and, despite Seward's rantings, were truly impartial.

The Trent Affair.   In November 1861, the rash action of a Union naval officer threatened to upset this neutrality. Learning that Davis was replacing the temporary commissioners he had sent to France and Britain by permanent envoys, John Slidell and James M. Mason, Union Captain Charles Wilkes decided to capture these diplomats en route. Off the shore of Cuba on November 8, 1861, his warship stopped the British merchant ship, the *Trent*, Union officers boarded and searched the vessel, and Mason and Slidell were unceremoniously removed, to be transported to Boston for imprisonment. When news of Wilkes's action, in clear violation of international law, reached Europe, hostility toward the Union government flared up. "You may stand for this," Prime Minister Palmerston told his cabinet, "but damned if I will!" The foreign minister, Russell, drafted a stiff letter demanding the immediate release of the envoys. It was clear that the Lincoln government faced a major crisis if it held its prisoners. After conferring with cabinet members and senators, Lincoln decided on Christmas day to release the Southern envoys. He would fight only one war at a time.

Even with the firm intention of remaining neutral, European powers found their patience tested as the American war stretched on without apparent chance of ending. International relations were disturbed, commerce was disrupted, textile manufacturing was suffering, and neither North nor South seemed able to achieve its goal. Increasingly, support built up in both France and Britain for offering mediation to the combatants, and such an offer inevitably involved recognition of the Confederacy as an independent nation. In September 1862, Palmerston and Russell agreed to explore a mediation plan involving France and Russia as well as Great Britain, but pro-Union members of the British cabinet, like the Duke of Argyll and George Cornewall Lewis, replied with strong arguments against mediation. Faced with dis-

"CAVALRY OFFICER" BY WINSLOW HOMER
Even after a year of combat, Americans, North and South, could not reconcile themselves to the fact that modern war requires regimentation. They continued to think of themselves as individualists, like this dashing union cavalry officer, sketched by Winslow Homer. *(Courtesy Cooper-Hewitt Museum, The Smithsonian Institution's National Museum of Design)*

sension within his unstable coalition and given no encouragement by Russia, Palmerston by October 1862 changed his mind and concluded that the European states must continue to be lookers-on till the war took a more decided turn.

Battles and Leaders

But on the battlefields in 1861 and 1862 there were no decided turns. Engagement followed engagement, campaign followed campaign, and neither side could achieve a decisive victory. The stalemate was baffling to armchair strategists, in both the South and the North, who had been sure that the war would be short and decisive, ending in an overwhelming victory for their own side.

Confederate war planners counted among their assets the fact that some of the best graduates of West Point led their armies and that President Davis himself had military training and experience. They believed that Southern men had more of a fighting spirit than Northerners, and they were probably correct in thinking that Southerners had more experience in handling firearms and were better horsemen. They knew that the Confederacy would generally act on the defensive and assumed that the offensive Union army would have to be at least three times as large as that of the South. Since Southern forces could operate on interior lines, they could move more quickly and easily than Union forces, which would have to travel longer distances. While recognizing the superiority of the Union navy, Southerners knew that the Confederacy had 3,500 miles of coastline, with innumerable hidden harbors and waterways through which shipping could escape. When Confederate strategists added to all these assets the fact that Southern soldiers were fighting on their home ground, where they knew every road and byway, they saw no reason to doubt ultimate victory.

But an equally good case could be made for the inevitability of a Union victory. The population of the Union in 1860 was about 20.7 million; that of the Confederacy, only 9.1 million. Moreover, 3.5 million of the inhabitants of the South were blacks, mostly slaves, who, it was presumed, would not be used in the Confederate armies. Along with this superiority in manpower, the North had vastly more economic

strength than the Confederacy. The total value of all manufactured products in all eleven Confederate states was less than one-fourth of that of New York alone. The iron furnaces, forges, and rolling mills in the United States were heavily concentrated in the North. The North in 1860 built fourteen out of every fifteen railroad locomotives manufactured in the United States. Northern superiority in transportation would more than compensate for Southern interior lines, as only 30 percent of the total rail mileage of the United States ran through the Confederacy. The Union navy, which experienced few defections to the South, was incomparably superior, and the blockade President Lincoln announced at the outbreak of hostilities would cut off, or at least drastically reduce, Southern imports from Europe. When Northern planners added to the advantages of their side the possession of the established government, the recognition of foreign powers, and the enormous enthusiasm of the people for maintaining the Union, they could not doubt that victory would be sure and swift.

Jomini's Game Plan. In fact, these assets substantially canceled each other during the first two years of the war and produced not victory but deadlock. As the armies engaged in complex maneuvers and in indecisive battles, Union and Confederate commanders largely employed the same strategic plans, for most had learned the art of war from the same teachers. In fifty-five of the sixty biggest battles of the war, the generals on both sides had been educated at West Point, and in the remaining five, a West Pointer led one of the opposing armies. At the military academy they had studied the theories of the French historian and strategist Baron Henri Jomini. Some read Jomini's works in the original French or in translation; more, doubtless, absorbed his ideas from the abridgement and interpretation of his work *Elementary Treatise on Advance-Guard, Outpost, and Detachment of Service of Troops* (1847), written by Dennis Hart Mahan, who for a generation taught at the academy and greatly influenced his students.

Although in fact a complex body of doctrine, subject to many differing interpretations, Jomini's

317.56
1.6
87.6

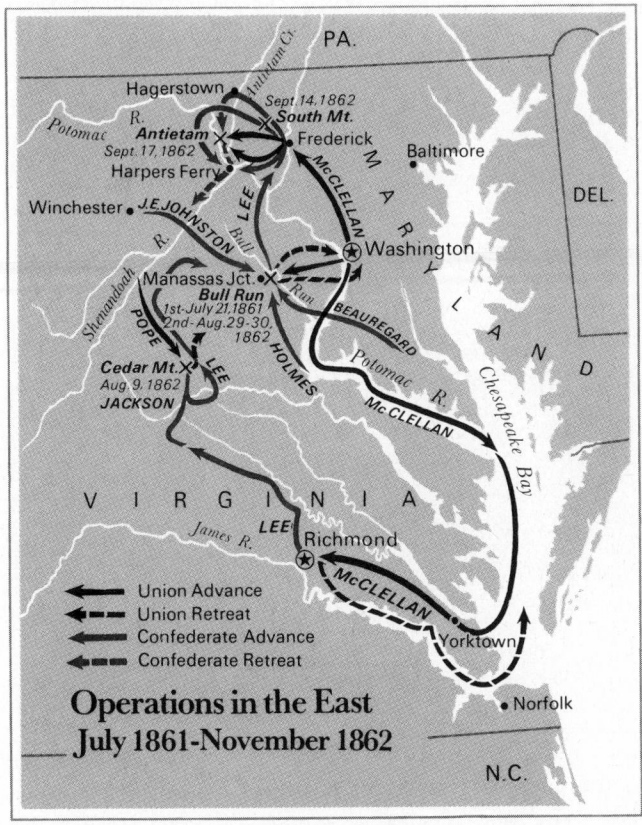

Operations in the East
July 1861–November 1862

**Legend (map):**
→ Union Advance
⇢ Union Retreat
→ Confederate Advance
⇠ Confederate Retreat

military theories as understood by American commanders stressed the importance of the conquest of territory and emphasized that the seizure of the enemy's capital was "ordinarily, the objective point" of an invading army. Jomini envisaged a battle situation in which two armies were drawn up in opposing lines, one offensive, and the other defensive, and he even prepared a set of twelve diagrams showing the possible orders of battle. In all twelve, a major determinant of victory was the concentration of force—the bringing to bear of a powerful, united force upon the enemy's weakest point. Warfare was thus something like an elaborate game of chess, an art that only professional soldiers could fully master.

Most of the military operations during the first two years of the Civil War can best be understood as a kind of elaborate illustration of Jomini's theories,

slightly modified to fit the American terrain. The first big battle of the war occurred on July 21, 1861, when Union General Irwin McDowell, under much pressure from Northern newspapers and much badgered by exuberant politicians in the Congress, reluctantly pushed his poorly organized army into Virginia. He expected to encounter the Confederates, under General Beauregard, near Centreville. In the ensuing battle of Bull Run (or Manassas), both armies tried to apply the same battle plan from Jomini's treatise; each attempted a main attack upon the enemy's left flank, to be followed by a secondary thrust at his center and right wings. If completely executed, the two plans would have had the amusing result of leaving each army in its opponent's original place. But the Confederates also followed another of Jomini's principles, that of concentration of force and, using the railroad, rushed General Joseph E. Johnston's troops from the Shenandoah Valley to join Beauregard's main force. The Union troops fought bravely and initially seemed to be carrying the day, but after Johnston's men were in position, the Union army was thrown back and then routed. Weary and disorganized, Federal troops limped back to the Potomac and to safety. The Confederates were almost equally demoralized by their victory and were unable to pursue. The South's easiest opportunity to follow Jomini's maxim and seize the enemy's capital had to be given up.

After this initial engagement, it was clear that both armies needed reorganization and training before either could attempt further campaigns. As a result, despite growing impatience for action, there was little significant military action during the rest of 1861, except for minor engagements in Kentucky and Missouri. During this period General George Brinton McClellan, who was credited with some overrated small successes in western Virginia, was summoned to Washington to bring order to the Union army. With enormous dash and enthusiasm, the young commander began to whip the Federal regiments into fighting shape. He insisted on careful drill and inspection; he demanded the best of food and equipment for his men; and he refused to move forward until his army was thoroughly prepared.

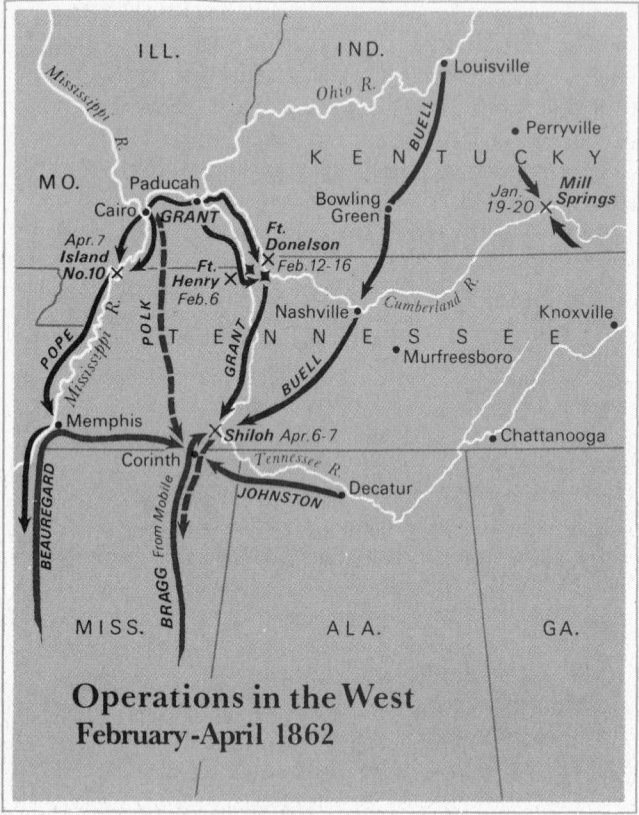

Operations in the West
February–April 1862

GENERAL GEORGE BRINTON MCCLELLAN
Union General McClellan, the "Little Napoleon" of the Civil War, seemed to have everything it took to make a great general. He was handsome and brave; he was a superb organizer and administrator; and he knew all that the books taught about the art of war. But, as Lincoln painfully found out, McClellan had one great fault: he had "the slows."   *(National Archives)*

The War in the West, 1862. By early 1862, Union armies, not merely those in the East but in all the theaters of war, were ready to advance, and, taking advantage of numerical superiority, Union commanders concentrated their forces on a series of weak spots in the Confederate defenses, just as Jomini had directed. In January, General George H. Thomas defeated a Confederate force at Mill Springs, Kentucky, and made a significant break in the Southern defense line west of the mountains. The next month General Ulysses S. Grant made an even more important breach in that line, when in collaboration with the Union gunboats on the Tennessee and Cumberland rivers, he captured Fort Henry and Fort Donelson, requiring the Confederate army in the latter fort to accept his terms of unconditional surrender.

The Southerners now had to abandon Tennessee.

Union armies under Grant and Don Carlos Buell pushed rapidly after them until checked at the battle of Shiloh (April 6–7). Dissatisfied with Grant's generalship, General Henry Wager Halleck, who was the Union commander for the entire western theater, took personal charge of the army after Shiloh. A dedicated disciple of Jomini, whose works he had translated, Halleck concentrated his force for a push on Corinth, Mississippi, in order to break the important rail connection that linked Memphis and the western portion of the Confederacy with the East.

The Peninsula Campaign. A Union advance in the eastern theater promised to be equally successful. After long delays, McClellan began his offensive against Richmond, not by going directly overland, but by transporting his troops to Fort Monroe, on the peninsula between the York and James rivers. Bitterly complaining because Lincoln violated the principle of concentration and held back 40,000 troops to defend Washington, McClellan nevertheless prepared to follow Jomini's maxims and seize the Confederate capital.

At this point in the gigantic, synchronized Union offensive, designed to crush the Confederacy, everything began to go wrong. The difficulties stemmed partly from human inadequacies. Although good theoreticians and able administrators, Halleck and McClellan were indecisive fighters. Halleck took nearly two months to creep from Shiloh to Corinth, stopping to fortify his position each night. By the time he reached his destination, the Southern army had moved south with all its provisions. Equally cautious was McClellan's advance on the Peninsula, where he allowed 16,000 Confederate soldiers under General John B. Magruder to hold up his magnificent army of 112,000 until the Confederates could bring reinforcements to Richmond. The trouble was partly that these Union campaigns required the coordinated movement of forces larger than anything seen before on the American continent, though few of the commanding officers had ever led anything larger than a regiment. But chiefly the Union failure was due to the fact that able Confederate generals had read the same books on strategy as the Union commanders and knew how to fight the same kinds of battles.

While McClellan slowly edged his way up the Peninsula, Confederate Commander Joseph E. Johnston, who had rushed in with reinforcements, kept close watch until the Union general injudiciously allowed his forces to be divided by the flooded Chickahominy River. Applying Jomini's principle of concentration on the enemy's weakest spot, Johnston on May 31–June 1 fell upon the exposed Union wing in battles at Fair Oaks (or Seven Pines), which narrowly failed of being a Confederate triumph. When Johnston was wounded in this engagement, President Davis chose Robert E. Lee to replace him.

Lee quickly revealed his military genius by showing that he knew when to follow Jomini's principles and when to flout them. Remembering from his days at West Point how slow McClellan was, Lee allowed "Stonewall" Jackson to take 18,000 men from the main army for a daring campaign through the Shenandoah Valley. Jackson defeated and demoralized the Union forces in the Shenandoah and so threatened Washington that Lincoln withheld reinforce-

UNION ORDNANCE READY FOR TRANSPORTATION FROM YORKTOWN
For McClellan's push up the Peninsula in the hope of capturing Richmond, the Union war department assembled the largest collection of men and materiel ever collected on the American continent. But, as events proved, Union generalship did not equal Union resources. (*National Archives*)

ments that he had promised McClellan. When Jackson had accomplished this objective, Lee reverted to the principle of concentration and ordered Jackson promptly to rejoin the main army before Richmond. The combined Confederate force fell upon McClellan's exposed right flank at Mechanicsville. Lee failed to crush McClellan; but in a series of engagements known as the Seven Days (June 25–July 1), he forced the Union army to beat a slow, hard-fought retreat to the banks of the James River, where it lay under the protection of Federal gunboats. Lee had saved Richmond.

The Confederate Counter-Offensive.   As the Union advances ground to a halt by midsummer, 1862, the Confederates planned a grand offensive of their own. In the West, two Southern armies under Generals Braxton Bragg and Edmund Kirby-Smith in August swept through eastern Tennessee; by September,

they were operating in Kentucky, where they were in a position to cut the supply line for Buell's army in Tennessee. The early phases of their offensive were brilliantly successful, but the campaign as a whole was fruitless because of a lack of coordination between the two Southern armies and because of Bragg's indecisiveness. After a bloody battle at Perryville (October 8), the Confederate forces withdrew toward Chattanooga, followed, at a respectful distance, by the Union army.

The more daring part of the Confederate offensive was in the East. While McClellan's army was slowly being withdrawn from the Peninsula, Lee turned quickly upon Union forces in central Virginia under the braggart General John Pope, and concentrating his entire strength upon this segment of the Federal army, scored a brilliant Confederate victory in the second battle of Bull Run (August 29–30). Free then to push into the North, Lee crossed the Potomac

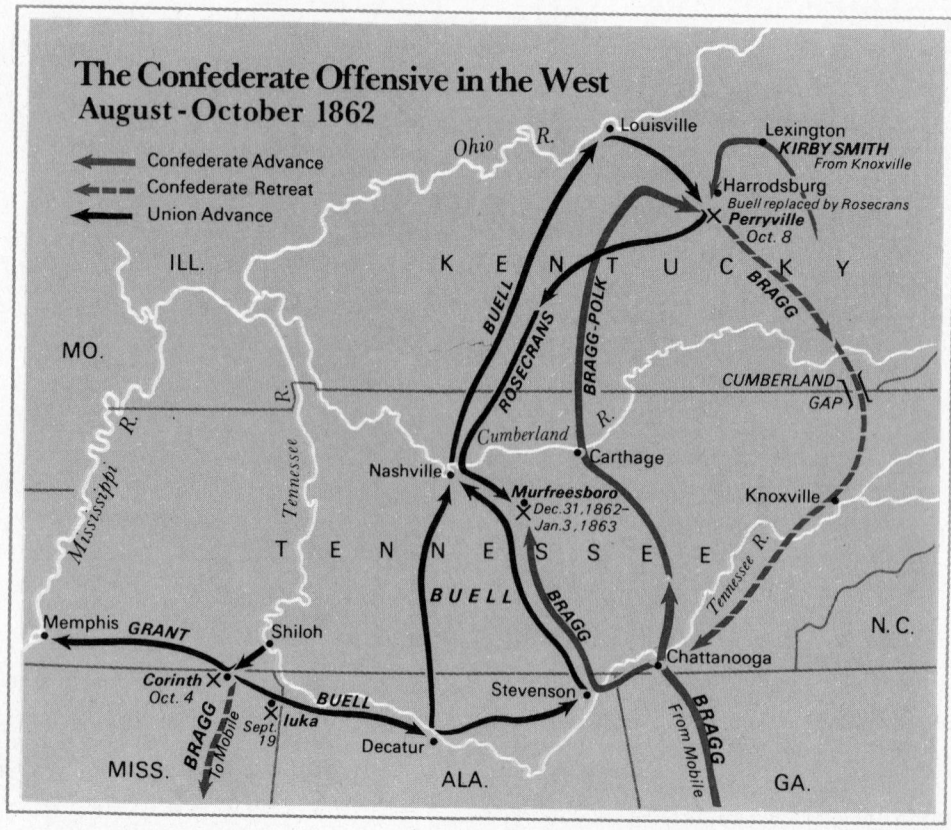

The Confederate Offensive in the West
August - October 1862

into Maryland, where he hoped to supply his ragged army and to rally the inhabitants of that state to the Confederate cause.

Lee's invasion of Maryland ended with the battle of Antietam (September 17), an indecisive engagement whose very inconclusiveness clearly demonstrated the impossibility of ever ending the war so long as it was fought by the conventional rules. Union General McClellan, again in command, moved slowly to catch up with Lee's army, because he wished to concentrate all his forces for an attack. Lee in turn waited in a defensive position behind Antietam Creek at Sharpsburg, Maryland, because he too needed to concentrate his troops, a portion of whom had been sent on a successful expedition to capture Harpers Ferry. When McClellan was finally ready to take the offensive, he followed one of Jomini's battle plans precisely, and Lee defended his position by the same rules. The result was the bloodiest day of the Civil War. In areas of the battlefield like the cornfield, the Dunker church, the Bloody Lane, and Burnside's bridge, men fell as in a slaughterhouse. By the end of the day, there were more than 25,000 casualties, with at least 5,000 dead. The next day an eyewitness noted "the most appalling sights upon the battle-field . . . the ground strewn with the bodies of the dead and the dying . . . the cries and the groans of the wounded . . . the piles of dead men, in attitudes which show the writhing agony in which they died—faces distorted . . . begrimed and covered with clotted blood, arms and legs torn from the body or the body itself torn asunder."

Quietly Lee slipped back into Virginia, and McClellan did not pursue him. The Confederate offensive was over, and with it ended an era. If Jomini's strategy could only lead to stalemate, it was time for both Union and Confederacy to experiment with new ways of waging war.

CHRONOLOGY

1861 Secession of remaining states of Deep South (Texas, Louisiana, Mississippi, Alabama, Georgia, and Florida).
Jefferson Davis begins serving as president of the Confederate States of America.
Abraham Lincoln inaugurated as president of the United States of America.
Firing on Fort Sumter precipitates war.
Secession of border slave states (Virginia, North Carolina, Tennessee, and Arkansas).
Union army routed at first battle of Bull Run (Manassas).
McClellan heads Union Forces.
Trent affair threatens to change European neutrality.

1862 Both Union and Confederacy adopt paper money.
Union general, U. S. Grant, captures Fort Henry and Fort Donelson.
Grant defeated at Shiloh.
Battle of the ironclads: *Virginia (Merrimack)* vs. *Monitor.*
McClellan's Peninsula campaign brings Union army to outskirts of Richmond, the Confederate capital.
Robert E. Lee becomes commander of Army of Northern Virginia.
Confederate victory at second battle of Bull Run.
Stalemate between Lee and McClellan at Antietam.
Confederate invasion of Kentucky.
Lincoln issues preliminary Emancipation Proclamation.
Confederate victory at Fredericksburg.

SUGGESTED READINGS

There are two excellent guides to the vast literature on the causes of the Civil War: Howard K. Beale, "What Historians Have Said about the Causes of the Civil War," in *Theory and Practice in Historical Study* (Social Science Research Council *Bulletin*, No. 54 [1946], 55–102), and Thomas J. Pressly, *Americans Interpret Their Civil War* (1954). Kenneth M. Stampp, *The Imperiled Union* (1980), offers an insightful analysis of these conflicting interpretations. Edwin C. Rozwenc, ed., *The Causes of the American Civil War* (1972), and Kenneth M. Stampp, ed., *The Causes of the*

Civil War (1974), contain extensive extracts from writings by contemporaries and subsequent historians.

Peter J. Parish, *The American Civil War* (1975), is the best one-volume history. *The Civil War and Reconstruction* (1969), by J. G. Randall and David Donald, is more comprehensive and has a fuller bibliography. Of the older large-scale studies, James Ford Rhodes, *History of the United States from the Compromise of 1850...*, Vols. 3–5 (1895–1904), remains valuable. The fullest modern account is Allan Nevins, *The War for the Union* (4 vols., 1959–71), a work of enormous scholarship, which, however, concentrates on the North. Bruce Catton, *The Centennial History of the Civil War* (3 vols., 1961–65), is eloquent and imaginative.

Mark M. Boatner, III, *The Civil War Dictionary* (1959), is a useful, accurate reference work. For maps, see Vincent J. Esposito, ed., *The West Point Atlas of American Wars* (2 vols., 1959).

The best Civil War anthologies are Henry S. Commager, ed., *The Blue and the Gray* (2 vols., 1950), and William B. Hesseltine, ed., *The Tragic Conflict* (1962). Francis T. Miller, *The Photographic History of the Civil War* (10 vols., 1911), offers the most complete pictorial coverage, but the photographs are poorly reproduced. Better pictorial histories, using modern photographic techniques, are David Donald, ed., *Divided We Fought* (1952), and Richard M. Ketchum, ed., *The American Heritage Picture History of the Civil War* (1960).

On the Sumter crisis, see David M. Potter, *Lincoln and His Party in the Secession Crisis* (1942), Kenneth M. Stampp, *And the War Came* (1950), and Richard N. Current, *Lincoln and the First Shot* (1963).

The best history of the Confederacy is Emory M. Thomas, *The Confederate Nation, 1861–1865* (1979). The fullest life of the Confederate president is Hudson Strode, *Jefferson Davis* (3 vols., 1955–64); the most recent is Clement Eaton, *Jefferson Davis* (1977). Students will learn much from Rembert W. Patrick, *Jefferson Davis and His Cabinet* (1944). Three Confederate diaries are invaluable: May B. Chesnut, *A Diary from Dixie*, ed. by Ben A. Williams (1949); John B. Jones, *A Rebel War Clerk's Diary* (2 vols., 1866); and Robert G. H. Kean, *Inside the Confederate Government*, ed. by Edward Younger (1955).

Abraham Lincoln has been the subject of many distinguished biographies. The best one-volume life is Stephen B. Oates, *With Malice Toward None* (1977); Benjamin P. Thomas's *Abraham Lincoln* (1952) is also valuable. The fullest and most flavorful of the biographies is Carl Sandburg, *Abraham Lincoln: The War Years* (4 vols., 1939). The most scholarly and critical is *Lincoln the President* (4 vols., 1945–55), by J. G. Randall and Richard N. Current. Several volumes of essays deal with important and controversial aspects of Lincoln's career: Richard N. Current, *The Lincoln Nobody Knows* (1958); David Donald, *Lincoln Reconsidered* (1956); Norman A. Graebner, ed., *The Enduring Lincoln* (1959); and J. G. Randall, *Lincoln the Liberal Statesman* (1947). See also Edmund Wilson's thoughtful essay on Lincoln in his *Patriotic Gore* (1962). The diaries of three of Lincoln's cabinet officers are indispensable: Howard K. Beale, ed., *The Diary of Edward Bates* (1933); David Donald, ed., *Inside Lincoln's Cabinet* (Salmon P. Chase) (1954); and Howard K. Beale and Alan W. Brownsword, ed., *Diary of Gideon Welles* (3 vols., 1960).

The standard work on Anglo-American relations remains Ephraim D. Adams, *Great Britain and the American Civil War* (2 vols., 1925). Frank L. Owsley, *King Cotton Diplomacy* (1959), David P. Crook, *The North, the South, and the Powers* (1974), and Brian Jenkins, *Britain and the War for the Union* (1974), are also valuable. Lincoln's role in foreign policy is overdramatized in Jay Monaghan, *Diplomat in Carpetslippers* (1945). For correctives, see Glyndon G. Van Deusen, *William Henry Seward* (1967), Martin B. Duberman, *Charles Francis Adams* (1961), and David Donald, *Charles Sumner and the Rights of Man* (1970). Franco-American relations are admirably covered in Lynn M. Case and Warren F. Spencer, *The United States and France: Civil War Diplomacy* (1970), and Daniel B. Carroll, *Henri Mercier and the American Civil War* (1971).

On social and economic conditions, see Paul W. Gates, *Agriculture and the Civil War* (1965), and Mary E. Massey, *Bonnet Brigades: American Women and the Civil War* (1966). Developments on the Southern home front are sketched in Charles W. Ramsdell, *Behind the Lines in the Southern Confederacy* (1944), and Bell I. Wiley, *The Plain People of the Confederacy* (1943). Emerson D. Fite, *Social and Industrial Conditions in the North during the Civil War* (1910), remains the best survey. For the continuing debate on the effect of the war on Northern economic growth, see Ralph Andreano, ed., *The Economic Impact of the American Civil War* (1962), and David T. Gilchrist and W. David Lewis, eds., *Economic Change in the Civil War Era* (1965).

Studies dealing with other aspects of the Civil War are listed at the end of the following chapter.

CHAPTER 19

Experimentation
1862–1865

At the outset of the Civil War both President Lincoln and President Davis assumed that the conflict would be a limited and relatively brief one, waged in a conventional fashion by armies in the field and having little impact on the economic, social, and intellectual life of their sections. The events of 1861–62 proved these expectations utterly wrong. It slowly became clear that to carry on the war Americans, in both North and South, had to break with tradition and engage in broad experimentation. They had to try new forms of government action, new modes of social and economic cooperation, and new patterns of thought.

Since the Union was ultimately victorious, it would be easy to conclude that Northerners were more willing to experiment, better able to mobilize all their resources, for what has been called the first modern war. But such a judgment makes the historian the camp follower of the victorious army. The record shows, instead, that both the Confederacy and the Union attempted innovations that for the time were daringly original. It also shows that both sides during the final years of the war resorted to much the same kinds of experimentation.

Evolution of a Command System

The bloody and indecisive campaigns of 1861 and 1862 made innovators out of both Union and Confederate soldiers. Experience under fire convinced them not to follow Jomini's tactics. The French writer had conceived of a tactical situation where infantrymen, drawn up in close, parallel lines, blazed away at each other with muskets capable of being loaded perhaps twice a minute and having an effective range of one hundred yards. But Civil War soldiers were equipped with rifles which not only were more quickly loaded but had an effective range of about eight hundred yards. In Jomini's day the offensive force had the great advantage; rushing forward with bayonets fixed, charging troops could break the defenders' line before they had time to reload. In the Civil War, on the other hand, the advancing force was exposed to accurate fire during the last half-mile of its approach. In consequence, nine out of ten infantry assaults failed, and the Civil War soldier had little use for his bayonet—except perhaps as a spit on which to cook meat.

Soldiers on both sides rapidly learned how to make defensive positions even stronger. At the beginning of the war, most military men were scornful of breastworks and entrenchments, arguing that they simply pinned down a defending force and made it more vulnerable to a charge. When Lee, upon assuming command of the Army of Northern Virginia in 1862, ordered his men to construct earthworks facing McClellan's advancing troops, Confederate soldiers bitterly complained and called their new general the King of Spades. But when they saw how entrenchments saved lives, they changed their tune, and Lee became to the Confederate common soldier "Marse Robert," the general who looked after his men's welfare. What Confederate generals started, Union commanders imitated. By the end of 1862, both armies dug in wherever they halted. Using spades and canteens, forks and sticks, soldiers pushed up improvised earthworks and strengthened them with fence rails and fallen logs.

Experience also quietly killed off Jomini's view that warfare was restricted to professionals. In the early days of the conflict, commanders believed warfare should not injure civilians. When McClellan's army pushed up the Peninsula, the general posted guards to keep his soldiers from raiding Confederate farmers' cornfields. Similarly Halleck permitted slaveowners to search his camp in order to reclaim their runaway slaves. By the end of 1862, such practices vanished. Soldiers joyfully foraged through civilians' watermelon patches, cornfields, and chicken roosts, while their officers ostentatiously turned their backs. Northern generals exhibited a growing reluctance to permit the recapture of fugitive slaves who had fled to the Union lines. As early as May 1861, General Butler at Fort Monroe, Virginia, refused to return three such fugitives on the ground that they were contraband of war. "Contrabands" became a code name for escaped slaves, and in 1862 the Federal Congress showed what it thought of Jomini's notion of limited warfare by prohibiting any Federal military officer from returning runaways.

Lincoln Takes Command. The deadlock of 1861–62 also brought about a transformation of the command systems of both Union and Confederate armies. Because the Union lost so many battles during the first two years of the conflict, Lincoln was forced to experiment first. His initial venture came in mid-1862. Since he distrusted McClellan's capacity to keep an eye on the general progress of the war while also leading a campaign to capture Richmond, he brought in Halleck from the West to serve as his military adviser and gave him the grand title of general in chief. The position was not a viable one, for it placed Halleck in conflict with the other generals, especially McClellan; it also often put him at odds with Secretary of War Stanton, and exposed him to what he called the "political Hell" of pressure from congressmen. In addition, Halleck's slowness, his indecisiveness, and his rigid adherence to Jomini's principles made him hostile to all innovation, and Lincoln soon concluded that he was of little more use than a clerk.

Seeing no alternative, Lincoln again tried to direct military operations himself. In the eastern theater he replaced McClellan, after his failure to follow up his partial success at Antietam, with that bumbling incompetent, Ambrose E. Burnside. Burnside led the Army of the Potomac into the battle of Fredericksburg on December 13, 1862, one of the most disastrous, and surely the least necessary, Federal defeats of the war. Replacing Burnside with "Fighting Joe" Hooker, a boastful egotist fond of the bottle, brought no better luck to the Union cause. The battle of Chancellorsville (May 1–4, 1863) was still another Confederate victory—but one won at a great price, for "Stonewall" Jackson was accidentally fired upon by his own Southern soldiers and mortally wounded.

Still trying to direct military operations himself, Lincoln watched anxiously as Lee in midsummer of 1863 began his second invasion of the North, this time pushing into Pennsylvania. When Hooker appeared unable or unwilling to pursue the Confederates, Lincoln replaced him with the shy, scholarly George Gordon Meade, who assumed command of the army only three days before the climactic battle of Gettysburg (July 1–3, 1863). Rushing all available forces to that Pennsylvania town, Meade succeeded in turning back the invaders. At last the Army of the

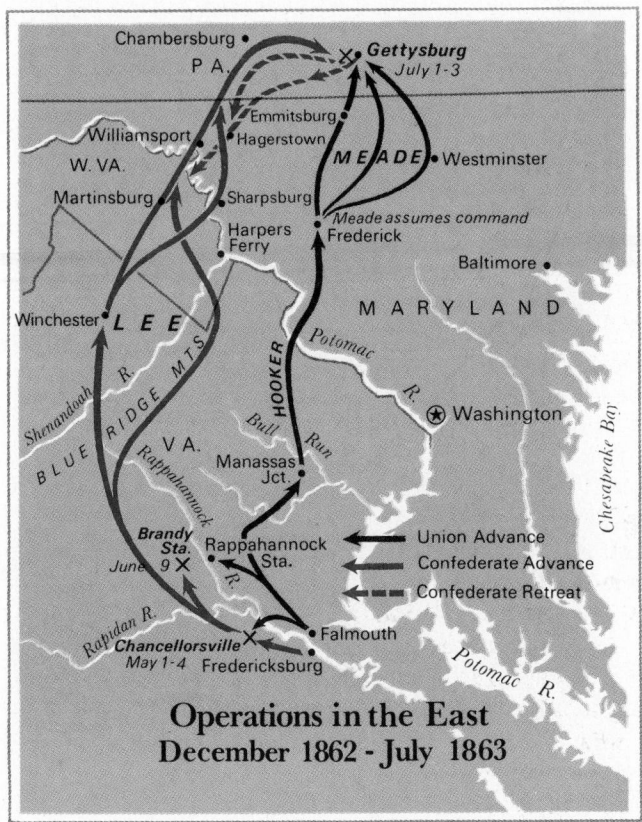

Chambersburg •

P A.

✗✗ **Gettysburg**
July 1-3

Emmitsburg •
Hagerstown •

Williamsport •

W. VA.

M E A D E • Westminster

Martinsburg •

Sharpsburg •

Harpers
Ferry

Meade assumes command
Frederick •

Baltimore •

M A R Y L A N D

Winchester • **L E E**

Potomac

☆ Washington

Shenandoah R.

BLUE RIDGE MTS.

Rappahannock

VA.

Bull Run

Manassas
Jct. •

Chesapeake Bay

**Brandy
Sta.**
June 9 ✗

Rappahannock
Sta.

➤ Union Advance
➤ Confederate Advance
➤ Confederate Retreat

Rapidan R.

Chancellorsville ✗
May 1-4

• Falmouth

Fredericksburg

Potomac R.

Operations in the East
December 1862 - July 1863

Potomac had won a victory—but Meade failed to pursue, and Lee's army recrossed the Potomac to safety. "We had them within our grasp," Lincoln lamented. "We had only to stretch forth our hands and they were ours. And nothing I could say or do could make the Army move."

When Lincoln tried personally to plan strategy for the trans-Appalachian theater of war, he was no more successful. After the battle of Perryville, it was clear that Buell must be replaced, and Lincoln chose W. S. Rosecrans. Lincoln urged him to push on to Chattanooga, the rail hub of the Confederacy, but en route Rosecrans encountered Bragg's army in the bloody and indecisive battle of Murfreesboro (December 30, 1862–January 2, 1863). Though Rosecrans claimed victory, his army was so badly mauled that he could not advance for another six months. Finally, in June 1863 he maneuvered the Confederates out of

Chattanooga, but in pursuing Bragg's army he received a smashing defeat at Chickamauga (September 19–20). Only the rocklike determination of General George H. Thomas prevented the reverse from becoming a rout, and Rosecrans's army limped back into Chattanooga. Disoriented by defeat, Rosecrans, as Lincoln said, behaved "like a duck hit on the head," and allowed Bragg to besiege the city.

Farther west, Lincoln's personal direction of the Union armies proved equally ineffectual. Here the main objective was Vicksburg, the last major city on the Mississippi River still in Confederate hands; when it fell, the eastern part of the Confederacy would be severed from the trans-Mississippi region.

Grant's Success at Vicksburg. Grant commanded the Union forces in this area after Halleck went to Washington, and William Tecumseh Sherman was his ablest lieutenant. After a frontal assault on the almost impregnable bluffs of Vicksburg failed to drive out the Confederates, commanded by General John C. Pemberton, Grant, without aid from Washington, devised a bold new strategy. Using the navy's gunboats and transports to run his ammunition and supplies past the Vicksburg batteries, he marched his army to a point on the west bank below the city, staged a rapid amphibious crossing, and before the Confederates could recover from their surprise, pushed inland. To the dismay of Washington, he thus abandoned his base of supplies, announcing that he planned to live on the countryside. First he struck at Jackson, the capital of Mississippi, to drive back the small Confederate force General Joseph E. Johnston had collected there, and then he turned on Pemberton's army and forced it into Vicksburg. After two ill-advised assaults, the Union army settled down to besiege the city, while from the river the Union gunboats kept up a constant bombardment. As civilians in the city took to caves for safety and as starvation made mule meat a delicacy, Pemberton fought back as well as he could, but on July 4, 1863—the day after Gettysburg—he had to surrender his army and the city.

When the news reached Washington, Lincoln, who had distrusted Grant's strategy, wrote the general a handsome apology: "I now wish to make the

MAJOR GENERAL ULYSSES SIMPSON GRANT, U.S.A., IN THE
FALL OF 1863

Grant lacked the polish of McClellan, the brilliance of
Sherman, and the flamboyance of Sheridan. But he had
one quality more important than any of these. As Lincoln concisely put it: "I can't spare this man—he fights."
(Library of Congress)

Operations in the West, 1863
The Vicksburg Campaign

←	Union Advance
←	Confederate Advance
⇠	Confederate Retreat

personal acknowledgment that you were right, and
I was wrong." The president was happy to be proved
wrong, for Grant's success meant that he finally had
a general who knew how to plan a campaign and fight
it. Putting Grant in command of all the troops in
the West, Lincoln directed him to relieve the army
cooped up in Chattanooga. Quickly Grant and Sherman came to the rescue, opened up a line of communication to the starving Union troops in Chattanooga, now commanded by Thomas instead of the
inept Rosecrans, and brought in reinforcements. On
November 23–25 the combined forces routed Bragg's
encircling army and forced it back into Georgia.

Two New Systems of Command. This further victory gave Lincoln a solution to the problem of command, which had so long vexed him. Early the next

year he brought Grant to Washington, where he
received the rank of lieutenant general, and assigned
him to command all the armies of the United States.
Initially Washington observers thought the burden
might be too much for this "short, round-shouldered
man," of whom they now received their first glimpse.
One observer reported that the new lieutenant general "had no gait, no *station*, no manner, rough, light-brown whiskers, a blue eye, and rather a scrubby
look withal . . . rather the look of a man who did, or
once did, take a little too much to drink." But appearances were deceiving, for in the next few days Grant
set forth a broad strategy for winning the war. Taking
advantage of Northern superiority in manpower, he
planned a simultaneous advance of all Union armies,
so that the Confederates must divide their forces or
else leave their territory open to invasion. The idea

of involving all the Federal forces at once made sense to Lincoln. "Oh, yes! I can see that," he exclaimed. "As we say out West, if a man can't skin he must hold a leg while somebody else does." Accepting Grant's plan, Lincoln created a modern command system for the United States army, with the president as commander in chief, Grant as general in chief, and Halleck as essentially a chief of staff, while Stanton as secretary of war ably supported all the others.

Meanwhile the Confederate command system was also evolving through experimentation. The tremendous victories won by Lee and the Army of Northern Virginia obviated the need for constant changing of command in the East, but by 1863 it was evident that there must be a reorganization of Confederate commanders in the West. Davis instituted what was, in effect, a theater command system, with Lee in control of the forces in Virginia, Joseph E. Johnston, now recovered from his wound, in command of the troops between the mountains and the Mississippi River, and Edmund Kirby-Smith in charge of all troops in the vast trans-Mississippi region.

The new system was only partially successful. Made a kind of super-commander of the trans-Mississippi theater, which was becoming increasingly isolated as Union forces captured point after point along the Mississippi, Kirby-Smith did an effective job of recruiting and reorganizing the troops in his region. He stepped up trade with Mexico, so that impressive amounts of European munitions and supplies were brought in by way of Matamoros. So strengthened, "Kirby-Smithdom," as it was popularly called, fared better than most of the rest of the South, but Kirby-Smith did little to make the vast resources of his command available to the government at Richmond.

In the central theater a strong Confederate command system failed to emerge. Johnston claimed he did not know the extent and nature of his duties. Repeatedly he asked whether he was supposed to take field command of the widely separated armies of Bragg, near Chattanooga, and of Pemberton, at Vicksburg, or was merely to serve as adviser to those generals. Knowing that both were protégés of the president, he did not dare give a positive order to either. In consequence, he made only a feeble effort to replace the unpopular Bragg and diverted a few

of his troops to support Pemberton. Unable to persuade Pemberton to leave Vicksburg while there was still time, Johnston watched in impotent impatience as the Confederate army was cornered and starved into surrender.

The brilliant successes of Lee and his lieutenants in the eastern theater allowed the Army of Northern Virginia to operate pretty much as it wished, without much regard for the needs of the Confederacy elsewhere. Lee, who had direct access to President Davis, resisted any attempt to weaken his force. In mid-1863, rather than attempt to relieve Vicksburg, Lee deliberately chose to stage a new invasion of the North, in the vain hope that it would relieve pressure on Confederate armies elsewhere. The result was the defeat at Gettysburg and the capture of Vicksburg.

Even so, Lee was by 1864 the only Confederate commander who retained the confidence of the country and of his troops. As Southern defeats became more numerous than victories, a strong demand swelled up in the Confederate Congress for coordinated direction of all the Southern armies, and men naturally looked to Lee. The general was, however, averse to these broader responsibilities and did all that he could to discourage the plan. When the Congress in January 1865 passed an act requiring the appointment of a commander in chief of all the armies, it had Lee in mind, and Davis named him. In accepting the new position, Lee made it clear that he would continue to be essentially a theater commander, responsible only to Davis. The Confederacy thus reached Appomattox without ever developing a truly unified command system, comparable to that of the Union.

The Naval War

In naval warfare necessity compelled the Confederates to take the lead in experimentation. Southerners were not a seagoing people, with a tradition of shipbuilding. Secretary of the Navy Stephen R. Mallory had initially not a single ship at his command. He had to improvise, and he did so with imagination and remarkable success.

In the early months of the war the long Southern

coastline seemed to be at the mercy of the Union fleet, which could pick the most vulnerable points for attack. In November 1861, a Union flotilla commanded by Flag Officer Samuel F. DuPont routed the weak Confederate defenders of Port Royal Sound, and Federal troops occupied Beaufort and the adjacent South Carolina Sea Islands. The victory gave the vessels in the Atlantic blockading fleet a much needed fueling station, and it also brought freedom to the numerous slaves of the area. In February and March 1862, another Union expedition easily reduced Confederate positions on Roanoke Island and at New Bern, North Carolina, and enabled the Federal blockaders to keep a closer watch on Hatteras Sound. David G. Farragut's fleet in April 1862 helped capture New Orleans, the Confederacy's largest city.

By this time the Confederacy had greatly strengthened its coastal defenses, and further Union successes came slowly and at great cost. In April 1863 the Confederates repelled a vast Union armada, commanded by DuPont, which tried to capture Charleston. That citadel of secession remained in Confederate hands until nearly the end of the war, when Sherman's advance compelled Southern troops to abandon it. Equally effective were the Confederate defenses of Wilmington, North Carolina, which became the main Southern port on the Atlantic through which supplies from Europe were imported. Not until January 1865 could Federal troops capture Fort Fisher, the principal defense of Wilmington. The powerfully protected harbor of Mobile remained in Southern hands until August 1864, when the sixty-three-year-old Admiral Farragut, lashed in the rigging of his flagship so that he would not fall to his death if wounded, led his fleet past the defending Confederate forts to stop the last remaining major Southern port on the Gulf.

Innovations in Naval Warfare. To supplement the coastal batteries that protected these and other harbors, the Confederate navy experimented with new weapons. They used torpedoes extensively for the first time in warfare. These "infernal machines," constructed of kegs, barrels, and cans filled with explosives, were sometimes anchored at the entrance of

Southern harbors, at other times were turned loose to float with the tide toward attacking Union vessels, and on still other occasions were propelled at the end of a long pole by a small boat, whose crew was willing to undertake the suicidal risk. Even more risky were the several Confederate experiments with submarine warfare. The most successful of these novel vessels was the *H. L. Hunley*, propelled under water by a crank turned by its eight-man crew. After four unsuccessful trials, in which all members of the crews were lost, the *Hunley* in February 1864 sank the Union warship *Housatonic* in Charleston harbor, but the submarine itself was lost in the resulting explosion.

Quickly comprehending that the Confederacy could never build as large a fleet as the Union, Secretary Mallory early in the war urged the construction of iron-armored ships, against which the wooden vessels of the North would stand no chance. Despite shortages of iron and lack of rolling mills, the Confederacy developed a surprising number of these vessels. The most famous of the Confederate ironclads was the *Virginia*, originally the United States warship *Merrimack*, which the Federals sank when they abandoned Norfolk navy yard at the beginning of the war. Raised and repaired, the *Virginia* had her superstructure covered with four-inch iron plate, and she carried a cast-iron ram on her prow. On March 8, 1862, just as McClellan began his campaign on the Peninsula, the *Virginia* emerged and began attacking the wooden vessels of the Union fleet at Hampton Roads. In the first day's action she destroyed two of the largest ships in the squadron and ran a third aground. Reappearing the second day, she found her way barred by a curious Union vessel, the *Monitor*, which looked like a tin can on a raft. Belatedly contracted for by the slow-moving Union navy department, the *Monitor*, designed by John Ericsson, was a low-lying ironclad with a revolving gun turret. The battle between the *Virginia* and the *Monitor* proved a draw, but the Confederate ship had to return to Norfolk to repair her defective engines. Two days later, when forced to abandon Norfolk, the Southerners ran the *Virginia* ashore and burned the vessel to prevent its capture. The South's most promising hope for breaking the blockade was lost.

MAKING GUNS FOR THE NEW MONITORS AT PITTSBURGH, PENNSYLVANIA

The success of the North was due in considerable measure to its economic superiority over the South. The Fort Pitt ironworks at Pittsburgh, which manufactured guns for the fleet of monitors, had their counterparts in a dozen other Northern cities. Confederate ordnance depended almost entirely upon imports from Europe and the output of the Tredegar ironworks in Richmond. *(Courtesy, Carnegie Library of Pittsburgh)*

Mallory was equally prompt in purchasing or commissioning conventional vessels for the Confederate navy, ships designed not to combat Union warships but to harass the United States merchant marine. The most successful of these vessels was the C.S.S. *Alabama*, built to Southern specifications at the Laird shipyards in Liverpool and commanded by Raphael Semmes. Ranging over the Atlantic, Indian, and Pacific oceans, the *Alabama* between 1862 and 1864 hunted down and destroyed sixty-nine Union merchantmen, valued at more than $6 million. Not until nearly the end of the war could the Union navy corner and sink the raider. By this time, however, the *Alabama*, along with other Confederate cruisers,

had virtually exterminated the United States carrying trade.

However imaginative and innovative, Confederate navy officials could not keep pace with the growth of the Union navy, under the slow but honest direction of Gideon Welles. Drawing upon the vast industrial resources of the North and upon the experience of its seagoing population, Welles was able to build up the United States navy from its 42 active vessels in 1861, only 26 of which had steam power, to 671 ships in December 1864, of which 71 were ironclad. Navy personnel rose from 7,400 at the start of the war to 68,000 at its end. Superbly equipped and managed, the Union fleet maintained an ever-tightening blockade of the Southern coast. According to the best, but not wholly reliable, statistics, the Union fleet captured not more than 1 in 10 blockade runners in 1861, and not more than 1 in 8 in 1862. But by 1864 they caught 1 in 3, and by 1865 every other one.

The Wartime Economy

Inevitably these huge military and naval operations put a heavy strain upon the economic resources of the combatants. In the Confederacy one result was a sharp shift in the nature of Southern agriculture. When the outbreak of war cut off Northern markets and the blockade increasingly sealed off European outlets for cotton and tobacco, farmers, at the urging of the Confederate and state governments, turned to producing grain and other foodstuffs. Cotton production in the South dropped from 4 million bales in 1861 to 300,000 in 1864.

In the North, too, farmers began producing more grain. Partly because of inflation, the price of wheat rose from 65¢ a bushel in December 1860 to $2.26 in July 1864, and farmers, especially in the Middle West, saw a chance to make money. At first the labor shortage kept them from expanding their acreage, for many farmhands enlisted in the Union army at the outbreak of the war, but machines soon made up for the absent men. One of Cyrus Hall McCormick's reapers could replace from four to six farmhands, and McCormick sold 165,000 of his machines during the war.

Industry in both the Union and the Confederacy also grew. As the Union blockade cut off imports, Southern factories had a virtual monopoly in that region, and the demands of the army and the needs of the civilians provided an insatiable market. It is hard to measure Southern industrial growth, both because there was no Confederate census and because inflation affected all prices, yet there are some clues to show that manufacturing could be very profitable. For instance, the 1862 conscription acts exempted the owners of certain basic industries provided that their annual profits were no more than 75

percent. Under the astute management of Joseph Anderson, the Tredegar Iron Works at Richmond, the largest privately owned factory in the South and the primary source for Confederate cannon, made profits of 100 percent in 1861 and of 70 percent in 1862.

Northern manufacturing was equally profitable, especially when it produced items needed for the army. With the demand for uniforms, woolen mills, which had averaged dividends of only 9 percent for the years before the war, by 1865 were able to pay 25 percent dividends, and the number of woolen mills more than doubled. Investors were willing to pour money into such industries more confidently because Congress raised tariffs to levels that virtually excluded competing European products. War demands made the mass production of ready-made clothing profitable, and the army's need for shoes speeded the introduction of Gordon McKay's machine for sewing soles to uppers. Simultaneously, in an unrelated development, the discovery of oil at Titusville, Pennsylvania, in 1859, led to a wartime boom in the new petroleum industry.

Structural Changes in the Two Economies. These changes had an important impact on the structure of the American economy. The increase in the number of factories, particularly in the Confederacy, encouraged entrepreneurship. In the North, men like John D. Rockefeller and Andrew Carnegie, who started their fortunes during the war, continued to dominate the industrial scene after 1865. When the South began rebuilding its industry in the 1870s and 1880s, it looked for leadership to its wartime entrepreneurs and to the Confederate commanders who likewise had experience in directing the labor of large numbers of men. The war also encouraged the growth of large, rather than small, factories. Obliged to contract for huge shipments, both Union and Confederate governments naturally turned to the manufacturing companies financially and physically able to handle them. The selective process was accelerated because larger firms could pay an agent in Washington or Richmond who understood the requirements of the army and navy—as well as those of influential congressmen and bureaucrats.

Most important of all, the wartime experience changed attitudes toward the role of the national government in the economy. Since the destruction of the Second Bank of the United States in the Jackson era, the national government had done little to regulate or control the economy, but during the war both the Union and the Confederate governments took steps that affected every branch of economic life. In passing the Homestead Act of May 20, 1862, which offered any citizen 160 acres of the public domain after five years of continuous residence, the Union Congress signaled its intention henceforth to give more attention to the nation's farmers, as it did in creating a federal Department of Agriculture that same year. The Morrill Act of 1862, giving vast tracts of the public domain to endow agricultural (land-grant) colleges, was further evidence of the same purpose. Both governments found it necessary to regulate transportation, especially railroads, during the war. Davis, despite his strict interpretation of the Confederate Constitution, urged his Congress to finance the construction of some missing links in the Southern rail system. Lincoln in July 1862 signed the Pacific Railroad Act, giving enormous tracts of the public land to support the construction of a transcontinental rail route.

In both the United States and the Confederacy, private citizens became aware, often for the first time, of the economic impact of their national governments. In the Confederacy, the Impressment Act of March 1863 authorized government agents to seize civilians' food, horses, wagons, or other supplies if required for the army and to set an arbitrary price for the confiscated goods. In the Union the creation of a new national banking system in 1863 (amended and strengthened in 1864) meant, among other things, that a uniform national currency began to replace the dozens of issues by local banks. Citizens, paying national taxes in national currency, grew accustomed to the idea that their national government would henceforth play a positive role in the economic life of the country.

Inflation and Its Consequences

During the desperate final years of the Civil War, both Union and Confederate Treasury Departments had to experiment with new ways to finance the war. Both imposed broad excise duties. The Union internal revenue act of July 1, 1862, has been fairly characterized as an attempt to tax everything. Duties were imposed upon all sorts of manufactures, with a fresh duty levied each time the raw material underwent a new process. In a carriage, for instance, the leather, the cloth, the wood, and the metal would each be taxed; then the manufacturer was taxed for the process of putting them together; the dealer was taxed for selling the carriage; and the purchaser, having paid a sufficient price to cover all these duties, was taxed in addition for ownership. Heavy duties fell upon luxuries, like billiard tables and yachts, and taxes upon professions and occupations covered, as Representative James G. Blaine said, "bankers and pawn brokers, lawyers and horse-dealers, physicians and confectioners, commercial brokers and peddlers." Ultimately these taxes brought in about 21 percent of the total wartime expenditures of the Union government.

The Confederacy moved more slowly, but on April 24, 1863, it too adopted a comprehensive tax measure, which included an income tax, occupational and license taxes ranging from $40 for bowling alleys to $500 for bankers, and what a later generation would call an excess profits tax. A unique feature of the Confederate legislation was the tax-in-kind, which compelled producers of wheat, corn, oats, potatoes, sugar, cotton, tobacco, and other farm products to pay one-tenth of their crop each year to the government. A last, desperate attempt in March 1865 to tax all coin, bullion, and foreign exchange was made too late to have any effect. All told, the Confederacy raised only about 1 percent of its income from taxes.

The sale of bonds contributed little more to the Confederate treasury. Values were so uncertain in the wartime South that investors were afraid to tie up their money in such fixed investments, and doubts spread as to when and whether the Confederate government would even pay the interest on its obligations. In the Union, on the other hand, bonds became a major source of revenue. Unable initially to sell bonds even at a discount, Secretary Chase appointed his friend, Jay Cooke, the Philadelphia banker who also had an office in Washington, special agent of the Treasury Department. Using high-pressure advertising, Cooke launched an extensive propaganda campaign, extolling the merits of the "five-twenties" (bonds bearing 6 percent interest, which could be paid off at the expiration of five, and must be redeemed in twenty, years). He was so successful that between 600,000 and a million citizens were persuaded to invest in the public debt, and the entire loan of half a billion dollars was oversubscribed. But in 1864, as the war stretched on endlessly and victory appeared nowhere in sight, the market for bonds collapsed. Resigning for political reasons, Chase left office at an opportune moment to preserve his reputation as a financier, and Cooke went with him. Chase's successor, William Pitt Fessenden, could only raise money through short-term loans at an exorbitant rate of interest. Not until the very end of the war, when victory was obviously near, did the sale of Union bonds pick up, and Cooke, reappointed special agent, attracted large additional numbers of investors.

The Resort to Paper Money. Necessarily, therefore, both governments continued to depend upon

paper money. The Union treasury, which had cautiously issued its first greenbacks in 1862, continued to print more and more during the rest of that year and during 1863 as well, until most of the $450 million authorized by Congress was in circulation. The value of the greenbacks gradually declined. A Union treasury note with a face value of one dollar was worth 99.86¢ in gold in 1862, but by 1864 it was worth only 62.66¢ and by early 1865, 50.3¢. In the Confederacy, where the printing presses never stopped, paper money had even less value. Perhaps $2 billion in unredeemable paper was issued in all. A Confederate treasury note for one dollar, worth 82.7¢ in gold in 1862, dropped to 29¢ in 1863 and to 1.7¢ in early 1865. In a desperate attempt to check the slide, the Confederate Congress in February 1864 undertook a partial repudiation of these notes, but the confusing and complex legislation was badly administered and served further to undermine trust in the government and its money. Having lost the confidence of the country, Memminger resigned in the summer of 1864—at about the same time that Chase left the Union Treasury Department. His successor, the South Carolina banker and businessman George A. Trenholm, could devise no better solution for the Confederacy's financial woes than to urge citizens to donate to the government their money, jewels, gold and silver plate, and public securities.

The excessive amount of paper money was only one of many factors that produced runaway inflation in both the North and the South. With importations

UNION PAPER MONEY:
A "GREENBACK"
Secretary Chase decided to print Union legal-tender notes with a patented green ink. Consequently they became known as "greenbacks."

largely cut off, in the North by the highly protective tariff and in the South by the Union blockade, with the productive labor force sharply reduced because of the number of men in military service, and with a huge portion of all goods required to supply the armies and navies, civilians had to expect shortages and high prices.

Profits and Deprivation. In both sections there were some who profited from the wartime economy. War contracts helped pull the Union economy out of a sharp depression, and higher prices spurred on manufacturers, who could now look for higher profits. The demand for grain, along with the Homestead Act, encouraged new settlers to begin farming, and the development of new industries, like petroleum, made for quick fortunes. The wartime boom in the North had a hectic quality about it, and men spent their easily earned money quickly lest it be worth less in the future. Many of the new rich were extravagant and hedonistic. Censoriously the New York *Independent* asked in June 1864:

Who at the North would ever think of war, if he had not a friend in the army, or did not read the newspapers? Go into Broadway, and we will show you what is meant by the word "extravagance." Ask [A. T.] Stewart [the department-store owner] about the demand for camel's-hair shawls, and he will say "monstrous." Ask Tiffany what kinds of diamonds and pearls are called for. He will answer "the prodigious," "as near hen's-egg size as possible," "price no object." What kinds of carpetings are now wanted? None but "extra." . . . And as for horses the medium-priced five-hundred-dollar kind are all out of the market. A good pair of "fast ones" . . . will go for a thousand dollars sooner than a basket of strawberries will sell for four cents.

But not all elements in the North shared in this wartime prosperity. Wages lagged sadly behind prices, so that in real income a worker between 1861 and 1865 lost 35 percent of his wages. Women, who composed one-fourth of the nation's manufacturing force in 1860, were especially hard hit. As more and more wives and mothers found it necessary to work, since soldiers could only send them a pittance for support, employers actually cut their wages. Even the United States government participated in this practice. At the Philadelphia armory, the government

in 1861 paid a seamstress 17¢ for making a shirt; three years later, when prices were at their highest, it cut the wage to 15¢. Meanwhile private contractors paid only 8¢.

Suffering in the North was, however, relatively minor when compared to that in the South. To be sure, residents of some parts of the agricultural South who were never disturbed by Union troops had only minor shortages to complain of. As imported goods disappeared from the grocers' shelves, they resorted to sassafras tea and to "coffee" made of parched rye, okra seeds, corn, and even sweet potatoes, the grounds of which were said to form a remarkable cleaning agent for curtains and carpets. Since salt was in short supply, meat could not be preserved, and Southerners ate more chicken and fish. As clothing wore out, they increasingly turned to homespun, and velvet draperies and brocaded rugs found new use as gowns and overcoats.

The thousands of Southerners in the path of the armies had to think not just of shortages but of survival. Hundreds of families fled before the invading Union armies, often attempting to take their slaves with them, but nowhere could these refugees find assurance of safety. Their lives took on a desperate, nightmarish quality, and merely existing from one day to the next was a struggle. There was never enough of anything, including food. Recalling these unhappy days, one writer declared that "the Confederacy was always hungry."

The greatest destitution appeared in towns and cities, where supplies had to be brought in over the rickety Southern railroad system. White-collar workers, especially those on fixed salaries from the government, were particularly hard hit. The celebrated diary of J. B. Jones, a clerk in the Confederate War Department at Richmond, is a melancholy record of shortages and high prices. In May 1864 he reported that beans in Richmond were selling for $3 a quart, meal for $125 a bushel, and flour $400 a barrel. Richmond, he observed, was an astonishingly clean city, since "no garbage or filth can accumulate." The citizens of the Confederate capital were obliged to be "such good scavengers" that there was "no need of buzzards."

Deprivation was the more painful because, as in

the North, some made enormous profits from the war. The blockade runner, who preferred to bring in compact, expensive items like silks and jewels rather than bulky supplies for the army, often reaped fantastic profits. Speculators flourished. As early as the winter of 1862, the governor of Mississippi learned that the families of volunteers in his state were seriously suffering for want of corn and salt, while rich planters held back their ample supply of both commodities, waiting for the inevitable rise in prices. Even more remunerative was trading with the enemy, a practice completely illegal but tacitly condoned by both Confederate and Union officials. Southern women and men who were initiated into the mysteries of the trade bought up as much cotton as they could find in their neighborhoods and took it to convenient exchange points like Memphis and Natchez to sell to the Yankees for coffee, clothing, and luxuries. Late in the war they accepted payment in United States greenbacks, which Southerners valued more than their own depreciated money.

Conscription and Conflict

Along with economic inequity, the unfairness of conscription was the subject of bitter complaints on the part of both Northerners and Southerners during the Civil War. The Confederate conscription act of 1862 ostensibly made all able-bodied white males between the ages of eighteen and thirty-five equally eligible for military service, but the Southern Congress promptly began exempting large categories of men.

As men rushed to enter "bombproof" occupations and claim exemptions, the outcry against the Confederate conscription system grew louder. One of the most vociferous critics was Governor Joseph E. Brown of Georgia, who protested, "The conscription Act, at one fell swoop, strikes down the sovereignty of the States, tramples upon the constitutional rights and personal liberty of the citizens, and arms the President with imperial power." After attempting unsuccessfully to induce the Georgia supreme court to declare conscription unconstitutional, Brown pro-

ceeded to undermine the policy by naming his supporters to state jobs exempt from military service. According to some estimates he put 15,000 able-bodied Georgians into this exempt category; certainly he created 2,000 justices of the peace and 1,000 constables, none of whom had to serve in the army. Less prominent than Brown but equally potent were the critics who complained that conscription was class legislation that benefited the educated and the wealthy. They raised especial objection to the so-called "twenty-nigger" provision, which clearly favored planters at the expense of farmers. "Never did a law meet with more universal odium than the exemption of slave owners," wrote Senator James Phelan of Mississippi to President Davis. "It has aroused a spirit of rebellion . . . and bodies of men have banded together to desert."

Despite intense criticism and dubious results, the Davis administration continued conscription, for it saw no other way to raise the needed number of men. Indeed, as the war progressed, it was obliged to experiment with even more stringent legislation. In a new conscription act of February 17, 1864, the Confederate Congress declared that all white males between the ages of seventeen and fifty were subject to the draft, with the seventeen-year-old boys and the men above forty-five to serve as a reserve for local defense. As a concession to small planters, the act exempted one farmer or overseer for every plantation with fifteen slaves, but it abolished most other exemptions, on the theory that once skilled laborers were in the army the government could detail them to the forges and factories where they were most needed. Total mobilization of manpower was, however, far beyond the competence of the shaky Confederate government, and in practice the industrial-detail system never worked. As the Confederacy scraped the bottom of the barrel, more and more white Southerners began thinking about the one group of able-bodied males who did not serve in the armies, the Negroes.

In the North, too, conscription evoked bitter criticism. The first effective Northern draft act, passed by the Union Congress on March 3, 1863, was patently unfair. Declaring that all able-bodied males between the ages of twenty and forty-five (except for certain high governmental officials and the only sons of widows and infirm parents) were liable to military service, the act promptly contradicted itself by permitting those who could afford to do so to hire substitutes. In an effort to keep the price of substitutes down, it also permitted a man to purchase outright exemption from military service for $300.

As in the South, there was immediate and widespread hostility toward conscription. The system favored the wealthiest citizens and the most prosperous sections of the country. A well-to-do man like George Templeton Strong of New York, for example, did not dream of serving in the army; he paid $1,100 for a substitute, "a big 'Dutch' boy of twenty or thereabouts," who, as Strong remarked complacently, "looked as if he could do good service." Rich towns and counties raised bounty funds to encourage volunteering, so that none of their citizens would have to be drafted, and as the war progressed, they offered higher and higher bounties. The volunteers they sought were by no means all local residents who needed a little financial inducement; many of them were professional bounty hunters, who went from place to place, enlisting, receiving bounties, and promptly deserting. Perhaps the record for bounty jumping was held by one John O'Connor, who when arrested in March 1865 confessed to thirty-two such desertions.

Part of the outcry against conscription in the North stemmed from the inequity of the quotas the president was authorized to announce for each state, presumably giving credit for the number of volunteers it had previously supplied. The Democratic governor of New York, Horatio Seymour, engaged in acrimonious correspondence with Lincoln and finally forced the president to admit that the quota assigned to the Empire State was excessive. Such concessions, however, came too late to placate those threatened by the draft. In Wisconsin, Kentucky, and Pennsylvania, in Troy, Newark, and Albany, there was outright resistance to the enrolling officers, and in several instances Federal troops had to be brought in to quell the insurgents. None of these outbreaks compared in extent or ferocity to that in New York City, where the drawing of the first draftees' names triggered a three-day riot (July 13–15, 1863) by a mob of predominantly Irish workingmen. Turning first against the enrollment officers and the police, the rioters then exhibited their hostility toward the rich by plundering fine houses and rifling jewelry stores. Toward Negroes, whom the rioters feared as economic competitors and blamed for the war and hence for conscription, the mob acted with hideous brutal-

THE NEW YORK DRAFT RIOTS: BATTLE IN SECOND AVENUE AND 22ND STREET AT THE UNION STEAM WORKS, JULY 14, 1863
Conscription triggered resistance in the North. The largest riot was in New York City, where Federal troops, fresh from the Gettysburg campaign, had to be called in to restore order. *(The New York Public Library)*

ity. After sacking and looting a Negro orphan asylum they chased down any blacks unwary enough to appear on the streets and left those they could capture hanging from lampposts. The Union government had to rush in troops from the Gettysburg campaign to stop the rioting and disperse the mob.

Despite all resistance, Lincoln's government continued conscription because, as in the Confederacy, there seemed to be no other source for soldiers. Even so, the draft remained cumbersome and often ineffectual. In 1864, for instance, 800,000 names were drawn, but so many were exempted because of health or occupation and so many other hired substitutes or paid the commutation fee that only 33,000 were actually inducted into the army. As conscription proved both unfair and ineffective, citizens in the North, like those in the South, began to think of the value of black soldiers.

Steps Toward Emancipation

Just as the Negro played a central part in causing the Civil War, so was he to play a major role in determining its outcome. At the outset there was a tacit agreement that the Civil War was to be a white man's fight, and both Union and Confederate governments in 1861 refused to accept black regiments. In the Confederacy during the first two years of the war, virtually nobody questioned the correctness of this decision. After all, as Vice-President Alexander H. Stephens announced, slavery was "the real 'cornerstone' " upon which the Confederate States had been erected, and few Southern whites could even contemplate the possibility of putting arms into the hands of slaves or of freeing blacks who became soldiers.

In the Union, on the other hand, there were from the beginning powerful voices urging the emancipation of slaves and the enlistment of black men in the army. Frederick Douglass, the leading spokesman of blacks in the North, constantly insisted: "Teach the rebels and traitors that the price they are to pay for the attempt to abolish this Government must be the abolition of slavery." Abolitionists, white

and black, repeatedly instructed Lincoln that he could win the war only if he emancipated the slaves. Senator Charles Sumner of Massachusetts visited the White House almost daily in his efforts to persuade Lincoln that emancipation was the *"one way to safety,* clear as sunlight—pleasant as the paths of Peace."

So influential was this antislavery sentiment that several of the president's subordinates who fell into disfavor with the administration tried to appeal to it. But President Lincoln, aware of the dangerous complexity of the issue, patiently overruled each of these subordinates, declaring that emancipation was a question "which, under my responsibility, I reserve to myself."

Nonmilitary Employment of Blacks.   Unwillingness to arm or emancipate the slaves did not signify any reluctance to employ blacks in nonmilitary service. Slaves were the backbone of the Confederate labor force. Had blacks not continued to till and harvest the grain, the Confederacy could never have fielded so large an army. Equally important was the role played by blacks, slave and free, in the industrial production of the Confederacy. In the Tredegar Iron Works, for example, half the 2,400 employees were blacks; they included not merely unskilled workers but puddlers, rollers, and machinists. Blacks also performed indispensable service for the quartermaster and commissary departments of the Confederacy, serving as teamsters, butchers, drovers, boatmen, bakers, shoemakers, and blacksmiths, and they were nurses in many Confederate hospitals.

So essential was Negro labor to the existence of the Confederacy that President Davis had to ensure that enough blacks were available for this service. From the beginning of the war, Confederate authorities from time to time compelled slaves to work on fortifications, and some states, notably Virginia, moved promptly to require owners to lease their slaves to the government when needed. But the Confederate government itself did not act until March 1863, when the Confederate Congress, despite much opposition from planters, authorized the impressment of slaves, whose owners were to receive

A BLACK FAMILY ON THE J. J. SMITH PLANTATION, BEAUFORT, SOUTH CAROLINA, 1862.
(Library of Congress)

valuable assets. Robert Smalls and his brother, who were slaves in Charleston, South Carolina, in May 1862 daringly seized the Confederate sidewheel steamer *Planter*, navigated it out of the harbor ringed with Confederate guns, and delivered it to the blockading Union fleet.

Debate Over Emancipation in the North. When the war appeared to have reached a stalemate, Northern sentiment in favor of freeing and arming the slaves grew. Republican congressmen were ahead of the president on these questions. As early as August 1861, they had passed an act declaring that slaves used to support the Confederate military were free. In March 1862 Congress forbade the return of fugitive slaves by the military. And on July 17, 1862, in a far-reaching confiscation act, it declared that slaves of all persons supporting the rebellion should be "forever free of their servitude, and not again [to be] held as slaves." These measures were, however, poorly drafted and not readily enforced, so that they had little practical consequence. More effective was the act of April 16, 1862, abolishing slavery in the District of Columbia.

But powerful forces in the North were opposed to emancipation. The border states, where slavery still prevailed, were of such uncertain loyalty that they might try to break away from the Union if emancipation became a Northern war aim. In the free states, anti-Negro prejudice was rampant, and many feared that emancipation would produce a massive migration of blacks to the North, where they would compete with white laborers for jobs. Belief in the inferiority of the Negro race was general, and the experience of Union soldiers in the South often strengthened this stereotype, for the fugitives who fled to their camps were mostly illiterate, ragged, and dirty.

During the initial stages of the war Lincoln, who hated slavery, could move toward emancipation only in a circuitous fashion. In early 1862 he made an earnest, though ultimately unsuccessful, plea to the border states to devise plans of gradual, compensated emancipation, for which he promised federal financial assistance. At the same time, he took anti-Negro sen-

$30 a month. In February 1864 it permitted military authorities to impress more slaves, with or without the consent of the owners.

Meanwhile the Union was also making full use of the labor of blacks. As slaves fled from their masters to the camps of the Union army, they were put to use as teamsters, cooks, nurses, carpenters, scouts, and day laborers. Perhaps half a million blacks crossed over to the Union lines, and nearly 200,000 of these performed labor for the army. Many of these "contrabands" brought with them valuable information about the disposition of Confederate troops and supplies. Occasionally some brought even more

FERROTYPE OF SERGEANT J. L. BALLDWIN OF COMPANY G, 56TH U.S. COLORED INFANTRY

Early in the war even President Lincoln thought "that the organization, equipment and arming of negroes, like other soldiers, would be productive of more evil than good." But after the Emancipation Proclamation the Union government began systematically to recruit for colored military units. By the end of the war 178,895 black soldiers were serving in the Union armies, and they saw action in Virginia, South Carolina, Florida, Mississippi and elsewhere. "The emancipation policy and the use of colored troops," Lincoln declared, were "the heaviest blow yet dealt to the rebellion." *(Chicago Historical Society)*

timent into account by favoring plans to colonize freedman in Central America and in Haiti.

By the fall of 1862, however, Lincoln felt able to act decisively against slavery. By failing to adopt his program of gradual emancipation, the border states had lost their chance. Blacks showed little interest in his plans for colonization, which in any case were poorly thought out and could only lead to disaster. As casualties mounted, Northern soldiers, without necessarily shedding their prejudices against Negroes,

came to think it was time to enroll blacks in the army. But most influential in changing Lincoln's mind was his grim recognition after eighteen months of combat that the war could not be ended by traditional means. "We . . . must change our tactics or lose the war," he concluded.

Waiting only for McClellan to check Lee's invasion at Antietam, Lincoln issued, on September 22, 1862, a preliminary emancipation proclamation announcing that unless the rebellious states returned to their allegiance he would on January 1, 1863, declare that "all persons held as slaves" in the territory controlled by the Confederates were "then, thenceforward, and forever free." Since the president justified his action on the ground of military necessity, it was appropriate that the definitive Emancipation Proclamation at the beginning of the new year officially authorized the enrollment of black troops in the Union army.

Promptly the War Department began to accept Negro regiments. These were not, to be sure, the first black soldiers to serve in the war, for a few Negroes had been enrolled without permission from Washington in the Federal forces on the Sea Islands of South Carolina, in Louisiana, and in Kansas, but now large numbers of blacks joined the army. They were enrolled in segregated regiments, in nearly all cases with white officers, and they received less pay than did white soldiers. By the end of the war, the number of Negroes in the Union army totaled 178,895—more than twice the number of soldiers in the Confederate army at Gettysburg.

At first most Union officials thought black regiments would be useful only for garrison duty, but in bitterly contested engagements such as Fort Wagner and Port Hudson, Miliken's Bend and Nashville, they demonstrated how well they could and would fight. The battle record of these black troops did much to change popular Northern stereotypes of the Negro. In the early stages of the war, cartoonists and caricaturists portrayed blacks as invisible men; their faces were vague and featureless blobs of black, hardly human. But with emancipation and the enrollment of Negroes in the army, war artists began to take a closer look, to depict blacks with distinctive, recognizably human features, and finally, in a kind of per-

CHANGING NORTHERN IMAGES
OF THE BLACK MAN

The Dis-United States: A Black Business

Teaching the Negro Recruits the Use of the Minié Rifle

The Escaped Slave in the Union Army

verse tribute to their merit, to sketch them with Nordic profiles.

The South Moves Toward Emancipation. Meanwhile, and much more slowly, sentiment was growing in the Confederacy for the military employment of blacks. Support for arming the slaves emerged first in those areas scourged by Northern armies. After Grant's successful Vicksburg campaign, the Jackson *Mississippian* boldly called for enrolling slaves as soldiers in the Confederate army. Though other Mississippi and Alabama newspapers echoed the call for black recruits, the most powerful voice for arming the slaves was that of General Patrick R. Cleburne, who witnessed how easily the powerful Union army broke the thin Confederate line at Chattanooga. Seeing no other source of manpower, Cleburne, together with his aides, addressed a long letter to General Joseph E. Johnston, who had succeeded Bragg as commander of the army of Tennessee, urging "that we immediately commence training a large reserve of the most courageous of our slaves, and further that we guarantee freedom within a reasonable time to every slave in the South who shall remain true to the Confederacy in this war."

So drastic a proposal was bound to rouse strong opposition, and President Davis, upon learning of Cleburne's letter, ordered it suppressed. But the subject would not die. As Union armies moved closer to the Confederate heartland, Virginia editors also began to urge arming the blacks, and at an October 1864 meeting Southern governors proposed "a change of policy on our part" as to the slaves. Finally, on November 7, 1864, President Davis, in a deliberately obscure message to Congress, put himself at the head of the movement. Urging further impressment of blacks for service with the army, Davis argued that the Confederate government should purchase the impressed slaves.

However obscurely phrased, Davis's proposal clearly looked toward the end of slavery, and it at once encountered powerful resistance. Davis, said his enemies, proposed the confiscation of private property; he was subverting the Constitution. His plan would be a confession to the world of the South's

weakness. It would deplete the labor force needed to feed the army. And most frightening of all, it would arm black men, who at best might desert to the Union armies and at worst might use those arms against their masters.

Despite all opposition, the Confederate government pushed ahead with the plan, for it had no other reservoir of manpower. In February 1865 the scheme received the backing of General Lee, who wrote that employing blacks as soldiers was "not only expedient but necessary" and announced plainly that "it would be neither just nor wise . . . to require them to serve as slaves." The next month the Confederate Congress passed, by a very close vote, an act calling for 300,000 more soldiers, irrespective of color. No provision was made in the act to free blacks who enrolled, but the Confederate War Department in effect smuggled emancipation into the measure through the orders it issued for its enforcement. Promptly the recruiting of black troops began, and some black companies were raised in Richmond and other towns. By this time, however, it was too late, even for such a revolutionary experiment, and none of the black Confederate soldiers ever saw service.

Europe and the War

Though the Union and Confederate governments moved toward emancipating and arming the blacks because of military necessity, both recognized how profoundly their actions affected the continuing struggle for European recognition and support. Well-informed Americans were aware of the intensity of European antislavery sentiment. But so long as neither government took a bold stand against the South's peculiar institution, European antislavery leaders were puzzled and divided by the war. Lincoln's Emancipation Proclamation ended the confusion. European antislavery spokesmen soon recognized that the proclamation marked a new era. Within three months after the final Emancipation Proclamation was issued, fifty-six large public meetings were held in Great Britain to uphold the Northern cause.

Union diplomacy had need of such popular support, for there still lurked the possibility of European intervention in the war. Though the gravest threat had passed in the fall of 1862, before the full effect of the Emancipation Proclamation could be sensed abroad, the French emperor continued to contemplate the advantages that might come of meddling in American affairs. Hoping that a divided United States would assist enterprise of establishing a puppet empire under the Emperor Maximilian in Mexico, Napoleon in February 1863, when Northern military fortunes were at their nadir after Fredericksburg, offered to mediate between the two belligerents. Shrewdly judging that Great Britain and Russia were not behind the French move, Secretary of State Seward spurned the offer.

More dangerous to the Union cause than Napoleon's clumsy diplomacy were the warships being built for the Confederacy in British shipyards. Supplying either belligerent in a war with armed ships was contrary both to international law and to British statutes, but through a loophole in the law it was legal to sell separately unarmed vessels and the armaments that would convert them into men of war. In March 1862 the ship that became the C.S.S. *Florida* sailed from a British shipyard, and in July of that year the more powerful *Alabama* set forth to begin her depredations. Even as these raiders swept the Union merchant marine from the high seas, a more formidable Confederate naval threat, this time to the blockade itself, was being forged in the form of two enormous ironclad steam rams under construction at the Laird yards in Liverpool.

The British government wished to observe its neutrality laws, but the legal machinery was slow and cumbersome. When Union minister Charles Francis Adams called the attention of the foreign office to the rams, Lord Russell replied that he could not act to detain them unless there was convincing evidence of Confederate ownership. Adams and his aides rushed to secure affidavits to prove that the vessels were intended for the Confederacy, but British law officers were unconvinced. Finally, in utter exasperation, Adams on September 5, 1863, sent Russell a final warning against permitting the ships to sail, adding: "It would be superfluous in me to point out to your Lordship that this is war." Fortunately, two days before receiving Adams's ultimatum, Russell had already decided to detain the rams, and the Confederates' final hope of breaking the blockade was lost.

With that crisis, the last serious threat of European involvement in the American war disappeared. So indifferent, or even hostile, to the Southern cause was the British cabinet that late in 1863 Confederate Secretary of State Benjamin ordered Mason, his envoy, to leave London on the grounds that "the Government of Her Majesty [Queen Victoria] ... entertains no intention of receiving you as the accredited minister of this government."

Keenly aware of the influence that emancipation had exerted in uniting European opinion against the South, President Davis sought similarly to capitalize on the actions that the Confederate States took against slavery during the final months of the war. In January 1865 he sent Duncan F. Kenner, one of the largest slaveholders in Louisiana, on a secret mission to Europe, authorizing him to promise the emancipation of the slaves in return for European recognition and aid to the Confederacy. The experiment came too late, for now it was evident that Northern victory was inevitable. Neither the French nor the British government expressed interest in Kenner's proposal.

Wartime Politics in the Confederacy

The military and diplomatic advantages resulting from emancipation were to a considerable extent counterbalanced by its political disadvantages. In the Confederacy there had been from the beginning of the war a sizable disloyal element. Unionism was strong in the Upper South, in the mountain regions, and in some of the poorer hill counties. As the war progressed, some of these disaffected Southerners joined secret peace societies, such as the Order of the Heroes, which had its following in the Carolinas and Virginia. Disloyalty extended into the ranks of the Confederate army, especially after conscription was initiated, and desertion was widespread. About one out of every nine soldiers who enlisted in the Confederate army deserted. Sometimes they formed guerrilla bands that preyed equally upon Confederate and Union sympathizers. When halted by an enrolling officer and asked to show his pass to leave the army, a deserter would pat his gun defiantly and say, "This is my furlough."

Probably no action of the Davis administration could have won over these actively disloyal citizens, but the policies of the Confederate government alienated also a large number of entirely loyal Southerners. Some of these critics complained that President Davis was timid and tardy. He was sickly, neurasthenic, and indecisive, they said; he could not tolerate strong men around him and relied for advice upon sycophants; he did not know how to rouse the loyalty and the passions of the Southern people; he lacked courage to put himself at the head of the Southern armies and lead the Confederacy to victory.

A much larger group of Confederates censured their president for exactly opposite reasons. Davis's plan to arm and free the slaves reinforced their conviction that he intended to undermine the principles upon which the Confederacy had been founded. Conscription, they argued, had begun the subversion of state sovereignty, guaranteed by the Constitution. They found evidence of Davis's dictatorial ambitions in his requests that Congress suspend the writ of habeas corpus, so that the disloyal could be arrested and imprisoned without trial. Grudgingly Congress agreed to the suspension for three limited periods, but late in 1864 it rejected Davis's appeals for a further extension on the ground that it would be a dangerous assault upon the Constitution. Although infringements of civil liberties were infrequent in the Confederacy and no Southern newspaper was suppressed for publishing subversive editorials, the critics warned that Davis was reaching after imperial powers. Leading this group of Davis's critics was none other than the vice-president of the Confederate states, Alexander H. Stephens, who spent most of the final years of the war not in Richmond but in Georgia, stirring up agitation against the president's allegedly unconstitutional usurpation of power and simultaneously complaining of Davis's "weakness and imbecility."

The congressional elections of 1863, held after Southerners had begun to realize the gravity of their defeats at Gettysburg and at Vicksburg, greatly strengthened the anti-Davis bloc. During the following year, the president was often able to muster a majority in Congress only because of the consistent support of representatives from districts overrun or threatened by advancing Federal armies. In some instances these districts were unable to hold regular elections in 1863 and their incumbent congressmen, chosen in the early days of complete commitment to the Confederate cause, remained in office; in any case, representatives from these occupied regions had little to lose from measures that taxed and bled the rest of the Confederacy. But by the desperate winter of 1864–65, not even this support could give Davis control of Congress. Now in a majority, his critics refused his request for control over the state militias and rejected his plea to end all exemptions from conscription. Even as Sherman's army advanced through the Carolinas, Congress endlessly debated his plan for arming the slaves. It passed, over Davis's opposition, an act creating the post of general in chief, advising the president to name Lee. Fearful of attacking the president directly, congressional critics began investigations of several of his cabinet officers, and they introduced resolutions declaring that the resignation of Secretary of State Judah P. Benjamin, Davis's closest friend and most trusted adviser, would be "subservient of the public interest." Secretary of War Seddon also came under fire, and when the Virginia delegation in Congress called for his resignation, he felt obliged to leave the cabinet. In January 1865, for the first and only time, the Confederate Congress overrode a presidential veto.

Wartime Politics in the North

Meanwhile in the North, Abraham Lincoln and his government were subjected to the same kinds of criticism. Pro-Confederate sympathy was strongest in the states of the Upper South that remained in the Union, in those parts of the Old Northwest originally settled by Southerners, and in cities like New

York, where the Irish immigrant population was bitterly hostile to blacks. Northerners joined secret societies, such as the Knights of the Golden Circle and the Order of American Knights, devoted to bringing about a negotiated peace, which inevitably would entail recognizing Confederate independence. Though most members of these secret "Copperhead" organizations intended nothing more subversive than replacing a Republican administration with a Democratic one, some of the leaders were ready to accept a dissolution of the Union. Some idea of the extent of disaffection in the North can be gained from the figures on desertion. One out every seven men who enlisted in the Union armies deserted.

Much of the criticism of the Lincoln administration came from those who were entirely loyal to the Union but who deplored the measures the president took to save it. They bitterly complained when Lincoln, without waiting for congressional approval, suspended the writ of habeas corpus so that suspected subversives could be arrested without warning and imprisoned indefinitely. Though Chief Justice Roger B. Taney protested against the unconstitutionality of these arrests, Lincoln refused to heed his objections, and more than 13,000 persons were thus arbitrarily imprisoned. Critics also complained when the Lincoln administration curbed the freedom of the press. Because of the publication of allegedly disloyal and incendiary statements, the Chicago *Times*, the New York *World*, the Philadelphia *Evening Journal*, and many other newspapers were required to suspend publication for varying periods of time.

Lincoln's Emancipation Proclamation, followed by the arming of black soldiers, gave his critics further evidence of his ambition to become dictator and of his diabolical plan to change the purpose of the war. So unpopular was the policy of emancipation that Lincoln's preliminary proclamation, together with the inability of Union generals to win victories, seriously hurt his party in the congressional elections of 1862. In virtually every Northern state there was an increase in Democratic votes. The Republican majority in Congress was now paper-thin, and the administration kept that lead only because the army interfered in the Maryland, Kentucky, and Missouri elections. Just as Jefferson Davis's control of the Confederate Congress after 1863 depended upon the votes of border state representatives, so Abraham Lincoln's majority in the Union Congress rested upon the support of representatives from the same region.

Republican Criticism of Lincoln. If Democrats complained that Lincoln acted arbitrarily and too swiftly, critics within his own party held that he was too slow, too cautious, and too indecisive. His own attorney general, Edward Bates, felt that Lincoln had the ability to cope with "neither great *principles* nor great *facts*." He lacked "practical talent for his important place," concluded Senator Sumner, since in inertia and indecisiveness he resembled Louis XVI more than any other ruler in history.

So widespread was dissatisfaction with Lincoln that when Congress reassembled in December 1862, after the fiasco at Fredericksburg, the Senate Republican caucus tried to force the president to change his cabinet. Just as Davis's critics made Benjamin their target, so Republican senators blamed Secretary of State Seward for the weakness of the Lincoln administration and the maladministration of the war. By forcing Seward's resignation, they hoped to make Chase, who had fed them stories of Lincoln's incompetence, in effect premier. Deeply distressed by this maneuver, Lincoln thwarted it with great adroitness, by securing Seward's resignation and forcing Chase also to offer his. Announcing that either resignation would leave his cabinet unbalanced, he declined them both. His cabinet remained intact, and the president remained responsible for Union policy.

Such sleight of hand was not enough to make dissent within Lincoln's own party disappear, and there gradually emerged two rival Republican factions, the Conservatives (or Moderates) and the Radicals (or "Jacobins," as their enemies called them). Represented by Seward in the cabinet and by Senator James R. Doolittle of Wisconsin in Congress, the Conservatives continued to think the war could be won by conventional means, and were opposed to such experiments as emancipation, the arming of

"PRESIDENT LINCOLN WRITING THE PROCLAMATION OF FREEDOM," BY DAVID GILMOUR BLYTHE: A NORTHERN VIEW

A Northern artist shows Lincoln consulting the history of the United States, United States court decisions, Daniel Webster's views of the Constitution, and other documents in preparing his Emancipation Proclamation. A bust of the ineffectual President Buchanan hangs by a noose from the book case. *(Library of Congress)*

"LINCOLN WRITING THE EMANCIPATION PROCLAMATION," BY ADALBERT VOLCK: A SOUTHERN VIEW

A Confederate caricaturist depicts Lincoln with his foot on the Constitution, sitting beneath a painting of slave insurrection in Santo Domingo, as he dips his pen into an inkwell held by Satan to draft the procalmation of freedom. *(Courtesy, Museum of Fine Arts, Boston)*

slaves, and the confiscation of rebel property. The Radicals, on the other hand, represented by Chase in the cabinet and by Sumner and Thaddeus Stevens in the Congress, were eager to try more drastic experiments; they demanded that the entire Southern social system be revolutionized, that Southern slaveholders be punished, and, increasingly, that blacks should have not merely freedom but civil and political equality.

Lincoln refused to align himself with either faction and tried to be even-handed in distributing federal patronage to both. He shared the desire of the Conservatives for a speedy peace and a prompt reconciliation between the sections, but he recognized that in casting about for votes to carry through their plans, they would be "tempted to affiliate with those whose record is not clear," even persons infected "by the virus of secession." As for the Radicals, he conceded that "after all their faces are set Zionwards," but he objected to their "petulant and vicious fretfulness" and thought they were sometimes "almost *fiendish*" in attacking Republicans who disagreed with them. For his neutrality, the president gained the distrust and abuse of both factions.

The Election of 1864. The schism within the Republican party was the more serious because the presidential election of 1864 was approaching. In General George B. McClellan the Democrats had a handsome, glamorous candidate, and they had a powerful set of issues. They could capitalize upon war weariness. They made much of Lincoln's arbitrary use of executive power and the infringement of civil liberties. They objected to the unfairness of the draft. They showed how the Republican Congress had benefited the Northeast by enacting protective tariffs, handing out railroad subsidies, and creating a national banking system. Endlessly the Democrats rang the changes on the anti-Negro theme, charging that the Lincoln administration had changed a war for Union into a war for emancipation. If Lincoln was reelected, they charged, Republicans were planning to amalgamate the black and white races; the word "miscegenation" made its first appearance in an 1864 campaign document.

MCCLELLAN POSTER

Both war Democrats and peace Democrats attended the national party convention that assembled in Chicago on August 29, 1864. To please the former the convention chose as the Democratic presidential candidate General George B. McClellan, who favored vigorous prosecution of the war and claimed that he could be more effective than Abraham Lincoln. To placate the peace Democrats the convention adopted a platform calling for a cessation of hostilities and condemning "four years of failure to restore the Union by the experiment of war." With the nominee facing one direction and the platform slanting in another, the Democratic drive for the presidency was probably doomed from the start, but the victories of Union armies in the South cinched the reelection of Abraham Lincoln. *(Smithsonian Institution, Division of Political History)*

Even in the face of such powerful opposition, the Republicans in the winter of 1863–64 divided sharply when Lincoln in December 1863 announced a plan for reconstructing the Southern states. Promising amnesty to all Confederates except a few high government officials, the president proposed to reestablish civilian government in the conquered areas of the South when as few as 10 percent of the number of voters in 1860 took an oath swearing future loyalty to the United States Constitution and pledging acceptance of emancipation. Fearing that this program would replace the antebellum leadership in control of the South and would leave freedmen in peonage, the Radicals pushed through Congress the Wade-Davis bill, requiring that over half the number of 1860 voters in each Southern state swear allegiance and participate in drafting a new constitution before it would be readmitted to the Union. When Lincoln killed this measure, passed at the very end of the 1864 congressional session, by a pocket veto, Radicals were furious. Senator Benjamin F. Wade and Representative Henry Winter Davis, the sponsors of the vetoed bill, issued a manifesto, accusing the president of "usurpations" and claiming that he had committed a "studied outrage upon the legislative authority of the people."

Because Lincoln had control of the federal patronage and of the party machinery, he was readily renominated in June 1864 by the Republican national convention, which selected Andrew Johnson of Tennessee as his running mate, but the unanimity of the vote was only a façade. After an unsuccessful attempt to run Chase as a rival to Lincoln, some ultra-Radicals had already thrown their support to a third-party ticket headed by General Frémont, who had been hostile to the president since his removal from command in Missouri. Other Radicals tried, even after Lincoln had been renominated, to persuade the party to pick a new candidate. As late as September 1864 a questionnaire sent to Republican governors, leading editors, and prominent congressmen elicited a virtually unanimous response that if Lincoln could be persuaded to withdraw from the race, Republicans should name another standard-bearer. As Massachusetts Governor John A. Andrew

JEFF DAVIS'S NOVEMBER NIGHTMARE
A Northern cartoon shows Lincoln's reelection in 1864 as evidence that there would be no letting up in pressure upon the Confederacy. *(Library of Congress)*

expressed the general sentiment, Lincoln was "essentially lacking in the quality of leadership." So bleak was the outlook that the president himself a few weeks before the elections conceded that McClellan was likely to win.

Northern Victory

Until the fall of 1864, then, the wartime history of the United States and of the Confederate States moved in parallel lines as each government improvised experiments that might lead to victory. But in the finals months of the struggle the course of the two rivals markedly diverged. Increasing dissension and disaffection marked Jefferson Davis's last winter in office, while Abraham Lincoln won triumphant reelection in November 1864. By April 1865 the Confederacy was dead, and a month later Davis was in irons, like a common criminal, at Fort Monroe. The Union was victorious, and Lincoln, killed by the bullet of the mad assassin John Wilkes Booth, lived in memory as the nation's martyred president who freed the slaves and saved the Union.

Campaigns in the East, 1864–1865. The very different fates of the Lincoln and Davis administrations were decided, in large part, on the battlefield. When Grant became general in chief of the Union armies in 1864, he determined to make his headquarters not in Washington but with the often-defeated Army of the Potomac. Working closely with Meade, the actual commander of that army, he developed a plan for pushing Lee back upon the defenses of Richmond. Checked in the bloody battle of the Wilderness (May 5–7), Grant did not retreat, as previous Union generals had done, but pushed around Lee's right flank, attempting to get between him and the Confederate capital. Checked again at Spotsylvania (May 8–12), Grant again did not retreat but sent word to Washington: "I propose to fight it out along this line if it takes all summer."

After a disastrous direct assault on the Confederate lines at Cold Harbor (June 3), Grant again skill-

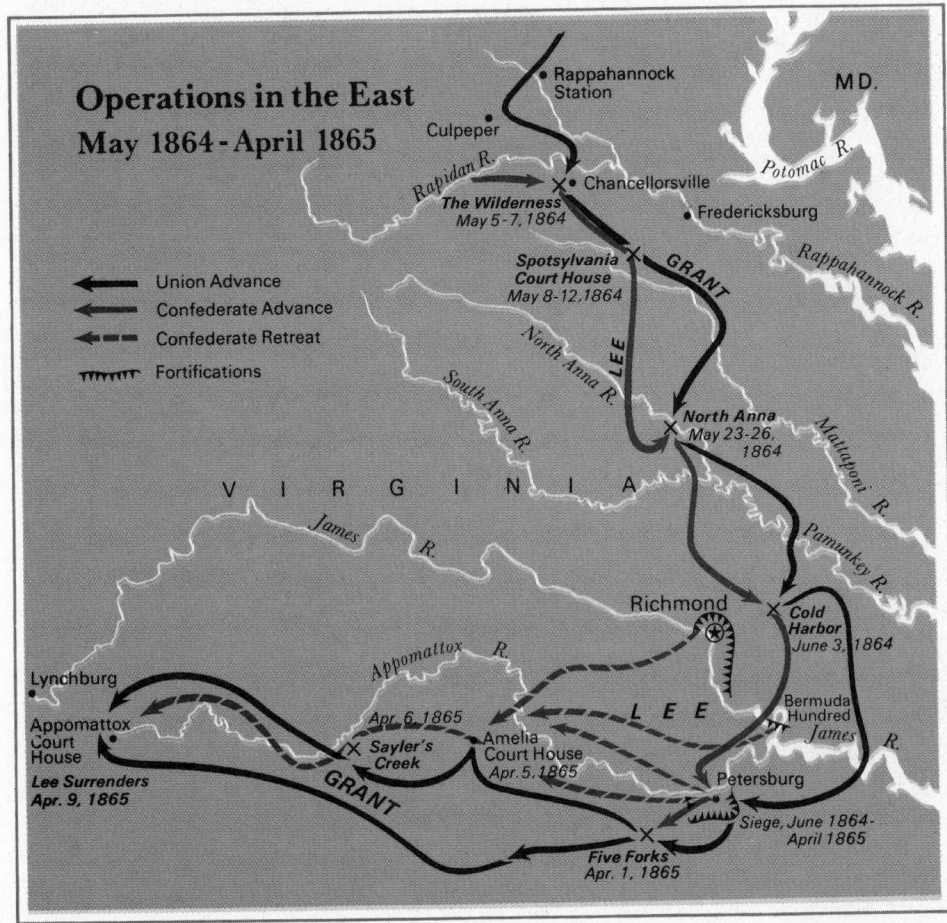

fully maneuvered around Lee's right flank, crossed the James River, and joined the Union troops already there under General Butler. He then instituted what became known as the "siege" of Petersburg and Richmond—incorrectly so, since the two cities were not fully surrounded and since supplies continued to come in from the South and West. But as Grant's lines constantly lengthened, he cut these access routes one by one. Pinned down before Richmond, Lee remembered "Stonewall" Jackson's brilliant diversionary campaign of 1862 and sent what men he could spare under Jubal A. Early into the Shenandoah Valley. Though Early achieved initial success and even pushed on to the outskirts of Washington, Grant did not loosen his grip on Richmond. Instead he sent brash, aggressive Philip H. Sheridan to the Shenandoah Valley, ordering him not merely to drive out the Confederates but to devastate the countryside so that thereafter a crow flying over it would have to carry its own rations. Sheridan followed his orders

explicitly, and Early's army was smashed. More than ever before, the fate of the Confederacy was tied to Richmond and to Lee's army.

Campaigns in the West, 1864–1865. Meanwhile, on May 7, 1864, Sherman began his slow progress through northwestern Georgia, opposed by the wily Joseph E. Johnston, who made the Union troops pay for every foot they advanced. But as Sherman neared the railroad hub of Atlanta, President Davis, who had never trusted Johnston, removed the general and put John B. Hood in command. In a series of attacks upon overwhelmingly superior Union forces—exactly the sort of engagement Johnston had so skillfully avoided—Hood was defeated; and on September 2 Sherman occupied Atlanta. News of the victory reached the North just before the presidential election and made a farce of the Democratic platform's assertion that the war was a "failure."

Next, casually dispatching Thomas to fend off

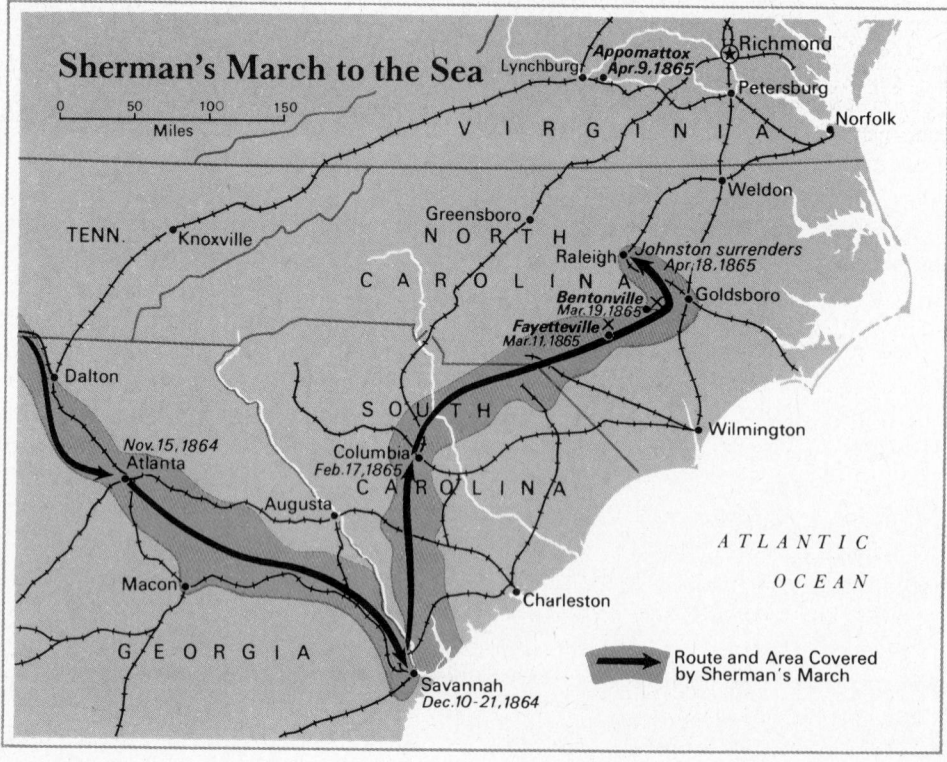

Sherman's March to the Sea

Route and Area Covered by Sherman's March

A DEAD CONFEDERATE SOLDIER AT FORT MAHONE, NEAR PETERSBURG, VIRGINIA, APRIL 2, 1865 In the final bloody battles of the war the Confederacy lost men who could not be replaced. "Where is this to end?" asked General Josiah Gorgas. "No money in the Treasury—no food to feed Gen. Lee's army—no troops to oppose Gen. Sherman—what does it all mean . . . ? Is the cause really hopeless?" *(Library of Congress)*

Hood and to hold Tennessee, Sherman turned his back on the smoking ruins of Atlanta and set out on a march toward Savannah and the sea, where he knew that a Union fleet was waiting with supplies.* Meeting only desultory resistance, Sherman's men cut a swath through central Georgia, destroying railroads, military supplies, and even many private houses. Sherman's objective was as much psychological as military. "I can make the march," he had promised Grant, "and make Georgia howl!"

Offering captured Savannah to Lincoln as a Christmas present, Sherman turned his army north, pushing aside the depleted Confederate forces, again under the command of Johnston. His men took Co-

lumbia, South Carolina, which was burned either by intention or by accident, and drove on into North Carolina. Grant, meanwhile, clamped down ever tighter on Richmond. At last, on April 2, 1865, Lee found his position untenable, and warning President Davis and his government to flee, he tried to lead his ragged troops to join Johnston's dwindling force. Cut off by Grant, he had no alternative but to surrender, and on April 9 at Appomattox Court House he told his weary, hungry men to lay down their arms. On April 18 Johnston followed by surrendering to Sherman (although the final terms were not agreed on until April 26). When the news reached the trans-Mississippi region, Kirby-Smith capitulated in June. The war had lasted almost precisely four years.

The Union cause, and the Lincoln administration, were the beneficiaries of these victories. The critics of the government had been most vocal, their opposi-

* Attempting to force Sherman to turn back, Hood invaded Tennessee but was checked in the battle of Franklin (November 30, 1864) and routed in the battle of Nashville (December 15–16).

tion most powerful, in the heartbreaking summer months of 1864, when Grant seemed to be getting nowhere in Virginia and Sherman appeared unable to bag his enemy in Georgia. Northern morale and support for the president mounted perceptibly at the news of Sherman's success at Atlanta and of Farragut's victory at Mobile Bay. Conversely, support for Davis's administration dwindled and critical voices became louder as Confederate reverse followed reverse. In a certain sense, then, victory begot victory, and defeat defeat.

Why the North Won the War. Yet this is circular reasoning and does not explain the final Union triumph after so many earlier Confederate successes. For a fuller understanding one must turn to the slow but steady mobilization of the North's infinitely superior economic resources and to the gradual erosion of those in the South. The effect of Northern economic and industrial superiority was not fully felt until after more than two years of war; it took time to award contracts, to expand factories, to recruit skilled laborers, and to deliver the products. But by 1863, observers noted that Lee's veterans invading Pennsylvania looked like a gaggle of "barefooted, ragged, lousy, [but] disciplined, desperate ruffians," so badly supplied and so poorly fed that their line of march was "traceable by the deposit of dysenteric stool the army leaves behind it." By 1863 the Union armies, on the other hand, were so completely equipped that their paraphernalia became a hindrance. When Northern soldiers advanced, they shucked off layers of greatcoats, blankets, and other unnecessary supplies. Nowhere was Northern economic superiority more evident by the end of the war than in its transportation system. By that time Southern railroads simply had worn out. In the Union, on the other hand, some 5,000 more miles of railroad were in operation in 1865 than at the start of the war—a figure that does not include the numerous military railroads operated in the South—and, under the necessity of linking up with the newly authorized Union Pacific Railroad, Northern lines all converted to a standard rail gauge.

But supplies do not fight wars, nor do trains; men do. From the start the overwhelming numerical preponderance of the Northern population counted heavily against the Confederacy, and during the conflict that advantage increased. During the four years of war more than 180,000 male immigrants of military age settled in the North, while there was virtually no immigration to the Confederacy. In addition, the black population of the country became another vast source of Union manpower. Confederates dared not tap this source until their cause was already lost.

But men, no matter how numerous, fight well only if ably led by their military commanders and inspired by their political leaders. It would be hard to argue that Northern generalship was superior to that of the South. While Grant has his admirers, to most students Robert E. Lee is the greatest Civil War commander. Nor is it easy to maintain that the political leadership of the North was markedly superior. Later generations, recalling the eloquence of the Gettysburg Address and the mystical beauty of the second inaugural address, have found it difficult to remember that for most of his administration Lincoln was considered uninspiring and ineffectual. Had Lincoln been defeated for reelection in 1864, he would doubtless be rated as an honest but unsuccessful president. On the other hand, had the Southern states been able to win their independence, Jefferson Davis would undoubtedly rank as the George Washington of the Confederacy.

There were, of course, important differences between the two wartime presidents, but these were of less significance than the differences in the political systems in which they had to work. Like many more recent emerging nations, the Confederacy tried to present a façade of unity to the world. It was a one-party, or more properly, a no-party state. Southerners feared that party divisions would suggest they were less than unanimous in seeking independence. The most careful analysis of the voting records of Confederate congressmen has been able to show, at most, only incipient party lines. Small temporary factions rather than permanent political parties dominated Congress. President Davis's enemies were many, and they were constantly attacking him from all directions, like a swarm of bees; his friends were divided, and he could never rally them into a unified cohort.

"GENERAL ROBERT E. LEE LEAVING THE MCLEAN HOUSE AFTER THE SURRENDER AT APPOMATTOX, 1865" BY A. W. WAUD

After accepting Grant's terms of surrender, Lee stepped out to the porch of the McLean House and signaled his orderly to bring up his horse. While the animal was being bridled, one of Grant's aides remembered, Lee "gazed sadly in the direction . . . where his army lay—now an army of prisoners. He thrice smote the palm of his left hand slowly with his right fist in an absent sort of way." Then he mounted, and Grant saluted him by raising his hat. "Lee raised his hat respectfully, and rode off at a slow trot to break the sad news to the brave fellows whom he had so long commanded." *(Library of Congress)*

As with the Congress, so with the people. It is safe to guess that if at any point the voters of the Confederacy had been asked to endorse their president or to topple him, Davis would have received overwhelming support. But lacking political parties, Southerners had no way of making this sentiment felt.

In the Union, on the other hand, the two-party system remained active. The Democrats remained a formidable, if not always united, force throughout the war. They came close to winning a majority in Congress in the 1862 elections; even in 1864 McClellan received 45 percent of the popular vote—at a time when the strongest opponents of the Republican party were still out of the Union and, of course, not voting. Such a powerful opposition party compelled the Republican factions, however bitterly at odds with each other, to work together. Conservatives and Radicals might disagree over slavery, emancipation, and reconstruction, but they all agreed that any Republican administration was better than a Democratic one. It was, then, the absence of political machinery in the South that weakened Davis's regime and rendered him unable fully to mobilize the material and spiritual resources of the Confederacy. And it was the much maligned two-party system that allowed Lincoln, despite quarrelsome and impassioned attacks from fellow Republicans, to experiment boldly and to grow into an effective wartime leader.

CHRONOLOGY

1863   Lincoln issues final Emancipation Proclamation.
Confederates defeat Union army under Hooker at Chancellorsville.
Lee's invasion of the North checked by Union army under Meade at Gettysburg.
Grant captures Vicksburg.
Draft riots in the North.
Confederate army under Bragg defeats Union forces at Chickamauga.
Union victory at Chattanooga (Lookout Mountain and Missionary Ridge).
Lincoln offers lenient reconstruction program.

1864   Grant named Union general in chief.
Grant's direct advance on Richmond checked at the Wilderness, Spotsylvania, and Cold Harbor.
Grant moves south of James River to begin "siege" of Petersburg.

Sherman pushes back Confederates under Joseph E. Johnston and captures Atlanta.
Farragut captures Mobile.
Lincoln reelected president over Democrat McClellan.
Sherman marches from Atlanta to the sea.

1865   Sherman pushes northward through South Carolina and North Carolina.
Lee gives up Petersburg and Richmond, and Confederate government flees.
Lee surrenders at Appomattox. Johnston surrenders to Sherman. Kirby-Smith surrenders Confederate forces west of the Mississippi.
Lincoln assassinated; Andrew Johnson becomes president.

SUGGESTED READINGS

The studies listed at the end of the previous chapter continue, for the most part, to be pertinent to the topics discussed in the present chapter.

Of the enormous literature on the military operations during the Civil War, only a few of the most important titles can be listed here. On the Northern armies, the most comprehensive works are Kenneth P. Williams's five-volume study, *Lincoln Finds a General* (1949–59), and Bruce Catton's absorbing trilogy: *Mr. Lincoln's Army* (1951); *Glory Road* (1952); and *A Stillness at Appomattox* (1953). Among the best biographies of Union generals are Warren W. Hassler, Jr., *General George B. McClellan* (1957); Bruce Catton, *Grant Moves South* (1960), and *Grant Takes Command* (1969); and Lloyd Lewis, *Sherman* (1932).

The most elaborate account of military operations from a Southern point of view is Shelby Foote, *The Civil War* (3 vols., 1958–74). Douglas S. Freeman, *Lee's Lieutenants* (3 vols., 1942–44), is an important examination of Confederate commanders in the eastern theater, while western operations receive excellent treatment in Thomas Connelly, *Army of the Heartland* (2 vols., 1967–71). Among the most significant biographies of Confederate generals are Douglas S. Freeman, *R. E. Lee* (4 vols., 1934–35),

Frank E. Vandiver, *Mighty Stonewall* (1957), and Grady McWhiney, *Braxton Bragg and Confederate Defeat* (1969).

On the recruitment of the Northern armies, see Fred A. Shannon, *The Organization and Administration of the Union Army* (2 vols., 1928), and Eugene C. Murdoch, *One Million Men: The Civil War Draft in the North* (1971). Adrian Cook, *Armies of the Street* (1974), is the definitive treatment of New York City draft riots. A. B. Moore, *Conscription and Conflict in the Confederacy* (1924), is still the best study of its subject.

Two books by Bell I. Wiley provide a fascinating social history of the common soldier of the Civil War: *The Life of Johnny Reb* (1943), and *The Life of Billy Yank* (1952).

The best accounts of Civil War naval operations are Virgil C. Jones, *The Civil War at Sea* (3 vols., 1960–62), and Bern Anderson, *By Sea and by River* (1962). See also John Niven's fine biography, *Gideon Welles: Lincoln's Secretary of the Navy* (1973).

On the function played by political parties in the Union and the Confederacy, see Eric L. McKitrick's brilliant essay, "Party Politics and the Union and Confederate War Efforts," in William N. Chambers and Walter D. Burnham, eds., *The American Party Systems* (1967), pp. 152–81. The story of Confederate politics has to be pieced together from Wilfred B. Yearns, *The Confederate Congress* (1960); Thomas B. Alexander and Richard E. Beringer, *The Anatomy of the Confederate Congress* (1972); Frank L. Owsley, *State Rights in the Confederacy* (1925); Georgia L. Tatum, *Disloyalty in the Confederacy* (1934); and James Z. Rabun, "Alexander H. Stephens and Jefferson Davis," *American Historical Review*, 58 (1953), 290–321. On Union politics, see William B. Hesseltine, *Lincoln and the War Governors* (1948); T. Harry Williams, *Lincoln and the Radicals* (1941); Grady McWhiney, ed., *Grant, Lee, Lincoln and the Radicals* (1964); Hans L. Trefousse, *The Radical Republicans* (1969); James A. Rawley, *The Politics of Union* (1974); and William F. Zornow, *Lincoln and the Party Divided* (1954). For conflicting interpretations of the amount of disaffection and disloyalty in the North, see Wood Gray, *The Hidden Civil War* (1942), George F. Milton, *Abraham Lincoln and the Fifth Column* (1942), and Frank L. Klement, *The Copperheads in the Middle West* (1960).

Benjamin Quarles, *The Negro in the Civil War* (1953), is a comprehensive study. James M. McPherson, ed., *The Negro's Civil War* (1965), is a valuable set of documents, skillfully interwoven. Bell I. Wiley, *Southern Negroes, 1861–1865* (1938), is the standard account; on Confederate moves toward emancipation it can be supplemented by Robert F. Durden's excellent study, *The Gray and the Blacks* (1972). The early chapters of Leon F. Litwack, *Been in the Storm So Long* (1979), superbly recapture the activities and attitudes of slaves during the war. Benjamin Quarles, *Lincoln and the Negro* (1962), and John H. Franklin, *The Emancipation Proclamation* (1963), are both valuable. James M. McPherson, *The Struggle for Equality* (1964), is a fine account of abolitionists' efforts during the war and afterward. The authoritative account of Negro troops in the Union army is Dudley T. Cornish, *The Sable Arm* (1956).

For varying explanations of the collapse of the Confederacy, see Henry S. Commager, ed., *The Defeat of the Confederacy* (1964); David Donald, ed., *Why the North Won the Civil War* (1960); Charles H. Wesley, *The Collapse of the Confederacy* (1922); and Bell I. Wiley, *The Road to Appomattox* (1956).

CHAPTER 20

Reconstruction
1865–1877

"A house divided against itself cannot stand," Abraham Lincoln prophesied in 1858. The Civil War proved that the United States would stand, not as a loose confederation of sovereign states but as one nation, indivisible. Never again would there be talk of secession. The war also ended slavery, the most divisive institution in antebellum America. Weakened by the advances of the Union armies and undermined by Lincoln's Emancipation Proclamation, slavery received its death blow in February 1865, when the Congress adopted the Thirteenth Amendment, outlawing slavery and involuntary servitude. Ratified by three-fourths of the states, the amendment became a part of the Constitution in December 1865.

But the Civil War did not settle the terms and conditions on which the several states, sections, races, and classes would live in the firmly united "house." Those problems formed the agenda of the Reconstruction era, one of the most complex and controversial periods in American history. During these postwar years some basic questions had to be answered: What, if any, punishment should be imposed on Southern whites who had supported the Confederate attempt to disrupt the Union? How were the recently emancipated slaves to be guaranteed their freedom, and what civil and political rights did freedmen have? When and on what conditions were the Southern states so recently in rebellion to be readmitted to the Union—that is, entitled to vote in national elections, to have senators and representatives seated in the United States Congress, and, in general, to become once more full-fledged, equal members in the national body politic?

The initial moves to answer these questions came from the president, whose powers had been greatly expanded during the war years. President Lincoln in December 1863 announced a generous program of amnesty to repentant rebels and inaugurated a plan for reorganizing loyal governments in the South when as few as 10 percent of the voters in 1860 were willing to support them. After the assassination of Lincoln in April 1865, President Andrew Johnson, his successor, continued the process of Reconstruction under a similar plan. Johnson, like Lincoln, expected Southern whites to take the lead in establishing new state governments loyal to the Union. To initiate the process he appointed a provisional governor for each of the former Confederate states (except those where Lincoln had already initiated Reconstruction) and directed them to convene constitutional conventions. These were expected to adopt the Thirteenth Amendment ending slavery, nullify or repeal the ordinances of secession, and repudiate state debts incurred for the prosecution of the war. By early 1866 each of the states that had once formed the Confederacy completed most of these required steps, and the president viewed the process of Reconstruction as concluded. He recommended that the senators and representatives chosen by these reorganized governments be promptly given their rightful seats in Congress.

From the outset presidential Reconstruction had its critics. Congress, which had jealously watched the executive branch augment its power during the war, was ready to reassert its equality, if not its hegemony. Unlike President Lincoln, Andrew Johnson, a Tennessee Democrat and former slaveholder, had no popular mandate, and the taciturn, inflexible, and pugnacious new occupant of the White House did not understand that politics is the art of compromise.

After an initial attempt to cooperate with the new president, Republican leaders in 1866 began to devise their own plans for Reconstruction. The first congressional plan was embodied in the Fourteenth Amendment to the Constitution, which made it clear that blacks were citizens of the United States and tried to define the rights and privileges of American citizens. When the Southern states refused to ratify this amendment, congressional Republicans moved in 1867 to a more stringent program of reorganizing the South by requiring Negro suffrage. Under this second plan of congressional Reconstruction, every Southern state (except for Tennessee, which had been readmitted to the Union in 1866) received a new constitution that guaranteed to men of all races equal protection of the laws, and between 1868 and 1871 all were readmitted to the Union. Republican governments, which depended heavily on Negro votes, con-

trolled these states for a period ranging from a few months in the case of Virginia to nine years in the case of Louisiana.

Paths Not Taken

Contemporaries called this the period of Radical Reconstruction or, very often, Black Reconstruction, and it is easy to understand why many Americans of the 1860s and '70s viewed these changes as little short of revolutionary. To their Constitution, which had not been altered since 1804, were added during the five years after the Civil War the Thirteenth Amendment, ending slavery, the Fourteenth Amendment, defining the rights of citizens, and the Fifteenth Amendment (1870), prohibiting discrimination in voting on account of race or color. The national government, so recently tottering on the edge of defeat, was now more powerful than in any prevous point in American history. The Southern ruling class of whites, lately in charge of their own independent government, were petitioners for pardon. More than 3 million blacks, slaves only a few months earlier, were now free, entitled to the same privileges as all other citizens. Americans fairly gasped at the extent and the speed of the transformation wrought in their society, and it is hardly surprising that most subsequent historians accepted this contemporary view of the Reconstruction era as one of turbulent disorder.

Without denying that real and important changes did occur during the Reconstruction period, it might help to put these into perspective by inventing a little conterfactual history, a recital of conceivable historical scenarios that were never acted out. For instance, it would be easy to imagine how the victorious North might have turned angrily on the prostrate South. In 1865 Northerners had just finished four years of war that cost the Union army more than 360,000 casualties. To destroy the Confederacy required Americans of that and subsequent generations to pay in taxes at least $10 billion. Northerners had reason to believe, moreover, that their Confederate opponents had prosecuted the war with fiendish barbarity. Sober

RUINS OF RICHMOND
When the Confederate government evacuated Richmond on April 3, 1865, orders were given to burn supplies that might fall into the enemy's hands. There were heavy explosions as ironclads, armories, and arsenals were blown up. The next morning, as the fires spread, a mob of men and women, whites and blacks, began to plunder the city. *(Library of Congress)*

Union congressmen informed their constituents that the Confederates employed "Indian savages" to scalp and mutilate the Union dead. Reliable Northern newspapers told how in April 1864 General Nathan Bedford Forrest and his Confederates overran the defenses of Fort Pillow, Tennessee, manned by a Negro regiment, and, refusing to accept surrender, deliberately beat, shot, and burned their prisoners. The influential *Harper's Weekly Magazine* carried apparently authentic drawings of a goblet that a Southerner had made from a Yankee soldier's skull and of necklaces made of Yankee teeth that Southern ladies wore. When Union armies liberated Northern prisoners from such hell-holes as Andersonville, Georgia,

pictures of these half-starved skeletons of men, clad in grimy tatters of their Union uniforms, convinced Northerners that Jefferson Davis's policy had been "to starve and freeze and kill off by inches the prisoners he dares not butcher outright."

After the murder of Abraham Lincoln by the Southern sympathizer John Wilkes Booth, an outraged North could easily have turned on the conquered Confederacy in vengeance. The victorious Northerners might have executed Jefferson Davis, Alexander H. Stephens, and a score of other leading Confederates and might have sent thousands more into permanent exile. The triumphant Union might have erased the boundaries of the Southern states and divided the whole region into new, conquered territories. They might have enforced the confiscation acts already on the statute books and have seized the plantations of rebels, for distribution to the freedmen.

No such drastic course was followed. With the exception of Major Henry Wirtz, commandant of the infamous Andersonville prison, who was hanged, no Confederate was executed for "war crimes." A few Southern political leaders were imprisoned for their part in the "rebellion," but in most cases their release was prompt. To be sure, Jefferson Davis was kept in prison for two years at Fort Monroe, and he was under indictment for treason until 1869, when all charges were dropped. His case was, however, as unusual as it was extreme, and one reason for the long delay in bringing him to trial was the certainty that no jury, Northern or Southern, would render an impartial verdict. There was no general confiscation of the property of Confederates, no dividing up of plantations.

Equally conceivable is another scenario—another version of history that did not happen—this time featuring the Southern whites. For four years Confederate citizens had been subjected to a barrage of propaganda designed to prove that the enemy was little less than infernal in his purposes. Many believed the Southern editor who claimed that Lincoln's program was "Emancipation, Confiscation, Conflagration, and Extermination." According to the North Carolina educator Calvin H. Wiley, the North had "summoned to its aid every fierce and cruel and licentious passion of the human heart"; to defeat the Confederacy it was ready to use "the assassin's dagger, the midnight torch, . . . poison, famine and pestilence." Such charges were easy to credit in the many Southern families that had relatives in Northern prison camps, such as the one at Elmira, New York, where 775 of 8,347 Confederate prisoners died within three months for want of proper food, water, and medicine. The behavior of Union troops in the South, especially of Sherman's "bummers" in Georgia and the Carolinas, gave Southerners every reason to fear the worst if the Confederate government failed.

It would therefore have been reasonable for Confederate armies in 1865, overwhelmed by Union numbers, to disband quietly, disappear into the countryside, and carry on guerrilla operations against the Northern invaders. Indeed, on the morning of the day when Lee surrendered at Appomattox, Confederate General E. P. Alexander advocated just such a plan. He argued that if Lee's soldiers took to the woods with their rifles, perhaps two-thirds of the Army of Northern Virginia could escape capture. "We would be like rabbits and partridges in the bushes," he claimed, "and they could not scatter to follow us." The history of more recent wars of national liberation suggests that Alexander's judgment was correct. At the least his strategy would have given time for thousands of leading Southern politicians and planters, together with their families, to go safely into exile, as the Tories did during the American Revolution.

But, once again, no such events occurred. Some few Confederate leaders did go into exile. For instance, General Jubal A. Early fled to Mexico and thence to Canada, where he tried to organize a Southern exodus to New Zealand; but finding that nobody wanted to follow him, he returned to his home and his law practice in Virginia. A few hundred Confederates did migrate to Mexico and to Brazil. But most followed the advice of General Lee and General Wade Hampton of South Carolina, who urged their fellow Southerners to "devote their whole energies to the restoration of law and order, the reestablishment of agriculture and commerce, the promotion of education and the rebuilding of our cities and dwellings which have been laid in ashes."

Still a third counterfactual historical scenario comes readily to mind. Southern blacks, who had been for generations oppressed in slavery, now for the first time had disciplined leaders in the thousands of Negro soldiers who had served in the Union army. They also had arms. Very easily they could have turned in revenge on their former masters. Seizing the plantations and other property of the whites, the freedmen might have made of the former Confederacy a black nation. If the whites had dared to resist, the South might have been the scene of massacres as bloody as those in Haiti at the beginning of the nineteenth century, when Toussaint L'Ouverture and Dessalines drove the French out of that island.

Many Southern whites feared, or even expected, that the Confederacy would become another Santo Domingo. They were much troubled by reports that blacks were joining the Union League, an organization that had originated in the North during the war to stimulate patriotism but during the Reconstruction era became the bulwark of the Republican party in the South. The secrecy imposed by the League on its members and its frequent nocturnal meetings alarmed whites, and they readily believed reports that the blacks were collecting arms and ammunition for a general uprising. Fearfully, Southern whites read newspaper accounts of minor racial clashes. Indeed, whites were told, racial tension was so great that blacks "might break into open insurrection at any time."

But no such insurrection occurred. Though the freedmen unquestionably coveted the lands of their former masters, they did not seize them. Indeed, black leaders consistently discouraged talk of extra-legal confiscation of plantations. Nor did freedmen threaten the lives or the rights of whites. One of the earliest black political conventions held in Alabama urged a policy of "peace, friendship, and good will toward all men—especially toward our white fellow-citizens among whom our lot is cast." That tone was the dominant one throughout the Reconstruction period, and in many states blacks took the lead in repealing laws that disfranchised former Confederates or disqualified them from holding office.

The point of these three exercises in counter-factual history is, of course, not to argue that the Civil War brought about no changes in American life. The preservation of the Union and the emancipation of the slaves were two consequences of incalculable importance. It is, instead, to suggest the inadequacy of conventional accounts of the Reconstruction period as a second American Revolution. During these postwar years there were swift and significant alterations in the society of the South, but the shared beliefs and institutions of the American people, North and South, black and white, set limits to these changes.

Constitutionalism as a Limit to Change

One set of ideas that sharply curbed experimentation and political innovation during the Reconstruction period can be labeled constitutionalism. It is hard for twentieth-century Americans to understand the reverence with which their nineteenth-century ancestors viewed the Constitution. That document, next to the flag, was the most powerful symbol of American nationhood. Tested in the trial of civil war, the Constitution continued to command respect approaching veneration during the Reconstruction era.

State Rights. Among the most sacrosanct provisions of the Constitution were those that separated the powers of the state and the national governments. Although the national government greatly expanded its role during the war years, Americans still tended to think of it as performing only the specific functions enumerated in the Constitution, which granted it virtually no authority to act directly on any individual citizen. The national government could not, for instance, prevent or punish crime; it had no control over public education; it could not outlaw discrimination against racial minorities; and it could not even intervene to maintain public order unless requested to do so by the state government. Virtually everybody agreed, therefore, that if any laws regulating social and economic life were required, they must be the work of state and local, not of national, government.

Nobody, consequently, even contemplated the possibility that some federal agency might be needed to supervise the demobilization after Appomattox. Everybody simply assumed that after some 200,000 of the Union army volunteers bravely paraded down Pennsylvania Avenue on May 23–24, 1865, and received applause from President Johnson, the cabinet, the generals, and the members of the diplomatic corps, the soldiers would disband and go back to their peaceful homes. This is precisely what they did. Of the more than one million volunteers in the Union army on May 1, 1865, two-thirds were mustered out by August, four-fifths by November. To the demobilized soldiers, the United States government offered no assistance in finding jobs, in purchasing housing, or in securing further education. It paid pensions to those injured in the war and to the families of those who had been killed, but beyond that it assumed no responsibility. Nor did anybody think of asking the national government to oversee the transition from a wartime economy to an era of peace. Without notice the various bureaus of the army and navy departments by the end of April 1865 simply suspended requisitions and purchases, government arsenals slowed down their production, and surplus supplies were sold off.

Hardly anybody had the thought that the national government might play a role in rebuilding the wartorn South. The devastation in the South was immense and ominous. The Confederate dead totaled more than a quarter of a million. In Mississippi, for instance, one-third of the white men of military age had been killed or disabled for life. Most Southern cities were in ruins. Two-thirds of the Southern railroads were totally destroyed; the rest barely creaked along on worn-out rails with broken-down engines. But none of this was thought to be the concern of the United States government.

The failure of the national government to come to the rescue was not caused by vindictiveness. To the contrary, Union officials often behaved with marked generosity toward Confederates. After Lee's hungry battalions surrendered at Appomattox, Grant's soldiers freely shared with them their rations. All over the South, Federal military officials drew on the full Union army storehouses to feed the hungry. But beyond these attempts to avert starvation the Federal government did not go, and very few thought that it should. Not until the twentieth century did the United States make it a policy to pour vast sums of money into the rehabilitation of enemies it had defeated in war.

Rebuilding had, therefore, to be the work of the Southern state and local authorities, and this task imposed a heavy tax on their meager resources. In Mississippi, one-fifth of the entire state revenue in 1866 was needed to provide artificial limbs for soldiers maimed in the war. For the larger tasks of physical restoration, the resources of the South were obviously inadequate. Borrowing a leaf from antebellum experience, Southern governments did the only thing they knew how to do—namely, they lent the credit of the state to back up the bonds of private companies that promised to rebuild railroads and other necessary facilities. Since these companies were underfinanced and since the credit of the Southern state governments after Appomattox was, to say the least, questionable, these bonds had to be sold at disadvantageous prices and at exorbitant rates of interest. In later years, when many of these companies defaulted on their obligations and Southern state governments had to make good on their guarantees, these expenditures would be condemned as excessive and extravagant, and Democrats blamed them on the Republican regimes established in the South after 1868. In fact, however, the need for physical restoration immediately after the war was so obvious and so pressing that nearly every government, whether controlled by Democrats or Republicans, underwrote corporations that promised to rebuild the region.

The Freedmen's Bureau. Even in dealing with the freedmen—the some 3 million slaves emancipated as a result of the war—the United States government tried to pursue a hands-off policy. Few influential leaders, either in the North or in the South, thought that it was the function of the national government to supervise the blacks' transition from slavery to freedom. Even abolitionists, genuinely devoted to the welfare of blacks, were so accustomed to thinking of the Negro as "God's image in ebony"—in other words, a white man in a black skin—that they had no plans for assisting him after emancipation. In 1865 William Lloyd Garrison urged the American Anti-Slavery Society to disband, since it had fulfilled its function, and he suspended the publication of *The Liberator*. Sharing the same point of view, the American Freedmen's Inquiry Commission, set up by the Union War Department in 1863, unanimously opposed further governmental actions to protect the blacks. "The negro does best when let alone," argued one member of the commission, Samuel Gridley

Howe, noted alike for his work with the deaf, dumb, and blind and for his hostility to slavery; "We must beware of all attempts to prolong his servitude, under pretext of taking care of him. The white man has tried taking care of the negro, by slavery, by apprenticeship, by colonization, and has failed disastrously in all; now let the negro try to take care of himself."

But the problem of the care of the freedmen could not be dismissed so easily. Wherever Union armies advanced into the South, they were "greeted by an irruption of negroes of all ages, complexions and sizes, men, women, boys and girls . . . waving hats and bonnets with the most ludicrous caperings and ejaculations of joy." "The poor delighted creatures thronged upon us," a Yankee soldier reported, and they insisted: "We'se gwin wid you all." "What shall be done with them?" commanders in the field plaintively wired Washington.

The administration in Washington had no comprehensive answer. Initially it looked to private philanthropic organizations to rush food, clothing, and medicine to the thousands of blacks that thronged in unsanitary camps around the headquarters of each Union army. The New England Freedmen's Aid Society, the American Missionary Association, and the Philadelphia Society of Friends promptly responded, but it was soon clear that the problem was too great for private charity.

Gradually sentiment grew in the North for the creation of a general "Emancipation Bureau" in the federal government—only to conflict directly with the even stronger sentiment that the national government had limited powers. Out of this conflict emerged the Freedmen's Bureau Act of March 3, 1865. Congress established, under the jurisdiction of the War Department, the Bureau of Refugees, Freedmen, and Abandoned Lands and entrusted to the new agency, for one year after the end of the war, "control of all subjects relating to refugees and freedmen." To head the new organization, Lincoln named Oliver O. Howard, a Union general with paternalistic views toward blacks.

At first glance, the Freedmen's Bureau seems to have been a notable exception to the rule that the national government should take only a minor, passive role in the restoration of the South. Howard had a vision of a compassionate network of "teachers, ministers, farmers, superintendents" working together to aid and elevate the freedmen, and, under his enthusiastic impetus, the bureau appointed agents in each of the former Confederate states. The most urgent task of the bureau was issuing food and clothing, mostly from surplus army stores, to destitute freedmen and other Southern refugees. This action unquestionably prevented mass starvation in the South. The bureau also took the initiative in getting work for freedmen. Fearful on the one hand that Southern planters would attempt to exploit and underpay the freedmen, troubled on the other by the widespread belief that blacks, once emancipated, were not willing to work, the bureau agents brought laborers and landlords together and insisted that workers sign labor contracts.

No part of the bureau's work was more successful than its efforts in the field of education. The slow work of educating the illiterate Southern blacks had already begun under the auspices of army chaplains and Northern benevolent societies before the creation of the bureau. Howard's bureau continued to cooperate with these agencies, providing housing for black schools, paying teachers, and helping to establish normal schools and colleges for the training of black teachers. All these educational efforts received an enthusiastic welcome from the freedmen. During the day classrooms were thronged with black children learning the rudiments of language and arithmetic; in the evenings they were filled with adults who were "fighting with their letters," learning to read so that they would not be "made ashamed" by their children. "The progress of the scholars is in all cases creditable and in some remarkable," reported one of the teachers. "How richly God has endowed them, and how beautifully their natures would have expanded under a tender and gentle culture."

Even more innovative was the work of the bureau in allocating lands to the freedmen. During the war many plantations in the path of Union armies had been deserted by their owners, and army commanders like Grant arranged to have these tilled

PRIMARY SCHOOL IN CHARGE OF MRS. GREEN, VICKSBURG, MISSISSIPPI
Freedmen were avid for learning. In schools sponsored by the Freedmen's Bureau, grandparents sat alongside toddlers, as all sought knowledge.

by the blacks who flocked to his camp. The largest tract of such abandoned land was in the Sea Islands of South Carolina, which were overrun by Federal troops in the fall of 1861. Though speculators bought up large amounts of this land during the war, sizable numbers of black residents were able to secure small holdings. When General W. T. Sherman marched through South Carolina he ordered that the Sea Islands and the abandoned plantations along the river banks for thirty miles from the coast be reserved for Negro settlement and directed that black settlers be given "possessory titles" to tracts of this land not larger than forty acres. The act creating the Freedmen's Bureau clearly contemplated the continuation of these policies, for it authorized the new bureau to lease confiscated lands to freedmen and to "loyal refugees." The bureau could also sell the land

to these tenants and give them "such title thereto as the United States can convey."

But if the Freedmen's Bureau was an exception to the policy of limited federal involvement in the reconstruction process, it was at best a partial exception. Though the agency did invaluable work, it was a feeble protector of the freedmen. Authorized to recruit only a minimal staff, Howard was obliged to rely heavily on Union army officers stationed in the South—at just the time when the Union army was being demobilized. Consequently the bureau never had enough manpower to look after the rights of the freedmen; toward the end of its first year of operation it employed only 799 men, 424 of whom were soldiers on temporary assigned duty. Important as the work of the bureau was in Negro education, its chief function was to stimulate private philanthropy in this field. In providing land for the freedmen, the bureau was handicapped because it controlled only about 800,000 acres of arable land in the entire South, enough at best for perhaps one black family in forty. Moreover, its efforts to distribute lands to the Negroes were repeatedly undercut both by the Congress and the president. The very wording of the act creating the bureau suggested congressional uncertainty about who actually owned deserted and confiscated lands in the South. President Johnson issued pardons to Southerners that explicitly included "restoration of all rights of property." In October 1865 the president directed Howard to go in person to the Sea Islands to notify blacks there that they did not hold legal title to the land and to advise them "to make the best terms they could" with the white owners. When blacks bitterly resisted what they considered the bureau's betrayal, Union soldiers descended on the islands and forced blacks who would not sign labor contracts with the restored white owners to leave. Elsewhere in the South the record of the bureau was equally dismal.

In short, belief in the limited role to be played by the national government affected the rehabilitation of the freedmen, just as it did the physical restoration of the South and the demobilization in the North. The United States government was supposed to play the smallest possible part in all these matters,

A GROUP OF FREEDMEN IN RICH-MOND, VIRGINIA, 1865

A central problem of Reconstruction years was the future of the freedmen. Nobody had made any plans for a smooth transition from slavery to freedom. Consequently, when emancipation came, as one former slave recalled, "We didn't know where to go. Momma and them didn't know where to go, you see, after freedom broke. Just like you turned something out, you know. They didn't know where to go." *(Library of Congress)*

and its minimal activities were to be of the briefest duration.

It is certain that most whites in the North and in the South fully approved these stringent limitations on the activities of the national government. What the masses of freedmen thought is harder to determine. On the one hand stands the protest of Sea Island blacks when they learned they were about to be dispossessed: "Why, General Howard, why do you take away our lands? You take them from us who have always been true, always true to the Government! You give them to our all-time enemies! That is not right!" On the other is Frederick Douglass's reply to the question, "What shall we do with the Negroes?" The greatest black spokesman of the era answered: "Do nothing with them; mind your business, and let them mind theirs. Your *doing* with them is their greatest misfortune. They have been undone by your doings, and all they now ask and really have need of at your hands, is just to let them alone."

Laissez-Faire as a Limit to Change

Along with the idea of limited government went the doctrine of laissez-faire ("let things alone"), which sharply limited what the government could do to solve economic problems that arose after the Civil War. Except for a handful of Radical Republicans, such as Charles Sumner and Thaddeus Stevens, most congressmen, like most academic economists, were unquestioning believers in an American version of laissez-faire. Though they were willing to promote economic growth through protective tariffs and land grants to railroads, they abhorred governmental inspection, regulation, and control of economic activities. These matters were ruled by the inexorable laws of economics. "You need not think it necessary to have Washington exercise a political providence over the country," William Graham Sumner, the brilliant professor of political and social science, told his students at Yale. "God has done that a great deal better by the laws of political economy."

Reverence for Private Property. No violation of economic laws was deemed more heinous than interference with the right of private property—the right of an individual or group to purchase, own, use, and dispose of property without any interference from governmental authorities. There was consequently never a chance that congressmen would support Thaddeus Stevens's radical program to confiscate all Southern farms larger than 200 acres and to divide the seized land into 40-acre tracts among the freedmen. "An attempt to justify the confiscation of Southern land under the pretense of doing justice to the freedmen," declared the New York *Times*, which spoke for educated Republicans, "strikes at the root of all property rights in both sections. It concerns Massachusetts quite as much as Mississippi."

Informed opinion in the North held that the best program of Reconstruction was to allow the laws of economics to rule in the South with the least possible interference by the government. Obsessed by laissez-faire, Northern theorists left out of their calculations the physical devastation wrought in the South by the war, and they did not recognize how feeble were the section's resources to rebuild its economy. Even excluding the loss of property in slaves, the total assessed property evaluation of the Southern states shrank by 43 percent between 1860 and 1865.

Southern Economic Adjustments. Northern pundits also failed to take into account the psychological dimensions of economic readjustment in the South. For generations Southern whites had persuaded themselves that slavery was the natural condition of the black race, and they truly believed that their slaves were devoted to them. But as Union armies approached and slaves defected, they were compelled to recognize that they had been living in a world of misconceptions and deceits. So shattering was the idea that slaves were free that some Southern whites simply refused to accept it. Even after the Confederate surrender, some owners would

not inform their slaves of their new status. A few planters angrily announced they were so disillusioned that they would never again have anything to do with blacks, and they sought, vainly, to persuade European immigrants and Chinese coolies to work their fields.

Even those whites who overtly accepted the reality of emancipation betrayed the fact that, on a deeper emotional level, they still could only think of blacks as performing forced labor. "The general interest both of the white man and of the negroes requires that he should be kept as near to the condition of slavery as possible, and as far from the condition of the white man as is practicable," explained Edmund Rhett of South Carolina. "Negroes must be made to work, or else cotton and rice must cease to be raised for export." The contracts that planters in 1865, under pressure from the Freedmen's Bureau, entered into with their former slaves were further indications of the same attitude. Even the most generous of these contracts provided that blacks were "not to leave the premises during work hours without the consent of the Proprietor," that they would conduct "themselves faithfully, honestly and civilly," and that they would behave with "perfect obedience" toward the landowner.

Blacks, too, had difficulties in adjusting to their new status that were never anticipated by the devotees of laissez-faire. *Freedom*—that word so often whispered in the slave quarters—went to the heads of some blacks. A few took the coming of "Jubilee," with the promise to put the bottom rail on top, quite literally. Nearly all blacks had an initial impulse to test their freedom, to make sure it was real. During the first months after the war there was, then, much movement among Southern blacks. "They are just like a swarm of bees," one observer noted, "all buzzing about and not knowing where to settle."

Much of this black mobility was, however, purposeful. Thousands of former slaves flocked to Southern towns and cities where the Freedmen's Bureau was issuing rations, for they knew that food was unavailable on the plantations. Many blacks set out to find husbands, wives, or children, from whom they had been forcibly separated during the

CELEBRATION FOR NEWLY MAR-
RIED BLACK COUPLES
Legally slaves could not
marry. When blacks became
free, they sought to regularize
their marital arrangements
and to legitimatize their children. Many Southern states
passed blanket laws for this
purpose, but thousands of
Negroes desired formal wed-
ding ceremonies. *(The New
York Public Library)*

slave days. A good many freedmen joined the general movement of Southern population away from
the seaboard states, devastated by war, and migrated
to the Southwestern frontier in Texas. Most blacks,
however, did not move so far but remained in the
immediate vicinity of the plantations where they
had labored as slaves.

The reluctance of freedmen in 1865 to enter
into labor contracts, either with their former masters
or with other white landowners, was also generally
misunderstood. Most blacks wanted to work—but
they wanted to work on their own land. Freedmen
knew that the United States government had divided
up some abandoned plantations among former slaves,
and many believed that on January 1, 1866—the anniversary of their freedom under Lincoln's Emancipation Proclamation—all would receive forty acres and
a mule. With this prospect of having their own farms,
they were unwilling to sign contracts to work on
somebody else's plantation.

Even when the hope of free land disappeared,
freedmen were averse to signing labor contracts
because, as has been noted, so many white landowners expected to continue to treat them like slaves.
Especially repugnant was the idea of being again

herded together in the plantation slave quarters,
with their communal facilities for cooking and washing and infant care, and their lack of privacy. Emancipation did much to strengthen the black family.
Families divided by slave sales could now be reunited. Marital arrangements between blacks, which
had had no legal validity during slavery, could be
regularized. Freedmen's Bureau officials performed
thousands of marriage ceremonies, and some states
passed general ordinances declaring that blacks who
had been living together were legally man and wife
and that their children were legitimate. This precious
new security of family life was not something blacks
were willing to jeopardize by returning to slave quarters. Before contracting to work on the plantations,
they insisted on having separate cabins, scattered
across the farm, each usually having its own patch for
vegetables and perhaps a pen for hogs or a cow.

When these conditions were met, freedmen in
the early months of 1866 entered into labor contracts,
most of which followed the same general pattern.
Rarely did these arrangements call for the payment
of wages, for landowners were desperately short of
cash and freedmen felt that a wage system gave
planters too much control over their labor. The most

common system was sharecropping. Although there were many regional and individual variations, the system usually called for the dividing of the crop into three equal shares. One of these went to the landowner; another went to the laborer—usually black, though there were also many white sharecroppers in the South; and the third went to whichever party provided the seeds, fertilizer, mules, and other farming equipment.

For the planter this system had several advantages. At a time when money was scarce, he was not obliged to pay out cash to his employees until the crop was harvested. He retained general supervision over what was planted and how the crop was cultivated, and he felt he was more likely to secure a good harvest because the freedmen themselves stood to gain by a large yield. Blacks, too, found the sharecropping system suited to their needs. They had control over how their crops were planted and when

they were cultivated and harvested. They could earn more money by working harder in the fields.

The Breakup of the Plantation System. To some observers the disappearance of the slave quarters and the resettling of families in individual, scattered cabins seemed to mark a revolution in the character of Southern agriculture. According to the United States census, the number of Southern landholdings doubled between 1860 and 1880 and their average size dropped from 365 acres to 157 acres. In fact, the census figures were misleading, because the census takers failed to ask farmers whether they owned their land or were sharecroppers. An examination of tax records, which show land ownership, in the representative state of Louisiana helps correct the distortion of the census. Between 1860 and 1880 in Louisiana the number of independently owned farms of less than 100 acres actually dropped by 14

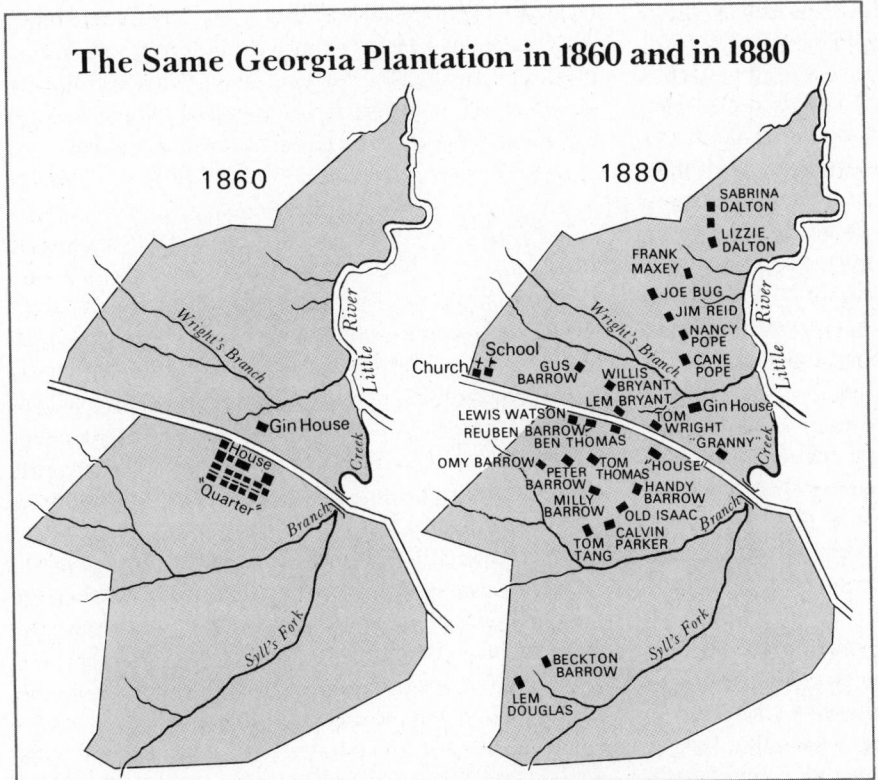

THE SAME GEORGIA PLANTATION IN 1860 AND 1880
Before the Civil War slave quarters were located close together, all near the white master's house, so that he could impose order and prevent secret meetings of the blacks. After emancipation freedmen insisted upon scattering out over the plantation, so that each family could have its own house and some privacy.

percent, while during the same period the number of plantations increased by 287 percent. By 1900 plantations of 100 acres or more encompassed half the cultivated land in the state, and more than half the farmers were not proprietors.

If the postwar period did not see the breakup of large plantations, it did bring some significant changes in ownership and control of the land. Hard hit by debt, by rising taxes, and by increasing labor costs, many Southern planters had to sell their holdings, and there was an infusion of Northern capital into the region after the war. More tried to cling to their acres by going heavily into debt. Since the banking system of the postwar South was inadequate, the principal source of credit was the local merchant, who could supply both the landowner and his sharecroppers with clothing, shoes, some food, and other necessities to tide them over the lean months between the planting of the tobacco or cotton crop and its harvest. On each sale the merchant charged interest, to be paid when the crop was sold, and he also charged prices ranging from 40 percent to 110 percent higher for all goods sold on credit. It is hardly surprising that those planters who could afford to do so set up their own stores and extended credit to their own sharecroppers, and quite soon they discovered they were making more profits on their mercantile enterprises than from farming. Planters who could not make such arrangements frequently had to sell their lands to the neighborhood merchant. It is not accidental that in William Faulkner's fictional saga of Southern history the power of planter families like the Compsons and the Sutpens diminished during the postwar years, while the Snopes family of storekeepers, hard-trading, penny-pinching, and utterly unscrupulous, emerged prosperous and successful.

It would be a mistake, however, to accept the novelist's hostile characterization of the Southern merchant without reservation. If the storekeeper insisted on a crop-lien system, which required the farmer legally to pledge that the proceeds from his crop must go first to pay off his obligation to the merchant, it was because he was aware that, as in both 1866 and 1867, crops throughout the South could fail. And if the merchant urged farmers to forget about soil conservation, diversification, and experimentation with new crops, it was because he knew that the only way to pay his own debts was to insist that his debtors must raise cotton and tobacco, for which there was a ready cash market.

Thus merchants, landowners, and sharecroppers, thus white Southerners and black Southerners, became locked into an economic system that, at best, promised them little more than survival. At worst, it offered bankruptcy, sale of lands, and hurried nocturnal migrations in an attempt to escape from a set of debts in one state with but little more than the hope of starting a new set in another.

By the 1880s, then, the South had become what it remained for the next half-century, the economic backwater of the nation. In 1880 the per capita wealth of the South was $376, that in the states outside the South $1,086. Yet it was this impoverished region that had to deal with some of the most difficult political and racial problems that ever have confronted Americans. In attacking these problems, Southerners, black and white, could expect no assistance from the government, since such intervention would violate the immutable laws of laissez-faire economics.

Political Parties as a Limit to Change

Of the institutions that checked radical change during Reconstruction, none were more influential than the national political parties. The fact that both parties were conglomerates of disparate and often competing sectional and class interests meant that party policy had to be arrived at through compromise and concession. In that process extreme and drastic measures were nearly always screened out.

Nationally the Democratic party during the postwar years was torn by two conflicting interests. On the one hand, Democrats sought the immediate readmission of the Southern states under the governments President Johnson had set up. Controlled by whites hostile to the Republican party, these states would surely send Democrats to Congress and support Democratic candidates in a national election.

Even during the 1850s, the South had increasingly become a one-party region; now the goal of a solidly Democratic South appeared within reach. On the other hand, too enthusiastic advocacy of the Southern cause could hurt Democrats in the North by reviving talk of disloyalty and the Copperhead movement during the war. To minimize the effectiveness of such attacks, Democrats had no choice but to urge restraint on their colleagues in the former Confederacy.

Among Republicans, similar constraints operated to dampen any ideas of taking vengeance on the South or of encouraging blacks to seize control of that region. From its inception the Republican party had been an uneasy admixture of antislavery men, former Whigs, disgruntled Democrats, and Know-Nothings. How tenuous were the ties that bound these groups together became evident in the factional disputes that racked Lincoln's administration, and for the party it was a bad omen that the sharpest disagreements among Republicans concerned Lincoln's plan to reorganize the Southern state governments.

Presidential Reconstruction. During the first year after Lincoln's death, quarrels among Republicans were somewhat muted because practically all members of the party joined in opposing President Johnson's program of Reconstruction. Followed by only a handful of Conservative Republicans, including Secretary of State Seward and Navy Secretary Gideon Welles, Johnson began to work closely with the Democrats of the North and South. He announced that the Southern states had never been out of the Union, and he insisted that, under the provisional governments he had set up, they were entitled to be represented in Congress.

It is easy to understand why almost all Republicans whether they belonged to the Radical or the Moderate factions, rejected the president's argument. Members of both wings of the party were outraged when the Southern elections in 1865, held at the direction of the president, resulted in the choice of a Confederate brigadier-general as governor of Mississippi, and they were furious when the new Georgia legislature named Alexander H. Stephens, the vice-president of the Confederacy, to represent that state in the United States Senate.

What made these newly elected Southern officials more threatening to Republicans was the fact that (though many had been Whigs before the war) they clearly contemplated allying themselves with the Democratic party. However much Republicans disagreed among themselves, they all agreed that their party had saved the Union. They believed, with Thaddeus Stevens, "that upon the continued ascendancy of that party depends the safety of this great nation." Now that ascendancy was threatened. What made the threat so grave, and so ironic, was the fact that when the Southern states were readmitted to the Union they would receive increased representation in Congress. Prior to the ratification of the Thirteenth Amendment, only three-fifths of the slave population of the South had been counted in apportioning representation in the House of Representatives; but now that the slaves were free men, all would be counted. In short, the Southern states, after having been defeated in the most costly war in the nation's history, would have about fifteen more representatives in Congress than they had had before the war. And under the president's plan, all of the Southern Congress unquestionably would be Democrats.

Equally troubling to Republicans of all factions was the fear of what white Southerners, once restored to authority, would do to the freedmen. The laws that the Southern provisional legislatures adopted during the winter of 1865–66 gave reason for anxiety on this score. Not one of these governments considered treating black citizens just as they treated white citizens. Instead, the legislatures adopted special laws, known as the Black Codes, to regulate the conduct of freedmen. On the positive side, these laws recognized the right of freedmen to make civil contracts, to sue and be sued, and to acquire and hold most kinds of property. But with these rights went restrictions. The laws varied from state to state, but in general they specified that blacks might not purchase or carry firearms, that they might not assemble after sunset, and that those who were idle or unemployed should "be liable to imprisonment, and to hard labor, one or both, . . . not exceeding twelve months." The Mississippi code prohibited blacks from renting or leasing "any lands or tenements except in incorporated cities or towns." That of South Carolina forbade blacks from practicing "the art, trade or business of an artisan, mechanic or shopkeeper, or any other trade, employment or business (besides that of husbandry, or that of a servant)." So clearly did these measures seem designed to keep the freedmen in quasi-slavery that the Chicago *Tribune* spoke for a united, outraged Republican party in denouncing the first of these Black Codes, that adopted by the Mississippi legislature: "We tell the white men of Mississippi that the men of the North will convert the state of Mississippi into a frog-pond before they will allow any such laws to disgrace one foot of soil over which the flag of freedom waves."

The Fourteenth Amendment. Unwilling, for all these reasons, to recognize the regimes Johnson had set up in the South, all Republicans easily rallied in December 1865, when Congress reassembled, to block seating of their senators and representatives. All agreed to the creation of a special joint committee on Reconstruction to handle questions concerning the readmission of the Southern states and their further reorganization. In setting up this committee, congressional Republicans carefully balanced its membership with Radicals and Moderates. If its most conspicuous member was the Radical Stevens, its powerful chairman was Senator William Pitt Fessenden, a Moderate.

Congressional Republicans found it easier to unite in opposing Johnson's plan of Reconstruction than to unite in devising one of their own. Recognizing that it would take time to draft and adopt a constitutional amendment and then to have it ratified by the requisite number of states, congressional leaders early in 1866 agreed on interim legislation that would protect the freedmen. One bill extended and expanded the functions of the Freedmen's Bureau, and a second guaranteed minimal civil rights to all citizens. Contrary to expectations, Johnson

vetoed both these measures. Refusing to recognize that these measures represented the wishes of both Moderate and Radical Republicans, the president claimed that they were the work of the Radicals, who wanted "to destroy our institutions and change the character of the Government." He vowed to fight these Northern enemies of the Union just as he had once fought Southern secessionists and traitors. The Republican majority in Congress was not able to override Johnson's veto of the Freedmen's Bureau bill (a later, less sweeping measure extended the life of that agency for two years), but it passed the Civil Rights Act of 1866 over his disapproval.

While relations between the president and the Republicans in Congress were deteriorating, the joint committee on Reconstruction continued to meet and consider various plans for reorganizing the South. With its evenly balanced membership, the committee dismissed, on the one side, the president's theory that the Southern states were, in reality, already reconstructed and back in the Union. On the other side, it discarded the theory of Thaddeus Stevens that the Confederacy was conquered territory over which Congress could rule at its own discretion, and it rejected Charles Sumner's more elaborate argument that the Southern state governments had committed suicide when they seceded, so that their land and inhabitants now fell "under the exclusive jurisdiction of Congress." More acceptable to the majority of Republicans was the "grasp of war" theory advanced by Richard Henry Dana, Jr., the noted Massachusetts constitutional lawyer, who was also the author of *Two Years before the Mast.* Dana argued that the federal government held the defeated Confederacy in the grasp of war for a brief and limited time, during which it must act swiftly to revive state governments in the region and to restore promptly the constitutional balance between national and state authority. Dana's theory was an essentially conservative one, in that it called for only a short period of federal hegemony and looked toward the speedy restoration of the Southern states on terms of absolute equality with the loyal states.

Finding in Dana's theory a constitutional source of power, the joint committee after much travail pro-

RECONSTRUCTION: UNCLE SAM VISITS THE SHOP OF
A. JOHNSON, TAILOR

Taking off from Andrew Johnson's frequent bragging
about his humble origins as a tailor, this cartoon shows
the president and Secretary of State Seward busily
mending Uncle Sam's coat, badly torn by the recently
ended Civil War. *(American Antiquarian Society)*

duced the first comprehensive congressional plan
of Reconstruction in a proposed Fourteenth Amendment to the Constitution, which was endorsed by
Congress in June 1866 and submitted to the states
for ratification. Some parts of the amendment were
noncontroversial. All Republicans accepted the opening statement of the amendment; "All persons born
or naturalized in the United States, and subject to
the jurisdiction thereof, are citizens of the United
States and of the State wherein they reside." There

was also no disagreement about the provision declaring the Confederate debt invalid.

All the other provisions, however, represented
a compromise between Radical and Moderate Republicans. For instance, Radicals wanted to keep
all Southerners who had voluntarily supported the
Confederacy from voting until 1870, and the arch-
Radical Stevens urged: "Not only to 1870 but 18,070,
every rebel who shed the blood of loyal men should
be prevented from exercising any power in this Government." Moderates favored a speedy restoration
of all political rights to former Confederates. As a
compromise the Fourteenth Amendment included a
provision to exclude high-ranking Confederates from
office but one that did not deny them the vote.

Similarly, the Fourteenth Amendment's provisions to protect the freedmen represented a compromise. Radicals like Sumner (who was considered
too radical to be given a seat on the joint committee) wanted an unequivocal declaration of the right
and duty of the national government to protect the
civil liberties of the former slaves. But Moderates
drew back in alarm from entrusting additional authority to Washington. The joint committee came
up with a provision that granted no power to the
national government but restricted that of the states:
"No State shall make or enforce any law which shall
abridge the privileges and immunities of citizens
of the United States; nor shall any State deprive any
person of life, liberty, or property, without due process of law; nor deny to any person within its jurisdiction the equal protection of the laws."

Finally, another compromise between Radicals
and Moderates resulted in the provision of the
amendment concerning voting. Though Sumner and
other Radicals called Negro suffrage "the essence,
the great essential," of a proper Reconstruction policy, Conservatives refused to give to the national
government power to interfere with the state requirements for suffrage. The joint committee thereupon devised a complex and, as it proved, unwork-
able plan to persuade the Southern states voluntarily
to enfranchise blacks, under threat of having reduced
representation in Congress if they refused.

The efficacy of the Fourteenth Amendment as a

"RETURN OF THE PRODIGAL SON —NEW VERSION"
In this Republican view of Reconstruction, the Northern Democrat urges Mrs. United States to welcome the return of the South as the prodigal son. But the South is unregenerate and tells their mother: "Yes, by the thunder, I've come back, and d'ye hear? Hurry up them cakes and hot whiskey, and don't let us see any darn'd niggers around." (*American Antiquarian Society*)

program of Reconstruction was never tested because of the outbreak of political warfare between President Johnson and the Republican party, which had elected him vice-president in 1864. During the summer of 1866, Johnson and his friends tried to create a new political party, which would rally behind the president's policies the few Conservative Republicans, the Northern Democrats, and the Southern whites. With the president's hearty approval, a National Union Convention held in Philadelphia in August stressed the theme of harmony among the sections. The entry into the convention hall of delegates from Massachusetts and South Carolina, arm in arm, seemed to symbolize the end of sectional strife. The president himself went on a "swing around the circle" of leading Northern cities, ostensibly on his way to dedicate a monument to the memory of another Democrat, Stephen A. Douglas. In his frequent public speeches he defended the constitutionality of his own Reconstruction pro-

gram and berated the Congress, and particularly the Radical Republicans, for attempting to subvert the Constitution. In a final effort to consolidate sentiment against the Congress, he urged the Southern states not to ratify the proposed Fourteenth Amendment. With the exception of Tennessee, which was controlled by one of Johnson's bitterest personal and political enemies, all the former Confederate states rejected the congressional plan.

The Second Congressional Program of Reconstruction. When Congress reassembled in December 1866, the Republican majority had therefore to devise a second program of Reconstruction. Cheered by overwhelming victories in the fall congressional elections, Republicans were even less inclined than previously to cooperate with the president, who had gone into political opposition, or to encourage the provisional regimes in the South, which had rejected their first program. Republican suspicion that Southern whites were fundamentally hostile toward the freedmen was strengthened by reports of a race riot in Memphis during May 1866, when a mob of whites joined in a two-day indiscriminate attack on blacks in that city, and of a more serious affair in New Orleans four months later, when a white mob, aided by the local police, attacked a black political gathering with what was described as "a cowardly ferocity unsurpassed in the annals of crime." In New Orleans 45 or 50 blacks were killed, and 150 more were wounded.

Once again, however, the Republican majority in Congress found it easier to agree on what to oppose than what to favor in the way of Reconstruction legislation. Stevens urged that the South be placed under military rule for a generation and that Southern plantations be sold to pay the national debt. Sumner wanted to disfranchise large numbers of Southern whites, to require Negro suffrage, and to create racially integrated schools in the South. Mod-

erate Republicans, on the other hand, were willing to retain the Fourteenth Amendment as the basic framework of congressional Reconstruction and to insist on little else but ratification by Southern states.

The second congressional program of Reconstruction, embodied in the Military Reconstruction Act of March 2, 1867, represented a comprise between the demands of Radical and Moderate Republican factions. It divided the ten former Confederate states that had not ratified the Fourteenth Amendment into five military districts. In each of these states, there were to be new constitutional conventions, for which black men were allowed to vote. These conventions must draft new constitutions that had to provide for Negro suffrage, and they were required to ratify the Fourteenth Amendment. When thus reorganized, the Southern states could apply to Congress for readmission to the Union.

The radical aspects of this measure, which were pointed out by Democrats during the congressional

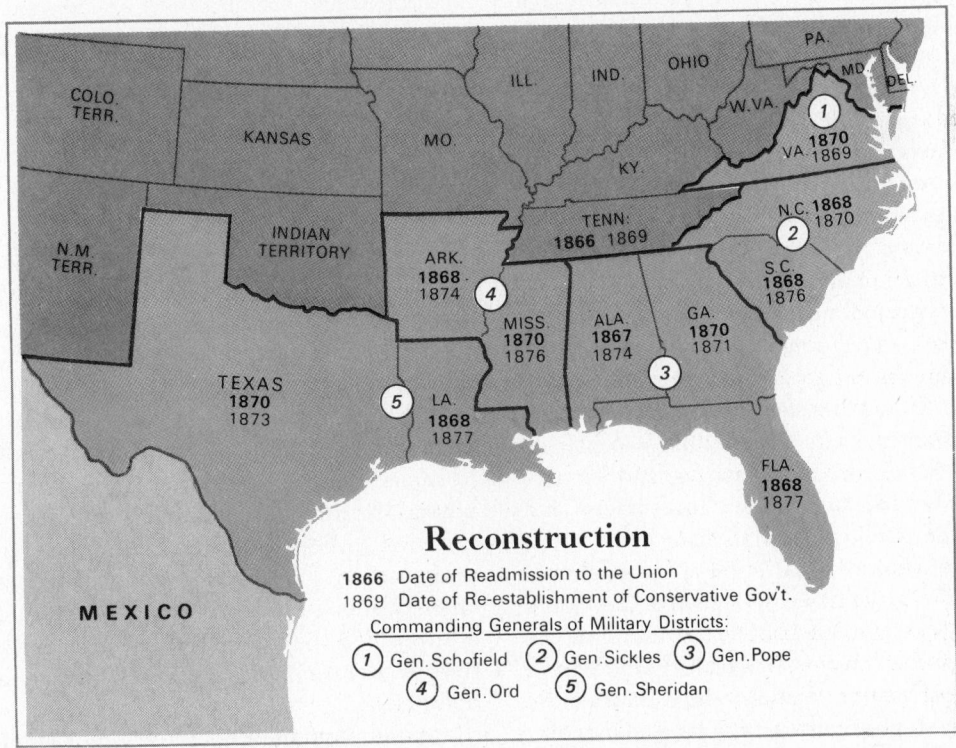

Reconstruction

1866 Date of Readmission to the Union
1869 Date of Re-establishment of Conservative Gov't.
Commanding Generals of Military Districts:
(1) Gen. Schofield   (2) Gen. Sickles   (3) Gen. Pope
(4) Gen. Ord   (5) Gen. Sheridan

debates and were denounced by President Johnson in his unsuccessful veto of the act, were easy to recognize. In particular, the requirement of Negro suffrage, which Sumner sponsored, seemed to Radicals "a prodigious triumph."

In fact, however, most provisions of the Military Reconstruction Act were more acceptable to Moderate than to Radical Republicans. The measure did nothing to give land to the freedmen, to provide education at national expense, or to end racial segregation in the South. It did not erase the boundaries of the Southern states, and it did not even sweep away the provisional governments Johnson had established there, though it did make them responsible to the commanders of the new military districts. So conservative was the act in all these respects that Sumner branded it as "horribly defective."

Intent on striking some kind of balance between the Radical and Conservative wings of the Republican party, the framers of the Military Reconstruction Act drafted the measure carelessly, and it promptly proved, as Sumner had predicted, "Reconstruction without machinery or motive power." Facing the acceptance of military rule or Negro suffrage, the provisional governments in the South chose the former, correctly believing that army officers were generally in sympathy with white supremacy. To get the Reconstruction process under way, Congress had therefore to enact a supplementary law (March 23, 1867), requiring the federal commanders in the South to take the initiative, when the local governments did not, in announcing elections, registering voters, and convening constitutional conventions. During the summer of 1867, as the president, the attorney general, and Southern state officials tried by legalistic interpretations to delay the Reconstruction program, Congress had to pass two further supplementary acts, explaining the "true intent and meaning" of the previous legislation.

With these measures, the fabric of congressional Reconstruction legislation as it affected the South was substantially completed. Both the first and the second congressional plans of Reconstruction were compromises between the Radical and the Moderate factions in the Republican party. The Radicals' insistence on change was essential in securing the adoption of this legislation, but the Moderates blocked all measures that would have revolutionary social or economic consequences in the South.

Impeachment. The same need to compromise between the factions of the Republican party dictated the policy of Congress toward the president during the Reconstruction years. Almost all Republicans were suspicious of the president and were fearful that he intended turning the South over to Confederate rule. Most were angered by Johnson's repeated veto messages, assailing carefully balanced compromise legislation as the work of Radicals and attacking the Congress itself as an unconstitutional body, since it refused to seat congressmen from all the states. Republicans of both factions were, therefore, desirous of keeping a close eye on the president and were willing to curb executive powers that had grown during the war. In 1867, fearing that Johnson would use his power as commander in chief to subvert their Reconstruction legislation, Republican factions joined to pass an army appropriations bill that required all military orders to the army, including those of the president himself, to go through the hands of General Grant. Suspecting that Johnson wanted to use the federal patronage to build up a political machine of his own, they adopted at the same time the Tenure of Office Act, which required the president to secure the consent of the Senate not merely when he appointed officials but when he removed them.

Up to this point the Republicans in Congress were prepared to go in striking unanimity—but no further. When Radical Republican James M. Ashley in January 1867 moved to impeach the president, he was permitted to conduct a seriocomic investigation of Johnson's alleged involvement in Lincoln's assassination, his purported sale of pardons, and other trumped-up charges; but when Ashley's motion reached the floor of the House of Representatives Moderate Republicans saw that it was soundly defeated.

A subsequent attempt at impeachment fared

better, but it also revealed how the Radical and Moderate factions checked each other. In August 1867 President Johnson suspended from office Secretary of War Edwin M. Stanton, whom he correctly suspected of having collaborated closely with the Radicals in Congress, and, as required by the Tenure of Office Act, he asked the Senate to consent to the removal. When the Senate refused, the president removed Stanton and ordered him to surrender his office. News of this seemingly open defiance of the law caused Republicans in the House of Representatives to rush through a resolution impeaching the president, without waiting for specific charges against him to be drawn up.

The trial of President Johnson (who was not present in court but was represented by his lawyers) was not merely a test of strength between Congress and the chief executive, but between the Radical and the Moderate Republicans. Impeachment managers from the House of Representatives presented eleven charges against the president, mostly accusing him of violating the Tenure of Office Act but also censuring his repeated attacks upon the Congress. With fierce joy Radical Thaddeus Stevens, who was one of the managers, denounced the president: "Unfortunate man! thus surrounded, hampered, tangled in the meshes of his own wickedness—unfortunate, unhappy man, behold your doom!"

But Radical oratory could not persuade Moderate Republicans and Democrats in the Senate to vote for conviction. They listened as Johnson's lawyers challenged the constitutionality of the Tenure of Office Act, showed that it had not been intended to apply to cabinet members, and proved that, in any case, it did not cover Stanton, who had been appointed by Lincoln, not Johnson. When the critical vote came, Moderate Republicans like Fessenden voted to acquit the president, and Johnson's Radical foes lacked one vote of the two-thirds majority required to convict him. Several other Republican Senators who for political expediency voted against the president were prepared to change their votes and favor acquittal if their ballots were needed.

Nothing more clearly shows how the institutional needs of a political party prevented drastic

"AWKWARD COLLISION ON THE GRAND TRUNK COLUMBIA RAILROAD"
This cartoon depicts presidential and congressional Reconstruction as two engines going in opposite directions on the same rails. Andrew Johnson, driver of the locomotive "President," says: "Look here! One of us has got to back." But Thaddeus Stevens, driver of the locomotive "Congress," replies: "Well, it ain't going to be me that's going to do it, you bet!" *(Library of Congress)*

change than did this decision not to remove a president whom a majority in Congress despised, hated and feared. The desire to maintain the unity of the national Republican party, despite frequent quarrels and incessant bickering, overrode the wishes of individual congressmen. Moderate Republicans felt that throughout the Reconstruction period they were constantly being rushed from one advanced position to another in order to placate the insatiable Radicals. With more accuracy, Radical Republicans perceived that the need of retaining Moderate support prevented the adoption of any really revolutionary Reconstruction program.

Racism as a Limit to Change

A final set of beliefs that limited the nature of the changes imposed upon, and accepted by, the South during the Reconstruction period can be labeled racism. In all parts of the country, white Americans looked with suspicion and fear on those whose skin was of a different color. For example, in California white hatred built up against the Chinese, who had begun coming to that state in great numbers after the discovery of gold and who were later imported by the thousands to help construct the Central Pacific Railroad. White workers resented the willingness of the Chinese to work long hours for "coolies'" wages; they distrusted the unfamiliar attire, diet, and habits of the Chinese; and they disliked all these things more because the Chinese were a yellow-skinned people. Under the leadership of a newly arrived Irish immigrant, Dennis Kearney, white laborers organized a workingman's party, with the slogan, "The Chinese must go."

The depression of 1873 gave impetus to the movement, for day after day thousands of the unemployed gathered in the sand lots of San Francisco to hear Kearney's slashing attacks on the Chinese and on the wealthy corporations that employed them. In the summer of 1877 San Francisco hoodlums, inspired by Kearney, burned 25 Chinese laundries and destroyed dozens of Chinese houses. Politically the movement was strong enough to force both major parties in California to adopt anti-Chinese platforms, and California congressmen succeeded in persuading their colleagues to pass a bill limiting the number of Chinese who could be brought into the United States each year. Since the measure clearly conflicted with treaty arrangements with China, President Rutherford B. Hayes vetoed it, but he had his secretary of state initiate negotiations leading to a new treaty that permitted the restriction of immigration. Congress in 1882 passed the Chinese Exclusion Act, which suspended all Chinese immigration for ten years and forbade the naturalization of Chinese already in the country.

Northern Views of the Black Race. If white Americans became so agitated over a small number of

"THE MARTYRDOM OF ST. CRISPIN"

Racism in postwar America took many forms. Here the artist Thomas Nast shows the obviously 100 percent American "St. Crispin," the patron saint of shoemakers, threatened by the cheap labor of Chinese immigrants. (*American Antiquarian Society*)

Chinese, who were unquestionably hard-working and thrifty and who belonged to one of the most ancient of civilizations, it is easy to see how they could consider blacks an even greater danger. There were more than 3 million Negroes, most of them recently emancipated from slavery. The exploits of black soldiers during the war—their very discipline and courage—proved that Negroes could be formidable opponents. The fact that blacks were no longer portrayed as invisible men but now, in photographs and caricatures, had sharply etched identities exacerbated, rather than allayed, white apprehensions. More clearly than ever before Negroes seemed distinctive, alien, and menacing.

Most American intellectuals of the Civil War generation accepted unquestioningly the dogma that blacks belonged to an inferior race. Though a few reformers like Charles Sumner vigorously attacked this notion, a majority of even philanthropic Northerners accepted the judgment of the distinguished Harvard scientist Louis Agassiz that while whites during antiquity were developing high civilizations "the negro race groped in barbarism and never originated a regular organization among themselves." Many credited Agassiz's conjecture that Negroes, once free, would inevitably die out in the United States. Others reached the same conclusion by studying the recently published work of Charles Darwin, *Origin of Species* (1859), and they accepted the Darwinian argument that in the inevitable struggle for survival "higher civilized races" must inevitably eliminate "an endless number of lower races." Consequently the influential and tenderhearted Congregational minister Horace Bushnell could prophesy the approaching end of the black race in the United States with something approaching equanimity. "Since we must all die," he asked rhetorically, "why should it grieve us, that a stock thousands of years behind, in the scale of culture, should die with few and still fewer children to succeed, till finally the whole succession remains in the more cultivated race?"

When even the leaders of Northern society held such views, it is hardly surprising that most whites in the region were overtly anti-Negro. In state after state whites fiercely resisted efforts to extend the political and civil rights of blacks, partly because they feared that any improvement of the condition of Negroes in the North would lead to a huge influx of blacks from the South. At the end of the Civil War only Maine, New Hampshire, Vermont, Massachusetts, and Rhode Island allowed Negroes to have full voting rights, and in New York blacks who met certain property-holding qualifications could have the ballot. During the next three years in referenda held in Connecticut, Wisconsin, Kansas, Ohio, Michigan, and Missouri, constitutional amendments authorizing Negro suffrage were defeated, and New York voters rejected a proposal to eliminate the property-holding qualifications for black voters. Only in Iowa, a state where there were very few blacks, did a Negro suffrage amendment carry in 1868, and that same year Minnesota adopted an ambiguously worded amendment. Thus at the end of the 1860s most Northern states refused to give black men the ballot.

In words as well as in votes, the majority of Northerners made their deeply racist feelings evident. The Democratic press constantly cultivated the racial fears of its readers, and they regularly portrayed the Republicans as planning a "new era of miscegenation, amalgamation, and promiscuous intercourse between the races." From the White House, denouncing Republican attempts "to Africanize the [Southern] half of our country," President Andrew Johnson announced: "In the progress of nations negroes have shown less capacity for self-government than any other race of people. . . . Whenever they have been left to their own devices they have shown an instant tendency to relapse into barbarism." Even Northern Republicans opposed to Johnson shared many of his racist views. Radical Senator Timothy O. Howe of Wisconsin declared that he regarded "the freedmen, in the main . . . as so much animal life," and Senator Benjamin F. Wade of Ohio, whom the Radical Republicans would have elevated to the presidency had they removed Johnson, had, along with a genuine devotion to the principle of equal rights, an incurable aversion to blacks. Representative George W. Julian of Indiana, one of the few Northern congressmen who had no racial prejudice, bluntly told his colleagues in 1866: "The real trouble is that *we hate the negro*. It is not his ignorance that offends us, but his color. . . . Of this fact I entertain no doubt whatsoever."

Both personal preferences and the wishes of constituents inhibited Northern Republicans from supporting measures that might alter race relations. When Sumner sought to expunge federal laws that recognized slavery or to prohibit racial discrimination on the public transportation in the District of Columbia, his colleagues replied: "God has made the negro inferior, and . . . laws cannot make him equal." Such congressmen were hardly in a position to scold the

South for racial discrimination or to insist on drastic social change in that region.

Southern Views of the Black Race. If racism limited the innovation that Northerners were willing to propose during the Reconstruction period, it even more drastically reduced the amount of change that white Southerners were prepared to accept. The note of racial bigotry runs through both the private correspondence and the public pronouncements of Southern whites during the postwar era. "Equality does not exist between blacks and whites," announced Alexander H. Stephens. "The one race is by nature inferior in many respects, physically and mentally, to the other. This should be received as a fixed invincible fact in all dealings with the subject." A North Carolina diarist agreed: "The Anglo-Saxon and the African can never be equal . . . one or the other must

fall." Or, as the Democratic party of Louisiana resolved in its 1865 platform: "We hold this to be a Government of white people, made and to be perpetuated for the exclusive benefit of the white race; and . . . that people of African descent cannot be considered as citizens of the United States, and that there can, in no event, nor under any circumstances, be any equality between the white and other races." The Black Codes were the legal embodiment of these attitudes.

These racist views shaped the attitudes of most Southern whites toward the whole process of Reconstruction. They approved of President Johnson's plan of Reconstruction because it placed government in the Southern states entirely in the hands of whites. They rejected the Fourteenth Amendment primarily because it made blacks legally equal to whites. They watched with incredulity bordering on stupefaction

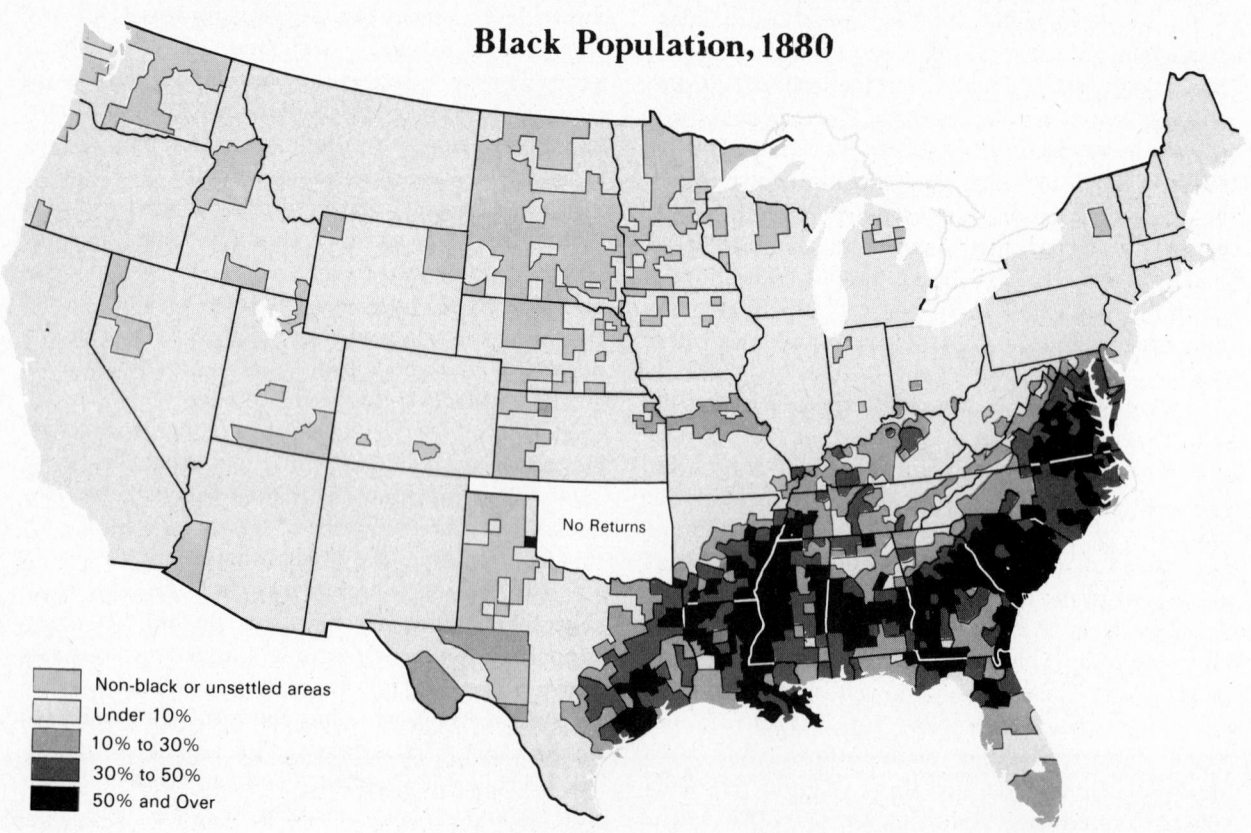

Black Population, 1880

No Returns

Non-black or unsettled areas
Under 10%
10% to 30%
30% to 50%
50% and Over

as Congress passed the 1867 Military Reconstruction Act, for they simply could not believe that the freedmen were to vote. Stunned, they saw army officers supervise the process of voter registration, a process that excluded many prominent whites who had participated in the Confederate government but included more than 700,000 blacks, who formed a majority of eligible voters in South Carolina, Florida, Alabama, Mississippi, and Louisiana. Knowing that these Negro voters were well organized by the Union League, often with the assistance of agents of the Freedmen's Bureau, whites were more apathetic than surprised when the fall elections showed heavy majorities in favor of convening new constitutional conventions.*

With hostile and unbelieving eyes, most Southern whites observed the work of these conventions, which between November 1867 and May 1868 drafted new constitutions for the former Confederate states. To Southern whites unaccustomed to seeing blacks in any positions of public prominence, the presence of freedmen in these conventions meant that they were Negro-dominated. In fact, except in the South Carolina convention, in which blacks did form a majority, only between one-fourth and one-ninth of the delegates were Negroes. Whites ridiculed the Negro members' ignorance of parliamentary procedures, and they laughed sardonically when they read how the "coal black" temporary chairman of the Louisiana convention put a question by asking those who favored a motion "to rise an stan on der feet" and then directing "all you contrary men to rise."

The reactions of Southern whites to the constitutions these conventions produced were also determined by their racial prejudice. Generally they denounced these new charters as "totally incompatible with the prosperity and liberty of the people." In fact the constitutions, often copied from Northern models, were generally improvements over the ones they superseded. In addition to requiring Negro suffrage (as Congress had directed), they promised all citizens of the state equality before the law. They reformed

financial and revenue systems, reorganized the judiciary, improved the organization of local government, and, most important of all, instituted a state-supported system of public education, hitherto notably lacking in most Southern states.

The Reconstruction Governments in the South.

Because these constitutions guaranteed racial equality, Southern whites tried, without great success, to block their ratification. In Alabama, whites boycotted the ratification election; in Mississippi, they cast a majority of votes against the new constitution. In Virginia, ratification was delayed because the conservative army commander of that district discovered that there was no money to hold an election, and in Texas all moves toward the creation of a new government lagged several months behind those in the Eastern states. Despite all the foot-dragging, new governments were set up, and in June 1868 Congress readmitted representatives and senators from Alabama, Arkansas, Florida, Georgia, Louisiana, North Carolina, and South Carolina. Two years later the reconstruction of Virginia, Mississippi, and Texas was completed, and in early 1870 these states were also readmitted. Meanwhile Georgia experienced one further reorganization after the legislature of that state attempted to exclude Negroes who had been elected to that body. But by 1871, when Georgia senators and representatives again took their seats in Congress, all the states of the former Confederacy had undergone the process of Reconstruction and had been readmitted to the Union.

With bitter hostility, most Southern whites witnessed this reorganization of their state governments, and the name "Black Reconstruction," which they gave to the ensuing period of Republican ascendancy in the South, reveals the racial bias behind their opposition. In fact, these Southern state governments were not dominated by Negroes, and the proportion of offices held by blacks was smaller than the percentage of blacks in the population. Only in South Carolina did blacks dominate the state legislature. No Negro was elected governor, though there were black lieutenant governors in South Carolina, Louisiana, and Mississippi. Only in South Carolina was

*The Texas election was not held until February 1868. Tennessee had no election, because it had already been readmitted to the Union.

COLORED RULE IN A RECON-
STRUCTED (?) STATE

As postwar racism mounted,
cartoonists no longer depicted
Negroes as handsome, intelligent fighters for freedom but
painted them as grotesque
and animal-like. In addition
to perpetuating racial stereotypes, this drawing of
Thomas Nast's exaggerates
the number and influence of
blacks in the Southern legislatures. *(American Antiquarian Society)*

there a black state supreme court justice. During the
entire Reconstruction period only two blacks, Hiram
R. Revels and Blanche K. Bruce, both from Mississippi and both men of exceptional ability and integrity, served in the United States Senate, and only
fifteen blacks were elected to the House of Representatives.

Even to the most racist Southern whites it was
obvious that most of the leaders of the Republican
party in the South, and a large part of the Republican
following as well, were white. To those white Republicans born in the North, racists gave the label Carpetbaggers, because they allegedly came South with
no more worldly possessions than could be packed
into a carpetbag, or small suitcase, ready to live on
and to exploit the prostrate region. The term, with
its implication of corruption, was applied indiscriminately to men of Northern birth who had lived in the

South long before the war as well as to newly arrived
fortune hunters, many of them recently discharged
Union army officers.

Southern-born white Republicans were called
Scalawags, a term that cattle drovers applied to "the
mean, lousy and filthy kine that are not fit for butchers or dogs." Again the term was used indiscriminately. Southern racists applied it to poor hill-country
whites, who had long been at odds with the planters
in states like North Carolina and Alabama and now
joined the Republican party as a way of getting back
at their old enemies. But other Scalawags were members of the planter, mercantile, and industrial classes
of the South; many of these were former Whigs who
distrusted the Democrats, and they felt at home in a
Republican party that favored protective tariffs, subsidies for railroads, and appropriations for rebuilding
the levees along the Mississippi River. A surprising

number of Southern-born white Republicans were former high-ranking officers in the Confederate army, like General P. G. T. Beauregard and General James Longstreet, who knew at first hand the extent of the damage wrought by the war and were willing to accept the victor's terms without procrastination.

Bitterly as they attacked these white Republicans, Southern Democrats reserved their worst abuse for Negroes, and they saw in every measure adopted by the new reconstructed state governments evidence of black incompetence, extravagance, or even barbarism. In truth, much that these state governments did supplied the Democrats with ammunition. The postwar period was one of low political morality, and there was no reason to expect that newly enfranchised blacks would prove any less attracted by the profits of politics than anybody else. Petty corruption prevailed in all the Southern state governments. Louisiana legislators voted themselves an allowance for stationery—which covered purchases of hams and bottles of champagne. The South Carolina legislature ran up a bill of more than $50,000 in refurbishing the statehouse with such costly items as a $750 mirror, $480 clocks, and 200 porcelain spittoons at $8 apiece. The same legislature voted $1,000 to the Speaker of the House of Representatives to repay his losses on a horse race.

Bad as these excesses were, Southern Democrats were angered less by them than by the legitimate work performed by the new state governments. Unwilling to recognize that Negroes were now equal members of the body politic, they objected to expenditures for hospitals, jails, orphanages, and asylums to care for blacks. Most of all they objected to the creation of a public school system. Throughout the South there was considerable hostility to the idea of educating any children at the cost of the taxpayer, and the thought of paying taxes in order to teach black children seemed wild and foolish extravagance. The fact that black schools were mostly conducted by Northern whites, usually women, who came South with a reforming mission, did nothing to increase popular support; too many of the teachers stated plainly and publicly their intention to use "every endeavor to throw a ray of light here and there,

among this benighted race of ruffians, rebels by nature." Adding to all these hostilities was a fear that a system of public education might some day lead to a racially integrated system of education. These apprehensions had little basis in fact, for during the entire period of Reconstruction in the whole South there were significant numbers of children in racially mixed schools only in New Orleans between 1870 and 1874.

The Ku Klux Klan. Not content with criticizing Republican rule, Southern Democrats organized to put an end to it. Theirs was a two-pronged attack. On the one hand, they sought to intimidate or to drive from the South whites who cooperated politically with the Republican regimes; on the other, they tried to terrorize and silence blacks, especially those active in politics. Much of this pressure was informal and sporadic, but much was the work of racist organizations that sprang up all over the South during these years. The most famous of these was the Ku Klux Klan, which originated in 1866 as a social club for young white men in Pulaski, Tennessee. As the Military Reconstruction Act went into effect and the possibility of black participation in Southern political life became increasingly real, racists saw new potential in this secret organization with its cabalistic name and its mysterious uniforms of long flowing robes, high conical hats that made the wearers seem preternaturally tall, and white face masks.

In 1867 the Klan was reorganized under a new constitution that provided for local dens, each headed by a Grand Cyclops, linked together into provinces (counties), each under a Grand Titan, and in turn into realms (states), each under a Grand Dragon. At the head of the whole organization was the Grand Wizard, who, according to most reports, was former Confederate General Nathan Bedford Forrest. Probably this elaborate table of organization was never completely filled out, and certainly there was an almost total lack of central control of the Klan's activities. Indeed, at some point in early 1869 the Klan was officially disbanded. But even without central direction its members, like those of the Order of the White Camellia and other racist vigilante groups, continued in their plan of disrupting the new Republican regimes in the South and terrorizing their black supporters.

Along with other vigilante organizations, the Klan was an expression of the traditional racism of Southern whites. They were willing to accept the defeat of the Confederacy, and they were prepared to admit that slavery was dead; but they could not bring themselves to contemplate a society that would treat blacks and whites as equals. As a group of South Carolina whites protested to Congress in 1868: "The white people of our State will never quietly submit to negro rule. . . . We will keep up this contest until we have regained the heritage of political control handed down to us by honored ancestry. That is a duty we owe to the land that is ours, to the graves that it contains, and to the race of which you and we alike are members—the proud Caucasian race, whose sovereignty on earth God has ordained."

The appeal was shrewdly pitched, for the Southern racist knew how to reach his Northern counterpart. Joined together, their fears of men with darker skins helped to undercut the Reconstruction regimes in the South and to halt any congressional efforts at further innovative Reconstruction legislation.

The Restoration of "Home Rule"

The effectiveness of these limitations on social and political experimentation in the South became evident as early as the fall congressional elections in 1867, which the Democrats won by a landslide. Responding to the popular mood of conservatism, the Republican party in 1868 passed over Radical candidates for the presidency, like Benjamin F. Wade, and nominated Ulysses S. Grant, whose affiliation with Republicans was of recent date but whose broad popular appeal as a military hero was unrivaled. Elected by a surprisingly narrow margin over former Governor Horatio Seymour of New York, the Democratic candidate, Grant shrewdly sized up the attitude of the country toward Reconstruction and in his inaugural address announced his policy: "Let us have peace."

Just what he meant was not immediately clear.

Some thought the new president was addressing the white Ku Kluxers who were trying to overthrow the Reconstruction governments in the South; others believed that he was speaking to Northern Radicals who wanted to bring about further changes in Southern society. As it proved, Grant had both extremes in mind. On the one hand, the president warmly supported the immediate and unconditional readmission of Virginia to the Union, even though Radicals like Sumner warned that the Virginia legislature was "composed of recent Rebels still filled and seething with that old Rebel fire." On the other, Grant was outraged by the terrorism rampant in the South, and he insisted that Congress pass a series of Enforcement Acts (1870–71) enabling him to crush the Ku Klux Klan. Under this legislation, the president proclaimed martial law in nine South Carolina counties where white terrorists were most active, and federal marshals arrested large numbers of suspected Klansmen in North Carolina, Mississippi, and other Southern states. In brief, then, Grant's policy was to warn Southern whites that the national government would not tolerate overt violence and organized military activity—but to let them understand that at the same time they would not be harassed if they regained control of their state governments through less revolutionary tactics.

The "Redemption" of the South. Quickly accepting the hint, Southern whites promptly undertook the restoration of what they euphemistically called "home rule"—which meant the rule of native white Democrats. Aware of Northern sensitivities, they now downplayed, when possible, the more brutal forms of terrorism and outright violence. White Republicans were subjected to social pressure and economic boycott; many fled the South, and others joined the Redeemers (as the advocates of home rule and white supremacy liked to call themselves). Redeemers exerted economic pressure on blacks by threatening not to hire or extend credit to those who were politically active.

In several states whites organized rifle clubs, which practiced marksmanship on the outskirts of Republican political rallies. Usually blacks were cowed by these tactics. In a few cases, however, when they organized and tried to defend themselves, there occurred what Southern newspapers called "race riots"—a better term would have been "massacres," for the more numerous and better armed whites overpowered the blacks and slaughtered their leaders. In state after state Republican governors appealed to Washington for additional federal troops, but Grant, convinced that the public was tired of "these annual autumnal outbreaks" in the South, refused.

In consequence of Grant's policy, the Redeemers quickly gained power in Virginia, North Carolina, Tennessee, and Georgia. In 1875 they won control of Alabama, Mississippi, Arkansas, and Texas, and early in 1877 they ended Republican rule in Florida. By the end of Grant's second administration, South Carolina and Louisiana were the only Southern states with Republican governments.

The Election of 1876. The fate of these two remaining Republican regimes in the South became intricately connected with the outcome of the 1876 presidential election. The Democratic nominee, Samuel J. Tilden, undoubtedly received a majority of the popular votes cast—though, equally undoubtedly, thousands of blacks who would have voted for his Republican rival, Rutherford B. Hayes, were kept from the polls. But Tilden lacked one vote of having a majority in the electoral college unless he received some of the votes from South Carolina, Florida, and Louisiana, all of which submitted to Congress competing sets of Democratic and Republican ballots. (There was also a technical question of the eligibility of one Republican elector from Oregon.)

Consequently when Congress assembled in December 1876 it confronted a crisis. If it decided to accept the disputed Democratic electoral votes, Republican control of the White House would be broken for the first time in a quarter of a century and the Reconstruction of the South would be ended. If Congress accepted the Republican electoral votes, that decision would run counter to the will of a majority of the voters in the country.

To resolve the impasse required a compromise—not a single compromise, but a complicated, interlocking set of bargains. After intricate and secret

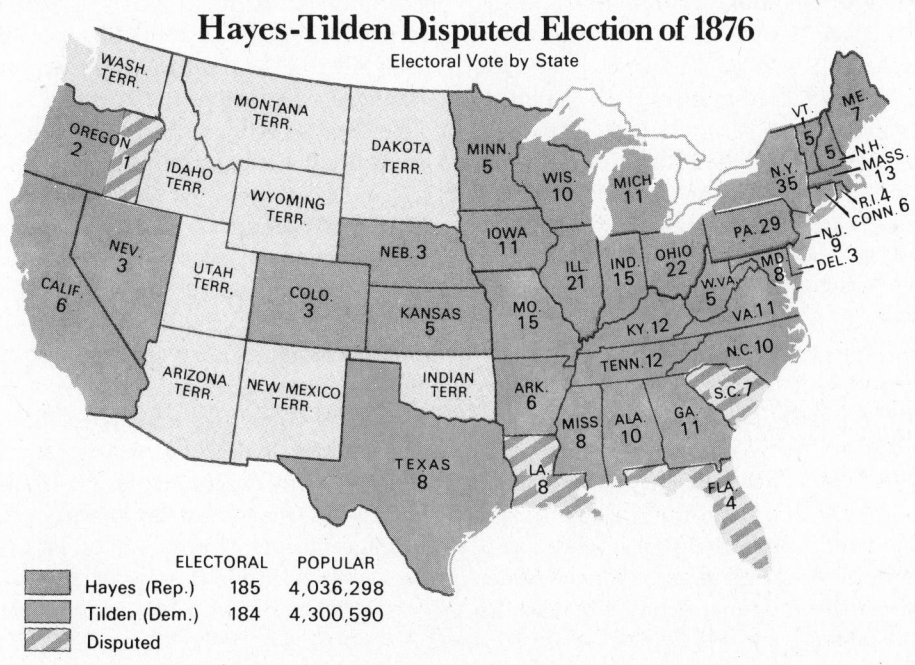

Hayes-Tilden Disputed Election of 1876
Electoral Vote by State

	ELECTORAL	POPULAR
Hayes (Rep.)	185	4,036,298
Tilden (Dem.)	184	4,300,590
Disputed		

negotiations, several agreements were reached. First, Congress decided that the disputed electoral votes should be referred to a special electoral commission, which should consist of five members from the House of Representatives, five members from the Senate, and five associate justices from the Supreme Court. This body was composed of eight Republicans and seven Democrats, and on every disputed ballot the commission ruled in favor of Hayes by that same vote. In consequence of these decisions, Tilden's electoral vote remained at 184, while Hayes's slowly mounted to 185. In March 1877, for the fifth time in succession, a Republican president was inaugurated.

Democrats reluctantly accepted the election of Hayes because of some other bargaining that took place while the electoral votes were being counted. One set of compromises came to be known as the Wormley agreement, because it was negotiated in the luxurious Washington hotel owned by the Negro restaurateur James Wormley. Representing Hayes at these sessions were Senator Sherman, Representative Garfield, and other prominent Republicans. Across the table sat Southern Democratic leaders, including Senator John B. Gordon, the former Confederate General who now represented Georgia in Congress, and L. Q. C. Lamar, once Confederate minister to Russia, who was senator from Mississippi. The Republicans promised the Southerners that, if allowed to be inaugurated, Hayes "would deal justly and generously with the south." Translated, that meant that Hayes would withdraw the remaining federal troops from the South and acquiesce in the overthrow of the Republican regimes in South Carolina and Louisiana. The Southerners found the terms acceptable, and they promptly leaked the news of the agreement, so as to protect themselves from charges that they had betrayed their section.

Behind the Wormley agreement lay other, less formal, compromises. Hayes's backers promised that the new president would not use federal patronage in the South to defeat the Democrats. They further pledged that he would support congressional appropriations for rebuilding levees along the flood-ridden Mississippi River and for constructing a transconti-

nental railroad along a Southern route. In return, Southerners agreed to allow the Republicans to elect Garfield Speaker of the new House of Representatives, with the power to determine the membership of congressional committees. More important, they promised to protect the basic rights of blacks, as guaranteed in the Thirteenth, Fourteenth, and Fifteenth Amendments to the Constitution.

Once Hayes was inaugurated, virtually all these informal agreements were flouted by both sides. Hayes, for his part, ordered the removal of federal troops from the South and did appoint a Southerner, former Confederate David M. Key, to his cabinet as postmaster general. But two-thirds of the federal officeholders in the South remained Republicans. Hayes changed his mind about supporting a Southern transcontinental railroad alleging that federal funding would lead to corruption.

Southern Democrats for their part reneged on their promise to support Garfield for Speaker, and, once the House was organized under Democratic leadership, they eagerly joined in an investigation of alleged fraud in Hayes's election. Only a very few Southern Democratic politicians, like Governor Wade Hampton of South Carolina, remembered their promises to respect the rights of blacks. Instead, almost all took the final withdrawal of federal troops from the South as a signal that the Negro, already relegated to a position of economic inferiority, could be excluded from Southern political life.

Disfranchisement of Blacks.   Southern whites had to act cautiously, so as not to offend public opinion in the North or to invite renewed federal intervention, but they moved steadily and successfully to reduce Negro voting. One of the simplest devices was the poll tax, adopted by Georgia in 1877 and quickly copied by other Southern states. To Northerners the requirement that a voter had to pay $1 or $2 a year did not seem unreasonable, yet in fact, since three-fourths of the entire Southern population had an average income of only $55.16 in 1880, the poll tax was a considerable financial drain, especially to poverty-stricken blacks. More imaginative was the "eight

"WE'LL SHOW YOU WHEN WE COME TO VOTE"
The attitude of Northern women contributed to the declining interest in the problems of the South. Many women who had loyally supported the war and emancipation felt that they, as well as the freedmen, should have been enfranchised under the Reconstruction amendments to the Constitution. In 1869 Elizabeth Cady Stanton, Susan B. Anthony, and others organized the National Woman Suffrage Association to promote a sixteenth amendment to the Constitution, enfranchising women. *(American Antiquarian Society)*

box" law, adopted by South Carolina in 1882 and imitated by North Carolina and Florida. Under this system ballots for each contested race had to be deposited in separate boxes. Thus a voter must cast in one box his ballot for governor, in another box his ballot for sheriff, and so forth. The system frustrated the illiterate Negro voter, who could no longer bring to the polls a single ballot, marked for him in advance by a Republican friend. To make the task of semi-literate voters more difficult, election officials periodically rearranged the order of the boxes. Still another device, which did not become popular until the late 1880s, was the secret, or Australian, ballot. Ostensibly introduced in the South, as in the North, in order to prevent fraud, the secret ballot actually discriminated heavily against blacks, for as late as 1900 the number of illiterate adult Negro males ranged from 39 percent in Florida to 61 percent in Louisiana.

Despite all these devices, Southern blacks continued to vote in surprising numbers. In the 1880 presidential election, for example, more than 70 percent of the eligible Negroes voted in Arkansas, Florida, North Carolina, Tennessee, and Virginia, and between 50 percent and 70 percent voted in Alabama, Louisiana, South Carolina, and Texas. To the Redeemers these black voters posed a double threat. They were numerous enough that ambitious Northern Republicans might be tempted again to try federal intervention in state elections, with the hope of breaking the now solidly Democratic South. Even more dangerous was the possibility that poor whites in the South, whose needs for public education and welfare the business-oriented Redeemers consistently neglected, might find common cause with their black peers.

The Redeemers saw both these dangers materialize after 1890. Shortly after the Republicans gained control of the House of Representatives in 1889, Representative Henry Cabot Lodge of Massachusetts introduced a strong bill for federal control of elections, which was promptly christened the Force Bill. Though Democrats in the Senate defeated Lodge's bill in January 1891, Redeemers saw in it a threat to renew "all the horrors of reconstruction days." Their fear was doubtless the greater because the almost simultaneous rise of the Populist movement threatened, as never before, to split the white voters of the region. Appealing to farmers and small planters, the Populist party was the enemy of lawyers and bankers and of the rising commercial and industrial spokesmen of the "New South." Some of the Populist leaders, like Thomas Watson of Georgia, were openly critical of the Redeemers' policy of repressing the blacks and seemed to be flirting with the Negro voters.

Faced with this double threat, Southern states moved swiftly to exclude the Negro completely and permanently from politics. Mississippi led the way

with a constitutional convention in 1890 that required voters to be able to read and interpret the Constitution to the satisfaction of the white registration officials. It is not hard to imagine how difficult even a graduate of Howard University Law School would have found the task of satisfactory constitutional exegesis. In 1898 a Louisiana constitutional convention improved on the Mississippi example by requiring a literacy test of all voters except the sons and grandsons of persons who voted in state elections before 1867. Since no Louisiana Negroes had been permitted to vote before that date, this provision allowed illiterate whites to vote, while the literacy test excluded most Negro voters.

State after state across the South followed, or elaborated on, these requirements. South Carolina held a disfranchising convention in 1895. North Carolina amended its constitution to limit suffrage in 1900. Alabama and Virginia acted in 1901–2, and Georgia adopted a restrictive constitutional amendment in 1908. The remaining Southern states continued to rely on the poll tax and other varieties of legislative disfranchisement. When opponents of these measures accused their advocates of discriminating against the Negroes, Carter Glass of Virginia replied for his entire generation: "Discrimination! Why that is precisely what we propose; that exactly is what this convention was elected for."

It took time, then, for the complete working out of the political compromises of the Reconstruction era. Not until the end of the nineteenth century did white Southerners receive the full price they had exacted in permitting the election of Rutherford B. Hayes. But by 1900 that payment had been made in full. The Negro was no longer a political force in the South, and the Republican party was no longer the defender of Negro rights.

CHRONOLOGY

1865 Lincoln assassinated; Andrew Johnson becomes president.
Johnson moves for speedy, lenient restoration of Southern states to Union.
Congress creates Joint Committee of Fifteen to supervise reconstruction process.
Thirteenth Amendment ratified.

1866 Johnson breaks with Republican majority in Congress by vetoing Freedmen's Bureau bill and Civil Rights bill. Latter is passed over his veto.
Congress approves Fourteenth Amendment and submits it to states for ratification.
Johnson and Republicans quarrel. Republicans win fall congressional elections.
Ku Klux Klan formed.

1867 Congress passes Military Reconstruction Act over Johnson's veto. (Two supplementary acts in 1867 and a third in 1868 passed to put this measure into effect.)
Congress passes Tenure of Office Act and Command of Army Act to reduce Johnson's power.

1868 Former Confederate states hold constitutional conventions, for which former slaves are allowed to vote, and adopt new constitutions guaranteeing universal suffrage.
Arkansas, Alabama, Florida, Georgia, Louisiana,
North Carolina, and South Carolina readmitted to representation in Congress. Because of discrimination against Negro officeholders, Georgia representatives are expelled. (State is again admitted in 1870.)
President Johnson impeached. Escapes conviction by one vote.
Republicans nominate Ulysses S. Grant for president; Democrats select Governor Horatio Seymour of New York. Grant elected president.

1869 Congress passes Fifteenth Amendment and submits it to states for ratification.

1870 First Ku Klux Klan (or Enforcement) Act gives Grant power to move against white terrorists in South. A second act in 1871 further strengthens president's hand.

1872 Grant reelected president.

1876 Republicans nominate Rutherford B. Hayes for president; Democrats nominate Samuel J. Tilden. Tilden secures majority of popular vote but electoral vote is in doubt because of disputed returns from three Southern states.

1877 After elaborate political and economic bargaining, Congress creates an electoral commission, which rules that all disputed ballots belong to Hayes, who is inaugurated president.

SUGGESTED READINGS

The Civil War and Reconstruction (1969), by J. G. Randall and David Donald, continues to be useful, especially for its full bibliography. Three modern treatments of the postwar period are John H. Franklin, *Reconstruction after the Civil War* (1961), Kenneth M. Stampp, *The Era of Reconstruction* (1965), and Rembert W. Patrick, *The Reconstruction of the Nation* (1967).

The best account of steps taken during the Civil War to reorganize the Southern states is Herman Belz, *Reconstructing the Union* (1969). William B. Hesseltine, *Lincoln's Plan of Reconstruction* (1960), argues that Lincoln had not

one but many approaches to Reconstruction, all of them unsuccessful. Peyton McCrary, *Abraham Lincoln and Reconstruction* (1978), is the authoritative account of developments in Louisiana, where Lincoln's experiment in Reconstruction was most fully tested.

Robert W. Winston, *Andrew Johnson, Plebeian and Patriot* (1928), is the best of several unsatisfactory biographies of that president. More valuable are the markedly favorable estimates of Johnson's program in George F. Milton, *The Age of Hate* (1930), and Howard K. Beale, *The Critical Year* (1930), and the strongly critical analyses in

Eric L. McKitrick, *Andrew Johnson and Reconstruction* (1960), LaWanda Cox and John H. Cox, *Politics, Principle, and Prejudice* (1963), and W. R. Brock, *An American Crisis* (1963).

Four major studies of postwar constitutional changes are Harold M. Hyman, *A More Perfect Union* (1973), Stanley I. Kutler, *Judicial Power and Reconstruction Politics* (1968), William Gillette, *The Right to Vote* (1965), and Charles Fairman, *Reconstruction and Reunion* (1971).

George R. Bentley, *A History of the Freedmen's Bureau* (1955), is a standard work, but it should be supplemented by William S. McFeely, *Yankee Stepfather: General O. O. Howard and the Freedmen* (1968), and Louis S. Gerteis, *From Contraband to Freedman* (1973).

Leon Litwack, *Been in the Storm So Long* (1979), is a masterful account of the transition from slavery to freedom. Four state studies of black responses to emancipation are especially valuable: on South Carolina, Willie Lee Rose, *Rehearsal for Reconstruction* (1964), and Joel Williamson, *After Slavery* (1965); on Alabama, Peter Kolchin, *First Freedom* (1972); and on Mississippi, Vernon L. Wharton, *The Negro in Mississippi* (1947).

Fred A. Shannon, *The Farmer's Last Frontier* (1945), and E. Merton Coulter, *The South during Reconstruction* (1947), give good general accounts of economic changes in the postwar South. Recently these changes have been reappraised by historians and economists using sophisticated quantitative methods: Stephen J. DeCanio, *Agriculture in the Postbellum South* (1974); Robert Higgs, *Competition and Coercion: Blacks in the American Economy* (1977); and Roger Ransom and Richard L. Sutch, *One Kind of Freedom: The Economic Consequences of Emancipation* (1977). For a thoughtful evaluation of this new literature, see Harold D. Woodman, "Sequel to Slavery: The New History Views the Postbellum South," *Journal of Southern History*, 43 (1977), 525–54. On the alleged breakup of the plantation system, see Roger W. Shugg, *Origins of Class Struggle in Louisiana* (1939), and on the continuing dominance of the planter class, see Jonathan M. Wiener, *Social Origins of the New South* (1978).

Two articles provide the best brief introduction to the modern interpretation of Reconstruction politics: Larry G. Kincaid, "Victims of Circumstance: An Interpretation of Changing Attitudes toward Republican Policy Makers and Reconstruction," *Journal of American History*, 57 (1970), 48–66, and Michael L. Benedict, "Preserving the Constitution: The Conservative Basis of Radical Reconstruction," *ibid.*, 61 (1974), 65–90. See also Hans L. Trefousse, *The Radical Republicans* (1969), David Donald, *The Politics of Reconstruction* (1965), and Michael L. Benedict, *A Compromise of*

Principle (1974). Among the fullest biographies of Radical leaders are Fawn M. Brodie, *Thaddeus Stevens* (1959), David Donald, *Charles Sumner and the Rights of Man* (1970), and Benjamin P. Thomas and Harold M. Hyman, *Stanton* (1962).

David M. DeWitt, *Impeachment and Trial of Andrew Johnson* (1903), is the standard account, strongly pro-Johnson in tone. Michael L. Benedict's book of the same title (1973) is a useful, anti-Johnson corrective. The best explanation of why impeachment occurred when it did is to be found in Hans L. Trefousse, *Impeachment of a President* (1975).

On American racial attitudes, George M. Fredrickson, *The Black Image in the White Mind* (1971), is excellent. On Northern racism, see V. Jacque Voegeli, *Free but Not Equal* (1967), and Forrest G. Wood, *Black Scare* (1968). A thoughtful and provocative essay is C. Vann Woodward, "Seeds of Failure in Radical Race Policy," *American Philosophical Society Proceedings*, 110 (1966), 1–9.

On the work of the Reconstruction governments in the South, see W. E. B. DuBois, "Reconstruction and Its Benefits," *American Historical Review* (1910), 781–99, and DuBois, *Black Reconstruction* (1935). The best accounts of Reconstruction in individual states are Francis B. Simkins and Robert H. Woody, *South Carolina during Reconstruction* (1932), Jerrell H. Shofner, *Nor Is It Over Yet: Florida in the Era of Reconstruction* (1974), Thomas B. Alexander, *Political Reconstruction in Tennessee* (1950), James W. Garner, *Reconstruction in Mississippi* (1901), and Joe G. Taylor, *Louisiana Reconstructed* (1974).

On the education of blacks after the war, see Henry A. Bullock, *A History of Negro Education in the South* (1967), William P. Vaughn, *Schools for All* (1974), and Roger A. Fischer, *The Segregation Struggle in Louisiana* (1974).

Southern white resistance to the Reconstruction process is the theme of Michael Perman, *Reunion without Compromise* (1973). Allen W. Trelease, *White Terror* (1971), is a harrowing account of white vigilantism, as carried on by the Ku Klux Klan and less formally organized groups.

On Grant's presidency the best, but not entirely satisfactory, account is William B. Hesseltine, *Ulysses S. Grant, Politician* (1935). William Gillette, *Retreat from Reconstruction* (1980), is the best account of Grant's Southern policy.

C. Vann Woodward, *Reunion and Reaction* (1951), is a highly original reexamination of the compromises of 1876–77. On the Redeemer regimes, see Woodward's authoritative *Origins of the New South* (1951). The best study of the disfranchisement of blacks is J. Morgan Kousser, *The Shaping of Southern Politics* (1974).

"Westward the Course of Empire Takes Its Way" by Emanuel Leutze. Courtesy of National Collection of Fine Arts, Smithsonian Institution

From Eden to Babylon

Just as the Civil War required Americans to reconsider the meaning of national loyalty, so it compelled them to rethink the bases of a good society. Before the war their vision of America was primarily agrarian. Most of the inhabitants of the United States lived on farms, planatations, and ranches. Of course there were bustling cities, but most city dwellers had been born in the countryside, whether in the United States, Ireland, Germany, or England. It was natural, then, that when mid-century Americans portrayed themselves, it was as farmers, herdsmen, trappers, and explorers —not as businessmen, factory laborers, or clerks.

Just before the outbreak of the war Emanuel Leutze accurately recaptured the Americans' definition of themselves in *Westward the Course of Empire Takes Its Way*, which filled a six-hundred-square-foot panel in the rotunda of the national Capitol. It was not a great painting, not even a good painting; in it, as one contemporary remarked, "confusion reigns paramount." But it did serve to perpetuate the myth that Americans were a people close to the land, who drew their strength from nature.

Nature had a special place in the thought of antebellum Americans. The most influential American philosophical work published in the first half of the nineteenth century was Ralph Waldo Emerson's essay on that topic. "Nature," to Emerson and the thousands who read his essays and heard him lecture, included those "essences unchanged by man: space, the air, the river, the leaf." It was to be distinguished from "art," the imposition of man's will upon nature that resulted in "a house, a canal, a statue, a picture." "Nature," then, had emotional and moral primacy over "art," and most Americans believed, with Emerson himself, that by shedding all artifice man could again become part and parcel of nature itself.

A self-taught Massachusetts painter, Erastus Salisbury Field, perfectly recaptured the spirit behind Emerson's ideas. With only three months of informal training as an artist, Field personified the spirit of spontaneity and improvisation that Emerson extolled. More important, his early paintings showed an attachment to, and a meticulous interest in, nature. The land he portrayed was a tidied-up, New England version of Leutze's sprawling continent. Field's *The Garden of Eden* did not have a specifically American setting, though his neatly paired animals of peculiar anatomy and his trees with their improbable fruit might have flourished in America, if anywhere. There is, however, a distinctively American note in Field's treatment of nudity in the Garden of Eden: a clump of strategically placed lilies preserves Adam's modesty, and Eve lurks behind some unlikely blossoms. Clearly for Field, as for Emerson, man is at his best when most closely linked to nature, in a scene unmarred by human artifice or ingenuity.

"The Garden of Eden" by Erastus Salisbury Field. M. and M. Karolik Collection, Museum of Fine Arts, Boston

"Proposed Arcade Railroad Under Broadway" by Samuel B.
B. Nowlan. Yale University Art Gallery, Mabel Brady
Garvan Collection

During the Civil War years Americans' perception of the good society dramatically changed. The
war may not have stimulated economic growth, but
it did promote mechanization. Steam power largely
replaced horse power and water power. Machines
of ever increasing complexity, with fascinating
gears and gauges, replaced men. The vast foundries
and rolling mills that had turned out cannons during the war were diverted to the production of
structural iron girders, and later steel beams, which
made possible a new American architecture. No
longer was it necessary to erect buildings out of
huge piles of masonry, and no longer was it dangerous to build them too high. Using steel beams,
innovative architects like Louis Sullivan invented
the skyscraper, a triumphant fusing of form and
function. Imaginative engineers, like Samuel B. B.
Nowlan of New York, foresaw the day when whole
cities would be made of steel, and Nowlan's sketch,
Proposed Arcade Railroad under Broadway, looked
ahead to a new era in urban design.

Postwar Americans found the new technology exhilarating to the point of intoxication. Gone now was the day when Erastus Field portrayed man in the bosom of nature. Instead, looking forward to the Centennial Exposition in Philadelphia, the aging Field painted his *Historical Monument of the American Republic*. Field's picture showed America as wholly urban, entirely built over with huge towers, with round or octagonal sides, rising in diminishing stages. The central and tallest tower commemorated Abraham Lincoln and the Constitution. Near the top, several of these towers were joined together with vaulting steel bridges, along which steam railroad trains puffed. As a significant reminder of Civil War days, soldiers paraded the avenue in front of Field's monumental vision of America as Babylon.

By 1876, then, Field's ideas, like those of most Americans, had completely shifted. Rural peace paled beside the attractions of mechanized urban life. The machine was now the magnet of the American mind. When the novelist William Dean Howells visited the Centennial Exposition, he, like thousands of other Americans, was most impressed by the gigantic Corliss engine, which gave power to the 8000 other machines, large and small, that sewed cloth, printed newspapers, made shoes, and pumped water on the thirteen-acre Exposition grounds. After comparing the displays of painting and sculpture with the Corliss engine, Howells concluded: "It is in these things of iron and steel that the national genius most freely speaks."

"Historical Monument of the American Republic" *by Erastus Salisbury Field. Museum of Fine Arts, Springfield, Massachusetts, The Morgan Wesson Memorial Collection*

"Max Schmitt in a Single Skull" by Thomas Eakins. Metropolitan Museum of Art, Alfred N. Punnett Fund and Gift of George D. Pratt, 1934

The greatest painter of the postwar period, Thomas Eakins of Philadelphia, shared Howells's admiration of the machine and his respect for the scientific knowledge that it represented. Just as the Corliss engine was "an athlete of steel and iron, without a superfluous ounce of metal on it," so a painting, thought Eakins, should be lean and objective. In order to portray the human figure scientifically, he studied anatomy at Jefferson Medical College. Eakins also linked painting with mathematics, because both were disciplines in which "the complicated things are reduced to simple things."

Eakins's portrait, Max Schmitt in a Single Skull, shows how perfectly he fused art, anatomy, and the mathematics of perspective. More subtly it also speaks of the changed values of postwar American society. In decisive contrast to the absence of all man-made artifacts in Leutze's painting and in Field's The Garden of Eden, a superb steel bridge is a vital part of Eakins's portrait. More emphatically than any number of words, the presence of that bridge shows that, by the end of the Civil War era, Americans had come to think of nature as something to be spanned, conquered, and controlled.

CHAPTER 21

National Problems

1865–1877

The Civil War strongly encouraged the sentiment of nationalism among Northerners. The primary Northern war aim was not to guarantee equal rights to all men nor even to end slavery; it was to preserve the Union. By that often repeated phrase, men and women of the war years meant something more than merely maintaining the country as a territorial unit. Attached to the idea of union was an almost mystical sense of the wholeness of the American people. Americans viewed themselves as a chosen people, selected to conduct an experiment in self-government, to be a test case as to the viability of democratic institutions. As Lincoln declared, the United States was nothing less than "the last, best hope of earth."

That faith in the special destiny of the United States gave courage and hope to Northerners during the darkest hours of the war. Defeats on the battlefield, properly understood, were the fire that served to burn away the dross and impurities in American life. As the Reverend Marvin R. Vincent of Troy, New York, announced: "God has been striking, and trying to make us strike at elements unfavorable to the growth of a pure democracy; and . . . he is at work, preparing in this broad land a fit stage for a last act of the mighty drama, the consummation of human civilization." A similar inspiration moved Julia Ward Howe to draw on the imagery of the Book of Revelation in composing the most powerful and popular battle hymn ever written:

*Mine eyes have seen the glory of the coming of the
    Lord:*
*He is trampling out the vintage where the grapes of
    wrath are stored;*
*He has loosed the fateful lightning of his terrible
    swift sword:*
His truth is marching on.

Northerners believed that the Union would emerge from the war more powerful, more cohesive than ever before. They expected that the United States would no longer be a confederation or a union of states but, in the fullest sense a nation. A small shift in grammar tells the whole story. Before the Civil War many politicians and writers referred to

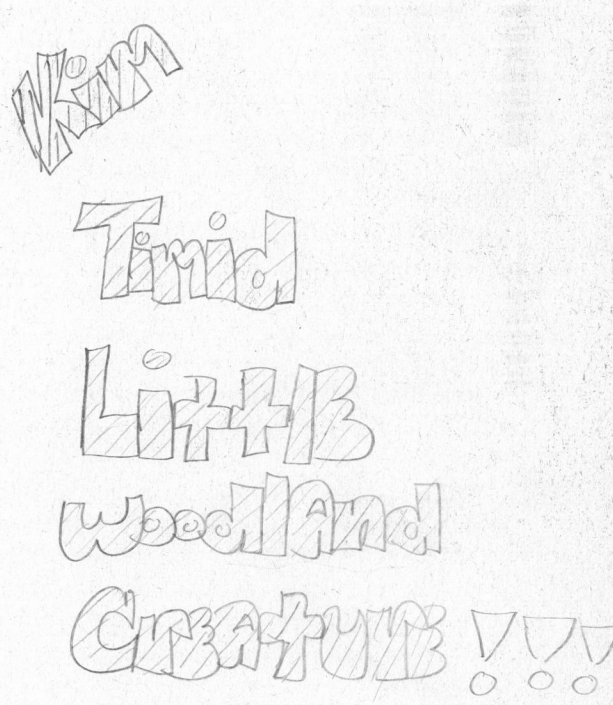

the United States in the plural, but after 1865 only a pedant or the most unreconstructed Southerner would have dreamed of saying "the United States are."

The word "nation" came easily now to American lips. Unlike his predecessors who generally avoided the term, Lincoln regularly referred to the United States as a nation. For example, he used the word no fewer than five times in his brief Gettysburg Address, most eloquently in the concluding pledge: "... that this nation, under God, shall have a new birth of freedom." In 1865 when Republicans agreed to establish a weekly journal that would reflect their views, they called it, as a matter of course, *The Nation*, and it became, as it has remained, one of the most influential periodicals in the country. In 1867 when Sumner took to the lecture circuit to supplement his senatorial salary, he chose for his topic, "Are We a Nation?" The answer, he believed, was obvious. Americans were "one people, throbbing with a common life, occupying a common territory, rejoicing in a common history, sharing in common trials." Never again should any "local claim of self-government" be permitted "for a moment [to] interfere with the supremacy of the Nation." He concluded: "Such centralization is the highest civilization, for it approaches the nearest to the heavenly example."

Political theorists as well as public men in the postwar generation exalted American nationalism. In 1865 Orestes Brownson, the former Jacksonian spokesman, published the first book-length contribution to the bibliography of American nationalism, *The American Republic: Its Constitution, Tendencies, and Destiny*. "Nations are only individuals on a larger scale," Brownson argued, and his treatise was designed to resolve the identity crisis of the Civil War by persuading the American nation to "reflect on its own constitution, its own separate existence, individuality, tendencies, and end." Even more soaring were the claims of the Reverend Elisha Mulford's *The Nation: The Foundations of Civil Order and Political Life in the United States* (1870). The nation, Mulford argued in terms of Hegelian philosophy, was a mystic body, endowed with a spirit and a majesty of its own. "The Nation" he concluded, "is a work of God in history. ... Its vocation is from God, and its obligation is only to God."

American Diplomacy

This mood of high nationalism helps explain American expansionism in the decade after the Civil War. Hardly a year passed without some significant American diplomatic move, either to assert the hegemony of the United States in the Western hemisphere or to annex new territory.

These foreign policy initiatives received considerable popular support. After Appomattox there was a general feeling that the United States, with a million seasoned veterans under arms, was in a position to humiliate the French Emperor Napoleon III, to have a showdown with Great Britain, and to pick up any adjacent territory that it pleased. The old spirit of Manifest Destiny, quiescent during the war, sprang to life again. Even those who feared it anticipated its triumph. The more optimistic rejoiced in the prospect. Advocating the annexation of both Haiti and the Dominican Republic and hoping for the future acquisition of the Kingdom of Hawaii, President Johnson's 1868 annual message to Congress concluded: "The conviction is rapidly gaining ground in the American mind that with the increased facilities for intercommunication between all portions of the earth the principles of free government, as embraced in our Constitution, if faithfully maintained and carried out, would prove of sufficient strength and breadth to comprehend within their sphere and influence the civilized nations of the world."

If the accomplishments of American foreign policy did not live up to Johnson's predictions, they were, nevertheless, considerable. From the point of view of national security the most important feat was Seward's success in getting French troops removed from Mexico. Introduced into Mexico during the Civil War, ostensibly to compel the bankrupt Mexican government of President Benito Juarez to pay its debts, French troops in 1864 provided the

THE LAST ACT OF THE MONROE DOCTRINE

Reflecting exuberant postwar American nationalism, this artist in 1866 predicts the simultaneous expulsion of the French (personified by an effete Emperor Maximilian) from Mexico and of the British (represented by a corpulent John Bull) from Canada. *(American Antiquarian Society)*

support for the installation of the Archduke Maximilian of Austria as emperor of Mexico. Unable to do more than protest against this violation of the Monroe Doctrine while the war was going on, Seward adopted a more vigorous tone after Appomattox. Yet, knowing the French emperor was a proud and volatile man, he refrained from direct threats and allowed Napoleon to discover for himself how expensive, unpopular, and unsuccessful his Mexican adventure was proving. By 1867 Napoleon finally decided to cut off further financial support for Maximilian's shaky regime and, under steady American pressure, withdrew his troops. Captured by Juarez's troops, Maximilian was shot by a firing squad on June 19, 1867.

A second diplomatic achievement of the Reconstruction years was the settlement of the *Alabama* claims—claims of American shippers against the British government for damages that British-built Confederate raiders inflicted during the war. Im-

mediately after the war it probably would have been possible to clear up this controversy speedily and inexpensively, had not the British government haughtily denied that it had violated international law in permitting Confederate raiders to be built in its shipyards. With delay, American grievances festered. Sumner, the powerful chairman of the Senate Committee on Foreign Relations, began to argue that the British owed not merely repayment for actual damages done by the *Alabama* and other vessels; they were also responsible for protracting the war, for the "immense and infinite" cost of the entire last two years of the conflict. The failure of Reverdy Johnson, Seward's special envoy to Great Britain, to secure an apology or expression of regret from the stubborn British government further exacerbated American feelings. Not until after Grant put Hamilton Fish in charge of the American State Department and not until after there was a change of government in Great Britain could a settlement be worked out.

In the Treaty of Washington of 1871 Great Britain admitted negligence in permitting the Confederate cruisers to escape and expressed regret for the damages they had caused; and the United States tacitly abandoned the extravagant claims put forward by Sumner and agreed that the amount of damages should be assessed by a commission of arbitration representing five nations. Ultimately damages to American shipping were estimated at $15.5 million and the British government paid this amount. More important than any monetary settlement was the precedent set for arbitrating international disputes, and the Treaty of Washington paved the way for the rapprochement of the two greatest English-speaking nations. Not until the two world wars of the twentieth century would the full consequences of this development emerge.

Apart from the almost unnoticed American occupation of the Midway Islands in August 1867, the sole territorial acquisition of the United States during the Reconstruction era was the purchase of Alaska. Seward's 1867 treaty to purchase Russian America for $7.2 million brought under the American flag new territory one-fifth as large as the entire continental United States, a land of vast natural and mineral resources and of obvious strategic importance for the future of the United States in the Pacific. Nevertheless there was little popular enthusiasm for the purchase. Newspapers called Alaska "a national icehouse" consisting of nothing but "walrus-covered icebergs." Congressmen were equally unenthusiastic. Yet after much grumbling the Senate finally ratified the treaty and the House reluctantly appropriated the money for the purchase. Seward's success was due in part to his ability to convince senators that Alaska had vast hidden natural resources; in part it was due to the judicious payments of money to American congressmen by the Russian minister in Washington. More influential than either of these factors, however, was the general feeling that rejecting the treaty would alienate Czar Alexander II, who alone of the important European rulers had been sympathetic to the Union cause during the Civil War.

Nothing came of other postwar plans for ex-

RUSSIAN AMERICA—CANVASSING THE STATE TICKET
Critics of the purchase of Alaska in 1867 called the Russian territory "Seward's Icebox" or Andrew Johnson's "Polar Bear Garden."   (American Antiquarian Society)

pansion. Each of them ran into snags that made American diplomats draw back. For instance, the desire of many United States politicians, including Grant, Fish, and Sumner, to annex Canada had to be abandoned when it became clear that the British would not withdraw without a fight. Grant's plan to acquire the Dominican Republic aroused the opposition of Sumner, who considered himself the senatorial voice of the blacks and wanted the island of Santo Domingo to become not an American possession but the center of "a free confederacy [of the West Indies], in which the black race should predominate." Seward's proposal for the purchase of the Danish West Indies was pigeonholed by the Senate when those unfortunate islands were visted by a hurricane, a tidal wave, and a series of earthquake shocks.

It would, however, be a mistake to put too much stress on these idiosyncratic factors that stopped American expansion, for there were broader forces at work. The American people, exhausted by four years of fighting, were not prepared to support a vigorously nationalistic foreign policy if it threatened another war. Northern businessmen felt that it was more important to reduce taxes and to return to a sound monetary policy than to engage in foreign adventures. Because of the difficulties of racial adjustment in the South, increasing numbers of politicians hesitated before agreeing to annex additional populations of dark-skinned inhabitants. During Johnson's administration, many Republicans opposed all Seward's plans for expansion because they might bring credit to that unpopular president. During Grant's tenure, disaffected Republicans, who by 1872 joined the Liberal Republican party and opposed Grant's reelection, had similar motives for blocking his diplomatic schemes. More important than any of these factors, however, was the general awareness that the American people had plenty of room for expansion closer to home, in the lands still occupied by the Indians.

Indian Wars

At the end of the Civil War most of the Great Plains and the Rocky Mountains belonged to native Americans, whom whites labeled "Indians." The term itself was a revelation of white misperceptions. Of course everyone had known for centuries that native Americans were not kin to the inhabitants of India, which Columbus and the other Spanish explorers thought they had reached. But even in the last half of the nineteenth century most whites still did not understand that "Indians" consisted of numerous culture groups at least as different as the inhabitants of the nations of Europe. Native American peoples ranged from the peaceable Pueblos of the Southwest to the fierce and devious Crows, who ranged over Wyoming and Montana. The Diggers of Utah, who barely subsisted by grubbing roots from the arid soil, were "Indians," as were the members of the Five

Civilized Nations—the Cherokees, Choctaws, Chickasaws, Creeks, and Seminoles, transplanted from the Southeast in Andrew Jackson's day—who had developed a sophisticated agricultural economy in the Indian Territory (later to become the state of Oklahoma).

Whites labeled all these diverse people Indians—meaning really "Wild Indians." President Lincoln voiced the general paleskin view of the redface. To leaders of several western native American nations who visited the White House in March 1863, just after the bloody battle at Fredericksburg, the president announced, with no intentional irony: "We are not, as a race, so much disposed to fight and kill one another as our red brethren."

Native Americans During the Civil War. Union leaders took advantage of the opportunities presented during the Civil War to limit the rights of native Americans and to restrict their territories. The divided loyalties of the Five Civilized Nations between Union and Confederacy led, after Union victory, to a renegotiation of the treaties governing the Indian Territory, and the native Americans were forced to give up huge tracts of land and to grant a right of way to railroads crossing the territory.

Far to the north, when wartime inefficiency and delay, along with the endemic corruption of the Indian Bureau, kept promised supplies from the Oglala Sioux, the Indians in desperation took to the warpath and threatened white settlements in Minnesota. Lincoln appointed John Pope, fresh from his defeat at the second battle of Bull Run, to command the armed forces in the Northwest, and the general announced that he would deal with the Sioux "as maniacs or wild beasts, and by no means as people with whom treaties or compromises can be made." When the Sioux surrendered in September 1862, about 1,800 were taken prisoner and 303 were condemned to death. Against the strong objections of local authorities, President Lincoln commuted the sentences of most, but he authorized the hanging of 38—the largest mass execution in American history.

In 1864 warfare spread to the Central Plains, after the discovery of gold in Colorado and the opening of the Pike's Peak trail led to an influx of whites. Since

EXECUTION OF THE THIRTY-EIGHT SIOUX INDIANS

The victims of outrageous frauds on the part of government agents, the Sioux in Minnesota began committing minor depredations on the property of white settlers. Inevitably conflict escalated, and soon the state began to fear a widespread Indian rebellion, perhaps organized by Confederate agents. General John Pope, whom Lincoln sent to Minnesota in 1862, promised to "exterminate the Sioux." By October he had taken more than 1,500 Indian prisoners, and 303 of these were scheduled for execution. Appalled, Lincoln reduced the sentences of most, but on December 26, 38 Sioux Indians were hanged at Mankato—the largest official mass execution in American history. *(Library of Congress)*

the regular army was fighting the Confederacy, maintaining the peace was the job of the poorly trained Colorado territorial militia. On November 29, 1864, a group of Colorado volunteers, under the command of Colonel John M. Chivington, a former minister, fell on Chief Black Kettle's unsuspecting band of Cheyennes at Sand Creek in eastern Colorado, where they had gathered under the protection of the governor. "As an act of duty to ourselves and civilization,"

they slaughtered about 150 native Americans, mostly women and children.

Indians' Struggle for Survival, 1865–1877. Soon the entire Plains became a battlefield, and for nearly two decades after the Civil War hardly a year passed without significant encounters between United States soldiers, now released from the battlefields of the South, and Indian warriors. Often the native Americans were the victors, for the United States army, loaded with heavy supply trains, was unable to fight a guerrilla war. In 1866, for instance, when army officers attempted to establish a series of forts along the Bozeman Trail, linking the North Platte River with the newly opened mines of Montana, the Sioux opposed them every step of the way, and on December 21, led by Chief Crazy Horse, they exterminated a band of eighty soldiers commanded by the boastful Captain William J. Fetterman.

More familiar is the fate, ten years later, of George Armstrong Custer, the golden-haired boy-general of the Civil War who had won several victories over Southern Plains Indians. The survey of the route of the newly chartered Northern Pacific Railroad and the discovery of gold in the Black Hills brought whites into the lands of the Cheyenne and the Sioux. Since the Black Hills were the sacred dwelling place of the Sioux gods, Sitting Bull and Crazy Horse resisted white encroachments with all their power. General Philip H. Sheridan, who now commanded the United States army in the West, planned to force concessions by capturing the large Indian encampment on the Little Bighorn River (which the native Americans called Greasy Grass). A three-prong attack was mounted, but Custer, leading one of the columns, reached the encampment first and ordered his men to advance. As the white soldiers charged, Chief Low Dog called to his men: "This is a good day to die; follow me." They did, and within an hour on June 25, 1876, not merely "Long Hair" (as the Indians called Custer) but all of his men were killed.

The Defeat of the Native Americans.

Despite such transient victories, the native Americans were finally overcome. In part, their defeat was the consequence of superior white force and resources. In the protracted wars, which cost, according to the Commissioner of Indian Affairs, $1 million and the lives of twenty-five white soldiers for each native American warrior killed, the Indian nations were bled of their best leaders. But the building of two transcontinental railroads—the Union Pacific and the Northern Pacific—ultimately did more to defeat the Indians than the campaigns of the soldiers. The rail lines, and the

MAJOR GENERAL GEORGE ARMSTRONG CUSTER, U.S.A.
Made a brigadier general in the Union army at the age of only twenty-four, Custer was the personification of youthful impetuosity. Tall, slender, and lithe, with piercing blue eyes and long golden hair (which, however, he cut after the war), he dashed ahead of Grant's army in April 1865 and, by blocking Lee's further retreat, helped bring about the Confederate surrender at Appomattox. The same tactics served him far less well in the subsequent Indian wars in the West. On June 26, 1876, instead of waiting for reinforcements, he precipitated a battle with a well-armed force of between 2,500 and 4,000 Indians on the Little Big Horn River. Custer and all of the 215 men he led were killed. *(National Archives)*

permanent settlements built along them, disrupted the traditional migrating patterns of the Plains Indians. The slaughter along these railroads of hun-

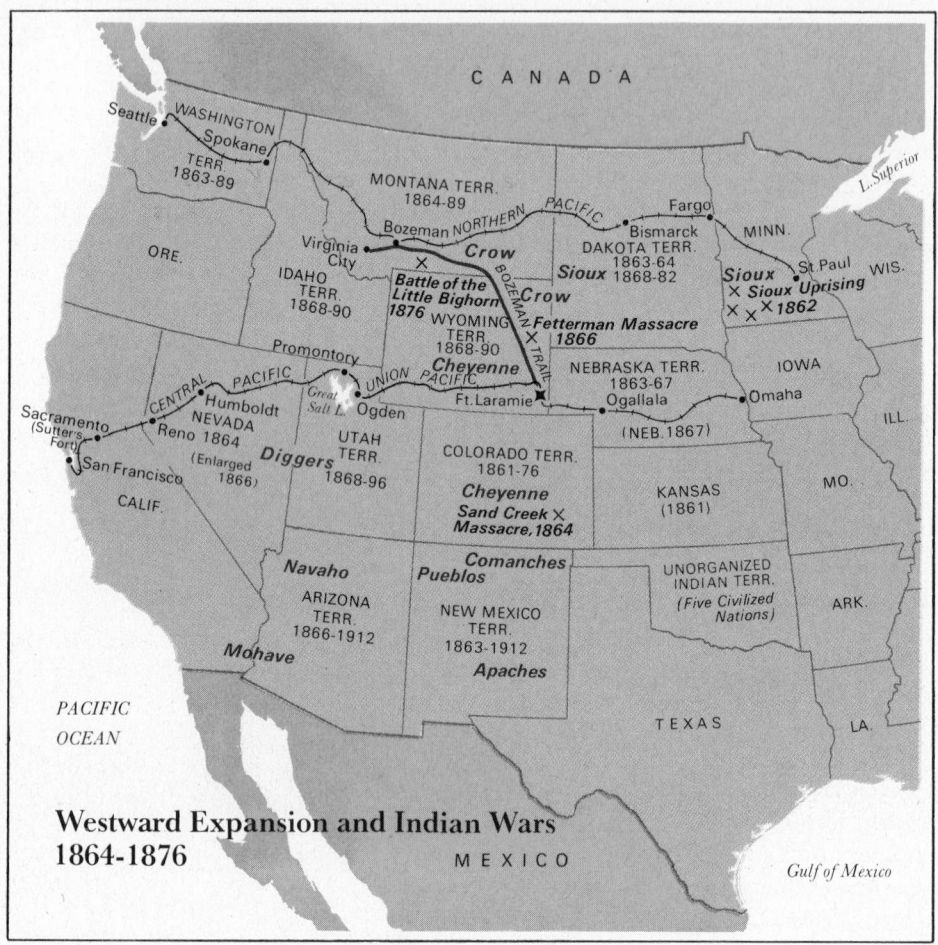

Westward Expansion and Indian Wars 1864-1876

dreds of thousands of bison, the chief food supply for the nomadic Indians, brought an end to the restless hunting life that had characterized the native Americans of the Plains.

As the proud and brave nations that had once dominated the American continent were defeated by the white man's arms, deprived of their lands by the white man's settlements, and debauched by the white man's alcohol, humanitarians across the country became aware that they were witnesses to what Helen Hunt Jackson called *A Century of Dishonor*—the title of her 1881 book, which reviewed the shabby record of government dealings with the Indians. But how this

record could be reversed was by no means clear. Probably a majority of white Americans favored confining the Indians to ever-smaller reservations in the most arid lands of the West, where they would surely and swiftly become extinct.

The only alternative reformers could suggest was to transform native Americans into homogenized citizens of the Republic. One means to this end, embodied in the Dawes Severalty Act of 1887, was to divide Indian lands into small holdings, vesting in each native American head of family the title to 160 acres. (That process incidentally freed vast areas hitherto under Indian control for white settlement.) Along with this plan went that proposed by President Merrill E. Gates of Amherst College, who told the Lake Mohonk Conference of the Friends of the Indians:

To bring him out of savagery into citizenship we must make the Indian more intelligently selfish before we can make him unselfishly intelligent. We need to *awaken in him wants....* Discontent with the teepee and the starving rations of the Indian camp in winter is needed to get the Indian out of the blanket and into trousers,—and trousers with a pocket in them, and with *a pocket that aches to be filled with dollars.*

Even the friends of the native Americans, then, saw as the only solution to the "Indian problem" assimilation or extermination.

Toward a National Economy

As the native Americans were pushed back, white settlers rushed in to occupy their lands. In 1860 the western frontier of settlement lay near the Missouri River, and between eastern Kansas and California there were hardly any white inhabitants except in the Mormon settlement in Utah and in the Spanish-speaking community at Santa Fe. Thirty years later, immigrants pushing west into the Great Plains and Rocky Mountain region and pushing east from California formed a virtually uninterrupted pattern of settlement across the continent. In 1890 the superintendent of the United States census announced—a bit prematurely—that the frontier was gone: "Up to

WAGON TRAIN CROSSING THE PLAINS DURING THE 1870s
For able-bodied single men a pack train was the most efficient way of moving West. But for families, undertaking a trip that might last from three to five months, a wagon train was more practicable. The covered wagon, or prairie schooner, usually pulled by oxen, had iron tires four inches wide and held up to 7,000 pounds. Such a wagon allowed a family to bring along its cherished possessions, and it also offered a place where the pregnant mother could rest, the children could sleep, or a sick member of the family could recuperate. *(University of Washington)*

SIOUX INDIAN ENCAMPMENT, DAKOTA TERRITORY, 1891
The Sioux, led by such chiefs as Crazy Horse and Sitting Bull, fiercely resisted white settlement of the northern Great Plains. *(Library of Congress)*

and including 1880 the country had a frontier settlement, but at present the unsettled area has been so broken into by isolated bodies of settlement that there can hardly be said to be a frontier line."

Westward Expansion. To some extent the peopling of the West was triggered by the passage in 1862 of the Homestead Act, which offered free of charge to any citizen who was over twenty-one or the head of a family 160 acres of public lands if he resided on them for five continuous years. As an alternative, a homesteader could purchase his land from the government for $1.25 an acre after six months' residence. Between 1862 and 1900 about 400,000 families received free homesteads under this program, but the dream that

free public land would siphon off industrial workers from the overcrowded cities of the East was not realized. Very few urban artisans could afford to transport themselves and their families to the frontier, pay the necessary fees at the land office, to construct a cabin, to purchase the necessary tools and seeds, and buy food during the long growing season before the wheat or corn was harvested. Even fewer knew how to farm. Consequently the great majority of homesteaders were men and women who had spent all their earlier years on the land. Even experience was no guarantee of success, for fully two-thirds of all homestead claimants before 1890 failed at the venture.

Most settlers in the West did not stake claims under the Homestead Act but continued, as they had always done, to purchase land directly from the government. Thousands more bought land from the railroad companies, which received from state and national governments enormous tracts of land, equal to more than twice the acreage made available to homesteaders. For instance, Congress gave the Union Pacific and the Central Pacific lines ten square miles of public land for every mile of track completed in the states, twenty square miles for every mile built in the territories.

The growth of western settlements was part of the general increase in the national population. During the decade from the end of the Civil War to 1876, when the Republic celebrated its centennial year, the population of the United States jumped by 30 percent, from 35.7 million to 46.1 million. During these same years more than 3 million immigrants, mostly from Europe, poured into the country.

Economic Growth.   Along with the increase in population came fantastic economic growth. Between 1866 and 1876 the number of bushels of corn produced in the United States increased by 100 percent. Railroad mileage increased by 111 percent. The production of bituminous coal increased by 163 percent. Almost no steel was manufactured in the United States at the end of the Civil War; 390,000 tons were made ten years later.

Growth strengthened the tendency to consolidate the American economy into one huge functional unit. This had been the dream of some businessmen long before the war, but after 1865 for the first time the necessary preconditions for economic integration existed. Never before had the United States had a national currency, and earlier businessmen had been obliged to settle their obligations with an assortment of state bank notes, local script, and coin; but passage of the National Banking Act of 1864 created a uniform circulating medium. Banks chartered by the national government were allowed, in return for purchasing government bonds, to issue the new national bank notes supplied by the federal comptroller of the currency. A tax placed on state bank notes in 1865 ensured that these national bank notes would thereafter have no competition.

For the first time, too, the United States after 1865 was bound together by a modern communications network. Before the Civil War, a number of rival telegraph companies had been constructing lines, but their efforts had been sporadic and uncoordinated. Thanks in part to the extensive military use of the telegraph during the war, the Western Union Telegraph Company grew strong enough to absorb smaller rivals, extended a line across the continent to San Francisco, and secured a virtual monopoly in the field. Western Union made it possible for a citizen in almost any part of the country to communicate almost instantaneously with his fellows in any other part of the reunited nation. After Alexander Graham Bell invented the telephone in the 1870s, and particularly after he demonstrated the miraculous ability to transmit the human voice by electrical current at the great Centennial Exhibition at Philadelphia in 1876, a second communications network appeared. By the 1880s most city physicians had telephones, and during President Hayes's administration an instrument was installed in the White House. The telephone was still such a novelty that, when it rang, the president himself was likely to pick up the receiver.

An improved transportation network also cemented the nation together. A transcontinental railroad, long advocated but repeatedly postponed because of sectional controversies, received the support of Congress in 1862, when it incorporated the Union Pacific Railroad Company. Financed by vast tracts of public lands, the Union Pacific began constructing a line from western Iowa to join the Central Pacific Railroad, which was pushing eastward from San Francisco. In 1869 the two roads met at Promontory Point, Utah, and it became possible to move passengers and freight by rail from the Atlantic Ocean to the Pacific. Less dramatic but more economically significant was the simultaneous coordination and consolidation of rail lines in more settled areas. Before the Civil War, there had been eleven different rail gauges in use on northern roads; President Lincoln's choice of the 4-foot 8½-inch gauge for the Union Pacific led to the standardization of all roads at this width. Before the war, rail travel from New York to Chicago had been barely possible by using eight or ten independent

The completion of a national system of transportation and communication encouraged the sale of nationally known, brand-name products. One of the first of these was Pears Soap, the nationally circulated advertisements for which managed simultaneously to titillate and to convey the impression of purity and cleanliness.   *(Culver Pictures, Inc.)*

lines, with repeated transfers. In 1869 Commodore Vanderbilt consolidated the New York Central and the Hudson River railroads to give continuous service from New York to Buffalo, and five years later he completed arrangements with western railroads to offer through service to Chicago. At about the same time the Pennsylvania Railroad, the Erie Railroad, and the Baltimore and Ohio Railroad also completed connections with Chicago.

Economic Consolidation.

A national communications and transportation network encouraged businessmen to seek national markets for their products. Business consolidation, already under way before the war, proceeded rapidly, and a striking number of new entrepreneurs—"robber barons," as later critics called them—were men whose wartime experience had taught them the advantages of technological innovation and large-scale management. For instance, Andrew Carnegie, who came to the United States as a poor Scottish immigrant and trained himself to become a skilled telegraph operator, served during the war as aide to Thomas A. Scott, the assistant secretary

of war in charge of all government railroads and transportation lines. From this vantage point, Carnegie shrewdly foresaw the postwar expansion and reorganization of the railway system, and he invested his early savings in the company that owned the patents for Pullman sleeping cars. When these cars became standard equipment on railroads, Carnegie was on his way to acquiring his huge fortune, with which he subsequently helped build the steel industry in the United States.

John D. Rockefeller, the pious young Baptist from Cleveland, Ohio, got his start through handling wartime government contracts for hay, grain, meat, and other commodities. Quickly he learned how a company that was managed with order and enterprise could drive inefficient competitors out of business, and he decided to apply this lesson to the new petroleum industry. Astutely recognizing that the way to dominate the industry was to control the refining process, Rockefeller in 1863 constructed the largest refinery in Cleveland, and two years later he built a second one. His brother, William, developed the eastern and the export market for their products. Enlisting Harry M. Flagler as a partner in 1867, Rockefeller worked systematically to cut costs and to nationalize an industry hitherto unstandardized and intensely competitive. By 1870 Rockefeller's company, Standard Oil of Ohio, made its own barrels, built its own warehouses, and owned its own fleet of tankers. Because of the volume of his business, Rockefeller was able to force the railroads to give his firm lower rates, or rebates, on all his shipments. Then, as his power grew, he compelled the railroads to turn over to Standard Oil "draw-backs," or a portion of what other oil companies had to pay in the way of freight. As a consequence of these business practices, which were at once shrewd and unscrupulous, Standard Oil by 1880 controlled 95 percent of the refining business of the country and practically all the transportation of oil, whether by pipeline or railroad.

PETROLEUM GALLOP
Petroleum seized the American imagination. Poets waxed rhapsodic about the soft kerosene light that was weaving a "golden web" over all America. The refrain of a popular song was "Oil on the Brain." The cover of this sheet music, by the pseudonymous "Oily Gammon"— i.e., bacon—captures the frenetic spirit of the oil fields. *(American Antiquarian Society)*

PIONEER RUN, 1865
The discovery of petroleum in western Pennsylvania led to its rapid and wasteful exploitaiton. Not more than one well out of twenty was properly sunk and carefully managed. *(Courtesy, American Petroleum Institute)*

While industry was expanding to reach a national market, other segments of the economy were becoming integrated into the national system. In the post–Civil War years a huge western range-cattle industry became the prime supplier of beef for the East, and also for Europe. Even before the Civil War, cattle raising had become a major occupation in the Great Plains area, stretching from Texas to Canada. There hardy cattle, descendants of Mexican longhorns, fed on open ranges. At yearly roundups calves were branded so that their owners could identify them, and cowboys selected the strongest steers for the long drive east. Since the war cut off markets for Texas cattle, herds became uncomfortably large, and as soon as peace was restored Texas cattlemen renewed their annual drive of cattle at an unprecedented scale. Initially these vast herds headed for the railhead at Sedalia, Missouri, where they could be transported to Chicago, St. Louis, and other eastern markets, but when the Kansas Pacific Railroad reached Abilene, Kansas, in 1867, cattlemen found a shorter, safer route to market. From Texas alone, 35,000 head of cattle came to the new railhead in its first year of operation; 350,000 in 1869; and 700,000 in 1871. Thereafter, as the national rail network extended farther west, Wichita and Dodge City came to rival, if not to replace, Abilene. These were rowdy frontier towns, where the cowboys, black as well as white, lonely after long months on the range, could let off steam in the dance halls, the saloons, and the red-light districts. But these cattle towns also served a basic economic function by tying the range cattle industry into the national economy.

Farmers, too, became part of that national network in the postwar era. The first few years after the war were boom times for northern and western farmers. With the growth of American cities, the domestic demand for grain constantly increased, and at the

TRANSPORT OF TEXAS BEEF ON THE KANSAS-PACIFIC RAILWAY, ABILENE
Beginning in 1867 Abilene, Kansas, became the principal railhead to which Texas ranchers brought their long-horn cattle, after the long drive, for shipment to the East. By 1871, 1,460,000 head of cattle were shipped out of Abilene. (Library of Congress)

same time Great Britain was becoming more dependent on American harvests. By 1880, for the first time, the value of American wheat and flour exports nearly equaled that of exported cotton.

Heartened by rising prices, northern and western farmers expanded their operations. Using new and improved farm machinery, such as Cyrus Hall McCormick's reaping machine, they were able to cultivate and harvest large crops with fewer workers. Since this machinery was expensive and since it operated best on large, level tracts of land, small, self-sufficient farmers, chronically short of cash, were at a disadvantage. The future seemed to belong to large producers, and confident western farmers went heavily into debt to buy more land and better machines. More than in any previous era they were now tied into a national market economy. Their fortunes depended not alone on the land, the weather, and their efforts, but on the grain elevators, the railroads, and the national and international markets.

Inevitably the movement toward a national economy in the post–Civil War decades encountered opposition. It rapidly became evident that complete integration could be achieved only at enormous economic, social, and psychological costs. Not even the business interests of the Northeast, which were the primary beneficiaries of a national economic system, unanimously favored such integration. If New York City grew because of the increasingly centralized financial and transportation networks, that growth was at the expense of such former rivals as Boston and Philadelphia. If Standard Oil profited from Rockefeller's nationalization of the refining industry, hundreds of less efficient oil companies were forced into bankruptcy. If mass production of nails at Andrew Carnegie's J. Edgar Thompson steel mill made building construction cheaper and safer, it also cost local blacksmiths and ironmongers their markets.

Politics in the Gilded Age

These economic and social tensions rarely surfaced as political issues during the Gilded Age—so-called from the novel by Mark Twain and Charles Dudley Warner, which depicted the boom-and-bust mental-

"BOSS TWEED" BY THOMAS NAST
Thomas Nast's caricatures of the corrupt William M. Tweed of New York were devastatingly effective. When the "Boss" fled the United States to escape prosecution, a Spanish immigration official identified him on the basis of Nast's drawings, and he was sent back to New York to serve his prison sentence. *(American Antiquarian Society)*

ity of businessmen of the post–Civil War era and the complaisance of the politicos who served these speculators. This was a period of low public morality in the United States, and few citizens were willing to entrust serious decisions to public officials—whether national, state, or local—tainted by favoritism, fraud, and bribery.

Scandals and Corruption. Disrespect for government mounted during the 1870s, when reformers and crusading newspaper editors started to expose startling scandals. The earliest revelations concerned New York City, which had fallen under the control of "Boss" William Marcy Tweed, who proceeded joyfully to loot the taxpayers. Tweed's ring began construction of a new county courthouse, on which $11 million was spent. Nearly $3 million went to a man named Garvey for plastering; after the amount of his fees leaked out, he became known as the "Prince of Plasterers." Tweed approved the purchase of so many chairs, at $5 each, that if placed in line they would have extended seventeen miles. In 1871 when the New York *Times* began to expose the ring's padded bills, faked leases, false vouchers, and other frauds, the attention of the whole nation was attracted, and when *Harper's Weekly* started carrying Thomas Nast's devastating caricatures of the Boss, Tweed's face became more familiar to Americans than that of any other man except Grant.

Soon revelations about the national government began to make equally fascinating reading. Shortly before the 1872 election, the New York *Sun*, a Democratic paper, exposed the workings of the Crédit Mobilier, the construction company that the Union Pacific Railroad Company paid to build its transcontinental route. Investigation proved that members of the Crédit Mobilier were also members of the board of directors of the Union Pacific, who were thus paying themselves huge profits. What was even more damaging was the revelation that, in order to avert public inquiry, the Crédit Mobilier offered stock to Vice-President Schuyler Colfax, Representative (and future president) James A. Garfield, and other prominent politicians. They were allowed to "purchase" the stock on credit, the down payment being "earned" by the high dividends that the stock began to pay.

Though Republicans found it advisable to drop Colfax from their ticket in 1872, scandal did not seriously touch the Grant administration until after the election. Then, in short order, stories of fraud began to appear about practically every branch of the executive offices. In the Treasury Department unscrupulous customhouse officers, especially in New York, preyed on importers. Merchants who failed to pay off the brigands had their shipments delayed, their imported goods subjected to minute, time-consuming inspection, and their crates and boxes that were not immediately removed from the docks stored at exorbitant rates. Corruption was rampant in the Navy Department, where political favoritism dictated everything from the employment of workers in the shipyards to the contracts for the construction of new vessels. Secretary of War William W. Belknap was proved to have accepted bribes from Indian traders, who had the exclusive and remunerative franchise to sell goods to Indians and soldiers at frontier posts.

Of all these scandals, the closest to the White House was the Whiskey Ring. In order to avoid heavy excise taxes, first levied during the war, whiskey distillers, especially those at St. Louis, had for years been conspiring with officials of the Internal Revenue Service. During Grant's administration they secured the cooperation of none other than Orville E. Babcock, the president's private secretary, who warned the swindlers whenever an inspection team was sent out from Washington. In return for his assistance, Babcock received such favors as a $2,400 diamond shirt stud, which he found defective and asked to have replaced with another, more expensive one, and from time to time the ministrations of a "sylph." When Grant first learned of the scandal, he urged, "Let no guilty man escape." But as it became clear that his close friends and his personal staff were involved, he did everything possible to block further investigation. When Babcock went on trial, the president of the United States offered a deposition expressing "great confidence in his integrity and efficiency." Babcock was acquitted, and Grant retained him on the White House staff.

Civil Service Reform. The desire to reduce political corruption led to the emergence of the civil service reform movement during the Gilded Age. Though voices had been raised against the spoils system long before the Civil War, it was not until after Appomattox that an organized reform drive appeared. Knowledge of widespread corruption among government officials, fear that President Johnson might convert the government bureaucracy into a tool to promote his renomination, and the example of the British system of appointing civil servants after competitive examinations gave strength to the movement. Early efforts to require federal appointees to pass competitive examinations failed in Congress, but the reformers, led by the politically ambitious George

IN MEMORIAM—OUR CIVIL SERVICE AS IT WAS
Thomas Nast proposes a substitute for Clark Mills's famous equestrian statue of Andrew Jackson, in Lafayette Square across from the White House. Nast incorrectly attributes to Jackson the phrase, "To the Victors belong the Spoils," which was a remark of William L. Marcy, a New York Democrat. *(Harper's Weekly, April 28, 1877)*

William Curtis, editor of *Harper's Weekly*, and by E. L. Godkin of *The Nation*, hoped for success under Grant's administration.

They were doomed to disappointment, for on this, as on all other controversial topics, Grant perfectly understood that compromise was the mood of the age, and he straddled. He made no mention of civil service reform in his first message to Congress, and Henry Adams—the son of Lincoln's minister to Great Britain and the grandson and great-grandson of American presidents—remarked in his supercilious way that Grant was inaugurating "a reign of western mediocrity." But when disgruntled civil service reformers began to talk loudly about joining the Liberal Republican movement, Grant moved swiftly to head them off. In 1871 he pressured Congress into creating the Civil Service Reform Commission, and he neatly co-opted his chief critic by naming Curtis chairman. Though the commission had little power and achieved less success, the move kept Curtis and a sizable number of reformers as supporters of Grant's reelection. Once the election was over, Grant lost interest in the commission and so blatantly violated its rules that Curtis had to resign.

Strengthened by the news of the scandals that rocked Grant's second administration, civil service reformers claimed some of the credit for the nomination of Hayes in 1876, but they found him as difficult to manage as Grant. On the one hand, the new president did take on the powerful political machine of New York's Senator Roscoe Conkling, and he succeeded in ousting some of Conkling's supporters, including future President Chester A. Arthur, from the New York customhouse. On the other hand, at election time the president wanted his own appointees to contribute to Republican campaign funds and to help organize Republican state conventions, much as their predecessors had done. "I have little or no patience with Mr. Hayes," exclaimed the reforming editor of the New York *Times*. "He is a victim of . . . good intentions and his contributions to the pavement of the road to the infernal regions are vast and various."

Hayes's successor, Garfield, gave civil service reformers little more satisfaction. With cruel accuracy one Massachusetts reformer characterized the new president as "a grand, noble fellow, but fickle, unstable, . . . timid and hesitating." Civil service reform advocates noted suspiciously that Garfield's vice-president was Arthur, named by the Republican national convention in a vain attempt to placate Conkling. Consequently reformers felt no special sense of victory when Garfield began to oust more of Conkling's "Stalwarts" from the New York customhouse. Conceited and imperious, Conkling resigned in a huff from the Senate and rushed to Albany seeking vindication through reelection. To his surprise, the removal of his friends from federal office undercut his support, and the New York legislature failed to send him back to the Senate. Shortly afterward, a crazed office seeker named Charles Guiteau assassinated Garfield, shouting that he was a Stalwart and rejoicing that Arthur was now president. Shocked by Garfield's assassination, Congress in 1883 passed the Pendleton Act, which required competitive examinations of applicants for many federal jobs. Though the measure covered only a fraction of all government employees, it was a genuine measure of civil service reform and permitted the emergence of a professional government bureaucracy.

Tariff and Currency Controversies

In addition to distrust of fraud and favoritism, there was a deeper reason why government, and in particular the national government, had so little to do with the basic economic problems of the Gilded Age. In dealing with economic issues, just as in dealing with those relating to the South and the freedmen, Americans were constrained by the doctrines of constitutionalism, by the belief that government had only fixed and enumerated powers. In the area of economics, only the tariff and the currency were clearly under the control of the national government. During the postwar years therefore disagreements over economic issues were usually voiced in connection with these two endlessly troublesome, highly technical questions, so complex that only a handful of congressmen fully understood them.

The Tariff Problem. Underlying debates on the tariff were basic questions whether the industrial sector of the economy should be favored at the expense of the exporting agricultural sector, whether the factories of the Northeast should benefit at the expense of the farmers of the South and West. These questions did not surface clearly, however, and during the debates the issue was rarely put in terms of free trade versus protection. Except for a few doctrinaire economic theorists, almost everybody during the Gilded Age recognized that some tariff barrier was needed to protect American industries from cheap foreign imports. The debates in Congress revolved about which industries and how much protection.

By 1865 almost everybody agreed that the high tariffs enacted during the Civil War, in part to protect heavily taxed American industry from untaxed foreign competition, needed modification. Hoping to make a reasonable adjustment, the New England economist David A. Wells, who was appointed Special Commissioner of the Revenue in 1866, drafted a bill to reduce duties on imported materials such as scrap iron, coal, and lumber, to eliminate arbitrary and unnecessary duties on items like chemicals and spices, and to make slight reductions in duties on most manufactured articles. Most lawmakers admitted the theoretical excellence of Well's bill—and most opposed the provisions that lessened or removed protection from their own constituents' businesses. Consequently Wells's bill was rejected, and during the next fifteen years there was no general revision of the tariff legislation.

The absence of general tariff acts did not mean that discussion of tariff rates was at an end. To the contrary, there was throughout the period an endless pulling and hauling between economic interests that stood to gain or lose from changes in duties on specific imported items. For example, during the war a considerable copper industry had grown up in Boston and Baltimore that smelted and refined Chilean ore, which paid a very low tariff duty. But in the late 1860s, the great copper mines around Lake Superior began to be worked on a large scale, and their owners asked Congress to protect their product by raising duties on imported ore. After sharp disagreement, in which President Johnson took the side of the refiners and most congressional Republicans the side of the ore producers, the tariff on copper ore was increased in 1869 to a point at which most of the eastern smelting firms had to go out of business.

Other tariff changes were the consequence of combined efforts by the producers and processors of raw materials. An 1867 act revising the duties on raw wool and on woolen cloth was drafted at a convention of wool producers and manufacturers at Syracuse, and it was lobbied through Congress by the indefatigable and effective secretary of the Wool Manufacturers' Association, John L. Hayes.

Some of the minor adjustments made in the tariff during the postwar years reflected political pressures. In a general way Republicans, with some notable exceptions, tended to favor high protective tariffs, and Democrats, especially those in the South who needed foreign markets for their cotton, wanted to reduce duties. But the issue was rarely clear-cut, for Democrats in manufacturing states like Pennsylvania were high-tariff men. Moreover, both parties tinkered with the tariff issue at election time. In 1872, for instance, the Republican party faced a split, when many tariff reformers in the Liberal Republican movement were preparing to join the Democrats. Attempting to check the bolt, the Republican-dominated Congress rushed through a bill reducing all duties by 10 percent. Once Grant was triumphantly reelected, the Congress promptly repealed the reduction. Again in 1883, when it seemed likely that in the next election Democrats would elect Grover Cleveland president and would win majorities in both houses of Congress, Republicans hurriedly enacted the first general tariff act since the Civil War. They claimed that it reduced duties by an average of 5 percent, but in fact the measure was so complex and so contradictory that nobody could predict its impact. John L. Hayes, now president of the United States Tariff Commission, gave the secret away when he explained, shortly after the passage of the 1883 act: "In a word, the object was *protection through reduction. . . .* We wanted the tariff to be made by our friends."

Debates Over Currency. The controversies over currency during the post–Civil War generation were more complex, but in general they illustrate the same tension between the needs of a national economy and the desires of local and special economic interests. Unless a historian is prepared to write a book about these monetary issues, perhaps he ought to confine his account to two sentences: During the generation after the Civil War there was constant controversy between those who wished to continue, or even to expand, the inflated wartime money supply and those who wanted to contract the currency. Most debtors favored inflation, since it would allow them to pay debts in money less valuable than when they borrowed it; and creditors favored contraction, so that the money they received in payment of debts would be more valuable than when it was loaned.

But those two sentences, accurate enough in a general way, fail to convey the full dimensions of the controversy. They make the whole argument seem a purely economic question of profit and loss. In fact, for many people the resumption of specie payments— that is, the redemption of the paper money issued by the United States government in gold, at face value— involved the sanctity of contracts, the reliability of the government's pledges, and the rights of private property. Indeed, the return to the gold standard seemed to have almost a religious significance. Probably most economists of the period shared the conviction of Hugh McCulloch, Johnson's secretary of the treasury, that "gold and silver are the only true measure of value. . . . I have myself no more doubt that these metals were prepared by the Almighty for this very purpose, than I have that iron and coal were prepared for the purposes for which they are being used." On the other hand, the advocates of so-called soft money argued that it was downright un-American to drive greenbacks out of circulation and return to the gold standard. "Why," asked the promoter Jay Cooke, "should this Grand and Glorious Country be stunted and dwarfed—its activities chilled and its very life blood curdled—by these miserable 'hard coin' theories, the musty theories of a bygone age?"

That two-sentence summary also ignores the fact that the currency controversy involved economic interests falling into more sophisticated categories than debtors and creditors. Merchants in foreign trade were ardent supporters of resumption because fluctuations in the gold value of United States paper money made the business of these importers and exporters a game of chance. On the other hand, many

American manufacturers, especially iron makers, were staunch foes of resumption because they needed an inflated currency to keep their national markets expanding.

Finally, that two-sentence summary does not indicate that attitudes toward these monetary policies changed over time. Throughout the postwar period farmers were mostly debtors, but they were primarily concerned with such issues as railroad regulation and until 1870 showed little interest in the currency. Creditor interests of the Northeast were indeed mostly supporters of resumption, but when the depression began, they unsuccessfully urged President Grant to sign a so-called Inflation Bill of 1874, which would have slightly increased the amount of paper money in circulation. In other words, they preferred mild inflation to economic collapse. Moreover, by the late 1870s, inflationists were no longer calling for additional greenbacks; instead, they joined forces with western mining interests to demand that the government expand the currency by coining silver dollars. When they discovered that, partly by oversight, partly by plan, the Coinage Act of 1873 had discontinued the minting of silver, they were outraged. Protesting the "Crime of '73," they demanded a return to bimetallism (both gold and silver being accepted in lawful payment of all debts) and the free and unlimited coinage of silver dollars.

With so many opposing forces at work, it is scarcely surprising that the history of currency policy and financial legislation in the postwar years is one of sudden fits and starts. Right after the war, Secretary McCulloch assumed that everybody wanted to return to specie payments promptly, and, as a means of raising the value of the paper currency, he quietly sequestered greenbacks paid into the United States treasury for taxes and for public lands. His mild contraction of the currency checked business expansion, and Congress forced him to desist. Subsequently the sequestered greenbacks were reissued, and in the total amount of $382 million they remained in circulation for the next decade.

In an indirect fashion, the currency became an issue in the presidential election of 1868. During the previous year, what became known as the Ohio Idea gained popularity in the Middle West. Critics of hard money objected to the government's practice of paying interest on the national debt in gold—which was, of course, much more valuable than greenbacks. Since the bonds had been purchased with greenbacks, they argued, it would be entirely legal and proper to pay their interest in the same depreciated currency. In this way the crushing burden of the national debt on the taxpayer would be reduced. So attractive was this argument that the Democratic national convention incorporated a version of the Ohio Idea in its 1868 platform, but it negated this move by nominating Governor Horatio Seymour of New York, an earnest hard-money man, for president. The Republican national convention, against the wishes of many western delegates, sternly rejected the Ohio Idea, and Grant was nominated with a pledge to reject "all forms of repudiation as a national crime."

Despite this commitment, Grant's administrations witnessed the completion of a series of compromises on currency. The new president announced that he favored a return to the gold standard; but at the same time he warned: "Immediate resumption, if practicable, would not be desirable. It would compel the debtor class to pay, beyond their contracts, the premium on gold . . . and would bring bankruptcy and ruin to thousands." But, lest anyone think that this last statement meant he desired further issues of paper money, Grant vetoed the Inflation Bill of 1874, against the advice of many of his advisers.

It was within this broad policy of affirmation checked by negation that John Sherman, the Senate expert on finance, persuaded Congress in 1875 to pass the Resumption Act, announcing the intention of the United States government to redeem its paper money at face value in gold on or after January 1, 1879. Ostensibly a victory for hard-money interests, the act was, in fact, a brilliant compromise. It did commit the United States to resumption—but only after a delay of four years. Sherman sweetened this pill for the silver mining interests by providing that "as rapidly as practicable" silver coins would be minted to replace the "fractional currency"—notes of postage-stamp size in 3, 5, 10, 15, 25, and 50-cent denominations—issued during the war. To placate the greenback interests in the South and West, Sherman's measure made it easier to incorporate national banks, which had the right to issue treasury notes, in those regions.

Though attempts were made after 1875 to repeal the Resumption Act, it was such a carefully constructed compromise that they all failed. Sherman, who became secretary of the treasury in President Hayes's cabinet, skillfully managed the transition in 1879 so that resumption took place without fanfare and without economic disturbance. The whole controversy over currency during the Gilded Age thus illustrates the tension between the needs of a national economy and the desires of local and special economic interests. The national policy of resumption, desired by most businessmen and needed if the United States was to play a part in world trade, was sustained; but local business interests were able to delay and modify implementation of the policy so that it did not impose too sudden or heavy a burden on groups adversely affected by hard money.

Discontent Among Farmers and Laborers

If the emergence of a national economy produced strains within the business community, it created severe problems for farmers and laborers, who felt that they were not fairly sharing its rewards. Discontent became vocal first among farmers. Even in the buoyant years immediately after the Civil War, the life of the northern and western farmer was often lonely and dull. On the western plains, where farmers lived miles from stores, schools, and churches, where there were often no near neighbors, and where there was no regular mail service, even the prosperous lived stunted lives. Perhaps farm women felt the isolation even more deeply than the men.

The Granger Movement.   In effort to remedy these problems, Oliver Hudson Kelley, a clerk in the United States Department of Agriculture, in 1867 founded a secret society called the Patrons of Husbandry. Kelley, who had lived in Massachusetts,

Iowa, and Minnesota and who had traveled extensively in the South after the war, knew at first hand the bleakness and the deprivation of rural living, and he wanted to give farmers all over the country a broader vision and a livelier social and intellectual life. The Patrons of Husbandry was intended to stimulate farmers' thinking through lectures, debates, and discussions, and it was designed to promote a sense of social solidarity through group singing, picnics, and other family entertainment. Each local unit of Kelley's society was called a Grange, and women as well as men belonged as equal members. So new was the whole idea to American farmers that the organization got off to a slow start, and at the end of 1868 only ten Granges had been established.

In the following year, when the price of farm commodities dropped sharply, agrarian discontent mounted, and by the mid-1870s about 800,000 farmers, mostly in the Middle West and South, joined the Granger movement. Though the Granges never abandoned their social and intellectual objectives, the meetings came increasingly to focus on economic issues important to farmers, such as the declining price of wheat and the mounting costs of railroad transportation. Forbidden by the constitution of the Patrons of Husbandry to engage in politics, the Grangers found it easy after the recital of the Grange litany and the standard literary or musical program to move that the meeting be adjourned; then, technically no longer Grangers but simply farmers gathered together, they discussed politics and endorsed candidates who favored the farmers' cause.

That cause embraced a variety of discontents with the operations of the national economy. Farmers in Iowa, Nebraska, and Kansas complained that it took the value of one bushel of corn to pay the freight charges for shipping another bushel to eastern markets; farmers in Minnesota and Dakota said the same of wheat. Middle Western farmers protested the policy of the grain elevators, used to store their wheat and corn until it could be picked up for rail shipment. Elevator operators frequently misgraded grain, offering the farmer with superior produce only the price for a lower grade, and the farmer usually had to accept, for he could not dump his grain on the ground.

THE GRANGER AT HOME AND ABROAD
The Patrons of Husbandry (the Grange) had a double function. Officially the organization was designed to promote better methods of agriculture and to improve the social and intellectual life of farmers. Unofficially Grangers often supported independent political candidates pledged to regulate rates charged by railroads and grain elevators.   *(American Antiquarian Society)*

Southern and western farmers also objected to the limited bank credit available in their regions. When the national banking system was set up, the war was still going on, and no provision was made for establishing national banks in the South. In the West there were few national banks because Congress required a minimum capital of $50,000, which few western towns could raise. Consequently the circulation of national bank notes, and hence the availability of loans, was grossly inequitable. Connecticut alone had more national bank notes in circulation than Michigan, Wisconsin, Iowa, Minnesota, Kansas, Missouri, Kentucky, and Tennessee.

Farmers' dissatisfaction with the national economy blended into a more general pattern of Middle

Western discontent. It was not farmers alone who objected to high and discriminatory railroad rates; businessmen in Middle Western cities and towns, especially those served by only one rail line, also protested. Because the railroads set rates that favored large grain terminals, wheat produced twenty miles from Milwaukee might be diverted to Chicago. Because railroads gave special preference to long-distance shippers, lumber merchants in Clinton, Iowa, found that Chicago lumber dealers could undersell them; trainloads of lumber rumbled in from Chicago on the way to central and western Iowa without even slowing down at Clinton. The inequities in the national banking system affected western businessmen at least as much as they did farmers, for the absence of credit crippled business expansion in the South and West.

Out of these general western grievances emerged what came to be known, somewhat inaccurately, as the Granger laws. Between 1869 and 1874, legislatures in Illinois, Iowa, Wisconsin, and Minnesota set maximum charges for grain elevators and railroads, and some of these states established regulatory commissions with broad powers. Though farmers supported this legislation, it was actually framed by western lawyers and pushed by western businessmen; only in Wisconsin were the Grangers the principal advocates of regulation. Promptly the railroad and grain elevator companies challenged the constitutionality of these acts, but the United States Supreme Court in *Munn* v. *Illinois* (1877) upheld the right of states to regulate railroads, even to the point of setting maximum rates. In the long run, state regulation of railroads and grain elevators proved ineffectual, and the Granger laws were repealed or modified. Nevertheless, their temporary success marked a victory for agrarian—and, in general, Middle Western—interests injured by the operation of the national economy.

Organization of Labor. Industrial laborers were slower than farmers to find spokesmen for their discontents with the national economy. Factory workers came from many national backgrounds and spoke many languages. In the decade after the Civil War more than 3.25 million immigrants, mostly from northern Europe, poured into the United States, and from these the labor force was largely recruited. By 1880, 87 percent of the inhabitants of Chicago, 84 percent of those in Detroit and Milwaukee, and 80 percent of those in New York and Cleveland were immigrants or the children of immigrants. Divided along ethnic and religious lines, they had little sense of workers' solidarity. Many members of the work force, moreover, regarded their status as transient; they hoped, unrealistically, to move west as homesteaders or, having made their fortunes, to return to their European homelands.

From such a fractured work force it was almost impossible for a meaningful national labor movement to emerge. One of the earliest efforts was the eight-hour movement, led by Ira Stewart, a Boston machinist who sought legislation to limit the work day to eight hours without reduction of wages. Under this pressure the United States established an eight-hour day for its employees in 1868, and legislatures in six states passed acts to make eight hours a legal day's work. In private industry these laws proved ineffectual because they instituted the eight-hour restriction only "where there is no special contract or agreement to the contrary." Consequently most businessmen required employees to agree to work longer hours as a condition of employment.

The National Labor Union, created in 1866 at a Baltimore conference of delegates from various unions, proved little more successful. It was headed by William H. Sylvis, a dedicated propagandist and a superb speaker, whose interests, however, were not

SPECIMEN DIAL FOR MECHANICSVILLE TOWN HALL—HANDS EMPLOYED TO WORK EIGHT HOURS ONLY

The eight-hour movement was the most popular of the early postwar labor reform drives. Its slogan was: "Eight hours work a day leaves eight for sleep and eight for play." (*American Antiquarian Society*)

in conventional labor issues like hours and wages but in cooperatives and currency reform. Sylvis recruited many members for the National Labor Union—it claimed 640,000 in 1868—but whether these were actual workingmen is questionable. A scornful observer remarked that the National Labor Union was made up of "labor leaders without organizations, politicians without parties, women without husbands, and cranks, visionaries, and agitators without jobs." After Sylvis's death in 1869, the organization began to decline, and it disappeared during the depression of 1873.

A more successful labor movement was the Knights of Labor, founded in 1869 by Uriah Stephens and other garment workers of Philadelphia. It grew slowly at first and, like the National Labor Union, received a serious setback in the depression. By the 1880s, however, its membership increased in a spectacular fashion as it attempted to create a broad union of all workingmen, skilled and unskilled. But its leadership, like that of the National Labor Union, was averse to discussing hours, wages, and working conditions and was reluctant to call strikes. After 1879, the General Master Workman of the Knights of Labor was the idealistic, eloquent, and neurasthenic Irishman Terence V. Powderly, who preferred to think of himself as the head of a national educational institution rather than of a labor union.

The tactics of the National Labor Union and of the Knights of Labor (and it must be remembered that only a small fraction of the industrial labor force ever belonged to either organization) did little to alleviate the day-to-day problems of working men and women: the long hours; the miserably low wages; the uncertainty of regular employment; the absence of health or accident insurance; the nonexistence of pension and retirement programs; the exploitation of child labor; and the blacklisting of employees who dared to speak out against such abuses.

Panic of 1873. These labor organizations were even less able to help in the severe depression that followed the Panic of 1873, precipitated by the failure of Jay Cooke and Company. Between 1873 and 1879 business activity in the United States declined by about one-third, and the number of bankruptcies doubled. Thousands of workers lost their jobs. During the winter of 1873–74 about one-fourth of all laborers in New York City were unemployed, and during the following winter the number increased to one-third. In this time of crisis the National Labor Union virtually collapsed, and many local unions disappeared as well. In New York City, for example, membership in all unions dropped from 45,000 in 1873 to 5,000 in 1877.

While private charities did what they could to relieve distress, nobody seemed to know how to end the depression. Informed opinion tended to view the panic and the subsequent unemployment and suffering as part of the natural workings of the national economic order, necessary to purge unsound businesses and speculative practices. Economists warned that "coddling" laborers would only retard this inevitable and necessary process. Blaming the depression on the wartime habit of looking to the federal government for leadership, Democratic Governor Samuel J. Tilden of New York called for a return to "government institutions, simple, frugal, meddling little with the private concerns of individuals . . . and trusting to the people to work out their own prosperity and happiness."

Those labor leaders who remained active were little more helpful. Many sought panaceas for the economic crisis. A writer in the *Radical Review* found the cause of the depression in the private ownership of land, which in his words, "begets . . . ground rent, an inexorable, perpetual claim for the use of land, which, like air and light, is the gift of Nature." In 1879 Henry George would make that proposition the basis for the economic system proposed in *Progress and Poverty*. Other labor voices supported the Socialist Labor movement, founded in 1874, which foresaw the ultimate overthrow of the capitalist system through a socialist revolution; it advocated, as interim measures to combat the depression, federal aid for education, industrial accident compensation, and women's suffrage. The movement attracted a minuscule following.

Some labor spokesmen sought the way out of the depression by supporting independent political parties pledged to protect labor's position in the national economy. There was considerable labor support for the Greenback, or National Independent, party, which was organized in 1874 at Indianapolis. The party's national platform opposed the resumption of specie payments and advocated further issues of paper money to furnish relief to the depressed industries of the country. That the Greenback party was not a labor movement exclusively is attested by the fact that its presidential candidate in 1876 was the eighty-five-year-old New York iron manufacturer, Peter Cooper. The 80,000 votes Cooper received came mostly from Middle Western farm states. In the congressional elections two years later, however, more laborers supported the National Independent party as it campaigned for government regulation of the hours of labor and for the exclusion of Chinese immigrants. Like other advocates of inflation, the party by this time had moved beyond favoring greenbacks and urged expansion of the currency through silver coinage. Candidates endorsed by the National Independent party received more than a million votes in the 1878 congressional elections.

Labor Unrest and Federal Intervention. Other laborers during the depression rejected politics in favor of direct action. With the collapse of the trade union movement, the "Molly Maguires," a secret ring that controlled the popular fraternal society, the Ancient Order of Hibernians, gained power in the anthracite coal region of Pennsylvania. Soon mine owners reported a "crime wave" in collieries, as the Mollies allegedly intimidated and even murdered bosses and superintendents they considered unfair. Eventually, on the dubious testimony of a paid infiltrator, a number of the ringleaders were arrested, and when twenty-four of them were convicted in late 1876, the disturbances ended.

Labor unrest reached its peak in 1877, the worst year of the long depression. Railroad managers precipitated a crisis when, without warning, they cut wages on most railroads east of the Mississippi River

by 10 percent. On July 17, the day after the cut became effective, workers on the Baltimore and Ohio Railroad went on strike, took possession of the railyards at various points, and refused to let any freight trains depart. Promptly employees of other eastern railroads also went on strike, and traffic on the four trunk lines connecting the Atlantic coast and the Middle West was paralyzed. Shortly afterward, the strike spread to some of the roads beyond the Mississippi and into Canada.

Local and state governments proved unable or unwilling to cope with the crisis. The governor of Maryland called out the state militia, but these civilian soldiers fraternized with their friends and relatives among the strikers. In Pittsburgh the strikers had the sympathy of the local government, for the city fathers had long felt that the Pennsylvania Railroad was discriminating against their city. Employees of nearby iron works joined the railroad men in blocking all traffic on the Pennsylvania. When the governor sent in state militia companies from Philadelphia to clear the tracks, they succeeded in dispersing a large mob by killing twenty-six persons, but their action roused so much additional hostility that the troops were obliged to retreat into the roundhouse, which the mob promptly surrounded and set on fire. The next morning the Philadelphia soldiers fought their way out of the roundhouse and retreated from the city, leaving it in control of a mob of strikers, sympathizers, and looters, who proceeded to destroy railroad property worth some $5 million.

To protect the national system of transportation so essential to the national economy, President Hayes sent in regular army troops. This was the first time in American history that the army had been used on any extensive scale to crush a labor disturbance. Promptly the army restored order, and the strike collapsed. Deeply disturbed members of the business community took steps to prevent any recurrence of such labor violence. State legislatures began passing conspiracy laws directed against labor organizations, and the courts began to invoke the doctrine of malicious conspiracy to break strikes and boycotts. Throughout the North the state militia, which had so often proved

THE GREAT RAILROAD STRIKE
Labor unrest mounted during the severe depression that began in 1873. The most severe outbreak of violence was in Pittsburgh, to which federal troops were dispatched after rioters set fire to the Pennsylvania Railroad roundhouse. *(The New York Public Library)*

untrustworthy during the 1877 crisis, was reorganized and given stricter training. Cyrus Hall McCormick personally purchased equipment for the Second Regiment of Illinois militia because it had "won great credit for its action during . . . disturbances and can be equally relied on in the future."

Thus labor protests failed at just the time when farmer protest movements won at least some temporary successes. The difference in outcome is attributable, in part, to the fact that there was a long history of agrarian discontent in the United States, and the Granger movement seemed as American as apple pie. Urban labor, labor unions, and massive strikes were, on the other hand, something novel to most Americans, and no doubt all three seemed the more dangerous since so many industrial laborers were immigrants with strange-sounding names and alien ways of behavior. In part, too, the differences stemmed from the fact that farmers and their allies lived in a distinct region of the United States, where they were strong enough to control local and state governments in the South and Middle West: industrial laborers were scattered geographically and the labor movement nowhere had political power commensurate with its numbers.

More important than either of these differences was the fact that agrarian discontent did not pose a basic threat to the structure of the national economy. The imposition of limits on the power of railroads and a few other monopolies was an idea that many businessmen also thought desirable. Labor unrest, on the other hand, appeared to strike at the heart of the national economic system. A popular Boston minister declared that the rioting of "the lawless classes at the bottom of our cities" had been instigated by "secret socialistic societies." The prominent financial editor, W. M. Grosvenor, spoke for much of the business community when he announced that "the light of the flames at Pittsburgh" portended "a terri-

ble trial for free institutions in this country." He warned: "The Communist is here."

The cumulative result of all these problems of the Gilded Age—of overseas expansion and Indian wars; of governmental corruption and tariff and currency controversies; of farmer movements and labor unrest—was to distract the attention of most Northerners from problems of the South. Increasing numbers of Americans came to understand that the basic tension between majority rule and minority rights was not something confined to relations between whites and blacks, or between Northerners and Southerners. The end of the era left Americans facing the unresolved problem of reconciling the centralizing, nationalizing tendencies in American life with the opposing tendencies toward localism, parochialism, and fragmentation.

THE EMANCIPATOR OF LABOR AND THE HONEST-WORKING PEOPLE

To terrified conservatives, like the cartoonist Thomas Nast, labor organizers were "Communists," with "foreign" ideologies, intent upon leading honest American working people to death and destruction. *(Harper's Weekly, February 7, 1874)*

CHRONOLOGY

1866 National Labor Union Formed.
Sioux Indians massacre Fetterman and troops.

1867 Maximilian's empire in Mexico falls.
Purchase of Alaska.
Patrons of Husbandry (the Grange) founded.

1868 Ulysses S. Grant elected president in contest with Democrat Horatio Seymour.

1869 Knights of Labor organized.
Union Pacific and Central Pacific link at Promontory Point to form first transcontinental railroad.

1870 Standard Oil Company of Ohio organized.

1871 Treaty of Washington, settling differences between United States and Great Britain, signed.
Tweed Ring scandals in New York City exposed.

1872 Crédit Mobilier scandals revealed.
Grant names G. W. Curtis to head Civil Service Commission.
Grant reelected over Horace Greeley, candidate of Liberal Republicans and Democrats.

1873 Coinage Act demonetizes silver in so-called Crime of '73.

Panic of 1873 begins long depression.

1874 Grant vetoes Inflation Bill.

1875 Specie Resumption Act provides for return to gold standard by 1879.

1876 Exposure of Whiskey Ring reveals further corruption in Republican administration.
Custer and his men slaughtered at battle of the Little Big Horn.
Centennial Exhibition opens in Philadelphia.
Republicans nominate Rutherford B. Hayes for president; Democrats nominate Samuel J. Tilden. Disputed returns leave outcome in doubt.

1877 Congress creates electoral commission, which rules that all disputed ballots belong to Hayes, who is inaugurated president.
In *Munn* v. *Illinois* Supreme Court upholds Granger legislation.
Nationwide railroad strike and ensuing violence lead to first significant use of federal troops to suppress labor disorders.

SUGGESTED READINGS

The best general treatment of social and economic change during the post–Civil War period is Allan Nevins, *The Emergence of Modern America, 1865–1878* (1927). There is an enormous amount of unassimilated data in Ellis P. Oberholtzer's *History of the United States since the Civil War,* Vols. 1–4 (1929–31).

Foreign affairs during the Reconstruction era are treated in Glyndon G. Van Deusen, *William Henry Seward* (1967), Allan Nevins, *Hamilton Fish* (1936), and David Donald, *Charles Sumner and the Rights of Man* (1970). Ernest N. Paolino, *The Foundations of the American Empire: William Henry Seward and U.S. Foreign Policy* (1973), and Milton Plesur, *America's Outward Reach* (1971), are both valuable. Adrian Cook's *The Alabama Claims* (1975), is authoritative. On expansionism, the standard work is A. K. Weinberg, *Manifest Destiny* (1935). For opposition to Manifest Destiny,

see Donald M. Dozer, "Anti-Expansionism during the Johnson Administration," *Pacific Historical Review,* 12 (1943), 253–76.

Wilcomb E. Washburn's *The Indian in America* (1975) is a superior, comprehensive work. *The American Heritage History of the Indian Wars* (1977), by Robert M. Utley and Wilcomb E. Washburn, is a spirited, illustrated account, chronicling the final defeat of the native Americans. Books that attempt to present the story from the Indian point of view include Dee Brown, *Bury My Heart at Wounded Knee* (1970); T. H. Fehrenbach, *Comanches* (1974); William Brandon, *The Last Americans* (1974); and, best of all, Angie Debo, *Geronimo* (1976). *The White Man's Indian* (1978), by Robert F. Berkhofer, Jr., is a fascinating analysis of whites' misperceptions of the native Americans. More conventional studies of Indian policy include David A. Nichols, *Lincoln and the Indians* (1978); Francis P. Prucha, *American Indian Policy in Crisis* (1975); and Loring B. Priest, *Uncle Sam's Stepchildren* (1975).

Edward C. Kirkland, *Industry Comes of Age* (1961), is an excellent account of the development of a national economy. *The Visible Hand* (1977), by Alfred D. Chandler, analyzes the managerial revolution that took place in American business. Two richly detailed studies of American industrial leaders are Allan Nevins, *Study in Power: John D. Rockefeller* (2 vols., 1953), and Joseph F. Wall, *Andrew Carnegie* (1970).

On the agricultural sector of the economy, see Fred A. Shannon, *The Farmer's Last Frontier* (1945). Walter P. Webb, *The Great Plains* (1931), contains a brilliant account of the settling of the trans-Mississippi West, and Robert F. Dykstra, *The Cattle Towns* (1968), is a fascinating study.

For a spirited, irreverent account of the politics of the Gilded Age, read Matthew Josephson, *The Politicos, 1865–1896* (1938). Two full studies of the corruption in New York City are *The Tweed Ring* (1966), by Alexander B. Callow, Jr., and *Boss Tweed's New York* (1965), by Seymour Mandelbaum. Ari A. Hoogenboom, *Outlawing the Spoils* (1961), is a model history of the civil service reform movement.

Three modern, sophisticated accounts of the currency controversy are Robert P. Sharkey, *Money, Class, and Party* (1959), Irwin Unger, *The Greenback Era* (1964), and Walter T. K. Nugent, *The Money Question during Reconstruction* (1967).

Solon J. Buck, *The Granger Movement* (1913), continues to be a standard work; but George H. Miller, *Railroads and the Granger Laws* (1971), shows the influence of western businessmen on the so-called Granger legislation. Samuel Rezneck, "Distress, Relief, and Discontent in the United States during the Depression of 1873–78," *Journal of Political Economy*, 58 (1950), 494–513, is exceptionally helpful, and there is much information about labor unrest in John R. Commons *et al.*, *History of Labor in the United States*, Vol. 2 (1918).

PART FIVE

John L. Thomas

Nationalizing
the Republic

1877–1920

As the American people completed their industrial revolution in the half-century following the Civil War, they continued to celebrate unprecedented growth even as they were driven to experiment with new ways of regulating it. In 1900 as in 1850 most Americans saw cause for national self-congratulation in the numerous signs of prosperity all around them: an improved standard of living; rapid population growth; the rise of great cities; and an ever-growing stock of consumer goods. More thoughtful observers, however, noted that all of these achievements had come at a high social price: the sudden uprooting of a rural people and the disruption of their communities; the forced mobility of new masses of underprivileged; deplorable working conditions for too many Americans; and the persistence of a conspicuously unequal distribution of wealth. Still, for most people caught up in America's industrial transformation the benefits of rapid material growth clearly outweighed its costs.

For economic growth continued to verify earlier predictions of unlimited betterment, and most Americans continued to believe in the cherished ideal of progress. The key concept in this doctrine of progress—freedom from external restraints on individual ambitions and energies—had survived the Civil War, if not unscathed at least largely intact. A simple faith in the individual continued to claim the allegiance of a majority of Americans in 1900 just as it had of an earlier generation.

Yet in spite of the optimistic mood of the country, reform-minded citizens in all walks of life by 1880 were beginning to note the signs of mounting social disorder. Under the triple impact of industrialization, modernization, and urbanization a growing number of leaders in all parts of the national community came to recognize the need for controls and system as new means of acquiring efficiency and stability. Businessmen sought consolidated power within their firms with which to improve their operations and increase their profits. Farmers quickly discovered an urgent need for better credit facilities and marketing mechanisms. Social theorists and urban reformers began to adjust their vision to the requirements of systematic planning. By 1890 what had

Overleaf: View of Waltham, Massachusetts, 1889, *(Photo by E. L. Sanderson, Courtesy of Waltham Historical Society)*

once been considered a self-regulating device for producing happiness automatically had come to be seen as a machine badly in need of repair if not of a complete overhaul.

Not all these would-be reformers of American society after 1890 agreed either on priorities or means. But the thrust of their ideas and programs pointed unmistakably toward the construction of a new national order. In historical terms this new vision seemed to repudiate the permissive philosophy of Thomas Jefferson and to refurbish the nationalist model of Alexander Hamilton. In the fields of law and constitutional theory, the change brought replacement of formal definitions of rights and duties with more flexible concepts of social utility, requiring new roles for lawyers and legislators alike. In social reform there was a new emphasis on training, expertise, and the predictive functions of science. In politics, the organizational revolution brought new styles of leadership and new approaches to the workings of government.

The distance the nation had traveled by 1920 could be measured in two widely different assessments of American politics and society, the first by the individualist prophet Ralph Waldo Emerson in the salad days of moral reform before the Civil War. Emerson located the national genius in the "wise man" with whose appearance "the state expires." "The tendencies of the times," Emerson predicted, "favor the idea of self-government, and leave the individual . . . to the rewards and penalties of his own constitution which works with more energy than we believe whilst we depend on artificial restraints." Three-quarters of a century later the progressive sociologist Charles Horton Cooley dismissed Emerson's self-enclosed individual as a moral abstraction unknown to history. "In a truly organic life the individual is self-conscious and devoted to his work, but feels himself and that work as part of a large joyous whole. He is self-assertive, just because he is conscious of being a thread in the great web of events." The story of the years separating the sage of Concord from the progressive social scientist is the account of the American discovery of the great social web and the multitude of connecting threads that composed it.

CHAPTER 22

Stabilizing the American Economy

In the first years of the Republic Alexander Hamilton predicted that industry and agriculture would advance together in the American march toward abundance. Hamilton's promise was echoed a few years later by Henry Clay in his prophecy of the eventual triumph of his American System, and it was repeated again and again in the years before the Civil War by businessmen and promoters eager to exploit the country's resources. It was not until the last decades of the nineteenth century, however, that the American people finally made good on Hamilton's initial promise. At the end of the Civil War the United States still stood on the edges of the modern industrial world, a hungry importer of capital, labor, and most of its technology. Thirty years later it had transformed itself into a major exporter of foodstuffs and the producer of a mammoth stockpile of industrial and consumer goods. Within a generation it had become one of the world's leading industrial powers.

Statistics, which Americans were just beginning to collect and interpret, told a story of unprecedented economic growth. The value of American manufactured products soared from $3 billion in 1869 to over $13 billion at the turn of the century. In the 1890s alone the national wealth climbed from $65 billion to $90 billion while national income rose from $12 billion to $18 billion. In the same years, production soared. The figures were startling.

Between the Civil War and 1900 the output of manufactured goods tripled; the product of the key, all-important steel industry jumped from 68,000 tons of finished steel in 1870 to 4.2 million tons in 1890. The national labor force rose sharply too, from 13 million to 19 million, and the percentage of the national income that went to pay wages increased from 37 percent to 47 percent.

It was figures like these that led Charles E. Perkins, president of the Chicago, Burlington, and Quincy Railroad, to ask his fellow-citizens, "Have not great merchants, great manufacturers, great inventors, done more for the world than preachers and philanthropists? . . . Can there be any doubts that cheapening the cost of necessaries and conveniences of life is the most powerful agent of civilization and progress?" Material progress, most Americans agreed,

CITY TRAFFIC IN THE NINETIES
Trolleys, horse-drawn cabs,
delivery wagons, and wary
pedestrians compete for space
on Chicago's Clark Street.
(Library of Congress)

came first because on it depended the intellectual and cultural achievements of their civilization. And material progress was the result of an industrial revolution that had changed the face of their society in less than a generation. What was this revolution? How did it happen? What forces accounted for it?

The Foundations of the American Industrial Revolution

Growth of Cities. A principal factor in the dramatic transformation of the United States in the last quarter of the nineteenth century was the unprecedented growth of American cities. An enormous demo-

graphic shift that had begun before the Civil War continued for the rest of the century. Native-born citizens and recently arrived immigrants crowded into metropolitan areas where they furnished huge new markets for consumer goods of all kinds, both basic necessities like food and clothing, and new products like sewing machines, typewriters, and cigarettes. By 1880 over a quarter of the nation's people lived in urban areas. In the remaining years of the century the urban population grew at the phenomenal rate of 6 percent per decade, until by 1900 a full 40 percent of the American people lived in cities. Even more important, they tended to concentrate in giant centers, like New York, Chicago, Philadelphia, and Detroit, where they quickly became dependent on a

BUILDING BROOKLYN BRIDGE
Dignitaries pose on the catwalk leading to the pier. *(Museum of the City of New York)*

steady supply of consumer goods provided by manufacturers, processors, and distributors. "We cannot all live in cities," Horace Greeley, the aging editor of the New York *Tribune,* complained to a younger generation headed toward the metropolis, "yet nearly all seem determined to do so. . . . 'Hot and cold water,' baker's bread, the theatre, and the streetcars . . . indicate the tendency of modern taste."

The cities, expanding at a pell-mell pace and pushing the boundaries of old commercial centers into surrounding suburbs along elevated railroad and trolley lines, became giant consumers of heavy industrial goods—electrical dynamos, telephone wire, lead pipe and copper tubing, streetcars and the motors to run them. American cities, whether subsidizing huge public constructions like John and Washington Roe-

bling's magnificent Brooklyn Bridge, or encouraging private ventures like architect Louis Sullivan's steel-framed Wainwright Building in St. Louis, provided an insatiable appetite for the products of the industrial machine. And with both labor and electric power available, major cities attracted new factories and quickly became producers as well as consumers of industrial abundance.

Railroads. Railroads also played a crucial role in developing a powerful national economy. They fed heavy industry with ever-larger orders for steel rails, machines, and equipment. In their search for the necessary capital, railroad leaders probed new investment markets in every sector of the economy, private and public. Soon the railroads linked the cities of the nation, first in a loose network and then in a tighter web that comprised a national market system. Here again statistics tell the story: 35,000 miles of track in 1865 had become 242,000 by 1897. At the end of the Civil War, railroads stopped just across the Mississippi, in Iowa and Missouri. By century's end there were no less than five transcontinental roads. Even more important was the rapid consolidation of the railroad empire east of the Mississippi where trackage, which had doubled in the 1870s, doubled again in the 1880s. By 1890 railroad transportation was dominated by a small group of integrated lines like the New York Central and the Pennsylvania roads in the Northeast, the Burlington system in the Midwest, and the Union Pacific, Northern Pacific, and Great Northern routes to the West Coast.

The railroads quickly acquired unsavory reputations which were usually well deserved. In the last quarter of the century they were accused—frequently with ample proof—of disregarding the safety and comfort of their passengers, jerry-building their roads, rigging rates that discriminated against small shippers, lobbying Congress for special legislation, and in general both preaching and practicing a philosophy of the public-be-damned. "They exact success, and do not cultivate political morality," complained Charles Francis Adams, Jr., a severe but judicious critic of the railroads.

The record of the railroads in establishing new national traffic patterns was nevertheless impressive. In 1865 they made up a collection of local systems without standard gauge or equipment and lacking

Principal Railroads, 1890

WRECK ON THE NEW YORK CENTRAL AT BATAVIA, NEW YORK, 1885
Passenger safety was not always a top priority for the nation's railroads. *(Photograph by P. B. Houseknecht, Library of Congress)*

even a common timetable. Twenty-five years later, without ever having given serious thought to public policy, they had provided for the country an immense system of rail lines. Across these tracks moved wheat, corn, and hogs from the Great Plains, cotton from the Mississippi Delta, lumber from Wisconsin and the Northwest, oil products from Pennsylvania, and coal from West Virginia and Kentucky—all in increasing quantity and with predictable regularity. With the development of the refrigerated car at the end of the century came meat from Chicago, Omaha, and Kansas City, and fruits and vegetables from California and Florida. Once this efficient distributing system had been equipped with instantaneous communication by the telegraph and the telephone, American businessmen were able to envision for the first time a national complex of business firms, practicing economies made possible by huge volume, and passing these savings along to consumers in all parts of the country in the form of lower prices. Both as economic

fact and organizational idea, the railroads dominated the development of the American economy.

Technology. Another powerful stimulant to economic growth was developing technology. The number of inventions mounted steadily after the Civil War, the annual total of patent applications reaching 25,000 in 1890. In 1871 the Hoe press and the Ingersoll air drill were invented, and three years later came the third rail for subways and elevated lines. Then in 1879 came the first railroad signal system; in 1883 in Chicago the first elevated electric railway, which defined the Loop; in 1886, alternating current. In every branch of industry and manufacturing—machine tools, steel, mining, flour-milling, lumbering—new inventions expanded productivity and reduced man-hours of labor.

Unlike twentieth-century technology, most of which is based on a "knowledge revolution," nineteenth-century inventions were developed by trial and error. The discovery and development of the Bessemer converter—the original key to making large quantities of steel—is an example. It was only after some clever guesswork and haphazard experimenting that Sir Henry Bessemer in England and William Kelly in the United States learned to force blasts of air into molten pig iron to burn out the carbon. With that discovery the modern science of metallurgy began. Important as the Bessemer process was in producing high-grade steel in large amounts, it was soon supplemented by the "open hearth" method powered by gas furnaces that eliminated the need for the air blast. Like many industrial improvements in the United States in the nineteenth century, steel technology originated in Europe but was quickly adapted to American conditions with the result that by the mid-1870s Bessemer mills in this country were producing 50 percent more steel than their British counterparts, a margin that widened every year as home-grown technological geniuses like Carnegie Steel's Captain "Bill" Jones designed more efficient layouts for mills and better ways of moving hot steel through them.

In every field American technology proved remarkably flexible in borrowing and improving foreign designs. Sometimes it provided a lighter and faster machine as in the textile industry; at other times it developed bigger and stronger machinery like the mammoth steam shovels needed for heavy construction. In oil it was the "cracking" process developed in the 1870s that allowed refiners to control various yields by altering the molecular structure of the petroleum. Often an invention broke a technological bottleneck that had blocked an entire process, as in the case of George Westinghouse's system for transmitting alternating current over long distances.

Technology and a new science of management worked together to improve the quality and performance of American labor. A huge pool of unskilled labor was still considered essential to American economic expansion, but the long-term trend pointed toward mechanization and, in the end, automation. Despite the willingness of native-born boys fresh from the farm and young immigrants just off the boat to feed the furnaces and work the lathes,

it was machinery that sent American productivity soaring, and consumption with it.

Capital Investment. Technology bred great expectations and a mounting hunger for capital. In the early years of the oil business, just after the Civil War, John D. Rockefeller was able to acquire a small refinery for $10,000 and a large one for $50,000. By 1910 the market value of Standard Oil was $600 million. Technology promised greater efficiency but also required increased investment that was readily forthcoming. In 1860 a total of $1 billion was invested in the nation's manufacturing plants, which turned out a collective product worth $1.8 billion and employed 4.3 million workers. By 1900 the size of the work force had grown fivefold and the total value of products nearly tenfold; at the same time, the amount of invested capital had multiplied twelvefold.

Here, in the sudden availability of massive amounts of capital, was one of the most striking features of the American Industrial Revolution. For the first seventy-five years of the nineteenth century, most of the capital for industrial investment had come out of the savings of the firms that used it. But the last half of the nineteenth century was a period of what economists call "capital deepening," when people reserved for savings and investment a much larger share of the gross national product. To put this new money to work, a host of new financial institutions appeared—commercial banks, savings banks, life insurance companies, and investment houses—to serve as intermediaries between the eager investor and the needy business firm. By 1900 the stock market had established itself as the main mechanism for exchanging securities and mobilizing the vast funds needed by new industrial firms. By the time the United States entered the First World War, Wall Street had succeeded in creating a genuine national market for capital.

The pace of the American Industrial Revolution was unregulated and hence uneven. For the first time a combination of potent economic forces was at work—a huge urban market, an efficient distribution system, a highly motivated workforce, and vast amounts of capital. All that was lacking was a public

EDGAR THOMSON STEEL WORKS, BRADDOCK, PENNSYLVANIA, 1908
Rapid industrialization was not gained without high ecological costs.   *(Library of Congress)*

policy that recognized the need for regulation and direction. Without that concern the transformation of the American economy was destined to be disorganized, at times chaotic.

Economic Instability.   The instability of the American economy in the last quarter of the nineteenth century was a hard-edged reality. The American economy swung like a pendulum from flush to hard times and back again. The Panic of 1873 plunged the country into six years of depression, with massive unemployment, wage cuts, and price declines. Following a short season of recovery, a second recession buf-

feted the economy in 1884 and again sent prices skidding and workers into the ranks of the unemployed. Once more, after a brief respite, the Panic of 1893 brought four more years of economic paralysis, from which the country recovered only at the end of the century.

All three depressions were triggered by financial panics—the collapse of the investment houses of Jay Cooke in 1873, of Grant and Ward in 1884, and of nearly the entire railroad empire in 1893. But satisfactory explanations of the causes of depressions were hard to come by. Whether they compared them to a swing of the pendulum, the breaking of a wave, or the onset of a fever, most American observers despaired of controlling the business cycle or of easing the effects of periodic slumps. Despite the lessons in the need for economic planning that the Civil War had taught, the great majority of Americans still believed in the self-regulating market, with which, conventional wisdom declared, government should not interfere. "Money-getters," P. T. Barnum admonished the politicians, "are the benefactors of our race." Stand aside and let them do their work!

The result of this popular belief in untrammeled business opportunity was a national government that frequently subsidized but seldom regulated. Politicians and businessmen alike predicted marvelous achievements for a new industrial statesmanship left to its own devices. Corporations, the wealthy ironmaster Abram S. Hewitt told the Chicago Board of Trade in 1885, were the "best friends" the American people had. Farseeing industrialists were now "doing the work which was done by Jefferson and Madison in the early years of the Republic." Sociologist William Graham Sumner, the great defender of American rugged individualism, amended this judgment only slightly. "The great leaders in the development of the industrial organization need those talents of executive and administrative skill, power to command, courage, and fortitude, which were formerly called for in military affairs and scarcely anywhere else."

As Gilded Age politicians deferred to such business leadership and extolled business values, the directive force of government tended to disappear in misty hopes for automatic prosperity. The great steel manufacturer and self-made man Andrew Carnegie explained the terms of the new social contract in a language that a business civilization instinctively understood. It would be a mistake, Carnegie insisted, for the American community to shoot its millionaires since, after all, they were the "bees" that made the most honey. "Under our present conditions the millionaire who toils on is the cheapest article which the community secures at the price it pays for him, namely, his shelter, clothing and food." Carnegie need not have worried: there would never be an open season on American millionaires.

Business Fills a Vacuum

Since the federal government was reluctant to assert its control over the economy, and state governments responded only gradually with piecemeal legislation, the job of providing a measure of economic stability fell to American businessmen. Blessed with organizational talent and energy, American businessmen were the first to respond to the challenge of disorder, even though they tended to concentrate on the specific problems confronting their own businesses. In the view of most businessmen, their needs did not require public policy but could be met by a set of limited private strategies to protect their own firms. Slowly a general pattern of self-regulation emerged, in response to threats to continuing prosperity.

The most obvious threat was a long-term drop in prices in the last decades of the nineteenth century. The wholesale price index sank from 100 in 1880 to 82 in 1890. Faced with recurrent panics and slumps, threatened by growing competition and the prospects of shrinking profits, the boldest of the nation's businessmen began to experiment with various ways of gaining greater control over their enterprises. Their experiments were improvised attempts at stability made by a business community suddenly confronted with severe problems but left to its own devices to find solutions. In deciding to demolish a small business economy with its free market system and to replace it with new combinations, American business leaders played—often without realizing it—a genuinely revolutionary role.

Cartels and Trusts. The earliest and simplest forms of consolidation, those requiring the least amount of change, were *cartels*. These were loose trade associations, or *pools*, of independent business firms joined together to dominate an industry. The organizer of the Wire Nail Association explained his case for a pool with disarming candor:

There is nail machinery enough in this country to produce four times as many nails as can be sold. When there is no pool the makers simply cut each other's throats. Some people think there is something wicked about pools. When we were trying to get up the nail pool, I talked

THE U.S. ECONOMY, 1873–1900

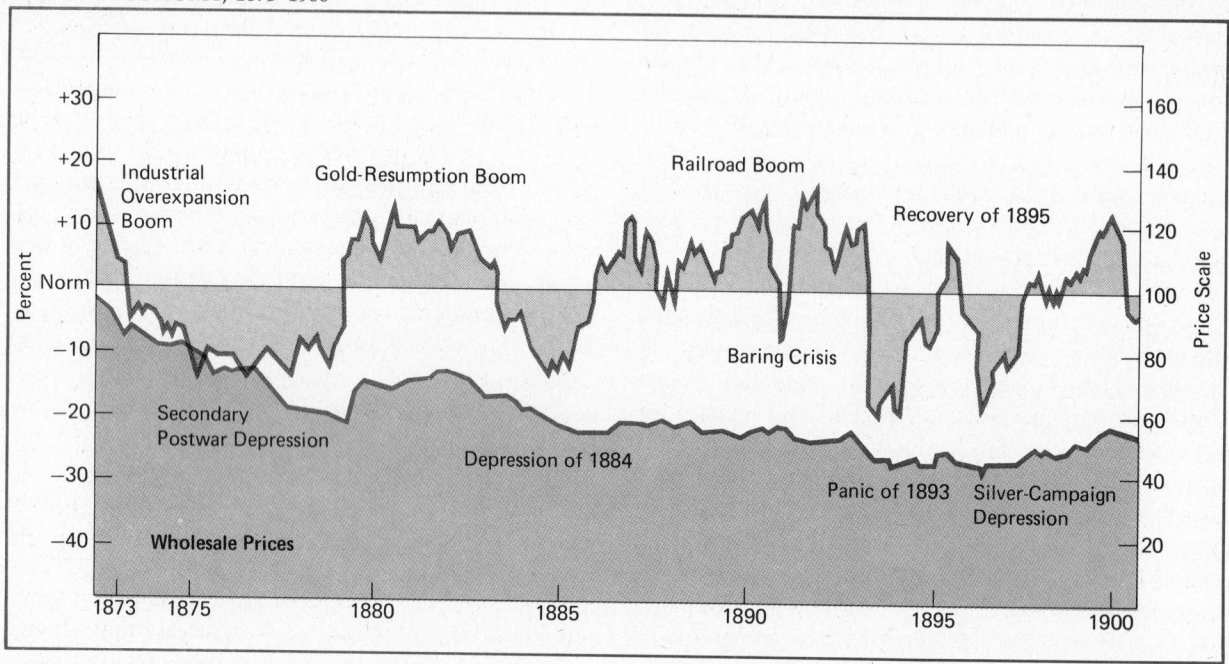

with directors of companies who held up their hands against going into any sort of combination. I said to them, "How much did you make last year?" "Not a cent." "Are you making anything now?" "No." "Well, what do you propose to do? Sit here and lose what capital you have got in the business. . .?" There is only one way to make any money in a business like the nail business, and that is to have a pool.

Pools attempted to meet the problem of overproduction and falling prices through gentlemen's agreements: competitors, while maintaining their independence, agreed among themselves to accept quotas and refrain from price-cutting. In organizing their pool in 1881 the whiskey distillers, for example, agreed that "only 28 percent of the full capacity shall be operated, and no stocking up beyond this amount under any circumstances." To tighten sagging steel prices, the steel rail manufacturers in 1887 formed the Steel Rail Association, which established a strict quota system and provided for a series of stiff fines for uncooperative members. Although the Steel Rail Association continually denied charges of price-fixing, it nevertheless enjoyed a period of remark-

able price stability thereafter.

Yet cartels had their drawbacks. They flourished in good times but fell apart under the pressure of recessions. Their agreements were unenforceable in the courts, and American consumers regarded them as an undue restraint of trade. Recognizing these limitations and sensitive to an aroused public opposition to secret agreements, pioneer organizers like John D. Rockefeller turned to "horizontal" combinations, or *trusts*. The trust was the brainchild of a member of Standard Oil's legal staff, the affable and shrewd Samuel C. T. Dodd, who patiently explained its advantages to hesitant colleagues. Since state laws prohibited outright ownership by one company of the stock of another, Dodd admitted, there was no foolproof way of consolidating, holding, and managing a string of separate companies.

But you could have a common name, a common office, and a common management by means of a common executive committee. . . . If the Directors of one of the companies and their successors shall be made Trustees of all such stock, you thus procure a practical unification of all the companies.

The idea worked. In 1882 forty-one stockholders in the Standard Oil Company of Ohio signed an agreement creating a board of nine trustees to whom they transferred all the properties and assets of their companies in exchange for trust certificates. The visible signs of this financial feat were 700,000 hundred-dollar certificates, the price of consolidated control over the American oil industry. The corporate spirit had wrought its first miracle.

Many trusts and *holding companies* (similarly integrated firms which were allowed to hold stock in other corporations), once they acquired formal control over production and prices, were content to operate as loose cartels, simply parceling out shares of the market without trying to impose a centralized management or authority. In such cases of partial consolidation the hoped-for efficiency and economies were not always forthcoming. But soon the largest and most powerful businesses began to follow the examples of Carnegie Steel Company and of Gustavus Swift in meatpacking, by achieving "vertical" integration of their industries. They sought to combine under single management all of the processes of production and distribution—from the sources of raw material to new marketing systems. More and more frequently after 1890 big business tried to secure control that extended "backward" to resources and transportation, as well as "forward" toward control of the market through research departments and central business offices.

The Merger Movement. In the last years of the nineteenth century the American economy entered a second phase of "horizontal" consolidation with the sudden growth of industrial and financial mergers that demolished the old brownstone order of Gilded Age capitalism and cleared the ground for twentieth-century skyscrapers housing new corporate giants. From one angle, the great merger movement at the turn of the century appeared to be a towering peak of corporate consolidations. The annual number of mergers traced a sharp trajectory from 69 in 1897 to 303 a year later to 1,208 in 1899, before leveling off in the next three years at between 350 and 425. By 1900 there were 73 so-called trusts, each with a capitalization of over $10 million, and two-thirds of them had been established within the previous three years.

Viewed negatively, the merger movement looked like nothing so much as a gigantic hole into which some 300 businesses tumbled each year, swallowed by huge new combinations like United States Steel and General Electric. United States Steel absorbed over 200 manufacturing and transportation companies, and swiftly gained control over two-thirds of the steel market. American Tobacco combined 162 independent companies and ruled all but 10 percent of the tobacco market. By 1904 the approximately 2,000 largest firms in the United States composed less than 1 percent of the total number of the nation's businesses yet produced 40 percent of the annual value of the nation's industrial goods. By 1910 *monopoly* (entire control of an industry by a single firm) and *oligopoly* (rule by a few large firms) had secured the commanding positions from which to dominate twentieth-century American life.

The merger movement that climaxed a half-century's search for economic order was both a logical outgrowth of rapid industrial development and at the same time an unsettling departure from remembered ways. It was natural for a new generation of promoters and investment bankers to see in industrial combination, if not the hand of God at least an inexorable law of nature at work ordering the business affairs of the world. Samuel C. T. Dodd, Rockefeller's counsel, warned of the futility of tinkering with the celestial machinery. "You might as well endeavor to stay the formation of the clouds, the falling of the rains, or the flowing of the streams as to attempt by any means or in any manner to prevent organization of industry, association of persons, and the aggregation of capital to any extent that the ever growing trade of the world may demand." And indeed, the success of mergers was hard to deny.

By 1895 the remarkable growth and sizable profits of Standard Oil, American Sugar Refining, and American Tobacco marked out what appeared to be a sure route to salvation through combination. Simply to ponder the scale of these new enterprises was exhilarating! The Federal Steel Corporation, Judge Elbert Gary boasted, "takes the ore from the ground, transports it, manufactures it into pig iron, manufactures pig iron into steel, and steel into finished products, and delivers those products." Even more impressive was the formation in 1901 of United States Steel, into which went not only some 200 manufacturing plants and transportation companies, but 1,000 miles of railroad, 112 blast furnaces, and 78 ore boats. Soon U.S. Steel was employing 170,000 workers as it gathered control over 60 percent of the country's steel. Its initial capitalization at $1.4 billion was three times the annual expenditure of the federal government.

Increased efficiency, elimination of waste, bigger shares of the market, and anticipated but often elusive economies of scale—all convinced adventurous businessmen of the need to pursue mergers. By 1910 mergers had spread to all the principal sectors of the economy. When the great wave of mergers receded in 1903, it left in its wake a new corporate capitalism—a system of mammoth integrated enterprises with interlocking structures, managed by professionals with newly acquired expertise, selling their increasing variety of products in shared markets at administered prices. The great merger movement declared the bankruptcy of old-fashioned, small-scale competition and announced the arrival of a modern corporate society in need of new definitions and values to replace the outworn Horatio Alger pieties of pluck and luck. In place of a host of small- and medium-sized businesses scrambling for a share of the market, there now stood huge unified structures. The corporate revolution was by no means over by 1914, and the nation throughout the Progressive years continued to support a dual economy of big and little businesses. But the central meaning of the merger movement was clear to most Americans: bigger was better.

Organizing the mergers and raising the capital to launch them became the specialty of investment bankers like J. P. Morgan and Jacob Schiff. Their role was critical, and they dominated the American economy at the turn of the twentieth century as they never would again. While taking a handsome slice of stock in the consolidations they created, they became powerful middlemen between a public eager to invest and an expansive business community. They arranged mergers and floated stock, established the workings of their new creations, and manufactured favorable

publicity. Their success could be read in the achievements of the House of Morgan, which by 1912, together with the Morgan-controlled First National Bank of New York and the Rockefeller-managed National City Bank, held 341 directorships in 112 national corporations worth $22.2 billion.

To the public the whole merger movement was personified in the investment banker, part savior of a threatened economy, part devil in disguise. An air of conspiracy characterized even the fictional portraits of the American businessman of the day—Van Harrington in Robert Herrick's *The Memoirs of an American Citizen*; Magnus Derrick in Frank Norris's *The Octopus*; Frank Cowperwood in Theodore Dreiser's trilogy of desire—as though to conceal embarrassing questions of right and wrong. For their everyday heroes, Americans might have preferred the inventor and the engineer—Thomas Edison, Alexander Graham Bell, George Westinghouse—but they also admired, feared, envied, and puzzled over the new captains of industry

TWO AMERICAN HEROES
Edward Steichen's portrait of J. Pierpont Morgan as the awesome financial wizard (left) contrasts sharply
with Thomas A. Edison in his laboratory in the legendary pose of the
native American genius (right). *(Left,
Collection, The Museum of Modern Art,
New York; right, Department of the Interior, National Park Service, Edison
National Historic Site)*

and the financial wizards who presumably ran the country: the awesome J. P. Morgan, the circumspect Jacob Schiff, and their clients and lesser breeds of big businessmen.

The leaders of the new corporate age, like their many admirers, were never entirely clear about their ultimate aims. Heavy capital investment, rapid plant expansion, increased production and reduced over-head, economies of scale, market control—all to what greater good? For profit, surely, and for rising quantities of consumer goods for more and more people. But beyond that? What did the manufacture and constant manipulation of consumer demand mean for individual freedom of choice? Was standardization of products and prices really so desirable? How were Americans to balance rising standards of living with loss of control over production? How could big business be called to account and made to deliver on its promise of economic security for all citizens? Were huge industrial and financial combinations compatible with

political democracy and social responsibility? These were questions that neither the corporate revolutionaries nor their uneasy admirers could quite answer. Such fundamental questions posed a continuing twentieth-century dilemma.

The Counterrevolution Fails

These same questions troubled the opponents of big business, whose numbers and influence also grew rapidly in the late nineteenth century. If the antimonopolists ultimately failed to stop economic concentration, it was not for lack of numbers. The antimonopoly army in the last quarter of the nineteenth century included at one time or another farmers and workingmen with their strong beliefs in equal opportunity; small businessmen with their individualist creed; and liberal publicists, country lawyers, clergymen, and academicians. Antimonopoly found a congenial home in the major protest parties of the period, from the Grangers and the Greenbackers of the 1870s, to the Populists of the 1890s.

The complaints of the antimonopolists were many and varied. Monopolies, it was widely held, misallocated and underused resources, and thus kept the nation's total output lower than it should have been. Trusts, it was said, tied the people's hands while they picked their pockets. They were inefficient and sheltered inefficient producers within huge integrated structures where their inefficiencies went undetected. If pools, trusts, and all other instruments of business collusion did not invariably raise prices, they at least had the power to do so at will. And that power had been acquired by driving out honest competitors.

The Case Against Monopoly.   The heart of the case against trusts and monopolies was the belief in a "natural development" that presumably had been violated. The chief spokesmen against business combination were three social prophets, Henry George, Edward Bellamy, and Henry Demarest Lloyd, whose bestsellers *Progress and Poverty* (1879), *Looking Backward* (1888), and *Wealth against Commonwealth* (1894) commanded national attention. For this trio of social reformers, as for countless other publicists and popularizers of the case against monopoly, "natural" economic growth meant a steady rate of development accompanied by full employment and widespread consumption. According to this reasoning, healthy societies like the United States enjoyed a "normal" pace of steady growth with which monopolies played havoc by accelerating the growth rate abnormally and stimulating a feverish speculation. If trusts, pools, holding companies, and all the other artificial contrivances could simply be dismantled and their special privileges annulled, the American economy would return to a steadier rate of "real growth" that would

spread the benefits of industrialism evenly throughout society.

The case against economic concentration rested on a set of moral assumptions that defined the good society and called upon Americans to recapture it. First came the distinction between the true producers of the world and the parasites who fed on them. Next, a faith in the natural cooperation and a sense of community inherent in a society of small producers. And finally, a moral economy derived from an eighteenth-century tradition of artisanship that established a just price and a fair wage with ethical precision. As Henry George explained in the opening of *Progress and Poverty*:

So long as all the increased wealth which modern progress brings goes but to build up great fortunes, to increase luxury and make sharper the contrast between the House

NEW YORK: WINTER AND SUMMER
Alfred Steiglitz's famous photograph of Fifth Avenue in a snowstorm (1892) contrasts with one of Madison Square Park cab stand in summer (1900). *(Left, The Metropolitan Museum of Art, Gift of J. B. Neumann, 1958; right, from the Clarence Davies Collection, Museum of the City of New York)*

of Have and the House of Want, progress is not real and cannot be permanent. The reaction must come.

Before 1890 public opposition to monopoly accomplished little. In the 1870s the Patrons of Husbandry, or the Grange, as the national farmers' organization was called, turned to politics in states like Illinois and Wisconsin, and together with shippers passed laws regulating the rates charged by railroads for hauling freight and storing grain. Although the Supreme Court originally upheld these so-called Granger laws in *Munn* v. *Illinois* (1877), nine years later in *Wabash, St. Louis & Pacific Railway Co.* v. *Illinois* a more conservative-minded majority declared that individual states could not regulate rates for interstate carriers.

Nor, on the federal level, was the Interstate Commerce Act (1887) much more successful in bringing the railroads to heel. The act prohibited pools, rebates, and rate discriminations, and set up a commission to investigate violations, but the commission's findings could be enforced only in the courts, a costly and cumbersome procedure. The Interstate Commerce Act marked the beginning of the American public's acceptance of the principle of government intervention, but it did not provide effective regulation. For that the country had to await Theodore Roosevelt's Square Deal.

By the time Congress responded to the public clamor to "do something about the trusts" by passing the Sherman Antitrust Act in 1890, more than a dozen states had already attempted some kind of antitrust legislation aimed at making restraint of trade "illegal, actionable, and indictable." Big business, however, countered these attempts at control by moving into more permissive states like New Jersey, where they secured generous enabling laws. Henry Demarest Lloyd, perhaps the severest critic of monopoly, complained that Standard Oil, in its bid for favors, had done everything to the legislature of Pennsylvania except refine it.

The Sherman Antitrust Act.   The Sherman Antitrust Act brought no antimonopoly millennium. The bill that John Sherman of Ohio introduced in the Senate quickly found its way to the Judiciary Committee, which rewrote it before sending it to the full Senate where it passed by a vote of 52 to 1. The House, in turn, passed the measure unanimously. The Sherman Act was an honest although confused, attempt to regulate the trusts. The long list of unanswered questions involving enforcement give big business ample leeway. The act declared "unreasonable restraint" illegal—but what did "unreasonable" mean? What constituted a monopoly? How much power over an industry spelled "control"? How, in short, was the government to proceed with the job of breaking up the trusts?

These questions the Sherman Act left to the government attorneys and judges, who at least during Cleveland's and McKinley's administrations in the 1890s were not disposed to stop the merger movement. Richard Olney, President Cleveland's waspish attorney general, spoke for big businessmen everywhere when he approved the Supreme Court's refusal to break up the sugar trust in the *E. C. Knight* case (1895). "You will observe that the government has been defeated in the Supreme Court on the trust question. I always supposed it would be, and have taken responsibility of not prosecuting under a law I believed to be no good." Labor unions, on the other hand, seemed to Olney and his masters thoroughly objectionable conspiracies against trade. When Eugene Debs's American Railway Union, in its epochal battle with the Pullman Company in Chicago in 1894, refused to move the mails, Olney drew up an injunction declaring the union in restraint of trade and successfully prosecuted Debs for contempt of court

in violating the injunction. On appeal, the Supreme Court upheld the application of the Sherman Act to labor unions.

The Sherman Act was successfully applied in two railroad cases in 1897 and in 1898, and again, more notably, in the *Northern Securities* case in 1904, which ended J. P. Morgan's dream of merging the Northern Pacific, Union Pacific, and Burlington railroads. Still, only eighteen cases were initiated in the first ten years following the passage of the act. And in the crucial *E. C. Knight* case, a poorly drafted government brief allowed a conservative Court to declare the American Sugar Refining Company—a trust controlling 98 percent of the industry—not technically in restraint of trade.

When Theodore Roosevelt took office in 1901, the fortunes of the antimonopolists appeared to improve. Moreover, Roosevelt's successor, William Howard Taft, continued to initiate suits against the trusts. The Sherman Act, besides breaking up the Northern Securities Company, was applied successfully in 1911 against the Standard Oil and American Tobacco companies. Yet by then it was clear that the act, far from achieving the results its framers had intended, was strengthening rather than checking the forces behind the merger movement. By admitting that not every restraint of trade was unreasonable, and by ruling cartel behavior unacceptable but full-blown mergers legitimate, the courts invited big business to abandon looser forms of organization for tighter and more controlled ones.

The spirit of antimonopoly survived down to the First World War. Gathering new coherence from the economic analysis and social ideas of several of President Woodrow Wilson's advisers, trust-busting supplied the impetus for the passage in 1914 of the Clayton Antitrust Act. Yet while the Clayton Act also defined certain unfair practices, like interlocking directorates and price discrimination, and a supplementary Federal Trade Commission Act provided for publicity and the prosecution of violators, the momentum of business combination was scarcely broken. The advantages of bigness now seemed unarguable, a fact attested to by the incorporation of the giant General Motors soon after the Clayton Act was passed. With few accomplishments to show for

BLACKFOOT INDIANS
In Glacier National Park,
Mont., in 1915. (Smith-
sonian Institution, National
Anthropological Archives)

forty years of continual agitation, the opponents of monopoly quit the field to await another call to battle in the waning years of the New Deal. The counter-attack against big business had failed.

The Farmers' Fight Against Disorder

Although American farmers refused to admit it, their problems in the last quarter of the nineteenth century were not very different from those confront-ing businessmen—enormously increased production, glutted markets, and falling prices. Just as technology was revolutionizing industrial production, so did mechanical reapers, harrowers, spreaders and har-vesters expand the farmers' productivity. With a traditional cradle scythe, a wheat farmer could cut two acres a day; with a self-raking reaper he could cut twelve. By 1880, 80 percent of American wheat

was being harvested by machine. The value of farm machinery, $42 million in 1870, exceeded $100 mil-lion thirty years later.

The Last Frontier. The key to agricultural surplus was the new land across the Mississippi, the Great Plains stretching westward from the tier of states along the river, across the Hundredth Meridian to the foothills of the Rockies. Only a generation earlier this huge area had been marked the "Great American Desert" on the most up-to-date map, but now it was being billed by promoters and boosters as the "Great Bread Basket of the World."

In the 1880s the Great Plains furnished a gigantic stage for the clash of four very different civilizations, each with its own receding frontier. The Indian wars of the late 1860s and 1870s together with the destruc-tion of the buffalo had already begun the work of confining the High Plains Indians—Apache, Hopi, and Comanche in the Southwest; Sioux, Blackfeet, Nez Percé, and Cheyenne in the North—to reserva-

Passing of the Frontier, 1870-1890

100°

Settled Area in 1870

Settled 1870-90

Unsettled in 1890 (Less than 2 people per square mile)

100°

tions. The misnamed "Battle" of Wounded Knee (1890), in which federal troops butchered two hundred Indian men, women, and children, was a fitting climax to twenty years of repression and extermination. The miner's frontier was also closing, after a thirty-year scramble up the California side of the mountains and down the other into Nevada, Colorado, Idaho, and Montana. By 1880 the lone "placer" miner, with his pick, shovel, and sluice box, was already retreating into myth as the heavy rockcrushers and trained engineers of the mining syndicates advanced. Five years later, the big cattle barons who had driven their herds up the Texas Panhandle to the railroad heads at Abilene, Dodge City, and Cheyenne, were enjoying one last year of magnificient open range before being defeated by the farmers with their barbed wire and the blizzard of 1886, which wiped out their herds.

The future lay with the farmers and their last frontier. The opening-up of the Great Plains reached its peak in the 1880s and 1890s, when the total amount of improved land in the United States doubled from 189 million to 414 million acres. Railroad agents, boasting of bonanza farms and the richness of the soil, and local chambers of commerce promising everything from a cure-all environment for the sickly to husbands for young women, seized control of the Great Plains through a land policy tailored to mythical yeoman farmers and a homestead law written for an earlier generation.

Settlers enticed across the ninety-eighth meridian found an environment different from any they had ever experienced. John Wesley Powell, the geologist and explorer of the High Plains, spent much of his career trying to tell Americans what it was like to farm land where less than twenty inches of rain fell annually. The choice, he explained, was between organizing what he called "this new industry of agriculture by irrigation" on the High Plains as a voluntary community of small holders, and a forced monopoly of "a few great capitalists, employing labor on a large scale, as is done in the great mines and manufactories of the United States." Few of his contemporaries, least of all the individualistic farmer, heeded Powell's predictions of an emerging agribusiness. Yet by 1900 the outlines of the new system were already clear.

One of the causes of a growing agricultural surplus was increasing crop specialization—wheat, hogs, and beef in the trans-Mississippi West; dairy products in the Old Northwest; and cotton in the South—encouraged by the railroads and new machinery. Even more important was a rising world demand for staples, which acted much like growing American cities in providing markets for industrial goods. In fact, the two developments were related. As American staples flooded Europe, prices for foodstuffs fell sharply there and land prices collapsed. The agricultural depression in Europe, beginning in the 1870s, drove millions of peasants and small farmers out of the countryside and into seaports, the first stopping point en route to American cities. Both in Europe and America, cheaper food hastened industrial transformation. In the United States, however, the farmers paid a large part of the bill by ensuring a favorable balance of trade with massive exports of staple crops at declining prices.

In one mood the American farmer could consider the move from subsistence farming to specialized commercial farming as progress toward a higher standard of living. But this advantage was soon offset by the staple-crop farmer's suspicions that he had become the prisoner of the market, locked into a price structure from which there was no ready means of escape. With the onset of the world agricultural depression in the 1870s the price curve for staple crops dropped precipitously, and the income of the farmer slid with it. Wheat fell from $1.19 a bushel in 1881 to a low of 49¢ in 1894. Corn fell in these same depression years from 63¢ a bushel to 18¢. Buying in a market protected by tariffs, and selling in an unpro-

tected one, the staple-crop farmer saw himself the victim of an absurd situation; he was forced to grow more and more in order to earn less and less. Why, he asked, as the producer of the largest share of the nation's abundance, should he sink deeper into the mire each year? A Kansas farmer in 1891 summed up these feelings of betrayal:

At the age of 52 years, after a long life of toil, economy, and self-denial, I find myself and family virtually paupers. With hundreds of hogs, scores of good horses, and a farm that rewarded the toil of our hands with 16,000 bushels of golden corn we are poorer by many dollars than we were years ago. What once seemed like a neat little fortune and a house of refuge for our declining years, by a few turns of the monopolistic crank has been rendered valueless.

Farmers as Businessmen. To put it another way, most American farmers were now businessmen in a business which was always unstable and at times hazardous. To increase output and cut costs, many staple-crop farmers, like their small-businessmen counterparts, borrowed heavily to buy machinery only to find themselves saddled with high interest rates. Tight money, the farmers reasoned, lay at the root of their troubles: as consumption fell, so too did prices. Bankers and eastern creditors might try to blame overproduction, but farmers in the West and South knew the problem was "under-consumption" and cursed both the "gold-bugs" and Wall Street.

Tight money and sharp price drops combined to drive the farmers into protest politics and third parties. Reform politics came first to the farmers of the Old Northwest in the aftermath of the Panic of 1873, as the Grangers began to experiment with cooperative storage and marketing schemes. At the same time, these midwestern farmers together with businessmen and shippers of the region conducted forays into state politics to force passage of railroad regulation. Yet significant rate regulation was slow in coming to the farmers. When it did, it was more a result than a cause of their improved bargaining power.

The 1880s saw the rapid growth of regional farm organizations like the Agricultural Wheel and the National Farmers Alliance, which joined in 1880 to form the powerful Southern Alliance with more than a million members. In the Great Plains states the Northern Alliance became the collective voice of staple-crop producers. Yet even though the West and South concurred in their diagnosis and prescription—opposition to the trusts, marketing cooperatives, and cheap money—only reluctantly could they agree to enter the political arena as a third party. Out of their agreement in Omaha in 1891 came the Populist crusade, which rallied the discontented with symbols of conspiracy and prophecies of decline, while making specific interest-group demands. Populism stirred profound convictions of betrayal.

The basic insight of American farmers throughout the nineteenth century was the moral primacy of agriculture. This view was stated most eloquently by William Jennings Bryan in his famous "Cross of Gold Speech" at the Democratic convention in 1896. "You come to us and tell us that the great cities are in favor of the gold standard," the Great Commoner thundered. "We reply that the great cities rest upon our broad and fertile prairies. Burn down your cities and leave our farms and your cities will spring up again as if by magic; but destroy our farms and grass will grow in the streets of every city in the country." Bryan confirmed the average farmer's own belief, borne out by the record, that the yeoman had indeed built America. He had cleared and cultivated the land, raised the foodstuffs, fed his own and other people throughout the world, and laid the material base on which a modern industrial society now rested. The land, in spite of the violence methodically visited upon it, remained foremost in the American moral imagination. "On the land we are born, from it we live, to it we return again—children of the soil as truly as is the blade of grass or the flower of the field," Henry George wrote. And his message reached millions of already converted farmers who sought only an endorsement of their faith.

The Farmer as Populist—A Holy War. Farmers knew that the land had produced the foodstuffs with which the United States paid for the European goods and capital needed to modernize. They lashed out with mounting frustration as an ungrateful urban society denied their achievements, ridiculed their proposals for reform, and mocked their provincial ways and narrow lives. Out of this massive loss of confidence came the politics of Populism. The Populists convened for the presidential election in 1892 determined to rescue the nation from moral as well as material ruin. "A vast conspiracy against mankind has been organized on two continents and is taking possession of the world," their St. Louis platform declared. "If not met and overthrown at once it forbodes terrible social convulsions, the destruction of civilization, or the establishment of an absolute despotism." With the coming of Populism, the American farmer's twenty-year crusade became a holy war.

By 1900, however, the predicted end of the world had failed to materialize. In the sharp upturn of the economy that opened the twentieth century, American farmers gave up their millennarian hopes for the more immediate gains furnished by rising farm incomes. The advantages of organization, consolidation, and integration, which were the same lessons being taught by big business, had now become too obvious for the farmer to ignore. He too could learn to read the statistics that told him what to do. The encouraging figures on production and price that he began to consult were being compiled by the Division of Statistics of the Department of Agriculture, whose other departmental divisions—soils, chemistry, and animal industry—were proof of the continuing bureaucratic revolution in American agriculture.

These figures, whether for soaring staple prices, declining shipping costs, or estimates of increasing staple production, continued to assure the farmer down to the First World War of the reality of his sudden prosperity. Between 1900 and 1910 the price of corn shot up from 35¢ to 52¢ a bushel, wheat from 62¢ to 91¢, as the wholesale farm price index jumped 50 percent and the average price of farm land doubled from $20 to $40 an acre. As staple-crop farmers remembered with chagrin, it had not been their frantic third-party politics that had accomplished all this; nevertheless the national economy was at last responding to their needs and demands. Just as American businessmen began the twentieth century by applying the lessons of consolidation, so American farmers were learning to follow seemingly simple

POPULIST COUNTRY
Beyond the 100th meridian rain was scarce, trees nonexistent, neighbors few, and life bleak. *(National Archives.)*

directives for finding safety in system and security in new organization.

Cooperatives. The most efficient of the early twentieth-century farm organizations were producers' cooperatives, which concentrated on solving the problems of prices and marketing. Except for their official nonprofitmaking status and their democratic voting procedures, cooperatives were really modern corporations as streamlined and efficient as their counterparts in business. They also came to rely on experts and specialists, trained managers and accountants, legal advisers, lobbyists, and public relations men. Like the integrated industrial firm, they also achieved forward integration by building their own facilities at railroad terminals and by writing ironclad contracts with their members, compelling them to hold their crops off the market until the price was right. By 1910 the antimonopoly scruples of big farmers were fast disappearing.

Prosperous farmers, like the big businessmen they were becoming, designed and built cooperatives as simple interest-group devices for solving particular problems. The Grangers, Knights of Labor, and Populists, who pioneered with commodity cooperatives, had hoped to preserve earlier conditions of independence and equality. The new farm cooperatives advertised no such grandiose social aims but were content, with the return of flush times, to perfect the means which the organizational revolution had assigned them. Their members were essentially agricultural trade-unionists who thought and behaved like cotton planters, corn-hog producers, dairy farmers. Why, they asked themselves, replace an economic system capable of producing the abundance that, however belatedly, was now being showered upon them?

The chief advocates of the bureaucratic revolution in American agriculture were not the staple-crop farmers in the trans-Mississippi West, but the dairy,

APPLE-PICKING IN WEST
VIRGINIA
Not all farming was mech-
anized by 1910. *(Photo by
Smith Brothers, October 1910,
Library of Congress)*

poultry, and fruit and vegetable farmers in the older
sections of the East and Northwest, and their competitors on the Pacific Coast, all of whose fortunes had
risen steadily with the growth of railroads and metropolitan markets. With the return of prosperity, these
groups put aside their interest in protest politics in
favor of scientific methods and interest-group associations.

Soon the cooperative marketing movement was
in full swing, and dozens of livestock unions, dairy-
men's leagues, grain exchanges, cotton cooperatives,
and tobacco pools were being founded each year. Cooperatives in turn spawned hundreds of new pressure
groups—the Farmers' Equity Union, the Farmers'
Mutual Benefit Association, the Farmers' Social and
Economic Union, the Farmers' Relief Association—all
of them proclaiming as their own the slogan of the
American Society of Equity: "What the farmer wants
to produce is not crops, but money." In 1912 cooperatives secured the blessing of the Department of Agriculture, which provided them with their own fact-

finding agency, the Bureau of Markets. Eight years
later the formation of the American Farm Bureau
Federation announced the arrival of modern agriculture as a national force. Although the chief gains in
numbers and influence were not to come until the
1920s, the commercialization of the American farmer
and his conversion to agribusiness had already been
accomplished.

The dramatic shift in farmers' thinking that came
with the return of prosperity after 1900 was expressed
in the changed outlook of one of the farmers' most
impassioned spokesmen. Returning home to the Middle Border in 1889 at the height of the agrarian distress, Hamlin Garland, still an unknown but aspiring young writer, found his old neighbors caught up
in social crisis and engaged "in a sullen rebellion
against government and against God."

Every house I visited had its individual message of sordid
struggle and half-hidden despair. . . . All the gilding of
farm life melted away. The hard and bitter realities came

back upon me in a flood. Nature was as bountiful as ever ... but no splendor of cloud, no grace of sunset, could conceal the poverty of these people; on the contrary, they brought out, with a more intolerable poignancy, the gracelessness of these homes, and the sordid quality of the mechanical routine of these lives. I perceived beautiful youth becoming bowed and bent.

Convinced that "men's laws" rather than God's were responsible for both "industrial slavery" and the degradation of the farmer, Garland brought to the Populists an enthusiasm for root-and-branch reform and an aesthetic theory of Veritism to match. Yet fifteen years later, with the Populist years a memory, Garland left the main travelled thoroughfares of agrarian protest for nostalgic excursions into the romantic highcountry of the Far Northwest, abandoning reform to settle for the promises of Theodore Roosevelt's Country Life Commission. The commission, itself proof of the revival of the farmers' influence, was appointed in 1908 and charged with the task of improving rural life in the United States. After taking the pulse of rural America and listening to a recital of its ailments, the commissioners concluded that what the farmer needed was simply to catch up with his city cousin, to "even-up" the distribution of amenities between city and country. This recovery, according to their diagnosis, involved agricultural credits, a highway program, rural free delivery, better schools, a country church movement to rescue lost sheep, and very little else. Prosperity had soothed old discontents. By 1910 Hamlin Garland's outraged cry for justice "for the toiling poor wherever found" had become a faint echo as American farmers moved into their golden age which statistics, government recognition, and their own pockets told them had come at last.

Workers and the Challenge of Organization

Of all the groups caught up in the American economic revolution of the late nineteenth century, industrial workers depended least on statistics to confirm what they already knew. And what they knew was that their rewards for tending the national indus-

trial machine hardly matched their services. Real wages rose 25 percent in the 1880s, but in 1882 Massachusetts's Commissioner of Labor Caroll Wright reported that male Fall River textile workers could not support their families unless their wives also worked. Data assembled in the last years of the century show that the work week for the "average" worker in industry was a little less than 60 hours, that the average wage for skilled workers was 20¢ an hour, and only half that amount for unskilled workers. Annual wages for most factory workers in 1900 came to an average of $400 to $500, from which a working family saved an average $30 per year. Nearly half the remainder was spent for food, another quarter for rent, and the balance for fuel, light, and clothing.

Earnings for workers in manufacturing continued to go up 37 percent between 1890 and 1914, but the cost of living between 1897 and 1914 climbed 39 percent. In spite of growing national wealth, American workers and their families managed on very narrow margins. Their share of the pie, though larger than it had been a half-century earlier, was still comparatively small. A statistical breakdown of national income, had they consulted it, would have strengthened their conviction that workers, too, had to organize for bargaining power. The richest tenth of the population received 33.9 percent of the nation's income, the poorest, 3.4 percent. The wealthier half of the population accounted for over 70 percent of all the country's income. The rich were certainly getting richer, while the American workers, if not absolutely poorer, were still not enjoying much of the wealth they were creating. Nor had they yet found the organizational power with which to counter the growing strength of American business. The growth of labor unions conspicuously failed to keep up with the expanding work force. In 1870 one in ten workers was a union member; in 1900, one in twelve.

Strikes and Work Stoppages. With or without union help, workers turned to the strike as their chief defensive weapon. There were 477 work stoppages in 1881, nearly 2,000 a decade later, and over 1,800 a year at the turn of the century. Strikes were usually responses to wage cuts. The Great Railroad Strike of 1877, the "Great Upheaval" on Jay Gould's Southwestern system in 1886, and the rash of railroad strikes culminating in the Pullman Strike in 1894, were all triggered by management's determination to slash wages. The pattern was the same in nearly every industry: strikes followed the attempt on the part of the employers to increase hours by "grinding" or "driving" workers beyond agreed-upon limits or, more frequently, to cut wages during recessions.

The attitude of many businessmen toward the "labor supply" before 1900 was apt to be that of the steelmaker who admitted to a congressional committee that "If I wanted boiler iron I would go out on the market and buy where I could get it the cheapest, and if I wanted to employ men I would do the same thing." The views of independent shop owners were often even more pronounced. "While you are in my workshop," one manufacturer told his workers, "you must conform to my rules. . . . You must not attempt to take the control of the workshop out of my hands." As for the notorious preference of American workers for "lager and leisure," Joseph Medill, publisher of the Chicago *Tribune,* warned his readers that this must be checked by teaching them that their "impecunious condition" was due entirely to their "improvidence and misdirected efforts. . . . The wage-classes cannot support in idleness a quarter of a million saloon-keepers . . . and at the same time hope to prosper themselves."

To correct such attitudes, the Knights of Labor president, Terence V. Powderly, proposed educating employers in the advantages of arbitration, and his own membership—some 700,000 strong in 1886—in the "folly of strikes." Education converted neither businessmen (who until late in the century were inclined to equate union leaders with secessionists in the War of the Rebellion) nor the leadership of the union locals. A series of strikes culminated in the disastrous contest with Jay Gould's Texas Pacific Railroad in 1886, and soon the Knights entered a period of sharp decline, a victim of business antagonism, craft union fears, and their own delusions of grandeur.

Labor Consolidation.   The American Federation of Labor (AFL), a flexible organization of craft unions formed in 1886, represented a new generation's ca-

pitulation to the corporate revolution. Workers too could learn the lessons of consolidation. Samuel Gompers, the founder and longtime president of the AFL, and his lieutenant, Adolph Strasser, readily confessed that their sole concern was for the skilled trades they represented and the immediate welfare of their members. Asked to define the "ultimate ends" of "pure and simple unionism," Strasser replied at once that the two terms were contradictory. "We have no ultimate ends. We are going on from day to day. We are fighting for immediate objects—objects that can be realized in a few years."

The new union leaders reminded businessmen that they too were "practical men," not closet theorists or reformers, but pragmatists and opportunists, like their employers, organizers with their eyes on the main chance. The distance the AFL had come from the cooperative industrial unionism of the Knights could be measured in Gompers's reply to Socialist Morris Hillquit, who was bent on discrediting his rival. Hillquit demanded to know whether the president of the AFL really believed that American workers received the "full product" of their labor. Gompers brushed aside the question as meaningless. "I will say," he replied, "that it is impossible for anyone to definitely say what proportion the workers receive as a result of their labor, but it is the fact that due to the organized labor movement they have received and are receiving a larger share of the product of their labor than they ever did in the history of modern society." Accused by irate socialists and labor radicals of having sold out the movement by refusing to develop a genuine social philosophy, Gompers and his craft unionists cheerfully admitted to a belief in half a loaf and a willingness to follow "the lines of least resistance."

"Least resistance" for organized labor as the twentieth century began meant accepting the merger movement and making bargains with big business. The trusts, Gompers announced, "are our employers, and the employer who is fair to us, whether an individual, or a collection of individuals in the form of a corporation or a trust, matters little to us so long as we obtain fair wages." As for the wage system on which capitalism rested, there was little, he thought, to be gained by quarreling with it or dreaming up substitutes. "The hope for a perfect millennium," Gompers told the U.S. Industrial Commission, "well, it don't come every night."

Enlightened Business. The American Federation of Labor, modest in its aims, overcame the resistance of employers only with difficulty and at some cost. Although membership grew from 140,000 at its founding in 1886 to over 2 million in 1914, less than a third of the country's skilled workers could be found in its ranks in 1900. When war broke out in Europe in 1914, only 15 percent of the nonagricultural workers in the United States were members of any union. They still faced obstacles such as the injunction and the yellow-dog contract, and small businessmen tried to stop them from unionizing. In 1903 the National Association of Manufacturers (NAM) formed and funded the Citizens Industrial Association to spread the gospel of the non-union "open shop" under the name "The American Plan." The success of their American Plan, conservative businessmen promised, would spell the doom of labor unions.

More enlightened leaders of business hoped to control labor through the concept of guided democracy. They stressed a paternal concern for the American worker along with arbitration schemes and appeals for "responsible leadership." "A man who won't meet his men half-way is a God-damn fool!" Mark Hanna, one of the new business leaders, announced in deriding the obstinacy of old-fashioned businessmen like George Pullman. For they recognized that labor's grievances were real and many of its demands legitimate—an acknowledgment that workers' needs for security and stability were not so very different from the needs of management. In 1900 progressive industrialists like George E. Perkins and financiers like J. P. Morgan struck a bargain with Gompers and founded the National Civic Federation on the proposition that labor, like business, must be encouraged to organize its interests and rally its forces for full participation in the new corporate society.

Any strategy for enlightened business interest required, first of all, vastly improved working conditions. Factory work was still alarmingly dangerous. A survey of industrial accidents for the year 1913 showed that some 25,000 workers had been killed on the job and another 750,000 seriously injured. Then there were the problems of incentive, alienation, and the loss of community resulting from increased scale and the impersonality of the factory. These were eloquently described to the Industrial Commission in 1899 by a veteran shoe worker, who recalled the days of a rough shop-floor socialism before the advent of the giant mechanized factory. "In these old shops, years ago," he told the commissioners, "one man owned the shop; and he and three, four, five or six others, neighbors, came in there and sat down and made shoes right in their laps, and there was no machinery. Everybody was at liberty to talk."

But could this idyll be recovered or recreated? "We do not want to go back to the time when we could do without the sewing machine or the machinery for manufacturing purposes, or the large aggregations of capital," the shoemaker replied, "but we want capital controlled in such a way that it will not result in the displacement of three-fourths of the population for the increased wealth of one-fourth of the population." In grudging admissions like this lay the secret of big business's success.

Working-Class Life. Workers packed in slums and ghettos of center cities knew precisely how far they stood from the margins of plenty. The quality of life in the working-class districts of most American cities was appalling. In 1915 President Wilson's Industrial Commission, still another investigatory body appointed to examine the causes of industrial unrest, concluded: "A large part of our industrial population are . . . living in actual poverty." Exactly what proportion of the nation's working class lived below the subsistence level the commissioners did not care to estimate. They added, however, "It is certain at least one-third and possibly one-half of the families of wage earners employed in manufacturing and mining earn in the course of the year less than enough to support them in anything like a comfortable and decent condition." Urban housing for new arrivals from Europe and the American countryside—whether

TWO DOCUMENTARY VIEWS OF URBAN POVERTY
Both artists and photographers aimed their message at
the American social conscience. The lithograph is John
Sloan's "Roofs, Summer Night"; the photograph of the
web of washlines criss-crossing a courtyard on the Lower
East Side's Thompson Street is by Jacob Riis, who illus-
trated his own exposé of urban poverty, *How the Other
Half Lives*. *(Left, Boston Public Library; right, photograph by
Jacob A. Riis, Jacob A. Riis Collection, Museum of the City
of New York)*

three-story wooden firetraps in South Boston or
dumbbell tenements on New York's Lower East Side
or dilapidated single-family shanties in Cincinnati,
St. Louis, or Chicago—was generally deplorable and,
worse still, expensive. Gas, water, electricity, sanitation, and transportation—all of the services needed
to make the life of city workers tolerable—were in
short supply and of poor quality as late as 1900.

The main surge in urban improvement began
with the new century, and within a decade municipal
services were improved, giving cities a public face-
lift and new vitality. But housing and personal standards of living improved much more slowly. The
public life of American cities responded to the work
of urban reformers with their vision of a rejuvenated
democratic purpose; yet blighted neighborhoods,
fractured communities, crumbling apartments, and
stunted lives continued as a stark reality for too many
American workers.

For recently arrived immigrants who endured
these conditions and who made up the major portion
of the industrial labor force by 1900, there was still
another and more subtle kind of exploitation in the

DUMBBELL TENEMENT
In New York City's teeming
Lower East Side most families
were crowded into the notorious "dumbbell' tenements,
seven or eight stories high.
Only one room in any apart-
ment in these wooden firetraps
received direct sun or air. All
the families on each floor
shared a toilet in the hall,
while in the oppressive heat
of July and August people fled
to fire escapes and roofs to
sleep.

cultural drive to "Americanize" them as quickly as possible. All of the ethnic groups arriving in such great numbers after 1880—Italians, Greeks, Poles, Russian Jews—were viewed at one time or another as potential bomb throwers in need of the saving word from "100 Percent" Americans. Where earlier generations had singled out the political party as the chief agent of cultural adjustment, reformers after 1880 emphasized the school. As one observer explained to the readers of *World's Work* in 1903, "There are many things in which, as a rule, the public consider that the public schools fail, but one thing that cannot be denied—and it is the greatest—is that these boys and girls of foreign parentage catch readily the simple American ideas of independence and individual work and, with them, social progress." "Social progress" in the half-century after 1880, meant vigorous Americanization: widespread literacy, technological education, elimination of child labor, cultural conformity, and last but not least, the cultivation in an aspiring working class of a hearty appetite for all the consumer goods produced by the huge American industrial machine.

Just as American businessmen after 1900 continued to form monopolies and oligopolies, and farmers launched their own organizational revolution, so the nation's industrial workers began to adjust their roles to the demands of corporate capitalism. In largely ignoring the alternative of socialism and in seemingly accepting their assignments, American workers added to the impression of inevitability created by the production statistics.

The Fruits of the Industrial Revolution

The economic transformation of the United States, like all revolutions, had unintended consequences. Used as an index of national prosperity, the statistics of growth seemed a simple instrument for measuring the accomplishments of a whole people. The national wealth, $16 billion in 1860, according to the estimate of government statisticians, had grown by 1900 to $88 billion, a per capita increase from $500 to $1,100. But these figures effectively masked differences of class, region, occupation, and the persistence of a grossly uneven distribution of income. Americans were being affected by the organizational revolution in drastically different ways.

Yet the American dream of 1900 remained what it had been a half-century earlier, a vision of a people uniquely equipped to create and enjoy abundance. Economic integration itself seemed convincing proof of the near approach of "the promise of American life." A national market had been built and the nation's shelves stocked with an incredible variety of goods. In this sense the economic well-being of the United States appeared to be exactly what a new generation of American businessmen pronounced it—a single economic system binding citizen and nation together in a network of mutual benefits.

But beneath the surface, as the new century began, lay not unity but multiplicity; not a single national purpose but competing and even warring interests; not pressures unifying American society but forces that threatened to fling it apart; not the conservation of national energies but their diffusion in politically volatile forms. Americans in the opening years of the twentieth century thus confronted a paradox capping a half-century of growth: the economic integration that had seemingly saved them from the waste of competition had set in motion cultural and political counterforces that threatened fragmentation, dispersion, diffusion, and isolation. To cope with these threats to national order, the American people would need new and more sophisticated concepts of social and political organization and the capacity somehow to use them.

CHRONOLOGY

1873   Panic of 1873 begins six years of depression.

1876   Alexander Graham Bell invents the telephone.

1877   Great Railroad Strike.

1879   Henry George's *Progress and Poverty* published. Thomas Alva Edison perfects the electric light bulb.

1880   Farmers' Agricultural Wheel and National Farmers' Alliance join together to form Southern Alliance.

1882   John D. Rockefeller's Standard Oil of Ohio consolidates American oil industry under Standard Oil Trust.

1883   Chicago builds first elevated electric railway. Brooklyn Bridge completed.

1884   Recession and unemployment jar the economy.

1886   AFL (American Federation of Labor) founded. The "Great Upheaval" stops work on Jay Gould's Texas Pacific railroad. George Westinghouse founds Westinghouse Electric Co. and subsequently perfects use of alternating current.

1887   Interstate Commerce Act passed to control railroads.

1888   Edward Bellamy's *Looking Backward* published.

1890   Sherman Anti-Trust Act passed in attempt to regulate monopolies in restraint of trade. Sherman Silver Purchase Act passed, resulting in depleted gold reserves. At "Battle" of Wounded Knee, South Dakota, federal troops massacre 200 Indians.

1891   Hamlin Garland's *Main-Travelled Roads* describes hardships of mid-western farmers' lives. Louis Sullivan's Wainwright Building completed in St. Louis.

1892   Populists organize; nominate General James B. Weaver for president at national convention in Omaha. Grover Cleveland elected president. Homestead strike in Carnegie steel mills.

1893   Financial panic sends U.S. economy into four years of depression. Repeal of Sherman Silver Purchase Act. Chicago World's Fair opens. Historian Frederick Jackson Turner in "The Significance of the American Frontier," announces closing of the frontier.

1894   Pullman strike broken by federal troops; Eugene V. Debs jailed. Henry Demarest Lloyd's *Wealth against Commonwealth*, exposé of Standard Oil Company, published.

1895 In *U.S.* v. *E. C. Knight Co.*, government defeated in antitrust suit against sugar monopoly.

1896 William McKinley elected president, defeating William Jennings Bryan and "Free Silver."

1900 McKinley reelected president, defeating Bryan once again.
National Civic Foundation established by labor leaders and industrialists.
Theodore Dreiser's *Sister Carrie*, naturalistic novel, causes literary stir.

1901 Theodore Roosevelt becomes president after McKinley assassinated.

United States Steel Corporation formed.

1903 Wright brothers make their first flight.
National Association of Manufacturers (NAM) formed.
Citizens Industrial Association formed to secure open shop in American industry.

1904 Case of *Northern Securities Co.* v. *U.S.* upholds government's case against railroad mergers.

1911 Triangle Shirtwaist Factory fire in New York City's East Side kills 146 women, leading to investigation and revision of state factory code.

SUGGESTED READINGS

There are two outstanding accounts of the organizational revolution in American society in the half-century after 1870. Brief but still the model for more recent interpretive work is Samuel P. Hays, *The Response to Industrialism* (1957). Robert Wiebe, *The Search for Order* (1968) traces the shift from small-town America to modern bureaucratic society in terms of political institutions and social values as well as economic reorganization. John A. Garraty, *The New Commonwealth, 1877–1890* (1968) focuses on the crucial decade of the 1880s. Ray Ginger, *The Age of Excess* (1965) is a lively and impressionistic survey, and so is Howard Mumford Jones, *The Age of Energy: Varieties of American Experience, 1865–1915* (1970).

The technical literature on the developing economy in this period is extensive. Among the most useful studies of aspects of American economic growth discussed here are Clarence D. Long, *Wages and Earnings in the United States, 1860–1900* (1960); Albert Rees, *Real Wages in Manufacturing, 1890–1914* (1961); Rendig Fels, *American Business Cycles* (1959): and Milton Friedman and Anna J. Schwartz, *A Monetary History of the United States, 1867–1960* (1963). The early chapters in Alfred D. Chandler, Jr., *Strategy and Structure: Chapters in the History of American Industrial Enterprise* (1966) provide a compact summary of the first phase of business concentration. Ralph L. Nelson, *Merger Movements in American Industry* (1959) gives a detailed account of the great merger movement at the end of the nineteenth century, and Hans B. Thorelli, *Federal Antitrust Policy: The Origination of an American Tradition* (1955) traces the origins and development of the countermovement against monopoly. These and other recent findings

are ably synthesized in Stuart Bruchey's brief but perceptive essay, *Growth of the Modern Economy* (1975) and in greater detail in W. Elliot Brownlee, *Dynamics of Ascent: A History of the American Economy* (1974).

The industrial transformation of the United States is characterized as a success story in Edward C. Kirkland's survey, *Industry Comes of Age: Business, Labor, and Public Policy, 1860–1897* (1961), which should be supplemented with Thomas Cochran, *The Inner Revolution* (1964). The development of the oil industry is exhaustively treated in Harold F. Williamson and associates, *The American Petroleum Industry* (2 vols., 1959–63), and Ralph W. Hidy and Muriel E. Hidy, *Pioneering in Big Business, 1882–1911: History of Standard Oil (New Jersey)* (1955). For changes in American banking practices in this period, see Fritz Redlich, *Molding of American Banking: Men and Ideas: Part II: 1840–1910* (1951), and for railroads, George R. Taylor and Irene Neu, *The American Railroad Network, 1861–1890* (1956), and Oscar O. Winther, *The Transportation Frontier: Trans-Mississippi West 1865–1890* (1964). Julius Grodinsky, *Transcontinental Railway Strategy, 1869–1893* (1962), analyzes the ideas and plans of the railroad builders and organizers; Lee Benson, *Merchants, Farmers, and Railroads* (1955), explores the movement for increased regulation; and Robert Fogel, *Railroads and American Economic Growth* (1964), offers an econometric revision of the role of the railroads in stimulating American economic growth. For an account of iron and steel, see Peter Temin, *Iron and Steel in Nineteenth-Century America: An Economic Inquiry* (1964).

The connections between economic theory and social policy are explored in Sidney Fine, *Laissez-Faire and the*

General Welfare State (1956). Richard Hofstadter, *Social Darwinism in American Thought* (1945), and Robert McCloskey, *Conservatism in the Age of Enterprise* (1951), are highly readable accounts of economic and social conservatism in the Gilded Age. James Weinstein, *The Corporate Ideal in the Liberal State, 1900–1918* (1960), is a carefully documented study of a central organizational concept and its wide social and political meanings. Irvin G. Wyllie's *The Self-Made Man in America* (1954), scrutinizes a resilient American myth, and Edward C. Kirkland's lively essays in *Dream and Thought in the Business Community, 1860–1900* (1956), describe the utopian musings of American businessmen.

Biographies of the leading figures in the American industrial transformation are legion. Among the best are three monumental studies: Joseph Wall, *Andrew Carnegie* (1970); Alan Nevins, *Study in Power: John D. Rockefeller, Industrialist and Philanthropist* (2 vols., 1953); and Matthew Josephson, *Edison* (1959). Frederick Lewis Allen, *The Great Pierpont Morgan* (1940), takes the measure of the great financier in a colorful portrait, and Edward C. Kirkland, *Charles Francis Adams, Jr., 1835–1915* (1965), gives sympathetic treatment to a frustrated planner and organizer. Keith Sward, *The Legend of Henry Ford* (1948), and Frank E. Hill, *Ford: The Times, the Man, the Company* (1954), provide useful estimates of the automative pioneer.

The recent literature on American urbanization is admirably synthesized in two recent studies: Howard Chudacoff, *Evolution of American Urban Society* (1975), and Zane Miller, *Urbanization of America* (1973). Constance Green, *The Rise of Urban America* (1965), and A. T. Brown, *A History of Urban America* (1967), are also helpful surveys. For a model study of urban spread in this period see Sam Bass Warner, *Streetcar Suburbs: The Process of Growth in Boston, 1870–1900* (1971). The pervasive antiurbanism of American intellectuals is documented in Morton and Lucia White, *The Intellectuals vs. the City* (1962). Charles N. Glab, ed., *The American City: A Documentary History* (1963), offers a wide range of source materials. David Ward, *Cities and Immigrants: A Geography of Change in Nineteenth-Century America* (1971), traces the patterns made by the new arrivals from Europe, and Stephen Thernstrom, *The Other Bostonians* (1973), and Howard Chudacoff, *Mobile Americans: Residential and Social Mobility in Omaha, 1880–1920* (1972), are two important studies of urban mobility.

The story of agrarian developments after the Civil War is told in Fred A. Shannon, *The Farmer's Last Frontier* (1963). Two older works—Solon J. Buck, *The Granger Move-*

ment (1913), and John D. Hicks, *The Populist Revolt* (1931)—are still useful surveys of their subjects. Irwin Unger, *The Greenback Era* (1964), and Walter T. K. Nugent, *Money and American Society, 1865–1880* (1968), examine monetary policy as it affected the farmer. For an illuminating discussion of agrarian politics in the South, see Theodore Saloutos, *Farmer Movements in the South, 1865–1933* (1960). Eric E. Lampard, *The Rise of the Dairy Industry in Wisconsin: A Study in Agricultural Change, 1860–1920* (1963), studies developments in a single industry, and Joseph C. Bailey, *Seaman A. Knapp* (1945), presents a profile of a "new" farmer. Harold Barger and H. H. Landsberg, *American Agriculture, 1899–1939: A Study of Output Employment and Productivity* (1942), traces the continuing rise of agricultural productivity in the early twentieth century. Allen G. Bogue, *Money at Interest: The Farm Mortgage on the Middle Border* (1955), offers a revisionist account of agrarian distress in that region. Grant McConnell, *The Decline of Agrarian Democracy* (1953), describes the growth of commercial farming, and Reynold M. Wik, *Steam Power on the American Farm* (1953), treats early technological change and its effect on American agriculture. The elimination of the Indian in the trans-Mississippi West is chronicled in two readable studies: Ralph K. Andrist, *The Long Death: The Last Days of the Plains Indians* (1964), and Dee A. Brown, *Bury My Heart at Wounded Knee* (1971).

Two brief surveys of American labor, Joseph G. Rayback, *A History of American Labor* (1959), and Henry Pelling, *American Labor* (1959), should be supplemented with the older but still valuable Norman J. Ware, *The Labor Movement in the United States, 1860–1896: A Study in Democracy* (1929). The conflict between the Knights of Labor and the new trade unions is explored in Gerald N. Grob, *Workers and Utopia* (1961). Philip Taft, *The A.F. of L. in the Time of Gompers* (1957), is an authoritative study of the organization in its formative years. Bernard Mandel, *Samuel Gompers, A Biography* (1963), and Stuart Bruce Kaufman, *Samuel Gompers and the Orgins of the American Federation of Labor* (1973), focus on the problems of leadership. The role of the immigrant in the American industrial revolution is explored in Charlotte Erickson, *American Industry and the European Immigrant* (1957), and Rowland Berthoff, *British Immigrants in Industrial America, 1790–1950* (1953). A brilliant article that points towards a new synthesis of cultural and labor history is Herbert G. Gutman, "Work, Culture, and Society in Industrializing America, 1815–1919," *American Historical Review* 78 (June 1973), 531–88.

Politics in the quarter-century following the Civil War gave Americans the sense of stability that their economic system lacked. The Jacksonian generation had first discovered in the political party the means of containing the disruptive forces of modern democracy. Now their sons, the professionals who ruled the Republican and Democratic parties after 1870, perfected this political machinery, which they proceeded to run with skill and zest until the end of the century.

They created a new political equilibrium. It depended, first of all, upon restoring a regional balance of power within both parties. Throughout the so-called Gilded Age* the Republicans sought to include both workers in the cities of the Northeast and farmers in the Midwest in their plans for economic development, and until the 1890s continued to dream of competing with the Democrats in the South. The Democrats were busy repairing the broad Jacksonian coalition of southern planters and northern city bosses that had been smashed by the war. The basic unit in this postwar party system was the state machine; both parties functioned as loose coalitions of autonomous state organizations. But states also comprised regions, each with its own cultural identity and economic interests which required careful tending. Increasingly after 1880 national tickets were arranged and party slates balanced with regional as well as state and city claims in mind.

The smooth operation of American politics in the Gilded Age also depended upon the mastery of a few basic rules. Chief among them was the axiom, accepted by politicians in both parties, that their organizations did not differ in class or economic interests, which were often quite similar, or even in general policies, which were frequently fuzzy: both parties were now financed by wealthy citizens whose opinions party leaders carefully acknowledged while maintaining an egalitarian posture before the rest of

The Politics of Reform

*In the title of their novel, *The Gilded Age* (1873), Mark Twain and Charles Dudley Warner coined the term that has been used to refer to the last third of the nineteenth century generally, connoting the wildly unstable, highly speculative economy of those years, and the flashy manners and loose morals that seemed so striking in American life then.

UNVEILING A STATUE
Patriotism and purity combined readily in the Gilded Age imagination. *(Pennell Collection, University of Kansas)*

the country. Both parties, in fact, were broadbased nonideological coalitions that appealed to businessmen, farmers, professionals, and workers. What separated Republicans and Democrats was not so much wealth or political principles or status as differing clusters of religious, ethnic, and cultural values.

One way of describing this difference between Republicans and Democrats is to use two religious terms—"pietistic" and "ritualistic"—which denote two poles in American thinking about religion and politics. *Pietism*, with its stress on personal purity, pointed toward a politics of morality. *Ritualism*, with its reliance on liturgy and ceremony, looked toward a politics of tradition and toleration. Pietistic thinking had dominated the original Whig party and its stepchild, the Republican party, before the Civil War. Party members were primarily Protestant, predom-

inantly of native stock or Anglo-Saxon descent, aggressively reform-minded, and eager to use government at all levels to enforce their behavioral standards on the rest of the community. George F. Hoar, a Republican senator from Massachusetts, drew on these pietistic sources when he described his party as filled with "the men who do the work of piety and charity in our churches, the men who administer our school systems, the men who own and till their own farms, the men who perform the skilled labor in the shops."

Given this image of Republicanism, it was easy for the party faithful to dismiss their Democratic opponents as "the old slave owner and slave driver, the saloon keeper, the ballot box stuffer, the Ku Klux Klan, the criminal class of the great cities, the men who cannot read and write." Despite the steady infiltration of the party by business interests after 1880, Republicans continued to attract a broad range of social moralists—prohibitionists, sabbatarians, blue law advocates, and moral reformers of every stripe. Only at the very end of the century had such evangelical types become marginal enough in the party as a whole for the managers to cast them aside as political liabilities.

The Democratic party with its "ritualistic" cast often seemed the opposite of the Republican. It embraced Catholics as well as Protestants, and professed a tolerance of immigrants who lacked the compulsive morality of the native-born. Democrats preached a "personal liberty" deemed safest when government was kept local and minimal, as the New York organization explained, drawing on the tradition of Andrew Jackson when it declared itself in 1881 "unalterably opposed to centralization of power in either state or federal governments." While Republicans expected all government to be generous and active, Democrats hoped to keep it grudging and stingy, if only to check the cultural imperialism as well as the appetite for patronage of its political foes. Thus the differences between the two parties in 1880 were real, but they derived from ethnic origins, religious backgrounds, and cultural outlook more than from economic interest.

Party managers also realized that the voters seldom approached political questions like the tariff or the currency as clear issues. Instead, party leaders considered them symbols that could be used to mobilize support for the party and its candidates. The skilled practitioners of Gilded Age politics had learned from the stormy debates of the Civil War years that the electoral behavior of most American voters was ultimately determined by images and impressions, prejudices and preferences. Voters might consider themselves both rational and informed, but no office seeker could ignore these vague but deeper forces at work in the political population.

This pattern of politics survived until the last decade of the century, when suddenly the very idea of party rule came under attack by a younger generation of political reformers. By 1890 rural Populists and urban progressives were challenging the code of the old professionals and forcing them to respond to new pressures. Out of their revolt came a transformation of politics that paralleled the revolution in the national economy and created new forms in the American political process and new ways of ordering it.

The Politics of Equilibrium

The Civil War shaped the thinking and molded the political behavior of Americans for a generation. Gilded Age politicians succeeded in tapping the emotions that had been engaged by the war. They were able, first of all, to inspire remarkably high levels of voting. In the six presidential elections between 1876 and 1896, an average of 78.5 percent of the eligible voters of the country actually voted, and an equally impressive 62.8 percent turned out for off-year elections. If political democracy is measured by a high rate of voter participation, then the Gilded Age, despite its glaring social and economic inequalities, remained flamboyantly, defiantly democratic.

The voting patterns remained consistent. Whether they marched to the polls behind candidates waving the "bloody shirt"—the radical Republicans' vengeful rhetoric aimed at keeping northern hostilities toward the South alive—or stirred to the memories of the Confederacy's Lost Cause, voters in all sections of the country kept alive the War Between the States even after the ideological struggles of Reconstruction had ended. Joining enthusiastically in campaigns that came complete with mounted military troopers and fancy drill teams, they made national elections extremely close. Sixteen states could always be counted on to go Republican; fourteen just as regularly voted Democratic. Presidential elections usually hung on the disposition of voters in five key states—Connecticut, New York, Indiana, Nevada, and California. Although the Republicans' grip on the presidency between 1872 and 1912, broken only by Grover Cleveland's two victories in 1884 and 1892, appeared to establish them as the majority party, in fact the Democrats controlled the House of Representatives with sizable majorities in seven out of ten

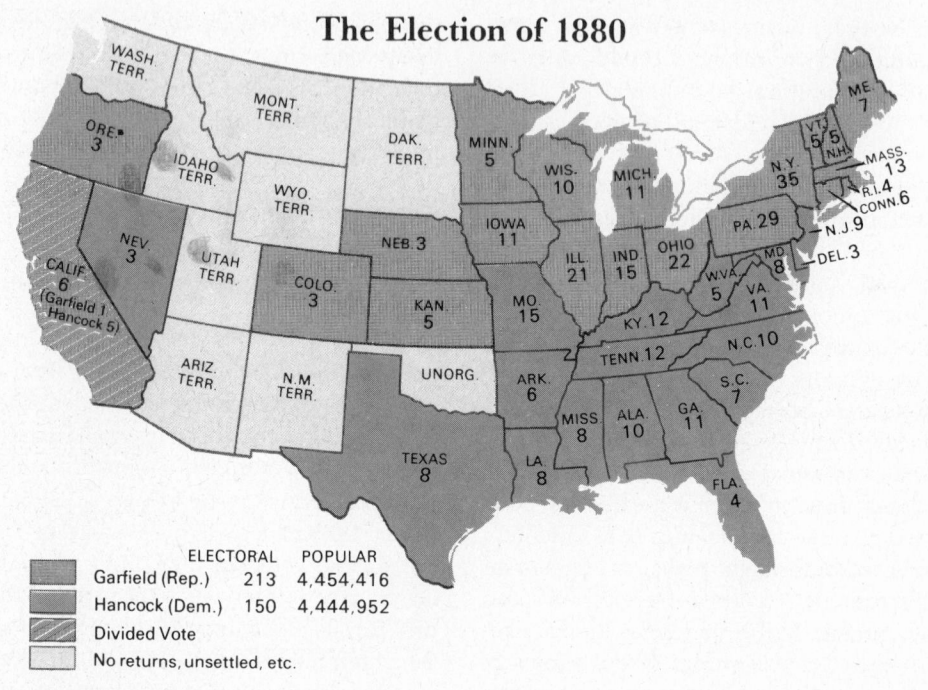

The Election of 1880

ELECTORAL	POPULAR
Garfield (Rep.) 213	4,454,416
Hancock (Dem.) 150	4,444,952
Divided Vote	
No returns, unsettled, etc.	

The Election of 1884

ELECTORAL	POPULAR
Cleveland (Dem.) 219	4,874,986
Blaine (Rep.) 182	4,851,981

congressional elections. Pluralities in key states were perilously slim, particularly in New York and Indiana. With such intense competition and close elections, winners were not only lucky but often surprised. In the three presidential contests in the 1880s the margin of victory was less than one percent. In the election of James A. Garfield in 1880 and Cleveland in 1884 less than twenty-five thousand votes separated the candidates, and in 1888 the winner, the Republican Benjamin Harrison, received fewer popular votes than did Cleveland, the loser.

Party Lines Drawn. Throughout the 1880s the two parties remained drawn up against each other like equally matched armies, their skirmishes resembling the engagements in the still familiar war. Famous military figures were featured in political rhetoric until well into the 1880s—in songs, war whoops, and speeches by bewhiskered colonels "late of the Confederate Army" or beribboned commissary generals of the Grand Army of the Republic. The median age of voters in the Gilded Age was thirty-seven, and so generally they had arrived at political maturity under the tutelage of fathers who had fought to preserve the "glorious Union" or to rescue a "prostrate nation." Ticket-splitting suggested a lack of patriotism, and the voter who switched parties was regarded as little better than a bounty jumper. Novelist Brand Whitlock remembered that in his youth being a Republican was "a fundamental and self-evident thing. . . . It was merely a synonym for patriotism, another name for the nation. . . . It was inconceivable that any self-respecting person should be a Democrat." Nor was it likely in the South, increasingly solid for the Democratic party, that a true gentleman would require any greater political comfort than that afforded by Bourbon conservatism.

Yet, for all its apparent stability, politics in this era was in the process of transformation, the same stage of transformation that small-scale entrepreneurial capitalism was undergoing. Newly arrived immigrants were urban consumers in need of jobs, favors, and services. Here was a vast human market in which a judicious investment of political capital could pay off handsomely. The new business of politics, unlike more established concerns, was open

IMMIGRANTS ARRIVING AT ELLIS ISLAND, NEW YORK CITY
New recruits for the American political army. *(Culver Pictures, Inc.)*

to new talent and offered unlimited opportunity of making good. As a go-getter, the professional politician—ward heeler, precinct captain, county chairman, state assemblyman, or senatorial aspirant—was a salesman who had to know the buying habits of every prospective customer in his territory.

George Washington Plunkitt, one of the leaders of New York City's Democratic organization Tammany Hall, described the political district in terms

BOSS POLITICS: PROGRESSIVE TARGET

Progressive reformers found it difficult to compete with the city boss whose services to his clients, like those of Tammany Hall, included free barbecues. *(Brown Brothers)*

familiar to every drummer out of New York or Chicago with a territory to cover, concluding: "If he holds his district and Tammany is in power, he is amply rewarded by a good office and the opportunities that go with it." The Gilded Age boss was the Horatio Alger rags-to-riches hero, in ward heeler's attire, sporting a campaign button. "Yes, many of our men have grown rich in politics," Plunkitt confided. "I have myself. I've made a big fortune out of the game, and I'm gettin' richer every day." The shortest route to success in the business of politics lay through the upstairs rooms at party headquarters where the sign over the door read "Never Closed."

The Urban Political Boss. Politics in the Gilded Age, from the city to the Senate, constituted a revitalized patronage society that bore some of the marks of its eighteenth-century ancestor. Under the guiding hand and sharp eye of the boss, political power was organized vertically within the machine in a hierarchical system of patrons and clients. The style of the Gilded Age boss was new and coarse, more personalized and direct than that of his gentleman predecessor. To reform critics like Moisei Ostrogorski, whose *Democracy and the Organization of Politi-*

cal Parties was a summary of the reformers' indictment of machine politics, the political boss was Machiavelli's prince come to life, an all-powerful leader, unsleeping, devious, and ruthless, who commanded through his "strength of will, his cleverness, his audacity and his luck." As Ostrogorski described the political boss:

To this one he lends a dollar; for another he obtains a railroad ticket without payment; he has coal distributed in the depth of winter; he makes gifts of other kinds; he sometimes sends poultry at Christmas time; he buys medicine for a sick person; he helps bury the dead by procuring a coffin on credit or half-price. He has a kind heart in virtue of his position and his position gives him the means of satisfying his need for kindness: the money which he distributes comes from the chest of the Machine; the latter has obtained it by the most reprehensible methods . . . but no matter. With this money he can also dispense an ample hospitality in the drinking-saloons. As soon as he comes in, friends known and unknown gather round him, and he treats everybody, he orders one drink after another for the company; he is the only one who does not drink; he is on duty.

The urban political machine's stock in trade was jobs and appointments, transit franchises, paving contracts, public construction bids, licenses, permits, and a hundred other salable items needed to conduct the business of the nation's cities.

The impulse motivating the city boss was essentially conservative: the need to bring a semblance of order to his fiefdom. "Politics ain't bean bag," Mr. Dooley, the creation of the humorist Finley Peter Dunne, observed from his Chicago saloon. "'Tis a man's game; an' women, childher an' pro-hybitionists do well to keep out iv it." The besetting sins of the reformer, the boss knew, were innocence and amateurism. "He hasn't been brought up in the difficult business of politics," Plunkitt of Tammany Hall complained, "and he makes a mess of it every time." From at least midcentury, bosses like New York City's William Marcy Tweed and Philadelphia's James McManes had watched the aimless spreading of their cities and understood the problem of managing them. Tweed frankly admitted that New York's population was "too hopelessly split into races and factions to govern it under universal suffrage, except by bribery of patronage and corruption." Their domains, the bosses realized, were fragmented like giant jigsaw puzzles. Only a professional could provide the liberal application of patronage to glue them together, even though his workmanship might be both slipshod and expensive. In New York City immediately after the Civil War, Boss Tweed secured a grip on the city government, built a mammoth new county courthouse, completed plans for Central Park, and began work on a city-wide transit system. All these achievements came at the cost of widespread corruption and an astronomical increase in the city's bonded debt.

Bosses seldom achieved the efficiency they sought. At best, they surrounded themselves with oligarchies that presided over loose federations of wards and precincts. Their failings in efficiency and accountability would provide progressive reformers with most of their ammunition in their attacks on the urban machines in the 1890s. But in the absence of a genuine science of administration and a corps of professional managers to apply it, the bosses, improvising lavishly and corruptly with materials at hand, at least gave their cities a minimum of order and services.

Patronage Politics in the States. By the 1880s political control of the states also had fallen to powerful bosses who built loyal organizations. Matt Quay in Pennsylvania, Tom Platt in New York, Nelson Aldrich in Rhode Island, William Vilas in Wisconsin, and George Hearst in California were typical of a new breed of party chieftains who conducted national business in Washington while keeping an eye on their cronies back home, mediating patronage quarrels, settling factional disputes, and smoothing discontents. In the 1870s such state bosses as Roscoe Conkling in New York and James G. Blaine, the "Plumed Knight" from Maine, were highly visible and colorful figures who cultivated the arts of demagoguery and personal leadership. By the 1880s, however, a new generation was taking over, quieter, more efficient, clever, cautious, and determined to avoid the feuds that had marred the rule of their predecessors. The key device for harmonizing party interests at the state level was the caucus where local nabobs, county chairmen, and state legislators gathered to stamp approval on the boss's choice of candidates. But the real work was often done in advance and on the sly. Michigan boss James McMillan explained to his supporters how his rise to the Senate only proved "what quiet work and an active continuance of party organization can accomplish. . . . When party organization is perfect, campaigns are more easily conducted and victory more certain."

Democratic party bosses won control over their states more slowly than Republicans, and, particularly in the one-party South, kept a looser grip on the party reins. Yet southern Democratic, or "Bourbon," conservatism soon became the model for Democratic stalwarts who continued to invoke the name of Jefferson in deploring the "spirit of centralization" while quietly employing just that principle in staffing and strengthening their organizations. In both parties, as in the business world after 1880, concentration was the order of the day.

A New Breed of Politicians. As late as 1880, however, much remained to be done. Democrats in that election year were entering the third decade of their prolonged tenure as an opposition party to the notorious Republicans, and were still saddled with un-

THE WOMAN'S SPHERE
For the Gilded Age politician the woman's proper occupations were domesticity and motherhood. *(Culver Pictures, Inc.)*

imaginative leadership, a negative program, and a philosophy of "go slow." The Republican party had also fallen on evil days. Republicans had spent the 1870s watching their share of the popular vote dwindle and their hopes for holding the South dim and then disappear. In 1880 the party was still torn by contending factions of "Stalwarts" taking their orders from New York's imperious Roscoe Conkling and "Half-Breeds" following paths blazed by James G. Blaine. These factional squabbles concerning patronage rather than matters of policy were serious enough to deadlock the Republican convention in

1880 and send delegates scurrying for a compromise candidate, James A. Garfield of Ohio. Democrats, having gone down to defeat with three civilian contenders since the war, decided to try their luck with the military, and nominated General Winfield Scott Hancock, the hero of Gettysburg.

For the professional politicians in both parties, politics could not be cut and trimmed by moral shears or patched together with the principles of reform. Dismissing reform as contrary to human nature and ridiculing its champions as long-haired men and short-haired women, the bosses snarled their defiance in crude and unambiguous language. Let the Civil Service reformers remain in their well-appointed parlors, Senator John J. Ingalls of Kansas declared, exchanging rumors of political misbehavior while sipping their lemonade. The real world, the Ingallses and Blaines and Conklings insisted, was their own world of cigar smoke and fifteen-dollar votes, rolling logs and brimming pork barrels.

As the presidential election of 1880 approached and neither party appeared to have an edge with the voters, the professionals' confidence in a robust style suddenly evaporated. Throughout the decade a new cautionary political style was unmistakable, and nowhere was it more in evidence than among a new breed of presidential contenders.

The Lost Decade

Novelist Thomas Wolfe once observed that for most Americans the Gilded Age presidents from Hayes to Harrison have become irretrievably lost;

their gravely vacant and bewhiskered faces mixed, melted ... together in the sea-depths of a past, intangible, immeasurable, and unknowable.... For who was Garfield, martyred man, and who had seen him in the streets of life? ... Who had heard the casual and familiar tones of Chester Arthur? And where was Harrison? Where was Hayes? Which had the whiskers, which the burnsides: which was which?

The oblivion to which these shadowy figures have been consigned is a result of the limited concept of the presidential office in the Gilded Age and the equally limited political imaginations of the men who filled it.

The Shadow Presidents. The principal task given to these presidents by party managers in the Congress was to get themselves elected without compromising their reputations by saying anything provocative and then to dispense patronage to the party worthies. Winning the presidency was not an easy task, especially when no clear-cut issues of public policy divided the two parties. James Bryce, the British minister in Washington who observed his first presidential election in 1884 in the contest between Blaine and Cleveland, was amazed to find that neither party had a distinctive platform. "Neither party has any principles, any distinctive tenets. Both have traditions. Both claim to have tendencies. . . . All has been lost, except office or the hope of it."

Once elected, the new president found the first order of business was handing out jobs, a process that was both complicated and time-consuming. Garfield, in his brief tenure in office, was exhausted by job-hunters, though he had been chosen by Republican leaders precisely for his sensitivity to the patronage demands of the party's warring factions. Soon after his inauguration in March 1881, Garfield's mutterings about party office-seekers swelled to a sustained wail: "My God! What is there in this place that a man should ever want to get into it?" He was not to remain in it long. In July 1881, as he was boarding a train in Washington for a well-earned vacation, he was shot in the back by a crazed government clerk who had been recently dismissed. Garfield lingered through the summer and died in September. "I am a Stalwart," Charles Guiteau had shouted as he fired at Garfield, "and Arthur is President now."

"My God! Chet Arthur!" was the response of liberal Republicans and Democrats alike at the prospect of four years of boss rule by a veteran spoilsman. Chester A. Arthur, former head of the New York

CAMPAIGN PROPAGANDA FOR THE CUSTODIAL PRESIDENCY
The "Grand National Republican Banner" provides the answer to Thomas Wolfe's question: "Which had the whiskers, which the burnsides: which was which?" *(Smithsonian Institution, Division of Political History)*

Custom House and follower of Roscoe Conkling, had been accorded second place on the ticket chiefly to placate New York's Stalwart faction, since Garfield was widely recognized as a protégé of Blaine and his Half-Breeds. Arthur, suave, accommodating, and thoroughly hardened to the work of dispensing patronage, presided genially over the staffing of the federal bureaucracy with party hacks even as he signed the Pendleton Act (1883) establishing an independent civil service commission whose work was to classify federal jobs and administer examinations. In two notable respects the new president confounded his critics: he urged the prosecution of those involved in the fraudulent Star Route postal contracts, and he vetoed an unprecedented $18 million Rivers and Harbors bill. The fact that the Star Route prosecutions failed and Congress passed the pork barrel appropriation over his veto in no way lessened the appreciation of liberals and reformers in both parties who agreed, upon his retirement, that Chet Arthur "had done well . . . by not doing anything bad."

In 1885 it was Grover Cleveland's turn to suffer the demands both of Democratic bosses clamoring for jobs, and civil service hopefuls bent on cleaning up the spoils system. Cleveland, like Garfield before him, endured a "nightmare" and complained constantly about "this dreadful, damnable office seeking." Cleveland's discomfort was the sharper because he had made his political fortune out of reform, first as the "Veto Mayor" of Buffalo, New York, where he got rid of corrupt street-cleaning and sewer contracts, and then in the governorship of New York where he quickly became known as the "Great Obstructionist" of the special interests. The "Big One," as the young Assemblyman Theodore Roosevelt called him, looked the part of the reform-minded man of integrity—a massive three hundred pounds of jut-jawed, rocklike imperturbability—who called for "the application of business principles to public affairs" and perfected the veto as his chief weapon.

The Republicans chose the perennial favorite James G. Blaine as their standard-bearer in 1884. This move made Cleveland the obvious "reform" preference of the Democrats along with those disaffected Republicans (the "Mugwumps") who bolted their party in the hope of destroying the spoils sys-

tem. Still, even in this election, genuine issues were difficult to discern. Blaine concentrated on the tariff issue and Cleveland stressed his leadership of a "far-reaching moral movement," which left the two candidates much like Tweedledee and Tweedledum. Both men, Bryce noted, openly declared their hatred of monopolies, their love of the flag, and their determination to defend the rights of Americans around the globe. Beyond these pronouncements neither was willing to venture, and it was only a question of time before the issues became personalized and cheapened.

The Republicans announced their discovery that Cleveland, that "libertine" and "moral leper," had fathered an illegitimate child in Buffalo. The Democrats produced the "Mulligan Letters" with their own disclosures of Blaine's corruption as Speaker of the House. Blaine's chances were further damaged by a fund-raising dinner at Delmonico's restaurant attended by such business luminaries as Jay Gould, John Jacob Astor, and sugar king Henry Havemeyer, and promptly denounced in the Democratic press as *The Royal Feast of Belshazzar Blaine and the Money Kings.* Then in the final days of the campaign, a misguided clergyman speaking at a Blaine rally in New York City referred to the Democratic party as the party of "rum, Romanism, and rebellion," a remark hardly designed to appeal to the city's working-class majority. Largely on the strength of these two mistakes Cleveland carried New York by 1,200 votes out of more than a million cast, and the country by the very slim margin of 25,000.

As president, Cleveland attempted to play the role of the realistic reformer. He admitted, however, that the "boss system" survived in American politics, and that since it did, it was a necessity—"a disagreeable necessity, I assure you"—for him to recognize it. This he did by doubling the number of jobs covered under civil service from 14,000 to 28,000, at the same time appointing his own people to all the jobs left untouched by the Pendleton Act. He had not been elected "merely for the purpose of civil service," he reminded his critics, and asked to be saved from "the misguided zeal of impracticable friends." No one could accuse Grover Cleveland of pandering to reform!

Benjamin Harrison, a prosperous railroad lawyer

1888 WOODCARVING OF BENJAMIN HARRISON
Folk artist and medium combine to catch the essential man. *(National Portrait Gallery, Smithsonian Institution, Washington, D.C.)*

scarcely the man to meddle in patronage matters; he preferred to leave them to congressional bosses who quickly exchanged some thirty thousand Democratic postmasters with Republicans.

Yet by 1890 the civil service principle had taken root in the federal bureaucracy, and it continued to grow until by 1900 there were one hundred thousand positions subject to the rules enforced by the Civil Service Commission. The gradual triumph of civil service affected the work of presidents quite directly. With fewer and fewer officeholders who could be dunned for contributions to the party coffers, it fell to the president as party leader to seek out wealthy donors—for Republicans the Rockefellers and the Jay Goulds, for Democrats the Levi Mortons and Henry B. Paynes—who now contributed the lion's share to the party's treasury. In this sense civil service reform strengthened the president's role as party leader.

The Custodial Presidency. In other respects, however, the Gilded Age presidents were content with their custodial role. The real power—to make budgets, authorize expenditures, and design legislation—remained with Congress, which in the 1880s was just beginning to modernize itself with an effective system of committees and chairmanships. With the great political questions of Reconstruction now dead letters, there seemed no compelling demand for presidential leadership. To congressional Republicans and Democrats alike, their president seemed simply a first-among-equals in constant need of advice and direction.

It was Grover Cleveland who defined the custodial presidency by insisting on the "entire independence" of the executive from the legislative branch. Cleveland's power lay in the veto with which he sought to make Congress accountable and the federal government honest, impartial, frugal, and not very energetic. His use of the negative was comprehensive: in his first term (1885–89) he vetoed three times as many bills as all his predecessors combined. Embedded in his veto messages was a social as well as a legal conservatism. In the aftermath of a series of devastating crop failures in the Texas Panhandle, Congress in 1887 passed the Texas Seed Bill appropriating the modest sum of $10,000 for seed grain for

from Indiana and grandson of "old Tippecanoe" President William Henry Harrison, narrowly defeated Cleveland in his bid for reelection in 1888 in what was probably the most corrupt presidential election in American history. He then announced that "Providence" had awarded his party a great victory. "He ought to know," snorted Matt Quay, the Republican boss of Pennsylvania, "that Providence hadn't a damn thing to do with it." Harrison, he added, would never know "how close a number of men were compelled to approach the gates of the penitentiary to make him President." Harrison, whose personality, one observer noted, had all the warmth of a "dripping cave," was needy farmers. The assumption that in times of distress the federal government could lend a helping hand aroused Cleveland's ire:

I do not believe that the power and duty of the General Government ought to be extended to the relief of individual suffering which is in no manner properly related to the public service or benefit. A prevalent tendency to disregard the limited mission of this power and duty should, I think, be steadfastly resisted, to the end that the lesson should constantly be enforced that though the people support the Government, the Government should not support the people.

Republican presidents were less doctrinaire, but they agreed that fashioning policies and programs was no part of their duties. None of the major pieces of Republican legislation passed during Harrison's administration (1889–93)—the Sherman Silver Purchase Act, the Sherman Antitrust Act, or the McKinley Tariff—bore the stamp of his design or the mark of his favor. Presidents of both parties were generally content with the narrow functions assigned them by antebellum tradition.

Thus Congress was the most visibly active branch of the federal government even though its pace, accelerating slightly, was still leisurely and its sense of itself as a national lawmaking body limited. The volume of congressional business had doubled from an average of 37,000 public and private bills per session in the 1870s to 74,000 by the mid-1880s. Gradually both houses of Congress were organizing themselves, modifying an older deliberative style and adapting it to the routine of new and stronger committees like the House's powerful Ways and Means Committee. By 1890 a Republican-dominated Senate was being managed by an informal but highly organized clique of a half-dozen senators who controlled all committee appointments. In the House both parties reluctantly were beginning to agree on the need for tightening rules and procedures. Slowly Congress was shedding its reputation for amateurism. The average length of congressional tenure increased. In the 1870s over half the membership in each session was new. During the 1880s only one member in three was newly elected, and a decade later only one in four. By the end of the century Congress was filled with seasoned professionals.

Still, Congress was slow to break with its past.

Senators and representatives still used Congress as the forum for debate among politicians whose connections with their local constituencies were all-important. Lawmaking under such circumstances tended to become an involved exercise in horse-trading by representatives of competing interests. Nowhere was this process more clearly shown than in the making of the tariff.

Tariff Making. The difficult and seemingly insoluble problem for the Congress after the Civil War was not raising revenue but spending it. There was a surplus of federal revenue every year between 1866 and 1893, and the average annual surplus in the 1880s was $100 million, with over half this amount coming from custom duties. To spend this enormous sum there was only pork barrel legislation and the patronage system that sluiced off some of the reserve into federal jobs, but with the passage of the Pendleton Act even this use of federal funds was restricted. The tariff had become an embarrassment, and complaints multiplied against the principle of protection that took from the poor consumer and gave to the already rich corporations. Republicans, suddenly in need of a strong defense of the tariff, took up James G. Blaine's cry that all the "wonders" of the previous twenty years were owing to high tariff schedules. Democrats gradually came to agree with Grover Cleveland that tariffs were "vicious, inequitable and illogical," and in need of amendment.

By the mid-1880s the tariff question had come to serve as a distinguishing symbol for Republicans and Democrats in much the way that the race issue had functioned during Reconstruction and the free silver cause would operate in the 1890s. Its significance was political rather than economic. Combined imports and exports accounted for less than 10 percent of the gross national product. What kept the economy going, it was clear, was a burgeoning domestic market. The tariff, to be sure, was important for particular economic interests—wool growers, steel manufacturers, sugar refiners—who stood to gain directly from high import barriers. It was also true that as the decade opened none of these interest groups had irrevocably tied themselves to either the Republican or the Democratic party. Yet five years later "protection" had become the watchword of a Republican party which increasingly catered to business and industry, and "a tariff for revenue only" the war cry of a Democratic party identified with farmers and urban consumers.

Tariff-making defied science, reason, and all but the most tireless lobbyists. Enacting a new tariff—upward with Republicans or downward with Democrats—was an elaborate three-act drama. The opening act was filled with a great number of speeches concerning the dangers to civilization lurking behind higher or lower schedules—the babble of the innocents. Act Two was set in the legendary smoke-filled room where the lobbyists held court and the amendments were drafted. The final act contrasted the embarrassment of the bill's original sponsors with the quiet satisfaction of special interest groups who had rewritten it. This ritual began in 1882 when President Arthur appointed a blue-ribbon Tariff Commission and charged it with finding ways to lower the schedules for those American industries long past infancy and no longer in need of paternal care. The Commission promptly obliged by drawing up a model bill that lowered the rates a general 20 percent. Once submitted to Congress, however, the carefully drafted bill lost whatever symmetry and harmony its drafters had originally claimed for it, and under the hammerings of the lobbyists and their representatives it was quickly reduced to rubble. Still dissatisfied with their demolition work, both House and Senate wrote separate bills and then joined forces and passed a "compromise" that raised the schedules on almost every product.

In all of the tariff contests between 1880 and 1900 the Democrats were consistently frustrated in their work for downward revision by their Republican foes. Both the McKinley Tariff (1890) and the Dingley Tariff (1897) legislated sizable increases in protection, and the Democrats could not prevent their enactment. From 1880 until Woodrow Wilson's first administration over thirty years later, Democrats failed to achieve a meaningful downward revision of the tariff schedules. The real significance of the debate over the tariff lay in the experience in national policy planning it provided. In invoking Hamilton in support of an active, interventionist state or in citing Jefferson in defense of limited government action, congressional debates brought the outlines of national policy into focus across the country.

Toward a National Policy. The same recognition of the need for new national controls lay behind the Interstate Commerce Act (1887). After the Supreme Court had invalidated a state attempt to regulate rates for interstate railroads in the 1886 *Wabash* case, the Senate appointed the Cullom Committee to investigate complaints against the railroads and to report on the feasibility of establishing a federal regulatory commission. The Cullom Committee was dominated by conservatives from both parties. Though anguished reactionaries like Senator Nelson B. Aldrich cried out that any regulation was tantamount to revolution, the Interstate Commerce Act was a conservative law. The Commission established by the law was empowered to forbid collusive manipulation by the railroads: rebates, rate discrimination, and railroad pools. But its supervisory powers were narrowly defined, and its decisions were subject to review in the courts. The Interstate Commerce Act was intended as a means of establishing national railroad policy, but the Commission itself never achieved that goal.

From the politics of this era came only the semblance, not the substance, of a national policy. Neither president nor Congress had a clear understanding of the powers needed by government to function effectively in national affairs. The concepts of a comprehensive national policy and executive leadership capable of effecting it did not emerge until the twentieth century. Meanwhile rapid industrialization was producing severe economic and social dislocation. Farmers were caught in a downward spiral of prices and credit. Industrial workers were locked in combat with management over wages, hours, and the right to organize. And small-town America, uneasy with the new secular political order, felt the stirrings of still another crusade for a Christian society. Ever since the Civil War farmers, laborers and moral reformers had been involved in third-party politics, but with scant success. Their main efforts—the Greenback Labor party and the Prohibition party—had never won more than 3.5 percent of the vote in a national election. Watching the repeated failures of these would-be reformers, the Republican and Democratic party bosses felt sure that the political stability they had achieved was permanent.

But there were deeper stirrings by 1890. In agrarian revolts in the countryside and civic campaigns in the cities, reformers were beginning to draw on the resources of two deep-lying traditions in American politics. The Populist movement in the trans-Mississippi West and in the South revived a millennial spirit that had erupted repeatedly in the past in moments of crisis. And by 1895, in the nation's cities, progressive reformers were challenging boss politics by drawing on the fears of the established elite groups, on business notions of efficiency and economy, and on the scientific ideas of a new generation of professionals and academics. Together in the midst of industrial strife and agrarian discontent, these two groups of reformers—Populists and urban progressives—shattered the confidence of professional politicians by confronting them with new interpretations of American life.

Conditions Without Precedent—the Populist Revolt

The first reform effort to challenge the political establishment of the late nineteenth century stemmed from a millennial outlook that had long flourished in a Protestant frontier democracy. This idea of reform was based on utopian blueprints for a world beyond politics in which power and strife were finally relinquished for the rule of "good men." The political pietists who dreamed of this utopia thought of politics in terms of personal good and evil, and defined their task as one of religious regeneration. Their language was openly evangelical. A new heaven on earth, they declared, awaited the coming of the new dispensation; social salvation required men of Old Testament vision who would lead true believers out of the political wilderness and into the promised land where they would need only the Lord to rule over them. Secular politics as practiced by the ungodly was an abomination, and political professionals were the willing instruments of the devil. Good politics was as simple and direct as the Golden Rule.

These political pietists demanded a complete change in the rule of conventional political behavior. In place of the easy tolerance of broker politics, they advocated cultural and political uniformity. Instead of competing interest groups, they proposed a national congregation of the right-minded. No more minor skirmishes between equally corrupt contestants, but the last mighty battle for the Lord. Pietism invited total participation at the grass roots, chiefly in the form of camp meetings of the faithful. The Populists sought to restore a lost community, to recover a preindustrial solidarity, and to return to old values. In its purest form, Populist pietism promised counterrevolution—the overthrow of the modern, secular, boss-run or bureaucratic state, and a return to the Golden Age.

The Populists' rejection of modernity, moreover, was matched by their economic program, which bore all the marks of small-scale entrepreneurial capitalism, with its hopes for the independent producer, steady growth rate, and voluntary cooperation. These hopes had once sustained the North and the Republican party in the war against slavery. Instead of the millennium of small producers, the Civil War, however, had brought business consolidation and the rule of the spoilsmen; the original vision had dimmed until it guided only such marginal groups as the prohibitionists and the Greenbackers. It was from the political margins, therefore, that the first calls for a "new politics" in the 1880s were heard—from Henry George's legion of "single-taxers," from the recruits to Edward Bellamy's "industrial army," and from converts to the "New Conscience" of the Social Gospelists preaching Christian cooperation. Their pietistic grievances centered on issues with social and cultural as well as economic meaning—cheap money, the power of monopolies, and Wall Street conspiracies—which underscored the isolation and insignificance of the little man in an increasingly impersonal society. It was in these attitudes of the economically and socially dispossessed, and particularly in the fears and frustrations of staple-crop farmers who

THE SOD-HOUSE FRONTIER
Picnicking in the front yard, Custer County, Nebraska, 1886. *(Solomon D. Butcher Collection, Nebraska State Historical Society)*

were certain they were being victimized by urban forces, that the deepest seedbed of Populism was to be found.

Regional Populism. Populist grievances were real enough. In the trans-Mississippi West they were the result of the hectic pace of unregulated economic development; in the South they were the product of a new feudal order complete with tenancy, a crop lien system, and a large submerged class of dirt-poor farmers, both black and white. In both regions exorbitant shipping charges, greedy middlemen, and extortionate mortgage rates were compounded after 1887 by a series of crop failures that sent land prices and farm income skidding. Years of retrenchment and retreat followed, and destitute farmers trekked back eastward from the sod-house frontier, leaving behind ghost towns with gilded opera houses and empty stores. Western Kansas lost half its population between 1882 and 1892, and South Dakota, some 30,000.

The number of prairie wagons lumbering back to Iowa from the Nebraska frontier in 1891 was estimated at 18,000. A sign on an abandoned farmhouse in Blanco County, Texas, in the drought year 1886 read: "200 miles to the nearest post office; 100 miles to wood; 20 miles to water; 6 inches to hell. God bless our home! Gone to live with the wife's folks." Populist Mary E. Lease put it this way:

We were told two years ago to go to work and raise a big crop, that was all we needed. We went to work and plowed and planted; the rains fell, the sun shone, nature smiled, and we raised the big crop they told us to; and what came of it? Eight-cent corn, ten-cent oats, two-cent beef, and no price at all for butter and eggs—that's what came of it. Then the politicians said that we suffered from overproduction.

Populism in the South, while plagued by many of the same problems, showed distinctive features. Tenancy and crop liens exploited an underclass of black and white farmers whose keen sense of their plight was checked by their fears of challenging an elite based on white supremacy. Western Populists risked little more than failure in organizing a third party. Southern farmers, in attacking the political establishment, put their personal security and sometimes their lives on the line.

In both regions, Populism emerged rapidly from a nonpartisan background in 1890 and drew into politics groups that previously had been inarticulate if not inert. Some of the new recruits were women: Mary Lease, who harangued audiences on the power of monopolies; Annie L. Diggs, a strict prohibitionist bent on saving the West from alcohol as well as from Wall Street; Sarah Emery, whose tract, *Seven Financial Conspiracies*, traced the national decline along a descending curve of democratic participation. For every seasoned veteran of third-party politics such as Minnesota's Ignatius Donnelly, "the Sage of Nininger," there were three new converts, like Georgia's Tom Watson, fired by Populist speeches for campaigns "hot as Nebuchadnezzar's furnace."

The atmosphere at Populist meetings was heavy with the spirit of revivalism—"a pentecost of politics," according to one observer, "in which a tongue of flame sat upon every man." Recruits, like converts, came from everywhere: farmers, hard-pressed local merchants, cattlemen, miners, small-town editors; men with chin whiskers, broad-brimmed hats and muddy boots, accompanied by wives "with skin tanned to parchment by the hot winds, with bony hands of toil, and clad in faded calico." Quickly they became stereotypes to the rest of the world—comic hayseeds to the political opposition, heroic figures in the folklore of Populism with nicknames to match: "The Kansas Pythoness," "Bloody Bridles," "Sockless Socrates." Behind the mask frequently appeared the original types, biblical figures like Senator William A. Peffer, a Topeka editor elected to the Senate, who reminded the writer Hamlin Garland of Isaiah with his full beard, steel-rimmed glasses, and frock coat, and the "habitual expression" of gravity on an otherwise inscrutable countenance. "He made a peculiar impression on me, something Hebraic," Garland recalled, "something intense, fanatical."

The Populist, or People's, party drew a strange variety of contrasting types into the reform movement. Southern Populists listened to the saving word not only from "Stump" Ashby, the Texas cowpuncher, and "Cyclone" Davis, toting his volumes of Jefferson, but also from such hard-hitting country editors as C. W. Macune, professional organizers such as North Carolina's Leonidas L. Polk, and Virginia patricians bearing the names of Page, Beverly, and Harrison. In Minnesota, Ignatius Donnelly's fiery campaign was offset by the sober advice of Charles H. Van Wyck, the party's candidate for governor in Nebraska, who singled out solid issues like railroad regulation for his campaign. For the most part, however, Populists were political innocents, and innocence was widely deemed a virtue. To eastern professionals in the two major parties, the Populists, gathered under banners urging the steadfast to vote as they prayed, presented the strange spectacle of an embittered interest group talking in tongues.

Building a National Party.   New to the work of organizing a national party, the Populists encountered formidable obstacles to building a platform that would advance farmers' interests and at the same time attract workers in the city. They discovered that appeals for votes could be made in two distinct ways. First, they could explain their problems as staple-crop farmers and call on the federal government for help. The second way was to avoid interest-group appeals altogether and to call on all those who lived by the sweat of their brow to join the crusade of "true producers" against the Money Power. It was the peculiar mark of Populism that it undertook both of these assignments at the same time.

The interest-group program of the Populists grew out of the reasoning of political leaders who urged the federal government to respond to the needs of all its citizens. They demanded a graduated income tax to lift the financial burden from farmers and workers; postal savings banks and a flexible currency; and a subtreasury plan for storing surpluses and issuing loans that would circulate like money. All of these demands, calling the federal government to the rescue, could be justified as protective measures for producers who lacked the security and the privileges accorded the more favored industrial interests.

Another different set of demands called for immigration restriction, punitive legislation against the Money Power, and farmer-labor cooperation, suggesting eternal brotherhood for the real producers of the nation. Party delegates to the Populist convention in Omaha in 1892 cheered lustily as their leaders denounced "governmental injustice," which was dividing the country into two great classes, "tramps and millionaires." To postpone the day of wrath, the Omaha party platform called for the people to seize power in a new constituent act:

Assembled on the anniversary of the birthday of the nation, and filled with the spirit of the grand general and chieftain who established our independence, we seek to restore the government of the Republic to the hands of the plain people with whose class it originated. . . . We declare we must be in fact, as we are in name, one united brotherhood of freemen.

In the ideal society envisioned by the Populists, righteousness would infuse God's chosen with high purpose. In the recesses of the Populist imagination lay hopes for a realm of harmony beyond politics, a haven where peace and virtue reigned supreme over a vast fee-simple empire of rejuvenated yeomen. The triumph of American justice would come only when the people had purified national life at the wellspring. Only a small part of such a gigantic task involved the passage of "wise and reasonable legislation." A much larger part involved a moral upheaval "to bring the power of the social mass to bear upon the rebellious individuals who thus menace the peace and safety of the state."

Populism transcended conventional politics in declaring itself "not a passing cloud on the political sky" nor a "transient gust of political discontent" but "the hope of realizing and incarnating in the lives of common people the fullness of the divinity of humanity." And with this shift in political perception came glimpses of catastrophe should the people's courage fail—the swift approach of the "last days," nightmare visions of "men made beastlike by want, and women shorn of the nobility of their sex" pouring through city streets past plutocrats who stand "grabbing and grinning" as the mob rushes to its destruction.

In this realm of the apocalyptic, the ordinary political rules no longer applied. If the crisis facing the nation could be reduced to a simple choice between justice and injustice, liberty and slavery, what was the need for complicated debates and sophisticated analysis? "The very fact of widespread suffering," a Nebraska Populist insisted, "is sufficient evidence that the whole system under which they have lived is a lie and an imposture." Once allow the people to destroy the Money Power, and politics as a selfish pursuit of wealth and power would disappear. Like the abolitionists before the Civil War, the Populists concentrated on issues that had symbolic as well as practical meaning—above all, the Money Question and Free Silver.

For western Populists particularly, "fusion" with the Democrats appeared increasingly attractive. In the presidential election of 1892, the Populist party won over a million popular votes and 22 electoral votes and sent a dozen congressmen to Washington while securing governors' chairs in Kansas, North Dakota, and Colorado. As the Panic of 1893 tipped the country into the deepest depression it had ever known, the Populists tried to reach into the industrial cities for support. But underfinanced, lacking a roster of appealing candidates, and beset with severe organizational and financial problems, the party made few electoral gains in 1894, even though it increased its total vote by nearly 50 percent. Fusion with the Democrats, two years later, seemed to be the only alternative to continued failure.

As the presidential election of 1896 approached, Populists split into two camps, one led by the fusionists eager to join the Democrats on the Free Silver platform, the other headed by diehard reformers who agreed with Ignatius Donnelly that while the Democratic party had learned a few of its lessons, Populists ought not to "abandon the post of teacher and turn it over to [a] slow and stupid scholar." For southern Populists, moreover, fusion seemed suicidal, since it meant rejoining the Bourbons, whose ranks they had so recently deserted. But for a majority of the delegates to the convention in St. Louis in 1896, a "Demopop" ticket headed by William Jennings Bryan seemed to offer the only sure passage out of the wilderness. Following a rancorous debate, in which it was charged that the People's party had become "more boss-ridden, gang-ruled, gang-gangrened than the two old parties of monopoly," the convention agreed to unite with their former enemies under the banner of Free Silver.

The Great Reversal: the Election of 1896

By 1896 the Democratic party was bitterly divided between agrarians and eastern business interests, and needed all the help it could get. Grover Cleveland's return to office four years earlier had begun with a depression and a series of industrial strikes that seemed to many Americans the opening shots in a class war. In 1892, the first of these upheavals came outside of Pittsburgh, at Homestead, Pennsylvania, when Andrew Carnegie sailed for Scotland and left Henry Clay Frick, his hard-driving manager and an implacable enemy of labor unions, in charge of his steel company.

Frick took advantage of his chief's absence by attempting to break the Amalgamated Iron and Steel Workers Union, which two years earlier had won a favorable wage settlement from the company. Frick decided on a wage cut to destroy the union. When Amalgamated refused his terms, he cut off negotiations and hired a private police force to take over the plant at Homestead. The union retaliated by calling a strike and prepared to repel the Pinkerton guards who had been sent by barge up the Monongahela River with orders to seize the plant. The invaders, some three hundred, were met with a hail of bullets from the workers lining the shore, and in the pitched battle that followed, were routed and their barges burned to the water line. But final victory, as Frick had foreseen, lay with the company, which prevailed on the governor of Pennsylvania to send the militia to open the plant. Frick's union-busting nearly cost him his life when a young anarchist, Alexander Berkman, attempted to assassinate him but bungled the

job. Frick's principle of the open shop emerged triumphant. After five months out on strike, the Homestead workers were forced to accept the harsh new terms of the settlement, suffering a defeat that ended effective organizing in the steel industry for nearly half a century.

The Pullman Strike. In the Pullman strike in 1894, Cleveland threw his weight on the side of management against the forces of organized labor. The Pullman strike, like the Homestead strike, was a response to the antiquated ideas of a businessman whose sense of duty to his employees included building them a model company town but did not extend to allowing them the right to negotiate their wages. When workers in the railroad car shops went on strike, George Pullman, president of the Pullman Palace Car Company and chief planner of the company town named after him, sent word to his managers to refuse to bargain, and to evict the strikers from their homes. Then

STRIKERS AND SOLDIERS:
HOMESTEAD AND PULLMAN
Strikers on the lookout for
Pinkertons at Homestead, 1892
(*left*). Federal troops at
Pullman, 1894 (*right*).
(*both, Library of Congress*)

in the late spring of 1894, Eugene V. Debs and his recently organized American Railway Union, fresh from a victory over the Great Northern Railroad, came to the rescue of the Pullman strikers with funds and an offer to help settle their grievances. When the company again declined to bargain, the ARU voted to boycott all Pullman cars by refusing to couple them to any trains, even those carrying the mail. The Pullman Company, with the support of the railroads' General Managers Association, seized on this issue to seek an injunction and the dispatch of federal troops to Chicago. Over the angry protests of Illinois Governor John P. Altgeld, President Cleveland obliged. Faced with a choice between the rights of labor and the rights of property, Cleveland sided with the men of property.

The Depression of 1893. In 1894 the American economy hit bottom. Five hundred banks closed their doors, sixteen thousand business firms collapsed, and

unemployment reached nearly 20 percent. New issues on the New York Stock Exchange plummeted from $100 million to $37 million, and 2.5 million jobless men tramped winter streets looking for work. Municipal governments and private charity organizations could not cope with the large numbers of destitute men who wandered aimlessly from city to city. Everywhere they found factory gates closed and long lines at the soup kitchens. Not since the dark days of the Civil War had the country seemed so threatened.

Workers met the depression and accompanying wage cuts with the only weapon at their disposal—the strike. In 1894 alone there were over 1,300 strikes. The mining industry was hit by a wave of strikes that rolled across the country from the coal fields in the East to Coeur d'Alene in Idaho, where besieged miners fought with sticks and dynamite, and Cripple Creek, Colorado, where armed deputies broke up demonstrations. For such acute economic distress

COXEY'S ARMY
Jacob Coxey's rag-tag Commonweal Army protesting in Pennsylvania for aid to the unemployed, 1894. *(Library of Congress)*

President Cleveland proposed the heroic remedies of self-denial and sacrifice.

The spectre of masses of starving men marching on the nation's cities to plunder and pillage in an uprising of the dispossessed assumed the shape of farce in the spring of 1894 with the arrival in Washington of Coxey's Army, a "petition in boots" come to the capital to ask for work. The leader of the few hundred jobless men who finally straggled into the city was the self-appointed "General" Jacob Coxey, a small-town businessman from Massillon, Ohio. Coxey simply wanted to present his plan for solving unemployment with a "good roads bill," which would finance public improvement with $500 million worth of government bonds. The Cleveland administration's reaction to this living petition was a measure of its fear of mass upheaval: Coxey's followers were dispersed and their leader jailed on a technicality, while rumors of revolution swept through the city.

Cleveland blamed the free silver forces for the depression. In 1890 Congress responded to the clamor of the silver interests and passed the Sherman Silver Purchase Act, which required the government to buy 4.5 million ounces of silver each month and to pay for it with treasury notes redeemable in gold or silver. The Sherman Silver Purchase Act precipitated a sudden rush on the gold reserves of the United States by investors frightened by high imports and falling crop prices. The gold reserves plunged from $190 million to $100 million in just three years. As the depression deepened Cleveland persuaded Congress to repeal the Silver Purchase Act. After a bitter struggle, Congress complied in 1893, but the repeal seriously weakened Cleveland's control over his own party. He had succeeded in limiting the flow of silver from the mines in the West but in doing so lost the support of the agrarian half of the Democratic party. By 1895 the president was complaining that there was "not a man in the Senate with whom I can be on terms of absolute confidence."

The Gold Standard: "A Crown of Thorns"? To check the drain on American gold, Cleveland issued government bonds at a generous interest rate to attract European investors. In calling on the banking syndicates of J. P. Morgan and August Belmont to market the bonds, Cleveland only compounded his political difficulties. The administration and the bankers, working together, arranged the sale of government bonds for gold on terms that allowed the banking houses to manipulate exchange rates in their own favor. To the Populists and to irate Democrats in the South and West, Cleveland's deal with the bankers was powerful proof of a Wall Street conspiracy to rig the economy against them.

The silverites proceeded to make the presidential election of 1896 a one-issue campaign. Silver and gold quickly became organizing symbols for diametrically opposed strategies for economic recovery. Financial policy was treated as sacred dogma and the opposing view denounced as anathema. Silver, according to its defenders, was the "people's" money, abundant, cheap and flexible. To businessmen and bankers gold was the only "honest" currency—solid and time-tested. Cleveland chose "sound money," the gold standard, and currency restriction as the only ethical course. William Jennings Bryan described gold as "a crown of thorns" for bankrupt farmers and western debtors, pressed on the brow of the honest laborer who was being crucified by the money lenders. In fact, Cleveland's monetary policy did aggravate the effects of the depression. But more important, it gave farmers a highly visible target for their grievances. South Carolina demagogue Ben Tillman denounced the president to his backcountry constituents as a Judas who had thrice betrayed the democracy. "He is an old bag of beef, and I am going to Washington with a pitchfork and prod him in his fat ribs."

Democrats gathered in Chicago for the convention of 1896 with similar intentions. Southern and western Democrats quickly realized that by repudiating Cleveland's policies and advocating the free and unlimited coinage of silver they had an opportunity to upstage the Populist party. Bryan immediately emerged as the choice of the agrarian wing of the party, which rode roughshod over the "sound money" advocates and drove them out of the convention to form their own splinter organization.

Bryan spoke the mood of his followers in sounding a new note of resistance:

We have petitioned, and our petitions have been scorned; we have entreated, and our entreaties have been disregarded; we have begged and they have mocked when our calamity came. We beg no longer; we entreat no more; we petition no more. *We defy them!*

The eastern press, both Republican and Democratic, replied with charges of anarchy and treason. "The Jacobins are in full control at Chicago," one editor announced. "No large political movement in America has ever before spawned such hideous and repulsive vipers." Both the promise and the danger of a Democratic victory seemed greater after the Populists' convention in St. Louis also endorsed Bryan for president. Not since 1860 had the fate of the nation appeared to hang in the balance of a single election. In 1896, as in 1860, the differences were sectional and economic, but they were also social and cultural, as two fundamentally opposed views of politics competed for the allegiance of the American voter.

Bryan and McKinley between them gave over nine hundred speeches in the campaign of 1896; the Republican from his front porch in Canton, Ohio, to throngs of admiring visitors shipped in by party managers, and the "Boy Orator of the Platte" at every whistlestop in the West where local leaders could collect a crowd. Their speeches riveted national attention on the money question, which quickly brought into focus cultural and social disagreements between urban and rural America. Bryan soon expanded his economic indictment of the Money Power to a plea for a national moral revival. Republicans, capitalizing on the gradual upturn in the economy late in the summer, continued to denounce the Democratic platform as "revolutionary and anarchistic . . . subversive of national honor and threatening to the very life of the Republic."

Bryan—A Crusading Prophet. A powerful orator and an appealing political personality, Bryan was new to the business of presidential campaigning, and in casting his party adrift from its eastern financial

CAMPAIGN STYLES: OLD AND NEW
Bryan barnstormed the country
in the time-honored political
fashion, while Republicans advertised McKinley with an icon
of prosperity. *(Left, Brown
Brothers; right, Division of Political
History, Smithsonian Institution)*

moorings, he was forced to improvise. The professionals, sensitive to the sound-money opinions of
their business backers and appalled by the prospect
of an inflationary free silver, withheld their support;
and Bryan rejected the limited offers of the few party
leaders who remained loyal. Sensing the need for new
rules and definitions, Bryan cast himself in the role
of the crusading prophet who could purify both his
party and his country—by eliminating corruption,
paring the campaign budget, purging the party of
hacks, and preaching principles rather than praising
men.

As the new leader Bryan appeared an avenging
angel of outraged American yeomanry, the people's
savior stopping his campaign train for just one more
sermon to his flock. To his listeners he invariably
apologized by confessing that "a large portion of my
voice has been left along the line of travel, where it is
still calling sinners to repentance." His speeches drew
on a fund of stock pietist images as he mixed indictments of the Money Power, the tariff, and the gold
standard with allusions to the Old Testament. His
message was always the same: the people must arise
in their majesty and smite the moneylenders, and
destroy their temple. Audiences came to know his
arguments by heart and gathered to hear confirmation
of their beliefs in the Protestant ethic of hard work
and a just reward. When their leader assured them
that "every great economic question is in reality a
great moral question," they understood instinctively
and they cheered. As Bryan preached the saving word
of free silver his audiences saw the stone suddenly
rolled away and "the door . . . opened for a progress
which would carry civilization up to higher ground."

Republicans, following the orders of such new managers as Mark Hanna of Ohio, willingly exchanged places with their rivals. Tossing aside their pietistic heritage as a burden, they embarked on a pragmatic course toward a coalition of business and labor in the cities where most of the votes lay. Their chosen candidate was McKinley, a born compromiser, bland, amiable, with no strikingly original ideas, but presumably plenty of common sense. To McKinley's front porch in Canton, Ohio, came some three-quar-

ters of a million people, carried there on nine thousand railroad cars paid for by the party, to stand behind a white picket fence and listen to homilies on the honest dollar and the full dinner pail.

"Live and Let Live" with McKinley. McKinley's image was the clever contrivance of Republican managers who recognized the liabilities of pietism in an age of secular industrial organization and the need for full-time professional organizers, effective propaganda, and a full treasury. During the campaign Republicans released an unprecedented flood of pamphlets, speeches, broadsides, and editorials that reached every corner of the country. All of them were carefully orchestrated to new themes of cultural and ethnic toleration, arranged to appeal to farmers and workers, small businessmen and big bankers, shippers and consumers, Catholics as well as Protestants, and a variety of ethnic groups to whom the gold standard was offered as the last best hope of democracy. McKinley himself summed up the new Republican message: "We have always practiced the Golden Rule. The best policy is to 'live and let live.'" With their candidate's blessing, Republicans turned their backs on their pietist past and squared to the task of engineering a broad social consensus.

Their success in the election was decisive. With 7 million popular and 271 electoral votes, McKinley swept the entire East and Middle West, carried California and Oregon, and held on to Minnesota, North Dakota, and Iowa. Bryan, with 6.5 million popular votes and 176 electoral votes, won the Solid South together with the plains and the mountain states. Beneath the regional features of the election of 1896 lay the deeper meaning of the political turnabout. With their votes, a majority of Americans declared their preference for toleration and accommodation.

The meaning of the Democrats' defeat was clear. The American electorate had repudiated the pietist countercrusade against modernism and secularism. Reforms there would undoubtedly be as the twentieth century opened, but they would not be the handiwork of millennial dreamers of purity and perfection. From now on, political parties would have to consider and cater to the wishes and prejudices of a multitude of

The Election of 1896

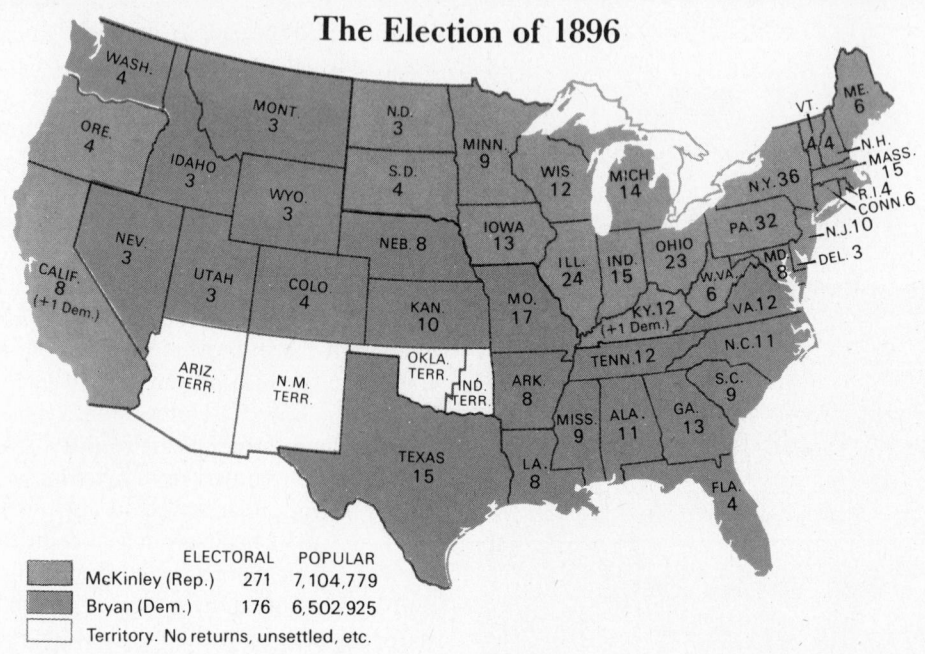

	ELECTORAL	POPULAR
McKinley (Rep.)	271	7,104,779
Bryan (Dem.)	176	6,502,925
Territory. No returns, unsettled, etc.		

social interests, welcoming newcomers from a wide variety of ethnic, cultural, and religious groups, meeting their demands, listening to their complaints, and serving their needs.

The election of 1896 also made it clear that the organizational revolution that was transforming business and finance had now invaded politics. Just as both houses of Congress were beginning to modernize their procedures for doing the nation's business, so the two principal parties had learned the importance of efficient organization, continuing communications, flexible and sophisticated candidates, and, above all, money with which to run their political machinery.

The Party System Realigned. Finally, and most significant for the immediate future, the election of 1896 broke the grip of party discipline and loyalty that had long been considered a permanent feature of American politics. The election freed the American party system for a long-term realignment of voting patterns that would reveal the average voter as con-

siderably more independent than the professionals had once assumed him to be.

Bryan had uncovered a latent American suspicion of politics, a set of misgivings that had been buried in the rubble of the Civil War. In his unsuccessful campaign, Bryan located this skepticism in the agrarian mind, attempted to exploit it, and failed. But by 1896 in the cities of the nation, new urban reformers were already experiencing a similar distrust of entrenched power and were beginning to experiment with still another form of politics. The political program of these new urban reformers, while it promised to end machine politics and return power to the people, envisaged not the rule of righteousness, but the triumph of the professionals. The vision of social reformers organizing in American cities after 1890 centered on an efficient, economically run "organic city" that was man-made rather than God-given. With the stirring of these reform hopes came a second and more potent challenge to the old politics, the challenge of progressivism.

CHRONOLOGY

1880 James A. Garfield elected president.

1881 Garfield assassinated; Chester A. Arthur becomes president.

1883 Pendleton Act establishes independent Civil Service Commission.

1884 Grover Cleveland elected president, defeating Republican James G. Blaine.

1887 Interstate Commerce Act attempts to control railroads.

1888 Benjamin Harrison narrowly defeats Cleveland and is elected president.

1890 Sherman Silver Purchase Act passed, resulting in depleted gold reserves.
Sherman Antitrust Act passed in attempt to regulate monopolies in restraint of trade.
McKinley Tariff raises duties to average 49.5 percent.

1892 Populists organize, nominate General James B. Weaver for president.
Grover Cleveland elected president.
Homestead strike in Carnegie steel mills.

1893 Financial panic sends U.S. economy into four years of depression.
Congress repeals Silver Purchase Act.

1894 Pullman strike broken by federal troops; Eugene V. Debs jailed.
"Coxey's Army" of unemployed marches on Washington.

1896 William McKinley elected president, defeating William Jennings Bryan and "Free Silver."

1897 Dingley Tariff raises duties to a new high of 57 percent.

SUGGESTED READINGS

An indispensable introduction to American politics and society from the end of the Civil War to 1900 is Morton Keller, *Affairs of State: Public Life in Nineteenth Century America* (1977). There are several useful guides to the politics of the Gilded Age. Leonard D. White, *The Republican Era, 1869–1901* (1958) examines the workings of the federal government. H. Wayne Morgan, *From Hayes to McKinley: National Party Politics, 1877–1896* (1969), concentrates on political organization. Daniel J. Elazar, *The American Partnership* (1962), treats federal-state relations in detail, and David J. Rothman, *Politics and Power: The United States Senate, 1869–1901* (1966), presents a fascinating account of the organizational changes in the upper house. Robert D. Marcus, *Grand Old Party: Political Structure in the Gilded Age, 1880–1896* (1971), analyzes the workings of the Republican party, and Horace Samuel Merrill, *Bourbon Democracy of the Middle West, 1865–1896*, gives a regional account of the Democrats for the same period. Vincent P. DeSantis, *Republicans Face the Southern Question* (1959) and Stanley P. Hirshson, *Farewell to the Bloody Shirt: Northern Republicans and the Southern Negro, 1877–1893* (1962), consider the race issue as it affected Republican strategy. Southern politics is perceptively treated in four important works: C. Vann Woodward, *The Origins of the New South, 1877–1913* (1951); Dewey W. Grantham, Jr., *The Democratic South* (1963); Albert D. Kirwan, *Revolt of the Rednecks: Mississippi Politics: 1876–1925* (1951); and Morgan Kousser, *The Shaping of Southern Politics: Suffrage Restriction and the Establishment of the One-Party South, 1880–1910* (1974). Mary R. Dearing, *Veterans in Politics* (1952), recounts the activities of Civil War veterans, and Marc Karson, *American Labor Unions and Politics, 1900–1918* (1958), discusses unions and politics in the opening years of the twentieth century.

A number of studies examine electoral behavior in crucial elections. Among the best are Paul W. Glad, *McKinley, Bryan, and the People* (1964); Stanley Jones, *The Presidential Election of 1896* (1964); J. Rogers Hollingsworth, *The Whirligig of Politics: The Democracy of Cleveland and Bryan* (1963). Two challenging studies, Paul Kleppner, *The Cross of Culture: A Social Analysis of Midwestern Politics, 1850–1900* (1970), and Richard J. Jensen, *The Winning of the Midwest* (1971), examine cultural factors operating in Midwestern politics during the Gilded Age and perhaps elsewhere as well.

Political biography abounds. Two of the best studies of Bryan are Paolo E. Coletta, *William Jennings Bryan: Political Evangelist, 1860–1908* (1964), and Paul Glad, *The Trumpet Soundeth: William Jennings Bryan and His Democracy, 1896–1912* (1964). For McKinley, see H. Wayne Morgan, *William McKinley and His America* (1963). On Cleveland, Horace Samuel Merrill, *Bourbon Leader: Grover Cleveland and the Democratic Party* (1957), supersedes Allan Nevins, *Grover Cleveland* (1932). Biographies of other important figures include numerous older works: Ray Ginger, *The Bending Cross: A Biography of Eugene V. Debs* (1948); Herbert Croly, *Marcus Alonzo Hanna* (1912); Nathaniel W. Stephenson, *Nelson W. Aldrich* (1930); Francis Butler Simkins, *Pitchfork Ben Tillman* (1944); Leland L. Sage, *William Boyd Allison* (1956); and Harry Barnard, *"Eagle Forgotten": The Life of John Peter Altgeld* (1938).

On the troubled 1890s, a good overview is Harold U. Faulkner, *Politics, Reform and Expansion, 1890–1900* (1959).

The intellectual and cultural climate of the decade is analyzed in the idiosyncratic and amusing Thomas Beer, *The Mauve Decade* (1952), and Lazar Ziff, *The American 1890s: Life and Times of a Lost Generation* (1966). For contemporary accounts that treat the social and cultural issues in nostalgic fashion, see Harry Thurston Peck, *Twenty Years of the Republic, 1885–1905* (1907), and the first volume of Mark Sullivan, *Our Times* (6 vols., 1926–35).

The effect of progressive reforms is described in Melvin Holli, *Reform in Detroit: Hazen Pingree and Urban Politics* (1969); James B. Crooks, *Politics and Progress: The Rise of Urban Progressivism in Baltimore, 1895–1911* (1968); and William D. Miller, *Memphis During the Progressive Era, 1900–1917* (1957). A good study of Tammany in this period is Nancy Weiss, *Charles Francis Murphy, 1858–1924: Respectability and Responsibility in Tammany Politics* (1968). Jack Tager, *The Intellectual as Urban Reformer: Brand Whitlock and the Progressive Movement* (1968), is a sharply etched portrait of a recognizable progressive type.

The Progressive Impulse

$\mathcal{I}$n 1915, as the progressive movement neared its zenith, a young professor of government at New York University, Benjamin Parke DeWitt, published an account entitled *The Progressive Movement*, in which he catalogued the political and social reforms in the United States in the two previous decades. DeWitt, an active progressive and a fervent admirer of Theodore Roosevelt, looked behind the campaigns and the elections and discovered three interlocking reform tendencies:

The first of these tendencies is found in the insistence by the best men in all political parties that special, minority, and corrupt influence in government—national, state, and city—be removed; the second tendency is found in the demand that the structure or machinery of government . . . be so changed and modified that it will be more difficult for the few, and easier for the many, to control; and finally, the third tendency is found in the rapidly growing conviction that the functions of government are too restricted and that they must be increased and extended to relieve social and economic distress.

DeWitt's analysis was accurate. The progressives believed that government at all levels was both inefficient and corrupt. Because it was corrupt it ignored the needs of the people. Therefore the people themselves had to seize the initiative in repairing the whole system. According to progressive logic, the first job was to remove unworthy and inept politicians and replace them with reliable public servants drawn from the popular ranks and equipped with the needed expertise. These new leaders would then see to it that government—city, state and national—performed an expanding range of tasks efficiently and responsibly. Progressives, in short, found in the idea of scientific government the materials for building a national reform movement.

A variety of forces shaped their movement. There was no single progressive type among the leaders or the rank and file; there was no typical age, status, background, religion, or education. The progressives were drawn from the mainstream of the native-born middle class that dominated American politics in the first two decades of the twentieth century. Educated, articulate, and eager to apply their ideas for reforming society and politics, they held no monopoly on political gentility and could be found in equal numbers in the reform wings of both the Republican and Democratic parties.

They had no uniform platform. They offered a wide array of reform proposals: initiative, referendum, recall, corporate regulation, child labor laws, tariff reform, city manager plans, zoning regulations, immigration restriction—even prohibition. Their priorities differed according to region and immediate interest. Farmers fought hard for regulation of railroad rates, but ignored the problem of industrial accidents. Southern progressives pushed for tariff and banking reforms, but disfranchised the blacks. Settlement-house workers grappled with the bosses for control of their cities, but neglected the problems of the small-town businessman.

With this great variety in progressivism from 1890 to 1914, it seems useful to analyze it, not as a movement at all, but rather as a patchwork of different interest groups who occasionally agreed on specific measures but were unable to combine behind a unified and coherent program. The progressives thought otherwise. They realized that the United States was entering a new era of economic and political consolidation, one that required new techniques for managing what all of them agreed was a flourishing national enterprise. Even though they admitted that there was much wrong with America, they saw little that could not be mended by using the authority of government and scientific efficiency. In the spirit of the Founding Fathers whose nationalism they so admired, progressive reformers, despite their differences, thought of themselves as the architects of a stable social order based on many of the principles that had guided their Federalist ancestors.

With their experiments in new political techniques, the progressives were innovators, but at a deeper level they were conservatives and restorationists. They picked up the promise of American life where their eighteenth-century forebears had dropped it—with the creation of a strong national government capable of harnessing and directing the energies of all its citizens. If part of the progressives' call for the people to take power back from their corrupt rulers seemed to invoke the spirit of Jefferson, the heart of

their program was the Hamiltonian demand for a new national leadership using the power of government to set priorities and provide direction. The ghosts of Hamilton and Jefferson fought over the progressive terrain just as the two statesmen had bitterly contested each other's principles a century earlier. To the delight of his many progressive admirers, Hamilton won the victory denied him during his lifetime. For in effect, if not in intent, progressivism marked the rebirth of original Federalist hopes for a managed republic in which men of talent and training guided the affairs of a prosperous people.

Cities in Revolt—the Rise of Urban Progressivism

The progressive search for order in a disordered world began in the city. Wherever urban reformers looked in the closing years of the century they saw disorganization and fragmentation. Wealthy neighborhoods with million-dollar mansions were set apart by parks and boulevards from teeming ghettos with dilapidated tenements and filthy streets, all too visible proof of the immense distances—social and psychological as well as economic and geographical—that separated the rich from the poor.

It was to close the distance between urban affluence and sprawling poverty that in 1889 Jane Addams, the pioneer settlement-house worker, moved into Hull House, a battered mansion on the corner of Polk and South Halstead streets in the heart of Chicago's Nineteenth Ward.

The streets are inexpressibly dirty [she reported], the number of schools inadequate, factory legislation unenforced, the street-lighting bad, the paving miserable and altogether lacking in alleys and smaller streets, and the stables defy all laws of sanitation. . . . Hundreds of houses are unconnected with the street sewer. . . . Back tenements flourish; many houses have no water supply save the faucet in the back yard; there are no fire escapes; the garbage and ashes are placed in wooden boxes which are fastened to the street pavements. . . . Our ward contains two hundred and fifty-five saloons; our own precinct boasts of eight. . . . There are seven churches and two missions in the ward.

In listing the needs of the Nineteenth Ward, Jane Addams summarized the main points in the urban progressive indictment of boss politics. Progressivism began as a spontaneous revolt of city-dwellers who were convinced that they had been short-changed in their share of the American social fund. The drive to clean up the nation's cities began with a pragmatic assessment of urban blight. Broad coalitions of voters demanded immediate solutions to a wide range of problems: they sought tax reforms, more effective health regulations, lower streetcar fares, better utility services, and efficient city governments free of corrupt bosses and predatory interests. The depression of the 1890s, by placing new burdens on consumers, bred a sense of urgency and focused public attention on the shortcomings of rule by the political machines.

The progressive attack centered on "invisible government," the alliance between municipal authorities and business interests. The connection between "corrupt government" and "corporate arrogance," which the progressives fought to destroy, was a simple one of mutual need. In attempting to modernize their cities, machine politicians had discovered in secret agreements with transit, utility, and construction interests a handy device for providing minimal service while lining their own pockets. At the same time, the new and unstable industries, involved with urban development, undergoing rapid reorganization and always short of funds, saw in monopoly franchises, wholesale bribery, and kickbacks a measure of certainty in an otherwise unpredictable world. By 1890 such bargains had been sealed in most of the major cities of the country. The only real loser in this arrangement was the public.

TENEMENTS, WASHINGTON, D.C.
Lewis W. Hine's famous photograph of the capital's black slums documents the urban progressive challenge. *(Lewis W. Hine, George Eastman House Collection)*

Thus progressivism began as a "people's movement" aimed at eliminating corruption and inefficiency. Cutting across class lines and fastening on specific issues like dangerous railway crossings, poor sanitation, or high streetcar fares, the progressive movement in its early years developed a style that was both democratic and moralistic. The twin devils in the reformers' morality play were the businessman and the boss. Lincoln Steffens, the dean of reform journalists, pronounced the American businessman "a self-righteous fraud." "I found him buying boodlers in St. Louis, defending grafters in Minneapolis, originating corruption in Pittsburgh, sharing with the bosses in Philadelphia, deploring reform in Chicago, and beating good government with corruption funds in New York." From the beginning, the progressives developed an antibusiness rhetoric that continued to obscure the real contributions of businessmen to urban reform.

Progressive Mayors.   The bosses offered even more enticing targets. Urban reformer Frederick C. Howe reported that Boss Cox of Cincinnati ruled his city "as a medieval baron did his serfs." The only remedy for boss rule lay in building citizens' coalitions to unite a fragmented community. "The very nature of city life," one progressive commentator pointed out, "compels manifold cooperation. The individual cannot 'go it alone'; he cannot do as he pleases; he must conform his acts in an ever increasing degree to the will and welfare of the community in which he lives." This concept of the organic city fitted neatly with the interests and ambitions of a new group of reform mayors in the 1890s who launched individual campaigns to overhaul their cities.

The first of these progressive mayors was Hazen Pingree, mayor of Detroit from 1889 to 1896, when he was elected governor. Pingree, a shoe manufacturer turned "reform boss," campaigned vigorously in all of the wards of the city, steering clear of controversial moral and religious questions like prohibition and parochial schools, and concentrating instead on the hard economic issues that would win him the broadest support. Pingree exposed bribery in a local electric company's dealings with his predecessors and em-

barked on an extensive program of school and park construction. After a prolonged battle with the transit and utility interests, he succeeded in reducing streetcar fares and gas rates while building the city's municipal lighting plant. During the depression in the 1890s he started programs of work relief for Detroit's unemployed and extended a variety of social service programs. Attacking Detroit's "invisible government" and replacing it with an efficient and responsive administration, Pingree set the pattern for his successors.

It remained for Tom Johnson, the mercurial mayor of Cleveland from 1901 to 1909, to exploit most fully a whole new range of possibilities for leadership. Johnson had made his fortune by reorganizing transit systems, and had been converted to reform after reading Henry George's *Social Problems.* After two successful terms in Congress as a reform Democrat, he returned to Cleveland to build a political coalition to fight Republican boss Mark Hanna and the transit interests. Energetic, tough-minded, and a consummate politician, down to the unlit cigar he waved while speaking from the nearest soapbox, Johnson borrowed the techniques of the machine politicians and improved on them. He inaugurated his reform program by arranging for a regulated system of prostitution free from police graft. Like Pingree, he threatened the transit interests with regulation. His most widely acclaimed achievement was the 3¢ fare, but he continued to agitate for municipal ownership of utilities, and provided his city with free public bathhouses, recreational facilities, and effective sanitary inspection.

Progressive mayors who launched their careers from a platform of pragmatic opposition to the "interests" were frequently driven to face broader questions of social welfare. Some mayors, like Pingree and Johnson, and later Brand Whitlock in Toledo, Ohio, and Mark Fagan in Jersey City, New Jersey, were forced to adjust to shifting economic interests within their reform coalitions and to support welfare measures that went far beyond the political and structural reforms they originally had called for. The "social justice" mayors, as they have been called, also came to question the value of strict party identification.

TROLLEY CAR AT BROADWAY AND 23RD STREET, 1901
For commuters and shoppers such as these New Yorkers, cheap transportation was a necessity. *(Photograph by Byron, The Byron Collection, Museum of the City of New York)*

Increasingly they came to rely on the advice and services of new nonpartisan experts in municipal management concerned with finding more efficient ways of running American cities.

Social Experimentation. "Streetcar politics" was only the most visible sign of the urban revival in the 1890s. City churches, keenly aware of their declining membership among the working class, responded to the crisis by developing the "institutional church" in lower-class neighborhoods. By providing services like lodging houses, reading rooms, recreational halls, and day nurseries, these church progressives hoped to spread the "social gospel" of Christianity. Then too, by 1890 groups of earnest young college graduates, many of them women, were moving into slums to live in settlement houses modeled on London's famed Toynbee Hall. By 1895 there were over fifty such settlements in major cities around the country, each with a staff of idealistic college graduates and seminarians.

Settlement-house workers were invariably young (most were under thirty), religious (predominantly Congregationalist and Presbyterian), college-educated, single, and overwhelmingly from middle-class families. For such young intellectuals and professionals, some of them with advanced training in the new social sciences taught in German universities, the city settlement offered an escape from gentility and from feelings of superfluousness, and provided the chance to practice new skills. Settlements freed them from what Jane Addams called "the snare of preparation" for unknown careers. More important, they developed a new and deeper understanding of the complex social and cultural relations that made up the modern city. Teachers, housing reformers, charity organizers, child labor opponents, health inspectors, and visiting nurses found a congenial home in the reform settlements, which seemed to them miniature models of the good society.

The progressive movement was not only a major effort in social engineering. It involved also a pro-

HENRY STREET SETTLEMENT HOUSE VISITING NURSE, NEW YORK, 1908

A short-cut leads over the roofs of the tenements. *(Photograph by Jessie Tarbox Beals, Museum of the City of New York)*

THE PROGRESSIVE SOCIAL WORKER'S CLIENTS

While social workers recognized that reforms ultimately depended upon the votes of men, they concentrated their efforts for immediate improvement on women and children. *(Both photographs, Lewis W. Hine, George Eastman House Collection)*

found intellectual revolution. The reformers came to understand the complexity and the interconnectedness of modern life. They experienced at first hand the difficulty of isolating the underlying causes of the problems they dealt with, and the futility of proposing simple solutions. Whether they were lawyers, engineers, clinicians, historians, sociologists, or economists, the progressives found themselves working with a new approach to knowledge which the philosopher John Dewey, one of their teachers, called "creative intelligence," and another powerful intellectual teacher, William James, called "pragmatism." James taught these young reformers to seek truth not in abstractions but in action. "How will truth be realized? What, in short, is truth's cash-value in experiential terms?" Truth was not a "stagnant property" inherent in an idea, as Emerson and the Transcendentalists had believed. Truth worked, James insisted.

"True ideas are those we can assimilate, validate, corroborate, and verify. False ideas are those we cannot."

John Dewey, whose interest in social reform was as strong as James's, traced this instrumentalist logic to its origins in Charles Darwin's evolutionary biology and in the new scientific way of thinking which did away with the old search for "absolutes and finalities." This new logic, Dewey told his progressive students, brought new intellectual responsibilities. Philosophy would hereafter have to deal with "the more serious of the conflicts that occur in life" and develop a method of "moral and political diagnosis and prognosis." Oliver Wendell Holmes, Jr., judge and legal instrumentalist, was even more specific. He taught the progressives that the true function of law was the expression not of abstract principles but of "accurately measured social desires."

By 1900 the settlement house had established itself as an indispensable laboratory of social experimentation. In devising urban programs and services, the progressives relied heavily on new methods of research and fact-gathering as essential to the work of reordering urban society. One of Jane Addams's first assignments was to collect and collate the raw data on the surrounding neighborhood; in 1895 *Hull House Maps and Papers* appeared as the first detailed account of an immigrant community published in the United States. In 1903 Lawrence Veiller and Robert W. De-Forest published their two-volume *Tenement House Problems,* an attempt to relate housing to the larger setting through statistics and first-hand observation. Perhaps the most ambitious project for studying the city in its entirety was the six-volume *Pittsburgh Survey* (1909-14) which treated politics, crime, prostitution, the family, housing, and working conditions as aspects of a functioning social organism.

Social surveys underscored the need for trained personnel and scientific management. The independent commission, staffed by trained professionals and given the power to revamp tax structures, regulate transit and utility rates, and provide efficient city services, quickly became an essential agency of effective urban reform. The multiplication of these commissions increased the demand for trained personnel. University education in these fields spread throughout the nation, and a new range of professions, each with its own organization, was created. By 1910 economists, political scientists, sociologists, tax reformers, charity organizers, settlement-house workers, and dozens of other specialized professions had formed national societies, each with its own publications and communications network. These national organizations, besides strengthening a sense of professional community among progressives, cemented an alliance with newly founded universities which provided the training and facilities for investigating urban problems. In Chicago, the residents of Hull House soon established close connections with William Rainey Harper's new University of Chicago through reform-minded academics like John Dewey, sociologists Albion Small and William I. Thomas, and political scientist Charles Merriam. In New York, economists and sociologists from Columbia University joined freelance writers and publicists in analyzing city problems and working out solutions. Settlement houses proved vital for young academicians by providing laboratories for testing new concepts of behavior, and by drawing them into the exciting world of business and politics beyond university walls.

Businessmen and academicians often parted company, however, on the question of how to apply the new critical spirit of reform. University scholars—historians, economists, and social theorists—now had sharp analytical tools for dissecting old conservative myths and challenging entrenched institutions. Historian Charles A. Beard was the best known of the young academicians who were beginning to question the hide-bound interpretations of American law and the Constitution as well as the ancestor-worship they encouraged. Beard's own Columbia University typi-

fied the new iconoclastic spirit. There, economist Edwin Seligman, the earnest advocate of the "New History," James Harvey Robinson, and pioneer students of administrative law such as Frank Goodnow were busy probing the economic roots of political behavior. At the same time, political scientist Arthur F. Bentley, in *The Process of Government* (1908), approached political decision-making as a complex process that was subject to the shifting forces of interest groups. At the University of Washington, radical historian J. Allen Smith, in a book entitled *The Spirit of American Government* (1907), dismissed the Constitution as a "reactionary document" designed to check the forces of democracy. After 1900 the alliance between highly critical academicians and their corporate financial supporters grew increasingly strained as the professors began to question the very business civilization on which their universities had come to depend.

Scientific Reform.   The universities also supplied a more conservative product. With the appearance of concepts of "social control" and "scientific efficiency," progressive reformers made contact with another reform tradition. This tradition was alien to the open tolerance of reform politicians and the democratic and humanitarian hopes of social workers, and concentrated instead on efforts to impose strict efficiency and economy. These business values and procedures assumed concrete shape for large numbers of progressives in the image of the modern corporation. The picture of the efficient, impersonal corporation was not drawn by businessmen alone. It was a widely accepted model of organization that appealed to intellectuals and professionals as well as to industrialists and financiers who recognized its uses in rebuilding American politics. The progressives' criticism of the trust was largely directed toward its misuse by unscrupulous promoters, not toward its seemingly rational structure. "The trust is the educator of us all," Jane Addams announced in explaining the need for new kinds of collective action. Seen in this light, the corporation appeared as a corrective of the waste and the inefficiencies of an earlier age, an actual model of social and political reform extendable, like the utopian communities before the Civil War, to a larger American society.

The "scientific" urban reformers believed that simply by tightening the system of expenditures, consolidating power in the hands of experts, and revising the political system without particular regard to human needs, they could manage the city. Good government, they reasoned, would be rigorously honest, determinedly efficient, resolutely frugal, and strictly accountable. But such scientific reform was a check on democratic participation. It limited the influence of uninformed voters, whose numbers it sought to reduce through literacy tests and tighter political registration laws.

These scientific reformers considered the city a challenge that was not very different from the challenges met by industrialists and financiers. Efficiency and economy came to be equated with business practices of budget-paring, cost-cutting, tax-trimming, and service-chopping according to the ledger-book ethics of corporation accountants. "Municipal government is business, not politics," read the slogan of the scientific reformers. The shaping power of the modern corporation in determining their outlook was reflected in their vocabulary, which developed a set of useful analogies. The mayor served as *chairman of the board* of an urban *corporation* comprised of big and little *stockholders,* who were expected to vote their *proxies* at *annual meetings* and accept their *dividends* without constantly interfering with the *managers* of the *enterprise.*

It was hardly a coincidence that the last years of the century, which saw the triumph of the corporation and the advent of scientific municipal reform, also witnessed the opening assault on the concept of a rational "public opinion," once considered the cornerstone of democratic politics. In dismissing ordinary public opinion as frivolous or perverse, scientific reformers demonstrated a distrust of democracy. The first order of reform business, insisted Frank Goodnow, an expert in administrative law and spokesman for the scientific reformers, was recruiting cadres of loyal and politically unambitious civil servants whose efficiencies would allow "the business and professional class of the community to assume care of the

public business without making too great personal sacrifice." For these good government advocates and business-dominated mayors who tried to clean up the cities after 1900, urban reform meant a chance for middle- and upper-class Americans, armed with new technical skills, to repossess the field of urban politics that an earlier generation had abandoned to the bosses.

Progressive businessmen and professionals shared a new set of values that reshaped their aims into concepts of system, control, stability and predictability. Charity organizers now realized the need for accurate data in drafting workable solutions to social disorganization. A giant lumber company like Weyerhaeuser came to appreciate the importance of planning and cooperation with the new experts in the Forestry Service. College professors and high school teachers recognized the need for professional solidarity to protect their rights. Public-service lawyers, like young Louis Brandeis, acknowledging the complexities of new legal relations, began to play the role of "counsel to the situation" in experimenting with new techniques of arbitration.

The social perceptions of this middle-class vanguard of the bureaucratic revolution stemmed from their sense of American society as a national collectivity in need of a new set of operating procedures. To implement their bureaucratic values progressive reformers centralized authority in a hierarchical order, concentrated decision-making power in an energetic executive, established impersonal relations in restructuring their organizations, and above all, planned for maximum efficiency.

The urban reform movement was therefore split between those who sought to extend popular influences in government and those whose programs limited popular participation. Reformers were faced with a choice between two widely divergent estimates of democracy and human nature. Some of them, like sociologist Edward A. Ross, frankly rejected the idea of democratic participation in favor of open elitism. Politically, Ross argued, democracy meant not the sovereignty of the average citizen, "who is a rather narrow, shortsighted, muddleheaded creature," but the "mature public opinion" of an educated elite. The case for democracy was most forcefully put by Brand Whitlock, novelist, social welfare reformer, and mayor of Toledo from 1905 to 1913, who defined the "city sense" as democracy and as "the spirit of goodwill in humanity," and predicted that cities would arise that would "express the ideals of the people and work wonderful ameliorations in the human soul."

The conservative bias of many progressive reformers could be clearly seen in their attacks on the boss and the machine while their real intentions were often obscured, even to themselves, by their seemingly democratic enthusiasm. "The people are finding a way," exclaimed progressive publicist William Allen White, who pointed in astonishment to the rapid growth of "fundamental democracy" throughout the country. A whole roster of progressive proposals for open government were billed as democratic devices for ensuring popular control at the grass roots. The direct primary and direct election of senators would release the stranglehold of the bosses on the electoral process. Referendum would send important questions of policy straight to the people over the heads of unresponsive legislators. Recall would return the power to remove officeholders to the voters, with whom it belonged.

Urban progressives were not hypocrites in advertising their reforms as democratic, but they did not always make it clear that by "the people" they meant, not the huddled masses in center cities, but solid citizens with sensible views and sober habits. Below the blaring trumpets of democracy could be heard, subdued but distinct, the progressive call for the politically vanquished to return to the fray armed with new weapons.

By 1900 a dual tradition had emerged, polarized around conflicting values of social efficiency and democratic liberation. These contrasting principles, which had combined briefly in the 1890s to challenge the politics of the bosses, would continue to diverge in the twentieth century, creating tensions within progressivism that would make it a confused yet creative movement.

The nerve center for urban progressivism after 1900 consisted of municipal leagues, civic federations, citizens lobbies, commercial clubs, and bureaus of municipal research. These civic groups provided forums for the lively exchange of ideas between academicians and businessmen eager to try out new ideas of efficiency and economy. From organizations like the National Municipal League and the National Civic Federation poured a flood of proposals and plans for repairing city government: home rule and charter revision; ballot reform and literacy tests; city-wide election schemes and city-manager plans, all of them aimed at the power base of the boss.

At first the reformers concentrated on improving procedures. They proposed segregated budgets for economy. They introduced time clocks, work sheets, job descriptions, and standardized salaries. They developed systematic ways of letting contracts to replace the old patronage system. But the heart of their reform program was the commission and city-manager plans, modelled on the corporation. Combining executive and legislative functions in a single board, the commission plan spread rapidly until by 1913 over 300 cities in the United States had adopted it. The city-manager plan, a refinement of the original commission idea, further consolidated decision-making in municipal government, and by the 1920s it too had been widely adopted.

Urban progressives never succeeded in putting the political boss out of business. Nevertheless, progressivism successfully challenged boss politics by confronting it with another way of doing the business of the city. The machine's power lay in the center city, with its immigrants and working classes. Middle-class reformers generally operated from power bases along the suburban periphery. Boss politics, for all its sins, was marked by a high degree of accountability and popular participation in the wards and precincts. Progressives tried to reduce direct popular involvement at both the voting and the officeholding level. Bosses were prodigal but democratic; reformers were economical and bureaucratic.

Progressive success was limited. All too often procedures changed but official policy did not. Still, if the boss and his clients proved adept at dashing the electoral hopes of reform candidates, they could no longer ignore the cries for more effective city government. The progressives' dream of a shiny, streamlined administrative model never materialized. Yet the modernizing of American cities proceeded with or without the politician's approval. In their partial overhaul of the nation's cities the progressives scored important gains for the new bureaucratic order.

The Man with the Muckrake

Many of these contradictions could be seen in the work of the muckrakers who supplied progressivism with an agenda. The name was affixed to a new brand of reform journalists by President Theodore Roosevelt, who complained that their relentless exposure of corruption in high places hindered rather than helped him in his work of improving American society. Comparing the group of headstrong publicists to John Bunyan's gloomy figure in *Pilgrim's Progress* who refused a celestial crown for a muckrake, the president denounced their "crude and sweeping generalizations" and their delight in pointing the finger of civic shame. For their part, the muckrakers—Lincoln Steffens, Ida Tarbell, Ray Stannard Baker, David Graham Phillips, and many less famous colleagues—accepted the label and wore it defiantly as proof of their devotion to the Jeffersonian principle of a free and vigilant press.

Muckraking was the product of two forces that had combined by the end of the nineteenth century: major advances in the technology of printing, which made it possible to produce inexpensive, illustrated, and popular magazines; and the simultaneous arrival on the metropolitan scene of reform reporters sensitive to the new social concerns of the middle-class reader and eager to exploit them. S. S. McClure, founder of *McClure's*, was one of the pioneer explorers of the lucrative field of reform journalism, and he was quickly joined by dozens of competitors drawn to social criticism by their keen sense of the market and the prospect of sizable profits. From the outset, muckraking proved that reform could be a paying proposition. Gathering a staff of trained, well-paid newspapermen, editors like McClure launched an attack on the underside of American life with articles on sweatshops, tainted meat, the white slave traffic, insurance company scandals, labor racketeering, city bosses, and high finance. Muckrakers happily compiled a list of all the social wrongs that their enlightened readers would presumably set right.

Muckraking offered both a new kind of factual reporting and an old form of moral publicity. Always extravagant and frequently sensational, the muckrakers perfected the uses of contrast and contradiction in pointing to the disparity between venerable American ideals and startling social facts. In an article for *Cosmopolitan* on child labor in southern cotton mills, for example, poet Edwin Markham depicted "The Hoe Man in the Making" in the faces of "ill-fed, unkempt, unwashed, half-dressed" children penned in the narrow lanes of the mills, little victims whose dreary lives mocked the "bright courtesy of the cultured classes." Social gospelist Ernest Crosby contrasted the appearance of a majestic United States Senate with the reality of a "House of Dollars," a political monopoly modeled on an industrial trust. Samuel Hopkins Adams explained the national failure to regulate the food and drug industries as the result of "private interests in public murder" when "everybody's health is nobody's business."

Muckraking thus presented a publicity technique rather than a philosophy, a popular journalistic style rather than a searching analysis. As social critics, journalists like Lincoln Steffens and David Graham Phillips were both tough-minded and factual, and romantic, moralistic, and sentimental. Like their millions of readers, they were the beneficiaries of a fundamental change in the idea of publicity, which they conceived of as an open-minded process of fact-gathering that reflected the shifting nature of social reality. Read in this subdued light, their articles could be considered wholesome remedies and useful correctives. Their work, the muckrakers insisted, was never done, since an unfolding social process required constant adaptation of old theories to new facts, accepted values to changed conditions.

Muckraking also tapped traditional morality while exploiting the time-honored role of the disinterested observer—the clear-eyed, hard-nosed investigator with a fierce desire to get all the facts and expose them to the sanitizing rays of publicity. Muckrakers liked to think of themselves as brave detectives, dashing from one hidden clue to another, looking for the fragments of information which, once collected and arranged, would tell reformers what to do next. There was a strong bias against party government in the muckrakers' view of American politics as well as a weakness for conspiratory interpretations. They believed the masses of American voters, once given the facts, would demand reform. Tell the people the truth, they said, and they would correct injustice forthwith. Conscience, duty, character, virtue—these were the watchwords of the muckrakers, and also a measure of their limited understanding of the problems confronting progressive America. Muckrakers identified the symptoms of disorder, but they could not isolate its causes or prescribe effective remedies. For these tasks a clearer understanding of the workings of modern industrial society was needed.

Progressivism Invades the States

After 1900 the progressives, building on urban achievements, set out to reform state politics. Beginning in 1900 with the first administration of Wisconsin governor Robert M. La Follette, reform swept across the country in the next decade transforming the conduct of state politics.

Although progressivism varied widely in the different sections of the country, there were enough similarities to give political reform at the state level the appearance of a national movement. In the South, progressives who had inherited a number of Populist grievances often wore the trappings of a redneck revolt against the business-minded Bourbons. By the opening years of the century one governorship after another was falling to economy-minded agrarians from upcountry or downstate. The southern rebellion

TWO PORT CITIES IN THE PROGRESSIVE AGE
Right, New Orleans docks in 1895. *Opposite,* San Francisco wharves in 1900. *(Right, Historic New Orleans Collection; opposite, National Archives)*

against the alliance of big business and Democratic politicians drew on popular sympathies and produced railroad and corporate regulation, antimonopoly laws, insurance company controls, and improved public education and child labor reforms—though all with the continuing disfranchisement of the black population.

Progressivism in the Midwest and on the Pacific Coast also grew out of a revolt, usually within the Republican party, which was perceived as too generous to railroads and corporations. Midwestern progressives drew more heavily from the arsenal of democratic political reforms—the initiative and the referendum, for example—than their counterparts in the East, who tended to rely more on administrative reforms. But everywhere the control of state legislatures by big business made an inviting target. In New Jersey state politics, corporate dominance by 1900 was all but complete. "We've got everything in the state worth having," a spokesman for corporate interests boasted. The legislature regularly elected two senators who represented the utility interests and the insurance companies; and the executive branch of the government was staffed by former employees of the Pennsylvania Railroad.

The governors who organized the revolts against these statehouse rings headed the cast of new progressive folk heroes. The most popular of the reform governors cast themselves as western heroes, riding into office with a mandate to clean up the state, setting about their task with grim determination, and moving on to bigger things when the job was done. Denied office by state party leaders, the reform governor collected his small band of insurgents and attempted, at first without success, to take over the party. To help in subsequent efforts he enlisted other mavericks and began to explore such electoral reforms as the primary system of party nomination and the direct election of senators, fixing his sights on the "interests" and eventually defeating party regulars.

Once elected, the progressive governor moved quickly to neutralize his opposition by absorbing some of them into his own reform coalition. He learned to wield patronage with a surprising ruthlessness, and with secure majorities in the legislature went to work on his reform program. This generally included strict regulation of railroads and public service corporations, a revamped tax structure, and major pieces of social legislation to improve working and living conditions in the state. After a hectic term or two in which he managed to complete at least part of this reform program, the progressive governor moved on to the United States Senate where he was joined by other like-minded rebels from similar backgrounds who had the same hopes of imposing their reform designs on national politics. The career of one such progressive hero, Robert M. La Follette, illustrates the main features of this legend of progressive reform.

"Battling Bob" La Follette.   La Follette, an intense, unsmiling, self-made man, was a small-town lawyer who struggled to the top of the political heap in Wisconsin. In his three terms as governor after 1900, he enacted a reform program that became the envy of progressives across the country. Born in Primrose, Wisconsin, in meager circumstances, young La Follette was a walking example of the Protestant ethic. He put himself through the state university at Madison by teaching school, and prepared himself for a career in politics by studying for the bar. At the University of Wisconsin he came under the reform influence of its president, John Bascom, who was just beginning to build a public service institution, a task that La Follette himself would complete a quarter of a century later.

Short, wiry, with a shock of bristling iron-gray hair, La Follette combined a rock-hard moralism with a combativeness hard to match. He won his first office as district attorney without the endorsement of the Republican machine, by barnstorming the county and haranguing rural voters on the need for integrity and independence. In 1884 he was elected, again without the support of party regulars, to the first of three terms in Congress, where he was the youngest member of the House. He was defeated for reelection in the Democratic landslide of 1890 and came home to a lucrative law practice.

The Republican party in Wisconsin, as in a number of other states, had been the effective instrument of the railroad and the lumber companies. Faced with a lawsuit against their corrupt state treasurers, the party bosses had sent an emissary to La Follette with a bribe to secure his influence with the judge, who happened to be his brother-in-law. La Follette promptly cried havoc and later reckoned the attempted bribe as the turning point of his career. "Nothing else ever came into my life that exerted such a powerful influence upon me as that affair." In exposing the machine's crime to the voters he effectively isolated himself from the party leaders and spent nearly a decade trying to collect enough votes from Scandinavian farmers and industrial workers in Milwaukee to overthrow the machine. By 1900 he had succeeded.

La Follette's victory won him instant national acclaim. After destroying the power of the old machine by winning over some of its leaders to his own cause, he set out to modernize Wisconsin. The "Wisconsin idea," as it came to be known, depended on a firm progressive majority in the state legislature, which the new governor secured by campaigning personally for his supporters and then holding them strictly accountable. Soon his enemies were complaining that he had made himself the boss of a ruthlessly efficient machine of his own. The substance of the Wisconsin idea consisted of a set of related reforms: a direct primary law, an improved civil service, a railroad rate commission, an equitable tax program, state banking controls, conservation measures, a water power franchise act, and protective labor legislation. At the center of La Follette's reform movement stood the independent regulatory commission, staffed by experts from the state university and given wide administrative latitude.

To his many admirers across the country, La Follette seemed a political anomaly, at once a popular leader with his feet firmly planted in the grass roots and an enthusiastic convert to scientific government. Exacting, fiercely partisan, and a powerful hater, he often viewed the world as a gigantic conspiracy

"BATTLING BOB" LA FOLLETTE CAMPAIGNING
La Follette was famous for his style of political barn-storming. *(State Historical Society of Wisconsin)*

against "Battling Bob." He kept ready for display at a moment's notice the image of the sea-green incorruptible who preached the virtues of direct democracy and constantly urged his followers to "go back to the people." "Selfish interests," he declared, "may resist every inch of ground, may threaten, malign and corrupt, they cannot escape the final issues. That which is so plain, so simple, and so just will surely triumph."

The other half of La Follette's reform equation, however, was filled with the facts and figures that his investigatory commissions collected. His own interminable speeches came loaded with statistics and percentages provided by a corps of tax experts, labor consultants, industrial commissioners, and social workers. He hammered these facts at the voters of Wisconsin in the belief that the people, once they learned their meaning, would hardly fail him. The

conflicting principles of popular democracy and government by an expert elite caused La Follette little distress. The expert commission, which was the key agency of the Wisconsin idea, secure above the battle of parties and interests, seemingly embodied the detachment and patriotism it was designed to foster in the people. La Follette's growing national reputation, in fact, rested on the belief he inspired that direct democracy and scientific government were not simply compatible but complementary.

State Progressive Reform. An important feature of progressive reform programs in the states was a package of new laws, drawn up by civic groups, women's organizations, and consumer interests that humanized working conditions. As late as 1900, over half of the states had no laws that established a minimum age for workers. By 1914 every state but one had set an age limit on the employment of children. In most states new laws for the protection of women in industry paralleled the drive to abolish child labor. Illinois led the way in 1892 by limiting hours for women. New York and Massachusetts followed, and then the movement spread rapidly westward. When the Supreme Court upheld the principle of state regulation of hours for women in the celebrated case of *Muller* v. *Oregon* in 1908, barriers collapsed. By the time America entered the First World War, thirty-nine states had written new laws protecting women or significantly strengthened old laws, while eight states had gone even further by passing minimum wage laws for women. Another feature of the progressive social reform program was the campaign for employers' liability laws and industrial accident insurance which did away with the worst of the abuses of the older doctrines of the "fellow servant" and contributory negligence. By 1916 nearly two-thirds of the states, reacting to mounting pressures from a progressive public, had established insurance programs.

Progressivism, taking different forms in different states, spelled a shift in power within the American political system. Cumbersome, interest-dominated legislatures gave way to a new public authority lodged in the executive and its supporting administrative agencies that were charged with discovering and then

SHUCKING OYSTERS, OYSTER
HOUSE, BALTIMORE, MARYLAND
After 1900 progressive legislation in the states was aimed at
protecting working women like
these. *(Culver Pictures, Inc.)*

serving the public interest. To justify their roles as custodians of the public interest, progressives unearthed a national-interest theory of politics as old as the Founding Fathers. "I would not be a dredger congressman, or a farm congressman, or a fresh-egg congressman," a typical progressive told his constituents in summoning up the spirit of Edmund Burke and virtual representation. "I would like to be an American congressman, recognizing the union and the nation." If warring economic and class interests were chiefly responsible for the lack of direction and the low tone of American politics, progressives reasoned, then it was wise to ignore them and appeal instead to a latent public virtue in the concept of citizenship. "Progressivism," another reformer added,

"believes in nationalism ... opposes class government by either business, the laboring class, or any other class." This tendency to reject interest-group government (government as a bargaining process between blocs of big business, big labor, and big agriculture) drove progressives to embrace the idea of leadership from above—from those "good men" in whom altruism presumably ran deeper than selfishness. "While the inspiration has always come from below in the advance of human rights," the California progressive William Kent insisted, the real accomplishments in improving American society must always be "the disinterested work of men who, having abundant means, have ranged themselves on the side of those most needing help." In the progressive interpretation of American politics, underdogs announced their needs but topdogs filled them.

Draped with the mantle of disinterested benevolence, state progressivism looked like nothing so much as a rebuilt model of Federalism, suitably modernized to fit an industrial society. Progressives, like their Federalist ancestors, feared the idea of party government and class division, and sought to take the politics out of American life in the name of scientific management. In place of eighteenth-century rule by republican notables, they substituted leadership by experts whose skills were to command the instant allegiance of all enlightened citizens. Most of the progressive political reforms aimed at securing stability and control. And in the same fashion, the progressive social justice programs initiated by the states were designed to strengthen corporate capitalism by giving government the power to reassign responsibilities and temper the harshness of the American industrial environment. To carry out their policies at the national level, the progressives looked to the figure of the new statesman, and in Theodore Roosevelt they found their earthly paragon.

Theodore Roosevelt: The Progressive as Hero

In September 1901 President William McKinley died in Buffalo of an assassin's bullet, and Theodore Roosevelt, "this crazy man," as Republican managers thought him, was catapulted from the vice-presidency into the post of national leader. Blueblood, historian, student of the classics, amateur naturalist, cowpuncher, and Rough Rider, Roosevelt at forty-two appeared to millions of admirers as the last of the universal men, but to uneasy Republican bosses such as Mark Hanna, as "that damned cowboy."

With an audible sigh of relief Old Guard Republicans heard the new president announce his intentions "to continue, absolutely unbroken, the policy of President McKinley." McKinley had meant high tariffs, the gold standard, a not-too-vigorous prosecution of the trusts, and just the right amount of impe-

rial ambition. The prospect of a continuing custodial presidency reassured those congressional standpatters who feared above all a rambunctious executive. Yet within the year, Roosevelt had begun to challenge congressional authority, and by the time he retired from his second term in March 1909, he had succeeded in creating a national progressive movement, reinvigorating American foreign policy, and laying the foundations of the twentieth-century welfare state.

A Patrician Cowboy. Roosevelt was the product of patrician New York society, the son of a banker-philanthropist who had dabbled in genteel reforms and organized the city's upper-class contribution to the Union cause during the Civil War. A graduate of Harvard, where he amused his classmates with his odd earnestness and vibrancy, young Roosevelt immediately settled on a life of politics among the 'kittle-kattle" of spoilsmen and mugwumps. He held the comfortable classes chiefly responsible for the moral chaos of Gilded Age politics, and with a highly developed sense of noblesse oblige, entered the New York State Assembly as a representative from one of the city's wealthy Republican districts.

In the Assembly, where he served a single term from 1882 to 1884, he displayed the singular mixture of social conservatism, pugnacity, and political acumen that was to become his distinguishing mark. In 1886 he accepted the Republican nomination in the three-way mayoralty race in New York City and ran a respectable third behind Democratic winner Abram S. Hewitt and single-taxer Henry George. The 1880s also saw the growth of a sizable body of Roosevelt's historical writing—*The Winning of the West*, a biography of Gouverneur Morris, and another of Thomas Hart Benton—in which Roosevelt proclaimed his unqualified approval of the nationalist designs of the Federalists, denounced Jefferson as a humbug and a hypocrite, and hymned the glories of westward expansion and the fulfillment of America's continental destiny.

When his first wife died in 1884, Roosevelt retired to the frontier he had described so eloquently, finding solace in Dakota ranch life filled with cowboys, frontier justice, and manly virtues. As a steadfast but unpredictable young Republican, he was appointed to the United States Civil Service Commission by President Benjamin Harrison in 1889, and served in Washington in a blaze of publicity until 1895, when he returned to New York to head the Board of Police Commissioners. Here he made another name for himself as a result of late-night prowls with his friend, journalist Jacob Riis, in futile attempts to enforce the city's blue laws. McKinley rewarded such energy by appointing him assistant secretary of the navy, despite Roosevelt's outspoken views on behalf of American military power.

The Spanish-American War in 1898 drew Roosevelt out of the shadows of appointive office and into the limelight of electoral politics. As self-appointed leader of the Rough Riders, the First Regiment of the United States Cavalry Volunteers, he caught the fancy of a jingoistic public that followed with keen interest his dramatic if somewhat superfluous exploits in charging up San Juan Hill, pausing now and then to exult over all "those damned Spanish dead" as he rallied his own disorderly troops.

Disembarking to the tune of "There'll Be a Hot Time in the Old Town Tonight," he was promptly elected governor of New York and as quickly upset party bosses by taking a firm progressive stand on a state factory inspection act and on another law regulating the hours of state employees. "If there is going to be any solution of the big social problems of the day," he warned his supporters, "it will come, not through a sentimental parlor socialism, but through actually taking hold of what is to be done working right in the mire." Republican leaders in New York responded by lifting their governor out of the mire of reform politics and into the clean and safe office of the vice-presidency. Their hopes for squelching the exuberant progressive were curtailed when an assassin's bullet put Roosevelt in the White House.

Roosevelt as President. Americans soon learned what kind of president they had acquired, for Roosevelt had strong opinions on every conceivable subject and delighted in publishing them in pungent and readable phrases. The objects of his scrutiny ranged from the novels of Emile Zola (which he generally disliked) to the "full baby carriage" (which he heartily endorsed); and his advice ranged from conduct becoming football players and would-be-reformers ("Don't flinch, don't foul, hit the line hard!") to what one observer called an "unflagging approval of the Ten Commandments." A vigorous intellectual, with interests in birds and political bosses, trusts and big game, divorce and "practical idealism," Roosevelt collected facts and ideas which he regularly assembled in print—not writing with a pen, as one reader put it, so much as charging with it.

Roosevelt's forceful and sometimes contradictory opinions revealed two distinct personalities. The first one was described by a New York politician as "the most indiscreet guy I ever met," the keeper of the national conscience always ready to speak his mind. This public Roosevelt served as the confident spokesman of an aggressive American nationalism—prophet of a coming Anglo-Saxon supremacy, celebrant of military valor, unblushing advocate of power politics, and a true believer in the American mission to order the affairs of the rest of the world. The national hero, "Teddy"—a name he disliked—looked the part. With pince-nez adorning a bulbous nose, toothy grin stretched in a near grimace, a full square face with its several chins resting on heavyset shoulders, a reedy voice and pump-handle gestures, he was a cartoonist's dream.

In the role of the mad American of his generation, as he has been called, Roosevelt could and frequently did talk great nonsense. He lashed out with equal contempt at "radical fanatics" and the "lunatic fringe" of soft-headed reformers. "Sentimental humanitarians" he denounced as "a most pernicious body, with an influence for bad hardly surpassed by that of the professional criminal classes." He stressed the importance of "good blood" flowing through the veins of well-bred, self-denying gentlemen. He predicted race suicide for any of the world's people who preferred "effeminacy of character" to the "rougher and manlier virtues." For handling mobs he recommended "taking ten or a dozen of their leaders out, standing . . . them against a wall, and shooting them dead." For anarchists and socialist agitators he had a similar prescription—troops supplied with real bullets and "the most wholesome desire to do them harm." Americans, whether delighted or appalled by such balderdash, recognized in Roosevelt the authentic American hero, the compulsive man of action who shot from the hip and whose motto read: "Get action; do things; be sane."

The other Roosevelt, unlike the trigger-happy dispenser of justice, was a thoughtful if highly partisan student of American history with a keen appreciation of the original work of the Founding Fathers. Young progressives entering the political arena after 1900 with credentials from the new universities brought with them training in such new disciplines as economics and sociology. But for the slightly older progressive leaders, the study of history was still the

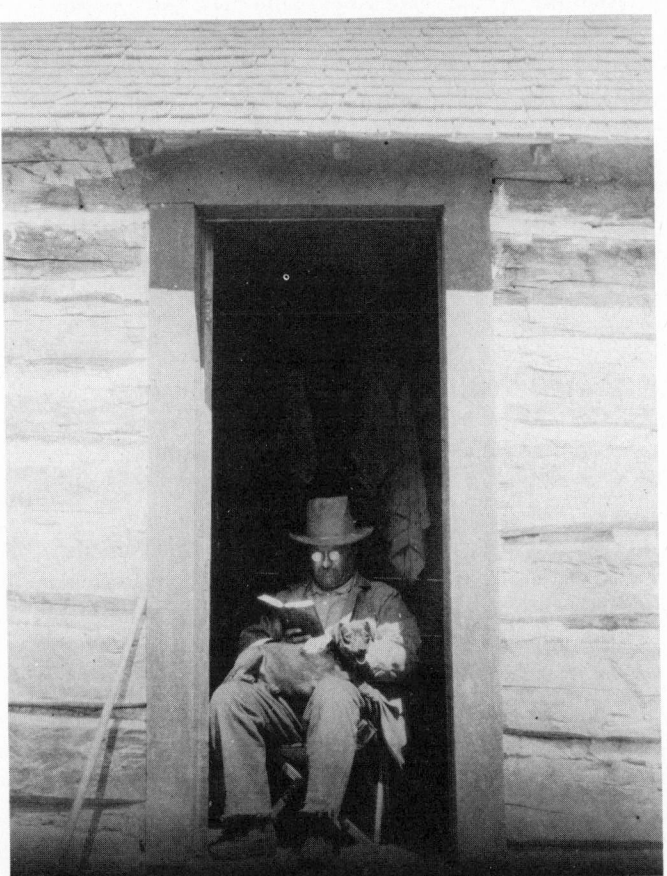

THE TWO SIDES OF THEODORE ROOSEVELT
Surrounded by the paraphernalia of patriotism, Roosevelt campaigns in New Castle, Wyoming, in 1903. The more reflective man appears in the doorway of his Dakota ranch-house. *(Above, Library of Congress; left, Theodore Roosevelt Collection, Harvard College Library)*

primary tool for examining American society. Despite the rapid growth of the "scientific" monograph, much of the popular history written after 1880 continued to be the work of gentlemen amateurs like Roosevelt or his friends Henry Adams and retired industrialist James Ford Rhodes, who measured the achievements and noted the shortcomings of nineteenth-century American democracy. The thrust of much of this popular history was toward political nationalism and social conservatism, whether in John Fiske's admiring account of the Founding Fathers, or Henry Adams's search for the principles of scientific government in his magnificent nine-volume history of the administrations of Jefferson and Madison, or in Roosevelt's own hymns to national valor in *The Naval War of 1812* and *The Winning of the West.*

Roosevelt's Political Philosophy. This reflective, history-minded Roosevelt was the first president after Lincoln and the last of the moderns with an understanding of the eighteenth century. Beneath his dramatic account of America's rise to greatness lay a clear grasp of the original Federalist design and the men who fashioned it. National greatness, it seemed to Roosevelt, was based, just as it had been in the past, on the "power to attain a high degree of social efficiency," by which he meant "love of order" and the "capacity to subordinate the interests of the individual to the interests of the community." The Federalists, he believed, led by such farseeing nationalists as Hamilton and Gouverneur Morris, had tried to teach the first Americans the same lessons that his own generation had just learned, that "the sphere of the State's action may be vastly increased without in any way diminishing the happiness of either the many or the few."

The American people, Roosevelt was convinced, had been given the wrong directions by a demagogic Jefferson and had drifted steadily toward the Civil War even as they had expanded and enriched their domain. From Jefferson and his Jacksonian heirs they had acquired the illusions that little government was needed and that the moral order was self-regulating. Despite their magnificent material accomplishments in filling out a continent and building an industrial

empire, the American people had failed to devise the political means of managing it. Only briefly during Lincoln's wartime administrations had Americans caught a glimpse of true national unity. With the onset of the Gilded Age, the original statesman's question "Will it work?" had been replaced by the huckster's demand "Does it pay?" and the national energy had been squandered in money-grubbing. One fact was clear at last—Americans had to "abandon definitely the *laissez-faire* theory of political economy, and fearlessly champion a system of increased Governmental control."

The opening years of the twentieth century, Roosevelt believed, represented "an era of federation and combination" that had been foreshadowed by the age of the Founding Fathers. The president, like his Federalist teachers, deplored class politics and called for the rule of enlightened men of integrity, whom he always identified with the better half of the Republican party. But wherever found, the disinterested patriot held the key to the future. By the time Roosevelt took over the presidency in 1901, he had acquired a clear definition of his role as general manager of the United States even though the details of his plan for its "orderly development" emerged only gradually from the recesses of his conservative mind.

"Wise Radicalism and Wise Conservatism"—the Square Deal

Roosevelt as president firmly established the regulatory principle as the foundation of administrative government. What he and the country came to call the Square Deal as he campaigned for reelection in 1904, began as a loose collection of proposals for directing national economic development. Roosevelt had inherited from Gilded Age Republicanism an Old Guard of conservatives. They had built their stronghold in the Senate where they kept firm control over the lawmaking process and saw to it that presidents followed their dictates. Roosevelt was immediately forced to bargain with their leader, Senator Nelson W. Aldrich of Rhode Island, and to agree to keep his hands off the tariff question in exchange for a limited freedom to pursue his plans for intervention elsewhere. These concerns, like those of his progressive followers, first centered on the trusts.

Trust-Busting. Roosevelt shared the progressives' ambivalence toward big business. "Nothing of importance is gained," he admitted, "by breaking up a huge interstate and international organization which has not offended otherwise than by its size. . . . Those who would seek to restore the days of unlimited and uncontrolled competition . . . are attempting not only the impossible, but what, if possible, would be undesirable." He believed that it was their behavior rather than their size that constituted the test of their utility, and he declared it the duty of the government to require trusts to operate "in the interest of the general public." To prevent them from fixing prices and manipulating the market, he proposed a watchdog agency modeled on the Interstate Commerce Commission, a body appointed by him and staffed with "trained administrators, well known to hold the scales exactly even in all matters." After a sharp skirmish with big business and its defenders in Congress, he succeeded in 1903 in establishing the Bureau of Corporations within the new Department of Labor and Commerce to police business practices and report its findings to the public.

Publicity formed the keystone of Roosevelt's regulatory program, and he quickly perfected the art of disclosure in launching a series of actions under the Sherman Antitrust Act. He advised the beef trust of his strictly honorable intentions to "Destroy the Evils in Trusts, But Not the Prosperity," and he insisted publicly on settling with the Northern Securities Company, the United States Steel Company, and the American Tobacco Company "the absolutely vital question" of federal power to regulate the trusts. It was essential, he announced, for the president and his administrators to maintain "strict supervision" of big business and see that it did not go wrong.

To make good on his promise Roosevelt gave the signal to the Department of Justice in 1902 to move against J. P. Morgan's railroad combine, the Northern Securities Company. Morgan, he recalled with relish, "could not help regarding me as a big rival operator who intended to ruin all his interests." But it was power that interested the president, who considered the clash with Morgan a dynastic one of rival sovereignties. The Supreme Court, in upholding the government's case against the railroad merger in *Northern Securities Co.* v. *United States* in 1904, gave Roosevelt his precedent. In the *E. C. Knight* case (1895), he announced with obvious satisfaction, the Court had erroneously decided that the federal government lacked the power to break up dangerous combinations. "This decision I caused to be annulled." He did not add what soon became obvious—that he had not at the same time checked the force of the merger movement.

Roosevelt's views on organized labor mirrored his convictions on big business: the ultimate test for both sides was a willingness to provide order and stability of their own volition. If trusts threatened the balance of economic power with irresponsible behavior, Roosevelt reasoned, labor could prove disruptive and greedy. If there were "good" and "bad" trusts, there were also dependable labor leaders like Samuel Gompers and dangerous visionaries like Eugene Debs. In either case it was the president who had to distinguish legitimate demands from crackpot notions. The only standard he could finally invoke was conduct. "Where in either one or the other, there develops corruption or mere brutal indifference to the rights of others, and short-sighted refusal to look beyond the moment's gain, then the offender, whether union or corporation, must be fought."

The test of Roosevelt's opinion of unions, strikes, and injunctions came early in the first administration, when the United Mine Workers struck against the anthracite coal operators, a confrontation that alarmed the whole country and gave Roosevelt welcome public support. The miners, led by the canny union leader John Mitchell, demanded a pay increase and an eight-hour day along with acknowledgment of their right to organize the coal industry. George Baer, president of the Reading Railroad, bungled the case for the coal operators from the outset. Baer proclaimed it his "religious duty" to defeat the strikers, insisting that "the rights and interests of the laboring men will be protected and cared for—not by labor agitators, but by Christian men to whom God in his infinite wisdom has given control of the property interests of the country."

Roosevelt, his hand strengthened by the obstinacy of the operators, moved quickly by calling for an investigation by his labor commissioner and using the findings to force the coal companies to compromise. When they refused, he ordered both parties to a conference in Washington, where the operators, under the presidential threat to send in troops, finally agreed to an arbitration panel. The Anthracite Coal Strike Commission awarded a 10 percent pay increase and a reduction of hours to the miners while refusing their demand for the closed shop. Once again, as in regulating the trusts, it was principle and procedure—the orderly disposition of grievances by disinterested men—that most concerned the president.

New Consumer Legislation. Roosevelt's theory of expanded executive power developed from his belief that only "a great exertion of federal authority" could meet the needs of all the people. The most vulnerable members of a largely unregulated commercial society were American consumers. In the field of consumer legislation as in his dealings with big business and labor, Roosevelt assumed the leadership of forces that had already begun to organize by 1900. The Pure Food and Drug Law, passed in 1906, was the result of a carefully orchestrated public outcry and shrewd presidential direction. The law, limited though it was, capped a strenuous campaign for effective legislation by Harvey Wiley, chief chemist of the Department of Agriculture, who twice had seen his recommendations accepted in the House only to languish in the Senate, where the food and drug interests held court. Aided by a series of lurid exposés furnished by the muckrakers, Roosevelt finally collected the votes he needed to prohibit the manufacture and sale of misbranded or adulterated foods and drugs, a limited power wielded cautiously ever since.

Support for the Meat Packing Act (1906) also came from consumers, many of whom learned of the appalling conditions in the industry from Upton Sinclair's sensational novel, *The Jungle.* In attacking the packers Sinclair traced the shipment, from prairie to slaughterhouse, of cows "that developed lumpy jaw, or fell sick, or dried up of old age," carcasses "covered with boils that were full of matter." Though annoyed by Sinclair's fictionalized account, Roosevelt promised him action. An investigation verified most of Sinclair's charges in a fact-studded report which Roosevelt, in a calculated piece of blackmail, threatened to release unless the packers accepted minimum regulation. The final bill, like most of the Square Deal legislation, represented a series of compromises—increased appropriations for inspection in exchange for the removal of inconvenient requirements for enforcement—and left the matter of appeal to the courts in what Roosevelt called "purposeful ambiguity." Once the industry had accepted the principle of federal regulation, the big packers welcomed those requirements that could be expected to drive out their small competitors. For his part the president was perfectly willing to compromise on details in order to gain the principle of federal control.

In his willingness to sacrifice specifics for the precedent, Roosevelt frequently disappointed his more determined progressive supporters who complained that he gave in too easily on points that might have been won. In the tug of war over the Hepburn Act (1906) regulating railroad rates, his critics appear to have won their case. In 1903 the Elkins Act, a piece of legislation supposedly prohibiting discriminatory rebates to favored shippers, had been drafted by the railroad senators who refused to grant the government effective control over rate-making. Roosevelt now meant to acquire this authority. An administration measure passed by the House was designed to strengthen the Interstate Commerce Act by giving it genuine power to fix rates and make them stick. In the Senate, however, Roosevelt's plan met the stubborn opposition of Aldrich and the railroad senators who decided to teach him a lesson. Aldrich and his conservatives quickly bottled up the bill in committee where they conducted interminable hearings for the benefit of its enemies.

Roosevelt tried a second time with another bill, this one sponsored by Representative William P.

Hepburn of Ohio. This was an even more moderate measure empowering the ICC to set reasonable rates after hearing complaints from shippers. Once again Aldrich stepped in, sent the bill to the Senate floor without endorsement, and looked on with detachment as one amendment after another stripped the bill of its original intent. In the end Roosevelt failed to rally a successful coalition of faithful Republicans and disgruntled Democrats, but managed to win over enough moderate Republicans to force Aldrich to a compromise. The final version of the Hepburn bill increased the powers of the ICC but left intact the injunction against enforcing new rates in cases that were under court appeal. At best, Roosevelt had won a very limited victory.

A Formula for Conservation.   In the case of conservation, the last main item on the Square Deal agenda, compromise again weakened principle. Though Roosevelt himself was a nature lover and preservationist by inclination, he abandoned the tradition of Thoreau and naturalist John Muir for a developmentalist strategy designed for multiple use of the nation's natural resources. Calling on citizens to look ahead to "the

CHICAGO STOCKYARDS STRIKE
Police guard an overturned meatwagon.   (*Chicago Historical Society*)

days of our children," he warned against the waste and destruction that would "result in undermining . . . the very prosperity" that ought to be passed on to them "amplified and developed." Yet his formula for conservation remained the same as that for other national needs: expert advice from scientists committed to development rather than preservation, much publicity, and permissive government oversight of private interests.

These long-term limitations were obscured for the moment in the flurry of executive actions during Roosevelt's second term as he added 43 million acres to the national forests, withdrew from entry over 2,500 water power sites and 65 million acres of coal lands, and established 16 national monuments and 53 wildlife refuges. The issue of conservation assumed a crucial symbolic significance in Roosevelt's mind as he found himself blocked by Congress from pursuing other social justice goals. He turned to the management of natural resources as "the fundamental problem which underlies almost every other problem in national life," the acid test of federal power. He flouted the congressional will with a "midnight proclamation" that set aside twenty-three new forest reserves and then threw down his challenge: "If Congress differs from me . . . it will have full opportunity in the future to take such positions as it may desire anent the discontinuance of the reserves." While Congress fumed, he moved rapidly ahead with plans for building a conservation empire consisting of bureaus and commissions filled with geologists, hydrologists, foresters, and engineers taking their orders from Gifford Pinchot, his volatile but capable chief forester. In 1908, sensing widespread public interest, Roosevelt called a National Conservation Congress, which was attended by forty-four governors and over five hundred conservation experts.

Yet in spite of its appearance as a popular crusade, Roosevelt's conservation program was less a grass-roots movement to save the environment than an executive scheme for national resource management imposed from above. The president envisioned a grand design in which irrigation, flood control, forestry, and reclamation would be "interdependent parts of the same problem" of regional development. He was forced to settle for much less. Government experts and lumber company executives shared a strong distaste for the ideas of the preservationists. The new federal agencies, understaffed and underfinanced, soon found themselves dependent on the goodwill of the very private interests they were charged with policing. Small operators, whose reputation for gouging the landscape was well earned, were sometimes driven out, but the large companies continued their policies of exploiting national resources under a government seal of approval. From the perspective of three-quarters of a century, Roosevelt's national conservation program, like the original Federalist partnership between wealth and government, appears to have identified with the welfare of powerful private interests.

The Limits of Neofederalism

Having retired from the presidency after two terms in office, Roosevelt embarked for Africa on a hunting trip in the spring of 1909, leaving in the White House his hand-picked successor, the ponderous William Howard Taft, to "carry on the work substantially as I have carried it on." In many ways the conservation issue symbolized both the partial success and the ultimate limitations of Roosevelt's attempt to forge a new national purpose. The key to his plan was teaching the American electorate the meaning of national unity and strong government, an educational task he performed admirably for seven years.

The conservation campaign, which slowly moved to the center of the progressive consciousness, meant a fight against sectionalism, state rights, business interests, and a Congress that gave them all voice. To check these divisive forces and hold the allegiance of his reform followers, Roosevelt had revitalized the presidential office and buttressed it with new concepts of civic duty and loyalty. "I believe in a strong executive; I believe in power," he announced, and he proceeded to use his power in ways that no president since Lincoln had contemplated. To aid him in his work of executive renovation, he drew heavily from the ranks of progressive experts and professionals whose cause of scientific government he championed with enthusiasm. His reform program, for all its timid approach to the regulatory principle and its deference to vested interests, marked at least a step toward the orderly republic he envisioned.

If Roosevelt's utopia lay well over the horizon in 1909, it was because he intentionally set conservative limits to the application of governmental power, and in the last analysis firmly believed in a guided democratic process. Although he chafed under the restraints placed on him by his party and a laggard Congress, he managed both of them with consummate skill, alternately bullying and cajoling both, but breaking with neither. In negotiating for his limited reforms he was willing more often than not to take the shell and leave the kernel, concerned as he was with winning a principle. Yet his presidency was no mere exercise in educational politics. Roosevelt wanted results that the country would accept, and to get them he willingly used traditional and even conservative political methods. When he left office, the results were clear. He had raised his office to its twentieth-century position of dominance. He had laid the foundation for a governmental bureaucracy and collected the presumably disinterested professionals to run it. And finally, he had preached with unflagging zeal the virtues of altruism, integrity, and service as indispensable to the new citizenship.

Further than this neither Roosevelt nor the nationalist-minded progressives could go. Roosevelt spoke for progressives across the country in demanding the return to service of "the man of business and the man of science, the doctor of divinity and the doctor of law, the architect, the engineer, and the writer," all of whom owed a "positive duty to the community, the neglect of which they cannot excuse on any plea of their private affairs." The ordinary citizen, "to whom participation in politics is a disagreeable duty," had long since been defeated by an organized army of political hacks. Now, Roosevelt and the progressives believed, it was time to try the extraordinary citizen wherever he could be found. Neither he nor they would have been surprised to learn that the average citizen was taking less rather than more interest in politics. Voter turnout, which in the Gilded Age had averaged nearly 80 percent in presidential years and 60 percent in off-years, fell a full 15 percent after 1900. Whether they were disenchanted with the prospects of a managed republic that the progressives promised them or simply because they were discovering their more pressing concerns outside the political arena, the fact was that fewer Americans were troubling themselves with the duty of taking what Roosevelt called "their full part in our life."

Here indeed lay the outermost reaches of Roosevelt's progressive domain. If Jefferson's political formula had long since proved hopelessly inadequate for managing an industrial republic, his original estimate of the diverse sources of American energy had not. Jefferson had counted the advantages as well as the dangers of sectional division, religious variety, ethnic diversity, and even class disagreement. With Roosevelt's retirement in 1909, these forces of social and political pluralism began to take revenge on his promise of national unity, first shaking the party structure, and then disrupting the national social consensus which Roosevelt and his followers had attempted to construct. In a suddenly revived Democratic party the American people would find a different variety of progressive reform, and in Woodrow Wilson a very different kind of leader.

CHRONOLOGY

1889 Jane Addams founds Hull House; beginning of settlement-house movement.
Hazen Pingree elected mayor of Detroit; first progressive mayor.

1890 Muckraking photo-journalist Jacob Riis publishes *How The Other Half Lives* depicting life in New York's slums.

1893 First issue of *McClure's* magazine.
Conference for Good City Government inaugurates urban progressive reform movement.

1899 John Dewey's *School and Society*, pioneer progressive education tract.

1900 Robert La Follette elected to his first of three terms as progressive governor of Wisconsin.
William McKinley reelected president, defeating William Jennings Bryan.

1901 Theodore Roosevelt becomes president after McKinley assassinated.
Tom Johnson elected mayor of Cleveland.

1902 Roosevelt launches antitrust action against Northern Securities Company.
Roosevelt settles anthracite coal strike through arbitration.

1903 Bureau of Corporations established within new Department of Labor and Commerce.

1904 Roosevelt elected, defeating Democrat Alton B. Parker and Socialist Eugene V. Debs.
Case of *Northern Securities Co.* v. *U.S.* upholds government's case against railroad mergers.
Lincoln Steffens' *The Shame of the Cities* published.

1906 Upton Sinclair's novel *The Jungle* published.
Meat Packing Act passed.
Pure Food and Drug Act passed.
Hepburn Act passed, strengthening powers of Interstate Commerce Commission.
John Spargo's *The Bitter Cry of Children*, exposé of child labor, published.

1907 Financial panic; Roosevelt turns to J. P. Morgan and the bankers for help.
William James' *Pragmatism* published.

1908 Supreme Court upholds state regulation of working hours for women in *Muller* v. *Oregon*.
Roosevelt convenes National Conservation Congress.
William Howard Taft elected president, defeating Bryan and Debs.

1911 Frederick Winslow Taylor's *Principles of Scientific Management*, pioneer work in industrial efficiency.
"Dissolution" of Standard Oil and American Tobacco trusts.

SUGGESTED READINGS

An assessment of progressivism properly begins with Benjamin Parke DeWitt, *The Progressive Movement* (1915), a contemporary account that emphasizes structural reforms. John Chamberlain, *Farewell to Reform: The Rise, Life and Decay of the Progressive Mind in America* (1932), records the New Deal disillusionment with early twentieth-century reform nostrums, and Otis L. Graham, Jr., *An Encore for Reform: The Old Progressives and the New Deal* (1967), explains the opposition of many of the progressives to later and (to them) more drastic reforms. Harold U. Faulkner, *The Quest for Special Justice, 1898–1914* (1931), defines the movement as a liberal response to social problems incident to rapid industrialization and urbanization. Read together, George E. Mowry, *The Era of Theodore Roosevelt, 1900–1912* (1958), and Arthur S. Link, *Woodrow Wilson and the Progressive Era, 1900–1917* (1954), provide an excellent survey of the politics of the Progressive period. Robert H. Wiebe, *Businessmen and Reform* (1962), and Gabriel Kolko, *The Triumph of Conservatism* (1963), make parallel observations concerning the role of businessmen in the progressive enterprise but draw different conclusions. Recent interpretive essays include William L. O'Neill, *The Progressive Years: America Comes of Age* (1975); Lewis L. Gould, ed., *The Progressive Era* (1973); and David M.

Kennedy, ed., *Progressivism: The Critical Issues* (1971).

Local politics continues to attract the attention of historians, and the recent literature on bosses and machines is impressive. Alexander B. Callow, Jr., *The Tweed Ring* (1966) and Seymour J. Mandelbaum, *Boss Tweed's New York* (1965) offer penetrating analyses of machine politics in New York, and so does Theodore J. Lowi, *At the Pleasure of the Mayor: Patronage and Power in New York City, 1898–1958* (1964) for a later period. For Chicago, Harold F. Gosnell, *Machine Politics: Chicago Model* (1935), is still useful but should be supplemented with Lloyd Wendt and Herman Kogan, *Bosses in Lusty Chicago: The Story of Bathhouse John and Hinky Dink* (1943), and Joel A. Tarr, *A Study of Boss Politics: William Lorimer of Chicago* (1971). Other big American cities are analyzed in Zane L. Miller, *Boss Cox's Cincinnati* (1968); Lyle Dorsett, *The Pendergast Machine* (1968); and Walton E. Bean, *Boss Ruef's San Francisco* (1952).

Still the best discussions of muckraking are two older works: Louis Filler, *Crusaders for American Liberalism* (1938), and C. C. Regier, *The Era of the Muckrakers* (1932), which should be supplemented by David M. Chalmers, *The Social and Political Ideas of the Muckrakers* (1964). Peter Lyon, *The Life and Times of S. S. McClure* (1963), and Harold S. Wilson, *McClure's Magazine and the Muckrakers* (1970), provide readable accounts of the career of the pioneer muckraking editor. Arthur Weinberg and Lila Weinberg, eds., *The Muckrakers* (1961), and Harvey Swados, ed., *Years of Conscience: The Muckrakers* (1962), cover a wide range of muckraking reporting. For the autobiographical accounts of two of the leading journalists, see Lincoln Steffens, *The Autobiography of Lincoln Steffens* (1931), and Ida M. Tarbell, *All in the Day's Work* (1939).

There are several good state studies of progressivism—among them George E. Mowry, *The California Progressives* (1951); Robert S. Maxwell, *La Follette and the Rise of Progressivism in Wisconsin* (1956); Herbert Margulies, *The Decline of the Progressive Movement in Wisconsin, 1890–1920* (1968); Ransom E. Noble, *New Jersey Progressivism before Wilson* (1946); Richard M. Abrams, *Conservatism in a Progressive Era: Massachusetts Politics, 1900–1912* (1964); Hoyt L. Warner, *Progressivism in Ohio* (1964); Irwin Yellowitz, *Labor and the Progressive Movement in New York State, 1897–1916* (1965); Robert F. Wesser, *Charles Evans Hughes: Politics and Reform in New York State, 1905–1910* (1967). David Thelen, *Robert La Follette and the Insurgent Spirit* (1976), is a brief biography of an influential Progressive leader.

Biographies of other major political figures in the Progressive era are numerous. For Roosevelt, see the lively but biased Henry Pringle, *Theodore Roosevelt: A Biography* (rev. ed., 1956); also consult the more judicious William H. Harbaugh, *The Life and Times of Theodore Roosevelt* (1961), the brief but perceptive essay by John Morton Blum, *The Republican Roosevelt* (1954), and George E. Mowry, *Theodore Roosevelt and the Progressive Movement* (1946). G. Wallace Chessman, *Theodore Roosevelt and the Politics of Power* (1969) is a short, balanced account. Edmund Morris, *The Rise of Theodore Roosevelt* (1979), is a highly readable account of Roosevelt's pre-presidential years. On Taft, Henry Pringle, *The Life and Times of William Howard Taft* (2 vols., 1939) completes his account of the two Republican presidents; a more useful study is Donald E. Anderson, *William Howard Taft* (1973). Norman Wilensky, *Conservatives in the Progressive Era: The Taft Republicans of 1912* (1965), is a good study of the Republican regulars, and James Holt, *Congressional Insurgents and the Party System, 1909–1916* (1969), covers the careers of leading Insurgents. Biographies of other important figures include Alpheus T. Mason, *Brandeis: A Free Man's Life* (1946); Paolo E. Coletta, *William Jennings Bryan* (3 vols., 1964–69); Lawrence W. Levine, *Defender of the Faith: William Jennings Bryan, The Last Decade* (1965); Dexter Perkins, *Charles Evans Hughes and American Democratic Statesmanship* (1956); Richard Lowitt, *George W. Norris: The Making of a Progressive* (1963); John A. Garraty, *Right-Hand Man: The Life of George W. Perkins* (1960); Richard Leopold, *Elihu Root and the Conservative Tradition* (1954); M. Nelson McGeary, *Gifford Pinchot: Forester-Politician* (1960).

Progressive issues have been exhaustively treated in numerous recent works. James H. Timberlake, *Prohibition and the Progressive Crusade, 1900–1920* (1963), explores connections between progressive politics and moral reform. Jack Holl, *Juvenile Reform in the Progressive Era* (1971), examines a hitherto neglected aspect of progressivism. The progressive concern with eugenics and birth control is described in Donald K. Pickens, *Eugenics and the Progressive Era* (1971); Mark H. Haller, *Eugenics: Hereditarian Attitudes in American Thought* (1963); and David Kennedy, *Birth Control in America: The Career of Margaret Sanger* (1970). C. Roland Marchand, *The American Peace Movement and Social Reform, 1898–1918* (1973), traces the varied fortunes of the progressive advocates of peace. Changing patterns of morality emerge clearly from William L. O'Neill, *Divorce in the Progressive Era* (1967), and crucial developments in progressive education from Lawrence Cremin, *The Transformation of the School: Progressivism in American Education, 1876–1956* (1961). Samuel P. Hays, *Conservation and the Gospel of Efficiency* (1959), provides a revisionist account of the conservation movement, and James Penick, Jr., *Progressive Politics and Conservation: The Ballinger-Pinchot Affair* (1968), effectively recounts an imbroglio. Albro Martin, *Enterprise Denied: Origins of the Decline of American Railroads, 1897–1917* (1971), reverses a number of long-held assumptions about the regulation and management of railroads in the Progressive era. Mary O. Furner, *Advocacy and Objectivity: A Crisis in the Professionalization of American Social Science, 1865–1905* (1975), treats perceptual contradictions inherited by Progressives.

The intellectual climate of Progressivism has been described in several excellent studies. David Noble, *The Paradox of Progressive Thought* (1958), is a stylistically dense but highly rewarding examination of representative progressive intellectuals and professionals. Charles Forcey, *The Crossroads of Liberalism: Croly, Weyl, Lippmann and the Progressive Era, 1900–1925* (1961), offers a lively account of three leading Progressive publicists. Edward Moore, *American Pragmatism* (1950), is useful for understanding the reform outlook of the Progressives. Robert W. Schneider, *Five Novelists of the Progressive Era* (1965), examines the connection between reform and new American fiction. Frederic C. Jaher, *Doubters and Dissenters: Cataclysmic Thought in America, 1885–1918* (1964), traces a persistent theme of apocalypticism in a handful of nay-sayers in the Progressive years. Thomas F. Gossett, *Race: The History of an Idea in America* (1963), and I. A. Newby, *Jim Crow's Defense* (1965), follow the history of another tenacious and socially destructive myth. The best introduction to the writing of Progressive history is Richard Hofstadter, *The Progressive Historians* (1968). R. Jack Wilson, *In Quest of Community: Social Philosophy in the United States, 1860–1920* (1968), and Jean B. Quandt, *From the Small Town to the Great Community* (1970), give accounts of still another central Progressive concept. Samuel J. Konefsky, *The Legacy of Holmes and Brandeis* (1956), examines the instrumentalist heritage. Samuel Haber, *Efficiency and Uplift: Scientific Management in the Progressive Era, 1890–1920* (1964), explains the many uses of Taylorism in reshaping Progressive values. For perceptive discussions of three key intellectuals, see David Riesman, *Thorstein Veblen: A Critical Introduction* (1963); Ralph Barton Perry, *The Thought and Character of William James* (2 vols., 1935); and Sidney Hook, *John Dewey: An Intellectual Portrait* (1939).

Reflections—something illuminating, always entertaining—on the meaning of Progressivism by two active Progressives are collected in William Allen White, *The Autobiography of William Allen White* (1946), and Frederic C. Howe, *The Confessions of a Reformer* (1925).

In 1910 Theodore Roosevelt, after a year's trek through Africa and the capitals of Europe, returned home to a rebellion in his own party. Once he learned of the widening rift between President William Howard Taft's supporters and his own leaderless progressive contingent, Roosevelt moved quickly to return the Republican party to his original vision of a unified national purpose. In a speech in 1910 dedicating a state park in Osawatomie, Kansas, where John Brown had fought with Missouri ruffians a half-century earlier, he gave his program a name—the "New Nationalism." In part, Roosevelt's speech owed its clarity to his recent reading of Herbert Croly's *The Promise of American Life,* a progressive's indictment of American political drift with which the former president fully agreed. But in a broader sense both Croly's lengthy analysis and the call to action at Osawatomie summed up arguments for an organized national society that Roosevelt had formulated years before.

He was not calling for "overcentralization," Roosevelt told his Kansas audience, but for "a spirit of broad and far-reaching nationalism" to guide the American people as a whole. His New Nationalism, which put national needs ahead of sectional interests and private advantage, would bring an end to "the utter confusion that results from local legislatures attempting to treat national issues as local issues." After listing the many unfinished tasks awaiting federal action Roosevelt drove home his point with a comparison that he hoped would still be familiar to the few aging veterans of the Civil War in the crowd. "You could not have won simply as a disorderly mob," the Rough Rider reminded them. "You needed generals; you needed careful administration of the most advanced type. . . . You had to have the administration in Washington good, just as you had to have the administration in the field. . . . So it is in our civil life."

Unfortunately for Roosevelt, administration of the most advanced type was not yet a fact, as the man who was to be his chief rival in the election of 1912 already sensed. Woodrow Wilson, a Southerner and a Democrat, drew on both these traditions in sounding the principal countertheme of progressivism. As

Progressives and the Challenge of Pluralism

TWO VIEWS OF NEW YORK AT THE
OPENING OF THE CENTURY
The New York Stock Exchange
on Wall Street contrasts with
Mulberry Street on the Lower
East Side. *(Library of Congress)*

a former professor of political science and president of Princeton, currently the reform governor of New Jersey, Wilson was fully Roosevelt's match as a historian and intellectual. In examining the American political and social system in 1910 he came closer to understanding the complex play of social forces at work in the country than either of his Republican rivals.

Roosevelt's New Nationalism called for the reordering of American priorities and the acquiring of new habits and duties. The "New Freedom"—as Wilson came to call his vision—offered another view of progressivism as a liberation movement. Wilson pictured an open, complex society, composed of immigrants and women as well as native-born white males, Catholics and Jews as well as Protestants, reformers as well as professional politicians, and vi-

sionaries of all sorts as well as political realists. In the election year of 1912, these broader strokes of Wilson's New Freedom seemed to present a truer picture of the complexity of American life in the early years of the twentieth century than did the views of Roosevelt and the New Nationalists. But it remained to be seen whether the Democratic party, emerging from sixteen years of enforced retirement, could succeed in turning these various energies into a political program.

Changing the Progressive Guard

By 1910 it seemed that reform had slowed. Congress, with a bipartisan faction of conservatives in both houses, was in no mood to finish the work of building a national banking system or designing a program of business regulation. And a watchful conservative Supreme Court stood ready to check any further advances toward the social service state.

Of all the branches of the federal government, the Supreme Court was the least responsive to the problems confronting industrial society and the most alert to the dangers of curtailing corporate privilege. Although it agreed to Roosevelt's breaking up of the Northern Securities trust and the oil and tobacco monopolies, the Court was much less enthusiastic about the new progressive forms of administrative regulation and the use of commissions to make and enforce rulings. The struggle for administrative effectiveness after 1890 often seemed to be waged between a handful of conservative justices clinging tenaciously to the right of judicial review and a clique of frustrated congressional reformers hoping to strengthen the administrative arm of the federal government. To these reformers the Supreme Court's stubborn defense of its prerogatives seemed an act of usurpation, taking away from federal agencies like the Interstate Commerce Commission the power to do their job. Progressives remembered, too, that the Supreme Court had recently declared a federal income tax unconstitutional, and had set severe limits on the powers of the states to enact social legislation.

Justice Holmes and the Court. The spirit of progressivism invaded the Supreme Court with the appointment of Oliver Wendell Holmes. He was chosen by Roosevelt in the hope that he would reeducate his senior colleagues in the uses of judicial restraint and bring a more enlightened view of the regulatory power to the Court. Holmes considered the Constitution, not a yardstick for measuring for shortcomings of imperfect laws, but a flexible instrument for providing for the "felt necessities" of the modern age. The life of the law, he was convinced, was inherent in its utility and function. Those of his colleagues on the bench who still professed a belief in higher law, Holmes dismissed as willing captives of "that naïve state of mind that accepts what has been familiar and accepted by them and their neighbors as something that must be accepted everywhere." As for himself, the outspoken newcomer admitted, "I . . . define truth as the system of my limitations and leave absolute truth for those who are better equipped."

Holmes explained his belief in the necessity of social experimentation in the famous *Lochner* case in 1905, a decision overturning a New York law that reduced the work week for bakers to sixty hours. In a five-to-four decision, the majority of the Court declared that the law was another "meddlesome interference with the rights of individuals" and thus unconstitutional. In his dissent, Holmes lectured his fellow justices on the dangers of intruding their laissez-faire views into the law. The Constitution, he declared, had not been intended "to embody a particular economic theory, whether of paternalism and the organic relation of the citizen to the state or of laissez-faire." Instead it was made for people who frankly differed, and "the accident of our finding certain opinions natural and familiar, or novel and even shocking, ought not to conclude our judgment upon the question whether statutes embodying them conflict with the Constitution of the United States." In a series of similar dissents during the next two decades, Holmes—together with Justice Louis Brandeis, who joined the liberal side of the Court in 1916 —argued for restraint on the judicial activism of a conservative majority concerned with slowing the progressive drift toward a managed society.

Political Conflicts Under Taft.

Congress, frequently divided within itself after 1909, could make little headway against such certainty of conservative purpose. Both the House and the Senate witnessed a

WILLIAM HOWARD TAFT
Taft preferred conservative Republicans to crusading Insurgents. *(Library of Congress)*

series of sharp encounters between aggressively reform-minded Insurgents and standpat conservatives over tariffs, conservation, and governmental reorganization. Without the leadership of the president, who backed the majority of Republican regulars, the reformers lost heart.

Meanwhile Taft's political lethargy and his ineptitude made an inviting target for the barbs of Republican reformers like La Follette. Though he came recommended by Roosevelt as a thorough-going reformer, Taft lacked his predecessor's concern with strengthening the federal government, as well as the former president's skill in managing his party. Ponderous, stubborn, unschooled in the arts of political persuasion and wholly lacking in Roosevelt's popular appeal, Taft quickly made it clear that he was no crusader.

Taft's administration, accordingly, was punctuated by a series of political explosions. The first one was touched off by the Pinchot-Ballinger struggle over conservation policy. Gifford Pinchot, chief of the U.S. Forest Service, "Sir Galahad of the Woods," as his numerous enemies called him, accused Taft's secretary of the interior, Richard Ballinger, of neglecting his duties. More specifically, Pinchot accused him of unsavory conduct in validating the Bering River coal claims that had mysteriously come into the possession of the Morgan-Guggenheim syndicate. Although a congressional investigation cleared Ballinger of any hint of fraud, and though the feisty and self-righteous Pinchot overplayed his hand by appealing to the American public at large, Ballinger felt obliged to resign. Taft, who had supported Ballinger, lost face and with it the loyalty of a sizable group of Roosevelt progressives.

In his handling of the tariff question, Taft only compounded his problems. After promising downward revision of the schedules, he backed away from the ensuing congressional struggle and looked on as the protectionist forces of Aldrich and the Old Guard loaded the original bill with higher schedules. Then, to the amazement of the progressive Insurgents, the president hurried to their midwestern camp, where he proclaimed the now unrecognizable Payne-Aldrich Act the "best tariff ever passed by the Republican party."

Roosevelt: The Bull Moose Candidate. Roosevelt watched Taft's mismanagement of his party with growing disdain. "A lawyer's administration," he snorted, was proving itself "totally unfit" to lead the country. For like-minded progressives who had recently formed the Progressive Republican League, there were two choices. The first was to appeal to Roosevelt to intervene in party councils in their behalf and help them replace Taft with a candidate of their choosing; the second, and more desperate, strategy was to bolt the Republican party altogether and set up an independent reform party. By 1912 Republican progressives remained sharply divided on this question.

As the election year approached, Roosevelt himself was undecided about the best course. On the one hand, he was convinced that under the Taft regime there had been little attention paid to the "needs of the country." On the other, he was dubious of the success of any movement on his own behalf, and confessed to little enthusiasm for "staggering under a load on my shoulders through no fault of my own."

Whether he knew it or not, Roosevelt had practically declared his availability with his "New Nationalism" speech at Osawatomie. The New Nationalism, composed of schemes for the improved regulation of corporations, physical evaluation of railroads, a graduated income tax, a refurbished banking system, labor legislation, the direct primary, and a corrupt practices act, seemed challenging to his progressive followers but nothing less than revolutionary to the Old Guard. Far from closing the breach between the two wings of the Republican party, the New Nationalism speech in effect threw down the gauntlet to Taft and his conservatives.

When Taft refused to step out of Roosevelt's way and Senator Robert La Follette entered a rival bid for the nomination, Roosevelt, who distrusted Taft and heartily disliked La Follette, decided to run. But Taft regulars, with a secure hold on southern "rotten boroughs," put them to good use against their old adversary. Roosevelt's hopes at the convention rested on some 252 contested seats, at least 100 of which he needed in order to win the nomination. With the credentials committee and the whole party apparatus in the hands of the regulars, he succeeded in winning only 14 of them. Consulting hurriedly with his financial backers, George W. Perkins and Frank Munsey, who promised to see him through, Roosevelt agreed to bolt and call his own convention and launch an independent Progressive party.

The loyal ten thousand who gathered in the Chicago Auditorium in August 1912 to hear their leader pronounce himself as fit as a "Bull Moose" and to sing with him the "Battle Hymn of the Republic" comprised a motley collection of mavericks and reformers, nationalists and big businessmen, social workers and intellectuals, all determined to stand with the "Colonel" at Armageddon. Conspicuously absent were most of the original liberal Insurgents, who declined to make a risky investment in third-party politics. Although the vibrant spirit of the old progressivism was evident at Chicago, winning the necessary votes, as Roosevelt and his advisers realized, would prove difficult. As Roosevelt intoned the Eighth Commandment and called down divine judgment on his Republican betrayers, he must have known that a Democratic victory was all but inevitable.

Wilson—The Shining Knight of Progressivism. Yet if fortune was about to shine its face on the Democrats in the election of 1912, it gave no sign. Democrats had their own liabilities, chief among them their titular head and perennial candidate, William Jennings Bryan, who had labored sixteen years to undo the damages of his ill-fated experiment in pietistic politics. In the center ring at the 1912 Democratic convention stood "Champ" Clark, Speaker of the House and veteran southern leader of the party, who had the support of the agrarian wing; William Randolph Hearst, the demagogic publisher and pseudo-reformer; and Woodrow Wilson, the shining knight of New Jersey progressivism. Fresh from a series of legislative encounters that had seen the passage of a direct primary law, railroad regulation, workmen's compensation, and a corrupt practices act, Wilson represented the hopes of urban progressives in the East.

The Democratic convention in Baltimore was every bit as uproarious as the Republican convention. Clark, armed with preconvention pledges, jumped out to an early lead, which he maintained until the Wilson contingent finally caught up. On the forty-sixth ballot, after endless maneuvering and a final

The Election of 1912

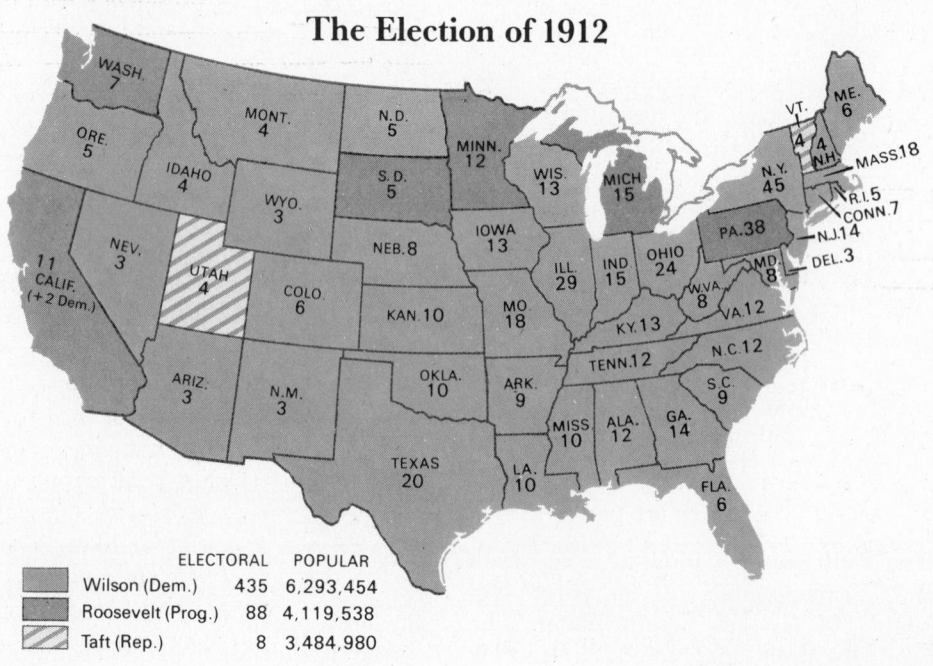

	ELECTORAL	POPULAR
Wilson (Dem.)	435	6,293,454
Roosevelt (Prog.)	88	4,119,538
Taft (Rep.)	8	3,484,980

WOODROW WILSON CAMPAIGNING, 1912
Although his style differed markedly from Theodore Roosevelt's, Wilson was an effective and persuasive speaker. *(Brown Brothers)*

agreement between southern agrarians and northern city bosses, the deadlock was broken and Wilson won the nomination. Before they adjourned, Democrats patched up their differences in a platform that roundly condemned Republican centralization—as Democratic platforms had unfailingly done since Reconstruction—and advertised its own brand of progressivism guaranteed to lower the tariff and break up the trusts, give the banks back to the people, and destroy all special privilege.

But the heart of the Democratic promise in 1912 lay in its candidate's call for liberation from the rule of big business and big government. Taft's official Republicanism, Wilson predicted, would spell continuing business domination, while Roosevelt's plan for monitoring the trusts simply added the powers of the government to those of the monopolists. Wilson pictured Democratic deliverance as "coming out of the stifling cellar into the open" where people could "breathe again and see the free spaces of the heavens." Remove the restrictions on private enterprise, Wilson warned, so that the younger generation would never become "the protégé of benevolent trusts," but

would be free to go about making of their own lives what they wished.

Wilson won the presidency with 6,286,214 popular votes—42 percent—and 435 electoral votes. Even with the split among Republicans, who gave Taft some 3.5 million votes, and Roosevelt's Progressive party, which garnered over 4 million, Wilson's victory was impressive. It remained to be seen whether the new president represented a new kind of leadership.

President Wilson: Schoolmaster to the Nation. If the intellectual sources of Roosevelt's New Nationalism lay in the eighteenth-century world of the Founders, the roots of Woodrow Wilson's New Freedom were firmly planted in nineteenth-century morality. Wilson, who was born in 1856 in Staunton, Virginia, grew up in the heart of the Confederacy, briefly attended Davidson College, and graduated from Princeton in 1879. After a year spent studying the law, for which he had no particular liking, he turned to his real interest, political science and history, studying with the great institutionalist historian Herbert Baxter Adams at the Johns Hopkins University and earning a doctorate there in 1886. Then came several years of climbing the academic ladder, with appointments at Bryn Mawr, Wesleyan, and Princeton, where he taught for twelve years before becoming its president in 1902. Wilson's books, polished though not sparkling works of political science and history, made a varied collection: *Congressional Government* (1885); an extended essay, *The State* (1889); a history of the Civil War Years, *Division and Reunion* (1893); the five volume *History of the American People* (1902); and *Constitutional Government in the United States* (1908).

By temperament as well as training, Wilson was an academician, an educator-scholar who felt a calling to instruct a progressive generation in the science of good government. As schoolmaster to the nation, he looked the part—with a lean, angular face, a long aquiline nose adorned by a pince-nez, full pursed lips, and eyes that seemed to look through his visitors rather than at them. Distant, formal, somewhat austere in his relations with the public, he often appeared correct but cold. He recognized this deep reserve in himself and thought it a weakness. "I have a sense of power in dealing with men collectively," he once confessed, "which I do not feel always in dealing with them singly." There was little familiarity in the man and no feelings of camaraderie. As president of Princeton, governor of New Jersey, and chief executive, Wilson was a man one worked *for* but not *with*. Both as a pedagogue and an administrator, he had a problem not so much in disciplining his followers, at which he excelled with a frosty politeness, as in controlling his own high-voltage temper and his tendency to bristle when challenged. When opposition to his plans mounted, as it did in a serious struggle over the graduate school at Princeton, Wilson would dig in his heels, personalize the conflict, and impute malice to his opponents while avowing the purity of his own motives.

At his best, however, Wilson was a superb leader, directing the work of his subordinates with cool precision, holding their loyalty with ideals, and winning the American public over with his moral authority. On the few occasions when his self-confidence flagged in the face of enemy attack, he could be petty and vindictive. But at all times, he lived the role of the statesman as educator, standing before and slightly above the American people to whom he sought to teach effective government.

Some of the lessons Wilson taught were curiously old-fashioned and abstract—moral precepts rather than practical proposals. For him, words like "liberty," "justice," and "progress" still retained their mid-nineteenth-century clarity, connected as they were in his mind with the Christian principles of "obligation," "service," and "righteousness" that his father had preached from his Presbyterian pulpit. These moral abstractions were the skeletal truths around which Wilson packed such flesh-and-blood meaning as fitted his southern Democratic heritage. His intellectual origins predisposed him to an individualistic and pluralistic view of American politics, one in which John Stuart Mill's definition of liberty as the absence of external restraint ideally held true. A southern upbringing also left him with a generally unenlightened view of race and a quiet respect for the reasoning on social questions that had once upheld the Confederacy.

Wilson sensed clearly that American life in the opening years of the twentieth century remained too amorphous, its forms too complex to be encased in a formula like the New Nationalism. "The life of the nation has grown infinitely varied," he reminded his fellow Democrats in pointing to a flourishing cultural and ethnic diversity. In his view, the most urgent American reform task was releasing the creative impulses of a free people. Nations, he argued with strict Jeffersonian logic, are renewed from the bottom up, from "the great struggling unknown masses of men" at the base of society.

If America discourages the locality, the community, the self-contained town, she will kill the nation. A nation is as rich as her free communities.... The welfare, the very existence of the nation rests at last upon the great mass of the people; its prosperity depends upon the spirit in which they go about their work in the several communities throughout the broad land.

What the nation needed most, Wilson firmly believed, was to listen to the counsel of the working men and women of the country.

Americans—New and Old

Many of the men and women who did the daily work of the nation were recent arrivals from Europe. The decade after 1900 saw the climax of a century-long European exodus in the cresting of a wave of new immigrants from new sources. Until roughly 1890 the great majority of immigrants had come from northern and western Europe. Although these early newcomers had produced fears and problems of cultural identity for native-born Americans, these paled beside those accompanying the so-called "new immigration." In the first place, the very number of new immigrants overwhelmed the nativists. Statistics confirmed their worst fears: in the quarter-century before the First World War, 18 million new arrivals poured down the gangplanks, 80 percent of them from southern and eastern Europe. In the first decade of the century alone some 5.8 million people arrived from Austria-Hungary, Spain, Italy, and Russia.

Another set of figures reinforced the fears of the nativists. In the peak year of 1882, when more than three-quarters of a million immigrants had disembarked at Atlantic ports, a third of their numbers had come from Germany, while Italy sent only 32,000 people and Russia not quite 17,000. The peak year in the progressive era, 1907, reversed this balance: Germany sent only 37,000, while Italy dispatched 285,000 of its citizens; the Austro-Hungarian empire, another 338,000; and Russia together with the Baltic states, still another 250,000 people. For the entire period, the Italians headed the list of European immigrants with 3 million. Next came the Jews, most of them from Russia, numbering about 2 million, followed by a million Poles by 1914. These three main groups, together with Magyars, Greeks, Armenians, Syrians, and Turks, attested to the results of leaving the gates ajar.

A Bewildering Ethnic Variety. Four out of five of the new arrivals settled in industrial cities in the Northeast and the Midwest in areas where jobs could

OLD AND NEW IMMIGRATION, 1871–1920

PASSENGERS WHO MISSED THE MAYFLOWER
Left, immigrants on the steer-age deck. Right, Lewis Hine's "Madonna of Ellis Island."
(Left, Photograph by Byron, The Byron Collection, Museum of the City of New York; right, The Metropolitan Museum of Art, Gift of Clarence McK. Lewis, 1954)

be found. Their collective impact on these cities became clear to progressives when they suddenly realized that 75 percent of the populations of New York, Chicago, Cleveland, and Boston were immigrants or children of immigrants. Like it or not, progressives faced a bewildering ethnic and religious variety in the unmistakable presence of many new people eager to get ahead in their new home.

Economic opportunity magnetized the new immigrants as it had the old, drawing them off worn-out lands and out of the ghettos of European port cities into an American setting of deprivation that at first seemed all too familiar. Once arrived, they started at the bottom of the occupational ladder doing the nation's dirty work—construction, mining, smelting, factory work, and domestic service. They usually settled in tight ethnic communities near their work, finding security in an enforced segregation. This pat-

tern of inner-city concentration fed old-stock American fears even as it removed the "foreigners" from the suburban field of vision. Frequently, too, the newcomers elbowed their predecessors out of their neighborhoods, sending them further out along the city's extremities.

Old-stock Americans tended to assign the new arrivals a national identity that most of them did not yet possess. The vast majority of the "new immigrants" came from provincial cultures that had long been narrowed to the locale, the region or the village. However compact and homogeneous the immigrant enclaves in American cities appeared to outsiders, they were in fact splintered ethnic and religious clusters, each neighborhood boasting its own churches and patron saints, feast days, and civic associations.

Packed into slums, exploited by native-born employers and their own contractors alike, harassed

Italy and the Pan-Hellenic Union, and a variety of social agencies and immigrant aid societies. Edward Corsi, who later became President Herbert Hoover's commissioner of immigration and naturalization, recalled the clotted tenement-house life of New York's East Harlem with "five thousand human beings in one city street, as many as fifteen to a four-room flat; two, three, and even four hundred to a tenement intended for fifty." Twenty-seven nationalities all told, including Chinese laundrymen, Syrian shopkeepers, and gypsy phrenologists. On the East River there were Italians; along Pleasant Avenue, Poles, Austrians and Hungarians; over on the West side, Jewish shopkeepers besieged by Turks and Spaniards. And driving them all before them, the blacks. Old-stock Americans lived in lonely social islands in this sea of immigrants, "like refugees in exile."

Corsi's East Harlem boasted a lusty popular culture—not the imposing façades of opera houses, theaters, and hotels—but Old World pageants in cafés, rathskellers, spaghetti houses, cabarets, and dance halls. "We have Yiddish theaters and Italian marionette shows," Corsi boasted, "not to mention movie and vaudeville houses. Our secondhand book shops are as good as those of Paris. So are our music stores."

by nativist groups and earlier arrivals, fighting among themselves for a foot on the economic ladder, millions of the new immigrants at first lived marginal lives close to the edges of defeat. The going rate for piecework in New York's garment industry was 8¢ an hour. Steel workers in Pittsburgh sweated a sixty-hour week for $12.50. A husband-and-wife team on Tenth Street on the Lower East Side of New York in 1900 could expect $3.75 for every thousand cigars they wrapped. By working fifteen hours a day the two of them could turn out three thousand cigars. Leisure for educational and cultural pursuits was a scarce commodity in America's Little Italys and Little Warsaws.

Slowly these immigrant communities gained a measure of stability. Neighborhoods built lively subcultures through their churches, foreign language newspapers, service organizations like the Sons of

The "New Immigration"—Unassimilable? Mystified and a little frightened by the variety of immigrant life, most progressive Americans took refuge in increasingly irrelevant schemes for "Americanizing" the new arrivals. At dockside, civic aid societies handed out pamphlets printed in English admonishing the newcomers to be "honest and honorable, clean in your person, and decent in your talk"; but these instructions scattered in the swirl of numbers like so many pious hopes. Advocates of immigration restriction agreed with Theodore Roosevelt in deploring the "tangle of squabbling nationalities" as "the one certain way of bringing the nation to ruin," yet the fact remained that hyphenated Americanism—Italian-Americanism, Greek-Americanism, Polish-Americanism—was the only avenue to full citizenship. Even the hopeful immigrant Israel Zangwill, looking ahead to the day of total assimilation, described a

The Lower East Side

The Jewish Immigrant
District of New York City
1910

Galician Jews
(From Southeast Poland)
— ·— Hungarian Jews
- - - Rumanian Jews
—·—·— Levantine Jews
*(From E. Mediterranean
Seacoast)*
——— Russian Jews

dream rather than a reality. The composer-hero of Zangwill's popular play *The Melting Pot* hears the melodies for his "American symphony" in the "seething crucible—God's crucible," where a new amalgam, "the coming superman," is being forged over divine fires. Yet Zangwill told progressive audiences what they wanted to hear, not what they saw around them.

A clearer view of the forces of cultural pluralism came from the more reflective of the immigrants themselves, who exposed the progressive idea of complete Americanization as the myth it really was. "There is no such thing as an American," a Polish priest told the genteel social worker Emily Greene Balch. Poland, he explained, was a nation, but the

United States was simply a country—in the beginning an empty land open to all comers in turn. Immigrants, according to the recently arrived Mary Antin, who later published a vivid account of the immigrant's hardships, were just people who had missed the *Mayflower* and taken the next available boat.

 A growing number of young progressive intellectuals responded with enthusiasm to this concept of cultural diversity and ethnic pluralism. In the excitement of cultural variety they found escape from stifling middle-class gentility. Randolph Bourne, a young radical student of John Dewey's at Columbia University, found a title for this diversity—"Trans-National America"—and hailed the United States as the "intellectual battleground of the world . . . a cosmopolitan federation of national colonies, of foreign cultures, from whom the sting of devastating competition has been removed."

Bourne's concept of America as a world federation in miniature ran headlong into the barrier of ethnic fears. The concept of the "new immigrants" took on a variety of ugly shapes. Immigrants, some said, were dangerously illiterate and culturally deprived; they brought with them either an unenlightened Catholicism or private visions of the destruction of free society; they were doomed to a permanently inferior place in the Darwinian scale of races and could never master the skills democracy demanded. Amateur and professional sociologists consulted the numbers and predicted "race suicide." Sociologist Franklin Giddings announced hopefully if somewhat ambiguously that the "softening" of the traits of "preeminently an energetic, practical people" would continue as Mediterranean instincts insinuated themselves into the American character until the original Baltic and Alpine stock had become transformed into "a more versatile, a more plastic people," at once gentler and more poetic. Gidding's prophecy raised the inevitable question that a progressive reformer put in an article in *Charities:* "Are we not, most of us, fairly well satisfied with the characteristics, mental and physical, of the old American stock? Do we not love American traits as they are?"

The Dillingham Commission, a joint House-Senate inquiry appointed by Theodore Roosevelt in 1907, underscored these progressive anxieties by making an official distinction between the already assimilated "old immigration" and the presumably unassimilable "new immigration." The commission took four years to complete its report, which filled forty-two volumes. Although it collected much useful information on the work patterns and living conditions of immigrants, the Dillingham Commission assumed from the beginning the need to check the flow of new arrivals, if not by means of a literacy test, then through a quota system. When Congress obliged by passing a literacy bill in 1913, Taft vetoed it in deference to Republican employers who still sought cheap labor. But the idea of a quota system survived, and was made into law in a later period. The Dillingham Report marked a reversal in American attitudes toward cultural minorities: by 1910 the hopes of the immigration restrictionists soared as the more tolerant aims of the pluralists flickered and died.

Wholesale Discrimination against Blacks. In the case of black Americans, white fears produced an even harsher reaction. The progressive generation had inherited from the late nineteenth century most of the ingredients of a racist myth, and improved the formula of exclusion with new "scientific" evidence of the biological inferiority of the black race. Not surprisingly, the opening years of the twentieth century saw the nearly total disfranchisement of black voters in the South. The techniques for denying them the vote varied from state to state: poll taxes, grandfather clauses, literacy tests, white primaries—all served effectively throughout the South to bar the great majority of blacks from the polls. Southern liberals and progressives often justified the exclusion with a variant of the argument northern reformers used to exclude the immigrant—that good government required the political removal of the untrained, the inferior, and the unfit.

Most northern liberals continued to regard the black as a peculiarly southern problem, despite mounting evidence to the contrary. But it was South Carolina's racist demagogue Ben Tillman who probed the softest spot in the progressives' plan for political improvement—the lack of moral certainty. "Your slogans of the past—brotherhood of man and father-hood of God—have gone glimmering down the ages," he chortled. A progressive age, lacking the moral absolutes that once guided the abolitionists, readily accepted the racist conclusions presumably proved by its up-to-date science.

In the opening decade of the twentieth century, however, statistics obscured the long-term effects of the Industrial Revolution on southern blacks, most of whom were tied to the land by tenancy and share-cropping. In 1900 there were less than 1 million blacks north of the Mason-Dixon Line, and thirty years later, a full 80 percent of the black community still lived in the South. Nevertheless, the intervening years saw a net gain to northern cities of 1.4 million migrants from the South as the often illusory lure of economic opportunity and personal freedom drew blacks north-ward. Herded into big-city ghettos—New York's black community numbered 70,000 by the turn of the century—they were met with wholesale discrimina-tion. As lynchings in the South slowly declined, their northern counterpart, race riots, increased—in the small Indiana town of Greensburg in 1906; in Spring-field, Illinois, two years later; and in explosive racial tensions in New York, Chicago, Philadelphia, and most of the major industrial cities of the North. Blacks paid a high price for their escape from sharecropping.

Booker T. Washington and W. E. B. Du Bois.   Black American leaders attempted to counter discrimina-tion and economic exploitation with two strategies, neither of them very successful in overcoming white progressive prejudices. The official black spokesman, the "office broker for the race" as admiring white liberals called him, was Booker T. Washington. The son of a slave, Washington learned the gospel of self-help at Hampton Institute in Virginia and put it into practice at Tuskegee, Alabama, where he founded the Normal and Industrial Institute for Negroes. There he trained thousands of young men and women in the industrial and domestic arts. Washington ex-plained his philosophy in a famous address at the Atlanta Exposition in 1895: he urged his black lis-teners to strike their roots in southern soil by "mak-

RURAL VIRGINIAN FAMILY
In 1900 most black American families, like this one, still lived in the rural South.
(Library of Congress)

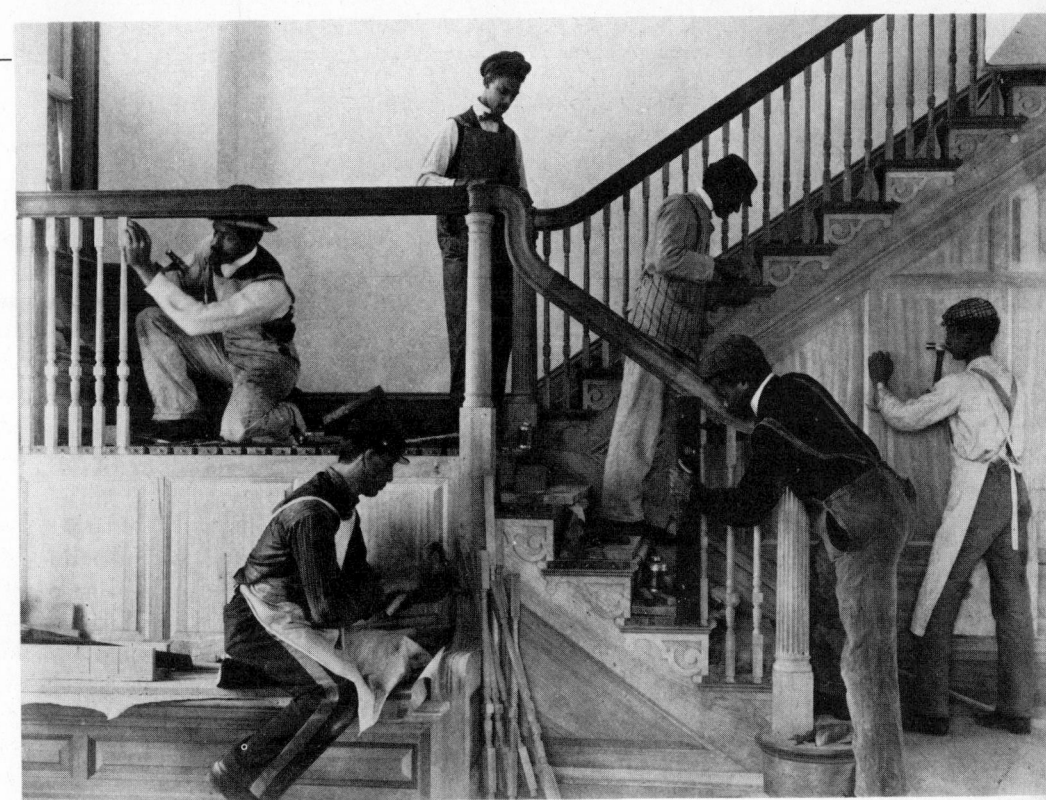

BLACK WORKERS TRAINING
The photographer Frances Benjamin Johnston posed this picture of a carpentry class at Hampton Institute to illustrate the kind of "useful" vocational training for blacks offered at the school.
(Library of Congress)

ing friends in every manly way of the people of all races by whom we are surrounded." To whites he offered the same suggestion, urging them to cast down their buckets among a race "whose habits you know, whose fidelity and love you have tested." Publicly, Washington continued to disclaim the vote for southern blacks, explaining in his autobiography *Up from Slavery* (1901) that "the opportunity to freely exercise such political rights will not come in any large degree through outside or artificial forcing, but will be accorded to the Negro by the Southern white people themselves." Privately and often secretly, however, Washington supported many of those blacks calling for stronger measures.

Most white liberals took Booker T. Washington to their hearts as a "credit to his race," although not all of them approved of Theodore Roosevelt's inviting him to lunch at the White House. Washington became the symbol of the "good Negro" who knew his place and aspired only to keep it—the man of sorrows

who accepted the fact of racial prejudice while rejecting all of its assumptions, and labored patiently to lift his people the few notches a dominant white society allowed. The question Washington's program did not address, however, was the one that muckraker Ray Stannard Baker asked in his pessimistic comment on American race relations, *Following the Color Line* (1908): "Does democracy really include Negroes as well as white men?"

By 1900 black progressive William E. B. Du Bois, together with several northern liberals of both races, had concluded that until blacks gained full political rights, democracy would never be theirs. The northern black leadership in the big cities appealed to a constituency different from Booker T. Washington's, and presented another approach to black advancement. Du Bois, a New Englander and a graduate of Harvard, had followed the typical progressive route to professionalism by studying in Berlin before returning to an academic career at Atlanta University in 1897. Like his counterparts among white liberals, he recognized the pressing need for accurate data on the actual living conditions of blacks, particularly in urban America. To provide some of the evidence, Du Bois pioneered with a sociological study of the Philadelphia blacks, in which he gave a clear picture of life in the ghetto. In *The Souls of Black Folk* (1903) he appealed to latent black solidarity by criticizing Washington's "gospel of work and money." Washington's doctrine, complained Du Bois, "has tended to make the whites, North and South, shift the burden of the Negro problem to the Negro's shoulders and stand aside as critical and rather pessimistic spectators; when in fact the burden belongs to the nation." In place of accommodation and outmoded programs for industrial arts, Du Bois suggested the cultivation of a black intellectual and cultural elite, the "Talented Tenth," and called for immediate plans to mobilize a black political vanguard. In this early and optimistic phase of his career before the First World War, Du Bois developed an unmistakable progressive program aimed at substituting "man-training" for money-making, and at fostering "intelligence, broad sympathy, knowledge of the world" in a new elite.

Although Washington's accommodationist tactics and Du Bois's elitist strategies complemented each other in theory, a bitter rivalry for the limited support available developed between the Tuskegee machine and the Niagara Movement of northern radicals agitating for full political and social equality for blacks. By the time the National Association for the Advancement of Colored People was founded in 1909 through the joint efforts of white neo-abolitionists Mary Ovington and Oswald Garrison Villard and the black followers of Du Bois, neither a moderate nor a militant approach to the "race problem" had succeeded in denting the prejudices of most white Americans. Actively or passively, they continued to support strict segregation and the fiction of "separate but equal."

The Jeffersonian tradition of decentralization and localism worked to the distinct disadvantage of black Americans throughout the progressive period. It perpetuated sectional patterns of discrimination and fostered a national disregard for what was quickly becoming the fundamental challenge of the twentieth century. The progressive compromise with bigotry and prejudice blocked any real hopes for a federal program to give blacks their political rights or to open the door to economic opportunity. Progressivism, for all its liberating idealism, rested on unspoken racist assumptions and condoned discrimination that had changed little since the Civil War.

The Rise of Social Feminism

The arrival of large numbers of American women on the social and industrial scene after 1900 also disrupted nationalist-progressive plans for completing the ordered society. The percentage of working women rose most spectacularly in the first decade of the century. Gainfully employed women between the ages of sixteen and forty-four composed 21 percent of the country's work force in 1910. Their rapid recruitment into industry effectively dismissed the question of their suitability for factory and office work, and raised a series of new issues. Were there certain "natural" occupations for women? Did they have the right to organize? to strike? For a raw industrial society which had yet to fashion *any* labor policy, these questions became increasingly urgent and were raised after 1910 in a militant fashion by a small group of women workers.

Even more difficult for American men in the progressive age was the question of the proper role and acceptable behavior of the "New Woman," the young, educated, unmarried woman in revolt against a smothering gentility and the prospects of perpetual domesticity. At first, feminist protests did not appear to threaten the ideology of progressivism. Some of the most articulate new feminists echoed progressive demands for greater efficiency in managing American society. Radical feminist Charlotte Perkins Gilman, for example, indicted the American home for its shocking waste of human energies. The home, she scoffed, was a case of arrested development. "Among the splendid activities of our age it lingers on, inert and blind, like a clam at a horse race." By reducing

TWO VIEWS OF WORKING WOMEN
The prettified portrait of a New England shoe factory worker recalls a lost 19th century idyll which the poster of the Women's Trade Union League of Chicago lampoons. *(Left, Photograph by Frances Benjamin Johnston, Library of Congress; right, Drawing by Luther D. Bradley, State Historical Society of Wisconsin)*

the wife to a "social idiot" and subjecting the child to the constant care of an ignorant "primeval mother," the home acted as the chief deterrent to progress.

Equally subversive of the progressive program for social order was the feminist theme of liberation that Jane Addams and the legions of settlement-house women sounded in announcing the need for new socially creative outlets. Addams cited not simply the inefficiencies of family arrangements, but the waste of individual lives in enforced domesticity. In her widely read account of social settlements, *Twenty Years at Hull House,* she acknowledged the conditions in urban slums as needing correction, but she stressed the "subjective necessity" for useful work to fill the

empty lives of educated women languishing in the family circle. While admitting the need to expand all aspects of social democracy, Addams was concerned that the feminine personality, denied a full range of experience, would wither and die. Where efficiency-minded reformers like Gilman called for better organization of public resources, Jane Addams and her colleagues emphasized the release of vital creative energies.

Yet viewed as either an efficiency or a liberation movement, the new feminism collected little ideological power. Even in its attempts to improve the lot of working women, the feminist movement did not challenge corporate capitalism or even the profit motive. Its capacity to unsettle an American male order stemmed from a different source. Nineteenth-century women had concentrated for the most part on removing legal barriers to full citizenship—on winning the vote and acquiring the right to hold and bequeath property, and otherwise to stand equal before the law. The new social feminists read Ibsen, Nietzsche, Bergson, and Freud, and absorbed a set of entirely new intellectual arguments for their self-realization. The emphasis on the unconscious and the irrational that swept across the Atlantic at the turn of the century gave women as well as men new standards of social and sexual behavior not yet legitimized in the moral politics of progressivism. It was precisely here that the challenge of feminism was so disquieting.

The revolt began inauspiciously as an uprising of young educated women against the male-imposed definition of female duty as circumscribed by hearth and home. One of the leaders of this feminine revolt, appropriately named Lydia Commander, pointed to the decline of the Victorian ideals of humility, obedience, and self-sacrifice once "assiduously cultivated as the highest womanly virtues." Now, she declared, these qualities had fallen from grace, and the "principle of self-development" reigned supreme. Gone too, feminists agreed, was the old-fashioned notion of female innocence. "What good does it do her?" snapped Charlotte Gilman.

Women's Organizations.   One of the outlets for the growing social concerns of women was the Women's Club movement, which provided a useful if somewhat limited perspective on the problems of industrial society. The General Federation of Women's Clubs grew rapidly from an initial membership of twenty thousand in 1890 to nearly a million twenty years later. The clubs were thoroughly genteel organizations, devoted, at least in the beginning, chiefly to self-culture. At no time did the federation encourage a high degree of political consciousness. Nevertheless, individual branches took up issues like factory inspection and child labor, lobbied for criminal justice reforms, and even experimented with tenement-house improvements. In a variety of "study groups,"

middle-class women discovered an expanding range of problems: the poor quality of municipal services, urban political graft, the need for pure food and drug laws, conservation, and, belatedly, the importance of the vote for women.

Women's clubs popularized rather than initiated reforms. Ultimately their most important contribution lay in their support, however tardy, for women's suffrage. Neither innovative nor consistently liberal, the General Federation of Women's Clubs did, however, succeed in shifting the interests of well-to-do women from the home to national social concerns.

A second and more sharply focused women's organization, which gave a practical point to the humanitarian concerns of the women's clubs, was the National Consumers' League. Modeled on English precedents, the NCL grew out of the early work of the patrician charity organizer Josephine Shaw Lowell, who had taken up the cause of New York City's working girls late in her career. Out of her efforts in the 1890s came a small group of upper-class women who decided to use their buying power to enforce an enlightened labor policy on the city's employers. As the consumer movement spread to other cities, a national league was formed in 1899, with the remarkable administrator, Florence Kelley, to head it. The daughter of an abolitionist congressman, trained at Cornell University and later in Zurich, a socialist, a superb lobbyist, and Illinois's first factory inspector, Florence Kelley brought impressive credentials and skills to her job. Under her firm guidance the National Consumers' League grew rapidly until it numbered sixty local branches in twenty states, all applying the league's White Label to approved products.

The league specialized in protective legislation for women and children, lobbying successfully for the Ten-Hour Law in Oregon and retaining Louis Brandeis to argue its constitutionality before the Supreme Court. The league also joined the campaign for establishing the Children's Bureau within the Department of Labor; and it helped its sister organization, the National Child Labor Committee, to press Congress for a child labor law. Working together in a new spirit of professionalism, the social feminists recruited such dedicated administrators as Frances Perkins and Pauline and Josephine Goldmark, who would carry their crusade against child labor and social abuse into the 1920s. These women reformers, adept in bureaucratic methods but free from the profit motive, were experimenting with an alternative to what feminist Rheta Childe Dorr called the "commercial ideal" of American business.

Settlements. The same distaste for the business world also characterized the settlement house. In contrast to England, where young men from Oxford and Cambridge took the lead in founding settlements in London's East End, women dominated the American wing of the movement from the outset. The settlements themselves stood in the middle of sprawling slums and quickly became focal points for the public activities of their inhabitants. To the busy complex at Hull House, for example, or to New York's Henry Street Settlement, or Boston's South End House, came children of the neighborhood to nurseries and playgrounds, their mothers for classes in hygiene and domestic economy, and, in the evenings, men for lessons in English and discussions of politics.

The impulse behind settlements was religious though not sectarian, and the atmosphere in all of them—Graham Taylor's Chicago Commons, New

LEWIS HINE'S CHILDREN

The pioneer documentary photographer Lewis W. Hine (1874–1940) had acquired a degree in sociology from Columbia when in 1908 he joined the staff of the National Child Labor Committee as investigator-photographer. Hine's primary subjects throughout the progressive years remained children and immigrants whose drab lives and harsh routines he caught with unforgettable clarity. (*Both photos, George Eastman House, Inc.*)

EAST SIDE SETTLEMENT CLASS, CIRCA 1910
A settlement teacher and her pupils. *(Brown Brothers)*

York's University Settlement, Kingsley House in Pittsburgh—was redolent with Christian ethics. Inevitably the earnestness of young college women bent on lifting the tone of immigrant neighborhoods with lectures on Ruskin and displays of reproductions of pre-Raphaelite paintings was met with sneers. Economist and social critic Thorstein Veblen dismissed the settlements as "consistently directed to the incubation, by precept and example, of certain punctilios of upper-class propriety." But it was not long before the settlement-house workers learned to estimate the needs of their neighbors more accurately, and cultural uplift gave way to hard practicality.

The restless energies of the residents combined with their vagueness about political means gave the settlement house all the features of a full-fledged alternative to progressive bureaucracy. Turnover remained high in the settlement houses, which were often mere collecting points for members whose jobs as teachers, social workers, visiting nurses, architects, and planners kept them out in city streets. For both men and women reformers, settlements provided halfway houses between the closed intellectual communities of the college or university and the specialization of a professional career. Settlement houses made possible fluid arrangements of work and leisure based on shared commitments to solving social problems.

Education formed the core of settlement-house work. Initially the educational process was conceived as a one-way street of instruction and learning which would lead immigrants toward citizenship. It was quickly redefined as a mutual learning experience, one that involved genuine exchange and not simply bestowal of education. As Jane Addams explained to an increasingly receptive public, "A settlement is a protest against a restricted view of education." The settlement-house workers' guide was the educational theory of John Dewey, which defined learning as social experience, and suggested ways of unifying settlements and the life of the community.

When the women first founded their settlements, they carefully avoided clashes with the city bosses on the theory that urban politics was hopelessly corrupt and that their own task lay elsewhere. Soon, however, they came to agree with Jane Addams that "to keep aloof from it [politics] must be to lose one opportunity of sharing the life of the community." Still, they found it difficult and often impossible to work with the unsympathetic ward bosses, who distrusted them as do-gooders and rivals for the affections of their clients. Cooperation turned to confrontation over matters of garbage removal, street lighting, police protection, or the location of a neighborhood park. The boldest of the residents opposed the bosses, but the contest was unequal, as Jane Addams learned in trying to unseat Alderman Johnny Powers in Chicago's Nineteenth Ward. She attacked Powers with every argument she could muster and capped her indictment with the charge that although he dispensed free turkeys at Christmastime, he gave notoriously poor service on the other 364 days of the year. But turkeys continued to turn the political trick, and the likes of Johnny Powers generally held onto their fiefdoms.

Struggling to fend off the counterattacks of the politicians, the settlement-house women deliberately turned their institutions into public forums where social and political opinions of every kind could be aired. Chicago Commons, for example, featured a weekly "Free Floor Discussion" billed as "self-conscious democracy," in which a labor leader, a college professor, an anarchist, and a businessman discussed the future of capitalist society. From these discussions the women themselves learned valuable political lessons as the logical thread connecting reform to the vote became too obvious to ignore: women needed the vote to make good on their promise to improve American life. Without the franchise they had little more than moral suasion, while their enemies—the crooked contractors and sweatshop owners—used their votes "to hold in terror" over the politicians. By 1910 mounting frustrations were beginning to lead many of the settlement-house women to join the drive for women's suffrage.

The Suffragists Divided.   The two main groups in the suffrage movement after 1912 were the staid and cautious National American Woman's Suffrage Association, headed by Carrie Chapman Catt, and its more militant offshoot, the National Woman's Party, organized by the formidable Quaker agitator, Alice Paul. Suffragists presented two basically different and even contradictory arguments. The first was well suited to the progressive political temper, and was summed up by Mary Putnam Jacobi, a veteran suffragist and leading woman doctor:

No matter how well born, how intelligent, how highly educated, how virtuous, how refined, the women of today constitute a political class below that of every man, no matter how base born, how stupid, how ignorant, how vicious, how poverty-stricken, how brutal.

The second suffragist argument singled out the special interests and capabilities of women in need of recognition. According to this reasoning, women were uniquely endowed with human qualities and, if franchised, could soften the rigors of industrial society and nurse the American polity back to health. Such was Jane Addams's explanation for the feminine political role: "If women have in any sense been responsible for the gentler side of life which softens and blurs some of its harsher conditions, may not they have a duty to perform in our American cities?" In justifying their claim to the vote, middle-class women could take their choice between a demand for simple justice and the promises of a regenerative creed.

Idealistic or purely practical, the case for women's suffrage was strengthened by the more glaring absurdities of its male opponents. One of them, a worried military officer, warned against the "dilution with the qualities of the cow, of the qualities of the bull upon which the herd's safety must depend."

The suffrage movement gathered momentum at the state level. In 1910 the state of Washington gave the vote to women, and the next year, California succumbed to a high-pressure campaign and also awarded women the vote. In 1912 Arizona, Kansas, and Oregon capitulated as Theodore Roosevelt's Bull Moose party, despite its leader's initial reservation, adopted a plank calling for national suffrage.

In the presidential election of 1912 a more militant strategy emerged, which concentrated on congressional and presidential candidates, few of whom were particularly sympathetic to the suffrage cause. The leader of a small band of radicals working at the national level who began to take direct action was Alice Paul, a grimly determined feminist who had earned a doctorate at the University of Pennsylvania and had spent five years in England studying suffragette Emmeline Pankhurst's disruptive tactics before returning home to try them out for herself. Intense, untiring, a stickler for principle and an able tactician, Alice Paul promptly singled out Woodrow Wilson and the occasion of his inauguration for a giant protest parade, involving five thousand women, which ended in a near riot. Then, applying the idea of the

English suffragettes, she organized an aggressive and highly verbal lobby, which soon became the National Woman's Party, dedicated to direct action. The National American Woman's Suffrage Association, stung by the success of its more militant rival, began to revive under Mrs. Catt's leadership, and a reorganized board of directors redoubled its efforts to reach women at the state and local levels.

By 1917, as the country prepared for war, Wilson's administration faced two groups of political feminists with distinctly different views of the world conflict: a small organization of militants who bitterly protested American participation in the war and demonstrated against "Kaiser Wilson" with marches and hunger strikes; and a much larger group of moderates who supported the war in the belief that peace would bring victory to women as well as to the cause of democracy. In June 1919 Congress rewarded the patience of the moderates by passing the Nineteenth Amendment which gave the vote to all adult Americans regardless of sex. Yet the cause of democracy and reform, American women would learn, was not

Woman Suffrage Before the 19th Amendment

Equal Suffrage (With Date Voted)
Partial Woman Suffrage
No State-Wide Woman Suffrage

SUFFRAGETTE AT WORK
(Brown Brothers)

to be advanced by their sudden invasion of the polls. Women, their arguments to the contrary notwithstanding, did not compose an interest group with special needs and talents, nor did their demands for their share of political responsibility alter the course of progressivism. Proposals for a comprehensive recasting of industrial society and for the complete reordering of American priorities were put forward only by the socialists.

Paradise Lost: Socialism in America

American socialism in the years before the First World War was a lively and varied critique of the capitalist system presented by an inventive but faction-ridden party, drifting steadily away from its nineteenth-century revolutionary moorings. Despite its official collectivist ideology, American socialism in action kept alive a Jeffersonian tradition that defied the bidding of progressive nationalists. In its best days between 1900 and 1914, the socialist movement was a volatile combination of regional groups. Party members included industrial workers in the cities of the Northeast, members of older ethnic groups in the urban enclaves of the upper Midwest, agrarians with memories of Populism in the Plains states, hard-bitten miners and lumber stiffs from the Rocky Mountains and the Pacific Northwest, and a cadre of college-trained intellectuals preaching everything from gradualist Fabianism and Christian Socialism to revolution-for-the-hell-of-it. If socialists never quite lived up to their reputation as the chief American menace to law and order, they nevertheless presented a case against corporate capitalism that progressives found deeply disturbing.

Socialism as a political force dated from the turn of the century. In 1901 disgruntled members of the tiny Socialist Labor party, fed up with the dictatorial ways of its hard-lining Marxist leaders, bolted, and, collecting other splinter groups like Eugene V. Debs's Social Democratic party, formed the Socialist Party of America. The 94,000 votes Debs won in the presidential election of 1900 marked the beginning of a shift among the majority of American socialists toward the moderate center. They also drifted toward

a theory of nonviolent parliamentary socialism, a move that was not always clear to the embattled participants themselves.

The Two Faces of Socialism. American socialism showed two faces. To progressive outsiders it was a menace to their capitalist system. According to the socialists, capitalism was traveling a historically determined route to oblivion, destroying small-scale enterprise, saturating international markets, and establishing spheres of influence and imperialist bastions along the way. Most progressives took comfort in the conviction that class war did not in fact appear likely. Yet to most Americans the very vehemence of socialist prophesying suggested a conspiracy of malcontents and political madmen. The progressives prepared to deal with the enemy in the best way they knew how, by intimidation and suppression.

To socialists themselves, American development seemed a baffling exception to the doctrines of economic determinism. Their list of unanswered questions lengthened as American capitalism continued to display surprising powers of accommodation. Did the immediate goals of shorter hours and improved working conditions strengthen class solidarity, or did they simply adjust workers to a wage system in which they had no power? Could socialists accomplish more through political action—by running candidates of their own—or was such politicking tantamount to betraying the interests of the working class? Was the overthrow of the capitalist order imminent, or would the takeover come only gradually following the education of the workers? The socialists' failure to reach agreement on such matters was seen by most progressives as proof of the absurdity of their ideas but also as a warning to a society willing to tolerate them.

Gradually the center of the Socialist party was occupied by solid and sensible moderates—men like Milwaukee's shrewd tactician, Victor Berger; New York's scarred veteran of innumerable ideological campaigns, Morris Hillquit; and the "Pennsylvania Dutchman," James Hudson Maurer, who hoped for an alliance with the major trade unions. This moderate center hoped to educate the country away from its capitalistic habits with the lessons of evolutionary socialism. The moderates were bitterly attacked by diehard members of the militant Socialist Labor party, and also by their own left wing, which had converted to industrial unionism and direct action. In the years after 1900 the Socialist party, far from solving its theoretical and organizational problems, kept on dividing into camps of pragmatists and doctrinaires, opportunists and "impossibilists."

The "Wobblies". Of all the dissident left-wing socialist groups, the most alarming to progressives was the Industrial Workers of the World (IWW), a faction of militant industrial unionists led by the charismatic "Big Bill" Haywood. The "Wobblies," as they were dubbed by a derisive but apprehensive American public, rejected all forms of political action and recommended strikes and sabotage as the only way to make the world over. The IWW aroused fear and resentment far out of proportion to its membership, which was mostly made up of unskilled and migratory workers. The Wobblies saw their mission as the total destruction of capitalist exploitation and the forming of the new society "within the shell of the old." Progressives shuddered at the prospect.

During their brief and stormy existence, the Wobblies waged a desperate struggle for survival. Although they scored short-lived victories in strikes in the Pennsylvania steel town of McKees Rocks in 1907 and again in the Lawrence, Massachusetts, mills in 1912, they lacked the funds and the organization for sustained membership drives and strikes. Their myth of the "general strike" and the vision of "one big union" served chiefly to rally the spirits of marginal men who dreamed of participatory democracy among the disinherited. At no time did the Wobblies threaten the American capitalist order.

Seen in perspective, the Wobblies represented the last futile attempt of a nineteenth-century producerist mentality to recover an imaginary world without politics, where abundance automatically rewarded the natural cooperation of free men. "Big Bill" Haywood could have been speaking for progressives when he confessed his hopes for the elimination of politics:

I have had a dream that I have in the morning and at night and during the day, that there will be a new society sometime in which there will be no battle between capitalist and wage-earner . . . there will be no political government

... but ... experts will come together for the purpose of discussing the means by which machinery can be made the slave of the people instead of part of the people being made the slave of machinery.

Ironically, it was a progressive majority bent on finding another way of transcending politics with the rule of the experts that clubbed the Wobblies' dream to death.

Moderate socialists were burdened with many of the same liabilities that the radicals faced—a tradition of local autonomy, fierce rivalries for leadership, and a host of competing views on the meaning of history. Somehow Eugene Debs retained the leadership of this splintered party. Tall, angular, with a shambling gait and an easygoing manner, Debs served the party faithfully as a national walking-delegate, captivating hundreds of thousands with homely speeches filled with allusions to America's past. His were the home-grown talents of the moral agitator, his heroes the abolitionists Wendell Phillips and William Lloyd Garrison. A spellbinder with no large fund of useful ideas, Debs was nevertheless an able conciliator and a durable campaigner. In 1904 he won some 400,000 votes for his party, and four years later, duplicated the feat with a whirlwind tour by rail across the country in his "Red Special," giving as many as twenty speeches a day. The big leap in Socialist party totals, however, came in 1912 when voters gave Debs nearly a million votes in his fourth try for the presidency.

Socialism as a Dissenting Party.   The chief socialist contribution to the American pluralist tradition was the example it set of the open society it sought to create. The Socialist party remained a model of pluralism in action—a loosely organized, tactically divided community in general agreement on condemning capitalism but unable to unite on the question of how to replace it. These disagreements crystallized in the lives of young academics, artists, and intellectuals who were drawn to socialism as much by its promise of cultural revolution as by its economic platform. Socialist intellectuals made it clear that they opposed both the moral pieties of progressivism and the bureaucratic collectivism of party centrists. They made their spiritual home in the Intercollegiate Socialist Society (ISS), the brainchild of novelist Upton Sinclair, which was composed primarily of students and their teachers, artists and intellectuals. The membership rolls of the ISS listed some of the most impressive and varied talent in the country, and offered a range of criticism extending from the moderate Fabianism of John Spargo to the proto-communism of Louis Budenz; the civil liberties of Roger Baldwin and Alexander Meiklejohn to the protest fiction of Ernest Poole and Zona Gale; the progressivism of defectors like Walter Lippmann to the pacifism of A. J. Muste and Jessie Wallace Hughan. Connecting these diverse personalities was a strong distaste for the commercial spirit, an abiding fear of privilege, and not much more.

The striking variety of American socialism, its shifting assessment of ends and means, and its inventiveness in tapping the rich reserves of American dissent made it a lively if not ultimately powerful opponent of progressivism. Despite occasional successes at the local level, the Socialist party was never a major political force even before the First World War. Perhaps its greatest days were spent in vocal but isolated opposition to that war and to the destructive mindlessness of superpatriots. Its most effective role, like the role of the Populist party before it, was largely educational. It taught, more by example than design, the uses of a secular, imaginative, permissive society. In doing so it supplied useful correctives for a compulsive progressive order from which Americans might have profited. Its disruption and decline with the coming of the war dealt a major setback to the Jeffersonian tradition which Woodrow Wilson was pledged to preserve.

The New Freedom

Woodrow Wilson, like Theodore Roosevelt before him, believed in a strong presidency. In the course of his scholarly career he had made an extensive examination of American institutions and political leadership. His training at Johns Hopkins had come at a time when political scientists were beginning to turn away from their preoccupation with constitutional questions and definitions of sovereignty but had not yet acquired the economic and sociological skills to examine the way institutions actually function. "My purpose," Wilson announced in one of his books, "is to show . . . our constitutional system as it looks in operation." Yet the workaday reality of American politics was precisely what his analysis always lacked—the linking of larger social forces with political action. Despite repeated promises to "look below the surface" of American institutions, Wilson was at his best in expounding a philosophy of politics that his rival Theodore Roosevelt would have endorsed: "All the country needs is a new and sincere body of thought in politics, coherently, distinctly, and boldly uttered by men who are sure of their ground." Like Roosevelt, Wilson believed that the key to effective democratic government rested in the hands of a powerful and energetic president who offered "the best chance for leadership and mastery."

Wilson's Program. Wilson, then, favored strong executive leadership yet felt a contradictory urge to dismantle federal power and liberate the energies of a free people. These seeming contradictions—strong presidential authority and the reduction of regulatory power—were linked in his mind by the figure of the national leader, like the great English prime minister William Gladstone, who could sense the aspirations of the common people and give them voice as commands to the legislature. But more would be required than sensing the "generous energies" of citizens. The federal government, in particular the executive office, had its uses, as he understood. The real question was whether it could be used to eliminate business coercion, break up clusters of privilege, restore competition, and rescue the little man from the grip of impersonal economic forces. For this work, Wilson needed a man with a better understanding of social and economic forces than he himself possessed.

The chief architect of the New Freedom was Louis Brandeis, the nation's leading progressive lawyer, who had made a career of challenging big business. In the course of this combat, Brandeis had worked out a complete alternative to Roosevelt's New Nationalism. His program rested on the conviction, reached after watching corporate capitalists play loosely with other people's money, that the country

was drifting toward oligarchy. Financial power, he warned, would soon become political despotism through the same process that had made Caesar master of Rome. In referring to the fate of Rome, Brandeis touched a sensitive Democratic nerve in Wilson, who also feared monopoly but had not yet devised an effective method of controlling it.

Brandeis supplied the guiding concepts for Wilson's first administration. The core of Brandeis's program was a dismantling operation that would ensure the survival of regulated business competition by shoring up the small business, breaking up new conglomerates, returning the market to free enterprise, dispersing wealth more widely, and reaching out a helping hand to the workingman.

Out of the collaborative thinking of Wilson and Brandeis came the New Freedom's arraignment of monopoly, and a distinction between acceptable and antisocial business behavior, which recalled Roosevelt's program. Big business, Wilson agreed, was natural and thus inevitable, but trusts were artificial and wholly undesirable. "A trust is an arrangement to get rid of competition, and a big business is a business that has survived competition by conquering in the field of intelligence and economy," the president announced in explaining how it was that he could support big business yet oppose monopoly. Wilson was also sure that Roosevelt's scheme of a regulatory commission to oversee the operations of big business was impractical. "As to the monopolies, which Mr. Roosevelt proposes to legalize and welcome, I know that they are so many cars of juggernaut, and I do not look forward with pleasure to the time when juggernauts are licensed and driven by commissioners of the United States." But could the New Freedom offer a better solution? Was the destruction of monopoly really feasible?

Before Wilson tackled the trusts, he decided to make good on the perennial promise to lower the tariff. Calling Congress into special session and breaking precedent by appearing in person, he called for immediate downward revision. The Underwood Tariff rode through the House quickly, but in the Senate it ran into a barrier erected by Republicans and Democrats representing the sugar and wool interests. Wielding patronage adroitly, Wilson turned aside the attacks of the protectionists. The Underwood Tariff lowered duties an average of 10 percent, placed the manufactured goods of the trusts on the free list, and added a small income tax to compensate for the loss of revenue.

Tariff reform tested Wilson's skills as an honest broker, but banking reform strained them to the limit. Most Americans were primarily interested in obtaining more credit than the eastern banking establishment was currently providing. But there were also vestiges of Andrew Jackson's Bank War in the struggle between big bankers in the East, with their plans for a central banking system under their direct control, and smaller regional bankers, who sought freedom from Wall Street in a decentralized system. Ranged somewhere between these contenders was a third group of progressives in both parties who wanted a genuinely national system under government management that would ensure stability.

Federal Control of Currency.   The Federal Reserve Act (1913) was another compromise between conflicting interest groups with diametrically opposed notions of what the country needed. Establishing twelve districts, each with a member-owned and member-directed Federal Reserve Bank, the act provided a certain degree of decentralization and autonomy. But the creation of a new national currency—Federal Reserve notes—and a supervisory seven-member board in Washington gave the federal government an effective instrument of monetary control.

Big bankers need not have fretted, however. Much depended on the willingness of the Federal Board to interpret its powers generously. The urge to regulate the financial machinery of the nation would not be a very vigorous one for another two decades. The immediate effect of the Federal Reserve Act was to strengthen rather than weaken the control of New York banks by consolidating their partnership with the government. As a stabilizing device for corporate capitalism involving a minimum amount of government interference and direction, the Federal Reserve System worked with reasonable efficiency. As a "democratic" reform designed to parcel out financial power to the people, it was an illusion. The gain for monetary efficiency was immediate, but the demo-

cratic social goals would be postponed for a later generation to achieve.

Wilson's experience with the trusts also ended in compromise. The confusions of a quarter-century's attempted enforcement of the Sherman Act had made clarification essential. The question was how to proceed. What degree of monopolistic control was permissible, and what constituted undue restraint? The Clayton Act, as originally drafted in 1914, had tried to answer this question with a long list of "thou shalt nots." The bill listed unfair trade practices in tedious and confusing detail. Continuing debate, however, and the anguished cries from big business made it increasingly obvious that a complete list of forbidden practices was an impossibility. Yet if it was impossible to specify each and every example of wrong conduct, the only alternative lay in vesting a regulatory commission with the discretionary power to make concrete applications of a very general rule. Here was the course Roosevelt and the New Nationalists had advised all along—regulation rather than proscription and dismantlement.

In reluctantly agreeing to the commission proposal, Wilson endorsed administrative government which he had earlier dismissed. His intentions in securing passage of the supplemental Federal Trade Commission Act in 1914 closely paralleled Roosevelt's aim to create an objective body of dispassionate experts whose judgments would rest on scientifically assembled evidence.

As a regulatory agency empowered to mediate conflicts between public needs and private economic opportunity, the Federal Trade Commission disappointed its progressive champions. During the First World War its functions in checking business concentration were drastically curtailed, and after the war even its fact-finding powers brought down the wrath of big business and of Congress itself. Congressional conservatives demanded an investigation of its methods. The courts, in a series of adverse decisions, stripped the FTC of its power to define unfair practices. Business simply defied it by denying it access to company records and ignoring its rulings. Government by commission in the 1920s provided no cure for a new rash of financial consolidations.

In other areas of national life as well, Wilson's

dream of liberating the energies of "the great struggling unknown masses of men" ended in perplexity and defeat. Not the "people" of his earlier progressive imaginings but highly organized interest groups —exacting, clamorous, selfish—descended on Washington seeking protection and advancement of their affairs. In some cases Wilson's administration proved generous: for newly organized farmers, rural credit facilities; for labor, a federal employees' compensation act; for consumer groups, a National Child Labor Act (promptly declared unconstitutional). But there were limits to Wilson's receptivity to interest-group politics. He disapproved of women's suffrage, and he refused to lift the burden of antitrust suits from the backs of labor organizations. He also tacitly supported the secretary of the interior and the postmaster general in maintaining segregation in their departments, and only reluctantly reversed himself when liberals objected. Not all interests, it was clear, could command the attention of a broker president.

Wilson's Program: More, Not Less, Government.

By 1916, as Americans watched the war in Europe settle into a protracted and bloody stalemate, the Wilson administration had largely completed its progressive program. The president's initial promise of reversal and restoration had not been fulfilled. In each of his major attempts at reform—lowering the tariff, building the Federal Reserve System, controlling the trusts—the president, although he preferred to disperse power, had been driven in exactly the opposite direction. He had created a Tariff Commission to systematize the nation's trade policies, a Federal Reserve Board to manage the monetary affairs of the country, a Federal Trade Commission to police big business.

The meaning of these reforms was unmistakable. *More*, not *less*, government; an increase rather than a decrease in governmental agencies; a greater instead of a lesser reliance on experts and bureaucratic procedures; and a supportive relationship rather than a supervisory one between government and the large organized interest groups it presumably sought to regulate in the name of the people. And presiding over this expanded system of government agencies and bureaus was a president fully as powerful as the most ambitious New Nationalist could have wished.

CHRONOLOGY

1896   Supreme Court in *Plessy* v. *Ferguson* establishes "separate but equal" doctrine whereby separate facilities for blacks and whites are declared constitutional.

1899   National Consumers' League founded.

1901   Socialist party of America organized.
Booker T. Washington's autobiography *Up From Slavery* published.

1902   Oliver Wendell Holmes appointed to Supreme Court by Roosevelt.

1903   W. E. B. Du Bois' *The Souls of Black Folk* published.

1904   Theodore Roosevelt elected president.
Anna Howard Shaw becomes head of National American Woman Suffrage Association.

1905   *Lochner* v. *New York*; Supreme Court declares unconstitutional a state law regulating work hours for bakers.

Niagara Movement formed to agitate for integration and civil rights for blacks.
Industrial Workers of the World (IWW) formed.

1907   Dillingham Commission investigates "new" immigration problem.

1908   William Howard Taft elected president, defeating William Jennings Bryan and Eugene Debs.

1909   Payne-Aldrich Tariff raising rates to protect eastern manufacturers provokes opposition of South and Midwest.
National Association for the Advancement of Colored People (NAACP) founded.

1910   Woodrow Wilson elected New Jersey governor.
Roosevelt's "New Nationalism" speech at Osawatomie, Kansas.
Women enfranchised in state of Washington.

1911   Triangle Shirtwaist Factory fire in New York City's East Side kills 146 women, leading to investigation and revision of state factory code.

1912   Woodrow Wilson elected president, defeating
Republican regular Taft, Progressive "Bull
Moose" Theodore Roosevelt, and Socialist
Eugene Debs.
Lawrence (Massachusetts) Strike against American
Woolen Company led by IWW.
Radical National Women's Party under Alice Paul
formed.

1913   Federal Reserve System created.
Underwood Tariff lowers duties.

1914   Clayton Antitrust Act passed.
First World War begins in Europe.
Federal Trade Commission created to regulate
business practices.

1916   Louis Brandeis appointed to Supreme Court.

1919   Congress passes Nineteenth Amendment giving
vote to women; ratified in following year.

SUGGESTED READINGS

Two good general introductions to the study of immigration and assimilation are Maldwyn A. Jones, *American Immigration* (1960), and Leonard Dinnerstein and David Reimers, *Ethnic Americans: A History of Immigration and Assimilation* (1975). The hostile reactions of native Americans is chronicled in John Higham, *Strangers in the Land: Patterns of American Nativism* (1955), and Barbara Solomon, *Ancestors and Immigrants* (1965). Their conclusions are documented in Stanley Feldstein and Lawrence Costello, eds., *The Ordeal of Assimilation* (1974), and Leonard Dinnerstein and Frederic C. Jaher, eds., *The Aliens: A History of Ethnic Minorities in America* (1970). Oscar Handlin, *The Uprooted* (2d ed., 1973), though challenged on many points by more recent studies, is nevertheless a classic; also see Philip Taylor, *The Distant Magnet* (1971), particularly for the European setting. Milton Gordon, *Assimilation in American Life: The Role of Race, Religion and National Origins* (1964), and Nathan Glazer and Daniel Moynihan, *Beyond the Melting Pot: Negroes, Jews, Italians and Irish of New York City* (1963), correct old American myths of easy assimilation.

The literature on specific minorities is extensive. Among the best collective portraits are Moses Rischin, *The Promised City: New York's Jews, 1870–1914* (1970); Arthur S. Goren, *New York Jews and the Quest for Community: The Kehillah Experiment, 1908–1922* (1970); Irving Howe, *World of Our Fathers: The Journey of the East European Jews to America and the Life They Found and Made* (1976); Humbert Nelli, *The Italians of Chicago, 1880–1920* (1970); Richard Gambino, *Blood of My Blood* (1974); Roger Daniels, *The Politics of Prejudice* (1968); Stanford M. Lyman, *Chinese Americans* (1974); Stephan Thernstrom, *The Other Bostonians: Poverty and Progress in the American Metropolis, 1880–1970* (1973).

August Meier, *Negro Thought in America, 1880–1915* (1963), is the best general assessment of black aspirations and programs during these years. George Fredrickson, *The Black Image in the White Mind, 1817–1914* (1972), contains several enlightening chapters on responses of the whites to the "race problem," and Jack Temple Kirby, *Darkness at the Dawning: Race and Reform in the Progressive South* (1972), gives an accurate estimate of the social price of progressive reform. The story of Harlem is well told in Gilbert Osofsky, *Harlem, The Making of a Ghetto, 1890–1930* (1966). For the Chicago equivalent, see Allan H. Spear, *Black Chicago* (1967). Louis R. Harlan, *Booker T. Washington: The Making of a Black Leader, 1856–1901* (1972), is a definitive account of the early years of that leader, and Elliot M. Rudwick, *W. E. B. DuBois: Propagandist of the Negro Protest* (1969), analyzes the early contributions of a mercurial black progressive. Organizational problems and institutional developments are thoroughly covered in Charles F. Kellogg, *NAACP: A History of the National Association for the Advancement of Colored People, 1909–1920* (1970); Nancy Weiss, *The National Urban League, 1910–1940* (1974); and Joyce Ross, *J. E. Spingarn and the Rise of the NAACP* (1972).

Two readable surveys of women's rights and social feminism are Eleanor Flexner, *Century of Struggle: The Woman's Rights Movement in the United States* (1959) and Lois Banner, *Women in Modern America* (1974). Aileen Kraditor, *The Ideas of the Women's Suffrage Movement, 1890–1920* (1965), is indispensable for understanding the ideology but should be supplemented by Alan P. Grimes, *The Puritan Ethic and Woman Suffrage* (1967). William O'Neill presents an impressive range of individual portraits in *Everyone Was Brave: The Rise and Fall of Feminism in America* (1969). David Morgan, *Suffragists and Democrats: The Politics of Woman Suffrage in America* (1972), thoroughly analyzes political developments. For a useful study of the problem of work, see Robert Smuts, *Women and Work in America* (1959).

American socialism has been fully treated in a number of solid monographs: Ira A. Kipnis, *The American Socialist Movement, 1897–1912* (1952); Howard Quint, *The Forging of American Socialism* (1953); David Shannon, *The Socialist Party of America: A History* (1955); James Weinstein, *The Decline of Socialism in America* (1967); and Daniel Bell, *Marxian Socialism in the United States* (1967). Donald D. Egbert and Stow Persons, eds., *Socialism and American Life* (2 vols., 1952), contains much useful documentary material. John H. M. Laslett, *Labor and the Left: A Study of Socialist and Radical Influences in the American Labor Movement, 1881–1924* (1970), explains a limited socialist impact on American workers. David Hereshoff, *American Disciples of Marx: From the Age of Jackson to the Progressive Era* (1967), covers a range of contributors to American socialism.

A brief but excellent survey of the rest of the radical spectrum is contained in John P. Diggins, *The American Left in the Twentieth Century* (1973). Melvyn Dubofsky, *We Shall Be All: A History of the Industrial Workers of the World* (1969), is a brilliant history of the movement; Paul F. Brissenden, *The IWW: A Study of American Syndicalism* (1919), provides useful documentation in addition, and Patrick Renshaw, *Wobblies: The Story of Syndicalism in the United States* (1967), is also valuable. Joseph R. Conlin, *Big Bill Haywood and the Radical Union Movement* (1969), improves on "Big Bill's" *Autobiography* (1929). Christopher Lasch, *The New Radicalism in America, 1889–1963* (1965), presents a persuasive indictment of cultural radicalism in the Progressive era.

On the intellectual and cultural transformation of American society after 1912 Henry F. May, *The End of American Innocence* (1959), is now standard. Lawrence Veysey, *The Emergence of the American University* (1970), analyzes the institutional growth of American higher education, and Richard Hofstadter and Walter Metzger, *The Development of Academic Freedom in the United States* (1955), recounts the struggle for academic autonomy. Joseph Blau, *Men and Movements in American Philosophy* (1952), covers the contributions of the pragmatists, and Nathan G. Hale, Jr., *Freud and the Americans: The Beginnings of Psychoanalysis*

in America, 1876–1917 (1971), is a detailed discussion of the development of Freudianism in the United States. Literary histories of the Age of Realism are numerous. Still the best discussions of important writers are Alfred Kazin, *On Native Grounds* (1942), and two volumes by Maxwell Geismar, *Rebels and Ancestors: The American Novel, 1890–1915* (1953), and *The Last of the Provincials: The American Novel, 1915–1925.* Jay Martin, *Harvest of Change: American Literature, 1865–1914* (1967), is a generally informative survey with good discussions of Henry James and Henry Adams. Michael Millgate, *American Social Fiction* (1964), traces the rise of a genre. Kenneth S. Lynn, *William Dean Howells: An American Life* (1970), is a sympathetic if critical assessment of a fractured artistic sensibility.

For illuminating discussions of significant contributors to the Progressive reform outlook, see two particularly valuable studies: Daniel M. Fox, *The Discovery of Abundance: Simon Patten and the Transformation of Social Theory* (1967), and Barry D. Karl, *Charles E. Merriam and the Study of Politics* (1974). James Gilbert, *Designing the Industrial State: The Intellectual Pursuit of Collectivism in America, 1880–1940* (1972), is an informative study.

Indispensable for an understanding of Wilson and the New Freedom is the magisterial Arthur S. Link, *Wilson* (5 vols., 1947–65), although the hostile John Blum, *Woodrow Wilson and the Politics of Morality* (1956), and John A. Garraty, *Woodrow Wilson* (1956), offer critical insights unavailable to the sympathetic Link; so does the psychoanalytical portrait, Alexander and Juliette George, *Woodrow Wilson and Colonel House: A Personality Study* (1956). William Diamond, *The Economic Thought of Woodrow Wilson* (1943), examines the shaky theoretical underpinnings of the New Freedom, and Melvin Urofsky, *Big Steel and the Wilson Administration* (1969), canvasses aspects of the Wilsonian labor policy.

Biographies of other important figures during the New Freedom years include Dorothy Rose Blumberg, *Florence Kelley: The Making of a Social Pioneer* (1966); Charles Larsen, *The Good Fight: The Life and Times of Ben Lindsey* (1972); Julius Weinberg, *Edward Alsworth Ross and the Sociology of Progressivism* (1972); Robert C. Bannister, *Ray Stannard Baker: The Mind and Thought of a Progressive* (1966); and H. C. Bailey, *Edgar Gardner Murphy* (1968).

For most of the nineteenth century, Americans managed their affairs with no general foreign policy save that of Washington's determination to avoid entangling alliances. The defeat of Napoleon and the brilliant success of the American peace commissioners in 1815 following a nearly disastrous war with England brought a strong conclusion to an era of diplomatic defeat for the new nation perched precariously on the rim of the Atlantic world and subject to the buffetings of the two major European powers, Britain and France. After 1815 geographical isolation and ideological separation gave the American people an open continental field to explore and exploit without interference. By the middle of the nineteenth century George Washington's prediction of a separate American destiny had seemingly come true. Secure on its own continent, its dominance of the Western Hemisphere guaranteed by British sea power, the United States turned inward to explore its hinterland and develop its resources.

A favorable international climate together with unlimited opportunity at home fostered extravagant versions of an American "Manifest Destiny," which at one time or another pointed to the annexation of Canada, the acquisition of Cuba, and the taking of "all Mexico." Expansionists such as the naval officer and oceanographer Matthew Fontaine Maury, who plotted to colonize Mexico with ex-Confederates, dreamed of the Caribbean as an American lake, or the Mississippi Valley as the center of a vast heartland empire reaching eastward across the Atlantic and westward to China shores. But these flickering dreams of empire, like the extravagant reckonings of farmers, businessmen, and shippers who visualized vast profits to be found in untapped foreign markets, were hopeful predictions rather than policy directives. In spite of sporadic American interest in the fate of republican movements in Europe, Manifest Destiny remained primarily an article for home consumption—exuberant, aggressive, but not really intended for export. The slavery problem also checked the American expansionist appetite after the Mexican War; the debate over the future of slavery in the newly opened territories monopolized national attention and absorbed the nation's political energies.

The Path to Power

American Foreign Policy 1890–1917

By the last quarter of the nineteenth century, however, a series of developments abroad began to draw the United States into the vortex of international power politics. The most important was the sudden imperialist scramble of the major European powers—first Britain, then France, Germany, and Russia—to carve out generous colonies for themselves in Asia and Africa. American diplomats in the field and politicians in Washington watched with growing apprehension as the European powers, following the lead of business investments, rushed for possessions and spheres of influence in the undeveloped regions of the world.

Still, in the course of his inaugural address in 1885, President Grover Cleveland contented himself with only the briefest word on American foreign policy. The genius of American institutions and the real needs of the people, Cleveland explained, required a "scrupulous avoidance of any departure from that foreign policy commended by the history, the traditions, and the prosperity of our Republic." In case his audience might have forgotten that traditional policy, he restated it clearly. "It is the policy of independence, favored by our position. . . . It is the policy of peace suitable to our interests. It is the policy of neutrality, rejecting any share in foreign broils and ambitions upon other continents and repelling their intrusion here."

This traditional passivity was reflected in the dilapidated foreign-policy establishment over which the president presided. A casual and still largely amateur operation, the diplomatic service had no effective fact-gathering apparatus; and although it boasted a handful of able diplomats, it was saddled with a great many nonentities and friends of influential politicians. Most of the useful information trickling back to Washington from European capitals came from cosmopolitan private citizens personally concerned with the shifting scenes of international politics. Until 1890 Europe appeared willing to take this American profession of disinterest at face value and considered the United States a second-class power. The diplomatic corps resident in Washington was not on the whole a distinguished one, and on more than one occasion a European state simply neglected to fill a vacant post in this country that had come to seem superfluous.

Yet at the very moment when Cleveland spoke the platitudes that had passed for a foreign policy throughout the nineteenth century, new forces were beginning to collect around a different set of propositions drawn directly from the study of European imperialist adventures. Lord Bryce, whose perceptive analysis of American government and society, *The American Commonwealth*, appeared in 1888, noted the difference between those who shaped foreign policy in England and their counterparts in the United States. In America, Bryce explained, "there are individual men corresponding to individuals in that English set, and probably quite as numerous." There were a sizable number of journalists of real ability, a handful of literary men, and not a few politicians who understood the mechanisms of international power politics. But these Americans remained isolated and disorganized for the most part, vulnerable constantly to public pressures and mass opinion, as the "first set" in England clearly was not. "In England the profession of opinion-making and leading is the work of specialists; in America . . . of amateurs." By the time Bryce published this observation, however, a small group of like-minded amateurs concerned with foreign affairs was already at work in Washington building the intellectual foundations for a foreign-policy establishment and calling for a more vigorous pursuit of world power.

The Origins of American Expansionism

By 1890 it began to dawn on the small number of Americans concerned with the conduct of foreign policy that the United States was in danger of being left far behind in the race for territory and markets. Looking back on the last decade of the nineteenth century, rabid expansionist Senator Albert J. Beveridge summed up the lessons taught the American people as trustees "under God" of world civilization: "He has made us the master organizers of the world to establish system where chaos reigns." Not all

SENATOR BEVERIDGE'S "TRUSTEES" PACIFYING THE PHILIPPINES
(*Library of Congress*)

Americans in 1900 agreed with Beveridge that destiny had mapped an imperial course for their country, but it had become clear that they could no longer view the international scene with indifference. In some way, it seemed, the United States would have to catch up with its European rivals.

A second force pushing the United States into the imperialist melee—a concern with world markets—was not so easy to analyze. After 1875 American businessmen, bankers, industrialists, and shippers began to call for more ready access to the markets of the world. Their demands were given dramatic point by the erratic development of the domestic market—the repeated depressions and gluts—and doubts as to its capacity to absorb American manufactured goods and staples. But the size of the American market in the undeveloped areas of the globe remained quite small as late as 1900, despite increasingly noisy demands for enlarging it. The state of overseas markets fur-

nished a focus for popular debate around which both expansionists and antiexpansionists, interventionists and isolationists argued the proper role for the United States. No one denied the importance of foreign markets in the American economy and their importance too in spreading the blessings of democracy. But did the search for markets necessarily mean intervention in the domestic affairs of undeveloped and politically unstable countries? Did it require outright annexation? Were markets for the investment of capital fundamentally different from markets for manufactured or staple goods? And, most troublesome of all, how could the spokesmen for new and bigger markets catch and hold the attention of an unresponsive federal government?

Conditions in the United States also helped focus attention on possibilities abroad. The 1890s were years of severe economic disorder, rising class conflict, political instability, and intellectual discord. The cumulative effect of these tensions and struggles was a growing popular belief that the United States had reached maturity as a fully developed modern nation. Whether or not they read the historian Frederick Jackson Turner's famous warning in 1893 of the consequences of the closing of the frontier, many Americans were well aware of the passing of an era in which free land and geographical mobility had been all-important. Viewed as a fact or a symbol of America's vast, seemingly limitless possibilities, the frontier had dominated the American imagination for two centuries. The announcement of its closing reinforced a widely shared sense of irreversible change. For the generation of the 1890s, the extension of the frontier concept into territories overseas quickened the old sense of mission and enterprise, and released pent-up feelings of humanitarianism, as though the answer to a loss of certainty at home was a vigorous pursuit of democratic purpose abroad.

Pacifism or Power?   In these shifting circumstances abroad and at home, a struggle developed for control of an emerging American foreign policy. The contestants played a variety of roles in the quarter-century before American entrance into the First World War. Some were upholders of international law or preachers of pacificism. Others were advocates of national power or defenders of American honor. Yet beneath the diversity lay two conflicting formulations of American power and responsibility.

The first view of the nature of power and of America's future was forcefully summarized by Captain Alfred Thayer Mahan, naval strategist and geopolitical theorist, in his *The Interest of America in Sea Power, Present and Future* (1897). Since governments, Mahan argued, could not be expected to act on any ground except national interest, it followed that patriotism and the will to fight were indispensable attributes.

Not in universal harmony, nor in any fond dream of unbroken peace, rest now the best hopes of the world. . . . Rather in the competition of interests, in that reviving sense of nationality . . . in the jealous determination of each people to provide first for its own . . . are to be heard the assurance that decay has not touched yet the majestic fabric erected by so many centuries of courageous battling.

William Jennings Bryan most effectively expressed the second and opposing view of the American mission in limiting the nation's role to that of moral preceptor. Nations, Bryan insisted, redeem only by force of example. "Example may be likened to the sun, whose genial rays constantly coax the buried seed into life, and clothe the earth, first with verdure, and afterward with ripened grain; while violence is the occasional tempest, which can ruin, but cannot give life."

Until 1900 Mahan's invitation to national greatness took precedence over Bryan's warnings of its eventual costs. Mahan had spent most of his career wandering about the world observing the patterns of European imperial politics. Now his warning to Americans was unequivocal. The United States, he announced, must develop an aggressive expansionist foreign policy based on naval supremacy and undisputed control of the world's sea lanes, a vigorous development of foreign markets, and an energetic cultivation of all the domestic spiritual resources needed to promote the national mission overseas. In a Darwinian world of warring nations, he argued, the United States must organize itself into a spiritual and military garrison ready to defend its interests with power. Mahan did not deny the existence of a universal law of conscience, but he anchored it in the concept of the national state fully apprised of its duty and prepared to perform it. In his view, the "evils of war" paled before the dangers of "moral compliance with wrong." In the last analysis, all depended on the willingness of the American people to take up their appointed tasks as the democratic saviors of civilization. "Whether they will or no, Americans must now begin to look outward."

Architects of Empire.   Mahan's arguments, which won him enthusiastic support in England and Germany, were also warmly received by a small circle of influential Americans whose own examination of the international situation in the 1890s led them to conclude that the United States should take its place among the imperialist powers. "You are head and shoulders above us all," wrote Theodore Roosevelt in promising Mahan to do all he could "toward pressing your ideas into effect." Other important converts to

THE GREAT WHITE FLEET
In 1907 President Roosevelt
dispatched the new American
navy on a world cruise as a
display of American strength.
(Brown Brothers)

the captain's expansionist doctrines joined in: John Hay, soon to become McKinley's secretary of state; the freewheeling romantic reactionaries Brooks and Henry Adams, and their protégé, Senator Henry Cabot Lodge; young, aggressive cosmopolitans like the diplomat Richard Olney and staid conservatives like lawyer Joseph Choate; academic popularizer John Fiske, with his own version of Manifest Destiny; and the social-gospeler Josiah Strong, whose best-selling *Our Country* (1885) argued the Christian evangelist's case for spiritual renewal through expansion. The views of these would-be architects of American empire were expressed with increasing frequency in metropolitan newspapers and liberal journals which called for a more generous appraisal of American capabilities. And when the test of strength came between imperialists and anti-imperialists over a "large policy" for the United States, these spokesmen for expansion would prove to be particularly effective.

In the meantime, American diplomacy continued to heat up. A series of minor crises early in the 1890s served notice of America's intention to take a firmer hand in managing foreign policy by asserting national interest and defending national honor whenever the opportunity arose. In Samoa, threat of a German protectorate brought United States naval forces steaming into the harbor at Apia—in time to be destroyed by a typhoon. In Chile, a barroom brawl in-

volving American sailors ended in an American ultimatum to Valparaiso. And in 1895 a boundary dispute between England and Venezuela—an unstable, improvident state—called forth a declaration of American power in the Western Hemisphere. "Today," Richard Olney, Cleveland's secretary of state, boasted to the startled British, "the United States is practically sovereign on this continent, and its fiat is law upon the subjects to which it confines its interposition . . . its infinite resources combined with its isolated position renders it master of the situation and practically invulnerable against any or all other powers." By 1896 events like these, minor irritations evoking a disproportionate American belligerence, paved the way for a popular crusade on behalf of Cuban independence.

President McKinley's "Wonderful Experience"

In 1895 the Cuban revolution against Spain, which had been smoldering for nearly a quarter of a century, flared once again, and Spain sent fifty thousand soldiers to extinguish it. American sympathies, a mixture of genuine outrage and "jingo" bluster, instinctively went to the underdogs, who were widely credited with the intent to establish a Yankee-style

"THE SPANISH BRUTE ADDS MUTILA-
TION TO MURDER"

The jingoistic tone of the American press during the Spanish-
American War is revealed in
this cartoon.   *(Culver Pictures,
Inc.)*

republic. The Cuban insurrectionists responded to
this encouragement by dispatching a high-powered
lobby to New York City with orders to raise money
and goodwill while keeping William Randolph
Hearst's and Joseph Pulitzer's reporters well supplied
with atrocity stories. Soon the Cuban revolutionaries
in New York began to receive help from unexpected
quarters—from Latin American trading interests, promoters of an isthmian canal, a variety of patriotic
groups, and even trade unions. Carefully orchestrated
"spontaneous" rallies across the country whipped
up enthusiasm for American intervention. Democrats
and Populists vied with their Republican rivals in
denouncing Spain and demanding a declaration in
support of the insurrectionists. It was obvious to the
incoming McKinley administration that the president
would have to move quickly to avoid capture by a
bellicose public mood.

Annexation or "Cuba Libre."   As late as 1896, however, the exact meaning of this public clamor over the
fate of Cuba was not altogether clear. To the small
group advocating the "large policy," intervention
in the island seemed a foregone conclusion. Roosevelt, who admitted to being "a quietly rampant 'Cuba
Libre' man," told Mahan that intervention was inevitable if the United States was to retain its self-
respect. Many expansionists agreed: the Cuban affair
would be a heaven-sent opportunity to annex Hawaii.
As for Cuba itself, no one could predict. Even Roosevelt, though he angrily dismissed "the craven fear
and brutal selfishness of the mere money-getters"
who opposed American intervention, doubted the
wisdom of annexing Cuba "unless the Cubans wished
it." "I don't want it to seem that we are engaged
merely in a land-grabbing war," he explained. Until
war was actually declared, there was little support

for the idea of permanent United States involvement in the island even among the most vocal of the interventionists.

In the fiercely contested presidential election of 1896, the issue of Cuba had given way to domestic problems of free silver and the tariff. It took the renewed campaigns of the Cuban revolutionaries in December 1896, and the murder of their leader, Maceo, to raise the ire of the American public once more. This time the response was different. Instead of planned demonstrations and organized rallies, there were loud outbursts of protest all over the country, genuinely spontaneous meetings in which businessmen joined patriots and humanitarians in demanding an end to Spanish rule. McKinley's administration now had to contend with a powerful popular indignation.

At this point, Spain added fuel to the interventionist fire when her troops on the island began brutally herding Cubans into makeshift camps, where they died by the thousands. Meanwhile, an irresolute government in Madrid continued to agonize over the dwindling number of options left to it. The decaying Spanish monarchy, torn by rival factions of liberals and conservatives, unable to pacify the island but unwilling to give it up, temporized hopelessly. Confusion was nearly as great within the McKinley administration, as the president found himself caught in an intense crossfire between Republican expansionists crying for justice at the point of an American sword, and his conservative business backers fearful of the effects of a war on business recovery. As popular pressure for intervention rose alarmingly, McKinley was also driven to temporize, publicly demanding promises of instant reform from Madrid while desperately reining in the most radical members of his party with promises of his own.

War with Spain. By 1897 the horrors of Spain's reconcentration program in Cuba had forced the president to press for even firmer Spanish concessions. Then a series of incidents brought relations between the two countries to the breaking point. First came the release of an indiscreet letter from Depuy de Lôme, the Spanish minister in Washington, to his government in which he ungenerously—but not inaccurately—described McKinley as "weak" and "a bidder for the admiration of the crowd." Then came the explosion in Havana harbor that destroyed the American battleship *Maine*. There were rumors everywhere that Spain had engineered the explosion—this "gigantic murder" of innocent American sailors, as Senator Lodge put it. At last, the expansionist jingoes had an aroused American public crying for retaliation in the name of justice and democracy.

McKinley's dilemma grew more painful as conflicting reports of Spanish intentions came flooding into Washington, accounts of the ministry's total intransigence on the one hand, and assurances of its willingness to comply with demands for full self-government for Cuba on the other. Given the choice between waiting and taking immediate action, McKinley finally decided to act. Two days after Spain had agreed to his demands for an immediate armistice and an end to reconcentration—while still declining to grant Cuban independence—the president sent a message to Congress requesting authority to intervene and to restore peace in the island. By the time word of Spain's partial compliance reached Washington it was too late. Intervention, McKinley knew, was tantamount to war, and Congress made the decision official on April 19, 1898, by declaring that a state of war existed. Lacking a clearly defined set of goals and the means of achieving them, caught in a domestic political crossfire, McKinley accepted the prospect of what Secretary of State John Hay called "a splended little war" for no particularly compelling reasons of national interest.

In the brief war that followed, the United States made short work of Spain's decrepit navy and demoralized army. Commodore George Dewey's Asiatic squadron quickly demolished the monarchy's Pacific fleet in the battle of Manila Bay, and the Atlantic squadron as easily penned up Admiral Cervera's ships in Santiago and systematically destroyed them. Spanish troops scarcely did any better when they fought the poorly trained, badly equipped, and disorganized American forces. After endless confusion, General William R. Shafter finally succeeded in assembling some eighteen thousand troops for an invasion of Cuba and managed to land his army, complete with press corps, foreign dignitaries, and well-wishers, near Santiago. There Colonel Roosevelt and his Rough Riders, a flamboyant cavalry regiment recruited from the cattle ranges and mining camps of the West, seized the lion's share of the glory of what the colonel called a "bully fight," the capture of San Juan Hill. The battle of Santiago capped the successes of the navy, and American soldiers settled in on the jungle heights above San Juan, where more of them died from disease than in actual combat. A small expeditionary force dispatched to nearby Puerto Rico encountered no real resistance. In August 1898, its meager military resources entirely spent and its morale shattered, Spain gave up and signed the peace protocol.

The Philippines—"Those Darned Islands." The problem of disposing of the remnants of the Spanish empire caught McKinley by surprise. In the case of Cuba, Congress in an unaccountable burst of self-

denial had rushed through the Teller Amendment, declaring the island free and independent and disavowing any American intentions of annexing it. Not for conquest nor for empire had American soldiers fought so bravely, but, as one Republican senator put it, "for humanity's sake . . . to aid a people who have suffered every form of tyranny and who have made a desperate struggle to be free." Within a year these professions of altruism had been cast to the winds.

The new question of the Philippines together with the old problem of Hawaii added to McKinley's worries. "If old Dewey had just sailed away when he smashed the Spanish fleet, what a lot of trouble he would have saved us," the president grumbled, confessing that he "could not have told where those darned islands were within 2,000 miles." But with Spain's collapse the barriers to American empire also began to fall, both within the administration and in the nation at large, as groups once hostile to the idea of acquiring new territory began to have

second thoughts. Business opinion, banking and mercantile interests, church organizations, and even social reformers joined in calling for the retention of
the Philippines, if not as a permanent possession,
at least as a temporary way station on the route to
Asian markets.

When the Senate came to debate the question
of annexation, the opponents of the new imperialism argued strenuously that "political dominion"
was not commercially necessary and that, in any case,
both the Constitution and the Declaration of Independence forbade it. Under the Declaration, Senator
George F. Hoar told his colleagues, "you can not
govern a foreign territory, a foreign people, another
people than your own . . . you can not subjugate
them and govern them against their will, because
you think it is for their good. . . ." But the logic of
expansion ran against the anti-imperialists. If, in order to secure commercial opportunity, the United
States needed political stability in Hawaii and the
Philippines, annexationists argued, then why not

go the whole way and at the same time lift untutored
peoples to the level of democratic self-government?
McKinley spoke the public mood in presenting a
narrow range of choices. It would be "cowardly and
pusillanimous," he insisted, for the United States
"to turn the islands back to Spain, giving them power
again to misrule the natives." Equally "despica-
ble" was the notion of handing them over to England or allowing Japan to take them by default.
"There is only one logical course to pursue," Mc-
Kinley announced:

Spain has shown herself unfit to rule her colonies, and
those [that] have come into our possession as a result of
war, must be held, if we are to fulfill our destinies as a
nation . . . giving them the benefits of a christian civilization which has reached its highest development under
our republican institutions.

The problem of ruling the Philippines admitted
of no such simple solution as McKinley proposed.
Before war with the United States broke out Spain

had finally suppressed an insurrection of Filipino patriots fighting for independence by bribing their leader, General Emilio Aguinaldo, to leave the islands. Admiral Dewey, following his smashing naval victory, brought Aguinaldo back to Manila to help fight the Spanish in exchange for a vague promise of eventual independence. But when it became clear that the United States had no intention of relinquishing control of his country, Aguinaldo and his followers took up arms again, this time against their former allies, and in the course of a savage four-year guerilla war, killed more than four thousand American soldiers before surrendering and swearing allegiance to the American flag.

As the debate over the peace terms intensified, there emerged a small vocal group of "anti-imperialists," as they styled themselves, hastily assembled and ranged along a broad spectrum of opinion. The nucleus of this anti-imperialist opposition was comprised of a group of venerable mid-nineteenth-century liberals whose advanced age and distrust of mass democratic politics constituted their distinguishing mark and their chief liability. Veteran antislavery campaigner Carl Schurz was seventy-one; free trader Edward Atkinson, seventy-three; Republican maverick George F. Hoar, seventy-four; steelmaker Andrew Carnegie, sixty-five. Most of the anti-imperialists were on the margins of their parties and the government, respected but minor figures who held long and honorable records in the cause of dissent against the Gilded Age. As imperial ambition swept up the majority of their countrymen, they found themselves severely handicapped by their self-denial. "Who will embarrass the government by sowing seeds of dissatisfaction among the brave men who stand ready to serve and die, if need be, for their country?" McKinley demanded of a cheering crowd in Omaha in the heartland of America. "Who will darken the counsels of the republic in this hour, requiring the united wisdom of all?" Against such expansionist ardor the anti-imperialists could not prevail. Unskilled in the new arts of mass propaganda, advocating a negative program, often distrustful of the democratic forces supporting the president, they were quickly outmanned and outmaneuvered by the expansionists.

Some anti-imperialist arguments expressed racist doubts about the wisdom of incorporating dark-skinned, unschooled peoples. Others appealed to the Constitution and the spirit of the Founding Fathers in denying Congress the power to govern other people against their wills. With social scientist William Graham Sumner, a loyal few railed against the prostitution of statesmanship to mere party interest. But the core of their case against empire was the charge that in betraying the cherished principles of the Declaration of Independence, their country had abandoned the moral law. Charles Eliot Norton, professor of the arts at Harvard, framed the indictment most eloquently:

We believe that America had something better to offer to mankind than those aims she is now pursuing, and we mourn her desertion of her ideals which were not selfish nor limited in their application, but which are of universal worth and validity. She has lost her unique position as a potential leader in the program of civilization, and has taken up her place simply as one of the grasping and selfish nations of the present day.

A few of the older anti-imperialists looked back to a less complex world of a half-century earlier, when the United States, as one traditionalist put it, was "provincial, dominated by the New England idea." These patriarchs, however, were joined by younger pragmatic critics of imperialism, like William James, who deftly probed the false "realism" of the expansionists and dissected their specious arguments. As the bloody and inconclusive pacification campaign in the Philippines dragged on and the freedom fighter Emilio Aguinaldo gave American troops a lesson in jungle warfare, James centered his own attack on the American penchant for substituting "bald and hollow abstractions" for the "intensely living and concrete situation." An unchecked appetite for power, he scoffed, had caused the country to "puke up its ancient soul . . . in five minutes without a wink of squeamishness."

Could there be a more damning indictment of that whole bloated idol termed "modern civilization" than this amounts to? Civilization is, then, the big, hollow, resounding, corrupting, sophisticating, confusing torrent of mere brutal momentum and irrationality that brings forth fruits like this?

Until the Philippine insurrection revealed the shallowness of American professions of benevolence, the opponents of expansion made very little headway against the winds of imperial destiny. McKinley, after wrestling with his conscience, announced that "without any desire or design on our part," the war had brought new duties to "a great nation." Accordingly, he instructed his peace commissioners to stand firm against any and all Spanish protests over the dismantling of her empire. By the terms of the peace treaty signed late in 1898, Spain agreed to dismemberment, relinquishing Cuba, the Philippines, Puerto Rico, and Guam.

Colonial Fruits of War. In the Senate the treaty was taken in hand by the Republican faithfuls—Lodge, Spooner, Nelson, and Beveridge—who were aided in their work by Bryan's odd notion that the course of empire could only be determined in the presidential election of 1900. The majority of senators agreed with Beveridge in striking a balance between the immediate material rewards of expansion and long-term spiritual gains. "It is God's great purpose," Beveridge declared, "made manifest in the instincts of the race whose present phase is our personal profit, but whose far-off end is the redemption of the world and the Christianization of mankind." Despite the warnings of the anti-imperialists that the nation was descending from the "ancient path" of republican rectitude into the "cesspool" of imperialism, the Senate voted 57 to 27 to accept the treaty. Hawaii became an incorporated territory under the Organic Act of 1900. Guam was acquired as a naval station administered by the Navy Department. And Puerto Rico, under the Foraker Act (1900) was attached as unincorporated territory with an elective legislature and a governor appointed by the president.

With the gathering of the colonial fruits of war with Spain and the arrival of Theodore Roosevelt in the White House, the initiative in formulating foreign policy fell to the activists who agreed with the president that the aggressive pursuit of national interest afforded the only sound base for a democratic foreign policy. "If we stand idly by," Roosevelt warned as the century opened, "if we seek merely swollen, slothful ease and ignoble peace, if we shrink from the hard

FOR PRESIDENT!

ROOSEVELT THE MILITARIST
A cartoonist for the Atlanta *Constitution* caricatured Roosevelt's militarism and chauvinism in the campaign of 1904.

contests where men must win at hazard of their lives and the risk of all they hold dear, then the bolder and stronger people will pass us by. . . . Let us therefore boldly face the life of strife." Strife marked and often marred Roosevelt's conduct of foreign policy from first to last—in Cuba and Panama and throughout Latin America, and in American dealings with China and Japan. National interest in the Roosevelt years came to mean national egotism.

In Cuba the occupation by American forces continued as the United States launched a program of administrative and public health reforms that culminated in a successful campaign against yellow fever. The Platt Amendment in 1901 drew even tighter the "ties of singular intimacy" between the

United States and the island by providing for American intervention in case an unstable new government failed to protect life, liberty, and property. With the help of some heavy pressure on the Cuban leadership, this provision was written into the constitution of the new republic in 1901 and incorporated into the treaty between Cuba and the United States two years later. By 1903 the United States, in spite of earlier disavowals, had established a virtual protectorate on the island and reserved to itself the right to intervene in the internal affairs of its neighbor, a privilege it would invoke with regularity in the next half-century.

In the Philippines the establishment of American control awaited the outcome of Aguinaldo's insurrection, which dragged on until March 1901, when the native leader was captured and his scattered forces surrendered. Under the terms of the Philippine Organic Act of 1902, the United States provided for a bicameral legislature and a governor with broad executive powers appointed by the president. Although there would be a gradual loosening of the governmental reins in the Philippines for the next three

decades, full independence would not be achieved until 1946.

The turn of the century marked the final achievements of American expansion. Within a decade the dreams of a handful of "large policy" advocates had become a reality. The United States, without actually willing it, had acquired an imperial base for commercial and ideological expansion throughout the world.

Open and Closed Doors: Progressive Foreign Policy under Roosevelt and Taft

If a "splendid little war" had suddenly thrust the United States into the ranks of the world's big powers, its aftermath taught corrective lessons on the limits of American influence. The United States proved a slow and often stubborn pupil in the school of international power politics, and as late as 1914, when war broke out in Europe, it still had much to

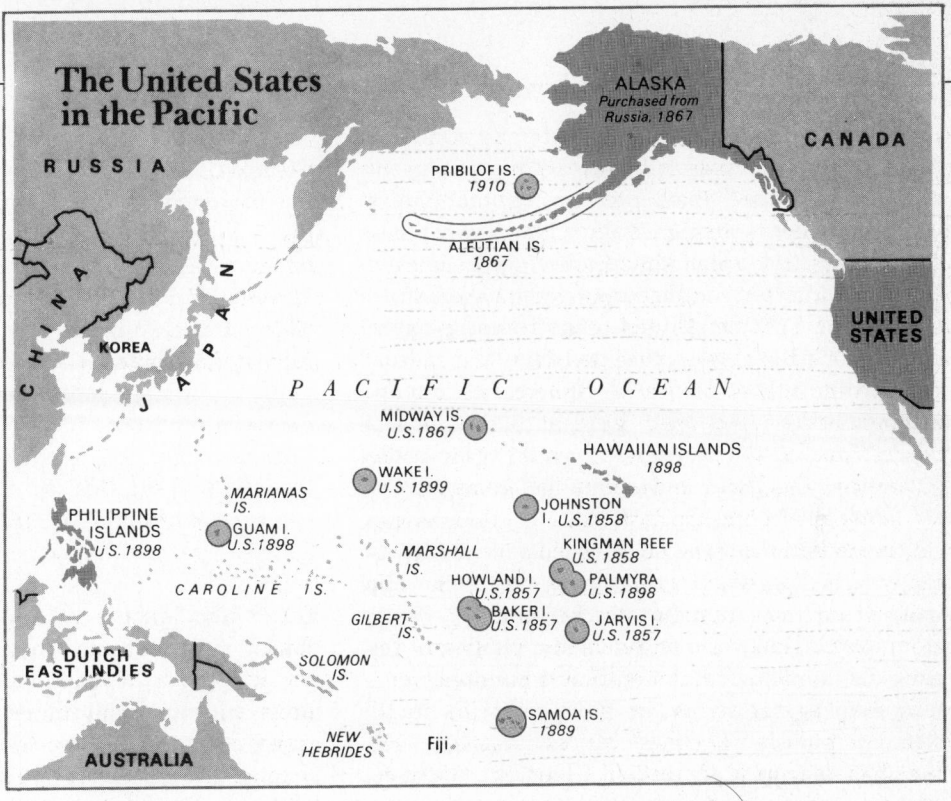

The United States in the Pacific

RUSSIA

ALASKA
Purchased from
Russia, 1867

CANADA

CHINA

JAPAN

KOREA

PRIBILOF IS.
1910

ALEUTIAN IS.
1867

UNITED
STATES

P A C I F I C   O C E A N

MIDWAY IS.
U.S.1867

HAWAIIAN ISLANDS
1898

MARIANAS
IS.

WAKE I.
U.S.1899

JOHNSTON
I. U.S.1858

PHILIPPINE
ISLANDS
U.S.1898

GUAM I.
U.S.1898

KINGMAN REEF
U.S.1858

MARSHALL
IS.

HOWLAND I.
U.S.1857

PALMYRA
U.S.1898

C A R O L I N E   I S.

GILBERT
IS.

BAKER I.
U.S.1857

JARVIS I.
U.S.1857

DUTCH
EAST INDIES

SOLOMON
IS.

NEW
HEBRIDES

Fiji

SAMOA IS.
1889

AUSTRALIA

learn about world affairs and the proper role of a democracy in managing them.

An "Open Door" in China. American education in the limits of power began in China at the turn of the century. The dream of a China market, rich and limitless, was older than the nation itself; it had been a prime motive for original explorations and for the search for the fabled Northwest Passage. After the Revolution the dream became a reality as the new nation began to open markets in the Far East to compensate for the loss of old ones. Success in these distant markets in the subsequent age of clipper ships continued to feed American hopes for gaining untold riches in the Orient. Still, by the end of the century less than 2 percent of the foreign trade of the United States involved China, and it was with expectations of increasing this slim total that commercial and banking interests, concession hunters, and investment seekers nervously watched European in-

fluence mount in the Far East. The fatal weakness of the Manchu dynasty had become apparent in China's disastrous war with Japan in 1894–95. By 1900 Germany, France, Russia, and Japan had secured generous "spheres of influence" in China together with exclusive economic "concessions" to develop these areas through long-term leases and special trading privileges. If the United States intended to establish its own foothold on the Chinese mainland, it would have to move quickly.

Once again, as in the case of the Monroe Doctrine seventy-five years earlier, American and British interests coincided on the point of equal trading rights and market opportunity for all nations. And once again the British Foreign Office proposed a joint statement, only to be told by the McKinley administration that the United States preferred to make its own unilateral pronouncement. The result of this decision was a series of notes dispatched to the European capitals and Tokyo by Secretary of State John

Hay. The Open Door note embodied three principles. Nations with spheres of influence in China: (1) promised to respect the "vested interests" of other nations within their own spheres; (2) agreed to allow Chinese customs officials to continue to collect duties in every sphere of interest "no matter to what nationality it may belong"; (3) pledged not to discriminate against competitor nations in levying port dues and railroad rates within their respective spheres of interest. Though he received what were at best equivocal replies from all the recipients, Secretary Hay boldly announced the "final and definitive" acceptance of the principles of the Open Door.

Hay's optimism was soon tested severely by the Boxer Rebellion, a series of militant antiforeign riots that cut off the international community in Peking from the outside world and invited a retaliatory rescue expedition (including twenty-five hundred American soldiers fresh from the Philippines) to lift the siege and punish the Chinese nationalists. Once again the road lay open to further Chinese concessions leading to the dismantlement of the empire. Now Hay was forced to write a second circular note, this one announcing simply that the United States intended to maintain the territorial integrity of the Chinese empire. Here was a sharp departure in American diplomacy—not simply a commitment to preserving equal economic opportunity on the mainland, but a pledge to uphold the sovereignty of China.

The Open Door, it was clear, would control imperialistic ambitions exactly to the extent that Britain and the United States wanted. Events soon disillusioned American policy-makers. The Chinese empire lay in shambles, its days numbered before revolution toppled the dynasty in 1911. England, accepting the inevitable, hastened to make overtures to Japan, acknowledging that country's predominant interests on the mainland. Meanwhile the rivalry between Russia and Japan over mining and railroad concessions in Manchuria led to the outbreak of war. Japan, in a series of smashing victories, played to perfection the role of "underdog" so appealing to Americans, and forced Russia to accept the mediational offices of President Roosevelt, who suddenly appeared in the unfamiliar guise of peacemaker.

The Portsmouth Treaty.   Although the Portsmouth Treaty (1905), which Roosevelt forced on an unhappy but thoroughly beaten Russia, established Japan as the dominant power in the Far East, the principles of the Open Door were not advanced. In a secret agreement in 1907, Russia and Japan agreed to divide Manchuria, Mongolia, and Korea into spheres of influence with "special interests." Roosevelt reluctantly recognized Japan's special interests in Manchuria in the Root-Takahira Agreement (1908), thus presiding over the ceremonial closing of the Open Door. Admitting that the Open Door principle was "an excellent thing" so far as it could be upheld by general diplomatic agreement, Roosevelt nevertheless confessed that the policy simply disappeared once a nation like Japan chose to disregard it. In this sense, the Open Door ended in failure.

Intervention in North Africa.   In the Moroccan crisis of 1905–6 Roosevelt managed to salvage at least some aspects of an Open Door policy while improving on his record as peacemaker. The crisis grew out of conflicting French and German interests in North Africa, a clash in which the United States, according to Roosevelt's secretary of state, Elihu Root, was not justified in taking "a leading part." Nevertheless, Roosevelt broke a tradition of nonintervention by actively directing the Algeciras Conference (1906). The settlement, as he intended, checked German penetration in North Africa momentarily, united France and England in solid opposition to the Kaiser, and reaffirmed for the United States the principles of the Open Door. Roosevelt, who already distrusted German military power, boasted of having stood the Kaiser on his head "with great decision." Yet imperial Germany soon righted itself, and it was clear that Roosevelt's departure from a century-long tradition of nonentanglement in European affairs was not soon to be repeated.

Intervention in the Caribbean.   No such doubts about the American role of policeman inhibited progressive foreign policy in the Caribbean. Here economic interests and preponderant power combined in a shortsighted policy of constant intervention that

Detail from "Stag at Starkey's" by George W. Bellows. The Cleveland Museum of Art, Hinman B. Hurlbut Collection

The great Chicago architect, Louis Sullivan, summed up the meaning of the twentieth-century city for a progressive generation of Americans when he defined it as a scene of "strife" —at once an "arena" for contending social energies and the center of a new democratic culture. For Sullivan a "culture of democracy" meant a "culture of action." His tall office buildings, as he called them, embodied the "mobile equilibrium" that symbolized for him the fusion of individual genius and the massed energies of a whole people. The architect, he explained, "causes the building by acting on the body social" following a design "struck out at a single blow." As for the building, "the force and power of altitude must be in it, the glory and pride of exaltation must be in it. It must be every inch a proud and soaring thing, rising in

Art as Urban Experience

sheer exaltation that from bottom to top it is a unit without a single dissenting line." Sullivan's own buildings with their sharp verticality, contrasting piers and planes, hard-edged mouldings and exuberant ornamentation represented the encased energy and power of "becoming" which their creator identified with the democratic spirit and the city.

American artists in the opening years of the century shared Sullivan's vision of the city as the focus of national life and the center of a new culture. For Robert Henri and his "black gang" of realists who gloried in the name of the Ashcan School, New York City served as a backdrop for an exciting procession of urban scenes and types which they recorded in the documentary style they had perfected as newspaper illustrators—swirling crowds on gusty street corners, slum kids swimming in the East River, working girls drying their hair on a sunny tenement roof, ragamuffins gaily dancing the two-step on a crowded pavement—all the "drab, happy, sad, and human" moments in the life of the metropolis. Henri's student, John Sloan, took West Fourteenth Street for his reporter's beat and painted the energy he discovered in ordinary people and familiar neighborhood scenes. George Bellows extended the idea of energy from subject to slashing technique in his famous *Stag at Sharkey's* with its two faceless fighters straining against each other. "Who cares what a prize fighter looks like," Bellows exclaimed. "It's his muscles that count."

"Cliff Dwellers," by George W. Bellows, Los Angeles County Museum of Art

"Election Night in Herald Square" by John Sloan. Memorial Art Gallery of the University of Rochester, R. T. Miller Fund

"Steaming Streets" by George W. Bellows. Santa Barbara Museum of Art

The New York Eight were boisterously democratic and proletarian in sympathy. "A child of the slums will make a better painting than a drawing room lady gone over by a beauty shop," insisted George Luks, the most colorful and obstreperous of the Eight. In the city's "incredible panorama" of clattering els and gigantic excavations, towering skyscrapers and shabby tenements, vaudeville houses and open-air markets, the Eight discovered an infinitely renewable America. "What a mistake we have made in life seeking for the finished product," Henri scoffed. "A thing that is finished is dead." To the Ashcan School, as to Louis Sullivan, the city promised a democratic immortality.

Another group of younger and more adventurous American artists fresh from encounters with European postimpressionism, who exhibited at Alfred Stieglitz's Photo-Secession Gallery at 291 Fifth Avenue, also responded to the clashing energies of the city which they caught and fixed in abstract patterns and bold colors. Like the Ashcan School, the new abstract painters sought vitality in

"Hammerstein's Roof Garden" by William J. Glackens. Whitney Museum of American Art

"Hester Street" by George Luks. The Brooklyn Museum, Dick S. Ramsay Fund

"Rush Hour, New York" by Max Weber. National Gallery of Art, Washington, D. C., Gift of the Avalon Foundation

their work in the conviction, as Stieglitz put it, that "it is the spirit of the thing that is important. If the spirit is alive, that is enough for me." But John Marin, Georgia O'Keeffe, Marsden Hartley, Max Weber, Arthur Dove and the other modernists gathered at 291 to celebrate, not the Eight's triumph of life over art, but the liberating forces of the aesthetic experience itself. The modernists, unlike the Ashcan School, were defiantly *avant garde*, and the freedom they sought was freedom from the conventions of pictorial art and the chance to experiment with new forms with which to record a kaleidoscopic urban world. "I see great forces at work, great movements," John Marin declared, "the large buildings and the small buildings, the warring of the great and the small. . . . While these powers are at work . . . I can hear the sound of their strife, and there is a great music being played."

The modernists, in the spirit of the progressives who often failed to understand them, approached their art as a process of experimentation and research, one demanding innovative technique and bold improvisation. "There was life in all these new things," Marsden Hartley explained in recalling the years before the First World War. "There was excitement, there was healthy revolt, investigation, discovery, and an utterly new world out of it all." Art, as the modernists conceived it, was what the instrumentalist John Dewey called "a process of doing or making," a confrontation with partially disorganized nature with its "breaks and reunions" that plunged the viewer into "the ongoing world around him." The young abstract painters were struck with the action, clash, and tension of city life which they captured in new dynamic patterns quite unlike the static forms of such European cubists as Georges Braque and Juan Gris. The futurist

"Lower Manhattan" by John Marin. Collection, The Museum of Modern Art, New York, Lillie P. Bliss Bequest

"Battle of Lights, Coney Island" by Joseph Stella. Yale University Art Gallery, Gift of the Collection of the Society Anonyme

Joseph Stella found the most powerful image of conflicting urban forms in the Brooklyn Bridge, with its "massive dark towers dominating the surrounding tumult of surging skyscrapers . . . the eloquent meeting point of all the forces arising in a superb assertion of their powers, an apotheosis." His *Coney Island*, an arrangement of splinters of light, Stella entitled *Battle of Lights*. Georgia O'Keeffe confessed to a fascination with New York's skyscrapers and determined to make her flowers "big like the huge buildings going up. People will be startled and look."

With the arrival of the twentieth century, the city came to dominate the imagination of artists and architects who continued to seek in it the source of a vital American art.

"Black Spot No. 2" by Georgia O'Keeffe. Private Collection

would leave a legacy of ill will and distrust. In Latin America interference in the internal affairs of unstable governments quickly became a pattern. Behind this pattern lay rapidly expanding American economic interests, not just in trade, but in banking, investments, and the development of natural resources, all of which seemingly required a favorable political climate and the willingness of Caribbean governments to grant generous concessions to the United States.

Trouble began in that "infernal little Cuban republic," as Roosevelt called it, in admitting to a recurrent urge to "wipe its people off the face of the earth." Four years after the removal of American forces in 1902, the troops were back again for another attempt at restoring order. A policeman's lot, the president agreed, was not a happy one. "All that we wanted from them was that they would behave

themselves and be prosperous and happy so that we would not have to interfere." Instead, the Cubans persisted in playing at revolution and "may get things into such a snarl that we have no alternative save to intervene—which will at once convince the suspicious idiots in South America that we do wish to interfere after all, and perhaps have some land hunger." The president neglected to add that it was not land hunger but the drive to establish economic dominance in Latin America that dictated his interventionist strategy.

A habit of constantly intervening in the domestic affairs of neighbors to the south required an explanation, and Roosevelt provided this in the famous "corollary" to the Monroe Doctrine in his annual message to Congress in 1905. The occasion once again, as in Cleveland's administration ten years earlier, was a fiscal crisis in Venezuela, where a chronically un-

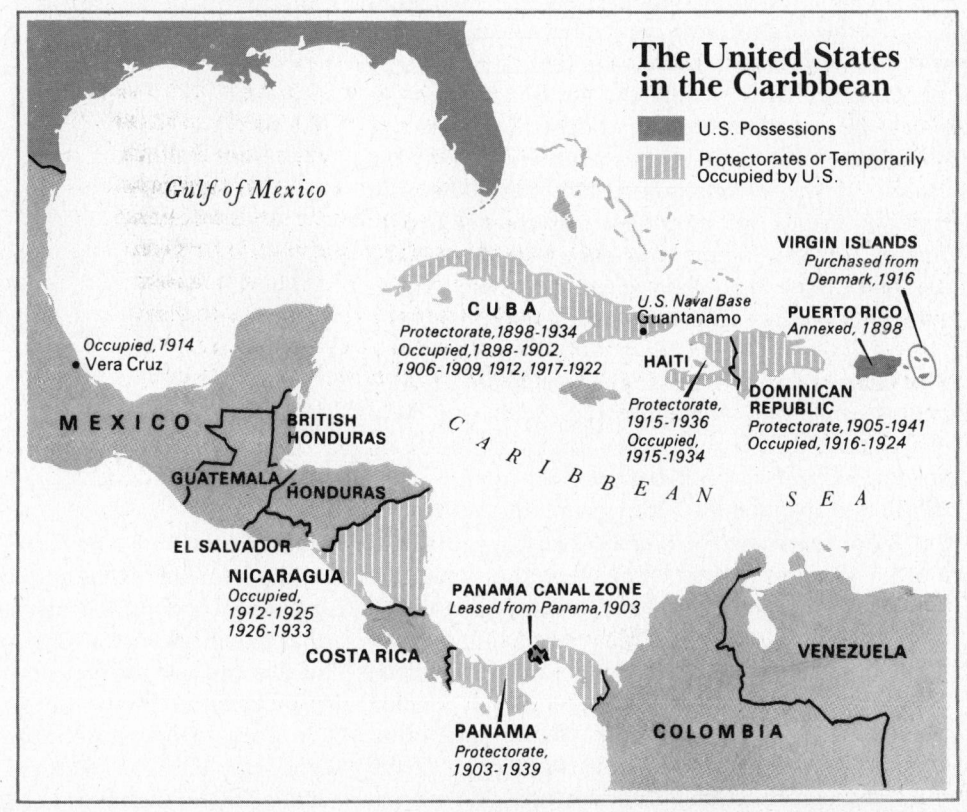

stable and corrupt dictatorship refused to honor its debts. In 1903 Germany tried to nudge the Venezuelan government toward a more conciliatory stance by bombarding Fort San Carlos, and was dissuaded from taking further measures only by prompt American condemnation of the "outrage." To forestall similar European moves to protect investments, Roosevelt offered his corollary. "Chronic wrongdoing," he admitted, would inevitably invite retaliation from "civilized" nations determined to protect their investments in Latin America. Since the Monroe Doctrine effectively prevented European powers from intervening directly, the United States, "however reluctantly," might be forced to step in "in flagrant cases of such wrongdoing or impotence." In short, Latin America properly belonged within the sphere of influence of the United States, which would undertake the work of an "international police power."

The meaning of the Roosevelt corollary became clear in the Dominican Republic in 1905 when, after considerable urging from the United States, the Dominican government agreed to request American assistance in straightening out its finances—advice which the president, despite congressional reservations, was more than happy to provide. With the control of the Dominican customhouse safely in American hands, the United States succeeded in preventing German intervention once again but at the cost of a policy that would continue to breed hemispheric ill will throughout the twentieth century.

The Panama Canal Affair.   The problem of Panama and securing American rights to an isthmian canal offered the clearest example of a foreign policy based on narrow and shortsighted national interest. The decision to abandon the Nicaraguan route, which had intrigued Americans for over a century, was made as a result of high-powered lobbying on the part of the New Panama Canal Company, the successor of the defunct French company that had tried and failed to build a Panamanian canal. A combination of French adventurers and American entrepreneurs succeeded in convincing Roosevelt, Mark Hanna, and other Republican leaders of the distinct advantages of the route through the Colombian province of Panama.

DIGGING THE PANAMA CANAL
Roosevelt poses at the controls of a giant steamshovel in Panama. *(The Bettmann Archive, Inc.)*

With the help of a few carefully placed investments in the future of their party, they managed to win congressional support for their lucrative deal. By 1902 all that remained was to convince the inept government of Colombia of the benefits about to be conferred on it by civilization.

For a while negotiations proceeded smoothly. The Hay-Herran Treaty of 1903 tendered to the United States the rights to a canal zone six miles wide for the price of $10 million plus an annual rental of $250,000. Then suddenly Colombian patriots, preparing to overthrow a corrupt dictator and realizing that they were being swindled, forced the Colombian Senate to withdraw the treaty.

Roosevelt duly denounced his new opponents as "inefficient bandits" and "contemptible little creatures" who were willfully blocking the march of progress across the hemisphere. With his initial scheme now frustrated, the president agreed to an alternative plan for a pocket revolution engineered by the promoters of the canal and a handful of native *insurrectos,* who proceeded to establish Panamanian independence from Colombia with the blessings of the United States and the help of its navy. The new state of Panama, after hasty recognition by the United States, obliged her benefactor by granting the terms for the canal that Colombia had just refused. Roosevelt had his canal project, the Panamanian patriots their revolution, and the promoters their profits. Roosevelt never ceased defending his part in the affair. "If I had followed traditional conservative methods I would have submitted a dignified state paper of probably two hundred pages to Congress and the debates on it would have been going on yet; but I took the Canal Zone and let Congress debate; and while the debate goes on the Canal does also."

Roosevelt's Style of Diplomacy. With this bald assertion of presidential and national power Roosevelt drew together the strands of his diplomacy. In the first place, his diplomatic style was a highly personal one which assumed that most of the issues in foreign affairs were best handled, as he said, "by one man alone." Although he used his secretaries of state, John Hay and Elihu Root, effectively on occasion, just as often he bypassed them completely and seldom gave them credit for decisions he rightly or wrongly considered his own. Resolved to play the lone hand, he fumed at the constant interference of the Senate and its tampering with what he considered an executive prerogative. Deliberative bodies, he insisted, were virtually useless when there was "any efficient work" to be done. It was for the president alone to take charge of foreign policy in the same way that he took

the lead in formulating domestic priorities of reform and reorganization. His aim in intervening in Latin American affairs, he later wrote, was to wake up the American people "so that they would back a reasonable and intelligent foreign policy which would have put a stop to the crying disorders at our very doors."

"Crying disorders"—here was the link between domestic progressive reform and foreign policy. Order and stability in Asia, Roosevelt was to learn, lay beyond the reach of American power. In Europe, where his leverage was greater, he could mix balance-of-power diplomacy with hopes for a perpetual Anglo-American ascendancy throughout the world. But it was at home in the Western Hemisphere that the benefits of order and system seemed to him greatest, and he did not hesitate to seek them for American business.

Although it fell to Roosevelt to preside over the transformation of territorial imperialism into a policy of economic penetration, his language betrayed an ignorance of his historical role. He spoke constantly of "honor, territorial integrity and vital interests" as the only basis for an American foreign policy. There were higher things in life, he kept insisting, than the enjoyment of material comforts or the pursuit of wealth. "It is through strife, or the readiness for strife, that a nation must win greatness." And greatness for Roosevelt was primarily spiritual. His speeches rang with the clichés of "righteousness" and "duty" as he combined moralism and nationalism in a blend of power politics that glossed over the hard economic motives he never clearly acknowledged.

The central theme running through his foreign policy pronouncements was the danger that American preoccupation with domestic prosperity would turn right-minded citizens into a mere "assemblage of well-to-do hucksters" who cared for nothing beyond their own borders. But to argue the case for an aggressive foreign policy purely in terms of altruism was to ignore the very economic forces that increasingly controlled the making of American foreign policy: investment opportunities, concessions, corporate resource development, and other forms of economic penetration, all requiring political and economic stability essential to the effective exploitation of colonial economies. Roosevelt's rhetoric concealed the fact that as president he became, if not the captive, at least the confederate of the very economic forces he presumably distrusted.

Taft's "Dollar Diplomacy."   The Taft administration substituted dollars for bullets and displayed no such squeamishness in acknowledging the reality of economic imperialism. Taft's choice of a secretary of state, corporation lawyer Philander C. Knox, was itself proof of the growing intimacy between the investment community in Wall Street and the State Department. Knox, who was given a much freer hand in formulating policy than Roosevelt had accorded his predecessors, was the chief architect of Taft's program of "dollar diplomacy." Dollar diplomacy, a form of democratic state capitalism, used American export capital together with preponderant political and military power to give force, as Taft put it, "alike to idealistic humanitarian sentiments, to the dictates of sound policy and strategy, and to legitimate commercial aims."

Dollar diplomacy extended the principles of domestic progressivism to the conduct of foreign policy. Investment capitalists were encouraged to proceed with the economic penetration of undeveloped areas under conditions of stability and profitability provided by the government. "In China," Taft told Congress in citing his favorite example, "the policy of encouraging financial investment to enable that country to help itself has had the result of giving new life and practical application to the open-door policy." Taft's administration was committed to encouraging the use of American capital in China to promote "those essential reforms" that China had pledged to the United States and to the other major powers. Here for congressional approval was a "new diplomacy," practiced by a foreign service "alert and equipped to cooperate with the businessmen of America," and dedicated to "improved governmental methods of protecting and stimulating it."

Taft's open avowal of the economic motive did not alter the pattern of American success and failure—conspicuous success in attracting investment in nearby Latin America, where the bankers were more than willing to go, and nearly total failure in the Far East, where they were not. In attempting to open China once more to American capital, Taft met the determined resistance of British, French, and German bankers, who excluded the Americans from a consortium to finance and build the Hukuang Railway in China, an ill-considered project that was never completed. By applying heavy diplomatic pressure on the Chinese emperor, Knox succeeded in gaining admission to the consortium. But he needlessly made trouble for himself by another poorly conceived experiment in state capitalism in Manchuria. Like Hay's original plan, the Taft administration's attempt to pry open the door for American capital ended in failure.

No such difficulties were encountered in Latin America, where American capital continued to pour in. Here a combination of supersalesmanship and regular government intervention to protect American investments—in Nicaragua, Guatemala, Honduras, and Haiti—kept the gates open.

Taft's foreign policy concerned itself with Latin America and the Far East to the virtual neglect of Europe. In warning against an exclusive concern with the Far East, progressive writer Herbert Croly (who had also presumed to advise Roosevelt in *The Promise of American Life*) predicted the early arrival of an international system of major powers that might force the United States to interfere "in what may at first appear to be a purely European complication." When that time came, Croly hastened to add, American policy-makers ought to meet it with "a sound, well-informed, and positive conception of American national interest rather than a negative and ignorant conception." Taft, however, preferred to keep his distance. The legal framework for dollar diplomacy was provided by the progressive faith in arbitration with which Taft hoped to defuse international crises in much the same way that boards of mediators in domestic affairs depoliticized economic conflict. Twenty-five arbitration treaties had been signed in the last days of the outgoing Roosevelt administration, and Taft sought to apply the same principle to all "justiciable" issues. The Senate, however, proceeded to eliminate the procedures for discussion and consultation in every case in which the United States might be presumed to have an interest. Nevertheless, the arbitration scheme lived on as a progressive panacea, drawing the attention of Woodrow Wilson and his secretary of state, the "Prince of Peace," William Jennings Bryan. There would be continuities as well as new departures in the missionary diplomacy of Woodrow Wilson.

"The Organized Force of Mankind"—Wilsonian Diplomacy and World War

At first Wilson appeared to represent a new constituency in American foreign policy. The years after 1900 saw peace groups, proponents of arbitration, and other idealists combine in a broad coalition behind the principles of missionary diplomacy, moral publicity, and open covenants. In repudiating both Roosevelt's role of big brother to the oppressed and Taft's dollar diplomacy, Wilson entered office with an appeal to national altruism which warmed the hearts of moralists everywhere. "My dream is that as the years go on and the world knows more and more of America," the president told a Fourth of July audience in 1914, "it . . . will turn to America for those moral inspirations which lie at the basis of all freedoms . . . and that America will come into the full light of day when all shall know that she puts human rights above all other rights and that her flag is the flag not only of America but of humanity." Yet three months earlier Wilson had ordered the occupation of Vera Cruz to vindicate American honor.

One of the paradoxes of American foreign relations in the early years of the twentieth century was that both of the widely divergent formulations of policy—national egotism and national altruism—led directly to similar involvements of the United States throughout the world and to forcible intervention in the affairs of neighboring states almost constantly. Both the demands of national interest and the less precise requirements of moral mission

ended in the application of raw power. By 1917 America's arrival as a world power had been clearly established, but it remained to be seen how that power would be used in reordering a world at war. Americans joined the fighting still seeking an answer to this question.

Like most Americans before 1914, Woodrow Wilson had given little serious attention to the specifics of an American foreign policy. Diplomatic questions had not figured prominently in the campaign of 1912, and to their solution Wilson brought only the conventional wisdom of an active peace movement in the United States concerning the exportability of the American democratic way. During his two terms, Wilson often served as the mouthpiece of this movement and took many of its principles for his own, fashioning them into an alternative to balance-of-power politics.

By 1914 a belief in the imminent arrival of an age of international harmony had become a staple item in the progressive intellectual stock. Progressive reformers, intellectuals, and professionals put their faith in improved worldwide communications, an international technology, and the uses of arbitration as the instruments of a new moral order. The peace movement in the United States was comprised of a variety of groups and interests: church-affiliated peace societies and new secular foundations like Andrew Carnegie's Endowment for International Peace; students of international law intent on constructing new legal frameworks; preachers of disarmament; and prophets of a vast people-to-people crusade. Common to many of these peace advocates was a peculiarly American set of assumptions that defined peace as an adjunct to domestic progressive reform.

Arbitration: The Key to World Order.   There was, first of all, the belief that the path to world order had been discovered by the United States as it progressed from a loose federation of sovereign states to a genuine union of all the people. From like beginnings, the promoters of peace reasoned, might well come one world of harmony and democratic striving. Associated with this golden vision of an Americanized world order was a tenacious faith in arbitration itself as a key mechanism for resolving tensions and potential conflicts. This mechanism could take various forms: the International Court at the Hague; a body of international law; or bilateral "cooling off" treaties.

These progressive beliefs led Wilson to accept the views of the peace advocates. His language, like Roosevelt's, was unrelievedly abstract. But whereas Roosevelt, a self-declared "realist," spoke of national duty, honor, and integrity, Wilson translated these terms into the language of altruism. Narrowly construed national interest he denounced as "selfishness" and the rule of unbridled materialism. "Balance of power," in his mind, meant unstable coalitions of aggressive interests. The outlook of "average" people the world over, on the other hand, was becoming "more and more unclouded" as national purposes fell more and more into the background and the "common purpose of enlightened mankind" took their place. He spoke of the time, not far distant, when these "counsels of plain men" would come to replace the "counsels of sophisticated men of affairs" as the best means of securing peace. Then the statesmen of the world would be forced to heed the "common clarified thought" or be broken.

Here in a preliminary formulation lay Wilson's plan for an alternative system of world politics, which had begun to take shape in his mind even before war broke out in Europe. Wilson's magisterial language was equal to his vision as he took on what his critics called his "papal role" in dispensing a humanitarian theology. "I do not know that there will ever be a declaration of independence or grievances for mankind," he told an audience at Independence Hall in Philadelphia in 1914, scarcely a week before the outbreak of war, "but I believe that if any such document is ever drawn it will be drawn in the spirit of the American Declaration of Independence, and that America has lifted high the light which will shine unto all generations and guide the feet of mankind to the goal of justice and liberty and peace." The president, noted the acerbic editors of the *New Republic*, uttered nothing that might sound trivial at the Last Judgment.

The first fruits of this Wilsonian "missionary" spirit were bitter ones for the promoters of dollar diplomacy. Wilson quickly dashed the hopes of the outgoing Taft administration for continued investment in China by rejecting a scheme for railroad financing as a violation of Chinese sovereignty. In the delicate negotiations over the Panama Canal tolls he argued that American exemption from payment showed a "dishonorable attitude," and at the risk of dividing his own party he secured a repeal. Then in October 1913, in an address in Mobile, Ala. that became famous, he completed the reversal of dollar diplomacy by promising to emancipate Latin America from its "subordination" to "foreign enterprise."

Intervention in Mexico. Yet in Latin America, where the interests of business were real and compelling, Wilson found it impossible to reverse his predecessors' policy of intervention, and his formal disavowal of American interference ended in bitter irony. In fact, under Wilson the United States intervened in the affairs of its neighbors more often than ever before. There was a military occupation of Haiti in 1915; financial supervision in the Dominican Republic in 1916; renewed controls in Cuba in 1917; and minor meddling in behalf of American investors throughout the Caribbean. Moralistic though he frequently was, Wilson was not blind to the operation of economic motives nor deaf to the appeals of American entrepreneurs. His difficulties in Latin America resulted in large part from his tendency to identify the beneficent workings of American capital with the welfare of "the submerged eighty-five per cent" of native populations to whom he wanted to bring the blessings of parliamentary democracy.

Mexico tested Wilson's theories of moral diplomacy and found them wanting. In 1911, following a long period of oppressive rule, moderate constitutionalists led by Francisco Madero overthrew Mexican dictator Porfirio Diaz. The new government received prompt recognition from the Taft administration. Then, less than two years later, Madero himself fell victim to a counterrevolutionary coup directed by one of his lieutenants, Victoriano Huerta, who murdered his former chief and seized the presidency. This was the situation confronting Wilson as he took office.

Wilson, outraged by Huerta's brutality, lost no time in denouncing him as a thug and a butcher, and refused to recognize his government. His refusal to accord recognition rested partly on genuine moral revulsion but also on the knowledge that England had recognized Huerta's dictatorship in hope of gaining further economic concessions. Wilson meant to check England's pretensions by toppling Huerta. Although economic and strategic concerns usually appeared on the periphery of Wilson's moral vision, they were never quite out of sight. He continued to insist that the United States must never abandon morality for expediency. But in Mexico, profits for American investors and parliamentary democracy for the Mexican people seemed to him wholly compatible.

Wilson was determined to replace Huerta with the moderate rule of Venustiano Carranza, another constitutionalist who had succeeded in rallying popular opposition to the dictator. The president seized the occasion for overthrowing Huerta when a boatload of American sailors was arrested and unlawfully detained in Tampico. Wilson demanded an immediate apology. When Huerta predictably refused to concede to a government which had refused to recognize him, Wilson ordered the occupation of Vera Cruz, an exercise that cost the lives of nineteen Americans and a great many more Mexicans. Under heavy pressure from the United States, and besieged by the forces of Carranza's constitutionalists, Huerta resigned and fled to Spain in 1914. Yet Carranza's liberal regime was no more willing to tolerate American intervention than the deposed dictator had been. Only a timely offer of the ABC Powers (Argentina, Brazil, and Chile) to mediate the dispute allowed Wilson to withdraw American forces and save face.

The second act of the Mexican crisis opened with the attempt of Pancho Villa, a bandit leader and an unsavory associate of Carranza, to overthrow his chief and take power for himself by provoking a war with the United States. Wilson very nearly obliged him. On January 10, 1916, Villa and his band stopped a train at Santa Ysabel in the northern provinces, took seventeen Americans off, and shot sixteen of them. Then in March, Villa raided the tiny New Mexico town of Columbus, burned it to the ground and killed nineteen more American citizens. Wilson responded, as Villa had hoped he would, by dispatching General John J. Pershing and his troops on a punitive expedi-

MEXICAN-AMERICAN RELATIONS, 1916–1917
Pancho Villa's raid on a New Mexico town and his murder of American citizens called for a U.S. punitive expedition led by General John J. Pershing. *(Both, Library of Congress)*

tion. Pershing chased the bandit chief some three hundred miles back into Mexico without managing to catch him. Carranza demanded the immediate withdrawal of Pershing's expeditionary force. Faced with the near certainty of war with Germany, Wilson could only comply. In 1917, as Villa roamed the Mexican countryside and an unstable Carranza government lurched toward yet another constitutional crisis, Wilson had nothing to show for his five-year labors. Now, however, his attention was fixed on Europe.

War in Europe.   The outbreak of the First World War in the summer of 1914 caught the Wilson administration and the entire country by surprise. At first the news that Austria had invaded tiny Serbia occasioned little more than traditional American sympathy for the underdog. Since neither European nor American diplomats yet realized the scope of the coming catastrophe, it was not difficult for Wilson to declare American neutrality and call on all citizens to remain "impartial in thought as well as in action." Behind the proclamation of neutrality lay the president's conviction that the war would be a short one ending in a settlement that the United States, from its Olympian station above the battle, could help arrange. And behind that unwarranted assumption lay still another belief that America could play an effective role in creating a new moral order.

As the war dragged into its second year, all of Wilson's hopes for remodeling the world of power politics came to hinge on a doctrine of neutrality that itself rested on two misconceptions. First, developments quickly showed that the United States was not and could not be unconcerned with the outcome of the war. As shrewd observers had pointed out before the war broke out, England, in upholding the European balance of power for a whole century, had directly contributed to American growth and well-being. And Germany, at least since 1890, had consistently threatened American security with a belligerent new diplomacy, an arms buildup, and a frightening doctrine of militarism. An Anglo-German conflict was thus bound to affect the United States in crucial ways.

The first year of the war drove this lesson home. England increasingly monopolized access to informa-

tion defining the meaning of the war and skillfully manipulated its advantage until the president and his advisers came to argue, as one of them put it, that "Germany must not be permitted to win this war." By 1915 the administration began, not always consciously, to act on that assumption. The American economy was placed at the disposal of the Allies, who despite the embarrassing presence of Imperial Russia, were presumed to be fighting autocracy and militarism in the name of democracy and freedom. Trade with the Allies was proclaimed "legal and welcome." When Allied credit soon evaporated, American bankers rushed to the rescue with credits and loans that totaled $2.5 billion by the time the United States entered the war in 1917. Wilson continued to press both England and Germany for a settlement of the war, but when neither side agreed, he tended to excuse the former and blame the latter for the disatrous military stalemate.

The Lusitania Incident.   The second misconception underlying Wilson's doctrine of neutrality stemmed from his failure to understand the logic of total war or to acknowledge the effect of modern technology. The submarine had made the traditional rights of neutrals obsolete. Both combatants, as they grappled for an economic stranglehold on the other, were driven to resort to novel practices that were clear violations of the established rules of war. England extended the right of naval search to new lengths and established a policy of blockade that virtually extinguished the rights of neutrals. Yet diplomatic exchange with England settled into a predictable pattern of violation, protest, discussion, and eventual resumption of the objectionable practice.

With Germany, on the other hand, the exchange grew brittle, and Wilson's language increasingly terse. The use of submarines, which struck without warning or provision for the safety of passengers and crew, touched a raw nerve in the American people. When in May 1915 a German U-boat torpedoed without warning the British liner *Lusitania* with the loss of 128 American lives, Wilson initiated an angry dialogue that grew more and more strident in the next year and a half. Germany quite correctly pointed out that the ship was carrying contraband of war, but that

PRESIDENT WILSON CONSIDERS HIS DWINDLING OPTIONS
(Library of Congress)

fact hardly weakened Wilson's determination to apply the old rules. For the president, the sinking of the *Lusitania* was proof of the practical impossibility of using submarines "without disregarding those rules of fairness, reason, justice, and humanity, which all modern opinion regards as imperative." In deciding to hold Germany "strictly accountable," Wilson put the United States on a collision course.

In the meantime, following the *Lusitania* incident, Germany said it would comply with Wilson's terms. Then in 1916, the German attack on the unarmed French passenger ship *Sussex* in the English Channel

resulted in injury to American citizens, and the meaning of "strict accountability" suddenly became clear to the president. Submarine warfare, he informed Germany, "of necessity, because of the very character of the vessels employed," was "incompatible" with the "sacred immunities of noncombatants." Unless the imperial government agreed to abandon its methods forthwith, the United States would have no choice but to sever relations. Germany agreed to discontinue the practice, but only if the United States could force England to lift the blockade. Until then the German government reserved the right to rescind its pledge. The president's options were dwindling fast.

Wilson's growing indignation reflected another, more personal anxiety. For three years he had continued to pile on to the conventional concept of neutral rights a heavy load of moral principles. Now he was forced to admit that the United States might not be able to impose its will on warring Europe without joining the Allies. A nation that had been "too proud to fight" and that had reelected him on the slogan "He kept us out of war" now faced the prospect of securing a "peace without victory" only by becoming a participant. As he became aware of this, Wilson began to redefine America's mission as nothing less than the building of a system of collective security to replace the collapsed system of balance of power. If compelled to fight, the United States would fight for utopia.

A New World Order. In January 1917, a week before Germany announced its decision to resume unrestricted submarine warfare, Wilson described his vision of a new world order to the Senate. The United States, prepared by "the very principles and purposes" of its humanitarian policy, must rebuild the machinery of diplomacy. Its terms for peace must "win the approval of mankind" and not merely "serve the several interests and immediate aims of the nations engaged." Wilson proposed a perpetual league of peaceful nations as an integral part of the peace settlement, a collective instrument which he described as "so much greater than the force of any nation now engaged or any allegiance hitherto projected" that governments and their leaders would instinctively bend to its dictates. The future of the

LIBERTY LOAN DRIVE
The American people prepare
for war. *(Brown Brothers)*

world would thus come to depend, not on a balance of power, but on a community of opinion; not on "organized rivalries," but on "organized peace." Wilson proposed, in short, a concert of moral force made up of peoples who, with open covenants openly arrived at, would enforce their collective will for national self-determination, democratic government, and lasting peace. To skeptical senators, particularly those in the Republican ranks, Wilson explained that his were at once "American principles" and "the principles of all mankind."

A week later the German imperial government renewed its submarine attacks in a desperate gamble to win the war before the United States could enter. In March, German submarines without warning sank four unarmed American merchantmen, and on April 2, 1917, Wilson appeared before a joint session of Congress to request that it accept the war that had been "thrust" upon the United States. By a vote of 82 to 6 in the Senate and 373 to 50 in the House, Congress agreed to the presidential request.

The United States, its citizens would learn from a year and a half of war and another year of peace-making, had arrived at a position of world power that very few of them could have envisioned thirty years earlier. Their country had gone to war with Spain on the flimsiest of pretexts and built an empire on its victory. But in the intervening years, most Americans, far from embracing imperial responsibilities, had neglected the chores of maintaining an empire, and, except in their own hemisphere, had forgotten their regenerative mission. Now as their president called on them to fight another and infinitely greater war, they turned to him for a sense of direction and for a definition of their moral commitment.

The president, for his part, having determined that war was the only option left open to him, made a prophecy to the nation and a private confession in considering his course. "We are at the beginning of an age," he told the country, "in which it will be insisted that the same standards of conduct and responsibility for wrong done shall be observed among nations and their governments that are observed among individual citizens of civilized states." But privately, in the solitude of the White House on the eve of his appearance before Congress, he admitted to fears about the unintended and uncontrollable effects of going to war. "Once lead this people into war," he told Frank Cobb, the editor of the New York *World,* "and they'll forget there ever was such a thing as tolerance. To fight you must be brutal and ruthless, and the spirit of ruthless brutality will enter into the very fibre of our national life, infecting Congress, the courts, the policeman on the beat, the man in the streets." The meaning of Wilson's prophecy of a new international morality awaited the outcome of the war, but his prediction of the domestic dangers involved in fighting it soon proved all too accurate.

CHRONOLOGY

1895 United States intervenes in boundary dispute between Britain and Venezuela as Secretary of State Richard Olney declares nation "practically sovereign on this continent."
Spain sends troops to quell Cuban revolution.

1896 Cuban rebel leader Maceo murdered, resulting in American popular support for Cuba.
William McKinley elected president.

1897 A letter from Spanish minister to Washington, Depuy de Lôme, in which he called McKinley "weak" and "a would-be politician" is intercepted, worsening American and Spanish relations.
U.S. battleship *Maine* explodes in Havana harbor.

1898 Spanish-American War: United States acquires Philippines, Puerto Rico, and Guam, and annexes Hawaii.

1899 Hay's "Open Door" notes to world powers calling for "equal and impartial trade" in China and preservation of "Chinese territorial and administrative" integrity.
Senate ratifies peace treaty with Spain.
United States, Germany, and Great Britain partition Samoa.

1900 Foraker Act establishes civil government in Puerto Rico.
Organic Act incorporates Hawaii as a territory of the United States.
McKinley reelected president, defeating Bryan once again.
Boxer Rebellion in China.

1901 Platt Amendment authorizes U.S. intervention in Cuba.
Theodore Roosevelt becomes president after McKinley assassinated.
Hay-Pauncefote Treaty with Great Britain gives United States sole right to build, control, and maintain neutrality of an isthmian canal in Central America.
Philippine Organic Act passed, making Philippine islands an unorganized territory of the U.S.

1902 United States returns civil government to Republic of China.

1903 Hay-Herran Treaty with Republic of Colombia giving United States 99-year lease on Canal Zone is rejected by Colombia.
Roosevelt aids revolt in Panama.

Hay-Bunau-Varilla Treaty gives United States full sovereignty in Canal Zone.
United States-Cuba reciprocity treaty forms close economic ties between both countries.

1904 Roosevelt "corollary" to Monroe Doctrine.
Roosevelt elected, defeating Democrat Alton B. Parker and Socialist Eugene V. Debs.

1905 Roosevelt mediates in Russo-Japanese War.

1906 American troops intervene in Cuba to restore order.
Algeciras Conference with Roosevelt's help settles French-German conflict in Morocco.

1908 William Howard Taft elected president, defeating Bryan and Debs.
Root-Takahira Agreement; United States recognizes Japan's interests in Manchuria.

1909 Taft inaugurates "Dollar Diplomacy" in China and Latin America.
United States intervenes in Haitian and Nicaraguan finances.

1911 Marines sent to Nicaragua.

1912 Woodrow Wilson elected president, defeating Republican regular William Howard Taft, Progressive "Bull Moose" Theodore Roosevelt, and Socialist Eugene V. Debs.

1914 First World War begins; Wilson declares American neutrality.
Wilson orders occupation of Vera Cruz, Mexico.
Panama Canal opened.

1915 United States troops occupy Haiti.
United States recognizes Carranza government in Mexico.
Germans declare unrestricted submarine warfare and sink *Lusitania* with loss of American lives.
Preparedness movement.

1916 Wilson reelected, narrowly defeating Charles Evans Hughes.
House-Grey Memorandum on United States' efforts for negotiated peace.
American troops occupy Dominican Republic.
General John J. Pershing's expedition into Mexico.

1917 Germans resume unrestricted submarine warfare and United States enters war.
Purchase of Danish Virgin Islands.

SUGGESTED READINGS

The boundaries of scholarly criticism of American foreign policy after 1890 are established in two different surveys. George F. Kennan, *American Diplomacy, 1900–1950* (1951), points to consistently unprofessional and uninformed leaders as the chief difficulty, while William Appleman Williams, *The Tragedy of American Diplomacy* (1959), cites economic expansion as the source of a peculiar kind of American imperialism. Robert E. Osgood, *Ideals and Self-Interest in America's Foreign Relations* (1953), evaluates the assumptions of both parties to the great debate over means and ends. Richard W. Leopold, *The Growth of American Foreign Policy* (1962), is an excellent survey, which should be combined with John A. S. Grenville and George B. Young, *Politics, Strategy, and American Diplomacy. . . . 1873 –1917* (1966). Two other readable accounts of the emergence of an American foreign policy are Foster R. Dulles, *America's Rise to World Power, 1898–1954* (1955), and for background Richard W. Van Alstyne, *The Rising American Empire* (1960). Rubin F. Weston, *Racism in U.S. Imperialism: The Influence of Racial Assumptions on American Foreign Policy, 1893–1946* (1972), examines race prejudice as a component of U.S. foreign policy. William Appleman Williams, *The Shaping of American Diplomacy* (1956), is a highly useful source.

The origins of the American expansionism in the 1890s are carefully examined in Walter LaFeber, *The New Empire: An Interpretation of American Expansion, 1860–1898* (1963), and Milton Plesur, *America's Outward Thrust, 1865– 1890* (1971). David Pletcher, *The Awkward Years: America's Foreign Relations under Garfield and Arthur* (1962), offers a meticulous analysis of early fumblings in the 1880s.

There are several excellent studies of the rising diplomatic crisis in the 1890s—among them Ernest R. May, *Imperial Democracy: The Emergence of America as a Great Power* (1961), and the same author's exploratory essay, *American Imperialism: A Speculative Essay* (1968); H. Wayne Morgan, *America's Road to Empire: The War with Spain and Overseas Expansion* (1965); David Healy, *United States Expansionism: The Imperialist Urge in the 1890's* (1970). The influence of the navy and the role of Mahan are explored in Peter Karsten, *The Naval Aristocracy* (1972), and William Livezey, *Mahan on Sea Power* (1947). Charles H. Brown, *The Correspondents' War: Journalists in the Spanish-American War* (1967), covers the reporters' beat. Robert L. Beisner, *The Anti-Imperialists, 1898–1900* (1968), and E. Berkeley Tompkins, *Anti-Imperialism in the United States: The Great Debate, 1890–1920* (1970), assess the arguments and futile

activities of the opponents of expansionism. Leon Wolff, *Little Brown Brother* (1961), gives an outraged account of the Philippine insurrection and the American pacification program.

Areas of growing American interest and control have been well covered in a number of careful monographs: Merze Tate, *The United States and the Hawaiian Kingdom* (1965); Howard F. Cline, *The United States and Mexico* (1953); A. Whitney Griswold, *The Far Eastern Policy of the United States* (1938); Charles Vevier, *The United States and China, 1906–1913* (1955); Charles E. Neu, *The Troubled Encounter: The United States and Japan* (1975); and Samuel F. Bemis, *The Latin American Policy of the United States* (1967). John Hay's intentions in announcing the Open Door policy are thoroughly canvassed in Tyler Dennett, *John Hay* (1933), and the unforeseen results in Marilyn B. Young, *The Rhetoric of Empire: American China Policy, 1893–1901* (1968); Warren Cohen, *America's Response to China* (1971); Thomas McCormick, *China Market: America's Quest for Informal Empire, 1893–1901* (1967); Jerry Israel, *Progressivism and the Open Door: America and China, 1905–1921* (1971); and Paul A. Varg, *The Making of a Myth: The United States and China, 1899–1912* (1968). Other detailed studies of aspects of progressive foreign policy include Charles E. Neu, *An Uncertain Friendship: Theodore Roosevelt and Japan* (1967); Akira Iriye, *Across the Pacific: An Inner History of American–East Asian Relations* (1967); and Edward Berbusse, *The United States in Puerto Rico* (1965).

On Roosevelt's foreign policy formulations, Howard K. Beale, *Theodore Roosevelt and the Rise of America to World Power* (1956), is still standard; see also Raymond A. Esthus, *Theodore Roosevelt and the International Rivalries* (1970). Robert A. Hart, *The Great White Fleet: Its Voyage Around the World* (1965), is a highly readable account of Roosevelt's colorful gesture. Dwight C. Miner, *Fight for the Panama Route* (1966), tell a complicated story well, and Akira Iriye, *Pacific Estrangement: Japanese and American Expansion, 1897– 1911* (1972), explains Roosevelt's many problems in that area. Walter V. Scholes and Marie V. Scholes, *The Foreign Policies of the Taft Administration* (1970), analyzes the workings of Dollar Diplomacy, and Dana G. Munroe, *Intervention and Dollar Diplomacy in the Caribbean, 1900–1921* (1964), examines its consequences. Sondra R. Herman, *Eleven Against War: Studies in American Internationalist Thought, 1898–1921* (1969), studies a variety of peace types, and Bradford Perkins, *The Great Rapprochement: England and the United States, 1895–1914* (1968), is indispensable for understanding American attitudes toward the First World War.

The most comprehensive discussions of Wilsonian diplomacy from a presidential perspective are to be found in the volumes of Link's *Wilson*. P. Edward Haley, *Revolution and Intervention: The Diplomacy of Taft and Wilson with Mexico, 1910–1917* (1970), is an even-handed examination of Mexican policy, and so is Robert Freeman Smith, *The U.S. and Revolutionary Nationalism in Mexico, 1916–1932* (1972), for the later period. Robert E. Quirk, *An Affair of Honor: Woodrow Wilson and the Occupation of Veracruz* (1962), criticizes the President for his misguided actions in that unfortunate affair, and Clarence C. Clendenen, *The United States and Pancho Villa* (1961) is adequate. Hans R. Schmidt, *The United States Occupation of Haiti, 1915–1934* (1971), surveys the problems presented by the unstable republic in the Progressive search for order in the Caribbean. Harley Notter, *The Origins of the Foreign Policy of Woodrow Wilson* (1937), tests the theoretical underpinnings of Wilsonian diplomacy.

Neutrality and American intervention in the First World War fascinated a Depression generation preparing for war and produced a number of notable accounts, from the acerbic Walter Millis, *The Road to War* (1935), to the scholarly Charles Seymour, *American Neutrality, 1914–1917* (1935), and Edwin Borchard and W. P. Lage, *Neutrality for the United States* (1940). More recent literature on Wilsonian neutrality and its premises is extensive. Among the best accounts are Ernest R. May, *The World War and American Isolation, 1914–1917* (1959); John M. Cooper, Jr., *The Vanity of Power: American Isolation and the First World War, 1914–1917* (1969); Ross Gregory, *The Origins of American Intervention in the First World War* (1971); Daniel M. Smith, *The Great Departure: The United States in World War I, 1914–1920* (1965); and Carl P. Parrini, *Heir to Empire: U.S. Economic Diplomacy, 1916–1923* (1969). Link's *Wilson* contains a meticulous account of the gradual shift in the President's assessment of the war, and Edward Buehrig, *Woodrow Wilson and the Balance of Power* (1955), examines his various strategies.

CHAPTER 27

Progressivism and the Great War

By the time the United States entered the war in April 1917, the European powers were rapidly approaching exhaustion. After three years of stalemate, Germany was suffering from starvation and the collapse of civilian morale. Austria-Hungary managed to continue the war only by imposing martial law. Russia, crippled by astronomical losses that had led to the overthrow of the czarist regime a month earlier, stood on the brink of a second Bolshevik revolution. France, its national will shattered, faced widespread mutiny in her armies. England, having sacrificed an entire generation of young men to German machine guns since 1914, was beset with severe manpower shortages both at home and in the field.

Slaughter on the Western Front

The original predictions of both sides—Germany's for a six-week war and the Allies' plan for rolling back the enemy on two vast fronts—had long since been buried under mounds of casualties. Shared strategic obsessions with artillery barrages and massed infantry assaults on entrenched positions had created a war of appalling senselessness and butchery. Two million casualties on the Western Front in 1916 had failed to move the line of advance for either side, and the war had descended once again into the trenches that stretched in an unbroken line from the sea to the mountains. A week after Wilson asked for a declaration of war in April 1917, the British launched still another frontal attack in Belgium on the Ypres sector of the front, and in five days gained 7,000 yards at the appalling cost of 160,000 dead and wounded.

Although the United States entered the war late and suffered proportionately fewer losses, the meaning of the slaughter lingered in the American imagination for a generation. In a scene in F. Scott Fitzgerald's *Tender Is the Night*, one of the characters leads a party of sightseers across the Somme Valley after the war. "See that little stream," he says. "We could walk to it in two minutes. It took the British a whole month to walk to it—a whole empire walking very slowly, dying in front and pushing forward behind.

SAYING GOOD BYE...
War Department photograph,
1917. *(National Archives)*

And another empire walked very slowly backward a few inches a day, leaving the dead like a million bloody rugs." American soldiers in the last year of the war followed the footsteps of their British and French predecessors. In joining the Allies, the United States committed its forces to a war in which the ultimate loser was the side that won the most battles. Woodrow Wilson's hopes for a just peace died along with more than 100,000 American soldiers on the Western Front.

It took eight months for American troops to join the fighting on the Western Front in effective numbers and nearly a year before they were decisively engaged in helping to turn back the final German offensive. In the meantime the Allied cause hung in the balance. In November 1917 Lenin and the Bolsheviks overthrew the provisional revolutionary government of Russia, established a party dictatorship, and took Russia out of the war, releasing badly needed German divisions for a last offensive on the Western Front. In the spring drive along the Somme beginning in March 1918, the Germans routed the British and penned up the French, but without making a decisive breakthrough.

In May and June the American Second Division was dispatched to the Marne, where it bolstered sagging French defenses. In the first big American engagements of the war, United States forces halted

AMERICAN SOLDIERS IN FRANCE
Elderly French couple welcomes American doughboys.
(National Archives)

a German advance at Chateau-Thierry and slowly drove the enemy out of Belleau Wood. These American actions were only preliminaries to the great Allied counteroffensive, which in late summer began to push the German army relentlessly back to its frontier. By September the American commander, General John J. Pershing, who had stubbornly held out for an independent command, had over half a million men at his disposal, a number that would double by the end of the war two months later. In October, Pershing, in concert with British and French offensives elsewhere along the line, opened a massive American drive out of the Argonne Forest aimed at the railhead at Sedan—the last sustained American action of the war.

On November 3 Austria-Hungary collapsed, and on the same day the German navy mutinied at Kiel, thus raising the specter of another communist revolution. Six days later a general strike in Germany led by the Independent Socialists forced the Kaiser to abdicate, and a coalition of socialists and liberals proclaimed a republic, which forty-eight hours later accepted Wilson's Fourteen Points as the basis for

an armistice. The Great War was over.

The American entry, it was immediately clear, had brought desperately needed troops and supplies to the Allies at a critical moment. American troops provided the preponderance of power needed to win the war. Equally important was the role of the United States in replenishing stockpiles of food and materiel with its "bridge of ships," replacing the merchantmen sunk by German submarines, and experimenting successfully with the convoy system of protecting Allied shipping, which in the last analysis saved the Allies. The American contribution was essential, and it came at a crucial time. Yet despite the provisional German acceptance of the Fourteen Points as the agenda for peacemaking, the American war effort had not wiped out national fears and hatreds embodied in wartime secret agreements and arrangements among the Allies, nor had it established the moral climate either at home or in Europe that Wilson knew was essential to lasting peace.

With the American entrance, a conflict that had already grown fiercely ideological became a crusade for democracy and national regeneration. All the

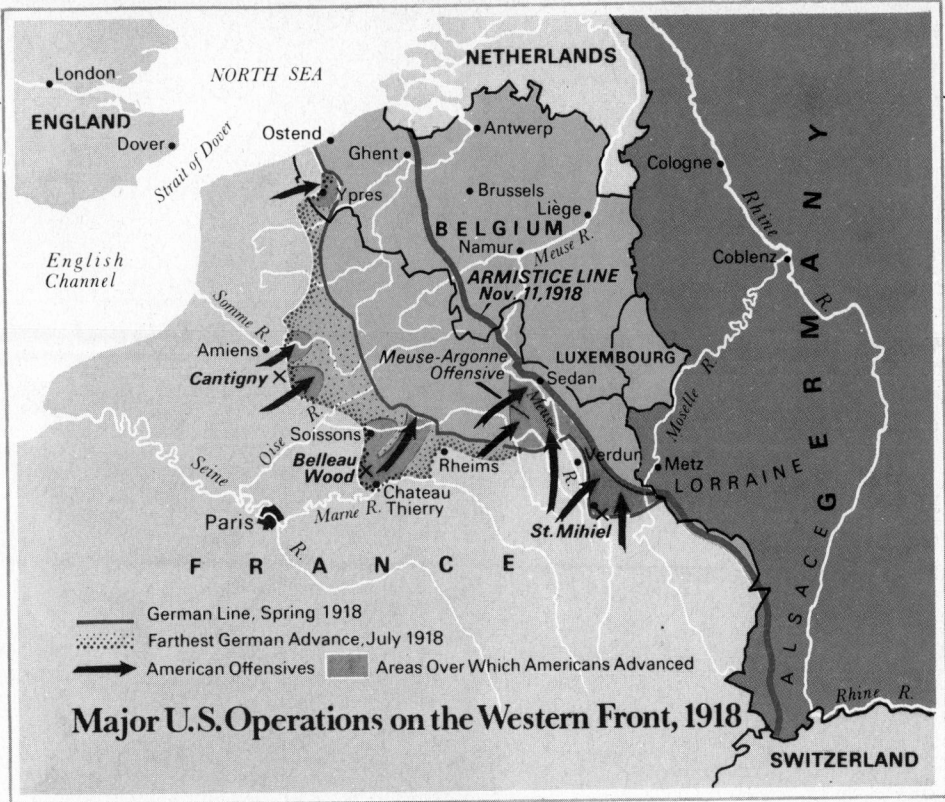

Major U.S. Operations on the Western Front, 1918

German Line, Spring 1918
Farthest German Advance, July 1918
American Offensives
Areas Over Which Americans Advanced

powers had secured control over the actions and opinions of their civilian populations as they accepted the logic of total war. But the United States entry completed an ideological shift for the Allies by defining the war in moral as well as political terms, as a struggle between the forces of peace and democracy and the dark powers of militarism. In submitting his Fourteen Points, and by explaining American war aims as "the right of those who submit to authority to have a voice in their own government" and "a universal dominion of right by . . . a concert of free peoples," Wilson unconsciously hardened the resolve of his allies to seek an unconditional surrender and a punitive peace. Perhaps the greatest irony of the First World War lay in the president's determination to inject into it a democratic ideology which in the end would make his own role as the evenhanded peacemaker impossible.

Total war also imposed an organizational logic on the participants, all of whom were forced to adjust to the national need for centralization and control. Early in the war, Germany recruited civilian administrators for its War Raw Materials Department, which established efficient mechanisms for allocating manpower, arms, and equipment. England organized its dwindling resources under the Defense of the Realm Act, which provided for full mobilization of all available manpower. France, its northern industrial provinces lost for the duration, used the powers of government to relocate factories and regulate the production of food. Once in the war, the United States followed the same pattern in building a war machine, enlisting civilians in the war effort, and improvising the bureaucratic controls demanded by the emergency. By the time the war ended in November 1918, Wilson's administration had completed an organizational revolution and brought the power of government into nearly every phase of American life.

War and the Health of the State

For some progressives, the coming of the war seemed a heaven-sent opportunity to realize the American promise. The war, they confidently predicted, would bring genuine national unity and an end to class and

OVER THERE
Left, Fifteenth Regiment on Fifth
Avenue. *Right,* American field
hospital in church ruins at Neuilly
near the Argonne Forest. *(Left,
Library of Congress; right, State Historical Society of Wisconsin)*

ethnic division. It would discredit dangerous radicalism by infusing the citizens of the nation with a new
spirit of patriotism. The demands of the war would
also destroy all selfish materialism and preoccupation
with profits and replace both with the higher goals
of service and sacrifice. National preparedness and
mobilization, central features of the New Nationalism, would foster moral virtue and civic purity in
soldiers and civilians alike. Those progressives who
continued to define their basic purpose as creating a
new American morality and citizenship saw in the
impending war effort the outlines of what one of
them called a "true national collectivism" based on
efficiency, social control, altruism, and revised moral
purpose.

On a more practical plane many more progressives responded enthusiastically to the organizational
and reform challenges furnished by the war. Those
reformers who saw their work as a form of moral
cleansing—of vice, alcohol, and prostitution—viewed
the war as a chance to purify democracy at home
while saving it abroad.

The war advanced the progressives' hopes in a
number of important ways. The preparedness campaign furthered the ideal of universal military service
as a school of citizenship. Americanization programs
aimed at controlling the immigrant took on new life.
Prohibitionist hopes soared, and women's suffrage
suddenly seemed possible. City planners, social justice workers, child labor reformers, and other pro-

gressive humanitarians warmed to the prospects of a domestic reformation in the midst of foreign war.

The war seemed to hold the greatest promise for progressives in administration and public service—those reformers who sought to join Roosevelt's New Nationalist emphasis on efficiency, administrative centralization, and executive power with Wilson's New Freedom faith in fact-finding, voluntary cooperation, and democratic participation. "We must speak, act, and serve together," Wilson reminded the nation. Efficiency quickly became the watchword for a new managerial elite that descended on Washington with proposals for a planned war effort. Wesley C. Mitchell, a professor-turned-bureaucrat who joined the Division of Planning and Statistics of the War Industries Board, explained the appeal of government service to the professionals and businessmen who signed up for the duration. "Indeed I am in a mood to demand excitement and make it up when it doesn't offer of itself. I am ready to concoct a new plan for running the universe at any minute." Efficiency as the dominant progressive ideal attached itself to the image of the war machine turning out men and military equipment automatically without the interference of politics and partisanship.

Regulations and Controls. American performance fell far short of the progressive ideal. The most urgent task for Wilson's war state was mobilizing industry. Even before war was declared, Congress established the Council of National Defense, an advisory body composed of cabinet members and industrial and labor leaders charged with taking an inventory of national resources. Out of the council's preliminary survey came the War Industries Board, which attempted—at first without success—to control production, arrange purchases, allocate scarce resources, and regulate labor relations. The War Industries Board failed to function effectively until Congress overhauled it, conferring near-dictatorial powers on the president. Wilson, in turn, brought Wall Street banker Bernard Baruch to Washington to head the agency early in 1918, and gave him sweeping powers to establish priorities and increase production. Baruch's agency, however, was hampered in its work throughout the war by inadequate information. By the end of the war, the War Industries Board was just beginning to unsnarl the problems of production.

In addition to regulating industry Wilson moved quickly to bring food and transportation under control. To head the Food Administration, he appointed Herbert Hoover, who used his powers under the Lever Act to extend government control over staples. Hoover's problems were complicated by poor harvests, and he was forced to experiment with price fixing and a massive consumer education campaign to limit consumption. His strategy succeeded, first in doubling and then in trebling the amount of food that could be exported to starving Europe. Hoover's efficient management of food production represented the chief accomplishment of wartime progressivism.

Managing the nation's railroads proved even more difficult than increasing food production. At first Wilson experimented unsuccessfully with a voluntary system under the Railroads War Board. Attempts to increase rolling stock and equalize traffic broke down completely in December 1917. Congress demanded an investigation, out of which came a

THE WAR ON THE HOME FRONT Victory gardens were one way Americans at home could contribute. *(Brown Brothers)*

revised United States Railroad Administration with effective power. Gradually the Railroad Administration extricated itself from confusion, and by the end of the war it too, like the War Industries Board, was beginning to function efficiently.

The Fuel Administration, headed by progressive Harry A. Garfield, followed Hoover's lead in the Food Administration by seeking to increase coal production with price supports fixed to guarantee profits, and, less successfully, with schemes for systematizing production and distribution on a national scale. Shipping presented Wilson's administration with its most severe problem. Here the challenge was deceptively simple—to build or commandeer ships faster than German U-boats could sink them. The solution, the Emergency Fleet Corporation—originally an offshoot of the United States Shipping Board—failed. Divided leadership played havoc with planning, and the heads of the competing agencies spent half the war quarreling over priorities and programs. Wilson finally removed them and put the competing interests under a single director. By September 1918 the Emergency Fleet Corporation had built only 500,000 tons of new shipping, less than German submarines had sunk in an average month in early 1917.

The labor policy of the Wilson administration was aimed at including the workingman in the wartime partnership with business and government—as a junior partner, but one entitled to a fair share of war prosperity. Yet here too success came slowly. Not until April 1918 did Wilson move to establish the National War Labor Board, with the power to adjudicate disputes between labor and management. Under the direction of former President Taft and progressive labor lawyer Frank P. Walsh, the National War Labor Board heard over a thousand cases during the war involving three-quarters of a million workers. In general, Wilson's labor policy was a generous one designed to tolerate if not encourage unions, establish an eight-hour day, avert strikes through arbitration, and sanction limited increases in wages.

Overall, the wartime effort in planning was hardly an unqualified success. Lacking an effectual bureaucracy at the outset, Wilson's administration necessarily fumbled and improvised, dispersing

ACETYLENE WELDER
Women contributed significantly to the war effort with new kinds of work. *(National Archives)*

rather than centralizing power through a host of overlapping and competing agencies. Not surprisingly, confusion and inefficiency resulted, as bureaucrats painfully groped their way toward centralization, learning slowly from their many mistakes. When the armistice came, the American war machine was just beginning to produce at a level approaching full capacity.

The most important consequence of the national war effort was the completion of the alliance between big business and the government. This collaboration was inevitable since it was only from within the consolidated national industries that the needed managerial talent could be recruited by the government. To Washington, accordingly, came the leaders of business and industry, primed with patriotism, but also determined to advance the interests of their sector which they quickly identified with the national good. Wilson's appointment of Bernard Baruch was only the most visible symbol of this new alliance. From the ranks of railroad management, from big steel, the machine tool industry, finance and banking came the self-appointed leaders of national mobilization, all bringing, along with expertise, demands for stability and predictability in their industries which could only be furnished by the government.

Corporate War Profits.   Big business profited from the war directly and indirectly—directly, in the form of arrangements like the cost-plus contract which guaranteed high levels of profit; indirectly, in the education its leaders received in the uses of government power. Labor fared less well. The cost of living, soaring on the crest of wartime inflation, more than doubled between 1913 and 1920 and cut deeply into wage increases. Farmers benefited from a substantial rise in real income during the war, a gain that would quickly disappear with the return of peace. But corporate profits skyrocketed in the years between 1914 and 1919, increasing threefold by the time the United States entered the war and leveling off in the following years at an annual increase of 30 percent. Gains in the steel industry ranged from 30 to 300 percent. In the lumber industry they averaged 17 percent; in oil, 21 percent; in copper, 34 percent. Even with the moderate excess-profits tax and steeper levies on higher incomes, the war made an estimated 42,000 millionaires. If the progressive programs of Theodore Roosevelt and Woodrow Wilson had sought, at least in part, a more equitable distribution of American wealth, the war tended to reverse the effects of their efforts by piling up profits in the upper reaches of the economy.

The progressive plans for constructing an effective system of bureaucratic management also came to little. American governmental bureaucracy in 1917 was still in its infancy. The handful of federal agencies at the policy-making level—the Federal Reserve Board, the Federal Trade Commission, and other fledgling agencies—had yet to assert their powers

fully. Inevitably, the wartime administrative apparatus creaked and strained under the pressures of mobilization. Ambitious reorganizational schemes were never carried out. Programs broke down. Authority almost always overlapped, and agencies collided over matters of precedence and priority. By a method marked by more trial and error than most progressives expected, the United States moved hesitantly from administrative chaos to at least some bureaucratic order at war's end.

If the gains for the federal bureaucracy brought by the war proved partial and in some cases temporary, the same was not true of the wartime campaign for loyalty and uniformity. Here the original progressive dream of an aroused and patriotic citizenry turned into a chauvinist nightmare, and the country experienced a crisis of civil liberties.

Repression and Hysteria.   The American people responded to the war with a spontaneous burst of nationalist fervor, which triggered a chain reaction of repression and hysteria. In the first months of the war hundreds of thousands of self-styled patriots banded together in vigilante-like groups bearing impressive titles—the American Defense Society, the National Security League, the American Anti-Anarchy Association, even the Boy Spies of America—and dedicated to hunting out heresy wherever they found it. The leaders of these grass-roots purges were usually the leading men in local communities—businessmen, professionals, and merchants—who combined more useful work for the Red Cross and Y.M.C.A. with the witch-hunting escapades common to superpatriots in any age. Wilson's administration, unable or unwilling to check such popular excesses, joined in purging dissent. The result was a fevered public uprising against nonconformity of all kinds and the ruthless suppression of American liberties.

The war hysteria fed a progressive appetite for national unity that had gone unchecked by a tradition of civil liberties. The absence of a libertarian concern with protecting basic freedoms—the central weakness in the progressive program—made a domestic war on liberalism all but inevitable. Patriots and vigilantes equipped with ropes, whips, and tar and feathers

WORLD WAR I RECRUITMENT POSTER
(National Archives)

ment agents rounded up 113 officers and organizers of the IWW and impounded five tons of books and pamphlets with which to arraign and convict them.

Out of these acts of suppression came loose national organizations and federations, perversions of the original progressive consumer and reform leagues, dedicated to rooting out subversion and punishing disloyalty. With support from local and state law-enforcement agencies, the National Security League and the Council of Defense fixed on new targets—the Non-Partisan League in North Dakota, intent on nothing more seditious than interest-group politics, and the People's Council of America for Peace and Democracy, a group of pacifists widely condemned as "traitors and fools." Within six months of Wilson's declaration of war, a rigid censorship combined with political repression had reached into the American press, schools and universities, the churches, and even the new movie industry.

A Pyramid of Repression. This mass popular reaction formed the base of a pyramid of repression supporting a middle range of official and semiofficial bodies, from citizens' councils to state administrative agencies such as the Minnesota Commission of Public Safety, which became a model for the rest of the country. Other states passed criminal syndicalism laws aimed primarily at left-wing dissenters but designed as dragnets for a variety of nonconformists as well. Soon the traditional American distinction between public and private had dissolved in a welter of competing patriotic agencies.

The apex of this national system of extralegalism was completed by the federal government itself with a multiplicity of agencies and activities, chief among them the Committee on Public Information headed by progressive journalist George Creel and charged with mobilizing public opinion behind the war. Perfecting the progressive technique of moral publicity, Creel encouraged a voluntary censorship program, and turned to the new public relations industry for a national cadre of opinion-shapers who launched a propaganda campaign of frightening proportions.

Another weapon in the government's domestic arsenal was an administrative technique inherited

enjoyed a ritualistic field day complete with flag-kissing ceremonies and forced declarations of loyalty. The victims of this reign of terror were mainly marginal people, uneducated or disaffected, isolated and without power. In Bisbee, Arizona, the "best" people rounded up some twelve hundred striking miners led by the Industrial Workers of the World ("Wobblies,") piled them into freight cars, and hauled them across the state line into the desert, where they were left stranded. In Montana, a mob dragged the IWW organizer Frank Little out of his boardinghouse and hanged him from a railroad trestle. Soon the federal government itself joined in the campaign to crush radical dissent: in September 1917, Justice Depart-from prewar progressivism—deportation of undesirable aliens and radicals. The deportation procedure was a simple administrative process. The decision to deport someone was made not by the courts but by magistrates. As a result, maximum freedom was provided for administrators and minimum safeguards for the rights of the accused. This original procedure for the swift removal of undesirables had been created by the Immigration Act of 1903, and the war simply gave widened scope for these summary actions.

The main contributions of the federal government to the repression of basic liberties were the Espionage Act of 1917 and the Sedition Act of 1918, twin declarations of bankruptcy, like the Federalist Alien and Sedition Acts, by a society that had reached the limits of toleration. The Espionage Act levied fines up to $10,000 and twenty years in prison for anyone convicted of causing insubordination, mutiny, or disloyalty in the armed forces by "false reports or false statements." The law also empowered the postmaster general to withhold mailing privileges to newspapers and periodicals deemed subversive, a power that Wilson's appointee, Albert S. Burleson, turned into a formidable weapon against dissent. With Wilson's knowledge, if not always with his approval, Burleson wielded discretionary power with a vengeance in banning socialist periodicals such as *The Masses* and Victor Berger's *Milwaukee Leader*; he even banned a single-tax journal for suggesting that more revenue be raised through taxation. Eugene Debs was convicted and sentenced to ten years in prison under the Sedition Act for telling a socialist audience that the master class causes wars while the subject class fights them. But most of the victims of such heresy-hunting were ordinary people guilty of nothing more scurrilous than the opinion that John D. Rockefeller was a son of a bitch who helped start a capitalist war.

The Sedition Act of 1918 was designed to close the few loopholes in the Espionage Act through which thousands of "spies" and "traitors" were presumed to have escaped. The new law provided punishment for anyone who should "utter, print, write or publish any disloyal, profane, scurrilous, or abusive language about the form of government in the United States, or the uniform of the Army or Navy" or any sentiments intended to bring the government or the military "into contempt, scorn, contumely, or disrepute." More than 1,500 Americans were tried and over 1,000 convicted under these laws. As Senator Hiram Johnson pointed out, this meant simply, "You shall not criticize anything or anybody in the Government any longer or you shall go to jail."

Administrative Agencies. In part, the war hysteria of the years 1917–19 was simply an aberration, a brief departure from good sense, and a betrayal of progressive ideals. But at a deeper level the excesses were growths—malignant, to be sure—of progressivism itself. Discretionary power vested in administrative agencies, which was a progressive innovation, provided flexibility and promptness but at the expense of more deliberate regular processes amenable to judicial oversight. Devised for the purpose of freeing policy-making and administrators from constant interference by the legislature, the progressive device of administrative government had its merits. Applied not to administrative procedures but to the ideas and opinions of citizens, the new process revealed the evils of government action cut adrift from accountability and control.

At times the war crisis lowered the principle of administrative autonomy to the level of license. In the case of Postmaster General Burleson, for example, even the president was unable to check misguided enthusiasm and the personal conviction that no American should ever be allowed "to say that this Government got into the war wrong. . . . It is a false statement," Burleson fumed, "a lie, and it will not be permitted." Such arbitrary power lodged either in the federal bureaucracy or in the lower echelons of state and local administrations inevitably fostered an alarming national irresponsibility by subjecting opinion and expression to the whims and caprices of petty officials freed entirely, as one of them boasted, from "exaggerated sentimentalism [or] a misapplied reverence for legal axioms."

It would have been difficult in any case for Wilson's administration to have curbed the patriotic passions of an American generation preoccupied with rescuing national unity from a vigorous cultural pluralism. But the wartime policy of the federal government was tantamount to issuing hunting licenses to superpatriots to track down and destroy dissent—in pacifists, liberal reformers, socialists, anarchists, and also in many cultural as well as political radicals opposed to the war. These dissenters were not simply outside the mainstream of the war effort. They were part of a more general movement, growing quickly after 1900, of what might be called cultural radicalism—a movement running counter to progressivism with deep roots in America's prewar experience. By 1917 a major shift in the artistic and intellectual life of the country had long been evident in a series of clashes, some symbolic and others real, between an inherited system of truth and the powerful, diverse forces of cultural modernism.

The Little Rebellion: Progressivism and the Challenge of Culture

On February 17, 1913, the International Exhibition of Modern Painting opened in the cavernous Sixty-Ninth Regiment Armory in New York City. To the music of a military band, beneath rafters festooned with huge banners and pine boughs, visitors strolled through a maze of sixteen hundred paintings, drawings, prints, and pieces of sculpture. The Armory Show, two years in the planning, took for its motto "The New Spirit," which was emblazoned on a mammoth replica of the Massachusetts Pine Tree Flag, a message that many American viewers translated as "the harbinger of universal anarchy."

The exhibition had originally been conceived as a strictly American affair, and it was actually dominated numerically by American work, which made up three-quarters of the show. The initial plans, however, had been scrapped for the more ambitious idea of a vast international retrospective tracing the rise of modernism from its nineteenth-century sources in Goya, Ingres, and Delacroix, through the French realist Courbet, to impressionism and the bewildering canvases of post-impressionists, expressionists, and cubists. It was not the dark, looming shapes of the American painter Albert Pinkham Ryder that outraged patrons, or the realistic cityscapes of the "New York Eight," with their conventional images and

brushwork, but what one critic called "the imported ideology" of the new European artists—Picasso, Matisse, Brancusi, Picabia, Léger, Rouault, Kandinsky, Duchamp, and Lehmbruck. Their collective impact carried the force of revolution. Staid art critic Kenyon Cox admitted to spending "an appalling morning" at the show, where he had witnessed the "total destruction of the art of painting. . . . To have looked at it is to have passed through a pathological museum where the layman has no right to go. One feels that one has seen not an exhibition, but an exposure."

The Armory Show collected into a single public image the disparate meaning of European modernism. In the bold thin colors of Matisse's *The Red Studio* or the splashes of one of Kandinsky's *Improvisations* or the frozen motion of Duchamp's *Nude Descending a Staircase*, Americans viewed the results of a perceptual revolution that had transformed the European intellectual and artistic world and that had now arrived in the United States. Here were visible effects of a general revolt against nineteenth-century positivism—in Nietzsche, Bergson, Sorel, Freud, Ibsen, Strindberg—the all too apparent fruits of recent explorations into the unseen, unknown, irrational, and relative, yielding new definitions of time, space, energy, force, and will. For those progressives who chose to examine the work of the modernists, the Armory Show took on the dimensions of a social crisis.

An Artistic Revolution.   The crisis rose directly out of the challenge to the comfortable realism and moralism of the average educated American, who firmly believed in the solidity of the objective social world and in the power of "good art," whether in print or on canvas, to represent it. Socially useful art, most progressives believed, was the art of representation. Progressivism was nourished by a strong sense of social reality—the belief that the world, after all, consisted of commonplace and everyday occurrences strung in orderly and predictable sequences. Progressivism, born in the country and moved to the city, relied upon the moral code of an earlier agrarian society to make otherwise bewildering problems manageable. There was also a lingering idealism in the progressive outlook—Theodore Roosevelt called

THE ARMORY SHOW MAKES NEWS
Marcel Duchamp's cubistic "Nude Descending a Staircase" was one of the European paintings in the 1913 exhibit that outraged critics and viewers and inspired this *Chicago Record-Herald* cartoon "The Rude Descending a Staircase— Rush Hour on the Subway." *(Philadelphia Museum of Art: Louise and Walter Arensberg Collection)*

SEEING NEW YORK WITH A CUBIST

The Rude Descending a Staircase
(Rush Hour at the Subway)

it "practical idealism"—that combined easily with newly discovered techniques of social analysis. These two halves of the progressive persuasion were held together by the belief that science and the scientific method, baffling as they might seem to the layman, would ultimately establish the unity of truth and the fact of progress.

These social opinions supported a set of aesthetic preferences. The progressives' favorite novelist was the reliable William Dean Howells, once, like so many of them, a young man from the provinces come to the metropolis to make his way. Howells built a career and a considerable fortune as a novelist and an editor with his cautious, sensitive probings of modern issues: divorce and the disintegration of the family; economic inequality and the insecurities of a commercial existence; the decline of an older business ethic in a new world of bigness. All of these perplexities Howells weighed in terms of the loss of certainty among small-town Americans and the hope that it might somehow be restored. In his portraits of the puzzled editor Basil March in *A Hazard of New Fortunes* and of the confused businessman in *The Rise of Silas Lapham,* Howells offered recognizable modern types, and progressive readers could find in his fiction their own problems framed and finally solved. And when realism paled, there was always fantasy and that favorite fictional hero, Owen Wister's "Virginian," the unassuming yet self-assured cowboy undefiled by a corrupting commercialism.

Tolerance of the excessive, the outsized, and the grotesque was strictly limited by a psychology that insisted on the rational, the measurable, the predictable. Whatever lay beyond these borders—Frank Norris's study of regression and bestialism in *McTeague,* Henry James's subtle studies of corruption, Mark Twain's experiment in determinism in *The Mysterious Stranger,* Theodore Dreiser's frank exploration of sexuality in *Sister Carrie*—was ignored or rejected as unhealthy or unclean.

In the visual arts, informed opinion had reluctantly come to terms with the "Ashcan School" of New York painters, among them John Sloan, George Luks, and George Bellows, whose realistic paintings of street scenes and city types (see color insert) drew from the same sources as those of progressive reformers and writers. The "New York Eight" as they were also called, sought to encompass the whole city scene with their illustrator's techniques and documentary style. Most progressives understood and accepted the social realism of the Eight, for it was directly involved with the pictorial aspects of twentieth-century urban life. "The tramp sits on the edge of the curb," the Eight's spokesman, Robert Henri, explained. "He is huddled up. His body is thick. His underlip hangs. His eyes look fierce. . . . He is not beautiful, but he could well be the motive for a great and beautiful work of art." Progressives engaged in similar explorations of city life agreed with Henri, for they shared his insistence on "fundamental law" and those axioms "controlling all existence." By 1910 realism had broken the Genteel Tradition's grip on the American imagination without, however, dissolving its view of objective reality.

It was just this sense of the manageability of their world that gave progressives the confidence to reform and improve it. Experimenting with the new tools of social analysis helped sharpen the progressive method, but it also strengthened the belief that the world was plastic after all and could be molded into a controlled environment. The recent knowledge explosion in American universities had shaken but not destroyed the progressive faith in the belief that the great facts in life were simple.

It was this conviction that art and politics amounted to the same thing that had made the Armory Show such a troubling spectacle for most American viewers. It threatened not simply their aesthetic preferences but their belief in the possibilities of planning and social control. The "detestable things" wrought by Picasso, Matisse and Duchamp—"degraded, indecent, and insane," they were called—disclosed the lurking presence of the unpredictable and ungovernable, of flux and formlessness. A Matisse painting reminded humorist Gelett Burgess of the havoc a "sanguinary" girl of eight, "half-crazed with gin," might wreak on a blank wall with a box of crayons. In choosing a revolutionary theme for their exhibition, the organizers of the Armory Show were only following the path their European counterparts had taken for over a century; but American viewers took their political challenge literally. As one hostile critic announced: "The exploitation of a theory of discords, puzzles, ugliness, and clinical details is to art what anarchy is to society and the practitioners need not so much a critic as an alienist [psychiatrist]." Artistic madness would surely lead to barbarism.

There was a natural flow of criticism from aesthetic into political channels. "The United States is invaded by aliens," warned archconservative Royal Cortissoz, "thousands of whom constitute so many acute perils to the health of the body politic. Modernism is of precisely the same heterogeneous alien origin and is imperiling the republic of art in the same way." The Armory Show, Cortissoz warned, was dominated "by types not yet fitted for their first papers in aesthetic naturalization—the makers of true Ellis Island art."

Proletarian Art—The Paterson Pageant. Modernism in the Armory Show presented most viewers with a symbolic dilemma: how to ensure the improvement of American society without underwriting revolution. Once again, as in all other matters American, it was Theodore Roosevelt who had the last word. "It is vitally necessary," the retired president reminded his followers, "to move forward to shake off the dead hand of the reactionaries; and yet we have to face the fact that there is apt to be a lunatic fringe among votaries of any forward movement." Still, the problem remained—how to give support to the sane and deny it to the dangerous. The political evidence was obvious. In New York City on a June evening in 1913, less than four months after the Armory Show, 1,000 silk workers from Paterson, New Jersey, stepped off the ferry and marched in a solid phalanx up Broadway and into Madison Square Garden. There, before a crowd of 15,000 they proceeded to reenact the events of their prolonged strike against the mill owners. Spectators witnessed a new form of proletarian art—social drama as participatory ritual.

The Paterson Pageant was the brainchild of young radical journalist John Reed and a handful of socialist intellectuals and artists who dreamed of fashioning a new mass art out of working-class griev-

ances and the formal protest of the intellectuals. The Paterson strike had been triggered by the decision of the mill owners to increase the workload for unskilled silk weavers and dyers already living on the edge of destitution. Most of the workers in the Paterson dye houses and mills, some 25,000 in all, were new immigrants from Italy, Russia, and eastern Europe, a large number of them young girls earning an average wage of $6 or $7 a week. The IWW entered the town in the winter of 1913 to help organize this unpromising material around the immediate issues of shorter hours and higher wages. "Big Bill" Haywood, fresh from his triumph in the Lawrence, Massachusetts, textile workers' strike, joined the young Wobbly agitator Elizabeth Gurley Flynn and the romantic syndicalist Carlo Tresca in teaching the Paterson workers that it was "far better to starve fighting than to starve working." By February they had succeeded in uniting the unskilled workers and shutting down the town.

The AFL, in trying to break the strike with its skilled workers, fed the progressive tendency to identify the immigrant with radicalism. Yet throughout the spring the ranks of the strikers held firm. The mill owners fought back, stirring up hatred of "outside agitators" and enlisting the police in their efforts to break the strike. "There's a war in Paterson," John Reed reported to his fellow artists and intellectuals in Greenwich Village. "But it's a curious kind of war. All the violence is the work of one side—the Mill Owners."

Reed had reason to know. Like many of the Village socialists and radicals, he had made the Sunday excursion to Paterson to see for himself the clash between the workers and the bosses. He had been jailed, and then returned to New York to compose his indictment of the owners for Max Eastman's *The Masses.* A cultural radical without as yet any clear sense of ideological direction, Reed dreamed of rallying artists and intellectuals to the side of the strikers as the beginning of a permanent alliance for the radical reconstruction of American life. This was the idea he brought back to socialite Mabel Dodge's salon, the gathering place of New York's radical writers and intellectuals. Out of the sessions at Mabel

Dodge's came the plans for a gigantic pageant to raise
money for the strike fund and to educate liberals in
the lessons of working-class solidarity. Reed threw
himself headlong into the project, spending eighteen
hours a day on the script, drilling a thousand amateur
performers into a theatrical company, designing the
massive sets with artist John Sloan and stage designer
Robert Edmond Jones. By June he was ready, Sloan's
huge factory scenes and red curtains in place, and his
cast primed for performance.

The pageant caught the spirit of solidarity that
Reed had sensed in Paterson. As it opened, throngs of
workers moved down the center aisle to linger in
front of the huge gray mills before entering to the
sound of whirring machinery. Suddenly the chant
began—"Strike! Strike!"—growing louder and more
insistent until the workers came pouring out of the
factory doors, and life moved outside the empty, dark

mills. In front of these dead industrial husks, the workers reenacted the scenes of the strike—mass picketing, police harassment, the clash between strikers and scabs in which a worker was killed, and finally the climactic funeral procession.

The audience, many of them workers admitted at 25¢ a seat, joined in booing the police, chanting strike slogans, and lustily singing the "Internationale." For a brief moment it seemed that Reed and the radical cultural critics had succeeded in forging new weapons for social justice out of the materials of mass art.

But life did not imitate art, and the pageant brought a cresting of radical hopes that quickly receded. The spectacle, originally intended to replenish the strike fund, actually yielded a check for $150. The 24,000 strikers who had not participated began to question the dubious honors bestowed on them by the intellectuals. "Bread was the need of the hour," Elizabeth Gurley Flynn complained, "and bread was not forthcoming." The gulf between art and politics could not be bridged by mere ceremony. The skilled workers broke ranks during the summer and returned to the mills. Then the mill owners, in a series of shop-by-shop settlements that conceded nothing to the unskilled workers, shattered their morale and routed the IWW leadership. By summer's end the Paterson workers were back on the job on their employers' terms. John Reed's script for the oppressed workers of America acting out "the wretchedness of their lives and the glory of their revolt" had failed to close the distance between the intellectual vanguard and the working class.

Artists and Scientists: Critics of Progressivism

Other critics of progressivism before the First World War perceived different divisions in American society and suggested other ways of closing them. In 1914 Walter Lippmann published his *Drift and Mastery*, and a year later Van Wyck Brooks his caustic essay, *America's Coming-of Age*. Both demanded a reassessment of progressives' aims and aspirations. Lippmann and Brooks represented a new intellectual type, the

liberal publicist directing criticism toward the progressive elite. Neither journalists in a traditional sense nor philosophers, they saw themselves as cultural and social commentators whose task it was to direct the flow of American life through channels of publicity and informed criticism toward new national goals. They sought to lift their roles as critics to the realm of public power through their analysis of American society.

Brooks's Critique. Van Wyck Brooks, a recent graduate of Harvard where he had studied under philosophers William James and George Santayana, was the chief spokesman for the "little renaissance" in American art and culture that swept across the country after 1912. By the time Brooks issued his challenge to progressivism the signs of cultural rebellion were everywhere. Brooks joined the expanding circle of artists and intellectuals in Greenwich Village after a brief teaching career at Stanford and the Worker's Educational Association in Cambridge, England. In the Village he met Walter Lippmann, who urged him to contribute to the literary renaissance by scrutinizing the "noble dream" of American democratic culture in the light of the "actual limitations of experience." Brooks promptly obliged with what he called an address to his own "homeless generation" of intellectuals and would-be critics.

Brooks discerned a basic American duality in the cultural split between "highbrow" and "lowbrow"; a fatal division, he said, that had paralyzed the creative will of the nation for over a century. The American impasse, Brooks argued, stemmed from the conflict between transcendental theory and the "catchpenny realities" of a business civilization. Between these poles lay a cultural wasteland in which no true community could thrive. Brooks traced the roots of this American schizophrenia to the original sin of Puritanism, "the all-influential fact in the history of the American mind." To Puritanism could be attributed both the "fastidious refinement" of current tastes and the "opportunism" of American moneymakers.

Like the progressive historian Vernon L. Parrington, who was already at work compiling the materials for the first volume of his *Main Currents of American Thought* which would document this view, Brooks presented his authors in sets of paired opposites: Jonathan Edwards and Benjamin Franklin; Henry Wadsworth Longfellow and Mark Twain; James Russell Lowell and Walt Whitman, figures on opposite sides of a chasm between literate and illiterate America. Throughout the nineteenth century the divorce of the real and the ideal, Brooks complained, had resulted in an "orgy of lofty examples, moralized poems, national anthems and baccalaureate sermons" until the average citizen was now "charged with all manner of ideal purities, ideal honorabilities, ideal femininities, flagwavings and skyscrapings of every sort." In the meantime the American landscape had become a stamping ground for every greedy commercial impulse of every last businessman who held that "society is fair prey for what he can get out of it."

Brooks pointed to the shortcomings of the progressive approach to reform. Progressivism, for all its moral certainties and good government ideals, had failed to solve the fundamental problem of modern industrial society—the "invisible government" of business and the profit motive. So far, the efforts of well-meaning progressive reformers to change American priorities had added up to nothing. Progressivism simply consolidated the rule of "commercialized men." Of what use was it, Brooks demanded, to tinker with political mechanisms or "do any of the other easy popular contemporary things" unless the quality of American life could also be improved?

Here Brooks reached the core of his critique. Meaningful betterment of American society would require more than rationalizing a business system, more than the cheerful cooperation of business and government, whether in the name of the New Nationalism or the New Freedom. Nothing would suffice now but the massive shift of American energies from business and politics to psychology and art. Otherwise progressivism would fail in its regenerative mission. When the First World War broke out, Brooks still hoped for the cultural rebellion for which he spoke. Three years later, American entrance into the war broke these hopes on the rocks of the war state.

Lippmann's Analysis. Walter Lippmann also discerned a split in twentieth-century American life that progressivism had failed to repair, but his definition concerned the conflict between Victorian silences—what he called the "sterile tyranny of taboo"—bequeathed by the nineteenth century, and his own generation's desire "to be awake during their own lifetime." "Drift" was the result of the rule of old bogeys. Mastery meant applying the scientific method to politics. Like Brooks, though for different reasons, Lippmann faulted the progressives for their lack of rigorous thought. The New Nationalism, although it had examined some of the worst abuses of industrialism, still spoke the language of the old moralists. The New Freedom continued to make false promises of a return to free competition. "You would think that competitive commercialism was really a generous, chivalrous, high-minded stage of human culture," Lippmann scoffed, instead of "an antiquated, feeble, mean, and unimaginative way of dealing with the possibilities of modern industry." Lippmann agreed with Brooks on the need for relocating American energies outside politics, but he differed dramatically on the means. Unlike Brooks and the cultural radicals, he championed the cause of business consolidation and the rule of industrial statesmen who would transcend politics by lifting decision-making out of the marketplace to the level of scientific management. Whereas the cultural radicals hoped to destroy the rule of big business, Lippmann sought to rationalize and reform it. His aim was to create a truly cooperative society, neither strictly capitalistic nor wholly collectivist, but a new commonwealth comprised of managers, workers, and consumers, each applying the instruments of measurement and control provided by modern science.

The Seven Arts and The New Republic. If American entry into the First World War threatened Van Wyck Brooks's plans for reconstructing American culture, it brought a welcome test for Lippmann's pragmatic liberalism and his design for a businessmen's government. Brooks deplored the war as a betrayal of his dreams; Lippmann embraced it as a challenge. By 1917 these two critiques of progressivism had been institutionalized in two very different magazines: *The Seven Arts*, which Brooks and his cultural radical friends Randolph Bourne and James Oppenheim founded in 1916 and nursed through a year of precarious existence; and *The New Republic*, which Lippmann together with liberal nationalists Herbert Croly and Walter Weyl had launched in 1914. The war records of these two magazines testified to the divergent fates of cultural radicalism and liberal nationalism under emergency conditions.

The Seven Arts lasted just a year before succumbing to the fervor of the patriots. Brooks's mantle fell on the diminutive figure of Randolph Bourne, who more clearly than any of the other opponents of the war saw the coming defeat of "that America of youth and aspiration" standing below the battle. In "War and the Intellectuals," the most scathing of his attacks on Lippmann and the prowar liberals, Bourne ridiculed the "war technique" of liberal reform that had led the intellectuals to the illusion that they had willed the war "though sheer force of ideas." In welcoming the war, Bourne charged, *The New Republic* editors allied themselves with the least democratic forces in American society, those primitive interests that still were trumpeting notions of the national state and the doctrines of economic privilege. The war, Bourne concluded, provided an escape for progressives who had become prisoners of their own fantasies of the ordered society. The collapse of *The Seven Arts* after a year of lonely opposition to the war and Bourne's untimely death marked the end of the cultural radical attempt to reconstruct progressivism by supplying it with higher values.

Lippmann and the other editors of *The New Republic* continued to cling to the belief that they could help direct a democratic war and write a liberal peace. The American entrance, Lippmann explained soon after Wilson's declaration of war, would prove "decisive in the history of the world," since the United States could now proceed to "crystallize and make real the whole league of peace propaganda." Nor did he fear the effects of a war psychology on the prospects of liberalism. In October 1917 he offered his services to the administration and was appointed secretary of The Inquiry, Wilson's hand-picked body of experts charged with preparing the American agenda for the peace table. Herbert Croly, who remained in his editorial post at *The New Republic*, quickly grew disillusioned as he realized the nature

of the liberal impasse both at home and abroad. Lippmann's hopes for a liberal peace remained high. But eighteen months later, discouraged by the president's failure at Versailles, and dubious now about the uses of war as a means of social reconstruction, Lippmann joined those "tired radicals" seeking to defeat the treaty.

The Ordeal of Woodrow Wilson

In his address to Congress on January 8, 1918—the low point in the American war effort—Woodrow Wilson outlined the steps the United States and the Allies would have to take in order to ensure a postwar world "made fit to live in." Wilson presented his Fourteen Points as a blueprint for peacemaking drawn to his own progressive specifications. Central in his thinking was the principle of "open covenants openly arrived at," the extension to international politics of the New Freedom idea of moral publicity. A counterweight to this first point in Wilson's moral scales was the fourteenth, calling for "a general association of nations . . . formed under specific covenants for the purpose of affording mutual guarantees of political independence and territorial integrity to great and small states alike." The main substantive points in Wilson's utopian calendar included a general disarmament, complete freedom of the seas, an equitable adjustment of colonial claims in the interests of the peoples involved, and a series of specific provisions for setting national boundaries in Europe on the basis of the language spoken in each region. These were the lofty terms that Wilson, in the face of mounting opposition from his war partners, intended to impose at the peace table.

Problems with the Fourteen Points. In attempting to achieve his aims, Wilson was driven by circumstance, as well as by his own intensely moral nature, to make several costly miscalculations. Part of his trouble lay in the Fourteen Points themselves. What, for example, did his principle of national self-determination mean, and by what general formula could it be applied? What adjustments might be needed

PRESIDENT WILSON EMBARKS
FOR PARIS, DECEMBER 1918

(Brown Brothers)

when linguistic nationalism failed to coincide with economic viability or military aims? Then, how could a new Soviet regime with an exportable totalitarian ideology be given "an unhampered and unembarrassed opportunity" for political development? How, in short, could Wilson, as the representative of the only disinterested power at the peace table, establish in each and every instance his claim to be the enlightened conscience of mankind?

A related set of problems concerned Wilson's political position at home. Who but himself—the president—he asked, could convert the Allies to his program and ensure the triumph of collective security? Determined to play the dominant role at the Paris conference, he insisted on making his peace program a partisan issue in the fall elections of 1918 by warning that a Republican victory would be a repudiation of his leadership and vision. Republicans, who had already grown restive under the nonpartisan war policy, now retaliated by accusing Wilson him-

self of partisan dealings. In 1918 the Republicans regained control of both houses of Congress. If their victory did not quite mean a vote of no confidence, it did serve notice on Wilson that the spirit of party politics had been revived and would be decisive in settling the fate of his peace program.

Even more serious was Wilson's refusal to include Republican leaders among his advisers at the peace conference. Former President Taft, Charles Evans Hughes, and a number of other Republican notables had expressed cautious interest in the idea of a League of Nations, and Wilson's calculated exclusion of these men isolated him from the moderate Republican internationalism he so desperately needed. On the eve of his departure for Europe in December 1918, there were already ominous signs of a growing presidential detachment from the realities of domestic politics, as Wilson began to retreat into the recesses of his moralistic nature. "Tell me what is right," he urged his advisers as he prepared for the

THE COUNCIL OF FOUR

From left to right: Vittorio Orlando of Italy, David Lloyd George of England, Georges Clemenceau of France, Woodrow Wilson.   *(National Archives)*

conference, "and I'll fight for it." Wilson fought tenaciously, even heroically, for his Fourteen Points against overwhelming odds. But in forgetting the first rules of politics and ignoring the domestic disarray he had left behind, he fatally compromised his position.

Problems in Paris.   In David Lloyd George of Great Britain, Georges Clemenceau of France, and Vittorio Orlando of Italy, the president confronted national leaders who, as he came to realize with chagrin, spoke for their countrymen as he could not. The Allies had

suffered grievously during the war, and their leaders could count on unwavering support at home for a punitive peace, one that would assign all the war guilt to Germany, strip it of all its colonial possessions, exact enormous reparations, and provide all the necessary safeguards against future aggression. To counter these narrow nationalistic aims, Wilson brought with him to Paris only the Fourteen Points and his vision of a new concert of power. Despite his initial popularity with the peoples of Europe, his lone voice became lost in the clamor of competing nationalisms. The American story of the peace deliberations was one of mounting frustration and a forced retreat from idealism.

The first of the Fourteen Points to be jettisoned was the utopian concept of "open covenants." Soon after the opening of the conference the plenary sessions gave way first to a Council of Ten dominated by the heads of state and their foreign ministers, and then to a Council of Four composed of Wilson, Lloyd George, Clemenceau, and Orlando, meeting behind closed doors. The press, barred from working sessions, became almost wholly dependent on news releases handed out after each plenary session. Wilson added to his problems of communication by withdrawing coldly from his colleagues on the council and ignoring most of his advisers, who also complained of his aloofness. Removed from presidential oversight, the American staff floundered in confusion. Wilson, announcing that he had no desire "to have lawyers drafting the treaty of peace," played a lone hand at Paris and quickly exhausted his reserves of moral capital.

On a few of the specific issues of the peace settlement Wilson was partially successful in moderating the extortionate demands of his partners. After an epochal battle of wills with the cynical Clemenceau, who likened his adversary to Jesus Christ and Moses bearing the Ten Commandments, Wilson forced France to agree to a multinational defense pact, but at the cost of the immediate return to France of Alsace-Lorraine, French occupation of the Rhineland, and huge reparations to be paid by Germany. On the question of the former German colonies he abandoned the principle of "impartial adjustment" but salvaged his plan for a mandate system under League auspices. For Poland he secured a corridor to the sea at the expense of linguistic nationalism, and in constructing a new Austria from the dismembered Austro-Hungarian empire, he presided over the transfer of some 200,000 German-speaking people to Italy. When he refused to agree to a similar transfer of a strip of the Dalmatian coast, he precipitated a major crisis by appealing for self-restraint directly to the Italian people over the heads of their representatives, a blunder that only hardened Italian resolves and further discredited him with his colleagues at the

peace table. Self-determination of peoples speaking the same language—a legacy of nineteenth-century romantic nationalism—was honored in the breach at Paris as often as it was successfully applied.

But it was on the question of reparations that the president suffered his sharpest defeat. France originally suggested the preposterous figure of $200 billion, and England seemed unwilling to settle for much less. Clemenceau and Lloyd George, bowing to heavy pressure from their respective publics, overrode Wilson's objections to such crippling demands and forced him to accept the inclusion of civilian damages and military pensions in the final assessment on Germany. The president, pushed beyond the limits of endurance, had become ill and confused. He agreed to the principle of massive repayments and allowed the fixing of the specific amount to be postponed. The Council of Four provided for a Reparations Commission, which in 1921 set the indemnity at $56 billion without regard to Germany's ability to pay or to the political consequences for the struggling new German republic.

The League of Nations. Throughout the agony of daily defeat Wilson was sustained by his hopes for the League of Nations and the work of drafting the covenant of the League. The League, he told himself, would correct the mistakes and make good the deficiencies of the peace settlement to which it must be firmly tied. By tying the League closely to the treaty, the president hoped to circumvent his congressional opponents by presenting them with a complete package that they would have to accept or reject as a whole. He never seriously considered that they might succeed in destroying his great work.

It was Article X of the League Covenant that became the great symbolic issue that eventually wrecked his dream. Article X provided that

the members of the League undertake to respect and preserve as against external aggression the territorial integrity and existing political independence of all the Members of the League. In case of any such aggression or in case of any threat or danger of such aggression the Council shall advise upon the means by which this obligation shall be fulfilled.

For Wilson, Article X represented the triumph of moral force. The details of applying sanctions against future offenders concerned him less than the simple recognition by the nations of the world of his principle of collective security. This principle, at least, he had managed to rescue from the ruins of the treaty, and he meant to defend it at all costs.

In part, the League of Nations, on which Wilson pinned all his hopes, represented the progressive idea of commission government applied to the field of international politics. Like a federal commission designed to free policy-making from the whims of politicians, the League, with its various branches and agencies, would provide the means of defusing international crises and resolving conflicts through arbitration. But in another and more profound sense Wilson's League was simply the application of inherited nineteenth-century liberal principles and a doctrine of progress.

In the president's mind the League embodied old truths and moral principles, particularly the belief that as American institutions and ideas reformed the rest of the world and as the beneficent workings of trade and commerce gathered peoples together in harmony and abundance, the old selfish national interests would die out. Ultimately a worldwide legal community would rise in place of the discredited system of balance of power. Wilson, having witnessed four years of international slaughter and having seen embittered nationalists at Versailles impose a savage, punitive peace on Germany, was convinced that the time had finally come for building such an international moral order. While he was willing to concede much—and in fact had conspicuously failed to control the peace conference—he was not prepared to compromise on the League of Nations or on the question of the role his country would have to play in its creation.

Wilson's utopian commitment led him to overlook two fundamental problems. The first resulted from attaching the League to the peace treaty. A second problem was that of intent. Was the League intended simply to enforce a victor's peace, or would it work to adjust shifting balances of national power,

incorporate new members including the defeated nations, and underwrite orderly change and development? No amount of Wilsonian rhetoric about "the general moral judgment of mankind" could obscure the basic uncertainty of purpose in the president's attempt to replace power relations with moral force.

The Red Scare.   Wilson returned to the United States in the summer of 1919 and found a nation already in the throes of reaction. The shadow of the Russian Revolution, which had fallen over the peace table, now lengthened across the Atlantic. The threat of revolution strengthened the forces of reaction everywhere in Europe as conservatives rushed to defend their states from the Bolshevik menace. To Americans, the Soviet challenge seemed particularly frightening because it threatened their own revolutionary tradition. Here was no mere political rebellion and rearrangement, sensibly completed and solicitous of property rights and personal liberties, but instead a vast social upheaval with a collectivist ideology that was the antithesis of Western capitalist democracy. The American response to the new Soviet regime was twofold: an abortive attempt to strengthen the counterrevolutionary forces in Russia by landing American troops (soon withdrawn) at Murmansk and Vladivostok, and the tendency at home to see "Reds" everywhere. By the summer of 1919 the "Red Scare" had taken full possession of the public imagination as a wartime fear of subversion was suddenly transformed into a dread of imminent revolution. Liberal ideas, whether in art or politics, were met with strident protests against nonconformity and demands for unconditional loyalty.

Wilson also felt the force of a congressional reaction that had been building since the armistice. Mobilization for war had concentrated power in the executive branch of the government, thus completing the political cycle that had begun with Theodore Roosevelt's presidency. But now, with reconversion and demobilization, the political pendulum began to swing the other way, as Congress moved firmly to reassert its control over foreign affairs as well as domestic policy.

Republicans Oppose Wilson. Congressional resurgence had already acquired a highly partisan cast with the revival of the Republican party, which with forty-nine seats in the Senate now enjoyed a two-vote margin over its rival. Given an opportunity to check Wilson's power by modifying the terms of American participation in the new League of Nations, Republicans could scarcely be expected to resist. Republican leaders were also preparing to roll back wartime controls and curb the regulatory power of federal agencies, whose activities they now tended to equate with socialism. The League was only the most obvious issue with which the Republican party aimed to establish itself in the majority once again.

Yet on the question of acceptance of Wilson's treaty and American participation in the League of Nations, the Republican members of the Senate remained divided. On the right of the party stood some dozen or fifteen "irreconcilables," isolationists opposed to nearly any continued international involvement. At the other end of the spectrum were the "mild reservationists," supporters of the League in principle but concerned with the extent of Wilson's commitment to collective security and anxious to limit it. Ranged between these two ideological poles were the "strong reservationists," making up the majority faction and led by Senator Henry Cabot Lodge. Lodge combined a cordial hatred for the president with a narrow nationalism that had not changed since the Spanish-American War. The "strong reservationists" were willing to consider United States participation in the League only on their own terms, and they were fully prepared to force on Wilson significant reservations limiting American commitments and making Congress rather than the president the final judge of their applicability.

Within his own party, Wilson could count on solid internationalist support, but it was clear at the outset of the struggle that he would have to win a sizable number of moderates away from Lodge in order to gain acceptance of his League of Nations. By July 1919, Wilson faced a formidable but not an impossible task, one that would require great patience and even greater flexibility.

For his part, Lodge followed a clever strategy contrived to exploit every advantage over his adversary. He packed the Senate Foreign Relations Committee with his followers; he conducted interminable hearings that gave a voice to every conceivable opponent of the League; he courted right-wing businessmen like Henry Clay Frick and Andrew Mellon; and he loaded the treaty down with amendments. By fall his original forty-five amendments had been reduced to fourteen reservations, one for each of Wilson's initial Fourteen Points. The first reserved to the United States the sole right to decide whether it had fulfilled its obligations under the covenant, and gave the power of withdrawal from the League to Congress. The second, directed at the controversial Article X, was also aimed at Wilson's greatest weakness. It provided that the United States would accept no obligation to enforce the collective-security provisions of the covenant without the consent of Congress in each and every case. Other reservations rejected any mandates assignable to the United States, reserved the right to determine which questions involving American interests might be submitted to the League, and withdrew the Monroe Doctrine from the international arena. Taken together, Lodge's reservations were significant but not crippling modifications, as the subsequent history of the League would show.

Yet, as Lodge hoped, Wilson believed otherwise. He consistently refused to make a realistic assessment of the situation. He was unwilling to discuss the specific circumstances under which the United States might be called on to apply sanctions—either economic or military—against other nations because he was convinced that full discussion in the forum of the League would make sanctions unnecessary. For him the real question was simple: Was the United States prepared to make the significant moral gesture toward peace and international security? Would the American people see to it that the Senate carried out its obligation? Although the actual fight in the Senate grew complicated with proposals and counterproposals, amendments, reservations, and interpretations, the president's position remained essentially the one he had taken in presenting the treaty to the Senate:

"The stage is set, the destiny disclosed.... We cannot turn back. We can only go forward, with lifted eyes and freshened spirit, to follow the vision."

Wilson's own vision led him away from Washington on an eight-thousand-mile tour of the nation, during which he gave forty speeches explaining to the American people the importance of the League to their future security and welfare. In taking his case to the country, Wilson was violating one of his own precepts. "The Senate," he once wrote, "is not . . . immediately sensitive to [public] opinion and is apt to grow, if anything, more stiff if pressure of that kind is brought to bear upon it." Now President Wilson ignored Professor Wilson's stricture. His tour of the nation carried him further and further away from political reality and the problem of securing the consent of the Senate. Although he referred frequently to specific issues and explained the limited nature of the American commitment, it was to the theme of moral principle that he returned repeatedly:

You have no choice, my fellow citizens.... You cannot give a false gift.... Men are not going to stand it.... There is nothing for any nation to lose whose purposes are right and whose cause is just.... The whole freedom of the world not only, but the whole peace of mind of the world, depends upon the choice of America.... I can testify to that.... The world will be absolutely in despair if America deserts it.

Worn out and distraught, collapsing under the weight of his moral mission, Wilson suffered a stroke in Pueblo, Colorado, on September 26, 1919, and was rushed back to Washington where a week later a second stroke left him paralyzed. Wilson in effect had spoken his last word on the treaty. Desperately ill, he was physically isolated from his followers and advisers, and locked in a private moral world. Loyal Democrats received their presidential orders: vote to reject the treaty with the Lodge reservations. On November 19, 1919, the treaty with the reservations failed of adoption by a vote of 39 for and 55 against, with the Democrats dutifully joining the irreconcilables to defeat it. Wilson still hoped to make the presidential election of 1920 the occasion of a giant referendum on the League, but his advisers, along with more objective observers, knew the fight was over. The president's dream was dead.

Domestic discord in the year 1919 mirrored the collapse of Wilson's moral world. A calendar of violence marked the decline of original progressive hopes:

In January, shipyard workers in Seattle struck for higher wages, organized a general strike, and paralyzed the city. At the request of the mayor the federal government sent in the Marines.

In May, 400 soldiers and sailors sacked the offices of the socialist newspaper, the New York *Call* and beat up the staff.

In the summer, race riots erupted in 25 cities across the country; the most serious outbreak was in Chicago where 38 were killed and over 500 injured.

In September, the Boston police force struck for the right to unionize, and the city experienced a wave of looting and theft until leading businessmen and Harvard students restored order.

In September, 350,000 steelworkers struck for the right to unionize and for an eight-hour day.

In November, a mob in Centralia, Washington, dragged IWW agitator Wesley Everett from jail and castrated him before hanging him.

In December, agents of the Labor Department rounded up 249 Russian communists and deported them to Finland.

There were Americans in 1919 who recalled Wilson's definition of the progressive task six years earlier as "the high enterprise of the new day.... Our duty is to cleanse, to reconsider, to correct the evil without impairing the good, to purify and humanize every process of our common life without weakening or sentimentalizing it." For those who remembered, there could be little doubt that the new day had ended.

CHRONOLOGY

1913   Armory Show in New York City.
Paterson strike.

1914   First World War begins; Wilson declares American neutrality.
"Ludlow Massacre"; National Guard attacks tent colony of strikers in Ludlow, Colorado, killing 11 women and 2 children.

1915   Germans declare unrestricted submarine warfare and sink *Lusitania* with loss of American lives.

1916   Wilson reelected, narrowly defeating Charles Evans Hughes.
House-Grey Memorandum on United States efforts for negotiated peace.

1917   Germans resume unrestricted submarine warfare and United States enters war.
Russian Revolution; "February Revolution" establishing provisional government; "October Revolution" engineered by Bolsheviks.
Draft Act.
Espionage Act.
Purchase of Danish Virgin Islands.
Creation of War Industries Board.
First Pulitzer prizes awarded.

1918   Wilson's Fourteen Points outlining administration's peace aims.
United States troops at Belleau Wood.
Saint Mihiel salient, first United States offensive.
Meuse-Argonne offensive.
Sedition Act providing severe penalties for expressing "disloyal" opinions.
Armistice; Germany defeated.

1919   *Schenck* v. *U.S.*, upholding Espionage Act and government curtailment of free speech during wartime.
Abrams v. *U.S.*, upholding Sedition Act.
Eighteenth Amendment (Volstead Act) prohibits sale or manufacture of alcoholic beverages.
Steel strike.
Race riots in Chicago, East Saint Louis, and Washington.

1920   Great Red Scare.
Defeat of Versailles Treaty by Senate.
Nineteenth Amendment gives vote to women.
Warren G. Harding elected president, defeating James M. Cox and Eugene Debs.

SUGGESTED READINGS

Three good surveys of the military conduct of the war are Edward M. Coffman, *The War to End Wars: The American Military Experience in World War I* (1968); Hanson W. Baldwin, *World War I* (1962); and Russell F. Weigley, *The American Way of War* (1973). Fredric L. Paxon, *American Democracy and the World War* (3 vols., 1936–48) provides massive treatment of the war years at home and in the field. John G. Clifford, *The Citizen Soldiers: The Plattsburg Training Camp Movement, 1913–1920* (1972), describes the preparedness movement.

Immediately following the war the participants on the home front took the measure of their difficulties and accomplishments in numerous monographs useful for their impressions: Benjamin Hibbard, *Effects of the Great War upon Agriculture in the United States and Great Britain* (1919); Grosvenor Clarkson, *Industrial America in the World War* (1923); Gordon Watkins, *Labor Problems and Labor Administration in the United States during the World War* (1920); George Creel, *How We Advertised America* (1920). More recent studies are at once more accurate, better balanced, and generally critical. Robert Cuff, *The War Industries Board* (1973), discusses in detail the overwhelming problems confronting the board, and Charles Gilbert, *American Financing of World War I* (1970), carefully analyzes a difficult subject. Frank L. Grubbs, Jr., *The Struggle for Labor Loyalty: Gompers, the A. F. of L., and the Pacifists, 1917–1920* (1968), describes the war efforts of labor leaders. Theodore Saloutos and John D. Hicks, *Agricultural Discontent in the Middle West, 1900–1939* (1951), contains an account of the growing plight of the farmers, as the opening section of George Soule, *Prosperity Decade* (1947), does for the American economy as a whole. Daniel R. Beaver, *Newton D. Baker and the American War Effort, 1917–1919* (1966), surveys the contributions of a great organizer. George T. Blakely, *Historians on the Homefront: American Propagandists for the Great War* (1970), is an unsettling account of misplaced patriotism. Seward W. Livermore, *Politics Is Adjourned: Woodrow Wilson and the War Congress, 1916–1919* (1966), recounts the fate of wartime bipartisanship.

The years since World War II have seen a growing number of incisive studies of American civil liberties during and after the First World War. Beginning with Zechariah Chafee, *Free Speech in the United States* (1941), the list includes Harry N. Scheiber, *The Wilson Administration and Civil Liberties, 1917–1921* (1960); Donald M. Johnson, *The Challenge to American Freedoms* (1963); H. C. Peterson and Gilbert Fite, *Opponents of the War, 1917–1918* (1957); William Preston, Jr., *Aliens and Dissenters: Federal Suppression of Radicals, 1903–1933* (1963); Robert K. Murray, *Red Scare: A Study of National Hysteria, 1919–1920* (1955); and Paul L. Murphy, *The Meaning of Freedom of Speech . . . Wilson to FDR* (1972). Stanley Cohen, *A. Mitchell Palmer* (1963), paints a portrait of a national villain.

For the effects on the social and cultural life of Americans during the war, see the selections in David F. Trask, ed., *World War I at Home: Readings on American Life, 1914–1920* (1969), and Arthur S. Link, ed., *The Impact of World War* (1969). Paul A. Carter, *The Decline and Revival of the Social Gospel* (1954), traces the history of a key religious concept through the war, and Ray Abrams, *Preachers Present Arms* (1933), describes the recruitment of segments of the ministry to the war state. A. Hunter Dupree, *Science and the Federal Government* (1957), considers how war cements ties between government and the scientific community. Arthur Waskow, *From Race Riot to Sit-In, 1919 and the 1960's* (1966), and William Tuttle, Jr., *Race Riot; Chicago and the Red Summer of 1919* (1970), analyze the most serious of the racial disturbances during and after the war. Robert L. Friedheim, *The Seattle General Strike* (1964) dissects an important event. Wesley M. Bagby, *The Road to Normalcy: The Presidential Campaign and Election of 1920* (1962) opens the political door on the Twenties.

The immediate shock of war as experienced by artists and intellectuals is described in Stanley Cooperman, *World War I and the American Novel* (1967), and its lingering effects in Malcolm Cowley, *Exiles Return: A Literary Odyssey of the 1920's* (1951), and Frederick J. Hoffman, *The 20's* (1955).

There are two good discussions of American art in the early twentieth century: Sam Hunter, *American Painting and Sculpture* (1959), and Barbara Rose, *American Art Since 1900: A Critical History* (1967), which should be read together with her *Readings in American Art Since 1900: A Documentary Survey* (1968). John I. H. Bauer, *Revolution and Tradition in Modern American Art* (1967) provides useful commentary on the Ashcan School. For the Armory Show, see Milton Brown, *The Story of the Armory Show* (1963), and also the best brief discussion of its revolutionary meaning for American art, Meyer Schapiro, "Rebellion in Art," in Daniel Aaron, ed., *America in Crisis* (1952). The confused response of one practitioner of the strenuous life can be found in Theodore Roosevelt, "A Layman's Views of an Art Exposition," *Outlook* 29, March 9, 1913.

The best approach to the intellectual history of the Progressive years is through the writers themselves. Significant works of social and political analysis, now considered classics, include Jane Addams, *Twenty Years at Hull House* (1910); Randolph Bourne, *Youth and Life* (1913) and a collection of Bourne's war pieces, *War and the Intellectuals* (1964), edited by Carl Resek; Louis Brandeis, *Other People's Money* (1914); Van Wyck Brooks, *America's Coming of Age* (1915); Charles H. Cooley, *Human Nature and the Social Order* (1922); Herbert Croly, *The Promise of American Life* (1909); John Dewey, *School and Society* (1899); W. E. B. DuBois, *Souls of the Black Folk* (1903); Charlotte Perkins Gilman, *Women and Economics* (1898); Walter Lippmann, *Drift and Mastery* (1914); John Reed, *Insurgent Mexico* (1914) and *Ten Days That Shook the World* (1919); Walter Weyl, *The New Democracy* (1912).

On the diplomacy of war and peacemaking, Arno J. Mayer, *Political Origins of the New Diplomacy, 1917–1918* (1959) and *Politics and Diplomacy of Peacemaking: Containment and Counterrevolution at Versailles, 1918–1919* (1967), are both ponderous and provocative. N. Gordon Levin, *Woodrow Wilson and World Politics: America's Response to War and Revolution* (1968), focuses on the presidential strategies as does Warren Kuehl, *Seeking World Order: The United States and World Organization to 1920* (1969). Two works by Thomas A. Bailey, *Woodrow Wilson and the Lost Peace* (1944) and *Woodrow Wilson and the Great Betrayal* (1945), detail Wilson's tragic postwar course. On the opposition to the League, Ralph A. Stone, *The Irreconcilables: The Fight Against the League of Nations* (1970), is admirable, and John Garraty, *Henry Cabot Lodge* (1953), offers a sympathetic but not uncritical appraisal of Wilson's archenemy. On Soviet-American relations, see George F. Kennan, *Russia Leaves the War* (1956), and *The Decision to Intervene: Prelude to Allied Intervention in the Bolshevik Revolution* (1958). Peter G. Filene, *Americans and the Soviet Experiment* (1967), and Christopher Lasch, *The American Liberals and the Russian Revolution* (1962), consider the varied American reactions to the Revolution. Betty M. Unterberger, *America's Siberian Expedition* (1956), explains the failure of that misguided action. Lawrence E. Gelfand, *The Inquiry: American Preparations for Peace, 1917–1919* (1963), is an account of the role of the president's advisers at Versailles. Paul Birdsall, *Versailles: Twenty Years After* (1973), assesses the peacemaking from the perspective of a later crisis.

PART SIX

Robert H. Wiebe

Modernizing the Republic

1920 to the Present

*T*he First World War shattered some hopes beyond repair. Never again would a cultural vanguard expect a sweeping, almost spontaneous revolution in values with such happy zest as the Greenwich Village radicals did on the eve of the war. Never again would Americans bring such a shining optimism to international affairs as they did when Woodrow Wilson called them to battle for universal democracy and justice. A certain faith in the world's moral wholeness and its natural improvement had been irreparably lost. Yet these casualities of the war were themselves an important preparation for the nation's future. As the high ideals of the progressive years faded, Americans entered the 1920s with a sharper focus on material goals. The greater willingness of Americans to find salvation through the economy set them on the path into the modern era.

The core of America's modern state was a national political economy that acquired its basic form in the 1920s. Beginning with the industrial consolidations of the late nineteenth century, the main subdivisions of the economy—the business of production and distribution, the centers of finance, skilled labor, and commercial agriculture—had become increasingly organized, increasingly committed to nationwide cooperation, and increasingly alert to the usefulness of the government in Washington. The First World War accelerated these trends. By the middle of the 1920s, the national government adopted a consistent policy of support for these organized groups, and the components of America's modern political economy fell into place. Although the operations of the political economy grew vastly more complex during the next five decades, its essential character did not change.

Along with this national system came four primary problems that have shaped modern American history. The dramatic occurrences of the modern era—the Great Depression, the Second World War, the onset of the Cold War, and the social and political upheaval of the 1960s—affected both the substance of these problems and their solutions; so in a much smaller way did the changes of presidents and political parties in Washington. But as the nation swung from prosperity to depression, from peace to war, and from confidence to doubt, it was always this set of four problems that gave continuity to America's development.

First, *How should Americans maintain a strong economy?* In the 1920s the new national system seemed quite capable of running itself. Without direction, however, the economy ended in depression, and a majority of Americans turned for help to the national government. For a quarter of a century after

Overleaf: Photograph of Lake Michigan shore near Chicago, 1949. *(Photograph by Lil and Al Bloom. Chicago Historical Society)*

the Great Crash of 1929, the nation's leaders sought a generally acceptable means of using the government's powers. Not until the early 1950s did Republicans and Democrats alike come to rely on Washington's fiscal authority, particularly the huge national budget, to guarantee a steady, healthy economy.

A fiscal solution gained bipartisan approval partly because it promised maximum government support for the economy with minimum interference in private affairs. A similar combination of support and restraint was the solution to a second primary problem in modern America: *How should political authority be divided between the national and local levels of American life?* What made this problem so acute was a growing separation between the two spheres. National politics concentrated more and more exclusively on national economic issues. Local politics, on the other hand, continued to be concerned with a variety of traditional ethnic and cultural issues. Different leaders, different standards, and different needs at the two levels threatened to disrupt government. During the 1930s the Democratic party under Franklin Roosevelt tacitly agreed that national leaders would have a free hand in devising general economic policy and local leaders a wide discretion in setting rules for their cultural and ethnic domains. In 1953, as the Republican Dwight Eisenhower entered the White House, this compromise seemed even sturdier than it had been under the Democrats.

Its economy made America the world's most powerful nation, yet America's tradition held it aloof from international commitments. Hence a third primary problem: *How should the United States exercise its great power in world affairs?* In resolving this problem, Washington initially sought to maintain international stability with as few formal obligations as possible. The worldwide depression of the 1930s destroyed this web of arrangements, and to protect its global interests against the challenge of military imperialism, the United States entered the Second World War. Only in response to international communism, however, did the United States develop a long-range, systematic pattern of commitments that by midcentury spread American power around the world.

A fourth primary problem involved personal rather than public issues. *What values should govern the individual in modern society?* Some Americans adapted their values to fit the specialized occupations they held in the modern economy. Others, finding little prestige in their routine jobs, looked elsewhere for meaning in their lives. Many wondered if they could even survive as individuals in an impersonally organized society. Such a mixture of perceptions demanded an equally rich variety of solutions. On the anvil of depression, war, and postwar uncertainty, Americans hammered out an array of answers for the individual that expressed the cultural diversity prevailing at midcentury.

By the early 1950s, an initial round of asking and answering was completed. In the process Americans had greatly increased the burdens on their national government. What happened in Washington intimately affected the network of solutions that had been reached, and any number of actions there might unravel the entire pattern, forcing a new search for answers. During the late 1950s and 1960s, the policies of the national government did precisely that. A drive for uniform, national racial and cultural standards, highlighted by the movement for black rights, disrupted the balance between national and local power. An attempt to determine the destiny of Indochina, which produced the Vietnam War, eroded popular support for the global containment of communism and national revolutions. These conflicts, in combination with deepening doubts about the future of the individual, triggered an open revolt against America's national leaders, first among well-to-do youths and then among millions of wage earners and townspeople throughout the land.

Early in the 1970s, while Washington's leaders were fashioning a new balance between national and local authority and exploring alternatives to containment, the economy fell on its hardest times since the Great Depression. International forces caused the greatest disturbance, and no purely American policy could tame them. Prolonged economic difficulties weakened the American people's confidence and cohesion sufficiently to reopen a whole range of questions about the modern state. As the nation entered the 1980s, all four primary problems still challenged American society as its citizens prepared to write another chapter of their modern history.

A confusing set of popular images has obscured the importance of the 1920s. On the one hand, they are pictured as the Roaring Twenties of a new technology, a new prosperity, and a new faith in the future. On the other hand, they appear as fearful years of repression at home and isolationism in world affairs. From hindsight after the Crash of 1929, the twenties seemed no more than a strange interlude, a decade of illusions that ended in depression and forced the nation to start over in its quest for a healthy society.

The actual history of the 1920s is more sensible, more subtle, and more interesting than these images would suggest. First, significant charges occurred in the course of the decade. Although cries of fear dominated the early twenties, voices of confidence increasingly prevailed after 1924, giving the late twenties a distinctive tone of affirmation. Second, different Americans experienced the decade in very different ways. Those who identified their future—and America's future—with a new national economy tended to be far more optimistic and expansive, both at home and abroad, than those whose lives were still rooted in their local societies and who gained relatively little from the national system. Third, and most important, depression did not destroy the foundations laid in the 1920s. The outlines of the economy, the obligations of the government, the divisions in society, and the commitments in world affairs that evolved during the twenties marked the emergence of modern America and set the framework for developments in later decades.

The Emergence of the Modern State

Vicious Years, 1920–1924

Rarely had Americans faced such a lackluster pair of presidential candidates as they did in 1920. Rather than gambling on a strong chief executive, both major parties nominated political mediocrities, both, as it happens, from Ohio. For the Democrats, Governor James M. Cox offered the best alternative to the stricken but still ambitious President Woodrow Wilson. Adding a dash of color to Cox's candidacy, the Democrats nominated jaunty, young Franklin D.

A LOSING CAUSE
Voters found neither "pep" nor "punch" in the League issue, and Harding demolished Cox in the presidential election of 1920.   *(The Bettmann Archive, Inc.)*

Roosevelt as his running mate. The Republicans, in order to break a convention deadlock, selected weak, affable Senator Warren G. Harding, and for vice-president the inconsequential governor of Massachusetts, Calvin Coolidge. As the candidates traded platitudes, the tide that had been flowing against the Democrats since 1918 was ready to sweep the Republicans to power. Soured by the disruptions of the war and the disillusionments of the peace, 61 percent of the voters chose the amiable Harding over Cox, who carried no state outside the South. Thus

after the interruption of Wilson's presidency, the Republican majority that had dominated American politics from 1894 to 1930 firmly reestablished itself.

Antiradicalism.   Harding, a decent man, came to office with vague impulses toward creating a quiet national harmony. "America's present need," he had declared during the campaign, "is not heroics, but healing; not nostrums, but normalcy." For many Americans, however, there could be no healing without major surgery first. Movements against disruptive radicals, labor unions, and immigrants, which had originated early in the century and swelled during the war, were cresting, and neither Harding nor his successor Coolidge had the will or the strength to check these repressive forces. Fulfilling this agenda of repression gave the early twenties their angry, fearful cast.

Fears of a Bolshevik revolution in America, touched off by the Russian upheaval of 1917, had subsided before Harding's election. During the Red Scare of 1919-20, a host of private vigilantes and public officials moved with devastating effect against organized radicalism. They completed the destruction of the Industrial Workers of the World (IWW), ransacked offices of the Socialist party, and even stopped legally elected Socialists from taking their seats in the U.S. House of Representatives and the New York Assembly. Wilson's attorney general, A. Mitchell Palmer, twice ordered extensive raids on America's fledgling Communist party and came very close to annihilating it. Eventually, the absence of real revolutionaries overcame the public's nightmares of a Bolshevik under every bed. When Palmer predicted that there would be massive bombings on May Day of 1920 and nothing happened, the scare rapidly subsided, and with it ended one phase of antiradicalism.

Nevertheless, a more general antiradicalism remained during the early twenties. One of its victims was the Non-Partisan League, an alliance of respectable farmers, lawyers, and merchants in the Northwest, who won control of the North Dakota government and tried to use state funds to aid local farmers. In 1921 and 1922 a group of bankers boycotted the League and succeeded in undermining its "socialist" program. Such groups as the American Legion imposed provincial, patriotic textbooks on the public schools, and forced the firing of liberal teachers. Officials in the Navy Department even campaigned against an imaginary "spider web" of women's organizations that were said to be subverting the nation's fighting spirit. "America," evangelist Billy Sunday proudly declared, "is not a country for a dissenter to live in."

Antiradicalism also merged with the drives against organized labor. Immediately after the war, businessmen and their allies created "open shop" committees throughout the nation to smash the unions. Although Samuel Gompers, the president of the American Federation of Labor (AFL), and most other labor leaders were vigorous antiradicals, they still could not protect their own unions from sweeping charges of socialism and un-Americanism. The steel companies made particularly effective use of antiradicalism as they crushed an ambitious drive to organize workers in their industry in 1919. Two years later the biggest meat packers cleared the unions from their plants. Conservative judges issued blanket injunctions that prohibited a variety of strikes, including ones by the coal miners in 1919 and the railway shopmen in 1922. Under these blows, union membership fell from a peak of over 5 million in 1920 to about 3.6 million in 1923, and union morale suffered even more than statistics could reveal.

Bigotry of the Twenties. Whatever Americans feared or strongly disliked in the early twenties, they called alien. It was an oppressive climate for immigrants, who, in addition to their ordinary social and economic problems, faced widespread charges that their alien influences were permanently corrupting American society. Even before the war a growing number of "native Americans"—white Protestants with northern and western European ancestors—became convinced that they needed special protection against the deluge of Catholics and Jews from southern and eastern Europe. Some accused the immigrants of flooding the labor market and lowering the American standard of living. Others, citing the newcomers' support of political bosses, declared them unfit to vote. Advocates of Prohibition condemned

their saloons, and urban reformers condemned their living habits. By 1920 innumerable Americans were justifying these prejudices with racial theories that categorized the "dirty little dark people" of southern and eastern Europe as a genetically inferior breed who were mongrelizing the American population.

Despite a minority of Americans who defended both the immigrants and the American tradition of open gates, public debate in the early twenties focused on the best techniques for restricting the immigrant flow. The government's first attempt, the Literacy Test of 1917, had failed because, contrary to common prejudice, most immigrants could read and write. Consequently the opponents of immigration shifted to a more effective device, setting annual immigration quotas by nationality. In 1921 Congress used 3 percent of the number of foreign-born in the 1910 census as the basis for each European country's quota. Then in the comprehensive National Origins Act of 1924, Congress substituted even lower quotas as an interim measure until experts could prepare the long-range solution, an annual limit of 150,000 immigrants divided according to the presumed percentage of each European nation's historical contribution to the white population in the United States.*

The justification of these laws was explicitly racial and defensive. Appropriately, they passed at a time when there was a considerable amount of anti-Semitism throughout American society. At each stage in the legislative sequence, Congress discriminated more harshly against southern and eastern Europe, where by far the largest number of potential immigrants lived. Not only did the act of 1924 place a ceiling on immigration that was less than one-fifth of the normal prewar flow; it assigned the English, Germans, and Scandinavians higher quotas than they were able to fill and almost closed the door on the Italians, Polish, and Russians. In a direct slap at the Japanese, the law totally excluded Asiatics. Seldom had Congress managed to embitter so many people here and abroad with a single law.

*The complicated calculations on national origins were not completed until 1929. The system then went into effect and remained the fundamental law on immigration until 1965, when Congress in a new law used the nation's need for skills as the basis for deciding who should be admitted.

THE KKK ON THE MARCH
At its height in the early 1920s, the Klan used this kind of pomp and mystery to attract new members, focus attention on its activities, and intimidate its enemies. *(The Bettmann Archive, Inc.)*

The Ku Klux Klan. The Ku Klux Klan came to embody all the bigotry of the early twenties. In 1920 two talented promoters, Edward Clarke and Elizabeth Tyler, took charge of a small southern organization with a name made famous in the days of Reconstruction. By capitalizing on the attractions of its fraternal secrecy, white-hooded ritual, and elaborate titles, they built the Ku Klux Klan into a nationwide organization of about 4 million members by 1924. Its primary enemies were alienism and immorality, and in fighting them, the Klan often resorted to intimidation and violence. The fiery cross and the midnight whipping became its symbols of justice.

Basically the Klan was a collection of local organizations that adapted their purposes to fight the particular enemies of each community. In the Oklahoma oil fields, a local "Klavern" boasted of transforming " 'no counts' of men and females . . . almost [into] a 'Sunday-School class.' " Its counterpart in Calypso, North Carolina, announced, "All the Catholic gold in the universe can't buy our manhood and our liberty." In Denver, the Klan opposed labor unions and welfare programs. But the Klan also stretched its influence into state and national politics. Early in the 1920s, its leaders claimed political control of states as varied as Oklahoma, Oregon, and Indiana. The Klan's national spokesmen supported every campaign against radicals and immigrants, and Klansmen paraded in the streets of the nation's capital. At the Democratic convention of 1924, a resolution condemning the Klan, which narrowly lost, almost tore the party apart.

In spite of a vigorous national opposition, the Klan remained a formidable presence in American politics. It represented only an exaggerated, somewhat disreputable, version of a common impulse. It longed openly for a mythical America of hardworking, church-going, small-town citizens, all white, Anglo-Saxon, and Protestant. The same themes of a lost virtue and a lost unity were woven throughout the movements against radicals, unions, and immigrants. Klansmen, like other Americans in all walks of life, expected public policy to reflect their cultural, moral visions, and to a striking degree by 1924 these expectations were fulfilled.

Yet this very success was a primary reason why these grim assaults dwindled so rapidly at mid-decade. After all, the battle against radicals, unions, and immigrants had largely been won. In 1924 the national government abandoned the cause of antiradicalism, and by 1928 thirty-four states allowed the feeble Communist party a place on their ballots. Pressure on the public schools lifted. At the annual meeting of the American Legion in 1925, one officer complained that "Americans have become apathetic to the monotonous appeal of the patriotic exhorter." Vigilante activities also declined dramatically. Between 1922 and 1926, the American Civil Liberties Union reported, the number of disrupted public meetings dropped from 225 to 21. By 1925 the Klan, king of the vigilantes, was suffering acute demoralization from exposés of corruption and the conviction of Indiana's leading Klansman, David Stephenson, for the sex murder of his secretary. Membership fell from 4 million in 1924 to 200,000 in 1928.

Much had changed between the early and the late twenties. In 1921, in the last public furor of the Red Scare, two immigrant anarchists, Nicola Sacco and Bartolomeo Vanzetti, were tried for the murder of a paymaster in South Braintree, Massachusetts. In a courtroom echoing with antiradical rhetoric, the two anarchists were convicted and sentenced to death. For years, legal appeals delayed their execution. The bias of the trial, and the dignity and eloquence of the prisoners during their long ordeal, attracted a wide range of sympathizers, who fought fervently for their pardon. But in August 1927, as large crowds here and abroad mourned in public, Sacco and Vanzetti died in the electric chair. The burden of protest had shifted. Now the conservatives were on the defensive. Prominent citizens who had once screamed "Bolshevik!" remained remarkably quiet while an embarrassing legacy from the recent past ran its course; they had largely lost interest in immigrants and radicals.

The Modern Political Economy, 1920–1929

Paralleling the angry trends of the early twenties were fundamental changes in social and economic organization that prepared the way for America's future. None of the changes individually made the headlines; in combination they completed an organizational revolution that had been under way for more than a generation. Since the turn of the century, national groups in business, labor, agriculture, finance, and the professions had been forming—lumber companies, retail druggists, railroad workers, investment bankers, civil engineers, and the like. Each group was organized according to the special economic function it performed, and each of them wanted to stabilize its own sphere with its own rules. Each expected long-range planning to increase its efficiency and its income. Each recognized the importance of linking its activities with the activities of other groups around it. Taken together, they created a new national system of specialized organizations that were integrated by a common national outlook, a common concern for the vigor of the whole economy, and a common belief in the value of cooperation and coordination.

Business in the Twenties. The most successful means of business stabilization was oligopoly, the domination of an industry by a few large firms. By 1920 oligopolies controlled almost every basic industry that needed a heavy investment of capital. In railroading, for example, a handful of corporations, approximately equal in strength, divided the nation's territory among themselves. In the automobile industry, Ford and General Motors set the standard for a competitive, expanding market. In steel, one huge firm, United States Steel, rose above the other corporations—called Little Steel—to become the industry's leader. No matter what the variation, however, oligopoly always simplified the problems of industrial coordination by limiting the number of companies that had to agree on a common business policy. Buccaneers of business like Jay Gould and John D. Rockefeller no longer ran these industrial giants. Now management teams, working through elaborate corporate structures, coordinated the nation's big business.

In industries such as clothing manufacture, building construction, and most branches of retailing, where capital demands were less and many small firms competed, trade associations were an alternative way of minimizing competition. About two thousand trade associations already existed in 1920, and they continued to multiply. With activities ranging from secret price-fixing pacts to occasional lunch meetings, the trade associations shared a belief that pooling information would stabilize their industries and increase their profits. Although they seldom coordinated business affairs as effectively as the oligopolies did, the trade associations still moved in the same general direction of cooperation and planning.

Most businessmen expected wage earners to play their part in these coordinating programs. Unlike the captains of industry of the late nineteenth century, who had usually treated wage earners much as they did hunks of ore or gears in the machinery, the modern business managers considered laborers as humans whose efficiency would increase as their morale and incentive improved. Specialists in personnel policy organized company recreational programs, prepared chatty company bulletins, and invited workers to suggest improvements in the firms' procedures. Large corporations in particular sponsored shop committees, company unions, and employee representation plans—"the world's greatest democracy," boasted the president of Standard Oil of Indiana. More and more of the unions in the AFL and the Railroad Brotherhoods adapted to such company policies in an effort to salvage a place for themselves in the

twenties. Under an accommodating new president, William Green, the AFL in 1925 listed the improvement of industrial productivity among its primary objectives. "[The] new, suave, discreet unionism," one commentator noted late in the 1920s, "talks the language of the efficiency engineer and busies itself about ways and means of increasing output."

For good reason, successful commercial farmers regarded themselves as businessmen. As chemical fertilizers and the gasoline engine were revolutionizing agriculture, only the wealthy investor, using the latest improvements on a large scale, could expect to profit from modern farming. These "agribusinessmen," like their industrial counterparts, wanted to coordinate their affairs, and they too organized. Local farm bureaus distributed information about scientific farming techniques, and through the national organization, the American Farm Bureau Federation, lobbied for favorable government policies. Other farmers—in dairying, for example—formed cooperative marketing associations. Groups of commercial farmers behaved so much like any other business organization that the same men who had staffed Bernard Baruch's War Industries Board in 1918 could become the most prominent agricultural advisers of the twenties.

Bankers acted as auxiliaries to these various business groups. The wizards of Wall Street no longer dominated American business as they had twenty years earlier. Not only did the regional structure of the new Federal Reserve System encourage financial decentralization, but an increasing number of important corporations also gained control over their own banking. During the 1920s, companies as diverse as Eastman Kodak, Aluminum Corporation of America, Ford, and Sears, Roebuck routinely financed business expansion from their own vast profits. Banks too, as agencies of service, organized themselves in subdivisions that matched the needs of their business clients. The professions formed a second band of auxiliaries to business. Legal specialties in such areas as contracts, taxation, and labor policy were growing alongside modern industry. A variety of engineers, economists, statisticians, psychologists, sociologists, and educators also became willing helpers to the nation's business. Where an important profession, such as research chemistry, was not adequately developed, powerful industries encouraged its growth.

The New National Economy. Changes in government trailed close behind the organization of these economic interests. Because the new network of groups was national in scope and outlook, only the government in Washington could meet its needs. In the broadest sense, the national government was expected to facilitate the work of private groups, smooth cooperation among them, and surround them with a favorable legal framework. During the early twenties, one after another of the government's offices shaped its policies to serve the new national economy. Herbert Hoover, as secretary of commerce (1921–29), the most important cabinet official of the decade, led his department in its efforts to help manufacturers standardize the production of items ranging from wood screws to fan belts; to distribute business statistics for the trade associations; to enable the major broadcasting companies to stabilize the new radio industry; and at every opportunity, to publicize the virtues of business cooperation.

Less dramatically, other departments expanded their services to commercial farmers, hydroelectric power companies, and private industries in food, mining, and lumber. Each of the independent regulatory commissions, so vital to progressive reform, found a way to assist business coordination. Through the Transportation Act of 1920, the Interstate Commerce Commission received extensive authority over almost all areas of the railroad industry, and it used these broad powers to encourage oligopoly and an assortment of cooperative agreements. By 1925 the Federal Trade Commission was specializing in conferences for trade associations. Because the Federal Reserve Board in Washington proved to be ineffective, the New York Regional Board coordinated national banking policy.

The Supreme Court endorsed all of these developments. First, it sanctioned oligopolies. In *United States* v. *United States Steel Co.* (1920), the Court allowed the nation's largest corporation to dominate its in-

dustry as long as some competitors survived. Then, after considerable hesitation, the Court in the *Maple Flooring Manufacturers' Association* case of 1925, declared that trade associations, like oligopolies, were legal if they did not eliminate competition in their areas of business. The Justice Department advised the trade associations on how best to stay inside the law. Meanwhile, the Court limited the constraints the labor unions might impose on business. Led by its new chief justice, William Howard Taft, whom Harding appointed in 1921, the Court sharply restricted organized labor's right to picket and boycott, and it watched approvingly as the lower courts expanded the use of injunctions against striking workers. In addition, the Supreme Court overturned a national child labor law in *Bailey* v. *Drexel Furniture Co.* (1922) and a state minimum wage law in *Adkins* v. *Children's Hospital* (1923).

The national economic system could not function without the government's assistance, and by 1925 the public accepted an increase of 250 percent over the 1915 level of the budget of the federal government. Hence, what appeared to be an economic system was broader than that. At the center of the national system was production and distribution, with agriculture connected at the side and labor linked below, and bankers and professionals contributing specialized services while government wrapped the system in protective rules, expert counsel, and helpful mediation. As Hoover, the leading proponent of this national political economy, envisaged the system, it was a "third alternative" to laissez-faire capitalism and state socialism, a voluntary, cooperative commonwealth that followed the scientific principles of coordination and efficiency.

A Consumer Paradise. By the mid-1920s the new national system was in place and performing miracles. After a sharp recession in 1921–22, the gross national product (GNP) climbed 5 percent a year, and during the decade manufacturing output rose 64 percent. The leaders of the boom were the automobile and construction industries. Both the number of automobile sales and the value of construction more

BACKGROUND TO THE AUTOMOBILE REVOLUTION

Early in the twentieth century even Ford cars were the luxuries of the few who could hire chauffers and mechanics. Inadequate roads and open bodies restricted the automobile to fair weather recreation. Only with the arrival of mass production did the car become a basic part of American life. *(Left, Ford Archives, Henry Ford Museum, Dearborn, Michigan; center, Automotive History Collection, Detroit Public Library; right, Courtesy Ford Motor Company)*

than tripled between 1915 and 1925, and these economic leaders created benefits widely for such related industries as steel, petroleum, rubber, and cement. By the end of the twenties the number of registered cars almost equaled the number of families. America's passionate love affair with the automobile had commenced.

Cars, roads, and houses were nationally visible benefits. So was a second category of consumer products that relied on the spread of electricity. Midwestern utilities magnate Samuel Insull pioneered in selling metered electrical service to households, and other companies soon recognized the genius of his scheme. By the end of the twenties, two out of three households had electricity, in contrast to one out of five before World War I. Into their new electrical outlets, Americans plugged lamps, refrigerators, washing machines, and toasters, each a marvel in the twenties. Above all, electricity brought the radio. In November 1920 the crackling sounds of America's first radio station, KDKA of East Pittsburgh, opened a modern era of personal mass communication. By 1923 over five hundred broadcasting stations with much-improved equipment were in operation. Electrical technology also created a new lord of the entertainment world, motion pictures, which grew from a scattering of nickelodeon shows and occasional full-length features to a systematized $2 billion industry with a steady flow of films. By 1929 more than 80 million people were going to the movies each week.

To countless Americans all of this created a consumer paradise. Abandoning the time-honored rules to buy cautiously, fear debt, and save each small surplus, they made consumer credit a national necessity, and it soon became available through a great variety of convenient outlets. But how the economy worked impressed some people even more than how much it produced. A broad range of manufacturing plants, following the lead of Henry Ford, introduced the moving assembly line, a revolution in factory proce-

dure. Through electricity in industry and the gasoline engine in agriculture, the amount of horsepower per worker rose well over 50 percent during the twenties. As a consequence of these changes, output per working hour increased an astonishing 35 percent, almost twice the gains of the previous decade. America, it seemed, had answered all the riddles of economic growth. Throughout the decade, a stream of delegations came from abroad in hopes of discovering the secret of American productivity.

Contemporaries declared the arrival of a "New Era." "The first responsibility of an American to his country," announced one newspaper, "is no longer that of a citizen, but of a consumer." Former critics of American society now became its ardent champions. Socialism was "reactionary," said John Spargo, once a leader of the Socialist party, and American capitalism offered "the greatest hope for mankind." As the number of strikes declined drastically, praise for the nationwide sport of cooperation filled the air.

"I can find no historic parallel, outside of the great religious revivals, with which [the New Era] has much in common," marveled a veteran of the social gospel. "Thru business...," another publicist promised even more grandly, "the human race is to be redeemed." From the vantage point of the Great Depression that followed, it would be easy to ridicule the grandiose claims: poverty on the verge of abolition, a chicken in every pot and two cars in every garage, anyone with self-discipline and common sense a millionaire. Yet during the late twenties, innumerable Americans were believers.

Divided Politics in the New Era, 1924–1929

Scandals. The first political test of confidence in the New Era came with revelations that President Harding, who had made some excellent appointments, had also made some disastrous ones. First, a friend of Harding's attorney general, Harry Daugherty, was caught accepting bribes to protect his clients from federal prosecution, and he committed suicide. Then Charles Forbes, a chance acquaintance whom Harding appointed director of the Veterans' Bureau, and Thomas Miller, the alien property custodian, were indicted and jailed for extensive frauds. Most sensational of all, a long congressional inquiry in 1923 and 1924 exposed a crude string of bribes and backroom deals behind the leasing to private concerns of government oil lands on Teapot Dome in Wyoming and Elk Hill in California. Two oil men, Harry Sinclair and Edward Doheny, had bought the leases from Secretary of Interior Albert Fall for almost half a million dollars in cash, bonds, and cattle. As a consequence of the "Teapot Dome Scandal," Fall, whose lean frame, broad-brimmed hat, and drooping handlebar moustache made him look for all the world like a Hollywood sheriff, was convicted of bribery and became the first cabinet officer in history to serve a prison sentence. Harding's close associate Daugherty barely escaped being the second.

The ineffectual Harding had sensed disaster. "I

have no trouble with my enemies...," he told a newsman, "[but] my God-damn friends... keep me walking the floor nights!" In August 1923, while touring the western states, a despondent Harding died of a heart attack. Vice-President Calvin Coolidge, an obscure politician of no apparent talents, suddenly inherited the mess. In 1924, as accounts of more corruption oozed to the surface, the Republicans faced an additional challenge when a collection of dissident farm spokesmen, union officials, socialists, and reformers revived the Progressive party and nominated for president the tough old liberal, Robert La Follette. His strongest appeal would be to normally Republican voters.

But Coolidge, who believed that most problems would disappear if left alone, waited and won. The Teapot Dome scandal had come to light in a time of anxiety over oil shortages. New discoveries of oil in Oklahoma and California eliminated those worries. While "Silent Cal" was demonstrating the old-fashioned Yankee virtue of tight-lipped integrity and tight-fisted frugality, his political opponents were destroying themselves. The Democratic convention of 1924, torn between an eastern urban bloc and a southern and western rural bloc, exhausted itself casting an incredible 103 ballots before nominating the drab Wall Street lawyer, John W. Davis. After selecting La Follette, the Progressive coalition dissolved in quarrels. Coolidge, who had no trouble gaining the Republican nomination, swamped Davis that November, 382 electoral votes to 136. Although La Follette received an impressive personal tribute of almost 5 million popular votes, he carried only Wisconsin.

Coolidge and the Congress. Coolidge's triumph coincided with a new calm in national affairs. Indeed, few presidents have encountered as meek a Congress as Coolidge faced after 1924. Liberal opponents such as Senator William Borah of Idaho and Senator George Norris of Nebraska won occasional skirmishes but no important campaigns. The president's Bureau of the Budget, relying on the advice of the United States Chamber of Commerce, decided on the level of government spending, and congressional appropriations were an almost perfect carbon for the

A COUNTRY BOY IN THE WHITE HOUSE
As President Coolidge presided over a business civilization, he shrewdly used his rural origins to suggest old-fashioned simplicity and honesty. *(From Stephan Lorant's The Glorious Burden)*

bureau's recommendations. In 1926 even the controversial tax program of Secretary of the Treasury Andrew Mellon was enacted. To release more money for private investment, Congress lowered the rate of income tax for the very wealthy from 46 percent to 26 percent, and cut inheritance taxes in half. As Coolidge neatly explained to the nation, "The business of government is business."

The only significant signs of a congressional rebellion came over farm policy. Commodity prices, which had fallen precipitously in 1921, revived sluggishly during the 1920s. In 1929 net farm income was still $3 billion lower than it had been in 1919. During the early twenties the farm lobby won an array of laws from Congress, including higher tariffs, tighter regulation of the grain exchanges and the stockyards, and easier credit for commercial farmers. When none of these helped very much, sentiment shifted toward the proposals of the persistent George Peek, a manufacturer of agricultural equipment who crusaded for agricultural reforms throughout the twenties. Seal off the domestic market with high tariffs, Peek told the farmers, and sell what you can in this protected market. Then have the government buy the surplus, dump it abroad at the best price, and tax the farmers a small amount to cover any losses.

In Washington, Peek's plan became the McNary-Haugen bill. First in the West and then in the South, Peek gathered enough support to push a McNary-Haugen bill through Congress twice, in 1927 and again in 1928. Twice Coolidge vetoed it. Yet by 1928 the actual difference between the farm lobby and the Coolidge administration was not very great. The administration's solution, which was enacted into law in 1929, also sought to regulate the marketing of agricultural products. When prices fell, commodity cooperatives would receive temporary government payments while they stored their products. As prices improved, the cooperatives would gradually sell their surplus and repay the government. In fact, the second McNary-Haugen bill included this scheme. Therefore, considerable optimism prevailed in 1929 when Congress created the Federal Farm Board, with an unprecedented $500 million in government credit to help the cooperatives market their products at the best prices.

Local Politics. Beneath the smooth surface of national politics, a very different spirit was bubbling in local affairs. In the best years of the New Era, the annual income of about two-thirds of the nation's families fell below $2,500, which experts considered adequate in the twenties. These families had only an indirect stake in the economic system that was forming on the national level. Most wage earners were not union members, and most farmers never joined the agricultural organizations. Very small businesses everywhere—the neighborhood grocer, the second-hand store, the repair shop—belonged to no economic league or trade association. Even a number of those Americans who were somewhat better off remained outside the New Era's organizational structure. The United States Chamber of Commerce discouraged membership in towns under 5,000, and businessmen there kept largely to themselves. The Chicago Bar Association, the strongest of its kind in the nation, enrolled only half of the city's licensed lawyers in the late twenties.

For most of these Americans, a neighborhood or a community bounded their lives. They cared very much about jobs and income, but they tried to manage such problems locally. Their networks were personal ones, woven through families, friendships, and local business contacts. They reinforced these strands with a high degree of cultural consciousness. Outside the cities, that usually meant pride in being white, Anglo-Saxon, and Protestant. These same qualities were also important in the cities, but there a great variety of groups were trying to preserve their ethnic differences. Black, brown, yellow, or white skin; Italian, Polish, German, or Irish ancestors; Catholic, Protestant, or Jewish religion—all drew critical social lines.

Such tight local attachments made any kind of broad political organization extremely difficult. The Ku Klux Klan and the Anti-Saloon League were exceptions early in the twenties, but both collapsed after 1924. Equally important, few people in national affairs seemed to care any more about the cultural and moral standards that still mattered a great deal to millions of Americans. Although former members of the Klan did not discard their old beliefs about foreigners, Catholics, and radicals, no strong voice spoke for them in Coolidge's Washington. They became what the Klan had always claimed to be, an "Invisible Empire."

Local politics remained the one natural center for this mixture of economic, cultural, and moral concerns. Local politics dominated innumerable county organizations in which friendship and family ties, not efficiency and expertise, determined who would receive most of the jobs and favors. In the wards of the large cities, similar private bargains tied individuals, families, and cultural groups into little political alliances.

Another set of private bargains entwined government officials with a web of criminal activities in prostitution, gambling, and bootlegging. The boxer, Billy Conn, growing up on the streets of Pittsburgh, was twenty years old before he realized that the police were paid by the city government. On a large scale, these many personal arrangements became political machines which thrived during the 1920s. Though they were known by the names of the bosses —Tom Pendergast in Kansas City, Big Bill Thompson in Chicago, Ed Crump in Memphis, Frank Hague in Jersey City, and James Michael Curley in Boston— their roots were decentralized and popular.

Prohibition as a Rallying Point.   During the New Era it required an exceptionally powerful force to draw these insular, local alliances into national affairs. The strongest magnet was the Eighteenth, or "Prohibition," Amendment, which banned the production and sale of liquor. Put into effect in January 1920 and enforced by the strict Volstead Act, the Eighteenth Amendment began its career in an atmosphere of high optimism. Drinking, declared William Jennings Bryan, was as dead an issue as slavery. But countless Americans decided otherwise. Continuing demand in the big cities and a considerable market elsewhere in the nation created a massive business out of illicit production and distribution. As one investigating commission ruefully noted, "Few things are more easily made than alcohol." A little machinery and a bathtub transformed any thirsty citizen into a distiller. Moreover, the long boundary of the United States provided many unpatrolled areas where illegal importers could smuggle liquor into the country. Rumrunners trucked it in from Canada and Mexico, and ferried it in small boats to isolated coves along both coasts. To police these many violations, the Treasury Department employed about 2,000 officials. Herbert Hoover later estimated that effective enforcement would have required at least 250,000.

Millions of Americans considered Prohibition an

insufferable violation of their rights. Not only did the "wets" make a joke of the law in their neighborhoods and communities; they increasingly demanded action from state and national governments. In 1923 New York repealed the state law that enforced Prohibition. By 1930 six other states had followed New York's lead. With equal fervor, millions of locally oriented "drys" regarded Prohibition as the keystone of American morality. Not only did they give teeth to Prohibition in their localities; they sponsored stern laws to uphold the "noble experiment." In Michigan a fourth offense under the Prohibition law meant life imprisonment. Basically the story of Prohibition was this stream of local passions pouring through the nation and battling in the name of irreconcilable truths.

National vs. Local Politics.   From these same sources came the emotions that made Alfred E. Smith the most controversial politician of the 1920s. A capable governor of New York who very much wanted to be president, Al Smith touched the nerve centers of local politics. He was a Catholic, a wet, the son of an immigrant, and a self-taught politician who wore Tam-

many Hall's traditional brown derby askew and spoke in the accents of Manhattan's East Side streets. The thought of Al Smith in the White House roused feelings of wonder and horror across the nation. Self-conscious ethnic groups in the northern cities who were Catholic and wet gave him their fanatical devotion. White Protestant Democrats in the rural South who were dry looked on Smith as the Antichrist. At the Democratic convention of 1924, Smith's friends and enemies fought over his nomination to the point of exhaustion before turning to John W. Davis. But in 1928, in the absence of a serious competitor, southern delegates finally allowed Smith's nomination for president, though with the most profound misgivings.

The election of 1928 provided a unique meeting ground for the conflicting spirits of national and local politics. To oppose Smith, the Republicans chose Herbert Hoover, by all odds the outstanding leader of the modern political economy. After an impressive early success in business, Hoover won renown during the First World War as an administrator, first of international relief, then of agriculture. There had been talk of Hoover as president in 1920. Instead, he had

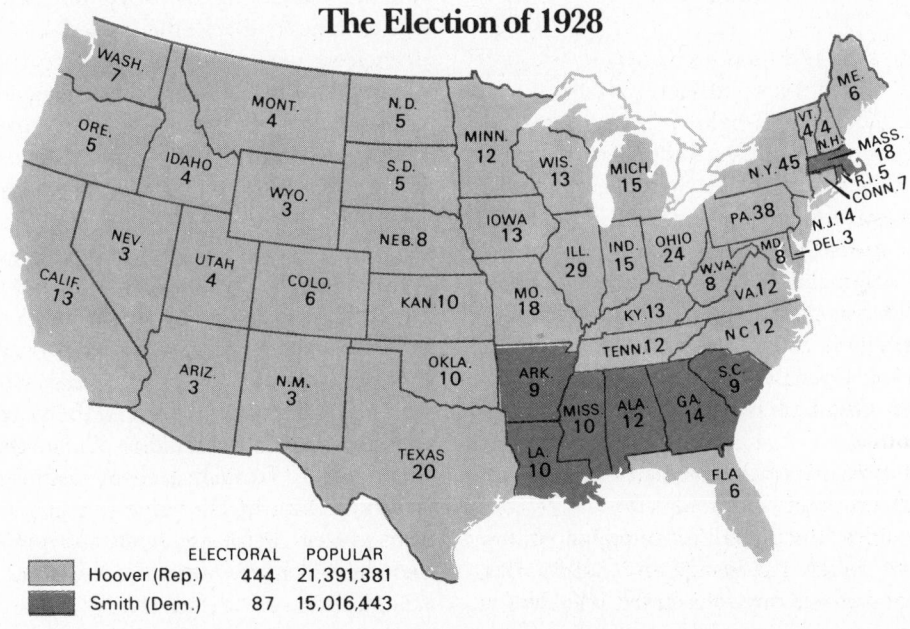

The Election of 1928

	ELECTORAL	POPULAR
Hoover (Rep.)	444	21,391,381
Smith (Dem.)	87	15,016,443

on the cover is the LIFE magazine, with text: Amusement News, Personalit[ies] Sport, LIFE, 15 Cents, June 21 1928, EAST SIDE, WET'S SIDE, IN THIS ISSUE: WILL ROGERS ON AL SMITH

AL SMITH ON THE COVER OF "LIFE" MAGAZINE, 1928
Loyal to Tammany and hostile to Prohibition, Al Smith could never escape the image of the New York ward boss who had made good. *(Culver Pictures, Inc.)*

served in the cabinets of Harding and Coolidge, and made himself the unofficial center of the executive branch: "Secretary of Commerce and assistant secretary of everything else." He was serious and shy, extremely proud and highly ambitious. Too formidable for Coolidge, who disliked him, and too independent for many professional politicians, who preferred a weaker man, Hoover still went after the nomination with absolute confidence in his ability to be president. Successful Americans overwhelmingly supported him. Of those listed in *Who's Who,* for example, 87 percent endorsed his candidacy.

Al Smith sought to pitch his campaign at the level of national policy. An essentially conservative man who later opposed the New Deal, the Demo-cratic candidate thought of himself as an eminently qualified leader for the system, not as a product of New York City's Lower East Side. To oversee his campaign, Smith selected a prominent executive in General Motors, John J. Raskob, rather than a professional politician. The partisans of local politics, however, would not let Smith rise above his origins. In November 1928 Smith's name on the ballot drew large, jubilant majorities in the industrial cities, but it also sent millions of Protestant townspeople to the polls with a religious commitment to Hoover and put seven formerly Democratic southern states in the Republican column. Hoover, the shining symbol of the New Era prosperity, swept to victory with 444 electoral votes against Smith's 87.

A New International Order, 1920–1929

Americans looked at the world beyond the nation's boundaries through approximately the same lenses they used in domestic life. Despite the recent war, no deep traditions or crucial issues of security restricted their international relations. As the world's most powerful nation, largely self-sufficient and invulnerable to serious attack, the United States had a range of choices, including the choice of withdrawal, that no other Western nation enjoyed. Hence, few Americans found any need to alter their everyday domestic standards when they considered an external world. Europeans called Americans naïve. Most Americans regarded themselves as lucky.

Appropriately, then, America's foreign relations in the twenties revealed roughly the same chronological pattern as its domestic affairs. The early years were defensive and agitated; by mid-decade the tone had mellowed considerably, and national leaders increasingly sought to extend the new national system abroad. But to millions of Americans, what lay outside their familiar territory appeared even less inviting late in the decade than it had before. Distant lands, except perhaps for ethnic homelands, promised only trouble. Here lay the roots of American isolationism.

Disengagement. In 1920 disillusionment with the First World War prevailed almost everywhere. A fear of Bolshevism and an aversion to immigrants went hand in hand with the widespread desire to insulate America from a sick, corrupt European society. After the Senate finally rejected the League of Nations in March 1920, few Americans mourned its fate. Under Harding, separate peace treaties were made with each of the defeated Central Powers which excluded any mention of international enforcement. By 1921 the army and navy together shrank to less than 250,000 men. A year later the Fordney-McCumber Act threw up the high tariff barriers that Wilson and the Democrats had lowered in 1913. A refusal to recognize the Soviet Union hardened into national policy. Americans, it seemed, wanted walls to protect them against everything foreign—people, goods, ideas, and responsibilities.

Yet disengagement after the war was not a simple process. American soldiers who had entered Siberia in a muddled attempt to counter the Bolsheviks lingered there until 1920 in an equally muddled attempt to counter Japanese influence. Until 1923 the United States also kept a token force in Germany's occupied Rhineland provinces, more to temper French belligerence than to punish Germany. Despite cries of outrage from America's former allies, the United States insisted on the repayment of large loans that had been made during the war. Because the European debtors tried to link their payments to the United States to the amount of reparations they were collecting from Germany, the United States once more found itself tangled in the issues that had defeated Wilson at Versailles.

The most substantial progress toward disengagement—the Washington Conference Treaties of 1921–22—also proved to be the first steps toward a new international order. One step leading to the Washington Conference resulted from the postwar passion for disarmament, most effectively voiced by liberal Senator Borah. A second step was brought about by the rising tension with Japan that had run as a minor theme throughout the war and the debate over Versailles. Not only were American leaders worried about Japan's imperial ambitions on the mainland of

Asia, and possibly in the Philippine Islands, but they also fretted over Japan's longstanding defensive alliance with Great Britain, which linked a European friend to an Asian rival. With the Far East in mind, Charles Evans Hughes, Harding's austere and able secretary of state, used the growing concerns over a worldwide naval armaments race as justification for calling an international conference.

Washington Conference Treaties. During the winter of 1921–22, representatives from industrial nations with interests in East Asia (except for the Soviet Union) met in Washington. To everyone's surprise, Hughes insisted that the delegates act as well as talk. Consequently the Washington Conference produced three important agreements. All of them sought in some way to freeze the existing balance of power and privileges in East Asia. One, the critical Four-Power Treaty of nonaggression among the United States, Japan, Great Britain, and France, superseded the troublesome Anglo-Japanese Alliance. A second agreement, the Five-Power Treaty, added Italy to the big four and established tonnage limitations on major warships according to a ratio approximating the current strength of these nations. Finally, the Nine-Power Treaty committed all imperial nations to the principle of equal opportunity inside an independent China—the American doctrine of the "Open Door."

On the one hand, these treaties reflected America's inward-turning, defensive impulses. They pulled the United States away from a naval confrontation with Japan, and they included no provisions for enforcement. On the other hand, they acknowledged a crucial interconnection among the world's industrial nations, a mutual dependence that required negotiation, coordination, and a broad structure of rules. These were precisely the principles of the voluntary, cooperative commonwealth that was forming inside the United States. Hughes, a cool conservative during the angry postwar years, had made the first important move in extending America's new national system abroad.

Cooperation Abroad. In the same spirit of coordination and stabilization, Americans responded to the

European crisis of 1923 and 1924. When Germany defaulted on its reparations and French troops occupied the industrial nerve center of the Ruhr, the German economy toppled. France, too, was shaky. Through the Dawes Plan of 1924, the United States unofficially took the lead in negotiating large private loans to revive Germany. Simultaneously, J. P. Morgan and Company arranged a loan to France on the understanding that it would not disrupt the fragile German recovery. As Germany again began paying reparations, the former Allied Powers then made some payments on their war debts, and the United States did not press them very hard for more. Without a formal government commitment, the United States presided over a complex process of international stabilization, much as the government in Washington was attempting to do at home.

These initial efforts to create international order remained basic to American policy. The Young Plan of 1929 reformulated the Dawes Plan in hopes of managing war debts and reparations far into the future. A year later the London Naval Conference expanded the scope of the Washington Conference naval agreement to cover a full range of warships. In addition, the United States diverted France's proposal in 1927 for a bilateral treaty into a general, multilateral declaration against war. More than sixty nations eventually ratified the Kellogg-Briand Peace Pact of 1928, which took its name from the principal negotiators, Coolidge's Secretary of State Frank B. Kellogg and France's Foreign Minister Aristide Briand. "An international kiss," snorted Missouri's flinty Senator James Reed. Nevertheless, the pulls of a popular isolationism would allow no greater American involvement in global enforcement. When the Coolidge administration recommended that the United States join the World Court, the League of Nations' weak judicial arm, the Senate attached so many special conditions to America's participation that the other members of the World Court refused the terms.

As the financial plans for Europe demonstrated, American policy-makers saw an intimate connection between international stability and economic expansion. Each, they thought, could be made to serve the other. At home or abroad, of course, the modern political economy was a profit system. Herbert Hoover's Department of Commerce invested heavily in gathering data and distributing publicity on foreign markets for American business. When American diplomats failed to break the European petroleum monopoly in the Middle East, the government allowed American oil companies to conduct their own diplomacy, with Washington's approval. At the same time, in Latin America the United States tried to preserve the near monopoly of American companies against their European competitors. Yet foreign trade remained about 5 percent of the national income during the twenties, and foreign investments never reached 3 percent of the nation's total assets. It was difficult to argue that the health of the American economy required drastic diplomatic measures abroad. Hence, within the limits of the voluntary cooperative system, Washington's leaders tried to assimilate business expansion into what they thought was a healthy international order.

As American bankers arranged loans with foreign governments, especially in Latin America, the State Department experimented with the kind of soft, indirect supervision that the government was exercising in domestic economic affairs. After evaluating the loans, the department gave judgments of "objection" or "no objection." Hoover's attempt to restrict these loans to "reproductive purposes"—that is, for economic growth rather than for fat salaries or swollen armies—also echoed the principles of America's new national system, but his efforts failed. In almost all cases, the government had "no objection."

Hoover was more successful in helping to discourage the use of military force to collect American debts. In general, Washington was gradually repudiating the "Roosevelt corollary" to the Monroe Doctrine, which had made the United States a policeman over Latin America's unstable, defaulting governments. The best evidence of a changing approach came from the long, difficult negotiations with Mexico over the rights of American corporations in its oil industry. President Coolidge dispatched the adroit banker Dwight Morrow as ambassador, and won a settlement of the oil controversy in 1928.

In all, American foreign policy by the late twenties was a relatively benign form of economic imperialism. The United States used its great power quite cautiously and supplied most of it to stabilize and systematize international relations. From the vantage point of the Second World War and the Cold War, the policy may have looked woefully deficient in treaties binding America to a military version of collective security. But neither Hughes nor Hoover should be faulted for failing to predict the Great Depression and the rise of aggressive governments in Japan and Germany. No one did—or could. Yet the nation's policy-makers did suffer from another form of shortsightedness. By envisioning a global spread of America's new national system, they not only revealed a familiar bit of American arrogance, but they also failed to recognize the profound differences between a domestic and a world political economy. Internationally, there was no counterpart to the supervising government in Washington, nor was there any working set of rules to govern worldwide conflicts. Moreover, the United States had deliberately turned its back on one of the major powers, the Soviet Union. A realistic world order simply could not ignore Russia. These crucial flaws of vision remained to bedevil American leaders when the comforting hand of prosperity no longer supported their new international order.

Depression, 1929–1932

Hoover had served at the creation of a new order at home and abroad, and as president, he presided over its triumph. By 1929 countless Americans were convinced that they were riding an escalator of unlimited progress, and they anticipated, along with Hoover, "the day when poverty will be banished from this nation." A wealthy minority expressed this happy faith by investing in the stock market. If tomorrow would inevitably be more prosperous than today, why not buy some of tomorrow at today's prices? This reasoning had already pushed up prices on the New York Stock Exchange by 40 percent in 1927, then another 35 percent in 1928, to heights that bore no relation to the actual growth of the nation's production. Yet the Great Bull Market charged heedlessly onward. With scarcely a pause, stock prices

continued to climb week after week until by September 1929 they stood at a dizzying 400 percent above their level of only five years earlier.

Spasms of doubt shook the stock market in September and early October. Then on October 23, 1929, confidence died. For almost a week the stock exchange was a mad scene of frantic sellers, elusive buyers, and exhausted clerks struggling to record the wreckage. By October 29, all the paper profits of 1929 had been lost. Early in November the gains of 1928 disappeared, and during the summer of 1930 those of 1927 dissolved. Finally, on June 8, 1932, the stock market hit bottom, 50 percent below its modest level at the time of Coolidge's inauguration.

INDEX OF COMMON STOCK PRICES, 1924–1932

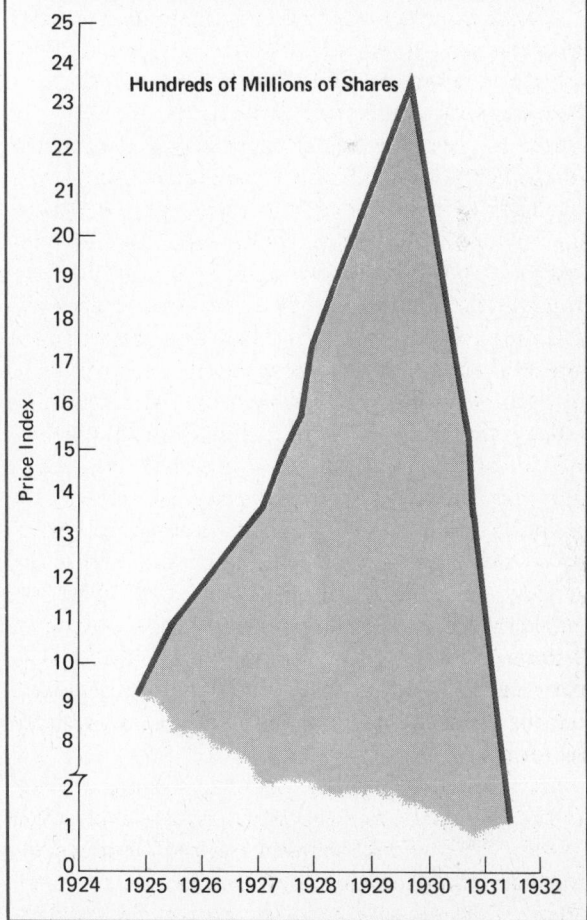

The Great Depression. The collapse of the Great Bull Market triggered the Great Depression. Consumption dropped. Businesses retrenched. As marginal enterprises in farming, banking, and business failed, they caused a further tightening and a new wave of bankruptcies. During the first three years after the Crash, the economy, like a tin can in a vise, was relentlessly squeezed to half its size. Some indicators—such as labor income, salaries, and national income—fell somewhat less than 50 percent; others, such as industrial production, manufacturing wages, dividends, and farm income, somewhat more. For people living through these years, there seemed to be no bottom at all.

The human costs were incalculable. Dramatic headlines told about the fall of the mighty—such as the utilities king, Samuel Insull, and the New York banking baron, Charles Mitchell—whose empires of speculation crumbled. Later studies argued that

STUDIES IN DESPAIR

The human effects of the Great Depression were crushing and numbing. No place to go, nothing to do. Urban workers hunted for jobs until they were drained of hope. Rural families sat helplessly as poverty enveloped them. With whatever scraps they could find, the homeless built their own shelters and survived for another day. *(Left, and center, Library of Congress; right, Museum of the City of New York)*

the most severe anxieties struck white-collar males, whose sense of personal worth depended entirely on their jobs and earnings. But the most crushing burdens of depression fell on the poor. Millions already living on the edge of poverty could afford no decline in farm income, no shorter hours of work. And the unemployed, about one-third of the labor force by early 1933, soon had nothing. "Folks that ain't never been poor," said one struggling housewife, "don't know nothin' a-tall about doing on nothing." The chicken once promised for every pot had gone into charity's soup kettle, and each year longer and longer lines of hungry, bewildered people formed in front of it with their empty bowls.

Why the depression was so deep and the fall so prolonged remain mysteries, and an inventory of economic weaknesses in 1929 does not solve the puzzle. Speculative stock levels comparable to the Great Bull Market became commonplace after midcentury.

The unequal distribution of income was a chronic problem of the modern age, in good times and bad. The apparent excesses of consumer credit in the twenties formed a mere puddle next to the ocean of consumer credit that later floated American prosperity. The faulty banking system was as strong as it had been since 1913 and sturdy enough to stand until early 1933. Agriculture dragged, but then the American economy always had significant soft spots. A longer list would tell more of the same.

We do know that 1931 was as critical a year as 1929. Early in 1931 the economy was improving, and the crisis looked similar to many other sharp downturns. Because farm prices had fallen much farther than wages, most urban consumers actually benefited. An intelligent person with money to invest in business or the stock market could find a variety of attractive prospects at home and abroad. Yet the consumers and the investors clutched their money.

By summer the Great Depression was sweeping Europe, and the American economy was sliding toward new depths. Curiously, Hoover and Franklin Roosevelt both sensed the profound importance of this paralyzing irrationality. Roosevelt called it "unreasoning fear." How else could one explain a drop of 95 percent in private investment while most indicators were declining about 50 percent?

President Hoover's initial responses to the depression were clear and firm. If the principles behind the New Era were correct, as everyone seemed to believe, Americans should use them to recover prosperity. "Progress is born of cooperation," the president reminded the nation. "The Government should assist and encourage these movements of collective self-help by itself cooperating with them." For business, Hoover sponsored meetings at the White House to establish common industrial policies. For labor, he won a promise from business leaders to spread the work in their firms rather than simply fire some percentage of their employees. For agriculture, the new Federal Farm Board issued large amounts of credit so that the commodity cooperatives could keep their products off the market and halt the decline in farm prices. For hard-pressed Americans everywhere, Hoover made the president's office the coordinator of private relief. Between 1929 and 1932, donations for relief increased about eightfold, a remarkable accomplishment by any previous standard. Viewing the economy as a national system, he was the first president in history to attack depression systematically.

The Deepening Depression.   But Hoover, like the economy, took a grim turn downward in the middle of 1931. As his sense of control over affairs began to slip, he grew more rigid, more persecuted by the specter of vast, oppressive forces. The White House became a funeral parlor. The president, never a charmer, looked, as one visitor remarked, as if a rose would wilt at his touch. In that mood, Hoover called together the villains of Wall Street who, in the president's view, had fed the Great Bull Market instead of facilitating legitimate business. When he demanded that they make massive new investments, they stalled. Finally Hoover accepted the necessity of an emergency government credit agency, the Reconstruction Finance Corporation (RFC), which in 1932 invested $1.5 billion in private enterprise. Meanwhile, to ease the pressures on international finances, he issued a moratorium on the payment of war debts.

By 1932 the president's policies lay in shambles. The exceptionally high Hawley-Smoot Tariff, which Hoover had signed in 1930, was intensifying worldwide depression. Employers discarded their programs for spreading the work, and unemployment shot above 12 million. Local relief funds, both public and private, evaporated. Abhorring the thought of federal relief, Hoover fought with Congress, which the Democrats now controlled, and eventually approved an inadequate law that authorized some

THE GREAT ENGINEER

A man of extensive ability and little charm, President Hoover gave an impression of cold detachment during the agonies of depression. *(The Bettmann Archive, Inc.)*

new public works and modest loans to the states for relief.

As commodity prices continued to fall, the Federal Farm Board simply ran out of credit. Farmers burned their corn and left their cotton unpicked because it no longer paid them to market the crop. In some midwestern county seats, silent men with hunting rifles closed the courts so that their mortgages could not be foreclosed. When thousands of jobless veterans marched to Washington asking for early payment of bonuses for their services in the First World War, President Hoover thought he heard revolution in their cries for a little cash, and in July 1932 he allowed the army to drive them away. By the end of the year 20 percent of the banks that had been operating in 1929 were closed. As tremors shook the entire banking system, Hoover hardened the convictions he had held in October 1929: "We have been fighting for four years to preserve the system of production and distribution from . . . [the] failure of the financial and credit system."

During the New Era relatively little was expected of the president as an individual. The modern political economy was, after all, a complex impersonal system, not the product of a particular administration, and it appeared to operate on its own momentum. But when the thoroughly national system broke down, only the national government had the scope and authority to repair it. Because the executive branch dominated the national government, people naturally looked there for help. Atop the executive branch stood the president, and the longer the depression lasted, the more he alone seemed the one person who could lead them out of the wilderness. Hoover was judged by new, demanding standards, and the popular verdict condemned him. By 1932 millions who had no other place to turn were blaming Hoover in a bitter, personal way for their troubles. A brave new leader with a magic touch, those same millions wanted desperately to believe, might still transform the toad of depression into a dazzling prince of prosperity.

CHRONOLOGY

1920   Warren G. Harding elected president.
        Transportation Act gives ICC extensive authority over railroads and other means of transportation.
        Ku Klux Klan revitalized.

1921   First bill restricting immigration by national quotas passed.

1922   Fordney-McCumber Act reestablishes high tariff.
        Washington Conference Treaties limit naval tonnage among major powers.
        Supreme Court overturns a national child labor law.

1923   Supreme Court overturns a state minimum wage law.
        President Harding dies; Calvin Coolidge becomes president.

1924   Dawes Plan negotiates loans to revive Germany.
        National Origins Act further limits immigration by quotas.

        Teapot Dome and other Harding administration scandals exposed.
        Coolidge elected president.

1927   Sacco and Vanzetti executed.

1928   Stock market boom begins.
        Kellogg-Briand Pact outlaws war.
        Second McNary-Haugen bill to regulate the marketing of agricultural products passed but vetoed.
        Herbert Hoover elected president over Al Smith.

1929   Congress creates Federal Farm Board.
        Young Plan reformulates Dawes Plan to manage war debts.
        Stock market crash begins the Great Depression.

1930   Smoot-Hawley Tariff raises protective barriers.

1932   Reconstruction Finance Corporation invests $1.5 billion in private enterprise.

SUGGESTED READINGS

John D. Hicks, *Republican Ascendancy, 1921–1933* (1960), is a good general guide to national politics. Robert K. Murray, *The Harding Era* (1969), and Donald R. McCoy, *Calvin Coolidge* (1967), generously assess these presidents and their policies, and Burl Noggle, *Teapot Dome* (1962), covers the major scandal of their administrations. David Burner's perceptive study, *The Politics of Provincialism* (1967), recounts the pulling and hauling in the Democratic party during the New Era. An interesting picture of the politics of natural resources emerges from Donald C. Swain, *Federal Conservation Policy, 1921–1933* (1963), and Norris Hundley, Jr., *Water and the West* (1975). Gilbert C. Fite's *George W. Peek and the Fight for Farm Parity* (1954) analyzes the politics of commercial agriculture.

For the limitations of liberal reform, see LeRoy Ashby, *The Spearless Leader: Senator Borah and the Progressive Movement in the 1920s* (1972), Richard Lowitt, *George W. Norris: The Persistence of a Progressive, 1913–1933* (1971), and Arthur Mann, *LaGuardia: A Fighter against His Times, 1882–1933* (1959). In *Seedtime of Reform* (1963), on the other hand, Clarke A. Chambers discovers a maturing process during the twenties. For the decisions of the Supreme Court, see Paul L. Murphy, *The Constitution in Crisis Times, 1918–1969* (1972). George B. Tindall's *The Emergence of the New South, 1913–1945* (1967) sets that region in a national context.

The most provocative interpretation of "The Age of Corporate Capitalism" appears in William Appleman Williams, *The Contours of American History* (1961), which may be supplemented with James Gilbert, *Designing the Industrial State* (1972). Thomas C. Cochran, *American Business in the Twentieth Century* (1972), gives a clear overview of its subject. The final section in Alfred D. Chandler, *The Visible Hand* (1977), analyzes the managerial structure of the giant corporations, while Louis Galambos, *Competition and Cooperation: The Emergence of a National Trade Association* (1966), traces the pattern of organization among the scattered firms in cotton textiles. Allan Nevins and Frank Ernest Hill, *Ford: Expansion and Challenge, 1915–1933* (1957), covers the peak years of the flivver king's career. On labor, the best study is Irving L. Bernstein's *A History of the American Worker, 1920–1933: The Lean Years* (1960). Grant McConnell's *The Decline of Agrarian Democracy* (1953) centers on the American Farm Bureau Federation.

The best introduction to the ethnic and cultural issues of the twenties is John Higham's excellent *Strangers in the Land* (1955), which deals with American nativism to 1925.

Paul A. Carter, *Another Part of the Twenties* (1977), also comments generally on these issues. David M. Chalmers, *Hooded Americanism* (1965), is a lively history of the Ku Klux Klan, and Kenneth T. Jackson, *The Ku Klux Klan in the City, 1915–1930* (1967), is an important supplement to the story. G. Louis Joughlin and Edmund M. Morgan, *The Legacy of Sacco and Vanzetti* (1948), remains the richest account of events surrounding the trial of these men. The rise and fall of the "noble experiment" is traced skeptically in Andrew Sinclair, *Prohibition: The Era of Excess* (1962), and sympathetically in Norman H. Clark, *Deliver Us From Evil* (1976). Joseph R. Gusfield, *Symbolic Crusade* (1963), explores the emotional force behind Prohibition, and Norman F. Furniss, *The Fundamentalist Controversy, 1918–1931* (1954), reviews the antimodernist legislative campaigns. How cultural issues have translated into politics is described generally in Oscar Handlin, *Al Smith and His America* (1958), and more specifically in J. Joseph Huthmacher, *Massachusetts People and Politics, 1919–1933* (1959). See in addition Humbert S. Nelli, *The Business of Crime* (1976).

L. Ethan Ellis, *Republican Foreign Policy, 1921–1933* (1968), is a sound introduction to the postwar years. However, the most influential work on America's international affairs is William Appleman Williams, *The Tragedy of American Diplomacy* (rev. ed., 1962), an essay on the dominance of economic expansion in the nation's foreign policy. Two excellent books, Joan Hoff Wilson's *American Business and Foreign Policy, 1920–1933* (1971), and Michael J. Hogan's *Informal Entente: The Private Structure of Cooperation in Anglo-American Economic Diplomacy, 1918–1928* (1977), further explore the process of economic expansion, and so, in a particular case, does Gerald D. Nash, *United States Oil Policy 1890–1964* (1968). Stephen A. Schuker, *The End of French Predominance in Europe* (1976), is a complicated but rewarding account of the issues surrounding the Dawes Plan.

A clear, reliable survey of United States policy in East Asia is presented in Warren I. Cohen, *America's Response to China* (1971). Akira Iriye's *After Imperialism: The Search for a New Order in the Far East, 1921–1933* (1965) locates American policy in an international setting. The postwar treaties on Asia are covered in Thomas H. Buckley, *The United States and the Washington Conference, 1921–1922* (1970), and Raymond G. O'Connor, *Perilous Equilibrium: The United States and the London Naval Conference of*

1930 (1962). Keith L. Nelson, *Victors Divided: America and the Allies in Germany, 1918–1923* (1975), is a careful study. Peter G. Filene's *Americans and the Soviet Experience, 1917–1933* (1967) traces responses from the Bolshevik Revolution to America's recognition of the Soviet Union. In *Herbert Hoover's Latin American Policy* (1951), Alexander DeConde finds a liberalizing trend.

John Kenneth Galbraith's *The Great Crash, 1929* (rev. ed., 1972) is an interesting essay, but Lester V. Chandler, *America's Greatest Depression* (1970), and Peter Temin, *Did Monetary Forces Cause the Great Depression?* (1976), are more authoritative. Arthur M. Schlesinger, Jr., *The Crisis of the Old Order* (1957), the first volume of his *The Age of Roosevelt*, evokes the desperate confusion of depression. More on its human meaning can be found in Federal Writers' Project, *These Are Our Lives* (1939), and Studs Terkel, *Hard Times: An Oral History of the Great Depression* (1970). David Burner, *Herbert Hoover: A Public Life* (1979), is the standard account of his career to 1933; Joan Hoff Wilson's *Herbert Hoover: Forgotten Progressive* (1975) provides another interesting evaluation of that controversial president. J. Joseph Huthmacher and Warren I. Susman (eds.), *Herbert Hoover and the Crisis of American Capitalism* (1973), adds the spice of debate. Fuller accounts of government policy during Hoover's administration appear in Albert U. Romasco, *The Poverty of Abundance* (1965), and Jordan A. Schwarz, *The Interregnum of Despair* (1970).

CHAPTER 29

The Modern State in Crisis

As president, Franklin Roosevelt accomplished less than his contemporaries imagined but more than his later critics claimed. Neither in domestic nor in foreign policy did the Roosevelt administration start with a basically new orientation. Behind the early New Deal at home and the initial responses to Japanese, German, and Italian militancy abroad lay the familiar principles of the twenties. As the crises refused to lift, however, the national government adapted. In 1935 it began accumulating new responsibilities for an economy that would not revive. After 1939, in a world that would not stay at peace, the United States began shifting from its policy of international stabilization to a military involvement in global conflict. Unresolved crises demanded new departures, and the Roosevelt administration took them. Yet its natural pace was a cautious one, and it tried hard to maintain continuity with past traditions. Looking back on this process, some historians wondered if any significant changes had actually occurred. They had—not revolutionary, but important ones, step by step. As a consequence, the nation in 1941 was pointed in a new direction without a compass: prosperity had returned, but the government had no program for sustaining it. War had come, but the Roosevelt administration had no goal beyond winning it. There were still years of groping ahead.

The New Deal Arrives, 1933–1934

Almost everybody except Herbert Hoover expected 1932 to be a Democratic year. The leading contender bore a magic name in American politics. Franklin D. Roosevelt, a distant cousin of Theodore, had been assistant secretary of the navy in the Wilson administration, then the vice-presidential candidate in the futile Cox campaign of 1920. A year later an attack of poliomyelitis paralyzed him from the waist down. With dedicated assistance from his wife Eleanor and his aide Louis Howe, Roosevelt returned to politics, resisted the Republican tide in 1928 to become governor of New York, and began gathering delegates for the 1932 national convention. A bargain with John Nance Garner of Texas, which made "Cactus Jack" his running mate, sealed Roosevelt's nomination. Demonstrating the dramatic flair that animated his entire career, Roosevelt flew to the convention, stood erect at the podium, the weight of his body supported by his powerful arms, and thrilled the hall with a ringing acceptance speech. The rest was easy. On the waves of public sentiment that repudiated his predecessor, Roosevelt received 472 electoral votes to the hapless Hoover's 59.

Roosevelt's Administration.   Roosevelt's margin of 17 percent in popular votes, duplicating Hoover's margin of victory in 1928, represented the greatest party reversal in presidential history. The reversal in presidential character was just as striking. Hoover, one associate remarked, "didn't like the human element." Roosevelt reveled in it. Not only did he mix easily with all kinds of people, but he also made them feel that intuitively he sympathized with them. Hoover, taking no one's counsel, thought he knew what the nation wanted. Unlike Hoover, Roosevelt welcomed the challenge of selling his programs to a demoralized nation. A master of popular phrasing and simple analogies, Roosevelt's strong, warm voice

reached into millions of American homes through radio "fireside chats" that were bits of genius in the use of a mass medium. Where Hoover cast somber eyes downward, the tilt of Roosevelt's chin and the cocky angle of his cigarette holder invariably gave the sense of a man looking upward. Always he radiated confidence.

Promising a "New Deal" with "bold experimentation" for a devastated land, Roosevelt attracted a swarm of newcomers to Washington, a curiously mixed but effective group of advisers. As secretary of the treasury, Roosevelt selected his close friend and neighbor from Hyde Park, Henry Morgenthau, whose conscientiousness and loyalty made him indispensable to the president. For secretary of agriculture, Roosevelt appointed Henry A. Wallace, the son of Harding's secretary of agriculture, whose broad liberal vision compensated for his occasional inattention to practical matters. Another liberal Republican, Harold Ickes, became secretary of the interior and watched over his domain with a fierce jealousy and a scrupulous honesty. From his New York administration, Roosevelt brought both the first woman to hold a cabinet post, Frances Perkins, to become secretary

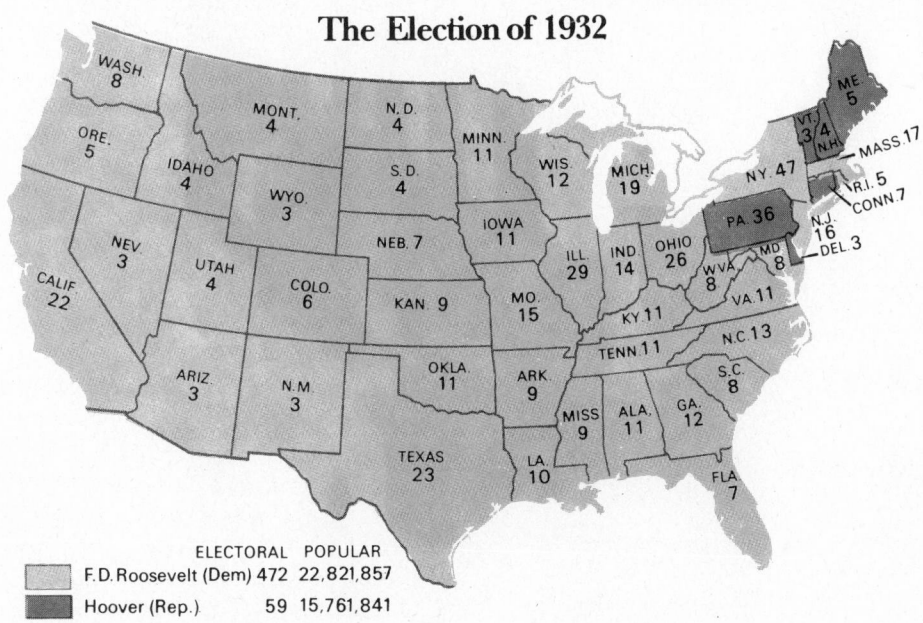

The Election of 1932

	ELECTORAL	POPULAR
F.D. Roosevelt (Dem)	472	22,821,857
Hoover (Rep.)	59	15,761,841

of labor, and the tough, dedicated administrator of relief, Harry Hopkins. All of them served to the end of Roosevelt's presidency.

The new administration also drew people who had never before influenced government policy: an obscure Montana professor named M. L. Wilson with a proposal for limiting agricultural production; Raymond Moley, Rexford Tugwell, and Adolf Berle of Columbia University, the "brains trust" of Roosevelt's 1932 campaign, with ambitions to improve the economy's organization; social workers with plans to aid the unemployed, the disabled, and the aged; and many more. Together, this patchwork of people comprised the "New Dealers." During Roosevelt's long tenure this term became part of Americans' everyday language—used with affection by some and with hatred by others to express their strong feelings about Roosevelt and his administration.

An open president gave some people the impression of a soft one, but beneath Roosevelt's easy public style and gracious private manner lay a keen, calculating mind that always sought to direct people and events. The din of demands around his powerful office never ruffled him. Moreover, Roosevelt brought to office a firm faith in the basic principles of the new national system. He wanted business to organize, industry by industry; and agriculture, commodity by commodity. With help from an efficient labor force and a supporting network of finance, he believed private groups could generate prosperity through their own natural patterns of cooperation. The government had only to assist them in regaining their strength and finding their proper places in the system. Roosevelt would experiment—but within these boundaries. Not surprisingly, the new president selected equally orthodox men for the crucial admin-

CLOSED
Once the pillars of economic stability, the banks became a symbol of national catastrophe as the entire financial structure collapsed in 1933. (*N.Y.* Daily News *photo*)

istrative posts of the early New Deal: Hugh Johnson and Donald Richberg in business affairs, George Peek and Chester Davis in agriculture, Jesse Jones for the Reconstruction Finance Corporation (RFC), and Lewis Douglas for the Bureau of the Budget. In fact, these appointments gave a slightly conservative cast to Roosevelt's initial list of lieutenants.

Roosevelt's very first problem—the collapse of the banking structure—fell upon him as he entered the White House. He responded with a fine sense of style and an instinctive moderation. During the worst winter of depression, 1932–33, accumulating panic spread from banks in the agrarian regions toward America's financial centers. State after state closed their banks until on March 4, 1933—inauguration day itself—the pressure finally overwhelmed the main citadels of national finance, New York and Chicago. As those doors closed, the entire system stopped. Borrowing an adman's phrase, Roosevelt immediately declared a nationwide "Bank Holiday," dispatched expert teams to classify all banks as either strong, wavering, or hopeless, and started a transfusion of over a billion dollars from the RFC into the banking system. The president spoke soothing words to the nation; in less than two weeks 90 percent of the frozen deposits were again available to customers, and money all over the country came out of the mattresses to fill the banks. It was an exemplary performance in the service of a free-enterprise financial system, and Wall Street joined Main Street in cheering the president.

Roosevelt's treatment for the banking emergency revealed the broad strategy of the New Deal's first months. Among the many popular prescriptions for halting an apparently endless economic decline, none appealed more to the Roosevelt spirit than a nationwide surge of activity that headed upward instead of downward. Mobilize confidence, synchronize energy, and prosperity would return because throughout the land people would suddenly behave as if it *were* returning. To a president who told Americans "that the only thing we have to fear is fear itself," that kind of grandiose bootstraps operation made perfect sense. As Roosevelt took office, he called Congress into special session, plied it with proposals, and during a whirlwind "Hundred Days" guided through fifteen major laws. They seemed to cover everything: unemployment relief, agricultural aid, mortgage supports, industrial cooperation, banking reforms, and still more.

The NRA and the AAA.   From this array of legislation two measures formed the heart of the early New Deal. One was the National Industrial Recovery Act of June 1933. Its most important provisions authorized each specialized segment of business to prepare a code of self-governance, and established the National Recovery Administration (NRA) to supervise the process. As chief of the NRA, the president chose General Hugh Johnson, a brash, noisy veteran in public affairs, who immediately launched a circus of a campaign to rally all Americans behind his program. Through parades, speeches, and assorted hoopla, Johnson made the Blue Eagle, the NRA's emblem of cooperation, almost synonymous with the New Deal itself, and he counted on public opinion to make it almost synonymous with Americanism. "When every American housewife understands that the Blue Eagle on everything that she permits to come into her home is a symbol of its restoration to security," the general roared in characteristic bombast, "may God have mercy on the man or group of men who attempt to trifle with this bird."

In the NRA's first four months, business groups wrote over seven hundred constitutions to govern their affairs. Where one or more large firms dominated an industry, the NRA relied on them to prepare the codes; where no firm dominated an industry, the NRA turned to a trade association. Although the codes varied from industry to industry, they usually included some agreement on prices, wages, and the acceptable limits of competition. The only integration among them was a common commitment to stabilization, a common freedom from antitrust prosecution, and a common dependence on the industrial groups themselves to regulate their own members. Johnson exalted the spirit of cooperation and swore at the "slackers," but never coerced the businessmen.

Section 7a of the National Industrial Recovery Act authorized workers to organize and bargain in

THE BALLYHOO OF THE EARLY NEW DEAL
At the heart of the National Recovery Administration was the hope that a great publicized surge of confidence would lift the nation out of depression. *(United Press International, Inc.)*

their own behalf, and some labor leaders, notably John L. Lewis of the United Mine Workers, acted as though the government was now their sponsor: "THE PRESIDENT WANTS YOU TO JOIN THE UNION!" Neither "union" nor "bargaining," however, had yet acquired a clear legal meaning. Company unions, many little organizations representing fractions of an industry's employees, and countless techniques for consultation between managers and workers fitted these elastic terms. The Roosevelt administration did not encourage an independent labor movement. When Ickes established the Labor Policy Board in the oil industry, for instance, he selected a company unionist, an independent unionist, and an economist. In fact, labor representation rarely served on the governing boards that policed the industrial codes.

The second basic law of the early New Deal was the Agricultural Adjustment Act of May 1933. A grab bag of alternatives, it included provisions for almost every farm program that had been proposed in this century: marketing agreements, commodity loans, export subsidies, government purchases, and—reminiscent of William Jennings Bryan—even currency inflation. To these familiar devices, the government added a favorite in New Deal circles, production restrictions, aimed at reducing agricultural surpluses at their source. During its first months the Agricultural Adjustment Administration (AAA) used production restrictions as a way of getting emergency cash relief to the countryside. In midseason farmers were paid to plow under their crops and slaughter their livestock, a bitter expedient with so much hunger in the nation. After 1933 the AAA expected each farmer growing a particular crop to reduce production by a nationally fixed percentage.

The long-term goal of the new law was to increase farm income to a level of "parity," or equality with the farmers' purchasing power just before the

First World War. To achieve parity, AAA relied on the organized farmers in each subdivision of agriculture to select the program appropriate to their product. George Peek and Chester Davis, who headed the AAA, were old friends of the farm associations and worked easily with them, especially the American Farm Bureau Federation. What looked like a concentration of power in Washington, therefore, was actually a scattering of powers among commercial farmers. Aside from temporary government coercion to limit the production of cotton and tobacco, the New Deal's farm policy preserved the essentials of the New Era. The national government delegated most of its authority to farm groups so that they could make their own decisions and largely administer them.

Financial Regulation. Elsewhere in the New Deal the same bustle, the same openness, and the same principles prevailed. Like Hoover, Roosevelt and many of his advisers considered finance particularly guilty of causing the depression. "The money changers have fled from their high seats in the temple of our civilization," the president bitingly said of the bankers in his inaugural address. While congressional investigations were revealing how bankers had speculated with their own institution's deposits, new laws sought to hold finance within proper bounds. Through the Glass-Steagall Act of 1933, Congress required banks to separate their investment in securities from normal commercial banking. The next year it placed the stock exchange under the regulation of the Securities and Exchange Commission (SEC). In 1935 Congress outlawed holding companies that had been formed in the 1920s for no other purpose than the sale of stock, and it gave the SEC authority to dissolve other questionable holding companies.

Aside from these punishments for past sins, however, finance received an impressive array of government assistance. The Reconstruction Finance Corporation pumped loans into the nation's solvent banks. In 1933 Congress created the Federal Deposit Insurance Corporation so that ordinary citizens would no longer lose their savings when a bank failed. New executive agencies, especially the Farm Credit Administration and the Home Owners Loan Corpora-

A GRAND SMILE AND A BUSTLE OF ACTIVITY
Opening the presidency to a flow of visitors and newsmen, Roosevelt demonstrated how effectively a dynamic style of leadership could raise public confidence. *(From Stefan Lorant's* The Glorious Burden*)*

tion, underwrote farm and housing mortgages. In 1935, when Congress consolidated the regulatory powers of the Federal Reserve System in a centralized board of governors, the government had completed a national framework of supports around American finance. The effect of these laws was to place both the prestige and the credit of the government behind the everyday decisions of private bankers. Within a short time, even the SEC was depending on the more enlightened brokers and financiers themselves to stabilize the stock exchanges. As Chairman William O. Douglas stated in 1938, "Government regulation at its best should be residual."

Public Relief.   The New Deal responded to the problem of unemployment and relief with an equally restrained use of government power. To generate new jobs, Congress appropriated $3.3 billion for the Public Works Administration (PWA) as part of the National Industrial Recovery Act of 1933. Secretary Harold Ickes, its director, vowed that no corruption would tarnish the PWA and spent the funds with a miser's caution. The Civilian Conservation Corps (CCC), one of the most popular measures of the "Hundred Days," functioned like an army summer camp for unemployed young men, who labored at a variety of valuable tasks in reforestations, soil conservation, and flood control. But in 1933 the CCC gave only a few weeks of work to about 2 percent of the unemployed.

PLANTING FOR THE FUTURE
By linking work relief with the preservation of natural resources, the Civilian Conservation Corps (CCC) became one of the New Deal's most popular measures. *(U.S. Forest Service)*

Although Roosevelt showed none of Hoover's reluctance to use federal funds for the destitute in 1933, he shared a common belief that only desperate circumstances could justify national money for relief. The New Deal's first relief agency was appropriately named the Federal Emergency Relief Administration (FERA). During 1933 and 1934 Congress voted relief funds as if each new contribution would surely be the last. When an initial appropriation of $500 million for FERA proved inadequate, Roosevelt drew an additional $400 million from Ickes's PWA for a hastily devised program, the Civil Works Administration (CWA). In February 1934 Congress finally authorized more funds for FERA. Harry Hopkins, Roosevelt's administrator of relief, employing a small staff, relied on private groups and local governments to distribute most of the money. "Nothing in the new federal act was meant to change that local responsibility, nor did the federal administration have any intention of doing so," an expert on public relief concluded. To the starving, all that mattered was that a little help had finally come.

The Tennessee Valley Authority.   The most daring government venture of the early New Deal was the Tennessee Valley Authority (TVA). Its origins lay in a long, inconclusive debate during the 1920s over the disposition of a dam at Muscle Shoals, Alabama, that the government had started to build in wartime but never completed. When Henry Ford, widely regarded in the 1920s as a great public benefactor, offered to lease and develop it, Senator George Norris of Nebraska, a tenacious old progressive, skillfully blocked the proposal and in time convinced a majority of his colleagues that the government itself should develop the dam. During the 1920s, however, no one anticipated the vast undertaking ahead. Beginning in 1933, Muscle Shoals became merely the point of departure for a new concept in regional rehabilitation, which soon gained international fame. The Tennessee Valley Authority, with sweeping administrative powers over a domain that wound through seven southern states, embarked on two decades of activity that created a network of dams and canals, rejuvenated the

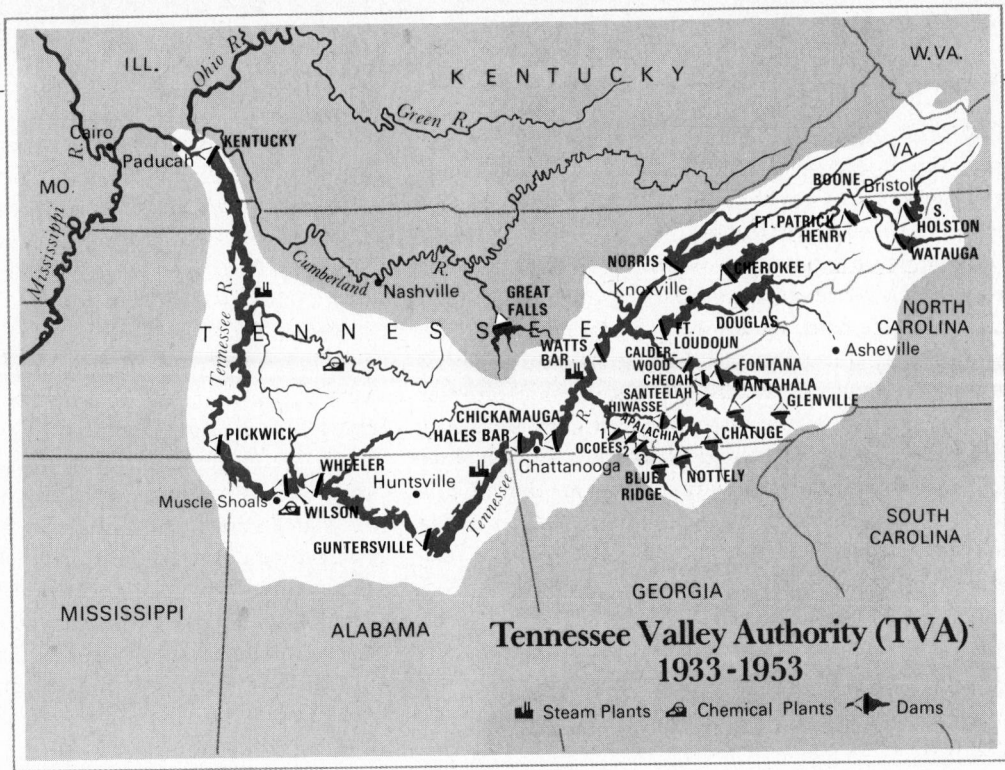

Tennessee Valley Authority (TVA)
1933-1953

Steam Plants   Chemical Plants   Dams

soil and protected it against floods, and harnessed electric resources to service millions of homes and thousands of new businesses.

From the outset, the TVA challenged the customary rights of private enterprise by selling the electric power it generated. Because of this, conservatives probably hated it as much as any New Deal program. Nevertheless, the TVA had not completely abandoned the principles of the New Era. The regional concept itself was a way of avoiding distant direction from Washington. At every step the TVA's directors worked through the existing organized groups in their region. Chambers of commerce, leagues of bankers, commercial farming associations, and their local associates from the Department of Agriculture and the state agricultural colleges channeled the TVA's information, chose its demonstration farms, and distributed many of its political benefits. The same local groups were the TVA's primary allies in the long legal battle with the private utility companies over the issue of public electricity, a battle that the TVA did not fully win until 1939. Even such a striking depar-

ture as TVA, in other words, cooperated as closely as it could with the established private interests in the area.

In 1934, shortly before Raymond Moley left the New Deal to become its conservative critic, he commented, "This administration is as far from socialism or communism as any group ever assembled in a national government." The sheer quantity of government activities during 1933 and 1934 misled a good many people into believing that profound changes were under way. Despite the broadened range of government services, however, the fundamentals of the New Era remained intact. Subsequent speculation about a critical moment in March 1933, when American society might have taken a radical turn, made little sense because the nation's leaders in March 1933 had no radical intentions. With fresh faces and tactics, through experiments and expedients, the New Deal fought to preserve a particular political economy that had formed during the 1920s and that continued to shape national policy after five grinding years of depression.

The New Deal at the Crossroads, 1935–1936

But the New Deal was not working. By late 1934 the NRA was a shambles, the victim of the businessmen's self-serving codes, widespread violations of these same rules, and bitter criticism from almost every section of American society. Now it was the National Run Around. The administration's own review board condemned the NRA, and Roosevelt himself lost interest in the grand experiment.   The depression refused to lift. Though unemployment declined from the darkest months of early 1933, it was about as bad as it had been the day Roosevelt was elected. Net farm income was a dismal 50 percent of its level in 1929, and the food shortages—caused by a cruel drought on the Great Plains, choking the farmers in vast clouds of topsoil that swept across the region—accounted for most of the price increases since 1933.

Because the AAA operated through landowners, not tenant farmers, sharecroppers, or farm laborers, its benefits scarcely touched the bottom rungs of agriculture. Only corporate profits were making strong gains in 1934.

Formulas for Prosperity.   As confidence in the New Deal dwindled, millions of angry suffering Americans appeared to be finding new leaders and new causes. From Louisiana came the shrewd, flamboyant Huey Long, who promised to make "every man a king." By appealing to the forgotten poor whites of his state, Long not only became governor in 1929 but actually ruled Louisiana through an extensive, ruthless political machine. After his election to the Senate in 1930, the Louisiana "Kingfish" used it as a forum to spread the gospel of Share Our Wealth, a simple, sweeping program that would expropriate the wealth of the very rich in order to provide all families with a $5,000 homestead and an annual income of

NATURE'S VENGEANCE
Bad agricultural practices and bad weather combined in 1934 to turn the Great Plains into a suffocating, impoverishing Dust Bowl.   *(USDA photograph)*

about $2,500, a glorious vision at depression prices.

From a suburb of Detroit came the rich radio voice of a Catholic priest, Father Charles Coughlin, who blasted Wall Street, called for the nationalization of the banks, and demanded an immediate, massive monetary inflation. From Long Beach, California, came Dr. Francis E. Townsend, who envisaged prosperity to everybody through monthly government payments of $200 for each unemployed person over sixty. By requiring the pensioners to spend their $200 within the month, the Townsend Plan promised to revitalize the entire economy. All three campaigns were rapidly accelerating in late 1934 and early 1935.

Long, Coughlin, and Townsend spoke the language of local politics, where the appeal of a popular, commonsense economics had always remained strong. As years of depression eroded hopes and evaporated resources in countless neighborhoods and communities, the people whose lives were rooted there desperately sought ways of bringing opportunity back to their localities. To many of them, the neat, mechanical answers of Share Our Wealth, inflation, and old-age pensions sounded just right. In the tradition of free silver in the 1890s and radical antimonopoly in the progressive years, these proposals promised at a stroke to give ordinary Americans a decent life without elaborate laws or government regimentation.

No one ever knew how many Americans accepted these formulas for prosperity. Though Long, Coughlin, and Townsend each claimed millions of adherents, none formed an effective organization. The imposing façades of Long's Share Our Wealth clubs, Coughlin's National Union for Social Justice, and Townsend's Old Age Revolving Pensions club covered a thoroughly scattered, locally oriented following that defied a head count. Nor could the New Dealers calculate the number of workers who had given up on the system and were ready for a revolution. Here also the signs were ominous. During 1934 an upheaval of strikes, involving over 7 percent of the labor force, shook the nation. Longshoremen in San Francisco, teamsters in Minneapolis, and textile workers along the East Coast were embroiled in particularly bloody conflicts that had radical overtones.

SENATOR HUEY LONG OF LOUISIANA
Long, Roosevelt's most powerful critic, expressed the anger and frustration of poor people who had not benefited from the early New Deal. *(Culver Pictures, Inc.)*

Partly because no one could estimate the strength of these rumbling movements, they sent tremors of anxiety throughout Washington's offices. Yet late in 1934 the New Deal had stalled. No one considered another gigantic starting up. Roosevelt could gamble only once on that strategy. The next round would have to address specific popular needs.

Relief and Old-Age Insurance. In January 1935 Roosevelt headed the New Deal into fresh winds by calling for a huge work relief program and a comprehensive social security measure. Three months later, Congress established the Works Progress Administration (WPA). The very size of the appropriation indicated how central the New Deal considered relief. With almost $5 billion, or ten times the amount originally given to FERA, the WPA absorbed close to half of the government's total expenditures. Like its predecessors, the act claimed to be a temporary measure. By 1935, however, very few people thought that local or private contributions could ever again carry the burdens of relief in a depression. Harry Hopkins, who administered the WPA, now emerged as Roosevelt's most powerful lieutenant. Through his large staff, the WPA supervised an extraordinary variety of projects, ranging from theatrical productions to road repairs, and on the average employed over 2 million people who would otherwise have been jobless. Although WPA wages could not match Huey Long's proposal of $2,500 per person, they were a blessed step above nothing.

The Social Security Act of August 1935, more cautious in approach, was an equally striking innovation with a more lasting influence. It established a national system of old-age insurance that was funded by a tax on workers' wages and an equivalent tax on their employers. The act also taxed employers to finance state programs for unemployment compensation, and it offered the states matching grants to aid dependent mothers and children and the disabled. In all, the Social Security Act was a conservative version of the schemes for social insurance that had been discussed since the early 1900s. The new taxes fell heavily on the poor. Welfare payments varied widely from state to state. By linking retirement pensions to employment, as one study summarized it, Social Security chose "to accept private industry's judgment of a person's worth." The poorest Americans, who had no wages to tax or whose jobs fell outside the scope of the law, received no protection at all. Nevertheless, if the act did not equal the generosity of the Townsend Plan, it coped with the same ills. Moreover, Social Security was an expandable formula, and later Congresses gradually extended its range until by the 1970s it covered almost all employees and many more of life's hazards.

Liberal congressmen produced the third basic law, which the president after months of hesitation finally endorsed. Passage of the National Labor Rela-

tions Act—the Wagner Act—in July 1935 marked another startling shift in New Deal policy. Before 1935 the government had considered labor primarily as a dependent part of industry. With the Wagner Act, however, the New Deal committed itself unequivocally to supporting unions that were independent of management. The Wagner Act outlawed company unions and any form of company discrimination that might inhibit workers from joining an independent union. The National Labor Relations Board (NLRB), which was created to administer the law, could conduct an election among a company's employees to ensure their free choice of a bargaining agent, and it could compel employers to comply with the new rules.

Passionate Reactions.   The first important consequence of these three unprecedented acts was a powerful release of emotions. During 1935 and 1936, the New Deal, and above all Roosevelt himself, generated both nationwide hope and hatred that would run like a high-voltage charge through the next generation of American politics. If the New Deal neither cured the depression nor saved the nation from suffering, it communicated a humane concern when no one else seemed to care. "I do think that Roosevelt is the biggest-hearted man we ever had in the White House," declared one typical citizen. The legislation of 1935, which offered millions of hard-pressed Americans a bit of help, simultaneously held out the promise of much more to come. Moreover, it offered a promise of dignity. The WPA gave people real jobs, not charity. Social Security raised miraculous visions of a decent life in old age. The Wagner Act told countless wage earners that through their own organization they could command respect as full-fledged citizens. In one worker's words, "Roosevelt is the only president we ever had that thought the Constitution belonged to the poor man too."

What gave hope at the bottom of society spread horror at the top. Among many people with a strong stake in the existing system—bankers, lawyers, corporation executives, and doctors—the new laws created images of a chaotic society where government was pitting the masses against everyone else's privileges. Year after year, their inability to explain what had gone wrong with the economy or predict what the government would do next had been deepening their frustration. Conservative doubts about the New Deal in 1933 turned into charges of incompetence in 1934, then outright hatred in 1935. No more irrational but much more powerful than the millions who loved Roosevelt, the wealthy foes of the New Deal had the means of making their feelings heard. They spoke from chambers of commerce and bar, medical, and banking associations. They formed new organizations such as the American Liberty League, which spent millions to discredit the New Deal. Through newspapers, radio, and venomous little rumors ("Polio? Syphilis!"), they mounted a furious assault on "that man in the White House" even more than on his administration.

National-Local Compromise. Such an intense involvement with Roosevelt tended to obscure a second basic issue that accompanied the New Deal's economic policy. In destitute localities everywhere, the prospect of any assistance, of course, was a godsend. But how would it be distributed? By the efficiency standards of a distant bureaucracy or the personal judgments of local politicians? As the battles over Al Smith demonstrated, the Democratic party had been collecting a particularly combustible mixture of ethnic groups during the twenties. The elections of 1932 and 1934 added even more urban cultural blocks to the party's new majority. If the government's programs interfered with the sensitive local standards of these groups, the New Deal coalition might disintegrate. The Long and Coughlin movements, in the tradition of local politics, appealed directly to the Democratic majority's racial and religious feelings.* But the Roosevelt administration, national and economic in orientation, hoped to avoid all issues that might disturb these local cultures.

*Long himself was assassinated at the Louisiana State House in September 1935. Others, notably the Reverend Gerald L. K. Smith, tried to reach his national audience through religious and racial prejudice.

After 1929 opponents of Prohibition argued persuasively that liquor production would generate more jobs. The national Democratic party led the campaign for the Twenty-First Amendment, which in December 1933 repealed the Eighteenth and left the rules governing alcohol to local choice. Overjoyed to have Prohibition behind them, the New Dealers expected to concentrate exclusively on the problems of depression. It never dawned on them, for example, to revive the old progressive wars against immigrant radicals or prostitution. Though Roosevelt selected the first woman to hold a cabinet post, neither Frances Perkins nor Roosevelt's active wife, Eleanor, nor anyone else in the New Deal wanted to revive the movement for women's rights. By 1935 these crusades were over, and no one in the Roosevelt administration was recommending a new one.

Yet in many ways, the New Dealers were impressively liberal on matters of race and religion. Secretary of the Interior Harold Ickes was a veteran member of the National Association for the Advancement of Colored People. Eleanor Roosevelt spoke eloquently for racial and religious equality. In the 1940s Henry Wallace became one of the most prominent white champions of black rights. The president himself appointed a Jew as secretary of the treasury, an ironic reply to the anti-Semitic hallucination about a Jewish plot to control world finance. Perhaps most impressive of all, the New Deal tried to reverse the long, cruel trend of native American impoverishment and tribal disintegration. In the late 1920s government reports began to reveal the rampant white greed and injustice that under the terms of the old Dawes Act of 1887 had transformed tribal lands into the private property of its members. In 1934, spurred on by John Collier, the New Deal's director of Indian affairs, Congress passed the Indian Reorganization Act, which enabled nations of native Americans to re-create communal control over their lands, and offered some assistance toward tribal self-sufficiency. Throughout the thirties, the zealous Collier scrambled for money to implement this program.

By inclination, however, the leading New Dealers ignored ethnic problems as much as they could. They wanted to frame public policy in economic, not ethnic, terms and that desire led them to compromise with the values of their local constituents. In return for the right to formulate broad economic policy, national Democratic leaders would allow local politicians to distribute public funds in their own areas by their own standards. New Deal money in the South underwrote white Protestant cultures. When white landlords needed cheap labor at harvest time, for example, local WPA administrators released workers from the public payroll. In the large cities government funds passed through urban politicians to the interested families and cultural groups. In only five of the forty-eight states did the WPA bypass the established local powers. Moreover, when Congress rejected an amendment to the Wagner Act that would have required racial equality on the job, the New Deal left the issue of bias in the unions to the labor leaders themselves. The immediate responses to these policies were politically heartening. Enthusiasm for the New Deal ran very high in the South. In such cities as Pittsburgh and Kansas City, the New Deal's relief laws shored up the existing political machines, and in Chicago, WPA funds actually saved the budding Democratic organization of Mayor Edward Kelley. These beneficiaries ranked among the Roosevelt administration's most dedicated supporters. Across the country organized labor declared Roosevelt its champion.

The primary political test of the New Deal's methods came in the elections of 1936. Roosevelt's Republican opponent was the honest, uninspired governor of Kansas, Alfred Landon. Coughlin, Townsend, and the remnants of Long's legions gathered to form the Union party and nominate Representative William Lemke of North Dakota for president. Although Coughlin personally promised 9 million votes for Lemke and the *Literary Digest* predicted Landon's election (from a poll of those still able to afford telephones), most people expected Roosevelt to win. The margin of victory, however, would serve as the critical index to the New Deal's success. The most optimistic estimate came from James Farley, Roosevelt's political aide and postmaster general, who dared to guess that the president would carry every state except Maine and Vermont. Then in November exactly that happened. Along with huge Democratic

majorities in Congress—75 senators and 333 representatives—the election gave Roosevelt a breathtaking 523 electoral votes to a mere 8 for Landon. The woebegone Union party did not even collect a million popular votes, and Coughlin announced his retirement from politics.

The Democratic conquest of 1936 ratified the New Deal's policies in two crucial and interrelated areas. First, it placed responsibility for the national economy squarely in the lap of the government. After 1936 Washington became the guarantor of the nation's economic welfare, and the popular economics of people like Long, Coughlin, and Townsend never again won a mass following. The business leadership of the New Era and the NRA was thoroughly repudiated. Wealthy haters of Roosevelt had to bide their time and fight another day. Second, the landslide of 1936 justified the New Deal's balance between national and local power. Broad economic policy from Washington and local control over cultural matters proved a brilliantly successful formula. As the election confirmed this long-range formula of responsibility and power, it also solidified the core of a new and enduring Democratic majority that had been forming since 1930. To the solid South were added the nation's industrial centers, where the party's greatest strength came from the relatively poor, the Catholics, the Jews, and the blacks. Other voters would slip away from the Democrats after 1936, but the heart of their support held quite firm for decades to come.

The New Deal Loses Its Way, 1937–1939

At the peak of his popularity, Roosevelt turned to America's faltering economy with renewed confidence. The president's first objective had already been dictated by the Supreme Court. In the tense climate of 1935 and 1936, as the New Deal was expanding its scope, the Court grew increasingly rigid. A bare majority of five justices attacked the national government's primary source of power over the economy, regulation of interstate commerce. Mining and farming, in the Court's view, were local, not interstate, activities. By implication, these interpretations jeopardized a full range of the New Deal's policies in industry and agriculture. Moreover, a narrow construction of interstate commerce automatically cast doubts on the government's authority to regulate labor-management relations through the Wagner Act, and to tax employers and employees through the Social Security Act.

FDR vs. the Supreme Court. The most publicized of the Court's many decisions during 1935 and 1936 were the *Schechter* case (1935), which struck down the National Recovery Administration (NRA), and *United States* v. *Butler* (1936), which invalidated the tax on food processing in the Agricultural Adjustment Act. Neither decision crippled the New Deal. The NRA, a loosely worded delegation of powers to the executive that all nine justices condemned, was already dead by 1935. The Court's judgment merely gave it a decent burial. Following the *Butler* decision Congress continued the New Deal's farm program of restricted production under the guise of soil conservation. But the Court's willingness to assault two such important laws, along with so many other threatening precedents in 1935 and 1936, forced a confrontation between the Roosevelt administration and the Supreme Court. As the president stated, the New Deal could not function with a "horse and buggy" conception of interstate commerce.

Reading his victory in 1936 as a mandate to storm this conservative outpost, the Supreme Court, Roosevelt submitted a judiciary reorganization bill to Congress in February 1937. The president requested the right to enlarge the Court from nine to a maximum of fifteen members if those justices over seventy years old did not voluntarily resign. If, as Chief Justice Charles Evans Hughes stated, the Constitution was what the Court made it, Roosevelt would remake the Court. But the president pretended that the issue was judicial efficiency rather than judicial interpretation. The existing Court, he claimed, could not manage its heavy load of work, a charge that the magisterial Hughes easily refuted. To this deviousness, Roosevelt added an unusual ineptness. When Congress rebelled at his plan, Roosevelt refused to negotiate. Although liberal congressmen were prepared to impose extensive restrictions on the Court through constitutional amendment, the president held stubbornly to his own unacceptable scheme. Meanwhile, the Court defused the central issue through an abrupt change in constitutional law. By a vote of five to four, the Court in *NLRB* v. *Jones and Laughlin Steel* (1937) upheld the Wagner Act with a broad interpretation of interstate commerce. Then, by a larger margin, the Court validated the Social Security Act. "A switch in time saved nine," the wags declared. The president's campaign looked more and more like a personal war against the Court. Defensively, he gave the public "solemn assurance" that he did not seek "the destruction of any branch of government or any part of our heritage of freedom." It did no good. After 168 days of exhausting, bitter battle, Roosevelt's bill was defeated.

In the end the conservatives did lose their judicial stronghold. A rapid sequence of retirements and deaths between 1937 and 1941 enabled the president to select seven associate justices and a chief justice. By the time of *United States* v. *Darby* (1941), the New Deal Court had authorized sweeping powers over interstate commerce and approved all the principal legislation that still mattered. But the price of victory was high. Roosevelt's clumsy attack on the Court tarnished his reputation as a leader. Instead of pitting the New Deal against the Court, his course set Congress against the president. In the future even Democratic congressmen would feel much freer to vote against the president.

The Strengthening Labor Movement. Nevertheless, the Court battle was only one part of a complex process leading to the New Deal's decline. At least as much strain in the New Deal coalition came from the labor movement. As the Wagner Act passed in 1935, the labor movement split into warring camps. John L. Lewis, president of the powerful United Mine Workers, led a group of dissident unions out of the craft-oriented AFL in order to organize the semiskilled and unskilled workers in the major mass-production industries. The rebels eventually formed the Congress of Industrial Organizations (CIO), while the skilled trades remained in the AFL. Looking at the leaders of the two organizations, there seemed to be no contest. Lewis's dramatic flair and imaginative leadership made him a national attraction in the mid-1930s second only to Roosevelt, and the shaggy giant of the CIO appeared capable of demolishing the AFL's mild little William Green with words alone. "Explore the mind of Bill Green," the advocates of labor compromise had suggested to Lewis. "I have done a lot of exploring in Bill's mind," Lewis declared, "and I give you my word there is nothing there." But the AFL proved to be a resourceful enemy that mobilized local opposition to the CIO, collaborated with employers who were fighting the new unions, and helped antiunion congressmen brand the CIO a communist organization.

In addition, the CIO faced a formidable challenge from the unorganized industries themselves.

VIOLENCE IN THE FACTORIES
The drives to organize America's mass production industries exposed the raw nerve of class conflict, as they pitted workers against both employers and their allies in local government. *(United Press International, Inc.)*

From the docks of San Francisco to the textile mills in North Carolina, employers murdered, gassed, beat, and intimidated their workers in order to demoralize them and to block the CIO's unionizing efforts. The first crisis in this rough, uncertain struggle began in December 1936, when workers at a number of General Motors affiliates sat inside the company plants to gain recognition for their new organization, the United Auto Workers (UAW). Ignoring court orders to evacuate the buildings, receiving supplies from their friends outside, and turning back the police in "The Battle of the Running Bulls," the auto workers, with the help of cooperative state and national politicians, achieved the CIO's first great victory. In February 1937, General Motors and UAW signed a peace pact. Illegal sit-down strikes quickly spread nationwide.

Meanwhile, a CIO drive in the steel industry won a second stunning success. In March 1937, U.S. Steel, the very symbol of antiunionism in America's mass production industries, ended a bitter strike by recognizing the steelworkers' union. Almost all the corporations in "Little Steel," however, adamantly refused to follow suit, and bloody counterattacks stalled the organizing campaign there. In the "Memorial Day Massacre" outside Republic Steel's plant in Chicago, for example, police shot into a fleeing crowd, killing or wounding dozens of strike sympathizers. In fact, there was an epidemic of industrial violence in 1937.

The turmoil of sit-down strikes and local warfare broke an uneasy truce over labor policy within the Democratic party. While an exasperated Roosevelt condemned management and labor alike by declaring "a plague on both your houses," Democratic factions in Congress angrily debated the sins of employers and unions. Fortunately for the CIO, a partisan National Labor Relations Board (NLRB) continued to fight vigorously in behalf of the new unions. By 1941, with almost 10 million members divided between the AFL and the CIO, the union movement had safely passed the first round of crisis. In the process, however, it had made a host of enemies, Democrats as well as Republicans.

Growing hostility to the labor movement decreased the likelihood that the government would assist other Americans to organize in their own behalf. Tenant farmers, for example, were particularly in need of the government's help. Always the poor relations in an era of commercial agriculture, they had suffered cruelly from depression and drought in the 1930s. In 1935, when some of them formed the Southern Tenant Farmers' Union, landlords and sheriffs crushed their organization. When reformers in the Department of Agriculture argued the tenants' cause, they were fired.

Principal New Deal Measures, 1935–1938

Works Progress Administration (WPA)	May 1935
Wagner Act, creating the National Labor Relations Board (NLRB)	July 1935
Social Security Act	August 1935
Bankhead-Jones Farm Tenancy Act, creating the Farm Security Administration (FSA)	July 1937
Fair Labor Standards Act	June 1938

The first serious attempt to reverse this tide was the Bankhead-Jones Farm Tenancy Act of 1937. Through a new agency, the Farm Security Administration (FSA), the law provided credit with which tenants could purchase the farms they were working. In addition, the FSA explored ways to develop a diversified, cooperative community life for small farmers and to protect the interests of the forgotten farm laborers. The FSA was one logical extension of the New Deal's innovations in 1935, a rural counterpart of the program for organized labor. But in 1937, the opposition of the established agricultural organizations and the flagging reform spirit in Congress kept the FSA budget small and the agency's future precarious.

The only solid expansion of the New Deal came in the Fair Labor Standards Act of 1938. After much wrangling, Congress established a minimum wage level and an official rate of time-and-a-half for overtime work, and it abolished child labor. With wholesale exemptions in agriculture, special dispensations for southern employers, and minimum wage scales that were meager even by a depression standard, this law, like the Social Security Act, was neither general in its coverage nor generous in its provisions. Yet in combination with Social Security and WPA, the Fair Labor Standards Act reinforced a fundamental new assumption: the national government should protect the economic welfare of its poorer citizens.

The Rise of Special Interests. By 1938 the New Deal was obviously drifting. Its thin list of accomplishments in two years reflected the sharp decline in Roosevelt's authority. On Capitol Hill, an informal coaliton of Republicans and conservative, largely southern Democrats moved into the vacuum of leadership. A defensive league, it concentrated primarily on opposing "socialist" measures that would enlarge the national government's responsibilities, or "giveaway" programs that would expand its services. In the spirit of the 1920s, many of the opposition still equated prosperity with a self-regulating economy. In 1938, when the president proposed a bill for executive reorganization to manage the government's broadening obligations, the conservative coalition—with cries of dictatorship—defeated the measure. And when Roosevelt tried to "purge" a few prominent opponents in his own party during the off-year elections of 1938, his failure only emphasized before the public the president's diminishing power.

Most fundamental of all its problems, the New Deal lacked a clear purpose. When the New Deal changed course in 1935, it abandoned the vision of the economy that had dominated public policy since the First World War. During the 1920s and early 1930s, policy-makers sought harmony among the nation's big economic units: business, labor, agriculture, and finance. With encouragement from Washington, it was assumed that business would lead the other units in a coordinated march to prosperity. By 1935 it was no longer possible to picture the economy as big interdependent blocs. More and more little economic units came to Washington demanding their own programs to serve their own interests.

There were no more NRAs for all of American business. Instead, Congress in 1935 created "little

NRAs" for coal, for trucking, and through an inter-state oil compact, for petroleum. Two new laws strengthened the rights of small businessmen. The Robinson-Patman Act of 1936 sought to protect independent retailers against such huge chains as A & P and Woolworth, and the Miller-Tydings Act of 1937 legalized "fair trade" agreements, or fixed retail pricing, in behalf of similar small firms. Between 1934 and 1937 special legislation responded to particular agricultural interests such as cattle grazers, cotton and tobacco growers, and dairy farmers. The labor movement not only sharpened the distinction between the unorganized and the organized, but also highlighted the very different grievances separating carpenters from steelworkers from longshoremen from hatmakers—a decentralization of interests far greater than just a division between the AFL and the CIO.

Only the hub in Washington connected these many spokes of special interest. Economic policy was now government policy. But no one in the New Deal had a sensible strategy for integrating these economic fragments. Since the beginning of the New Deal, some voices advocated national planning. Yet their statements were studies in vagueness. Reach "a reasonable meeting of minds," the historian Charles Beard proposed; "coordinate private industry" with public enterprises like TVA, the philosopher John Dewey suggested. The president had authorized the Justice Department to bring more antitrust suits against big business. Yet Roosevelt never longed for the old days of small-unit competition, and the administration's new antitrust policy did not try to destroy giant corporations.

Some advisers recommended a closer alliance between the New Deal and the unions, but Roosevelt neither understood organized labor's raw battles nor trusted John L. Lewis, its outstanding leader. Marriner Eccles, the chairman of the Federal Reserve Board, wanted to regain prosperity through government spending. But Roosevelt retained a traditional faith in balanced budgets. He even contributed to a new economic crisis in 1937 by sharply reducing the government budget when, in fact, only a radical increase in government spending would have worked. The budgets of the thirties were simply too small a frac-

tion of the economy's total activities, and the New Deal was attempting to move a boulder with a stick. Although Roosevelt was profoundly disturbed by the vision of "one-third of a nation ill-nourished, ill-clad, ill-housed," he did not know how, in the long run, to solve the problem. By 1939 the weight among the president's domestic advisers had shifted well to the left of the balance in 1933, but liberals no more than conservatives knew how to manage America's fragmenting economy.

Because the New Deal failed to accomplish everything did not mean that it accomplished nothing. Taking office in 1933, Roosevelt set out to save a crumbling American system, and he succeeded. Through new departures in 1935, the New Deal generated popular hopes where despair had prevailed, and it did so with only modest changes in the distribution of power among private groups. The Roosevelt administration did not seize leadership of the economy; it inherited the role in a depression that private initiatives could not budge. Perhaps it is enough to say that in crisis the New Deal had the wit to start the political economy in a fresh, more promising direction.

International Disintegration, 1931–1939

Abroad as at home, the United States developed a system in the 1920s based on certain general rules. The most important rule was that international peace be maintained. A second was that as the world's greatest economic power, the United States would rely on investment and trade, not force of arms, to further its global interests. These rules were challenged by the Great Depression.

By 1931 the pall of depression had spread worldwide. The German economy was virtually bankrupt, the British credit system was tottering, and the foundation beneath every other industrial nation was badly shaken. Economic nationalism thrived, as government after government moved to protect its weakened domestic economy from outside competition. Some powers—notably Japan, Germany, and Italy—also tried to renew their economic strength through military imperialism. Where they conquered, they assimilated, absorbing governments and integrating dependent economies into their own. The United States, always a formidable competitor in a strictly economic contest, was not even allowed into these spheres. In the broadest sense, the international military crisis that culminated at Pearl Harbor was a conflict between these rival forms of imperialism: the one based on peace, the economic persuasion of foreign governments, and competition; the other predicated on war, domination, and monopoly.

The first of the military imperialists to strike was Japan. When depression pinched its lifelines of commerce, Japan looked more avidly than ever to its most natural area for economic expansion, the Asian mainland. But Japan could expect little profit in China as long as it was plagued by civil wars and carved into many spheres of foreign influence. In September 1931, Japan's Kwantung Army, which was stationed in Manchuria, took the initiative by seizing all of this rich province in northern China. Twelve months later, Manchuria became the Japanese puppet state of Manchukuo.

Only a year before the Manchurian assault, Hoover's Secretary of State Henry L. Stimson had thought of Japan as a stabilizing force in East Asia, a "buffer state" between the United States and a chaotic China. Outraged, Stimson now hastened to find some way of thwarting Japan through collective international action. As an outsider, however, the United States could not collaborate effectively with the League of Nations. And the Nine-Power Treaty on the Open Door in China, a vague document at best, contained no sanctions against a violator. Wanting at least to threaten Japan with a stronger American policy, Stimson was blocked by President Hoover, who publicly renounced either economic or military sanctions against Japan. What emerged was a purely American statement of principle. The Hoover-Stimson Doctrine of 1932, relying on the Kellogg-Briand Peace Pact's repudiation of war, stated that the United States would refuse to recognize any treaty that impaired the sovereignty of China or infringed on the Open Door policy.

An even more formidable imperialism emerged in Germany. Against a background of economic pros-

THE ORIGINAL FASCIST
A boastful Benito Mussolini promised military glory to an Italian nation beset by serious economic problems. *(United Press International, Inc.)*

tration, the National Socialist party worked its way into the German government early in 1933, established its leader, Adolf Hitler, as dictator, and proceeded to eliminate its opponents. For a time, outsiders refused to take the militaristic pomp, the crude racism, and the ranting speeches of the Nazis seriously. But the new government proved ingenious in attracting German loyalties and mobilizing the country's resources. As the Nazis consolidated their power at home, they also asserted it abroad. Hitler, repudiating the Versailles Treaty as a "stab in the back," left the League in 1933 and two years later announced that Germany would rearm. As a minor accompaniment, Italy also joined the new imperialists. Benito Mussolini, a fascist who had risen as Italy's dictator in 1922, longed to dominate the Mediterranean but lacked the power. In October 1935, hoping to distract Italians from their economic woes at home, the opportunistic Mussolini settled for an invasion of the independent African state of Ethiopia.

America's Response. Franklin Roosevelt entered office sharing the general commitment of the twenties to international stabilization. Yet he showed even less inclination than Hoover toward international cooperation. As Hoover was leaving the White House in 1933, he wanted the United States to take the lead at a forthcoming London Economic Conference, the last faint hope for a collective approach to the world's financial crisis. Although Roosevelt sent a delegation to London, he disrupted the conference by refusing America's cooperation. Meanwhile, the new president took the United States off the gold standard, tinkered for a while with the international value of the dollar, and generally let it be known that the United States would solve its depression alone. The only nod toward international cooperation came from those Democrats who argued that an increased flow of trade would relax international tensions and improve the prospects of world peace. With Secretary of State Cordell Hull in command, Congress passed the Reciprocal Trade Agreement Act of 1934, enabling the State Department to negotiate lower tariffs with one nation at a time. Eventually the United States signed many such agreements, but they had no appreciable effect on the state of world diplomacy.

Following an old American tradition, Roosevelt rejected America's involvement in European affairs and concentrated on the Western Hemisphere. The most heralded part of the administration's policy toward Latin America completed a process that had begun in the twenties: the United States formally abandoned any authority to intervene in a Latin American state. With his uncanny talent for the right phrase and gesture, Roosevelt declared a "Good Neighbor Policy" and in 1936 made an unprecedented, highly successful tour of Latin America. Beneath the new surface, however, the old substance held quite firm. The United States still sought to consolidate its hemispheric authority. In 1933, when a revolutionary government arose in Cuba, for example, the Roosevelt administration undermined it through nonrecognition, then supported the military regime of Fulgencio Batista. The Cuban economy fell even further under American control and the State Department pursued reciprocal trade agreements with special zeal in Latin America.

Military Actions. In 1936 the pace of military imperialism quickened. In May, Italy annexed Ethiopia as a colony. Two months later, civil war in Spain offered Mussolini another chance to extend Italy's influence in the Mediterranean. Between 1936 and 1938, Italian military intervention on behalf of General Francisco Franco's army, more than matching the assistance that France and the Soviet Union gave to the Spanish Republicans, made a critical difference in the war. By 1939 Franco's reactionary Falange ruled Spain. In 1936 German troops occupied the Rhineland provinces, which the Versailles Treaty had demilitarized. Then in March 1938, demanding the political unification of all German people, Hitler sent his soldiers into Austria, and Germany annexed it. By an alliance in 1939, the Rome-Berlin Axis was forged between those two dictatorships. Across the Pacific, Japan in 1936 discarded the international agreements that limited the size of its navy. A year later, after a vain attempt to make a vassal of China's most successful warlord, Chiang Kai-shek, Tokyo released its impatient army to conquer all of China. By October 1938, Japan occupied China's most important cities.

In response to these waves of violence, each threatened nation set its own course. The League of Nations' futile attempt to impose economic sanctions against Italy merely exposed the League's helplessness. No European power had the energy to confront Japan. Britain and France, though fretful about their own imperial interests in Asia, neither condoned nor seriously challenged Japan's conquests. The Soviet Union and France were particularly vehement in condemning Hitler's advances, yet neither trusted the other sufficiently to take an effective joint stand. Moreover, both Hitler and Mussolini, by keeping the hopes for compromise alive with hints of moderation, discouraged a collective retaliation. It was British Prime Minister Neville Chamberlain who most earnestly explored these prospects of a peaceful settlement. When Hitler demanded the Sudetan territory of Czechoslovakia, Chamberlain carried the primary burdens of diplomacy that culminated in the Munich Conference of September 1938. At Munich, England and France averted war by agreeing that Germany and its Central European

PEACE IN OUR TIME

As British Prime Minister Neville Chamberlain waved a copy of the Munich agreement with Adolf Hitler, he fanned the last spark of hope that another world war could be avoided. *(Wide World Photos, Inc.)*

allies could divide about one-third of Czechoslovakia among themselves. Chamberlain returned to London promising "peace in our time."

Spheres of Influence. Americans reacted to the accelerating pace of military imperialism along lines that roughly approximated their national or local orientations toward domestic affairs. Those who understood their own society as a system of interest groups also tended to see the world as interrelated national interests and international spheres of influence. Many of them believed that the United States and Latin America formed one sphere of reciprocal interests, with the United States investing in the Latin American economies, processing their raw materials, and selling finished products in their markets. Early in the thirties, some of these Americans were willing to accept Japan and Manchuria as a similar sphere. The more vigorously the new imperial systems grew, however, the more they seemed bent on absorbing the whole world. If Japan controlled all China, would its sphere not expand throughout the western Pacific

and Southeast Asia? If Germany dominated Europe, how could it possibly be excluded from the Western Hemisphere? Worries about adequate territory for American trade and investment rose sharply after 1936. By lumping all of the expansive powers together as "fascist," Americans increasingly found themselves pondering the ultimate danger. Could America itself survive in a world of fascist spheres?

The other, far more popular line of reaction turned inward. The more violent the world became, the more intensely some Americans felt a chasm between their lives and the bloody struggles abroad. As one isolationist baldly stated it for millions of others, "Europe's quarrels are not ours." Where ethnic loyalties did give local Americans attachments abroad, they usually strengthened the case against a confrontation with fascism. Catholics could identify much more readily with Franco than with his anti-clerical enemies. Italian Americans rarely demanded war with Mussolini, and Irish Americans rarely sided with the British against any opponent. Reinforcing the urge toward separation, a committed band of liberals branded war the "enemy of democracy," and that viewpoint found a wide audience through the investigations of Senator Gerald Nye's subcommittee, which blamed bankers and munition makers for America's entry into the First World War.

As these sentiments deepened, Congress translated them into law. The Tydings-McDuffie Act of 1934, which set a schedule for attaining independence for America's Philippine colony, promised to remove a particularly dangerous outpost of responsibility. The Johnson Debt-Default Act of 1934, establishing the narrowest possible definition of America's friends and enemies abroad, denied credit to any foreign government that had not honored its war debt. Then between 1935 and 1937, Congress enacted major neutrality laws to close off the routes that had led into the previous war. It embargoed arms and munitions to belligerents, banned using American vessels to ship them, prohibited arming American merchant ships, and proscribed extending credit to belligerents. Later, the neutrality laws would be ridiculed as a scheme to "Keep America Out of the First World War." Americans, not yet knowing any other war, praised these laws as their protection against the madness of a world in arms. A final step in this sequence barely failed. In 1938, when Congress debated the "Ludlow amendment," requiring a national referendum to declare war, only heavy pressure from the White House kept it from passing.

Most Americans concentrated their feelings of horror on Japan and Germany. The full-scale invasion of China in 1937 gave Americans their first appalling revelations of what a modern air force could do to an urban population. On the eve of the Second World War, the Japanese bombing of China's cities produced the same kind of humanitarian outcry in America that bayoneted babies had roused during the First World War. Although most Americans would not realize until the mid-1940s how literally the Nazis sought to exterminate the Jews, news about mass arrests and concentration camps increasingly identified Hitler's anti-Semitism as a threat to all civilized values. Japan and Germany, a majority of Americans concluded, were the centers of an insane barbarism.

A PRELUDE TO MODERN AIR WAR
To horrified Americans in 1937, this scene in Shanghai symbolized the savagery of Japanese imperialism. *(Wide World Photos, Inc.)*

Roosevelt moved with the dominant currents of opinion. Although in private he despised the Axis dictators, he seldom said anything in public on foreign affairs. Among the neutrality laws, the president seriously contested only the Ludlow amendment. His one clear goal was to tighten the bonds with Latin America. As Germany and Japan became more menacing, the United States sponsored agreements in 1936 and 1938 that made an external threat to one nation in the hemisphere the common concern of them all. At least the United States would protect the "American sphere." In October 1937, Roosevelt did use the suggestive word "quarantine" in a speech on the evils of war and aggression. But when commentators took it to imply coercion or collective action against the fascist powers, the president angrily denied any such thought. After the Munich Conference of 1938, Roosevelt wired congratulations to the leaders in England and France for their efforts to keep the peace.

World War, 1939–1941

In March 1938, Hitler devoured the rest of Czechoslovakia and hungrily eyed the former German territories under Polish rule. As Chamberlain's illusion of peace dissolved, Britain and France committed themselves to a defense of Poland and frantically prepared for war. Then in August 1939, Germany and the Soviet Union, Europe's most relentless foes, shocked the world by signing a nonaggression pact. With the Nazi army prepared to strike at Poland, all eyes fixed on Berlin.

The invasion came in September 1939. As Hitler prepared to divide Poland with the Soviet Union, Britain and France declared war on Germany. That winter the world waited. Then in April 1940, Germany began a lightning sweep through Western Europe, taking Norway, Denmark, the Netherlands, and Belgium. By June, France itself had fallen. Only England remained. German bombers devastated its cities and German submarines squeezed its lifeline of supplies, apparently in preparation for an invasion of the British Isles.

THE NAZI MENACE
Through public demonstrations of Germany's mobilized martial spirit, Hitler tried to awe his opponents into submission even before he struck. *(The Bettmann Archive, Inc.)*

While Germany was swallowing Europe, Japan extended its authority southward into French Indo-China—ostensibly to tighten the blockade of China but actually to control a new area rich in natural resources. Just ahead lay the precious oil and rubber of Southeast Asia. In September 1940, Japan joined the Axis powers in a defensive Tripartite Pact. It was a tentative connection. Many Japanese leaders never trusted Hitler or wanted their nation's destiny tied to a European power. Yet from the outside, Tokyo's link with Berlin and Rome verified the impression of a unified fascist force rolling toward global domination.

At the outbreak of war America hugged its shore. In 1939 the United States induced the nations of Latin America to join it in declaring a huge neutrality zone between Europe and the Western Hemisphere. Although England and France purchased war materials in the United States, the terms were "cash and carry." By law, Americans could provide neither credit nor shipping for a belligerent. Almost everyone hoped a major war would never develop. Once again, Hitler shattered other people's dreams with the conquest of Western Europe. Germany's *blitzkrieg*—lightning war—that eliminated in weeks the Western Front of the entire First World War and set Hitler astride Europe, erased the lingering images of war as a titanic struggle between massed lines of troops. While squadrons of planes fought for air supremacy in "the Battle of Britain," the United States no longer seemed so distant or so safe from Germany's might. In 1940 the proportion of Americans who wanted to seal themselves from the war was shrinking. A majority held tight to their desire for peace, but an increasing number of them believed that the United States should support Britain's resistance to Hitler. The rough guideline became "all aid short of war."

Roosevelt's Unprecedented Third Term. As the war raged, the nuances in Roosevelt's thinking grew ever more critical, for in an emergency the president had immense power over foreign policy. Early in his career, Roosevelt came to believe that a great power such as the United States should play an important role in world affairs. His background and training equated Anglo-American culture with civilization, and his instincts told him that Germany was the nation's enemy. Unlike many of his contemporaries, Roosevelt never questioned either the wisdom or the justice of America's entry into the First World War. As foreign affairs occupied more and more of the president's attention, these attitudes increasingly shaped American policy. Characteristically, Roosevelt avoided hard commitments as long as he could, and in the process kept personal control over the government's decisions.

If Roosevelt had doubts about running for reelection, world crisis resolved them. By 1939 the nation's parlor game was guessing whom the president might designate as his successor. But by keeping a serene silence, Roosevelt held the spotlight on himself and at the last minute allowed the Democratic convention of 1940 to nominate him for an unprecedented third term. That prospect stirred all the latent emotions about Roosevelt the aspiring dictator and Roosevelt the indispensable man. As the president knew very well, he himself would be the issue of the 1940 campaign. This time, the Republicans selected a candidate able to challenge Roosevelt.

Wendell Willkie, a former utilities executive who had once led the fight against the TVA, was an inspired amateur in national politics. Liberal enough to attract independent voters yet conservative enough to satisfy most opponents of the New Deal, Willkie eagerly took on "the Champ" in a vigorous presidential campaign. With arms akimbo and eyes sparkling, he became the first Republican candidate in twenty years to elicit a warm popular response as he toured the nation. "Well, muss my hair and call me Willkie!" a common saying in 1940, expressed an easy affection that no American had bestowed on solemn Herbert Hoover or bland Alfred Landon. Moreover, some former allies of the president, including John L. Lewis and Vice-President Garner, deserted him, while many conservative Democrats talked as if they might when Roosevelt selected the liberal Henry Wallace to replace Garner.

Nevertheless, the New Deal's combination of national aid and local autonomy continued to be an extremely successful formula, and war-related de-

TAKING ON THE CHAMP
Although he lost the election to Roosevelt in 1940, Wendell Willkie won countless admirers for his enthusiasm, vitality and human warmth. *(Wide World Photos, Inc.)*

mands were finally lifting the depression. Willkie's chances lay in foreign affairs. Here, however, the Republican's enthusiasm for resisting fascism at least matched the president's. When fierce debates surrounded a bill to create America's first peacetime draft, Willkie supported it. In September 1940, when the president announced an exchange of fifty old American destroyers for the lease of British bases in the Western Hemisphere, Willkie also approved this clear commitment to the British cause. Then at the last moment, Roosevelt gave the guarantee most Americans wanted desperately to believe: "Your president says this country is not going to war." By 449 electoral votes to Willkie's 82, "the Champ" won four more years.

U.S. Aid to Britain. After the election, the politician who had promised peace became the president who prepared for war. By the winter of 1940–41, Britain's dwindling assets in the United States could not begin to pay for the war materials it needed. Describing the United States as the "arsenal of democracy," Roosevelt proposed that Britain have an almost unlimited access to American production and credit. An "America First" movement, which had opposed his reelection, fought frantically against the legislation. Lend-lease, its enemies cried, was a Grim Reaper's AAA that would "plow under every fourth American boy." Publicly, Roosevelt tried to calm these fears of war. In private, he knew that as Congress debated, secret Anglo-American staff meetings were sketching the outlines for a joint wartime strategy. In March 1941, Congress passed the open-ended Lend-Lease Act, wiping out the last traces of American neutrality.

During the twentieth century American policymakers had acquired the habit of a quiet collaboration with the British. Informal Anglo-American understandings underwrote the plans in the twenties for international stabilization. In the thirties, Washington tested the winds of resistance to military imperialism by checking first with London. From that perspective Britain was already a tacit ally in 1939, and the events of early 1941 only strengthened these deep, traditional ties. Not surprisingly, therefore, dramatic changes in the European war did not alter the commitment to Britain. In 1941 the Royal Air Force was winning the battle of Britain, and Hitler turned eastward. With feeble assistance from their Italian ally, the Nazis conquered the Balkans. Then in June 1941, Hitler launched the fateful thrust of the war, an attack into Russia. The Nazi-Soviet Pact of 1939 had been a calculated expedient between enemies, enabling Hitler to dominate the heart of Europe, and the Russians to seize a portion of Poland, the Baltic states of Latvia, Lithuania, and Estonia, and a slice of Finland. Now the Nazis were ready to smash their last great opponent on the continent, and the German war machine rumbled across a broad eastern front against Russia's primary cities.

As determined as ever to supply their English ally, American convoys carried their lend-lease cargoes closer and closer to the British Isles. In April 1941, the United States extended its patrols to the mid-Atlantic. Then in July, following Germany's invasion of Russia, American convoys moved a big step closer to the English ports by escorting the supplies as far as Iceland. A month later, Roosevelt astonished the nation by meeting with British Prime Minister Winston Churchill on an American cruiser off Newfoundland, where the two leaders prepared an "Atlantic Charter" of postwar principles. Meanwhile, the American navy expanded its protection to cover British merchant ships as well as American, and along the Atlantic sea lanes, the two nations collaborated in locating and attacking German submarines. In September, one German submarine, as it fled from the U.S.S. *Greer*, fired at the American destroyer. Roosevelt, pretending that the submarine had been the aggressor and likening German power to a "rattlesnake" that was coiled to strike at the Western Hemisphere, authorized American ships to "shoot on sight." By October, Congress allowed convoys to land in Britain. "All aid" to Britain could not stop "short of war."

Pearl Harbor.   During these crucial months of 1940 and 1941, Asian affairs appeared to be far less important. Most Americans agreed that Japanese imperialism posed some kind of threat, but few could define it. Fewer still in 1940 believed that Japan would dare to fight the United States. Roosevelt largely left the negotiations with Japan to his crusty secretary of state, Cordell Hull, who in turn relied on the rigid, moralistic Stanley Hornbeck, a state department expert on Asian matters. Hull demanded that Japan honor the Nine-Power Treaty on the Open Door, which, in effect, required a withdrawal from the mainland of Asia. As leverage, the United States imposed an increasingly tight embargo on trade with Japan. During most of 1941, conciliatory forces in the Japanese government under Prince Fuminaro Konoye, the prime minister, sought some way of mollifying the United States short of a Japanese capitulation. Although Konoye would not reopen the question of Manchuria, he proposed a Japanese military withdrawal elsewhere on the Asian mainland in exchange for a friendly Chinese government and American economic cooperation. But Hull was unrelenting. Before serious negotiations could begin, he insisted, Japan must accept the Open Door throughout the area of Japanese expansion.

By the summer of 1941, the two nations were drifting toward a war neither one wanted. In July, Japan completed its occupation of French Indochina, and Roosevelt retaliated by freezing Japanese assets in the United States. Washington was now in the curious position of battling Japanese imperialism to defend European imperialism in Southeast Asia. Appraising their limited resources, Japan's leaders realized that if they had to fight the United States for their empire, the time had come. Though Prince Konoye continued to explore various formulas of compromise, his authority at home was waning. In October 1941, the militant Hideki Tojo replaced Konoye as prime minister, and Japan prepared for war. Washington, sensing much deeper trouble in Asia than it had expected, finally gave hints of flexibility in November. It was too late.

Because American intelligence had broken Japan's secret code, Washington knew that a Japanese

PEARL HARBOR
(National Archives)

attack of some kind was pending. Roosevelt's inner circle guessed that it would strike in Southeast Asia. For two reasons, no one seriously considered Hawaii. First, American policy-makers to the very end underrated Japan as a second-class power with more bluff than nerve. Second, American intelligence intercepted so many clues leading in so many directions that it made no sense from any of them. At dawn on December 7, as waves of Japanese planes roared across the naval base at Pearl Harbor, Hawaii, and crippled America's Pacific force, no one was ready.

A stunned nation officially went to war.

Within days, the attack on Pearl Harbor clarified issues around the world. Britain immediately joined the United States against Japan. Unpredictable as always, Hitler, who had no obligation to act, decided to declare war on the United States, and Italy followed suit. Hence, a surprise attack precipitating an unwanted war became the event that dissolved America's doubts and propelled it into global conflict. The vast long-range consequences of the plunge would take years to unfold.

CHRONOLOGY

1931   Japan occupies Manchuria.

1932   Hoover-Stimson Doctrine refuses recognition of
           Japanese conquests.
           Franklin D. Roosevelt elected president.

1933   Nationwide "Bank Holiday."
           Federal Deposit Insurance Corporation guarantees
               depositors' savings.
           Agricultural Adjustment Act passed.
           Civilian Conservation Corps formed.
           National Industrial Recovery Act creates National
               Recovery Administration and Public Works
               Administration.
           Tennessee Valley Authority established.
           Prohibition repealed.

1934   Reciprocal Trade Agreement passed.

1935   Supreme Court broadens attacks on New Deal
               legislation.
           Social Security establishes old-age, other social
               insurance programs.
           Wagner Act affirms collective bargaining rights,
               sets up NLRB.
           Works Progress Administration increases funds
               for relief of unemployed.

Hitler announces Germany's intent to rearm.
Italy invades Ethiopia.

1936   Roosevelt reelected president.
           Spanish Civil War erupts.
           Wave of sit-down strikes begins.

1937   U.S. Steel recognizes CIO.
           Law to reorganize Supreme Court fails.
           Japan invades China.

1938   Fair Employment Practices Act establishes
               minimum wage, outlaws child labor.
           Munich Conference attempts to appease Hitler by
               surrendering Czechoslovakia.

1939   Germany invades Poland, starting Second
               World War.

1940   Japan joins Axis Powers.
           Roosevelt elected to a third term.

1941   Congress approves Lend-Lease, American
               supplies to Allies.
           Japan attacks Pearl Harbor; United States enters
               war.

SUGGESTED READINGS

William E. Leuchtenburg, *Franklin D. Roosevelt and the New Deal, 1932–1940* (1963), is an outstanding survey. For a more critical appraisal, see Paul K. Conkin, *The New Deal* (rev. ed., 1975). Volumes 2 and 3 of Arthur M. Schlesinger, Jr., *The Age of Roosevelt—The Coming of the New Deal* (1958) and *The Politics of Upheaval* (1960)—provide a thorough and readable account of Roosevelt's first administration. The initial problem he encountered is detailed in Susan Estabrook Kennedy's *The Banking Crisis of 1933* (1973). Robert F. Himmelberg, *The Origins of the National Recovery Administration* (1976), analyzes the complex background to NRA.

For the history of NRA and its aftermath, the most valuable work is Ellis W. Hawley's *The New Deal and the Problem of Monopoly* (1966). Van L. Perkins, *Crisis in Agriculture* (1969), covers the beginning of the Agricultural Adjustment Administration. On the most innovative New Deal policy, C. Herman Pritchett, *The Tennessee Valley Authority* (1943), supplies basic information; Phillip Selznick, *TVA and the Grass Roots* (1949), discusses the Authority's social orientation; and Thomas K. McCraw, *TVA and the Power Fight, 1933–1939* (1971), traces the principal challenge to its program. Grace Abbott, *From Relief to Social Security* (1966), records the story of public assistance; and Roy Lubove, *The Struggle for Social Security, 1900–1935* (1968), explains the origins of the Social Security Act. Michael E. Parrish, *Securities Regulation and the New Deal* (1970), is an illuminating monograph on that area of public policy; and Kenneth R. Philp, *John Collier's Crusade for Indian Reform, 1920–1954* (1977), is the basic study of another area.

The battle over the Supreme Court that opened Roosevelt's second administration is reported in Joseph Alsop and Turner Catledge, *The 168 Days* (1938). On the struggles of organized labor, the best survey is Irving Bernstein's *A History of the American Worker, 1933–1941:Turbulent Years* (1970). Sidney Fine, *Sit-Down* (1969), captures the drama of a crucial strike in the automobile industry; and Jerold S. Auerbach, *Labor and Liberty: The La Follette Committee and the New Deal* (1966), examines one form of government assistance to the new unions. For the curious story of labor's outstanding leader, see Melvyn Dubofsky and Warren Van Tine, *John L. Lewis* (1977). The bottom of the rural economy is explored in David E. Conrad, *The Forgotten Farmers: The Story of Sharecroppers in the New Deal* (1965), in Pete Daniel, *The Shadow of Slavery: Peonage in the South, 1901–1969* (1972), and most feelingly in James Agee and Walker Evans, *Let Us Now Praise Famous Men* (1941). Sidney Baldwin's *FSA* (1968) is an appealing history of the New Deal's major effort to help the rural poor. Two interesting studies—Paul Conkin, *Tomorrow a New World: The New Deal Community Program* (1959), and Jane DeHart Mathews, *The Federal Theater, 1935–1939* (1967)—suggest the breadth of interests affected by the New Deal. Barry Dean Karl, *Executive Reorganization and Reform in the New Deal* (1963), and Richard Polenberg, *Reorganizing Roosevelt's Government: The Controversy over Executive Reorganization, 1936–1939* (1966), discuss an important political contest in the late thirties. These studies along with two other fine books—Richard S. Kirkendall's *Social Scientists and Farm Politics in the Age of Roosevelt* (1966) and James T. Patterson's *Congressional Conservatism and the New Deal* (1967)—help to explain the decline of reform.

On Roosevelt himself, the best study for the New Deal years is James MacGregor Burns, *Roosevelt: The Lion and the Fox* (1956). Frank Freidel's massive biography, *Franklin D. Roosevelt* (4 vols. to date, 1952–73), has carried FDR through his first critical months in the White House. Additional insights into the Roosevelt household appear in Alfred B. Rollins, Jr., *Roosevelt and Howe* (1962), and Joseph P. Lash, *Eleanor and Franklin* (1971). Among the many published journals and memoirs by participants in the New Deal, Raymond Moley's critical *After Seven Years* (1939) and Rexford G. Tugwell's appreciative *The Democratic Roosevelt* (1957) are especially useful. J. Joseph Huthmacher, *Senator Robert F. Wagner and the Rise of Urban Liberalism* (1968), Paul A. Kurzman, *Harry Hopkins and the New Deal* (1974), and George Martin, *Madam Secretary: Frances Perkins* (1976), are complimentary accounts of these important officials. Otis L. Graham, Jr., *An Encore for Re-*form (1967), explores the generally unfavorable responses of the old progressives to the New Deal, and George Wolfskill, *The Revolt of the Conservatives* (1962), describes the outrage of the American Liberty League.

Local politics is an elusive subject. James Patterson, *The New Deal and the States* (1969), analyzes one source of resistance to national power. John M. Allswang's *A House for All People: Ethnic Politics in Chicago, 1890–1936* (1971) sketches an interesting picture for one big city, and Arthur Mann's *La Guardia Comes to Power: 1933* (1965) explores the roots of an important election in New York City. The relation between the New Deal and the local bosses is considered in Bruce M. Stave, *The New Deal and the Last Hurrah: Pittsburgh Machine Politics* (1970), Lyle W. Dorsett, *The Pendergast Machine* (1968), and Charles H. Trout, *Boston, the Great Depression, and the New Deal* (1977). Charles J. Tull, *Father Coughlin and the New Deal* (1965), and T. Harry Williams, *Huey Long* (1969), examine the New Deal's leading competitors in local politics, and David H. Bennett, *Demagogues in the Depression* (1969), chronicles their decline. The cultural values of the New Dealers themselves are summarized in E. Digby Baltzell, *The Protestant Establishment* (1964).

America's reaction to the early imperialist crisis in Asia is explored in Sara R. Smith, *The Manchurian Crisis, 1931–1932* (1948), Richard N. Current, *Secretary Stimson* (1954), and Robert H. Ferrell, *American Diplomacy in the Great Depression: Hoover-Stimson Foreign Policy, 1929–1933* (1957). Dorothy Borg's *The United States and the Far Eastern Crisis of 1933–1938* (1964) continues the story into the full-scale Sino-Japanese War. The best discussion of the London Economic Conference appears in Frank Freidel's *Franklin D. Roosevelt: Launching the New Deal* (1973). The title of Arnold A. Offner's *American Appeasement: United States Foreign Policy and Germany, 1933–1938* (1969), indicates the author's approach to the years when Hitler was consolidating power. Alton Frye, *Nazi Germany and the American Hemisphere, 1933–1941* (1967), minimizes Hitler's transatlantic ambitions. Lloyd C. Gardner's *Economic Aspects of New Deal Diplomacy* (1964) emphasizes an insatiable urge for profits. David H. Culbert, *News for Everyman: Radio and Foreign Affairs in Thirties America* (1976), brings a new perspective to the decade's developments.

The most thorough account of diplomatic events leading to the Second World War is the two-volume study by William L. Langer and S. Everett Gleason, *The Challenge to Isolation, 1937–1940* (1952) and *The Undeclared War, 1940–1941* (1953), a detailed justification of American policy. Robert A. Divine's two volumes, *The Illusion of Neutrality* (1962) and *The Reluctant Belligerent* (1966), are only slightly more critical. On the other hand, Charles A. Beard's *President Roosevelt and the Coming of the War, 1941* (1948) indicts FDR for maneuvering the nation into war, and Bruce M. Russett's thin but thoughtful essay, *No Clear and Present Danger* (1972), dismisses the claims of a fascist threat to the United States. Manfred Jonas, *Isolation in America, 1935–1941* (1966), presents the basic facts about the domestic opposition to the government's policies, and Warren F. Kimball, *The Most Unsordid Act: Lend-Lease, 1939–1941* (1969), discusses the issue that aroused the fiercest resistance. James R. Leutze, *Bargaining*

for Supremacy: Anglo-American Naval Collaboration, 1937–1941 (1977), traces secret adjustments of power preceding the war. The narrow American vision is revealed in Paul W. Schroeder's *The Axis Alliance and Japanese-American Relations, 1941* (1958) and Charles E. Neu's *The Troubled Encounter: The United States and Japan* (1975). The official in Tokyo who tried to broaden Washington's view is the subject of Waldo H. Heinrichs, Jr., *American Ambassador: Joseph C. Grew and the Development of the United States Diplomatic Tradition* (1966). Roberta Wohlstetter, *Pearl Harbor: Warning and Decision* (1962), analyzes the controversy surrounding the Japanese strike at Hawaii.

The Second World War greatly accelerated America's modernization, most noticeably in Washington. In both foreign and domestic affairs the national government shifted dramatically from a rather detached and tentative role of manipulator to a central one of manager and financier. Once the United States assumed a complex array of global responsibilities during the war, it never relinquished them. Once government spending dominated the domestic economy, that power remained in Washington. Although the war tremendously expanded the national government, policy-makers struggled for almost another decade determining how to translate this enormous authority into systematic international and national policies.

Since the 1920s two crucial questions had been unanswered: How should the United States respond to the threat of hostile powers abroad? and how could it maintain prosperity at home? By 1954 policy-makers had answered these questions. A global military strategy was established to contain communism. At home, the health of the modern political economy depended on framing the national budget, funding the national debt, and adjusting the national monetary controls so that Washington satisfied a host of clients and maintained a steady prosperity. These were long-range commitments that set patterns into the 1980s.

As America became stable in these two areas, however, the country grew unstable in a third crucial area, the relationship between national and local affairs. The New Deal's compromise presupposed a far less dominant government in Washington than the giant that began to emerge in the 1940s. Increasingly, racial and cultural issues that had been hidden in America's communities and neighborhoods flowed toward the hub of national power where they came into sharp conflict with national beliefs and aspirations.

The Second World War, 1941–1945

Between December 1941 and May 1945, the United States, unlike its allies, was continuously engaged in two very different wars. In the Pacific theater of war,

CHAPTER 30

A Global Setting for the Modern State

where victory hinged on control of the seas, the United States fought almost alone. In the European theater, where victory could be won only on the continent, the United States contributed to a complex, collective effort.

During the early months of the war, both theaters offered a dismal picture of retreat and jeopardy. Japanese units swept away the remnants of resistance in Southeast Asia, occupying the Netherlands East Indies (Indonesia), capturing the British base at Singapore, and penetrating to the frontiers of India. Japan's naval victory in the Java Sea assured its control of the western Pacific. In May 1942 the remnants of America's small, isolated force in the Philippines surrendered to the Japanese. Across a vast expanse from the tip of the Aleutian Islands near Alaska through the central Pacific to the mountain passes of Burma, imperial Japan dominated. From beleaguered China, General "Vinegar Joe" Stillwell, America's adviser to Chiang Kai-shek, summarized the first round of the Asian War: "We got a hell of a beating."

In Europe, Germany's successes were even more ominous. Its fleet of submarines, which had been held in check before December 1941, unleashed a

SIEGE OF LENINGRAD
Their city surrounded by German troops, citizens of Leningrad dip water from a broken main. More than 600,000 died of starvation during the two-year siege. *(Wide World Photos, Inc.)*

devastating attack on the Allies' Atlantic supply lines. In the early months of the war, they roamed along the American coast and into the Caribbean, as the United States had not yet developed an effective counterattack to the elusive submarine. Nor could American shipyards yet replace the tonnage lost at sea. Meanwhile, Nazi mechanized divisions under General Erwin Rommel drove across North Africa into Egypt, threatening the Suez Canal. Above all, a renewed offensive in Russia spread German troops from the outskirts of Leningrad in the north to the gates of Stalingrad in the south. Into the late fall of 1942, the greatest disaster, a Soviet collapse, loomed as a strong possibility.

Establishing War Strategy. How could the United States best use its massive resources to alter the balance of the war? In broad strategic matters, the answers came quickly and clearly. The European theater had priority over the Pacific. Food and war materiel, which under lend-lease had been moving to Russia before Pearl Harbor, were the immediate contributions that the United States could make to Soviet survival. Despite the menace of the German submarines, which took a terrible toll along the icy routes in the North Sea, the quantity of these supplies slowly increased. Finally, to relieve the pressure on the Soviet army, American and British forces had to launch a "second front" as soon as possible somewhere in the west.

The men who ultimately made these decisions were President Roosevelt and Prime Minister Winston Churchill, Britain's brilliant, calculating war leader. Their personal collaboration had begun at the Atlantic Conference of August 1941, which declared to the world that the United States and Great Britain stood together against the Axis. From December 1941 to January 1943, through a series of private meetings, the two men grew closer. Although Russia's fate also hung on the decisions that Roosevelt and Churchill made, the Soviet Union remained a distant ally, declaring its needs and awaiting a response from the Western powers.

The initial American impulse was to open at least a token second front in Western Europe during 1942. But no one had anticipated the complexities of global warfare. Although the United States pushed the German submarines away from its coast, the Nazis more than held their own during 1942 in the battle for the Atlantic sea lanes. Without guaranteed supplies, the Allies would never breach the coast of France. And such crucial items as landing craft were still very scarce. Moreover, the Pacific war also demanded attention, especially because the attack on Pearl Harbor gave it a special importance to so many Americans.

The United States began to stabilize its position against the weaker but more remote foe in Asia. Because Congress had authorized a program of naval construction well before Pearl Harbor, the American fleet was able to return in strength to the Pacific less than a year after Japan's devastating attack. In May 1942, even as Japan was overrunning the Philippines, a successful American assault on Japanese shipping in the battle of the Coral Sea secured Australia. A month later, a Japanese naval force was repulsed at the battle of Midway, west of Hawaii. Then in November 1942, the American navy won a three-day encounter off the Solomon Islands near Australia, and the balance of sea power shifted back to the United States. Meanwhile, with an eye to morale back home, American forces in August launched small, difficult counteroffensives at Guadalcanal in the Solomon Islands and on the far larger, contested island of New Guinea.

Sobered by the complications of a global war, Roosevelt and his advisers abandoned plans for a quick attack on France and accepted Churchill's alternative of a North African campaign. In November, 1942, Operation Torch under General Dwight D. Eisenhower invaded French Morocco and Algiers. As the British General Bernard Montgomery pushed Rommel's *Afrika Korps* from the east, Eisenhower's troops swept westward. By May 1943 they had eliminated Axis power throughout North Africa.

During the North African campaign, the tide of battle began to shift around the world. The Soviet Union had already won the pivotal engagement of the European war. Hitler, in an effort to crack Russia's resistance before another winter froze his army

IN THE PACIFIC
Victory in the Pacific theater required dominance both on the sea and in the air. Although aircraft carriers were very vulnerable to enemy bombers, they transported the navy's indispensable air cover. Once in command of the sea lanes, the navy supported American ground forces in their bitter battle for the Pacific islands. From bases in the South Pacific islands, these grim crewmen took their chances in bombing Japan itself. *(Opposite, National Archives; left, Photoworld; below, Photo by Lt. Wayne Miller, U.S.N.R., from National Archives)*

in place, gambled recklessly on an assault against Stalingrad. During the winter's war of 1942–43, a relentless Soviet counterattack not only saved Stalingrad but actually cost Germany half a million troops. The following summer the Soviet army took the initiative against its weakened, overextended German enemy and began the drive westward toward Berlin. In the southwest Pacific, American forces cut the first wedge through the enemy perimeter north of Australia, placed the Japanese on the defensive, and charted the winding trail of island conquests that led to Japan itself. In the summer of 1943, radar and long-range air patrols finally tipped the balance against the German submarines in the battle of the Atlantic.

The Tide Turns in Europe. When the United States and Great Britain bypassed France for North Africa in 1942, Soviet Premier Josef Stalin was again promised a second front in Europe for the following year.

World War II
Europe and North Africa

The Axis Powers in Europe
Areas Under Maximum Axis Control, 1942
Major Allied Offensives
Air Attacks on Germany

SOVIET UNION

CASPIAN SEA

Moscow

Leningrad

Aug.-Dec., 1942
Stalingrad

Farthest German Advance

Limit of

FINLAND

SWEDEN

NORWAY

BALTIC SEA

NORTH SEA

GREAT BRITAIN

IRELAND

London
Dunkirk

DENMARK

Berlin

GER.

1945
1945

Warsaw

POLAND

1944
1945

Prague
CZECHOSLOVAKIA

Vienna

AUSTRIA

SWITZ.

Kiev

1943

UKRAINE

1943

CRIMEA
Yalta

BLACK SEA

RUMANIA
1944

HUNGARY
1945

YUGOSLAVIA

1944

BULGARIA
1944

ALBANIA

GREECE

AEGEAN SEA

TURKEY

IRAN

IRAQ

SYRIA

TRANS-JORDAN

SAUDI ARABIA

CYPRUS

PALESTINE
SUEZ CANAL

Trieste

ADRIATIC SEA

Monte Cassino
Salerno

Rome
Anzio
Naples

Jan. 1944

CORSICA

SARDINIA

ITALY

Palermo
Sept. 1943
SICILY

CRETE

MEDITERRANEAN SEA
or

MEDITERRANEAN

Tripoli

1943

LIBYA

El Alamein
Cairo

1942

EGYPT

Paris

NORMANDY
June 6, 1944

BRITTANY

1944-45

BELG.

NETH.

Lux.

FRANCE

Vichy

VICHY

Farthest German Advance

1944-45

Aug. 1944

SPAIN

PORTUGAL

Strait of Gibraltar

SP. MOROCCO

Casablanca

MOROCCO

Nov. 1942

Oran

1942

Algiers

ALGERIA

KASSERINE PASS
Feb. 14-22, 1943

Limit of

Bizerte
July 1943

Tunis

TUNISIA

MALTA

Farthest German Advance

1943

1942-1943

1944-45

ATLANTIC OCEAN

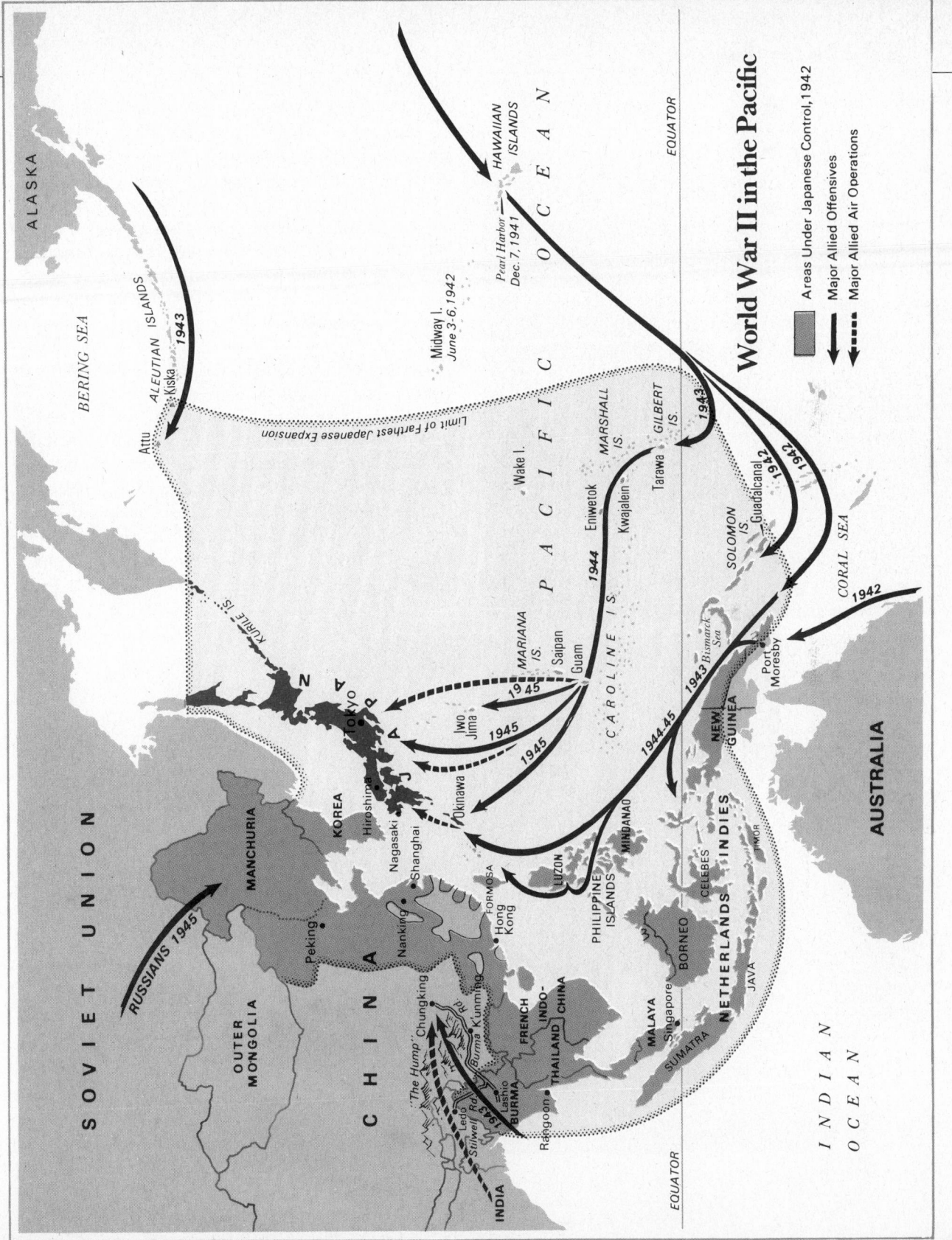

World War II in the Pacific

Areas Under Japanese Control, 1942

→ Major Allied Offensives

⇢ Major Allied Air Operations

ALASKA

BERING SEA

ALEUTIAN ISLANDS
Kiska 1943
Attu

SOVIET UNION

OUTER MONGOLIA

MANCHURIA

KOREA

RUSSIANS 1945

CHINA

Peking

Nanking
Shanghai

Chungking

"The Hump"

Kunming

Ledo
Stilwell Rd.
Lashio
Burma Rd.
BURMA
Rangoon
THAILAND
FRENCH INDO-CHINA

INDIA

Hong Kong

FORMOSA

Hiroshima
Nagasaki

J A P A N

TOKYO

KURILE IS.

Iwo Jima
1945

Okinawa
1945
1945

Limit of Farthest Japanese Expansion

MARIANA IS.
Saipan
Guam
1944

Wake I.

Eniwetok
Kwajalein
MARSHALL IS.

Midway I.
June 3-6, 1942

Pearl Harbor
Dec. 7, 1941

HAWAIIAN ISLANDS

EQUATOR

P A C I F I C   O C E A N

CAROLINE IS.

GILBERT IS.
Tarawa
1943

SOLOMON IS.
Guadalcanal
1942

Bismarck Sea
1943

NEW GUINEA

1944-45

Port Moresby
1942

CORAL SEA
1942

PHILIPPINE ISLANDS
MINDANAO
LUZON

BORNEO

CELEBES

NETHERLANDS INDIES

TIMOR

JAVA

SUMATRA

MALAYA
Singapore

AUSTRALIA

INDIAN OCEAN

EQUATOR

But in 1943 Churchill once more convinced Roosevelt to postpone an attack on France. That July, in the most dubious strategic decision of the war, an Allied force landed in Sicily, then in September, crossed into Italy. Nothing in the campaign went well. Although Italy immediately surrendered, German troops filled the vacuum from the north, fortified the critical mountains and passes, and stalled the large Allied army. Stalin, whose soldiers continued to bear the primary burden of the ground war against Germany, was furious.

Not until June 6, 1944, did the United States and Britain finally establish a successful second front in France. By then, Rome had fallen, and the Soviet army had reached Poland. The systematic bombing of Germany, after accomplishing relatively little in 1943, was now devastating its cities. The Allies commanded the air, and American supplies flowed across the Atlantic. While feints to the northern coast of France confused Germany's waiting army, Operation

INCHING UP THE ITALIAN PENINSULA
Climate and terrain contributed to the endless frustrations of the Italian campaign. *(U.S. Army Photograph)*

THE INFANTRYMAN'S WAR
Behind every move on the generals' maps lay a terrible price in human suffering. This soldier, wounded by shrapnel, receives a transfusion of blood plasma as a Sicilian family looks on. *(U.S. Army Photograph)*

Overlord struck the beaches of Normandy on June 6 in the greatest amphibious assault in history. After six weeks of struggle, the Allies broke through Germany's coastal defenses, opening northern France to the Allied army. In August another force invaded southern France, and that same month Paris fell.

Hitler's last thrust came a week after Overlord when the first rocket-launched bombs whined across the English Channel. In September the silent and more deadly V-2 rockets, replacing the V-1 "buzz bombs," hit London. They brought terror to England but no success for the Nazis. That same month British and American troops entered Germany. The Russian army pressed through Poland and the Balkans. Except for a desperate Nazi counterattack at the German-Belgian border—the "battle of the Bulge" in December 1944—Germany's army collapsed inside the Allied vise. By the end of April, Russian troops were fighting in the streets of Berlin. Hitler, ill and deranged, committed suicide in a hidden bunker in Berlin, and German officers formally capitulated on May 7, 1945, to the Allied command.

Russian lives and American productivity had been the basic contributions to victory in Europe. About 16 million citizens of the Soviet Union died in the conflict with Germany. By contrast, British losses were about 500,000 and American losses in both theaters of war about 300,000. The United States served as the arsenal of the Allied cause. By 1942, America's war production equaled the combined output of the Axis powers; by 1944, it doubled the enemy's total. When Germany could no longer slow the delivery of American goods, the Nazis were doomed to fall beneath the crushing weight of war materiel.

Bloody Advances in the Pacific. While American troops fought through the Italian mud in 1943, the pace of the Pacific war remained slow. That November, on the assumption that only an occupation of Tokyo itself could end the war, naval forces under Admiral Chester Nimitz and a combination of American, Australian, and New Zealand ground forces under General Douglas MacArthur began a grim, two-pronged assault toward the Japanese mainland. Nimitz's command has to regain control over the myriad islands in the central Pacific. Bloody links lay in the chain ahead: Tarawa in the Gilbert Islands, Saipan in the Marianas, Iwo Jima, and then Okinawa at the tip of Japan's homeland. From the south, MacArthur's command had to hack its way through the jungles of New Guinea and converge with Nimitz's forces on the Philippines.

Early in 1944, as America's production expanded to serve both the European and Pacific wars, the drive to Japan gained momentum. By summer, the United States controlled the central Pacific. Then in October, with General MacArthur dramatically leading his troops to the site of a humiliating defeat early in the war, American forces invaded the Philippines. That same month, in the battle of Leyte Gulf, Japanese naval power was destroyed. Fierce Japanese resistance continued to keep casualties high. As late as March 1945, a month's fight for the tiny, desolate island of Iwo Jima left 20,000 Americans dead and wounded. But Japan now lay open to systematic bombing. Napalm raids burned its compact cities, one by one. In March 1945 a single attack on Tokyo killed more than 80,000 inhabitants. When Germany surrendered in May 1945, an utterly exposed Japan was already tottering.

Strangely enough, the climactic blow of the Asian war had been in preparation even before Pearl Harbor and had been originally aimed at Germany, not Japan. In 1939 refugee physicists from Europe, fearing the potential of Germany's military technology, began urging the American government to explore the possibility of an atomic bomb before the Nazis could develop it. Within a year the awesome project was under way. In utmost secrecy, groups of scientists at separate laboratories struggled against time to master the secrets of the atom. They learned to control a chain reaction of atomic fission so that it would generate enormous power which they then translated into a technically practical military device. In July 1945 the task was finally completed at a lonely center in Los Alamos, New Mexico, under the direction of physicist J. Robert Oppenheimer. By then, however, Germany had fallen. A new, inexperienced president, Harry S Truman, sat in the White House. An array of military and civilian advisers counseled the pres-

D-DAY
Taking cover behind barriers that had blocked their landing craft, these Allied soldiers fought for a piece of the Normandy beaches. *(Robert Capa/Magnum Photos, Inc.)*

THE BATTLE OF BRITAIN
Shelter from the deadly crash of German bombs was daily routine in London during 1940. Here a tube station was converted to a bomb shelter. *(United Press International, Inc.)*

ident to use the new weapon against Japan, and Truman agreed. On August 6 a single bomb demolished the city of Hiroshima, immediately killing about 80,000 people and maiming and poisoning thousands more. Three days later, just as the Soviet Union declared war on Japan, a second bomb razed Nagasaki. On August 14 Japan capitulated.

Postwar International Planning for Peace, 1945

On the very eve of Japan's surrender, Roosevelt set the nation's course in world affairs. As in domestic affairs, he was an inspired spokesman of hope, not only for Americans, but also for yearning people throughout the world. Even before Pearl Harbor, Roosevelt and Churchill had sketched ideals for the postwar world in the Atlantic Charter, which drew heavily on the Wilsonian principles of political self-determination, free economic exchange, and international cooperation. Roosevelt's broad goal of the "Four Freedoms"—freedom from want and fear, freedom of speech and religion—became international bywords.

As an architect of national policy, however, Roosevelt seemed vague. He willingly committed himself to the Allied policy of fighting until the Axis admitted "unconditional surrender." In the process he put aside most long-range problems of the postwar world in favor of dealing with the short-term needs of a military victory. Unlike Churchill and Stalin, Roosevelt had almost no traditional and realistic goals for his country in the postwar world. Moreover, he had no inclinations to develop any. In his wartime exchanges with Churchill and Stalin, Roosevelt chided the British on the sins of their empire, talked of future Soviet-American cooperation, but whenever possible avoided specific commitments. The only heritage Roosevelt could draw on was the pattern of international stabilization and mediation that had formed in the 1920s and foundered in the 1930s. This flexible American model for the postwar world emphasized diplomacy. Instead of territorial maps, Roosevelt concentrated on mechanisms for international coordination and quiet cooperation between nations.

International Organizations. In preparation for a global postwar coordination, the Roosevelt administration moved decisively to create new international organizations. At the Bretton Woods Conference of 1944, the United States took the initiative in developing a program for international monetary stabilization. The American dollar became the basis for most monetary transactions. To facilitate international finance, the conference planned two new agencies—the World Bank, which would help to regularize transactions among the industrial powers, and the International Monetary Fund, which would issue loans to the poorest nations. At the same time, the Roosevelt administration led the movement for another attempt at worldwide collective security.

Secretary of State Cordell Hull, a devoted Wilsonian, deserves the primary credit for negotiating a postwar United Nations (UN). Recalling Wilson's disaster, the secretary wooed the Senate and included prominent Republicans in the planning of a new league. At every opportunity, Hull pressed America's wartime allies for firm commitments to an international organization. When the secretary retired in 1944, the hardest work had been done. Despite British fears for its empire and Soviet fears for its security, their representatives joined delegates from forty-six other nations in San Francisco to found a world organization. Overcoming final Soviet resistance, the delegates signed the charter of the United Nations in June 1945. In July the United States Senate overwhelmingly approved America's participation.

Changing Soviet-American Relations. Between the Bolshevik Revolution of 1917 and the German invasion of Russia in 1941, Soviet-American relations were an almost unrelieved story of mutual hostility. Until 1933 the United States did not even recognize the Soviet Union. Americans responded with disgust to the Nazi-Soviet pact of 1939 and the Russian war against Finland that winter. Even after the United

THE YALTA CONFERENCE
Flanked by Churchill on his right and Stalin on his left, an ill and weary Roosevelt prepared to negotiate the preliminaries for a postwar settlement. *(Imperial War Museum)*

States and the Soviet Union became wartime allies, their early exchanges were sometimes sharp, especially over the delays on a second front.

In November 1943, at the depths of Russia's wartime doubts, Roosevelt opened a dialogue with the Soviets when Stalin, Churchill, and he held their first joint meeting in Tehran, Iran. As their conversations ranged over the second front in Europe, Russia's entry into the Asian war, and punishment for Germany, Roosevelt responded to Stalin's proposals in encouraging tones. During their second meeting, at the Black Sea port of Yalta in February 1945, Roosevelt renewed his conciliatory efforts. At the very end of the European war, when Churchill argued for troop movements that would place the Western powers, not the Soviet Union, in Berlin and the Balkans, Roosevelt refused to play military chess with Stalin. It was not a case of a politically minded Churchill and a militarily minded Roosevelt; the president simply had different political objectives.

Nevertheless, Roosevelt knew that at best he had only narrowed, not closed, the gap between the United States and the Soviet Union. In the modern American tradition, a tacit Anglo-American alliance remained the crucial means for informal international cooperation. Although Roosevelt twitted Churchill about the British empire, he used none of his wartime leverage to alter Britain's colonial policies. Churchill —but not Stalin—was informed about the atomic bomb as it was being developed. If Soviet-American relations deteriorated, American diplomats seemed to feel, the United States could always rely on this Anglo-American basis for a broad structure of international cooperation.

What part the military would play in these postwar schemes puzzled Roosevelt just as it did other Americans. Almost every prominent citizen interpreted the confrontation with fascism as a lesson on power. In the past, they argued, the nation's diplomacy had depended far too much on moral principles and good intentions. The ultimate guarantee of a just cause was an adequate military force and the will to use it. Blaming the Second World War on the failure of democratic nations before 1939 to confront the fascist aggressors, Americans made "Munich" and "appeasement" synonymous with diplomatic suicide.

Roosevelt envisaged "four policemen"—Great Britain, the Soviet Union, the United States, and China—maintaining the postwar peace. But he also expected each policeman to patrol his natural region of influence, a division that might draw the United States back to its old role as the great power of the Western Hemisphere. Even during the war, the presence of American troops abroad had seemed unnatural. Almost everyone expected the soldiers to come home and stay home after the war, an assumption that Roosevelt himself expressed to Stalin at Tehran. For emotional as well as logistical reasons, therefore, Americans increasingly favored a powerful air force to provide a maximum of protection with a minimum of involvement. As the fighting came to an end, Chief of Staff General George C. Marshall was planning the nation's postwar defense in these terms. But no one had a clear picture of what the United States would be defending or against whom.

The Cold War, 1945–1950

The man who took Roosevelt's tentative, flexible mechanisms for international stabilization and shaped them into hard policy came to the White House with almost no knowledge of foreign affairs. Harry S Truman was an able Missouri judge who had entered the Senate in 1935 and built a reputation for hard work, party loyalty, and stubborn determination. At the 1944 convention, Democratic leaders selected the reliable, unobtrusive Truman to replace Vice-President Wallace, whose desire to expand the New Deal and usher in the "century of the common man" had alienated the conservative Democrats. Yet no one— including Truman himself—thought of the little man from Missouri as a possible president. Senator Robert Taft of Ohio once said, in rejecting the office, that the vice-president had nothing to do except "inquire about the president's health." Truman did not even do that.

Truman as a Cold War Leader.   On April 12, 1945, only a few weeks after his fourth inauguration, Franklin Roosevelt died. Millions mourned in public; thousands celebrated in their private clubs; and Truman, no more prepared than the nation, suddenly found himself the chief executive.

Within two years after Truman took office, the United States and the Soviet Union were engaged in a "Cold War" along a line approximating the locations of their victorious armies in the summer of 1945. Though no experienced observer expected a smooth transition from war to peace, relatively few people anticipated such bitter animosity. Although the United States and the Soviet Union both seemed to desire some accommodation, the two nations found it impossible to compromise on a set of basic problems. The underlying causes of the rift were extremely complex, and for decades reasonable people would differ sharply over their meaning. The immediate source of conflict, however, was obvious to everyone. What should be the postwar disposition of Germany and Eastern Europe?

At the Yalta Conference, in February 1945, Roosevelt, Churchill, and Stalin took an initial step toward resolving this complicated package of problems. Stalin stated the Soviet position in detail: for Germany, which had invaded Russia twice in thirty years, he demanded a harsh settlement. He insisted that Germany be stripped of the potential to make war and that it send massive reparations in machinery and labor to the Soviet Union. In Eastern Europe, which had been Germany's avenue for invasion, Stalin wanted friendly governments from Poland in the north to the boundary of Greece in the south. Where Stalin was rigid and determined, Roosevelt, who was by then gravely ill, was vague and agreeable. The president seemed to accept Stalin's argument that these measures were essential to Russian security. It was Churchill, not Roosevelt, who futilely resisted $20 billion as an estimate for German reparations. Again it was Churchill, more than Roosevelt, who forced the insertion of the words "free and unfettered elections" into the Yalta agreement on the postwar Polish government. Neither Churchill nor Roosevelt challenged a general Soviet sphere of influ-

…ce covering Hungary, Rumania, Bulgaria, and Yugoslavia.

All parties regarded the agreements at Yalta as no more than the outline for a later settlement. But instead of proceeding toward a full-scale peace treaty, the Soviet Union and the United States each began reshaping the Yalta decisions to suit its own ends. Stalin made it clear that his candidates would have to be elected in Poland. Truman not only attacked Russia's coercion of Poland; he challenged the entire concept of a Soviet sphere in Eastern Europe. Meanwhile, the United States reconsidered the plans for a harsh peace in Germany. As a temporary measure, Germany had been divided into American, British, French, and Russian zones of military occupation. By treating these zones as self-contained administrative units, the United States was able to shield the western industrial portions of Germany from most Soviet demands for reparations.

By summer, Soviet-American tensions were so high that any meeting between Stalin and Truman was in doubt. In July 1945, however, the two did confer at Potsdam. Although they issued bland statements of unity and Stalin renewed a promise to declare war on Japan, it was an unhappy conference for both leaders. The crucial exchanges concerned Germany. Unable to find a common ground, the great powers accepted the separate ground that each one already held. The Soviet Union could set its own policy in the Eastern zone of Germany; the United States, Great Britain, and France would determine policy in their Western zones. The divisive issue of German reparations was cast vaguely into the future. After Potsdam, neither Truman nor Stalin sought another summit meeting.

RETURNING FROM THE POTSDAM CONFERENCE
Friends from their congressional days, Harry Truman and James Byrnes joined again as president and secretary of state to help fashion the postwar world. *(United Press International, Inc.)*

The Iron Curtain Falls. There were many other sources of Soviet-American friction in 1945 and 1946. At the San Francisco conference to found the United Nations, the Russian delegates came close to disrupting the proceedings. The Soviet Union continued to view the UN as a league of potential enemies and often obstructed its work. Moreover, to contest American and British influence in the Middle East, Russia kept its troops in Iran and withdrew them early in 1946 only after strong protests. On its part, the United States abruptly ended economic aid to the Soviet Union after Germany's defeat, despite Russia's desperate need for assistance. Bluntly, Truman made any future aid dependent on a Soviet acceptance of American policies. In addition, the United States excluded Russia from the occupation government of Japan, as it already had from the occupation government of Italy.

Yet each of these problems by itself was either negotiable or tolerable. Only the issues of Germany and Eastern Europe defied any accommodation. In what Soviet officials construed as an assault on their vital interests, the Truman administration pursued a policy of reconciliation with Germany and demanded independent governments throughout Eastern Europe. The German zones rapidly became permanent Eastern and Western spheres; the Soviet Union tightened its authority over Poland and the Balkans. "From Stettin in the Baltic to Trieste in the Adriatic," Churchill declared in a speech of March 1946 at Fulton, Missouri, "an iron curtain has deceded across the Continent." More and more stories of mass killings, deportations, and labor camps filtered through that curtain. Although there were moments of hope for a year after the Potsdam conference, the main trend in Soviet-American relations ran strongly toward suspicion and anger. By late 1946 even the occasional hopes disappeared.

American Rationale for Confronting Soviets. What led the United States to confront the Soviet Union in Europe? The answer has four parts. The most elusive but perhaps the most important element was a powerful tradition of mutual distrust. There was a natural inclination in both the United States and the Soviet Union to regard the other nation as the "communist" or "capitalist" enemy. During the war, people had become accustomed to thinking of the world as composed of two diametrically opposed philosophies—fascism and democracy. Now, by substituting "communism" for "fascism," many Americans assumed a simple response to a bewildering snarl of global problems. At the founding of the UN, the influential Republican senator, Arthur Vandenberg, noted in his diary, "The basic trouble is that we are trying to unite two incompatible ideologies." Moreover, because both Soviet and American leaders viewed their counterparts as inherently expansionist, feelings of distrust easily turned into fears of aggression. There was little to choose between Hitler and Stalin as mass murderers. But Stalin, ruling a decimated land in 1945, showed little urge for expansion beyond Eastern Europe. It was the United States that filled the great vacuums of power in the Pacific, the Middle East, and Western Europe. Nevertheless, as power met power in the middle of Europe, each nation assumed the worst of the other.

The second reason why the United States confronted the Soviets concerned American expectations following a victory. The United States, never before paramount above all other nations, assumed it would control the terms of a postwar settlement. An "American century" was dawning, declared the prominent publisher Henry Luce. Policy-makers could hardly resist acting as lords of the domain. After the war the United States made its own decisions on distributing American food abroad instead of relying on a neutral international relief agency (UNRRA), and Washington treated both the World Bank and the International Monetary Fund as instruments of American policy. Under the Baruch Plan of 1946, the United States offered to internationalize the control of atomic power only if America retained an indefinite monopoly and was assured that no other nation was developing its own atomic weapons. The Soviet Union hotly rejected the plan as no bargain at all. In this climate of national self-confidence, most Americans assumed that an able president could manage any international problem. Such a high level of popular expectations and low level of popular patience contributed to a hard line in foreign affairs in 1945 and 1946.

The third element in America's postwar policy was Truman's personal inclination toward a hard line. By temperament he was a fighter. Reporting his first sharp exchange with Soviet Foreign Minister Molotov, Truman wrote with obvious relish, "I gave it to him straight 'one-two to the jaw.'" The same man who thoroughly enjoyed a "Give 'em hell, Harry" political campaign at home found it natural to "get tough" with the Russians abroad. In a characteristically Truman manner, the president wrote his secretary of state in January 1946, "I'm tired of babying the Soviets." Moreover, Truman took pride in his ability to reach a decision promptly, then hold to it firmly. After a meeting with J. Robert Oppenheimer over the moral implications of the atomic bomb, the president snapped: "Don't ever bring the damn fool in here again. He didn't set that bomb off. I did. This kind of snivelling makes me sick." With the unyielding Russians on one side and the pugnacious Truman on the other, the possibilities of a compromise were always slender.

Truman's advisers made the fourth contribution to America's postwar foreign policy. In his first months as president, Truman turned everywhere for advice on foreign affairs. The group of counselors whom he inherited from Roosevelt could not look at Truman without seeing the giant shadow of FDR behind him. Understandably the new president allowed them to drop away one by one. Harry Hopkins, Roosevelt's most intimate aide, and Henry Wallace, now secretary of commerce, were particularly unhappy about Truman's hard line with Stalin. By the fall of 1945, Hopkins lamented that "we are doing almost everything we can to break with Russia, which seems so unnecessary to me." After a long period of strain, Wallace finally cut ties with the Truman administration in a major speech of September 1946: "'Getting tough' never brought anything real and lasting—whether for schoolyard bullies or businessmen or world powers. The tougher we get, the tougher the Russians will get."

Truman had better luck with his former political associates from Congress. One of these, James F. Byrnes, became secretary of state in July 1945. Following an impressive career in Congress, on the Supreme Court, and as "assistant president" in charge of America's wartime mobilization, Byrnes took his new office on the assumption that he himself, rather than Truman, really should have been Roosevelt's successor. Though Byrnes was a firm anticommunist, he was also a bargainer, and he kept an element of flexibility in America's relations with the Soviet Union.

The State Department in the Cold War.   Discreetly at hand stood a third group of advisers, whose base of operations was the State Department. As America's world affairs increasingly demanded a wider range of diplomatic services, the State Department emerged as a significant center of government power, with extensive connections in those business, mili-

tary, and publishing circles that affected its work. The expanding department attracted an able and strong-minded set of leaders, including W. Averell Harriman, the son of a railroad magnate and ambassador to Great Britain and the Soviet Union; George Kennan, a career diplomat with special talents as a writer and planner; and Dean Acheson, a wellborn lawyer who had found his true calling in the State Department. Through such men as Harriman, Kennan, and Acheson, the department offered Truman something that his other advisers failed to provide: the outlines for a systematic world policy.

As the leaders in the State Department interpreted Soviet behavior, the Russians were following a long-term plan to destroy all capitalist societies. Communist ideology made them fanatics. Despite the needs of their war-ravaged nation, Soviet officials kept a large army mobilized after Germany's surrender. State Department leaders thought that if weakness in a neighboring country gave the Russians the opportunity, they would seize it. The Soviet army had already attempted such a probe in Iran. From its base in Central Europe, the Soviet Union could strike the devastated, chaotic nations of Western Europe at any time. To counter this broad threat, the United States, too, needed a long-term plan. American power had to meet Soviet power on a global scale. Otherwise, as Harriman warned, the Russians would pursue their goal of world domination by continuing to build "tiers [of satellites], layer on layer," until they crushed the forces of freedom. Only firmness could stop them. As the history of fascism proved, appeasement merely whetted a dictator's appetite.

The Truman Doctrine and the Marshall Plan.   With the United States hesitating at an important crossroads in its foreign policy, Truman was ready to follow the State Department's guidance. In January 1947, Byrnes was replaced as secretary of state by General George Marshall, a man of flawless integrity but limited imagination who, like Truman, relied heavily on the judgment of Assistant Secretary Dean Acheson. In February, one of Roosevelt's four policemen, Great Britain, greatly weakened by its war effort, informed Washington that it was retiring from the force. American, not British, aid would have to save the conservative government in Greece, which was racked with civil war. President Truman, addressing Congress in March on aid to both Greece and Turkey, dramatically announced the new "Truman Doctrine." "At the present moment in world history nearly every nation must choose between alternative ways of life," Truman declared. One way of life was freedom and democracy. Communism, according to Truman, was the alternative:

The second way of life is based upon the will of a minority forcibly imposed upon the majority. It relies upon terror and oppression, a controlled press and radio, fixed elections, and the suppression of personal freedoms. I believe that it must be the policy of the United States to support free people who are resisting attempted subjugation by armed minorities or by outside pressure.

Meanwhile, the State Department was preparing strategy for a general European defense "against totalitarian pressures." Through the Marshall Plan, which took shape in the summer of 1947, America eventually sent more than $12 billion in American aid to its European allies and enabled their shattered economies to achieve a minor miracle of recovery. The Marshall Plan brought the United States an extraordinary amount of goodwill in Western Europe. Moreover, in July 1947 Washington made a formal commitment to rehabilitate West Germany as part of a "free Europe." Though the communist nations of Europe were officially invited to participate in the Marshall Plan, participation would require Russia to break its security system for Eastern Europe. As American leaders expected, the Russians refused and demanded that their European allies refuse as well. Hungary, in May, then Rumania in December, fell totally under Soviet control. American trade with the Soviet Union, which had flourished in 1946, dwindled to a trickle.

Czechoslovakia Falls; Berlin Stands. In Czechoslovakia—the very symbol of a liberated Europe—political turmoil in February 1948 allowed the Communist party to take power. Communications across the Iron Curtain virtually ceased. That spring, rumors

THE BERLIN AIRLIFT
In 1948 the Berlin airlift expressed America's resolve to keep any further European territory from communist control. *(Walter Sanders/LIFE Magazine © 1948 Time, Inc.*

raced through Washington that a real war was imminent. Instead, between April and June 1948, the Soviet Union cut the transportation lines to Berlin, which lay deep within the Russian sector of Germany. Berlin, like the country as a whole, was administered through zones. Now the American, British, and French zones within Berlin were under siege. The United States responded with an impressively organized airlift that brought essential supplies to the citizens in these isolated zones. In May 1949, the Russians finally abandoned the blockade. More than any other event, the Berlin blockade seemed to verify the Truman administration's warnings about Soviet aggression. Domestic opposition to the Cold War collapsed, and anti-Soviet sentiments spread in Western Europe.

The U.S. as a World Peace Power. Riding the momentum of these changes at home and abroad, the Truman administration completed negotiations for the North Atlantic Treaty, a pact of mutual assistance among twelve nations that was signed in April 1949.* Although the wording of the treaty was general, almost everyone interpreted it as the guarantee of American military support in case of a Soviet attack in Europe. In January 1949, Dean Acheson, the primary architect of Truman's European program, became secretary of state and received proper credit for this sweeping commitment of American power. Meanwhile, the Federal Republic of Germany evolved from the Western zones of occupation and was set on its way to independence. To each of these steps, the Soviet Union responded with a countermeasure: the German Democratic Republic in the East, then the Warsaw Pact which formed a league of Russia's European satellites.

With breathtaking speed, the United States had fundamentally changed its role as a peacetime world power. During the rise of fascism in the 1930s, the United States had withdrawn more and more tightly into the Western Hemisphere. Now through the Truman Doctrine, the United States made an open-ended offer of assistance to nations everywhere in the world. Instead of demanding payment of its war debts, as the United States had done after the First World War, the government devised the Marshall Plan to underwrite the economies of Western Europe. In 1940 even the fall of continental Europe had not brought the United States into the Second World War; in 1948 danger to the single city of Berlin threatened to trigger a third world war. In 1927 Americans

had shied away from a simple bilateral treaty with France renouncing war; in 1949 the North Atlantic Treaty placed eleven other nations under the shelter of American power.

In spite of these profound changes, however, the United States still did not have a clear and detailed foreign policy. What areas of the world did the Truman Doctrine cover? Under Acheson's guidance, the Truman administration concentrated on Europe and left the rest of the world in limbo. How did the United States plan to defend the nations that fell under its protection? No one expected American troops to be stationed throughout the world. Some people, including the influential columnist Walter Lippmann, hoped that American economic aid would enable groups of nations to organize their own regional leagues of defense. In his inaugural address of 1949, President Truman encouraged this kind of vision. "Point Four" of that address raised the possibility of exporting more technological skills and fewer weapons to the world's needy nations.

Communist Gains. Two critical events of 1949 underlined the importance of these unresolved problems. One occurred in Asia; the other, in the Soviet Union.

In Asia, Mao Tse-tung's communists poured out of Manchuria, drew popular support as they moved, and swept through China, driving Chiang Kai-shek's tattered remnants to the island of Formosa (Taiwan). That civil war had been brewing during the years of the Chinese resistance to Japan. At times Chiang, America's East Asian ally in the Pacific war, seemed more concerned about his domestic enemy than his foreign foe. Even before the end of the Second World War, American officials began their futile attempts to mediate between Chiang's nationalists and Mao's communists. Special American missions including a highly publicized one in 1945–46 under General Marshall, warned Chiang about the corruption in his government, dangled the prospect of economic assistance before the two camps, and struggled to arrange a truce between their armies. Unwilling to force concessions from Chiang, yet unable to intervene effectively in his behalf, the United States invested some

*The eleven other nations were Belgium, Canada, Denmark, England, France, the Netherlands, Iceland, Italy, Luxembourg, Norway, and Portugal. Soon Greece, Turkey, and West Germany joined.

military aid and much larger amounts of hope in his cause. By 1949 the Truman administration could only take comfort in the fact that nobody had guessed right on China. Stalin, like Truman, had bet that Chiang would win.

As the world's preeminent power, many argued, America could have saved China from communism. By a reasonable construction of the Truman Doctrine, they said, the United States should have. Instead, a vast territory and huge population had fallen to the enemy. Adding China to the Soviet sphere in Eastern Europe produced an appalling total effect. Simple maps blocked out the recent losses, and simple arithmetic summarized the human costs. In 1949, when Congressman Richard Nixon of California totaled the peoples inside and outside the communist domain, he concluded that "in 1944 . . . the odds were 9 to 1 in our favor. Today . . . the odds are 5 to 3 against us."

Before the communist victory in China, Americans had been comforted by the belief that people elsewhere, once free to choose, would select something similar to American democracy. The struggle against evil persisted, but as that sturdy liberal senator, Robert Wagner of New York, said, "History is on our side." In the administration's most cogent justification for the Truman Doctrine, George Kennan of the State Department outlined what would happen if the United States applied steady, patient pressure along the perimeter of the communist sphere. In time, the communist domain would erode from its own weakness, and gradually more and more people would select freedom. But the communist revolution in China struck at the heart of this faith. For another quarter-century, the United States not only refused to recognize the communist government of China; many Americans also clung to the belief that the Chinese, given a choice, would still follow the old warlord Chiang.

The second critical event of 1949 was the detonation of an atomic bomb by the Soviet Union. Since 1945, the American monopoly in atomic weapons had enabled the United States to expand its international commitments without spreading its military forces abroad. The Truman Doctrine seemed to say that American aid alone would protect its ____ American possession of the bomb would deter a large-scale Soviet intervention. A few months before the Soviets' atomic test, Secretary Acheson told the Senate Foreign Relations Committee that the North Atlantic Treaty Organization (NATO) would require no more than token American soldiers in Europe. Truman gave this claim the ring of truth in 1949 by insisting on a reduced military budget. No American leader seriously contemplated using the bomb; just having the bomb was enough.

How thoroughly the United States had relied on its monopoly in atomic weapons became clear after that monopoly was broken. Suddenly the United States seemed terribly vulnerable. America's new security program for Europe no longer had teeth. In the scramble for alternatives, some government officials actually did suggest a preemptive atomic strike at the Soviet Union. Moreover, if Soviet society was inherently inferior, as Americans had been repeatedly told, how had it manufactured its own bomb so soon? Spies must have stolen American secrets. The Federal Bureau of Investigation proceeded to uncover the communists Julius and Ethel Rosenberg, who were charged with passing information about the bomb to the Soviet Union. They were found guilty, and executed. Judge Irving Kaufman, who sentenced the Rosenbergs to death in 1951, expressed the anger of a nation that had been stripped of its primary protection:

Your conduct in putting into the hands of the Russians the A-bomb . . . has already caused, in my opinion, the Communist aggression in Korea, with the resultant [American] casualties exceeding fifty thousand and who knows but that millions more of innocent people may pay the price of your treason. Indeed, by your betrayal you undoubtedly have altered the course of history.

Containment, 1950–1953

The Korean War, which began in June 1950, completed America's global policy of "containment." As the problems of 1949 demonstrated, neither the geographical extent of America's anticommunism nor the methods of enforcing it had been carefully examined.

LIFTING OFF THE WOUNDED IN KOREA
This contrast between a modern war technology and an agrarian culture would be repeated again and again after mid-century. *(Official U.S. Air Force Photo)*

The Shifting Front in Korea

June 1950

September 1950

November 1950

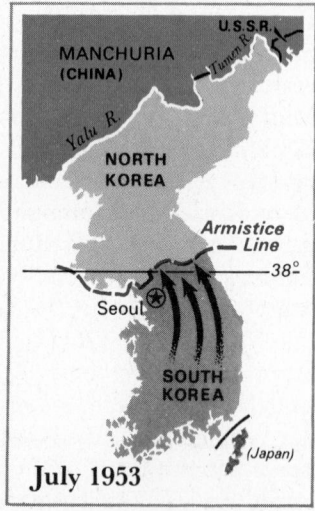

July 1953

Without firm solutions on both of these issues, the United States would continue to stumble from incident to incident. Appropriately, the place of decision was East Asia, where the Chinese Revolution had just forced Americans to rethink both the scope and the tactics of their foreign policy.

The Korean War.   In 1945, during the Soviet Union's brief war against Japan, Russian troops moved across Manchuria into the Korean peninsula before American troops could land from the sea. The two armies hastily agreed to occupy northern and southern halves of the peninsula, divided at the thirty-eighth parallel, until their governments could settle the fate of this Japanese territory. As so often happened after the war, delays, Soviet-American tensions, and then the Cold War transformed a momentary convenience into a permanent solution. Under the auspices of the UN, which assumed responsibility for a Korean settlement, the United States backed one government in South Korea. The Soviet Union sponsored a rival government in North Korea. Each Korean government claimed the whole of the peninsula, and each was itching to fight for it. Because Korea had little significance in the complex contest between the Soviet Union and the United States, neither power closely supervised its dependent government before 1950.

As if in spite, the Korean pawns moved themselves in June 1950. Under circumstances that remain obscure, the two Korean armies clashed, and the superior Northern force began rolling southward. Although the Truman administration had not prepared for a crisis in Korea, it was ready to act. After sending the South Koreans light reinforcements from Japan, the United States took advantage of Russia's absence from the Security Council of the United Nations to place America's cause under the authority of the UN. On June 27, the Security Council endorsed UN intervention. Officially, therefore, the United States did not fight a war in Korea; it cooperated in a UN police action.

Within a few days American military power under General Douglas MacArthur did reverse the battle and drove the North Korean army past the thirty-eighth parallel back through its own territory to the Chinese border. The original purpose of the war had been protection of South Korea's territory. Now the goal seemed to be unification of the entire Korean peninsula. In November large Chinese reinforcements surprised the American forces and pushed them once again below the thirty-eighth parallel. By early 1951 the war settled into a grudging, bloody struggle along the original boundary. Shortly after the inauguration of President Dwight Eisenhower in 1953, an armistice between the opposing armies more or less reestablished the division at the thirty-eighth parallel. A formal peace never came. Over a million Koreans and Chinese and about 23,000 Americans had died in the conflict.

Though this stalemate war aroused widespread resentment in the United States, the range of opposition was quite narrow. Critics filled the air with might-have-beens and should-have-beens that censured Truman and Acheson as shortsighted, fumbling leaders, but they almost never questioned the appropriateness of American military intervention. Nor did the administration's critics rally much support for a big war against either China or Russia. The center of such ambitions was the imperious General MacArthur, whose belligerent and insubordinate behavior after China's entry into the war forced Truman to recall him from Korea in April 1951 and relieve him of his command. As the hero of two wars and the successful director of America's occupation government in postwar Japan, MacArthur received an adoring welcome home after his recall. As the advocate of Asian conquest, however, MacArthur won no important endorsements. The Korean War was thoroughly unpopular but the majority of Americans ratified the president's policy in fighting it.

The elections of 1952 endorsed both the policy behind the war and its unpopularity. According to the opinion polls, only one in four Americans thought that the United States was winning the Cold War. Nevertheless, neither the Republicans nor the Democrats broke from the administration's Korean policy. Both General Eisenhower, the Republican presidential candidate, and his opponent, Adlai Stevenson, supported the concept of a limited war. Both promised to settle it as promptly as possible. After declaring that he would "go to Korea" himself in an effort to end the fighting, Eisenhower took office in a climate of expectations that he, far better than Truman, could make Truman's policy work.

The Free World. With the Korean War came answers to the two most perplexing questions in America's international affairs. What was the scope of America's anticommunist policy? and What were the best means of implementing it? After several years of hesitation, the government interpreted the words in the Truman Doctrine literally: any nation willing to cooperate with America's worldwide anticommunist policy became a member of the "free world." Some of these members, such as England and Canada, were old and trusted democratic friends. Others were recent enemies. West Germany was now preparing to enter NATO. In 1951, over the vehement protests of the Soviet Union, the United States signed a formal peace with Japan and incorporated it, along with Australia, New Zealand, and the Philippines, in America's expanding scheme of defensive alliances. Still other members of the free world, such as Spain and South Korea, were authoritarian states. As John Foster Dulles, the Republican party's leading expert on foreign affairs, said to the dictatorial government of South Korea, its nation formed one "part in the great design of human freedom." Even a desire to remain neutral in the Cold War indicated an indifference to "human freedom."

Officially every member of the free world had equal importance in America's global policy. Before June 1950, both General MacArthur in Japan and Secretary Acheson in Washington had suggested that South Korea fell outside America's primary line of defense. War followed, and the government vowed never to repeat the mistake. Viewing the communist camp as one interrelated whole and the free world as another, American policy-makers interpreted a weakness in either bloc as the sign of greater changes to come. Yugoslavia's refusal to accept Soviet dictation after 1948, for example, kindled hopes for the liberation of all Eastern Europe. Korea, as the expression

went, pointed like a dagger at Japan. Clusters of free nations were likened to rows of dominoes, where the tipping of one into communism toppled the rest. From these concerns came the cardinal rule that would dominate the next two decades of American foreign policy: the free world must not relinquish a single additional piece of territory. No more Munichs; no more Chinas.

Just as firmly, the United States resolved the problem of tactics. Containment depended primarily on military power. Years of debate about the best way of assisting friendly nations ended in a resounding victory for military aid, which Congress not only increased but also distributed throughout the free world. In Western Europe, the United States pressed its allies, including West Germany, to rearm and merge their military strength. At home, the United States embarked on a long-range program of military preparedness that included the development of tactical units against local aggression, elaborate surveillance systems to gather military intelligence, and the construction of a far more lethal nuclear weapon, the hydrogen bomb. In addition, it explored better means for delivering a nuclear attack by air, from the sea, and through a network of foreign bases. Lacking a monopoly of nuclear weapons, America sought a clear military advantage over the Soviet Union, because ultimately, the proponents of containment argued, communist totalitarianism would respond only to power. The Department of Defense, which the National Security Act of 1947 had created to coordinate the army, navy, and air force, participated closely in decisions on foreign affairs. And the Central Intelligence Agency (CIA), which had also been established by the National Security Act, came of age as an important intelligence-gathering agency and center of secret international operations.

The New Consensus. "Containment" was a popular policy. Intellectuals, horrified by the communist controls over free expression, welcomed the new policy. National leaders who thought naturally in terms of long-range planning and stability admired containment as an example of sound international management. Under the containment policy, corporations with foreign interests received more consistent government support than ever before. Almost by definition, the links between American business and a foreign nation strengthened the cohesion of the free world. Cultural and religious groups whose compatriots abroad were persecuted under communism supported containment with a particular zeal. Finally, containment appealed to the powerful American tradition of personal courage. As statesmen of the Cold War from Arthur Vandenberg to Richard Nixon said, it took "guts" to hold the line.

Government officials, citing the alternative of total war, called containment a moderate policy. Yet no one could deny that it was an astonishing departure from the past. Instead of designing mechanisms for international stability and quietly working them from a distance, the United States threw itself into the intricacies of global politics. Daily, Washington monitored the domestic affairs as well as the foreign policies of nations around the world. American aid shored up friendly governments from Latin America to Southeast Asia. American power subverted unfriendly governments—in Iran in 1953, in Guatemala in 1954. Soon the United States developed a system of alliances that encircled the globe. The old distinctions between economic and military imperialism that had defined friends and enemies in the 1930s no longer made sense in the 1950s, when dollars, guns, and ideas merged in a continuous, worldwide struggle.

International spheres became elaborate systems of power dividing the world into free and communist halves. In response to almost every international issue, the United States applied one basic test. What would help the communists and what would strengthen anticommunism? Critics abroad considered that test too narrow to deal with the world's diversity. America, they complained, was the first nation in history to move directly from childhood to senility in its foreign policy. But Americans replied that the solution to all other problems hinged on the outcome of this global contest. There would be ample time to test these conflicting viewpoints, because

the United States had set its course in world affairs for the next twenty years.

From Wartime Prosperity to Peacetime Management, 1941–1945

The Second World War solved the depression. Before the war was over, net farm income almost doubled, and corporate profits after taxes climbed 70 percent. From a total of over 8 million unemployed in 1940, the curve dropped below a million by 1944. Moreover, an abundance of jobs and an industrial wage scale that rose 24 percent drew into the labor market an additional 7 million workers, half of whom were women. There had been no economic boom like it in American history.

The Wartime Boom.   Economic organization for a worldwide conflict required an extraordinary expansion of government power. Washington suddenly teemed with hundreds of thousands of new arrivals who jammed themselves into cubbyhole offices with a bewildering array of alphabet labels. The main divisions of the government bureaucracy matched the major functions of the modern economy. The War Production Board, the Office of Price Administration, the War Manpower Commission, the Office of Defense Transportation, and the War Food Administration each had broad authority to manage its subdivision of the economy. Beginning in October 1942, the skillful South Carolina politician James Byrnes ruled these agencies through the Office of Economic Stabilization, and subsequently through the Office of War Mobilization.

The problems that most bedeviled the wartime agencies were allocating scarce resources, and controlling inflation. Because the United States was blessed with an abundance of natural resources, it had enough raw materials for most wartime programs. When a shortage of rubber created a crisis, the rapid development of synthetic rubber soon resolved it. The shortage of skilled labor, however, defied solution. Not only did the armed services absorb over 15

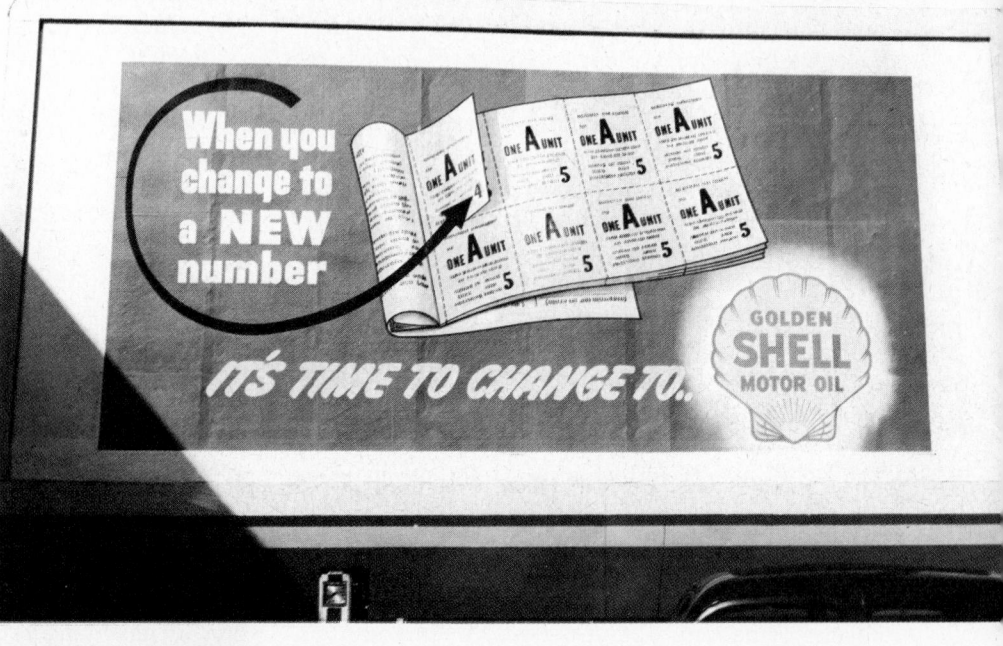

GAS RATIONING BOOKLET ON A WARTIME BILLBOARD
(Library of Congress)

PATRIOTISM AT RECESS
Money and morale went hand in hand in the campaign to draw Americans of every age into the war effort. School-children bought War Stamps, and when their books were full turned them in for War Bonds. *(Library of Congress)*

million men and women, but civilians could not resist hopping from job to job in search of better wages. "Stabilization," or job-freeze, orders from Washington had little effect on labor turnover, and Roosevelt's proposal in 1944 to draft workers into an industrial army collapsed in the face of united opposition from employers and unions alike.

Prices soared during the early months of the war. The Office of Price Administration (OPA), under the able but politically obtuse economist Leon Henderson, lacked the power to control inflation because Congress refused to check the rise of agricultural prices. Only late in 1942, when Byrnes took charge of the entire mobilization program, did a semblance of order begin to emerge. By mid-1943, a broad legal ceiling over prices, wages, and rents finally stopped the upward spiral. Although the cost of living increased about 33 percent during the war, relatively little of that occurred after the summer of 1943.

Finance posed another basic wartime problem. Though more than half the costs of war accumulated as a national debt, massive new funds still had to be raised. The answer came in the revolutionary Revenue Act of 1942, which established America's modern structure of taxation. The heart of the measure was a steeply graduated income tax that for the first time covered most middle-income and lower-income groups. As a result, the number of families paying income tax quadrupled, and by 1945 revenues from the tax were an astronomical twenty times above their level in 1940. To ease the pain yet increase the flow, the government took most of these taxes directly from the paychecks rather than demand them in a lump once a year.

Inside the intricate framework of wartime rules, extreme decentralization prevailed. The tax laws contained numerous loopholes for the wealthy. Thousands of local draft boards decided who should fill the quotas for military service. To get the planes and tanks and beef and wheat it needed, the government simply offered to pay a lot of money. It signed lucrative contracts with individual companies guaranteeing costs, profits, and large tax write-offs. Companies negotiated these contracts through the various bureaus of the wartime government, then fought with one another for the labor and raw materials all of them needed. After the government allowed farm prices to skyrocket for a year, it continued to subsi-

SILENCE MEANS SECURITY

RECOVERY OF THE NATIONAL ECONOMY

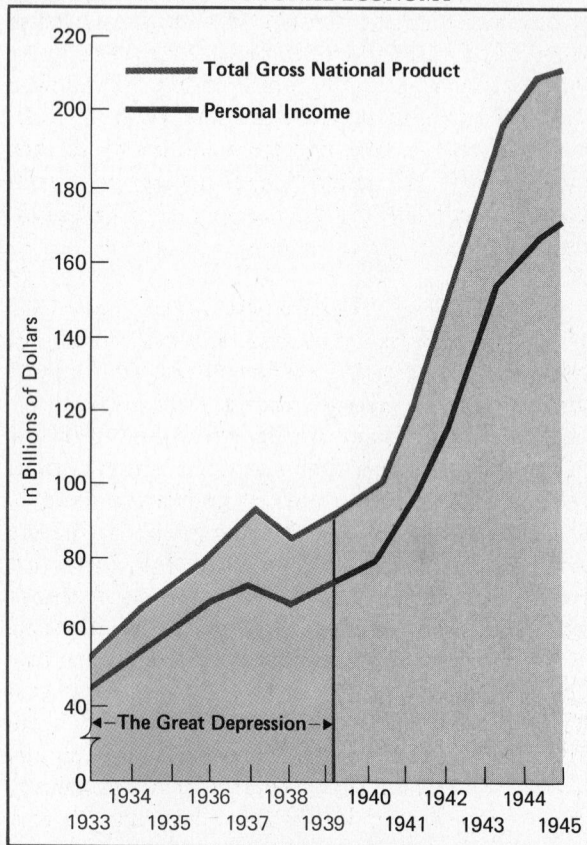

dize many farmers at a level above the market price for their products. Even the unpopular OPA, which rationed such scarce commodities as gasoline, meat, shoes, and sugar among a nation of grumbling consumers, exercised little control over the widespread violation of its rules. The government's chief administrators intervened only when the many small decisions below them had created a hopeless mess.

In the wartime scramble for advantage, the strong reaped the greatest benefits. In 1940 the 100 leading companies manufactured 30 percent of the nation's output. By 1943 the 100 leaders produced 70 percent. The conservative coalition in Congress grew larger and bolder. As the unemployed came back to work, Congress in 1942 terminated the WPA. Calling the

Farm Security Administration a "communist" center, its congressional opponents abolished the agency's social programs for the rural poor. Despite President Roosevelt's efforts, Congress lightened the tax burden on the rich in 1943.

The one child of the thirties to thrive during the war was the union movement. In 1941, two more citadels of the open shop—Ford and the corporations in "Little Steel"—surrendered. During the war itself union membership rose 40 percent. Even more important, many employers, in an effort to hold their workers and maintain production, actually bargained with the unions for the first time. Yet here also the conservatives had their say. Although the number of strikes remained quite low between 1941 and 1945, important ones in the coal and railroad industries during 1943 triggered an angry public reaction, and Congress responded with the Smith-Connally Act, which authorized the president to postpone a strike for thirty days and seize a plant that had been struck. Strikers could be fined and imprisoned.

Above all, the conservatives fought every executive agency that tried to make economic plans for the postwar years. Not one of them survived the congressional budget cuts. As the war drew to a close, the only significant preparation for peace was the Servicemen's Readjustment Act of 1944, popularly known as the GI Bill, which provided unemployment compensation, medical care, mortgage funds, and educational subsidies for the returning veterans. An ailing Roosevelt did nothing to arrest the confusion. Investing all his energies in world problems, the president left the home front to his subordinates. Except in military affairs, Roosevelt had lost almost all influence in Congress by late 1943. When the Democrats nominated him for a fourth term in 1944, he campaigned listlessly against Thomas E. Dewey, the smooth, capable Republican governor of New York. Although Roosevelt's percentage of the popular vote declined, he still won handily, 439 to 99 electoral votes. Perhaps the nasty Democratic comment that no one wanted "little Tom Dewey sitting on two Washington telephone books" at the peace conference captured the essence of Roosevelt's strength. At a grand juncture in world affairs, the president had an appropriately grand international prestige. But domestically, America had no leader at all entering 1945.

"To Err Is Truman." Upon Roosevelt's death in April 1945, Harry Truman was left to preside over the nation's transition to peace. The most experienced leader would have had difficulty guiding America's economy out of the war. Lost in a maze of complex problems, "quick and brittle" in his decisions, Truman simply foundered. Even before Japan surrendered in August 1945, he could not withstand the popular pressures for a rapid demobilization of the armed forces and a rapid dismantling of most wartime regulations. Industries now made their own decisions in their own behalf, and during the first postwar year corporate profits shot up 20 percent.

Labor discontent spread across the nation. By January 1946, 3 percent of the labor force, including auto, steel, electrical, and packinghouse workers, were simultaneously on strike. When a new round of strikes occurred that spring, a furious president went before Congress to threaten the railroad workers with an army draft even though the railroad brotherhoods had already canceled the strike. Of the wartime controls, only those governing prices remained, and a feud between the president and Congress needlessly allowed these to end all at once in June 1946, producing the highest rate of inflation in the nation's history. Farm prices rose almost 14 percent in a month and nearly 30 percent before the end of the year. As the saying went, "To err is Truman." "Had enough?" asked the Republican campaign slogan.

Apparently many Americans had, for the off-year elections of 1946 cost the Democrats 11 seats in the Senate and 54 in the House. When the Eightieth Congress convened in 1947, the Republicans were the majority party for the first time since Hoover's administration. With the cooperation of conservative Democrats, they could even override the president's veto. Yet the Eightieth Congress had little to offer as an alternative to Truman's erratic policies. Its primary contribution was the Taft-Hartley Act of 1947, a culmination of the congressional antagonism toward unions that had been growing for a decade. A complicated law, Taft-Hartley required financial reports from the unions, restricted their political activities, and prohibited a list of "unfair" labor practices. It also empowered the president to postpone a major strike for an eighty-day "cooling-off" period and allowed state governments to pass antiunion "right to work" laws. But despite these new rules and the howls they brought from the unions, labor-management relations proceeded much from the same after Taft-Hartley as before.

Decentralization. The last years of the New Deal left a confusing legacy of more and more economic interests seeking their own fortunes in Washington. And during the Second World War innumerable special interests fought for the government's favors. The stakes were high, the rules loose, and the results chaotic. Each economic interest grew accustomed to caring for itself in the Washington jungle. By the end of the war, the big economic blocs of an earlier era were in thorough disarray. Such broad organizations as the U.S. Chamber of Commerce, the National Association of Manufacturers, and the American Bankers Association, once the voices of basic economic groups, now spoke for no one in particular. The American Farm Bureau Federation was rapidly losing strength, and the Department of Agriculture came to rely less and less on it to administer the government's farm programs.

As the AFL and the CIO began making peace and preparing for their merger in 1955, both organizations experienced a similar decentralization. Strong industrial unions in the CIO exercised the same kind of independence that the affiliates of the AFL had long enjoyed, and the central headquarters of neither union had much success in trying to discipline such stubborn organizations as the Longshoremen and the Teamsters. Even the oligopolies were less integrated than they had once been. The latest wave of corporate consolidations, which eventually produced such conglomerates as Litton Industries, Textron, and Kaiser Industries, favored purely financial combinations of distinct and often very different kinds of business firms.

Paralleling the fragmentation of interests, a permanent professional bureaucracy formed in Washington to deal with each specialized subdivision of the economy. During the war the government bureaucracy swelled to four times its size in 1939. In the hubbub of crash programs and quick decisions, no one closely supervised its myriad economic activities. Even after demobilization, more than twice as many civilian employees worked for the government as before the war. A job in Washington was no longer a stopover, as it tended to be in the twenties, or a cause, as many considered it in the thirties. Now it was a career. Experienced administrators grew accustomed to running their own little domains and protecting them from higher authorities. Almost every office along the miles of Washington corridors was linked to some private group and a few friendly congressmen. In sum, these many alliances between public officials and private interests made a broad public policy extremely difficult to create.

As the pattern of decentralization developed, the economic importance of the national government loomed larger than ever. No one could miss the intimate connection between government policy and the nation's phenomenal economic growth during the war. America's gross national product (GNP) rose a breathtaking 67 percent. Government expenditures accounted for an equally astonishing 40 percent of the total GNP. Government became an everyday term to designate this huge center of money and power. In the Full Employment Act of 1946, Congress accepted the government's responsibility for maintaining a healthy economy. But Congress carefully avoided specifying how. This sprawling, government-oriented economy had been changing too rapidly, and neither the Democrats nor the Republicans had found a satisfactory technique for managing it.

The Election of 1948. Although most Democratic leaders prayed that Truman would not run for president in 1948, he did. With little choice, less enthusiasm, and no hope, the national convention dutifully nominated him. The odds against Truman's success were prohibitive. Immediately after his nomination, two additional parties formed to attract the votes of dissident Democrats. The Progressive party, in the tradition of American parties with that name, depended on the reputation of one man, Henry Wallace, who symbolized New Deal liberalism at home and accommodation with the Soviet Union abroad. In Birmingham, Alabama, a new state-rights Democratic party—the Dixiecrats—attracted southern leaders who

The Election of 1948

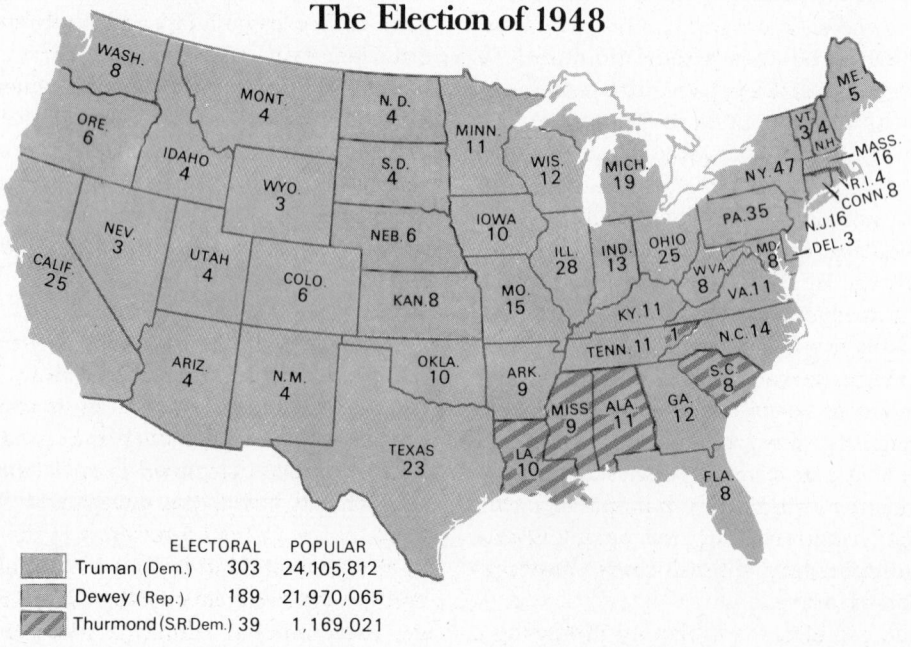

	ELECTORAL	POPULAR
Truman (Dem.)	303	24,105,812
Dewey (Rep.)	189	21,970,065
Thurmond (S.R.Dem.)	39	1,169,021

thought their enemies from the northern cities were dominating the regular party and who feared an assault on southern race relations. The Dixiecrats nominated Governor J. Strom Thurmond of South Carolina and dreamed of carrying the entire South. The Roosevelt coalition, it seemed, was crumbling. Above all, Truman faced a formidable Republican opponent in Governor Dewey of New York, who had done better against the indomitable Roosevelt in 1944 than any of the three Republican candidates who had preceded him. The only argument among the experts was the margin of Dewey's victory.

Truman made fools of the experts in 1948 because he responded so shrewdly to the prevailing disorganization in political and economic affairs. In a nation of innumerable scattered interest groups, no one knew how to provide effective leadership. Using a carefully devised strategy, the president shifted the blame for weak leadership to the Republican majority in the Eightieth Congress, which he scorned as the "Do-Nothing Congress." After the nominating conventions, he called Congress into special session and challenged the Republicans to enact their program. Of course little happened. The general paralysis in public policy appeared to be specifically a Republican malady.

Without a systematic program of his own, Truman compiled a long list of favors and promises. He reminded the unions that he had vetoed the Taft-Hartley Act of 1947 and that Republican votes had overridden him. He reminded business groups of tax benefits and government contracts. He promised subsidies to everything a farmer could produce. He recommended enlarging the TVA, increasing public housing, and broadening Social Security. He favored government aid to education. At the national convention in 1948, with Mayor Hubert H. Humphrey of Minneapolis leading the drive, the Democrats committed themselves to federal laws against job discrimination, lynching, and poll taxes. Truman not only endorsed this platform; he took the cause to Harlem, where no presidential candidate had ever campaigned. Even more striking, the president embarked in 1948 on the long, difficult course of desegregating the armed forces.

Dewey took the high road, blandly promising a sound, sane administration. But Truman, the bantam rooster from Missouri, fighting his way through an arduous cross-country campaign, ran for president like a county politician. His remark to one audience summarizes his campaign: "Vote your own interests." In 1948 Truman's provincial style was highly effective. Meanwhile, the deepening Cold War with the Soviet Union eroded the appeal of the Progressives and made Wallace appear to be the candidate of the Communist party. On election day, only a stubborn handful voted the Progressive ticket. Thurmond kept only the four southern states that he had controlled in July. Truman, with 303 electoral votes to Dewey's 189, scored the most stunning upset in modern politics and instantly joined America's folk heroes in the grand old tradition of the underdog triumphant.

Truman's victory demonstrated how many groups now looked to the national government for assistance. His second term revealed the constraints on responding to these groups. Truman gave his many promises a name, the "Fair Deal," but few of them survived the next four years. Congress rejected federal aid to education, national health insurance, and civil rights legislation. Although the president held to his purpose of desegregating the armed forces, he did not lead a general campaign for black rights. As a result, most of Thurmond's Dixiecrats returned to the regular Democratic party. The laws that did pass minimized the national government's influence in guiding social change. The Housing Act of 1949 allowed local governments and private groups to decide who would benefit from public housing in their areas. Simply, government subsidies to hospitals and medical research were controlled by local medical establishments.

Government and the Economy. The politics of the late forties made three points clear. First, nothing could relieve the government of its responsibility for general economic maintenance. Second, innumerable interest groups demanded special benefits from the government. Third, the government had to satisfy these groups without interfering in their daily affairs. Immediately at hand lay the ideal means for fulfilling all three requirements: the government's expanding fiscal powers. Although national expenditures dropped with the end of the war, they still remained six or seven times greater than in the 1930s, and double the percentage of the GNP under the New Deal. The tax laws now bound almost all Americans into the government's financial network. By 1946 the national debt had also risen sevenfold above the level of 1939, and funding this giant debt automatically made the government a dominant force in the nation's credit system. Moreover, the Federal Reserve's board of governors in Washington exercised an important general control over the nation's monetary affairs.

Adjusting the national budget, funding the national debt, regulating national monetary policy—here were precisely the mechanisms that suited the postwar economy. The fiscal machinery operated effectively no matter how many interest groups sought benefits in Washington, for fiscal management stood aloof from the political distribution of special favors. Hence, fiscal management minimized government interference with private groups or individuals. Yet it profoundly affected the whole economy. If the economy faltered, the government could ease credit, lower taxes, and increase its deficit. If an economic boom threatened inflation, the government could tighten credit, raise taxes, and shrink the deficit.

Truman, however, was not qualified to shape the government's fiscal powers into an acceptable public policy. Much as Roosevelt had, he disliked budget deficits and periodically led stern attacks on government spending. His narrow secretary of the treasury, John Snyder, regarded the national debt as simply an unfortunate government expense. Moreover, the Korean War in 1950 brought sharp inflation and growing frustration over international affairs. In 1951 and 1952, evidence of corruption among Truman's associates and in the Justice Department sullied the administration's reputation. According to opinion polls in 1952, fewer than one in four Americans approved of Truman's presidency.

The Election of 1952.   To obtain broad bipartisan approval for a policy of fiscal controls required a new president with a fresh start. Looking toward the 1952 elections, the Republicans vowed that this time they, and not the Democrats, would name the new presi-

dent. The two outstanding candidates for the Republican nomination were the brusque, efficient Robert Taft, son of a president and leader of his party in the Senate, and Dwight D. Eisenhower, hero of the Second World War and favorite of the party's moderates. Taft had established a long record of opposition to Washington bureaucracies and government inter-

DWIGHT D. EISENHOWER
In Ike, the Republicans finally found a winner. A war hero with such a smile was unbeatable in the fifties. *(United Press International, Inc.)*

ference with business. However, as a practicing politician, he accepted the primary results of the New Deal and acknowledged a government responsibility to protect the economy. Eisenhower, on the other hand, had established his record in the army, where he had demonstrated an impressive talent for diplomacy as well as command. These qualities mattered very much at a tense, critical time in world affairs, and they contrasted with Taft's tendency to favor blunt, unilateral actions abroad.

In a bitter contest, Eisenhower defeated Taft for the Republican nomination in 1952. Despite Taft's impressive strength among party regulars, the Republicans could not resist an immensely popular war hero. The Democrats had more difficulty finding a candidate. A folksy campaign by the liberal Tennessee senator Estes Kefauver, replete with handshakes, barbecues, and coonskin caps, gave him an early lead in a crowded field, but Truman withheld his blessing. Instead, the Democrats finally drafted the circumspect governor of Illinois, Adlai E. Stevenson. That fall, against an eloquent but outclassed Stevenson, Eisenhower transformed his radiant smile, unaffected manner, and shining reputation into an overwhelming 442 electoral votes to Stevenson's 89.

Eisenhower's Support for Local Control. By November it was becoming clear that Eisenhower, even more than the conservative Taft, retained a nostalgic attachment to an earlier age. An army career had spared Eisenhower the kinds of policy adjustments that Taft had been making in the 1930s and 1940s. He prized individualism and visualized its operation through private groups—political, industrial, church, school, labor.

"It has been a group effort, freely undertaken, that has produced the things of which we are so proud," Eisenhower announced, and he expected his administration to serve this "American way of life." "Free enterprise," "private initiative," and the dangers of "regimentation" peppered his conversations. He regarded TVA as "creeping socialism." On election night, 1952, when Eisenhower finally broke loose from the happy mob, his first telephone call was to Herbert Hoover.

Eisenhower gathered so many wealthy opponents

of the New Deal into his cabinet that it was popularly described as "nine millionaires and a plumber"— and the "plumber," Secretary of Labor Martin Durkin, soon resigned. In its first months, the new administration seemed bent on reversing the flow of the past twenty years in domestic affairs. It wanted the rich deposits of oil just off America's shores to belong to the states, not the national government, and in 1953 Congress passed a law providing for this. Eisenhower also proposed distributing federal revenues to the states. In cooperation with Secretary of the Treasury George Humphrey, the president set out to slash the national budget and minimize the government's influence in the economy. Eisenhower had no disagreement with the statement of Secretary of Defense Charles E. Wilson, former president of General Motors, that "what was good for our country was good for General Motors, and vice versa." Nor did he object when Secretary of Commerce Sinclair Weeks tried to fire the chief of the Bureau of Standards for reporting that a commercial battery additive, AD-2X, was useless. Secretary Weeks thought it should be allowed a "test of the marketplace."

Nevertheless, Eisenhower's attempt to revive the past quickly failed. Private groups welcomed favors, but almost none of them wanted responsibilities. Bipartisan leagues of businessmen, union leaders, and professionals demanded more money and more assistance, not less, from Washington. The farm associations were horrified when Eisenhower recommended phasing out their subsidies.

Public confidence broke during a recession in 1953 and 1954. When Eisenhower responded with a firm assurance of no more New Deals and a willingness to wait for prosperity's return, he met a fearful nationwide cry. Reluctantly but realistically, the president reconsidered. By March 1954 the Eisenhower administration had committed itself to protecting the economy with fiscal countermeasures, and when the recession had passed, the president gave due credit to the "workings of the fiscal system."

A stamp of approval from impeccably conservative Republicans largely ended debate over the government's new approach to economic maintenance. By 1954 substantial majorities in Congress stood ready to support the economy by adjusting taxes and federal spending. The Treasury Department and the Federal Reserve both agreed that they should handle the national debt and regulate interest rates so that credit would expand in a weak economy and contract during inflation. In fact, the secretary of the treasury now ranked with the secretaries of state and defense as primary government leaders. Many people accepted these fiscal techniques almost immediately because they seemed so neutral. They did not inhibit the stream of favor-seeking and favor-dispensing that flowed through Washington's busy offices. Liberals could still plan to expand government services, and conservatives could still hope to preserve the government's detachment. For the Invisible Hand that had guided Hoover's cooperative commonwealth in the 1920s, the national government of the 1950s substituted the Barely Visible Hand of fiscal manipulation.

Local Politics Comes to Washington, 1941–1954

While leaders in Washington were grappling with the problems of the economy, the racial and cultural concerns of local politicians rose into the sphere of national affairs. For a time, it had appeared that the informal bargain between the New Dealers and local Democrats might keep the two levels separate. But the Second World War blurred the boundaries. As the power of the national government rapidly expanded, it inevitably became entangled in local politics.

Concentration Camps.   The most shocking example of government intervention occurred on the West Coast immediately after the Japanese attack at Pearl Harbor. A large majority of whites along the West Coast had nursed a traditional hostility toward Asiatics. After the surprise attack on American territory, they readily believed rumors of a Japanese seditious "fifth column" in the United States that was planning extensive sabotage and communicating with enemy submarines off America's shore. The government, they cried, must destroy the danger from within. These popular, bipartisan emotions found a willing

PRISONERS

With pride as their only defense, these Japanese-Americans await shipment to one of the wartime concentration camps.   *(National Archives)*

servant in Lieutenant General John DeWitt, who headed the army's Western Defense Command. Responding to DeWitt's request, Washington gave the general broad powers in February 1942 to solve the Japanese problem as he chose.

At the outset, DeWitt planned to use stronger measures against the 40,000 alien Japanese (immigrants who by law were denied the right to become American citizens) than against the 70,000 who were American citizens by birth. But that distinction quickly disappeared. Early in 1942 DeWitt ordered all Japanese Americans along the coast of Washington, Oregon, and California and in southern Arizona to abandon their homes. From temporary stockades, they were transported to ten inland centers where the Army Relocation Authority guarded them for the duration. In *Korematsu* v. *United States* (1944), the Supreme Court upheld these policies on grounds of national security. Along with their liberty, Japanese Americans lost about $350 million in property and income.

Concentration camps for 110,000 Japanese Americans were an embarrassment to the Roosevelt administration, which was simultaneously fighting to empty the Nazi concentration camps in Europe. Officially the Japanese Americans were in "relocation centers." After the initial wave of panic passed, government officials discussed ways of reversing their policy and releasing the prisoners. Once again, local hostilities prevailed. The Roosevelt administration was told that no communities would accept the Japanese Americans. As a compromise, the army during 1943 and 1944 issued individual leaves to 35,000 imprisoned Japanese Americans. Finally, in January 1945 the prison gates were opened to everyone.

Meanwhile, in response to the desperate wartime need for unskilled labor, the United States in 1942 negotiated an agreement with Mexico for the importation of *braceros*, or temporary workers. Los Angeles, booming with war contracts and bursting with new arrivals, was a favorite destination for both legal and illegal immigrants from Mexico. City officials did nothing to ease their transition. Ethnic tensions simmered in the overflowing metropolis until finally the local hostility toward Chicanos erupted in "zoot suit" riots, which in most cases meant the beating of young Mexican Americans.

The Mobilization of Blacks. The broadest challenge to the rules of local politics came from black Americans. Between the two world wars, racial problems that had once been considered peculiarly southern spread nationwide. Close to a million blacks left the South during the 1920s, almost double the number who had emigrated in the previous decade. Even in the depression, when the unemployed crowded the large cities, 400,000 more came North. Then during the early 1940s alone, another million responded to the wartime jobs that beckoned from Los Angeles to Boston. By 1950 approximately one-third of America's black population lived outside the South.

In two important respects, the northern urban experience altered black attitudes. First, it encouraged their assertiveness. During the same years that whites argued over what percentage of which race should be allowed to immigrate, urban blacks were also showing a stronger racial consciousness. Claude McKay, Langston Hughes, Countee Cullen, and other contributors to the "Harlem Renaissance" of the 1920s wrote eloquently about the black spirit. Early in the twenties, millions of blacks found inspiration in the African nationalism of Marcus Garvey, an immigrant from Jamaica whose Universal Negro Improvement Association promised racial glory in the Empire of Africa.* Second, the northern urban experience stimulated a national movement for black rights. Its primary organization was the National Association for the Advancement of Colored People (NAACP), and the primary spokesman was Walter White, a talented writer and persistent lobbyist who in 1931 began his twenty-four year tenure as national secretary for the NAACP. When it became clear that only the national government could significantly improve the position of blacks in America, the NAACP pressed two kinds of arguments on the government's leaders. One, appealing to their conscience, demanded racial equality. The other, appealing to their political interests, offered to trade black votes for black rights. Unlike the southern cotton fields, the northern cities lay in competitive, two-party states with large electoral votes, and the NAACP tried to convince the Democratic party in particular that urban blacks could tip the balance in these states.

The New Deal's response was extremely disappointing. In matters of personal discrimination, Roosevelt's circle responded with sensitivity and imagination. In 1939, for example, when world-famous contralto Marian Anderson was denied the use of Constitution Hall in Washington because she was

---

*Garvey's conviction in 1923 for mail fraud disorganized his movement, and nothing comparable arose to take its place.

Black Population, 1920-1930

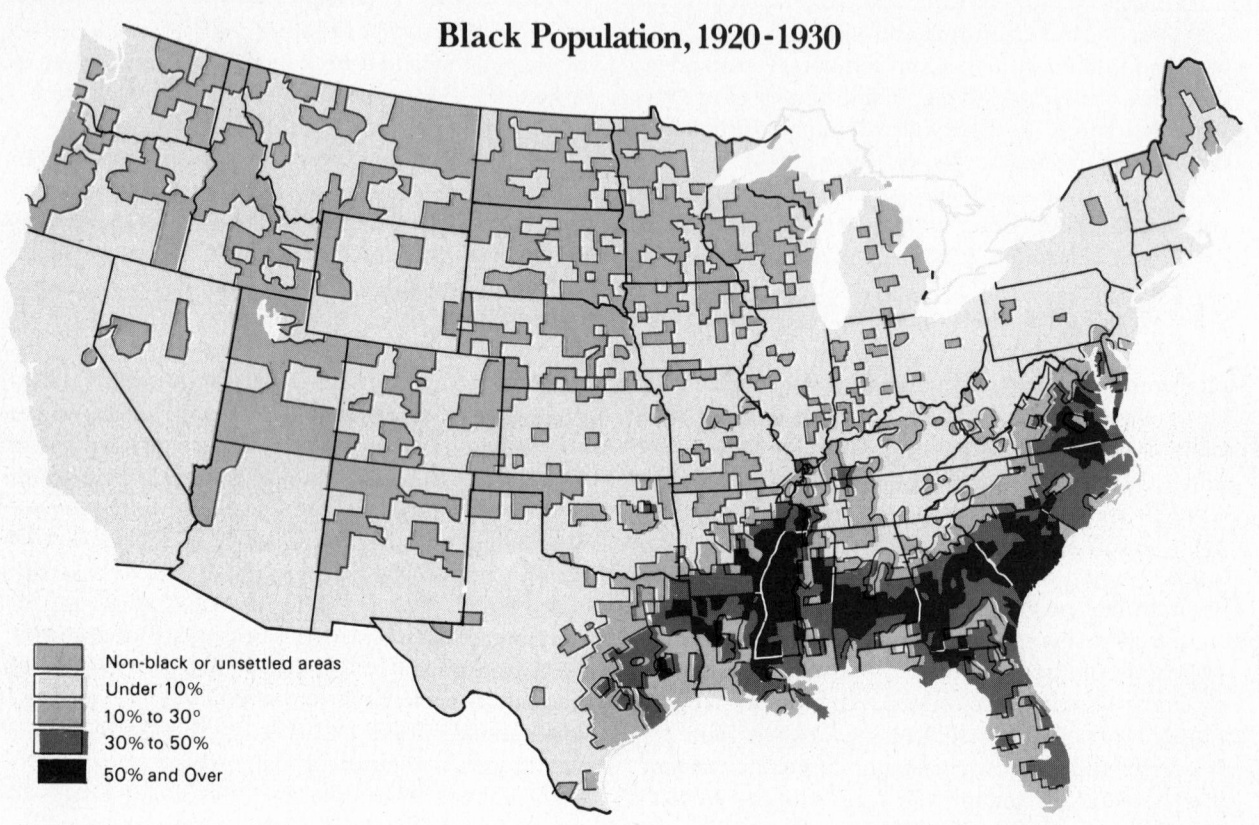

Non-black or unsettled areas
Under 10%
10% to 30°
30% to 50%
50% and Over

black, Harold Ickes arranged for a dramatic concert at the steps of the Lincoln Memorial. But in basic matters of civil and economic rights, the Roosevelt administration changed very little. It refused to take a strong stand against lynching. Without specific rules against discrimination, the New Deal's policies sometimes resulted in even fewer jobs for blacks. Its agricultural programs in the South were administered through white channels and did nothing to loosen the bonds of black peonage. In the Department of Agriculture, black county agents who complained about white favoritism were fired. Although blacks did benefit from national relief, they often stood last in line. The New Deal left blacks to fight for their share through local politics, where their rewards were meager.

With these frustrations as background, A. Philip Randolph, the shrewd president of the Brotherhood of Sleeping Car Porters, introduced a new tactic in the fight for black rights. Early in 1941, as the economy was mobilizing for war, Randolph rallied blacks throughout the nation for a mass march on Washington that would publicize America's racial discrimination around the world and possibly disrupt the early stages of war production. Randolph's price for canceling the march was President Roosevelt's intervention in behalf of black workers. Despite his irritation at Randolph's threat, Roosevelt on June 25, 1941, issued a precedent-setting executive order that banned discriminatory hiring "because of race, creed, color, or national origin," both within the national government and throughout its expanding network of war-related contracts. The executive order also established the Fair Employment Practices Committee (FEPC) to oversee these rules.

But it was the need for labor, not the weak FEPC,

VARIETIES IN BLACK LEADERSHIP

A flourishing black culture in the 1920s spread in many directions. Langston Hughes's softly singing poetry was one voice in the Harlem Renaissance. Black nationalism found a spectacular leader in the fiery Marcus Garvey. A. Philip Randolph, who organized the black railroad workers in the 1920s, won a striking victory for fair employment practices from President Roosevelt in 1941. Marching in suit and tie, he continued the drive for black rights at the Democratic convention of 1948. *(Right, National Portrait Gallery, Smithsonian Institution, Gift of W. Tjark Reiss in memory of his father; below, "Marcus Garvey in Regalia, 1924," Van Der Zee; left, United Press International, Inc.)*

that expanded economic opportunities for blacks during the war. Both in the war industries and in the armed services, Jim Crow rules weakened slightly under the pressure of an increasingly severe manpower shortage. However, racial tensions were mounting, especially over access to housing and public facilities in the swollen industrial areas of the large cities. During the summer of 1943 these emotions exploded from coast to coast in a series of violent racial encounters.

The worst of the riots occurred in Detroit, a primary center of war production, where 500,000 newcomers, including 60,000 blacks, had been squeezed in since 1940. On a hot Sunday in June 1943 a fight between teenage whites and blacks ignited two days of guerrilla warfare and widespread looting. Twenty-five blacks and nine whites were killed, hundreds wounded, and millions of dollars in property lost. By then, some Democrats were openly worrying about "the Negro vote." Yet every national election between 1936 and 1944 seemed to verify the political wisdom of Democratic policies. If blacks were really discontented, why did they vote as heavily Democratic as any other urban group? Wait until after the depression, the Roosevelt administration had told its black critics. Wait until after the war, it told them in the early 1940s.

After the war, black leaders insisted that the time was now. They had two reasons to feel some optimism. First, they were mobilizing far more support. During the war, membership in the NAACP rose from 50,000 to 450,000, and a growing number of northern whites joined the blacks in the fight for equal rights. This alliance produced a string of FEPC laws in New York, New Jersey, Massachusetts, Connecticut, and other states, and prepared the ground for a national campaign against racial discrimination. Second, the election of 1946, which returned Republican majorities in several northern states that had previously been Democratic, gave new force to the old argument of the NAACP. Black votes might indeed make the critical difference in a closely balanced national election.

Some claimed that in fact black votes did tip the scales for Truman in 1948. Nevertheless, the president muted the issue of civil rights during his second term, and Adlai Stevenson, the Democratic candidate in 1952, spoke more moderately on the subject than Truman had done. The NAACP turned its energies to the Supreme Court. In *Smith* v. *Allwright* (1944), the Court had outlawed all-white primary elections in the South. Then in *Sweatt* v. *Painter* (1950), it broadened an earlier ruling against segregated professional schools. The NAACP, behind its chief counsel, Thurgood Marshall, quietly prepared a legal assault on all segregated facilities.

Anticommunism.   The issue that most disrupted the existing balance between national and local policies at midcentury was not black rights but anticommunism. A new wave of antiradicalism began to build after 1935, when enemies of the New Deal accused it of adopting communist ideas, and patriotic groups attacked the public schools for teaching radical doctrines. The House Committee on Un-American Activities, established in 1938, gave lurid publicity to the charge that communists dominated the new industrial unions. Congress captured the spirit of this vague antiradicalism in the Smith Act of 1940, which set criminal penalties for teaching or advocating violent revolution, or for belonging to an organization that did either. Despite America's wartime alliance with the Soviet Union, anticommunist rhetoric remained fairly common during the early 1940s, and immediately after the war the House Committee on Un-American Activities and numerous state antisubversive committees moved into action against an ever-widening range of expected dangers. For the next decade, clouds of uncertainty enveloped thousands of Americans who had once advocated a reform and left a record, or who had made an enemy. As one historian noted, "A perverse kind of democracy was practiced: all accusations, no matter from whom, were taken equally seriously." Reputations, friendships, and careers popped like bubbles at the prick of the charge, "Communist!"

In 1947 the Truman administration declared international communism the enemy of the United States. Prominent Americans of both parties echoed the alarm. Throughout the nation—in government, in the labor unions, in the communications industries, in public and private education—a variety of oaths and reviews screened those who were suspected of communist sympathies. The Justice Department, using both the Smith Act and a new Internal Security Act of 1950, prosecuted some members of the Communist party and forced the rest to disband. After a dramatic series of public hearings, Alger Hiss, once a respected official in the State Department, was convicted of perjury in January 1950 for denying that he had passed government information to a Soviet agent. In June came the shock of the Korean War, followed by arrests that eventually led to the execution of Julius and Ethel Rosenberg as Soviet spies. America seemed to be a monolith of anticommunism.

But within this apparent consensus lay two profoundly different kinds of anticommunism. One, which appeared in strength around 1947, sought to defend the United States against an international challenge: the Soviet Union, the league of communist countries it headed, and the espionage system it directed. Abroad, this anticommunism tried to contain the power of the Soviet Union. At home, it concentrated above all on communists in government, because the enemy's agent at a crucial spot in the government could seriously damage the nation's defense. Hence, the revelations about Alger Hiss greatly aggravated these worries.

The other anticommunism expressed the fears and frustrations of the average American. To them, communism concerned with local affairs was a pervasive web of dangers that might appear in the guise of atheism, sexual freedoms, strange accents, civil rights, or whatever most threatened a particular group's sense of security. Although this anticommunism was also concerned with national defense and international conflict, it equated these issues with threats to local cultural and moral standards. The actual sources of danger might well be some of the leaders in national politics. Splintered, diffuse, and eruptive, this was the truly popular anticommunism.

These two anticommunisms, one emphasizing power and the other emphasizing sin, were distinctly different. From a national vantage point, the many state and local committees that in the name of anti-communism attacked textbooks and library catalogues and civil libertarians were part of an aimless witch-hunt. What possible relevance could these matters have to an international contest with Soviet communism? As one lawyer summarized the work of the Broyles Commission in Illinois, it "almost completely skirted . . . the operations of the Communist party in Illinois," and it failed totally "to cover evidence of actual subversion within the state." But such committees in Illinois, California, New York, Maryland, and elsewhere were not looking for that kind of communism. As the Broyles Commission stated, "Liberalism" was its enemy, and the educational system, the commission's primary target, was an excellent place to begin the battle. Sophisticated "Eastern internationalists" in the State Department were an equally logical target.

McCarthyism.   In February 1950, a month after the conviction of Alger Hiss, an undistinguished first-term Republican senator from Wisconsin, Joseph McCarthy, elbowed forward to make anticommunism his personal crusade. For more than four years, this canny politician frightened government officials with charges of communist infiltration in their departments, staged melodramatic investigations of suspected enemy agents, exercised a powerful influence over government appointments, and won a nationwide following. McCarthy was the first politician to make effective use of national television, both in interviews and in broadcasts of his investigations. According to a poll early in 1954, three out of five Americans with an opinion about McCarthy favored his activities.

McCarthy opened his campaign by claiming he had a list of authentic communists who were still employed by the State Department. Some thought he said 205. The senator later settled on 57. During Truman's administration McCarthy continued a scattergun attack on the State Department and helped to make "communism" a noisy issue in the elections of 1952. After Eisenhower's inauguration, McCarthy broadened his anticommunist fire until finally he hit the army itself early in 1954. Few politicians cared to risk an encounter with the Wisconsin slugger,

SENATOR JOSEPH MCCARTHY
UNDER A HALO OF LIGHTS AND
HIS AIDE ROY COHN AT THE
ARMY-MCCARTHY HEARINGS
IN 1954
To millions of Americans in
the early fifties, these were
fearless patriots who defended
the nation against an in-
sidious network of commu-
nists. *(Wide World Photos, Inc.)*

because McCarthy quickly acquired a reputation for defeating his political enemies at the polls. Eisenhower also refused to engage him, saying privately, "I will not get into the gutter with that guy."

The key to McCarthy's success was his ability to use the national issue of communists in government as a source of strength in the Senate, and the local issue of domestic subversion as a source of strength among millions of citizens. McCarthy repeatedly claimed that the sole purpose of his investigations was the exposure of communists in government, and after the Hiss conviction, no one in Washington could lightly dismiss that possibility. As cool a head as Senator Taft endorsed McCarthy's freewheeling search for spies. When McCarthy failed to find any Soviet agents, however, he shifted his attack to the books that his suspects had written, the reforms that they had supported, and the people who had associated with them. McCarthy invariably identified communism as "Godless" and usually discovered its American disciples among the wellborn, well educated, and well placed.

Despite the special attention that McCarthy at-

tracted, others used even more extreme language. In 1952 Senator William Jenner of Indiana declared, "I charge that this country today is in the hands of a secret inner coterie which is directed by agents of the Soviet Union." Democrats, including Truman, made important contributions to the harsh anticommunist climate. What set "McCarthyism" apart was capacity to bring a rough-hewn version of local politics inside the national government. Violating the customary procedures of the Senate, McCarthy impugned the personal integrity of his critics and called them "gutless." The State Department, instead of selecting officials for their knowledge and skills, had to listen when it was told to "get rid of the alienminded radicals and moral perverts."

Years of such confusion in the standards of government eventually became intolerable. When McCarthy attacked the upper echelons of the army in 1954, his growing opposition in Washington began to organize. The senator and his aides did not fare well in a televised series of "Army-McCarthy" hearings. In August 1954 the Senate created a select committee to review charges of senatorial misconduct against McCarthy, and that December, by a vote of 67 to 22, his colleagues condemned him for his abuse of the Senate's rules. Without authority in the Senate, McCarthy faded into obscurity.

McCarthyism was simultaneously unique and representative. The special style of the Wisconsin senator and the special circumstances encouraging his success were passing matters. But the collision that McCarthyism caused between national and local politics would occur again and again in later years.

By 1954 the scope and significance of the national government had qualitatively changed since the 1920s. A long cycle of development had ended in the formulation of a worldwide policy for containing international communism and a fiscal system for managing the national economy. The centrality of the national government made it a magnet for almost every ambitious group in American society. If the government circled the globe to protect the American way from its international enemies, surely it also cared enough to defend the American way from its domestic enemies. If the national government could solve America's economic problems, surely it could also solve America's racial and cultural problems. The balance was tipping so rapidly toward Washington that the New Deal's compromise between national and local authority was in serious danger.

CHRONOLOGY

1941 Roosevelt bans racial discrimination in government and defense industry hiring.
      FDR, Churchill meet in Atlantic Conference to prepare Anglo-American alliance.

1942 Japanese Americans moved to "relocation centers."
      Revenue Act expands graduated income tax.
      Government wage, price, and rent controls established.
      Operation TORCH, Allied invasion of North Africa.
      American troops driven from Philippines.
      U.S. inflicts first major defeat on Japan at battle of Midway.

1943 Allied invasion of Italy.

1944 Operation OVERLORD, Allied invasion of France.
      Bretton Woods Conference on international monetary stabilization.
      Roosevelt reelected president, his fourth term.

1945 Yalta Conference.
      Roosevelt dies; Harry S Truman becomes president.
      UN charter signed by 47 nations.
      Germany surrenders.
      Potsdam Conference.
      U.S. drops atomic bombs on Hiroshima and Nagasaki in Japan.
      Japan surrenders.

1947 Truman Doctrine calls for containment of communism.
      Marshall Plan sends massive aid to Europe.
      Department of Defense and Central Intelligence Agency established by National Security Act.
      Taft-Hartley Act restricts actions of labor unions.

1948 Berlin blockaded by Soviets; U.S. organizes airlift.
      Truman elected president.

1949 NATO established.
      Soviet Union detonates atomic bomb.
      Communist government controls China.

1950 Alger Hiss convicted of perjury in relation to espionage charges.
      Senator Joseph McCarthy launches crusade against communists in government.
      Korean War begins.

1951 Twenty-Second Amendment limits presidents to two terms.

1952 Dwight D. Eisenhower elected president.

1953 Rosenbergs executed as spies.
      Armistice in Korea.

SUGGESTED READINGS

Gordon Wright, *The Ordeal of Total War, 1939–1945* (1968), gives an overview of the European theater during the Second World War. A. Russell Buchanan, *The United States in World War II* (2 vols., 1964), details America's military activities in both the European and the Pacific theaters; and Martha Byrd Hoyle, *A World in Flames* (1970), covers them more briefly. A famous naval historian, Samuel Eliot Morison, tells of the conflict at sea in *The Two-Ocean War* (1963). Morison's *Strategy and Compromise* (1958) and Kent Roberts Greenfield's *American Strategy in World War II: A Reconsideration* (1963) evaluate broad questions of military policy. Forrest C. Pogue, *George C. Marshall* (3 vols. to date, 1963–73), has followed the career of Roosevelt's chief of staff to 1945. Stephen E. Ambrose, *The Supreme Commander: The War Years of General Dwight D. Eisenhower* (1970), contains valuable insights. On foreign relations, Gaddis Smith's *Diplomacy during the Second World War, 1941–1945* (1965) is a convenient introduction. Herbert Feis, *Churchill, Roosevelt, and Stalin* (1957), and Robert Beitzell, *The Uneasy Alliance: America, Britain, and Russia, 1941–1943* (1972), examine the critical issues besetting the grand alliance.

Three fine books—Diane Shaver Clemens, *Yalta* (1970), Robert A. Divine, *Second Chance: The Triumph of Internationalism in America during World War II* (1967), and Michael Sherry, *Preparing for the Next War: American Plans for Postwar Defense, 1941–45* (1977)—chart paths into the postwar years. William Roger Louis, *Imperialism at Bay: The United States and the Decolonization of the British Empire* (1978), is also useful. For the development of the atomic bomb, see Richard G. Hewlett and Oscar E. Anderson, *The New World* (1962). Martin J. Sherwin, *A World Destroyed* (1975), and Barton J. Bernstein (ed.), *The Atom Bomb* (1976), explore its international implications.

Specifically on the president's leadership, the concluding volume of James MacGregor Burns's biography, *Roosevelt: The Soldier of Freedom* (1970), and Robert Dallek, *Franklin D. Roosevelt and American Foreign Policy, 1932–1945* (1979), are basic. Robert Divine's *Roosevelt and World War II* (1969) is a keen and generally favorable appraisal. Valuable material on two of Roosevelt's advisers appears in Robert E. Sherwood, *Roosevelt and Hopkins* (rev. ed., 1950), and John Morton Blum, ed., *From the Morgenthau Diaries: Years of War, 1941–1945* (1967). Lloyd C. Gardner, *Architects of Illusion: Men and Ideas in American Foreign Policy, 1941–1949* (1970), is a perceptive essay on the men who won

control of America's postwar foreign policy; and Thomas G. Paterson, ed., *Cold War Critics: Alternatives to American Foreign Policy in the Truman Years* (1971), is a collection of essays on the men who lost. Additional information on the shapers of American policy appears in George Curry, "James F. Byrnes," in Vol. 14 of *American Secretaries of State and Their Diplomacy* (1965), Robert H. Ferrell, *George C. Marshall* (1966), which is Vol. 15 of the same series, Gaddis Smith, *Dean Acheson* (1972), which is Vol. 16, and Arnold A. Rogow, *James Forrestal* (1964), a study of the first secretary of defense. The writings of participants themselves include these particularly useful books: Dean Acheson, *Present at the Creation* (1969), Lucius Clay, *Decision in Germany* (1950), George F. Kennan, *Memoirs, 1925–1950* (1967), and Arthur H. Vandenberg, Jr., ed., *The Private Papers of Senator Vandenberg* (1952).

The history of the Cold War is a caldron of controversy. Two judicious guides are John Lewis Gaddis, *The United States and the Origins of the Cold War, 1941–1947* (1972), which tends to justify American policies, and Walter LaFeber, *America, Russia, and the Cold War, 1945–1971* (1972), which tends to criticize them. For a pungent taste of the battle, however, read on the one hand Herbert Feis, *From Trust to Terror: The Onset of the Cold War, 1945–1950* (1970), the last in his series of volumes explaining modern American diplomacy; and on the other hand Gabriel Kolko, *The Politics of War: The World and United States Foreign Policy, 1943–1945* (1968), and Joyce and Gabriel Kolko, *The Limits of Power: The World and United States Foreign Policy, 1945–1954* (1972), a thorough condemnation of Washington's policies.

Several careful studies add substantially to our knowledge of the crucial issues dividing the United States and the Soviet Union: Lynn Etheridge Davis, *The Cold War Begins: Soviet-American Conflict over Eastern Europe* (1974), George C. Herring, Jr., *Aid to Russia, 1941–1946* (1973), Bruce Kuklick, *American Policy and the Division of Germany* (1972), and especially Thomas G. Paterson, *Soviet-American Confrontation* (1973). On problems that hardened the pattern of the Cold War, see Joseph I. Lieberman, *The Scorpion and the Tarantula: The Struggle to Control Atomic Weapons, 1945–1949* (1970), W. Phillips Davison, *The Berlin Blockade* (1958), and Robert E. Osgood, *NATO* (1962).

The origins and the course of America's postwar policy in East Asia are discussed in Akira Iriye's very perceptive *The Cold War in Asia* (1974), Kenneth E. Shewmaker's

Americans and Chinese Communists, 1927–1945 (1971), and Tang Tsou's *America's Failure in China, 1941–1950* (1963). For the background to the Korean War, see Leland M. Goodrich, *Korea: A Study of U.S. Policy in the United Nations* (1956). The policy struggles accompanying the war are discussed in John W. Spanier, *The Truman-MacArthur Controversy and the Korean War* (1959), and Trumbull Higgins, *Korea and the Fall of MacArthur* (1960). The indefatigable journalist I. F. Stone raises some intriguing questions in *Hidden History of the Korean War* (1952).

The domestic side of the Second World War has received much less attention from historians. Richard Polenberg, *War and Society: The United States, 1941–1945* (1972), provides a useful overview, and John Morton Blum, *V Was for Victory: Politics and American Culture during World War II* (1976), offers penetrating insights. Joel Seidman, *American Labor from Defense to Reconversion* (1953), deals primarily with government policy. On the other hand, William Henry Chafe, *The American Woman: Her Changing Social, Economic, and Political Roles, 1920–1970* (1972), includes a valuable discussion of women in the wartime economy. Roland A. Young, *Congressional Politics in the Second World War* (1956), reviews the legislative record. On specific laws, Davis R. B. Ross, *Preparing for Ulysses* (1969), explains the GI Bill, and Stephen K. Bailey, *Congress Makes a Law* (1957), analyzes the Full Employment Act.

A growing literature examines the place of racial minorities in modern America. Two surveys—John Hope Franklin, *From Slavery to Freedom* (3rd ed., 1969), and August Meier and Elliott M. Rudwick, *From Plantation to Ghetto* (rev. ed., 1970)—ably cover the years after 1920. Nathan Irvin Huggins, *Harlem Renaissance* (1971), minimizes the cultural significance of its subject. On the very different aspirations of Marcus Garvey and his followers, the best assessments are E. David Cronon, *Black Moses* (1955), and Thomas G. Vincent, *Black Power and the Garvey Movement* (1971). St. Clair Drake and Horace R. Cayton, *Black Metropolis* (2 vols., rev. ed., 1962), remains a valuable study of the Chicago ghetto. Raymond Wolters, *Negroes and the Great Depression* (1970), tells a grim story of the early thirties, and Dan T. Carter's smoothly written *Scottsboro* (1969) recounts the most notorious abuse of justice in the South during that decade. The most important organizations serving blacks are discussed in Langston Hughes, *Fight for Freedom: The Story of the NAACP* (1962), and Nancy J. Weiss, *The National Urban League, 1910–1940* (1974). Also see Walter White's autobiography, *A Man Called White* (1948). Richard M. Dalfiume's *Desegregation of the United States Armed Forces*

(1969), traces the most striking public gain for blacks during the Truman years. In *Black Bourgeoisie* (1957), E. Franklin Frazier offers a sharp analysis of relatively well-to-do blacks. Roger Daniels, *Concentration Camps, USA* (1971), is a brief study of the persecution of Japanese Americans during the Second World War; Jacobus ten Broek *et al.*, *Prejudice, War and the Constitution* (1954), provides many of the details; and Michi Weglyn, *Years of Infamy* (1976), expresses the feelings of the prisoners.

Although there is no authoritative account of Harry Truman's administration, Cabell Phillips, *The Truman Presidency* (1966), is a reasonable introduction. Merle Miller, *Plain Speaking: An Oral Biography of Harry S Truman* (1974), helps in understanding the president's quality of mind. A considerably more sophisticated study, Alonzo L. Hamby's *Beyond the New Deal: Harry S Truman and American Liberalism* (1973), analyzes the place of the Truman administration in a modern democratic tradition. A good place to begin exploring the election of 1948 is Samuel Lubell, *The Future of American Politics* (1952). Susan M. Hartmann, *Truman and the 80th Congress* (1971), covers important background in Washington. The meaning of Henry A. Wallace's third-party candidacy is evaluated in Norman D. Markowitz, *The Rise and Fall of the People's Century* (1973), and Allen Yarnell, *Democrats and Progressives* (1974). V. O. Key, Jr., *Southern Politics in State and Nation* (1949), is a mine of information on its subject, and Robert A. Garson, *The Democratic Party and the Politics of Sectionalism, 1941–1948* (1974) is a useful supplement. On particular areas of public policy, William C. Berman, *The Politics of Civil Rights in the Truman Administration* (1970), and Richard O. Davies, *Housing Reform during the Truman Administration* (1966), are both careful studies. Allen J. Matusow's *Farm Policies and Politics in the Truman Years* (1967) makes a thorough assessment in its field. More critical appraisals of the president appear in Barton J. Bernstein, ed., *Politics and Policies of the Truman Administration* (1970), especially the essays by Bernstein himself.

The best source on the growing Republican challenge to the Democrats is James T. Patterson's appreciative biography of Robert A. Taft, *Mr. Republican* (1972). Herbert S. Parmet, *Eisenhower and the American Crusades* (1972), is a good general account of the Eisenhower presidency, and Gary W. Reichard, *The Reaffirmation of Republicanism* (1975), contains a fuller examination of Eisenhower's early years in office. *The Ordeal of Power* (1963), a thoughtful appraisal of Eisenhower's presidency by Emmet John Hughes, is also most valuable on the early years. The momentous changes in the government's fiscal powers and policies are discussed in Herbert Stein, *The Fiscal Revolution in America* (1969). For a dissent from the new fiscal orthodoxy, see Milton Friedman and Anna J. Schwartz, *A Monetary History of the United States, 1867–1960* (1963).

No domestic subject since the New Deal has attracted such scholarly attention as the anticommunist issue after the Second World War. Robert Griffith and Athan Theoharis, eds., *The Specter: Original Essays on the Cold War and the Origins of McCarthyism* (1974), Earl Latham, *The Communist Controversy in Washington* (1966), and Walter Gellhorn, ed., *The States and Subversion* (1952), suggest the wide range of topics and interests that were involved. Athan Theoharis, *Seeds of Repression* (1971), and Richard M. Freeland, *The Truman Doctrine and the Origins of McCarthyism* (1972),

place a heavy responsibility for the rise of popular anticommunism on the Truman administration, and Alan D. Harper, *The Politics of Loyalty: The White House and the Communist Issue, 1946–1952* (1969), significantly tempers that judgment. Robert Griffith, *The Politics of Fear* (1970), analyzes McCarthy's sources of power in the Senate. In *The Intellectuals and McCarthy* (1967), Michael Paul Rogin blames conservative academicians for inflating the record of McCarthy's popular appeal, and Mary Sperling McAuliffe, *Crisis on the Left: Cold War Politics and American Liberals, 1947–1954* (1978), traces the capitulation of her subjects. On the most sensational espionage cases, see Walter and Miriam Schneir, *Invitation to an Inquest* (1965), which explores the Rosenberg case, and Allen Weinstein, *Perjury! The Hiss-Chambers Conflict* (1978).

Modern Culture

*T*he 1920s revolutionized the personal experiences of a great many Americans. The automobile, now within the range of the average person's pocketbook, dramatically expanded the scope of the immediate environment. People who had never traveled fifty miles from their home towns were now discovering a wider world and coming home with different points of view. Through extended and improved telephone services, they wove wider networks of family, friendship, and community ties. Radio and motion pictures, too, brought another dimension to their lives. The voices from the radio and faces on the screen generated a new environment, a synthetic world of familiarity and trust in which no personal participation was necessary, or even possible.

In a distinctively modern way, millions now felt more intimately involved with people they would never meet than with the people next door. Once this cultural revolution was under way, neither depression nor war significantly altered its course. Even in hard times, Americans clung tenaciously to their cars and telephones, and as soon as they could afford to, bought a second car and installed an extension phone. Although movie audiences declined slightly during the thirties, the sale of radios increased, and both media boomed in the forties.

Rapid standardization in production created an illusion of American homogeneity. By 1930 three automobile manufacturers—General Motors, Ford, and Chrysler—manufactured 83 percent of the nation's automobiles. Soon they would be synchronizing industry-wide changes in car styles.

The formation of the National Broadcasting Company in 1926 and the Columbia Broadcasting System in 1927 superimposed national network programming over the previously decentralized radio industry, and after 1927 the total number of stations declined. In the fall of 1931, one-third of the population listened weekly to the comedy, "Amos 'n' Andy." A flourishing industry of advertising had Americans everywhere humming the jingles for Campbell's soup and Rinso soap. Hollywood films issued from a handful of gigantic studios such as Warner Brothers and Metro-Goldwyn-Mayer.

THE PROUD CONSUMERS
In the 1920s the radio revolutionized mass communication in America as countless citizens gathered around their radio sets every evening to "tune in" to their favorite programs. (Brown Brothers)

Yet in important ways this standardizing process actually sharpened the division in American society. Among people who were already like-minded, it strengthened common, nationwide standards. Between groups with very different ways of life, however, it increased an awareness of competing values, hardened antagonistic stereotypes, and focused cultural conflicts on a national scale which in earlier times had been diffused across a more loosely integrated society. One common thread did run through almost all of these groups: a concern for the fate of the individual in an organized, mechanized society. Nevertheless, the many contrasting responses that evolved between 1920 and midcentury only accentuated the diversity in modern American culture.

Modern Values

Among the messages coming from America's modern centers of communication was a new model of the good life. As the modern state developed, it became more and more necessary for specialized tasks to be performed efficiently. Specialists in such business-related occupations as management, banking, merchandising, and advertising and in such professions as law, medicine, engineering, and economics became so important to the political economy that to achieve success in any of these careers was in itself to achieve prestige. In the 1920s approximately 3 million Americans had the skills, or the success, to belong to these high ranks. In addition, as the nation's population grew during the twenties from 106,466,000 to 123,077,000—or about 15 percent—the number of white-collar workers rose 40 percent to over 14 million. Many of these white-collar workers also thought of themselves as part of a specialized economic system.

Freedom to Enjoy. The greater the emphasis on occupational success, the less people felt bound by traditional rules of behavior. What happened away from work increasingly belonged to a separate realm of individual discretion. From this crucial division of occupational life from private life came a new, often exhilarating freedom to enter the consumer market and simply enjoy oneself. During leisure hours, clothes became a matter of personal taste rather than an expression of solid character. The styles of the 1920s emphasized the modern freedom: new colors and patterns for men's clothing, the departure of corsets and hobbling long skirts for women. Both men and women now smoked casually in public, and cigarette sales climbed 250 percent during the decade. The symbol of the exciting new freedom was the "flapper." With hair bobbed, face painted and cigarette in hand, she airily waved good-bye to yesterday's rules. Her flattened breasts, loose-fitting clothes, and short skirt gave her the appearance of a modern Peter Pan, seizing the pleasure of the moment in the spirit of eternal youth.

Nothing more clearly announced a new attitude toward private freedom than the changing responses of successful Americans to Prohibition. In 1920 most prominent citizens dutifully endorsed the Eighteenth Amendment. During the twenties, however, they increasingly defected to the opposition, and by 1932 about three-fourths of the readers of *Literary Digest*, a rough index to the opinion of successful Americans, favored repeal of Prohibition. Their reasoning was simple. By making illegal an act that millions refused to consider wrong, Prohibition artificially created a new class of criminals, spread disrespect for the law, and then increased taxes to pay for the enforcement of the law. On the surface, it was a weak argument. Many other unpopular laws increased the crime rate and were far more expensive to police. Because the enforcement of Prohibition was always haphazard, its cost had little effect on taxes. People who favored repeal assumed that the use of alcohol simply did not matter very much. Prohibition, according to the industrialist Pierre du Pont, was "a nuisance and menace"—or, more accurately, a menace *because* it was merely a nuisance. To him, and millions of others, drinking should be a question of individual choice.

As the areas of private discretion expanded, leisure in general came to have a new meaning. Leisure activities no longer had to be justified as morally beneficial but were simply considered good ways for people to release their tensions and return refreshed to their jobs. Between 1919 and 1929 Americans' expenditures for recreation more than doubled. The best expression of the new meaning of leisure was the annual vacation, a period of time set aside specifically for relaxation. Once the prerogative of a very small, prosperous minority, the annual vacation became widely accepted during the twenties. Early in the decade, according to a study by the sociologists Robert and Helen Lynd, most white-collar employees in Muncie, Indiana, assumed for the first time in their lives that they had a right to an annual vacation, and many received one with pay. Increasing numbers used the expanding National Park Service for those vacations. Parks were recognized as a valuable public facility, where the nation's city dwellers could turn once a year for their revitalization.

Changing Morals. A higher premium on personal freedom meant a lower premium on traditional morals. Although church membership increased a striking 31 percent between 1916 and 1926, so did the emphasis in white-collar congregations on a soothing, largely undemanding religion that stressed good human relations rather than sin and salvation. Not every liberal Protestant welcomed Bruce Barton's best-selling *The Man Nobody Knows* (1925), which transformed Jesus into a vigorous executive who had taken "twelve men from the bottom ranks of business and forged them into an organization that conquered the world." Nevertheless, few liberal Protestants during the twenties expressed much concern of any kind for theological details or even denominational distinction. To many of them, Catholicism now seemed less an evil religion than an odd but purely private choice. The anti-Catholic furor surrounding Al Smith's presidential campaign in 1928 simply made no sense from the new, liberal Protestant perspective.

Nor did the long-standing association between sex and sin. During the twenties, a variety of psychologists, including the American disciples of Sigmund Freud, told Americans to consider sex a human need to satisfy: the more complete the satisfaction, the healthier the individual. Repression and guilt only warped the personality. Public displays of affection did not, as in the past, imply loose morals. Even premarital sex was a legitimate subject for discussion. Margaret Sanger, America's pioneer advocate of birth control who had once been scorned in respected circles, now won the approval and even the financial support of many well-to-do Americans. Though too much "petting" remained a parental worry and any hint of "free love" was sharply condemned, sex emerged in the twenties as a subject for rational examination instead of moral taboo.

Urban Values in the Twenties.   The new values concerning recreation, religion, and sex found their strongest support in metropolitan areas. During the 1920s cities of 100,000 or over grew more than twice as fast as the population as a whole. White-collar workers, whose numbers were increasing at about the same rate, congregated in and around these cities and reinforced one another's values. An urban way of life became the ideal, and they used it to judge the rest of the nation. Instead of praising the education given at the little red schoolhouses in the countryside, urban educators recommended that these schools be consolidated to lower costs and modernize instruction. At the University of Chicago, sociologists declared the urban family emotionally healthier than the rural family. The farther that life was removed from the styles of the big city, the less attractive it appeared. The descriptions of the small town as a prison in Sherwood Anderson's *Winesburg, Ohio* (1919) and Sinclair Lewis's *Main Street* (1920) met a warm reception from urban readers.

The new urban standard was particularly hard in its judgment of the South. In 1925 Henry L. Mencken, critic, essayist, and high priest of the new urban culture, visited Dayton, Tennessee, to report on the trial of a high school biology instructor, John Scopes, who had broken a state law by teaching Darwin's theory of evolution. Because the trial pitted the famous criminal lawyer Clarence Darrow against William Jennings Bryan, the aging champion of evangelical Protestanism, it became a national spectacle.

An urban audience, unable to comprehend why anyone would legislate against science, treated the Scopes trial like a carnival of freaks. As Mencken described the "anthropoid rabble" of Tennessee protecting themselves "from whatever knowledge violated their superstitions" and climaxing an outdoor religious revival with a sex orgy, the modern carica-

ture of the South was taking shape. Sharecropping, soil leaching, and unmechanized farming retarded southern agriculture. A crude racism seemed to dominate its society, and a narrow Protestant theology seemed to tyrannize its spirit. Support for Prohibition and opposition to Al Smith thrived there. When Erskine Caldwell's *Tobacco Road* appeared in 1932, many Americans were already prepared to accept this account of a stunted life on Georgia's barren soil as a picture of the true South.

Modern Families and Careers

Modern values also reshaped the role of the family in American life. In the white-collar world around the cities, occupations were the primary source of men's prestige; their reputations were created in their offices. So extramarital sex, especially in the large cities, became increasingly acceptable. In Sinclair Lewis's *Babbitt* (1922), the hero could have a brief affair without damaging his career, even in the small fictional city of Zenith. Wives, however, were expected to counter their husbands' drift away from the family. Advertisements promised housewives miraculous results from better dinners, cleaner houses, or any number of enticing domestic surprises. Newspaper advice columns revealed how to soothe a tense, weary man at the end of the workday. Accompanying the new explicitness about sex, a thriving cosmetics industry encouraged wives to enhance their charms as a means of holding husbands within the home.

Changing Family Roles.   Unlike the nineteenth century wife who had been solemnly charged with preserving society's morals, her modern counterpart had no such high responsibilities. In a system of values that honored expertise, her talents as a homemaker could never compete with the claims of business and the professions despite the national promotion of a "science" of home economics. As women's traditional sphere shrank, however, other opportunities beckoned. "Bedroom towns"—the residential areas from which men commuted daily to their downtown offices—became uniquely female

Her first Cigarette

Her first Cocktail

Her first red kiss

Learning to flirt

A seasoned vamp

An accomplished necker

FLAMING YOUTH
featuring
COLLEEN MOORE

HOLLYWOOD DREAMS
Behind the fantasy of this movieland poster lay important changes in public behavior that sharpened the conflict between modern and traditional values and institutionalized the "adolescent rebellion." *(The Wisconsin Center for Theatre Research)*

domains, where women moved and talked and acted much as they chose during the daytime hours. Under radically less surveillance than their grandmothers had experienced, they purchased most of the food and clothing for their families, and consequently their preferences had a powerful influence on the local consumer market.

Modern mothers and fathers reared their children to enter the same kind of occupationally oriented world in which they lived. The home, it was assumed, could provide very little of the knowledge that children would later need to make their way in twentieth-century society. Modern Americans looked outside the home for expert advice on almost every subject, from the family car to balancing the family budget. In the *Reader's Digest*, founded in 1922, and *Time*, in 1923, parents could find convenient, expert summaries of the latest news about their contemporary world. Hence, as parents, they were expected to be intermediaries between their children and an array of specialists who claimed to know all about their children's psyches, health, and education.

Because parents had a relatively small part in equipping their children for successful adult careers, they had to prepare their sons and daughters to accept directions from outside the home. In the twenties and thirties parents were warned against the dangers of an excessive emotional attachment to their children or a domineering authority over them. Mothers heard about the perils of the Oedipus complex. Manuals on child care gave specific instructions on cuddling and comforting to avoid psychological "invalidism." Playwrights such as Sidney Howard and Tennessee Williams made the clutching, overbearing mother a central character in the American theater. In the movies of the 1930s and 1940s, such actors as Lewis Stone and Spencer Tracy modeled the modern role of the father: a superficially gruff, basically agreeable man who footed the bills, fussed with his pride, and eventually allowed the children to have their way.

The critical phase in the children's preparation for adulthood occurred during adolescence. Beginning in the 1920s, a well-developed and widely publicized youth culture provided adolescents with means of rebelling against their parents and declaring themselves ready for the occupational world. Along some sensitive frontier of values—sex during the 1920s, for example, or social reform during the 1930s —adolescents stepped just across the adult boundary and derided their lagging parents. They developed their own car culture of jalopies, drag racing, and mobile units for necking and drinking. Dividing the age groups further, adolescents adopted their own jargon, dances, and dress. Unlike the square dances and waltzes of the nineteenth century in which people of all ages participated, the Charleston in the 1920s and jitterbugging in the 1930s and 1940s required such limber joints that older people risked catastrophe if they tried them. Young men dressed in outlandish clothes that would have made their fathers look foolish. Young women chose sufficiently revealing ones to contrast their firm flesh with mothers' signs of age. Modern parents not only subsidized the youth culture; they were told to worry if their children did not fully participate.

Expanding Influence of the Schools.   At each stage in child-rearing, schools exercised a greater and greater influence. During the twenties and thirties, the public school system underwent a considerable expansion and adaptation. The elementary grades, which changed the least, increasingly served as feeders into the high schools, now important institutions in their own right. Enrollment in high schools doubled during the 1920s, and then rose another 50 percent during the 1930s. In 1920 one-sixth of America's adult population had high school diplomas; in 1940 one-half held them. Indeed, secondary education became so significant to white-collar families that some of them chose places to live on the basis of the local high school's reputation. The Winnetka System under Carleton Washburne, for example, made that Illinois community nationally famous. A major educational study in 1945 likened the modern high school to the old village church.

What modern families sought in a school system was a combination of instruction in the basic skills and socialization for modern America. The current trends in "progressive" education favored precisely

this combination. The modern high school tried to prepare young minds, as one committee of educational experts stated in 1929, "to be suited to the changing situations" of modern society. Therefore, the more progressive high schools taught general methods of thinking and a general open-mindedness rather than a specific body of truths and moral absolutes.

If young people could make a successful adjustment in high school, it was assumed, they would be prepared for a happy, rewarding life in modern America. Aptitude tests and counseling centers, both suddenly prominent in the high schools of the 1920s, guided them into the proper occupational areas or, for increasing numbers, to college for further specialization. Those who then entered the best white-collar occupations had the satisfaction of discovering that they had acquired a superior mental power. According to a variety of publicists during the twenties, individuals who mastered a specialty in business or the professions developed a general capacity for rational thought that placed them in a select minority. By implication, the majority of Americans, in Mencken's blunt but revealing term, were "boobs," a highly suggestive public that could be manipulated by a foresighted few.

Behaviorism as a Manipulative Force.   Along with this belief came a popular psychology called "behaviorism," which contained a simple, persuasive formula for mass manipulation. As psychologist John B. Watson explained the human personality, a clear stimulus produced a predictable response in the individual and when such stimuli were regularly repeated, a habit was established. With occasional reinforcement, this reaction became automatic. During the 1920s behaviorism became an article of faith among many Americans and gave them extraordinary confidence in their powers of social control. By using the right techniques, an expert in mass communication boasted, the rational minority could "regiment the masses according to our will without their knowing it."

A number of otherwise routine white-collar jobs, particularly selling, now seemed fraught with significance. The insights into mass manipulation even offered a fresh view of history. "Galileo failed because he was an investigator and not a salesman," one psychologist revealed in 1925. "Consequently, he could not get his goods marketed.... His competitors, Aristotle, Moses, and the church fathers, had monopolized the market, and their stockholders would not let him do business." Advertising developed into an especially honored field. A new group of experts in personnel management also used the same basic formula of mass manipulation to guarantee employers a loyal and productive work force.

Americans of many different persuasions accepted this assumption of a two-tiered society: a minority of manipulators and a mass to be manipulated. Neither liberal nor conservative, it simply came with America's modern values. What Republican businessmen in the 1920s applied to the sale of their goods, New Dealers in the 1930s applied to the sale of their reforms. By the Second World War, these habits of modern leadership were so ingrained that businessmen and reformers alike automatically went about the tasks of "selling" the war, "conditioning" the public for bad news from the battlefront, and experimenting with better ways to improve American "morale."

Response of the Traditionalists

From the lower of these two tiers, modern America looked quite different. Most people's jobs—in shops, on farms, in factories—did not belong in the specialized upper ranks of the economy and therefore brought very little national prestige. Moreover, mass communication made it impossible to ignore the disparity between their own lives and the lives of the most successful Americans. Millions of Americans with unskilled or routine jobs hoped that they, or their children, would eventually rise on the occupational ladder. Yet almost all of them found the modern values unacceptable to some degree. They lived by local values. In rural communities and city neighborhoods, people judged one another by family reputations, church preferences, work habits, and a variety

of other personal characteristics—standards that applied specifically to their own localities.

Local Values in a Modern Society. Resistance to the modern ways varied a great deal from place to place and even from person to person. During the twenties and thirties, in local pockets of opposition, particularly in the countryside, people repudiated the new values wholesale. Condemning the new liberalism in dressing, drinking, dancing, smoking, and sex, they refused to consider such behavior a matter of private choice and set firm rules against the modern hedonism. The most common agency of moral discipline was the church. A large majority of Protestant church members belonged to the evangelical denominations. Many Baptist and Methodist congregations, with a history of serious concern about their members' public behavior, banned the new ways as sins. Smaller bodies of Lutherans and Seventh-Day Adventists were even stricter about such practices as dancing and smoking.

From evangelical Protestantism came the political pressure behind Tennessee's anti-evolutionary law of 1925, which precipitated the famous Scopes trial. In other southern states as well, including Texas and Mississippi, state officials cooperated in keeping Darwin's theories out of the classroom. As the modern system parceled knowledge into a bewildering array of specialties, the Bible continued to provide local Americans with guidance for unifying and comprehending the basics of life. In the northern cities, the Catholic church often set its considerable weight against modern values, especially those on sex. As in the public schools in areas where evangelical Protestantism predominated, in the Catholic parochial system pupils were carefully instructed in religious morality. According to nationwide studies in the 1920s and 1930s, a majority of American schoolchildren were still receiving this kind of traditional, moral education.

Nevertheless, only a minority of Americans in a few localities totally rejected the new ways. A compromise between modern and traditional values was much more common. Almost all Americans wanted some share in the new culture, and a great many of

"CHURCH SUPPER," PAINTING BY JAMES B. TURNBULL

In reaction to modern values, millions of Americans idealized an older, simpler society that was rooted in the family, the church, and the community. *(Courtesy of Mr. & Mrs. Carroll Martin)*

them hoped to participate without feeling that it would corrupt them. At the beginning of the twenties, for example, sex was exploited so rampantly in motion pictures that a majority of state legislatures threatened to censor them. In 1922 the movie industry responded by creating the Hays Office, Hollywood's center for self-censorship, which designated what parts of the female anatomy had to be covered, decided what language was taboo, and determined justice must triumph in the end. These moral formulas created just the right aura of respectability. Without basically altering the movies, they appeased the critics and assured a mass audience.

Other mass media also enhanced their popularity by catering to traditional values. In magazines and newspapers, countless stories told of how the time-honored virtues of honesty, thrift, and perseverance had enabled ordinary people to weather their troubles and win in the end. To vast daytime audiences, such radio soap operas as "Ma Perkins' Family" and "Just Plain Bill" recounted the trials and tribulations of ordinary, small-town people who preserved their simple goodness under the most extraordinary hardships. Norman Rockwell's famous covers for the *Saturday Evening Post,* depicting the comforts of life in the family and the small town, ennobled many of the same traditional values.

In a traditional local setting, trusting other people

required a feeling of intimacy with them. Sunday supplements appealed to this need for intimacy with articles on the private lives and endearing habits of prominent Americans, and radio stations featured informal, personal interviews with a variety of otherwise anonymous leaders. The popularity of both Franklin and Eleanor Roosevelt benefited immeasurably from the warm, friendly personalities they communicated to a traditionalist public. The president's battle with polio, his hobbies, and his anecdotes, all gave indispensably human qualities to the nation's leader. Far more than had any other president's wife, Eleanor Roosevelt traveled throughout America to express her personal concern for the needs of its citizens. Her syndicated newspaper column, "My Day," an unpretentious account of her thoughts and affairs, significantly lessened the distance between the nation's First Lady and a large, attentive body of readers.

Conservative Responses to Depression. In the short run, the Great Depression contributed the most powerful, general force in behalf of traditional values. Immediately after the crash of 1929, Americans repudiated the twenties with such sweeping and intense rhetoric that its echoes still rang in the 1980s. People condemned the decade as frivolous, wasteful, and amoral, and believed that the economy could be revived through a reassertion of solid, old-fashioned common sense in their everyday lives. Skirt lengths dropped well below the knees, and women were lectured on their primary obligations inside the home. Public tolerance for innovative architecture, design, and music declined, and a simple realism in painting and sculpture became the vogue. After a burst of creativity in literature during the 1920s, the experimental novels of a major writer such as William Faulkner were largely ignored in the thirties, and Margaret Mitchell's nostalgic *Gone with the Wind* (1936) was the hit of the decade.

As Americans rejected the recent past, they looked back to earlier traditions that they could reaffirm. Thomas Jefferson and Walt Whitman, who were interpreted as simple, homespun democrats, enjoyed a surge of popularity. In *The Flowering of New England*

(1936), Van Wyck Brooks glorified the same antebellum literary heritage that he had dismissed so disdainfully twenty years before. A deepening sense of democracy at bay in a totalitarian world strengthened the conservative cast of this search for cultural roots. In direct contrast to the Wilsonian dream of democracy's global expansion, the nightmare of the thirties pictured America fighting firmly to preserve its traditions against the swelling currents of fascism and communism that were sweeping across Europe. Now was a time for bedrock values, not for trivial novelties. Then, as the Second World War revived the economy, the temporary constraints on cultural innovation disappeared, and traditionalists once again found themselves living in an atmosphere resonant with modern values.

The American Dream. Perhaps the most important need of those Americans whose jobs neither carried much prestige nor paid very well was some evidence that they could still succeed without abandoning their values. During the 1920s, an abundance of publicity assured them that the avenue upward was not only broad but especially well traveled by people of solid character and good habits. Salesmanship offered a particularly enticing route because it held out the prospect of success without a highly specialized training. Throughout the twenties, a popular passion for the salesman's skills was fed by numerous manuals, lectures, and correspondence courses that promised to reveal the secret of the art to any ambitious American. The example of certain businessmen encouraged hopes of an even more dramatic rise to riches. If immigrants such as utilities magnate Samuel Insull, banking king A. P. Giannini, and movie mogul Samuel Goldwyn could make it to the top, American society must still be rewarding the traditional virtues of hard work and high ambition.

No one's reputation benefited more grandly from such reasoning than Henry Ford's. Here was a country boy who had turned mechanical genius and dogged persistence into a fabulous fortune and international fame. He had mastered the modern economy so thoroughly that everyone came to him to learn the best techniques of mass production and distribution.

Yet he gave the appearance of a man who never capitulated to the slick ways around him. He attacked the evils of Wall Street, belittled the significance of higher education, and demanded strict moral standards from his workers. He could even give new values the sound of old truths: "One day some one brought to us a slogan which read: 'Buy a Ford and Save the Difference.' I crossed out the 'save' and inserted 'spend'—'Buy a Ford and Spend the Difference.' It is the wiser thing to do. Society lives by circulation, and not by congestion."

The depression irreparably damaged this American dream. After 1929 Ford's popularity declined drastically, and no businessman ever replaced him. Not even the prosperous 1940s revived the vision of a simple man's rise from humble origins to the pinnacle of the corporate system. The avenues to fame and fortune grew increasingly obscure. Dale Carnegie's phenomenally popular *How to Win Friends and Influence People* (1936), the counterpart for the 1930s of the salesmen's manuals of the 1920s, promised wonders for its readers if only they would master an elementary set of rules for tapping their inner resources. Yet unlike the literature of salesmanship, Carnegie's book was quite vague about where in modern society the ambitious but poor person should look for his success. A critical element of hope was dwindling in the lives of millions of Americans.

ERNEST HEMINGWAY PHOTOGRAPH BY MAN RAY, 1923
Hemingway's terse prose and lonely heroics had a powerful impact on modern literature. *(National Portrait Gallery, Smithsonian Institution, Washington D.C.)*

Dangers to the Individual

The dimming prospects for individual success were only one part of a large, complicated problem. How could people in any walk of life preserve their integrity in a nationalized, systematized society? Signs of a new concern for the individual were already appearing before 1920. The American Civil Liberties Union, which had originated as an emergency committee to defend dissenters during the First World War, remained after the war as a permanent center to protect the individual's freedom of speech, religion, assembly, and press under the First Amendment. Even before the war, America's most creative poets, Ezra Pound and T. S. Eliot, had moved to Europe, starting an exodus of young writers and artists who felt stifled by American culture. "A Lost Generation" was the way Gertrude Stein described these intellectual exiles. In 1920 America's greatest playwright, Eugene O'Neill, won the first of four Pulitzer Prizes for *Beyond the Horizon,* launching his long, agonizing exploration into the power of irrational forces over the individual's fate. From such scattered beginnings developed a broader and broader survey of the dangers for the individual in modern society.

The first danger to receive serious attention was the dehumanizing quality of modern society's organization. During the 1920s the best of the so-called antiwar novels—John Dos Passos's *The Three Soldiers* (1921), e e cummings's *The Enormous Room* (1922), and Ernest Hemingway's *A Farewell to Arms* (1929)—said relatively little about war itself. Instead, they used the war as a means of portraying the individual's jeopardy inside an impersonally mobilized society. In 1923 theater critics gave a warm reception to the American version of Karel Capek's play *R.U.R.*, introducing the robot as modern society's citizen, and to *The Adding Machine*, Elmer Rice's biting comedy on the effects of dull, routine work.

Of all the routine tasks in modern America, intellectuals considered work on the assembly line the most threatening to the individual. In fact, it was less wearing than harvesting fruit, less demanding than working in a sweatshop, and less dangerous than mining coal. But factory labor combined monotony and mechanization in a way that seemed especially dangerous to people who were already worried about modern society's depersonalization. After Sherwood Anderson had exposed the oppression of the small town in *Winesburg, Ohio*, he turned to the tyranny of the modern factory's assembly line. Henry Ford's plant produced cars at the price of humanity, the young pastor Reinhold Niebuhr bitterly recorded in his journal, and a company spokesman validated Niebuhr's fears: "[Ford] prefers machine-tool operators who . . . will simply do what they are told to do, over and over again from bell-time to bell-time. The Ford help need not even be able bodied." One of the most acclaimed scenes in an American movie was Charlie Chaplin's rebellion in *Modern Times* against the intolerable discipline of the assembly line and his glorious escape through a maze of giant gears and monstrous machinery. America's great challenge, the cultural critic Lewis Mumford wrote in 1934, was to make "the machine . . . our servant, not our tyrant." By the 1930s, it became commonplace for intellectuals to condemn everything about the factory as ugly and alien.

The Price of Success. Critics were also disturbed about an all-consuming passion for goods and money. The New Era, Suzanne La Follette acidly concluded, was testing the proposition "that human beings can live a generally satisfactory life . . . so long as they are kept powerfully under the spell of a great number of mechanical devices." During the 1920s old progres-

sives as dissimilar as the moralistic Westerner George Norris and the patrician Easterner Gifford Pinchot warned of the corrosive influence that the pursuit of money was having on American values. John Dos Passos made this corrupting passion a central theme in his powerful, rambling trilogy *USA* (1930–36). In the 1930s the nineteenth-century pioneers of corporate enterprise received the indelible label "robber barons."

No part of the nation's heritage suffered more severely at the hands of American writers than the success ethic, which such important novels as F. Scott Fitzgerald's *The Great Gatsby* (1925) and Theodore Dreiser's *An American Tragedy* (1925) attacked for its destructive effects on the individual. In *I'll Take My Stand* (1930), twelve southern intellectual writers, attacking the worship of money along with "the tempo of industrial life" and the cult of machinery, declared that their region's agrarian tradition offered the sole "defense of the individual" in modern America. To the surprise of both authors and publisher, the book won an enthusiastic national following.

As urgent as many of these critics sounded, they were rarely either desperate or radical. They located danger spots in America's industrial order. They usually cautioned the individual to keep a safe distance from modern society's most threatening centers. The individual's protection, in other words, was a calculated detachment. The clearest summary of this view appeared in Hemingway's *A Farewell to Arms*, in which Lieutenant Frederic Henry, an American who had volunteered for the Italian ambulance corps early in the First World War, watched the impersonal forces of the war devour more and more people around him. When they threatened to swallow him too, he deserted—a sane and courageous act, as Hemingway described it. Escaping to Switzerland, he found fulfillment briefly in a love affair with a nurse, Catherine Barkley. When her death left Frederic Henry absolutely alone, his core of inner strength enabled him to survive in an insensitive universe.

Calculated detachment, however, failed to satisfy a growing number of Americans who felt overwhelmed by the forces surrounding them. Their response to their feelings of powerlessness was an

CHARLIE CHAPLIN IN THE 1936 MOVIE "MODERN TIMES"
Charlie Chaplin, a Pied Piper for the working stiffs, romps through the dehumanizing machinery of a modern factory
(Culver Pictures, Inc.)

elaborate set of images and myths, a special culture of compensations that spun a dreamlike web of strength around the individual. During the depression, for example, a flood of advertisements promised men a way to achieve physical strength so great that no one would dare to challenge it. In the most famous of these appeals, a mail-order course in "Dynamic Tension," Charles Atlas, a huge man whose grotesquely developed muscles rippled from every ad,

disclosed that he had been "a ninety-seven-pound weakling" before he discovered the secret he would now divulge.

The new mass media presented a striking array of fantasies. Some were comic: Charlie Chaplin's carefree little tramp weaving his way among bullies and cops and puffing, pompous officials; a dutiful, intent Buster Keaton wheeling and spinning past impossible dangers to complete the appointed task;

the infinitely resilient pseudo-blacks in "Amos 'n' Andy," the most popular radio program of the 1930s, who were always scheming, always losing, but always ready to try again. Or the fantasies might be brutal. Following James Cagney's performance in the movie *Public Enemy* and Edward G. Robinson's in *Little Caesar*, an antihero cult developed in which the idol, with swaggering ruthlessness, cleared away every obstacle with a Tommy gun. The most popular fantasy of toughness continued to be the classic Western hero, brave and handsome, who killed faceless bad men in the good man's cause and faceless Indians in the white man's cause. During the Second World War, in the midst of bombs, tanks, and machine gun blasts, Hollywood's Westerner-as-GI even overcame the awesome threats of modern warfare.

Star Quality. America's new culture of compensation was also filled with images of an all-conquering power. As public restraints on the subject of sex relaxed, both the movies and the popular magazines spread a modern version of the traditional rags-to-riches tale. The hero in the nineteenth-century form of this tale had won the rich man's daughter through his sterling character and her father's approval. In the modern variation, however, physical charm alone catapulted the hero to the top. The rich man's daughter, finding the poor but virile man irresistible, convinced an angry father that she could not live without him. In the mirror image of this tale, a sexually charged Cinderella story, the poor but beautiful woman finally fell into the arms of a rich, adoring husband.

The "star" system that came to dominate the entertainment industry during the 1920s reflected this popular involvement with an all-conquering power. The stars themselves seemed to have such powers: the irresistible lover, Rudolph Valentino, thrilling millions of moviegoers; the "Galloping Ghost," Red Grange, scoring five touchdowns in one game; the courageous young Gertrude Ederle swimming the English Channel; even the publicized flagpole sitters staying awake and alive days on end.

Accentuating the personal qualities of success, Americans showed a strong preference for the idio-syncratic star who ignored many of the usual rules of the game. Fans loved the erratic slugger Jack Dempsey more than the boxing machine Gene Tunney, and the high-living, casual "Sultan of Swat," Babe Ruth, more than the intense, consistent batting champion Ty Cobb. In a crowded arena of eager competitors, success depended on a star's ability to attract public attention through a carefully staged, dramatic "event." J. Edgar Hoover, the perennially popular director of the Justice Department's Federal Bureau of Investigation, mastered the technique in a series of orchestrated manhunts for petty criminals, each of whom he spotlighted as "Public Enemy Number One," and an enthralled audience followed the real-life Hoover crime show, chapter by chapter.

Against this background Charles Lindbergh, the star of stars, rose to fame in the most dramatic event of the twenties. In May 1927, as liberally financed and elaborately organized competitors were stalled on the ground, this unknown pilot became the first person to complete a solo airplane flight from New York to Paris. Americans instantly made the quiet, handsome Midwesterner a national idol. Lindbergh's triumph, as millions interpreted it, was the accomplishment of an indomitable individual. Both literally and figuratively, the "Lone Eagle" had soared beyond the ordinary individual's constraints to purely personal success. Moreover, Lindbergh's sudden fame did not appear to affect his traditional virtues of modesty, simplicity, and self-reliance. Of all the stars, Lindbergh had the greatest popularity.*

The star system also encouraged Americans to picture themselves, or their children, leaping to fame and fortune. The entertainment world not only made its stars fabulously rich; it also seemed to reward them instantaneously. Stars, according to popular mythology, were "discovered." As the prospect of immediate success in business or the professions dimmed, boys dreamed of becoming athletes and girls actresses. The fewer alternatives they had, the

---

*The tragic kidnaping and death of Lindbergh's son produced a new surge of public interest in 1932. Then in 1941, Lindbergh's advocacy of a negotiated settlement with Hitler's Germany sharply diminished his popularity.

STARS

For Americans who felt trapped in modern society, the mass media offered visions of individual glory. Now the average American male could pretend he was Rudolph Valentino making love in "the Sheik's" exotic tent; feel the power of the bat as Babe Ruth sent one of his towering homers out of the park, or sit in the cockpit of Charles Lindbergh's "Spirit of St. Louis" and soar to fame as a transatlantic pilot. *(All, Brown Brothers)* more passionately they dreamed. In the late 1930s the black heavyweight boxing champion Joe Louis was almost worshiped in the black ghettos. In some urban neighborhoods, the kings of organized crime, who emerged in the 1920s with Prohibition, were equally compelling models of power and success.

The "Golden Years." One threat to the individual, the emptiness of old age, required a separate cluster of compensations. For two reasons, the problems of the aged were growing more severe in modern times. First, as the average life expectancy for an American rose from 47 years in 1900 to 58 years in 1950, the proportion of old people increased dramatically. Second, as the numbers increased, the sources of self-respect for the aged were shrinking. Wherever America's modern values prevailed, old people felt useless. Knowledge in a specialized society was supposed to be advancing too rapidly for an older generation to

master. Only the young could keep pace with America's highly technical and increasingly complex progress. As adults reached middle age, therefore, they had good reason to feel that their best years were behind them and that the future, which belonged to the young, opened a huge void before them.

Many older Americans earnestly set about the task of tricking the fates and staying young. The market thrived for bright clothes and beauty aids, cosmetic surgery and dentistry, wigs and elixirs. At the same time, a veil fell over the process of dying. Pictures of old people invariably showed them smiling, alert, and vigorous. A special literature, including Walter Pitkin's very popular *Life Begins at Forty* (1932), told Americans to think positively about their later years, and a multiplying number of settlements for old people, particularly in Florida and California, promised a happy, relaxed retirement for those who could afford to buy it. Despite these compensations, however, Americans occasionally heard a cry of resentment from their abandoned elders. During the 1930s the Townsend movement for old-age pensions, which drew its greatest strength from the retirement communities of California, was both an expression of economic need and a demand for attention. Although Social Security responded to the economic problem, nothing was done about the human importance of these forgotten Americans.

Answers for the Individual

During the twenties and thirties, the individual received a good deal of general advice and a variety of palliatives. But what failed to appear was a clear statement of the individual's situation and future prospects in modern society. A new round in search of an answer to this problem began rather vaguely in the depression, when a number of public leaders and intellectuals conceived of the individual as part of a broad social enterprise. New Deal enthusiasts attacked the evils of "rugged individualism" and foresaw a new age of social responsibility. The reputation of philosopher John Dewey, America's leading advocate of a social ethic, rose impressively during the

1930s. Moreover, as depression crippled America, one group of intellectuals looked abroad to the Soviet Union as a model of the healthy society. A few of them also took the next logical step and applied Karl Marx's theories of class conflict to American society. But in most cases, the affair between American intellectuals and the Soviet Union was a brief infatuation. Never willing to relinquish the individual in favor of the class, they were revolted by the bloody Soviet "purge" of the late thirties, and increasingly they became convinced that Americans would have to develop their own kind of social consciousness.

The Yearning for Unity.   At best, the search in the thirties offered a hope for the future, but not a solution for the times. John Steinbeck, who had once been attracted by Marxism and who continued to have a strong social conscience, captured this hope of the future at the end of his finest novel, *The Grapes of Wrath* (1939). Steinbeck told the grim story of an impoverished Oklahoma farm family, the Joads, tracing them from their uprooting early in the depression through their futile quest for a fresh start in California. Then on the last page of his otherwise tragic novel, Steinbeck suddenly shifted moods and in a few sentences sketched a vision of a new fellow feeling just beginning to surface in America.

For a great many Americans, that spirit of a collective endeavor finally arrived with the Second World War. In 1940 Hemingway's hero from the 1920s reappeared in *For Whom the Bell Tolls* as Robert Jordan, who was no longer alone because he had found a social commitment. This time Hemingway's hero was fighting in the Spanish Civil War. Instead of deserting, as Frederic Henry had done in *A Farewell to Arms*, Robert Jordon chose to die for human values in the battle against fascism. A year later, the former pacifist Robert E. Sherwood, winner of four Pulitzer Prizes, announced his conversion to the same crusade in his play *There Shall Be No Night*.

After the attack on Pearl Harbor in December 1941, the sense of a shared enterprise spread throughout America. In ways that no government propaganda could have achieved, all kinds of people linked all kinds of activities to a common cause: welding for

"*Joe, yestiddy ya saved my life an' I swore I'd pay ya back. Here's my last pair of dry socks.*"

(By Permission of Bill Mauldin and Wil-Jo Associates, Inc.)

the war effort, waking an hour early for the car pool, keeping tin cans for the scrap-metal drive, saving war stamps for a war bond. Nothing eliminated the conflicts in a complex society, yet to a remarkable degree, whatever an American did had a larger social meaning. Factories, rather than dreary mills of oppression, were now pictured as vibrant centers of cooperation. Intellectuals wrote confidently about "the public interest" as if everyone understood its meaning. For a brief period, the individual seemed to require no special reinforcements. Even in the midst of military combat, Bill Mauldin's extremely popular cartoons of the GIs Willie and Joe pictured them slogging through the muck of war with their sense of reality and their instinct for survival firmly intact.

Then as soon as the war ended, the spirit of a common cause dissolved. The news told only of selfish strikers, business profiteers, and greedy farmers. The government seemed no more than an arena for squabbling interests. Where were the truly national goals? According to *The Best Years of Our Lives,* one of Hollywood's most acclaimed movies of the 1940s, the returning soldiers had to fight still another battle at home to preserve their dignity in an ungrateful society. In fact, what had the war meant? In its aftermath, total war raised questions about the threat of a technological barbarism that could no longer be attributed simply to the evils of fascism.

In these sobering postwar years, the place of the individual in modern American society could be defined in four separate ways. Though each of the four was different, all dealt in some way with the clash between modern and traditional values, and all responded in some fashion to the problems and hopes of the vulnerable individual. Taken together these four answers outlined the central issues in modern American culture.

The Achieving Individual. One answer was for the individual to learn the rules of the modern occupational system, abide by them, and succeed. The wartime economy had intensified the demand for greater numbers of specialists with higher levels of skill, and immediately after the war Americans turned to the schools to fill this demand. Bands of citizens campaigned to improve instruction in the basic skills. Funds flowed freely into the entire educational system. Between 1945 and 1950, expenditures in the public schools more than doubled; even more impressive, enrollment in higher education doubled. Just as the importance of the high school had dominated the 1920s and 1930s, so the importance of higher education dominated the years after the Second World War. Now only colleges and graduate schools could satisfy a complex economy's need for specialized training. The greatest single impetus to college enrollment came from the GI Bill of 1944, which eventually subsidized the education of about 8 million former servicepeople. Along with the sheer numbers it funded, the GI Bill helped to democra-

tize opportunities in higher education and hence in the upper ranks of business and the professions as well.

In *Death of a Salesman* (1949), the young playwright Arthur Miller created a brilliant morality tale of why and how to use these broadening opportunities. Miller's drama was immediately acclaimed as one of America's greatest plays. Through the story of Willy Loman, it provided an excruciating lesson on how to fail in modern America. Willy lived by a weakened, vulgarized version of the traditional American dream of success. In the 1920s, when salesmanship had seemed the right avenue to wealth and importance, Willy chose that career with visions of a swift rise. Instead, he became trapped in the endless, weary rounds of meager sales, humiliating failures, and interminable debts. Willy desperately hoped that his sons, who idolized him, could still realize his dream of quick riches, and he taught them the only values he knew: a personal style, a winning appearance, and an eye for the main chance would achieve the miracle of success. Under their father's guidance, Biff and Hap approached manhood athletic, shallow, and morally stunted. Biff, discovering the fraud of Willy's life, turned in impotent rage on his father. Hap became a petty cheat. Willy, broken and psychotic, fulfilled his dream by committing suicide, under the pathetic delusion that his life-insurance payment would somehow catapult Biff to greatness.

During the hopeful years, while Willy and the boys were polishing the car and talking of Biff's future as an athlete, Bernard, the scrawny kid next door, mooned over the popular Loman boys. But Bernard was also winning the highest grades in his high school class. Bernard went to school to learn a speciality and returned a self-possessed, well-balanced adult, who was sufficiently eminent as a young lawyer to argue a case before the Supreme Court. His father, Charley, cool and clear-eyed, had simply relinquished his son to America's system of specialized occupations. "And you never told him what to do, did you?" a bewildered Willy asked his neighbor. "You never took any interest in him." An embittered Biff plagued Willy. Charley, on the other hand, enjoyed an easy, warm relationship with the adult Bernard, who dropped by whenever his busy schedule allowed. Bernard's success explained Willy's failure. Modern America's avenue upward had been there all the while, but Willy's dream had hidden the only legitimate path to success.

The Humanistic Individual. The second of the postwar answers acknowledged that the individual would have to find an anchor of values outside of science. Like the earlier critics of America's machine culture, a variety of intellectuals, educators, and publicists now warned that science and technology by themselves were amoral. Each person, they said, must find the fundamental principles in civilized life, and only the humanists—the philosophers and poets and theologians—could lead that search.

The quest for basic values was a nationwide preoccupation in the late forties. Some scholars explored the American past to discover its essentially American qualities, giving special attention to such brooding spirits as Thoreau, Melville, and the Puritans. Others examined the far richer resources of the Western tradition. Adults enrolled in well-attended classes on the "Great Books" of Western civilization. In colleges throughout the country, new and often required courses tried to distill wisdom not only from a long span of time but also from a breadth of subjects such as an interdisciplinary examination of American culture or a humanistic understanding of science. The most intriguing innovation in college education was Chancellor Robert Hutchins's program at the University of Chicago that integrated the entire subject matter of the undergraduate curriculum in a unified course of study.

The fascination with fundamentals produced a strong reaction against the pragmatist's faith in an experimental, evolving truth. John Dewey, who more than any other intellectual leader was identified with a scientific method in ethics, became a particular target of attack in the late 1940s. Dewey's old friends, such as philosopher Sidney Hook, joined his old enemies, such as journalist Walter Lippmann, in condemning the effects of scientific relativism. Dewey's critics wanted certainties in place of his open-ended pursuit of truth. In foreign policy, for example, they sought to define a single unwavering "national interest" to guide America's international affairs. In civil liberties, they assigned to the freedoms of the First Amendment an absolute, timeless meaning that no judiciary, they asserted, should ever alter.

The critics of scientific relativism accused its adherents of arrogance as well as fuzziness. The human mind, they claimed, was incapable of solving all of the world's problems through a scientific method. This line of opposition, which acquired the name of realism, found its most effective spokesman in Reinhold Niebuhr, a theologian who in his own career had moved from an optimistic Christian socialism to the humbling doctrines of Martin Luther. Niebuhr believed that ultimate truth is beyond the human reach in God's inscrutable wisdom. Therefore, all actions reflect an inevitable human fallibility, and all choices involve moral risks. Nevertheless, people cannot throw up their hands and quit. Individuals have a moral responsibility to choose among alternatives and to act on their choices. The necessity of choosing from an inherently imperfect knowledge defined the human predicament. Niebuhr, supporting the containment of international communism, lectured Americans that "It is not easy . . . for an adolescent nation, with illusions of childlike innocency to come to terms with the responsibilities and hazards of global politics," yet meet them it must. Americans had to abandon their simple faith in manmade progress, meet each situation as it arose, and, without arrogance, commit themselves to a course that held the best promise of fulfilling their moral obligations. Niebuhr's complex commandments were praised more than they were studied. But in the simplified image of the sober individual strengthened through self-knowledge and humility, his message had a remarkably wide appeal during these anxious years.

The Heroic Individual. The third of the postwar answers was a defiant statement in behalf of the sovereign individual. Setting the individual at odds with modern society, it told him to overcome the dangers around him through his interior powers. In a few instances, this answer was addressed to the specialist. Ayn Rand's best-selling novel *The Fountainhead* (1943), for example, glorified the right of the creative professional to discard society's ordinary rules in order to realize his genius, and in the postwar years, Rand cults mushroomed on college campuses. Usually, however, the hero had no special training and no resources except his hard, inner core. During the forties, a mass audience learned about this type of hero through a host of movies, particularly those starring Humphrey Bogart, and through a flood of inexpensive paperbacks that suddenly deluged drugstores and newsstands.

Soon after the publication of his first book in 1947, Mickey Spillane became undisputed king of the new paperback market. In less than a decade, 30 million copies of his novels had been sold, a record that far surpassed any competitor's. Spillane's hero was a tough, resourceful private detective named Mike Hammer, who radiated an irresistible power. Good people willingly helped him; weak ones crumbled before him. Beautiful, sensuous women, looking past his lumpy face to the inner man, desired him. Though often battered, he always survived through a "gimmick" or a bit of Hammer luck. Enemies understood that nothing would deter him. When Hammer set upon organized crime, for example, the entire Mafia quaked, for they knew that he would bring them a personal, bloody justice.

Although Spillane drew on a full tradition of fantasies about the all-conquering individual, he more than any of his predecessors gave them a contemporary urban setting. The metropolis, Mike Hammer declared, was a formless "monster," teeming with ominous forces. City culture was dehumanized and city government corrupt. In the urban jungle, Spillane's hero had no alternative but to devise his own code of values. It required an exceptional courage, an extraordinary effort of will, to break free from this threatening human mass. Those who succeeded, however, became true individuals and survived. Obviously, Spillane's message had touched a popular nerve. The number of his imitators even

more than the sale of his books indicated that his, of all the postwar answers, found the widest audience.

The Desperate Individual.   The fourth of the postwar answers was the acceptance of despair that threatened to destroy the individual. In the late forties, Americans were listening for the first time to those Europeans who had already peered inside a soulless society and found no individuals there. Franz Kafka's nightmares of man as vermin, of a nameless subject wandering through a fathomless system to a death he came to welcome, were suddenly relevant. A much larger public responded so attentively to the accounts of a devouring social organization in Aldous Huxley's *Brave New World* (1932), Arthur Koestler's *Darkness at Noon* (1941), and George Orwell's *1984* (1949) that their contents became clichés. Because Orwell and Koestler were describing communist totalitarianism, Americans had a choice of reading their books as justifications for a free Western society. Instead, many Americans used them as a frame of reference for discussing the dangers in their own lives.

The Second World War, as it was viewed in retrospect, contributed significantly to this new spirit of despair. The best of the American war novels— Norman Mailer's *The Naked and the Dead* (1948), Irwin Shaw's *The Young Lions* (1948), and James Jones's *From Here to Eternity* (1951)—did not simply surround their characters with danger, as the war novels of the 1920s had done. Now individuals were sucked into the very center of destruction, and all characters were equally exposed to the stray bullet. No personal choice or inner strength affected these human specks that were being tossed by the fates.

Above all, "The Holocaust" and "The Bomb" posed the most profoundly disturbing problems of the postwar years. After Germany's surrender in 1945, the numbing facts about the Nazi's Jewish policy began to filter back to the United States. Rationally and efficiently, the German government had applied the best techniques of modern organization to systematically destroy 6 million human beings. Had the Germans, in the process, revealed an es-

HIROSHIMA, 1945
Was modern society on the brink of suicide? The awful power of the atomic bomb raised fundamental questions about the meaning of science, progress, and civilization. *(U.S. Air Force)*

sential truth about the impersonal mobilization of power in modern society? Also in 1945, American atomic bombs demolished the Japanese cities of Hiroshima and Nagasaki. Through the development and use of the bomb, scientific genius and human annihilation were juxtaposed so sharply, the concept of civilization was so directly challenged, and the terrors of nuclear death were so vividly imprinted

on the minds of Americans, that even the most resolute Americans were unable to express its import.

The uniquely American way of expressing despair about the individual's lot appeared in a new image, "the Southern." In 1949 the Southerner William Faulkner, with his finest writing already behind him, received the Nobel Prize for literature. He had recently risen to public prominence, and a favorite

Eric Simmons/Stock, Boston

The meaning of art in modern America expanded and blurred. A profusion of photographs, illustrations, movies, buildings, landscapes, fashions, and handicrafts hopelessly muddied the traditional questions about the appropriate subjects of art, the necessary training for artists, and the proper cultivation of the viewers. Could advertising qualify as art? Were the creators of comic strips artists? Did mass production destroy artistic taste or generate new forms of democratic art? Yet the endless quarreling over these unanswerable questions could not hide the timeless qualities of the debate. Now as before, each aspiring artist tried to determine *what* people saw and *how* they saw it. Each of these many images promised its viewers a special insight into what was real, rather than merely superficial or transient. And these competing visions of reality, in turn, reflected the main lines of tension in modern American culture.

Varieties of Reality

Images, like other modern goods, were mass distributed and, however unwittingly, Americans consumed them along with the myriad products of their society. As Americans took sides in a cultural conflict, therefore, they received images that helped them to understand their choices. During the 1920s and 1930s, for example, an aversion to city life was visualized in small groups of country people: a warm family gathering, an easy intimacy among friends, a mutual support between generations. The images of urban-industrial progress, on the other hand, were oriented toward things rather than people. Long, dramatic views of a factory, skyscraper, or center of a city communicated the expansive grandeur of American technology. Americans came to know these images so well that in the 1960s environmentalists needed only a slight shift in focus to make ironic statements about modern progress. A tip of the camera accentuated the smoke belching from the factory. A longer view of the city juxtaposed its skyline with urban blight. By the sixties, the country town was slipping from memory, and the visual alternative to the city leaped past civilization to the wilderness. The image of pure nature, however, was a study in contemporary American frustration, for it also offered no human comfort. As soon as people entered the virgin wilderness, they defiled it.

For Americans without personal knowledge of small-town life, Norman Rockwell's famous drawings defined it as simple, friendly, and unaffected. In this fashion, Rockwell's imaginary town became part of modern America's reality. In contrast to Rockwell's cozy, vibrant town, the untouched wilderness had no place for people. Beneath this beautiful vision ran an undercurrent of hopelessness about modern American society.

Samuel M. Vauclain—William Hazlett Upson—James Warner Bellah
Wesley Stout—Eleanor Mercein—Samuel Crowther—Booth Tarkington

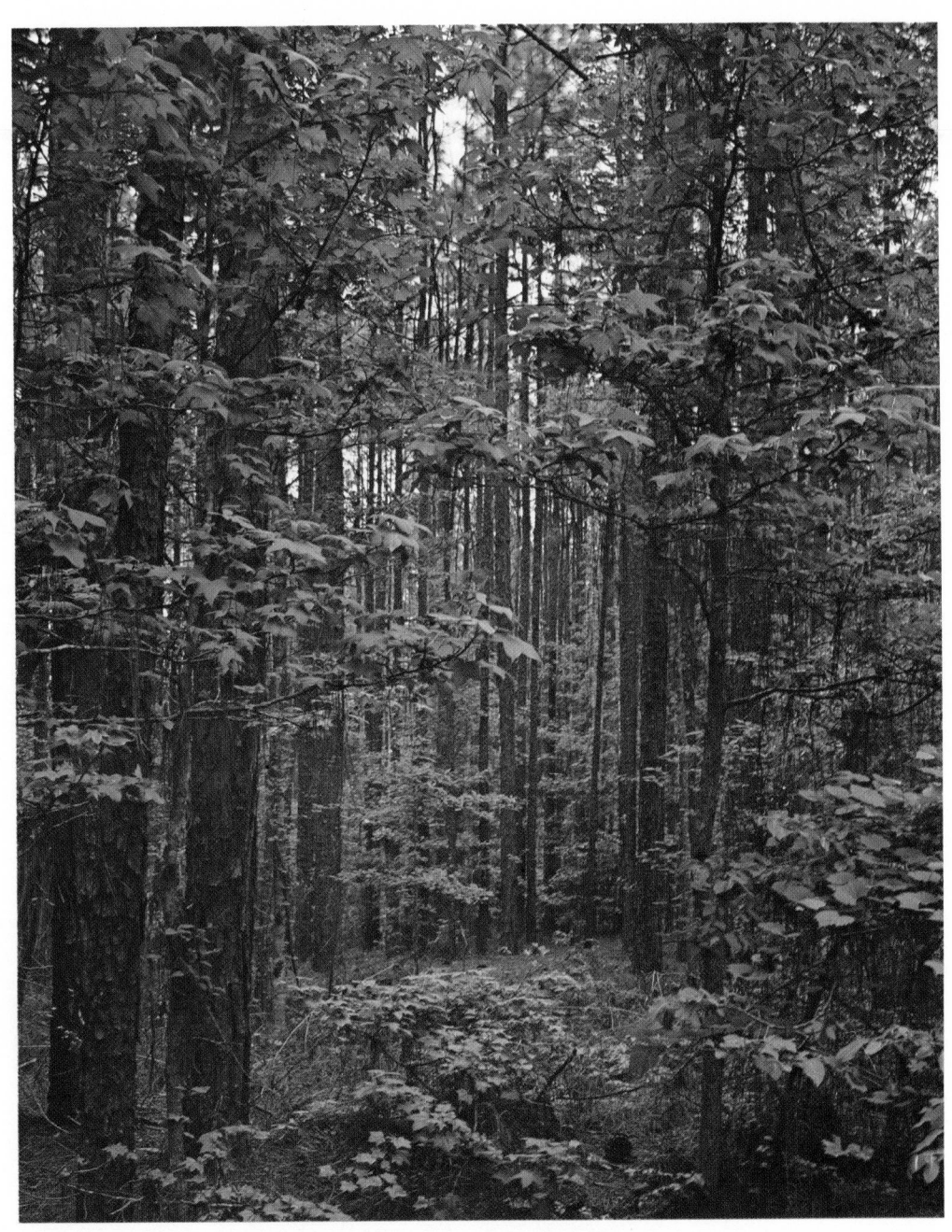

Erich Hartmann/Magnum Photos, Inc.

Another group of artists sought reality in a complex relation between the emotions of the viewers and the essential components of what they saw. They probed the same subjects of nature and urban-industrial society, but they rephrased these issues in abstract images. The flowering of American abstraction came in the years after the Second World War when Willem de Kooning was expressing the dynamism of modern life in rugged blocks and explosive colors, and the controversial Jackson Pollock was extending visual horizons with his flowing lines and subtle uses of depth. Then in the 1960s, as many Americans rebelled against the clutter and complexity around them, painters of the minimalist and op art schools responded to these new yearnings with simple geometric abstractions.

Abstract artists, like other modern experts, developed techniques of expression that required special training simply to understand, let alone to use. Among their strongest defenders were professional and business people whose own success depended on expertise. Every subdivision of knowledge, they assumed, had special rules for understanding. But modern abstractionists, unlike the pioneers of the Armory Show in 1913, reached a nationwide audience. For millions of skeptical Americans abstract art was an incomprehensible jumble of shapes and colors. In art as in other areas of knowledge, they demanded a commonsense reality that anyone could grasp.

"Gotham News 1955" by Willem de Kooning. Albright-Knox Art Gallery, Buffalo, New York, Gift of Seymour H. Knox, 1955

"Number 3, 1950" by Jackson Pollock. Private Collection

"House by the Railroad" by Edward Hopper. The Museum of Modern Art

Willem de Kooning, a major contributor to America's renaissance in painting after the Second World War, gave new vitality to the European cubist tradition. More innovative than de Kooning, Jackson Pollock was particularly ingenious in adapting modern technology to his art, as the aluminum paint on this canvas demonstrates. In the 1960s the trends moved away from Pollock's complexity toward a simple, almost photographic reality. The reputation of Edward Hopper, whose best paintings had been completed three decades earlier, rose impressively. Almost no signs of life intruded on Hopper's brilliant, haunting scenes, and the loneliness of his stark art touched widespread anxieties about the individual's survival during the sixties.

Sex and violence—sometimes singly, sometimes in combination—dominated the popular arts after the Second World War. Mass-marketed stereotypes of sex and beauty reached their peak with the era of Marilyn Monroe, who exercised an extraordinary influence over American dreams and behavior. The vision of history's most horrible weapon as an awesome fantasy of color and clouds greatly strengthened the modern connection between violence and beauty.

The popular arts satisfied these demands. Through constant repetition the popular arts drilled a few simple images of truth and beauty into the American consciousness. The most familiar of all was the smooth, sexy, welcoming woman. From the Hollywood vamp of the twenties to the Petty girl of the forties to the *Playboy* centerfold of the six-

ties, a composite model of female beau... men's assumptions about women and w... sumptions about themselves. The popula... celebrated the virtues of certain occupati... the auspices of the New Deal, for exam... murals and bas-relief sculptures glorifi... labor with scenes of proud, muscular...

women in the fields and factories. During the Second World War these handsome titans became soldiers and sailors. In fact, the Second World War introduced an elaborate aesthetic of violence that made instruments of destruction into objects of beauty: first the gleaming fleets of battleships and bombers, then the eerie majesty of the atomic bomb's mushroom cloud. The beauty of violence remained after the war as an important theme of the popular arts. A particularly striking example appeared in the climactic scene of the movie *Bonnie and Clyde*, which transformed the mutilation of the heroine's body into an arresting, slow-motion dance of death.

Subway Graffitti. Was it art or vandalism? The answer lay in the cultural standards of the beholder.

Naar/Alskog/Photo Researchers, Inc.

In reaction against these mass-produced images, some Americans swung to the other extreme and praised the beauty of almost anything unique. The market for handicrafts and homemade art objects thrived during the 1960s and 1970s. What popular primitivism lacked in refinement it contributed in personal expression, and its proponents contrasted the reality of a rough-hewn people's art with the artificiality of a slick commercial art. The urge for self-expression also spread into "street art," a new public outlet for the emotions of assertive, often angry city dwellers. None of the older art forms had to give way for the newcomers. A contemporary people's art simply added to the artistic variety of modern America.

intellectual game of the late forties was unraveling the family histories in Faulkner's "Yoknapatawpha County," the fictional Mississippi setting for his greatest works. A year earlier, the young Tennessee Williams had been awarded a Pulitzer prize for *A Streetcar Named Desire*, which with another dramatic success in the 1940s established him as a leading playwright. These two, along with other gifted southern writers such as Carson McCullers and Flannery O'Connor, created a shockingly new American image.

Understanding the Southern depended on an appreciation of the Western, for intentionally or not, the Southern was a systematic attack on America's oldest myth of individual strength. In the Western, one man entered an open plain that was as stripped of constraining institutions as he himself was of a constraining past. There he confronted a direct challenge, and by a clear moral choice he overcame it. He was the pure individual: a man alone, a man of simple, sovereign convictions, a man of action whose problem, once met, dissolved in a cleansing rite of violence. Not only had the movies, the radio, comics, and pulp fiction expanded the audience for this myth since the 1920s; such thoughtful writers as Hemingway had borrowed from it. The Western hero continued to stand tall in postwar America.

Like the Western, the Southern also used a regional sterotype to communicate a national message. Just as countless Americans associated the West with a new, formless land, many regarded the South as a decaying, backward region. This popular caricature helped southern writers reach a national audience. In contrast to the Western's openness, the world of the Southern was a suffocating prison—a town or household or room in which the inmates were held by invisible shackles they could never break. Dreams and memories bound them to the dead as well as the living. Unlike the direct challenge in the Western, the hovering, atmospheric problems in the Southern were impalpable. The Southern world was filled with human vulnerability. Children were caught in a whirl of adult terror and adults locked in a desperate battle for sanity; amorality was in power and sadism at large; bodies were deformed and brains addled. In these struggles, contrary to the gun fights of the Western, women managed more effectively than men. Maleness and impotence were common companions in the Southern.

Where the Western hero acted, the characters in the Southern talked. They stabbed one another with words, searched in vain for the meaning of their lives through words, and covered their own anguish with words. Occasionally someone's hopelessness or passion would explode in violence, but violence only complicated the problems that no one would ever resolve. In *A Streetcar Named Desire*, Tennessee Williams let loose a caricature of the Western hero, the physical-sexual-nonverbal Stanley Kowalski, and he wrecked the fragile human defenses around him. Perhaps only a small minority listened carefully to the agonizing message of the Southern. Nevertheless, an exceptionally talented cluster of American writers were finally probing fundamental questions about the individual's chances for survival.

At midcentury one phase in the creation of modern culture was ending. An elaborate framework of modern values relating to occupational specialization, personal freedom, and mass manipulation lay across the top of American society. Beneath it a complex pattern of traditional values simultaneously resisted and assimilated these modern ways. The long overlapping frontier between the two spheres did not alter their basically antagonistic orientations. Hence, the range of answers to a problem common to both—the fate of the individual—revealed a wide diversity of standards, aspirations, and doubts. A distant viewer might well wonder if Arthur Miller's Bernard, Reinhold Niebuhr's Moral Man, Mickey Spillane's Mike Hammer, and Tennessee Williams's Stanley Kowalski all belonged to the same human race. To maintain the uneasy coexistence among these conflicting beliefs required a good deal of mutual tolerance—or mutual indifference. Whether an increasingly nationalized American society would contain such leeway became one of the crucial questions for the next quarter-century to resolve.

SUGGESTED READINGS

Modern culture is explored broadly in Daniel J. Boorstin, *The Americans: The Democratic Experience* (1973). William E. Leuchtenburg, *The Perils of Prosperity, 1914–32* (1958), has particularly revealing chapters on the consumer culture of the twenties and the changes in values accompanying it, subjects that are also covered in Frederick Lewis Allen's *Only Yesterday* (1931). Isabel Leighton, ed., *The Aspirin Age* (1949) contains a lively set of essays on the twenties. There are perceptive analyses of the new sexual morality in Christopher Lasch's *The New Radicalism in America [1889–1963]* (1965) and Paul Robinson's *The Modernization of Sex* (1976). Robert H. Elias, *Entangling Alliances with None* (1973), probes the meaning of individualism in the twenties. The city's dominance in twentieth-century society is discussed generally in Zane L. Miller, *The Urbanization of Modern America* (1973), and more interpretively in Sam Bass Warner, Jr., *The Urban Wilderness* (1972). Some effects of urbanization on suburban values appear in Peter J. Schmitt, *Back to Nature* (1969). Carl Bode, *Mencken* (1969), assesses the leading spokesman for the new urban culture. An intriguing section in Gilman M. Ostrander, *American Civilization in the First Machine Age: 1890–1940* (1970), defines the place of youth in modern society, and John R. Seeley *et al.*, *Crestwood Heights* (1956), examines the importance of the schools in modern suburban life. Three books evaluate women's part in the new culture. William L. O'Neill, *Everyone Was Brave: The Rise and Fall of Feminism in America* (1969), and William Henry Chafe, *The American Woman* (1972), trace the decline of earlier trends toward emancipation, while J. Stanley Lemons, *The Woman Citizen: Social Feminism in the 1920s* (1973), concentrates on women's continuing action after the First World War. In *Birth Control in America* (1970), David M. Kennedy adds a critical analysis of Margaret Sanger's career.

Several books illuminate the values of important institutions and occupations. James W. Prothro, *Dollar Decade* (1954), summarizes the attitudes of businessmen during the twenties. Otis Pease, *The Responsibilities of American Advertising* (1958), and Stuart Ewen, *Captains of Consciousness* (1976), provide contrasting interpretations of a particularly thriving field. The engineer's dedication to business values is the subject of Edwin T. Layton, Jr., *The Revolt of the Engineers* (1971), and the social scientists' dedication to the same values is the subject of Loren Baritz, *The Servants of Power* (1960). Roy Lubove, *Professional Altruists* (1965), describes the businesslike efficiency of social

workers. The section on the United States in Reinhard Bendix's *Work and Authority in Industry* (1956) investigates the strategy of the new specialists in personnel management. Also see Milton Derber, *The American Idea of Industrial Democracy, 1865–1965* (1970). The effects of the new culture on education are analyzed in Patricia Albjerg Graham, *Progressive Education from Arcady to Academe: A History of the Progressive Education Association, 1919–1955* (1967), August Hollingshead, *Elmtown's Youth* (1949), and Solon Kimball and James E. McClellan, Jr., *Education and the New America* (1962). Christopher Jencks and David Riesman, *The Academic Revolution* (1968), explores the modern university. Barry D. Karl, *Charles E. Merriam and the Study of Politics* (1974), and Fred H. Matthews, *Quest for an American Sociology: Robert E. Park and the Chicago School* (1977), discuss a new breed of academic entrepreneurs.

Traditional values in modern America have attracted less scholarly attention. Two interesting books analyze these values under challenge: Ray Ginger's *Six Days or Forever? Tennessee v. John Thomas Scopes* (1958) and Don S. Kirschner's *City and Country: Rural Responses to Urbanization in the 1920s* (1970). *Middletown* (1929) and *Middletown in Transition* (1937), classic studies of Muncie, Indiana, by Robert S. and Helen Merrell Lynd, reveal a mixture of traditional and modern values. Donald B. Meyer, *The Positive Thinkers* (1965), examines modern variations on the traditional doctrine of self-help. Other books cast light on traditional values through the study of popular heroes. In *The Hero* (1959), Kenneth S. Davis discusses the fame of Charles Lindbergh. Reynold M. Wik, *Henry Ford and Grass-Roots America* (1972), explains the automobile magnate's powerful appeal, and Keith T. Sward, *The Legend of Henry Ford* (1948), contrasts the public image with the actual record. Robert Sklar, *Movie-Made America* (1975), interprets the development of a new mass medium, and John G. Cawelti, *Adventure, Mystery, and Romance* (1976), anatomizes the most popular forms of fiction.

The best account of modern relativism is Morton G. White, *Social Thought in America: The Revolt against Formalism* (rev. ed., 1957). Three excellent books discuss early discontents with relativism and various quests for certainty: Donald B. Meyer, *The Protestant Search for Political Realism, 1919–1941* (1960), Edward A. Purcell, Jr., *The Crisis of Democratic Theory: Scientific Naturalism and the Problem of Values* (1973), and David A. Hollinger, *Morris R. Cohen and the Scientific Ideal* (1975). Another group of valuable books explores the intellectual consequences of the Great De-

me
te   le(l')   lui
nous   la(l')   leur   y   en   Verb
vous   les

Affirmative imperative

            moi
Verb le   lui
     la   nous   y   en
     les   vous
            leur

pression: Arthur A. Ekirch, *Ideologies and Utopias: The Impact of the New Deal on American Thought* (1969), R. Alan Lawson, *The Failure of Independent Liberalism, 1930–1941* (1971), Richard H. Pells, *Radical Visions and American Dreams: Culture and Social Thought in the Depression Years* (1973), William Stott, *Documentary Expression and Thirties America* (1973), and Frank A. Warren III, *Liberals and Communism: The "Red Decade" Revisited* (1966). John P. Diggins, *Up from Communism* (1975), follows the evolution of four intellectuals from radicalism to reaction. James Hoopes, *Van Wyck Brooks* (1977), examines one intellectual's quest for cultural roots. Other studies trace ideas in creative writing. Alfred Kazin, *On Native Grounds: An Interpretation of Modern American Prose Literature* (1942), is a stimulating essay. Frederick J. Hoffman, *The Twenties* (rev. ed., 1966), discusses American fiction in an artistically critical decade. The strains of both modern society and depression are revealed in Maxwell Geismar's *Writers in Crisis: The American Novel, 1925–1940* (1942), and Daniel Aaron's *Writers on the Left* (1961). Thomas R. West, *Flesh of Steel* (1967), deals with the effects of the machine on the literary imagination. Of course, the creative writers themselves remain our indispensable

sources. The best survey of the fine arts is Oliver W. Larkin, *Art and Life in America* (rev. ed., 1960). On architecture, see John Burchard and Albert Bush-Brown, *The Architecture of America* (1961).

The ferment in values after the Second World War has yet to find a historian. Something of the concern for the individual is communicated in two important sociological studies, David Riesman *et al., The Lonely Crowd: A Study of the Changing American Character* (1950), and C. Wright Mills, *White Collar: The American Middle Class* (1951). Alexander Meiklejohn, *Free Speech and Its Relation to Self-Government* (1948), and Hans J. Morgenthau, *In Defense of the National Interest* (1951), illustrate the demand for fixed values. Also see Carl L. Becker, *Freedom and Responsibility in the American Way of Life* (1945). Robert M. Hutchins, *The Conflict in Education in a Democratic Society* (1953), and Arthur E. Bestor, Jr., *Educational Wastelands: The Retreat from Learning in Our Public Schools* (1953), discuss the place of fundamentals in education. The new tough-minded approach to social values is revealed in Arthur M. Schlesinger, Jr., *The Vital Center* (1949), Max Ascoli, *The Power of Freedom* (1949), and Reinhold Niebuhr, *The Irony of American History* (1952).

CHAPTER 32

The Consequences of Modernization

The process of modernization that dominated American history during the second quarter of the twentieth century was also a process of nationalization. National politics drew more and more problems into its orbit. National values dominated in such critical areas as the meaning of success and the rearing of children. National security preoccupied Americans in a tumultuous world of hot and cold wars. By the early 1950s, these nationalizing forces had integrated American society far more tightly than ever before. But the hope that integration meant unity and that a united American society guaranteed a smooth, stable progress proved to be illusory. Instead, nationalization created a critical imbalance in the lives of a growing number of Americans. New national rules in racial and cultural affairs threatened the traditional local autonomy of millions of white citizens. Other Americans rebelled against the nation's global involvements, particularly its war in Vietnam. Still others believed that nationalization was crushing them as individuals.

"National" usually meant "the national government." As Washington became the mecca for modern society's ambitions, it also became the focus for modern society's discontents. Even those who feared for their survival as individuals increasingly blamed their problems on the policies of the national government. During the late 1960s, a powerful surge of these many emotions poured into national politics and precipitated a crisis. The nation's political leaders, who had been coasting on a wave of confidence, could not grasp what had gone wrong, and at the end of the sixties, it was still not clear that they would be able to surmount the crisis.

Unity and Progress

The 1950s, like the 1920s, were years of fulfillment. As the bitter strikes and angry rhetoric of the postwar years subsided, so did most worries about a selfish, fragmented society. Despite two recessions during the decade, the GNP rose by 50 percent, and the economy spread out a feast of goods and services. Echoing the claims of the 1920s, publicist Peter Drucker told

Americans that their society had passed *"beyond Capitalism and Socialism."* Once again, millions believed that they had not only solved the major problems of the past but had also learned how to manage the problems of the future.

This sense of control over America's destiny came from three primary sources: the resurgence of mass consumerism, faith in the experts, and confidence in government management.

A Consumer Society.   After the frustrations of the Great Depression and the shortages of the Second World War, the consumer extravaganza of the 1950s gave Americans the most persuasive evidence that theirs was a progressive, democratic society. The sheer quantity of goods and services suggested a more egalitarian consumer market. Because agricultural productivity increased dramatically, doubling the yield of wheat and cotton and trebling the yield of corn per acre in the quarter-century after the war, food remained abundant and cheap. By the 1950s, leisure activities were absorbing 15 percent of the GNP. Between 1945 and 1957, the amount of consumer credit rose a breathtaking 800 percent, and as it swelled, it brought the full paraphernalia of revolving charge accounts, easy payment plans, and credit cards.

The use of light, relatively inexpensive materials such as plastics and aluminum became widespread. Not only did these new materials expand the range of inexpensive goods; they created a mass market for cheap imitations of goods that had once been luxury items. Most American women could now afford to wear nylon stockings whereas once only a few could afford silk ones. Although industry's policy of "planned obsolescence" caused an accumulation of consumer trash and inadequate repair services—it was cheaper to buy a new product than to have the old one repaired—Americans of the 1950s appeared quite willing to tolerate these side effects.

The nationwide rush to the suburbs gave further evidence of a democratized consumer society. During the depression and war years, the number of new dwellings had averaged about 300,000 a year. During the fifties, the annual average ran almost four times

higher, and the demand for suburban housing seemed insatiable. By 1960 more than one in three Americans lived in suburbs—as many as lived in the cities. Instead of relying on the services of the inner city, as did the "bedroom towns" of the 1920s, the suburbs of the 1950s provided an increasingly self-contained life. Business firms, following the rush to the suburbs, displayed their wares along miles of commercial avenues and inside countless shopping plazas. By the late 1960s, there were even more jobs in the suburbs than in the cities.

In its broad effects, the consumerism of the fifties appeared to be drawing Americans closer together. A network of highways was quickly spreading across the nation. Between 1946 and 1956, state governments tripled their investment in road construction, and the Federal Highway Act of 1956 committed the national government to subsidizing over 40,000 miles of superhighways that would connect America's major cities. In the high-powered postwar cars, Americans greatly expanded their range of travel. The airplane shrank distances even more dramatically. Between 1947 and 1957, as passenger service grew fourfold, the airlines became a normal, accepted means of travel. Most impressive of all, television was transformed from a curious new toy into a staple of the American home. Fourteen thousand families had TV sets in 1947; ten years later 35 million families owned them. By driving, flying, or simply watching at home, Americans, it was assumed, were discovering one another. Nobody, no place, needed to be strange or distant in a land of rapid transportation and instant communication.

Moreover, Americans appeared to unite just by acting as consumers. Common cars and clothes, common houses and vacations, common foods and recreations, gave the impression of a single national commitment to the same good life. In 1933 the Roosevelt administration had issued a 3¢ postage stamp to symbolize unity in a society of large, economic blocs: a farmer, a businessman, a laborer, and a housewife, each in distinctive dress, marched shoulder to shoulder "in common determination." In the consumer society of the 1950s, a comparable image of unity would have shown an assortment of shoppers in the same style of clothes filling their carts with the same standardized products. Consumerism and the American way of life had become almost synonymous.

Social and Scientific Expertise. Faith in the experts provided a second source of public confidence in the fifties. Following the awesome discoveries in atomic physics, the mass distribution of "wonder drug" antibiotics, and the conquest of poliomyelitis, scientists had reached a new peak of prestige. Millions of Americans now made the astonishing assumption that they had an inalienable right to good health. More eagerly than ever, Americans also looked to the nation's experts for personal happiness. Psychoanalysis achieved its pinnacle of popularity. Counseling specialists and home beautification advisers, tourist handbooks and sports manuals flourished. "Culture vultures" joined record and book clubs, studied brochures on the mysteries of painting and subscribed to theater series so that they could experience the best of the arts. After a partial eclipse during the depression, advertising and public relations returned to public favor and sugarcoated the work of the experts. Scarcely a government program appeared without an attractive acronym like HUSKY, SHAPE, or VISTA. Farm subsidies became thrifty investments in a "soil bank," and the recession in 1953 a "rolling readjustment."

Faith in the experts also expressed itself in an intensified campaign to improve the educational system during the 1950s. Attacking the vagueness of the schools' "life-adjustment" programs, reformers demanded rigorous instruction in basic skills. Curricular "tracks" in the best suburban and private schools were linked so well with higher education that the brightest high school students, especially in science and mathematics, were able to prepare themselves for advanced college work. Between 1940 and 1960, the cost of educating students in the public schools more than quadrupled, and expenditures per student in higher education rose more than sixfold. Scientists and engineers seemed in dangerously short supply; as a result, with the National Defense Education Act of 1958, the national government invested

in their education. In all, another impressive vote of confidence was cast for the social value of expertise.

The distinctive new element in the 1950s was a faith in the unique powers of massed expertise. An increasing number of Americans looked on the experts as a vast, national pool of skills that could be used in various combinations to suit particular problems. Scientifically coordinated teams, rather than just scientifically trained individuals, held the key to the future. It required a team of specialists to harness the atom, to operate on the human heart, to measure public opinion, or to run a giant corporation. Moreover, these teams now had a marvelous new technological aid, the computer, which promised impartial answers to the world's most complicated questions. No lone genius could match the scientific range of computerized team research.

The modern faith in science, management, and success merged the public responses to America's space program. In 1957, the Soviet Union shocked Americans with the successful launching of a small "Sputnik" spacecraft that circled the globe in outer space. In 1961, after considerable public discussion about the weaknesses in American policy and technology, President John Kennedy countered the Soviet challenge by promising to place a man on the moon before 1970. Amply financed and widely publicized, the Mercury program to orbit the earth, the Gemini program to maneuver in space, and the Apollo program to reach the moon filled the 1960s with televised countdowns, blastoffs, reentries, and splashdowns. Americans of all ages watched with fascination as scurrying teams of specialists readied the crafts and clicking computers monitored their flights. The climax of the Apollo program occurred on July 20, 1969, as Neil Armstrong descended to the surface of the moon before a billion television witnesses, declaring that he had taken "one small step for man, one giant leap for mankind."

In the midst of these extremely intricate operations sat the crews of astronauts, the group heroes of the 1960s. Even their personalities seemed to merge into a composite of the healthy, balanced American male. Various Americans saw what they

THE SPACE AGE
Old myths of adventure and new marvels of technology combined to give America's space program enthusiastic public support during the 1960s. Here astronauts L. Gordon Cooper, Jr., and Charles Conrad, Jr., practice insertion into the Gemini 5 spacecraft. *(NASA)*

terparts in the 1960s were cheered for achieving glory through an incredibly complicated team effort.

Government at Work. A third source of confidence during the fifties was government management. The popular faith in government management derived from a modern sense of the nation's wholeness, and in this vision of wholeness Washington was the natural overseer of America's welfare. Clearly the government's most important obligation was to maintain a healthy economy. Beyond that broad obligation, however, effective government management did not require systematic plans for the entire nation. On the contrary, the government devoted most of its energies to responding to the endless demands of private groups. The standard formula was to give something to all of them without capitulating fully to any one of them.

Under President Dwight Eisenhower's light rein, the government followed this guideline at a cautious pace, and its unspectacular course actually contributed to a feeling of security among the nation's major interest groups. Many businessmen who had once been mortal enemies of a big bureaucracy enjoyed easy and profitable relations with the government of the fifties. For example, the New Deal's bitter foe, the electric power industry, found the Eisenhower administration very cooperative and received, among other favors, the Atomic Energy Act (1954), which subsidized the private development of nuclear power. After frightening talk in 1953 of a free market for agricultural products, farm groups soon learned that their subsidies would not disappear. In 1956 an additional form of federal support was introduced: the soil bank, a government program that paid farmers to remove land from cultivation. For those scientifically advanced farmers who could grow more and more on less and less acreage, the soil bank proved a bonanza. The merger of the AFL and the CIO in 1955 under a tough, conservative president, George Meany, strengthened the somewhat wobbly political position of a third set of interests, organized labor. Although most unions were unenthusiastic about the Eisenhower administration, the AFL-CIO continued

wanted in the flight of the astronauts: the interplanetary Western, the verification of a science-fiction future, the triumph of ordinary American virtues, or the waste of national resources. For a good many people, however, the astronauts exemplified the values of massed expertise. In the 1920s, the nation had idolized Charles Lindbergh as the "Lone Eagle" who transcended his impersonally organized society. Inside the fantastic gear of the space explorer, his counto have many allies in Congress. Minor restrictions on their financial affairs in the Landrum-Griffin Act of 1959, which like the earlier restrictions in the Taft-Hartley Act, scarcely affected the union's policies.

Appropriately, government policies came to reflect the rising importance both of the experts and of mass consumerism. By the early 1950s, physicists, chemists, biologists, engineers, hospital administrators, and a host of other scientific groups had become part of the Washington establishment, and government expenditures for scientific research and development skyrocketed from $74 million in 1940 to $7.3 billion in 1960. Other professionals ranging from archivists and advertising specialists to experts in race relations and traffic management found places for themselves in the government bureaucracy.

No one coordinated Washington's vast apparatus of government. On paper it looked as though the executive branch was the center of control. In 1950 Congress added to the executive's powers by giving the president the right to appoint his own chairman to the independent regulatory commissions. Now each new administration could have an immediate influence on the policies of the "Big Six": the Civil Aeronautics Board, the Federal Communications Commission, the Federal Power Commission, the Federal Trade Commission, the Interstate Commerce Commission, and the Securities and Exchange Commission. Then in 1953, the new Department of Health, Education, and Welfare (HEW) combined a great variety of services and programs under one executive chief. Nevertheless, the larger the executive branch grew, the more its authority was scattered among innumerable offices and subdivisions. As powerful a politician as President Eisenhower's principal domestic aide, Sherman Adams, could do no more than respond to the issues of government one at a time as they came to him. Fortunately for the president, the tests of good management required only a strong economy and a satisfied constituency of private interest groups. By these standards, the government functioned very well during the 1950s. Although Americans grumbled about incompetent bureaucrats, they generally approved the results of bureaucratic government.

World Order

In foreign policy, as in domestic affairs, the United States presented a new face of national unity and common purpose during the fifties. After the Korean War, no significant group of Americans challenged the basic outlines of the nation's containment policy. Both Republicans and Democrats defined international communism as a worldwide conspiracy that was directed from its headquarters in Moscow. The United States, they told the nation, must gird for a long, taxing struggle against the enemy.

Containment Through Military Might. The consensus on foreign policy covered strategy as well. The proponents of containment envisaged a worldwide league of so-called free nations encircling communist territory and sealing off its avenues of expansion. To complete the circle, the United States negotiated a variety of agreements with nations outside Europe. The most ambitious of these was the Southeast Asia Treaty Organization (SEATO) of 1955, which allied France, Great Britain, and the United States with Australia, New Zealand, Pakistan, the Philippines, and Thailand. In addition, the United States encouraged its allies in the Middle East to form the Central Treaty Organization (CENTO) of 1959.* As some critics promptly noted, neither organization was strong or comprehensive. Of the countries on the mainland of Southeast Asia, only Thailand entered SEATO. Only one Arab nation belonged to CENTO. Nevertheless, in combination with the North Atlantic Treaty Organization (NATO), these treaties formed a symbolic global ring around the communist domain.

America's reliance on military power to contain communism went almost unchallenged. Although Democrats and Republicans hotly debated the adequacy of each other's defense proposals, they were trying to prove themselves even more committed than their opponents to military preparedness. The Eisenhower administration, borrowing a term from women's fashions, proposed a "New Look" in Amer-

*The members of CENTO were Great Britain, Iran, Pakistan, and Turkey.

ica's military program. Politically, it appealed to the economy-minded, who were promised, in Secretary of Defense Charles Wilson's blunt phrase, "more bang for the buck." But militarily, the New Look represented only a slight shift away from ground and naval forces in favor of air and missile power. Some critics of the New Look, such as Professor Henry Kissinger of Harvard University, charged that the Eisenhower administration's heavy reliance on nuclear weapons removed too much flexibility from the nation's military policy and left it unable to meet a variety of small, local communist thrusts. Other critics, including Senator John Kennedy of Massachusetts, warned of a general decline in the nation's military power. Not many Americans paid attention to these complaints.

People's confidence in containment was based on a broad faith in government management and massed expertise. The wonders of science figured just as prominently in international as in national affairs. The latest developments in ballistic missiles, supersonic jets, and nuclear-powered submarines became common topics of conversation and standard symbols of American defense. Under President Eisenhower, the United States established a worldwide, electronic Distant Early Warning System (DEW Line) that would alert the nation's military power in case of an enemy attack. Under President Kennedy, a "Hot Line" was installed in 1963 to provide instant communication between the White House and the Kremlin in case of the ultimate emergency. Abroad as at home, skillful managers plus modern technology equaled national security.

The Economics of Peace. But foreign and domestic affairs were linked by much more than this abiding faith in managers and experts. Military expenditures now dominated the national budget. The size of these expenditures alone, fluctuating at about 60 percent of the government's total costs, made them crucial to maintaining a healthy economy. Directly or indirectly, the military program financed the research behind America's most important technological innovations. Moreover, such giant corporations as General Electric, General Motors, and Douglas Air-

craft subcontracted portions of their military work to smaller companies. If the government were to terminate a big defense contract, it might send shock waves through a large section of the economy and undo the government's efforts to sustain prosperity.

A former general first popularized the phrase that most Americans used to describe these arrangements. President Eisenhower, always unhappy over the accumulation of power in Washington and always skeptical of budget demands from the military, devoted part of a farewell address in January 1961 to warn the nation about this "military-industrial complex." During the sixties, more and more Americans came to picture the military-industrial complex as a diabolical force directing the nation's foreign policy. Actually, the government awarded military contracts in the same piecemeal fashion as it did the rest of its benefits, and the military-industrial complex remained much too decentralized to act in concert. But the sum of its influences was profound. In the past, mobilizing the nation for war had disrupted the economy. Now disarming the nation for peace threatened to disrupt the economy even more.

Along with the military industrial complex, "multinational" corporations also strengthened the connection between the domestic economy and world affairs. Before the Second World War, almost all the subdivisions that American corporations established abroad had remained small dependent outposts of the parent companies. After the war, corporate expansion entered a new phase. American industries, from soft-drink makers to automobile and electronics manufacturers, gravitated to the capital-poor nations where production costs were low, governments encouraging, and ready markets inviting. Even more important than the sheer quantity of foreign subsidiaries was the fact that an increasing proportion of them duplicated the parent company's full corporate structure and dropped roots in the societies where they were planted. By the 1950s these corporate offshoots were thriving on every continent. Still tied to their parent companies in the United States yet assimilated into the lives of foreign nations, they gave a new transnational cast to the American economy.

Multinational corporations were only the most

striking part of a massive business expansion after the Second World War. In 1946 America's private investments abroad approximated their level in 1929. During the next decade, foreign investments tripled. By the end of the 1960s, they stood almost ten times higher than in 1946. Much of this money was spent in search of minerals that the United States either lacked or used at a faster rate than it produced. Oil alone accounted for more than a third of these investments. Overall, the American economy was becoming increasingly dependent upon foreign resources and markets and upon government policies in countries around the world.

A clear purpose in international affairs, a managerial approach to international problems, and a growing economic stake in international stability all contributed to the continuity in American foreign policy during the Eisenhower and Kennedy administrations. John Foster Dulles, who as secretary of state between 1953 and 1959 was largely responsible for the conduct of American policy, moved naturally with these currents. His experience in diplomacy began in 1907. As Eisenhower commented, only half in jest, "Foster has been studying to be secretary of state since he was five years old." During his legal career Dulles had worked sympathetically with some of America's most internationally oriented businessmen. Moreover, he was adamantly anticommunist.

U.S. Brinkmanship in the Fifties. Foreign affairs continued to follow the primary rule of the Truman years: Lose no more people or territory to communism. Secretary Dulles firmly believed that the United States must convince the Soviet Union of America's willingness to risk total war in behalf of containment. Behind America's policy, Dulles pointedly reminded the world in January 1954, lay a "great capacity to retaliate, instantly, by means and at places of our own choosing." The first test of the secretary's "brinkmanship" began only a few months later in 1954. China opened a bombardment of several tiny islands less than ten miles from its coast. Chiang Kai-shek, over a hundred miles away on Formosa (Taiwan), had

fortified these islands as his outposts. In the Formosa Resolution of January 1955, Congress authorized the president to protect both Formosa and these offshore islands. At that time and again in 1958, America's leaders seriously discussed the possibility of thermonuclear war over a few rocky islands in the Formosa Strait named Quemoy and Matsu. There was "an even chance," Dulles thought, of maintaining peace or going to war. But China did not press the attack on the islands and the principle of containment was preserved.

Far closer to home, another crisis arose in 1959, when an intensely nationalistic and charismatic Cuban, Fidel Castro, toppled the dictator Fulgencio Batista and set about breaking Cuba's economic dependence on the United States. Castro's assertiveness and Washington's hostility to his revolution produced a quick rupture. The Eisenhower administration established the main lines of a policy that the Kennedy administration continued after 1960: an economic boycott of Cuba, an attempt to isolate it politically in the Western Hemisphere, and encouragement for Cuban counterrevolutionaries. There were also secret American plans to assassinate Castro. Castro came to rely much more on Soviet assistance than he had anticipated, and soon the Cuban government formally committed itself to communism. Not only had the cardinal rule of containment been violated; the breach had occurred just off the Florida coast.

Castro became an American obsession. President Kennedy, who controlled his administration's foreign policy and shared Dulles's commitment to containment, entered office in 1961 with a powerful urge to eliminate Castro. When the CIA promised a successful counterrevolution in Cuba if it could only land a cadre of Castro's opponents on the island, Kennedy allowed the CIA to train a small army of Cuban exiles in preparation for such an attack. On April 17, 1961, an ill-equipped force of 1,400 emigrés made a disastrous landing in Cuba at the Bay of Pigs, where the invaders and America's reputation promptly sank together. As sponsor of the invasion, the United States was guilty of violating another nation's basic rights. As manager of America's foreign policy, the

FIDEL CASTRO AND NIKITA KHRUSHCHEV
It was a happy moment for Castro and Khrushchev but an ominous one in Washington, where their embrace was interpreted as a grave threat to containment. *(Wide World Photos, Inc.)*

president was vulnerable to charges that he had done either too much or too little in assisting the emigré army.

The Bay of Pigs was background to a much graver crisis a year later. After the Cuban exiles' attack, both Castro and Soviet Premier Nikita Khrushchev, a tough but erratic gambler, calculated that missile bases in Cuba would improve their bargaining positions with the United States. Secretly a flow of Soviet materials and technicians began to arrive in Cuba. American intelligence learned about the missile sites in 1962 as they were being constructed. Neither Kennedy nor Secretary of Defense Robert McNamara considered Cuban missiles a threat to America's military security. In a global scale of power, their meaning was "psychological and political." Rejecting advice to bomb the sites at once, the president announced on October 22, 1962, that the United States would set a naval blockade around Cuba and demanded an immediate halt to the missile traffic. The

world held its breath. A day after the blockade went into effect a dozen Soviet supply ships stopped in their courses, then turned for home. Russia dismantled the bases, America promised to honor Cuba's sovereignty, and in the United States, Kennedy emerged from the ordeal a hero.

Khrushchev also designated another point of international crisis. The rough-hewn Soviet premier came to full power in 1958 determined to break the stalemate of the Cold War. He especially bridled at the impasse over a divided Germany. In an effort to force both the diplomatic recognition of East Germany and a new settlement for Berlin, Khrushchev not only threatened to restrict Western access to the city, but he declared that the Soviet Union and East Germany might have to decide Berlin's future by themselves. Off and on between 1958 and 1962, Berlin, that isolated Western outpost, once again became a potential center of war. The peak of danger occurred in the summer and fall of 1961, when the communists

THE BERLIN WALL
With the wall came the threat of war.   *(U.S. Army Photo)*

erected a wall across Berlin to seal off their section of the city and so prevent dissidents from leaving. "The threat is worldwide," President Kennedy told the nation, and he made preliminary moves toward war mobilization by calling up military reserves, increasing civil defense, and reinforcing the American garrison in Berlin. Although the Berlin Wall remained, the crisis passed. By 1962 neither side wished to press the other on the issue of Berlin.

In each area of crisis—the Far Eastern offshore islands, Cuba, and Berlin—the United States sought to preserve the status quo. Indeed, American policy expressed a general opposition to major changes and upheavals. In 1958 the urge to maintain the status quo led Eisenhower to land 14,000 American troops in Lebanon, in an attempt to keep the bitter, tangled rivalries of the Middle East from toppling govern-

ments that were friendly to the United States. Between 1960 and 1964, a similar impulse lay behind the financial and diplomatic assistance that the United States gave to a United Nations police force in the Congo (Zaire), where a chaotic civil war was racking this former Belgian colony. American policy was accurately described as antirevolutionary. In even broader terms, it was antidisruptive. In July 1956, for example, fiery President Gamal Nasser of Egypt vented his anger at the Western powers by seizing the Suez Canal. From a mixture of motives and a mistaken impression that the United States would support them, England, France, and Israel coordinated military forces in October to humble Nasser and retake the canal. The United States, however, broke from its allies. Coldly cooperating with the Soviet Union, the Eisenhower administration worked through the United Nations to halt the war and return the canal to Egypt.

The strong desire to stabilize international affairs tempered America's foreign policy throughout the Eisenhower and Kennedy years. Despite loose Republican promises during the 1952 campaign to "roll back the iron curtain" in Europe and "unleash" Chiang Kai-shek's army on China, the Eisenhower administration carefully avoided either course. When East Germans rioted in 1953 and Hungarians revolted against their government in 1956, the United States did nothing to provoke a wider conflict. In East Asia, the United States made an explicitly defensive treaty with Formosa in 1955, and on several other occasions Secretary Dulles assured Americans that the leash on Chiang Kai-shek was very tight indeed.

Hope for Peaceful Coexistence.   The longer America's containment policy lasted, the more it seemed to be a ceaseless international game played according to a careful set of rules. The first, tentative moves to regularize the competition of the Cold War occurred soon after President Eisenhower took office. Stalin's death in 1953, coinciding with a new administration in Washington, reopened the possibility for the first positive exchange between the Soviet and American governments since 1947. Very gingerly, diplomats from the two superpowers began to explore a number of delicate problems, including a settlement for Germany and a limitation on armaments. In 1955 they actually signed a peace treaty for Austria.

The symbol of hope for a new era of "peaceful coexistence" was the summit conference between Soviet and American heads of state, comparable to the ones Roosevelt, Churchill, and Stalin had held during the Second World War. Worldwide pressures for such a conference grew too strong for either great power to resist. In July 1955, for the first time in ten years, the president of the United States and the premier of the Soviet Union, along with their counterparts from Britain and France, sat down together at a meeting in Geneva. Less formally, Eisenhower and Khrushchev met again at Camp David, Maryland, in September 1959. Although Americans spoke optimistically about a new "spirit of Geneva" in 1955 and then a new "spirit of Camp David" in 1959, the next two summit conferences were disasters. Just before an eagerly anticipated meeting at Paris in 1960, an American U-2 spy plane was downed far inside Russia and its pilot, Francis Gary Powers, was displayed to the world as proof of America's hostile intentions. Khrushchev's angry attacks on Eisenhower wrecked the Paris meeting. Then at Vienna in 1961, the distrust between Khrushchev and Kennedy ruined the chances for an effective conference. For a time, the vogue of the summit ended.

Nevertheless, the underlying forces for stabilization continued to operate. Both the United States and the Soviet Union found the management of their international spheres a complicated, frustrating, and expensive task. Both had little success appealing to the so-called neutral countries outside the two spheres. Both were deeply committed to providing consumer satisfactions at home. Moreover, as the weapons of nuclear annihilation piled higher and higher in the arsenals of both nations, their leaders were to some degree sobered by the incredible power they could unleash. "We have arrived at that point," Eisenhower acknowledged in 1954, "where war does not present the possibility of victory or defeat." His counterpart in the Soviet Union, Georgi Malenkov, who had succeeded Stalin, had already admitted as much a year earlier. Each of these parallel develop-

ments applied a slight brake of caution to the diplomacy of the Cold War. Gradually the trends seemed to be moving from a volatile Cold War to a predictable Cold Peace.

Presidential Leadership

Each additional step in the process of modernization placed a heavier burden of management on the president. After the Great Depression, the responsibility for maintaining a sound economy never left the White House. During the 1940s, world war and cold war placed the president at the center of America's international security, with responsibility for life and death around the world. By the 1950s the president alone seemed capable of ensuring the nation's unity, stability, and progress.

Changes in the Presidency. Under this massive weight of responsibilities, the meaning of the presidency changed in two important respects. First, the office was separated from the normal patterns of electoral politics. Beginning with Eisenhower's triumph in 1952, the vote for president no longer followed the same curve as the nationwide vote for other Democratic and Republican candidates. Franklin Roosevelt's rising and falling majorities had roughly paralleled the majorities of the Democratic party. Even Harry Truman's surprising victory in 1948 had coincided with a similar Democratic revival. After 1952, however, the presidential vote set a course of its own. In 1954 the Democrats recaptured both houses of Congress and continued to hold them, usually by substantial majorities. By contrast to this steady, partisan line, the presidential returns swung in big loops every four years that expressed the public's specific choices between candidates.

As Americans detached their president from normal party politics, they were developing a new relation with him that had relatively little to do with the electoral process. Its crucial components were television and national opinion polls. The president spoke directly to all the people through television; they responded directly to him through opinion polls.

A presidential election was merely the most formal and dramatic moment in a continuous dialogue. Between elections, a string of opinion polls charted results that were widely interpreted as substitute elections, measuring the success of the nation's leader. Any overwhelming endorsement of the president, such as Eisenhower's runaway victories in the 1952 and 1956 elections or Kennedy's impressive ratings in the opinion polls of 1961 and 1962, became a sign of national strength. By the same token, a sharp drop in Truman's ratings during 1951 and 1952 signaled a severe national problem. Americans, in other words, made their month-by-month judgments of the president into a bedside graph of America's health.

The second significant change in the presidency involved the requirements for effective national leadership. The complex nature of the president's tasks forced him to act as a mobilizing leader for the whole nation and, at the same time, as a cautious manager of America's intricate foreign and domestic affairs. As early as the 1930s, Roosevelt had understood the need to be both inspiring and moderate. FDR, however, served during a bitterly partisan period when no one could hope to transcend parties and represent all the people. Moreover, his leadership was identified not with steady management but with great emergencies: depression, then war. Truman was the last of the openly partisan presidents. The Missouri scrapper seldom allowed anyone to forget that he was a Democrat, and his quick temper, sharp tongue, and unpredictable ways clashed with the image of a smooth manager.

Nonpartisanship in the Presidency. Eisenhower was the first to meet the modern demands on the president. The general's background allowed him to appear a man above the clamor of special interests. Each landmark in his military career—wartime commander of the Allied armies of Europe, chief of staff, and commander of NATO's forces—suggested the highest level of nonpartisanship. Even as president, Eisenhower liked to think of himself as a nonpartisan leader. He projected an instinctive fairness that promised to reunite the nation after the harsh years of

Truman and McCarthy. Although his temper and tongue could match Truman's, Eisenhower held them in public. Eisenhower never mastered the art of a formal television speech, but he was irresistibly attractive in casual shots. His incomparable smile, strong stride, and easy yet authoritative manner made him everybody's Ike. In a special sense, Eisenhower seemed able to speak to all Americans at home and speak for them abroad.

Eisenhower strengthened his position as national leader by delegating much of the controversial work of his administration. While his secretary of state used the militant language of the Cold War, the president spoke in a moderate, conciliatory tone. The world identified Dulles with "brinkmanship." It identified Eisenhower with "Atoms for Peace," a program to share America's scientific knowledge that the president first proposed in 1953 and then elaborated in 1955. In election years Eisenhower relied almost always on broad, bland pronouncements. Vice-President Richard Nixon was the administration's partisan voice, and every two years he flayed the Democrats with rawhide campaign rhetoric.

The Eisenhower formula was unbeatable. In the campaign of 1956, the Democrats again set the cultivated phrasemaker, Adlai Stevenson of Illinois, against the president, and again Eisenhower easily defeated him, 457 electoral votes to 73. As long as Eisenhower remained in the White House, no one else seemed very important as a national leader. However, at the nominating conventions of 1960, Richard Nixon and John Kennedy came to prominence. Vice-President Nixon, borrowing a reflected glory from the nation's one indispensable leader, became the president's natural successor. Muting his earlier partisanship, Nixon conducted his campaign like the heir apparent who would continue the policies of Eisenhower's popular rule. The Democrats, sensing the need for a new name to replace Stevenson, chose the youthful Senator Kennedy from Massachusetts, whose well-organized and liberally financed primary campaign gave him a considerable edge over his competitors. In the closest presidential race since the late nineteenth century, the inexperienced Kennedy won, receiving a scant 100,000 votes more than the uninspired Nixon.

The Election of 1960

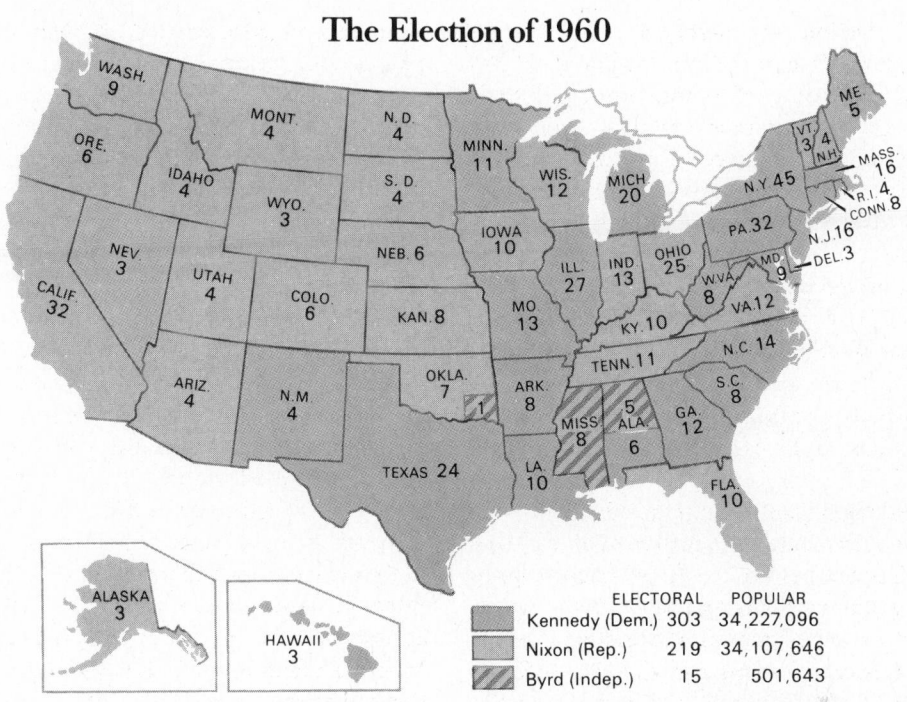

	ELECTORAL	POPULAR
Kennedy (Dem.)	303	34,227,096
Nixon (Rep.)	219	34,107,646
Byrd (Indep.)	15	501,643

Kennedy's New Frontier.   When Kennedy entered the White House in 1961, the modern role of the president was already well defined. In place of his predecessor's nonpartisan background, Kennedy's large family fortune conveyed a similar detachment from the scramble of economic interests. In place of Eisenhower's reputation for fairness, Kennedy's record of personal courage in the Second World War suggested that he, too, would make a strong, even-handed leader. Kennedy, like his immediate predecessors, tried to balance militancy and moderation in his foreign policy. After the Cuban missile crisis of 1962, for example, came the Test Ban Treaty of 1963, in which the Soviet Union and the United States agreed to stop contaminating the atmosphere with their nuclear tests.

Kennedy's most impressive contributions to the new leadership involved the intangibles of vitality and charm. By the end of the Eisenhower years, many Americans were mourning a loss of national energy. The economy was sluggish. The launching of the Sputnik satellite suggested that American science was losing in competition with the Russians, and Khrushchev's humiliation of Eisenhower at the Paris summit meeting suggested that the United States was also losing the initiative in foreign affairs.

As the youngest elected president in history, Kennedy at forty-three radiated vigor. By sponsoring a wide assortment of studies and reports, the new president imaginatively associated his office with the definition of broad national goals. Kennedy recognized that Americans of all types and ages would look on a journey to the moon as a truly national undertaking. The organization of the Peace Corps in 1961, through which American volunteers took their skills to the world's poor nations, had a comparable appeal. Appropriate to his administration's image of youthful adventure, Kennedy identified his presidency with explorations of the New Frontier.

The handsome, erect Kennedy made a striking appearance on television, as he had already demonstrated in his televised debates with Nixon during

HUMANIZING THE WHITE HOUSE
Through his family as well as
his presidential style, John Kennedy sent sparks of vitality and
hope across the country. In 1962,
five-year-old Caroline and two-
year-old John, Jr., dance to their
father's clapping. *(United Press
International, Inc.)*

the 1960 campaign. As president, Kennedy continued to excel in both formal and informal uses of the medium. At times, his private affairs seemed to loom larger across the nation than his public actions. Through the eager cooperation of the news industry, the president and his stunningly attractive, photogenic family entered everybody's lives: Jack and his wife, Jackie, their children, Caroline and John Jr., the president's brother, Bobby, and the rest of the vibrant Kennedy clan.

Nothing better illustrated this intimate bond between Kennedy and the public than America's response to the president's assassination in Dallas on November 22, 1963. For a long, mournful weekend, the nation immersed itself in every detail of the tragedy and its aftermath. Through television, Americans traced the president's motorcade, saw Kennedy jarred by an explosion of shots, shared the vigil outside the

hospital, witnessed the incredible murder of the prime suspect, Lee Harvey Oswald, and then followed the doleful state funeral through the gray streets of Washington. No event had ever been so thoroughly national and yet so intensely personal. Almost two decades later, with important questions about the assassination still unanswered, millions could re-create those "six seconds in Dallas" as if their lives, too, had hung in the balance. In memory, Kennedy's popularity soared. A majority of Americans, in a Gallup poll in 1976, judged him the greatest of all American presidents.

After Kennedy's successor, Lyndon B. Johnson, had been in office only a few months, the Democratic party nominated him for a presidential term in his own right. Although Johnson had neither the towering prestige of Eisenhower nor the brilliant charm of Kennedy, he did have a long record of moderate congressional management and by 1964 a brief but striking record of presidential leadership. To challenge Johnson in 1964, the Republicans selected the deeply conservative senator from Arizona, Barry Goldwater. Goldwater represented a wing of the Republican party that opposed city bosses and government bureaucrats, labor unions and farm subsidies, welfare payments and poverty programs. That fall, the Arizona senator, an honest, articulate man, spoke his mind freely. He promised thorough, drastic changes in government policy, including a considerably more aggressive foreign policy. Johnson skillfully kept his campaign within the standard presidential mold of dynamic temperateness. If anyone had doubted the popular appeal of the modern presidential model, this election must have settled the issue. The contest between Johnson's image of unifying moderation and Goldwater's image of factional extremism was remarkably clear: Johnson received the largest proportion of popular votes in presidential history, 43 million to Goldwater's 27 million.

The Crisis in National-Local Relations

There was such optimism in the fifties in the powers of national management that some Americans came to believe that every problem had a national, managerial solution. But as the national government enlarged the scope of its responsibilities, it generated new problems. The first sign of these unexpected consequences appeared in an increasingly angry clash between an expansive national government and a threatened world of local white power.

One of President Eisenhower's earliest appointments was a new chief justice of the Supreme Court. He chose the affable California Republican, Earl Warren, who had been an extremely popular governor and the party's vice-presidential candidate in 1948. Warren, classified a "liberal Republican," was a skilled mediator who had no record of interest in social experimentation. He had even participated in the drive to intern Japanese Americans during the Second World War. His appointment seemed to augur a safe, middle-of-the-road Court.

The Court and Segregation. When Earl Warren became chief justice in 1953, the most significant issue pending before the Supreme Court was racial segregation in the public schools. Precedents that challenged the doctrine of "separate but equal" educational facilities for blacks had been accumulating for more than a decade, but the Supreme Court had phrased them in cautious, narrow terms. Many observers expected a similar wording from the moderate new chief justice. Instead, in the unanimous decision of *Brown* v. *Board of Education* (1954), Warren boldly declared separate educational facilities inherently unequal and inhumane. The long legal march of the National Association for the Advancement of Colored People had reached its objective. At a stroke, the Court undercut the entire structure of Jim Crow laws.

JIM CROW IN THE FORTIES
The first target in the campaign for black rights was the elaborate caste system of the South.   *(Magnum Photos, Inc.)*

INTEGRATING LITTLE ROCK HIGH SCHOOL
President Eisenhower's unprecedented use of military power in 1957 did not change the
basic pattern of segregation in the southern states. *(Wide World Photos, Inc.)*

Few successful white Americans could debate Warren's conclusions. In their occupational world, distinctions based on skin color had no logical justification, and a rigid structure of Jim Crow drinking fountains and bus seats seemed absurd. In the postwar years, segregation had become an obvious affront to America's modern values. At home, it clashed with the ideal of an open society, in which citizens were free to acquire all the skills they could learn and buy all the goods they could earn. Abroad, it jeopardized America's chances of bringing people with brown or black or yellow skin into a worldwide anticommunist league. Prominent southern liberals increasingly joined the critics of segregation. By the 1950s nationally minded Americans regarded Jim Crow as an anachronism that a modern society could no longer tolerate.

They considered education an excellent place to begin racial desegregation. Because successful Americans based their own careers on specialized skills, they immediately recognized the serious consequences of an inferior education. Moreover, they believed that completely dismantling the caste system would require slow, careful adjustments over many years. If children in integrated schools grew up free of prejudice, these new generations, coming one after another, would eventually eliminate the last traces of racial hate. Time and the power of education lay on the side of progress. In this spirit of optimistic caution the Supreme Court declared in the second *Brown* decision of 1955 that school desegregation should proceed "with all deliberate speed."

During the next decade, the conflicts over racial segregation reinforced these initial desires to abolish it. It was the opponents of segregation who could almost always claim to be law-abiding, orderly, and moderate. Southern whites, on the other hand, threw all manner of legal obstacles in the path of integration, ranging from the groundless constitutional doctrine of "state interposition" between the national government and its citizens, to the substitution of private segregated schools for the public system. With increasing firmness, the federal courts removed each one. In 1957, when Governor Orval Faubus of

Arkansas defied a court order to desegregate Little Rock High School, it required a wall of soldiers to protect the thin line of black students from a menacing crowd of adult whites. Individual blacks faced a comparable experience as they tried to enter the state universities in Alabama and Mississippi. In 1957 and 1960 Congress passed two mild civil rights laws that allowed the federal courts to intervene in behalf of disfranchised blacks. A number of southern politicians reacted as if the right to vote were a subversive doctrine.

Black Protest. During the same years, blacks and whites also confronted each other directly over segregation. Blacks took the initiative, and their movement quickly became identified with the particular style of an intense, eloquent young minister from Montgomery, Alabama—Martin Luther King, Jr. Not yet twenty-seven years old, he emerged in 1955 as the nationally publicized leader of a local boycott against Montgomery's segregated buses. Through words and example, King provided blacks with a creative combination of the Christian love that their churches taught, the strategy of peaceful mass resistance that the Hindu, Mahatma Gandhi, had formulated, and the self-discipline that relatively well-to-do blacks had long used to defend their rights in America's caste system. While King was inspiring his fellow blacks with appeals for nonviolent direct action, he was also attracting wide support among whites committed to orderly behavior and peaceful change. Increasingly King was heralded as an American statesman.

In 1960 black students throughout the cities of the South applied King's tactics in a dramatic wave of "sit-ins" that desegregated numerous restaurants, then a variety of other public accommodations. The following year the Congress on Racial Equality (CORE), another organization of peaceful resistance, sponsored black and white "freedom riders" on a harrowing bus trip into the South that publicized the illegal segregation in interstate travel. This pillar of Jim Crow also toppled. As in the case of Little Rock, the violent responses to these protests strengthened the bond between white and black moderates.

In 1963, when King led a movement against segregation in Birmingham, Alabama, national television vividly recorded the cattle prods, fires hoses, and snarling dogs that local police used to intimidate blacks. Murders relating to the civil rights movement that year in Birmingham and the next summer in Mississippi could not be prosecuted in the southern courts. King's Southern Christian Leadership Conference (SCLC) and its offspring, the Student Non-Violent Coordinating Committee (SNCC), seemed the embodiment of rationality in contrast to the revived Ku Klux Klan, the raucous rhetoric of local southern politicians, and the partiality of southern white courts.

MOBILIZING FOR CIVIL RIGHTS
Eloquence, courage, and ingenuity made Martin Luther King, Jr., an extraordinary public leader. In this 1966 photo he was speaking at the Antioch Baptist Church in Camden, Ala. *(Bob Adelman/Magnum Photos, Inc.)*

White sympathy for King's inspired moderation continued to rise in the summer of 1963 when a quarter-million Americans, including a significant minority of whites, dramatized the plight of the blacks by marching peacefully through Washington and gathering at the Lincoln Memorial. There they heard King's moving message of hope: "I have a dream that one day [in the deep South] ... little black boys and black girls will be able to join hands with little white boys and white girls and walk together as sisters and brothers."

Executive Leadership. What was missing was strong political leadership. The White House had largely held aloof from the civil rights movement. President Eisenhower, who later cursed his choice of Earl Warren as chief justice, stated privately "that the Supreme Court decision [on school desegregation] *set back* progress in the South at least fifteen years.... We can't demand *perfection* in these moral questions." No one was less happy than Eisenhower when the posturing Governor Faubus forced the president to intervene in little Rock. Kennedy was equally cautious as he began his term. Despite campaign promises to end racial discrimination in public housing with "a stroke of the presidential pen," he delayed almost two years before signing the appropriate executive order, and then it covered only future public housing. Finally, Kennedy delivered an important address in support of black rights and called for new legislation in blacks' behalf. However, Kennedy's pressure on Congress still lagged behind his words.

Lyndon Johnson filled the void in leadership. Always a restless soul, he had left the Texas hills as a youth, entered Congress in the 1930s, then moved up to the Senate in 1949. During Eisenhower's two terms, Johnson was generally regarded as the most powerful Democrat in Washington. An exceptionally skillful legislative director, he combined a relentless energy, a keen understanding of politics, and a driving ambition for greatness. A good many people were surprised in 1960 when Johnson accepted the nomination for vice-president. But the shrewd Texan, who had watched Nixon step from vice-president to the Republican presidential nomination, knew just what he was doing.

By temperament, Johnson was always prepared to lead. With Kennedy's grave scarcely sealed in November 1963, the new president was already mobilizing for action, and during his first two years in office he compiled an astonishing record. Some of the measures he sponsored had originated with the Kennedy administration. Others were Johnson's own. Declaring a "War on Poverty," the president convinced Congress to invest billions of dollars in training the unemployed, supporting community development, reviving impoverished regional economies, and expanding educational services in the slums. As headquarters for this war, Congress in 1964 created the Office of Economic Opportunity (OEO). In addition, the Education Act of 1965 marked the beginning of massive federal aid to the public and parochial schools. Finally, after decades of discussion, medical insurance (Medicare) was instituted for the elderly who were collecting Social Security benefits.

In each of these two extraordinary years, President Johnson guided an important civil rights law through Congress. In the Civil Rights Act of 1964, the national government became involved in almost every area of the expanding movement for equality: voting, public accommodations, schools, employment. Under the Civil Rights Act of 1965, which concentrated on the franchise, the national government could act as official registrar for black voters in the South. Under the provisions of the new law, the lists of eligible black voters rapidly expanded. Johnson, who cherished the tradition of the New Deal, assumed his administration could facilitate the rise of black Americans much as the Roosevelt administration had assisted the poor thirty years earlier. In effect, the War on Povery was a selective antidepression program, and a high proportion of the impoverished Americans it was designed to help were blacks. The Civil Rights Acts of 1964 and 1965 completed a framework for racial reform that in many ways resembled the New Deal's labor policies of the late 1930s. They established uniform rules, centralized the administration of these rules, and relied on a sympathetic federal judiciary to enforce them.

"WE SHALL OVERCOME"
President Lyndon Johnson's enthusiasm for racial equality is apparent in this scene as he reaches out to black children and their parents. *(Lyndon Baines Johnson Memorial Library)*

Local Values and Desegregation. Johnson's legislative success ended one phase of the movement for black rights. Its rationale had actually been stated in 1944 by Gunnar Myrdal's *An American Dilemma*, which dominated the understanding of race relations for the next twenty years. In this thorough study that Myrdal prepared for the Carnegie Foundation, the Swedish scholar defined antiblack prejudice as the one great contradiction to the "American creed," a nationally accepted set of beliefs in equality, opportunity, and justice for everybody. Behind the civil rights movement lay a faith that this American creed would inevitably triumph over its antiblack contradictions. The Warren Court depended on the creed to give social authority to its legal rulings against segregation. Martin Luther King depended on the creed as a national white conscience that his strategy of civil disobedience could stir. The Johnson administration depended on the creed to rally the people who were still resisting a national program to eliminate racial inequalities from American life.

Because of their common faith in the creed, a disciplined black minority and a well-to-do white minority had been able to work together in the cause of black rights. As a climax to the biracial civil rights movement, whites enthusiastically applauded in 1964 when King rose in Oslo to receive the Nobel Prize for Peace.

But contrary to the hopes of those in the civil rights movement, millions of whites understood the American creed not as a common system of national values but as a justification for their particular set of local values. Turning inward, they continued to be concerned only with their own family groups, cultural identities, and special local ways. In the 1960s about half of America's white wage earners still lived in "ethnic, religious, and social enclaves relatively untouched by [the postwar years] and emphatically personal in character." Attempts to draw local Americans into a uniform system of national rules arrived like an enemy invasion. In most cases they could not grasp the legal and bureaucratic procedures behind such rules. As a study in 1970 revealed, a majority of Americans were "functionally illiterate" in the face of tax forms, insurance claims, credit contracts, and similar fine print. In the 1950s and 1960s, plans for urban improvement seldom took into account the local ways of life they were disrupting. The acronym for one local organization spoke the feelings of innumerable Americans from the inner city: SOUR—Stamp Out Urban Renewal. Similar suspicions and resentments defeated a majority of local referenda on fluoridating water systems during these same years. In the countryside as well as the city, it was becoming harder each year for Americans to protect their local networks.

In many localities skin color was a primary means of establishing protective barriers. White wage earners, who increasingly worked with people of other colors, still refused to accept such people in their neighborhoods, schools, parks, and taverns. During the fifties these insular feelings exploded in anger throughout the South, where the civil rights movement first concentrated. But temperatures were also rising in the North. During the 1950s every northern city suffered from a housing shortage that dated from the slowing of home construction late in the 1920s. Indeed, there was a growing pressure on all kinds of city resources, partly as a result of new migrations. Rural blacks and whites who had been replaced by mechanical cotton pickers, consolidated farms, and mechanized coal mining poured into the city slums. So did Mexican Americans and Puerto Ricans, who were trying to escape their own grinding poverty. In a crowded arena of competitors, racial antagonisms turned into hate. When King took his civil rights campaign north in 1964, the ferocity of the white reaction matched anything he had encountered in the South.

Other Challenges to Local Power. By itself, the civil rights movement would have tipped modern America's delicate balance between national and local authority. Establishing national rules in such an extremely sensitive area of local white privilege guaranteed revolt in many localities. But civil rights did not come alone. A broader movement for national uniformity accompanied the movement for

black rights and threatened an array of traditionally local powers. Because the Supreme Court figured so prominently in this nationalizing process, the Warren Court came to symbolize a wholesale assault on local America. "Impeach Earl Warren" became a popular slogan of resistance. Between 1956 and 1966, the Court significantly narrowed the local power to censor obscenity. Beginning with the *Mallory* decision of 1956 and culminating in the *Escobedo* and *Miranda* decisions of 1964 and 1966, it set standards of police procedure to protect the rights of suspected criminals. In 1962 and 1964, the Court outlawed prayers and Bible readings in the public schools. Through *Baker* v. *Carr* (1962) and *Reynolds* v. *Sims* (1964), the Court also required the creation of state election districts that would approximate the rule of "one person, one vote."

Each of these changes challenged an established local right. Censorship of movies, pornography, and schoolbooks was widely used to preserve local values. As the fear of street crime spread in the cities, many people thought they would not be able to walk in their neighborhoods if the police were hobbled in pursuit of suspected criminals. Religion, many Americans continued to believe, belonged in the schools just as it did in the home. Establishing election districts that underrepresented the cities was the customary way for voters and politicians to ensure that the state legislature would protect the rights of small towns against outside intrusions. In some instances, city-dwellers used the same device against the suburbs.

The period of acute crisis in local power began in 1957. That year, Congress passed the first civil rights law since Reconstruction, federal troops entered Little Rock to enforce school desegregation, and the Warren Court embarked on its most active period. By 1965 the local barriers against national power appeared to be smashed. Washington officials were registering black voters in the rural South. The Warren Court had defined its broad national domain. As local governments complained of a budget squeeze, fresh funds for the war on poverty were bypassing almost all of the white neighborhoods in favor of the people economically below them. Not only did the public welfare rolls swell enormously in the mid-1960s, but some agents of OEO were even encouraging welfare recipients to demand more. Until 1964 the president and Congress indicated from time to time that they had not completely forsaken the old balance. But when President Johnson called for a Great Society in January 1965, he officially committed his administration to a vigorous national management of matters that once were privileges of localities. That year Congress responded with large majorities for the president's program.

Nationally oriented Americans had convinced themselves that their understanding of equality, opportunity, and justice was everybody's American creed. As they used this creed to make national policy, they assumed that no one would seriously question the new policy's impartiality. Bursts of opposition, they believed, were only temporary interruptions in the march toward nationwide acceptance. But this nationalizing process had the opposite effect. Instead of creating a nonpolitical consensus, it ignited fresh political conflicts. By 1965 not a great deal had actually changed. Only a small percentage of black children attended integrated classes. Many communities still found ways of keeping Christianity in and "alien" books out of their schools. Police procedures altered very little. Nevertheless, when locally oriented whites saw a solid phalanx in the national government arrayed against them, they prepared to fight for their traditional rights.

The Decline of Containment

A second crisis in Washington's management occurred in international affairs. Here also the nation's leaders tried to impose their understanding of events on people who lived by very different values. In this case, it was the doctrine of containment that clashed with people's aspirations, and it was a variety of nations throughout the world that challenged America's right to thwart their own distinctive ambitions.

From the beginning, containment was a specifically American policy. Relatively few other nations gave anticommunism the same overriding importance that the United States assigned to it. The more

the Cold War stabilized and America's European allies became economically independent, the more they followed their own interpretation of world affairs. France led the resistance. By refusing to join the European Defense Community (EDC) in 1954, France destroyed America's plans for a thoroughly integrated continental military force. After 1958 the government in Paris, under its imperious president, Charles de Gaulle, furnished a center for continuing European criticism of American policy. More subtly, Japan also maneuvered for greater independence from the United States. No sooner had the American occupation ended in 1951 than Japan sought full control over its own territory and policies. Here, as in Western Europe, desire to trade with communist nations contributed to the tension, for the United States opposed almost all economic relations between the two international spheres.

Containment versus Nationalism. Although the world's agrarian nations had a meager share in the prosperity of the 1950s, many of them, too, were marking their own separate paths. The electric names in Africa and Asia were those of fervent nationalists such as Gamal Nassar of Egypt, Kwame Nkrumah of Ghana, Jawaharlal Nehru of India, and Sukarno of Indonesia. In a variety of ways, these leaders struggled to develop their nations without sacrificing their independence to either side in the Cold War. Extremely sensitive to pressures from the great powers, they retaliated in anger when the United States or the Soviet Union appeared to dangle economic aid as an incentive to enter their camps. Because the United States was allied with their former imperial masters in Europe, the recently emancipated colonies especially set themselves against American domination in the future.

In the face of these nationalist assertions, John Foster Dulles held tenaciously to the principles of containment. Eisenhower's secretary of state threatened France with an "agonizing reappraisal" of American support, and he condemned the trend toward neutralism among the agrarian nations. As far as possible he minimized the importance that such countries as India and Pakistan, or Greece and Turkey, assigned to their own feuds. After Dulles's retirement in 1959, however, the monolithic conceptions of the Cold War began to erode. With Kennedy's inauguration, officials in Washington began exploring ways of responding to the diverse ambitions of many nations. The new president, who expected to build his reputation in foreign affairs, encouraged fresh ideas about America's policies. He promised to accept the new nations of Africa and Asia on their own terms and to negotiate with the established nations as equals. In 1961 Kennedy announced the "Alliance for Progress" with Latin America that would use economic aid from the United States to improve the quality of life in the Western Hemisphere. The Peace Corps also placed individual human needs above international military policy.

Nevertheless, in the day-to-day conduct of foreign affairs, Kennedy, his primary adviser on foreign policy, McGeorge Bundy, and his secretary of state, Dean Rusk, gave priority to the containment of international communism. During the 1960 campaign Kennedy had claimed that Soviet technological advances had outstripped those of the United States, creating a "missile gap." Though no one ever found the gap, the new president "initiated the largest and swiftest military buildup in America's peacetime history." Through a flexible military power, Kennedy envisaged a new American mastery in the global battle against communism. In Latin America, American policy was not the implementation of the Alliance for Progress but the isolation of Castro's Cuba and the insulation of other countries against similar revolutions. Aid from the United States reflected the degree of a Latin American nation's commitment to anticommunism.

Involvement in Vietnam. Under Kennedy's successor, even the exploration of alternatives dwindled. Johnson came to office in 1963 with a long-standing dedication to containment, and he showed little patience with new ideas on world policy. He was the first president in at least fifteen years to give domestic issues clear precedence over international affairs. The new president assumed that it would be enough to give support to requests from the Pentagon and the State Department; they would manage international problems while he concentrated on domestic policy.

With this cast of mind, Johnson met the primary international challenge of his administration, a civil war in Vietnam. America's involvement in Vietnam dated from 1950, when the United States supplied aid to the French in their attempt to recapture their Indochinese colony. Despite this aid and an immense commitment of men and resources, France lost the battle of the jungles to Ho Chi Minh's nationalist army, and in 1954 an international conference at Geneva created three independent states from the former French territory: Laos, Cambodia, and Vietnam. Vietnam was temporarily divided between a communist north and a noncommunist south pending national elections and unification.

As France was facing defeat, the Eisenhower administration considered, then rejected, American intervention in the war. After 1954, however, the United States assumed responsibility for containing communism throughout Indochina. One-third of the foreign aid for 1955 went there, and, as Dulles explained, the Southeast Asia Treaty Organization in 1955 provided a "cover" over Indochina to protect it against international communism. With American support, the leaders in the southern portion of Vietnam repudiated the Geneva plan for national elections and established a permanent state in the south. As Kennedy took office, the anticommunist governments in both South Vietnam and neighboring Laos were in jeopardy. South Vietnamese guerrillas who had been fighting the corrupt government in Saigon consolidated their forces as the National Liberation Front (NLF). Kennedy responded by expanding America's covert military assistance, including the use by American and South Vietnamese aircraft of napalm bombs on suspect villages, the extensive spraying of dioxin—"most poisonous of all chemicals"—to defoliate guerrilla shelter, and the organization of raids inside North Vietnam, where some of the rebels were trained and supplied. The conflict in Laos stabilized, but not the one in South Vietnam. The more American the war in Vietnam became, the broader the guerrilla resistance to Saigon grew.

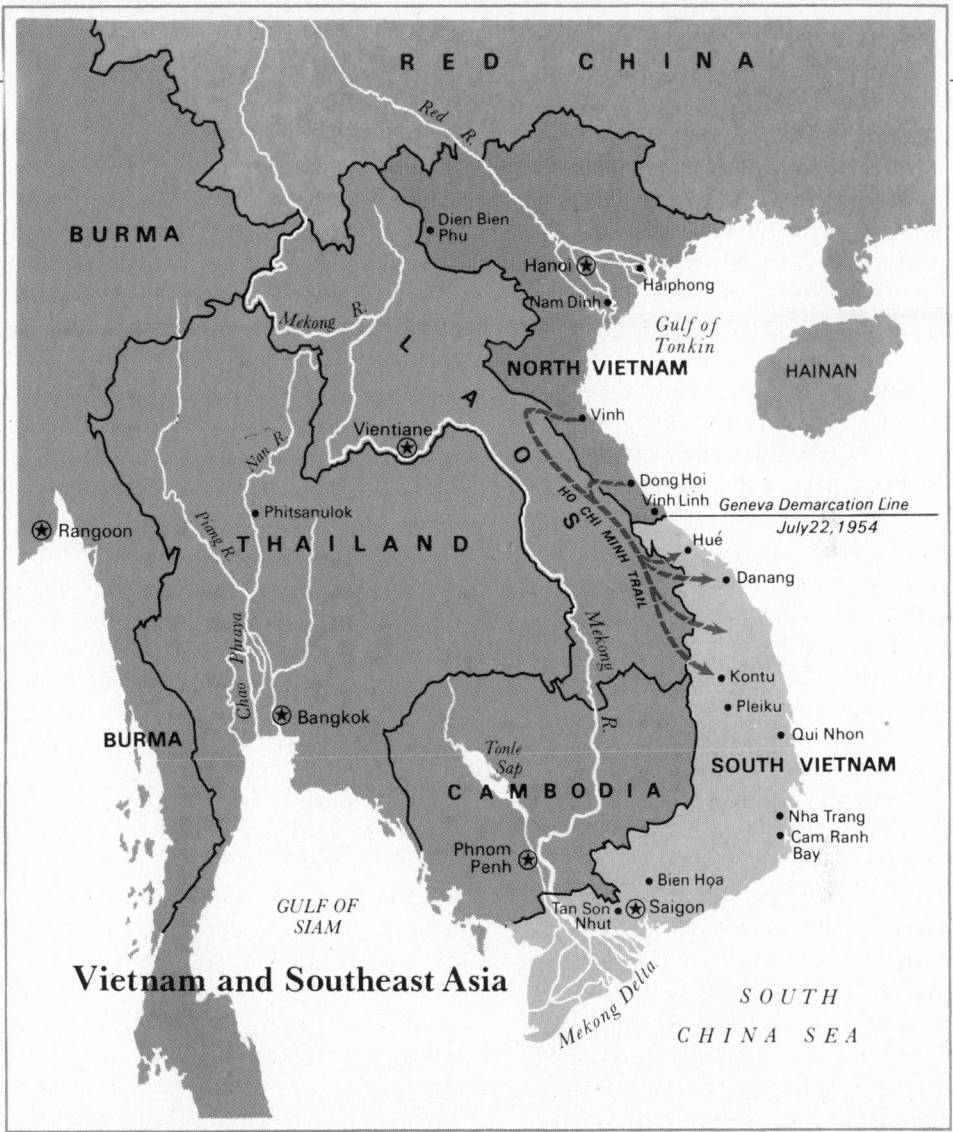

Vietnam and Southeast Asia

Johnson's Strategy. Johnson escalated America's involvement into a major war. In 1964 he inflated a small naval encounter off the Vietnamese coast as a calculated attack by North Vietnam on an American ship, and in the "Gulf of Tonkin" Resolution the Senate granted the president wide discretion in defending America's forces in Vietnam. Starting seriously in 1965, Johnson enlarged the American contingent in Vietnam until by 1968 it exceeded half a million men. Under the code name Operation Rolling Thunder, massive bombing raids struck North Vietnam, which now sent its own troops into the south. Squads of American planes bombed the winding jungle trails of Indochina in an attempt to block the flow of troops from the north. Johnson abruptly dismissed each overture to compromise.

Johnson's plan in Vietnam grew out of his central assumption about America's containment policy. As Kennedy's military adviser General Maxwell Taylor stated it, the communists had to be taught that a war for national liberation was "costly," not "cheap." Or in Dulles's words of 1954, communist guerrillas had to "suffer damage outweighing any possible gains from aggression." Johnson's strategy was to increase the level of punishment until the price of continuing the war became too high and the enemy would quit. Because the guerrilla foe was so difficult to locate, the military relied on broad coverage rather than precise assaults and inevitably took a terrible toll of civilian deaths and injuries in the process. Meanwhile, the Johnson administration issued optimistic statements about the progress of the war.

The Vietnamese did not respond according to plan. Neither North Vietnam nor the NLF weakened under increasing attack. During January and February of 1968, in a dramatic demonstration of their continuing strength, the communists launched the "Tet offensive" into major cities of South Vietnam that had been considered well beyond the reach of the guerrilla armies. Even before the Tet offensive, American opposition to the war had been rising. Like Hoover's prosperity, Johnson's victory in Vietnam stayed just around the corner too long. In the jargon of the sixties, the "credibility gap" had spread too wide. Saigon eventually reported a count of communist casualties that exceeded the total Vietnamese population.

As the military draft quotas mounted each year in the United States, so did the number of evaders. In 1968 draft resistance erupted nationwide. J. William Fulbright, the chairman of the Senate Foreign Relations Committee, who had once trusted Johnson to conduct the war in his own way, became one of its sharpest critics, and a growing body of disillusioned Democrats sided with Fulbright against the president. With the Tet offensive, television coverage and news dispatches increasingly emphasized the futility and brutality of the war. "Bombing, bombing! Why do

WAR IN VIETNAM
Who was the enemy in Vietnam? Perhaps this Vietnamese woman knew, but increasing numbers of Americans could not say. *(Philip Jones Griffiths/Magnum Photos, Inc.)*

you always write 'bombing'?" an angry officer demanded at a military briefing for reporters in Saigon. "It's air support, not bombing!" (Reporters called these sessions the "five o'clock follies.") On March 31, 1968, a frustrated Johnson turned the corner. Before a nationwide television audience, he announced an end to the escalation of the war and a new willingness to negotiate. Then in a stunning postscript, the subdued president said that he would not seek reelection.

Once a popular faith in containment would have strengthened American support for the war. By the late 1960s, however, the Vietnam crisis just accelerated the general decline of America's global policy. Communism, according to the logic of containment, was a single international system directed from Moscow. Yet throughout the 1960s, astonished Americans had been learning more and more about the bitter hostility between China and the Soviet Union. The Soviet-Chinese feud not only shattered a cardinal principle behind the Cold War; it also contributed to Americans' growing awareness that they lived in a highly diverse, subdivided world.

The Vietnam war hastened the decline of containment. Foreign governments that had been harboring resentment against the United States used the war as an occasion to express these feelings and declare their independence of Washington. Even former imperialists in Western Europe joined in the worldwide criticism of American policy in Vietnam. No nation altered its basic relations with the United States. But the American isolation that resulted from its Vietnam policy did hurry the international decentralization that had been under way for more than a decade.

By 1968 the American policy of containment was disintegrating. As the Vietnam War demonstrated, containment could not deal effectively with the rising nationalist passions among the world's agrarian peoples. Nor could it respond adequately to the growing independence among the world's industrial nations. In the early fifties containment had appeared to be a model of global management. Now this outworn policy, which the United States seemed unable to use or to abandon, had become a manager's nightmare.

The Lament
of the Individual

Meanwhile a third crisis was brewing among the very Americans who were supposed to be the primary beneficiaries of modern society. In the 1950s a minority of well-trained and well-paid people, holding jobs with national prestige in business and the professions, presumably had reached the top in American society. Yet the same nationalizing forces that gave them power and prestige also shrank their importance as individuals. The more systematized American society became, the less significant, or even distinguishable, any one person was in its operations. Perhaps, as the most critical voices of the late forties had implied, there really were no individuals in a modern bureaucratic society.

During the 1950s people praised the unifying effects of mass consumerism. They expected the computer to make sense out of the complex social problems around them. Sufficient megatons of "nuclear deterrent," they said, would preserve the free world. Publicist Peter Drucker asked Americans to picture the industrial enterprise as their social model. According to economist John Kenneth Galbraith huge "countervailing powers," or nationwide interest groups, maintained a healthy balance in the American capitalist system.

But where were the individuals in this scheme of abstractions? Such popular novels and movies as *On the Beach* and *Fail-Safe*, which portrayed life in a thermonuclear age, touched people's deep fears that the world would die in its contaminated atmosphere or that a flaw in a computer would trigger the ultimate holocaust. The audience for a dehumanizing science fiction expanded. The most intriguing new American writer of the 1950s, J. D. Salinger, and the most talented new American dramatist of the 1960s, Edward Albee, both emphasized the individual's agonizing, inescapable vulnerability in modern society. Many young writers accentuated the individual's isolation by using ordinary conversation as a way of hiding rather than communicating their characters' feelings. Only when the characters talked to themselves in lonely, interior monologues did they honestly express their emotions. Such novelists as Saul Bellow and Joseph Heller relieved the individual's preposterous fate in modern society with a wild laughter.

The Demise of the Hard-Work Ethic.   The malaise that these writers expressed was also affecting attitudes toward work. During the 1950s employers noted that white-collar employees were inquiring more often about fringe benefits like vacations, company cars, and retirement plans than they were about the challenges of the job itself. By the 1960s many corporations were discovering a new problem of morale among those executives who ran the company's daily affairs. Rising rates of absenteeism and declining rates of efficiency expressed the refusal of "middle managers" to devote themselves to jobs that were no longer rewarding. Indeed, white-collar efficiency had become a pervasive problem. Studies revealed that, on the average, an office of white-collar employees worked only about 50 percent of the time they spent in the office. In the fifties large audiences followed the television series *Ben Casey* in which the utterly dedicated doctor-hero never shed his white coat or left his patients. By the 1960s Ben Casey had become a grind. Somewhere outside of the job lay an elusive something called "fulfillment," and more and more Americans set out to find it.

It was a wide-ranging quest. Some cultivated their avocations instead of their vocations. It became increasingly common for well-to-do Americans to find their primary satisfactions in boating or bridge or travel or tennis. Leisure became something much more basic in life than simply time to recuperate. A cult of the wilderness came into vogue. The people who embraced this way of thinking condemned the artificiality of modern society and praised the value of living close to nature. The glorification of nature was in part a reaction against the biological devastation that an indiscriminate use of insecticides was causing throughout America. In a chilling best-seller, *Silent Spring* (1962), Rachel Carson eloquently publicized this modern blight. Reaction against the taste and quality of mass-produced goods helped to generate an interest in personal craftsmanship. Beginning with the modest "do-it-yourself" kits of the 1950s, handcrafts became increasingly important in the lives of white-collar Americans.

The most general expression of the individual's modern quest was a nationwide fascination with personal power. Books coached Americans on games of "one-upmanship" in their everyday relations with friends and acquaintances. Commentators and historians praised the "strong" presidents. Because the preoccupation with personal power was a mass phenomenon, it found a variety of popular outlets. The crunching game of football arrived as America's leading sport. Its competitors adapted as best they could: through shortened fences and livelier balls in baseball, the "big game" in tennis, the "dunk" in basketball, and the "power play" in hockey. High-speed auto racing attracted more and more fans. By the 1960s everybody's car could be a personal vehicle of power: Cougar, Wildcat, Thunderbird, Stingray, Mustang. Promises of personal power suffused the advertising of everything from perfumes to breakfast foods. The theme of personal power saturated the movies and television, not only in the James Bond shows and their many "superspy" imitators, but just as thoroughly in the children's cartoons and the movies' technicolor shots of mutilation and bloodshed.

Counterculture.   Against this background of doubting and searching, bands of well-to-do white youths came into the streets as the hippies, flower children, dropouts, and rebels of the 1960s. Though a minority of their age group, they were so visible and so audible that they always seemed far more numerous than they were. They clustered in the parks to smoke and to sing. They crowded the sidewalks around college campuses. They became the most committed white partisans of black rights and the bulwark of a marching, chanting peace movement. Beginning with the free speech movement at Berkeley in 1964 and culminating in the nationwide activities of Students for a Democratic Society (SDS), their protest groups rallied many more young people behind specific campaigns for student rights and social justice. Suburban high school students copied both their programs and their tactics. By 1967 and 1968, student strikes were commonplace. So were colonies of young people, including swarms of teenage runaways, who experimented with communal life, drugs, and poverty. In the late 1960s the largest of these colonies occupied much of the Haight-Ashbury district of San Francisco.

In many ways these young dissenters were acting out just one more variation of the modern adolescent rebellion. All the standard elements of the past forty years were there. Increasingly, hard rock set a musical barrier between the generations. Trust no one over thirty, the rebels declared. Even their primary areas of rebellion—dress, language, drugs, and sex—were the familiar ones from the 1920s. When young people in the 1960s wore workclothes or exotic clothes or no clothes, screamed four-letter words, substituted narcotics for alcohol, and claimed the right of sexual intercourse on demand, they were extending the very domains of personal freedom that well-to-do Americans of four decades earlier had explored.

This noisy rebellion made a penetrating commentary on contemporary life. It focused on the most sensitive problems of the individual in modern society. In response to a dehumanizing bureaucracy, the young dissenters assaulted the nation's important institutions: the government, the political party, the corporation, and the university. Some of them pointedly rejected the products of these institutions—the government's laws, the party's candidates, the corporation's goods, the university's degrees—and many more young people cheered them on. Rather than postpone gratifications in the name of a career, the young dissenters wanted the good life now. In response to feelings of loneliness, they emphasized community and loyalty and love. Craftsmanship, nature, and a "whole earth" were sacred causes. A few rebels tried to build an entire life around these values in self-sufficient rural communes. Young radicals even reflected their society's preoccupation with power. The abuse of power, they claimed, lay at the root of America's social evils. "Power to the people" would bring a new era of justice.

As they probed their doubts about their parents' lives, the young rebels divided the older generations. A minority defended the right of their sons and daughters to a dissenting life-style. Often these adults

PEACE AND FREEDOM
Shortly after this lively scene outside the 1968 Democratic convention, Chicago police attacked the demonstrators, the Democrats nominated Hubert Humphrey, and the youth movement turned sour. *(United Press International, Inc.)*

found courage to act out their own feelings. Some marched for civil rights and peace. Others, acknowledging the need for a new intimacy in human relations, experimented with "encounter" and "sensitivity" groups and greater sexual freedom. A few joined the youthful dropouts. But a majority of adults opposed the new youth movement. By making public their private anxieties, the young rebels threatened the balance that older people were trying to maintain between adult responsibility and adult discontents. The more extreme the rebellion, the more widespread the opposition became. By 1970 the young radicals had lost almost all their sympathizers.

Women's Rights.   The most lasting outgrowth of the rebellious sixties was a revived movement for women's rights. After a promising search for new directions in the 1920s, the women's movement had collapsed in the depression. Although during the forties women poured into the labor market to stay, and during the fifties, expanded the range of their public activities, the question of basic rights remained

dormant. Only in their private world away from work did women enjoy anything approximating the freedom of men. As dressing styles, leisure activities, and public behavior increasingly became "unisex," men continued to keep the best jobs. By the 1960s close to half of the women in America held paying jobs, partly because more than one-third of the marriages in America ended in divorce. Most women received lower salaries or wages than men did for the same work, and an even larger proportion of women were blocked somewhere along the ladder of promotion in their occupations. Meanwhile, women's responsibilities at home scarcely changed. The widespread concerns about individual fulfillment, the anxieties about powerlessness, and the increasing doubts about the quality of American consumerism, had particularly sharp application in the lives of women.

In 1963 Betty Friedan's *The Feminine Mystique* broke the silence. By the end of the decade, a host of books and articles had appeared that analyzed the evils of sexism. The drive for black rights contributed a vocabulary to communicate women's feelings of

SISTERHOOD
The women's movement, the last great outpouring of the sixties, raised fundamental questions about sexual discrimination and human fulfillment. *(John Olsen, Time-Life Picture Agency)*

oppression, and the inspiration for the acronym of a new pressure group, the National Organization for Women (NOW), which appeared in 1966. ("What do you want?" the civil rights marchers chanted. "FREEDOM!" "When do you want it?" "NOW!") One portion of the swelling movement explored the myriad psychic and cultural ways in which women were bound into the role of "the second sex." Consciousness-raising activities that ranged from public bra-burnings to private seminars sought to define women's special needs and give them outlets. A second portion of the movement concentrated on women's economic plight, and this agenda met far less resistance from men. Gender, like race or culture, was irrelevant to the skills standards that prevailed in most white-collar occupations. Here women's demands for an equal opportunity was an irrefutable claim. Quite promptly, both the federal courts and the national executive committed themselves to enforcing equal access to jobs, and equal pay for equal work. Although extensive discrimination against women remained, an important start had been made.

Counterattack

Early in 1968 the forces of protest and reform seemed on the verge of capturing the national government. The summer before, a quarter-million Americans had marched quietly through Washington in behalf of peace in Vietnam. Both their number and their discipline gave the movement a new respectability. The inheritor of this strength was a thoughtful, enigmatic Democratic senator from Minnesota, Eugene McCarthy, who in November 1967 opened his campaign for president on a peace platform. In January and February 1968, as the Tet offensive exposed the military failure of America's policy in Vietnam, McCarthy was touring New Hampshire in preparation for the first presidential primary. That March, the quixotic candidate no one had taken seriously received almost as many votes as President Johnson himself.

Within a few weeks after the New Hampshire primary, Johnson quit the race. A second peace candidate, Robert Kennedy, entered the lists. The boyish Bobby Kennedy, who had been attorney general in John Kennedy's administration and then senator from New York, attracted an even more zealous following than his older brother had, and a majority of Americans assumed that in time he also would be president. The favorite of the youth movement, however, was still McCarthy. His willingness to fight a lonely battle and his cool, moral style converted tens of thousands of college students, "Clean for Gene" with shaves and neckties, into his campaign workers. Meanwhile, through sit-ins, rallies, and strikes, radical students were applying heavy pressure on the major universities to support a variety of causes for social justice.

Black Despair and Black Power. Actually, the ground beneath the reform movement was already eroding. In April 1968, a sniper killed Martin Luther King as he stood on the balcony of a Memphis hotel. At the news of his assassination, black ghettos across the country erupted in violence. In death as in life, King could not channel the emotions of the northern ghettos toward peaceful resistance. Although King gathered many loyal partisans in the northern cities, he also encountered a very different, angry spirit, especially among younger blacks. This, in a broad sense, was the spirit of Black Power.

At one level, Black Power was a reasoned explanation of American race relations. In 1967 Stokely Carmichael and Charles Hamilton used the phrase to define an alternative strategy to that of the American creed. Whites did not really believe in equality and justice for all, they argued. On the contrary, white values created a self-serving institutional structure that made blacks a colonial people inside American society. Only a racially proud movement that was exclusively black could hope to break these institutional shackles. At another, more popular level, however, Black Power was a volatile expression of ghetto frustrations, a release of raw feelings that struck in fury at the most immediate sources of oppression, sometimes in the ghettos themselves.

Less than a week after the adoption of the Civil Rights Act of 1965, the ghetto area of Watts in Los Angeles exploded in riot and flames. More black riots scorched almost every major city during the next three years, burned miles of the Detroit ghetto in 1967, and spread nationwide at the word of King's murder in 1968. Meanwhile, new black leaders were demanding exclusive control over the movement for black rights and draining support from King's biracial civil rights campaign. In place of King's cause, the spreading spirit of Black Power strengthened such groups as the ascetic, business-minded Black Muslims and the militant, socially minded Black Panthers. Middle-class whites were left in confusion. Some of them still read the autobiographies of Malcolm X and Claude Brown as moving accounts of how individual blacks had survived against extraordinary odds. The rise of the individual from poverty to success was also a triumph according to white values. But the slashing ghetto despair in which people burned their own homes belonged to an alien, terrifying world.

White Retaliation. The people who could best appreciate this rage were locally oriented whites, who were also rising in retaliation against outside domination. As the national threats to local power intensified, these whites struck back along two lines. One was an attempt to reassert control over what they regarded as their own local institutions. In the northern cities, they fought against the racial integration of the schools, especially when integration meant busing black and white children. Numerous white Catholics in New Orleans, Philadelphia, and Boston actively resisted their church's policies of integration. Urban politicians attacked the local agencies of OEO and lobbied in Washington to disband it. In the towns as well as the cities, bumper stickers reading "Support Your Local Police" signaled a growing opposition to judicial restraints and supervisory review boards. The Crime Control Act of 1968, which generally endorsed strong police action, was considered a significant victory in this cause. In many white communities Mayor Richard Daley of Chicago became

LOCAL AMERICA STRIKES BACK
The assault on traditional values and local rights triggered a nationwide response in the late sixties. In Cocoa Beach, Florida, marchers show their disdain for antiwar demonstrations. *(Flip Schulke, LIFE Magazine © 1967 Time, Inc.)*

an instant hero when he reportedly instructed the police to maim looters and kill arsonists during a ghetto riot.

The second line of counterattack was aimed at the youth rebellion. In the tradition of community control, locally oriented whites set out to suppress a wide range of unacceptable behavior. "Sideburns . . . shall not extend lower than the bottom of the ear opening and shall be of uniform width," the regulations of the Louisville Fire Department stated. "Beards, goatees or any other extraneous facial hair will not be permitted." Opinion polls showed consistently large majorities favoring severe punishment for drug users, including marijuana smokers. Although the Vietnam War was unpopular throughout the United States by 1968, waving a Viet Cong flag or burning an American one, as television reported some radicals doing, ranked as a far greater evil than the war itself. By local values, affluent students had no right to insult their nation or squander its educational privileges. The New York police who cracked heads while breaking a campus strike at Columbia University in 1968, the townsmen who took a crowbar to the flower children, or the construction workers who roamed lower Manhattan beating up long-haired youths were expressing the feelings of innumerable fellow citizens. In May 1970, when four students at Kent State University were killed for no apparent reason by the National Guard, a nationwide poll tallied four out of five Americans on the side of the guardsmen.

What happened at Kent State typified what was happening throughout the country at the end of the decade. University administrators relied more and more on the local police to control student unrest. Law enforcement agencies killed, jailed, or scattered the leadership of a small, militant black power organization, the Black Panthers. After 1967, the peace marches in Washington were battling, antagonistic affairs, and the peace organizations, always a quarreling lot, fragmented. Occasionally a happy episode broke the pattern. In the summer of 1969, "the nation of Woodstock," perhaps 400,000 young people, gathered at White Lake, New York, for a rock festival and a holiday frolic. But a few months later in Alta-

mont, California, an attempt to repeat the joys of Woodstock dissolved in violence.

These rising waves of anger swept over the presidential campaign of 1968. In June, while celebrating an important victory in the California primary, Robert Kennedy was killed by a moody young Jordanian, Sirhan Sirhan. The shock of a second Kennedy assassinated only two months after King's murder, and in the train of so much public violence, spread the numbing sense that society was consuming itself through paroxysms of hate. Eugene McCarthy, now the sole leader of the peace movement, unaccountably allowed his own drive for the presidential nomination to lose momentum. That August in Chicago, while policemen were banging their way through a park full of young demonstrators outside convention headquarters, the Democrats nominated a very different Minnesota politician, the talkative, middle-of-the-road vice-president, Hubert Humphrey. The most vital force in the fall campaign was Governor George Wallace of Alabama, candidate of the American Independent party. As the advocate of "poor folks" against invading bureaucrats and decent citizens against subversive youths, Wallace gave local whites their first authentic spokesman in a presidential contest since Al Smith. Even more impressive than the 10 million votes Wallace eventually received, the nationwide enthusiasm for Wallace's cause revealed the depth of America's discontent.

In general, harsh and negative feelings dominated the campaign of 1968. Richard Nixon, who had returned to win another Republican nomination, promised to impose law and order on a permissive society. The Democrat Humphrey likened the peace marchers to the appeasers of Hitler. In striking contrast to the fifties and early sixties, no one spoke any longer for a common American purpose. America's nationalizing trends had divided people into hostile camps, and for a time no national manager could win the confidence of a broad majority. Except for the economy, which remained strong, the old problems of modernization had simply returned in new forms. As they converged in the politics of the late sixties, some Americans wondered if their society could survive the onslaught.

CHRONOLOGY

1952	Dwight D. Eisenhower elected president.
1953	Department of Health, Education, and Welfare formed.
1954	Atomic Energy Act subsidizes private development of nuclear energy.
	Brown v. *Board of Education* outlaws segregation of schools.
1955	Formosa Resolution authorizes president to protect Formosa.
	Southeast Asia Treaty Organization formed.
	Summit meeting at Geneva among leaders of United States, Soviet Union, and Great Britain.
	Merger of AFL and CIO, with George Meany as president.
1956	Federal Highway Act authorizes building of superhighways.
	Eisenhower reelected president.
1957	Federal troops enforce school desegregation in Little Rock, Arkansas.
	Soviet Union launches Sputnik.
1958	National Defense Education Act.
1959	U.S. encourages formation of CENTO by Middle Eastern allies.
	Castro comes to power in Cuba.
1960	John F. Kennedy elected president.

1961	Peace Corps organized.
	American-backed invasion of Cuba at Bay of Pigs fails.
	Berlin Wall erected.
1962	Cuban missile crisis.
1963	Test Ban Treaty between United States and Soviet Union.
	Kennedy assassinated; Lyndon B. Johnson becomes president.
1964	Johnson announces national War on Poverty.
	Free speech movement at Berkeley.
	Major Civil Rights Act passed.
	Johnson elected president.
1965	Johnson sends American combat troops to Vietnam; bombing of North begins.
	Second major Civil Rights Act passed.
	Ghetto riots in Watts section of Los Angeles.
1966	National Organization for Women founded.
1968	Martin Luther King, Jr., and Senator Robert Kennedy assassinated.
	Richard M. Nixon elected president.
1969	U.S. puts first man on the moon.
1970	Four students killed by the National Guard at Kent State University.

SUGGESTED READINGS

William E. Leuchtenburg, *A Troubled Feast: American Society since 1945* (rev. ed., 1979), is a lively introduction to the postwar years. The confidence of the 1950s glows from *U.S.A., the Permanent Revolution* (1951) by the editors of *Fortune* and from *The Big Change* (1952) by Frederick Lewis Allen. From a more critical perspective, five books help in assessing the political economy. C. Wright Mills, *The Power Elite* (1956), explores what later came to be called the military-industrial complex. Grant McConnell, *Private Power and American Democracy* (1966), and Theodore J. Lowi, *The End of Liberalism* (1969), analyze the dangers to the public interest from pressure-group politics. John Kenneth Galbraith, *The New Industrial State* (1967), examines the influ-

ence of corporate managers in national economic policy, and Harry Braverman, *Labor and Monopoly Capital* (1974), examines the influence of the corporate system on the working lives of its employees.

The history of politics during the confident years focuses largely on the presidency. Charles C. Alexander, *Holding the Line: The Eisenhower Era, 1952–1961* (1975), and Peter Lyon, *Eisenhower* (1974), cover the general's two terms. Marquis W. Childs, *Eisenhower: Captive Hero* (1958), gives valuable background. See also Sherman Adams, *Firsthand Report* (1961), the memoir of Eisenhower's primary domestic aide. On John Kennedy and his administration, Theodore C. Sorensen, *Kennedy* (1965), and Arthur M.

Schlesinger, Jr., *A Thousand Days* (1965), are appreciative assessments by insiders. Bruce Miroff, *Pragmatic Illusions: The Presidential Politics of John F. Kennedy* (1976), emphasizes Kennedy's limitations. In *The Promise and the Performance: The Leadership of John F. Kennedy* (1975), Lewis J. Paper tries to find a middle ground. Doris Kearns's controversial *Lyndon Johnson and the American Dream* (1976) helps to explain that powerful chief executive. For legislation during the fifties and sixties, James L. Sundquist, *Politics and Policy: The Eisenhower, Kennedy, and Johnson Years* (1968), is indispensable. *The Life of Adlai E. Stevenson* (1976–77), a two-volume biography by John Bartlow Martin, sympathetically examines the hero of the liberals who twice lost to Eisenhower. Theodore H. White's *The Making of the President, 1960* (1961) includes shrewd observations on Nixon's losing campaign. Barry Goldwater speaks for himself in *The Conscience of a Conservative* (1960). In a deceptively entitled study, *The Revolt of the Moderates* (1956), Samuel Lubell explains moderate voting behavior that affected presidential politics. Richard E. Neustadt, *Presidential Power* (1960), is an analysis of leadership that reputedly influenced John Kennedy. Insights into the political turmoil of the late sixties appear in Eric F. Goldman, *The Tragedy of Lyndon Johnson* (1969), Tom Wicker, *JFK and LBJ* (1968), Arthur Schlesinger, Jr., *Robert Kennedy and His Times* (1978), and Lewis Chester *et al., An American Melodrama: The Presidential Campaign of 1968* (1969).

Donald R. Matthews, *U.S. Senators and Their World* (1960), and William S. White, *Citadel: The Story of the U.S. Senate* (1957), contain interesting material on another center of political power. John D. Weaver, *Warren* (1967), and Leo Katcher, *Earl Warren* (1967), praise the controversial chief justice, and Milton R. Konvitz, *Expanding Liberties* (1966), evaluates some of the Warren Court's important decisions. How the national government has affected modern urban affairs is analyzed in Mark I. Gelfand, *A Nation of Cities* (1975). A crucial new political bloc is examined in Robert Gilpin and Christopher Wright, eds., *Scientists and National Policy-Making* (1964), and Don K. Price, *The Scientific Estate* (1965).

John W. Spanier, *American Foreign Policy since World War II* (rev. ed., 1973), is a clear, largely favorable summary. On the internationalization of American business, see Raymond Vernon, *Sovereignty at Bay: The Multinational Spread of U.S. Enterprise* (1971), and Mira Wilkins, *The Maturing of Multinational Enterprise: American Business Abroad from 1914 to 1970* (1974). In *The Politics of Oil*, Robert Engler examines some effects of internationalization. Paul Y. Hammond, *Organizing for Defense* (1961), discusses the

place of the military in twentieth-century America. Maxwell D. Taylor, *The Uncertain Trumpet* (1960), is a prominent general's critical appraisal of the Eisenhower years that influenced the Kennedy administration; Richard A. Aliano, *American Defense Policy from Eisenhower to Kennedy* (1975), sides with Eisenhower. The sources and consequences of America's military foreign policy are explored in Richard J. Barnet, *Roots of War* (1972), and Alexander L. George and Richard Smoke, *Deterrence in American Foreign Policy* (1974).

Michael A. Guhin, *John Foster Dulles* (1972), praises one architect of American foreign policy for his flexibility, and Herman Finer, *Dulles over Suez* (1964), gives a detailed account of the international furor that the secretary of state raised in 1956 and 1957. A dangerous issue that spanned the Eisenhower and Kennedy administrations is examined in Jack M. Schick, *The Berlin Crisis, 1958–1962* (1971). Richard J. Walton's *Cold War and Counterrevolution* (1972) takes a negative view of Kennedy's foreign policy. The decline of Kennedy's Alliance for Progress is traced in Jerome Levinson and Juan de Onís, *The Alliance That Lost Its Way* (1970). On the Cuban missile crisis, Graham T. Allison, *Essence of Decision* (1971), offers an intriguing set of alternative explanations, and Herbert S. Dinerstein, *The Making of a Missile Crisis: October 1962* (1976), tries to view the confrontation from Moscow's perspective.

George McTurnan Kahin and John W. Lewis, *The United States in Vietnam* (rev. ed., 1969), is a solid introduction to the war in Southeast Asia. Most writers on the war condemn the United States, and *The Indochina Story* (1970) by the Committee of Concerned Asian Scholars is a particularly striking example. Donald S. Zagoria, *Vietnam Triangle: Moscow, Peking, Hanoi* (1967), is one of the relatively few defenses of American policy. Henry Brandon, *Anatomy of Error: The Inside Story of the Asian War on the Potomac, 1954–1969* (1969), and Arthur M. Schlesinger, Jr., *The Bitter Heritage: Vietnam and American Democracy, 1941–1966* (1967), seek a middle ground. David Halberstam's fascinating *The Best and the Brightest* (1972) dissects the policy-making in Washington, and Frances Fitzgerald's excellent *Fire in the Lake* (1972) analyzes the consequences of this policy in Vietnam. J. William Fulbright, *The Arrogance of Power* (1967), expresses the opposition from Congress. A notorious massacre of civilians in Vietnam and the official attempts to hide it are exposed in Seymour M. Hersh, *My Lai 4* (1970).

The hopes and concerns of the civil rights movement are revealed in Martin Luther King, Jr., *Why We Can't Wait* (1964); Howard Zinn's account of young activists, *SNCC: The New Abolitionists* (1964); and two studies in public opinion by William Brink and Louis Harris—*The Negro Revolution in America* (1964) and *Black and White* (1967). Carl M. Brauer, *John F. Kennedy and the Second Reconstruction* (1977), analyzes a critical juncture in the movement. For background, see the first volume of Harvard Sitkoff's *A New Deal for Blacks: The Emergence of Civil Rights as a National Issue* (1978) and Charles F. Kellogg's *NAACP* (1967). The sources of black militancy emerge from *The Autobiography of Malcolm X* (1965), Charles V. Hamilton and Stokely Carmichael, *Black Power* (1967), Eldridge Cleaver, *Soul on Ice* (1968), and James Forman, *The Making of Black Revolutionaries* (1972). Claude Brown's *Manchild in the Promised Land* (1965) is an eloquent statement on life and survival in the ghetto. On the travail of civil rights leaders, see David L. Lewis, *King: A Critical Biography* (1970), and August Meier and Elliott Rudwick, *CORE* (1973), the account of an organization transformed by the sweep of events. *Report of the National Advisory Commission on Civil Disorders* (1968) and Robert M. Fogelson, *Violence as Protest* (1971), reflect the sense of complexity that came to surround the issue of black rights. Two important studies of poverty in America are Michael Harrington, *The Other America* (1962), and Harry M. Caudill, *Night Comes in the Cumberlands* (1963). Frances Fox Piven and Robert A. Cloward, *Regulating the Poor* (1971), is devastating on public policy.

The literature of the youth rebellion begins with Jack Kerouac's *On the Road* (1957) and more or less ends with Charles A. Reich's *The Greening of America* (1971). The world against which these youths rebelled is discussed in William H. Whyte, *The Organization Man* (1956), and Scott Donaldson, *The Suburban Myth* (1969). Theodore Roszak, *The Making of a Counter-Culture* (1969), and Richard Flacks, *Youth and Social Change* (1971), attempt to probe the rebellion's inner meaning. Philip E. Slater, *The Pursuit of Loneliness* (1970), contrasts the rebel culture with establishment culture. In *Young Radicals* (1968), Kenneth Keniston analyzes leaders in the rebellion. Kirkpatrick Sale, *SDS* (1973), is a sympathetic study of its most prominent campus organization. Four fine books add historical perspective: John P. Diggins, *The American Left in the Twentieth Century* (1973), Rosabeth Moss Kantor, *Commitment and Community* (1972), James Weinstein, *Ambiguous Legacy: The Left in American Politics* (1975), and Lawrence S. Wittner, *Rebels against War: The American Peace Movement, 1941–1960* (1969). Tom Wolfe's *The Electric Kool-Aid Acid Test* (1968) and Joan Didion's *Slouching Towards Bethlehem* (1968) comment on the culture of Haight-Ashbury.

Three outstanding books—Betty Friedan, *The Feminine Mystique* (1963), Kate Millett, *Sexual Politics* (1970), and Robin Morgan (comp.), *Sisterhood Is Powerful* (1970)—suggest the range and force of the women's movement. Peter G. Filene's *Him/Her/Self: Sex Roles in Modern America* (1975) is also useful.

Sources on the resistance to national liberalism and young radicalism are scattered. Arthur B. Shostak's *Blue-Collar Life* (1969) summarizes an array of studies on white urban wage earners and their families. Bennett M. Berger, *Working-Class Suburb* (1960), Herbert J. Gans, *The Levittowners* (1967), and William Kornblum, *Blue-Collar Community* (1974), add substantially to this analysis. Robert A. Caro, *The Power Broker: Robert Moses and the Fall of New York* (1974), Herbert J. Gans, *The Urban Villagers* (1962), and Sam Bass Warner, Jr., *The Urban Wilderness* (1972), include perceptive accounts of how government policies have damaged inner-city life. In *Small Town in Mass Society* (1958), Arthur J. Vidich and Joseph Bensman describe the defenses of townspeople against external authority. In *All Our Kin* (1974), Carol Stack explains the creative adaptations among poor black families. Peter Binzen, *Whitetown, U.S.A.* (1970), discusses urban dwellers in rebellion against government authority, and Numan V. Bartley, *The Rise of Massive Resistance* (1969), and Neil R. McMillen, *The Citizens' Council* (1971), trace an earlier rebellion in the South. The new explicitness about ethnic identities is explored in Michael Novak's *The Rise of the Unmeltable Ethnics* (1972).

By election time 1968, such broad, optimistic visions as John Kennedy's New Frontier and Lyndon Johnson's Great Society had dissolved into the past. The news was a daily bombardment of conflicts: teachers versus students, "hawks" versus "doves," professionals versus "hard hats," men versus women, whites versus blacks. Countless Americans were preparing for even more trouble. Elementary schools taught children to be wary of strangers, particularly the friendly ones. Gun sales continued to climb. So did the hiring of private police.

The attempt to resolve these problems during the administration of President Richard Nixon led to important changes in the 1970s and 1980s. A new formulation of minority rights eased the crisis in national-local relations. As the United States withdrew from Southeast Asia, Washington adopted a more circumspect approach to global issues that recaptured some of the detached, manipulative qualities of American diplomacy before the Cold War. Gerald Ford and Jimmy Carter, the presidents who succeeded Nixon, followed these departures with only minor modification. At the same time, they also found their administrations struggling with new problems bequeathed by the Nixon era. One was a bog of economic troubles in which America seemed mired at a critical point in its decline from global preponderance after the Second World War. Nixon's fall from power dramatically highlighted two additional problems: a waning authority among leaders of the political economy and a spreading hostility among the public toward vast bureaucracies. In these ways, around these issues, the early seventies marked a turn in modern American history. Contemporary society continues along the path that was set by the time of President Nixon's resignation in 1974.

A National-Local Balance

Richard Nixon first attracted national attention in the late 1940s as the congressman from California who helped to link the former State Department official Alger Hiss with communist espionage. That success, in addition to his reputation as a reliable Republican,

An Elusive Stability

made him a senator, then the vice-president under Dwight Eisenhower. After his narrow loss to John Kennedy in the presidential race of 1960 and his failure to become governor of California in 1962, Nixon suffered a temporary eclipse. But he fought tenaciously to win a second presidential nomination in 1968. This time, in another extremely close contest, he defeated both Democrat Hubert Humphrey and George Wallace, the third-party candidate.

Nixon took office under a cloud. A minority president and a stiff, uninspiring speaker, he also attracted particularly deep hostility from his opponents. Intellectuals nursed a hatred for "Tricky Dick" Nixon unlike anything a new president had faced in this century. In a short time, however, the shrewd chief executive was surprising enemies and friends alike with his political skills.

The first item on the new president's agenda was to adjust the balance between national and local power. Through policies that were sometimes called a "southern strategy" and sometimes considered as an appeal to the "silent majority," Nixon immediately set about allaying fears that the national government was antagonistic to local control. Washington dismantled the Office of Economic Opportunity (OEO), which had sponsored local black activities, and decentralized the administration for urban renewal. At the same time, programs of revenue sharing and grants to community groups gave local governments federal money to manage more or less as they chose. When a presidential commission recommended only minimal local supervision over pornography, Nixon dismissed its findings as "morally bankrupt." Attorney General John Mitchell publicized the administration's cooperation with local police forces, and in May 1970, when tens of thousands of antiwar protesters came to Washington, the Justice Department responded with mass arrests and makeshift detention corrals. Nixon, who had once been the partisan voice of the Eisenhower administration, now used Vice-President Spiro Agnew to heap scorn on "an effete corps of impudent . . . intellectuals," accuse the television networks of news distortion, and lock horns with such nationally prominent liberal newspapers as the New York *Times* and the Washington *Post*.

Nixon's Middle Ground.   Most critical of all, the new administration reshaped the Supreme Court. Four vacancies offered Nixon the best opportunity any president had had since Franklin Roosevelt's second term to recast the Court's philosophy. Beginning with a new chief justice, the politically astute Minnesota Republican Warren Burger, the president's appointments to the Court created a majority of justices who were unlikely to impose broad national rules over varied local practices. Nevertheless, as the record of the Burger Court demonstrated, the dominant trend in Washington was not an abdication of centralized power. Instead, the trend was to find a new balance between national and local authority. Although local police received wider latitude than before in dealing with suspected criminals, the legal protections against summary justice were modified, not destroyed. By establishing a woman's constitutional right to an abortion in *Roe* v. *Wade* (1973), the Burger Court actually extended the boundaries of national supervision, but the vagueness of that right encouraged strong resistance from abortion's many enemies.

The same search for a middle ground characterized the national government's approach to the conflict over minority rights. After the *Brown* decision of 1954, white attitudes toward blacks underwent a revolution. In spite of the violence of the late sixties, a huge majority of white Americans now favored racial equality in voting, employment, education, and everyday public life. During the 1970s whites came to accept the presence of blacks in a wide range of roles on television and in the movies, and their attitudes toward interracial mixing and marriages also softened considerably. On the strength of these sentiments, the courts pushed hard between 1968 and 1974 to eliminate the vestiges of legal segregation.

But there was no general support for an effective attack on black poverty, which increasingly became an urban problem. As waves of whites continued to move to the suburbs, the cities were left with increasing populations of poor blacks. Although the courts imposed citywide busing schemes to desegregate urban schools, they balked in *Milliken* v. *Bradley* (1974) at a plan for metropolitan Detroit that would have incorporated the suburban schools, 98 percent white, with the city schools, 65 percent black. "No single tradition in public education is more deeply rooted than local control over the operation of schools," Chief Justice Burger declared in the spirit of the old national-local compromise. The judiciary would "deprive the people of local control" if it imposed its authority across the jurisdictional boundaries of the metropolitan area. As quietly as possible, each administration in Washington worked piecemeal during the 1970s to implement affirmative action programs in employment and education. In *Bakke v. Board of Regents of California* (1978), the Supreme Court walked a tightrope, legalizing affirmative action but requiring a case-by-case analysis to determine its applicability. Even more quietly, Washington subsidized budgets of predominantly black cities such as Cleveland and Detroit. Between the late sixties and late seventies, the national government's contribution to these urban budgets rose from about 15 percent to well over 50 percent of their incomes. Nevertheless, as chronic inflation and unemployment beset the United States in the 1970s, blacks suffered disproportionately, and the prospects of more substantial help remained exceedingly slender.

Minority Rights in the Seventies. The economic prospects for Americans of Central and South American origins were even slimmer, both because of an additional language barrier and because more illegal than legal immigrants arrived from the nations to the south. In numbers no one could precisely specify, that flow increased drastically during the 1970s and spread from the traditional destinations in California and Texas to urban centers everywhere. Spanish signs multiplied in the inner-city stores, and bilingual education became an important issue in the city schools. Though these immigrants participated in the various affirmative action programs, they were only beginning to use group pressure for a larger share of urban jobs. Their most effective organization developed in California's "farm factories," where Mexican American labor supported a thriving commercial agriculture. Under the patient, persistent leadership of César Chavez, the United Farm Workers, which was formed in California during the sixties, rallied national support through boycotts of the sale of non-union lettuce and grapes. By the mid-seventies Chicano farm workers had a solid union base in areas where exploitation had long been a way of life.

The most successful new drive for minority

STRENGTH IN UNION
Through persistence and publicity, the moderate César Chavez organized Chicano laborers in California's "farm factories." *(George Ballis/ Black Star)*

The Election of 1968

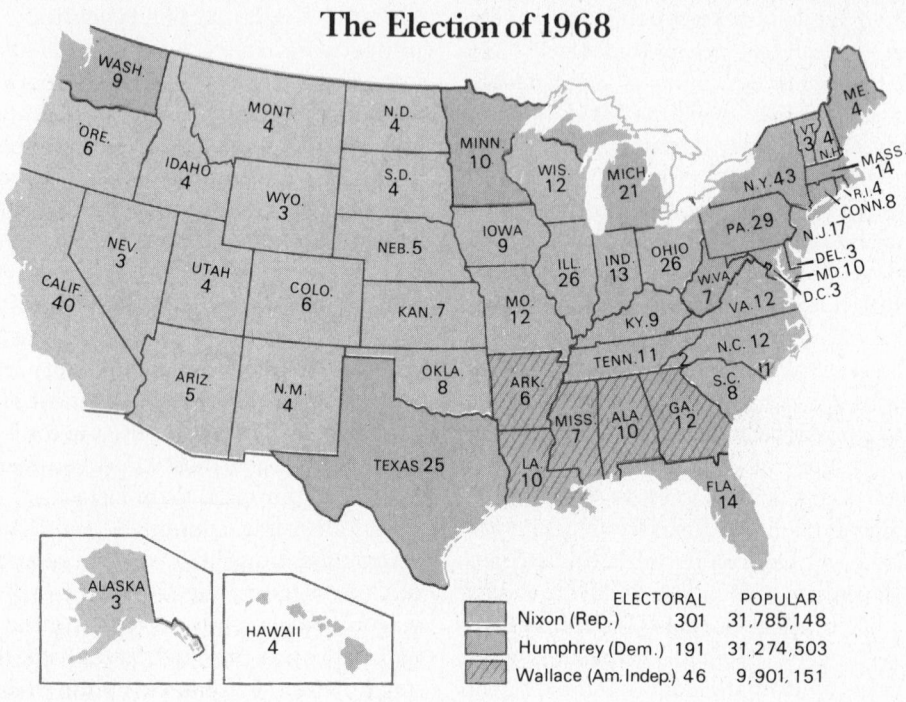

	ELECTORAL	POPULAR
Nixon (Rep.)	301	31,785,148
Humphrey (Dem.)	191	31,274,503
Wallace (Am. Indep.)	46	9,901,151

rights came from native Americans, who had watched their hopes for tribal autonomy crumble during the 1950s. In a mood for decentralization, the Republican Congress of 1953 declared an end to the national supervision of native Americans and placed their reservations under the laws of the individual states. The consequences were disastrous. The Klamath Nation in Oregon promptly lost its rich lumber resources, and the demoralized Menominee Nation in Wisconsin saw its small, tight economy disappear in a rush of panic sales. Not until the late sixties did a significant turn of fortunes occur. Adapting the protest tactics of the time, groups of native Americans, with the Sioux Nations in the forefront, occupied sites that symbolized the burial of their heritage beneath white civilization: Alcatraz Island, Mount Rushmore, Fort Sheridan, and, in 1973, in a bloody confrontation with law enforcement agents at Wounded Knee, South Dakota. By 1970 Washington was once again committed to assisting tribal autonomy. Overlapping these public and often violent protests, striking victories occurred in the courts. In a wave of separate actions that began in 1969 in the Alaskan hinterland

and which extended from the Northwest fisheries to the Maine woods, some native Americans transformed their endlessly violated treaties from another century into a legal basis for claiming important economic rights through the processes of law. As a whole, however, native Americans continued to suffer more severely from poverty and disease than any other cultural group in the United States.

During the 1970s these many, tentative adjustments reshaped the compromises between national and local power. Washington stepped carefully through such prickly fields as local censorship and police practices, and it cut back on the supervision of its economic aid to local economies. Particularly through the federal courts, however, national standards had an important balancing effect in the apportionment of economic rights and opportunities among minorities. Cautious accommodation was the watchword.

The crusades of the Great Society sounded only a faint echo in the seventies. The last man to raise their banner was George McGovern, a serious, liberal senator from South Dakota, who in 1972 won the

RICHARD NIXON
There was little warmth in his political style, but Nixon proved to be an extraordinarily successful president during his first term. *(Newsweek/Wally McNamee)*

A Flexible Diplomacy

Nixon's influence on the course of America's foreign affairs was equally basic. The bitter controversy over Vietnam continued as he took office in 1969, and the president knew that, one way or another, he had to end the war. To this task he brought two primary assumptions.

Nixon's Strategy in Vietnam. First, Nixon believed that the United States should be willing to punish the stubborn enemy considerably more than had been done during the Johnson administration. Initially he hoped that a more daring use of ground forces could still shift the military balance in Vietnam. Through invasions of Cambodia in 1970 and Laos in 1971, the American command tried to destroy the supplies and disperse the armies that the enemy was concentrating in South Vietnam. When a coup established a friendly government in Cambodia, the United States equipped its army. Now the Vietnamese conflict was openly an Indochinese war. But as America expanded the war, a guerrilla opposition also spread into Cambodia and Laos and left the balance of power in Vietnam unaffected. The longer Nixon managed the war, the more he came to rely on bombing raids that exceeded even the massive ones under Johnson.

Nixon's second assumption, which recalled Eisenhower's settlement of the Korean conflict, was that in an unpopular war most Americans would choose withdrawal of their own troops over a clear-cut military victory. As he expanded the scope of the Indochinese War, the president also reduced the number of American troops from over half a million in 1969 to under 100,000 in 1972. The South Vietnamese army, the president said, would soon be capable of fighting the ground war alone. Because these withdrawals significantly lessened American criticism of the war after 1970, they gave Nixon more time to reach some kind of settlement with the North Vietnamese. He needed the leeway, for the failure of his Indochinese strategy strongly argued for compromise. During the final months of Johnson's presidency, the United States and North Vietnam had opened a forum for these negotiations in Paris, and,

Democratic nomination for president following a string of successes in the primaries. Everything about McGovern's candidacy suggested danger to the emerging balance of the seventies. He wanted to revitalize the War on Poverty and expand the government's programs in behalf of black rights. His support among well-to-do college students was almost as enthusiastic as Eugene McCarthy's had been four years earlier. McGovern refused to endorse harsh measures against street crimes and drug violations, and he appeared indifferent to such issues as Bibles in the schools and the suppression of obscenity. In November 1972 only Massachusetts and the District of Columbia gave majorities to McGovern. With 521 of 538 electoral votes, President Nixon, a marginal leader less than four years before, scored one of the most impressive political victories of modern times. After 1972 every aspiring leader would mark the McGovern lesson well.

after 1969, delegates from the two nations used it alternately to storm at one another and to explore the possibilities of peace.

The crisis in the negotiations occurred just after the election of 1972, when the scale of America's air attacks implied that it might indeed try to bomb North Vietnam "back into the Stone Age." In January 1973 both sides modified their demands just enough to sign a peace agreement. In effect, the settlement allowed the war to continue without American troops. Through a tortured use of the language, Nixon was able to call the agreement "peace with honor," because technically it satisfied the standard rule of containment. No new territory had been relinquished to the communists. But the Indochinese paid an appallingly high cost in blood and misery for that honor. In two more years, even the illusion of containing communism dissolved. After appearing to hold their own against the communist armies, America's allies in South Vietnam and Cambodia collapsed abruptly in the early months of 1975. Suddenly communist governments ruled everywhere on the mainland of Southeast Asia except Thailand, and American power was eliminated. Hawks and doves alike agreed that the war had been the most disastrous in American history.

Breakthroughs with China and the Soviet Union. During the final years of the Indochinese War, the Nixon administration was also responding to the worldwide problem of containment's crumbling structure. Here it showed exceptional imagination. In the most important series of events during Nixon's presidency, the United States dramatically improved its relations first with China, then with the Soviet Union. The deepening hostility between China and Russia, and the desire in each of these two nations to devote more energy to internal affairs, raised the possibility that one or both of them might welcome an accommodation with the United States. Early in 1971, Nixon seriously began investigating the opportunity. Feelers indicated that China was receptive to an American overture. While leaders in Washington and Peking made small public gestures of modera-

tion, Nixon's adviser Henry Kissinger was meeting secretly in China with Premier Chou En-lai. In the summer of 1971, the president broke the astonishing news that he would visit China.

After turning its back on the People's Republic of China for more than twenty years, the United States acknowledged its existence with the chief executive's presence. The entire affair was international theater at its best. In a rush of discovery, millions of Americans learned something of the revolution that had been transforming the world's largest nation. Then they watched on television as their president crossed containment's invisible barrier in February 1972 to shake hands with the leaders of "Red China." Though relations between the two governments remained cautious, the United States accepted China in the United Nations and prepared the way for a broader interchange.

Also during 1971, the Nixon administration was moving silently toward détente—an easing of tension —with Russia. The Soviet premier, Leonid Brezhnev, who was anxious to limit the range of Russia's international involvements, willingly grasped a chance to lessen the tensions with his country's chief rival. Once again, private diplomatic discussions on the possible areas of agreement came first. Once again, the president surprised the world by announcing a visit to the Soviet Union in May 1972. Nixon picked up a thread that had been lost at the futile summit conferences of 1960 and 1961. Soon after his trip to China, he traveled to Moscow, where he had an extremely cordial meeting with the very officials whom Americans had recently considered the masterminds of international conspiracy.

Following the shock caused by this change of policy, the consequences of these new departures in foreign relations evolved slowly and unevenly. Closer relations with China came only after the death of Mao Tse-tung and an abrupt shift within the People's Republic toward modernization. In 1978 the United States formally recognized China, and during the next year another flurry of state visits inaugurated wider economic relations between the two nations, ranging from international credits to the distribution

REVOLUTION IN FOREIGN POLICY President Nixon, once an ardent enemy of all communist nations, changed the meaning of containment with his visit to China in 1972. *(Nixon Presidential Library)*

of Coca-Cola—"very refreshing," read a Chinese inscription on the familiar bottle. As the two governments exchanged ambassadors, they informally promised mutual caution on the issue of Taiwan, which China claimed as its own and the United States continued to support.

Détente with Russia carried greater significance for world peace and involved more complex world problems. At best, it promised an orderly competition between international opponents. The Soviet Union showed restraint during the settlement between its ally, North Vietnam, and the United States, and it remained aloof later in the seventies when American negotiators searched for peace in the Middle East. The United States, on its part, responded mildly to the expansion of Russian influence in Africa.

In treaty form, the spirit of détente translated into two agreements to regulate the weapons of war. Strategic Arms Limitation Talks (SALT), which began in 1969, produced the first treaty in 1972. This treaty

was ratified by the United States in the honeymoon atmosphere of Nixon's gala visit to Moscow. When SALT II reached the Senate in 1979, however, it met much stiffer resistance. Although SALT II, like its predecessor, provided for a method of balancing the growth of military power rather than a means of disarmament, it required a foundation of trust that was eroding in the late seventies. The heritage of Cold War hatreds, the tensions of global competition, and the publicized persecution of dissenters inside Russia kept accommodations with the Soviet Union extremely fragile. Then early in 1980, the Soviet's crude use of military power to crush its enemies in neighboring Afghanistan temporarily snapped that thread of accommodations. Interpreting the invasion of Afghanistan as a major international crisis, the Carter administration halted trade agreements with Russia, sponsored a boycott of the summer Olympic games in Moscow, and generally fanned the flames of antagonism between the two super powers.

The New Diplomacy

The new understandings with China and the Soviet Union, in turn, were part of an even broader reorientation of American diplomacy. The world's heterogeneity that the Kennedy administration recognized and the Johnson administration tried to ignore became the starting point in foreign relations during the Nixon administration. The new diplomacy relied on principles similar to those prevailing in America's domestic politics: bargain with one group at a time, work to minimize the friction among allies, make only short-term promises, and assume the need for continuing negotiations. In domestic affairs, Americans tested the effectiveness of these techniques by such traditional guidelines as the victory of a political party or a rise in the standard of living. In world affairs, however, Americans had no comparable way of calculating success or failure, and during the late

seventies, the arguments about foreign policy sounded more and more like quibbles.

Nixon's collaborator in this transformation was Henry Kissinger, a German-born professor from Harvard who first served as the president's adviser and then in 1973 became secretary of state. Kissinger personified the new diplomacy of evolving bargains and ad hoc arrangements. Under both Nixon and his successor, Gerald Ford, Kissinger was the man in motion, negotiating the Paris accord with North Vietnam, preparing the way for Nixon's visits to Peking and Moscow, shuttling between Israel and the Arab nations, touring the capitals of Europe, and searching for a settlement of the Cyprus War between Greece and Turkey.

The substance of the nation's foreign policy seemed to be Kissinger grappling with one problem after another. As a result, many Americans held this one man responsible for the ups and downs of world

NIXON AND KISSINGER
Starting as Nixon's adviser, Henry Kissinger became America's most prominent diplomat in the seventies.
(Nixon Presidential Library)

affairs. In the summer of 1974, when international problems appeared to be abating, Kissinger was acclaimed by the press as the one indispensable man in Washington. Six months later, when détente with the Soviet Union was losing its freshness, hostilities were threatening in the Middle East, and Southeast Asia was falling to the communist armies, disillusioned critics called the secretary of state an utter incompetent. In another six months, Kissinger was presiding over a historic agreement between Egypt and Israel, and once again his reputation soared.

Kissinger's incessant travels gave the impression that the United States was immersed in every one of the world's problems. Actually the trend ran in the opposite direction. During the era of containment, the slightest change anywhere on the globe had some meaning for America's anticommunist policy. Now each issue had to prove its own importance, and the United States remained passive in the face of events that once would have sounded the alarm in Washington. In 1975, for example, when the Organization of American States (OAS) in the Western Hemisphere lifted its boycott of Cuba, few Americans even knew about this break in the old chain of containment. Before 1980, President Jimmy Carter was especially open about the limitations of American power to shape destinies around the globe. Moreover, his administration gave cautious responses to a series of African upheavals and an outburst of war in 1979 among Vietnam, Cambodia, and China.

Selective Problem Solving. As a result of this selectivity, the new diplomacy sharpened the nation's focus on those problems that did receive Washington's special energies. None attracted greater attention than the efforts to stabilize relations in the Middle East. In a brief war in 1967, Israel expanded its domain over a broad stretch of Arab land. Although there were cheers in Tel Aviv, there were soon groans in Washington, for the United States was left as the defender of Israel's occupation and America's role as the arbiter of Middle Eastern conflicts was destroyed.

In 1973 a combination of Arab nations showed far greater military strength during another brief war to regain these lands. Secretary Kissinger labored mightily to facilitate cease-fire agreements between Israel and both Egypt and Syria in 1974, but the United States had no luck at all finding a comprehensive formula for a Middle Eastern peace. Then, in November 1977, Egypt's President Anwar el-Sadat, the moderate successor to Gamal Nasser, suddenly altered the focus with a surprising visit of goodwill to Israel and raised hopes for a separate Egyptian-Israeli accord. Twice the negotiations threatened to collapse; twice President Carter revived them with his personal diplomacy. In 1979, as Israeli troops prepared to leave Egyptian territory, Cairo became the first Arab capital to recognize the Jewish state. Yet once again, a victory for some marked a defeat for others. By evading the question of a homeland for 3 million dispossessed Palestinians, Egypt and the United States alienated even the conservative Arab nations and rallied new support behind Israel's bitter foe, Yasir Arafat, the leader of the Palestinian Liberation Organization (PLO).

Selective diplomacy in a cautious spirit gave many Americans a sense that the United States was losing control over its global interests. In its relations with the major industrial nations, the United States was no more than first among equals. Almost everywhere else, the tides of revolution ran steadily against American influence. Too often, Washington scrambled in confusion when a shift of power was occurring. The Iranian revolution of 1979 found the United States clinging to a repudiated Shah as he was being forced from the country. That same year in Nicaragua, Washington abandoned its client, General Somoza, only after the dictator had barricaded himself inside his own capital. John Kennedy's vision of "a critical and vigilant intelligence marching in advance of events . . . producing the events we want" seemed to mock an inept nation. In that mood, a growing number of political leaders turned to military might as the one source of national security firmly in America's own hands. SALT II, they cried, would seal America's doom as a declining power. Entering the 1980s, no trend in foreign affairs ran stronger than this tough, compensatory emphasis on arms in an unpredictable world.

A Stumbling Economy

As Nixon took office in 1969, the state of the economy remained America's primary source of confidence. On a long, rising curve across three decades, its performance had been impressive. In dollars adjusted for inflation, the median family income had doubled, and that astounding increase had released a torrent of private funds for the good life. Personal spending for recreation increased fivefold. Easy credit enabled thousands of people to buy now and refinance later. The proportion of Americans who continued from high school into college leaped from 1 in 8 in 1940 to 1 in 2 in 1970. The trajectory of the stock market for those thirty years shot skyward.

Worldwide Inflation. No sooner did Nixon enter the White House than trouble erupted. Its immediate origins traced back to the Johnson administration. Because Congress had lowered taxes just as the heaviest financing of the Vietnam War was about to begin, a surge of purchasing power was generated that practically guaranteed inflation, and prices were already rising sharply as Nixon became president. At the same time, the economy grew sluggish. Although the squeeze lessened temporarily in 1971, a full-scale crisis struck in 1973. Inflation took off at an annual rate of about 10 percent, unemployment mounted until it also approached 10 percent, the GNP slumped, and the stock market sank. A mold for the seventies was set.

The deeper cause of America's prolonged doldrums was linked to its declining place in the world economy. At the end of the Second World War, the United States accounted for well over half of the world's industrial production and came close to monopolizing the monetary resources for international trade. What it wanted it bought. Its economic decisions reverberated around the globe. As other nations cut into that industrial predominance, American spending never abated, and by the 1960s, the United States was suffering from an adverse international balance of payments. If America was no longer an economic demigod, however, it remained the king.

Then early in the 1970s, on an ominously falling curve, its percentage of the world's industrial production fell below 30 and its percentage of monetary reserves below 15. Hurting in international trade and investment, the United States still expected a lion's share of the world's raw materials for its sumptuous consumer markets at home. But other strong economies that no longer jumped in response to every turn in American policy were ready to bid for those limited resources.

In 1973 the competitors collided in the world market and inaugurated a new era in global economics. The wave of inflation that swept over the United States flooded the world, overwhelming all national economies, and bringing rates of increase elsewhere that were considerably higher than America's. Basic resources ranging from grains and sugar to oil and aluminum soared in price. The United States could not control any of them. When international inflation was superimposed on an American recession, the standard techniques of economic management no longer worked. Attacking the recession with greater budget deficits and lower interest rates risked an even wilder inflation. On the other hand, attacking inflation with steeper taxes and tighter credit risked an even deeper depression. The United States tossed in the same winds that were whipping the rest of the world, and nobody could find a pilot.

As the clouds gathered in 1971, President Nixon bought a little time with two dramatic moves. First, he abandoned the international monetary regulations dating from the Bretton Woods agreement of 1944 and let the value of the dollar abroad fall. Temporarily, cheaper dollars boosted American exports, although the sagging dollar soon became a part of America's difficulties. Second, the president imposed a sudden, nationwide freeze on wages and prices. With no long-range purpose behind the freeze, however, it simply delayed the explosion. Unfortunately for Nixon, he lifted the controls just as world inflation was about to skyrocket, and his brief success was immediately lost in the updraft.

President Ford took office in midflight. From the confusion of plans and counterplans that followed, a pattern for the 1970s emerged. Like Nixon before him and Carter after him, Ford began with the instinctive American assumption that he should get the economy rolling again. Yet opinion polls repeatedly verified that, in the pinch, an overwhelming majority of Americans chose inflation over unemployment as the central problem, and in this spirit Ford was soon vetoing government appropriations one after another. Between 1977 and 1978, President Carter repeated the same sequence, first attacking unemployment and then, as inflation exceeded 10 percent, trying instead to dampen economic growth. Nothing worked very well. During the 1970s the Consumer Price Index more than doubled while the sputtering economy suffered from chronic recessions. By the end of the decade, Washington's leader were hoping for minimum damage: how much inflation would it take to avoid depression, how much recession to slow inflation?

Energy Dependence. At the heart of the problem lay the sobering issue of energy. Before the 1970s the American economy floated on an abundance of cheap petroleum. A combination of four new developments abruptly ended this drift and threatened the economy. First, the major oil exporting countries, principally in the Middle East and Africa, took command of their own resources. Forming the Organization of Petroleum Exporting Countries (OPEC) in 1959, they educated themselves in the mysteries of international distribution, subordinated the giant oil companies to their control, and in 1974 shook the foundations of the world economy by quadrupling the price of oil.

Second, the Arab nations that dominated OPEC began using oil as a diplomatic weapon. During the winter of 1973–74, every important industrial nation except the Soviet Union suffered a frightening oil shortage when the producers stopped shipments in support of the Arab war against Israel. During the balance of the decade, threats of another halt in oil shipments sent tremors around the globe. Third, just as OPEC's power was crystallizing, American oil production peaked and started to decline. As recently

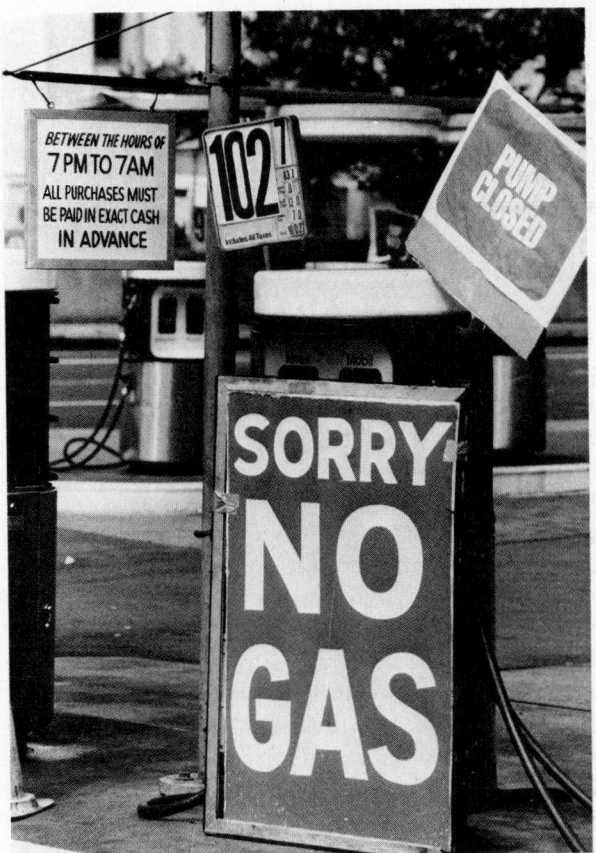

GAS CRISIS, 1979
Sudden shortages and steep price increases in a variety of basic resources became commonplace in the seventies. *(Alain Dejean/Sygma)*

as 1967, the United States had forestalled an Arab boycott by pointing to America's reserve of unused wells. By 1973, no longer possessing adequate domestic oil reserves, the United States stood exposed with the rest of the world. Fourth, America's general weaknesses in international trade and finance, developing at the same time as its vulnerability in oil, destroyed the possibility of American leadership among the industrial powers and left the major nations in the world competing with each other for the available oil.

Americans' initial response to the oil crisis was outrage mixed with disbelief. There were plenty of villains—Arab nabobs squeezing the world economy, oil companies profiting from the nation's hardship, politicians ignoring the danger signals, automobile companies evading the need for fuel economy—but there were no heroes. Although Carter did give energy the highest priority as he became president, neither his pallid assortment of development incentives and waste deterrents nor his clumsy dealings with Congress generated an effective policy. In their anger Americans dreamed of returning to national self-sufficiency. All the trends, however, made that an idle hope.

Between 1973 and 1978, while other industrial nations stabilized their oil imports, America's rose a staggering 42 percent. Its voracious economy was consuming one-third of the world's oil production, its government was marking time, and a majority of its citizens were denying that a real problem existed. Not until the summer of 1979, when the Iranian revolution precipitated another oil shortage, did the glimmerings of a new awareness appear. President Carter, reviving the theme of national crisis, preached the necessity of patience and sacrifice during a long period of austerity while America diversified its energy sources and halved its oil imports. Nevertheless, it was not at all clear who had the patience or who would sacrifice.

A Cloudy Horizon

If the radicals of the sixties trusted no one over thirty, an increasing number of Americans in the seventies wondered whether they could trust anyone at all. Worldwide terrorism—hijackings, bombings, assassinations—and violent domestic crimes were sensationalized in all the news media, and conveyed the persistent message that nobody was ever safe from random slaughter. In the name of entertainment, the use of violence in countless TV shows said it again. In addition, the nation's officials defenders of law and order, it seemed, were really specialists in deceit.

The Outrage of America. In 1971 the Pentagon Papers, a collection of classified documents that had been leaked to the press by Daniel Ellsberg, a consultant to the Department of Defense, exposed the government's secret maneuvers in Vietnam and its systematic lies about the Indochinese War. Each year brought more stories that discredited the agencies of law and order. President Johnson had approved a wiretap on Robert Kennedy, and President Nixon had authorized one on his own brother. The director of the FBI, J. Edgar Hoover, had waged a personal vendetta against Martin Luther King, Jr. The Bureau and military intelligence agencies had compiled mounds of dossiers on everybody from senators to singers, and the Internal Revenue Service had audited tax returns on the basis of citizens' political activities. Traditionally, Americans had enjoyed a bit of humbug now and then. It was funny, for example, to discover that the all-American housewife in a soap commercial was also a porno queen. But it was deadly serious business to learn that, in response to widespread contamination from the government's nuclear tests, President Eisenhower had instructed subordinates to "confuse" the public.

Some Americans slipped into a sense of helplessness. The computer, that miracle cure of the 1950s, only verified the intractability of the big problems: inflation and recession, crime and violence, domestic poverty and global hunger. The novelist Kurt Vonnegut captured the mood in an exchange between two middle-aged men who were pondering a prospective world population of 7 billion:

"I suppose they will all want dignity," I said.
"I suppose," said O'Hare.*

That same feeling of the individual trapped in a vast web of uncontrollable forces characterized the important writings of Joyce Carol Oates, John Cheever, and Joan Didion. The most popular movies alternated between fantasies of terror like *The Exorcist*

*From *Slaughterhouse-Five* by Kurt Vonnegut, Jr. © 1969, Delacorte Press/Seymour Laurence.

and *Jaws* and fantasies of escape like *Star Wars* and *Rocky*.

Other Americans tried to reassert tough, fundamental values. "Permissive" child-rearing fell into disrepute, and parents pledged their allegiance to maintaining clear authority and salutary discipline in the home. Hostility toward the rights of criminal suspects dominated the television dramas of the mid-seventies. At the end of the decade over five hundred state prisoners faced execution. A well-organized Right-to-Life movement fought abortions, and a well-publicized campaign under the leadership of the singer Anita Bryant opposed homosexuality. Late in the decade, conservatives broke the momentum of the drive toward an Equal Rights Amendment (ERA) for women, suspending it just a few states shy of victory.

Americans reserved their greatest indignation for defense of their rights as consumers. In 1965 a zealous young lawyer named Ralph Nader inspired a consumer movement with the publication of *Unsafe at Any Speed*, a detailed analysis of the dangers built into automobiles manufactured in Detroit. A shabby attempt by General Motors to discredit him only enlarged his fame. Nader's young volunteers—"Nader's Raiders"—rapidly produced a variety of additional exposés. By the 1970s innumerable journalists, scientists, and local committees were spreading the gospel of consumer standards, and new legal guidelines covered such areas as automobile safety, credit contracts, product labeling, and food adulteration. In spite of its popular base, however, the consumer movement never had a disciplined, focused strength. For example, the latest American right that was proclaimed—the right to good health—generated a consistent, broad support for a variety of national health plans that regularly appeared in Washington, but just as regularly died at the hands of lobbyists in

ROSALYNN CARTER AND BETTY FORD IN THE MIDST OF THE WOMEN'S MOVEMENT

A cause that once seemed certain of success was bogged down in controversy by 1980. *(United Press International, Inc.)*

NUCLEAR CONTROVERSY
The crisis at Three Mile Island in 1979 spurred a nationwide campaign against nuclear power.
(Arthur Grace/Sygma)

Congress. Consumers were everybody in general and nobody in particular—and exceedingly hard to organize.

The most positive attempts to reclaim some measure of lost control were the many efforts to repair the urban-industrial society's damage to the physical environment. Images of an uncontaminated earth where man and nature were once again in harmony aroused a deeply embedded set of emotions during the sixties and seventies. In a crescendo of cries, more and more Americans of all ages demanded relief from the dangers of chemical sprays, industrial wastes, and automobile exhaust. "Organic" foods and "recyclable" products became increasingly popular in the consumer market. The national government responded to the public's demands by establishing a series of antipollution standards—beginning with the Clean Air Act of 1963—to protect the atmosphere and the waterways, and both state and local laws supplemented the ecology movement.

Some progress was made, yet here too the problems came to outweigh the prospects. As the economy faltered, the arguments that environmentalism cut into jobs, profits, and energy development sounded more and more persuasive. Bureaucratic confusion between Washington's Environmental Protection Agency (EPA) and the regulatory offices in local government hampered the enforcement of the new laws. By the mid-seventies, unfolding revelations about the extensive dumping and the gruesome toxicity of industrial wastes dimmed people's hopes of ever undoing the damage.

Then in March 1979, a conjunction of faulty equipment, inadequate safety provisions, and bad judgment triggered a week of crisis at the nuclear power plant on Three Mile Island, Pennsylvania. The radioactive core of the plant heated toward catastrophe, lethal gas drifted through the area, and a hushed and helpless nation wondered if a massive accident might devastate the East. (By chance, a movie version of just such a crisis, *The China Syndrome*, was simultaneously playing before packed, rapt audiences across the country.) As the nuclear reactor finally cooled, so did the faith that government regulation could actually protect America from the worst environmental disasters.

The Leaders Fall.   One after another, these issues revolved in fretful circles around the question of trust, and in the modern state the center of that constellation was trust in the national government. Hence, the fall of the government's great men, coming in noisy sequence early in the decade, inevitably affected the malaise of the seventies. First came Abe Fortas, an associate justice of the Supreme Court whom President Johnson, in his final days, tried to make Earl Warren's replacement as chief justice. When a congressional inquiry in 1969 revealed that Fortas had profited unduly from his office, public pressure forced him to resign from the Court. Fortas was followed by another judge, Otto Kerner, a liberal Democrat with an unusually high reputation for integrity, who had chaired the important Presidential Advisory Commission on Civil Disorders. Found guilty of accepting bribes while he had been governor of Illinois, Kerner went directly from his place on the circuit court to jail.

Next came Vice-President Agnew, national champion of law and order and a favorite to win the Republican nomination for president in 1976. Early in 1973 the Justice Department reconstructed a long history of secret payments that engineering firms, in return for government contracts, had been making to Agnew throughout his rise in Maryland politics. Couriers had even sat in the vice-president's anteroom waiting to deliver the cash. After a frantic attempt to save his career, the vice-president suddenly resigned in October as part of a bargain with the Justice Department. Agnew received a light sentence for evading income tax, but avoided the much more serious penalties for extortion and bribery.

The Watergate Scandal.   The loss of the vice-president was stunning enough. Yet Agnew was only the prologue. As he fell, President Nixon himself was toppling. In June 1972, five men were arrested for burglarizing Democratic headquarters at the Watergate Apartments in Washington, D.C. After a flurry of attention, the story slipped from sight. Despite the clear connection between the burglars and the Republican Committee to Reelect the President, Nixon's Democratic opponent, Senator McGovern, could rouse little interest in the incident during the fall campaign. Then in the spring of 1973, one of the burglars decided to cooperate with the government investigators. As he was confessing, John Dean, a close presidential adviser, acknowledged his part in the incident. Behind these two, a long line of penitents began to form.

The stories they told spread in two directions. One traced a variety of activities through the executive's most powerful offices: the use of campaign contributions to win government favors, the illegal handling of those funds, devious techniques for making the president a millionaire, and assorted tactics of political sabotage to ensure Nixon's reelection. Although it was a sordid view through the keyhole of national politics, it attracted far less attention than the second trail of evidence, which carried the planning and suppressing of the Watergate burglary to Nixon's inner staff—John Dean, Attorney General John Mitchell, and a pair of hard, austere organization men, H. R. Haldeman and John Ehrlichman, who were the president's principal domestic aides. Would the trail lead to the president's desk?

For more than a year, Nixon fought to block the investigation. In public, the president repeatedly declared his innocence. In private, he plotted ways of obstructing a grand jury under the tenacious judge, John Sirica, and a Senate investigating committee under the skeptical old-timer, Sam Ervin of North Carolina. Forced to accept a special Watergate prosecutor within the Justice Department, Nixon in October 1973 fired the first one, Archibald Cox of the Harvard Law School, because Cox was preparing to sue for evidence that the president would not relinquish. Cox's replacement, the conservative Houston lawyer Leon Jaworski, proved just as dogged and carried his demand for the evidence to the Supreme Court.

The evidence in question lay in a vault of tapes recording almost every conversation that had been held in President Nixon's private office. These tapes, which Nixon strangely chose to preserve rather than destroy, eventually wrecked his defenses. Someone tried erasing portions of the tapes. The White House issued an edited transcript of parts of them. Finally, the president decided to withhold them altogether. But in July 1974 the Supreme Court unanimously awarded the tapes to Judge Sirica's grand jury and, through the grand jury, to the public. As the House of Representatives was preparing to vote articles of impeachment against the president, Nixon acknowledged much of what the tapes would verify about his intimate involvement in the Watergate affair. Admitting the facts but denying any guilt, Nixon resigned as president on August 9, 1974.

(Copyright 1972 Los Angeles Times. Reprinted with permission)

"He says he's from the phone company . . ."

This last and mightiest fall set the most astonishing of precedents. After receiving 97 percent of the electoral vote, the president—the indispensable leader—had been driven from office in midterm. Moreover, his replacement had been elected to no office higher than representative from the Fifth Congressional District of Michigan. Gerald Ford, whom Nixon selected in 1973 to replace the departed Agnew, had a mandate for national leadership only from the two houses of Congress.

Nevertheless, for two reasons the transition was remarkably smooth. First, the Watergate crisis was widely interpreted in personal terms. The news media focused on the individual, Richard Nixon, and interpreted his disgrace as a lesson to prove that even the most exalted would suffer for the sin of pride.*

If Nixon was the problem, then Ford was a fine solution. With an open, amiable, and unaffected manner, he offered a perfect contrast to Nixon. In his initial address, he promised to represent almost everyone except atheists, and he began his presidency with a cautious, congressional style of leadership, offering a little for this group, a little for that one. Well before Nixon's resignation, only about one in four Americans was supporting his presidency. When opinion polls showed three out of four behind the new president, Ford had weathered the crisis.

A subtler but equally important reason for the smooth transition was a nationwide cynicism about all Washington politics. Assuming the worst, Americans generally concluded that they were getting it. When a poll showed that a majority of people believed that Nixon was lying about Watergate, for example, four out of five also judged him no more corrupt than his predecessors. In the bicentennial year, a meager 17 percent of Americans expressed respect for the United States Congress.

The sour sentiments generated by Watergate

*Many people who subscribed to this interpretation sharply criticized President Ford late in 1974 for issuing a blanket pardon to Nixon while associates like Mitchell, Haldeman, and Ehrlichman were about to go to prison. At the very least, the argument went, Nixon should confess his guilt in order to earn that pardon.

washed over Nixon's successors. By no standards was either Ford or Carter an outstanding president. Both appealed to the voters as plain, honest men with a small-town folksiness who could bring a fresh, commonsensical approach to the national government's cluttered complexity. Carter, a former governor of Georgia, added the moral tone of evangelical Christianity and the attraction of having had absolutely no connection with Washington—assets that brought him from obscurity through an impressive record in the Democratic primaries of 1976 to a close victory over Ford that November.

Neither president surrounded himself with notable talents, neither developed a strong relation with Congress, and neither mastered the art of inspiring public leadership. Their televised debates during the 1976 campaign were models of dull competence. But both Ford and Carter faced almost insoluble problems. Each was commanded to spin the gold of American prosperity from the straw of worldwide stagnation, to control global affairs in spite of America's waning international authority, and to elevate the national spirit through political institutions in which Americans had little faith. Small wonder that after a few months in office the approval ratings of both fell and stayed low even during times when they were relatively skillful. The longer President Carter held office, the more difficulty he had in sustaining his popularity. Although he overcame a mismanaged challenge from Senator Edward Kennedy of Massachusetts and won renomination for president in 1980, Carter commanded little respect among his party's leaders or the voters at large. The Republicans, therefore, approached the election of 1980 with high optimism. To oppose Carter, they selected Ronald Reagan. A former movie actor with a charming public manner, Reagan had been a controversial but politically successful governor of California, and had built his base in the conservative wing of the Republican party. He championed traditional values in an appeal to local Americans, free enterprise in an appeal to wealthy Americans, and a tough, aggressive foreign policy in an appeal to those who were frustrated by

THE WINNERS

The dramatic results of the 1980 Presidential campaign was a landslide victory for the Republican candidates, Ronald Reagan and George Bush, who carried 44 states with 489 electoral votes. Democrat Jimmy Carter carried 6 states and the District of Columbia with 49 electoral votes. *(Michael Evans/Sygma)*

the limits of America's international power. It seemed like a winning combination. The chances were excellent, however, that the next president, like his predecessors, would get caught between the expanding scope of public problems and the shrinking government authority to solve them.

Disenchantment with The National System. After six decades, the problems of America's modern state looked very similar to its earlier problems in broad outline but were very different in detail. The issue of a strong economy remained at the center of American life, and so did the obligation of public officials to oversee it. Governments at all levels had grown so luxuriantly that they took a third of the nation's personal income in taxes and also accounted for a third of the nation's personal income in salaries, wages, and other payments. The techniques of economic management, however, roused fierce debate. Washington's standard fiscal formulas seemed inadequate, yet no substitute materialized to take their place. Most Americans, without easing their demands for prosperity and services, insisted on lower taxes and smaller bureaucracies. In hard times, the voters wanted more services for less money, and political leaders no longer had a clear mandate for fulfilling their economic responsibilities.

The revolt against taxes and rules was part of a general reaction against elite authority that spread well beyond the government. Confidence in all major institutions—corporations, universities, medicine, law—dropped drastically during the seventies. *The Screwing of the Average Man* was author David Hapgood's summary of these feelings. As the specialized national system appeared more ominous and less competent, a growing variety of Americans looked elsewhere for satisfaction. Interest in mysticism, astrology, and supernatural forces thrived. Alternative routes to good health—from special diets to faith healing to the Laetrile cure for cancer—increasingly competed with traditional medicines. The deeper the disenchantment with an impersonal structure of expertise, the stronger became the attraction of America's local, personal ways. Late in the seventies, millions, both white and black, thrilled to the story of *Roots*, which traced the history of a black family from its African home through generations of American slavery. Innumerable Americans began their own search for family and ethnic ties that could give life meaning apart from the hierarchical world of skills and careers.

The values of the national system emphasized planning for the future. Appropriately, the increasing skepticism about the system went hand in hand with a widespread caution about the future. In diverse ways, Americans were resisting long-term commitments. More and more pairs of people were substituting tentative living arrangements for marriages, and the practice spread from the young to older age groups. By the late seventies, courts were struggling to devise a new subdivision of the law that would cover these ad hoc partnerships. At the bicentennial, the birthrate reached its lowest level in American history. Such a large percentage of voters avoided party labels and declared themselves independents that each election became a surprise package of special whims. Commentators used such labels as "privatism" and "narcissism" to describe these trends. In the gradual development of modern culture, they belonged with the continuing defense of the individual against a rationalized, routinized society. More and more Americans were trying to fashion lives that would maximize personal pleasure and personal growth by minimizing their formal ties in an imponderable society.

A growing aversion to constraints and commitments cast the nation's foreign policy in a haze of uncertainty. Clearly Americans now viewed world affairs with a greater impatience, a lower tolerance for the ceaseless volatility of life around the globe. On the one hand, that short of fuse set off a string of crude, irritable explosions. After the oil embargo of 1973–74, a number of writers and officials suggested a little gunboat diplomacy to seize the resources America wanted. In response to President Carter's moderate treaty with Panama, by which America would gradually relinquish American control over the Canal Zone, a senator concluded that the United States had a right to keep it because "we stole it fair and square." In 1980, when Iranian revolutionaries seized more than fifty American hostages and held them month after month to protest United States' imperialism, many Americans responded chillingly with demands to "nuke Iran," and Carter mounted an unsuccessful American military expedition to try to free the prisoners.

On the other hand, impatience generated a kind

of indifference. As national revolutions unraveled America's network of global connections, there was a powerful urge to stay clear of these eruptions and avoid "another Vietnam." Carter's tendency to lecture the world on human rights but to do very little about them expressed a prevailing mood of restless withdrawal that made the formation of consistent policies very difficult. In foreign as in domestic affairs, the binding, integrating forces of conformity and containment that materialized in the early 1950s were loosening to the point where all the major problems of modern society—economic management, national-local balance, individual fulfillment, and international order—awaited a new and more penetrating comprehension in the 1980s.

CHRONOLOGY

1971 Classified documents about Vietnam War, the Pentagon Papers, leaked to the press.

1972 Nixon visits China and Soviet Union.
SALT treaty signed to balance the growth of military power.
Five men arrested burglarizing Democratic Watergate headquarters.
Nixon reelected president.

1973 American withdrawal from Vietnam.
Roe v. *Wade* establishes women's constitutional right to abortion.
Senate Watergate Committee begins hearings.
Vice-President Agnew resigns after charges of bribe-taking; Gerald Ford appointed to succeed him.

Arab oil boycott creates energy shortage.

1974 Worst economic recession since 1930s.
Nixon resigns the presidency; Ford becomes president.
Ford pardons Nixon.

1975 Government in South Vietnam falls.

1976 Jimmy Carter elected president.

1979 United States formally recognizes China.
President Carter mediates in Egyptian-Israeli peace settlement.
Accident at Three Mile Island nuclear power plant.

1980 Ronald W. Reagan elected president.

SUGGESTED READINGS

Three interesting books attempt general interpretations of contemporary American politics: David Knoke, *Change and Continuity in American Politics* (1976), Everett Carll Ladd, Jr., and Charles D. Hadley, *Transformations of the American Party System* (rev. ed., 1978), and Kevin P. Phillips, *The Emerging Republican Majority* (1969). Accounts of Richard Nixon include a favorable one in Earl Mazo and Stephen Hess, *Nixon* (1968), and an unfavorable one in Garry Wills, *Nixon Agonistes* (1970). In *Kissinger* (1974), Marvin and Bernard Kalb raise Nixon's reputation in foreign affairs by deflating claims that Kissinger dominated the president. Tad Szulc, *The Illusion of Peace: Foreign Policy in the Nixon Years* (1978), is harsher still on Kissinger. Kissinger defends himself in his memoir, *White House Years* (1979).

Harland B. Moulton's *From Superiority to Parity: The United States and the Strategic Arms Race, 1961–1971* (1973) discusses some preliminary moves toward détente. On the Middle East, William B. Quandt, *Decade of Decision: American Policy toward the Arab-Israeli Conflict, 1967–1976* (1977), and Robert W. Stookey, *America and the Arab States* (1975), are especially useful. Recent interest in the office of the chief executive has generated a variety of books, including George E. Reedy, *The Twilight of the Presidency* (1970), Arthur M. Schlesinger, Jr., *The Imperial Presidency* (1973), which is sharply critical of Nixon, and Otis L. Graham, Jr., *Toward a Planned Society: From Roosevelt to Nixon* (1976), which also faults Nixon for disrupting the evolution of national planning. The Watergate affair elicited its own special group of studies. Carl Bernstein and Bob Woodward, the reporters who helped to expose the affair, tell a fascinating tale of investigation and deception in *All the President's Men* (1974). Their sequel, *The Final Days* (1976), deals with Nixon during the year before his resignation. Among the many memoirs by participants, John Dean's *Blind Ambition* (1976) is particularly enlightening. Jonathan Schell, *The Time of Illusion* (1976), also illuminates the Watergate period. The conservative senator who led an early investigation into the mess is the subject of Dick Dabney's *A Good Man: The Life of Sam J. Ervin* (1976).

A number of fine books argued the need for reconsideration after the sixties. Alexander M. Bickel, *The Supreme Court and the Idea of Progress* (1970), explores the limitations of the judiciary, Andrew Hacker, *The End of the American Era* (1970), the limitations of Washington's managerial leadership, Robert L. Heilbroner, *An Inquiry into the Human Prospect* (1974), the limitations of the world economy, and E. F. Schumacher, *Small Is Beautiful* (1973), the limitations of giant enterprise. Other studies continue the pattern of criticism at the end of the seventies: Barry Commoner, *The Poverty of Power* (1976), David Halberstam, *The Powers That Be* (1979), on the news empires, Christopher Lasch, *The Culture of Narcissism* (1978), William Ophuls, *Ecology and the Politics of Scarcity* (1977), and Peter Steinfels, *The Neoconservatives* (1979). Daniel Bell, on the other hand, is quite confident about America's future in *The Coming of Post-Industrial Society* (1973). On two controversial issues, Martin Hoffman's *The Gay World: Male Homosexuality and the Social Creation of Evil* (1968) presents the case for homosexuals, and David F. Musto's *The American Disease* (1973) traces the history of federal policy on narcotics.

Matt S. Meier and Feliciano Rivera, *The Chicanos: A History of Mexican Americans* (1972), is a general account of an increasingly important minority in American life. Also useful is Julian Samora, *Los Mojados: The Wetback Story* (1971). Wilcomb E. Washburn, *Red Man's Land, White Man's Law* (1971), details a record of mass injustice, D'Arcy McNickle, *Native American Tribalism* (1973) helps to explain the culture of recent protests, and Vine Deloria, Jr., *Behind the Trail of Broken Treaties* (1974), expresses the spirit of contemporary militancy. For a general survey and extensive bibliography, see Wilcomb Washburn's *The Indian in America* (1975). The essays in Michael V. Namorato, ed., *Have We Overcome?* (1979), assess the state of black rights, and Anthony Downs, *Opening Up the Suburbs* (1973), discusses race and social policy.

Appendix

C A

C A

PACIFIC OCEAN

Tacoma• •Seattle
Olympia Spokane•
⊛ Mt. Rainier
14,410'
WASHINGTON
1889
Portland•
Columbia R.
⊛Salem
Willamette R.
OREGON
1859
SIERRA
Sacramento R.
Sacramento⊛
San
Francisco•
CALIFORNIA
1850
Mt. Whitney
14,495'

Helena⊛ MONTANA
Butte• 1889
Yellowstone R.
Missouri R.

IDAHO
⊛Boise 1890
Snake R.

R
O
C
K
Y
WYOMING
1890
Great
Salt
Lake
Salt Lake⊛
City
NEVADA 1896
1864 UTAH
Reno•
Carson
City

Cheyenne⊛

Denver⊛
COLORADO
1876
Pikes Pk.
14,110'

NORTH DAKOTA
1889 ⊛Bismarck

SOUTH ⊛DAKOTA
Pierre
1889

1867
NEBRASKA
Platte R.

Lincoln⊛

1861
K A N S A

Wichita•

Colorado R.
Grand
Canyon
ARIZONA
1912
Gila R. ⊛Phoenix
•Tucson

Santa Fe⊛
NEW MEXICO
1912

S
A
N
G
R
E
D
E
C
R
I
S
T
O

Canadian R.

Oklahoma
⊛City
O K L A H
1907

Ft
Worth•
1 8 4 5
T E X A S R.

M E X I C O

El Paso•
Pecos R.
Rio Grande

San
Antonio•

Austin
⊛
Colorado R.

Nueces R.

Inset — Alaska and Hawaii

SOVIET UNION 180° ARCTIC OCEAN
Pt. Barrow
International Dateline (U.S.S.R.)
(United States)
ARCTIC CIRCLE
Nome• Yukon R.
Attu•
BERING Fairbanks•
SEA Mt. McKinley
20,300'
ALEUTIAN Anchorage•
CANADA
Kodiak I. Juneau⊛
Unimak ALASKA
1959
180° PACIFIC OCEAN
0   600
Miles

KAUAI
NIIHAU
OAHU MOLOKAI
Honolulu⊛
PACIFIC LANAI MAUI
KAHOOLAWE
O C E A N
HAWAII
1959 •Hilo
HAWAII
0   150
Miles

ii

Norman Clark Adams

The United States of America

★★★★★★★★★★★★

⊛ National Capital   ⊛ State Capital   • Other Major Cities

1845   Date of Admission to the Union

0   100   200   300   400   500

Scale of Miles

PUERTO RICO   **VIRGIN ISLANDS**

San Juan

St. Thomas I.

St. Johns I.   (Br.)

St. Charlotte Amalie

0   100

Miles

St. Croix I.

CARIBBEAN SEA

A D A

Lake of the Woods

Lake Superior

Duluth

MINNESOTA 1858

St. Paul

Minneapolis

MICHIGAN

Lake Huron

Lake Michigan

1837

WISCONSIN 1848

Madison

Milwaukee

Grand Rapids

Lansing

Detroit

Lake Erie

Quebec

St. Lawrence R.

Montreal

Ottawa

1820 MAINE

Bangor

Eastport

Augusta

L. Champlain

Montpelier

VT. 179 N.H. 1788

Portland

Concord

Toronto

L. Ontario

Rochester

Buffalo

Albany

Hudson R.

MASS. 1788

Boston

Cape Cod

Providence

Hartford

R.I.1790

CONN.1788

1846 IOWA

Des Moines

Chicago

South Bend

Ft.Wayne

Toledo

Cleveland

1803 OHIO

Columbus

1818 ILLINOIS

Springfield

1816 INDIANA

Indianapolis

Cincinnati

PENNSYLVANIA

Harrisburg 1787

Pittsburgh

Philadelphia

Long Island

New York

Trenton

N.J. 1787

Delaware R.

Dover

DEL. 1787

Omaha

Kansas City

Jefferson City

St. Louis

MISSOURI 1821

Louisville

Frankfort

KENTUCKY 1792

Cumberland R.

Ohio R.

Wabash R.

WEST VIRGINIA 1863

Charleston

Washington D.C.

Baltimore

MD. 1788

Annapolis

Potomac R.

Richmond

VIRGINIA 1788

James R.

Norfolk

Roanoke I.

Cape Hatteras

ARKANSAS

Little Rock 1836

Memphis

Nashville

Knoxville

TENNESSEE 1796

Tennessee R.

NORTH CAROLINA

Raleigh

Charlotte 1789

APPALACHIAN MTS.

Mississippi R.

Birmingham

Atlanta 1788

1817 MISSISSIPPI

1819 ALABAMA

Jackson

Montgomery

Alabama R.

Pearl R.

GEORGIA

SOUTH CAROLINA 1788

Columbia

Charleston

Cape Fear

Savannah R.

Savannah

Sabine R.

1812 LOUISIANA

Baton Rouge

New Orleans

Houston

Tallahassee

FLORIDA

1845

Tampa

L. Okeechobee

Miami

BAHAMA ISLANDS

ATLANTIC OCEAN

Havana

CUBA

iii

Declaration of Independence

IN CONGRESS, JULY 4, 1776

THE UNANIMOUS DECLARATION OF THE THIRTEEN UNITED STATES OF AMERICA

When, in the course of human events, it becomes necessary for one people to dissolve the political bands which have connected them with another, and to assume, among the powers of the earth, the separate and equal station to which the laws of nature and of nature's God entitle them, a decent respect to the opinions of mankind requires that they should declare the causes which impel them to the separation.

We hold these truths to be self-evident: That all men are created equal; that they are endowed by their Creator with certain unalienable rights; that among these are life, liberty, and the pursuit of happiness; that, to secure these rights, governments are instituted among men, deriving their just powers from the consent of the governed; that whenever any form of government becomes destructive of these ends, it is the right of the people to alter or to abolish it, and to institute new government, laying its foundation on such principles, and organizing its powers in such form, as to them shall seem most likely to effect their safety and happiness. Prudence, indeed, will dictate that governments long established should not be changed for light and transient causes; and accordingly all experience hath shown that mankind are more disposed to suffer, while evils are sufferable, than to right themselves by abolishing the forms to which they are accustomed. But when a long train of abuses and usurpations, pursuing invariably the same object, evinces a design to reduce them under absolute despotism, it is their right, it is their duty, to throw off such government, and to provide new guards for their future security. Such has been the patient sufferance of these colonies; and such is now the necessity which constrains them to alter their former systems of government. The history of the present King of Great Britain is a history of repeated injuries and usurpations, all having in direct object the establishment of an absolute tyranny over these states. To prove this, let facts be submitted to a candid world.

He has refused his assent to laws, the most wholesome and necessary for the public good.

He has forbidden his governors to pass laws of immediate and pressing importance, unless suspended in their operation till his assent should be obtained; and, when so suspended, he has utterly neglected to attend to them.

He has refused to pass other laws for the accommodation of large districts of people, unless those people would relinquish the right of representation in the legislature, a right inestimable to them, and formidable to tyrants only.

He has called together legislative bodies at places unusual, uncomfortable, and distant from the depository of their public records, for the sole purpose of fatiguing them into compliance with his measures.

He has dissolved representative houses repeatedly, for opposing, with manly firmness, his invasions on the rights of the people.

He has refused for a long time, after such dissolutions, to cause others to be elected; whereby the legislative powers, incapable of annihilation, have returned to the people at large for their exercise; the state remaining, in the mean time, exposed to all the dangers of invasions from without and convulsions within.

He has endeavored to prevent the population of these states; for that purpose obstructing the laws for naturalization of foreigners; refusing to pass others to encourage their migration hither, and raising the conditions of new appropriations of lands.

He has obstructed the administration of justice, by refusing his assent to laws for establishing judiciary powers.

He has made judges dependent on his will alone, for the tenure of their offices, and the amount and payment of their salaries.

He has erected a multiude of new offices, and sent hither swarms of officers to harass our people and eat out their substance.

He has kept among us, in times of peace, standing armies, without the consent of our legislatures.

He has affected to render the military independent of, and superior to, the civil power.

He has combined with others to subject us to a jurisdiction foreign to our constitution, and unacknowledged by our laws, giving his assent to their acts of pretended legislation:

For quartering large bodies of armed troops among us;

For protecting them, by a mock trial, from punishment for any murders which they should commit on the inhabitants of these states;

For cutting off our trade with all parts of the world;

For imposing taxes on us without our consent;

For depriving us, in many cases, of the benefits of trial by jury;

For transporting us beyond seas, to be tried for pretended offenses;

For abolishing the free system of English laws in a neighboring province, establishing therein an arbitrary government, and enlarging its boundaries, so as to render it at once an example and fit instrument for introducing the same absolute rule into these colonies;

For taking away our charters, abolishing our most valuable laws, and altering fundamentally the forms of our governments;

For suspending our own legislatures, and declaring themselves invested with power to legislate for us in all cases whatsoever.

He has abdicated government here, by declaring us out of his protection and waging war against us.

He has plundered our seas, ravaged our coasts, burned our towns, and destroyed the lives of our people.

He is at this time transporting large armies of foreign mercenaries to complete the works of death, desolation, and tyranny already begun with circumstances of cruelty and perfidy scarcely paralleled in the most barbarous ages, and totally unworthy the head of a civilized nation.

He has constrained our fellow-citizens, taken captive on the high seas, to bear arms against their country, to become the executioners of their friends and brethren, or to fall themselves by their hands.

He has excited domestic insurrection among us, and has endeavored to bring on the inhabitants of our frontiers the merciless Indian savages, whose known rule of warfare is an undistinguished destruction of all ages, sexes, and conditions.

In every stage of these oppressions we have petitioned for redress in the most humble terms; our repeated petitions have been answered only by repeated injury. A prince, whose character is thus marked by every act which may define a tyrant, is unfit to be the ruler of a free people.

Nor have we been wanting in our attentions to our British brethren. We have warned them, from time to time, of attempts by their legislature to extend an unwarrantable jurisdiction over us. We have reminded them of the circumstances of our emigration and settlement here. We have appealed to their native justice and magnanimity; and we have conjured them, by the ties of our common kindred, to disavow these usurpations, which would inevitably interrupt our connections and correspondence. They, too, have been deaf to the voice of justice and of consanguinity. We must, therefore, acquiesce in the necessity which denounces our separation, and hold them, as we hold the rest of mankind, enemies in war, in peace friends.

We, therefore, the representatives of the United States of America, in General Congress assembled, appealing to the Supreme Judge of the world for the rectitude of our intentions, do, in the name and by the authority of the good people of these colonies, solemnly publish and declare, that these United Colonies are, and of right ought to be, FREE AND INDEPENDENT STATES; that they are absolved from all allegiance to the British crown, and that all political connection between them and the state of Great Britain is, and ought to be, totally dissolved; and that, as free and independent states, they have full power to levy war, conclude peace, contract alliances, establish commerce, and do all other acts and things which independent states may of right do. And for the support of this declaration, with a firm reliance on the protection of Divine Providence, we mutually pledge to each other our lives, our fortunes, and our sacred honor.

JOHN HANCOCK [*President*]
[*and fifty-five others*]

The Articles of Confederation and Perpetual Union

BETWEEN THE STATES OF NEW HAMPSHIRE, MASSACHUSETTS BAY, RHODE ISLAND
AND PROVIDENCE PLANTATIONS, CONNECTICUT, NEW YORK, NEW JERSEY,
PENNSYLVANIA, DELAWARE, MARYLAND, VIRGINIA,
NORTH CAROLINA, SOUTH CAROLINA, GEORGIA.*

ARTICLE 1.

The stile of this confederacy shall be "The United States of America."

ARTICLE 2.

Each State retains its sovereignty, freedom and independence, and every power, jurisdiction, and right, which is not by this confederation expressly delegated to the United States, in Congress assembled.

ARTICLE 3.

The said states hereby severally enter into a firm league of friendship with each other for their common defence, the security of their liberties and their mutual and general welfare; binding themselves to assist each other against all force offered to, or attacks made upon them, or any of them, on account of religion, sovereignty, trade, or any other pretence whatever.

ARTICLE 4.

The better to secure and perpetuate mutual friendship and intercourse among the people of the different states in this union, the free inhabitants of each of these states, paupers, vagbonds, and fugitives from justice excepted, shall be entitled to all privileges and immunities of free citizens in the several states; and the people of each State shall have free ingress and regress to and from any other State, and shall enjoy therein all the privileges of trade and commerce, subject to the same duties, impositions, and restrictions, as the inhabitants thereof respectively; provided, that such restrictions shall not extend so far as to prevent the removal of property, imported into any State, to any other State of which the owner is an inhabitant; provided also, that no imposition, duties, or restriction, shall be laid by any State on the property of the United States, or either of them.

If any person guilty of, or charged with treason, felony, or other high misdemeanor in any State, shall flee from justice and be found in any of the United States, he shall, upon demand of the governor or executive power of the State from which he fled, be delivered up and removed to the State having jurisdiction of his offence.

Full faith and credit shall be given in each of these states to the records, acts, and judicial proceedings of the courts and magistrates of every other State.

ARTICLE 5.

For the more convenient management of the general interests of the United States, delegates shall be annually appointed, in such manner as the legislature of each State shall direct, to meet in Congress, on the 1st Monday in November in every year, with a power reserved to each

*This copy of the final draft of the Articles of Confederation is taken from the *Journals,* 9:907–925, November 15, 1777.

State to recal its delegates, or any of them, at any time within the year, and to send others in their stead for the remainder of the year.

No State shall be represented in Congress by less than two, nor by more than seven members; and no person shall be capable of being a delegate for more than three years in any term of six years; nor shall any person, being a delegate, be capable of holding any office under the United States, for which he, or any other for his benefit, receives any salary, fees, or emolument of any kind.

Each State shall maintain its own delegates in a meeting of the states, and while they act as members of the committee of the states.

In determining questions in the United States, in Congress assembled, each State shall have one vote.

Freedom of speech and debate in Congress shall not be impeached or questioned in any court or place out of Congress: and the members of Congress shall be protected in their persons from arrests and imprisonments, during the time of their going to and from, and attendance on Congress, *except for treason,* felony, or breach of the peace.

ARTICLE 6.

No State, without the consent of the United States, in Congress assembled, shall send any embassy to, or receive any embassy from, or enter into any conference, agreement, alliance, or treaty with any king, prince, or state; nor shall any person, holding any office of profit or trust under the United States, or any of them, accept of any present, emolument, office or title, of any kind whatever, from any king, prince, or foreign state; nor shall the United States, in Congress assembled, or any of them, grant any title of nobility.

No two or more states shall enter into any treaty, confederation, or alliance, whatever, between them, without the consent of the United States, in Congress assembled, specifying accurately the purposes for which the same is to be entered into, and how long it shall continue.

No state shall lay any imposts or duties which may interfere with any stipulations in treaties entered into by the United States, in Congress assembled, with any king, prince, or state, in pursuance of any treaties already proposed by Congress to the courts of France and Spain.

No vessels of war shall be kept up in time of peace by any State, except such number only as shall be deemed necessary by the United States, in Congress assembled, for the defence of such State or its trade; nor shall any body of forces be kept up by any State, in time of peace, except such number only as, in the judgment of the United States, in Congress assembled, shall be deemed requisite to garrison the forts necessary for the defence of such State; but every State shall always keep up a well regulated and disciplined militia, sufficiently armed and accoutred, and shall provide, and constantly have ready for use, in public stores, a due number of field pieces and tents, and a proper quantity of arms, ammunition and camp equipage.

No State shall engage in any war without the consent of the United States, in Congress assembled, unless such State be actually invaded by enemies, or shall have received certain advice of a resolution being formed by some nation of Indians to invade such State, and the danger is so imminent as not to admit of a delay till the United States, in Congress assembled, can be consulted; nor shall any State grant commissions to any ships or vessels of war, nor letters of marque or reprisal, except it be after a declaration of war by the United States, in Congress assembled, and then only against the kingdom or state, and the subjects thereof, against which war has been so declared, and under such regulations as shall be established by the United States, in Congress assembled, unless such State be infested by pirates, in which case vessels of war may be fitted out for that occasion, and kept so long as the danger shall continue, or until the United States, in Congress assembled, shall determine otherwise.

ARTICLE 7.

When land forces are raised by any State for the common defence, all officers of or under the rank of colonel, shall be appointed by the legislature of each State respectively, by whom such forces shall be raised, or in such manner as such State shall direct; and all vacancies shall be filled up by the State which first made the appointment.

ARTICLE 8.

All charges of war and all other expences, that shall be incurred for the common defence or general welfare, and allowed by the United States, in Congress assembled, shall be defrayed out of a common treasury, which shall be supplied by the several states, in proportion to the value of all land within each State, granted to or surveyed for any person, as such land and the buildings and improvements thereon shall be estimated according to such mode as the United States, in Congress assembled, shall, from time to time, direct and appoint.

The taxes for paying that proportion shall be laid and levied by the authority and direction of the legislatures of the several states, within the time agreed upon by the United States, in Congress assembled.

ARTICLE 9.

The United States, in Congress assembled, shall have the sole and exclusive right and power of determining on peace and war, except in the cases mentioned in the 6th article; of sending and receiving ambassadors; entering into treaties and alliances, provided that no treaty of commerce shall be made, whereby the legislative power of the repective states shall be restrained from imposing such imposts and duties on foreigners as their own people are subjected to, or from prohibiting the exportation or importation of any species of goods or commodities whatsoever; of establishing rules for deciding, in all cases, what captures on land or water shall be legal, and in what manner prizes, taken by land or naval forces in the service of the United States, shall be divided or appropriated; of granting letters of marque and reprisal in times of peace; appointing courts for the trial of piracies and felonies committed on the high seas, and establishing courts for receiving and determining, finally, appeals in all cases of captures; provided, that no member of Congress shall be appointed a judge of any of the said courts.

The United States, in Congress assembled, shall also be the last resort on appeal in all disputes and differences now subsisting, or that hereafter may arise between two or more states concerning boundary, jurisdiction or any other cause whatever; which authority shall always be exercised in the manner following: whenever the legislative or executive authority, or lawful agent of any State, in controversy with another, shall present a petition to Congress, stating the matter in question, and praying for a hearing, notice thereof shall be given, by order of Congress, to the legislative or executive authority of the other State in controversy, and a day assigned for the appearance of the parties by their lawful agents, who shall then be directed to appoint, by joint consent, commissioners or judges to constitute a court for hearing and determining the matter in question; but, if they cannot agree, Congress shall name three persons out of each of the United States, and from the list of such persons each party shall alternately strike out one, in the petitioners beginning, until the number shall be reduced to thirteen; and from that number not less than seven, nor more than nine names, as Congress shall direct, shall, in the presence of Congress, be drawn out by lot; and the persons whose names shall be so drawn, or any five of them, shall be commissioners or judges to hear and finally determine the controversy, so always as a major part of the judges who shall hear the cause shall agree in the determination; and if either party shall neglect to attend at the day appointed, without shewing reasons which Congress shall judge sufficient, or, being present, shall refuse to strike, the Congress shall proceed to nominate three persons out of each State, and the secretary of Congress shall strike in behalf of such party absent or refusing; and the judgment and sentence of the court to be appointed, in the manner before prescribed, shall be final and conclusive; and if any of the parties shall refuse to submit to the authority of such court, or to appear or defend their claim or cause, the court shall nevertheless proceed to pronounce sentence or judgment, which shall, in like manner, be final and decisive, the judgment or sentence and other proceedings being, in either case, transmitted to Congress, and lodged among the acts of Congress for the security of the parties concerned: provided, that every commissioner, before he sits in judgment, shall take an oath, to be administered by one of the judges of the supreme or superior court of the State where the cause shall be tried, "well and truly to hear and determine the matter in question, according to the best of his judgment, without favour, affection, or hope of reward": provided, also, that no State shall be deprived of territory for the benefit of the United States.

All controversies concerning the private right of soil, claimed under different grants of two or more states, whose jurisdictions, as they may respect such lands and the states which passed such grants, are adjusted, the said grants, or either of them, being at the same time claimed to have originated antecedent to such settlement of jurisdiction, shall, on the petition of either party to the Congress of the United States, be finally determined, as near as may be, in the same manner as is before prescribed for deciding disputes respecting territorial jurisdiction between different states.

The United States, in Congress assembled, shall also have the sole and exclusive right and power of regulating the alloy and value of coin struck by their own authority, or by that of the respective states; fixing the standard of weights and measures throughout the United States; regulating the trade and managing all affairs with the Indians not members of any of the states; provided that the legislative right of any State within its own limits be not infringed or violated; establishing and regulating post offices from one State to another throughout all the United

States, and exacting such postage on the papers passing through the same as may be requisite to defray the expences of the said office; appointing all officers of the land forces in the service of the United States, excepting regimental officers; appointing all the officers of the naval forces, and commissioning all officers whatever in the service of the United States; making rules for the government and regulation of the said land and naval forces, and directing their operations.

The United States, in Congress assembled, shall have authority to appoint a committee to sit in the recess of Congress, to be denominated "a Committee of the States," and to consist of one delegate from each State, and to appoint such other committees and civil officers as may be necessary for managing the general affairs of the United States, under their direction; to appoint one of their number to preside; provided that no person be allowed to serve in the office of president more than one year in any term of three years; to ascertain the necessary sums of money to be raised for the service of the United States, and to appropriate and apply the same for defraying the public expences; to borrow money or emit bills on the credit of the United States, transmitting, every half year, to the respective states, an account of the sums of money so borrowed or emitted; to build and equip a navy; to agree upon the number of land forces, and to make requisitions from each State for its quota, in proportion to the number of white inhabitants in such State; which requisitions shall be binding; and, thereupon, the legislature of each State shall appoint the regimental officers, raise the men, and cloathe, arm, and equip them in a soldier-like manner, at the expence of the United States; and the officers and men so cloathed, armed, and equipped, shall march to the place appointed and within the time agreed on by the United States, in Congress assembled; but if the United States, in Congress assembled, shall, on consideration of circumstances, judge proper that any State should not raise men, or should raise a smaller number than its quota, and that any other State should raise a greater number of men than the quota thereof, such extra number shall be raised, officered, cloathed, armed, and equipped in the same manner as the quota of such State, unless the legislature of such State shall judge that such extra number cannot be safely spared out of the same, in which case they shall raise, officer, cloathe, arm, and equip as many of such extra number as they judge can be safely spared. And the officers and men so cloathed, armed, and equipped, shall march to the place appointed and within the time agreed on by the United States, in Congress assembled.

The United States, in Congress assembled, shall never engage in a war, nor grant letters of marque and reprisal in time of peace, nor enter into any treaties or alliances, nor coin money, nor regulate the value thereof, nor ascertain the sums and expences necessary for the defence and welfare of the United States, or any of them: nor emit bills, nor borrow money on the credit of the United States, nor appropriate money, nor agree upon the number of vessels of war to be built or purchased, or the number of land or sea forces to be raised, nor appoint a commander in chief of the army or navy, unless nine states assent to the same; nor shall a question on any other point, except for adjourning from day to day, be determined, unless by the votes of a majority of the United States, in Congress assembled.

The Congress of the United States shall have power to adjourn to any time within the year, and to any place within the United States, so that no period of adjournment be for a longer duration than the space of six months, and shall publish the journal of their proceedings monthly, except such parts thereof, relating to treaties, alliances or military operations, as, in their judgment, require secrecy; and the yeas and nays of the delegates of each State on any question shall be entered on the journal, when it is desired by any delegate; and the delegates of a State, or any of them, at his, or their request, shall be furnished with a transcript of the said journal, except such parts as are above excepted, to lay before the legislatures of the several states.

ARTICLE 10.

The committee of the states, or any nine of them, shall be authorized to execute, in the recess of Congress, such of the powers of Congress as the United States, in Congress assembled, by the consent of nine states, shall, from time to time, think expedient to vest them with; provided, that no power be delegated to the said committee, for the exercise of which, by the articles of confederation, the voice of nine states, in the Congress of the United States assembled, is requisite.

ARTICLE 11.

Canada acceding to this confederation, and joining in the measures of the United States, shall be admitted into and entitled to all the advantages of this union; but no other colony shall be admitted into the same, unless such admission be agreed to by nine states.

ARTICLE 12.

All bills of credit emitted, monies borrowed and debts contracted by, or under the authority of Congress before the assembling of the United States, in pursuance of the present confederation, shall be deemed and considered as a charge against the United States, for payment and satisfaction whereof the said United States and the public faith are hereby solemnly pledged.

ARTICLE 13.

Every State shall abide by the determinations of the United States, in Congress assembled, on all questions which, by this confederation, are submitted to them. And the articles of this confederation shall be inviolably observed by every State, and the union shall be perpetual; nor shall any alteration at any time hereafter be made in any of them, unless such alteration be agreed to in a Congress of the United States, and be afterwards confirmed by the legislatures of every State.

These articles shall be proposed to the legislatures of all the United States, to be considered, and if approved of by them, they are advised to authorize their delegates to ratify the same in the Congress of the United States; which being done, the same shall become conclusive.

Constitution of
the United States of America

PREAMBLE

We the people of the United States, in order to form a more perfect union, establish justice,
insure domestic tranquillity, provide for the common defense, promote the
general welfare, and secure the blessings of liberty to ourselves and
our posterity, do ordain and establish this CONSTITUTION
for the United States of America.

ARTICLE I

Section 1. All legislative powers herein granted shall be vested in a Congress of the United States, which shall consist of a Senate and a House of Representatives.

Section 2. The House of Representatives shall be composed of members chosen every second year by the people of the several States, and the electors in each State shall have the qualifications requisite for electors of the most numerous branch of the State Legislature.

No person shall be a Representative who shall not have attained to the age of twenty-five years, and been seven years a citizen of the United States, and who shall not, when elected, be an inhabitant of that State in which he shall be chosen.

Representatives and direct taxes shall be apportioned among the several States which may be included within this Union, according to their respective numbers, *which shall be determined by adding to the whole number of free persons, including those bound to service for a term of years and excluding Indians not taxed, three-fifths of all other persons.* The actual enumeration shall be made within three years after the first meeting of the Congress of the United States, and within every subsequent term of ten years, in such manner as they shall by law direct. The number of Representatives shall

NOTE: Passages that are no longer in effect are printed in italic type.

not exceed one for every thirty thousand, but each State shall have at least one Representative; *and until such enumeration shall be made, the State of New Hampshire shall be entitled to choose three, Massachusetts eight, Rhode Island and Providence Plantations one, Connecticut five, New York six, New Jersey four, Pennsylvania eight, Delaware one, Maryland six, Virginia ten, North Carolina five, South Carolina five, and Georgia three.*

When vacancies happen in the representation from any State, the Executive authority thereof shall issue writs of election to fill such vacancies.

The house of Representatives shall choose their Speaker and other officers; and shall have the sole power of impeachment.

Section 3. The Senate of the United States shall be composed of two Senators from each State, *chosen by the legislature thereof,* for six years; and each Senator shall have one vote.

Immediately after they shall be assembled in consequence of the first election, they shall be divided as equally as may be into three classes. The seats of the Senators of the first class shall be vacated at the expiration of the second year, of the second class at the expiration of the fourth year, and of the third class at the expiration of the sixth year, so that one-third may be chosen every second year; *and if vacancies happen by resignation or otherwise, during the recess of the legislature of any State, the Executive* thereof may make temporary appointments until the next meeting of the legislature, which shall then fill such vacancies.

No person shall be a Senator who shall not have attained to the age of thirty years, and been nine years a citizen of the United States, and who shall not, when elected, be an inhabitant of that State for which he shall be chosen.

The Vice-President of the United States shall be President of the Senate, but shall have no vote, unless they be equally divided.

The Senate shall choose their other officers, and also a President *pro tempore*, in the absence of the Vice-President, or when he shall exercise the office of President of the United States.

The Senate shall have the sole power to try all impeachments. When sitting for that purpose, they shall be on oath or affirmation. When the President of the United States is tried, the Chief Justice shall preside: and no person shall be convicted without the concurrence of two-thirds of the members present.

Judgment in cases of impeachment shall not extend further than to removal from the office, and disqualification to hold and enjoy any office of honor, trust or profit under the United States: but the party convicted shall nevertheless be liable and subject to indictment, trial, judgment and punishment, according to law.

Section 4. The times, places and manner of holding elections for Senators and Representatives shall be prescribed in each State by the legislature thereof; but the Congress may at any time by law make or alter such regulations, except as to the places of choosing Senators.

The Congress shall assemble at least once in every year, and such meeting *shall be on the first Monday in December, unless they shall by law appoint a different day.*

Section 5. Each house shall be the judge of the elections, returns and qualifications of its own members, and a majority of each shall constitute a quorum to do business; but a smaller number may adjourn from day to day, and may be authorized to compel the attendance of absent members, in such manner, and under such penalties, as each house may provide.

Each house may determine the rules of its proceedings, punish its members for disorderly behavior, and with the concurrence of two-thirds, expel a member.

Each house shall keep a journal of its proceedings, and from time to time publish the same, excepting such parts as may in their judgment require secrecy; and the yeas and nays of the members of either house on any question shall, at the desire of one-fifth of those present, be entered on the journal.

Neither house, during the session of Congress, shall, without the consent of the other, adjourn for more than three days, nor to any other place than that in which the two houses shall be sitting.

Section 6. The Senators and Representatives shall receive a compensation for their services, to be ascertained by law and paid out of the treasury of the United States. They shall in all cases except treason, felony and breach of the peace, be privileged from arrest during their attendance at the session of their respective houses, and in going to and returning from the same; and for any speech or debate in either house, they shall not be questioned in any other place.

No Senator or Representative shall, during the time for which he was elected, be appointed to any civil office under the authority of the United States, which shall have been created, or the emoluments whereof shall have been increased, during such time; and no person holding any office under the United States shall be a member of either house during his continuance in office.

Section 7. All bills for raising revenue shall originate in the House of Representatives; but the Senate may propose or concur with amendments as on other bills.

Every bill which shall have passed the House of Representatives and the Senate, shall, before it become a law, be presented to the President of the United States; if he approve he shall sign it, but if not he shall return it with objections to that house in which it originated, who shall enter the objections at large on their journal, and proceed to reconsider it. If after such reconsideration two-thirds of that house shall agree to pass the bill, it shall be sent, together with the objections, to the other house, by which it shall likewise be reconsidered, and, if approved by two-thirds of that house, it shall become a law. But in all such cases the votes of both houses shall be determined by yeas and nays, and the names of the persons voting for and against the bill shall be entered on the journal of each house respectively. If any bill shall not be returned by the President within ten days (Sundays excepted) after it shall have been presented to him, the same shall be a law, in like manner as if he had signed it, unless the Congress by their adjournment prevent its return, in which case it shall not be a law.

Every order, resolution, or vote to which the concurrence of the Senate and House of Representatives may be necessary (except on a question of adjournment) shall be presented to the President of the United States; and before the same shall take effect, shall be approved by him, or being disapproved by him, shall be repassed by two-thirds of the Senate and House of Representatives, according to the rules and limitations prescribed in the case of a bill.

Section 8. The Congress shall have power

To lay and collect taxes, duties, imposts, and excises, to pay the debts and provide for the common defense and general welfare of the United States; but all duties, imposts and excises shall be uniform throughout the United States;

To borrow money on the credit of the United States;

To regulate commerce with foreign nations, and among the several States, and with the Indian tribes;

To establish an uniform rule of naturalization, and uniform laws on the subject of bankruptcies throughout the United States;

To coin money, regulate the value thereof, and of foreign coin, and fix the standard of weights and measures;

To provide for the punishment of counterfeiting the securities and current coin of the United States;

To establish post offices and post roads;

To promote the progress of science and useful arts by securing for limited times to authors and inventors the exclusive right to their respective writings and discoveries;

To constitute tribunals inferior to the Supreme Court;

To define and punish piracies and felonies committed on the high seas and offenses against the law of nations;

To declare war, grant letters of marque and reprisal, and make rules concerning captures on land and water;

To raise and support armies, but no appropriation of money to that use shall be for a longer term than two years;

To provide and maintain a navy;

To make rules for the government and regulation of the land and naval forces;

To provide for calling forth the militia to execute the laws of the Union, suppress insurrections, and repel invasions;

To provide for organizing, arming, and disciplining the militia, and for governing such part of them as may be employed in the service of the United States, reserving to the States respectively the appointment of the officers, and the authority of training the militia according to the discipline prescribed by Congress;

To exercise exclusive legislation in all cases whatsoever, over such district (not exceeding ten miles square) as may, by cession of particular States, and the acceptance of Congress, become the seat of government of the United States, and to exercise like authority over all places purchased by the consent of the legislature of the State, in which the same shall be, for erection of forts, magazines, arsenals, dock-yards, and other needful buildings;—and

To make all laws which shall be necessary and proper for carrying into execution the foregoing powers, and all other powers vested by this Constitution in the government of the United States, or in any department or officer thereof.

Section 9. The migration or importation of such persons as any of the States now existing shall think proper to admit shall not be prohibited by the Congress prior to the year 1808; but a tax or duty may be imposed on such importation, not exceeding $10 for each person.

The privelege of the writ of habeas corpus shall not be suspended, unless when in cases of rebellion or invasion the public safety may require it.

No bill of attainder or ex post facto law shall be passed.

No capitation, or other direct, tax shall be laid, unless in proportion to the census or enumeration herein before directed to be taken.

No tax or duty shall be laid on articles exported from any State.

No preference shall be given by any regulation of commerce or revenue to the ports of one State over those of another; nor shall vessels bound to, or from, one State, be obliged to enter, clear, or pay duties in another.

No money shall be drawn from the treasury, but in consequence of appropriations made by law; and a regular statement and account of the receipts and expenditures of all public money shall be published from time to time.

No title of nobility shall be granted by the United States: and no person holding any office of profit or trust under them, shall, without the consent of the Congress, accept of any present, emolument, office, or title, of any kind whatever, from any king, prince, or foreign state.

Section 10. No State shall enter into any treaty, alliance, or confederation; grant letters of marque and reprisal; coin money; emit bills of credit; make anything but gold and silver coin a tender in payment of debts; pass any bill of attainder, ex post facto law, or law impairing the obligation of contracts, or grant any title of nobility.

No State shall, without the consent of Congress, lay any imposts or duties on imports or exports, except what may be absolutely necessary for executing its inspection laws: and the net produce of all duties and imposts, laid by any

State on imports or exports, shall be for the use of the treasury of the United States; and all such laws shall be subject to the revision and control of the Congress.

No State shall, without the consent of Congress, lay any duty of tonnage, keep troops or ships of war in time of peace, enter into any agreement or compact with another State, or with a foreign power, or engage in war, unless actually invaded, or in such imminent danger as will not admit of delay.

ARTICLE II

Section 1. The executive power shall be vested in a President of the United States of America. He shall hold his office during the term of four years, and, together with the Vice-President, chosen for the same term, be elected as follows:

Each State shall appoint, in such manner as the legislature thereof may direct, a number of electors, equal to the whole number of Senators and Representatives to which the State may be entitled in the Congress; but no Senator or Representative, or person holding an office of trust or profit under the United States, shall be appointed an elector.

The electors shall meet in their respective States, and vote by ballot for two persons, of whom one at least shall not be an inhabitant of the same State with themselves. And they shall make a list of all the persons voted for, and of the number of votes for each; which list they shall sign and certify, and transmit sealed to the seat of government of the United States, directed to the President of the Senate. The President of the Senate shall, in the presence of the Senate and House of Representatives, open all the certificates, and the votes shall then be counted. The person having the greatest number of votes shall be the President, if such number be a majority of the whole number of electors appointed; and if there be more than one who have such majority, and have an equal number of votes, then the House of Representatives shall immediately choose by ballot one of them for President; and if no person have a majority, then from the five highest on the list said house shall in like manner choose the President. But in choosing the President the votes shall be taken by States, the representation from each State having one vote; a quorum for this purpose shall consist of a member or members from two-thirds of the States, and a majority of all the States shall be necessary to a choice. In every case, after the choice of the President, the person having the greatest number of votes of the electors shall be the Vice-President. But if there should remain two or more who have equal votes, the Senate shall choose from them by ballot the Vice-President.

The Congress may determine the time of choosing the electors and the day on which they shall give their votes; which day shall be the same throughout the United States.

No person except a natural-born citizen, *or a citizen of the United States at the time of the adoption of this Constitution,* shall be eligible to the office of President; neither shall any person be eligible to that office who shall not have attained to the age of thirty-five years, and been fourteen years a resident within the United States.

In case of the removal of the President from office or of his death, resignation, or inability to discharge the powers and duties of the said office, the same shall devolve on the Vice-President, and the Congress may by law provide for the case of removal, death, resignation, or inability, both of the President and Vice-President, declaring what officer shall then act as President, and such officer shall act accordingly, until the disability be removed, or a President shall be elected.

The President shall, at stated times, receive for his services a compensation, which shall neither be increased nor diminished during the period for which he shall have been elected, and he shall not receive within that period any other emolument from the United States, or any of them.

Before he enter on the execution of his office, he shall take the following oath or affirmation:—"I do solemnly swear (or affirm) that I will faithfully execute the office of the President of the United States, and will to the best of my ability preserve, protect and defend the Constitution of the United States."

Section 2. The President shall be commander in chief of the army and navy of the United States, and of the militia of the several States, when called into the actual service of the United States; he may require the opinion, in writing, of the principal officer in each of the executive departments, upon any subject relating to the duties of their respective offices, and he shall have power to grant reprieves and pardons for offenses against the United States, except in cases of impeachment.

He shall have power, by and with the advice and consent of the Senate, to make treaties, provided two-thirds of the Senators present concur; and he shall nominate, and by and with the advice and consent of the Senate, shall appoint ambassadors, other public ministers and consuls, judges of the Supreme Court, and all other officers of the United States, whose appointments are not herein otherwise provided for, and which shall be established by law: but Congress may by law vest the appointment of such inferior officers, as they think proper, in the President alone, in the courts of law, or in the heads of departments.

The President shall have power to fill up all vacancies that may happen during the recess of the Senate, by granting commissions which shall expire at the end of their next session.

Section 3. He shall from time to time give to the Congress information of the state of the Union, and recommend to their consideration such measures as he shall judge necessary and expedient; he may, on extraordinary occasions, convene both houses, or either of them, and in case of disagreement between them, with respect to the time of adjournment, he may adjourn them to such time as he shall think proper; he shall receive ambassadors and other public ministers; he shall take care that the laws be faithfully executed, and shall commission all the officers of the United States.

Section 4. The President, Vice-President and all civil officers of the United States shall be removed from office on impeachment for, and on conviction of, treason, bribery, or other high crimes and misdemeanors.

ARTICLE III

Section 1. The judicial power of the United States shall be vested in one Supreme Court, and in such inferior courts as the Congress may from time to time ordain and establish. The judges, both of the Supreme and inferior courts, shall hold their offices during good behavior, and shall, at stated times, receive for their services a compensation which shall not be diminished during their continuance in office.

Section 2. The judicial power shall extend to all cases, in law and equity, arising under this Constitution, the laws of the United States, and treaties made, or which shall be made, under their authority;—to all cases affecting ambassadors, other public ministers and consuls;—to all cases of admiralty and maritime jurisdiction;—to controversies to which the United States shall be a party;—to controversies between two or more States;—*between a State and citizens of another State;*—between citizens of different States;—between citizens of the same State claiming lands under grants of different States, and between a State, or the citizens thereof, and foreign states, citizens or subjects.

In all case affecting ambassadors, other public ministers and consuls, and those in which a State shall be party, the Supreme Court shall have original jurisdiction. In all the other cases before mentioned, the Supreme Court shall have appellate jurisdiction, both as to law and fact, with such exceptions, and under such regulations, as the Congress shall make.

The trial of all crimes, except in cases of impeachment, shall be by jury; and such trial shall be held in the State where said crimes shall have been committed; but when not committed within any State, the trial shall be at such place or places as the Congress may by law have directed.

Section 3. Treason against the United States shall consist only in levying war against them, or in adhering to their enemies, giving them aid and comfort. No person shall be convicted of treason unless on the testimony of two witnesses to the same overt act, or on confession in open court.

The Congress shall have power to declare the punishment of treason, but no attainder of treason shall work corruption of blood, or forfeiture except during the life of the person attainted.

ARTICLE IV

Section 1. Full faith and credit shall be given in each State to the public acts, records, and judicial proceedings of every other State. And the Congress may by general laws prescribe the manner in which such acts, records, and proceedings shall be proved, and the effect thereof.

Section 2. The citizens of each State shall be entitled to all privileges and immunities of citizens in the several States.

A person charged in any State with treason, felony, or other crime, who shall flee from justice, and be found in another State, shall on demand of the executive authority of the State from which he fled, be delivered up, to be removed to the State having jurisdiction of the crime.

No person held to service or labor in one State, under the laws thereof, escaping into another, shall, in consequence of any law or regulation therein, be discharged from such service or labor, but shall be delivered up on claim of the party to whom such service or labor may be due.

Section 3. New States may be admitted by the Congress into this Union; but no new State shall be formed or erected within the jurisdiction of any other State; nor any State be formed by the junction of two or more States, or parts of States, without the consent of the legislatures of the States concerned as well as of the Congress.

The Congress shall have power to dispose of and make all needful rules and regulations respecting the territory or other property belonging to the United States; and nothing in this Constitution shall be so construed as to prejudice any claims of the United States, or of any particular State.

Section 4. The United States shall guarantee to every State in this Union a republican form of government, and shall protect each of them against invasion; and on application of the legislature, or of the executive (when the legislature cannot be convened), against domestic violence.

ARTICLE V

The Congress, whenever two-thirds of both houses shall deem it necessary, shall propose amendments to this Constitution, or, on the application of the legislatures of two-thirds of the several States, shall call a convention for proposing amendments, which, in either case, shall be valid to all intents and purposes, as part of this Constitution, when ratified by the legislatures of three-fourths of the several States, or by conventions in three-fourths thereof, as the one or the other mode of ratification may be proposed by the Congress; provided *that no amendments which may be made prior to the year one thousand eight hundred and eight shall in any manner affect the first and fourth clauses in the ninth section of the first article;* and that no State, without its consent, shall be deprived of its equal suffrage in the Senate.

ARTICLE VI

All debts contracted and engagements entered into, before the adoption of this Constitution, shall be as valid against the United States under this Constitution, as under the Confederation.

This Constitution, and the laws of the United States which shall be made in pursuance thereof; and all treaties made, or which shall be made, under the authority of the United States, shall be the supreme law of the land; and the judges in every State shall be bound thereby, anything in the Constitution or laws of any State to the contrary notwithstanding.

The Senators and Representatives before mentioned, and the members of the several State legislatures, and all executive and judicial officers, both of the United States and of the several States, shall be bound by oath or affirmation to support this Constitution; but no religious test shall ever be required as a qualification to any office or public trust under the United States.

ARTICLE VII

The ratification of the conventions of nine States shall be sufficient for the establishment of this Constitution between the States so ratifying the same.

Done in Convention by the unanimous consent of the States present, the seventeenth day of September in the year of our Lord one thousand seven hundred and eighty-seven and of the Independence of the United States of America the twelfth. In witness whereof we have hereunto subscribed our names.

[Signed by]
G° WASHINGTON
Presidt and Deputy from Virginia
[and thirty-eight others]

Amendments to the Constitution

ARTICLE I*

Congress shall make no law respecting an establishment of religion, or prohibiting the free exercise thereof; or abridging the freedom of speech, or of the press; or the right of the people peaceably to assemble, and to petition the government for a redress of grievances.

*The first ten Amendments (Bill of Rights) were adopted in 1791.

ARTICLE II

A well-regulated militia being necessary to the security of a free State, the right of the people to keep and bear arms shall not be infringed.

ARTICLE III

No soldier shall, in time of peace, be quartered in any house without the consent of the owner, nor in time of war, but in a manner to be prescribed by law.

ARTICLE IV

The right of the people to be secure in their persons, houses, papers, and effects, against unreasonable searches and seizures, shall not be violated, and no warrants shall issue but upon probable cause, supported by oath or affirmation, and particularly describing the place to be searched, and the persons or things to be seized.

ARTICLE V

No person shall be held to answer for a capital, or otherwise infamous crime, unless on a presentment or indictment of a grand jury, except in cases arising in the land or naval forces, or in the militia, when in actual service in time of war or public danger; nor shall any person be subject for the same offense to be twice put in jeopardy of life or limb; nor shall be compelled in any criminal case to be a witness against himself, nor be deprived of life, liberty, or property, without due process of law; nor shall private property be taken for public use without just compensation.

ARTICLE VI

In all criminal prosecutions, the accused shall enjoy the right to a speedy and public trial, by an impartial jury of the State and district wherein the crime shall have been committed, which district shall have been previously ascertained by law, and to be informed of the nature and cause of the accusation; to be confronted with the witnesses against him; to have compulsory process for obtaining witnesses in his favor, and to have the assistance of counsel for his defense.

ARTICLE VII

In suits at common law, where the value in controversy shall exceed twenty dollars, the right of trial by jury shall be preserved, and no fact tried by a jury shall be otherwise reexamined in any court of the United States, than according to the rules of the common law.

ARTICLE VIII

Excessive bail shall not be required, nor excessive fines imposed, nor cruel and unusual punishments inflicted.

ARTICLE IX

The enumeration in the Constitution, of certain rights, shall not be construed to deny or disparage others retained by the people.

ARTICLE X

The powers not delegated to the United States by the Constitution, nor prohibited by it to the States, are reserved to the States respectively, or to the people.

ARTICLE XI
[*Adopted 1798*]

The judicial power of the United States shall not be construed to extend to any suit in law or equity, commenced or prosecuted against one of the United States by citizens of another State, or by citizens or subjects of any foreign state.

ARTICLE XII
[*Adopted 1804*]

The electors shall meet in their respective States, and vote by ballot for President and Vice-President, one of whom, at least, shall not be an inhabitant of the same State with themselves; they shall name in their ballots the person voted for as President, and in distinct ballots the person voted for as Vice-President, and they shall make distinct lists of all persons voted for as President, and of all persons voted for as Vice-President, and of the number of votes for each, which lists they shall sign and certify, and transmit sealed to the seat of government of the United States, directed to the President of the Senate;—the President of the Senate shall, in the presence of the Senate and House of Representatives, open all the certificates and the votes shall then be counted;—the person having the greatest number of votes for President shall be the President, if such number be a majority of the whole number of electors appointed; and if no person have such majority, then from the persons having the highest numbers not exceeding three on the list of those voted for as President, the House of Representatives shall choose immediately, by ballot, the President. But in choosing the President, the votes shall be taken by States, the representation from each State having one vote; a quorum for this purpose shall consist of a member or members from two-thirds of the States, and a majority of all the States shall be necessary to a choice. And if the House of Representatives shall not choose a President whenever the right of choice shall devolve upon them, before *the fourth day of March* next following, then the Vice-President shall act as President, as in the case of the death or other constitutional disability of the President.

The person having the greatest number of votes as Vice-President shall be the Vice-President, if such number be a majority of the whole number of electors appointed; and if no person have a majority, then from the two highest numbers on the list the Senate shall choose the Vice-President; a quorum for the purpose shall consist of two-thirds of the whole number of Senators, and a majority of the whole number shall be necessary to a choice. But no person constitutionally ineligible to the office of President shall be eligible to that of Vice-President of the United States.

ARTICLE XIII
[*Adopted 1865*]

Section 1.   Neither slavery nor involuntary servitude, except as a punishment for crime whereof the party shall have been duly convicted, shall exist within the United States, or any place subject to their jurisdiction.

Section 2.   Congress shall have power to enforce this article by appropriate legislation.

ARTICLE XIV
[*Adopted 1868*]

Section 1.   All persons born or naturalized in the United States, and subject to the jurisdiction thereof, are citizens of the United States and of the State wherein they reside. No State shall make or enforce any law which shall abridge the privileges or immunities of citizens of the United States; nor shall any State deprive any person of life, liberty, or property, without due process of law; nor deny to any person within its jurisdiction the equal protection of the laws.

Section 2.   Representatives shall be apportioned among the several States according to their respective numbers, counting the whole number of persons in each State, excluding Indians not taxed. But when the right to vote at any election for the choice of Electors for President and Vice-President of the United States, Representatives in Congress, the executive and judicial officers of a State, or the members of the legislature thereof, is denied to any of the male inhabitants of such State, being twenty-one years of age and citizens of the United States, or in any way abridged, except for participation in rebellion, or other crime, the basis of representation therein shall be reduced in the proportion which the number of such male citizens shall bear to the whole number of male citizens twenty-one years of age in such State.

Section 3.   No person shall be a Senator or Representative in Congress, or Elector of President and Vice-President, or hold any office, civil or military, under the United States, or under any State, who, having previously taken an oath, as a member of Congress, or as an officer of the United States, or as a member of any State legislature, or as an executive or judicial officer of any State, to support the Constitution of the United States, shall have engaged in insurrection or rebellion against the same, or given aid or comfort to the enemies thereof. Congress may, by a vote of two-thirds of each house, remove such disability.

Section 4.   The validity of the public debt of the United States, authorized by law, including debts incurred for payment of pensions and bounties for services in suppressing insurrection or rebellion, shall not be questioned. But neither the United States nor any State shall assume or pay any debt or obligation incurred in aid of insurrection or rebellion against the United States, or any claim for the loss of emancipation of any slave; but all such debts, obligations, and claims shall be held illegal and void.

Section 5.   The Congress shall have power to enforce, by appropriate legislation, the provisions of this article.

ARTICLE XV
[*Adopted 1870*]

Section 1.   The right of citizens of the United States to vote shall not be denied or abridged by the United States or by any State on account of race, color, or previous condition of servitude.

Section 2. The Congress shall have power to enforce this article by appropriate legislation.

ARTICLE XVI
[*Adopted 1913*]

The Congress shall have power to lay and collect taxes on incomes, from whatever source derived, without apportionment among the several States, and without regard to any census or enumeration.

ARTICLE XVII
[*Adopted 1913*]

Section 1. The Senate of the United States shall be composed of two Senators from each State, elected by the people thereof, for six years; and each Senator shall have one vote. The electors in each State shall have the qualifications requisite for electors of [voters for] the most numerous branch of the State legislatures.

Section 2. When vacancies happen in the representation of any State in the Senate, the executive authority of such State shall issue writs of election to fill such vacancies: Provided, that the Legislature of any State may empower the executive thereof to make temporary appointments until the people fill the vacancies by election as the Legislature may direct.

Section 3. This amendment shall not be so construed as to affect the election or term of any Senator chosen before it becomes valid as part of the Constitution.

ARTICLE XVIII
[*Adopted 1919; Repealed 1933*]

Section 1. After one year from the ratification of this article the manufacture, sale, or transportation of intoxicating liquors within, the importation thereof into, or the exportation thereof from the United States and all territory subject to the jurisdiction thereof, for beverage purposes, is hereby prohibited.

Section 2. The Congress and the several States shall have concurrent power to enforce this article by appropriate legislation.

Section 3. This article shall be inoperative unless it shall have been ratified as an amendment to the Constitution by the legislatures of the several States, as provided by the Constitution, within

seven years from the date of the submission thereof to the States by the Congress.

ARTICLE XIX
[*Adopted 1920*]

Section 1. The right of citizens of the United States to vote shall not be denied or abridged by the United States or by any State on account of sex.

Section 2. The Congress shall have power to enforce this article by appropriate legislation.

ARTICLE XX
[*Adopted 1933*]

Section 1. The terms of the President and Vice-President shall end at noon on the 20th day of January, and the terms of Senators and Representatives at noon on the 3d day of January, of the years in which such terms would have ended if this article had not been ratified; and the terms of their successors shall then begin.

Section 2. The Congress shall assemble at least once in every year, and such meeting shall begin at noon on the 3d day of January, unless they shall by law appoint a different day.

Section 3. If, at the time fixed for the beginning of the term of the President, the President-elect shall have died, the Vice-President-elect shall become President. If a President shall not have been chosen before the time fixed for the beginning of his term, or if the President-elect shall have failed to qualify, then the Vice-President-elect shall act as President until a President shall have qualified; and the Congress may by law provide for the case wherein neither a President-elect nor a Vice-President-elect shall have qualified, declaring who shall then act as President, or the manner in which one who is to act shall be selected, and such persons shall act accordingly until a President or Vice-President shall have qualified.

Section 4. The Congress may by law provide for the case of the death of any of the persons from whom the House of Representatives may choose a President whenever the right of choice shall have devolved upon them, and for the case of the death of any of the persons from whom the

Senate may choose a Vice-President whenever the right of choice shall have devolved upon them.

Section 5. Sections 1 and 2 shall take effect on the 15th day of October following the ratification of this article.

Section 6. This article shall be inoperative unless it shall have been ratified as an amendment to the Constitution by the Legislatures of three-fourths of the several States within seven years from the date of its submission.

ARTICLE XXI
[*Adopted 1933*]

Section 1. The eighteenth article of amendment to the Constitution of the United States is hereby repealed.

Section 2. The transportation or importation into any State, Territory, or Possession of the United States for delivery or use therein of intoxicating liquors, in violation of the laws thereof, is hereby prohibited.

Section 3. This article shall be inoperative unless it shall have been ratified as an amendment to the Constitution by conventions in the several States, as provided in the Constitution, within seven years from the date of submission thereof to the States by the Congress.

ARTICLE XXII
[*Adopted 1951*]

Section 1. No person shall be elected to the office of President more than twice, and no person who has held the office of President, or acted as President, for more than two years of a term to which some other person was elected President shall be elected to the office of President more than once. But this article shall not apply to any person holding the office of President when this article was proposed by the Congress, and shall not prevent any person who may be holding the office of President, or acting as President, during the term within which this article becomes operative from holding the office of President or acting as President during the remainder of such term.

Section 2. This article shall be inoperative unless it shall have been ratified as an amendment to the Constitution by the legislatures of three-fourths of the several States within seven years from the date of its submission to the States by the Congress.

ARTICLE XXIII
[*Adopted 1961*]

Section 1. The District constituting the seat of Government of the United States shall appoint in such manner as the Congress may direct:

A number of electors of President and Vice-President equal to the whole number of Senators and Representatives in Congress to which the District would be entitled if it were a State, but in no event more than the least populous State; they shall be in addition to those appointed by the States, but they shall be considered for the purposes of the election of President and Vice-President, to be electors appointed by a State; and they shall meet in the District and perform such duties as provided by the twelfth article of amendment.

Section 2. The Congress shall have the power to enforce this article by appropriate legislation.

ARTICLE XXIV
[*Adopted 1964*]

Section 1. The right of citizens of the United States to vote in any primary or other election for President or Vice-President, for electors for President or Vice-President, or for Senator or Representative in Congress, shall not be denied or abridged by the United States or any State by reason of failure to pay any poll tax or other tax.

Section 2. The Congress shall have the power to enforce this article by appropriate legislation.

ARTICLE XXV
[*Adopted 1967*]

Section 1. In case of the removal of the President from office or of his death or resignation, the Vice President shall become President.

Section 2. Whenever there is a vacancy in the office of the Vice President, the President shall nominate a Vice President who shall take office upon confirmation by a majority vote of both Houses of Congress.

Section 3. Whenever the President transmits to the President pro tempore of the Senate and the Speaker of the House of Representatives his written declaration that he is unable to discharge the powers and duties of his office, and until he transmits to them a written declaration to the contrary, such powers and duties shall be discharged by the Vice President as Acting President.

Section 4.   Whenever the Vice President and a majority of either the principal officers of the executive departments or of such other body as Congress may by law provide, transmit to the President pro tempore of the Senate and the Speaker of the House of Representatives their written declaration that the President is unable to discharge the powers and duties of his office, the Vice President shall immediately assume the powers and duties of the office as Acting President.

Thereafter, when the President transmits to the President pro tempore of the Senate and the Speaker of the House of Representatives his written declaration that no inability exists, he shall resume the powers and duties of his office unless the Vice President and a majority of either the principal officers of the executive department[s] or of such other body as Congress may by law provide, transmit within four days to the President pro tempore of the Senate and the Speaker of the House of Representatives their written declaration that the President is unable to discharge the powers and duties of his office. Thereupon Congress shall decide the issue, assembling within forty-eight hours for that purpose if not in session. If the Congress, within twenty-one days after receipt of the latter written declaration, or, if Congress is not in session, within twenty-one days after Congress is required to assemble, deter-

mines by two-thirds vote of both Houses that the President is unable to discharge the powers and duties of his office, the Vice President shall continue to discharge the same as Acting President; otherwise, the President shall resume the powers and duties of his office.

ARTICLE XXVI
[Adopted 1971]

Section 1.   The right of citizens of the United States, who are eighteen years of age or older, to vote shall not be denied or abridged by the United States or by any State on account of age.

Section 2.   The Congress shall have power to enforce this article by appropriate legislation.

ARTICLE XXVII
[Sent to States, 1972]

Section 1.   Equality of rights under the law shall not be denied or abridged by the United States or by any State on account of sex.

Section 2.   The Congress shall have the power to enforce, by appropriate legislation, the provisions of this article.

Section 3.   This amendment shall take effect two years after the date of ratification.

Presidential Elections*

Election	Candidates	Parties	Popular Vote	Electoral Vote
1789	**George Washington**	No party designations		69
	John Adams			34
	Minor Candidates			35
1792	**George Washington**	No party designations		132
	John Adams			77
	George Clinton			50
	Minor Candidates			5
1796	**John Adams**	Federalist		71
	Thomas Jefferson	Democratic-Republican		68
	Thomas Pinckney	Federalist		59
	Aaron Burr	Democratic-Republican		30
	Minor Candidates			48
1800	**Thomas Jefferson**	Democratic-Republican		73
	Aaron Burr	Democratic-Republican		73
	John Adams	Federalist		65
	Charles C. Pinckney	Federalist		64
	John Jay	Federalist		1
1804	**Thomas Jefferson**	Democratic-Republican		162
	Charles C. Pinckney	Federalist		14
1808	**James Madison**	Democratic-Republican		122
	Charles C. Pinckney	Federalist		47
	George Clinton	Democratic-Republican		6
1812	**James Madison**	Democratic-Republican		128
	DeWitt Clinton	Federalist		89
1816	**James Monroe**	Democratic-Republican		183
	Rufus King	Federalist		34

*Candidates receiving less than 1% of the popular vote are omitted. Before the Twelfth Amendment (1804) the Electoral College voted for two presidential candidates, and the runner-up became vice-president. Basic figures are taken primarily from *Historical Statistics of the United States, 1789–1945* (1949), pp. 288–90; *Historical Statistics of the United States, Colonial Times to 1957* (1960), pp. 682–83; and *Statistical Abstract of the United States, 1969* (1969), pp. 355–57.

†"Min." indicates minority president—one receiving less than 50% of all popular votes.

Election	Candidates	Parties	Popular Vote	Electoral Vote
1820	**James Monroe**	Democratic-Republican		231
	John Q. Adams	Independent Republican		1
1824	**John Q. Adams** (Min.)†	Democratic-Republican	108,740	84
	Andrew Jackson	Democratic-Republican	153,544	99
	William H. Crawford	Democratic-Republican	46,618	41
	Henry Clay	Democratic-Republican	47,136	37
1828	**Andrew Jackson**	Democratic	647,286	178
	John Q. Adams	National Republican	508,064	83
1832	**Andrew Jackson**	Democratic	687,502	219
	Henry Clay	National Republican	530,189	49
	William Wirt	Anti-Masonic ⎫		7
	John Floyd	National Republican ⎭	33,108	11
1836	**Martin Van Buren**	Democratic	762,678	170
	William H. Harrison	Whig ⎫		73
	Hugh L. White	Whig ⎟		26
	Daniel Webster	Whig ⎬	736,656	14
	W. P. Mangum	Whig ⎭		11
1840	**William H. Harrison**	Whig	1,275,016	234
	Martin Van Buren	Democratic	1,129,102	60
1844	**James K. Polk** (Min.)*	Democratic	1,337,243	170
	Henry Clay	Whig	1,299,062	105
	James G. Birney	Liberty	62,300	
1848	**Zachary Taylor** (Min.)*	Whig	1,360,099	163
	Lewis Cass	Democratic	1,220,544	127
	Martin Van Buren	Free Soil	291,263	
1852	**Franklin Pierce**	Democratic	1,601,274	254
	Winfield Scott	Whig	1,386,580	42
	John P. Hale	Free Soil	155,825	
1856	**James Buchanan** (Min.)*	Democratic	1,838,169	174
	John C. Frémont	Republican	1,341,264	114
	Millard Fillmore	American	874,534	8
1860	**Abraham Lincoln** (Min.)*	Republican	1,866,452	180
	Stephen A. Douglas	Democratic	1,375,157	12
	John C. Breckinridge	Democratic	847,953	72
	John Bell	Constitutional Union	590,631	39
1864	**Abraham Lincoln**	Union	2,213,665	212
	George B. McClellan	Democratic	1,802,237	21
1868	**Ulysses S. Grant**	Republican	3,012,833	214
	Horatio Seymour	Democratic	2,703,249	80
1872	**Ulysses S. Grant**	Republican	3,597,132	286
	Horace Greeley	Democratic and Liberal Republican	2,834,125	66

*"Min." indicates minority president—one receiving less than 50% of all popular votes.

Election	Candidates	Parties	Popular Vote	Electoral Vote
1876	**Rutherford B. Hayes** (Min.)*	Republican	4,036,298	185
	Samuel J. Tilden	Democratic	4,300,590	184
1880	**James A. Garfield** (Min.)*	Republican	4,454,416	214
	Winfield S. Hancock	Democratic	4,444,952	155
	James B. Weaver	Greenback-Labor	308,578	
1884	**Grover Cleveland** (Min.)*	Democratic	4,874,986	219
	James G. Blaine	Republican	4,851,981	182
	Benjamin F. Butler	Greenback-Labor	175,370	
	John P. St. John	Prohibition	150,369	
1888	**Benjamin Harrison** (Min.)*	Republican	5,439,853	233
	Grover Cleveland	Democratic	5,540,309	168
	Clinton B. Fisk	Prohibition	249,506	
	Anson J. Streeter	Union Labor	146,935	
1892	**Grover Cleveland** (Min.)*	Democratic	5,556,918	277
	Benjamin Harrison	Republican	5,176,108	145
	James B. Weaver	People's	1,041,028	22
	John Bidwell	Prohibition	264,133	
1896	**William McKinley**	Republican	7,104,779	271
	William J. Bryan	Democratic	6,502,925	176
1900	**William McKinley**	Republican	7,207,923	292
	William J. Bryan	Democratic; Populist	6,358,133	155
	John C. Woolley	Prohibition	208,914	
1904	**Theodore Roosevelt**	Republican	7,623,486	336
	Alton B. Parker	Democratic	5,077,911	140
	Eugene V. Debs	Socialist	402,283	
	Silas C. Swallow	Prohibition	258,536	
1908	**William H. Taft**	Republican	7,678,908	321
	William J. Bryan	Democratic	6,409,104	162
	Eugene V. Debs	Socialist	420,793	
	Eugene W. Chafin	Prohibition	253,840	
1912	**Woodrow Wilson** (Min.)*	Democratic	6,293,454	435
	Theodore Roosevelt	Progressive	4,119,538	88
	William H. Taft	Republican	3,484,980	8
	Eugene V. Debs	Socialist	900,672	
	Eugene W. Chafin	Prohibition	206,275	
1916	**Woodrow Wilson** (Min.)*	Democratic	9,129,606	277
	Charles E. Hughes	Republican	8,538,221	254
	A. L. Benson	Socialist	585,113	
	J. F. Hanly	Prohibition	220,506	
1920	**Warren G. Harding**	Republican	16,152,200	404
	James M. Cox	Democratic	9,147,353	127
	Eugene V. Debs	Socialist	919,799	
	P. P. Christensen	Farmer-Labor	265,411	

*"Min." indicates minority president—one receiving less than 50% of all popular votes.

Election	Candidates	Parties	Popular Vote	Electoral Vote
1924	**Calvin Coolidge**	Republican	15,725,016	382
	John W. Davis	Democratic	8,386,503	136
	Robert M. La Follette	Progressive	4,822,856	13
1928	**Herbert C. Hoover**	Republican	21,391,381	444
	Alfred E. Smith	Democratic	15,016,443	87
1932	**Franklin D. Roosevelt**	Democratic	22,821,857	472
	Herbert C. Hoover	Republican	15,761,841	59
	Norman Thomas	Socialist	881,951	
1936	**Franklin D. Roosevelt**	Democratic	27,751,597	523
	Alfred M. Landon	Republican	16,679,583	8
	William Lemke	Union, etc.	882,479	
1940	**Franklin D. Roosevelt**	Democratic	27,244,160	449
	Wendell L. Wilkie	Republican	22,305,198	82
1944	**Franklin D. Roosevelt**	Democratic	25,602,504	432
	Thomas E. Dewey	Republican	22,006,285	99
1948	**Harry S Truman** (Min.)*	Democratic	24,105,812	303
	Thomas E. Dewey	Republican	21,970,065	189
	J. Strom Thurmond	States' Rights Democratic	1,169,063	39
	Henry A. Wallace	Progressive	1,157,172	
1952	**Dwight D. Eisenhower**	Republican	33,936,234	442
	Adlai E. Stevenson	Democratic	27,314,992	89
1956	**Dwight D. Eisenhower**	Republican	35,590,472	457
	Adlai E. Stevenson	Democratic	26,022,752	73
1960	**John F. Kennedy** (Min.)*	Democratic	34,226,731	303
	Richard M. Nixon	Republican	34,108,157	219
1964	**Lyndon B. Johnson**	Democratic	43,129,484	486
	Barry M. Goldwater	Republican	27,178,188	52
1968	**Richard M. Nixon** (Min.)*	Republican	31,785,480	301
	Hubert H. Humphrey, Jr.	Democratic	31,275,166	191
	George C. Wallace	American Independent	9,906,473	46
1972	**Richard M. Nixon**	Republican	45,767,218	520
	George S. McGovern	Democratic	28,357,668	17
1976	**Jimmy Carter**	Democratic	40,276,040	297
	Gerald R. Ford	Republican	38,532,630	241
1980	**Ronald W. Reagan**	Republican		
	Jimmy Carter	Democratic		

*"Min." indicates minority president—one receiving less than 50% of all popular votes.

Presidents and Vice-Presidents

Term	President	Vice-President
1789–1793	George Washington	John Adams
1793–1797	George Washington	John Adams
1797–1801	John Adams	Thomas Jefferson
1801–1805	Thomas Jefferson	Aaron Burr
1805–1809	Thomas Jefferson	George Clinton
1809–1813	James Madison	George Clinton (d. 1812)
1813–1817	James Madison	Elbridge Gerry (d. 1814)
1817–1821	James Monroe	Daniel D. Tompkins
1821–1825	James Monroe	Daniel D. Tompkins
1825–1829	John Quincy Adams	John C. Calhoun
1829–1833	Andrew Jackson	John C. Calhoun (resigned 1832)
1833–1837	Andrew Jackson	Martin Van Buren
1837–1841	Martin Van Buren	Richard M. Johnson
1841–1845	William H. Harrison (d. 1841) John Tyler	John Tyler
1845–1849	James K. Polk	George M. Dallas
1849–1853	Zachary Taylor (d. 1850) Millard Fillmore	Millard Fillmore
1853–1857	Franklin Pierce	William R. D. King (d. 1853)
1857–1861	James Buchanan	John C. Breckinridge
1861–1865	Abraham Lincoln	Hannibal Hamlin
1865–1869	Abraham Lincoln (d. 1865) Andrew Johnson	Andrew Johnson
1869–1873	Ulysses S. Grant	Schuyler Colfax
1873–1877	Ulysses S. Grant	Henry Wilson (d. 1875)
1877–1881	Rutherford B. Hayes	William A. Wheeler
1881–1885	James A. Garfield (d. 1881) Chester A. Arthur	Chester A. Arthur
1885–1889	Grover Cleveland	Thomas A. Hendricks (d. 1885)
1889–1893	Benjamin Harrison	Levi P. Morton
1893–1897	Grover Cleveland	Adlai E. Stevenson
1897–1901	William McKinley	Garret A. Hobart (d. 1899)
1901–1905	William McKinley (d. 1901) Theodore Roosevelt	Theodore Roosevelt
1905–1909	Theodore Roosevelt	Charles W. Fairbanks
1909–1913	William H. Taft	James S. Sherman (d. 1912)
1913–1917	Woodrow Wilson	Thomas R. Marshall
1917–1921	Woodrow Wilson	Thomas R. Marshall
1921–1925	Warren G. Harding (d. 1923) Calvin Coolidge	Calvin Coolidge
1925–1929	Calvin Coolidge	Charles G. Dawes
1929–1933	Herbert C. Hoover	Charles Curtis
1933–1937	Franklin D. Roosevelt	John N. Garner

Term	President	Vice-President
1937–1941	Franklin D. Roosevelt	John N. Garner
1941–1945	Franklin D. Roosevelt	Henry A. Wallace
1945–1949	Franklin D. Roosevelt (d. 1945)	Harry S Truman
	Harry S Truman	
1949–1953	Harry S Truman	Alben W. Barkley
1953–1957	Dwight D. Eisenhower	Richard M. Nixon
1957–1961	Dwight D. Eisenhower	Richard M. Nixon
1961–1965	John F. Kennedy (d. 1963)	Lyndon B. Johnson
	Lyndon B. Johnson	
1965–1969	Lyndon B. Johnson	Hubert H. Humphrey, Jr.
1969–1974	Richard M. Nixon (resigned 1974)	Spiro T. Agnew (resigned 1973); Gerald R. Ford
1974–1976	Gerald R. Ford	Nelson A. Rockefeller
1976–**1980**	Jimmy Carter	Walter F. Mondale
1980–	Ronald W. Reagan	George Bush

Growth of U.S. Population and Area

Census	Population of Contiguous U.S.	Percent of Increase Over Preceding Census	Land Area, Square Miles	Population Per Square Mile
1790	3,929,214		867,980	4.5
1800	5,308,483	35.1	867,980	6.1
1810	7,239,881	36.4	1,685,865	4.3
1820	9,638,453	33.1	1,753,588	5.5
1830	12,866,020	33.5	1,753,588	7.3
1840	17,069,453	32.7	1,753,588	9.7
1850	23,191,876	35.9	2,944,337	7.9
1860	31,443,321	35.6	2,973,965	10.6
1870	39,818,449	26.6	2,973,965	13.4
1880	50,155,783	26.0	2,973,965	16.9
1890	62,947,714	25.5	2,973,965	21.2
1900	75,994,575	20.7	2,974,159	25.6
1910	91,972,266	21.0	2,973,890	30.9
1920	105,710,620	14.9	2,973,776	35.5
1930	122,775,046	16.1	2,977,128	41.2
1940	131,669,275	7.2	2,977,128	44.2
1950	150,697,361	14.5	2,974,726*	50.7
†1960	178,464,236	18.4	2,974,726	59.9
1970	204,765,770 (including Alaska and Hawaii)			

*As remeasured in 1940.
†Not including Alaska (pop. 226,167) and Hawaii (632,772).

Index

ABC Powers (Argentina, Brazil, and Chile), 723
Aberdeen, Lord, 425
Abilene, Kan., and cattle industry, 570
Abolitionism: during Jackson's presidency, 351-352; radical, 391, 397-402; ethical basis of, 398; supporters of, 398-401; and freedom of speech, 401; public relations for, 401; nonresistance in, 401-402
Abolitionists: female, 402-404; political, 405; black, 406-407; and planter aristocracy, 416; and Texas, 422, 425; and British, 426; and John Brown, 456. *See also* Antislavery movement; Radical Republicans
Abominations, Tariff of, 347, 361
Abortion: controversy over, 925; Supreme Court on, 931
Abrams v. *U.S.*, 755
Academy of Fine Arts, Penn., 303
Acadia (Nova Scotia), British acquisition of, 105
Acadians, deportation of, 154
Acheson, Dean, 830, 836
Aconostota (Cunne Shote, Cherokee chief), *182*
Act Concerning Religion (1649), 85-86
Act of Settlement (1701), 113
Adams, Abigail, *241*
Adams, Brooks, 707
Adams, Charles Francis, 483, 511, 593
Adams, Henry, 573, 664, 707
Adams, Herbert Baxter, 678
Adams, John, 3, 196, 197, 200, 209, *268*, 275; quoted, 172, 203, 211, 226, 302, 237; and peace negotiations, *221*, 251; and Constitutional Convention, 226, 253; as vice president, 260; on paper money, 262; elected president, 268, 272; presidency of, 271; and election of 1800, 277; retirement of, 281; death of, 339
Adams, John Quincy, 280, 281, *346*, 358, 405; quoted, 297, 339; elected president, 344-346, 361; presidency of, 346; and territorial expansion, 418; and negotiations with Spain, 420; and Federalists, 422; in House of Representatives, 425; filibuster on Texas annexation, 435
Adams, Samuel, *193*, 197, 249; land bank support of, 161; and Congressional resolutions, 226; and Constitutional Convention, 253
Adams, Samuel Hopkins, 655
Adams, Sherman, 884
Adams-Onis Treaty (1819), 304, 418, 420, 435
Addams, Jane, 646, 649, 651, 652, 670; feminism of, 689; on women's suffrage, 693
Adelantados, 12
Adkins v. *Children's Hospital* (1923), 769
Admiralty courts, 98. *See also* Vice-admiralty courts
Adolescence, 861-862; and counterculture, 905

Advertising: in 1887, *568*; growth of, 857, 863; popular acceptance of, 882
Affirmative action programs, 915
Afghanistan, Soviet invasion of, 931
Africa, English trade with, 18
Africans: arrival in colonial America, 64; transplanted to colonies, 30, 126. *See also* North Africa
Afro-American culture: in Chesapeake area, 127; on Southern plantations, 327-332, 371
Agassiz, Louis, 400, 545
Aged: and revolving pension club, 795; and changing values, 871
Age of Reason (Paine), 292
Agnew, Spiro, 914; resignation of, 927, 931
Agricultural Adjustment Act (AAA) (1933), 790-791, 794, 812; and Supreme Court, 799
Agricultural Wheel, 607
Agriculture: colonial, 34; in south, 129-132, 318; eighteenth-century shifts in, 134-135; on frontier, *236*; nineteenth-century expansion of, 316; entrepreneurial character of, 317; and panic of 1837, 355-356; and industrial growth of 1840s, 410, 413; crop specialization, 607; bureaucratic revolution in, 609-610; impact of gasoline engine on, 771; during 1920s, 773; and Great Depression, 781, 782. *See also* Cotton; Farmers; Tobacco industry
Agriculture, Department of, 801
Aguinaldo, Gen. Emilio, 712, 714
Airplane industry, growth of, 881
Aix-la-Chapelle, Treaty of (1748), 151
Alabama: admitted to Union, 286, 341; Indians in, 323; secession of, 460, 461, 491; black suffrage in, 547; reconstruction of, 547, 555
Alabama, C.S.S. (confederate ship), 499, 511, 559
Alamance, Battle of, 181, 200
Alamo Mission, 423
Alaska, purchase of, 560, 584
Albany, N.Y., as state capital, 244
Albany Congress, 153, 154, 168, 197
Albany *Evening Journal*, 359
"Albany Regency," 344, 347, 359
Albee, Edward, 903
Albemarle, Carolina, Culpeper's Rebellion in, 111
Albemarle, Duke of, 56
Albemarle Sound, *56*, 57
Alcatraz, Native American occupation of, 916
Aldrich, Sen. Nelson, 625, 631, 664, 666, 667
Alexander, Gen. E. P., 527
Alexander II (czar of Russia), 560
Alexandria, Va., economic expansion of, 183
Algeciras Conference (1906), 716, 727
Alger, Horatio, 600, 624
Alien and Sedition Acts (1798), 271, 272

Allen, Ethan, 181, 292
"Alliance for Progress," 900
Allied Powers, U.S. joins, 731; war debt of, 777, 778. *See also* England; France; World War I; World War II
Altamont rock restival, 909
Altgeld, Gov. John P., 637
Aluminum Corporation of America, 768
Amalgamated Iron and Steel Workers Union, 636
"Amalgamationists," 401. *See also* Abolitionism
Amendments to Constitution, 255; First, 874; Fifth, 452; Eleventh, 272; Twelfth, 277, 303, 345; Thirteenth, 524, 525, 537, 555; Fourteenth, 525, 538-540; 555; Fifteenth, 525, 555; eighteenth, 755, 774, 859; Nineteenth, 694, 701, 755; Twenty-first, 797; Twenty-Second, 853
America: Spanish conquests in, *6*; and early cultural perceptions, 161-162; European image of, 163. *See also* British America; North America; Spanish America
"America First" movement, 809
American Bankers Association, 841
American Bible Society, 303, 396
American Board of Customs, 191, 200
American Civil Liberties Union, 767, 866
American Colonization Society, 391, 397
American Farm Bureau Federation, 610, 768, 841
American Federation of Labor (AFL), 612, 613, 616, 765; and Paterson strike, 744; modernization of, 768; vs. CIO, 800; merger with CIO, 841, 883, 910
American Federation of Labor-Congress of Industrial Organizations (AFL-CIO), and Eisenhower administration, 883-884
American Independent party, 909
Americanism, immigrant view of, 683-685
American Legion, 765, 767
American Liberty League, 797
American Missionary Association, 530
American Party, 356, 446. *See also* Know-Nothing party
American Plan, 613
American Philosophical Society, 200
American Railway Union, 604, 637
American Society for the Promotion of Temperance, 391
American Sugar Refining Co., 599; and Supreme Court, 604
American Sunday School Union, 391
American system: of Henry Clay, 344, 361, 590; of manufacturing, 411
American Tobacco Co.: and merger movement, 599; and T. Roosevelt's trust-busting, 665, 670
American Tract Society, 303, 391, 396

Amherst, Jeffrey, 154-156, 185
"Amos and Andy," 869
Ancient Order of Hibernians, 581
Anderson, Joseph, 500
Anderson, Marian, 847
Anderson, Maj. Robert, 472
Anderson, Sherwood, 860, 867
Andersonville, Ga., Confederate prison at, 526
Andover Theological Seminary, Mass., 393
Andrew, Gov. John A., 516
Andros, Edmund: governorship of, 97; rebellion against, 113
Anglican Church: and Quakers, 61; in Virginia, 83-85; compared with Puritanism, 87-89; dissent privileges of, 136; rejection of, 184; during Revolutionary era, 291
Anglo-American alliance, 817, 853
Annapolis Convention, 251, 272
Anthoniszoon, Cornelis, 16
Anthony, Susan B., 553
Anglo-Japanese Alliance, 777
Anthracite Coal Strike Commission, 666
Antiabolitionists, 400. *See also* Abolitionism
Antibiotics, introduction of, 882
Anti-Catholicism: Philadelphia riots, *374*; Know-Nothing movement, 438, 445-447, 457, 461
Anticommunism, 833, 837, 850-851; in Latin America, 900. *See also* Containment policy
Antietam, Battle of, 491
Anti-evolutionary law, Tennessee's, 863
Antifederalists, 255, 256-258
Anti-imperialists, 712
"Anti"-institutions, 395
Anti-Masonic party, 359, 360-362; evolution of, *340*; and election of 1832, 353; and Sabbatarian movement, 395
Antimonopoly, 601-602, 604
Antin, Mary, 685
"Antinomianism," 47
Antiradicalism, 764-765; of national government, 764, 767. *See also* Radicalism
Anti-Saloon League, 774
Antislavery movement: origins of, 242-243; and Missouri Compromise, 341-344; political, 405-406; in South, 416; during Civil War, 506. *See also* Abolitionism
Anti-Slavery Society, American, 399, 401-406
Antitrust legislation, 604, 630, 643, 699, 701
Antitrust policy: T. Roosevelt's, 665; Taft's, 604; F. Roosevelt's, 802
Antwerp, and English wool market, 17, 27
Apache Indians, 327, 605
Apollo space program, 882
Appalachian mountains, as frontier, 123
Appleton, Nathan, 440
Appomattox Court House, Lee's surrender at, 519, 522
Appropriations Act, 1851, 327
Arab nations: and foreign policy, 920; oil weapon of, 923, 931
Arafat, Yasir, 921
Arbitration, 612; as key to world order, 721-722
Architecture: of seventeenth century New England, 78; of colonial aristocracy, *107*, *108*, 109; of republican America, 245; federal, *250*, *262*; Jefferson on, *276*
Argentina, Spanish conquest of, 7, 27
Argyll, Duke of, 485
Aristocracy, Anglo-American, 100-109; trade as basis of, 102; political influence as basis of, 103-104; and wartime projects, 105-106; limits of social distinction of, 106; great landowners, 128; merchant, 134-135; planter, 415-416. *See also* Elite
Arizona, women's suffrage in, 694

Arkansas: admitted to Union, 315; importance of cotton in, 320; secession of, 471, 473, 491; reconstruction of, 547, 555
Armed forces, desegregation of, 843; and McCarthyism, 851-852
Arms limitations: and peaceful coexistence, 889; and Test Ban Treaty of 1963, 891
Armstrong, Neil, 882
Army: Continental, 210, 213, 214, 248-249; under Jefferson's Republicans, 279; Confederate, 476-480; Union, 470, 476-480; desegregation of, 843
Army purchasing agencies, 235. *See also* Munitions industry
Army Relocation Authority, 847
Arndt, Johann, 124
Arnold, Benedict, 210
Art: of mid-nineteenth-century, 379-382; as product, 381; as character shaper, 381-382; "primitive," *382*; modern, 741; and Progressivism, 741-744, 746; proletarian, 744-746; "little renaissance" in, 746. *See also* Folk art; Literature; Painting
Arthur, Chester A., 573; becomes president, 574, *627*, 643; patronage dispensed by, 628; Tariff Commission of, 631
Articles of Confederation, 224, 228; and nature of Union, 229-230; and disposition of western lands, 230-232; ratification of, 272
Artisans: in colonial America, 79; slave, 127-128; during Revolutionary era, 238; support for Constitution of, 257; and temperance movement, 396; and Nativism, 446; in Confederacy, 475
"Ashcan School," of painting, 743
Ashley, James M., 542
Ashley Cooper, Anthony, 56, 57-58, 59
Ashley-Locke "Fundamental Constitutions," 58
Asia, English trade with, 18
Asiatics, and immigration quotas, 544, 581, 765
Assemblies, colonial: and Stamp Act, 189-190; and Townshend duties, 193
Assembly line, 771; and importance of individual, 867. *See also* Industrialization
Assimilation: of native Americans, 565; of "new immigrants," 683-684
Astor, John Jacob, 334, 628
Astronauts, 882-*883*
Atchison, Sen. David R., 449
Akinson, Edward, 712
Atlanta, Ga., capture of, 518, 522
Atlantic Charter, 810, 825; and war strategy, 817, 853
Atomic bomb: development of, 823; dropped on Japan, 825, 876; and Soviet Union, 826; control of, 829; detonated by Soviet Union, 833
Atomic Energy Act (1954), 883, 910
"Atoms for Peace," 890
Attitudes: early American, 161-162; colonial, 204-205; revolutionary, 198-200, 203-205; republican, 238-243; toward material success, 309, 332, 336; toward work, 904. *See also* Values
Auburn system, 393
Audiencias, 10-11
"Augsburg Confession," 124
Australia, in World War II, 817; in SEATO, 884
Austria, and King George's War, 151
Austria-Hungary, immigrants from, 681; and First World War, 730
Austrian Succession, War of, 151, 168
Automobile, impact on culture, 857
Automobile industry: oligopoly in, 767-768; boom during 1920s, 769-770; mass production revolution in, 770; standardization in, 857

Axis powers, 804, 808. *See also* Germany; Italy
Aztecs, Spanish conquest of, 7, 13

Babcock, Orville E., 572
Bacon, Nathaniel, 110
Bacon's Rebellion, 76, 109, 110-111, 119
Baer, George, 665-666
Bailey v. *Drexel Furniture Co.* (1922), 769
Baker, Ray Stannard, 655, 687
Baker v. *Carr* (1962), 898
Bakke v. *Board of Regents of California*, 915
Balance of payments: effect of smuggling on, 157-158; adverse international, 922. *See also* Trade
Balboa, Vasco Nuñez de, 6, 26
Baldwin, Roger, 697
Baldwin, Theron, 372
Balkans, Nazi conquest of, 810
Ballinger, Richard, 677
Baltic, English trade with, 18
Baltimore, Md.: economic development of, 76, 183; in 1752, 134; copper industry in, 574
Baltimore, first Lord (George Calvert), 48
Baltimore, second Lord (Cecil Calvert), 48, *49*, 50, 62, 63, 64
Baltimore and Ohio Railroad, 414, 568, 581
Bankhead-Jones Farm Tenancy Act (1937), 801
"Bank Holiday," 789, 812
Banking industry: farmers' dissatisfaction with, 578; federal reserve system in, 699; and Great Depression, 781; collapse of, 788-789; New Deal regulation of, 791
Bank of North America, 249
Bank of the United States (BUS), First: Hamilton's creation of, 261-262; established, 272; under Jefferson's Republicans, 279; and Supreme Court, 290; expiration of, 300, 303
Bank of the United States (BUS), Second, 303; chartered by Congress, 303; Jackson's "War" on, 352-353, 699
Bankruptcies, during Great Depression, 780
Banks: in colonial America, 159-161; and laissez-faire capitalism, 356; state-chartered, 280; and Second Bank of the United States, 352; pet, 354; and Civil War bond issues, 481; national, 577; Federal Reserve, 699
Baptist Church: and revivalism, 370; and slavery, 416
Baptists: in Carolina settlements, 58; dissent privileges of, 136; Separatists, 184; growth in numbers of, 293; and antimission movement, 395; traditional values of, 863
Barbados, and Carolina settlements, 56, 57-58
Barbary pirates, 279
Barbary states, 279, 303; tribute demanded by, 250-251
Barlow, Joel, 260
"Barnburners" (Democratic faction), 440
Barnum, P. T., 597
Barrington, Lord, 195
Barrow, Bennet H., 329
Barton, Bruce, 859
Baruch, Bernard, 736, 738, 768, 829
Bascom, John, 658
Bates, Edward, 513
Batista, Fulgencio, 804, 886
Bauman, Leila T., 321
Bayard family, 111
Bay of Pigs fiasco, 434, 886-887, 910
Beals, Jessie Tarbox, 650
Beard, Charles, 652, 802
Beard, Mary, 652
Beauregard, Gen. P. G. T., 432, 472, 487, 549
Beecher, Catharine, 402
Beecher, Lyman, 364-365, 374, 391; and Sabbatarian movement, 393, 394, 395; as presi-

dent of Lane Theological Seminary, 401; family of, 402
Behaviorism, as manipulative force, 862–863. *See also* Management
Belcher, Andrew, 105
Belcher family, 109
Belgium, German invasion of, 807
Belknap, William W., 572
Bell, Alexander Graham, 567, 600, 616
Bell, John, 459, 470
Bellamy, Edward, 602, 616, 632
Belleau Wood, U.S. troops at, 732, 755
Bellow, Saul, 903
Bellows, George, 743
Belmont, August, 639
Benevolent Empire, 391–397
Benjamin, Judah P., 478, 483, 511, 512, 513
Bentley, Arthur F., 652
Benton, Thomas Hart, 352, 426, 661
Bergen, N. J., early settlement of, 53
Berger, Victor, 695, 740
Berkeley, Lord John, 59
Berkeley, Sir William, 37, 56, 103; and Bacon's Rebellion, 109; on school system, 117
Berkman, Alexander, 636
Berle, Adolf, 788
Berlin Airlift, *831*, 853
Berlin Wall, 887–*888*, 910
Bermuda: English settlement in, 25; economic base for, 26
Bermuda Company, 26
Bernard, Gov. Francis, 193, 195
Bessemer, Sir Henry, 595
Bessemer process, 595. *See also* Steel industry
Beveridge, Sen. Albert J., 704, 713
Bibb, Henry, 406
Bible: influence on education, 115; importance of, 291; and revivalism, 394
Bible Society, 303, 396
Biddle, Nicholas, 352, 353, 354
Bigelow, Jacob, 376
Bill of Rights: American, 259, 272; English, 113
Bills of credit: in colonial America, 159; post-Revolutionary, 235. *See also* Money; Paper money
Bimetallism, 576. *See also* Money
Bingham, George Caleb, 340
Birmingham, Ala., black protest in, 895
Birney, James G., 405, 428
Birth control movement, 860
Bison, slaughter of, 317, 327, 564
Black codes, 416, 537, 546; in Carolina settlements, 59. *See also* Racism
Blackfoot Indians, *605*
Black Hills, discovery of gold in, 563
Black Kettle (Cheyenne chief), 562
Black Muslims, 908
Black Panthers, 908, 909
Black Power, 907–908
"Black Republicans," 449, 466; and Brown's raid, 456. *See also* Republican party
Black rights: and New Deal, 797, 847–848; and Supreme Court, 850; during World War II, 850; and Jim Crow laws, 893–894; and Supreme Court, 893–894; movement for, 895–896; youth involvement in, 904; and Black Power, 907–908. *See also* Civil Rights movement
Blacks: in Spanish America, 15; in colonial America, 70, 101; in eighteenth-century America, 122, 126–128; northern, 126; Afro-American culture of, 330–332; and higher education, 369; church of, *371*; and colonization movement, 395; in abolition movement, 406–407; in Union army, *508*; changing northern images of, *509*; post-

Civil War attitudes toward, 529–530; adjustment as freedmen, 533; northern views of, 544–546; southern views of, 546–547; disfranchisement of, 552–554, 657; Sumner as champion of, 560; housing for, *647*; and Progressivism, 685–686; migration of, 686, 847; in Democratic party, 798. *See also* Slaves
Blacks, free: and immigration, 332; and Missouri Compromise, 343; and temperance movement, 396; southern, 416; excluded from Oregon Territory, 441; disfranchisement of, 552–554. *See also* Freedmen
Blaine, James G., 501, 625, 626, 628, 630, 643
Bland, Giles, 110
Blast furnaces, 159, 411
Blizzard of 1886, 606
Blockade: British, 297; during Civil War, 481, 498–500; and submarine warfare, 724, 727; Berlin, 831; Cuban, 887
Blodget, Samuel, 262
Blount, William, 260
Blythe, David Gilmour, 514
Board of Trade (*Casa de Contratación*), 10, 12, 26
Board of Trade and Plantations, 94, 95, 119
Bogart, Humphrey, 875
Boggs, Gov. L. W., 387
Bolivia, Spanish conquest of, 7, 26
Bolsheviks, 731, 755; fear of, 764, 777. *See also* Communism
Bonds, for financing Civil War, 481
Bonus Bill, 303
Boone, Daniel, 176, 179
Booth, John Wilkes, 517, 526
Borah, Sen. William, 772, 777
"Border Ruffians," 449, 474
Border states: and secession, 471–472, 473–474; division of, 473–475; importance of, 475–476; and gradual emancipation, 508; and wartime politics, 513. *See also specific states*
Boss rule, 628; and Progressive reform, 648, 654; and settlement house movement, 693; of 1920s, 774
Boston, Mass.: early town of, 30; early settlement of, 43; in eighteenth century, 123; Scotch-Irish in, 124; population growth of, 132; vice-admiralty courts in, 191; British troops sent to, 194, 200; in Revolutionary War, 211; British evacuation of, 213, 224; immigration to, 314; segregated schools in, 368; copper industry in, 574; immigration population of, 682; police strike in, 754; boss rule in, 774
Boston Massacre, *194*, 195, 200
Boston Tea Party, 196, 200
Bourbons, 635
Bourne, Randolph, 685, 747, 748
Bowdoin College, black students in, 369
Boxer Rebellion, 716, 727
Boycotts: by United Farm Workers, 915; of Olympic games, 919; Arab oil, 931
Boylston, Nicholas, *237*
Bozeman Trail, 563, *564*
Braceros, 847
Braddock, Maj. Gen. Edward, 154, 155
Bradford, William, 40, 41, 191
Brady, Mathew, 464–465
Bragg, Gen. Braxton, 490, 495, 496, 497, 522
"Brain trust," 788
Brandeis, Justice Louis, 653, 676, 690, 698, 701
Brandywine, Battle of, 216, 224
Brant, Joseph (Mohawk chief), *182*
Bray, Rev. Thomas, 137

Breckinridge, John C., 457, 458–459
Bretton Woods Conference (1944), 825, 853, 922
Brezhnev, Leonid, 918
Briand, Aristide, 778
Brinkmanship, 886–888, 890. *See also* Foreign policy
Britain: political system of, 141–143; French and Indian war, 150, *153*–156; War of Jenkins' Ear, 151; and balance of payments with colonies, 157–158; Confederation and, 251; and American Anglophobia, 418, 420; and Monroe Doctrine, 422; slave trade ended by, 425; and Texas, 425–426; and emancipation in West Indies, 434; and U.S. attempt to acquire Cuba, 434; Confederate warships built in, 511; nineteenth-century colonization efforts of, 704; and Versailles Treaty, 750–751; and Anglo-Japanese Alliance, 777; declares war on Germany, 807; U.S. aid to, 809–810; and Atlantic Charter, 810, 817, 825, 853. *See also* British America; Colonies; England; Great Britain; Revolutionary War
"Britain, battle of," 808, 824
British America: politics in, 5; contrasted with Spanish America, 11–13; peopling of, 22–23; government imposed on, 23; chronology for, 26–27; unicameral government, 63; in 1763, *175. See also* England
British Empire: American colonies in, 93–100; government of, 11–12; in late seventeenth century, 94; extent of, 174; economic expansion of, 182–184; reorganization of, 185; war debt of, 185; imperial debate, 206–209. *See also* Britain
British and Foreign Bible Society, 392, 393
Broadcasting, radio: first station in U.S., 770–771; in 1920s, 771, 857, *858*
Brooklyn Bridge, *592*, 616
Brooks, Sen. Preston, 450
Brooks, Van Wyck, 746–747, 748, 865
Brown, Charles Brockden, 272
Brown, Claude, 908
Brown, John, 461; and massacre at Pottawatomie Creek, 450; raid on Harpers Ferry, 456
Brown, Dr. John, 167
Brown, Joseph E., 504
Brown, William Wells, 406
Brown v. Board of Education (1954), 893–894, 896, 910, 914
Brown University, 118, 140, 200
Brownson, Orestes, 558
Broyles Commission, 851
Bruce, Blanche K., 548
Bryan, William Jennings, 617, 636, 643, 670, 700, 790; "Cross of Gold" speech, 608; and 1896 campaign, 639–*640*; and election of 1912, 678, 701; on foreign policy, 706; and election of 1900, 713; as secretary of state, 721; on Prohibition, 774; and Scopes trial, 860
Bryant, Anita, 925
Bryce, Lord James, 627, 704
Bubble Act (1741), 160
Buchanan, James: as secretary of state, 429; and Mexican War, 433; and Ostend Manifesto, 434; elected president, 448, 461; and Kansas crisis, 450, 451; and *Dred Scott* decision, 452; and secession of South Carolina, 460
"Bucktails" (Republican faction), 344
Budenz, Louis, 697
Budget, federal: during 1920s, 769; and New Deal, 802; and postwar economy, 844; military expenditures of, 885
Buell, Don Carlos, 488, 490, 495
Buena Vista, Battle of, 432

Buffalo, N.Y., Convention of the Free People of Color at, 407
Bulfinch, Charles, 245
Bulgaria, in Soviet sphere of influence, 828
Bulge, Battle of the, 823
Bull Run, First Battle of, 487, 491
Bull Run, Second Battle of, 490, 491
Bundy, McGeorge, 900
Bunker Hill, Battle of, 212, 224
Bunyan, John, 655
Bureau of Budget, and New Deal, 789
Bureau of Corporations, 665, 670
Bureaucracy: of Spanish empire, 9
Bureaucracy, federal: under Jefferson's Republicans, 279, 280; and First World War, 738, 740; decentralization of, 842; attitudes toward, 884; spreading hostility toward, 913
Bureau of Markets, 610
Burger, Warren, 914
Burgess, Gelett, 743
Burgh, James, 167
Burgoyne, Gen. John, 212, 215, 218
Burke, Edmund, 130, 186, 207, 660
Burleson, Albert S., 740
Burlington Railroad, 593
Burnside, Ambrose E., 494
Burr, Aaron, 286, 303
"Burrites," 281
Bushnell, Horace, 545
Business: and early labor movement, 583; laissez-faire approach to, 597; cartels in, 597; trusts, 598, 665; merger movement in, 599–601; failure of counterattack on, 601–605; and government regulation, 603; farmers in, 607–608; and union movement, 613; and urban reform, 648; academic interests of, 652–653; and T. Roosevelt's conservation campaign, 668; and Wilson's New Freedom, 698; and foreign policy, 705; during First World War, 735, 737–738; in Lippmann's analysis, 747; in 1920s, 767–769; and Supreme Court, 769; and Great Depression, 782; and New Deal, 801–802; and multinational corporations, 886. See also Economy; Industrialization; Management
Bute, Lord, 185, 186
Butler, Sen. Andrew, 450
Butler, Gen. Benjamin F., 494, 518
Byrd, Maria, *108*
Byrd, William, II, 100, *108*, 114
Byrd family, 106, 109
Byrnes, James F., *828*, 830, 838

Cabinet: Jackson's Kitchen, 349; of Pres. Davis, 470; Lincoln's, 513
Cabot, Sen. George, 268
Cabot, John, 16, 26
Cabot, Sebastian, 16, 26
Cabot family, 234
Cagney, James, 869
Caldwell, Erskine, 860
Calhoun, John C., 281, 299, *350*; and election of 1824, 344–346; and theory of nullification, 350; political role of, 357–358; *South Carolina Exposition and Protest*, 361; and Tyler administration, 425; and British role in Texas, 426; and election of 1844, 426–427; planning imperial expansion, 435; and Wilmot Proviso, 439; on Clay's 1850 resolutions, 443; and majority rule, 467
California: admitted to Union, 315, 440; and Manifest Destiny, 428–429; in 1840s, *429*; offer to purchase from Mexico, 430; and free soil, 439–442; gold rush in, 440, *441*, 461; as free state, 442; women's suffrage in, 694; oil discovered in, 772

Calvert, Cecil (Lord Baltimore), 48, *49*, 50, 62, 63, 64
Calvert, Leonard, 48, 50
Calvert family, 128; and Protestant Association, 112; religious toleration of, 85
Calvinism: in Massachusetts, 46; in New Amsterdam, 55; in colonial America, 86. See also Puritanism
Calvinists: seminaries organized by, 293; reaction to evangelical denominationalism, 293–294
Cambodia: invasion of, 917; collapse of, 918, 931
Camden, Battle of, 224
Cameron, Simon, 477–478
Campbellites, 294
Camp David, summit meeting at, 889
Camp meetings: Cane Ridge, 293, 303; popularity of, *370*; on frontier, 372; and Populists, 632. See also Revivalism
Canada: English settlement in, 25; French colonies of, 27; and Treaty of Paris, 156; ceded to Britain, 174; 1812 invasions of, 300–301; and expansionism, 560
Canal system: and agricultural expansion, 318–319; in 1840s, 413
Cane Ridge revival meeting, 293, 303
Canning, George, 422
Cape Ann, settlement of, 42, 43
Cape Cod, Pilgrims' landing at, 39
Cape Fear River, *56*, 57
Capek, Karel, 867
Capital: planning for, 264; burning of, 301; moved to Washington, D.C., 303
Capitalism: laissez-faire, 356, 769; and late nineteenth-century economy, 595; corporate, 600; wage system of, 612. See also Economy; Laissez-faire policy
Caribbean: Spanish conquest of, *6*; English settlement in, 25; and sugar trade, 183; and American exports, 183; and black riots, 329, 418; and expansionism, 417–418, 428, 430, 434, 435; Spanish War in, *714*; in twentieth-century, 716–718. See also West Indies; specific countries
Carlisle Commission, 217
Carmichael, Stokely, 907
Carnegie, Andrew, 500, 568, 571, 597, 636, 712
Carnegie, Dale, 866
Carnegie Steel Co., 599
Carolina (colonial): early settlement in, 55–59; royal charter for, 56–58, 64; religious toleration in, 58; economic basis of, 58–59; government of, 93; charter confiscated, 97, 119; separation of, 98, 168; rebellion in, 109, 111, 119; Fundamental Constitutions of, 119; Anglican Church in, 137
Carpetbaggers, 548
Carracks, Portuguese, *16*
Carranza, Venustiano, 723
Carroll, Father John, 272
Carson, Rachel, 904
Cartels, 597–599, OPEC, 923
Carter, Jimmy, 913, *929*; foreign policy of, 921; energy policy of, 924; election as president, *929*, 931; and human rights, 931
Carter, Landon, 130
Carter, Robert "King," 101
Carter, Rosalynn, *925*
Carter family, 106
Carteret, Sir George, 59, 98
Cartier, Jacques, 27
Cartwright, Peter, 372
Case de Contratación (Board of Trade), 10, 12
Cass, Lewis: and Mexican War, 433; and election of 1848, 434

Caste system, 894
Castro, Fidel, 886, *887*, 910; and missile crisis, 887; and Kennedy foreign policy, 900
Cathay, Company of, 19
Catholicism: in Latin America, 13; in Maryland, 48, 85; and Know-Nothing party, 445–446; and changing morals, 859; and traditional values, 863
Catholics: and naturalization, 125; and Protestant school reformers, 367; and Know-Nothing party, 438; and election of 1852, 445; and bigotry of 1920s, 766; in Democratic party, 798; and pre-World War II isolationism, 805; and black rights, 908
Catlin, George, 324
Catt, Carrie Chapman, 693, 694
Cattle industry, 570. See also Meat-packing industry
Caucus system, 269, 281
Censorship: during First World War, 739–740; in motion picture industry, 864; Supreme Court on, 898. See also Dissent
Centennial Exhibition at Philadelphia (1876), 567, 584
Central Intelligence Agency (CIA), creation of, 836, 853; and Bay of Pigs fiasco, 886–887
Central Pacific Railroad, 544, *564*, 567, 584
Central Treaty Organization (CENTO), 884, 910
Chamber of Commerce, U.S., 774
Chamberlain, Neville, 804–805, 807
Champlain, Samuel de, 27
Chancellorsville, Battle of, 494, 522
Channing, William Ellery, 377, 385
Chaplin, Charlie, 867, *868*
Chapman, Maria Weston, 402
Charles I (king of England), 23, 55, 64
Charles II (king of England), 55–56, 93; and William Penn, 61–62
Charleston (dance), 862
Charleston, S. C.: in eighteenth century, 123; slave market of, 126; vice-admiralty court in, 191; British capture of, 218, 224; state capital removed from, 244; and crisis over Fort Sumter, 472; during Civil War, 498
Charlestown, Mass., early settlement of, 43
Charles Town, S.C.: early town of, 30; early settlement of, 58; in late seventeenth century, 59
Chase, Salmon P., 405, 471, 480, 482, 502, 513, 515
Chase, Samuel, 288, 303
Chatham, Lard, 186. See Pitt
Chattanooga, Battle of, 522
"Chattel slavery," 37–38. See also Slavery
Chavez, Cesar, *915*
Cheever, John, 924
Chemical warfare, in Vietnam, 900
Cherokee Indians, 182, 288, 323, 561; and colonial expansion, 179–181; removal of, 325, 326; and Confederacy, 473
Cherokee War, 181
Chesapeake (American warship), 298
Chesapeake-Leopard affair, 303
Chesapeake region: early settlement in, 37, 48–51; indentured servants in, 68; demographic characteristics of, 68–69; and slave trade, 70; tobacco economy of, 75; demographic characteristics of, 81–82; Afro-American culture in, 126–127. See also Delaware; Maryland; Virginia
Cheyenne Indians, 563, 605
Chiang Kai-shek, 804, 816, 832, 886, 888
Chicago, Ill., immigrant population in, 591–592, 682; elevated electric railway in, 594, 616; race riots in, 686, 755; boss rule in, 774; 1968 Democratic convention in, *905*

Chicago, University of, 652, 874
Chicago Bar Association, 774
Chicago World's Fair, 616
Chicanos: during World War II, 847; labor organization of, 915
Chickamauga, Battle of, 495, 522
Chickasaw Indians, 323, 325, 561; and colonial expansion, 179-181; and Confederacy, 473
Child, Lydia Maria, 402
Child labor, abolished, 801, 812
Children: in seventeenth century, 69; in colonial America, 81; "halfway covenant" for, 135-136; in republican society, 240; and population growth, 312; and social reform, 651; and settlement house movement, 691-693; and national values, 880
Chile, Spanish conquest of, 7-8, 27
China: "Open Door" policy in, 715-716, 727; Boxer Rebellion, 716; Japan's invasion of, 804, 806, 812; civil war in, 832-833; Communist government in, 853; and principle of containment, 886; Cold War perceptions of, 903; détente with, 918, 919; recognition of, 931
China trade, furs for, 427; and "Open Door" policy, 715-716, 727
Chinese, protests against, 544; and racism, 581
Chinese Exclusion Act (1882), 544, 581
Chivington, John M., 562
Choate, John, 707
Choate, Rufus, 339
Choctaw Indians, 323; and colonial expansion, 179-181; and Confederacy, 473
Chou En-Lai, 918
Christianity: and Spanish empire, 13; and English exploration, 19; in colonial America, 82-91; trinitarians, 86; and social order, 372-374; and organized philanthropy, 392-393. *See also* Religion; *specific churches*
Christian Socialism, 695
Chrysler Corp., 857
Church of England, 38, 42, 43, 47, 48, 136. *See also* Anglican Church
Churchill, Winston, 2, 810; war strategy of, 817, 828; at Yalta Conference, *826*, 827
Church of Jesus Christ of Latter-Day Saints, 386. *See also* Mormonism
Church and State: in New England, 44-45; and Glorious Revolution, 141-142; and revivalism, 369. *See also* Revivalism
Cider tax, English (1763), 185
Cincinnati, Ohio, German immigration to, 313
Cincinnati, Order of, 237
Cincinnati, Society of, 263, 272
"Circular Letter," 193, 200
Cities: nineteenth-century growth of, 591-592; and need for reform, 646-648; Progressive mayors in, 648-649; and Progressive reform, 654-655; port, *656-657*; and literature, 875; and suburbanization, 881
Citizenship: as issue in Dred Scott case, 451-454; defined in Fourteenth Amendment, 539
Citizens Industrial Organization, 617
Civic groups, of Progressive era, 654
Civil Aeronautics Board (CAB), 884
Civilian Conservation Corps (CCC), 792, 812
Civil liberties, of abolitionists, 401; restricted during Civil War, 512, 513; defined in Fourteenth Amendment, 539; during First World War, 738-739. *See also* Dissent
Civil Rights Act (1866), 538, 555
Civil Rights Act (1965), 896, 908, 910
Civil rights laws (1957, 1960), 895
Civil rights movement: mobilizing for, 895; March on Washington, 896; and local values, 897; youth involvement in, 904. *See also* Black rights

Civil Service Commission, 628, 629, 643
Civil service reform: after Civil War, 572-574; Pendleton Act, 574; and role of president, 629
Civil Service Reform Commission, creation of, 573, 584
Civil War: significance of, 466-467; and border states, 471-476; crisis over Fort Sumter, 472; beginning of, 473; financing of, 480-482; diplomacy during, 482-485; *Trent* affair, 485; military theory in, 486-488; western campaigns of, *487*, 488, *495*, 518-520; eastern campaigns of, *487*, *495*, *517*-518; Peninsula campaign of, 488-490; Confederate counter-offensive, *490*-491; Seven Days in, 490; Command system of, 493-497; civilians during, 494; Grant's success at Vicksburg, 496; naval war, 497-500; Union blockade in, 499-500; inflation during, 501-504; paper money of, *502*; profits and deprivation during, 503-504; illegal trade during, 504; blacks in, 506-508; Europe during, 510; end of, 519-520; assessment of, 520; Native Americans during, 651-562. *See also* Reconstruction
Civil Works Administration (CWA), 792
Clarendon, Earl of, 56
Clark, George Rogers, 224, 260
Clarke, Edward, 766
Clay, Henry, 299, *345*, 470; quoted, 334; and Missouri Compromise, 342-343; "American System" of, 344, 361; on domestic improvements, 348; and Compromise of 1820, 351; and Bank of the United States, 352; and election of 1832, 353; political roles of, 357; effects Missouri Compromise, 361; and election of 1844, 426; in election of 1844, 427-428; and California's admission, 442; and 1850 Compromise, 442; predictions of, 590
Clayton Antitrust Act (1914), 604, 699, 701
Clean Air Act (1963), 926
Cleburne, Gen. Patrick R., 510
Clemenceau, Georges, *750*
Clergy: Anglican, 84-85; and colonial education, 118
Clermont (steamboat), 303
Cleveland, Grover, 621; and Sherman Act, 604; elected president, 616, 622, 623, 628, 643; patronage dispensed by, 628; and Congress, 629; on tariff, 630; reelection of, 636; and union movement, 636, 637; monetary policy of, 639; on foreign policy, 704
Cleveland, Ohio: urban progressivism in, 648; immigration population of, 682; federal subsidization of, 915
Clinton, George, 267
Clinton, Sir Henry, 218
"Clintonians" (Republican faction), 281
Clipper ships, *424*
Cloth industry, in Massachusetts Bay Colony, 71, 72. *See also* Textile industry
Clothing, and cultural change, 79, *80*, 859
Clothing industry, trade associations in, 768. *See also* Textile industry
Coal industry: post-Civil War growth in, 567; early labor organization in, 581; strikes in, 665-666; antiradicalism of, 765
Cobb, Frank, 726
Cobb, Howell, *469*
Cobb, Ty, 869
Coello, Alonzo Sanchez, 12
Coercive Acts (1774), 196, 200
Coexistence, peaceful, 88-89. *See also* Foreign policy
Cohens v. *Virginia*, 290

Cohn, Roy, *852*
Coinage Act (1873), 576, 584
Cold Harbor, Battle of, 517, 522
Cold War, 755, 827-833; "Iron Curtain," 828-829; American rationale for, 829-832; State Department, 830; Czechoslovakia falls, 831; and Marshall Plan, 831; Truman Doctrine, 831; Berlin Airlift, 831-832; and U.S. as world peace power, 832; communist gains, 832-833; and election of 1948, 843; and Berlin Wall, 887-888, 910; and peaceful coexistence, 888-889; Dulles and, 890; containment vs. nationalism, 899-900; heritage of, 919
Cole, Thomas, 381
Colfax, Schuyler, 572
Colleges: colonial, 118; increasing numbers of, 239; blacks in, 369; women, 369; postwar increase in demand for, 873; humanistic approach in, 874. *See also* Universities
Colleton, John, 56
Collier, John, 797
Collinson, Peter, 165
Colonies, American, financing of, 25; frontier characteristics, 67; demographic characteristics of, 68-70, 101, *178*; economic instability of, 70-76; cloth industry in, 71-72; fur trade in, 72; fishing industry in, *73*; tobacco industry in, 75-76; social instability of, 76; religion in, 82-91; administration of, 94; commercial regulation of, 95-96; aristocracy of, 100; provincial culture of, 113-118; German settlement in, *125*; slavery in, 126; legislatures of, 145; royal governors, 145, 197; pattern of politics in, 146; and balance of payments with Britain, 157-158; frontier expansion of, *177*; resistance of, 188-197, 206; British military authority in, 194; country-Whig tradition of opposition in, 204-205
Colonists: character of, 37; Pilgrims as, 42; recruitment of, 49
Colonization: of North America, 2; English, 19-20, 31; chronology for, 26-27, 64; patterns of, 30-31; and Virginia Company publicity campaign, 33. *See also* British America; Spanish America
Colonization movement, 395, 399
Colorado, discovery of gold in, 561
Columbia, S.C., burning of, 519
Columbia Broadcasting System (CBS), 857
"Columbian Magazine," *270*
Columbia University, 652; campus strike at, 909
Columbus, Christopher, 6, 10, 26
Comanche Indians, 605
Commander, Lydia, 690
Commerce: of colonial New England, 73-74; eighteenth century, 132-135; transoceanic, 147. *See also* Business; Trade
Committee on Public Information, 739
Committees of correspondence, 196, 200, 269
Common school movement, 240. *See also* Public school system
Common Sense (Paine), 199, 205, 210, 224
Commonwealth, concept of, 77
Communications: telegraph, 567; revolution in, 857; and FCC, 884. *See also* Media
Communism: in China, 833, 853; and anti-communism, 850; and containment policy, 884. *See also* Cold War; Containment policy
Communist nations, and trade, 899
Communist party, American, federal raids on, 764
Communists: conservatives' fear of, 583; deportation of, 754

Communitarianism, 404
Compensations, culture of, 868, 869
Compromise of 1820, 351
Compromise of 1850, 442-*444*, 461; and Whig
  division, 445; failure of, 456-461
Computer: introduction of, 882
Concentration camps: Nazi, 806; for Japanese-
  Americans, 846-847, 853
Concord, Battle of, 209, *210*, 212, 224
Confederate States of America: compared with
  Union, 466-467, 468-471; Constitution of,
  468-469; crisis over Fort Sumter, 472;
  Indian alliance with, 473; and importance of
  border states, 475; army of, 476-480;
  and financing of war, 480-482, 500; and
  European neutrality, 483-484; army of,
  494; command system of, 497; naval warfare
  of, 498-500; conscription under, 504, 510;
  and emancipation, 506; navy, 511; wartime
  politics in, 511-512, 521. *See also* South
Confederation: democratization of state legislatures in, 243-244; local factionalism during, 244; domestic weaknesses of, 249;
  international weakness of, 250-251. *See also*
  Republican Society
Confederation Congress, 248; and financial
  crisis, 249-250
Confederation of New England Colonies, 64
Conference for Good City Government, 670
Congo, the (Zaire), UN mission in, 888
Congregational Church, 89; and Great Awakening, 135; in New England, 136
Congregationalists: 1790 countermovement by,
  292; seminaries organized by, 293
Congress, Confederate, 470
Congress, U.S.: Constitutional provision for,
  254; first session of, 272; under Jeffersonian
  Republicans, 281; and Supreme Court,
  289-290; blacks in, 548; modernization of,
  629; vs. presidency, 630; and Roosevelt's
  conservation campaign, 668
Congress of Industrial Organizations (CIO):
  formation of, 799; vs. AFL, 800; unionizing
  efforts of, 800; merger with AFL, 841,
  883, 910
Congress on Racial Equality (CORE), 895
Congressional reconstruction: outline of, 524-
  525; radicalism of, 525-528; first plan of,
  538-540; second plan of, 540-542; implementation of, 547-549
Conkling, Sen. Roscoe, 573, 574, 625, 626, 628
Conn, Billy, 774
Connecticut (colonial): early settlements in,
  43-44; split from Massachusetts Bay Colony,
  48; Fundamental Orders adopted in, 64;
  puritanism in, 89; charter confiscated, 97,
  119; landowning aristocracy in, 101; education in, 115; Saybrook Platform in, 119,
  136; leadership in, 146-147; backcountry
  disorder in, 181
Connecticut (state): constitution for, 226,
  228; western claims of, *231*; Constitution
  ratified by, 258; religious liberty in, 293;
  negro suffrage in, 545
Connecticut Moral Society, 303
Conquistadores, 6, 7, 22
Conrad, Charles, Jr., *883*
Conscription: during Civil War, 478; Confeder-
  ate, 479; Union, 479-480; during Civil
  War, 504-506
Conscription Act (1862), 504
Conservation: of Square Deal, 666-668;
  Pinchot-Ballinger dispute, 677; and CCC,
  792, 812; and National Park Service, 859;
  EPA created, 926
Conservatives, Republican, 513. *See also*
  Republican party

Consignment system, of marketing tobacco,
  75-76, 131
Conspiracy laws, 581
Constitution, British, 141, 143, 166, 204
Constitution, federal, 248, 253; provisions of,
  254-256; Hamilton's broad construction of,
  265; Jefferson's strict construction of, 285;
  and social reform, 652
Constitution, U.S.S. (American frigate), 301
Constitutional Convention, 272; need for,
  246; Virginia Plan, 253-254; New Jersey
  Plan, 254; Federalist-Antifederalist debate,
  256-258
Constitutional conventions, in postwar South,
  547, 555
Constitutionalism, as limit to change, 528-532,
  574
Constitutional Union party, 458, 459
Constitutions, state, 224; drafting of, 226-227;
  as written documents, 227; fear of executive power expressed in, 227-228; and
  strengthening of the legislatures, 228;
  revision of, 245-246; ratification of, 272;
  in postwar South, 547, 555
Construction industry: trade associations in,
  768; boom during 1920s, 769-770
Consulado, 12
Consumer credit, 771; and Great Depression,
  781
Consumerism, 881-882; mass, 903; reaction
  against, 904; and consumer movement, 925
Consumer Price Index, during 1970s, 923
Consumer protection: during Eisenhower
  administration, 845; Nader's raiders, 925
Consumption: introduction of brand-name
  products, 568; 1920s patterns of, 769-772;
  and advertising, 857, 863, 882; mass, 881
Containment policy, 833-837; and Korean
  War, 835-836; and Free World, 836; attrac-
  tion of, 837; through military might, 884-
  885; and brinkmanship, 886; vs. nationalism,
  899-900; involvement in Vietnam, 900
Continental Army: creation of, 210; organiza-
  tion for war, 213; recruitment for, 214;
  and financial crisis, 248-249. *See also*
  Revolutionary War
Continental Association, 197, 200
Continental Congress, First, 196-197, 200;
  Declaration and Resolves of, 209
Continental Congress, Second, 209, 224;
  appointment of generals by, 213; and
  Articles of Confederation, 228-229
"Contrabands," 494
Convention of 1800, 303
Conway, Thomas, 217
"Conway Cabal," 217
Cooke, Jay, 502, 575, 596
Cooley, Charles Horton, 589
Coolidge, Calvin, 764, *773*; becomes president,
  772, 783; elected president, 772; relations
  with Congress, 772-773; foreign policy of,
  778
Cooper, Gordon, Jr., *883*
Cooper, James Fenimore, 381
Cooper, Peter, 581
Cooperatives, farmers', 609-611; and Federal
  Farm Board, 773
Copley, John Singleton, 237, 238
Copperhead movement, 513, 537
Copper industry, and tariff, 574
Coral Sea, Battle of, 817
Cornbury, Loard, 98-99, 104
"Corn Laws," 413
Corn production, post-Civil War growth in,
  567
Cornwallis, Lord, 218, 220, 224
Coronado, Vasquez, 7, 27

Corporate society, 600
Corporations: created during Confederation
  period, 239; early railroad, 414-415; and
  scientific reform, 652-653; multinational,
  885-886. *See also* Business; Joint-stock
  companies
Corresponding committees, 196, 200, 269
Corsi, Edward, 683
Cortés, Hernando, 7, 26
Cortissoz, Royal, 744
Cost of living: during World War II, 838;
  during 1970s, 923
Cotton: nineteenth-century rise of, 320;
  England's dependence on, 425; during Civil
  War, 483
Cotton, John, 77
Cotton gin, 272, 320
Coughlin, Father Charles, 795, 797, 798
Council of Fifty, Mormon, 388
Council of Four, *750*, 751
Council of the Indies, 10, 11, 26, 94
Council of National Defense, 736
Counterculture, 904-906
Country Life Commission, 611
Court system, in Puritan settlements, 45.
  See also Admiralty courts; Judiciary
Covered wagons, *427*, *565*
Cowboys, 570
Cowpens, Battle of, 224
Cox, Archibald, 927
Cox, George, 648
Cox, James M., 755, 763
Cox, Kenyon, 741
Coxey, Jacob, 638
Coxey's Army, *638*, 643
Craft, Ellen, 406
Craftsmen: during Revolutionary era, 238;
  support for Constitution of, 257. *See also*
  Artisans
Crash, of 1929, 762, 783. *See also* Great
  Depression
Crawford, William H., 281, 344-346
Crazy Horse (Sioux chief), 563, 566
Creek Indians, 287, 322, 323, 561; and colonial
  expansion, 179-181; and Confederacy, 473
Creel, George, 739
Creoles: in Spanish America, 14-15; environ-
  mentalist view of, 162
Crimean War, 484
Crime Control Act (1969), 908
"Crime of '73," 576, 584
Crittenden, Sen. John J., 460, 470
Critz, Jan de, 23
Croly, Herbert, 673, 720, 748
Cromwell, Oliver, 41, 55, 113, 223
Crop-lien system, 536, 633
Crosby, Ernest, 655
Crow Indians, 561
Crown Point, 154, 155
Crump, Ed, 774
Crystal Palace exhibition (1851), 411
Cuba: and War of Jenkins' Ear, 151; and Treaty
  of Paris, 156; as Spanish territory, 417;
  and Transcontinental Treaty, 418; illegal
  trade with, 425; and Manifest Destiny,
  428; attempts to acquire, 434, 435; revolu-
  tion of 1895 in, 707-708; occupation by
  American forces, 713; Spanish cession of,
  713; renewed controls in, 722; American
  troops intervene in, 727; refusal to recognize revolutionary government of, 804;
  economic boycott of, 886-887; and missile
  crisis, 887, 910
Cullen, Countee, 847
Cullom Committee, 631

Culpeper, John, 111
Culpeper's Rebellion, 111, 119
Cuming, Alexander, 180
cummings, e.e., 866
Curly, James Michael, 774
Currency: in colonial America, 159-161; national, 567; "hard vs. soft" money controversy, 575-576; Resumption Act, 576-577; advocacy of silver coinage, 581; federal control of, 699-700. *See also* Banking industry; Money
Currency Act (1751), 161, 168
Currency Act (1764), 189, 200
Curtis, Benjamin R., 452
Curtis, George William, 572-573, 584
Custer, George Armstrong, *563*, 584
Cuzco, Battle for, 7
Cyprus War, 920
Czechoslovakia: partitioning of, 805; Soviet control of, 831

Dakotas, Granger movement in, 577
Daley, Richard, 908-909
Dana, Richard Henry, Jr., 538
Danish West Indies, and expansionism, 560
Darrow, Clarence, 860
Dartmouth College, 118, 140; black student in, 369
Dartmouth College case, 239, 304
Darwin, Charles, 545, 651
Darwinism, and Scopes trial, 860
Daughterty, Harry, 772
Daughters of Liberty, 193
Daval, P. S., 433
Davies, Samuel, 139
Davis, Chester, 789, 791
Davis, Henry Winter, 516
Davis, Jefferson: in Mexican War, 432, 433; on Brown's raid, 456; and federal slave code, 456; inauguration of, *469*, 491; administration of, 470, 478, 483; and crisis over Fort Sumter, 472-473; and border states, 475; command system of, 497, 518; and Cleburne letter, 510; European mission of, 511; criticism of, 512; as prisoner, 517, 527; in assessment of Civil War, 520; northern view of, 526
Davis, John W., 772, 775
Dawes Plan (1924), 778, 783
Dawes Severalty Act (1887), 564, 797
D-Day, 823, *824*
Dean, John, 927
Debates: Lincoln-Douglas, 452-455, 461; Kennedy-Nixon, 891-892; Carter-Ford, 929
DeBry, Theodore, 7, 14
Debs, Eugene V., 604, 616, 637, 643, 665; and election of 1904, 670, 727; and Socialist party, 695; socialist leadership of, 697; and election of 1908, 700; and election of 1912, 701; convicted under Sedition Act, 740; and election of 1920, 755
Declaration of Independence, 211, 224; and American expansionism, 711
Declaratory Act (1766), 209
Deerfield, Mass., Indian attack at, 104
Defense Department, creation of, 836, 853
DeForest, Robert W., 651
de Gaulle, Charles, 899
Deism, 291
DeLancey, Stephanus, 106
DeLancey family, 198
Delaney, Martin, 407
Delavan, Edward C., 393
Delaware (colonial): early settlement in, 63; Scotch-Irish in, 124; and colonial expansion, 179-181
Delaware (state): constitution for, 226, 228,

246; Constitution ratified by, 258; and secession, 471, 473
"Demesne" farms, 50
Democracy, 141; and social reform, 653-654
Democratic party: evolution of, *340*; vs. national Republicans, 348; hard-money faction, 355-356; southern domination of, 356; and election of 1836, 423; and annexation of Texas, 425; and election of 1844, 426-428; and Mexican War, 433; and free soil, 439; and election of 1856, 448; and Lecompton Constitution, 450, 451; division of, 456-458, 461; and protective tariffs, 575, 630; during Gilded Age, 619-621; majority coalition of, 798; and international communism, 884; in 1950s, 889
Dempsey, Jack, 869
"Denization," 125
Denmark, German invasion of, 807
Denominationalism: sources of, 135-141; evangelical, 293-294. *See also* Religion
Depression: of 1839, 361; revivalism associated with, 375; of 1873, 544; of 1893, 637-638; conservative responses to, 865; and American Dream, 866. *See also* Great Depression; Panic; Recession Desegregation: and local values, 897; federal support of, 894-895, 910. *See also* Black rights
de Soto, Hernando, 7, 27
Despotism, democratic, 243-246
Détente, 918
Detroit, Mich.: surrender of, 303; immigrant populations in, 591-592; urban Progressivism in, 648; race riots in, 850, 908; federal subsidization of, 915
Dewey, Adm. George, 709, 712
Dewey, John, 650, 651, 652, 670, 685; and settlement house movement, 693; and economic policy, 802; and social responsibility, 871-872; scientific relativism of, 874
DeWitt, Benjamin Parke, 645
DeWitt, Gen. John, 846
Diaz, Porfirio, 722
Dickinson, John, 166, 193, 200, *208*, 209
Diderot, Denis, 165
Didion, Joan, 924
Digger Indians, 327, 561
Diggs, Annie L., 634
Dillingham Commission, 685, 700
Dingley Tariff (1897), 631, 643
Diplomacy: under Jefferson, 279; republican, 295-297; during Civil War, 482-485; and post-Civil War expansionism, 558; T. Roosevelt's style of, 719; "dollar," 720; missionary, 721-726; after World War I, 825; of Cold War, 889; Kissinger's, 920-921. *See also* Foreign policy
Diplomatic corps, at end of nineteenth century, 704
Disarmament, postwar passion for, 777. *See also* Arms limitations
Disciples of Christ, 294
Discrimination, racial: federal laws against, 843; and New Deal, 848; banned by F. D. Roosevelt, 853. *See also* Racism
Discrimination, sexual, in sixties, 906-907
Disease: in early settlements, 29, 32; yellow fever epidemic, 272; and Indian removal, 325; and Confederate Army, 520
Disfranchisement: of ex-Confederates, 539; of black voters, 552-554. *See also* Suffrage
Dissent: and Glorious Revolution, 142; religious, 184; centered in New England, 385; Mormonism, 386-391; during Civil War, 513; during World War I, 739-741; during 1920s, 764-765; in Soviet Union, 919; during 1960s, 904-907

Distant Early Warning System (DEW line), 885
District of Columbia: slavery in, 361, 405; slave trade in, 442, 444; slavery abolished in, 507
Dixiecrats, 842-843
Dodd, Samuel C. T., 598, 599
Dodge, Mabel, 744
Dodge City, Colo., cattle industry and, 570
Doheny, Edward, 772
Dollar, and international inflation, 922. *See also* Currency
Dominican Republic: and expansionism, 560; U.S. intervention in, 718; financial supervision of, 722; American troops occupy, 727
Dominion of New England, 96-98
Donelson, Fort, Grant's capture of, 488, 491
Donnelly, Ignatius, 634, 635
Doolittle, Sen. James R., 513
Dorr, Rheta Childe, 691
Dos Passos, John, 866, 867
Douglas, Lewis, 789
Douglas, Stephen, *455*, 540; and Mexican War, 433; and Compromise of 1850, 443; and popular sovereignty, 445; and Nebraska Territory, 447-448; and Kansas-Nebraska Act, 448; and Emigrant Aid Society, 449; and Lecompton constitution, 450-451; and *Dred Scott* case, 452; and debates with Lincoln, 452-455; political style of, 454-455; "Freeport Doctrine" of, 454-455; and election of 1860, 457, 458-459
Douglas, William O., 791
Douglas Aircraft, military contracts of, 885
Douglass, Frederick, 404, 406, 506, 532
Douglass, Dr. William, 143
Downing, George, 113
Draft, and Vietnam War, 902. *See also* Conscription
Draft Act (1917), 755
Drake, Francis, 18, 20, 22, 27
Dred Scott decision, 451-453, 461; reaction to, 452-453; and John Brown's raid, 456
Dreiser, Theodore, 600, 617, 743
Drowne, Shem, 144
Drucker, Peter, 880-881, 903
Du Bois, W. E. B., 686-688, 700
Duchamp, Marcel, 741-*742*
Dulany, Daniel, 199, 207
Dulles, John Foster, 836, 886, 890; China policy of, 888; and defense treaty with Formosa, 888; containment policy of, 899-900; and involvement in Indochina, 900
Dunmore, Lord Charles, 181
Dunne, Finley Peter, 625
du Pont, Pierre, 859
Du Pont, Samuel F., 498
Duquesne, Fort, 153-155
Durand, Asher B., 381
Durkin, Martin, 845
Dutch: New Amsterdam settlements of, 51-55; conflict with New England, 54
Dutch Reformed Calvinist church, 86
Dutch West India Co., 51, 55, 64
Dwight, Louis, 393
Dwight, Timothy, 241, 260

Eagle, symbolism of, 259
Earl, Ralph, 241, 255
Early, Jubal A., 518, 527
East Harlem, immigrant culture of, 683
East India Co., 18
Eastland Co., 18
Eastman, Max, 744
Eastman Kodak, 768
East St. Louis, race riots in, 755

Eccles, Marriner, 802
E. C. Knight case (1895), 604, 665
Economics, and politics, 663
Economy: Virginia settlement trade, 34–35; of
early settlements, 36, 50; colonial, 70–76,
128–135, 158–161; 1820–1860, 311; slavery
in, 327–329; agriculture dominating, 355;
of 1840s, 410–415; Civil War, 500–504;
laissez-faire policy, 532–536; post-Civil War
growth of, 567–568; brand-name products
in, 568; nineteenth-century consolidation of,
568–571; 1873–1900, 598; of 1920s, 767–
772; as profit system, 778; wartime boom,
837; and changing values, 865; government
management of, 883; dependent on foreign
resources, 886. *See also* Business; Depression; Inflation; Labor force
Ecuador, Spanish conquest of, 7, 27
Ederle, Gertrude, 869
Edgar Thomson Steel Works, *596*
Edison, Thomas, 600, *601*, 616
Education: in colonial America, 114–117; en-
vironmentalist theory, 162; during Revolutionary era, 239–240; first state board of,
365; working-class demands for, 365–367;
mid-nineteenth-century reform in, 366–367;
for women, 368–369; lyceum movement,
376–377; of blacks in South, 530; expanding
influence of schools, 862; and GI Bill, 873;
and expertise, 882; and desegregation, 894;
bilingual, 915. *See also* Public school system;
Universities
Edwards, Jonathan, 137, *138*, 168
Egypt: seizure of Suez Canal, 888; agreement
with Israel, 921, 931
Ehrlichman, John, 927, 928
"Eight box" law, 552, 553
Eight-hour movement, 579
Eisenhower, Gen. Dwight D., 817, *844*, 883;
and question of sovereignty, 761; and
Korean War, 835; elected president, 836,
844, 845, 910; economic policy of, 845–
846; support for local control, 845–846; on
Sen. McCarthy, 852; economic policy of,
883; military policy of, 884–885; on "military-industrial complex," 885; foreign policy
of, 886; arms policy of, 889; at summit conferences, 889; and opinion polls, 890; and
desegregation, 894, 910; and Civil Rights
movement, 896; and involvement in Vietnam, 900; and nuclear tests, 924
Election districts, Supreme Court on, 898
Elections, Congressional: in 1854, 446; in 1858,
451; in 1867, 550; of 1878, 581; of 1918,
749; of 1938, 801; of 1946, 850; in 1954,
889
Elections, presidential: of 1800, 275, 277; of
1816, 302; of 1820, 302; of 1824, 344; of
1828, *347–349*; of 1832, 353; of 1836, 423;
of 1840, *360–361*; of 1844, 426–428; of
1848, 431–432, 434, 439–440; of 1852,
445; of 1856, 448; of 1860, 456–461, *457*,
459; of 1864, 515–516; of 1868, 576; of
1876, *551*; key states in, 621; of 1880, *662*,
625–626; of 1884, *622*, 627; of 1888, 629;
of 1892, 608; of 1896, 636, 639, 641, *642*;
of 1912, 678, *678*; of 1920, 763–764, 783;
of 1924, 772; of 1928, 775–776; of 1932,
787; of 1936, 798; of 1948, 842; of 1952,
835–836, 844; in 1956, 890; of 1960, 890–
891, 914; of 1964, 893; of 1968, 909–910,
916; of 1972, 917
Electoral college: Constitutional provision for,
255; and Twelfth Amendment, 277; in
1828, *347*; in 1840, *360*; in 1844, *428*; in
1860, *459*; in 1876, *551–552*; in 1880, *622*;
in 1884, *622*; in 1896, *642*; in 1912, *679*; in
1928, *775*; in 1932, *787*; in 1948, *842*; of
1960, *891*; of 1968, *916*; of 1972, *917*
Electoral commission, Congress creates, 584
Electoral districts, in colonial America, 207
Electricity: Franklin's study of, 165; increase
in households with, 770; and TVA, 793
Electric light bulb, Edison perfects, 616
Electric power industry, and Eisenhower ad-
ministration, 883
Eliot, John, 114
Eliot, T. S., 866
Elite: in colonial America, 100; and colonial
rebellions, 109; merchant, 134–135; of
republican society, 234, 237; among
Jeffersonian republicans, 253; during
mid-nineteenth century, 334. *See also*
Aristocracy
Elitism, democratic participation vs., 653
Elizabeth I (queen of England), *17*, 20, 27
Elkins Act (1903), 666
Ellsberg, Daniel, 924
Elmira, N.Y., northern prison camp at, 527
Emancipation: in West Indies, 434; Union de-
bate over, 507–508; northern attitudes
toward, 544–546; southern attitudes toward,
546–547
Emancipation Proclamation, 491, 524; events
leading to, 506–507; preliminary, 508; effect
on southern whites, 533
Embargo Act (1807), 298, 303
Emergency Fleet Corporation, of First World
War, 737
Emerson, Ralph Waldo, 378–379, 466, 589,
650
Emery, Sarah, 634
Emigrant Aid Society, 449
Encomiendas, 12–13
Energy: and foreign dependence, 923; gas crisis,
923; demand for, 924. *See also* Petroleum
industry
Enforcement Acts (1870–1871), 550, 555
England: overseas expansion of, 16–21; Irish
colonization by, 24, 27; early settlements of,
30, *47*, 56; civil war in, 51, 64; and Rule
Britannia, 150–156; diplomatic isolation of,
218; and Spain in 1823, 422; and outbreak
of First World War, 724; and First World
War, 730. *See also* Britain; British America
English, and immigration quotas, 765
Enlightenment: impact of, 3; ideal of, 68;
Franklin as model thinker, 165–166; influ-
ence on republican society, 239
Entail, republicanism and 240
Entertainment industry. *See* Media
Environmental Protection Agency (EPA), 926
Epidemics, yellow fever, 272. *See also* Disease
Episcopalians, as social elites, 294
Equal Rights Amendment (ERA), 925
Era of Good Feelings, 302, 339, 361
Ericsson, John, 498
Erie Canal, 173, 194, 314, *318*, 414
Erie Railroad, 568
Ervin, Sam, 927
Escobedo decision (1964), 898
Eskimos, John White's sketches of, *18*
Espionage Act (1917), 740, 755
Essex decision, 296
Ethics: and scientific method, 874; hard-work,
904. *See also* Values
Ethiopia, invaded by Italy, 803
Europe: World War II campaigns in, *820*; and
Marshall Plan, 832
European antislavery sentiment, 510
European Defense Community (EDC), 899
European estates, compared with southern
plantations, 129–130
Evangelical movement: of eighteenth century,
135; post-Revolutionary, 293; and tradi-
tional values, 863. *See also* Revivalism
Evans, George Henry, 335
Everett, Wesley, 754
Exclusion Crisis, 61
Expansion: in 1760s, *177*; westward, 427, 566–
567; and Indian Wars, *564*. *See also* Frontier
Expansionism: in 1840s, 417–428; and slavery,
418–420; 1818–1848, *421*; annexation of
Texas, 422–426; justification for, 426; and
election of 1844, 426–428; after Civil War,
558–581; origins of, 704–707
Expansionists, and anti-expansionists, 467
Expertise, reliance on, 882–883
Exports: from colonies to Britain, 158–159; in
1840s, 413. *See also* Tariff; Trade
Extralegalism, national system of, 739. *See also*
Vigilante groups

Fabianism, 695, 697
Factionalism, local, 244. *See also* Sectionalism
"Factors," 131
Factories: Waltham system of, 411; in Confed-
eracy, 475; and introduction of assembly
line, 771; violence in, *800*; "farm," 915. *See
also* Industrialization; Manufacturing; Union
movement
Fagen, Mark, 648
"Fair Deal," 843
Fair Employment Practices Committee (FEPC),
848, 850
Fairfax, Lord, 128
Fair Labor Standards Act (1938), 801, 812
Fair Oaks, Battle at, 489
"Fair trade" agreements, 802
Falange, 804
Fall, Albert, 772
Fallen Timbers, Battle of, 272
Family income: during 1920s, 773; during
1960s, 922
Family life: in American colonies, 79–82; in
republican society, 240; and economic
growth, 311; slave, *331–332*; black, *507*,
534, 686; modern, 860–863. *See also* Chil-
dren; Women
Faneuil, Andrew, 106
Faneuil, Peter, *106*
Farley, James, 798
Farm Credit Administration, 791
Farmers: and paper money, 159, 235; and free
market, 312; and expansionism, 315–322;
lifestyle of, 316; and urbanization, 316;
demand for transportation, 318–320; and
post-Civil War economic growth, 570–571;
and currency controversy, 576; and Granger
movement, 577–579; and frontier, 606–607;
organization of, 607–608, 768; as business-
men, 607–608, 768; and populism, 608–609,
632–636; cooperatives of, 609–611; and
First World War, 738; and New Deal, 794,
801; government subsidization of, 839, 883.
See also Agriculture
Farmers' Equity Union, 610
Farmers Mutual Benefit Association, 610
Farmers' Relief Association, 610
Farmers Social and Economic Union, 610
Farm policy: during 1920s, 773; of New Deal,
790; "parity" in, 790–791
Farm Security Administration (FSA), 801, 840
Farragut, David G., 498, 520
Faubus, Gov. Orval, 894–895, 896
Faulkner, William, 536, 865, 876
Federal Communications Commission (FCC),
884
Federal Deposit Insurance Corporation (FDIC),
791, 812

Federal Emergency Relief Administration (FERA), 792
Federal Farm Board, 773, 782, 783
Federal Highway Act (1956), 881
Federalism: during Confederation, 228–230; Virginia Plan vs. New Jersey Plan, 254; debated at Constitutional Convention, 256–259; philosophy of Federalist papers, 257; paper money and, 280, 354–355; judicial review, 290; and state rights debate, 528–529; and Progressive movement, 646; and state progressivism, 661; neofederalism, 668–670. See also Sovereignty; State's rights
Federalist, The, 257, 265, 272, 278
Federalists: and Hamiltonian Program, 258; opposition to, 264–271; pro-British policies of, 268; split among, 271; leaders of, 280–281; and international relations, 296; demise of, 302; and Anglophobia, 418; J. Q. Adams as example of, 422; and War of 1812, 431
Federal Reserve Act (1913), 699, 701
Federal Reserve Board, 700, 760; during First World War, 738
Federal Reserve System, 768, 791. See also Banking industry
Federal Steel Corp., 599
Federal Trade Commission (FTC), 700, 701, 769, 884; during First World War, 738
Federal Trade Commission Act (1914), 604, 699, 701
Feke, Robert, 131, 164
Feminism: of mid-nineteenth century, 402–404; rise of, 688–690; and women's organizations, 690–691; and settlement house movement, 691–693; and suffragists, 693–695. See also Women's movement
Ferdinand II (king of Spain), 13
Ferdinand VII (king of Spain), 420
Fessenden, William Pitt, 502, 538, 543
Fetterman, Capt. William J., 563, 584
Feudalism, in British America, 48, 49. See also Aristocracy
Fillmore, Millard, 356; succession to presidency, 443, 461; and election of 1852, 445; and election of 1856, 446
Findley, William, 244
Finney, Charles Grandison, 373, 374, 375, 394, 398
"Fireside chats," Roosevelt's, 787
First National Bank of New York, 600
Fish, Hamilton, 559
Fisher, Samuel, 375
Fisher, Fort, Union capture of, 498
Fishing: and Plymouth Plantation, 40; in colonial America, 73; in eighteenth-century trade, 133
Fiske, John, 664, 707
Fitzgerald, F. Scott, 730, 867
Fitzhugh, George, 417, 435
Fitzhugh family, 106
Five Civilized Nations, 561
Five-Power Treaty (1921), 777
Flag, burning of, 909
Flagler, Harry M., 569
Fletcher, Gov. Benjamin, 104, 111, 137
Fletcher v. Peck, 290, 303
Florida: and War of Jenkins' Ear, 151; and Treaty of Paris, 156; ceded to Britain, 174; royal government of, 187; admitted to Union, 315; Indians in, 323; as Spanish territory, 417; ceded by Spain, 421; secession of, 460, 461, 491; black suffrage in, 547; reconstruction in, 547, 555
Florida, C. S. S., 511
Flying Cloud (clipper ship), 424
Flynn, Elizabeth Gurley, 744, 746
Folk art: weathervane, 144; snake device, 153;

wooden carving, 198; Thomas Jefferson's victory banner, 278; Liberty symbolized in, 282; Afro-American sculpture, 330; carving of President Jackson, 349; wooden sculpture of Stephen Douglas, 455; carving of Benjamin Harrison, 629
Food Administration, 736
Foraker Act (1900), 713, 727
Forbes, Charles, 772
Force Bill, 351, 361, 554
Ford, Betty, 925
Ford, Gerald, 913; and foreign policy, 920; economic policy of, 923; becomes president, 928, 931
Ford, Henry, 771, 792, 857, 865, 866
Ford Motor Co., 768, 770, 840
Fordney-McCumber Act (1922), 777, 783
Foreign policy: before Civil War, 309; in 1840s, 417–428; during nineteenth century, 703; "Open Door," 715–716, 727, 777; of 1920s, 776–779; after World War I, 825; U.S. as world peace power, 832; brinkmanship, 886–888; preservation of status quo, 888; peaceful coexistence, 888–889; Nixon's, 918–919. See also Diplomacy; Expansionism
Forestry Service, 653
Forests, and westward expansion, 317
Forges, in colonies, 159. See also Industrialization
Formosa (Taiwan): Chinese nationalist retreat to, 832; and principle of containment, 886; defense treaty with, 888
Formosa Resolution, 910
Forrest, Gen. Nathan Bedford, 526, 549
Fortas, Abe, 927
Foster, John, 46, 109
"Four Freedoms," 825
Fourier, Charles, 404
Four-Power Treaty (1921), 777
Fourteen Points, Wilson's, 748–750, 755
Fowler, Orson and Lorenzo, 377–378
Fox Indians, 326
France: and French and Indian war, 150, 153–156; and King George's War, 151; and Treaty of Paris, 156; territory in 1763, 175; and American Revolution, 217–218; Confederation and, 251; revolution in, 267; quasi-war with, 268, 270, 272; and Haitian revolution, 418; and Spain in 1823, 420; and U.S. attempt to acquire Cuba, 434; nineteenth-century colonization efforts of, 704; and First World War, 730; and Versailles Treaty, 750–751; German invasion of, 807; Allied invasion of, 823; in SEATO, 884; and Suez Canal, 888; and European Defense Community, 899; and partitioning of Indochina, 900
Franchise, in eighteenth-century America, 146. See also Suffrage
Francis, Guy, 234
Franco, Gen. Francisco, 804
Franklin, Battle of, 519
Franklin, Benjamin, 63, 153–154, 163–168, 181, 200, 211; western land speculation of, 179; quoted, 184; and peace negotiations, 221
Franklin, Temple, 221
Freake, John, 80
Fredericksburg, Battle of, 491, 494
Freedmen: and labor contracts, 534; civil liberties of, 539; disfranchisement of, 552–554. See also Blacks
Freedmen's Bureau, 529–532; education provided by, 530–531; marriages performed by, 534
Freedmen's Bureau Act (1865), 530, 555
"Freedom riders," 895

Freeman, Thomas, expedition of, 284
Freemasonic order, and Protestant revivalism, 446. See also Anti-Masonic party
Free Silver, 636, 643; Cleveland and, 638. See also Money
Free Soil movement, 439–442; and Mexican War, 434. See also Expansionism
Free Soil party, 405, 439, 440; and election of 1848, 406; black support for, 407; and Republican party, 448
Free speech movement, 904
Free world, 836. See also Containment policy
Frémont, Gen John C., 429, 474, 478, 516; in election of 1856, 448
French and Indian War, 153–156, 168; profits from, 104–106; effect on Anglo-American relations, 156
Freud, Sigmund, 859
Frick, Henry Clay, 636, 753
Friedan, Betty, 906
Fries, John, 271
Fries's uprising, 272
Frobisher, Martin, 18, 19
Frontenac, Fort, 154
Frontier: in eighteenth century, 122; after Seven Years' War, 176–179; and backcountry disorder, 181–182; Appalachian Mountains as, 187; farms on, 236; and religion, 293; in art, 381; last, 565, 605–607, 706
Frost, Robert, 310
Fugitive Slave Law (1793), 405
Fugitive Slave Law (1850), 407, 442, 443, 444, 461; and Dred Scott case, 451; Lincoln opposes repeal of, 454
Fulbright, J. William, 902
Full Employment Act (1946), 842
Fulton, Robert, 303
Fur trade: in colonial economy, 34, 72; and Plymouth Plantation, 40; Dutch in, 52–53; Carolinas in, 59; in eighteenth century, 133; and Indians, 181; in Pacific Northwest, 427

Gage, Thomas, 196, 212, 213
"Gag rules," 351–352, 405
Galbraith, John Kenneth, 903
Gale, Zona, 697
Gall, Franz Joseph, 377
Gallatin, Albert, 279
Galloway, Joseph, 197
Galloway's Plan of Union, 197, 200
Gandhi, Mahatma, 895
Gardoqui, Diego de, 251
Garfield, Harry A., 737
Garfield, James A., 552, 572, 573, 626, 627; assassination of, 574, 643; elected president, 623, 643; patronage dispensed by, 627
Garland, Hamlin, 610–611, 616, 634
Garner, John Nance, 808
Garnet, Henry Highland, 406, 407
Garrison, William Lloyd, 391, 399, 401, 529, 697; jailing of, 398–399
Garvey, Marcus, 847, 849
Gary, Elbert, 599
Gas crisis, 923. See also Petroleum industry
Gaspée (British naval schooner), 195–196, 200
Gates, Gen. Horatio, 217, 218
Gates, Merrill E., 565
Gemini space program, 882
General Electric Corp., 599; military contracts of, 885
General Motors Corp., 604, 845, 857, 925; and UAW, 800; military contracts of, 885
General Union for Promoting the Observance of the Christian Sabbath, 391
Genêt, Citizen, 267, 272
Geneva, summit meeting at, 889, 910

George, Henry, 580, 602, 608, 616, 632; as New York City mayoral candidate, 661

George I (king of England), 119

George III (king of England), 150, 156, 157, 162, 168, *186*, 203, 358; and British politics, 185–187; accedes to throne, 200; and Olive Branch Petition, 210; colonists' view of, 211

Georgia (colonial): early settlement in, 55; Anglican Church in, 137; voting requirements in, 146; established, 168

Georgia (state): constitution for, 227, 228, 246; western claims of, *231*; Constitution ratified by, 258; religious liberty in, 291; rise of cotton in, 320; Indians in, 323; secession of, 460, 461, 491; reconstruction of, 547, 555

Germain, Lord George, 214

German Democratic Republic, riots in, 888

Germans: eighteenth-century immigration of, 123–124; attitudes of, 125–126; mercenaries in American Revolution, 213; nineteenth-century immigration of, 312, 313–314; and immigration quotas, 765

Germantown, Battle of, 216, 224

Germany: nineteenth-century colonization efforts of, 704; and First World War, 724, 730; after First World War, 751; postwar loans negotiated for, 778; rise of aggressive government in, 779; military imperialism of, 802–803; sphere of influence of, 805, 806; nonaggression pact with Soviet Union, 807; and Pearl Harbor, 811; submarine warfare of, 816–817; surrender of, 823, 853; postwar policy of reconciliation with, 829; Berlin Wall erected, 887–*888*, 910

Gettysburg, Battle of, 494, 522

Gettysburg Address, 520, 558

Ghent, Treaty of, 301, 303, 357

Ghettos: workers in, 613–615; despair of, 908. *See also* Blacks; Immigrants; Race riots

Giannini, A. P., 865

GI Bill (Servicemen's Readjustment Act), 873

Gibraltar, problem of, 220

Giddings, Franklin, 685

Giddings, Joshua, 405

Gilbert, Sir Humphrey, 18, 19, 20, 22, 27

Gilded Age, 571

Gilman, Charlotte Perkins, 688, 689, 690

Gladstone, William, 698

Glass, Carter, 554

Glas-Steagall Act (1933), 791

Glorious Revolution, 94, 97, 119; and rebellion in colonies, 109; and extent of crown authority, 141; religious settlement after, 142; impact on colonies, 144

Godkin, E. L., 573

Gold, discovered in California, 440, 441, 461. *See also* Money

Goldmark, Josephine, 691

Goldmark, Pauline, 691

Goldsmith, Deborah, 382

Gold standard: national significance of, 575; return to, 576–577, 584; and Cleveland's money policies, 639; during New Deal, 804. *See also* Currency

Goldwater, Barry, 893

Goldwyn, Samuel, 865

Gompers, Samuel, 612, 613, 665, 765

Gooch, William, 99

"Good Neighbor Policy," 804

Goodnow, Frank, 652

Gordon, Sen. John B., 552

Gordon, Thomas, 204

Gorgas, Gen. Josiah, 478, 519

Gould, Jay, 628, 629, 768

Government: disrespect for, 571; and business, 653; Progressive view of, 654; progressive,

657–658; scientific, 658; management by, 883–884. *See also* Bureaucracy

Governors, royal colonial, 145, 197

Grandfather clause, 685

Grand Ohio Company, 187

Grange, "Red," 869

Granger laws (1869–1874), 579

Granger movement, 577–579, 584; success of, 582; antimonopolist sentiments of, 602; and railroad regulation, 603

Grant, Gen. Ulysses S., 488, 491, *496*; in Mexican war, 432; Vicksburg campaign of, 495–496; given command of Union Army, 496, 522; in assessment of Civil War, 520; and Lee's surrender, *521*; election as president, 550, 555, 584; Reconstruction program of, 550–551; reelected president, 555, 573, 584; and disaffected Republicans, 561; scandal associated with, 572; and civil service reform, 573; currency program of, 576

Grant and Ward, collapse of, 596

Granville, Earl of, 98, 128

Grasse, Marquis François de, 220

Great Awakening, 135, 151; events leading to, 137; effects of, 139–140; and denominationalism, 140; second, 292, 293. *See also* Revivalism

Great Britain: and claims against Confederate ships, 559; in CENTO, 884; in SEATO, 884; and Suez Canal, 888. *See also* Britain, England

Great Depression, 755; events leading to, 779; human suffering during, 780–781; and Europe, 782; deepening of, 782, 783; and local politics, 795; and international disintegration, 802

Great Migration, 24–25, 42–44, 90

Great Northern Railroad, 637

Great Plains, settlement of, 565

"Great Society," 913, 916

"Great Upheaval," 616

Greece: war for independence, 422; civil war in, 831

Greeley, Horace, 335, 360, 584, 592

Green, Duff, 426, 435

Green, William, 768, 800

Greenback Labor party, 631

Greenback movement, antimonopolist sentiments of, 602

Greenbacks, 502; in currency controversy, 576. *See also* Currency; Paper money

Greene, Nathanael, 218

Green Mountain Boys, 181

Greenough, Horatio, 381

Greensburg, Ind., race riots in, 686

Greenville, Treaty of (1795), 264, 272, 287

Greenwich Village, New York City's, 746, 760

Greenwood, John, 132

Greer, U.S.S. (American destroyer), 810

Grenville, Sir Richard, 22

Grimké, Angelina, 402–403

Grimké, Sarah, 402–403

Griswold, Roger, *266*

Gross national product (GNP): during 1920s, 769; during World War II, 842; of 1950s, 880. *See also* Economy

Grosvenor, W. M., 583

Grundy, Felix, 299

Guadalcanal, fighting for, 817

Guadalupe Hidalgo, Treaty of (1848), 433–434

Guadeloupe, and sugar trade, 157–158

Guam: Spanish cession of, 713; acquisition of, 727

Guatemala, 7, 26; "dollar diplomacy" in, 720; U.S. subversion in, 837

Guilford Courthouse, Battle of, 218, 224

Guinea Company, 18

Guiteau, Charles, 574, 627

Hague, Frank, 774

Haight-Ashbury district, 905

Haiti, revolution in, 329, 418, 527–528; "dollar diplomacy" in, 720; military occupation of, 722, 727

Hakluyt, Richard, 19, 20

Hakluyt, Richard (the Younger), 27

Haldeman, H. R., 927, 928

Hale, John P., 405

"Half-Breeds" (Republican faction), 626, 627

"Halfway covenant," 136

Halleck, Gen. Henry Wager, 488, 489, 494

Hamilton, Alexander, 249, 258, *261*, 303, 589, 631; *Federalist* papers of, 257; as secretary of treasury, 259; financial program of, 260–263, 272; political program of, 263–264; Republican's view of, 266; predictions of, 590; political philosophy of, 646; T. Roosevelt's view of, 664

Hamilton, Charles, 907

Hamlin, Hannibal, 458

Hampton, Gen. Wade, 527, 552

Hancock, John, 193, 194, 200

Hanna, Mark, 613, 641, 648, 661, 718

Harding, Warren G.: elected president, 755, 764, 783; death of, 772; foreign policy of, 777

Hard money: and Bank war of 1832, 352; Jackson's policy of, 354–355. *See also* Money; Paper money

Hard-work ethic, demise of, 904

Hariot, Thomas, 30

"Harlem Renaissance," 847

Harper, Robert Goodloe, 280

Harper, William Rainey, 652

Harpers Ferry, Va., Brown's raid on, 456, 461

Harper's Weekly Magazine, 526, 572, 573

Harriman, W. Averell, 830

Harrington, James, 222

Harris, Gov. Isham, 473

Harrison, Benjamin, 662; elected president, 623, 628–629, 643

Harrison, William Henry, 356, 425, 629; and War of 1812, 300–301; as general, 287, 322; as Whig candidate, 359; elected president, 362; death of, 435

Hartford, Treaty of (1650), 54

Hartford Convention, 302, 303

Harvard, John, 118

Harvard College, 117, 118, 140; founded, 64; black students at, 369

Hat Act (1732), 158

Haun's Mill, massacre at, 387

Havemeyer, Henry, 628

Haverhill, Mass., manufacturing at, 183

Hawaii: question of, 710; annexation of, 727

Hawkins, John, 18, 22, 27

Hawley-Smoot Tariff, 782, 783

Hawthorne, Nathaniel, 144, 381, 382, 469

Hay, John, 707, 719; and Spanish-American War, 709; and "Open Door" policy, 716

Hay-Bunau-Varilla Treaty (1903), 727

Hayes, John L., 575

Hayes, Rutherford B., 544, 551, 554, 584; election as president, 551–552, 555; and civil service reform, 573; response to railroad strike, 581

Hay-Herran Treaty (1903), 718–719, 727

Haynes, Lemuel, 292

Hay-Pauncefote Treaty (1901), 727

Haywood, "Big Bill," *696*, 744

"Headright" system, 35

Health, Education, and Welfare (HEW), Department of, 884

Hearst, George, 625

Hearst, William Randolph, 678, 701, 708

Heller, Joseph, 903

Hemingway, Ernest, *866*, 867, 872
Henderson, Leon, 838
Henri, Robert, 743
Henrico (Richmond), 34
Henry, Fort, Grant's capture of, 488, 491
Henry, Patrick, 184, 189, 190, 197, 199, 255; and Constitutional Convention, 253
Henry VII (king of England), 16
Henry VIII (king of England), 16, 24, 26, 87
Henry Street Settlement, 691
Hepburn, William P., 666-667
Hepburn Act (1906), 666, 670
Herkimer, Fort, 154
Herrick, Robert, 600
Hewitt, Abram S., 597, 661
Higginson family, 234
High schools, 862
Highways, interstate, 881, 910
Hill, Benjamin H., 469
Hillquit, Morris, 612, 695
Hillsborough, Lord, 193, 194, 195
Hine, Lewis W., 647, 650, 651, 682, 691
Hingham, Mass., first parish meeting house in, *88*
Hippies, 904
Hiroshima, atomic bomb dropped on, 825, 853, *876*
Hiss, Alger, 851, 913
History, and politics, 663-664
Hitler, Adolph, 803, 804, *807*; anti-Semitism of, 806; and Pearl Harbor, 811; suicide of, 823
Hoar, Sen. George F., 621, 711, 712
Ho Chi Minh, 900
Hoe press, 594
Holding companies, 599; outlawed by Congress, 791. *See also* Corporations
Holmes, Oliver Wendell, Jr., 651, 675-676, 700
Holy Alliance, and Spanish colonies, 420-422
Home Owners Loan Corporation, 791
Homer, Winslow, 485
Homestead Act (1862), 501, 503, 566; Lincoln endorsement of, 458
Homestead strike, 616, 636, 643
Homosexuality, controversy over, 925
Honduras, 7, 26; "dollar diplomacy" in, 720
Hood, John B., 518, 519
Hook, Sidney, 874
Hooker, "Fighting Joe," 494, 522
Hoover, Herbert, 683, 736, *782*, 787, 845; as secretary of commerce, 769; and Prohibition, 774; elected president, 775-776, 783; foreign policy of, 778, 803, 804; and Great Depression, 782
Hoover, J. Edgar, 869, 924
Hoover-Stimson, Doctrine of 1932, 803, 812
Hopi Indians, 605
Hopkins, Harry, 788, 792, 796, 830
Hornbeck, Stanley, 810
Horseshoe Bend, Battle of, 303
Housatonic (Union warship), 498
House of Burgesses, Virginia's, *145*, 189
House of Commons, British, 45, 141, *142*; and sugar trade, 158
House-Grey Memorandum, 727, 755
Household-family, 81. *See also* Family life
House of Lords, British, 141
House of Morgan, 600
House of Representatives, U.S.: Constitutional provision for, 255; blacks in, 548
Housing: nineteenth-century urban, 614, 615; for blacks, *647*
Housing Act (1949), 843
Houston, Sam, *423*, 433
Howard, Gen. Oliver O., 530, 532
Howard, Sidney, 861
Howe, Frederick C., 648

Howe, Julia Ward, 557
Howe, Louis, 786
Howe, Adm. Richard, Lord, 214
Howe, Samuel Gridley, 396, 529-530
Howe, Sen. Timothy O., 545
Howe, Sir William, 212, 213, 214, 218
Howells, William Dean, 743
Hudson Bay: expedition to, 27; British acquisition of, 105
Hudson River, 51
Hudson River Estates, in colonial New York, *103*
Hudson River School, *380*, 381
Hudson's Bay Company, in Oregon, 427
Huerta, Victoriano, 722
Hughan, Jessie Wallace, 697
Hughes, Archbishop John, 367, 446
Hughes, Charles Evans, 727, 749, 755, 799; as secretary of state, 777
Hughes, Langston, 847, 849
Huguenots, 58, 123
Hull, Cordell, 804, 810, 825
Hull, William, 300
Hull House, 646, 652, 670, 691
Human rights, 931
Hume, David, 257
Humphrey, George, 845
Humphrey, Hubert, 843, 905, 909, 914
"Hundred Days," Roosevelt's, 789-793
Hungary: in Soviet sphere of influence, 828; Soviet control of, 831; revolt in, 888
Hunley (Confederate warship), 498
Hunter, Robert, 99
Hunter, Robert Mercer Taliaferro, 483
Huron Indians, and colonial expansion, 179-181
Hutchins, Robert, 874
Hutchinson, Anne, 45, 47, 64, 90
Hutchinson, Gov. Thomas, 146, 160, 190, 196, 200, 209
Hutchinson family, 109
Huxley, Aldous, 875

Ickes, Harold, 787; and labor policy, 790; and PWA, 792; and NAACP, 797; and black rights, 847-848
Identity, American, 206
Ideology: of republicanism, 236, 239, 266; of Revolution, 203-205, 275; antislavery, 399; Republican antislavery, 454. *See also* Values
Illinois, admitted to Union, 286
Illinois Central Railroad, 443; Lincoln as lobbyist for, 453
Illiteracy: in early nineteenth century, 365; among Southern blacks, 553. *See also* Education
Immigrants: and factory labor shortage, 411; Irish, 420; in Democratic party, 621; at Ellis Island, *623*; early twentieth-century, 682-685; organizations of, 683; "new," 685; and antiradicalism, 764; and bigotry of 1920s, 765
Immigration: eighteenth-century, 123-126; stimulus to, 312-313; and Mormonism, 387; and Know-Nothing movement, 446; during Civil War, 520; Chinese Exclusion Act, 544, 581; post-Civil War, 567; and organization of labor, 579; and urban growth, 591; old and new, *681*
Immigration Act (1903), 740
Immigration quotas, 765, 783
Impeachment, of Pres. Johnson, 542-543
Imperialism: arguments for, 704-707; economic, 705, 778; support for, 712; in China, 777; rival forms of, 802-803; post-World War II, 829. *See also* Expansionism, Foreign policy

Imports, and iron industry, 412. *See also* Tariff, Trade
Impressment, of seamen: during King George's War, 153; British policy of, 296, 297
Impressment of slaves, during Confederacy, 507, 510
Incan empire, 7, 13
Income, average family: during 1920s, 773, during 1970s, 922
Income distribution, in mid-nineteenth-century, 333. *See also* Population density
Income tax, graduated: Populist demand for, 634; lowered rate for wealthy, 773; and Revenue Act, 838-839; and rich vs. poor, 840
Indentured servitude, 37, 68, 101
Independence, Mo., Mormon settlement near, 386
Independence Hall, *250*
Independent Treasury Act (1840), 362
India, English trade with, 18, 25
Indiana: admitted to Union, 286; and water transportation, 319; Ku Klux Klan, 766, 767
Indiana territory, 287
"Indian Problem," 565
Indian Removal Bill (1830), *326*
Indian Reorganization Act (1934), 797
Indians, American: in Spanish America, 13-16; of Chesapeake Bay area, 21; precolonial population distribution of, 29-30; in Pennsylvania, *31*; and Virginia settlements, 36; relations of colonists with, 41; and New Amsterdam, 53, 54; Dutch relations with, 54-55; and slavery, 59; and southern colonies, 76; French and Indian wars, 104-106, 153-156; and Bacon's Rebellion, 110; colonial attitudes toward, 162; and colonial expansion, 179-181; in Ohio Territory, 264; and westward expansion, 287; and economic growth, 312, 332; and agricultural expansion, 322; federal policy toward, 322-326; removal to Western territories, *326*; early reservations, 326-327; and art, 381; and Kansas Territory, 449; and Confederacy, 473; struggle for survival of, 562-563
Indian Territory, 561
Indian Wars, 561-565; and westward expansion, *564*
Indigo culture, 59, *102*; and slavery, 101, 126
Individual, in modern society, 873-877
Indochina: Japanese occupation of, 810, 816; partitioning of, 900. *See also* Vietnam
Industrial Commission, Wilson's, 613
Industrialization: and economic expansion, 182-183; and South, 322; of 1840s, 410-415; consequences of, 588; of nineteenth century, 590; and urban growth, 591-592; impact of railroads on, 592-594; and technology, 594-595; capital investment in, 595-596; and merger movement, 599; of agriculture, 605; and food availability, 607; fruits of, 615-616; effects on southern blacks, 686
Industrial Workers of the World (IWW), 696-698, 701, 754; formation of, 700; and First World War, 739; and Paterson strike, 744; destruction of, 764
Industry: impact of electricity on, 771; "planned obsolescence" in, 881. *See also* Factories; Manufacturing
Inflation: during Civil War, 501-504; after World War II, 841; and Korean War, 844; during 1970s, 915; worldwide, 922-923; and sense of helplessness, 924. *See also* Economy
Inflation Bill (1874), 576, 584
Ingalls, Sen. John J., 626

Ingersoll, Charles Jared, 364
Ingersoll air drill, 594
Inquiry, The, 748
Insull, Samuel, 770, 780, 865
Insurance programs: state, 659; Medicare, 896; proposed national health, 925-926
Intercollegiate Socialist Society (ISS), 697
Internal Revenue Act (1862), 501
Internal Revenue Service: and Whiskey Ring, 572; during Nixon administration, 924
Internal Security Act (1950), 851
International affairs: and Wilson's League of Nations, 752; precedent set for arbitrating, 560; and U.S. foreign policy, 755; 1920-1929, 776; 1931-1939, 802-807; after World War II, 825; humanistic approach in, 874; managerial approach to, 886, and containment, 899. See also Diplomacy, Foreign policy
International Exhibition of Modern Painting (1913), 741, 742, 743
International Monetary Fund (IMF), 825, 829
Interstate Commerce Act (1887), 603, 616, 631, 643; and Hepburn bill, 666-667
Interstate Commerce Commission, 665, 670, 769, 783, 884
Investment policy, in colonial America, 158. See also Joint-stock companies
Iowa: admitted to Union, 315; Negro suffrage in, 545; Granger movement in, 577
Iowa Territory, *421*
Iran: American subversion in, 837; in CENTO, 884; revolution in, 921, 924; And American hostages, 930
Ireland: colonized by England, 24, 27; eighteenth-century migration from, 123; famine in, 312
Irish: nineteenth century immigration of, 313-314; value priorities of, 336; and pre-World War I isolationism, 805
Iron Act (1750), 159, 168
Ironclads, 498
Ironclads, Battle of, 491
Iron Curtain, 828, 888
Iron industry: Saugus Ironworks, 71, *72*, 78; growth of, 158-159; in 1860, 411
Iroquois Confederacy, 30
Irving, Washington, 381
Isabella (queen of Spain), 13
Isolationism: pre-World War I, 724-725; roots of, 776; and ethnic groups, 805
Israel: and Suez Canal, 888; peace settlement with Egypt, 921, 931
Italians: and immigration quotas, 765; and pre-World War I isolationism, 805
Italy: immigrants from, 681; military imperialism of, 802-803; invasion of Ethiopia by, 803; reaction to Pearl Harbor attack, 811; Allied invasion of, 822, 853
Iwo Jima, Battle of, 823

Jackson, Andrew, 322, 621; elected president, 281, 347, 361; quoted, 299; invades Florida, 304, 420; Indian policy of, 325, 326; and election of 1824, 345; party politics of, 346-347; presidency of, 348; and tariff in South Carolina, 351; and election of 1832, 353; hard-money policy of, 354-355; Whig image of, *357*; Texas policy of, 423-425; and nullification crisis, 460; T. Roosevelt's view of, 664
Jackson, Helen Hunt, 564
Jackson, Thomas J. ("Stonewall"), 432, 478, 489
Jacobi, Mary Putnam, 693
Jacobites, 123
Jamaica, slave revolt in, 350, 397-398

James, Duke of York, 94
James, Henry, 743
James, William, 650, 670, 746
James I (king of England), *23*, 27, 75
James II (king of England), *94*, 109; accession of, 119; and Dominion of New England, 96-98
Jamestown, 32-36; early settlements of, 23, 26, 64; English colony established at, 27
Japan: opened to trade, 438, 461; and Portsmouth Treaty, 716; rise of aggressive government in, 779; military imperialism of, 802-803; Manchuria occupied by, 803, 812; sphere of influence of, 805; as threat, 806; and Tripartite Pact, 808, 812; Pearl Harbor attacked by, 810, 812; domination in Pacific of, 816; Soviet Union declares war on, 825; surrender of, 825, 853; and American foreign policy, 899
Japanese: and immigration quotas, 765; in wartime concentration camps, *846-847*, 853
Jarratt, Rev. Devereux, 139
Jarvis, John Wesley, 206
Jaworski, Leon, 927
Jay, John, 251, 254, 264; and peace negotiations, *221*; *Federalist* papers of, 257; British mission of, 267; retirement of, 280
Jay Cooke and Co., failure of, 580
Jay-Gardoqui Treaty (proposed), 272
Jay's Treaty (1795), 267-268, 272, 298
Jefferson, Thomas, 209, 211, 251, *277*, 410, 589, 631, 835; Statute of Religious Freedom of, 86; quoted, 205, 223 302; and Declaration of Independence, 211; during Revolution, 218; and penal codes, 240; on slavery, 243; *Notes on Virginia*, 245; and Confederation, 250, 252, 253; and Constitutional Convention, 253; on *Federalist* papers, 257; as secretary of state, 259; and quasi-war with France, 269; Monticello of, *276*; presidential style of, 278; political reform under, 279-280; politics of, 280-281; expansionism of, 282; and embargo, 298; elected president, 303; reelection of, 303; on Indians, 323; death of, 339; and Missouri Compromise, 342; and territorial expansion, 418; and Florida, 420; and proposed British-American declaration, 422; political philosphy of, 646; T. Roosevelt's view of, 664
Jeffersonianism, 416. See also Republican party
Jenkins, Capt. Robert, 151
Jenkins' Ear, War of, 151, 168
Jenner, Sen. William, 852
Jersey City, N.J., boss rule in, 774
Jerseys (colonial): early settlement of, 55, 59-61; unification of, 98
Jesuits, in colonial Maryland, 85
Jews: and naturalization; 125; value priorities of, 336; immigration of, 681; in Democratic party, 798; in Nazi concentration camps, 806
Jim Crow laws, 850, *893-894*
Johnson, Andrew: quoted, 369-370; as vice presidential candidate, 516; becomes, 522; Reconstruction program of, 524-525, 537, 546, 555; and Republican party, 540; impeachment of, 542-543, 555; racism, 545; expansionism of, 561; and tariff, 574
Johnson, Sen. Hiram, 740
Johnson, Hugh, 789
Johnson, Lyndon Baines, 896; *897*, becomes president, 892, 910; elected president, 893, 910; and civil rights movement, 896-897; domestic policy of, 899; and Vietnam War, 900-903, 910; quits 1968 presidential race, 903, 907; Great Society of, 913, 916; and wiretapping, 924

Johnson, Reverdy, 559
Johnson, Tom, 648, 670
Johnson, Sir William, 182
Johnson Debt-Default Act (1934), 806
Johnston, Albert Sidney, 390
Johnston, Frances Benjamin, 687
Johnston, Gen. Joseph E., 487, 489, 496, 497, 510, 518, 522
Joint Committee on Reconstruction, 538
Joint-stock companies: Drake's world voyage financed by, 18; financing of colonies by, 25; Virginia Company, 33, 34, 35; and Bubble Act, 160. See also Trade
Jomini, Baron Henri, 486-487
Jones, Capt. "Bill,", 595
Jones, James, 875
Jones, J. B., 503
Jones, Jesse, 789
Jones, Robert Edmond, 745
Journalism, 272; reform, 655-656. See also Media
Juarez, Benito, 558
Judicial review, origins of, 288-291. See also Sovereignty
Judiciary: in American colonies, 144; creation of federal, 260; Federalist view of, 271; manipulative tradition in, 290-291. See also Supreme Court
Judiciary Act (1789), 289
Judiciary Act (1801), 288
Julian, George W., 545

Kafka, Franz, 875
Kaiser, abdication of, 733
Kaiser Industries, 841
Kansas: crisis over, 434, 447-451; terrorism in, 450; admitted to Union, 451; and Negro suffrage, 545; Granger movement in, 577; population decreases in, 633; women's suffrage in, 694
Kansas City, Mo., boss rule in, 774
Kansas-Nebraska Act (1854), 447-448, *449*, 453, 461
Kansas Pacific Railroad, 570
Kant, Immanuel, 379
Kaufman, Irving, 833
Kearney, Dennis, 544
Kearny, Stephen W., 432
Keaton, Buster, 868
Keayne, Robert, 46
Kefauver, Estes, 845
Kelley, Edward, 798
Kelley, Florence, 690
Kellogg, Frank B., 778
Kellogg-Briand Peace Pact (1928), 778, 783, 803
Kelly, Abby, 402
Kelly, Oliver Hudson, 577
Kelly, William, 595
Kendall, Amos, 352
Kennan, George, 830, 833
Kennedy, Sen. Edward, 929
Kennedy, John Fitzgerald, 882, 921; on Eisenhower's military policy, 885; foreign policy of, 886; and Bay of Pigs fiasco, 886-887; at summit conference, 889; and opinion polls, 890; elected president, 890, 910; "New Frontier" of, 891-893, 913; assassination of, 892, 910; and Civil Rights movement, 896; and containment policy, 900
Kennedy, Robert, 907, 909, 924
Kenner, Duncan F., 511
Kent, William, 660
Kent State University, students killed at, 909, 910
Kerner, Otto, 927

Kentucky: admitted to Union, 260; and secession, 471, 475
Kentucky resolution, 272
Kentucky territory, and population growth, 236
Key, David M., 552
Khrushchev, Nikita, 891; and missile crisis, *887*; at summit conferences, 889
Kiefft, Willem, 54, 55
Kiel, German naval mutiny at, 733
King, Martin Luther, Jr., *895*; wins Nobel Prize, 897; campaign in North of, 898; assassination of, 907, 910; and FBI, 924
King, Rufus, 342, 343
"Kingfish." *See* Long, Huey
King George's War, 151–153, 168. *See also* Austrian Succession, War of the
King Philip's War, 106, 119
King's Mountain, Battle of, 218, 224
King William's War, 104, 119
Kirby-Smith, Gen. Edmund, 490, 497, 519, 522
Kirtland, Ohio, Mormon settlement at, 386
Kissinger, Henry, 885, 918, *920*
Klamath Nation, 916
Knight case (1895), 604, 665
Knights of the Golden Circle, 513
Knights of Labor, 580, 584, 612
Knowles, Comm. Charles, 153
Know-Nothing party, 438, 457; upsurge of, 445–447; significance of, 446–447; election victories of, 461. *See also* American party
Knox, Henry: as secretary of war, 263; and land speculation, 284
Knox, Philander C., 720
Knox, William, 208
Koestler, Arthur, 875
Konoye, Prince Fuminaro, 810
Korean War: beginning of, 833, 853; shifting front in, 834; armistice for, 834–835, 853; as UN police action, 835; and inflation, 844. *See also* Containment policy
Korematsu v. *United States* (1944), 847
Krimmel, John Lewis, 302
Ku Klux Klan, 549–550, 555, 774; revitalized, 766–767, 783, 895

Labor: in British empire, 22; in early settlements, 37, 50, 58, 59; and tobacco industry, 76; in colonial America, 79, 81; and colonial manufacturing, 158; and immigration, 313; agricultural, 316; and New England manufacturing, 411; in textile industry, 412–413; and white southerners, 416; and nativism, 446; during Civil War, 503; freedmen's, 534–535; and day-to-day problems, 580; nineteenth-century growth of, 590, 611; consolidation of, 612–613 (*see also* Union movement); and Progressive reform, 659; and coal industry strikes, 665–666; Supreme Court on, 676; and women, 688, 689; and First World War, 738; and assembly line methods, 771; and Great Depression, 781, 782; and racism, 798; and corporate profits, 841; and *braceros*, 847; monotony and mechanization in, 867; women in, 906–907. *See also* Industrialization; Servitude; Slavery
Labor, Department of, Children's Bureau in, 690
Labor and Commerce, Department of, Bureau of Corporations in, 665, 670
Laborers, unskilled: and economic growth, 312; during mid-nineteenth century, 334, 335
Labor movement: origins of, 579; and Panic of 1873, 580; and federal intervention, 581–583. *See also* Union movement
Labor relations, in republican society, 237–238

Labor unions: first, 580; and antiradicalism, 764. *See also specific unions*
Labrador, 26
Lafayette, Marquis de, *220*, 302
LaFollette, Robert M., 656, *659*, 670; career of, 658–659; and election of 1912, 677; and election of 1924, 772
La Follette, Suzanne, 867
Laissez-faire policy: as limit to change, 532–536; "third alternative" to, 769. *See also* Economy
Lake Erie, Battle of, 303
Lake Mohonk Conference of the Friends of the Indians, 565
Lamar, L. Q. C., 552
Landon, Alfred, 798
Land ordinances: and colonial land claims, 231–232; provisions of, 233
Land ownership: Indian attitudes toward, 29; in Virginia settlements, 35; in New England, 44; in Maryland settlements, 49–50; in New Amsterdam, 53–54; in Carolina settlements, 58; and family life, 81–82; and Anglo-American aristocracy, 100–102; freehold tenure, 128; great landowners, 128–129; plantations in South, 129–132; warrant system, 233; and immigration, 313; and agricultural expansion, 316, 317–318; and Freedmen's Bureau, 531; vs. sharecropping, 535; and Native Americans, 564; Homestead Act, 566; and populism, 633
Landrum-Griffin Act (1959), 884
Land surveys: Lewis and Clark expedition, *284*, 285, 303; federal support for, 316
Land system, federal, 317
Lane Theological Seminary, 401
Laos, invasion of, 917
Larkin, Thomas, 429, 432
Latin America: independence movement in, 11; T. Roosevelt's intervention in, 719; "dollar diplomacy" in, 720; U.S. monopoly in, 778; and Roosevelt's "Good Neighbor policy," 804; "Alliance for Progress" program, 900; containment policy and, 900. *See also* Spanish America
Laurens, Henry, 195, 221
Law: in early Virginia settlements, 34; in Puritan settlements, 45–46; in Pennsylvania settlements, 63; manipulative tradition in, 290–291; international, 484; new national organization of, 589; and national system of extralegalism, 739. *See also* Judiciary; Vigilante groups
Lawrence, Abbott, 377, 440
Lawrence, Kan., terrorism in, 450
Law school, first, 345
League of Augsburg, War of, 104
League of Nations, 749, 751–752, 803; Congressional attack on, 753–754; and international integration, 804
Lease, Mary E., 633, 634
Lebanon, American troops in, 888
Lecky, W. E. H., 123
Lecompton (Kansas) Constitution, 450–451, 461
Lee, Arthur, 249
Lee, Richard Henry, 197, 226, 249, 253, 255
Lee, Gen. Robert E., 491, 497, 508, 527; in Mexican war, 432; and Peninsula campaign, 489; as commander of Confederate army, 494; on black soldiers, 510; in assessment of Civil War, 520; surrender of, *521*
"Legend of Sleepy Hollow, The" (Irving), 381
Legislatures: unicameral, 63; colonial, 145; House of Burgesses, *145*, 189; and problem of sovereignty, 208–209; and state constitutions, 228; democratization of, 243–244

Leisler, Jacob, 111
Leisler's Rebellion, 111–112, 119
Leisure: modern concept of, 858–859; in consumer society, 881; attitudes toward, 904
Lemke, William, 798
Lend-Lease Act (1941), 809, 812
Lenin, V. I., 731
Leningrad, siege of, *816*
León, Ponce de, 26
Leopard (British man-of-war), 298
Levant Company, 18
Lever Act (1917), 736
Lewis, George Cornewall, 485
Lewis, John L., 790, 799, 800, 802, 808
Lewis, Meriwether, *285*
Lewis, Sinclair, 860
Lewis and Clark expedition, *284*, 285, 303
Lexington, Battle of, 209–210, 212, 224
Leyte Gulf, Battle of, 823
Liberalism, pragmatic, 747
Liberal Republican movement, 573, 575
Liberal Republican party, 561
Liberator, The, *399*, 529
Liberty: rhetoric of, 199; symbolism of, 259
Liberty party, 405; black support for, 407
Library of Congress, 303
Lima, Peru, 7
Lincoln, Abraham: on Mormons, 390; and debates with Douglas, 452–455; background of, 453; "House Divided" speech, 453–454; political style of, 454–455; and election of 1860, 457–459; elected as president, 459–460, 461; southern reaction to, 466; and secretary of state, 482–483; command system of, 494–495, 496–497; and slavery issue, 507; Emancipation Proclamation, 508, 510, 513, 522, 524; Republican criticism of, 513, 515; opposing views of, *514*; reelection of, 515–516, 517, 522; reconstruction plan of, 516, 522, 524; in assessment of Civil War, 520; assassinated, 522, 526, 555; nationalism of, 558
Lincoln, Gen. Benjamin, 218, *220*
Lindbergh, Charles, 869, *870*, 883
Lippmann, Walter, 697, 746, 747; and Wilson's board of experts, 748; on U.S. role in world affairs, 832; on scientific relativism, 874
Literacy tests: in Louisiana, 554; for black voters in South, 685; for immigrants, 765
Literature: "transcendental," 379; nationalism in, 558; of social reform, 602; and changing family roles, 861; conservative, 865; antiwar novels, 866–867; success ethic in, 867; yearning for unity in, 872; and Nazis, 875; paperback, 875; Second World War in, 875; South in, 877
Little, Frank, 739
Little Bighorn, Battle of, 563, 584
Little Rock, Ark., school desegregation in, *894*–896, 898, 910
Litton Industries, 841
Livingston, Robert, 104, 211, 285
Livingston, William, 243
Livingston family, 111, 198
Literacy law, in Massachusetts, 64
Lloyd, Henry Demarest, 602, 604, 616
Lloyd George, David, *750*
Localism, tendencies toward, 467, 583
Lochner case, 676
Locke, John, 56–58, 59, 165, 204, 239
Lodge, Sen. Henry Cabot, 554, 707, 709, 713, 753
Lok, Michael, 19
Lome, Depuy de, 709, 727
London, Bishop of, 85
London, Cheapside-Cornhill district of, *22*
London Economic Conference, 804

London Naval Conference, 778
Long, Huey, 794-795, 796, 797
Longfellow, Henry Wadsworth, 381
Long Island: early settlement of, 53; Battle of, 224
Longshoremen: striking, 795; in union movement, 841
Longstreet, Gen. James, 549
Loom, power, 411. See also Textile industry
Lopez, Narcisco, 434
Lords of Trade, 94, 119
Loudoun, Fort, 182
Loudoun, Lord, 154
Louis, Joe, 871
Louisbourg, Nova Scotia, 151-152, 154, 168
Louis XIV (king of France), 95
Louis XVI (king of France), 217, 272
Louisiana: admitted to Union, 286; rise of cotton in, 320; secession of, 460, 461, 491; black suffrage in, 547; reconstruction of, 547, 555
Louisiana Purchase, 284-286, 303, 420, 426
Lovejoy, Elijah P., 401
Low Dog (Sioux chief), 563
Lowell, James Russell, 381
Lowell, Josephine Shaw, 690
Lowell, Mass., and 1840s industrialization, 411
Lowell family, 234
Lower East Side, New York City's, 675, 684
Loyalists: and British policy during war, 214; departure of, 232
Luce, Henry, 829
Ludlow Amendment, 806, 807
Ludlow Massacre, 755
Luhan, Mabel Dodge. See Dodge, Mabel
Luks, George, 743
Lumber, in colonial trade, 40
Lumber industry, 653; and First World War, 738
Lundy, Benjamin, 423
Lusitania (British liner), sinking of, 724-725, 727, 755
Lutherans: in colonial America, 86; traditional values of, 863
Lyceums, 376-377
Lynchings: decline in, 686; federal laws against, 843; and New Deal, 848. See also Racism; Vigilante groups
Lynd, Robert and Helen, 859
Lyon, Matthew, 266, 270

MacArthur, Gen. Douglas, 823, 836; in Korea, 835; recalled, 835
McCarthy, Sen. Eugene, 907, 909
McCarthy, Sen. Joseph M., 851-853, 852, 890
McCarthyism, 851-853, 890
Macchu Pichu, 8, 9
McClellan, Gen. George Brinton, 488, 491, 494, 508; character of, 488; in Mexican War, 432; Peninsula campaign of, 489, 491; and election of 1864, 515, 521
McClure, S. S., 655
McClure's, 655, 670
McCormick, Cyrus Hall, 413, 500, 571, 582
McCullers, Carson, 877
McCulloch, Hugh, 575, 576
McCulloch v. Maryland, 290, 304, 353
Macdonough, Comm. Thomas, 303
McDowell, Gen. Irwin, 487
Maceo, Antonio, 709, 727
McGovern, Sen. George, 916-917, 927
McGuffey's readers, 367
McKay, Claude, 847
McKay, Gordon, 500
McKay's shipyard, 424
McKinley, William, 641, 643; and Sherman Act, 604; elected president, 617, 670, 727; re-elected, 617; assassination of, 617, 661; and

1896 campaign, 639-640; character of, 641; Cuban policy of, 709; on Philippines, 710-711; and "Open Door" policy, 715
McKinley Tariff (1890), 630, 631, 643
McLean, John, 452
McManes, James, 625
McMillan, James, 625
McNamara, Robert, 887
McNary-Haugen Bill, 773, 783
Macon, Nathaniel, 300
Macon's Bill No. 2 (1810), 298, 303
Macune, C. W., 634
Madero, Francisco, 722
Madison, James, 236, 244, 249, 251, 253, 280; on slavery, 243; and Confederation, 252, 253; and Constitutional Convention, 253-254; at Philadelphia Convention, 257; Federalist papers of, 257, 263; and Antifederalists, 259; Congressional power of, 265; elected president, 281, 303; and Nonintercourse Act, 298; presidency of, 302; reelected, 303; and Missouri Compromise, 342; and West Florida, 420; and proposed British-American declaration, 422; and majority rule, 467
Magruder, Gen. John B., 489
Mahan, Alfred Thayer, 706
Mahan, Dennis Hart, 486
Mailer, Norman, 875
Maine (colonial): Virginia Company settlement in, 32; during King George's War, 152; early settlement in, 32
Maine (state): admitted to Union, 315, 343, 361; and Negro suffrage, 545
Maine (American battleship), sinking of, 709
Maine law (1851), 397
Majority rule: in Compromise of 1850, 442-445; and election of 1860, 459; and secession crisis, 459-461; and minority rights, 467, 583; and reconstruction of South, 524-555. See also Federalism; Sovereignty
Malcolm X, 908
Malcomb, John, 207
Malenkov, Georgi, 889
Mallory, Stephen R., 497, 498, 499
Mallory decision (1956), 898
Management: and post-Civil War economy, 568; technology and, 595; vs. labor, 613; personnel, 863; government, 883-884; and national security, 885. See also Business
Manassas, First Battle of, 487, 491
Manassas, Second Battle of, 490, 491
Manchukuo, 803
Manhates Indians, 51
Manhattan Island, Dutch settlement of, 51, 64
Manifest Destiny: and war with Mexico, 428-434; phrase coined, 430; after Civil War, 558; and foreign policy, 703. See also Expansionism
Mann, Horace, 367, 377
Manorial system: in Maryland settlements, 49-50; in New York, 104; failure of, 129
Manufacturing: Anglo-American conflict over, 158-159; colonial origins, 183; of 1840s, 411-413; during Civil War, 486, 500; in late nineteenth century, 590; and working-class life, 613; and introduction of assembly line, 771. See also Factories; Industrialization; Labor; specific industry
Mao Tse-Tung, 832
Maple Flooring Manufacturers' Association case (1925), 769, 783
Marbury v. Madison, 289-290, 303
March, Basil, 743
Marcy, William L., 573
Marion, Francis, 218
Markham, Edwin, 655

Marne, Battle of, 731
Marshall, Gen. George C., 827, 830, 832
Marshall, John, 288, 289, 303; and Marbury v. Madison, 289-290; Constitutional nationalism of, 290; and Worcester v. Georgia, 323, 324
Marshall, Thurgood, 850
Marshall Plan, 831, 832, 853
Martinique, and sugar trade, 157-158
Martin's Hundred, 35
Martin v. Hunter's Lessee, 290
Marx, Karl, 335, 872
Mary I (queen of England), 17, 27
Maryland (colonial): Lord Baltimore's charter, 48; early settlements in, 48-51, 64; government of, 49; politics of, 50-51; religious toleration in, 51, 85-86; charter confiscated, 97, 119; aristocracy of, 103; rebellion in, 109, 112-113; schools in, 117; Anglican Church in, 137; colonial shipbuilding in, 158
Maryland (state): constitution for, 226, 228; western claims of, 230, 231; religious liberty in, 291; and secession, 471, 473-474
Mason, George, at Constitutional Convention, 253
Mason, James M., 485, 511
Mason-Dixon line, 63
Massachusetts (colonial): English settlement in, 25; early settlements in, 43-44; government in, 44-45; Puritanism in, 89; charter confiscated, 97, 119; rebellion in, 109, 113; education in, 115; and King George's War, 151; coinage of money in, 159; paper money in, 160; private land bank created in, 168; manufacturing in, 183; resistance in, 193
Massachusetts (state): constitution for, 224, 227, 228, 245; western claims of, 230, 231; Constitution ratified by, 258; religious liberty in, 293; urban centers of, 314; Whig interests in, 359; and 1840s industrialization, 411; and Mexican War, 430; and Negro suffrage, 545
Massachusetts Bay Colony: Plymouth in, 40; Puritans' Great Migration to, 42-44; school law in, 64; economy of, 71
Massachusetts Bay Company, 42-43, 64
Massachusetts General Court, 44; Anne Hutchinson trial, 47; sumptuary law of, 79-80; educational provisions of, 115-116; search warrants granted by, 156; land bank authorization of, 160
Massachusetts Province House, 144
Massachusetts State House, 245
Masses, The, 740, 744
Materialism, revivalism as response to, 375. See also Values
Mather, Cotton, 116
Mather, Richard, 46
Matsu, bombardment of, 886
Mauldin, Bill, 872
Maurer, James Hudson, 695
Maury, Matthew Fontaine, 703
Maximilian, Archduke (emperor of Mexico), 511, 558-559, 584
Mayflower (Pilgrim ship), 39, 41
Mayflower Compact, 41, 64
Mayhew, Jonathan, 150
Mayors, urban, and Progressivism, 648
May resolves (1776), 226
Maysville Road Bill, 348, 361
Meade, Gen. George Gordon, 432, 494, 517, 522
Meany, George, 883
Meat Packing Act (1906), 666, 670
Meat-packing industry: and consumer legislation, 666; strike in, 667; antiradicalism of, 765

Medell, Joseph, 612
Media: journals, 376–377; moralistic tracts, 396; press, 533, 545, 572, 573, 655–656, 708, 739–740, 754; radio, 770–771, 857, *858*; television, 852, 881, 889, 890, 891–892, 902–903, 929; revolution in, 857; motion pictures, 857, 869, 875; and contemporary values, 861–877; Federal Communications Commission, 884; and Nixon administration, 914; and Watergate crisis, 928. *See also* Newspapers; Press; Television
Medical insurance, proposed national, 925–926
Medicare, 896
Meiklejohn, Alexander, 697
Mellon, Andrew, 753, 773
Melville, Herman, 382, 460–461, 874
Memminger, Christopher G., 480, 482, 502
"Memorial Day Massacre," 800
Memphis, Tenn.: race riots in, 541; boss rule in, 774
Mencken, Henry L., 860, 862
Menominee Nation, 916
Mercantilism, 95–96; British enforcement of, 156; problems of, 157; and manufacturing, 158–159. *See also* Trade
Merchants: in colonial aristocracy, 102–103; New England, 74; social mobility, 109
Mercier, Henri, 484
Mercury space program, 882
Merger movement, 599–601
Merriam, Charles, 652
Merrimack (ironclad ship), 498
Mestizos, 15
Methodism: and Great Awakening, 135, 139; and revivalism, 370; and slavery, 416
Methodists, 184; growth in numbers of, 293; and revivalism, 372, 373; and anti-mission movement, 395; traditional values of, 863
Mexican-Americans: during World War II, 847; and urban pressure, 898; and farmworkers unions, 915
Mexican cession, *421, 432*
Mexican War, 410; beginning of, 428–430, 435; and Slidell's mission, 429–430; American troops in, *431*; major campaigns of, 431–432; occupation of capital, 433; and Treaty of Guadalupe Hidalgo, 433
Mexico: Cortés conquers, 26; and annexation of Texas, 422–426; and British role as mediator, 425; abolishes slavery, 435; U.S. intervention in, 722–724; oil controversy with, 778
Michigan: admitted to Union, 315; and Negro suffrage, 545
Middle class: and temperance movement, 396; and Black Power movement, 908. *See also* Aristocracy; Artisans; Labor; Social Organization
Middle East: English trade with, 18; U.S. involvement in, 778; CENTO in, 884
"Midnight judges," 288, 289
Midway Islands, Occupation of, 560, 817, 853
Migration: Great, 24–25, 42–44, 90; in mid-seventeenth century, 176; post-revolutionary, 283; covered wagons, *427*. *See also* Expansion; Immigration
Milan Decree (1807), 297
Milbourne, Jacob, 111
Military Reconstruction Act (1867), *541*, 542, 547, 555
Mill, John Stuart, 680
Millenialism, 294
Millenarianism, 698, 632
Miller, Arthur, 873, 877
Miller, Thomas, 772
Miller-Tydings Act (1937), 802
Milliken v. *Bradley*, 914

Millionaires: attitudes toward, 597; and First World War, 738
Mills, textile, 411. *See also* Textile industry
Milwaukee, Wisc., German immigration to, 313
Mind control, 377
Mingo Indians, and colonial expansion, 179–181
Minimum wage: and Supreme Court, 769, 783; legislation for, 801, 812
Mining industry: and frontier, 606; and working-class life, 613; strikes in, 637
Minnesota: admitted to Union, 315; and Negro suffrage, 545; Granger movement in, 577
Minority rights, in 1970s, 915–917. *See also* Sovereignty
Minuit, Peter, 51, 54
Miranda decision (1966), 898
Miscegenation, 332, 515, 545
"Missile gap," 900
Missionary work, 393, 394
Mississippi: admitted to Union, 286, 341; Indians in, 323; secession of, 460, 461, 491; Black Codes in, 538; black suffrage in, 547; reconstruction of, 547; black protest in, 895
Mississippi River, importance of, 285
Mississippi Territory, 287
Missouri, 339; admitted to Union, 315, 361; and secession, 471, 474–475; and Negro suffrage, 545
Missouri Compromise, 304, 341, 361, 418, 440, 451; and distribution of slaves, *419*; Douglas's view of, 447; declared unconstitutional, 452; and election of 1848, 439
Mitchell, Charles, 780
Mitchell, John, 665
Mitchell, John, 914, 927, 928
Mitchell, Margaret, 865
Mitchell, Wesley C., 735
Mobil Bay, Farragut's victory at, 520, 522
Moderate Republicans: and Lincoln, 513, 521; and Reconstruction legislation, 537–538, 540–542; and Johnson's impeachment, 542–543. *See also* Republican party
Modernism, cultural, 741–746
Modernization: consequences of, 588; effect of World War II on, 815; and traditionalists, 863–866; and literature, 867; and nationalization, 880. *See also* Industrialization
Mohawk Indians, 182
Molasses: in eighteenth-century trade, *133*; and Sugar Act, 189
Molasses Act (1733), 158, 168, 188
Mole, John, Esq., 134
Moley, Raymond, 788, 793
Moll, Hermann, 14
"Molly Maguires," 581
Molotov, Vyacheslav, 829
Monarchy: Spanish, 10; british, 141; republican fear of, 267. *See also* Sovereignty
Money: coinage of, 159; bills of credit, 159, 235; and farmers, 159, 235, 252; in colonial America, 159–161, 168, 189, 200; financing of American Revolution, 210, 235; and Continental Congress, 229; and decline of Confederation, 248–250; as cause of inflation, 248–250, 502–503; as cause of Shays's Rebellion, 252; federalism and, 280, 354–355; Jacksonian policy toward, 354–355; financing of Civil War, 482, 502; national currency, 567; and Sherman Silver Purchase Act, 638; and election of 1896, 639–640; international stabilization of, 825; and international inflation, 922. *See also* Banks; Currency; Hard-money; Paper money
Monitor (ironclad), 498
Monmouth, Battle of, 224
Monopoly: in colonial trade, 111; Protestant

program against, 112–113; in industry, 599; case against, 602; Supreme Court on, 675; and Wilson's New Freedom, 698
Monroe, James, 269, 280, 298; nominated for presidency, 281; elected president, 302, 303; reelection of, 304, 361; on Indians, 323; second inaugural address, 339; and foreign policy of 1820s, 418; and Transcontinental Treaty, 420; and proposed British-American declaration, 422; and Spanish America, 422
Monroe Doctrine: in 1840s, 417–428; events leading to, 420–422; Adams's role in, 422; Polk reformulation of, 435; Roosevelt corollary to, 717–718, 727, 778
Monroe-Pinckney Treaty (1806), 298, 303
Montcalm, Marquis Louis Joseph de, 156
Montesquieu, Baron de, 163
Montezuma (Aztec emperor), 7–8
Montgomery, Gen. Bernard, 817
Montgomery, Gen. Richard, 210, 224
Montgomery convention, 469. *See also* Confederate States of America
Monticello, *276*
Montreal, and Treaty of Paris, 156
Moore, Thomas, 279
Morgan, Daniel, 218
Morgan, J. P., *600*, 601, 604, 613, 639; and "Square Deal," 665; and panic of 1907, 670; and loan for France, 778
Morgenthau, Henry, 787
Mormonism: beginnings of, 386; persecution of, 386–390; migrations associated with, *389*; as a radical challenge, 390–391; and Protestant revivalism, 446
Mormon War, 390
Morrill Act (1862), 501
Morrill Tariff (1861), 481
Morris, Gouverneur, 253, 261, 661, 664
Morris, Robert, *249*, 284
Morris, Thomas, 405
Morrow, Dwight, 778
Morton, Levi, 629
Motion pictures: impact on culture, 857
Mott, Lucretia, 402
Mt. Rushmore, Native American occupation of, 916
Muckrakers, 655–656, 670; and consumer legislation, 666; and blacks, 687
"Mugwumps" (Republican faction), 628
Muir, John, 667
Mulford, Rev. Elisha, 558
Muller v. *Oregon*, 659, 670
"Mulligan Letters," 628
Multinational corporations, 885–886
Mumford, Lewis, 867
Munich agreement, 804–805, 812
Munitions industry: during Civil War, 480; and naval warfare, 499
Munn v. *Illinois*, 579, 603
Munsey, Frank, 677
Murfreesboro, Battle of, 495
Muscovy Company, 18
Mussolini, Benito, *803*, 804
Muste, A. J., 697
Myrdal, Gunnar, 897

Nader, Ralph, 925
Nagasaki, atomic bomb dropped on, 825, 853, 876
Napalm raids, in World War II, 823
Napoleon, and Louisiana Purchase, 420
Napoleon III, 483, 484, 558
Nashville, Battle of, 519
Nasser, Gamal, 888
Nast, Thomas, 544, 548, 571, 572, 573, 583
Natchez, Miss., as trading center, 287

National American Woman's Suffrage Association, 693, 694, 700

National Association for the Advancement of Colored People (NAACP), 797; founded, 688, 700; demands of, 847; membership in, 850; and *Brown* decision, 893

National Association of Manufacturers (NAM), 613, 841

National Banking Act (1864), 567

National Broadcasting Company, 857

National Child Labor Act, 700

National Child Labor Committee, 690

National City Bank, 600

National Civic Federation, 613, 654

National Civic Foundation, 617

National Conservation Congress, 668, 670

National Consumers' League (NCL), 690, 700

National Defense Education Act (1958), 882, 910

National Farmers Alliance, 607

National forests, 668

National Independent party, 581

National Industrial Recovery Act (1933), 789-790, 792, 812

Nationalism: Constitutional, 290; economic, 345, 347; encouraged by Civil War, 557-558; in literature, 558; American, 662; Roosevelt's "new," 673-674, 677, 700; African, 847. *See also* Federalism

Nationalization, 880

National Labor Relations Act (1935), 796, 799, 812

National Labor Relations Board (NLRB), 796, 800, 812

National Labor Relations Board v. *Jones and Laughlin Steel*, 799

National Labor Union, 579-580, 584

National Liberation Front (NLF), 900

National Municipal League, 654

National Organization for Women (NOW), 907, 910

National Origins Act (1924), 765, 783

National Park Service, 859

National party convention, 348. *See also* Politics

National Recovery Administration (NRA): established, 789; decline of, 794; and Supreme Court, 799

National Republican party, 347, 357, 359; evolution of, *340*; vs. Jacksonian Democrats, 348. *See also* Whigs

National security, 880, 885

National Security Act (1947), 836

National Socialist (Nazi) party, 803; anti-Semitism of, 875. *See also* World War II

National system, disenchantment with, 930. *See also* Sovereignty

National Union Convention, 540

National Union for Social Justice, 795

National Woman's Party, 693, 694, 701

National Women's Rights conventions, of 1850s, 404

Native Americans: during Civil War, 561-562; defeat of, 563-565; organization of, 916. *See also* Indians

Nativism: and anti-Catholic activities, 396; upsurge of, 445; and Know-Nothing party, 446; and election of 1860, 457; and early twentieth-century immigration, 681

Naturalization Law (1740), 125

Nauvoo, Illinois, *387, 389*

Navajo Indians, 327

Navigation Acts, 76, 96, 119, 125

Navy: under Jefferson's republicans, 279; and War of 1812, 295; Union vs. Confederate, 486; during Civil War, 497-500; and Grant's administration, 572; and Washington Confer-ence Treaties, 777, 783; and attack on Pearl Harbor, 811; in World War II, 817

Nazi (National Socialist) party, German, 803, 875

Nazi-Soviet Pact (1939), 810

Nebraska, Granger movement in, 577

Nebraska Territory, confrontation over, 447-448

Necessity, Fort, 153

Nelson, Adm. Horatio, 271

Neofederalism, limits of, 668-670

Netherlands: early settlements of, 30; North American colonies of, 51; German invasion of, 807. *See also* Dutch

Networks, broadcasting, 857

Neutrality, European, and Civil War, 483-485

Neutrality laws (1935 and 1937), 806

New Amsterdam: Dutch settlements in, 51-55, *52-53*; character of, 52; English capture of, 55. *See also* New York City

Newburgh conspiracy, 272

Newcastle, Duke of, 185, 186

New Deal: arrival of, 786; and Roosevelt's administration, 787-789; and NRA, 789-790; and AAA, 790-791; financial regulation under, 791; public relief provided by, 792; and TVA, 792-793, 812; dwindling confidence in, 794; stalled, 795; WPA of, 795-796, 812; and Social Security Act, 796; conservative doubts about, 797; and national-local compromise, 797; and Supreme Court, 798-799, 812; principal measures of, 801; and reform, 801; and special interests, 801-802; successful formula of, 808-809; and black rights, 847

New England (colonial): settlement of, 38, 44; Pilgrims in, 39-42; Puritan settlements in, 42-48; conflict with Dutch, 54; demographic characteristics of, 68, 69; economy of, 71-75; commercial system evolved in, 73-74; Puritanism in, 87-91; English origins of, *90*; landowning aristocracy in, 100-101; Great Awakening in, 135; "halfway covenant" in, 136; early settlement in, 179. *See also specific colonies*

New England: Federalism in, 298; industry in, 412; Know-Nothing party in, 446. *See also specific states*

New England, Council for, 41

New England, Dominion of, 119

New England Freedmen's Aid Society, 530

New England Non-Resistance Society, 402

"New Era," 772, 773, 774, 782, 783, 791, 798, 867

Newfoundland: and European fisherman, 16; English settlement in, 25; and John Cabot exploration, 26; British acquisition of, 105; and fishing rights, 220

New France, and Treaty of Paris, 156

"New Freedom," 674, 697-700, 735, 747

"New Frontier," 891-893, 913

New Haarlem, early settlement of, 53

New Hampshire (colonial), 97; royal charter for, 119; early settlements in, 179

New Hampshire (state): constitution for, 226, 228, 245, 246; and Negro suffrage, 545

New Harmony, Ind., socialist experiment in, 404

New Jersey (colonial): settlement of, 59-61; population of, 60; charter confiscated, 97, 119; division of, 119; unification of, 119; religious toleration in, 137; colonial ship-building in, 158; during American Revolution, 214

New Jersey (state): constitution for, 226, 228; Constitution ratified by, 258; enabling laws of, 604; state politics of, 657

New Jersey Plan, 254

New Mexico: statehood, 440; slavery in, 445; and popular sovereignty, 447

New Mexico Territory, and Compromise of 1850, 444

"New Nationalism," 673-674, 677, 700, 734, 747

New Netherlands: settlements in, 64; British capture of, 119. *See also* Manhattan

New Orleans, La., 287; and Treaty of Paris, 156; in early nineteenth century, *286*; Union capture of, 498; race riots in, 541

New Orleans, Battle of, 301, 303, 345

Newport, R.I.: early town of, 30; in eighteenth century, 123; decline of, 235

New Republic, The, 722, 748

New Spain, viceroyalty of, 10, *11*, 27

Newspapers: colonial, 189, 191, 193; in Republican society, 269; first daily, 272; Whig, 360; and religious revivals, 375; and *Dred Scott* decision, 452; during Civil War, 503; during Reconstruction, 533; and Black Codes, 538; on urban reform, 572; on civil service reform, 573; and muckraking tradition, 655-656; and changing values, 864. *See also* Journalism; Media; Press

New York (colonial): Dutch settlements in, 51-55; Dutch Church in, 86-87; royal governors of, 99; aristocracy of, 103-104; rebellion in, 109, 111-112; land ownership in, 129; religious toleration in, 137; during King George's War, 152; population growth in, 176; backcountry disorder in, 181

New York (state): constitution for, 227, 228, 245; western claims of, *231*; Constitution ratified by, 258; immigration to, 314; canal system of, 318-319; political machine in, 359; and Negro suffrage, 545

New York City: early town of, 30; in eighteenth century, 123, 132, *137*; British in, 224; after Revolution, *234*; relocation of capital from, 244; immigration to, 314; and cotton industry, 321; Five Points, *333*; educational reform in, 365-366; segregated schools in, 368; public school system in, 369; social reform in, 396; draft riots in, *505-506*; under "Boss" Tweed, 571; immigrant populations in, 591-592, 682; of late nineteenth century, *602-603*; cheap transportation in, *649*; in early twentieth century, *674-675*; Jewish immigrant district of, *684*; black community of, 686; race riots in, 686

New York Central Railroad, 568, 593

"New York Eight," 743

New York Public School Society, 366

New York Stock Exchange, *674*; and 1928 boom, 779, 783. *See also* Stock market

New Zealand, in SEATO, 884

Nez Percé Indians, 605

Niagara, Fort, 154, 155

Niagara (American vessel), *300*

Niagara Movement, 688, 700

Nicaragua: "dollar diplomacy" in, 720; marines sent to, 727; revolution in, 921

Nicholson, Francis, 111

Niebuhr, Reinhold, 867, 874, 877

Nimitz, Adm. Chester, 823

Nine-Power Treaty (1922), 777, 813, 810

Nixon, Richard, 837, 917, *920*; on communism, 833, as vice president, 890; and election of 1968, 909; elected president, 910, 916; re-election of, 917, 931; visit to China, 918, 919, 931; and foreign policy, 918-921; economic policy of, 922-923; and wiretapping, 924; and Watergate scandal, 927; resignation of, 928, 931; pardon for, 928, 931

Nonimportation Act (1806), 297

Nonintercourse Act (1809), 298, 303
Nonresistance, of abolition movement, 401–
402. *See also* Abolitionism
Norfolk, Va., economic development of, 76,
183
"Normal schools," 369
Normandy, Allied invasion of, 823, 824, 853
Norris, Frank, 600, 743
Norris, Sen. George, 772, 792, 867
North: blacks in, 126; revivalism in, 375; anti-
abolitionists in, 400; racism in, 544; nation-
alism in, 557; civil rights movement in, 898.
See also Union
North, Lord, *186*, 195; and Coercive Acts, 196;
conciliatory efforts of, 209
North Africa: U.S. intervention in, 716; World
War II in, 817, *820*, 853
North America: French claims of, 26; in 1763,
175; frontier expansion in, 177. *See also*
British America; Spanish America
North Atlantic Treaty (1949), 832, 853
North Atlantic Treaty Organization (NATO),
833, 884, 890
North Carolina (colonial), 56; voting require-
ments in, 146; backcountry disorder in, 181.
See also Carolinas
North Carolina (state): constitution for, 226,
228; western claims of, *231*; Constitution
rejected by, 258; Indians in, 323; secession
of, 471, 473, 491; reconstruction of, 547,
555; Ku Klux Klan in, 766
Northeast Railroad, 593
Northern Alliance, 608
Northern Pacific Railroad, 563, *564*, 593
Northern Securities Company, antitrust action
against, 665, 670, 675
Northern Securities Co. v. *United States* (1903),
604, 617, 665, 670
Northrup, Solomon, 406
Northwest Ordinance, 231, *233*, 272, 342
Norton, Charles Eliot, 712
Norway, German invasion of, 807
Nova Scotia: and early English colonization, 19;
English settlement in, 25; John Cabot ex-
plores, 26; in French and Indian War, 154;
and Treaty of Paris, 156
Noyes, John Humphrey, 404
Nuclear power: private development of, 883,
910; controversy over, 926, 931
Nullification: theory of, 349–351; crisis over,
460
Nye, Sen. Gerald, 806

Oates, Joyce Carol, 924
Oberlin College, 401; black students in, 369
"Occupancy laws," 317
O'Connor, Flannery, 877
O'Connor, John, 505
Office of Economic Opportunity (OEO), 896,
899, 908; dismantling of, 914
Officeholders, in British imperial system, 99–
100. *See also* Bureaucracy
Office of Price Administration (OPA), 838
Oglala Sioux Indians, 561. *See also* Sioux
Indians
Ohio: admitted to Union, 286; immigration to,
314; and water transportation, 319; and
Negro suffrage, 545
Ohio Idea, 576
Ohio territory, and Treaty of Greenville, 264
Ohio Valley, Indian rebellion in, 187
Oil: discovered in Pennsylvania, 500, 569; dis-
covered in Oklahoma, 772; foreign invest-
ment in, 886
Oil crisis, 924
Oil industry, Labor Policy Board in, 790; and
state rights, 845; and foreign dependence,

923. *See also* Petroleum industry; Standard
Oil Co.
Okinawa, occupation of, 823
Oklahoma: Indian removal to, 325–326; during
Civil War, 473; as Indian Territory, 561; Ku
Klux Klan in, 766; oil discovered in, 772
Old-age pensions, Townsend movement for, 871
Old Age Revolving Pensions club, 795
"Old Hickory," 345
"Old Republicans," 344, 345, 347. *See also*
Republican party
Old Ship Church, 88
Oligarchy, 141; planter, 415. *See also* Aristoc-
racy; Elite
Oligopoly: in industry, 599; of business, 767
Olive Branch Petition, 209, 210
Oliver, Andrew, 190
Olney, Richard, 604, 707, 727
Olympic games, boycott of, 919
"Omnibus Bill," 443
One hundredth meridian, *606*
Oneida experiment, 405
O'Neill, Eugene, 866
Onis, Luis de, 420
"Open hearth" method, 595
"Open Door" policy, 715–716, 727, 777
"Open shop" committees, 765
Operation Overload, 822–823, 853
Operation Rolling Thunder, 901
Operation Torch, 817, 853
Opinion polls: and presidential elections, 889–
890; and Kennedy presidency, 892; on drug
use, 909. *See also* Public opinion
Oppenheim, James, 747
Oppenheimer, J. Robert, 823, 829
Opposition, country-Whig tradition of, 204–205
Oral communication, in Afro-American culture,
332. *See also* Media
Order of American Knights, 513
Order of the Heroes, 511
Order of the Star-Spangled Banner, 445–446
Order of the White Camellia, 549
Oregon (territory), *421*; Russian traders in, 422;
American claims to, 426; and election of
1844, 426–427; and Manifest Destiny, 428–
429; controversy over, 430–432; Treaty with
Britain divides, 435; and antislavery, 440–
441
Oregon (state): admitted to Union, *315*; wo-
men's suffrage in, 694; Ku Klux Klan in, 766
Oregon Trail, 427
Organic Act (1900), 713, 727
Organic Act, Philippine (1902), 714
Organization of American States (OAS), 921
Organization of Petroleum Exporting Countries
(OPEC), 923
Orkney, Early of, 98
Orlando, Vittorio, *750*
Orphan courts, 82
Orwell, George, 875
Osborn, Sir Danvers, 99
Osceola (Seminole chief), 324
Ostend Manifesto (1854), 434, 435
Ostrogorski, Moisei, 624
Oswald, Lee Harvey, 892
Otis, James, 207, 241
Outewas Indians, *180*
Ovington, Mary, 688
Owen, Robert, 404

Pacific Ocean: Balboa's discovery of, 6; and
English exploration, 25; and Transcontinen-
tal Treaty, 420; U.S. possessions in, *715*;
World War II campaigns in, *821*
Pacific Railroad Act (1862), 501
Paine, Thomas, 199, 205, *206*, 210, 224,
292; quoted, 215

Painting: mid-nineteenth-century, *321*, 382;
Hudson River School, *380*, 381; modern,
741; "Ascan School" of, 743. *See also* Art
Pakistan, in CENTO and SEATO, 884
Palatinate Homelands, immigration from, 123,
125
Palestinian Liberation Organization (PLO),
921
Palmer, A. Mitchell, 764
Palmer, Elihu, 292
Palmerston, Lord, 484, 485, 486
Pamphleteers: colonial, 204, 207; English
government, 206
Panama, Spanish conquest of, 7
Panama Canal: negotiating for, 718; opened,
727
Pan-Hellenic Union, 683
Panic: of 1819, 304, 320, 339; of 1837, 320,
355–356, 361; of 1857, 415, 435; of 1873,
580–581, 584, 596, 607, 616; of 1893,
596, 616, 635, 643; of 1907, 670. *See also*
Depression
Pankhurst, Emmeline, 694
Paoli, Pascal, 205
Papacy: and Spanish crown, 13; and Treaty
of Tordesillas, 17
Paper money: in colonial America, 159–*160*;
Currency Acts, 161, 168, 189, 200; for
Revolutionary War, 210; issued by Continen-
tal Congress, *229*; during Revolutionary era,
235, 248; of Bank of the United States,
261–262; of state-chartered banks, 280;
Confederate, *482*, 491; during Civil War,
502; national significance of, 575. *See also*
Currency; Money
"Paper war," with colonies, 195
Paris, Treaty of (1763), 156, 174, 185, 200
Paris, Treaty of (1783), 272
Parish, Anglican, in Colonial Virginia, 83–84
"Parity," in agricultural policy, 790–791.
See also Farm policy
Parker, Alton B., 670, 727
Parliament, British: and Glorious Revolution,
109; House of Commons, *142*; Sugar and
Stamp Acts of, 187–188; colonial opposi-
tion to, 206–209
Parrington, Vernon L., 746
Parsons' Cause, 184, 189, 200
Party system, disintegration of, 446–447;
realignment of, 642. *See also* Politics
Paterson, William, 254
Paterson Pageant, 744–746
Patronage, Jefferson's view of, 280. *See also*
Spoils system
Patrons of Husbandry, 577. *See also* Granger
movement
Patroonships, 53
Paul, Alice, 693, 694, 701
Paxton uprising, 181, 200
Payne, Henry B., 629
Payne-Aldrich Act (1909), 677
Payne-Aldrich Tariff, 700
Peace, economics of, 885–886
Peace Corps, 891, 900, 910
Peace movement: of Progressive era, 721;
youth involvement in, 904
Pearl Harbor, attack on, 810–811, 812, 872
"Peculiar institution," 243
Peek, George, 773, 789, 791
Peffer, Sen. William A., 634
Pemberton, Gen. John C., 496
Penal system: during Revolutionary era, 240;
origins of, 392; Auburn system, 393; reform
of, 396
Pendergast, Tom, 774
Pendleton Act (1883), 574, 628, 630, 643
Penn, William, 59, 61–63, 163; and Charles

Penn, William (*continued*)
II, 61–62, 64; colonizing efforts of, 62–63; charter granted to, 119; quoted, 143
Penn family, 128
Pennsylvania (colonial): Indians in, 31; early settlements in, 55, 61–63; charter confiscated, 97, 119; religious toleration in, 137; factionalism in, 143; in French and Indian War, 154; Quakers in, 163; population growth in, 176; backcountry disorder in, 181; manufacturing in, 183
Pennsylvania (state): constitution for, 226, 228, 246; immigration to, 314; and water transportation, 319; Whig interests in, 359; discovery of petroleum in, 569
Pennsylvania, University of, 118
Pennsylvania Dutch, 123
Pennsylvania Railroad, 568, 581, 593
Pentagon Papers, 924, 931
Pepperrell, William, 151–*152*
Perfectionism, 396; of mid-nineteenth century, 402–404. *See also* Values
Perkins, Charles E., 590
Perkins, Frances, 691, 787, 797
Perkins, George E., 613
Perkins, George W., 677
Perry, Matthew C., 438, 461
Perry, Oliver Hazard, 300, 301
Perryville, Battle at, 490, 495
Pershing, Gen. John J., 723–724, 727; expedition into Mexico, 727; in First World War, 733
Peru: Spanish conquest of, 7, 26; viceroyalty of, 10–*11*, 27
Petersburg, seige of, 518, 522
Petroleum industry: during Civil War, 500; Rockefeller's domination of, 568–569; cracking process in, 595; trusts in, 599. *See also* Oil industry
Phelan, Sen. James, 504
Philadelphia: early town of, 30; Penn's map of, *62*; founding of, 63; in eighteenth century, 123, 132; Voltaire's view of, 163; vice-admiralty court in, 191; First Continental Congress in, 197; Second Continental Congress in, 209; British capture of, 217, 224; removal of national capital from, 278; and water transportation, 319; revivalism in, 373; anti-Catholic violence in, *374*; 1884 riot in, 446; Centennial Exhibition at, 567, 584; immigrant populations in, 591–592; race riots in, 686
Philadelphia (frigate), *295*
Philadelphia Convention: call for, 251–253; delegates to, 253. *See also* Constitutional Convention
Philadelphia-Lancaster turnpike, 272
Philadelphia Society of Friends, 530
Philip II (king of Spain), 17
Philippine Organic Act (1902), 714
Philippines: question of, 710; Spanish cession of, 713; Spanish war in, *714* acquisition of, 727; American troops driven from, 816, 853; in SEATO, 884
Phillips, David Graham, 655
Philipse, family, 111
Philips, Wendell, 407, 697
Philosophy: of achievement, 873–874; humanistic, 874; heroic, 874–875. *See also* Values
Phrenology, 377–378
Pickens, Fort, 472
Pickens, Francis, 472
Pickering, John, 288, 303
Pickering, Timothy, 280
Pierce, Franklin: and expansionism, 434; election as president, 445, 461; and Missouri Compromise, 448; and Kansas crisis,

450; Jefferson Davis in cabinet of, 456
Pietism, 135, 139, 620, 632
Pike, Albert, 473
Pike, Zebulon, *284*
Pike's Peak trail, 561
Pilgrims: Plymouth settlement, 38–42; legacy of, 42
Pinchot, Gifford, 668, 677, 867
Pinckney, Charles, 342
Pinckney, Thomas, 264
Pinckney, William, 298
"Pine tree shilling," 159
Pingree, Hazen, 648, 670
Pitkin, Walter, 871
Pitt, William, 186; war strategy of, 154–155; impact on colonies, 156; and Navigation Acts, 156; reforms of, 185
Pittsburgh, Pa., 319; railroad strike in, 581–*582*
Pittsfield, Mass., 412, *412–413*
Pizarro, Francisco, 7, 26
"Placemen," 205
Plains of Abraham, battle on, 155–156
"Planned obsolescence," policy of, 881
Plantations: early, 30; "hundreds," *35*; in South Carolina, 59; and slavery, 126–128; in South, 129–132; owners of, 130; economics of, 131; visitors' views of, *242*; cotton, *328*; life on, 330; as feudal manors, 417; breakup of, 535–536. *See also* Cotton; Slavery; South
Plan of Union, 168
Platt, Tom, 625
Platt Amendment (1901), 713, 727
Pledge of solidarity, *238*
Plessy v. Ferguson, 700
Plows, steel, 413
Plunkitt, George Washington, 623–624, 625
Pluralism, ethnic, 685
Plymouth: early settlement of, 23, 26
Plymouth Plantation, 39–42, *40*; economic basis of, 40; government, 41
Poe, Edgar Allan, 382
Poland: German invasion of, 807, 812; Yalta agreement on, 827; Soviet policy in, 828
Poles, immigration of, 681, 765
Police procedures: Supreme Court on, 898; and legislation, 908; and Nixon administration, 914
Poliomyelitis, conquest of, 882
Political bosses, in Gilded Age, 624. *See also* Boss rule
Political convention, first national, 359, 361
Political machines, of 1920s, 774. *See also* Boss rule
Political parties: emergence of, 258, 341; justification for, 344; as limit to change, 536–543; during Gilded Age, 619–621; third, 631, 643, 677–678, 695, 842–843, 909; effect of election of 1896 on, 641–642; muckrakers' view of, 656. *See also* Democratic party; Republican party; *specific parties*
Politics, American: origins of, 141–147; compared with British, 143–146; early patterns of, 146; popularization of, 198–200; caucus system, 269, 281; antebellum, *340*, 341; first national party convention, 348; of post-Civil War era, 571; new national organization of, 589; of equilibrium, 621–626; boss, 624 (*see also* Boss rule); and religion, 632; realignment of party system, 642; "streetcar," 649; patronage, 652; Progressivism in, 656–661; national-interest theory of, 660; local, 773–774, 775, 795; national vs. local, 775–777
Politics, British, 141–143; George III and, 185–187. *See also* Parliament

Polk, James K.: and English interests, 418; in election of 1844, 426; reformulation of Monroe Doctrine, 428; elected president, 428, 435; settlement of Oregon controversy, 430–432; and Mexican War, 430–434; and attempts to acquire Cuba, 434; and Wilmot Proviso, 439; and "Barnburners," 440; and Independent Treasury, 442
Polk, Leonidas, 634
Poll tax, 552, 685; federal laws against, 843
Pollution, as governmental problem, 926. *See also* Conservation
Polygamy, among Mormons, 388, 390
Pontiac (Ottawa chief), 181, 187, 200
Poole, Ernest, 697
Poor, in Democratic party, 798
Poor Richard's Almanac (Franklin), *164*
Pope, Gen. John, 940, 561, 562
Popish Plot, 61
Population density: Indian, 29–30; in 1810, *283*; in 1820, *312*; in 1860, *313*; of slaves, *419*; of blacks, *546*
Population growth: in early settlements, 50, 60–61, 63; of colonial era, 68–70; in eighteenth century, 122–123, 176–179; post-Revolutionary, 282; from 1820 to 1860, 312–314; of mid-nineteenth century blacks, 397; after Civil War, 567; in nineteenth-century cities, 591; during 1920s, 858
Populism, 554; origins of, 608, 632; regional, 633–634
Populist movement, 554
Populist party: antimonopolist sentiments of, 602; organized, 634–636, 643; and Progressives, 656
Pork barrel legislation, 628, 630
Pornography, commission on, 914
Port Royal, Nova Scotia, *56*, 57, 104
Portsmouth Treaty (1905), 716
Portugal: empire of, 9, *10*; early sailing vessels of, *16*; and Treaty of Tordesillas, 26
Potosí, silver mines at, *14*, *15*
Potsdam Conference, 828, 853
Pottawatomie Creek, massacre at, 450, 461
Pound, Ezra, 866
Poverty: in pre-Revolutionary towns, 132; urban, *614*; and Great Depression, 781; "War" on, 896, 910, 917
Powderly, Terence V., 580, 612
Powell, John Wesley, 606–607
Powers, Francis Gary, 889
Powers, Hiram, 380
Powers, Johnny, 693
Pragmatism, of William James, 650–652
"Prerogative courts," 144
Presbyterians: in Carolina settlements, 58; and Anglican church, 124; New Lights, 140, 184; 1790 countermovement by, 292; seminaries organized by, 293
Presidency: Constitutional provision for, 254–255; and spoils system, 280, 347, 470–471; and caucus system, 281; "Virginia Dynasty," 339; and two-party system, *340*; and national party convention, 348; vetoes and, 348, 555; Confederate, 469–470; shadow, 627–629; custodial, 629–630, 661; of T. Roosevelt, 668–669; dominance of, 783; and independent regulatory commissions, 884; changes in, 889–890; nonpartisanship in, 890; and television, 891–892; and Civil Rights movement, 896
Presidential Reconstruction, 537–538
Press: colonial, 204, 205, 207; in republican society, 269; and religious revivals, 375; abolitionist, *399*, 401, 529; and reaction to John Brown's raid, 456; during Civil War, 503; during Reconstruction, 533; racism in,

545; and Cuba's war for independence, 708; during First World War, 739–740; socialist, 740, 754. *See also* Dissent; Journalism; Media; Newspapers
Primaries: direct, 654; white, 685
Primogeniture, 82, 240
Princeton, Battle of, 215, 224
Princeton University, 118, 138, 140
"Principles of '98," 281
Printing, technology of, 655
Prison Discipline Society, 391
Privateers, during American Revolution, 214
Proclamation line, 200
Proclamation of Neutrality, 272
Proclamation of 1763, 187
Professionals: during First World War, 735; in Washington establishment, 884
Progressive party, 677–678, 842; in 1924 election, 772
Progressive Republican League, 677
Progressivism: origins of, 642; zenith of, 645; urban, 646–649; social experimentation associated with, 649–652; scientific reform associated with, 652–655; and politics, 656; and state reform, 659–661; of early twentieth century, 674; Wilson as representative of, 678; and blacks, 685–688; racist assumptions of, 688; and challenge of feminism, 688–690, 700; and women's suffrage, 695; and First World War, 733–735, 736; and artistic revolution, 741–744; and challenge of culture, 741–746; critics of, 746–748
Prohibition, 774–775, 859; repealed, 797
Prohibition party, 631
Promontory Point, Utah, 567, 584
Propaganda: pre-Revolutionary, 194; during Civil War, 525–527. *See also* Press
Property rights, and Reconstruction, 533. *See also* Land ownership
Prophet (Tenskwatawa), 287
Prostitution, regulation of, 648
Protectionism, and sectionalism, 349; Lincoln's endorsement of, 458. *See also* Tariff
Protestant Association, 112–113, 119
"Protestant work ethic" of Mormonism, 391
Protestant Irish, immigration of, 176. *See also* Scotch-Irish
Protestantism: and European politics, 17; evangelical, 863. *See also* Revivalism; *specific churches*
Providence Island Company, 26
Prussia, and King George's War, 151
Psychoanalysis, 882
Public opinion: and scientific reform, 653; and NRA, 789; and presidency, 889, 890, 892; and drug use, 909. *See also* Opinion polls
Public relations: and social reform, 385; of abolitionist movement, 401; popular acceptance of, 882. *See also* Media; Press
Public school system: beginnings of, 115–116, expansion of, 367; Freedmen's Bureau, 530–531; in South, 549; Americanization in, 615; increase in spending for, 873, 882. *See also* Education
Public Works Administration (PWA), 792
Pueblo Indians, 561
Puerto Ricans, urban migration of, 898
Puerto Rico: invasion of, 710; Spanish cession of, 713; acquisition of, 727
Pulitzer, Joseph, 708
Pullman Palace Car Company, 636; strike, 612, 616, 636–637, 643
Pure Food and Drug Act (1906), 666, 670
Puritanism, 22; and social order, 77, 79; character of, 87–89. *See also* New England
Puritans: compared with Pilgrims, 38; Great

Migration of, 42–44, 64, 90; New England settlements or, 42–48; early settlements of, 43–45; and importance of education, 115; legacy of, 746, 874
Putney, Vt., communitarian experiment at, 405

Quakers: in Puritan settlements, 47; in Jersey settlements, 59–60; and Pennsylvania settlements, 61–63; and naturalization, 125; mercantile aristrocracy of, 135; dissent privileges of, 136; symbolic importance of, 162–163; antislavery society of, 224, 243; and revivalism, 373; and slavery, 423
Quantrill, William C., 475
Quartering Act (1765), 192
Quay, Matt, 625, 629
Quebec: during King George's War, 152; British capture of, *155*–156, 168; royal government of, 187
Quebec Act (1774), 187
Queen Anne's War, 104, 109, 119
Quemoy, bombardment of, 886
Quota system, for immigration, 685

Racially mixed populations: in Spanish America, 15; fear of, 332, 515, 545
Race riots: in North, 686; post-First World War, 754, 755
Racism: of chattel slavery, 38; origins of, 308; and economic growth, 312; propagandized, 324, *325*; in Benevolent Empire, 397; among northern workers, 397; and nonresistance, 402; of planter class, 416; and California gold rush, 440; black codes, 537, 546; in North, 544–546; as limit to change, 544–550; in South, 546–547; and Ku Klux Klan, 550; of scientific Progressivism, 561; of scientific Progressivism, 685; and immigrant quotas, 765; in labor force, 798. *See also* Blacks; Jim Crow laws; Segregation
Radicalism: cultural, 741; and anti-radicalism, 764–765
Radical Republicans, 532; emergence of, 513, 515; and Lincoln's vetoes, 516; and Johnson's plan for Reconstruction, 537–538; and Fourteenth Amendment, 539–540; and Military Reconstruction Act, 541–542; and impeachment, 542–543
Radio, introduction of, 770–771; impact on culture, 857; and changing values, 864; "Amos and Andy," 869. *See also* Media
Railroad industry: post-Civil War growth in, 567; early strikes in, 581; impact of refrigerated car, 594; collapse of, 596; and consumer legislation, 666–667; antiradicalism of, 765; oligopoly in, 767; strikes in, 840
Railroads: in 1840s, 413–414; in 1860, *414*; trans-Appalachian, 414; and Compromise of 1850, 443; and Kansas, 447; and Lincoln-Douglas Debates, 454; transcontinental, 458; in Civil War, 501; impact on Plains Indians, 563–564; transcontinental, 567, 593; reorganization of, 568; farmers' dependence on, 571; and Granger movement, 579; and nineteenth-century industrialization, 592–594; in 1890, *593*; and Cullom Committee, 631; and Interstate Commerce Act, 643; during First World War, 736–737
Railway, elevated electric, 594
Raleigh, Sir Walter, *19*, 20, 22, 23, 27, 31; Virginia of, 20, *21*
Rand, Ayn, 875
Randolph, A. Philip, 848, 849
Randolph, Edmund, 269; at Constitutional Convention, 253
Randolph, George Wythe, 478

Randolph, John, 288, 341
Rappites, 404
Raskob, John J., 776
Ratification: of state constitutions, 246, 258; of federal Constitution, 256–257
Rationalism, religious, 291
Rationing, wartime, 838, 840
Ray, Man, 866
Raymond, Daniel, 342
Reagan, Ronald, 929
Reaping machines, 413, 571
Recession: during Eisenhower's administration, 845, 880; and sense of helplessness, 924. *See also* Depression
Reciprocal Trade Agreement Act (1934), 804, 812
Reconstruction: black codes of, 416, 537; Lincoln's program of, 516; Johnson's program for, 524–525; Radical, 525; limited by constitutionalism, 528–532; Freedmen's Bureau during, 529–532; limited federal involvement in, 531; as limited by economic theory, 532–536; limited by political parties, 536–543; political parties during, 536–543; Black Codes during, 537; presidential, 537–538; Fourteenth Amendment, 538–540; second Congressional program of, 540–542; limited by racism, 544–550; "Black," 547
Reconstruction Finance Corporation (RFC), 782, 783, 789, 791
Recreation, during 1960s, 922. *See also* Leisure
"Red China," 918. *See also* China
"Redeemers," in South, 550, 551, 554
"Redemptioners," German, 126
Rednecks, 656
Red Scare: after First World War, 752, 755; of 1920s, 764; and Sacco and Vanzetti trial, 767, 783. *See also* Communism; McCarthyism
Reed, Sen. James, 778
Reed, John, 744–746
Referendum, 654
Refining business, Rockefeller's domination of, 568–569. *See also* Petroleum industry
Reform movement: of Revolutionary era, 239–240; under Jefferson's Republicans, 279; centered in New England, 385; of pre-Civil War period, 385–386; Benevolent Empire, 391–397; Scientific, 652–655; progressive approach to, 659–661, 747. *See also* Social reform
Refrigerated railroad car, 594
"Regulators," 181, 200
Regulatory commissions, politics of, 884
Religion: and early colonization, 26; Pilgrims and Puritans, 38; Puritans', 42, 45–46; in Maryland settlements, 48; in Carolina settlements, 58; Quakers in Pennsylvania, 61–63 (*see also* Quakers); in colonial America, 82–91; Great Awakening, 135–140; denominationalism, 140–141; and King George's War, 151; republican, 291–294; mid-nineteenth-century revivalism, 369–371; and politics, 632; and expansionism, 707; during 1920s, 859; and humanism, 874. *See also* Values; Revivalism; *specific religions*
Religious Freedom, Act for Establishing (1786), 291
"Relocation centers," 847
Remond, Charles Lenox, 406, 407
Rensselaerswyck, 104
Reparations: after First World War, 778; after World War II, 827
Reparations Commission, 751
Representation: demand for, 199; virtual vs. actual, 206–207

Republican Committee to reelect the President, 927
Republicanism, 221–223; independent citizens, 222–223; equality, 223; need for virtue, 223; nineteenth-century image of, 620. *See also* Republican society
Republican party (Jeffersonian): emergence of, 265; ideology of, 266, 416; politics of, 280–281; expansionist aims of, 288; and religion, 291; diplomacy of, 295–299; and war in Europe, 296–298
Republican party: and election of 1824, 344–346; and nativism, 446; emergency of new, 446, 461; rise of, 448; and *Dred Scott* decision, 452; and convention of 1860, 457–458; antislavery principles of, 459, 460; factions during Civil War, 513; and Reconstruction, 537; and Johnson's Reconstruction program, 538; and impeachment, 542–543; Southern view of, 548; and Negro rights, 554; and protective tariffs, 575; during Gilded Age, 619–621; and Progressive revolt, 657; in Wisconsin, 658; and international communism, 884; and Goldwater candidacy, 893. *See also* "Black Republicans;" National Republicans; Old Republicans; Radical Republicans
Republican society: departure of Loyalists, 232; and social change, 236–238; and destruction of corporate privilege, 238–239; educational reform in, 239–240; family in, 240–242
Reservations, Plains Indians confined to, 606
Restoration, 93, 119
Resumption Act (1875), 576–577
Retailing, trade associations in, 768
Revels, Hiram R., 548
Revenue Act (1942), 838, 853
Revenue sharing, 914
Revere, Paul, 195, 204, 238
Revivalism: of eighteenth century, 138–140; post-Revolutionary, 293; mid-nineteenth-century, 369–376; social significance of, 370; in South, 371; in West, 372; and economic prosperity, 374–376; at populist meetings, 634. *See also* Religion
Revolution, American: ideals of, 3; legacy of, 712; interpretation of, 173; explanation of, 203; and religious liberty, 291
Revolution, of 1800, 275–281
Revolution, French, 267, 272
Revolution, Haitian, 329, 418, 527–528
Revolution, Russian, 731, 752, 755
Revolutionary War: events leading to, 209; shipping during, 210; northern campaigns, 211–215; British objectives in, 214; southern campaigns of, 218–220; economic effects of, 232–235; and slavery, 242–243
Reynolds v. *Sims*, 898
Rhenish Palatinate, immigration from, 123, *125*
Rhetoric: pre-Revolutionary, 199; patriotic, 339; antielitist, 359. *See also* Attitudes; Values
Rhett, Edmund, 533
Rhode Island (colonial): Roger Williams in, 47–48; English patent for, 48; charter granted to, 64; charter confiscated, 97, 119; religious toleration in, 137; voting requirements in, 146; paper money in, 161
Rhode Island (state): constitution for, 226, 228; western claims of, 230, *231*; Philadelphia Convention ignored by, 253; Constitution rejected by, 258; urban centers of, 314; and Negro suffrage, 545
Rhodes, James Ford, 664
Rice, Elmer 867

Rice culture: in South Carolina's economy, 59; and slave labor force, 101, 126
Richberg, Donald, 789
Richmond, Va.: early settlement at, 34; state capital removed to, 244; ruins of, *464–465, 526*; Lee's defense of, 490; during Civil War, 503; freedmen in, *552*
Right-to-Life movement, 925
Riis, Jacob, 614, 662, 670
Rio Grande River, as Texan border, 429, 430
Ritualism, 620
Roads, of 1840s, 319. *See also* Transportation
Roanoke settlement, 19, 20, 27, 30
"Roaring Twenties," 763
"Robber barons," 568, 867
Robinson, Edward G., 869
Robinson, Harriet, 402
Robinson, James Harvey, 652
Robinson-Patman Act (1936), 802
Rochambeau, Comte de, *220*
Rochester, N.Y., revivalism in, 373; Sabbatarian movement in, 394
Rockefeller, John D., 375, 500, 568, 571, 595; and trusts, 598, 616; and management, 768
Rockefeller, William, 569
Rockefeller family, 629
Rocketry, in World War II, 823
Rockingham, Marquess of, 186
Rockwell, Norman, 864
Rocky Mountain region, settlement of, 565
Roebling, John and Washington, 592
Roe v. *Wade*, 914, 931
Rome-Berlin Axis, 804
Rommel, Gen. Erwin, 817
Roosevelt, Eleanor, 786, 797, 865
Roosevelt, Franklin, *791, 827*; and question of sovereignty, 761; as vice-presidential candidate, 763–764; quoted, 782, 789; assessment of presidency of, 786; as governor of New York, 786; elected president, 787, 812; first administration of, 787–789; and early New Deal, 789–793; "Hundred Days" of, 789–793; and later New Deal, 795; reelection of, 798–799, 812; and Supreme Court, 799; antitrust policy of, 802; foreign policy of, 804, 808–809; "quarantine" speech of, 807; reelected to third term, 808–809, 812; war strategy of, 817, 822; "Four Freedoms" of, 825; at Yalta Conference, *826*, 827; fourth campaign of, 840, 853; death of, 853; popularity of, 865; and Democratic party, 889; leadership style of, 890
Roosevelt, Theodore, 628, *663*, 701, 752; Square Deal of, 603, 664–668; and Sherman Act, 604; becomes president, 617, 661, 670, 727; on muckrakers, 655; presidency of, 662–664; political philosophy of, 664; neofederalism of, 668–669; elected president, 670, 700, 726; "New Nationalism" of, 673–674, 677, 700; and election of 1912, 677; as Bull Moose candidate, 677–678; on immigrants, 683; Dillingham Commission appointed by, 685; view on presidency of, 698; expansionism of, 706; Cuban policy of, 708; and Battle of San Juan Hill, *711*; and foreign policy, 713; militaristic image of, *713*; as peacemaker, 716; and Monroe Doctrine, 717–718; diplomacy of, 719–720; "practical idealism" of, 741, 743; quoted, 744
Root, Elihu, 716, 719
Root-Takahira Agreement (1980), 716, 727
Rosecrans, W. S., 495, 496
Rosenberg, Julius and Ethel, 833, 851, 853
Ross, Edward A., 653

Ross, John (Cherokee chief), 473
Rough Riders, 662, 710, 711
Rousseau, Jean Jacques, 166
Royal Air Force, and Battle of Britain, 810
Royal Society in London, first American member, 114
Royall, Isaac, Jr., *131*
"Rule Britannia," 150–156
Rum, in eighteenth-century trade, *133*
Rumania: in Soviet sphere of influence, 828; Soviet control of, 831
"Running Bulls," Battle of, 800
Rush, Benjamin, *240*
Rush-Bagot convention, 304
Rusk, Dean, 900
Russell, Lord John, 468, 483, 485, 511
Russia: English trade with, 18; and Spain in 1823, 420; claiming Pacific monopoly, 422; Alaska purchased from, 560; immigrants from, 681; nineteenth-century colonization efforts of, 704; and Portsmouth Treaty, 716; and First World War, 730; revolution in, 731, 755; American troops in, 752. *See also* Soviet Union
Russians, and immigration quotas, 765
Russian territory, in 1763, *175*
Russo-Japanese War, 727
Rutgers University, 118, 140
Ruth, "Babe," 869, *870*
Ryder, Albert Pinkham, 741

Sabbatarian movement, 393–396
Sacco, Nicola, 767
Sac Indians, 326
Sadat, Anwar el-, 921
St. Augustine, Fla., and War of Jenkins' Ear, 151
St. Clair, Gen. Arthur, 264, 272
St. Domingue, slave revolt in, 329
St. Leger, Barry, 215–216
St. Louis, Mo., German immigration to, 313
St. Mary's (settlement), 49
Salem, Mass., early settlement of, 43
Salinger, J. D., 903
SALT (Strategic Arms Limitation Talks) I and II, 919, 921, 931
Salt Lake Valley, Mormon migration to, 388
Samoa, partitioning of, 707
Sand Creek, slaughter at, 562
Sandys, Sir Edwin, 35
Sandys, George, 113
San Francisco, Cal.: clipper ship travel to, 424; in Mexican War, 428–429
Sanger, Margaret, 859–860
San Ildefonso, Treaty of (1800), 285
San Jacinto, Battle of, 423
San Juan Hill, capture of, 710
Santa Anna, Antonio López de, 423, 430, 432
Santa Fe trail, 423
Santayana, George, 746
Santiago, naval battle at, 709
Santo Domingo: and sugar trade, 157–158; black insurrections in, 243; and expansionism, 560. *See also* Dominican Republic
Saratoga, Battle of, 217, 224
Saugus, Mass., ironworks in, 71, 72, 78
Savage, Edward, 259
Savannah, Ga., in eighteenth century, 123; British capture of, 214, 218; as colonial capital, 244; capture of, 519
Say and Sele, Lord, 77
Scalawags, 548
Scandinavia, emigration encouraged in, 312
Scandinavians, and immigration quotas, 765
Schechter case, 799
Schenk v. *United States*, 755

Schiff, Jacob, 600, 601
School, "moving," 116. *See also* Education
Schurz, Carl, 483, 712
Schuylet, Peter, *112*
Schuyler brothers, 106
Schuyler family, 111
Science: and Ben Franklin, 165; and Progressivism, 743, 746
Scientific reform, 652–655
Scientific relativism, 874
Scientific research, government involvement in, 884
Scopes, John, 860
Scotch-Irish: eighteenth-century immigration of, 123, 176; attitudes of, 124–125
Scots, immigration of, 176
Scott, Dred, 451–453
Scott, Thomas A., 568
Scott, Sir Walter, 381
Scott, Winfield, 360, 431; Mexican campaign of, 433, 435; nominated for presidency, 445
Sculpture: Afro-American, *330*; of mid-nineteenth century, 380. *See also* Folk art
Sea Islands, S.C., black settlement of, 531
Search warrants, 187
Sears, Roebuck Corporation, 768
Seattle, Wash., shipyard strike in, 754
Secession: and Compromise of 1850, 443; and election of 1860, 460; states involved in, *474*
Secoton, Indian village of, *20*
Sectionalism: during Confederation, 251; and Missouri Compromise, 342; and Republican unity, 344–346; and protective tariff, 349; and political parties, 361; and slavery, 417; and Texan independence, 423; and Ostend Manifesto, 434; and two-party system, 438; and election of 1848, 440; and Compromise of 1850, 443; and Lincoln's election, 466; and tariff, 574; and banking system, 578; and Progressive movement, 646; and Roosevelt's conservation campaign, 668. *See also* Frontier; North; South
Securities and Exchange Commission (SEC), 791, 884
Seddon, James A., 478, 512
Sedition Act (1798), 271, 279
Sedition Act (1918), 740, 755
Segregation: and Supreme Court, 893–894, 910; absurdity of, 894. *See also* Desegregation
Self-improvement, cult of, 376; mind control, 377; phrenology, 377–378; transcendentalism, 378–379
Seligman, Edwin, 652
Seminole Indians, 323, 420, 561; and Confederacy, 473
Seminole War, 303, 324
Semmes, Raphael, 499
Senate, U.S.: Constitutional provisions for, 255; blacks in, 548; direct election for, 654; and Watergate hearings, 927
Senates, state, 228, 246
Seneca Falls, N.Y., women's rights convention at, 404
Seneca Indians, and colonial expansion, 179–181
Separation of powers, principle of, 227
Separatists, Pilgrims as, 38–40, 41
Servicemen's Readjustment Act (GI Bill) (1944), 840
Servitude: indentured, 37, 68, 101; and colonial households, 81; in republican society, 237. *See also* Slavery
Settlement: in eighteenth century, 122; post-Revolutionary westward, 282–284; western, 565. *See also* Expansion

Settlement house movement, 649, 651, 691–693
Seven Arts, The, 747, 748
"Seven Days," in Civil War, 490
Seven Oaks, Battle at, 489
Seventh-Day Adventists, traditional values of, 863
Seven Years' War, 153, 168, 174. *See also* French and Indian War
Seville, *12*
Seward, William H., 359, 513, 537; and California's admission, 442; on antislavery, 443; and Pres. Taylor, 445; and Kansas-Nebraska Act, 447; and Republican party, 448; and Brown's raid, 456; and 1860 election, 457–458; as Lincoln's secretary of state, 471; foreign policy of, 482–484, 485; and Monroe Doctrine, 558–559; and claims against Confederate ships, 559; and Alaskan purchase, 560
Sex roles, idealized by art, 381
Sexual activity: and changing values, 860; in motion pictures, 864; and youth counter-culture, 905, 906
Seymour, Horatio, Gov., 505, 550, 555, 576, 584
Shafter, Gen. William R., 709
Shaftsbury, Earl of (Anthony Ashley Cooper), 57–58
Shakers, 404
Shakespeare, William, 33
Sharecropping, 535
Share Our Wealth program, 794–795
Sharpe, Gov. Horatio, 191
Shattuck, Jacob, 252
Shaw, Anna Howard, 700
Shaw, Irwin, 875
Shawnee Indians, 179–181, 322
Shays, Daniel, *252*
Shays's Rebellion, 252, 272
Shenandoah Valley, in Civil War, 489, 518
Sheridan, Gen. Philip H., 518, 563
Sherman, Sen. John, 552, 576, 577, 604
Sherman, Roger, 211, *255*
Sherman, Gen. William T., 495, 496, 498, 512, 531; in Mexican war, 432; march to sea, *518–519*, 522; "bummers" of, 527
Sherman Antitrust Act (1890), 603, 604, 616, 630, 643, 665, 699
Sherman Silver Purchase Act (1890), 616, 630, 638, 643
Sherwood, Robert E., 872
Shiloh, Battle of, 488, 491
Shipbuilding industry, growth of, 158–159
Shipping, colonial, 74. *See also* Trade
Shirley, Gov. William, 151, 154
Shoe industry, in American colonies, 183
Siberia, American troops in, 752, 777
Sidney, Algernon, 204, 222
Silk, in eighteenth-century trade, *133*
Silk industry, and Paterson strike, 744–*745*
Silliman, Benjamin, 377
Simms, William Gilmore, 381
Sinclair, Harry, 772
Sinclair, Upton, 666, 670, 697
Singapore, Japanese occupation of, 816
Single taxers, 632, 661
Sioux Indians: mass execution of, 561–562; plains warfare of, 563, 584; encampment, *566*; confined to reservations, 605
Sioux nation, 916
Sirhan, Sirhan, 909
Sirica, John, 927, 928
"Sit-ins," 895
Sitting Bull (Sioux chief), 563, 566
Skillin, Simeon, 198
Slater, Samuel, 272

Slave codes, 38, 327
Slaveholders: and Missouri Compromise, 448; among Indians, 473; exempted from conscription, 504. *See also* Aristocracy; South
Slave Power, 405, 407
Slavery: "chattel," 37–38; in Virginia settlements, 37–38; in Carolina settlements, 58–59; and tobacco economy, 76; social impact of, 101; in eighteenth-century America, 126–128; in Revolutionary era, 242–243; westward expansion of, 309; and agricultural expansion, 316; and King Cotton, 320; revolts against, 329; and political parties, 340; and Missouri Compromise, 341–344; and Benevolent Empire, 395; and northern industrial growth, 415; South as "slave society," 415–417; arguments in favor of, 417; decline in New World, 418; and territorial expansion, 418–420; and Monroe administration, 422; Mexico abolishes, 422–423; and British role in Texas, 425; and American values, 439; and election of 1848, 439; federal slave code, 456; Lincoln's policy on, 476; Emancipation Proclamation, 491, 506–507, 508; and Thirteenth Amendment, 524; effect on expansionism, 703
Slaves: in Spanish America, 15; in eighteenth century, 122, *133*; resistance of, 127; and economic growth, 312, 332; life style of, 327–332; religious practice of, 371; in West Indies, 415; geographical distribution of, *419*; and Polk's attempt to acquire Cuba, 434; fugitive, 426; and Webster-Ashburton Treaty, 435; and Compromise of 1850, 442, 443
Slave trade: beginnings of, 70; eighteenth-century, *133*; during Revolutionary era, 243; prohibited, 303; Britain's abolition of, 395, 425; movement to revive, 455
Slidell, John, 433, 483; Mexican mission of, 429, 435; and *Trent* affair, 485
Sloan, John, 614, 743, 745
Sloughter, Henry, 111
Slums, workers in, 613–615. *See also* Ghettos
Small, Albion, 652
Smallpox, 29. *See also* Disease
Smalls, Robert, 507
Smibert, John, 152
Smith, Alfred E., 775–776, 797, 859, 909
Smith, Rev. Gerald L. K., 797
Smith, Gerrit, 393
Smith, J. Allen, 652
Smith, J. J., *507*
Smith, Capt. John, 33, 35
Smith, Joseph, 386, *387–388*
Smith, Sir Thomas, 23, 32
Smith, William, 145
Smith Act (1940), 850
Smith v. Allwright (1944), 850
Smith-Connally Act (1943), 840
Smuggling, and balance of payments, 157–158
Snyder, John, 844
Social change: and Puritanism, 90–91; associated with republican society, 236; national government's influence on, 843
Social consciousness, 872
Social Democratic party, 695
Social drama, 744–746
Socialism: two faces of, 695–696; and Wobblies, 696; as dissenting party, 697; periodicals of, 740, 754
Socialist Labor movement, 580
Socialist Labor party, 695, 696, 700
Social organization: colonial, 77–82; of eighteenth century, 147; and Christianity, 372–374. *See also* Aristocracy; Elite; Middle class
Social reform: during Revolutionary era, 240;

Social reform (*continued*)
and public relations, 385; origins of, 391; organized philanthropy, 392; volunteer societies, 392–393; communitarianism, 404–405; and industrialism, 589; literature of, 602; settlement house movement, 649, 651, 691–693. *See also* New Deal; Progressivism

Social Security Act (1935), 796, 812; Supreme Court validates, 799

Society for the Propagation of the Gospel in Foreign Parts, 84, 137

Sociology, and politics, 663

Soft money, national significance of, 575. *See also* Money

Solomon Islands, Battle of, 817

Somoza, Gen. Anastasio, 921

Sons of Italy, 683

Sons of Liberty, 190, 195

SOUR (Stamp Out Urban Renewal), 898

South: colonial economy of, 75; plantations in, 129–132; economic effect of revolution on, 232, 234; agricultural shifts in, 318; mid-nineteenth-century economic growth of, 322; slave masters in, 327–330; and Missouri Compromise, 341–344; and nullification theory, 351, 361; churches in, 371; reaction to abolition in, 400; dominance class in, 416; and attempts to acquire Cuba, 434; disintegrating economic position of, 441; devastation in, 529; economic adjustments in, 533–535; postwar economy of, 536; as one-party region, 537; Reconstruction districts in, *541*; racism in, 546; Reconstruction governments in, 547; "Redemption" of, 550; populism in, 633; modern caricature of, 860; in literature, 876–877; integration in, 894–895; and Civil Rights movement, 895–896

South Carolina (state): constitution for, 226, 228, 246; religious liberty in, 291; and protective tariffs, 349–350; and nullification theory, 351, 361; secession of, 460, 461; Black Codes in, 538; black suffrage in, 547; reconstruction of, 547, 555

South Dakota, population decrease in, 633

Southeast Asia Treaty Organization (SEATO), 884, 900, 910

Southern Alliance, 607–608, 616

Southern Christian Leadership Conference (SCLC), 895

Southern Tenant Farmers' Union, 801

South Vietnam, collapse of, 918, 931. *See also* Vietnam War

Sovereignty: British and colonial rule, 23; Puritan, 45–46; colonial New England vs. Dutch, 54; and colonial insurrections, 109–110; in colonial America, 208–209; concept expressed in *Declaratory Act*, 209; Jefferson and Adams on, 209; and Federalist-AntiFederalist debate, 256; American fear of unchecked power, 438–439; Douglas's definition of, 457; and State Rights debate, 528–529; and tariff, 574–575; and currency, 575–577; government vs. business, 597; Progressive view of, 645; and arbitration, 721–722; and national economy, 761; and upheaval of the 1960s, 762; and New Deal, 792–793, 797; as issue in 1940s, 815; and centralization of authority, 853; and government management, 883; national vs. local, 914

Sovereignty, popular: Federalists' 257; and slavery prohibition, 444–445; Douglas's view of, 450, 453; and *Dred Scott* case, 452; and Southern interests, 455, 456

Sovereignty, state: in Confederation, 228, 230; and Wilmot Proviso, 439–440; and Con-

federate conscription, 479

Soviet-American relations: after World War II, 825–827; and Iron Curtain, 828–829; and Truman administration, 829–830. *See also* Containment policy

Soviet Union: refusal to recognize, 777, 779; nonaggression pact with Germany, 807; and German front, 817; World War II costs of, 823; Cold War with, 827–833, 903; sphere of influence of, 829; Communist ideology of, 830; in Korean War, 835; *Sputnik* launched by, 882, 910; Cuban turn to, 886; and Suez Canal, 888; détente with, 918, 919; Nixon visit, 918, 931

Space program, success of, 882–883, 910

Spain: empire of, 9–11, *10*; creates Council of the Indies, 26; and Treaty of Tordesillas, 26; early New World settlements, 55; and King George's War, 151; and War of Jenkins's Ear, 151; and Treaty of Paris, 156; territory in 1763, *175*; and American Revolution, 217–218; Confederation and, 251; and relations with early republic, 263–264; and westward expansion, 285; and Transcontinental Treaty, 418, 420; and Ostend Manifesto, 434, 435; immigrants from, 681; and 1895 Cuban revolution, 707–709, 727; Cuban reconcentration program of, 709; civil war in, 804, 812

Spanish America: colonization of, 5–9; extent of, 9; government of, 10–11; population of, 13–14; Creoles in, 14–15; chronology for, 26–27; independent republics of, 422

Spanish-American War: events leading to, 709; Philippine question 710–712; peace terms for, 712, 727; colonial fruits of, 713–714, 727

Spanish Succession, War of the, 104, 122, 151

Spargo, John, 670, 697, 771

Special interests: and Benevolent Empire, 395; ethnic vs. economic, 798; rise of, 801–802; and decentralization of government, 841–843

Specialization: crop, 607; growth of, 858; and success, 873

Specie circular, 354–355, 361; national significance of, 575

Spillane, Mickey, 875, 877

Spirit of American Government, The (Smith), 652

"Spoils" system, and Jacksonian Democrats, 347; and Lincoln election, 470–471; and civil service reform, 572; Mugwumps and, 628. *See also* Civil service reform; Political parties

Spooner, Sen., 713

Sports, popularity of, 904

Spotswood, Alexander, 99, 100

Spotsylvania, Battle of, 517, 522

Springfield, Ill., race riots in, 686

Spurzheim, Johann Gaspar, 377, *378*

Sputnik, launching of, 882–883, 891

"Square Deal," 664–668

Squatters, and government policy, 317. *See also* Land ownership

Stalin, Josef, 819; at Yalta Conference, 826, 827; and Potsdam Conference, 828

Stalingrad, Battle of, 819

"Stalwarts" (Republican faction), 574, 626, 627

Stamp Act (1765), 188, 189, 200; opposition to, 189–*191*, 193; resistance to, 206

Stamp Act Congress, 190, 208

Standard of living, of farmers, 607. *See also* Family income

Standard Oil of Ohio: organization of, 569, 584; prosperity of, 595; trust for, 599, 616;

exposé of, 602, 616; antitrust action against, 670. *See also* Oil industry

Stanton, Edwin M., 478, 494, 543

Stanton, Elizabeth Cady, 403, 553

Staple Act (1663), 119

Stark, John, 217

"Starving times," 23, 25–26, 39, 69, 77

State Department, in Cold War, 830. *See also* Foreign policy

State rights: and federalist program, 259; and Supreme Court, 290; and slavery, 344; and Mormonism, 390; and Constitutional limits, 528–529; and Roosevelt's conservation campaign, 668; and Dixiecrats, 842–843. *See also* Sovereignty

Steamboat, invention of, 303; and King Cotton, 320; in 1840s, 413

Steam power, 411, 413

Steel industry: post-Civil War growth in, 567; early growth of, 568; technological innovations in, 595; cartels in, 598; and union movement, 636, 840; and First World War, 738; 1919 strike in, 754, 755; antiradicalism in, 765; oligopoly in, 768; CIO drive in, 800

Steel Rail Association, 598

Steffens, Lincoln, 648, 655, 670

Steichen, Edward, 601

Stieglitz, Alfred, 602

Stein, Gertrude, 866

Steinbeck, John, 872

Stephens, Alexander H., 481, 506, 512, 526, 537, 546

Stephens, Uriah, 580

Stephenson, David, 767

Steuben, Baron von, *220*

Stevens, Thaddeus, 515, 532, 533, 537, 538, 539, 541, 543

Stevenson, Adlai, 835, 845, 850

Steward, Alvan, 405

Stewart, Ira, 579, 890

Stiles, Ezra, 179, 244

Stillwell, Gen. "Vinegar Joe," 816

Stimson, Henry L., 803

Stock market, establishment of, 595. *See also* New York Stock Exchange

Stoddard, "Pope" Solomon, 138

Stone, Lewis, 861

Stone, Lucy, 404

Stonites, 294

Story, Joseph, 377

Stoughton, Gov. William, *117*

Stowe, Harriet Beecher, 364, 402, *403*, 444, 461

Strasser, Adolph, 612

Strategic Arms Limitation Talks (SALT), 919, 931

Strickland, William, 134

Strikes: eighteenth-century, 132; post-Revolutionary, 238; women's, 402; nationwide railroad, 581–582, 616; of late nineteenth century, 611; Pullman, 612, 616, 636–637, 643; Homestead, 616, 636, 643; during 1894, 637; of United Mine Workers, 665–666; in Chicago stockyards, *667*; against American Woolen Company, 701; Paterson, 744–746; Seattle shipyard, 754; Boston police, 754; 1919 steel, 754, 755; decline in number of, 771; during 1934, 795; during 1937, 800; during World War II, 840, 841. *See also* Labor; Union movement

Strong, George Templeton, 505

Strong, Josiah, 707

Stuart, Charles, 398

Student Non-violent Coordinating Committee (SNCC), 895

Students, and 1960 presidential campaign, 907. *See also* Youth

Students for a Democratic Society (SDS), 904

Stuyvesant, Peter, *54–55*, 86

Submarine warfare: and blockade policies, 724; of First World War, 737, 755; of World War II, 810, 816–817, 819

Success ethic; and national values, 858, 880; in literature, 867. *See also* Values

Suez Canal, Egyptian seizure of, 888

Suffrage: in eighteenth-century America, 146; Fifteenth Amendment, 525, 555; disfranchisement of blacks, 553–554, 685; for women, *553*, 690, 693–695, 734; and scientific reform, 653; and civil rights legislation, 896

Suffragists, woman, 693–695

Sugar: and balance of payments problem, 157; in eighteenth-century trade, *133*; production, 157; and Haitian revolution, 418; in Cuba, 434

Sugar Act (1764), 187, 189, 200

Sugar trust, and Supreme Court, 604

Sullivan, Louis, 592, 616

Summit conference, Eisenhower-Krushchev, 889

Sumner, Sen. Charles, 450, 506, 513, 515, 532, 536; and Fourteenth Amendment, 538, 539; on Reconstruction legislation, 541, 542; on black inferiority, 545; and restoration of "Home Rule," 550; nationalism of, 558; and claims against Great Britain, 559–560

Sumner, William Graham, 532–533, 597, 712

Sumptuary law (1651), 79–80

Sunday, Billy, 765

Sunday School Union, 396

Sumter, Fort: crisis over, 472, 491

Supreme court: *Dartmouth College* case, 239; and *Marbury v. Madison*, 289–290; *Cohens v. Virginia*, 290; *Fletcher v. Peck*, 290; *McCulloch v. Maryland*, 290; *Martin v. Hunter's Lessee*, 290; *United States v. Peters*, 290; on Indian rights, 323–324; and territorial authority, 445; and *Dred Scott* case, 451–453; *Munn v. Illinois*, 579, 584, 603; *E. C. Knight* case, 604, 665; *Northern Securities Co. v. United States*, 604, 617, 665; *Wabash, St. Louis & Pacific Railroad Co. v. Illinois*, 603, 611; *Muller v. Oregon*, 659; and Progressivism, 675; Justice Holmes on, 675–676; *Lochner* case, 676; *Plessy v. Ferguson*, 700; *Abrams v. United States*, 755; *Schenk v. United States*, 755; *Adkins v. Children's Hospital*, 769; *Bailey v. Drexel Furniture Co.*, 769; *Maple Flooring Manufacturers' Association* case, 769, 783; oligopolies sanctioned by, 769; *United States v. United States Steel Co.*, 769; on labor, 783; and New Deal, 798–799, 812; FDR vs., 799–801; *NLRB v. Jones and Laughlin Steel*, 799; *Schechter* case, 799; *United States v. Butler*, 799; *United States v. Darby*, 799; *Korematsu v. United States*, 847; *Smith v. Allwright*, 850; *Sweatt v. Painter*, 850; *Brown v. Board of Education*, 893–894, 896, 910; on segregation, 893–894, 896, 910, 914; *Baker v. Carr*, 898; *Escobedo* decision, 898; *Mallory* decision, 898; *Miranda* decision, 898; *Reynolds v. Sims*, 898; on abortion, 914, 931; *Milliken v. Bradley*, 914; Nixon's, 914; *Roe v. Wade*, 914; *Bakke* decision, 915; on Nixon tapes, 928

Surinam (Dutch Guiana), *133*

Sussex (French passenger ship), German attack on, 725

Svinin, Pavel Petrovich, 301

Sweatt v. Painter (1950), 850

Swift, Gustavus, 599

Sylvis, William H., 579–580

Symbolism: severed snake, *153*; classic, *198*; eagle, *259. See also* Folk art.

Taft, Sen. Robert, 827, 844–845, 852

Taft, William Howard, 668, *676*, 749; and Sherman Act, 604; elected president, 670; attitude toward reformers, 676–677; and election of 1912, 677; elected president, 700, 727; dollar diplomacy of, 720; and National War Labor Board, 737; as chief justice, 769

Taft-Hartley Act (1947), 841, 853, 884

Taiwan. *See* Formosa

"Talented Tenth," 688

Tallmadge, James, Jr., 342

Tammany Hall, 623, 625. *See also* Boss rule

Taney, Roger B., 354, 513; and *Dred Scott* case, 451–452

Tappan, Arthur, 393, 398, 400, 401

Tappan, Lewis, 393, 394, 400

Tarbell, Ida, 655

Tariff: sugar, 158; of Abominations, 347, 361; and sectionalism, 349–350; and theory of nullification, 349–351; Walker, 442, 461; of 1867–1869, 574, 575; of 1883, 575; and Democratic party, 630; McKinley, 630, 631, 643; and Taft administration, 677; Wilson on, 698–699; Payne-Aldrich, 700; Fordney-McCumber Act, 777, 783; Hawley-Smoot, 782, 783; and policy of international stabilization, 804. *See also* Foreign policy; Trade

Tariff Commission, 700

Tarleton, Col. Banastre, 218

Tax(es) and taxation: by Anglican Church, 83; Stamp Act crisis, 188–191, 193, 200, 206; on tea, 196, 200; and Whiskey Rebellion, 263, 272; on state bank notes, 567; IRS, 572, 924; graduated income tax, 634, 773, 838–839, 840; and government's financial network, 844

Tax revolt, 930

Taylor, B. F., 400

Taylor, Frederick Winslow, 670

Taylor, Graham, 691

Taylor, Gen. Maxwell, 901–902

Taylor, Nathaniel William, 294

Taylor, Zachary, 356, 360, 431; and war with Mexico, 430, 435; elected president, 434, 439, 461; and sectionalism, 440; and divisions within Whig party, 442; and Seward, 443, 445

Tea Act (1773), 196, 200

Teamsters: striking, 795; in union movement, 841

Teapot Dome scandal, 772

Technology, and American ingenuity, 411; and post-Civil War economy, 568; nineteenth-century, 594–595; of war, 834; and national security, 885. *See also* Industrialization

Tecumseh (Shawnee chief), *287*, 300

Tehran Conference, 826, 827

Telegraph: economic development of, 567; and industrialization, 594

Telephone: economic development of, 567; and industrialization, 594; Bell invents, 616; impact on culture, 857

Television: "Army-McCarthy" hearings broadcast on, 852; development of, 881; and presidency, 889, 890, 891–892; and Vietnam War, 902–903; and presidential debates, 929. *See also* Media

Teller Amendment, 710

Temperance movement, 373, 396–397

Temperance Society, 396

Tenancy: British concept of, 128; American interpretation of, 129. *See also* Land ownership

Tenements: dumbbell, 614, 615; in Washington, D.C., *647. See also* Ghettos

Ten-Hour Law, 690

Tennent, Gilbert, 139

Tennessee: admitted to Union, 260; Indians in, 323; secession of, 473, 491

Tennessee Valley Authority (TVA), 792–793, 812, 845

Tenure of Office Act (1867), 542, 555

Terrorism, worldwide, 924

Test Ban Treaty (1963), 891, 910

"Tet offensive," 902, 907

Texas: admitted to Union, 315, 428, 435; rise of cotton in, 320; Indian policy of, 327; annexation of, 410, 418, 422–426; as Spanish territory, 417; and Louisiana Purchase, 420; and Britain, 425; proclaims independence, 435; and Clay resolutions, 442; secession of, 460, 461, 468, 491; reconstruction of, 547; and cattle industry, 570

Texas Pacific Railroad, 612

Texas Seed Bill (1887), 629–630

Textile industry: in American colonies, 183; and demand for cotton, 320–321; of 1840s, 411; women in, *412*; and election of 1848, 440; and Civil War, 483–485; nineteenth-century wages in, 611; strikes in, 795

Textron, 841

Thailand, in SEATO, 884

Thames, Battle of, 287, 303

Theocracy, Mormonism as, 388. *See also* Puritans

Thomas, Gen. George H., 488, 495, 496, 518

Thomas, William I., 652

Thompson, "Big Bill," 774

Thompson, Cephas, 289

Thompson, George, 400

Thompson, J. Edgar, 571

Thoreau, Henry David, 382, 667, 874

Three Mile Island nuclear plant, 926, 931

Thurmond, Gov. J. Strom, 843

Ticket-splitting, 623

Ticonderoga, Fort, 154, 155, 201, 224

Tilden, Samuel J., 551, 555, 580, 584

Tillman, Ben, 639, 685

Timber, in colonial economy. *See also* Lumber

Tippecanoe, Battle of, 287, 300, 303

Tithingmen, 80

Tobacco, as medium of exchange, 84

Tobacco industry: and colonial economy, 34; in colonial South, 75; overproduction in, 75; competition in, 76; and slavery, 101; "factors" in, 131; in eighteenth century, *133*; after Revolution, 234

Tocqueville, Alexis de, 308, 315, 316, 334, 369

Todd, John, 377

Tojo, Hideki, 810

Tonkin Resolution, 901. *See also* Vietnam War

Toombs, Robert, 442, 470, 472, 483

Tordesillas, Treaty of (1494), 17, 26

Tories, 203. *See also* Loyalists

Torpedoes, 498

Totalitarianism, in literature, 875

Toussaint L'Ouverture, 329, 527–528

Town meetings: in Dominion of New England, 97; in colonial New England, 100

Towns: cattle, 570; "bedroom," 860; suburban, 881

Townsend, Dr. Francis E., 795, 798

Townsend movement for old-age pensions, 871

Townshend, Charles, 186, 191

Townshend, George, 180

Townshend Acts (1767), 191, 192, 195, 200

Toynbee Hall, 649

Tracy, Spencer, 861
Trade: in Virginia settlements, 34-35; of Plymouth Plantation, 40; in Maryland settlements, 50; and Carolina settlements, 59; of Pennsylvania settlements, 63; "triangular," 74; mercantilism, 95-96, 156-159; as basis of Anglo-American aristocracy, 102; eighteenth-century Atlantic, *133*; sugar, 157-158; and Currency Act, 161; and Anglo-American trade acts, 192; post-Revolutionary War, 234-235; pre-War of 1812, *297*; opening of Japan for, 438, 461; and tariff question, 574-575; world markets and imperialism, 705; China, 715-716; and "Fair Trade" agreements, 802; with Communist nations, 899. *See also* Tariff
Trade associations, 768; and FTC, 769. *See also* Union movement
"Trail of Tears," 325
Transcendentalism, 379
Transcendentalists, 650
Transcontinental Treaty, 421. *See also* Adams Onis Treaty
Transportation: and colonial manufacturing, 158; and Mississippi River, 285, 303; and agricultural expansion, 316, 318-320, 413; in 1840s, 413; public transit, 648; airlines, 881; interstate highways, 881. *See also* Automobile industry; Railroads
Transportation Act (1920), 769, 783
Treasury Act (1840), 356
Treasury Department: established under Hamilton, 260-261; in Grant's administration, 572; and Prohibition, 774
Tredegar Iron Works, 473, *499*, 500, 506
Trenchard, John, 204
Trenholm, George A., 502
Trent affair, 485-486, 491
Trenton, Battle of, 215, 224
Tresca, Carlo, 744
Triangle Shirtwaist Factory fire, 617, 700
Tripartite Pact (1940), 808, 812
Trist, Nicholas, 433
Truman, Harry S., 823, *828*; becomes president, 827, 853; as Cold War leader, 827; and Potsdam Conference, 828; foreign policy of, 829-830; and transition to peace, 841; "Fair Deal" of, 843; and election of 1948, 843, 853; presidency of, 844; and Democratic party, 889; and opinion polls, 890
Truman Doctrine, 830-831, 832, 833, 836, 853. *See also* Containment policy
Trumbull, John, 166, 220
Trust-busting, 665-666. *See also* Antitrust policy; Corporations
Trusts, 598; and antitrust legislation, 603-604; progressives' criticism of, 652; Wilson on, 698, 699. *See also* Business
Tubman, Harriet, *406*
Tugwell, Rexford, 788
Tully, Cristopher, 412
Tunney, Gene, 869
Turkey: Greek war for independence from, 422; in CENTO, 884
Turnbull, James B., 864
Turner, Frederick Jackson, 335, 616, 706
Turner, Nat, 329, 397, 417; and insurrection in Virginia, 435
Tuskegee, Ala., Normal and Industrial Institute for Negroes at, 686
Twain, Mark, 365, 571, 619, 743, 747
Tweed, William M., *571*-572, 625
Two-party system: evolution of, *340*, 341; Whigs and, 356-361; limitations of, 361; and sectionalism, 438; in Union, 521
"Two Penny Acts" (1755, 1758), 184
Tydings-McDuffie Act (1934), 806

Tyler, Elizabeth, 766
Tyler, John, 356, 360; becomes president, 362, 425, 435; and West Indian emancipation, 425; and British role in Texas, 426; and election of 1844, 428

U-boats, and blockade policies, 724. *See also* Submarine warfare
Ulster, colonization of, 24-25
Un-American Activities, House Committee on, 850
Uncle Tom's Cabin (Stowe), 444, 461
Underground Railroad, 406, 407
Underhill, John, 54
Underwood Tariff, 698-699, 701
Unemployment: and depression of 1893, 638; Coxey's Army, *638*, 643; and Great Depression, 781, 782; during 1970s, 915. *See also* Labor
Union: compared with Confederacy, 466-467, 468-471; and crisis over Fort Sumter, 472; Indian alliance of, 473; and importance of border states, 475-476; army of, 476-480, 494, 504-506; and financing of war, 480-482; and European neutrality, 483-484; command system of, 496-497; naval warfare of, 498-500; and wartime economy, 500; conscription of, 504-506; and emancipation, 506; debate over emancipation in, 507-510; wartime politics in, 512-516; victory of, 516-521; two-party system in, 521; draft riots in, 522; and cost of war, 525; support for, 557. *See also* North
Union League, 528, 547
Union movement, in early nineteenth century, 335; and Cleveland administration, 604; and "American Plan," 613; Wobblies in, 696-697; and antiradicalism, 765; adapted to modern business, 768; and Supreme Court, 769; and New Deal, 790, 799-801; and Wagner Act, 796; racism in, 798; during World War II, 840; and Taft-Hartley Act, 841. *See also* Labor
Union Pacific Railroad, 563, *564*, 567, 572, 584, 593
Union party, 798
Unions, growth of, 611. See also Trade associations; *specific unions*
Unitarians, 294
United Auto Workers (UAW), 800
United Farm Workers, 915
United Mine Workers, 665-666, 790, 799
United Nations (UN): charter signed, 825, 853; Korean settlement of, 835
United States: 1803-1807, *285*; 1820-1860, *315*; 1820-1821, *343*. *See also* North America
United States v. *Butler*, 799
United States v. *Darby*, 799
United States v. *Peters*, 290
United States v. *United States Steel Co.* (1920), 769
United States Steel Corp., 600, 617, 768; and merger movement, 599; and T. Roosevelt's trust-busting, 665
Unity, symbolism for, 881
Universalists, 294
Universal Negro Improvement Association, 847
Universities: postwar increase in demand for, 873; blacks in, 895. *See also* Colleges
Upshur, Abel P., 425
Urbanization: and frontier expansion, 315; and agricultural expansion, 316; and industrial growth of 1840s, 410; in Northeast, 441; consequences of, 588. *See also* Cities; Industrialization

Utah Territory: Mormon occupation of, 388; and Compromise of 1850, 444; slavery in, 445; and popular sovereignty, 447
Utilities, public: and Progressive revolt, 657; and Eisenhower administration, 883
Utrecht, Treaty of (1713), 104
U-2 spy plane, shot down, 889

Vaca, Cabeza de, 7, 26
Vacation, annual, 859
Valdivia, Pedro de, 7-8, 27
Valentino, Rudolph, 869, *871*
Valley Forge, Washington at, 224
Values, American, 3; anti-authoritarianism, 99; republican, 221-223; Christian, 294; material, 309; sense of limitless possibility, 315; efficiency vs. community solidarity, 316; self-improvement, 376-379; sex roles, 381; perfectionism, 396, 402-404; fear of unchecked power, 438-439; antislavery, 439; dignity of labor, 439; American Dream of 1900, 616; modern society, 761-762; anti-communism, 850-851; modern, 858-860; changing, 859; and behaviorism, 862; local, 863; success ethic, 867; star quality, 869; youth culture, 871; social ethic, 871-872; yearning for unity, 872-873; modern vs. traditional, 873; achievement, 873-874; humanistic, 874; heroism, 874-875; modern, 877; national, 880; segregation, 894; team effort, 883; and desegregation, 897; demise of hard-work ethic, 904; personal power, 904; and counterculture, 905; white, 907; of national system, 930
Van Buren, Martin, 344, 347, 352, 425; as secretary of state, 348; during Jackson administration, 351; hard-money policy of, 354, 356; elected president, 354, 361, 435; Whig criticism of, 359; and election of 1840, 360; and election of 1844, 426; and election of 1848, 439, 440; and Free-Soil party, 461
Van Cortlandt, Pierre, 107
Van Cortlandt, Stephanus, 107
Van Cortlandt family, 109, 111
Van Cortlandt Manor, *107*
Vancouver Island, 431
Vandenberg, Arthur, 829, 837
Vanderbilt, Cornelius (Commodore), 568
Van Rensselaer, Kiliaen, 53
Van Wyck, Charles H., 634
Vanzetti, Bartolomeo, 767, 783
Veblen, Thorstein, 692
Veiller, Lawrence, 651
Venezuela, boundary dispute with England, 707, 727
Vera Cruz, occupation of, 721, 723, 727
Vermont (colonial): early settlement in, 129, 179; during King George's War, 152; back-country disorder in, 181
Vermont (state): admitted to Union, 260; and Negro suffrage, 545
Verrazano, Giovanni da, 26
Versailles Treaty: drawing up, 750-751; limitations of, 752; defeat of, 753-754, 755
Vesey, Denmark, 329, 343, 361
Veterans: Civil War, 529; of Second World War, 873
Vetoes, presidential: A. Johnson's, 555; Grant's, 576; Arthur's, 628; Cleveland's, 628, 629-630; Coolidge's, 773
Vice-admiralty courts, 144, 191, 196; customs cases in, 187
Viceroyalties, 10, *11*
Vicksburg, Grant's capture of, 495-496, 522
Victoria (queen of England), 484, 511
Victory gardens, *736*

Vietnam, *901*
Vietnam War, 762: origins of, 900; escalation of, 901; Tet offensive, 902; opposition to, 902, 907, 909; and containment policy, 903; and peace negotiations, 917–918; Nixon's strategy for, 917–918; collapse of Saigon, 918; financing of, 922
Vigilante groups: in backcountry, 181; during Revolutionary era, 256–258; and law, 291; racist, 549–550; during First World War, 738–739; and antiradicalism, 764; decline of, 767; and Great Depression, 783
Vilas, William, 625
Villa, Pancho, *723*
Villard, Oswald Garrison, 688
Villiers, Elizabeth, 98
Vincent, Rev. Marvin R., 557
Violence, and sense of helplessness, 924
Virginia (colonial), Raleigh's, 20, *21*; English settlement in, 25; early settlements in, 31–38; Jamestown settlement, *32–36*; as royal colony, 37; Northern Neck of, *56*, 64, 128; Indian rebellion in, 64; Anglican Church in, 83–85, 136–138; royal governors of, 99; aristocracy of, 103; rebellion in, 109, 110, 111; schools in, 117; House of Burgesses, *145*; voting requirements in, 146; leadership in, 146–147
Virginia (state): constitution for, 226, 228; western claims of, 230, *231*; Constitution ratified by, 258; religious liberty in, 291; antislavery movement in, 416–417; debates abolition of slavery, 435; secession of, 471, 473, 491; "reorganized," 475; West Virginia secession from, 475; reconstruction of, 547
Virginia (ironclad), 498
Virginia, University of, *276*
Virginia Company, 26, 27, 31–38, 52, 162; collapse of, 36–37; Pilgrims' charter from, 38–39, 41; charter of, 64
Virginia Plan, 253–254
Virginia resolution, 272
Virgin Islands, Danish, purchase of, 727, 755
Volck, Adalbert, 514
Volney, Comte de, 292
Volstead Act (1920), 755, 774
Voltaire, 162–163, 165, *166*
Voluntary organizations: for social reform, 393; of Progressive era, 654. *See also* Benevolent Empire
Volunteers, in Civil War, 477–478, 481
Vonnegut, Kurt, 924
Vote: in eighteenth century, 146; and southern blacks, 553–554; and Gilded Age, 621; and Supreme Court, 898. *See also* Suffrage

Wabash, St. Louis & Pacific Railway Co. v. Illinois, 603, 631
Wade, Sen. Benjamin F., 516, 545, 550
Wade-Davis bill, 516
Wagner, Sen. Robert, 833
Wagner Act (1935), 796, 812; Supreme Court upholds, 799
Wagon trains, *427*, *565*
Wainwright Building, St. Louis, 592, 616
Walker, David, 397
Walker, Leroy P., 477, 478
Walker Tariff, 442, 461
Wallace, George, 909, 914
Wallace, Henry A., 787, 797, 827, 830, 842; as vice presidential candidate, 808
Wall Street, 595
Walpole, Sir Robert, 122, 134, 151, 204
Walsh, Frank P., 737
Waltham system, 411
War debts, after First World War, 778
War of 1812, 410, 411; origins of, 295; declaration of, 299; major campaigns of, *299*; invasions of Canada, 300–301; Treaty of Ghent, 301; and Indians, 322; and 1840s foreign policy, 417–418; plans to seize East Florida, 420; and Federalist party, 431
"War Hawks," 281, 299
War of Jenkins' Ear, 151
War Industries Board, 736, 755, 768
Warner, Charles Dudley, 571, 619
Warner Brothers, 857
"War on Poverty," 896, 910, 917
Warr, Lord de la, 34
Warren, Earl, 893, 896, 898, 927
Warren, James, 241
Warren, Mercy Otis, *241*
Warren, Peter, 151–152
War tax, during Civil War, 481
Wartime profits: during Civil War, 504; and economic growth, 568–570; corporate, 738
Washburne, Carleton, 862
Washington, D.C., capital established at, 279; British burn, 301, 303; race riots in, 755
Washington (state), women's suffrage in, 693–694, 700
Washington, Booker T., 686–688, 700
Washington, George, 155, 213, *220*; Mount Vernon Plantation of, *130*; in French and Indian War, 153; as commander of Continental Army, 210, 213; election as president, 259; Farewell Address of, 268, 272; and land speculation, 284
Washington, Treaty of (1871), 560, 584
Washington Conference Treaties (1921–1922), 777, 783
"Washingtonian Societies," 397
Watergate scandal, 927–929, 931
Water power, in 1860s, 413
Watie, Gen. Stand, 473
Watson, John B., 862
Watson, Thomas, 554, 634
Watts, race riot in, 908
Waud, A. W., 520, 521
Wayne, Gen. Anthony, 264, 272
Ways and Means Committee, House, 630
Wealth: and emergence of aristocracy, 106–108; and social change, 237; inherited. *See also* Values
Weapons systems: atomic bomb, 823, 825, 826, 829, 833, 876; and Test Ban Treaty, 891, 910; "missile gap," 900
Weaver, Gen. James B., 616, 643
Webster, Daniel, 349, *354*; on Bank of the United States, 352; character of, 357; as Whig candidate, 359; as secretary of state, 425; and California's admission, 442; on Clay's 1850 resolutions, 443; and popular sovereignty, 445
Webster-Ashburton Treaty (1842), 425, 435
Weed, Thurlow, 359, 361, 448
Weld, Theodore Dwight, 398, 401
Welfare system: during Progressive era, 648; funding of, 898–899
Weeks, Sinclair, 845
Welles, Gideon, 499, 537
Wells, David A., 574
Werth, John, *476*
West: revivalism in, 372; promise of, 439; myth of, *877*. *See also* Frontier
West, Benjamin, 186, 221
Westchester, early settlement of, 53
Western Union Telegraph Co., 567
West Indians, in Carolina settlements, 58
West Indies: early British trade with, 18; and Carolina settlements, 56, 59; and sugar trade, 157–158; and slavery issue, 395; emancipation in, 434. *See also* Caribbean
Westinghouse, George, 595, 600, 616
Weston, Thomas, 39
Westover Estate, *108*
West Point Academy, influence on Civil War, 486
West Virginia, admitted to Union, 475
Weyerhauser (lumber company), 653
Weyl, Walter, 748
Whaling, in California, 423, 425
Wheat production, and industrialization, 605
Whig party: political theory of, 228; evolution of, *340*; emerging strength of, 356–357; constituency of, 358–360; philosophy of, 358, 620; and election of 1840, 360–361; and slavery, 416; Tyler disowned by, 425; Tyler's Texas policy, 426; and election of 1844, 426, 428; disintegration of, 438; and free soil, 439; and election of 1848, 440; divisions within, 442; collapse of, 445–447, 461; Whigs: Rockingham, 190; origins of name, 203; "Conscience," 439; "Cotton,: 440; and election of 1856, 447; and Republican party, 448
Whiskey Rebellion, 263, 272
Whiskey Ring, 572, 584
White, Hugh, 359
White, John, 18, 20, 30
White, Walter, 847
White, William Allen, 654
White-collar workers, 858; increase in numbers of, 860; and behaviorism, 862–863; and hard-work ethic, 904. *See also* Bureaucracy; Management
Whitefield, George, 138–*139*, 168
Whites, reaction to black rights movement, 908, 910
Whitlock, Brand, 623, 648
Whitman, Walt, 382, 471, 747, 865
Whitney, Eli, 272
Whittier, John Greenleaf, 381, 387, 390
"Whole earth," 905
Wholesale price index, in late nineteenth century, 597
Wichita, Kan., and cattle industry, 570
Wilderness, Battle of, 517, 522
Wiley, Calvin H., 527
Wiley, Harvey, 666
Wiley, Henry, 666
Wilkes, Capt. Charles, 485
Wilkes, John, 204, 205
Wilkinson, Gen. James, 186
Willamette Valley, 427
William Henry, Fort, 154
William and Mary, College of, *84*, 118
Williams, Roger, 45, 47, 64, 90, 113
Williams, Tennessee, 861, 877
Willkie, Wendell, 808
William III (king of England), 98, 111
Williamsburg, Va., 76, 244
Wilmot, David, 439
Wilmot Proviso (1846), 439–441, 442, 461
Wilson, Charles E., 845, 885
Wilson, James, 284; at Constitutional Convention, 253
Wilson, M. L., 788
Wilson, Woodrow, 631, 673, *679*, *725*, *748*, *750*; "new Freedom," of, 674, 697–700, 735; and election of 1912, 678, 701; elected president, 678, 701; written works of, 680; and interest-group politics, 700; progressive program of, 700; missionary diplomacy of, 721–726; doctrine of neutrality, 724; new world order of, 725; reelected, 727; Fourteen Points of, 748–750, 755; and Congressional opposition, 752–754
Winnetka System, 862
Winslow, Edward, *41*
Winthrop, John, *43*, 44

Winthrop, John, Jr., 71, *114*
Wire Nail Association, 597
Wirt, William, 353
Wirtz, Maj. Henry, 527
Wisconsin: admitted to Union, 315; and Negro suffrage, 545
Wisconsin, University of, 658
"Wisconsin idea," 658
Wise, John, 97
Wister, owen, 743
Witchcraft hysteria, 119
Wobblies, 696–698, 701; and First World War, 739; and Paterson strike, 744. *See also* Industrial Workers of the World
Wolfe, James, 154–156
Wolfe, Thomas, 626, 627
Wollaston, John, 139
Woman Suffrage Association, 553
Women: and colonization, 26; in American colonies, 69–70, 82; and republicanism, 240–242; in nineteenth-century labor force, 335; and education reform, 367; and higher education, 368–369, nineteenth-century image of, 381; in abolition movement, 402–404; in textile industry, *412*; in labor force during Civil War, 503; in Granger movement, 577; in Gilded Age, 626; in Populist movement, 634; and social reform, 651; minimum wage laws for, 660; working conditions of, 660; rise of feminism, 688–690; organizations for, 690–691; and settlement house movement, 691–693; and suffrage movement, 693–695; suffrage, 734; during First World War, *737*; first in U.S. cabinet, 787; in wartime workforce, *839*; and changing family roles, 860–861; in Southern novels, 877; abortion rights of, 914
Women's Club Movement, 690

Women's movement: during New Deal, 797; during 1960s, 906–907, NOW in, 907, 910
Wood, Thomas John, 431
Woodstock rock festival, 909
Wool, English market in, 16. *See also* Textile industry
Woolen Act (1699), 119, 158
Wool industry, underemployment in, 22
Wool production, and tariff, 575. *See also* Textile industry
Woolman, John, 329
Worcester v. *Georgia*, 323–324
Workers: and nativism, 446; strikes and work stoppages, 611–612; and consolidation of labor, 612–613; life style of, 613–615; and intellectual vanguard, 746. *See also* Labor
Working Men's party, of Philadelphia, 365
Works Progress Administration (WPA), 795–796, 812; terminated, 840
Work stoppages, 611. *See also* Strikes
World Bank, 825
World War I: begins, 701, 727, 755; *Lusitania* incident, 724; submarine warfare of, 724–726, 737; and new world order, 725; human casualties of, 730, 731; American involvement in, 730–731; major U.S. operations in, *733*, 733; mobilization for, 733–741; armistice, 733, 737; business interests during, 737–738; and grass-roots purges, 738; and social reconstruction, 748; and Wilson's Fourteen Points, 748–750
World War II, 755; events leading to, 807–811; Pacific theater, 815–816, 819, *821*, 823; European theater, 816, *820*; Stalin and Second Front, 821–822; Italian campaign, 822; German surrender, 823, 853; atomic bomb dropped, 825, 876; Japan surrenders, 825, 853

Wormley, James, 552
Wormley agreement, 552
Wounded Knee: massacre at, 606, 616; Native American occupation of, 916
Wren, Christopher, 84
Wright, Carroll, 611
Wright brothers, 617
Writs of assistance, 187
Wythe, George, 246

XYZ affair, 268, 271, 272

Yale College, 118, 119, 140
Yalta Conference, *826*, 827, 853
Yancey, William L., *469*, 483
"Yankees," 468
Yates, Abraham, 244
Yellow fever, 240. *See also* Disease
"Yeoman," 68
York (Toronto), American capture of, 301
Yorktown, Cornwallis's surrender at, 220, 224
Young, Brigham, 388, *390*
Young Plan (1929), 778, 783
Youth: culture of, 871; counterculture of, 904–906
Yugoslavia, in Soviet sphere of influence, 828, 836

Zangwill, Israel, 683, 684
Zenger, John Peter, 168
Zola, Emile, 662
"Zoot suit" riots, 847
Zouave regiments, in Civil War, 477